Seventh Edition

Essentials of Entrepreneurship and Small Business Management

Norman M. Scarborough

Presbyterian College

PEARSON

Boston   Columbus   Indianapolis   New York   San Francisco   Upper Saddle River
Amsterdam   Cape Town   Dubai   London   Madrid   Milan   Munich   Paris   Montréal   Toronto
Delhi   Mexico City   São Paulo   Sydney   Hong Kong   Seoul   Singapore   Taipei   Tokyo

Editor-in-Chief: Stephanie Wall
Acquisitions Editor: Sarah Parker McCabe
Director of Editorial Services: Ashley Santora
Editorial Project Manager: Claudia Fernandes
Editorial Assistant: Ashlee Bradbury
Director of Marketing: Maggie Moylan
Senior Marketing Manager: Nikki Ayana Jones
Marketing Assistant: Gianna Sandri
Senior Managing Editor: Judy Leale
Production Project Manager: Kelly Warsak
Operations Specialist: Cathleen Petersen
Creative Director: Blair Brown

Senior Art Director: Kenny Beck
Cover Designer: LCI Design
Cover Photo: Getty Images/Image Source
Permission Specialist: Brooks Hill-Whilton
Media Project Manager, Production: Lisa Rinaldi
Media Project Manager, Editorial: Allison Longley
Full-Service Project Management: Christian Holdener/S4Carlisle
  Publishing Services
Composition: S4Carlisle Publishing Services
Printer/Binder: Courier/Kendallville
Cover Printer: Lehigh-Phoenix Color/Hagerstown
Text Font: Times LT Std

Credits and acknowledgments borrowed from other sources and reproduced, with permission, in this textbook appear on appropriate page within text.

Library of Congress Cataloging-in-Publication Data
Scarborough, Norman M.
Essentials of entrepreneurship and small business management / Norman M. Scarborough. — 7th ed.
    p. cm.
ISBN-13: 978-0-13-266679-4
ISBN-10: 0-13-266679-0
  1. Small business—Management.   2. New business enterprises—Management.   3. Entrepreneurship. I. Title.
HD62.7.Z55 2013
  658.02'2—dc23
                                                                2012029306

10 9 8 7 6 5 4 3 2 1

ISBN 10:   0-13-266679-0
ISBN 13: 978-0-13-266679-4

To Cindy, whose patience is always tested during a writing project
of this magnitude. Your love, support, and understanding
are a vital part of every book. You are the love of my life.

—NMS

"May your own dreams be your only boundaries."

—The Reverend Purlie Victorious Judson,
in "Purlie," Broadway Theater, 1970

Brief Contents

Contents

Preface

What's New to This Edition?

Entrepreneurship is a fast-growing and ever-changing discipline. This edition includes many new features that reflect this dynamic and exciting field of study.

- Almost all of the real-world examples in this edition are new and are easy to spot because they are accompanied by an icon. These examples allow you to see how entrepreneurs are putting into practice the concepts that you are learning about in the book and in class. These examples are designed to help you to remember the key concepts in the course. The business founders in these examples also reflect the diversity that makes entrepreneurship a vital part of the global economy.

- I have added several new "Ethics and Entrepreneurship" features that give you the opportunity to wrestle with some of the ethical dilemmas that entrepreneurs face in business, including the controversial issues surrounding employers' responses to employees' postings on social media sites. Encouraging you to think about and discuss these issues now prepares you for making the right business decisions later.

- A new sample business plan that illustrates a business plan that was created using Palo Alto Software's Business Plan Pro (www.paloalto.com), the best-selling business planning software in the country, is included. Your instructor may have included the software as part of a bundled package. Many courses in entrepreneurship and small business management require students to write business plans. If creating a business plan is part of your class, you will find that having a model to guide you as you build your own plan to be quite helpful. This sample plan serves as a good model.

- This edition provides expanded and updated coverage of important topics such as using social media, including Facebook, Twitter, and YouTube, as guerrilla marketing tools, attracting capital using crowd funding, using "pop-up" stores to test potential permanent locations, identifying the factors that drive employee engagement, using colors, sound, scents, and lighting as "symbolics" to send important subconscious signals to customers, and others.

- To emphasize the practical nature of this book, I have updated the content of the very popular "Hands On: How To . . ." feature, which selects a concept from each chapter and explains how you can put it to practice in your own company. These features include topics such as how to "Be a Successful Innovator," "Launch a Lean Start-Up," "Select the Ideal Franchise—For You," "Increase Your Web Site's Conversion Rate," "Get a Bank to Say 'Yes' to Your Loan Application," and many others.

- Another feature that is popular with both students and professors is "You Be the Consultant." Every chapter contains at least two of these inserts that describe a decision that an entrepreneur faces and asks you to play the role of consultant and advise the entrepreneur on the best course of action. This feature includes the fascinating stories of how entrepreneurs came up with their business ideas (including Susan Gregg Koger, who used to play "dress up" in her grandmother's basement and now runs a vintage clothing company with $50 million in annual sales), taking a barbecue restaurant from social media zero to social media hero (Big Papa's BBQ in Denver, Colorado), helping entrepreneurs develop strategies for capitalizing on the growing opportunities in mobile commerce (Dungarees.net and Carolina Rustica), and looking for capital to fuel a successful clothing business in the aftermath of the turbulence in the financial markets (Kenneth Giddon of Rothman's). Each one poses a problem or an opportunity and includes questions that focus your attention on key issues and helps you to hone your analytical and critical thinking skills.

- This edition includes 11 new brief cases that cover a variety of topics (see the Case Matrix that appears on the inside cover). All of the cases are about small companies, and most are companies that you can research online. These cases challenge you to think critically about a variety of topics that are covered in the text—from developing a business strategy and building a brand to protecting intellectual property and financing a business. In two of these cases, the winners of a national case writing contest sponsored by Vision Forward's Hot Mommas Project tell their own inspiring entrepreneurial stories and how they struggled to overcome obstacles to achieve success.

- The content of every chapter reflects the most recent statistics, studies, surveys, and research about entrepreneurship and small business management. You will learn how to launch and manage their businesses the *right* way by studying the most current concepts in entrepreneurship and small business management.

Entrepreneurship has become a major force in the global economy. Policymakers across the world are discovering that economic growth and prosperity lie in the hands of entrepreneurs—those dynamic, driven men and women who are committed to achieving success by creating and marketing innovative, customer-focused new products and services. Not only are these entrepreneurs creating economic prosperity, but as social entrepreneurs many of them are also striving to make the world a better place in which to live. Those who possess this spirit of entrepreneurial leadership continue to lead the economic revolution that has proved time and again its ability to raise the standard of living for people everywhere. I hope that by using this book in your small business management or entrepreneurship class, you will join this economic revolution to bring about lasting, positive changes in your community and around the world. If you are interested in launching a business of your own, *Essentials of Entrepreneurship and Small Business Management* is the ideal book for you!

This seventh edition of *Essentials of Entrepreneurship and Small Business Management* introduces you to the process of creating a new venture and provides you with the knowledge you need to launch a business that has the greatest chance for success. One of the hallmarks of every edition of this book has been a very practical, "hands-on" approach to entrepreneurship. I strive to equip you with the tools you will need for entrepreneurial success. By combining this textbook with your professor's expertise, you will be equipped to follow your dreams of becoming successful entrepreneurs.

Other Text Features

- This edition once again emphasizes the importance of conducting a feasibility analysis and creating a business plan for a successful new venture. Chapter 4 offers comprehensive coverage of how to conduct a feasibility study for a business idea and then how to create a sound business plan for the ideas that pass the feasibility test. Your professor may choose to bundle Prentice Hall's *Business Feasibility Analysis Pro* or Palo Alto's *Business Plan Pro* software with this edition of *Essentials of Entrepreneurship and Small Business Management* at a special package price. These programs will guide you as you conduct a feasibility analysis or build a business plan.

- This edition features an updated, attractive, full-color design and a layout that includes an in-margin glossary and learning objectives and is designed to be user-friendly. Each chapter begins with learning objectives, which are repeated as in-margin markers within the chapter to guide you as you study.

- Chapter 2, "Inside the Entrepreneurial Mind: From Ideas to Reality," explains the creative process entrepreneurs use to generate business ideas and to recognize entrepreneurial opportunities. This chapter helps you learn to think like an entrepreneur.

- Chapter 9, "E-Commerce and the Entrepreneur," serves as a practical guide to using the Internet as a marketing and business tool.

- Chapter 13, "Sources of Financing: Equity and Debt," gives you a useful overview of the various financing sources that are available to entrepreneurs with plenty of practical advice for landing the financing you need to start or grow your business. Given the changes that have resulted from recent turmoil in the financial industry, this is a particularly important chapter.

- *Business Plan Pro*, the best-selling business planning software package from Palo Alto Software, is a valuable tool that has helped thousands of entrepreneurs (and students) to build winning business plans for their entrepreneurial ideas. Every chapter contains an updated *Business Plan Pro* exercise that enables you to apply the knowledge you have gained from this book and your class to build a business plan with *Business Plan Pro*.

Supplements

A useful companion Web site, www.pearsonhighered.com/scarborough, offers free access to learning resources including multiple-choice quizzes, Web essays, and links to relevant small business sites.

CourseSmart eTextbook—CourseSmart eTextbooks were developed for students looking to save on required or recommended textbooks. Students simply select their eText by title or author and purchase immediate access to the content for the duration of the course using any major credit card. With a CourseSmart eText, students can search for specific keywords or page numbers, take notes online, print out reading assignments that incorporate lecture notes, and bookmark important passages for later review. For more information or to purchase a CourseSmart eTextbook, visit www.coursesmart.com.

Essentials of Entrepreneurship and Small Business Management, 7/e, has stood the test of time and contains a multitude of both student- and instructor-friendly features. I trust that this edition will help you, the next generation of entrepreneurs, to reach your full potential and achieve your dreams of success as independent business owners. It is your dedication, perseverance, and creativity that keep the world's economy moving forward.

Acknowledgements

Supporting every author is a staff of professionals who work extremely hard to bring a book to life. They handle the thousands of details involved in transforming a rough manuscript into the finished product you see before you. Their contributions are immeasurable, and I appreciate all they do to make this book successful. I have been blessed to work with the following outstanding publishing professionals:

- Claudia Fernandes, my exceptionally capable project manager, who was always just an e-mail away when I needed her help with a seemingly endless number of details. She did a masterful job of coordinating the many aspects of this project. Her ability to juggle many aspects of multiple projects at once is amazing!

- Kelly Warsak, production editor, who skillfully guided the book through the long and sometimes difficult production process with a smile and a "can-do" attitude. She is always a pleasure to work with and a good friend.

- Zoe Milgram, photo researcher, who took my ideas for photos and transformed them into the meaningful images you see on these pages. Her job demands many hours of research and hard work, which she did with aplomb.

- Nikki Jones, marketing manager, whose input helped focus this edition in an evolving market.

I also extend a big "Thank You" to the corps of Prentice Hall sales representatives, who work so hard to get our books into customers' hands and who represent the front line in our effort to serve out customers' needs. They are the unsung heroes of the publishing industry.

Special thanks to the following academic reviewers, whose ideas, suggestions, and thought-provoking input have helped to shape this and previous editions of my two books, *Essentials of Entrepreneurship and Small Business Management* and *Effective Small Business Management: An Entrepreneurial Approach*. I always welcome feedback from customers!

Lon Addams, *Weber State University*

Sol Ahiarah, *Buffalo State College*

Professor M. Ala, *California State University–Los Angeles*

Annamary Allen, *Broome Community College*

Tammy Yates Arthur, *Mississippi College*

Jay Azriel, *York College of Pennsylvania*

Bruce Bachenheimer, *Pace University*

Kevin Banning, *University of Florida*

Jeffrey Bell, *Dominican University*

Tom Bergman, *Northeastern State University*

Nancy Bowman, *Baylor University*

Jeff Brice, *Texas Southern University*

Michael S. Broida, *Miami University*

James Browne, *University of Southern Colorado*

Rochelle Brunson, *Alvin Community College*

John E. Butler, *University of Washington*

R. D. Butler, *Trenton State College*

Pamela Clark, *Angelo State University*

Richard Cuba, *University of Baltimore*

Kathy J. Daruty, *Los Angeles Pierce College*

Gita DeSouza, *Pennsylvania State University*

Stuart Devlin, *New Mexico State University*

John deYoung, *Cumberland Community College*

Michael Dickson, *Columbus State Community College*

Judy Dietert, *Southwest Texas State University*

Robert M. Donnelly, *St. Peter's College*

Steve Dunphy, *Indiana University Northwest*

Art Elkins, *University of Massachusetts*

W. Bruce Erickson, *University of Minnesota*

Frances Fabian, *University of Memphis*

Jan Feldbauer, *Austin Community College*

George J. Foegen, *Metropolitan State College of Denver*

Caroline E. W. Glackin, *Delaware State University*

Stephen O. Handley, *University of Washington–Bothell*

Charles Hubbard, *University of Arkansas*

Fred Hughes, *Faulkner University*

Samira B. Hussein, *Johnson County Community College*

Ralph Jagodka, *Mt. San Antonio College*

Theresa Janeczek, *Manchester Community College*

Robert Keimer, *Florida Institute of Technology*

E. L. (Betty) Kinarski, *Seattle University*

Kyoung-Nan Kwon, *Michigan State University*

Dick LaBarre, *Ferris State University*

Paul Lamberson, *Riverton, Wyoming*

Mary Lou Lockerby, *College of DuPage*

Martin K. Marsh, *California State University–Bakersfield*

Charles H. Matthews, *University of Cincinnati*

John McMahon, *Mississippi County Community College*

Michael L. Menefee, *Purdue University*

Julie Messing, *Kent State University*

William Meyer, *TRICOMP*

Milton Miller, *Carteret Community College*

John Moonen, *Daytona Beach Community College*

Linda Newell, *Saddleback College*

Marcella Norwood, *University of Houston*

David O'Dell, *McPherson State College*

John Phillips, *University of San Francisco*

Louis D. Ponthieu, *University of North Texas*

Ben Powell, *University of Alabama*

Frank Real, *St. Joseph's University*

William J. Riffe, *Kettering University*

Matthew W. Rutherford, *Virginia Commonwealth University*

Joseph Salamone, *State University of New York at Buffalo*

Manhula Salinath, *University of North Texas*

Nick Sarantakes, *Austin Community College*

Khaled Sartawi, *Fort Valley State University*

Terry J. Schindler, *University of Indianapolis*

Thomas Schramko, *University of Toledo*

Peter Mark Shaw, *Tidewater Community College*

Jack Sheeks, *Broward Community College*

Lakshmy Sivaratnam, *Johnson Community College*

Bill Snider, *Cuesta College*

Deborah Streeter, *Cornell University*

Ethné Swartz, *Fairleigh Dickinson University*

Yvette Swint-Blakely, *Lancing Community College*

John Todd, *University of Arkansas*

Charles Toftoy, *George Washington University*

Barry L. Van Hook, *Arizona State University*

Ina Kay Van Loo, *West Virginia University Institute of Technology*

William Vincent, *Mercer University*

Jim Walker, *Moorhead State University*

Bernard W. Weinrich, *St. Louis Community College*

Donald Wilkinson, *East Tennessee State University*

Gregory Worosz, *Schoolcraft College*

Bernard Zannini, *Northern Essex Community College*

I also am grateful to my colleagues who support me in the often grueling process of writing a book: Foard Tarbert, Sam Howell, Jerry Slice, Suzanne Smith, Jody Lipford, Tobin Turner, and Cindy Lucking of Presbyterian College.

Finally, I thank Cindy Scarborough for her love, support, and understanding while I worked many long hours to complete this book. For her, this project represents a labor of love.

Norman Scarborough

Special Note to Students

I trust that this edition of *Essentials of Entrepreneurship and Small Business Management* will encourage and challenge you to fulfill your aspirations as an entrepreneur and to make the most of your talents, experience, and abilities. I hope that you find this book to be of such value that it becomes a permanent addition to your personal library. I look forward to the day when your personal success story appears on these pages.

Norman M. Scarborough
William Henry Scott III Associate Professor of Entrepreneurship
Presbyterian College
Clinton, South Carolina
nmscarb@presby.eduSpecial Note to Students

© Blend Images/Alamy

1

The Foundations of Entrepreneurship

Learning Objectives

On completion of this chapter, you will be able to:

1. Define the role of the entrepreneur in business in the United States and around the world.
2. Describe the entrepreneurial profile.
3. Describe the benefits and drawbacks of entrepreneurship.
4. Explain the forces that are driving the growth of entrepreneurship.
5. Explain the cultural diversity of entrepreneurship.
6. Describe the important role that small businesses play in our nation's economy.
7. Put failure into the proper perspective.
8. Explain how an entrepreneur can avoid becoming another failure statistic.

To succeed, your desire for success should be greater than your fear of failure.

—Bill Cosby

Do not follow where the path may lead. Go instead where there is no path and leave a trail.

—Anonymous

LO1

Define the role of the entrepreneur in business in the United States and around the world.

The World of the Entrepreneur

Welcome to the world of the entrepreneur! Around the world, growing numbers of people are realizing their dreams of owning and operating their own businesses. Entrepreneurship continues to thrive in nearly every corner of the world. Globally, one in nine adults is actively engaged in launching a business.[1] Research by the Kauffman Foundation shows that in the United States alone, entrepreneurs launch 565,000 businesses each month![2] This entrepreneurial spirit is the most significant economic development in recent business history. In the United States and around the globe, these heroes of the new economy are reshaping the business environment and creating a world in which their companies play an important role in the vitality of the global economy. With amazing vigor, their businesses have introduced innovative products and services, pushed back technological frontiers, created new jobs, opened foreign markets, and, in the process, provided their founders with the opportunity to do what they enjoy most.

Entrepreneurial activity is essential to a strong global economy. Many of the world's largest companies continue to engage in massive downsizing campaigns, dramatically cutting the number of employees on their payrolls. This flurry of "pink slips" has spawned a new population of entrepreneurs: "castoffs" from large corporations (in which many of these individuals thought they would be lifetime ladder climbers) with solid management experience and many productive years left before retirement. According to the Small Business Administration, during a recent one-year period, the largest companies in the United States *shed* 88,000 net jobs; during the same period, small businesses with fewer than 20 employees *created* 987,000 net jobs![3]

One casualty of this downsizing has been the long-standing notion of job security in large corporations. As a result, many people no longer see launching a business as being a risky career path. Having been victims of downsizing or having witnessed large companies execute layoffs with detached precision, these people see entrepreneurship as the ideal way to create their own job security and success! Rather than pursue corporate careers on graduation, many students are choosing to launch companies of their own. They prefer to control their own destinies by building their own businesses.

ENTREPRENEURIAL PROFILE: Michelle Jolliffe: Oh Fudge! Michelle Jolliffe moved from San Diego, California, to Tampa, Florida, to take a job managing a location for a national tax preparation service, but when she arrived, the job she was promised had evaporated. She found another job only to be laid off when a recession hit. "I finally decided to start a business of my own," she says. "I got tired of being laid off." Jolliffe decided to take her friends' advice and transform her hobby of making fudge into a business. Using her own capital, she launched Oh Fudge!, a small company located in a shopping mall that makes more than 50 delectable flavors of fudge, including cookies and cream, peanut butter, orange cream, bubble gum, and many others. Jolliffe, who also is earning a college degree in accounting, is committed to making her business a success. "Any venture for an entrepreneur is sink or swim," she says. "I don't want to do the 'sink' thing; I like a roof over my head."[4] ∎

The downsizing trend among large companies has created a more significant philosophical change. It has ushered in an age in which "small is beautiful." Twenty-five years ago, competitive conditions favored large companies with their hierarchies and layers of management; today, with the pace of change constantly accelerating, fleet-footed, agile, small companies have the competitive advantage. These nimble competitors can dart into and out of niche markets as they emerge and recede, they can move faster to exploit market opportunities, and they can use modern technology to create within a matter of weeks or months products and services that once took years and all the resources a giant corporation could muster. The balance has tipped in favor of small, entrepreneurial companies. Howard Stevenson, Harvard's chaired professor of entrepreneurship, says, "Why is it so easy [for small companies] to compete against giant corporations? Because while they [the giants] are studying the consequences, [entrepreneurs] are changing the world."[5]

One of the most comprehensive studies of global entrepreneurship conducted by the Global Entrepreneurship Monitor (GEM) shows significant variation in the rate of new business formation among the nations of the world when measured by total entrepreneurial activity or TEA (see Figure 1.1). The most recent edition of the study reports that 12.3 percent of the adult population in the United States—one in 8 people—is working to start a business. The GEM study also reports that globally men are twice as likely to start a business as women; that the majority of

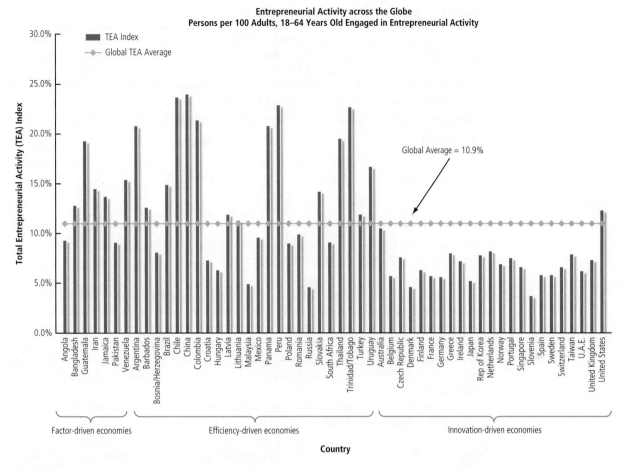

Entrepreneurial Activity across the Globe
Persons per 100 Adults, 18–64 Years Old Engaged in Entrepreneurial Activity

FIGURE 1.1

Entrepreneurial Activity across the Globe

Source: Adapted from Donna J. Kelley, Slavica Singer, and Mike Herrington, *Global Entrepreneurship Monitor 2011 Global Report*, Babson College, Universidad del Desarrollo, and Universiti Tun Abdul Razak, 2011, pp. 10–11.

entrepreneurs turn to family members, friends, and other informal investors for external capital; and that entrepreneurs are most likely to launch their companies between the ages of 35 and 44.[6] The health of the global economy and the level of entrepreneurial activity are intertwined. "The world economy needs entrepreneurs," says GEM researcher Kent Jones, "and increasingly, entrepreneurs depend on an open and expanding world economy for new opportunities and growth—through trade, foreign investment, and finance."[7]

The United States and many other nations are benefiting from this surge in global entrepreneurial activity. Eastern European countries, China, Vietnam, and many other nations whose economies were state controlled and centrally planned are now fertile ground for growing small businesses. Table 1.1 shows some of the results from a recent study by the U.S. Small Business Administration that ranks 71 nations according to the quality of the entrepreneurial environment they exhibit. Even in Afghanistan, a country torn by conflict and debilitated by an inadequate business structure, entrepreneurs of all ages are hard at work.

ENTREPRENEURIAL PROFILE: Mohammad Aqa Alawi In Bamiyan, an isolated and mountainous region in central Afghanistan, Mohammad Aqa Alawi, an 18-year-old student, recently completed an entrepreneurship class called Tashabos, which is sponsored by the Center for International Private Enterprise and is designed to help young people learn how to launch businesses. Alawi spotted a business opportunity in his small village, which has no electricity. Alawi built a hydroelectric turbine in the stream that runs through the village and generates enough electricity to power 20 homes. Alawi's initial investment to build the small power plant was 30,000 Afghanis (about $668), and his business generates 3,000 Afghanis (about $67) per month.[8] ■

TABLE 1.1 Entrepreneurship-Friendly Nations

Which nations provide the best environment for cultivating entrepreneurship? A recent study by the Small Business Administration ranked 71 countries on the quality of the entrepreneurial environment using the Global Entrepreneurship and Development Index (GEDI), an index that includes a variety of factors that range from the availability of capital and workforce quality to attitudes toward entrepreneurs and technology available. The maximum GEDI score is 1.0.

GEDI Score, Top Five Countries	GEDI Score, Bottom Five Countries
1. Denmark .76	67. Bolivia .16
2. Canada .74	68. Syria .16
3. United States .72	69. Guatemala .15
4. Sweden .69	70. Philippines .13
5. New Zealand .68	71. Uganda .10

Source: Zoltan J. Acs and Laszlo Szerb, *Global Entrepreneurship in the United States*, U.S. Small Business Administration, Office of Advocacy, September 2010, pp. 11, 16.

Wherever they may choose to launch their companies, these business builders continue to embark on one of the most exhilarating—and one of the most frightening—adventures ever known: launching a business. It's never easy, but it can be incredibly rewarding, both financially and emotionally. It can be both thrilling and dangerous, like living life without a safety net. Still, true entrepreneurs see owning a business as the real measure of success. Indeed, entrepreneurship often provides the only avenue for success to those who otherwise might have been denied the opportunity.

Who are these entrepreneurs, and what drives them to work so hard with no guarantee of success? What forces lead them to risk so much and to make so many sacrifices in an attempt to achieve an ideal? Why are they willing to give up the security of a steady paycheck working for someone else to become the last person to be paid in their own companies? This chapter will examine the entrepreneur, the driving force behind the U.S. economy.

LO2

Describe the entrepreneurial profile.

entrepreneur

one who creates a new business in the face of risk and uncertainty for the purpose of achieving profit and growth by identifying significant opportunities and assembling the necessary resources to capitalize on them.

What Is an Entrepreneur?

An **entrepreneur** is one who creates a new business in the face of risk and uncertainty for the purpose of achieving profit and growth by identifying significant opportunities and assembling the necessary resources to capitalize on them. Although many people come up with great business ideas, most of them never act on their ideas. Entrepreneurs do. In his 1911 book *The Theory of Economic Development*, economist Joseph Schumpeter said that entrepreneurs are more than just business creators; they are change agents in society. The process of creative destruction, in which entrepreneurs create new ideas and new businesses that make existing ones obsolete, is a sign of a vibrant economy. Although this constant churn of businesses—some rising, others sinking, new ones succeeding, and many failing—concerns some people, in reality it is an indication of a healthy, growing, economic system that is creating new and better ways of serving people's needs and improving their quality of life and standard of living. Schumpeter compared the list of leading entrepreneurs to a popular hotel's guest list: "always full of people, but people who are forever changing."[9]

Researchers have invested a great deal of time and effort over the last few decades trying to paint a clear picture of "the entrepreneurial personality." Although these studies have identified several characteristics entrepreneurs tend to exhibit, none of them has isolated a set of traits required for success. We now turn to a brief summary of the entrepreneurial profile.[10]

1. *Desire for responsibility.* Entrepreneurs feel a deep sense of personal responsibility for the outcome of ventures they start. They prefer to be in control of their resources, and they use those resources to achieve self-determined goals.

2. *Preference for moderate risk.* Entrepreneurs are not wild risk takers but are instead calculated risk takers. A study of the founders of the businesses listed as *Inc.* magazine's

fastest-growing companies found no correlation between risk tolerance and entrepreneurship. "The belief that entrepreneurs are big risk takers just isn't true," says researcher and former *Inc.* 500 chief executive officer (CEO) Keith McFarland.[11] Unlike "high-rolling, riverboat" gamblers, entrepreneurs rarely gamble. Their goals may appear to be high—even impossible—in others' eyes, but entrepreneurs see the situation from a different perspective and believe that their goals are realistic and attainable.

ENTREPRENEURIAL PROFILE: Richard Branson: Virgin Group Richard Branson, founder of Virgin Group, a diverse collection of more than 300 global companies, admits that most people believe that he has "an unusually high tolerance for risk." However, Branson says, "Our actions spring from another principle: Always protect the downside. It should be a guideline for every entrepreneur." Before Branson launched airline carrier Virgin Atlantic Airways, he created a contract with Boeing, the plane's maker, that minimized his risk. "We could hand the plane back at the end of the first year if people didn't like our business. If it didn't work out, it wasn't going to bring everything else crashing down." Virgin Atlantic Airways now generates profits of more than €45 million annually.[12] ∎

Like Richard Branson, entrepreneurs usually spot opportunities in areas that reflect their knowledge, backgrounds, and experiences, increasing their probability of success. One writer observes,

> Entrepreneurship is not the same thing as throwing darts and hoping for the best. It is about planning and taking calculated risks based upon knowledge of the market, the available resources or products, and a predetermined measure of the potential for success.[13]

In other words, successful entrepreneurs are not as much risk *takers* as they are risk *eliminators*, systematically removing as many obstacles to the successful launch of their ventures as possible. One of the most successful ways of eliminating risks is to build a solid business plan for a venture.

3. *Confidence in their ability to succeed.* Entrepreneurs typically have an abundance of confidence in their ability to succeed and are confident that they chose the correct career path. An American Express Open Ages Survey reports that 90 percent of baby-boomer business owners and 76 percent of Generation Y business owners said that their decision to go into business was the right one.[14] Entrepreneurs' high levels of optimism may explain why some of the most successful entrepreneurs have failed in business—often more than once—before finally succeeding. Entrepreneur Dal LaMagna failed in business 14 times before he finally achieved success with his personal care–tool venture, Tweezerman, which he built into a company with $30 million in annual sales and hundreds of employees worldwide.[15]

4. *Determination.* Some people call this characteristic "grit," the ability to focus intently on achieving a singular, long-term goal. Studies show that grit is a reliable predictor of achievement and success, whether the goal involves launching a successful business, winning the Scripps National Spelling Bee, or excelling in professional sports.[16] (One recent study concludes that top performance in the National Football League's Combine, in which players who are entering the league's draft perform short physical and mental tasks, has no "consistent statistical relationship" to subsequent performance in the league.) Successful entrepreneurs demonstrate high levels of determination, especially in the face of challenging circumstances. Perhaps that explains why more than 50 percent of the *Fortune* 500 companies were launched in either a recession, a "bear" market, or both.[17]

ENTREPRENEURIAL PROFILE: Gary Erickson: Clif Bar Gary Erickson started Clif Bar, a maker of nutritious, organic energy bars and snacks, during the recession of 1991 after the idea hit him while on a one-day, 175-mile bike ride with his friend Jay. "We'd been gnawing on 'other' energy bars all day," recalls Erickson. "Suddenly, despite my hunger, I couldn't take another bite. I thought, 'I could make a better bar than this.' That's the moment I now call 'the epiphany.'" After many hours spent in his mother's kitchen,

Erickson developed the energy bar (named after Erickson's father, Clifford) around which he and his wife, Kit (who is co-CEO), built a very successful company, now with annual sales of $235 million.[18] ■

5. *Desire for immediate feedback.* Entrepreneurs enjoy the challenge of running a business, and they like to know how they are doing and are constantly looking for feedback. "I love being an entrepreneur," says Nick Gleason, cofounder of CitySoft Inc., a Web site design firm based in Cambridge, Massachusetts. "There's something about the sheer creativity and challenge of it that I like."[19]

6. *High level of energy.* Entrepreneurs are more energetic than the average person. That energy may be a critical factor given the incredible effort required to launch a start-up company. Long hours and hard work are the rule rather than the exception, and the pace can be grueling. According to the American Express Open study, 66 percent of Generation Y business owners and 58 percent of baby-boomer owners work 10 or more hours a day and do so six days a week.[20] Will Schroter, an entrepreneur who has launched numerous companies, including Go Big Network, an online community for entrepreneurs, explains, "I'm working at 1:34 in the morning because that's what I do. I'm a start-up founder, and I don't sleep. Start-up founders don't sleep because the work of a start-up is never done." Only half joking, he adds, "Many years from now, when this start-up idea turns into a big company with lots of managers and bureaucracy, then I can sleep."[21]

7. *Future orientation.* Entrepreneurs have a well-defined sense of searching for opportunities. They look ahead and are less concerned with what they did yesterday than with what they might do tomorrow. Not satisfied to sit back and revel in their success, real entrepreneurs stay focused on the future. Alex Mashinsky (who says that he was "born into Communism, reared under Socialism, and now thrives under Capitalism") was a pioneer in Web-based communication and has seven start-ups in several industries under his belt. Always looking for the next opportunity, Mashinsky recently launched Transit Wireless, a company that is installing cell phone service in New York City's subway system.[22]

Entrepreneurs see potential where most people see only problems or nothing at all, a characteristic that often makes them the objects of ridicule (at least until their ideas become huge successes). Whereas traditional managers are concerned with managing available *resources*, entrepreneurs are more interested in spotting and capitalizing on *opportunities*. In the United States, 59 percent of those engaged in entrepreneurial activity are **opportunity entrepreneurs**, people who start businesses because they spot an opportunity in the marketplace, compared to **necessity entrepreneurs**, those who start businesses because they cannot find work any other way. (Australia, Belgium, France, and Norway lead the world in opportunity entrepreneurs.)[23]

Serial entrepreneurs, those who repeatedly start businesses and grow them to a sustainable size before striking out again, push this characteristic to the maximum. The majority of serial entrepreneurs are *leapfroggers*, people who start a company, manage its growth until they get bored, and then sell it to start another. A few are *jugglers* (or *parallel entrepreneurs*), people who start and manage several companies at once. *The Entrepreneur State of Mind* study reports that 54 percent of business owners are serial entrepreneurs.[24] "The personality of the serial entrepreneur is almost like a curse," admits one entrepreneurial addict. "You see opportunities every day."[25]

opportunity entrepreneurs
entrepreneurs who start businesses because they spot an opportunity in the marketplace.

necessity entrepreneurs
entrepreneurs who start businesses because they cannot find work any other way.

serial entrepreneurs
entrepreneurs who repeatedly start businesses and grow them to a sustainable size before striking out again.

ENTREPRENEURIAL PROFILE: Michael and Xochi Birch: Bebo In 2005, Michael and Xochi ("SO-chee") Birch launched a social networking site called Bebo (their second start-up) that, although a distant second to Facebook, proved to be extremely popular in Europe. Three years later, the Birches sold Bebo to AOL for $850 million, but their payday did not dampen their entrepreneurial aspirations. The Birches have since launched Monkey Inferno, a business incubator in San Francisco, and Jolitics.com, a political networking site based in Ireland, and have invested in more than 30 start-up companies. "I don't understand why you wouldn't want to launch a new start-up," says Michael. "Not many entrepreneurs really want to retire. There is a great sense of satisfaction in achieving something."[26] ■

It's almost as if serial entrepreneurs are addicted to launching businesses. "Starting a company is a very imaginative, innovative, energy-driven, fun process," says Dick Kouri, who has started 12 companies in his career and now teaches entrepreneurship at the University of North Carolina. "Serial entrepreneurs can't wait to do it again."[27]

8. *Skill at organizing.* Building a company "from scratch" is much like piecing together a giant jigsaw puzzle. Entrepreneurs know how to put the right people together to accomplish a task. Effectively combining people and jobs enables entrepreneurs to transform their visions into reality.

9. *Value of achievement over money.* One of the most common misconceptions about entrepreneurs is that they are driven wholly by the desire to make money. To the contrary, *achievement* seems to be entrepreneurs' primary motivating force; money is simply a way of "keeping score" of accomplishments—a symbol of achievement. What drives entrepreneurs goes much deeper than just the desire for wealth. Economist Joseph Schumpeter claimed that entrepreneurs have "the will to conquer, the impulse to fight, to prove oneself superior to others, to succeed for the sake, not of the fruits of success, but of success itself." Entrepreneurs experience "the joy of creating, of getting things done, or simply of exercising one's energy and ingenuity."[28]

Other characteristics that entrepreneurs tend to exhibit include the following:

High degree of commitment. Entrepreneurship is hard work, and launching a company successfully requires total commitment from an entrepreneur. Business founders often immerse themselves completely in their companies. Most entrepreneurs have to overcome seemingly insurmountable barriers to launch a company and to keep it growing. That requires commitment and fortitude. Many people dream of launching their own companies; entrepreneurs muster the commitment to actually do it.

Tolerance for ambiguity. Entrepreneurs tend to have a high tolerance for ambiguous, ever-changing situations, the environment in which they most often operate. This ability to handle uncertainty is critical because these business builders constantly make decisions using new, sometimes conflicting information gleaned from a variety of unfamiliar sources. Based on his research, entrepreneurial expert Amar Bhidé says that entrepreneurs exhibit "a willingness to jump into things when it's hard to even imagine what the possible set of outcomes will be."[29]

Flexibility. One hallmark of true entrepreneurs is their ability to adapt to the changing needs and preferences of their customers and the changing demands of the business environment. In this rapidly changing global economy, rigidity often leads to failure. Successful entrepreneurs learn to be masters of improvisation, reshaping and transforming their businesses as conditions demand. Research by Saras Sarasvathy, a professor at the University of Virginia's Darden School of Business, shows that entrepreneurs excel at effectual reasoning, which "does not begin with a specific goal." Instead, says Sarasvathy, "it begins with a given set of means and allows goals to emerge contingently over time from the varied imagination and diverse aspirations of the founders and the people they interact with. Effectual thinkers are like explorers setting out on voyages into uncharted waters." Entrepreneurs set goals, but their goals are flexible. Sarasvathy compares entrepreneurs to "iron chefs," who prepare sumptuous meals when handed a hodgepodge of ingredients and given the task of using their creativity to come up with an appetizing menu. Corporate CEOs, on the other hand, develop a plan to prepare a specific dish and then create a process for making that dish in the most efficient, expeditious fashion.[30]

Willingness to work hard. Entrepreneurs work hard to build their companies, and there are no shortcuts around the workload. In his book *Outliers: The Story of Success*, Malcolm Gladwell observes that the secret to success in business (or sports, music, art, or any other field) is to invest at least 10,000 hours practicing and honing one's skills. "What's really interesting about this 10,000-hour rule is that it applies virtually everywhere," says Gladwell. For instance, Mark Cuban, billionaire owner of the Dallas Mavericks of the National Basketball Association and founder of Broadcast.com, the leading provider of multimedia and streaming on the Internet (which he sold to Yahoo! for $5.7 billion), says that he worked for seven years without taking a day off to launch his first business, MicroSolutions, a computer systems integrator. Cuban spent his days making sales calls, and at night and on weekends he studied and practiced to learn everything he could about computers.[31]

Tenacity. Obstacles, obstructions, and defeat typically do not dissuade entrepreneurs from doggedly pursuing their visions. They simply keep trying. Noting the obstacles that entrepreneurs must overcome, economist Joseph Schumpeter argued that success is "a feat not of intellect but of will." Milton Hershey's first three candy-making businesses failed before he created the Lancaster Caramel Company, which became very successful and allowed him to build the chocolate manufacturing business that still carries his name and remains one of the best-known candy makers in the world.[32]

What conclusion can we draw from the volumes of research conducted on the entrepreneurial personality? Entrepreneurs are not of one mold; no one set of characteristics can predict who will become entrepreneurs and whether they will succeed. Indeed, *diversity* seems to be a central characteristic of entrepreneurs. One astute observer of the entrepreneurial personality explains, "Business owners are a culture unto themselves—strong, individualistic people who scorn convention—and nowadays, they're driving the global economy."[33] Indeed, entrepreneurs tend to be nonconformists, a characteristic that seems to be central to their views of the world and to their success.

As you can see from the examples in this chapter, *anyone*, regardless of age, race, gender, color, national origin, or any other characteristic, can become an entrepreneur (although not everyone should). There are no limitations on this form of economic expression. Entrepreneurship is not a mystery; it is a practical discipline. Entrepreneurship is not a genetic trait; it is a skill that most people can learn. It has become a very common vocation. The editors of *Inc.* magazine claim, "Entrepreneurship is more mundane than it's sometimes portrayed. . . . You don't need to be a person of mythical proportions to be very, very successful in building a company."[34] Figure 1.2 summarizes the factors that company founders say are most important to the success of their businesses.

FIGURE 1.2

Sources of Entrepreneurial Success

Source: Vivek Wadwha, Raj Aggarwal, Krisztina "Z" Holly, and Alex Salever, *The Anatomy of an Entrepreneur: Making of a Successful Entrepreneur*, Kauffman Foundation, November 2009 pp. 9–10.

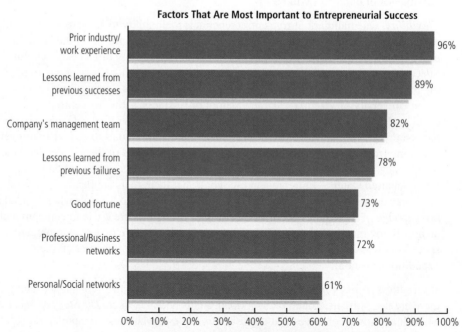

Factors That Are Most Important to Entrepreneurial Success

- Prior industry/work experience — 96%
- Lessons learned from previous successes — 89%
- Company's management team — 82%
- Lessons learned from previous failures — 78%
- Good fortune — 73%
- Professional/Business networks — 72%
- Personal/Social networks — 61%

Percentage of Respondents Ranking Factor as Important, Very Important, or Extremely Important

The Benefits of Entrepreneurship

Surveys show that owners of small businesses believe they work harder, earn more money, and are more satisfied than if they worked for someone else. Before launching any business venture, every potential entrepreneur should consider the benefits of small business ownership.

Opportunity to Create Your Own Destiny

Owning a business provides entrepreneurs the independence and the opportunity to achieve what is important to them. Entrepreneurs want to "call the shots" in their lives, and they use their businesses to make that desire a reality. "At a very early age, I decided that I don't want to work for somebody else," says Vivek Randive, CEO of Tibco Finance Technology, a company that provides a variety of business applications software. "Instead, I want to be the master of my own destiny."[35]

For many entrepreneurs, living where and how they choose is one of the principal benefits of controlling their destinies through business ownership.

Safari Surf School

ENTREPRENEURIAL PROFILE: Tyler and Tim Marsh: Safari Surf School After Tyler Marsh visited his brother, Tim, in Nosara, a small town in Costa Rica, he realized that he enjoyed living in a tropical paradise and decided to stay. The brothers started the Safari Surf School, which has grown into the premier surf school in Costa Rica. Even though it is located 30 miles off of the main paved road in the area, the surf school offers customers all of the comforts of home as well as amenities such as beautiful waterfalls, a sea turtle sanctuary, fresh fruit smoothies, and a gorgeous beach. Their business has been so successful that the Marshes recently purchased the hotel/restaurant/bar where their students stay. Tyler, who teaches surf lessons daily, says, "I can't think of it as work. I get to go surfing, and I meet fascinating people from every part of the world."[36] ∎

Like Tyler and Tim Marsh, entrepreneurs reap the intrinsic rewards of knowing that they are the driving forces behind their businesses.

Opportunity to Make a Difference

Increasingly, entrepreneurs are starting businesses because they see an opportunity to make a difference in a cause that is important to them. Known as **social entrepreneurs**, these business builders seek innovative solutions to some of society's most vexing problems. They use their skills not only to create profitable business ventures but also to achieve social and environmental goals for society as a whole. Their businesses often have a triple bottom line that encompasses economic, social, and environmental objectives. These entrepreneurs see their businesses as mechanisms for achieving social goals that are important to them as individuals. Whether it is providing low-cost, sturdy housing for families in developing countries or establishing a recycling program to preserve Earth's limited resources, these entrepreneurs are finding ways to combine their concerns for social issues and their desire to earn a good living.

social entrepreneurs entrepreneurs who use their skills not only to create profitable businesses but also to achieve economic, social, and environmental goals for the common good.

ENTREPRENEURIAL PROFILE: Dave Melton and Odes Armijo-Caster: Sacred Power Corporation Dave Melton spent 10 years working in a uranium mine on a Navajo Indian reservation in the Southwest to pay for his college education. In 2001, he and Odes Armijo-Caster launched Sacred Power Corporation, a company that designs, builds, and installs a variety of solar energy products for homes. One reason that Melton, a member of the Laguna tribe of the Navajo, started the business was to improve living conditions on the Navajo reservation, where 43 percent of the population lives in poverty and nearly 18,000 homes have no electricity. Sacred Power, now with more than $7 million in annual sales, has won four contracts from the U.S. Department of Agriculture's Rural Utilities Service to provide hybrid power generators to isolated homes on the Navajo reservation. Melton says that these homes "are so far off the grid that they would never get electricity from normal means. Children, who can now study by fluorescent lighting instead of kerosene lantern, will see their study habits improve 10-fold. The economic impact is immeasurable."[37] ∎

You Be the Consultant

Where Do Ideas Come From?

Successful entrepreneurs get the inspiration for their businesses from many sources, but most often their ideas come from a moment of frustration or discomfort. "There must be a better way," they think, and another business idea is born. "To find a good idea, talk to other people to learn about their stress points," says Derek Johnson, who launched a group text-messaging company after listening to a friend at the University of Houston describe the difficulty she was having messaging the members of her sorority about important announcements, dues, and meeting dates. E-mail, Facebook, and message boards were proving to be ineffective, but texting a large number of people required lots of work and time. Within months, Johnson, already a serial entrepreneur at age 25, had launched Tatango, a Web site that allows subscribers to send text messages from any computer or phone to groups ranging in size from just a few people to tens of thousands of people. "People will pay for products that fix problems, make life easier, or make it simpler," he observes. Tatango's subscription plans start at just $19 per month, and more than 2,500 clients already are using the service, generating more than $500,000 in sales for Johnson's young company.

Susan Gregg Koger traces the inspiration for her vintage clothing company to her grandmother's basement when she was a little girl playing "dress-up." "My Grandma had an amazing wardrobe in the 60s and 70s, some of which she kept, and I loved to imagine what her life was like when she wore those garments," says Susan. "The story behind vintage garments has always fascinated me." Throughout high school, Susan frequented thrift shops, estate sales, and garage sales looking for unique vintage clothing. "I couldn't pass up a great vintage find, even if it wasn't my size or style," she admits. By the time she left at age 17 for Carnegie Mellon University, Susan had amassed an extensive collection of vintage clothing. She convinced her boyfriend (now husband), Eric Koger, to build a Web site, Modcloth, through which she could sell some of her clothing collection—"a modest moneymaking hobby," she thought. "The customer service line listed on the Web site was actually my cell phone number," recalls Susan. She quickly discovered that there were many young women who, like her, wanted to express their personal style with unique, vintage clothing. When her inventory threatened to take over her dorm room, Susan and Eric moved their business into a house that served as their warehouse, their office, and their living space. By her senior year, Modcloth was attracting 60,000 visitors per month.

Susan graduated from Carnegie Mellon University in 2006 and decided to focus her attention on Modcloth full-time rather than pursue a career in the corporate world. She also realized the limitations that selling authentic vintage clothing imposed on her company's sales and reached out to independent clothing designers she found at the Magic Trade Show in Las Vegas to create garments that followed the look, feel, and style of the vintage items the company had always sold. "It was clear that the demand for our aesthetic was much greater than the supply of vintage clothing," says Susan. To finance the expansion of her company, she charged $50,000 of inventory and expenses to a credit card, borrowed money from family members, and took out a second mortgage on her house.

Although the business has grown—attracting 2 million visitors per month and generating annual sales of $50 million—Susan still selects most of the clothing, shoes, and accessories featured on the site and selects the company's designers. Eric is the company's CEO and manages the operational side of the business. The copreneurs recently closed a $50 million round of funding to expand the business, which now has more than 150 employees (and growing). Modcloth's future looks bright. Susan is integrating social commerce into the company's marketing plan to increase customers' ties to the company. Modcloth recently introduced a "Be the Buyer" feature that allows customers to vote on which styles actually go into production. The idea is to encourage customers to develop an emotional connection to Modcloth and to start conversations with other potential customers about the unique fashions the company sells. "There's a lot more coming," says Susan.

1. Explain how these entrepreneurs exhibit the entrepreneurial spirit.

2. Have you encountered a "stress point" recently or talked with someone who has? If so, is there a potential business opportunity present? How would you describe the opportunity?

3. What benefits do these entrepreneurs reap from owning their own businesses? What disadvantages do they face?

4. What career lessons can you learn from these entrepreneurs?

Sources: Based on Joel Holland, "What's Your Problem?," *Entrepreneur*, May 2010, p. 70; "Jennifer Wang, "Out of Her Closet, a $50 Million Business," *Entrepreneur*, September 2010, p. 52; and "A Thrifting Tale: Susan's Story," Modcloth, http://www.modcloth.com/about_us/susans-story.

Melton is one of millions of social entrepreneurs who have started for-profit businesses with a broader goal of making the world a better place to live.

Opportunity to Reach Your Full Potential

Too many people find their work boring, unchallenging, and unexciting. But not entrepreneurs! To them, there is little difference between work and play; the two are synonymous. Entrepreneurs' businesses become their instruments for self-expression and self-actualization. They know that the only boundaries on their success are those imposed by their own creativity, enthusiasm, and vision. Owning a business gives them a sense of empowerment. Barbie Dallman, who left the security (and the hassles) of corporate life at age 30 to start a résumé service, says, "Starting my own business was a spiritual awakening. I found out what was important to me—being able to follow my own interests."[38]

Opportunity to Reap Impressive Profits

Although money is not the primary force driving most entrepreneurs, the profits their businesses can earn are an important motivating factor in their decisions to launch companies. A recent survey by Wells Fargo reports that 72 percent of small business owners believe that they are in a better financial position running their own businesses than working for a company in the same field.[39] Most entrepreneurs never become superrich, but many of them do become quite wealthy. In fact, more than two-thirds of the billionaires on the *Forbes* list of the 400 richest Americans are first-generation entrepreneurs![40] People who own their own businesses are more likely to be millionaires than those who are employed by others. According to Russ Alan Prince and Lewis Schiff, authors of *The Middle Class Millionaire*, more than 80 percent of middle-class millionaires, those people with a net worth between $1 million and $10 million, own their own businesses or are part of professional partnerships. (They also work an average of 70 hours a week.)[41] Indeed, the typical millionaire's business is not a glamorous, high-tech enterprise; more often, it is something much less glamorous—scrap metal, welding, auctioneering, garbage collection, and the like.

Roku

ENTREPRENEURIAL PROFILE: Anthony Wood: Roku Serial entrepreneur Anthony Wood, now 45, started his first business, a company that sold computer software, while he was in high school. Since then, he has launched six companies, including his latest business, Roku (the name means "six" in Japanese), which sells a small device that allows customers to stream movies and television episodes from providers, including Netflix, Amazon Instant Video, Hulu Plus, the National Basketball Association, and Crackle, directly to their television sets via their home Internet connections. Wood invented the first digital video recorder and launched a company, ReplayTV, in 1997 to market the device just before the first TiVo came on the market. Before he had turned 30, Wood had sold for $36 million a software company that he had started, and a few years later, he sold ReplayTV to DirecTV for $110 million. For now, Wood has decided to retain control of Roku, which generates annual sales of more than $50 million.[42] ■

Opportunity to Contribute to Society and Be Recognized for Your Efforts

Playing a vital role in their local business systems and knowing that their work has a significant impact on the nation's economy is yet another reward for small business managers. Often, small business owners are among the most respected and most trusted members of their communities. Business deals based on trust and mutual respect are the hallmark of many established small companies. These owners enjoy the trust and recognition they receive from the customers and the communities they have served faithfully over the years. A recent Pew Research Center survey reports that small businesses make up the most trusted institution in the United States, ranking ahead of churches and colleges.[43]

Opportunity to Do What You Enjoy and Have Fun at It

A common sentiment among small business owners is that their work really isn't work. Most successful entrepreneurs choose to enter their particular business fields because they have an interest in them and enjoy those lines of work. They have made their avocations (hobbies) their vocations (work) and are glad they did! These entrepreneurs are living Harvey McKay's advice: "Find a job doing what you love, and you'll never have to work a day in your life." The journey rather than the destination is the entrepreneur's greatest reward. "Rather than have money be your primary motivator," says Tony Hsieh, CEO of online shoe retailer Zappos, a company that Hsieh sold to Amazon for $1.2 billion, "think about what you would be so passionate about doing that you'd be happy doing it for 10 years, even if you never made any money from it. *That's* what you should be doing. Your passion is what's going to get you through the hard times. Your passion is going to be contagious and rub off onto employees and have a ripple effect on customers and business partners as well."[44]

ENTREPRENEURIAL PROFILE: Kate Friedman: Atelier Shoes Kate Friedman is a self-admitted shoe aficonado with an eye for style. After long days at work as a corporate attorney, she often rewarded herself with a new pair of shoes. While on vacation, Friedman decided to combine her entrepreneurial interest with her love of shoes to create Atelier Shoes, an online business that allows customers to design their own shoes by selecting among 80 different materials for the exterior and interior uppers, heel, sole, foot bed, and even the label. Women also can attend a Shoe Party at a friend's house where they can see the variety of options up close and try on shoes before buying. Friedman spent months writing a business plan, sketching shoe designs, testing prototypes, and choosing fabric samples before launching her unique, custom-designed shoe company. "This is a creative outlet for me," Friedman says of her business. "It's the most fun I've ever had. It's very empowering. I like the problem solving. You can be nimble as a small business."[45] ■

Not only has Friedman found a way to earn a living, but, more important, she is doing something she loves!

The Potential Drawbacks of Entrepreneurship

Although owning a business has many benefits and provides many opportunities, anyone planning to enter the world of entrepreneurship should be aware of its potential drawbacks. Individuals who prefer the security of a steady paycheck, a comprehensive benefit package, a two-week paid vacation, and the support of a corporate staff probably should not go into business for themselves. Some of the disadvantages of entrepreneurship include the following.

Uncertainty of Income

Opening and running a business provides no guarantee that an entrepreneur will earn enough money to survive. Some small businesses barely earn enough to provide the owner-manager with an adequate income. In the early days of a start-up, a business often cannot provide an attractive salary for its owner and meet all its financial obligations, meaning that the entrepreneur may have to live on savings. The steady income that comes with working for someone else is absent because the owner is always the last one to be paid.

ENTREPRENEURIAL PROFILE: Thea Marx: Contemporary Western Designs Thea Marx, founder of Contemporary Western Designs, a company in Cody, Wyoming, that sells art, furniture, jewelry, and accessories by Western artists, did not draw a salary from her business for the first three years, choosing instead to reinvest everything that her company earned to finance its growth.[46] ■

Dewey Vanderhoff

Risk of Losing Your Entire Investment

Business failure can lead to financial ruin for an entrepreneur, and the small business failure rate is relatively high. According to research by the Bureau of Labor Statistics, 31 percent of new businesses fail within two years, and 51 percent shut down within five years. Within 10 years, 66 percent of new businesses will have folded.[47]

Before "reaching for the golden ring," entrepreneurs should ask themselves if they can cope psychologically with the consequences of failure:

- What is the worst that could happen if I open my business and it fails?

- How likely is the worst to happen? (Am I truly prepared to launch my business?)

- What can I do to lower the risk of my business failing?

- If my business were to fail, what is my contingency plan for coping?

Long Hours and Hard Work

Business start-ups often demand long hours from their owners. The average small business owner works 54 hours a week, compared to the 40.4 hours per week the typical U.S. production employee works.[48] In many start-ups, six- or seven-day workweeks with no paid vacations are the *norm*. In fact, a Gallup survey concludes that self-employed people "are most likely to work atypically long hours, in many cases upwards of 60 hours per week."[49] A recent survey by American Express found that only 46 percent of small business owners were planning to take a summer vacation of at least one week. The primary reason entrepreneurs don't take vacations? "Too busy."[50] The demands of owning a business make achieving a balance between work and life difficult for entrepreneurs. "When you own a business, it's full-time," says Lori Russell, co-owner with her husband, Marc Elliot, of Nature Connection, a gift shop in downtown Kalamazoo, Michigan. "I mean a 24-hour job. There are always things to be done. It's really hard to get away. We have sneaked away for a few weekends, but for two weeks? Never."[51]

Lower Quality of Life Until the Business Gets Established

The long hours and hard work needed to launch a company can take their toll on the other aspects of an entrepreneur's life. Business owners often find that their roles as husbands or wives and fathers or mothers take a backseat to their roles as company founders. In fact, according to a survey by American Express, 67 percent of entrepreneurs say that owning a business requires them to make sacrifices, most often in the areas of family relationships and friendships.[52] Holly Dunlap, 32-year-old designer of women's shoes, handbags, and party dresses that she sells through Hollywould, the boutique she founded with locations in New York City and Palm Beach, Florida, admits that she is married to her business. Her 14-hour workdays leave little time for lunch most days or for a quiet evening with friends. "As my mother has pointed out," she says, "businesses do not produce grandchildren."[53] Part of the problem is that more than half of all entrepreneurs launch their businesses between the ages of 25 and 39, just when they start their families. As a result, marriages, families, and friendships are too often casualties of small business ownership.

High Levels of Stress

Starting and managing a business can be an incredibly rewarding experience, but it also can be a highly stressful one. Entrepreneurs often have made significant investments in their companies, have left behind the safety and security of a steady paycheck, and have mortgaged everything they own to get into business. Failure may mean total financial ruin, and that creates intense levels of stress and anxiety! Sometimes entrepreneurs unnecessarily bear the burden of managing alone because they cannot bring themselves to delegate authority and responsibility to others in the company, even though their employees are capable.

Complete Responsibility

It's great to be the boss, but many entrepreneurs find that they must make decisions on issues about which they are not really knowledgeable. Many business owners have difficulty finding advisers. When there is no one to ask, the pressure can build quickly. The realization that the decisions they make are the cause of their company's success or failure has a devastating effect on some people.

Discouragement

Launching a business is a substantial undertaking that requires a great deal of dedication, discipline, and tenacity. Along the way to building a successful business, entrepreneurs will run headlong into many different obstacles, some of which appear to be insurmountable. In the face of such difficulties, discouragement and disillusionment are common emotions. Successful entrepreneurs know that every business encounters rough spots along the way, and they wade through difficult times with lots of hard work and an abundant reserve of optimism.

Despite the challenges that starting and running a business pose, entrepreneurs are very satisfied with their career choices. A Wells Fargo/Gallup Small Business Index survey reports that 83 percent of small business owners say that if they were choosing a career again, they would still become small business owners.[54] "I absolutely love what I'm doing," says Scott Badger, founder of KPI Direct, a consulting company that helps businesses create direct marketing programs. "I have no regrets."[55] Many entrepreneurs are so happy with their work that they want to continue it indefinitely. In fact, 47 percent of entrepreneurs polled in a recent survey say that they never intend to retire at all.[56]

LO4

Explain the forces that are driving the growth of entrepreneurship.

Behind the Boom: What's Feeding the Entrepreneurial Fire

What forces are driving this entrepreneurial trend in our economy? Which factors have led to this age of entrepreneurship? Some of the most significant ones include the following:

Entrepreneurs as heroes. An intangible but very important factor is the attitude that Americans have toward entrepreneurs. As a nation, we have raised them to hero status and have held out their accomplishments as models to follow. Business founders such as Bill Gates (Microsoft Corporation), Oprah Winfrey (Harpo Productions and OWN [the Oprah Winfrey Network]), Jeff Bezos (Amazon.com), Steve Jobs (Apple), and Mark Zuckerberg (Facebook) are to entrepreneurship what LeBron James and Peyton Manning are to sports.

Entrepreneurial education. Colleges and universities have discovered that entrepreneurship is an extremely popular course of study. Disillusioned with corporate America's downsized job offerings and less promising career paths, a rapidly growing number of students sees owning a business as their best career option. Growing numbers of students enroll in college knowing that they want to start their own companies rather than considering entrepreneurship as a possibility later in life; indeed, many are starting companies while they are in college. Today, more than two-thirds of the colleges and universities in the United States (more than 2,300) offer courses in entrepreneurship or small business, up from just 16 in 1970. More than 200,000 students are enrolled in entrepreneurship courses, and many colleges and universities have difficulty meeting the demand for courses in entrepreneurship and small business.[57]

Courtesy of Rent The Runway

ENTREPRENEURIAL PROFILE: Jennifer Hyman and Jenny Fleiss: Rent the Runway While in college, Jennifer Hyman came up with the idea for her designer clothing rental business, Rent the Runway, after she witnessed one of her sister's "closet full of clothes, but nothing to wear" moments during Thanksgiving break. When she returned to school, she shared her idea with a suitemate, Jenny Fleiss, and the two collegiate entrepreneurs soon were selling the concept ("Netflix meets fashion") to designers, customers, and potential financiers. They envisioned a Web-based business that would allow women to "constantly refresh their wardrobes and wear the latest designer fashions for all of the special occasions in their lives" by renting upscale dresses and accessories, says Hyman. In less than three years, Hyman and Fleiss have raised $31 million in two rounds of venture capital financing, hired 25 employees, and assembled an impressive inventory of more than 25,000 dresses from 95 designers, such as Vera Wang and Dolce and Gabbana. Women can play Cinderella for one night, wearing designer dresses for just a fraction of their cost. Customers simply select the dress they want, enter their size (a backup size comes free), and specify the rental date; returns are as easy as dropping the dress into a prepaid return envelope. Hyman and Fleiss say that Rent the Runway, which became cash-flow positive in less than one year, now has more than 1 million members.[58] ■

Demographic and economic factors. Nearly two-thirds of entrepreneurs start their businesses between the ages of 25 and 44, and the number of Americans in that age range currently is 85 million! In addition, the economic growth that spanned most of the last 25 years created a significant amount of wealth among people of this age-group and many business opportunities on which they can capitalize.

Shift to a service economy. The service sector accounts for 77.2 percent of the jobs and 76.7 percent of the gross domestic product (GDP) in the United States, both of which represent a sharp rise from just a decade ago.[59] Because of their relatively low start-up costs, service businesses have become very popular among entrepreneurs. The booming service sector continues to provide many business opportunities, from educational services and computer maintenance to pet waste removal and iPod repair.

ENTREPRENEURIAL PROFILE: Jay Shectman: You Ask, We Tutor When Jay Shectman was in the fifth grade, he was inspired by his siblings, who tutored other children after school. That experience inspired him to launch a tutoring business, You Ask, We Tutor!, designed to help struggling students when he was just 14 years old. Shectman employs only students because he believes that they can relate to his student customers better than adults can. Students schedule tutoring sessions online at the company's Web site, www .youaskwetutor.com. Now in college (studying entrepreneurship), Shectman says that his company's customers have a track record of more than 90 percent improvement in their classroom performances. Shectman recently was named the Young Entrepreneur of the Year by the National Federation of Independent Businesses and Visa Inc.[60] ▪

Technology advancements. With the help of modern business machines such as personal computers, laptop computers, smart phones, fax machines, copiers, color printers, answering machines, and voice mail, even one person working at home can look like a big business. At one time, the high cost of such technological wizardry made it impossible for small businesses to compete with larger companies that could afford the hardware. Today, however, powerful computers and communication equipment are priced within the budgets of even the smallest businesses. Although entrepreneurs may not be able to manufacture heavy equipment in their spare bedrooms, they can run a service- or information-based company from their homes—or almost anywhere—very effectively and look like any *Fortune* 500 company to customers and clients. Jimbo Wales, founder of Wikipedia, says, "Wherever my laptop is, that's my office."[61]

Independent lifestyle. Entrepreneurship fits the way Americans want to live—independent and self-sustaining. People want the freedom to choose where they live, the hours they work, and what they do. Although financial security remains an important goal for most entrepreneurs, many place top priority on lifestyle issues, such as more time with family and friends, more leisure time, and more control over work-related stress.

The Internet and cloud computing. The proliferation of the Internet, the vast network that links computers around the globe and opens up oceans of information to its users, has spawned thousands of entrepreneurial ventures since its beginning in 1993. **Cloud computing**, Internet-based subscription or pay-per-use software services that allow business owners to use a variety of business applications, from database management and inventory control to customer relationship management and accounting, has reduced business start-up and operating costs. Fast-growing small companies can substitute cloud computing applications for networks of computers and large office spaces, which allows entrepreneurs to build their companies without incurring high overhead costs.

cloud computing
Internet-based subscription or pay-per-use software services that allow business owners to use a variety of business applications, from database management and inventory control to customer relationship management and accounting.

Online retail sales, which currently account for 5 percent of total retail sales, are forecast to continue to grow rapidly (see Figure 1.3), creating many opportunities for Web-savvy entrepreneurs. Travel services, computer hardware and software, books, music, videos, and consumer electronics are among the best-selling items on the Internet, but entrepreneurs are learning that they can use this powerful tool to sell just about anything! In fact, entrepreneurs are using the Web to sell services such as tours to the sites of their favorite television shows and movies (including *Sex and the City* and *The Sopranos*) and pajama parties for women and products such as crocheted cotton thong underwear and recordings by musicians who perform for tips in the subway of New York City.[62]

FIGURE 1.3

U.S. Retail E-Commerce Revenues

Source: U.S. Online Retail Forecast, 2011 to 2016, Forrester Research, February 27, 2011.

Unfortunately, many small business owners have not yet tapped the power of the Internet. According to a study by Network Solutions, 56 percent of small businesses have Web sites, nearly double the number that had Web sites in 1997. Among those small companies that have created Web sites, only 18 percent actually offer customers the ability to pay for their purchases online.[63] Small companies that do conduct e-commerce typically reap benefits quickly, however, in the form of new customers and increased sales. These "netpreneurs" are using the Internet to connect more closely with their existing customers and, ultimately, to attract new ones.

ENTREPRENEURIAL PROFILE: Fan Bi and Danny Wong: Blank Label When Fan Bi, a college student at Australia's University of New South Wales, visited Shanghai, he discovered the joy of shopping for custom-made shirts in the city's famous fabric markets. "I used to buy dress shirts off the rack," says Bi, "but going to a fabric market, being measured, being able to choose different fabrics makes for a superior experience." Not only were the shirts Bi purchased of better quality than the off-the-rack shirts he had been purchasing, but they also were less expensive, which led Bi to an idea for a Web-based customized shirt company aimed at graduating college students who need professional wardrobes but who cannot afford luxury prices. While studying abroad at Babson College in Wellesley, Massachusetts, Bi met Danny Wong, a student at nearby Bentley University. Together, they teamed up with a programmer on the West Coast and launched Blank Label, a Web-based business that allows shoppers to select from existing shirts or to design their own ("Designed by you, stitched by us"). "You see a dress shirt on the left-hand side and then style options on the right-hand side," Bi says, describing the Web site. Customers can select the fabric, collar style and color, placket, cuff, pocket, buttons, monogram, and even a custom label—all for as little as $55! In less than 18 months, Bi and Wong sold more than 7,000 shirts and used the Internet almost exclusively to operate their company. "Thanks to the Internet, you can work with the best people in the world, not just the best people in your neighborhood," says Bi.[64] ∎

International opportunities. No longer are small businesses limited to pursuing customers within their own borders. The shift to a global economy has opened the door to tremendous business opportunities for entrepreneurs willing to reach across the globe. Although the United States is an attractive market for entrepreneurs, approximately 95 percent of the world's population lives outside its borders. The emergence of potential markets across the globe and crumbling barriers to international business because of trade agreements have opened the world to entrepreneurs who are looking for new customers. Whereas companies once had to grow into global markets, today small businesses can have a global scope from their inception. Called **micromultinationals**, these small companies focus more on serving customers' needs than on the countries in which their customers live. Small companies make up 97 percent of all businesses engaged in exporting, yet they account for only 31 percent of the nation's export sales.[65] Most small companies do not take advantage of export opportunities, often because their owners don't know how or where to start an export initiative. Although terrorism and regional recessions remain challenges to international trade, global opportunities for small businesses have a long-term positive outlook.

Although going global can be fraught with dangers and problems, many entrepreneurs are discovering that selling their products and services in foreign markets is really not so difficult. Small companies that have expanded successfully into foreign markets tend to rely on the following strategies:

- Researching foreign markets thoroughly
- Focusing on a single country initially
- Utilizing government resources designed to help small companies establish an international presence
- Forging alliances with local partners

ENTREPRENEURIAL PROFILE: John Hering: Lookout Mobile Security John Hering, the 26-year-old cofounder of Lookout Mobile Security, a San Francisco–based company that provides software that guards smart phones against attacks from viruses, malware, and spyware, says that he planned for the company to operate globally from its inception. After conducting extensive research on mobile security threats, Hering realized that the potential

micromultinationals
small companies that operate globally from their inception.

✔ You Be the Consultant

College: The Ideal Place to Launch a Business

For growing numbers of students, college is not just a time of learning, partying, and growing into young adulthood; it is fast becoming a place for building a business. More than 2,000 colleges and universities offer courses in entrepreneurship and small business management (an increase from just 200 schools in the 1970s) to more than 200,000 students, and many of them have trouble keeping up with demand for these classes. "Students used to come to college and assume that five to ten years down the road, they'd start a business," says Gerry Hills, cofounder of the Collegiate Entrepreneurs Organization. "[Today], they come in preparing to get ideas and launch."

Many collegiate entrepreneurs realize that if they are going to have a job when they graduate, it is likely to be one they have created for themselves. According to the latest outlook of the National Association of Colleges and Employers, only 24.4 percent of college graduates who applied for a job had one waiting for them after graduation. For a growing number of college students, landing a job in corporate America, starting on the bottom rung of an uncertain career ladder, has lost much of its allure. While studying at Harvard (where she majored in the history of science), Windsor Hanger worked in internships at *OK! Magazine* and at Bloomingdale's, which offered her a marketing position when she graduated. Hanger turned down the job offer, choosing instead to focus on the

business, *HerCampus*, an online magazine aimed at college women, that she had started with classmates Stephanie Kaplan and Annie Wang. "It's not a pure dichotomy anymore that entrepreneurship is risky and other jobs are safe, so why not do what I love?" she says. For their work at *HerCampus*, which is now profitable, Hanger, Kaplan, and Wang recently were named to *Inc.* magazine's "30 Under 30 Coolest Young Entrepreneurs" list.

Perhaps because of their stage in life, college entrepreneurs are particularly keen at spotting business opportunities. While Susie Levitt and Katie Shea were working as student interns on Wall Street, the two New York University students bonded over a common problem: they spent many hours a day on their feet, and the high-heel shoes that they wore made their feet ache. "Having lived in the city for four years as NYU students, we had developed a love-hate relationship with our pointy pumps and strappy stilettos," they write. Looking around at the thousands of professional women in New York City, "we realized that there was a huge need for lightweight, portable shoes that women could wear during their commute or after a long night on the town." An Internet search revealed nothing, and Levitt and Shea decided to create a product of their own. With $10,000, they launched FUNK-tional Enterprises LLC, a company that markets foldable, slipper-like shoes called CitySlips that come in a small carrying case that fits easily into a handbag, from their college dorm room. Returning for their senior year, they began building the framework of their company. Shea enrolled in a business plan writing class, leading them to enter their business plan in the Stern Business Plan Competition. The competition not only gave them excellent feedback about their idea but also opened the door to advice from experts in many different areas. Recognizing that they needed to protect their product idea, Levitt and Shea enrolled in an intellectual property class, where their professor helped them file a patent application. "We got free advice from lawyers who would have charged $500 to $700 an hour," says Levitt. Once they had designed a prototype shoe, Levitt and Shea used Alibaba, a Web site that lists thousands of global suppliers, and Skype to research potential suppliers. Within a year, they had imported 70,000 pairs from China. Shea and Levitt, both of whom come from entrepreneurial families, priced their flats affordably, starting at just $12.99 for a base version called AfterSoles and going up to $24.99 for their original CitySlips, which come in a multitude of colors. Annual sales of CitySlips recently passed the $1 million mark.

Budding entrepreneurs at a growing number of colleges can take advantage of a special programs designed to create a culture for entrepreneurship. According to one business writer, "With their focus on entrepreneurship and programs for developing solid, marketable business plans, business schools are becoming the twenty-first century version of the legendary Hewlett-Packard garage" (the company, like so many successful small businesses, started in a garage). A growing number of schools are offering on-campus business incubators that offering promising student

Courtesy of HerCampus.com

(continued)

You Be the Consultant (continued)

entrepreneurs amenities such as low-cost (sometimes free) office space, professionally appointed conference rooms, wireless Internet access, smart whiteboards, ample computer facilities, video-conferencing equipment, copiers, and a phone system that rings simultaneously land and smart phones so that no one misses an important business call. Presentations from entrepreneurs, venture capitalists, bankers, attorneys, and others help students define their business ideas and develop their business plans. "It's often over those late-night pizzas where the best ideas are born," says one official. One student entrepreneur in the program agrees: "A

lot of it is the community. Being around people in the [entrepreneurship] program inspires one to think about other opportunities out there. What I've learned here is how to plan, how to make a business actually work."

1. In addition to the normal obstacles of starting a business, what other barriers do collegiate entrepreneurs face?

2. What advantages do collegiate entrepreneurs have when launching a business?

3. What advice would you offer a fellow college student about to start a business?

4. Work with a team of your classmates to develop ideas about what your college or university could do to create a culture of entrepreneurship on your campus or in your community.

Sources: Based on David Whitford, "Can You Learn to Be an Entrepreneur?," *Fortune*, March 22, 2010, pp. 63–66; Hannah Seligson, "No Jobs? Young Graduates Make Their Own," *New York Times*, December 11, 2010, http://www.nytimes.com/2010/12/12/business/12yec.html; Glenn Rifkin, "A Classroom Path to Entrepreneurship," *New York Times*, May 1, 2008, http://www.nytimes.com/2008/05/01/business/smallbusiness/01sbiz.html?_r=1&pagewanted=print&oref=slogin; Joel Holland, "Putting Your School to Work," *Entrepreneur*, December 2009, p. 78; Max Raskin and Sommer Saadi, "Startup Fever: College Students Have It Bad," *Bloomberg Business Week*, October 19, 2010; "Susie Levitt of CitySlips on Zero to $1 M in Sales," *Teen Business Forum*, March 11, 2011, http://www.teenbusinessforum.com/interviews/susie-levitt-cityslips-million-sales-interview; Jared O'Toole, "Interview: Katie Shea and Susie Levitt of NYC Startup CitySlips," *Under 30 CEO*, http://under30ceo.com/interview-katie-shea-and-susie-levitt-of-the-nyc-startup-cityslips; and Jason Daley, "From the Blackboard to the Boardroom," *Entrepreneur*, April 2010, p. 58.

---

market for smart phone security was huge. He also discovered that the market was even greater outside the United States because smart phones are a more important part of people's lives in other countries. "For many people, [a smart phone] is the only computer they have," explains Hering. "We have customers in 170 countries. Our service is available on 400 mobile networks around the world." Lookout Mobile Services is growing rapidly, adding 1 million new users per month, and has attracted the attention of top venture capital firms.[66] ■

LO5

Explain the cultural diversity of entrepreneurship.

The Cultural Diversity of Entrepreneurship

As we have seen, virtually anyone has the potential to become an entrepreneur. Indeed, diversity is a hallmark of entrepreneurship. We now explore the diverse mix of people who make up the rich fabric of entrepreneurship.

Young Entrepreneurs

Young people are embracing entrepreneurship enthusiastically as a career choice. A recent survey by Junior Achievement reports that 51 percent of teens would like to own their own business someday.[67] Disenchanted with their prospects in corporate America and willing to take a chance at controlling their own destinies, scores of young people are choosing entrepreneurship as their initial career path. A recent Harris Interactive poll reports that 40 percent of young people between the ages of 8 and 24 already have started a business or would like to do so in the future.[68] Members of the Millennial generation (or Generation Y, those people born between 1982 and 2002), in particular, show high levels of interest in entrepreneurship. Many members of this diverse generation, 75 million strong, are deciding that owning their own companies is the best way to create job security and to achieve the balance between work and life that they seek. "People are realizing [that] they don't have to go to work in suits and ties and don't have to talk about budgets every day," says Ben Kaufman, founder of Mophie, a company (named after his golden retrievers, Molly and Sophie) that he started at age 18 while still in high school that makes iPod accessories such as cases, armbands, and belt clips. "They can have a job they like. They can create a job for themselves."[69] Because of young people such as Kaufman, the future of entrepreneurship looks very bright.

Women Entrepreneurs

Despite years of legislative effort, women still face discrimination in the workforce. However, small business has been a leader in offering women opportunities for economic expression through entrepreneurship. Increasing numbers of women are discovering that the best way to break the "glass ceiling" that prevents them from rising to the top of many organizations is to start their own companies. Women entrepreneurs have even broken through the comic strip barrier. Blondie Bumstead, long a typical suburban housewife married to Dagwood, now owns her own catering business with her best friend and neighbor Tootsie Woodly!

Although the businesses that women start tend to be smaller (the average revenue for women-owned companies is 27 percent of the average of men-owned businesses) and are far less likely to attract equity capital investments as those that men start, their impact is anything but small.[70] The more than 8.1 million women-owned companies in the United States employ more than 7.6 million workers and generate sales of nearly $1.3 trillion a year! Women now own 28.7 percent of all privately held businesses in the United States.[71] A study by Guardian Life Small Business Research Institute projects that women-owned companies will generate between 5 million and 5.5 million jobs in the United States by 2018, which represents more than half the total jobs that small companies will generate in that period.[72]

ENTREPRENEURIAL PROFILE: Simone Gonzales: Pleasure Doing Business After a summer internship during college in the fashion office at Bloomingdale's and a brief stint at Krishan Chaudry, a Los Angeles clothier, Simone Gonzales decided that she was ready to start a fashion business of her own. One day while walking in the Los Angeles garment district, she spotted some unusual elastic fabric that she purchased and transformed into a unique, banded tube skirt. Gonzales realized that she was on to something when she took her colorful creations to a friend's boutique and they sold quickly. "I searched the garment district and bought every elastic [fabric] in every color available," she says. Gonzales borrowed $10,000 from her mother and launched Pleasure Doing Business, which now employs 16 people, including her mother and

Photograph by Steven Michael Sims

"She's my hero. Life gave her lemons and she came up with pomegranate cranberry lemonade."

Source: © Chris Wildt/www.CartoonStock.com

father and an aunt, in a downtown studio. More than 100 retailers, ranging from small boutiques to well-known retailers such as Saks, Nordstrom, and Neiman Marcus, carry her company's chic, elasticized skirts, which start at less than $100. Pleasure Doing Business, which generates more than $2 million in annual sales, has expanded its product line to include dresses, blazers, tops, and tees, but elasticized skirts are the mainstay of the company's sales. Gonzales's brand has benefited from celebrities such as Rihanna, Heidi Klum, Elle Macpherson, Nicole Richie, and many others wearing her designs.[73] ■

Minority Enterprises

Another rapidly growing segment of the small business population is minority-owned businesses. Hispanics, African Americans, and Asians are the minority groups that are most likely to be entrepreneurs.[74] Hispanics, who now make up the largest minority population in the United States, own 8.5 percent of all businesses. African Americans, who make up about 13 percent of the U.S. population, own 7 percent of all businesses, and Asians own 5.9 percent of all businesses.[75] Minority-owned businesses have come a long way in the last two decades (see Figure 1.4), however, and their success rate is climbing.

ENTREPRENEURIAL PROFILE: Monique Péan: Monique Péan Fine Jewelry After Monique Péan graduated from the University of Pennsylvania, she worked on Wall Street, but her aspiration was to start a business that combined her love of jewelry and her passion for the environment. In 2006, she left Wall Street and launched Monique Péan Fine Jewelry, a company that makes high-quality, environmentally friendly jewelry that is inspired by indigenous cultures in the United States. She uses antique gemstones and recycled gold and platinum in her designs ("The production of one gold ring generates 20 tons of waste," she says). Péan's New York City–based company has won several awards for its innovative designs and its focus on the environment. Péan also started the Vanessa Péan Foundation in memory of her sister to provide scholarships for needy children in Haiti.[76] ■

Minority entrepreneurs own 22.4 percent of all businesses, and their economic impact is significant.[77] Minority-owned businesses generate $1.03 trillion in annual revenues and employ more than 5.9 million workers.[78] The future is promising for this new generation of minority

FIGURE 1.4

Growth in Minority-Owned Businesses since 2002

Source: Based on data from the U.S. Census Bureau, 2010.

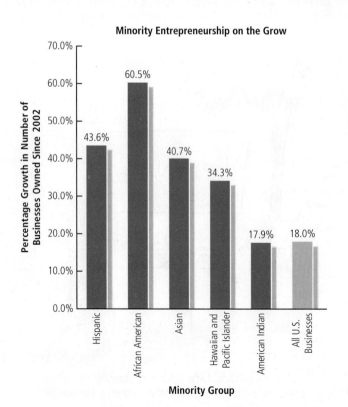

Minority Entrepreneurship on the Grow

entrepreneurs, who are better educated, have more business experience, and are better prepared for business ownership than their predecessors.

Immigrant Entrepreneurs

The United States has always been a melting pot of diverse cultures, and many immigrants have been drawn to this nation by its promise of economic freedom. Unlike the unskilled "huddled masses" of the past, today's immigrants, which make up 11.7 percent of the U.S. population, arrive with more education and experience and often a desire to start a business of their own. In fact, immigrants are significantly (2.2 times) more likely to start businesses than are native-born U.S. citizens.[79] Immigrant entrepreneurs founded 25.3 percent of all the technology and engineering companies started in the United States between 1995 and 2005.[80] Although many immigrants come to the United States with few assets, their dedication, hard work, and desire to succeed enable them to achieve their entrepreneurial dreams.

ENTREPRENEURIAL PROFILE: Patrick Lo: Netgear Inc. Patrick Lo moved to Hong Kong with his grandparents from his native China after his parents were sent to a labor camp. Lo studied hard and won a full scholarship to Brown University in Providence, Rhode Island, to study electrical engineering. After graduating in just three years, Lo went to work for Hewlett-Packard, where he built the Unix server division into a $200 million business. In 1996, Lo approached his bosses about starting a division to capitalize on the potential that the newly emerging Internet offered, but they rejected his idea. Lo quit and started his own company, Netgear, to sell hardware for connecting to the Internet with Mark Merrill and financing from his friend and former boss, Dominic Orr. After a slow start, Netgear hit its stride, and in 2006 Ernst and Young named Lo the Entrepreneur of the Year. Today, Lo is the CEO of the publicly traded company, which is a leading provider of networking products for individuals and small businesses.[81] ■

Part-Time Entrepreneurs

Starting a part-time business is a popular gateway to entrepreneurship. Part-time entrepreneurs have the best of both worlds: they can ease into business for themselves without sacrificing the security of a steady paycheck and benefits. The Internet (and particularly eBay) makes establishing and running a part-time business very easy; many part-time entrepreneurs run online businesses from a spare bedroom in their homes.

ENTREPRENEURIAL PROFILE: Clarissa Trujillo: Ugly Sweater Store After Clarissa Trujillo's husband received an invitation to an "ugly sweater" Christmas party, she launched the Ugly Sweater Store as an online, part-time business from her home. "The concept of an online ugly sweater store seemed simple, manageable, and fun," says Trujillo, who has a full-time job as a communications manager at a pharmaceutical company but had entrepreneurial aspirations for many years. She enjoys perusing her network of thrift stores and after-Christmas sales "with an expert eye for ugly." Trujillo's ugly sweaters sell for between $25 and $40 ("The uglier the sweater, the more it costs," she says), and unit sales have more than tripled in just three years. Thanks to the Internet, Trujillo has sold sweaters to customers in South Africa, Australia, and the United Kingdom. The Ugly Sweater Store saw sales increase after posting a video featuring a fictitious rapper, Lil' Ugly, who saves a boring holiday party with his ugly sweater.[82] ■

Photo courtesy of UglySweaterStore.com

A major advantage of going into business part-time is the lower risk in case the venture flops. Many part-timers are "testing the entrepreneurial waters" to see whether their business ideas will work, whether there is sufficient demand for their products and services, and whether they enjoy being self-employed. As they grow, many successful part-time enterprises absorb more of entrepreneurs' time until they become full-time businesses.

Home-Based Businesses

Home-based businesses are booming! More than 12 percent of the households in the United States operate home-based businesses, generating $427 billion a year in sales.[83] Fifty-two percent of all small businesses are home based, and half of these have at least one employee, which means that home-based companies employ 13.2 million workers (including the owner).[84] Several factors make the home the first choice location for many entrepreneurs:

- Operating a business from home keeps start-up and operating costs to a minimum.

- Home-based companies allow owners to maintain a flexible lifestyle and work style. Many home-based entrepreneurs relish being part of the "open-collar workforce."

- Technology, which is transforming many ordinary homes into "electronic cottages," allows entrepreneurs to run a wide variety of businesses from their homes.

- Many entrepreneurs use the Internet to operate e-commerce businesses from their homes that literally span the globe.

In the past, home-based businesses tended to be rather mundane cottage industries, such as making crafts or sewing. Today's home-based businesses are more diverse; modern "home-preneurs" are more likely to be running high-tech or service companies with annual sales of hundreds of thousands of dollars. Thirty-five percent of home-based businesses generate more than $125,000 in annual revenue, and 8 percent generate more than $500,000 in annual revenue.[85]

Family Businesses

family-owned business
one that includes two or more members of a family with financial control of the company.

A **family-owned business** is one that includes two or more members of a family with financial control of the company. Family businesses are an integral part of our economy. Of the roughly 28 million businesses in the United States, 90 percent are family owned and managed. These companies account for 62 percent of total employment in the United States and 78 percent of all new jobs, pay 65 percent of all wages, and generate 64 percent of the nation's GDP. Not all of them are small; 33 percent of the *Fortune* 500 companies are family businesses.[86]

"When it works right," says one writer, "nothing succeeds like a family firm. The roots run deep, embedded in family values. The flash of the fast buck is replaced with long-term plans. Tradition counts."[87] Indeed, the lifespan of the typical family business is 24 years.[88] Despite their magnitude, family businesses face a major threat, a threat from within: management succession. Only 30 percent of family businesses survive to the second generation, just 12 percent make it to the third generation, and only 3 percent survive into the fourth generation and beyond. Business periodicals are full of stories describing bitter feuds among family members that have crippled or destroyed once thriving businesses. The co-owner of one family business explains the challenges of operating a family business this way: "The best part is working with family. The worst part is working with family."[89] To avoid the senseless destruction of thriving family businesses, owners should do the following:

- Work to build positive relationships among family members both at and away from work

- Demonstrate respect for other family members' abilities and talents

- Separate responsibilities in the company based on each person's interests, abilities, and talents

- Develop plans for minimizing the potentially devastating effects of estate taxes

- Develop plans for management succession long before retirement looms before them

Copreneurs

copreneurs
entrepreneurial couples who work together as co-owners of their businesses.

Copreneurs are entrepreneurial couples who work together as co-owners of their businesses. Nearly 4 million couples operate businesses together in the United States, but unlike the traditional "Mom and Pop" (Pop as "boss" and Mom as "subordinate"), copreneurs "create a division of labor that is based on expertise as opposed to gender," says one expert.[90] Managing a small business with a spouse may appear to be a recipe for divorce, but most copreneurs say not. "There is nothing like sharing an intense, life-changing experience with someone to bring you closer," says Caterina Fake, who with her husband Sewart Butterfield launched Flickr, a photo-sharing Web site. "Late nights, early mornings, laughter, terror, white-knuckle meetings with people you desperately need to give you money, getting your first check from a paying user—how can you beat it?"[91] Successful copreneurs learn to build the foundation for a successful working relationship before they ever launch their companies. Some of the characteristics they rely on include the following:

- An assessment of whether their personalities will mesh—or conflict—in a business setting

- Mutual respect for each other and one another's talents

- Compatible business and life goals—a common vision

- A view that they are full and equal partners, not a superior and a subordinate

- Complementary business skills that each acknowledges and appreciates and that lead to a unique business identity for each spouse

- The ability to keep lines of communication open, talking and listening to each other about personal as well as business issues

- A clear division of roles and authority, ideally based on each partner's skills and abilities, to minimize conflict and power struggles

- The ability to encourage each other and to lift up a disillusioned partner

- Separate work spaces that allow them to escape when the need arises

- Boundaries between their business life and their personal life so that one doesn't consume the other

- A sense of humor

- The realization that not every couple can work together

Although copreneuring isn't for everyone, it works extremely well for many couples and often leads to successful businesses. "Both spouses are working for a common purpose but also focusing on their unique talents," says a family business counselor. "With all these skills put together, one plus one equals more than two."[92]

ENTREPRENEURIAL PROFILE: Rina and Will Stein: Philip Stein After Rina Stein sold a business she had started with a partner, she and husband Will Stein decided to become copreneuers and launch Philip Stein, a company that markets luxury watches to upscale retailers such as Neiman Marcus, Saks Fifth Avenue, and Bloomingdale's. The Steins handle separate aspects of their thriving business, which generates nearly $40 million in annual sales. Rina, who has extensive experience in the watch industry, manages product development and manufacturing, and Will handles the company's marketing efforts, traveling extensively to call on current and prospective clients. The Steins say that they have learned the art of compromising and often consult with their employees when the two of them disagree on a decision. "We're partners in life and in business," says Will.[93] ■

Corporate Castoffs

Concentrating on shedding the excess bulk that took away their flexibility and speed, many large American corporations have been downsizing in an attempt to regain their competitive edge. For decades, one major corporation after another has announced layoffs—and not just among blue-collar workers. According to placement firm Challenger, Gray, and Christmas, from 1990 to 1999, corporations laid off an average of 43,400 employees per month; from 2000 to 2009, the average was 95,900 layoffs per month.[94] Executives and production workers alike have experienced job cuts, and these corporate castoffs have become an important source of entrepreneurial activity. Some 20 percent of discharged corporate managers have become entrepreneurs, and many of those left behind in corporate America would like to join them.

Many corporate castoffs are deciding that the best defense against future job insecurity is an entrepreneurial offense. Accustomed to the support in the corporations they left, many corporate castoffs decide to purchase franchises, where there is a built-in management system already in place. *Entrepreneur* magazine surveyed the companies on its Franchise 500 list recently and discovered that 77 percent of franchisors report that "second-career executives" (i.e., corporate castoffs) were among the primary purchasers of their franchises.[95]

Corporate Dropouts

The dramatic downsizing of corporate America has created another effect among the employees left after restructuring: a trust gap. The result of this trust gap is a growing number of dropouts from the corporate structure who then become entrepreneurs. Although their workdays may grow longer and their incomes may shrink, those who strike out on their own often find their work more rewarding and more satisfying because they are doing what they enjoy. Other entrepreneurs are inspired to launch their companies after being treated unfairly by large impersonal corporate entities.

ENTREPRENEURIAL PROFILE: Petra Cooper: Fifth Town Artisan Cheese Petra Cooper was president of a $47 million division of a major publishing company in Toronto, and although she earned an impressive salary, she was bored. In 2003, she decided to launch a business and began researching ideas that interested her. A food enthusiast, Cooper settled on starting an artisanal cheese company in nearby Prince Edward County on beautiful Lake Ontario. Cooper knew nothing about dairies and cheese making and kept her day job for two more years, taking online courses and using vacations to study the art of making cheese. In June 2005, she purchased 20 acres in Prince Edward County and launched Fifth Town Artisan Cheese. After overcoming several start-up challenges, Cooper won three awards from the prestigious American Cheese Society, which led to a significant increase in sales. At the end of her second year of operation, Cooper was just $20,000 short of hitting her break-even point. "I still worry about the monthly budget," she says, "but things are good. You don't feel dead when you go to work everyday."[96]

Because they have college degrees, a working knowledge of business, and years of management experience, both corporate dropouts and castoffs may ultimately increase the small business survival rate. A study by Richard O'Sullivan found that 64 percent of people starting businesses have at least some college education, and 14 percent have advanced degrees.[97] Better-trained, more experienced entrepreneurs are more likely to succeed.

Retiring Baby Boomers

Because people are living longer and are remaining active as they grow older, the ranks of older entrepreneurs are growing. In fact, according to studies by the Ewing Marion Kauffman Foundation, the level of entrepreneurial activity among people ages 55 to 64 actually exceeds that of people ages 20 to 34 (see Figure 1.5 on page 26). Research by the Kauffman Foundation also reveals that the average age of the founders of technology companies in the United States is 39, with twice as many over age 50 as under age 25.[98] One advantage that older entrepreneurs have is wisdom that has been forged by experience.

ENTREPRENEURIAL PROFILE: Anita Crook: Pouchee Inc. At age 63, Anita Crook, who had been frustrated by not being able to find specific items in her purse, designed a pocketbook organizer and launched a company named after her invention, Pouchee, to market it. Crook started the business from her home in Greenville, South Carolina, with $10,000 from her savings and the confidence that she was not the only woman who faced the problem of a cluttered purse. Her instinct was correct, and Pouchee now offers 25 different purse organizers that are made from a variety of materials and include pouches for cell phones, makeup, credit cards, keys, and other items. Metal rings at the top allow a user to switch the organizer from one purse to another in just seconds. Crook, who has received a patent on the Pouchee, takes a selective marketing approach, selling at wholesale to more than 1,500 small boutiques (only one shop per ZIP code) across the United States and Canada. Annual sales continue to grow by 45 to 70 percent per year.[99]

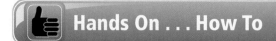

Hands On . . . How To

Launch a Successful Business While You Are Still in College

Collegiate entrepreneurs are becoming increasingly common as colleges and universities offer more courses and a greater variety of courses in the areas of entrepreneurship and small business management. Launching a business while in college offers many advantages, including access to research and valuable advice, but starting an entrepreneurial career also poses challenges, including a lack of financial resources, business experience, and time. What are some of the most common myths that prevent young people (not just college students) from launching businesses?

- **I don't have enough money to launch a business.** One of the greatest benefits of the shift in the United States to a service economy is that service businesses usually are very inexpensive to start. One young entrepreneur worked with a friend to launch a Web development company while in high school, and their total start-up cost was just $80.

- **I don't have enough time.** Many companies that have grown into very successful, mature businesses were started by entrepreneurs in their spare time. Everyone has the same 24 hours in a day. What matters is what you do with those hours.

- **I'm not smart enough to start a company.** SAT scores and grades have little correlation to one's ability to launch a successful business. Quite a few successful entrepreneurs, including Michael Dell (Dell Inc.), Richard Branson (Virgin), Walt Disney (Disney), Mark Zuckerberg (Facebook), and Debbi Fields (Mrs. Fields Cookies), dropped out of college to start their businesses.

- **I'm not majoring in business.** Success in entrepreneurship is not limited to students who earn business degrees. *Anyone* has the potential to be a successful entrepreneur. At the University of Miami, only 20 percent of the students who have participated in The Launch Pad, the school's start-up accelerator, have been business majors.

- **I'm not creative enough to come up with a good idea for a business.** As you will learn in Chapter 2, *everyone* has the potential to be creative. Some of the most successful businesses are the result of an entrepreneur who recognized a simple need that people had and created a business to meet that need.

- **I don't have any experience.** Neither did Bill Gates (Microsoft) and Michael Dell (Dell Inc.) when they launched their companies, and things worked out pretty well for both of them. Business experience can be an important factor in a company's success, but every entrepreneur has to start somewhere to gain that experience.

- **I might fail.** Failure *is* a possibility. In fact, the survival rate of new companies after five years is 51 percent. Ask yourself this: What is the worst that can happen if I launch a business and it fails? Entrepreneurs do not allow the fear of failure to stop them from trying to realize their dreams.

If you want to become a successful collegiate entrepreneur, what can you do to increase the chances of your success? The following tips will help.

Recognize That Starting a Business at an Early Age May Be to Your Advantage

Young people tend to be highly creative, and that can provide your company with a competitive advantage. In addition, young people often accomplish things simply because they don't know that they are not supposed to be able to do them!

Build a Business Plan

One of the best ways to lower the probability that your business will fail is to create a business plan. Doing so forces you to ask and then answer some tough questions about your idea and your proposed venture. "It's all about 'derisking' your idea," says Gregg Fairbrothers, who teaches entrepreneurship at Dartmouth's Tuck School of Business. "Identifying, unblinkingly, what could go wrong and taking whatever steps necessary to slash the odds that it will."

Use All the Resources That Are Available to You

Many colleges and universities now offer courses in entrepreneurship and small business management and have faculty members who are experts in the field. In many cases, the people who are teaching these classes are veteran entrepreneurs themselves with tremendous reservoirs of knowledge and experience. Some colleges provide special dorms for budding entrepreneurs that serve as business incubators. Smart collegiate entrepreneurs tap into the pool of resources that their campuses offer. Justin Gaither and Dan Thibodeau used the extensive network of contacts at the University of Miami's The Launch Pad to hone their idea for an online college roommate matching service. Their company, URoomSurf, now has 16 employees and 80,000 registered users.

Find a Mentor

Most young entrepreneurs have not had the opportunity to gain a wealth of business experience, but they do have access to mentors who do. Mike Brown, who recently won the top prize at the annual Global Student Entrepreneur Awards for his company ModBargains.com, a business that sells aftermarket products for modifying cars and trucks, says that his first boss, who owns several businesses, served as his mentor. ModBargains.com, which Brown started with fellow car enthusiast Ron Hay, now has more than 4,000 products available and has surpassed annual sales of $1 million.

Learn to Be a Guerrilla Marketer

Because they lack the deep pockets of their larger rivals, entrepreneurs must use their creativity, ingenuity, and street smarts to market their companies effectively. For example, the owner

(continued)

Hands On . . . How To *(continued)*

of a company that provided investigative services for law firms slipped his business cards into books in the legal section of the local library. Attorneys and paralegals doing research in the library assumed that other law firms used the company's services and began hiring the investigator. You will learn more about guerrilla marketing tactics in Chapter 8.

Learn to Be a "Bootstrapper"

Learning to start and manage a company with few resources is good training for any entrepreneur. In the early days of their start-ups, many successful entrepreneurs find creative ways to finance their businesses and to keep their operating expenses as low as possible.

Manage Your Time Wisely

Taking college classes and running a business places a large workload on any collegiate entrepreneur, one that demands good time management skills. The most successful entrepreneurs recognize the importance of controlling their schedules (as much as possible) and working as efficiently as they can.

Remember to Have Fun

College is supposed to be one of the best times of your life! Starting and running a business also can be one of the most rewarding experiences of your life. Doing both can double the fun, but it also can create a great deal of stress. Balance is the key.

Source: Based on Adam Bluestein and Amy Barrett, "Revitalize the American Dream: Bring on the Entrepreneurs!," *Inc.*, July/August 2010, pp. 76–88; David Whitford, "Can You Learn to Be an Entrepreneur?," *Fortune*, March 22, 2010, p. 66; Robert Sherman, "Student Entrepreneur Shares Hard-Won Lessons at YoungMoney.com," *Orange Entrepreneur*, Syracuse University, Fall 2007, p. 5; Daniel Jimenez, "The Best College Entrepreneurs of 2006," *Young Money*, July 2007, http://www.youngmoney .com/entrepreneur/student_entrepreneurs/070126; Michael Simmons, "Why Starting a Business Now May Be the Best Way to Achieve Your Dreams," *Young Money*, July 2003, http://www.youngmoney.com/entrepreneur/student_entrepreneurs/031010_01; and Scott Reeves, "How to Swing with Guerrilla Marketing," *Forbes*, June 8, 2006, http://www.forbes.com/2006/06/08/entrepreneurs-marketing-harley-davidson-cx_sr_0608askanexpert.html.

FIGURE 1.5

Entrepreneurial Activity by Age-Group

Source: Based on Kauffman Index of Entrepreneurial Activity, 1996–2010 Kauffman Foundation, 2011, p. 11.

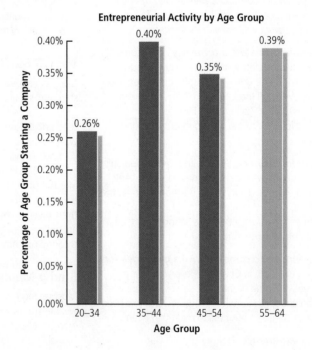

LO6

Describe the important role that small businesses play in our nation's economy.

small business

one that employs fewer than 100 people.

The Power of "Small" Business

Of the 28 million businesses in the United States, approximately 27.9 million, or 99.7 percent, are considered small. Although there is no universal definition of a small business (the U.S. Small Business Administration has more than 800 definitions of a small business based on industry categories), a common delineation of a **small business** is one that employs fewer than 100 people. They thrive in virtually every industry, although the majority of small companies are concentrated in the service and retail industries (see Figure 1.6). Although they may be small businesses, their contributions to the economy are anything but small. For example, small companies employ 49.2 percent of the nation's private sector workforce, even though they possess

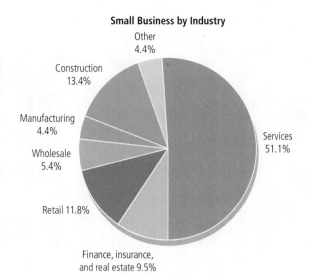

Small Business by Industry

Other
4.4%

Construction
13.4%

Manufacturing
4.4%

Wholesale
5.4%

Services
51.1%

Retail 11.8%

Finance, insurance,
and real estate 9.5%

FIGURE 1.6

Small Businesses by Industry

Source: Based on data from the U.S. Small Business Administration, 2009.

less than one-fourth of total business assets. Almost 90 percent of small businesses employ fewer than 20 workers, but small companies account for 43 percent of total private payroll in the United States. Because they are primarily labor intensive, small businesses actually create more jobs than do big businesses. In fact, between 1993 and 2009, small companies created 65 percent of the net new jobs in the U.S. economy.[100]

Researcher David Birch says that the ability to create jobs is not distributed evenly across the small business sector, however. His research shows that just 3 percent of small companies create 70 percent of the net new jobs in the economy, and they do so across all industry sectors, not just in "hot" industries. Birch calls these job-creating small companies **gazelles**, those growing at 20 percent or more per year for four years with at least $100,000 in annual sales. His research also identified "mice," small companies that never grow much and don't create many jobs. The majority of small companies are mice. Birch tabbed the country's largest businesses "elephants," which have continued to shed jobs for several years.[101]

Small businesses also produce 46 percent of the country's private GDP and account for 47 percent of business sales.[102] In fact, the U.S. small business sector is the world's third-largest "economy," trailing only the entire U.S. economy and China! One business writer describes the United States as "an entrepreneurial economy, a system built on nimble, low-overhead small companies with fluid workforces, rather than the massive conglomerates that upheld the economy for decades."[103]

Small companies also are incubators of new ideas, products, and services. Small firms actually create 16.5 times more patents per employee than large companies.[104] Traditionally, small businesses have played a vital role in innovation, and they continue to do so today. Many important inventions trace their roots to an entrepreneur, including the zipper, FM radio, the laser, the brassiere, air-conditioning, the escalator, the lightbulb, the personal computer, and the automatic transmission.

gazelles
small companies that are growing at 20 percent or more per year with at least $100,000 in annual sales; they create 70 percent of net new jobs in the economy.

Putting Failure into Perspective

Because of their limited resources, inexperienced management, and lack of financial stability, small businesses suffer relatively high mortality rates. As you learned earlier in this chapter, two years after start-up, 31 percent of small companies have failed, and after five years, 51 percent have failed.[105] Figure 1.7 shows the number of business births and the business terminations in recent years, clear evidence of the constant "churn" that exists as entrepreneurs create new businesses and others close. New companies that replace old ones with better ideas, market approaches, and products actually are a sign of a healthy, entrepreneurial economy.

Because they are building businesses in an environment filled with uncertainty and shaped by rapid change, entrepreneurs recognize that failure is likely to be part of their

LO7

Put failure into the proper perspective.

FIGURE 1.7

**Business Starts
and Closures**

Source: Based on data from
the U.S. Small Business
Administration, 2010.

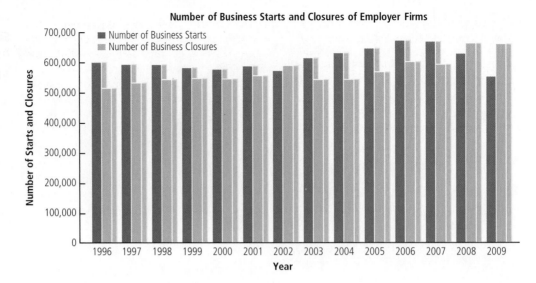

lives, but they are not paralyzed by that fear. "The excitement of building a new business from scratch is greater than the fear of failure," says one entrepreneur who failed in business several times before finally succeeding.[106] Entrepreneurs use their failures as a rallying point and as a means of refocusing their business ventures for success. They see failure for what it really is: an opportunity to learn what does not work! Successful entrepreneurs have the attitude that failures are simply stepping-stones along the path to success. Basketball legend Michael Jordan displayed the same attitude. "I've missed more than 9,000 shots in my career," he says. "I lost almost 300 games. Twenty-six times, I've been trusted to take the game-winning shot and *missed*. I've failed over and over and over again in my life. And that is why I succeed."[107]

Failure is a natural part of the creative process. The only people who never fail are those who never do anything or never attempt anything new. Baseball fans know that Babe Ruth held the record for career home runs (714) for many years, but how many know that he also held the record for strikeouts (1,330)? Successful entrepreneurs know that hitting an entrepreneurial home run requires a few strikeouts along the way, and they are willing to accept them. Failure is an inevitable part of being an entrepreneur, and true entrepreneurs don't quit when they fail. One entrepreneur whose business burned through $800 million of investors' money before folding says, "If you're an entrepreneur, you don't give up when times get tough."[108]

One hallmark of successful entrepreneurs is the ability to fail *intelligently*, learning why they failed so that they can avoid making the same mistake again. James Dyson, whose company makes one of the best-selling vacuum cleaners in the world, made 5,127 prototypes of his bagless vacuum cleaner before he hit on one that worked. "There were 5,126 failures," he says, "but I learned from each one. That's how I came up with a solution. So I don't mind failure."[109] Like Dyson, entrepreneurs know that business success depends on their ability not to avoid making mistakes but rather to be open to the lessons that each mistake teaches. They learn from their failures and use them as fuel to push themselves closer to their ultimate target. Entrepreneurs are less worried about what they might lose if they try something and fail than about what they might lose if they fail to try.

Entrepreneurial success requires both persistence and resilience, the ability to bounce back from failure. Thomas Edison discovered about 1,800 ways not to build a lightbulb before hitting on a design that worked. Walt Disney was fired from a newspaper job because, according to his boss, he "lacked imagination and had no good ideas." Disney also went bankrupt several times before he created Disneyland. R. H. Macy failed in business seven times before his retail store in New York City became a success. In the spirit of true entrepreneurship, these visionary business leaders refused to give up in the face of failure; they simply kept trying until they achieved success. When it comes to failure, entrepreneurs' motto seems to be, Failure is temporary; quitting is permanent.

ENTREPRENEURIAL PROFILE: Bill Bartmann: Bill Bartmann Enterprises Bill Bartmann, who founded Commercial Financial Services in the 1980s, built his company into one of the most successful small businesses in the United States. In 1998, Bartmann, who at the time was one of the wealthiest people in the country, lost everything—$3.5 billion—after Commercial Financial Services collapsed. Bartmann learned from his company's failure, and the tenacious entrepreneur launched another company, Bill Bartmann Enterprises, that has made consistent appearances on *Inc.* magazine's list of the 500 fastest-growing small companies in the United States. "I have always gotten back up after someone knocks me down," says Bartmann.[110] ■

How to Avoid the Pitfalls

LO8

Explain how an entrepreneur can avoid becoming another failure statistic.

Although failure can be a valuable part of the entrepreneurial process, no one sets out to fail in business. Now we must examine the ways to avoid becoming another failure statistic and gain insight into what makes a successful business.

Know Your Business in Depth

We have already emphasized the need for the right type of experience in the business you plan to start. Get the best education in your business area you possibly can *before* you set out on your own. Become a serious student of your industry. Read everything you can—trade journals, business periodicals, books, and research reports—relating to your industry and learn what it takes to succeed in it. Personal contact with suppliers, customers, trade associations, and others in the same industry is another excellent way to get that knowledge. Smart entrepreneurs join industry trade associations and attend trade shows to pick up valuable information and to make key contacts before they open their doors for business.

ENTREPRENEURIAL PROFILE: Steve Ells: Chipotle Mexican Grill Steve Ells has had a passion for food his entire life. As a child, while his friends watched cartoons, he watched cooking shows starring famous chefs Julia Child and Graham Kerr, the Galloping Gourmet. "In grammar school, I learned how to make hollandaise from my Mom, and in high school, I started throwing dinner parties and collecting cookbooks," he recalls. After graduating from the University of Colorado in Boulder, he enrolled in the Culinary Institute of America to refine his cooking skills. From there, he moved to San Francisco, where he worked at Stars, a restaurant that launched the careers of many renowned chefs, and learned the details of operating a restaurant. One day, while dining in a small taqueria in the Mission district of San Francisco, Ells noted the volume of customers the restaurant handled and the system it used to serve them extremely efficiently. Inspired by the experience, Ells decided to return to Denver, Colorado, where he launched the first Chipotle Mexican Grill in 1993 with the help of an $85,000 loan from his father. "My friends and family thought I was crazy," recalls Ells, "but I had a very clear vision of the way Chipotle was going to look and taste and feel. It was going to incorporate all of the things I had learned while at the Culinary Institute and at Stars." Ells's knowledge and experience in the restaurant industry has paid off. Today, Chipotle, a publicly held company, has nearly 1,100 restaurants and generates more than $1.8 billion in annual sales![111] ■

Develop a Solid Business Plan

For any entrepreneur, a well-written business plan is a crucial ingredient in preparing for business success. Without a sound business plan, a firm merely drifts along without any real direction. Yet entrepreneurs, who tend to be people of action, too often jump right into a business venture without taking time to prepare a written plan outlining the essence of the business. Not only does a plan provide a pathway to success, but it also creates a benchmark against which an entrepreneur can measure actual company performance. Building a successful business begins with implementing a sound business plan with laser-like focus.

A business plan allows entrepreneurs to replace sometimes faulty assumptions with facts before making the decision to go into business. The planning process forces entrepreneurs to ask and then answer some difficult, challenging, and crucial questions.

ENTREPRENEURIAL PROFILE: Tom Szaky: TerraCycle In his freshman year at Princeton, Tom Szaky created a business plan that helped him launch TerraCycle International, a company that uses red worms to compost food waste into potting soil and liquid all-natural fertilizers guaranteed not to burn plants. Szaky's ingenious plan was to sell waste disposal services to restaurants, schools, penitentiaries, and other institutions and to allow the worms to transform the waste into vermicompost, which the company turns into potting soil and fertilizers and sells to garden centers, nurseries, home superstores, and other retail outlets. Szaky's research told him that the organic segments of the fertilizer and potting soil industry are multi-billion-dollar businesses and have been growing at double-digit rates for the last several years. TerraCycle sells its all-natural plant foods and other products through retail outlets across the United States and is planning to expand into global markets as well. Szaky not only used his business plan to make TerraCycle a success but, in the early days of the company, also used it as a source of financing, entering numerous business plan competitions to win prize money that kept the young company afloat.[112] ∎

We will discuss the process of developing a business plan in Chapter 4.

Manage Financial Resources

The best defense against financial problems is to develop a practical information system and then use this information to make business decisions. No entrepreneur can maintain control over a business unless he or she is able to judge its financial health.

The first step in managing financial resources effectively is to have adequate start-up capital. Too many entrepreneurs start their businesses undercapitalized. One experienced business owner advises, "Estimate how much capital you need to get the business going and then double that figure." His point is well taken; it almost always costs more (and takes longer) to launch a business than any entrepreneur expects. Jake Burton, founder of Burton Snowboards, a company that dominates the snowboard industry with 58 percent market share, made that mistake when he started his now successful company in 1977 straight out of college. "I lost [my start-up capital] before I knew what had happened," he says. "I underestimated the cost and time it would take to get the business going."[113]

The most valuable financial resource to any small business is *cash*. Although earning a profit is essential to its long-term survival, a business must have an adequate supply of cash to pay its bills and obligations. Some entrepreneurs count on growing sales to supply their company's cash needs, but this almost never happens. Growing companies usually consume more cash than they generate, and the faster they grow, the more cash they gobble up! Business history is littered with failed companies whose founders had no idea how much cash their businesses were generating and were spending cash as if they were certain there was "plenty more where that came from." We will discuss cash management techniques in Chapter 13.

Understand Financial Statements

Every business owner must depend on records and financial statements to know the condition of his or her business. All too often, entrepreneurs use these only for tax purposes and not as vital management control devices. To truly understand what is going on in the business, an owner must have at least a basic understanding of accounting and finance.

When analyzed and interpreted properly, these financial statements are reliable indicators of a small firm's health. They can be quite helpful in signaling potential problems. For example, declining sales, slipping profits, rising debt, and deteriorating working capital are all symptoms of potentially lethal problems that require immediate attention. We will discuss financial statement analysis in Chapter 12.

Learn to Manage People Effectively

No matter what kind of business you launch, you must learn to manage people. Every business depends on a foundation of well-trained, motivated employees. No business owner can do everything alone. The people an entrepreneur hires ultimately determine the heights to which the company can climb—or the depths to which it can plunge. Attracting and retaining a corps of quality employees is no easy task, however. It remains a challenge for every small business owner. "In the end, your most dominant sustainable resource is the quality of the people you have," says one small business expert.[114] At Chipotle Mexican Grill, Steve Ells is quick to point to the company's dedicated 26,500 employees as one key to success. "We develop our people and promote from within," says Ells, pointing out that 90 percent of Chipotle's salaried managers and 95 percent of its hourly managers are promoted from within the company.[115] We will discuss the techniques of managing and motivating people effectively in Chapter 16.

Set Your Business Apart from the Competition

The formula for almost certain business failure involves becoming a "me-too business"—merely copying whatever the competition is doing. Most successful entrepreneurs find a way to convince their customers that their companies are superior to their competitors even if they sell similar products or services. It is especially important for small companies going up against larger, more powerful rivals with greater financial resources. Ideally, the basis for differentiating a company from its competitors is founded in what it does best. For small companies, that basis often is customer service, convenience, speed, quality, or whatever else is important to attracting and keeping satisfied customers. We will discuss the strategies for creating a unique footprint in the marketplace in Chapters 3 and 8.

Maintain a Positive Attitude

Achieving business success requires an entrepreneur to maintain a positive mental attitude toward business and the discipline to stick with it. Successful entrepreneurs recognize that their most valuable resource is their time, and they learn to manage it effectively to make themselves and their companies more productive. None of this, of course, is possible without passion—passion for their businesses, their products or services, their customers, and their communities. Passion is what enables a failed business owner to get back up, try again, and make it to the top! One business writer says that growing a successful business requires entrepreneurs to have great faith in themselves and their ideas, great doubt concerning the challenges and inevitable obstacles they will face as they build their businesses, and great effort—lots of hard work—to make their dreams become reality.[116]

Conclusion

As you can see, entrepreneurship lies at the heart of this nation's free enterprise system; small companies truly are the backbone of our economy. Their contributions are as many and as diverse as the businesses themselves. Indeed, diversity is one of the strengths of the U.S. small business sector. Although there are no secrets to becoming a successful entrepreneur, there are steps that entrepreneurs can take to enhance the probability of their success. The remainder of this book will explore those steps and how to apply them to the process of launching a successful business with an emphasis on building a sound business plan.

- Chapter 2, "Inside the Entrepreneurial Mind: From Ideas to Reality," explores the creative process that lies at the heart of entrepreneurship and offers practical tips on how you can stimulate your own creativity.

- Section 2, "Building a Business Plan: Beginning Considerations" (Chapters 3 to 7), discusses the classic start-up questions every entrepreneur faces, particularly conducting a feasibility analysis, developing a strategy, choosing a form of ownership, alternative methods for becoming a business owner (franchising and buying an existing business), and building a business plan.

- Section 3, "Building a Business Plan: Marketing Considerations" (Chapters 8 to 11), focuses first on creating an effective marketing plan for a small company. These chapters address creating an effective e-commerce strategy, establishing pricing and credit strategies, and penetrating global markets.

- Section 4, "Building a Business Plan: Financial Matters" (Chapters 12 to 14), explains how to develop the financial component of a business plan, including creating projected financial statements and forecasting cash flow. These chapters also offer existing business owners practical financial management tools and explain how to find the sources of funding, both debt and equity, necessary to launch a business.

- Section 5, "Putting the Business Plan to Work: Making the New Venture a Success" (Chapters 15 and 16), discusses how entrepreneurs can select the right location and layout for their businesses. This section also provides useful techniques for assembling a strong new venture team and leading its members to success and discusses the importance of creating a management succession plan to ensure that a company successfully makes the transition to the next generation of owners.

As you can see, the journey down the road of entrepreneurship will be a fascinating and exciting one. Let's get started!

Chapter Summary by Learning Objective

1. Define the role of the entrepreneur in business in the United States and around the world.

Entrepreneurship is thriving in the United States, but the current wave of entrepreneurship is not limited to the United States; many nations across the globe are seeing similar growth in their small business sectors. A variety of competitive, economic, and demographic shifts have created a world in which "small is beautiful."

Capitalist societies depend on entrepreneurs to provide the drive and risk taking necessary for the system to supply people with the goods and services they need.

2. Describe the entrepreneurial profile.

Entrepreneurs have some common characteristics, including a desire for responsibility, a preference for moderate risk, confidence in their ability to succeed, desire for immediate feedback, a high energy level, a future orientation, skill at organizing, and a value of achievement over money. In a phrase, they are tenacious high achievers.

3-A. Describe the benefits of entrepreneurship.

Driven by these personal characteristics, entrepreneurs establish and manage small businesses to gain control over their lives, make a difference in the world, become self-fulfilled, reap unlimited profits, contribute to society, and do what they enjoy doing.

3-B. Describe the drawbacks of entrepreneurship.

Entrepreneurs also face certain disadvantages, including uncertainty of income, the risk of losing their investments (and more), long hours and hard work, a lower quality of life until the business gets established, high stress levels, and complete decision-making responsibility.

4. Explain the forces that are driving the growth of entrepreneurship.

Several factors are driving the boom in entrepreneurship, including the portrayal of entrepreneurs as heroes, better entrepreneurial education, economic and demographic factors, a shift to a service economy, technological advances, more independent lifestyles, and increased international opportunities.

5. Explain the cultural diversity of entrepreneurship.

Several groups are leading the nation's drive toward entrepreneurship: young people, women, minorities, immigrants, part-timers, home-based business owners, family business owners, copreneurs, corporate castoffs, corporate dropouts, social entrepreneurs, and retired baby boomers.

6. Describe the important role that small businesses play in our nation's economy.

The small business sector's contributions are many. They make up 99.7 percent of all businesses, employ 51 percent of the private sector workforce, have created two-thirds to three-fourths of the net new jobs in the economy, produce 51 percent of the country's private GDP, and account for 47 percent of all business sales.

7. Put failure into the proper perspective.

Entrepreneurs recognize that failure is a natural part of the creative process. Successful entrepreneurs have the attitude that failures are simply stepping-stones along the path to success, and they refuse to be paralyzed by a fear of failure.

8. Explain how an entrepreneur can avoid becoming another failure statistic.

Entrepreneurs can employ several general tactics to avoid these pitfalls. They should know their

businesses in depth, prepare a solid business plan, manage financial resources effectively, understand financial statements, learn to manage people, set their businesses apart from the competition, and maintain a positive attitude.

Discussion Questions

1. What forces have led to the boom in entrepreneurship in the United States and across the globe?
2. What is an entrepreneur? Give a brief description of the entrepreneurial profile.
3. *Inc.* magazine claims, "Entrepreneurship is more mundane than it's sometimes portrayed . . . you don't need to be a person of mythical proportions to be very, very successful in building a company." Do you agree? Explain.
4. What are the major benefits of business ownership?
5. Which of the potential drawbacks to business ownership are most critical?
6. Briefly describe the role of the following groups in entrepreneurship: young people, women, minorities, immigrants, part-timers, home-based business owners, family business owners, copreneurs, corporate castoffs, corporate dropouts, social entrepreneurs, and retired baby boomers.

7. What is a small business? What contributions do they make to our economy?
8. Describe the small business failure rate.
9. Outline the causes of business failure. Which problems cause most business failures?
10. How does the typical entrepreneur view the possibility of business failure?
11. How can the small business owner avoid the common pitfalls that often lead to business failures?
12. Why is it important to study the small business failure rate and to understand the causes of business failures?
13. Explain the typical entrepreneur's attitude toward risk.
14. Are you interested in some day launching a small business? If so, when? What kind of business? Describe it. What can you do to ensure its success?

Business Plan Pro™ This book may include the best-selling business planning software *Business Plan Pro™* by Palo Alto Software, Inc. This software can assist you in four ways as you begin to build your business plan.

1. *Structure: Business Plan Pro™* provides a structure to the process of creating a business plan. There are general business plan standards and expectations, and *Business Plan Pro™* has a recognized and well-received format that lends credibility to your plan. A comprehensive plan that follows a generally recognized outline adds credibility and, if it is a part of the plan's purpose, of attracting financing.
2. *Efficiency: Business Plan Pro™* will save you time. Once you become familiar with the interface, *Business Plan Pro™* creates all the essential financial statements for you based on the information the software prompts you to enter. The software automatically formats the income statement, balance sheet, and the profit-and-loss statement.
3. *Examples: Business Plan Pro™* includes a variety of sample business plans. Seeing examples of other plans can be a helpful learning tool as you create a plan that is unique based on your product or service and your market.

4. *Appearance: Business Plan Pro™* automatically incorporates relevant tables and graphs into your text. The result is a cohesive business plan that combines text, tables, and charts to enhance the impact of your plan.

Writing a business plan is more than just creating a document. The process itself can be the most valuable benefit of all. A business plan "tells the story" about your business. It addresses why your business concept is viable, who your market is, what you offer to that market, why your offer represents a unique value, how you are going to reach customers, how your business is going to be funded, and, based on your projections, how it will result in financial success.

Creating a business plan is a learning process. For the start-up business, completing a business plan allows the entrepreneur to gain insight before the business launches. The current business owner benefits from writing a business plan to better address challenges and optimize opportunities. *Business PlanPro™* is a tool to assist with this process.

The *EasyPlan Wizard™* within the software guides you through the process by asking a series of questions to bring the vision of your business to paper. The wizard will skip from section to section as you build concepts about your business, the products and services you offer, the markets you will serve, and your financial information. You can use the wizard or follow the sections of the outline based on the guidance from each chapter. Both options will lead you through the entire process and help you create a comprehensive business plan.

At the end of each chapter in this book, you will find a *Business Plan Pro*™ activity that applies the concepts discussed in the chapter. These activities will enable you to build your plan one step at a time in manageable components. You will be able to assemble your plan in a way that captures the information you know about your business and also raise key questions that will push you to learn more in areas you may not have considered. *Business Plan Pro*™ will guide you through each step to complete your plan as you progress through this book. This step represents a critical step toward launching a business or establishing a better understanding of an existing business.

Business Plan Exercises

The following set of exercises leads you through the process of creating your own business plan. If you or your planning team does not have a business concept in mind, select a business idea and work through these steps. Future chapters will ask you to review, validate, and change this concept as needed.

On the Web

Visit the companion Web site designed for this book at www.pearsonhighered.com/scarborough. Find the cover of this book, the seventh edition of *Essentials of Small Business Management*, and click on the Companion Site link. Find the Business Plan Resource tab in the left-hand navigation. The information and links here will be a resource for you as you progress through each chapter to develop your business plan.

Sample Plans

Click on the Sample Plan Browser and review these two plans: The Supreme Courts and InteliChild.com.

- Compare the table of contents of each plan. What differences do you notice?
- Review the executive summary of each plan. What is the key difference in these two business concepts?
- What similarities do the plans share?
- What are common tables and charts within the text? What value do these tables and charts offer?

In the Software

Follow the instructions included on the CD to install *Business Plan Pro*™. After opening *Business Plan Pro*™—preferably on a PC with an Internet connection—open the Sample Plan Browser. The Sample Plan Browser allows you to preview a library of sample business plans. You will find numerous business plan examples ranging from restaurants to nonprofit organizations. A search tool will help sort through these plans based on a specific industry or key words. Don't be concerned about finding a plan that is identical to your business concept. Look for plans that contain parallel characteristics, such as a product or service plan, or one that targets consumers versus business customers. Review several of these plans to get a better idea of the outline and content. This may give you a clearer vision of how your finished business plan may look.

Building Your Business Plan

Open *Business Plan Pro*™ and select the choice that starts a new plan. Optional resources help you throughout the experience of creating a business plan. For example, the movie offers an animated and audio overview of the software. Using the *EasyPlan Wizard*™ asks about your start date, the title of your plan, and other basic information, such as the following:

- Do you sell products or services?
- Is your business a profit or a nonprofit organization?
- Is your business a start-up operation or an ongoing business?
- What kind of business plan do you want to create?
- Do you want to include the SWOT analysis?
- Will the business have a Web site?
- A series of revenue and expense questions structure the financial aspects of your plan with assistance throughout.
- Do you want to prepare a plan for three years (a standard plan) or a longer-term plan of five years?

Save these decisions by using the drop-down menu under File and clicking on Save or by clicking on the save icon at the top right of the menu bar. You can change your response to these decisions at any time. Review the plan outline by clicking on the Preview icon on the top of your screen or by clicking on File, Print, and then Preview within the Print window to see the outline of your business plan. *Business Plan Pro*™ will enable you to change and modify the plan outline in any way you choose as you progress through each chapter.

Beyond the Classroom . . .

1. Choose an entrepreneur in your community and interview him or her. What's the "story" behind the business? How well does the entrepreneur fit the entrepreneurial profile described in this chapter? What advantages and disadvantages does the owner see in owning a business? What advice would he or she offer to someone considering launching a business?

2. Select one of the categories under the section "The Cultural Diversity of Entrepreneurship" in this chapter and research it in more detail. Find examples of business owners in that category. Prepare a brief report for your class.

3. Search through recent business publications (especially those focusing on small companies) and find an example of an entrepreneur, past or present, who exhibits the entrepreneurial spirit of striving for success in the face of failure. Prepare a brief report for your class.

Endnotes

1. Donna Kelly, Niels Bosma, and Jose Ernesto Amoros, *Global Entrepreneurship Monitor 2010 Global Report*, Babson College, Universidad del Desarrollo, and Global Entrepreneurship Research Consortium, 2011, pp. 22–23.
2. Robert W. Farlie, *Kauffman Index of Entrepreneurial Activity 1996–2010*, Ewing Marion Kauffman Foundation, March 2011, p. 2.
3. *The Small Business Economy: A Report to the President* (Washington, DC: Small Business Administration, Office of Advocacy, U.S. Government Printing Office, 2010), p. 126.
4. Jeff Houck, "When the Going Gets Tough, the Tough Make Fudge," *Tampa Bay Online*, September 26, 2010, http://www2.tbo.com/content/2010/sep/26/tr-when-the-going-gets-tough-the-tough-make-fudge; "About Us," Oh Fudge!, http://www.ohfudgeinternational.com/about_us.html.
5. Howard H. Stevens, "We Create Entrepreneurs," *Success*, September 1995, p. 51.
6. Niels Bosma, Kent Jones, Erkko Autio, and Jonathan Levie, *Global Entrepreneurship Monitor 2007 Executive Report*, Babson College, London School of Business, and Global Entrepreneurship Research Consortium, 2008, pp. 6, 23; Erkko Autio, *2007 Global Report on High-Growth Entrepreneurship*, Babson College, London School of Business, and Global Entrepreneurship Research Consortium, 2008, p. 31; William D. Bygrave and Mark Quill, *2006 Financing Report*, Babson College, London School of Business, and Global Entrepreneurship Research Consortium, 2008, p. 4.
7. "Entrepreneurship Is Going Global," Babson College Newsroom, January 18, 2008, http://www3.babson.edu/Newsroom/Releases/GEM-2007-Global-Report.cfm.
8. "Tashasbos Students Create Successful Businesses in Afghanistan," *Overseas Report*, Center for Private Enterprise, Number 46, Fall 2010, pp. 1–2; Kim Bettcher, "Tashabos Students Create Successful Businesses in Afghanistan," Community of Young Entrepreneurs, December 15, 2010, http://www.reformsnetwork.org/youth/?p=925#more-925.
9. Thomas K. McCraw, "Mapping the Entrepreneurial Psyche," *Inc.*, August 2007, pp. 73–74.
10. David McClelland, *The Achieving Society* (Princeton, NJ: Van Nostrand, 1961), p. 16.
11. Rod Kurtz, "What It Takes," *Inc. 500*, Fall 2004, p. 120.
12. Richard Branson, "The Art of the Calculated Risk," *Entrepreneur*, November 1, 2010, http://www.entrepreneur.com/article/217479; "Frequently Asked Questions," Virgin Atlantic Airways, http://www.virgin-atlantic.com/en/jp/allaboutus/pressoffice/faq/pretaxprofits.jsp.
13. Evan T. Robbins, "E Is for Entrepreneurship," *Syllabus*, November 2002, p. 24.
14. "First Major Study on Gen Y and Boomer Entrepreneurs Shows Business Confidence and Different Appetites for Risk," American Express, April 26, 2007, http://home3.americanexpress.com/corp/pc/2007/geny.asp.
15. Alyson Shontell, "How 15 Failed Businesses Led One Founder to a Multi-Million-Dollar Success," *Business Insider*, December 29, 2010, http://www.businessinsider.com/how-15-failed-businesses-led-the-founder-of-tweezerman-to-a-multi-million-dollar-empire-2010-12.
16. Jonah Lehrer, "Measurements That Mislead," *Wall Street Journal*, April 2, 2011, http://online.wsj.com/article/SB10001424052748704471904576230931647955902.html; Jonah Lehrer, "Which Traits Predict Success? (The Importance of Grit)," *Wired*, March 14, 2011, http://www.wired.com/wiredscience/2011/03/what-is-success-true-grit.
17. Dane Stangler, *The Economic Future Just Happened*, Ewing Marion Kauffman Foundation, 2009, p. 4.
18. David Van Den Berg, "Recessions and Entrepreneurship," *Region Focus*, Fall 2009, pp. 12–14; Darren Dahl, "Clif Bar: How a Husband-Wife Team Built a $235 Million Empire," *AOL Small Business*, June 14, 2010, http://smallbusiness.aol.com/2010/06/14/clif-bar-how-a-husband-wife-team-built-a-235-million-empire; "Who We Are," Clif Bar, http://www.clifbar.com/soul/who_we_are.
19. Gayle Sato Stodder, "Goodbye Mom & Pop," *Entrepreneur*, May 1999, p. 112.
20. "First Major Study on Gen Y and Boomer Entrepreneurs Shows Business Confidence and Different Appetites for Risk," American Express, April 26, 2007, http://home3.americanexpress.com/corp/pc/2007/geny.asp.
21. Will Schroter, "Sleep Sounds Nice, but for Start-Up Founders, It's an Unaffordable Luxury," BizJournals.com, September 3, 2007, http://www.bizjournals.com/extraedge/consultants/go_big/2007/09/03/column10.html.
22. Eric Markowitz, "What It Takes to Become a Serial Entrepreneur," *Inc.*, September 23, 2010, http://www.inc.com/news/articles/2010/serial-entrepreneurs-share-insight-and-advice.html; "About Alex Mashinksy," http://www.mashinsky.com/who_is_alex_mashinsky.html.
23. Donna J. Kelley, Slavica Singer, and Mike Herrington, *Global Entrepreneurship Monitor 2011 Global Report*, Babson College, Universidad del Desarrollo, and Universiti Tun Abdul Razak, 2011, pp. 10–11.
24. Siamak Taghaddos, "Results Are In: Entrepreneur State of Mind 2010," *Grasslands: The Entrepreneurial Blog*, April 12, 2010, http://grasshopper.com/blog/founders/2010/04/12/results-are-in-the-entrepreneur-state-of-mind-2010.
25. Meg Cadoux Hirshberg, "Once More into the Breach," *Inc.*, September 2010, p. 41.
26. Jessi Hempel, "Social Network Pioneers Michael and XoChi Birch Cashed Out But Never Stopped Thinking about New Ventures," *Fortune*, November 15, 2010, p. 147; Maija Palmer, "New Lease on Life after Bebo," *Financial Times*, June 29, 2010, http://www.ft.com/cms/s/0/f9a9b81e-83a8-11df-b6d5-00144feabdc0.html#axzz1NHB3PbgK.
27. Stephanie Clifford, "They Just Can't Stop Themselves," *Inc.*, March 2005, p. 104.
28. Thomas K. McCraw, "Mapping the Entrepreneurial Psyche," *Inc.*, August 2007, p. 73.
29. George Gendron, "The Origin of the Entrepreneurial Species," *Inc.*, February 2000, p. 107.

30. S. K. Murphy, "Saras Sarasvathy's Effectual Reasoning Model for Expert Entrepreneurs," *SKMurphy*, February 7, 2010, http://www.skmurphy.com/blog/2010/02/07/saras-sarasvathys-effectual-reasoning-model-for-expert-entrepreneurs; Leigh Buchanan, "How Great Entrepreneurs Think," *Inc.*, February 2011, pp. 54–61.

31. Scott Edward Walker, "What Makes a Great Entrepreneur?," *Venture Beat*, January 17, 2011, http://venturebeat.com/2011/01/17/what-makes-a-great-entrepreneur; Steven Swinford, "Malcolm Gladwell Says That If You Want to Shine, Put in 10,000 Hours," *Sunday Times*, October 19, 2008, http://entertainment.timesonline.co.uk/tol/arts_and_entertainment/books/article4969415.ece.

32. "History: Milton S. Hershey," Hershey Entertainment and Resorts, http://www.hersheypa.com/town_of_hershey/history/index.html.

33. Dan Goodgame, "Our Roving Editor," *FSB*, April 2008, p. 10.

34. John Case, "The Origins of Entrepreneurship," *Inc.*, June 1989, p. 52.

35. Priya Jain, "Master of His Own Destiny," *Express Computer*, March 12, 2007, http://www.expresscomputeronline.com/20070312/technologylife03.shtml.

36. "I Started a Business in Paradise," *CNNMoney*, November 2, 2010, http://money.cnn.com/galleries/2010/smallbusiness/1010/gallery.best_places_paradise/3.html; "About Safari Surfing School," http://www.safarisurfschool.com/about.html.

37. Issie Lapowsky, "Entrepreneurs We Love: For Tackling Third World Poverty Here at Home," *Inc.*, December 2010/January 2011, p. 98; "New Mexico Success Story: Sacred Power Corporation," U.S. Small Business Administration, http://www.expresscomputeronline.com/20070312/technologylife03.shtml.

38. Gayle Sato Stodder, "Are You Satisfied?" *Entrepreneur*, October 1999, p. 86.

39. "Small Business," *Wall Street Journal*, December 16, 2010, p. B8.

40. "The Forbes 400: The Richest People in America," *Forbes*, http://www.forbes.com/wealth/forbes-400/list.

41. "Most Middle Class Millionaires Are Entrepreneurs," *Small Business Labs*, May 13, 2008, http://genylabs.typepad.com/small_biz_labs/2008/05/most-middle-cla.html; Thomas Kostigen, "The 'Middle Class Millionaire,'" *MarketWatch*, March 5, 2008, http://www.marketwatch.com/news/story/rise-middle-class-millionaire-reshaping-us/story.aspx?guid=%7B6CF2AF9B-7A4C-487E-8AD1-8B49A6A87104%7D.

42. Eric Markowitz, "Entrepreneurs We Love: Anthony Wood," *Inc.*, December 2010/January 2011, p. 96; Michael Hiltzik, "Roku Box Developer Has a Sixth Sense about Video," *Los Angeles Times*, October 13, 2010, http://articles.latimes.com/2010/oct/13/business/la-fi-hiltzik-20101013.

43. "Distrust, Discontent, Anger, and Partisan Rancor: The People and Their Government," Pew Research Center, April 18, 2010, http://people-press.org/2010/04/18/section-3-government-challenges-views-of-institutions.

44. Donna Fenn, "Tony Hsieh: How to Find the Perfect Business Opportunity," *BNET*, April 1, 2011, http://www.bnet.com/blog/entrepreneurs/tony-hsieh-how-to-find-the-perfect-business-opportunity/1735.

45. Sharon Gillen, "Entrepreneur Walks into Custom-Made Shoe Business," *Denver Business Journal*, May 23, 2010, http://www.bizjournals.com/denver/stories/2010/05/24/smallb1.html; "Online Design Studio Where Shoe Lovers Can Design Their Own Shoes," *Luxury Gifts*, May 22, 2011, http://www.luxurygive.com/online-design-studio-where-shoe-lovers-can-design-their-own-shoes.

46. Romy Ribitzky, "It Pays at the Top," *Portfolio*, April 20, 2011, http://www.portfolio.com/views/blogs/daily-brief/2011/04/20/ceos-earn-average-of-343-times-the-average-employee-salary.

47. "FAQs," U.S. Small Business Administration, 2010, http://web.sba.gov/faqs/faqIndexAll.cfm?areaid=24.

48. "Employment Situation Summary," Bureau of Labor Statistics, May 6, 2011, http://www.bls.gov/news.release/empsit.nr0.htm.

49. Lymari Morales, "Self-Employed Workers Clock the Most Hours Each Week," *Gallup*, August 26, 2009, http://www.gallup.com/poll/122510/self-employed-workers-clock-hours-week.aspx.

50. Shandra Martinez, "More Than Half of All Small Business Owners Won't Take Vacations This Summer, according to Survey," *MLive*, May 25, 2011, http://www.mlive.com/business/west-michigan/index.ssf/2011/05/more_than_half_small_business.html.

51. Shandra Martinez, "More Than Half of All Small Business Owners Won't Take Vacations This Summer, according to Survey," *MLive*, May 25, 2011, http://www.mlive.com/business/west-michigan/index.ssf/2011/05/more_than_half_small_business.html.

52. Rosa Alphonso, "Small Business Optimism Is on an Upswing, according to the OPEN from American Express Small Business Monitor," *American Express*, May 24, 2007, http://home3.americanexpress.com/corp/pc/2007/monitor.asp.

53. Stephanie Clifford and Rory Evans, "Romance: Love for the Workaholic," *Inc.*, February 2005, p. 53; April Y. Pennington, "Almost Famous," *Entrepreneur*, August 2005, p. 140.

54. Dennis Jacobe, "Most Small Business Owners Don't Plan to 'Fully' Retire," *Gallup*, March 10, 2008, http://www.gallup.com/poll/104866/four-smallbusiness-owners-dont-plan-retire.aspx.

55. Kristin Edelhauser Chessman, "Confessions of Workaholics," *Entrepreneur*, March 28, 2008, http://www.entrepreneur.com/worklife/healthandfitness/article191950.html.

56. Moe Bedard, "Wells Fargo Survey Says Business Owners Delaying Retirement," *LoanSafe*, August 31, 2010, http://www.loansafe.org/wells-fargo-survey-says-business-owners-delaying-retirement.

57. Judith Cone, "Teaching Entrepreneurship in Colleges and Universities: How (and Why) a New Academic Field Is Being Built," Ewing Marion Kauffman Foundation, http://www.kauffman.org/entrepreneurship/teaching-entrepreneurship-in-colleges.aspx.

58. Tricia Duryee, "Rent the Runway Gets $15 Million from Kleiner Perkins to be the Netflix of Fashion," *All Things Digital*, May 23, 2011, http://allthingsd.com/20110523/rent-the-runway-gets-15-million-from-kleiner-perkins-to-be-the-netflix-of-fashion; Tiffany Black, "30 under 30: Jennifer Hyman and Jenny Fleiss, Founders of Rent the Runway," *Inc.*, July 19, 2010, http://www.inc.com/30under30/2010/profile-jennifer-hyman-jenny-fleiss-rent-the-runway.html?nav=related.

59. "The Service Sector: Projections and Current Stats," Department for Professional Employees, AFL-CIO, May 2011, p. 1; "GDP Composition by Sector," *World Fact Book*, Central Intelligence Agency, https://www.cia.gov/library/publications/the-world-factbook/fields/2012.html.

60. "NFIB and Visa Announce 2009 'Young Entrepreneur of the Year' Winner," National Federation of Independent Businesses, June 25, 2009, http://www.nfib.com/press-media/press-media-item?cmsid=49403; "NFIB and Visa Announce 'Young Entrepreneur of the Year' Winner Jay Shechtman, Young Entrepreneur Foundation, July 15, 2009, http://youngentrepreneurfoundation.wordpress.com/2009/07/15/nfib-and-visa-inc-announce-2009-young-entrepreneur-of-the-year-winner-jay-schectman.

61. Jimbo Wales, "The Knowledge Maestro," *Fortune*, September 17, 2007, p. 36.

62. "Unusual Business News," May 2008, http://unusualbusinessnews.blogspot.com/search?updated-min=2008-01-01T00%3A00%3A00-08%3A00&updated-max=2009-01-01T00%3A00%3A00-08%3A00&max-results=32.

63. "Small Business Marketing: Social, Search Fastest-Growing Channels," *MarketingProfs*, March 17, 2011, http://www.marketingprofs.com/charts/2011/4643/small-business-marketing-social-search-fastest-growing-channels.

64. Joel Holland, "Dressed for Success," *Entrepreneur*, April 2011, p. 84.

65. *Report to the President on the National Export Initiative*, Export Promotion Cabinet, September 2010, p. 10.

66. Ryan Underwood, "Going Global: Made to Travel," *Inc.*, March 2011, pp. 96–98.

67. *Junior Achievement's 2010 Teens and Entrepreneurship Survey: Empowering Entrepreneurship Success*, Junior Achievement, p. 7.

68. "Business Ownership Is Attractive to a Substantial Amount of America's Young People, Survey Reveals," Ewing Marion Kauffman Foundation Youth Entrepreneurship Survey 2010, http://www.kauffman.org/entrepreneurship/youth-entrepreneurship-survey-2010.aspx.

69. Sharon Jayson, "Gen Y Makes a Mark, and Their Imprint Is Entrepreneurship," *USA Today*, December 8, 2006, http://www.usatoday.com/news/nation/2006-12-06-gen-next-entrepreneurs_x.htm; Donna Fenn, "30 under 30: Ben Kaufman," *Inc.*, July 2007, http://www.inc.com/30under30/2007/1-kaufman.html.

70. Renee Martin, "Women Entrepreneurs Close the Gap and Dream Big," *Forbes*, June 7, 2010, http://www.forbes.com/2010/06/07/small-business-loans-funding-forbes-woman-entrepreneurs-great-ideas.html.

71. *State of Women-Owned Businesses Report*, American Express Open, 2011, p. 2.

72. *Women Small Business Owners Will Create 5+ Million New Jobs by 2018, Transforming the Workplace for Millions of Americans*, Guardian Life Small Business Research Institute, December 2009, p. 3.

73. Erin Weinger, "Selling Short," *Entrepreneur*, April 2010, p. 19.

74. "Census Bureau Reports Minority Business Ownership Increasing at More Than Twice the National Rate," U.S. Census Bureau, July 13, 2010, http://www.census.gov/newsroom/releases/archives/economic_census/cb10-107.html.

75. "Census Bureau Reports Minority Business Ownership Increasing at More Than Twice the National Rate," U.S. Census Bureau, July 13, 2010, http://www.census.gov/newsroom/releases/archives/economic_census/cb10-107.html.

76. "10 Young Entrepreneurs to Watch," *Black Enterprise*, April 18, 2011, http://www.blackenterprise.com/2011/04/18/10-young-entrepreneurs-to-watch-out-for/?show=6; "Monique Pean," Monique Péan Fine Jewelry, http://www.moniquepean.com; "Expert Advice: Monique Péan, Eco Jewelry Designer," *Martha Stewart Weddings*, April 2011, http://thebridesguide.marthastewartweddings.com/2011/04/expert-advice-monique-pean-eco-jewelry-designer.html.

77. "Minorities in Business: A Demographic Review of Minority Business Ownership," *Small Business Research Summary*, Small Business Administration Office of Advocacy, April 2007, p. 1.

78. *Minorities in Business: A Demographic Review of Minority Business Ownership*, Small Business Administration Office of Advocacy, April 10, 2007, p. 27.

79. *2010 Kauffman Index of Entrepreneurial Activity*, Ewing Marion Kauffman Foundation, p. 10.

80. "Education, Entrepreneurship, and Immigration: America's New Immigrant Entrepreneurs, Part II," Ewing Marion Kauffman Foundation, http://www.kauffman.org/research-and-policy/education-entrepreneurship-and-immigration.aspx.

81. "Patrick C.S. Lo," *Forbes*, May 2011, http://people.forbes.com/profile/patrick-c-s-lo/56756; Mary Crane, "Out of China," *Forbes*, May 29, 2007, http://www.forbes.com/2007/05/21/outsourcing-entrepreneurs-immigrants-oped-cx_mc_0522entrepreneurs.html.

82. Jason Fell, "From the Trash Heap to Holiday Fashion Chic," *Entrepreneur*, December 14, 2010, http://www.entrepreneur.com/article/217746; Sara Glassman, "Sweater Season," *Star Tribune*, November 24, 2010, http://www.startribune.com/lifestyle/style/110416499.html.

83. "Key Statistics on the Growing Home-Based Business Market," *Home Business Magazine*, March 2010, http://www.homebusinessmag.com/newsstand/news/key-statistics-growing-home-based-business-market.

84. "Frequently Asked Questions: Advocacy Small Business Statistics and Research," Small Business Administration, 2011, http://web.sba.gov/faqs/faqIndexAll.cfm?areaid=24.

85. *Homepreneurs: A Vital Economic Force*, Small Business Index Research Note, Network Solutions, 2009, p. 6.

86. "Facts and Perspectives on Family Business around the World: United States," Family Firm Institute, http://www.ffi.org/genTemplate.asp?cid=186#us; "Facts and Figures: Family Business in the U.S.," *Family Business Magazine*, http://www.familybusiness.unh.edu/usefulinfo/FamilyBusinessFacts.pdf; "Family Business Statistics," American Management Services, http://www.amserv.com/familystatistics.html.

87. Erick Calonius, "Blood and Money," *Newsweek: Special Issue*, p. 82.

88. "Family Business Facts," University of St. Francis, Fort Wayne, Indiana, http://www.sfc.edu/business/fbc_facts.shtml.

89. *The MassMutual FamilyPreneurship Study*, MassMutual, March 2010, p.10.

90. Margaret Heffernan, "Copreneurs: Do You Really Want to Go into Business with Your Spouse?," *BNET*, July 15, 2010, http://www.bnet.com/blog/business-strategy/copreneurs-do-you-really-want-to-go-into-business-with-your-spouse/330; Udayan Gupta, "And Business Makes Three: Couples Working Together," *Wall Street Journal*, February 26, 1990, p. B2.

91. Pia Chatterjee, "Making Beautiful Start-Ups Together," *Business 2.0*, September 2007, p. 43.

92. Echo M. Garrett, "And Business Makes Three," *Small Business Reports*, September 1993, pp. 27–31.

93. Colleen Debaise, Sarah Needleman, and Emily Maltby, "Married to the Job (and Each Other)," *Wall Street Journal*, February 14, 2011, pp. R1, R4.

94. "Planned Job Cuts Drop to 10-Year Low of 34,768," Challenger, Gray, and Christmas, September 1, 2010, http://www.challengergray.com/press/PressRelease.aspx?PressUid=144.

95. "Franchise News," Liberty Tax Service, November 9, 2010, http://www.libertytaxfranchise.com/franchise-news.html?a=800156869.

96. Jena McGregor, "From Textbooks to Triple Cream," *Fortune*, February 19, 2010, p. 34.

97. *NFIB Small Business Policy Guide* (Washington, DC: NFIB Education Foundation, 2003), p. 21.

98. Dane Stangler, *The Coming Entrepreneurship Boom*, Ewing Marion Kauffman Foundation, June 2009, p. 4.

99. Deborah L. Cohen, "Grandmother Finds Business Idea in Her Purse," *Reuters*, September 8, 2010, http://www

.reuters.com/article/2010/09/08/us-cohen-column-pouchee-idUSTRE6873WY20100908.

100. *The Small Business Economy: A Report to the President* (Washington, DC: Small Business Administration, Office of Advocacy, U.S. Government Printing Office, 2010), p. 26.

101. "Cognetics Corporate Quiz," Cognetics, Inc., http://www.cogonline.com/IndexL.htm; Garry Powers, "Wanted: More Small, Fast-Growing Firms," *Business & Economic Review*, April–June 1999, pp. 19–22.

102. "FAQs," U.S. Small Business Administration, 2010, http://web.sba.gov/faqs/faqIndexAll.cfm?areaid=24.

103. Jason Daley, "The Entrepreneur Economy," *Entrepreneur*, December 2009, p. 54.

104. "FAQs," U.S. Small Business Administration, 2010, http://web.sba.gov/faqs/faqIndexAll.cfm?areaid=24.

105. "FAQs," U.S. Small Business Administration, 2010, http://web.sba.gov/faqs/faqIndexAll.cfm?areaid=24.

106. Michael Warsaw, "Great Comebacks," *Success*, July/August, 1995, p. 43.

107. Paige Arnof-Fenn, "Failing Your Way to Success," *Entrepreneur*, November 21, 2005, http://www.entrepreneur.com/worklife/worklifebalanceadvice/theentrepreneurslifecolumnistpaigearnoffenn/article81130.html.

108. Marc Gunther, "They All Want a Piece of Bill Gross," *Fortune*, November 11, 2002, p. 140.

109. Chuck Salter, "Failure Doesn't Suck," *Fast Company*, May 2007, p. 44.

110. Bill Bartmann and Darren Dahl, "How I Lost It All, and How I'm Getting It Back," *Inc.*, September 2010, p. 94.

111. Jessica Shambora, "Chipotle's Rise," *Fortune*, October 18, 2010, p. 72; "How It All Started," Chipotle, http://www.chipotle.com/en-US/chipotle_story/steves_story/steves_story.aspx; *Chipotle Mexican Grill Annual Report 2010*, p. 27.

112. "History," TerraCycle, http://www.terracycle.net/history.htm.

113. Dinah Eng, "Jake Burton: My Life as a Pioneer," *Fortune*, December 8, 2010, p. 72.

114. G. David Doran, Michelle Prather, Elaine Teague, and Laura Tiffany, "Young Guns," *Business Start-Ups*, April 1999, pp. 28–35.

115. *Chipotle Mexican Grill Annual Report 2010*, p. 5.

116. Rhonda Abrams, "Building Blocks of Business: Great Faith, Great Doubt, Great Effort," *Business*, March 4, 2001, p. 2.

2 Inside the Entrepreneurial Mind: From Ideas to Reality

Learning Objectives

On completion of this chapter, you will be able to:

1. Explain the differences among creativity, innovation, and entrepreneurship.

2. Describe why creativity and innovation are such an integral part of entrepreneurship.

3. Understand how the two hemispheres of the human brain function and what role they play in creativity.

4. Explain the 10 "mental locks" that limit individual creativity.

5. Understand how entrepreneurs can enhance the creativity of their employees as well as their own creativity.

6. Describe the steps in the creative process.

7. Discuss techniques for improving the creative process.

8. Describe the protection of intellectual property through patents, trademarks, and copyrights.

Innovation distinguishes between a leader and a follower.

—Steve Jobs

Failure: A man who has blundered but is not able to cash in on the experience.

—Elbert Hubbard

One of the tenets of entrepreneurship is the ability to create new and useful ideas that solve the problems and challenges people face every day. Entrepreneurs achieve success by creating value in the marketplace when they combine resources in new and different ways to gain a competitive edge over rivals. From Alexander Fleming's pioneering work that resulted in a cure for infections (penicillin) and the founders of the Rocket Chemical Company's fortieth try to create an industrial lubricant (WD-40) to Jeff Bezos's innovative use of the Internet in retailing (Amazon .com) and Ted Turner's around-the-clock approach to the availability of television news (CNN), entrepreneurs' ideas have transformed the world.

As you learned in Chapter 1, entrepreneurs can create value in a number of ways—inventing new products and services, developing new technology, discovering new knowledge, improving existing products or services, finding different ways of providing more goods and services with fewer resources, and many others. Indeed, finding new ways of satisfying customers' needs, inventing new products and services, putting together existing ideas in new and different ways, and creating new twists on existing products and services are hallmarks of the entrepreneur!

ENTREPRENEURIAL PROFILE: Jeff Skiba: Vomaris Innovations Jeff Skiba, a former medical consultant, began conducting experiments in his garage on the ability of electrical current to heal wounds. Within two years, he had launched a company, Vomaris Innovations, and won approval from the Food and Drug Administration (FDA) for an adhesive bandage equipped with microscopic batteries that passes a small amount of electrical current (just 1.2 volts) over the injured area. Although scientists do not fully understand how electrical current promotes healing, research shows that it does work; early clinical trials showed that Skiba's "electric bandage," called Prosit, accelerated healing for every patient in the sample. Prosit bandages also save money: healing a wound using standard bandages costs an average of $1,000 per wound, but Prosit bandages reduce that cost to just $140 per wound. Skiba has applied for FDA approval for an over-the-counter version of Prosit that will add to Vomaris's sales, which already exceed $2 million. ∎

Like many innovators, Skiba created a successful business by taking a common item, bandages, that had existed for many years and looking at it in a different way.

LO1

Explain the differences among creativity, innovation, and entrepreneurship.

Creativity, Innovation, and Entrepreneurship

According to the Battelle *R&D Magazine*, U.S. companies, government agencies, and universities invest nearly $400 billion annually in research and development (R&D).[1] Small companies are an important part of the total R&D picture. One study by the Small Business Administration reports that small companies produce 16.5 times more patents per employee than their larger rivals. Small businesses also produce more economically and technically important innovations than larger firms.[2] What is the entrepreneurial "secret" for creating value in the marketplace? In reality, the "secret" is no secret at all: it is applying creativity and innovation to solve problems and to exploit opportunities that people face every day. **Creativity** is the ability to develop new ideas and to discover new ways of looking at problems and opportunities. **Innovation** is the ability to *apply* creative solutions to those problems and opportunities to enhance or to enrich people's lives. Harvard's Ted Levitt says that creativity is *thinking* new things and that innovation is *doing* new things. In short, entrepreneurs succeed by *thinking and doing* new things or old things in new ways. Simply having a great new idea is not enough; transforming the idea into a tangible product, service, or business venture is the essential next step. As management legend Peter Drucker said, "Innovation is the specific instrument of entrepreneurs, the act that endows resources with a new capacity to create wealth."[3]

Successful entrepreneurs introduce new ideas, products, and services that solve a problem or fill a need. In a world that is changing faster than most of us ever could have imagined, creativity and innovation are vital to a company's success—and ultimate survival. That's true for businesses in every industry—from automakers to tea growers—and for companies of all sizes. A recent survey by IBM of chief executive officers (CEOs) from 60 countries across 33 industries identified creativity as the most important leadership competency required for success in the future.[4]

Although big businesses develop many new ideas, creativity and innovation are the signatures of small, entrepreneurial businesses. Creative thinking has become a core business skill,

creativity
the ability to develop new ideas and to discover new ways of looking at problems and opportunities.

innovation
the ability to apply creative solutions to problems and opportunities to enhance or to enrich people's lives.

and entrepreneurs lead the way in developing and applying that skill. In fact, creativity and innovation often lie at the heart of small companies' ability to compete successfully with their larger rivals. Even though they cannot outspend their larger rivals, small companies can create powerful, effective competitive advantages over big companies by "out-creating" and "out-innovating" them! If they fail to do so, entrepreneurs don't stay in business very long. Leadership expert Warren Bennis says, "Today's successful companies live and die according to the quality of their ideas."[5]

Sometimes innovation involves generating something from nothing. However, innovation is more likely to result in elaborating on the present, from putting old things together in new ways or from taking something away to create something simpler or better. Apple did not invent the digital music player, but Steve Jobs's company created a player that was easier to use and offered a "cool" factor that existing MP3 players did not have. One experimenter's research to improve the adhesive on tape resulted in a glue that hardly stuck at all. Although most researchers might have considered the experiment a total failure and scrapped it, this researcher asked a simple, creative question: What can you do with a glue when you take away most of its stickiness? The answer led to the invention of one of the most popular office products of all time: the Post-It note, a product that now includes more than 4,000 variations.

Some entrepreneurs stumble onto their ideas by accident but are clever enough to spot the business opportunities they offer.

ENTREPRENEURIAL PROFILE: Brian Levin: 3Perky Jerky Serial entrepreneur Brian Levin, who created the first text-message voting system (the one used on *American Idol*), and a friend were on a chairlift on the snowy slopes in Snowbird, Utah, one morning when Levin reached into his backpack for a package of beef jerky. Unfortunately, an energy drink had spilled onto the package, soaking the jerky, but Levin and his friend were hungry and ate it anyway. As they skied down the mountain, the duo experienced an energy boost. The jerky, now quite tender because of its soaking, had taken on the characteristics of the energy drink but had retained its peppery flavor. Inspired, Levin spent the next two years working with a food laboratory to refine a process for making an energy-boosting jerky around which he built a company to market the new product, which he named Perky Jerky. The company now generates annual sales of $7 million.[6] ∎

More often, creative ideas arise when entrepreneurs look at something old and think something new or different. Legendary Notre Dame football coach Knute Rockne, whose teams dominated college football in the 1920s, got the idea for his constantly shifting backfields while watching a burlesque chorus routine! Rockne's innovations in the backfield (which included the legendary "Four Horsemen") and his emphasis on the forward pass (a legal but largely unused tactic in this era) so befuddled opposing defenses that his teams compiled an impressive 105-12-5 record.[7]

ENTREPRENEURIAL PROFILE: Victor Li: Engineered Cement Composites More recently, Victor Li, a civil and environmental engineering professor at the University of Michigan, saw the sad—and dangerous—condition that the nation's bridges and highways are in (the average bridge in the United States is 43 years old, and nearly 27 percent of them are either structurally deficient or functionally obsolete) and realized that governments at all levels lacked the resources to upgrade them. "The only way is new technology," he says. Li developed a new version of a very old product—concrete. Li's concrete is superior because it is as strong as traditional concrete, but it is bendable and self-repairing! The bendable concrete is 40 percent lighter and 500 times more resistant to cracking than standard concrete. If the concrete does crack, the material, which includes calcium carbonate (the substance that makes up seashells), absorbs moisture, expands, reseals the cracks, and regains its original strength. Although Li's bendable concrete costs more to produce than traditional concrete, its longer life and lower maintenance cost result in a life cycle cost that is 50 percent less.[8] ∎

Entrepreneurship is the result of a disciplined, systematic process of applying creativity and innovation to needs and opportunities in the marketplace. It involves applying focused strategies to new ideas and new insights to create a product or a service that satisfies customers' needs or solves their problems. It is much more than random, disjointed tinkering with a new gadget.

Millions of people come up with creative ideas for new or different products and services; most of them, however, never do anything with them. Entrepreneurs are people who connect their creative ideas with the purposeful action and structure of a business. Thus, successful entrepreneurship is a constant process that relies on creativity, innovation, and application in the marketplace.

Innovation must be a constant process because most ideas don't work and most innovations fail. One writer explains, "Trial—and lots of error—is embedded in entrepreneurship."[9] Karen Anne Zien, cofounder of Polaroid Corporation's Creativity and Innovation Lab, estimates that for every 3,000 new product ideas, four make it to the development stage, two are actually launched, and only one becomes a success in the market. These new products are crucial to companies' success, however. According to Robert Cooper, a researcher who has analyzed thousands of new product launches, on average, new products account for a whopping 40 percent of companies' sales.[10] Still, successful entrepreneurs recognize that many failures will accompany innovations, and they are willing to accept their share of failures because they know that failure is merely part of the creative process. Rather than quit when they fail, entrepreneurs simply keep trying. While working as a textbook editor, James Michener had an idea for a book based on his experiences in the Solomon Islands during World War II. He sent the manuscript to a publisher and received the following note: "You are a good editor. Don't throw it all away trying to be a writer. I read your book. Frankly, it's not really that good." Michener persisted and went on to publish *South Pacific*, for which he won a Pulitzer Prize and which became the basis for one of Broadway's most successful musicals of all time.[11]

Entrepreneurship requires business owners to be bold enough to try their new ideas, flexible enough to throw aside those that do not work, and wise enough to learn about what will work based on their observations of what did not. We now turn our attention to creativity, the creative process, and methods of enhancing creativity.

Creativity—Essential to Survival

LO2

Describe why creativity and innovation are such an integral part of entrepreneurship.

In this fiercely competitive, fast-faced, global economy, creativity is not only an important source for building a competitive advantage but also a necessity for survival. When developing creative solutions to modern problems, entrepreneurs must go beyond merely relying on what has worked in the past. "A company that's doing all the things that used to guarantee success—providing quality products backed by great service, marketing with flair, holding down costs, and managing cash flow—is at risk of being flattened if it fails to become an engine of innovation," says one business writer.[12] Transforming their organizations into engines of innovation requires entrepreneurs to cast off the limiting assumptions, beliefs, and behaviors and to develop new insights into the relationship among resources, needs, and value. In other words, they must change their perspectives, looking at the world in new and different ways.

Entrepreneurs must always be on guard against traditional assumptions and perspectives about how things ought to be because they are certain killers of creativity. Such self-imposed mental constraints that people tend to build over time push creativity right out the door. These ideas become so deeply rooted in our minds that they become immovable blocks to creative thinking—even though they may be outdated, obsolete, and no longer relevant. In short, they act as logjams to creativity. That's why children are so creative and curious about new possibilities; society has not yet brainwashed them into an attitude of conformity, nor have they learned to accept *traditional* solutions as the *only* solutions. By retaining their creative "inner child," entrepreneurs are able to throw off the shackles on creativity and see opportunities for creating viable businesses where most people see what they've always seen (or, worse yet, see nothing). Creative exercises, such as the one in Figure 2.1, can help adults reconnect with the creativity that they exhibited so readily as children.

Many years ago, during an international chess competition, Frank Marshall made what has become known as one of the most beautiful—and one of the most creative—moves ever made on a chess board. In a crucial game in which he was evenly matched with a Russian master player, Marshall found his queen under serious attack. Marshall had several avenues of escape for his queen available. Knowing that the queen is one of the most important offensive players on the chessboard, spectators assumed that Marshall would make a conventional move and push his queen to safety.

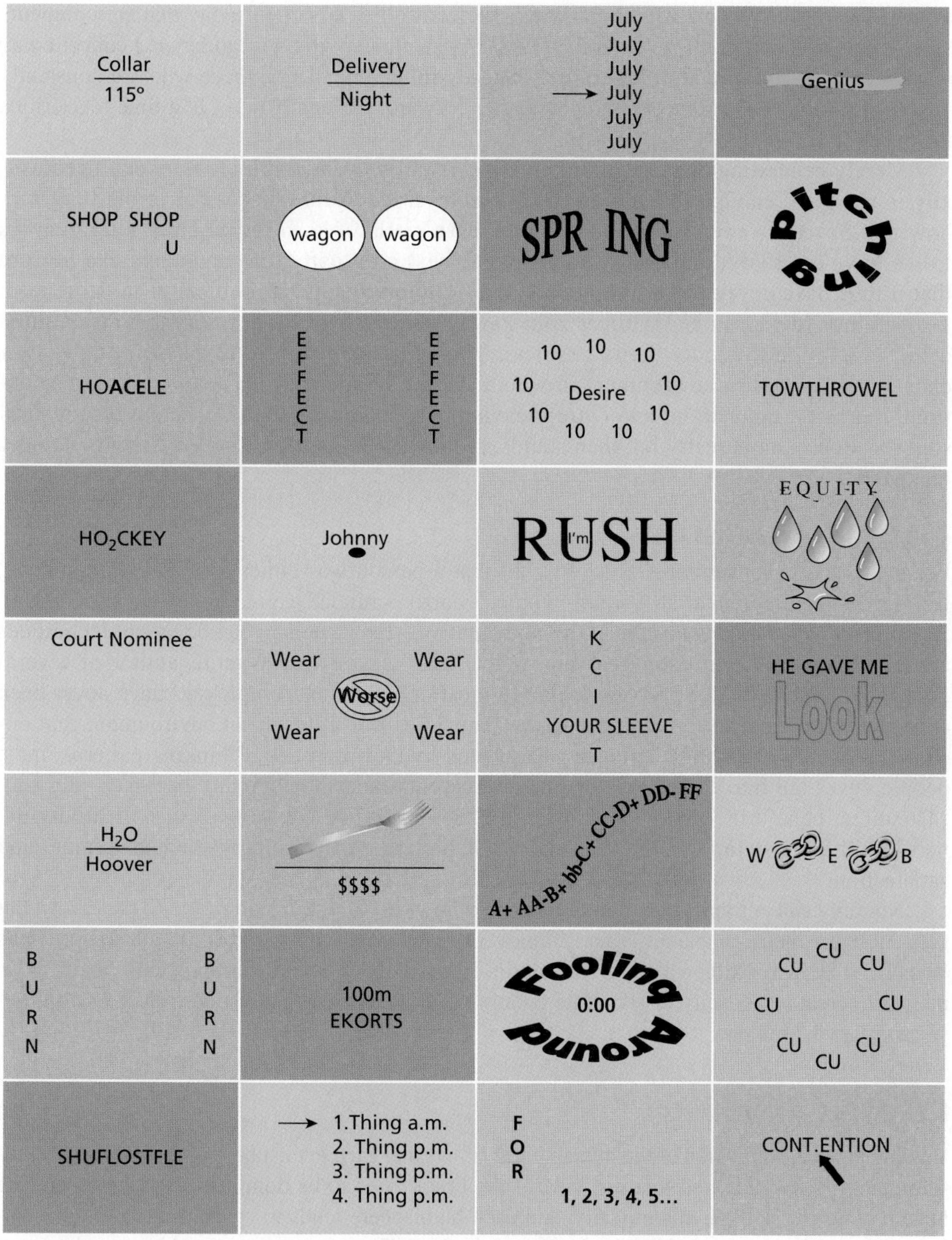

FIGURE 2.1

"How Creative Are You?"

Sources: Tery Stickels, "Frame Games," USA Weekend, August 12–14, 2005, p. 30; August 19–21, 2005, p. 18; June 13–15, 2003, p. 26; October 17–19, 2003, p. 18; October 31–November 2, 2003, p. 22; February 27–29, 2004, p. 18; May 14–16, 2004, p. 30; November 26–28, 2004, p. 18; August 20–22, 2004, p.15; October 22–24, 2004, p. 26; March 4–6, 2–5, p. 15; April 8–10, 2005, p. 23; May 6–8, 2005, p. 19; October 8–10, 2004, p. 19; January 23–25, 2004, p. 14.

Using all the time available to him to consider his options, Marshall picked up his queen—and paused—and put it down on the most *illogical* square of all—a square from which the queen could easily be captured by any one of three hostile pieces. Marshall had done the unthinkable! He had sacrificed his queen, a move typically made only under the most desperate of circumstances. All the spectators—even Marshall's opponent—groaned in dismay. Then the Russian (and finally the crowd) realized that Marshall's move was, in reality, a brilliant one. No matter how the Russian opponent took the queen, he would eventually be in a losing position. Seeing the inevitable outcome, the Russian conceded the game. Marshall had won the match in a rare and daring fashion: he had won by sacrificing his queen![13]

What lesson does this story hold for entrepreneurs? By suspending conventional thinking long enough to even consider the possibility of such a move, Marshall was able to throw off the usual assumptions constraining most chess players. He had looked beyond the traditional and orthodox strategies of the game and was willing to take the risk of trying an unusual tactic to win. The result: he won. Although not every creative business opportunity that entrepreneurs take will be successful, many who, like Frank Marshall, are willing to go beyond conventional wisdom will be rewarded for their efforts. Successful entrepreneurs, those who are constantly pushing technological and economic boundaries forward, constantly ask, "Is it time to sacrifice the queen?"

Merely generating one successful creative solution to address a problem or a need usually is not good enough to keep an entrepreneurial enterprise successful in the long run, however. Success—even survival—in the modern world of business requires entrepreneurs to tap their creativity (and that of their employees) constantly. Entrepreneurs can be sure that if they have developed a unique, creative solution to solve a problem or to fill a need, a competitor (perhaps one six times zones away) is hard at work developing an even more creative solution to render theirs obsolete. This extremely rapid and accelerating rate of change has created an environment in which staying in a leadership position requires constant creativity, innovation, and entrepreneurship. A company that has achieved a leadership position in an industry but then stands still creatively is soon toppled from its number one perch.

Can Creativity Be Taught?

For many years, conventional wisdom held that a person was either creative—imaginative, free-spirited, entrepreneurial—or not—logical, narrow-minded, rigid. Today, we know better. Research shows that *anyone* can learn to be creative. "Every person can be taught techniques and behaviors that help them generate more ideas," says Joyce Wycoff, author of several books on creativity.[14] The problem is that in most organizations, employees have never been expected to be creative. In addition, many businesses fail to foster an environment that encourages creativity among employees. Restricted by their traditional thinking patterns, most people never tap into their pools of innate creativity, and the company becomes stagnant. "The direct benefit of employee innovation is a competitive advantage," says creativity expert David Silverstein, "but the secondary benefits are greater employee empowerment and satisfaction."

Not only can entrepreneurs and the people who work for them learn to think creatively, but they must for their companies' sake! "Innovation and creativity are not just for artists," says Wycoff. "These are skills with a direct, bottom-line payoff."[15] Before entrepreneurs can draw on their own creative capacity or stimulate creativity in their own organizations, they must understand creative thinking.

LO3

Understand how the two hemispheres of the human brain function and what role they play in creativity.

Creative Thinking

Research into the operation of the human brain shows that each hemisphere of the brain processes information differently and that one side of the brain tends to be dominant over the other. The human brain develops asymmetrically, and each hemisphere tends to specialize in certain functions. The left brain is guided by linear, vertical thinking (from one logical conclusion to the next), whereas the right brain relies on kaleidoscopic, lateral thinking (considering a problem from all sides and jumping into it at different points). The left brain handles language, logic, and symbols; the right brain takes care of the body's emotional, intuitive, and spatial functions. The left brain processes information in a step-by-step fashion, but the right brain processes it intuitively—all at once, relying heavily on images.

Left-brain vertical thinking is narrowly focused and systematic, proceeding in a highly logical fashion from one point to the next. Right-brain lateral thinking, on the other hand, is somewhat unconventional, unsystematic, and unstructured, much like the image of a kaleidoscope, whirling around to form one pattern after another. It is this right brain–driven, lateral thinking that lies at the heart of the creative process. Those who have learned to develop their right-brain thinking skills tend to do the following:

- Always ask the question, "Is there a better way?"

- Challenge custom, routine, and tradition.

- Be reflective, often staring out windows, deep in thought. (How many traditional managers would stifle creativity by snapping these people out of their "daydreams," chastise them for "loafing," and admonish them to "get back to work?")

- Be prolific thinkers. They know that generating lots of ideas increases the likelihood of coming up with a few highly creative ideas.

- Play mental games, trying to see an issue from different perspectives.

- Realize that there may be more than one "right answer."

- See mistakes as mere "pit stops" on the way to success.

- See problems as springboards for new ideas.

- Understand that failure is a natural part of the creative process. James Dyson spent 15 years and nearly his entire savings before he succeeded in developing the bagless vacuum cleaner that made him rich and famous. "If you want to discover something that other people haven't," he says, "you need to do things the wrong way. You don't learn from success."[16]

- Have "helicopter skills," the ability to rise above the daily routine to see an issue from a broader perspective and then swoop back down to focus on an area in need of change.

- Relate seemingly unrelated ideas to a problem to generate innovative solutions.

ENTREPRENEURIAL PROFILE: Charles Kaman: Kaman Aircraft Company and Ovation Instruments After graduating from college, Charles Kaman worked in the helicopter division of United Aircraft Corporation, where he helped to design helicopters for the military. Using a homemade calculator he called the Aeronalyzer, Kaman developed several innovations in rotor and wing designs, in none of which his employer showed any interest. In 1945, with $2,000 and his idea for a new dual rotor system that made helicopters more stable and safer to fly, 26-year-old Kaman, also an accomplished guitarist, turned down an offer to join Tommy Dorsey's famous swing band and decided to pursue his innovative designs for helicopters and start the Kaman Aircraft Company in his mother's garage. Over the next 50 years, Kaman built his company into a billion-dollar aviation business, creating many important innovations along the way, including turbine engines; blades made of lightweight, sturdy composite materials; and remote-controlled helicopters. Kaman also maintained an avid interest in guitars and in 1964 began working with a small team of aerospace engineers to build a better acoustic guitar. Drawing on their experience of removing vibrations from helicopters, the team reverse-engineered a guitar with a bowl-shaped body made of composite materials that incorporated more vibration into the instrument, giving it a bolder, richer sound. "In helicopters, engineers spend all of their time trying to figure out how to remove vibration," Kaman said. "To build a guitar, you spend your time trying to figure out how to put vibration in." Kaman founded Ovation Instruments in 1966 and began selling the Balladeer, an acoustical guitar that immediately attracted attention for its superior tone and volume among musicians, including famous artists such as John Lennon, Glen Campbell, Bob Marley, Carly Simon, Jimmy Page, and Melissa Etheridge.[17] ■

Although each hemisphere of the brain tends to dominate in its particular functions, the two halves normally cooperate, with each part contributing its special abilities to accomplish those tasks best suited to its mode of information processing. Sometimes, however, the two hemispheres may even compete with each other, or one half may choose not to participate. Some researchers have suggested that each half of the brain has the capacity to keep information from the other! The result, literally, is that "the left hand doesn't know what the right hand is doing." Perhaps the most important characteristic of this split-brain phenomenon is that an individual can learn to control which side of the brain is dominant in a given situation. In other words, a person can learn to "turn down" the dominant left hemisphere (focusing on logic and linear thinking) and "turn up" the right hemisphere (focusing on intuition and unstructured thinking) when a situation requiring creativity arises.[18] To get a little practice at this "shift," try the visual exercises presented in Figure 2.2. When viewed from one perspective, the picture B on the right portrays an attractive young lady with a feather in her hair and a boa around her shoulders. Once you shift

FIGURE 2.2

What Do You See?

Sources: Thomas
W. Zimmerer and Norman
M. Scarborough, *Entrepre-
neurship and New Venture
Formation.* © 1995.
Reprinted by permission of
Prentice Hall, Inc., Upper
Saddle River, NJ.

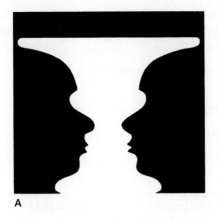

your perspective, however, you will see an old woman with a large nose wearing a scarf on her head! This change in the image seen is the result of a shift from one hemisphere in the viewer's brain to the other. With practice, a person can learn to control this mental shift, tapping the pool of creativity that lies hidden within the right side of the brain. This ability has tremendous power to unleash the creative capacity of entrepreneurs. The need to develop this creative ability means that exploring inner space (the space within our brains)—not outer space—becomes the challenge of the century.

Successful entrepreneurship requires both left- and right-brain thinking. Right-brain thinking draws on the power of divergent reasoning, which is the ability to create a multitude of original, diverse ideas. Left-brain thinking counts on convergent reasoning, the ability to evaluate multiple ideas and choose the best solution to a given problem. Entrepreneurs need to rely on right-brain thinking to generate innovative product, service, or business ideas. Then they must use left-brain thinking to judge the market potential of the ideas they generate. Successful entrepreneurs have learned to coordinate the complementary functions of each hemisphere of the brain, using their brains' full creative power to produce pragmatic innovation. Otherwise, entrepreneurs, who rarely can be accused of being "halfhearted" about their business ideas, run the risk of becoming "halfheaded."

How can entrepreneurs learn to tap their innate creativity more readily? The first step is to break down the barriers to creativity that most of us have erected over the years. We now turn our attention to these barriers and some suggested techniques for tearing them down.

✓ You Be the Consultant

Charles Darwin Was Right

The Great Recession took a toll on businesses of all sizes, but small companies, with their thin asset bases and limited access to capital, bore the brunt of the economic storm. Many of the weakest small companies did not survive. "The ghost of Charles Darwin [originator of the "survival of the fittest" theory] chased these weaker companies into oblivion," observes one entrepreneur. The owners of the small companies that did survive the economic turmoil responded quickly, remaking their businesses, launching new products, developing innovative business models, entering new markets, and implementing creative strategies. Bob Dimke, president of Lexington Manufacturing in Minneapolis, Minnesota, saw signs of the recession early on and anticipated that sales at his company, which supplies wood parts to manufacturers of doors, windows, cabinets, and other architectural features in homes, would be adversely affected as the housing market slowed. Dimke's forecast was correct; over two years, sales at Lexington Manufacturing declined by 25 percent. Fortunately, Dimke saw the interest in environmentally friendly products and began developing components for stylish fireproof doors made from wheatstraw fiber, which burns more slowly than wood fiber. The move paid off. Sales of fireproof door parts have doubled in just two years, filling the gap left by declining sales of the company's traditional wood parts. Dimke is now investing all of his R&D budget into products aimed at the fireproof market because of the potential that he sees there.

Garden Associates Landscape Architects

Dave Chewey, president of Garden Associates Landscape Architects, a company founded in 1990 in Somervillle, New Jersey, saw his company take a heavy blow from the collapse in the housing market. The company's target customers, upscale home owners, were cutting back expenditures on landscape services so much that the company's revenue plummeted 60 percent in just one year. Chewey's company, which did almost all its jobs within the immediate area, relies mostly on native plants, which require less maintenance because they are in their natural surroundings. Garden Associates also offered its clients instruction on rainwater recycling techniques to help them keep their landscapes healthy without spending a fortune watering them. With the dramatic sales slowdown, Chewey is looking for ways to reinvent his business to avoid "the ghost of Darwin."

Mike George Fitness System

Opened in 1995 in Chicago as an upscale fitness facility offering one-on-one instruction, Mike George Fitness System targeted well-to-do clients, who pay $1,000 per month for three one-hour customized training sessions each week. The company also offers a personal chef service that delivers customized meals to complement clients' fitness regimes. Founder Michael George says that his company's sales grew steadily until the Great Recession hit, when the flow of new customers dried up and many existing customers left. The result was a devastating 50 percent decrease in sales revenue in one year. "We have to look at our model and do something to change our ability to reach more people," says George.

Stone Hearth Pizza

Chris Robbins and Jonathan Schwarz opened the first Stone Hearth Pizza in 2005 in Belmont, Massachusetts, a suburb of Boston, as an upscale neighborhood dining spot that served fresh, oven-fired pizzas made with organic, locally grown ingredients. Within three years, the entrepreneurs had opened locations in nearby Needham and Cambridge. They were considering opening a fourth location when the recession hit and consumers reduced their expenditures on dining out. Robbins and Schwarz have read reports from industry associations that say that customers' inclination toward dining at home may be a permanent trend. Consumers spend about 44 percent of their food dollars outside the home, which represents a decrease from about 50 percent from just a few years ago. Some industry forecasts project restaurant sales growth in the near future of just 1 percent, less than the overall population growth rate.

Whole Foods Market, the upscale grocery chain, has approached Robbins and Schwarz about selling Stone Hearth Pizzas in the refrigerated foods section of their stores. They see the opportunity to diversify their business but realize that Whole Foods would pay wholesale prices for their pizzas.

1. "Small businesses can remake themselves faster than larger companies," says a small business consultant. Do you agree? Explain.

2. Select one of the three businesses featured above and use the creativity-stimulating techniques described in this chapter to generate ideas for transforming their businesses and getting them back on the pathway to profitability. Write a brief memo to the business owner(s) that describes your ideas.

Sources: Based on Suzanne Barlyn, "New and Improved," *Wall Street Journal,* April 23, 2009, http://online.wsj.com/article/SB124025160159735869.html; Ellen Gibson, "Eat-at-Home Trend Might Stay a While," *News Tribune,* January 24, 2011, http://www.thenewstribune.com/2011/01/24/1514577/eat-at-home-trend-might-stay-a.html; Kelly Spors, "Tough Times Call for New Ideas," *Wall Street Journal,* February 15, 2009, http://online.wsj.com/article/SB123466563957289181.html; and Gene Marks, "Why Most Small Businesses Will Beat the Recession," *Bloomberg Business Week,* January 8, 2009, http://www.businessweek.com/smallbiz/content/jan2009/sb2009015_212410.htm.

Barriers to Creativity

The number of potential barriers to creativity is virtually limitless—time pressures, unsupportive management, pessimistic coworkers, overly rigid company policies, and countless others. Perhaps the most difficult hurdles to overcome, however, are those that individuals impose on themselves. In his book *A Whack on the Side of the Head*, Roger von Oech identifies 10 "mental locks" that limit individual creativity:[19]

1. *Searching for the one "right" answer.* Recent research by Kyung Hee Kim, a professor at the College of William & Mary, shows that creativity (as measured by the Torrance Test of Creative Thinking) among both children and adults in the United States has declined markedly since 1990. The decline, which Kim says is "very significant," is particularly acute among the youngest segment of the population, children from kindergarten to sixth grade.[20] Part of the problem is that deeply ingrained in most educational systems is the assumption that there is one "right" answer to a problem. In reality, however, most problems are ambiguous. The average student who has completed four years of college has taken more than 2,600 tests; therefore, it is not unusual for this one-correct-answer syndrome to become an inherent part of our thinking. "Schools are educating creativity and innovation out of children," says Matt Goldman, a cofounder of the Blue Man Group, which recently started Blue School, a prekindergarten and elementary school that focuses on developing creativity in its students.

   Depending on the questions one asks, there may be (and usually are) several "right" answers.

   ENTREPRENEURIAL PROFILE: Ben Vigoda and David Reynolds: Lyric Semiconductor From their earliest days, computers have processed information using the binary code, a system that uses only zeroes and ones. However, Ben Vigoda and David Reynolds, the cofounders of Lyric Semiconductor, a small company based in Cambridge, Massachusetts, realized that there might be other ways for computers to process information. They have developed a semiconductor chip (the "brain" of any computer) that also uses values between zero and one, an advancement that has the potential to revolutionize computing. Lyric's probability-processing technology not only dramatically increases the speed with which a computer works, ranging from faster Google searches to speedier analysis of the human genome, but also can reduce the size of computers because fewer chips are needed to process a given amount of data. "We are changing something that's been true for 50 or 60 years," says Vigoda. Lyric's creative technology holds so much potential that venture capital firms and the U.S. Department of Defense have invested $20 million in the company, which recently was named one of the world's most innovative companies by *Technology Review* magazine.[21] ∎

2. *Focusing on "being logical."* Logic is a valuable part of the creative process, especially when evaluating ideas and implementing them. However, in the early imaginative phases of the process, logical thinking can restrict creativity. Focusing too much effort on being logical also discourages the use of one of the mind's most powerful creations: intuition. Von Oech advises us to "think something different" and to use nonlogical thinking freely, especially in the imaginative phase of the creative process. Intuition, which is based on the accumulated knowledge and experiences a person encounters over the course of a lifetime and which resides in the subconscious, can be unlocked. It is a crucial part of the creative process because using it often requires one to tear down long-standing assumptions that limit creativity and innovation.

   ENTREPRENEURIAL PROFILE: John Rogers and George Whitesides: mc10 For decades, logic dictated that the chips and circuits that served as the "brains" of computers and other electronic devices be placed on rigid circuit boards, but professors John Rogers and George Whitesides suspended traditional logic long enough to develop flexible, high-performance electronics with springy connectors made of gold wires that fit on stretchable silicon. Their innovative design removes the inherent limitations of rigid electronics and opens the door to an array of amazing applications in fields as diverse as medicine, energy, defense, manufacturing, and athletics. Their company, mc10, has attracted investments from venture capital firms, the Department of Energy, and the U.S. Navy and is developing a line of "smart" surgical tools, flexible solar modules for tents and unmanned aircraft, and a line of apparel for Reebok that includes wearable electronics that monitor athletic performance.[22] ∎

3. *Blindly following the rules.* We learn at a very early age not to "color outside the lines," and we spend the rest of our lives blindly obeying such rules. Sometimes, creativity depends on our ability to break the existing rules so that we can see new ways of doing things. Consider, for example, the top row of letters on a standard keyboard:

Q W E R T Y U I O P

In the 1870s, Sholes & Company, a leading manufacturer of typewriters, began receiving numerous customer complaints about its typewriter keys sticking together when typists' fingers were practiced enough to go really fast. Company engineers came up with an incredibly creative solution to eliminate the problem of sticking keys. They designed a *less* efficient keyboard configuration, placing the letters O and I (the fourth and fifth most commonly used letters of the alphabet) so that the weaker middle and ring fingers would strike them. By slowing down typists with this inefficient keyboard, the engineers solved the sticking keys problem. Today, despite the fact that computer technology has eliminated all danger of sticking keys, this same inefficient keyboard configuration remains the industry standard!

4. *Constantly being practical.* Imagining impractical answers to "what-if" questions can be powerful stepping stones to creative ideas. Suspending practicality for a while frees the mind to consider creative solutions that otherwise might never arise. Whenever Thomas Edison hired an assistant to work in his creative laboratory, he would tell the new employee, "Walk through town and list 20 things that interest you." When the worker returned, Edison would ask him to split the list into two columns. Then he would say, "Randomly combine objects from column A and column B and come up with as many inventions as you can." Edison's methods for stimulating creativity in his lab proved to be successful; he holds the distinction of being the only person to have earned a patent every year for 65 consecutive years![23]

   Periodically setting aside practicality allows entrepreneurs to consider taking a product or a concept from one area and placing it in a totally different application.

> **ENTREPRENEURIAL PROFILE: Richard Dyson: Dyson Airblade** Richard Dyson spent 10 years developing the motor that powers his unique bagless vacuum cleaner and finally came up with one that runs at 110,000 revolutions per minute, three times faster than competitors' motors. While studying ways to apply that same technology to another product, Dyson discovered that he could squirt air at 400 miles per hour through a tiny slot, creating an "air blade." Dyson asked himself, "How can we use this concept?" The creative answer he came up with: a revolutionary hand dryer for use in restrooms in which the blade safely wipes water off the hands in a mere 10 seconds rather than the average 40 seconds required for a traditional hand dryer. Not only do users get dry hands faster, but the device also cuts energy use by 75 percent.[24] ∎

5. *Viewing play as frivolous.* A playful attitude is fundamental to creative thinking. There is a close relationship between the "haha" of humor and the "aha" of discovery. Play gives us the opportunity to reinvent reality and to reformulate established ways of doing things. Children learn when they play, and so can entrepreneurs. Watch children playing, and you will see them invent new games, create new ways of looking at old things, and learn what works (and what doesn't) in their games.

   Entrepreneurs can benefit from playing in the same way that children do. They, too, can learn to try new approaches and discover what works and what doesn't. Creativity results when entrepreneurs take what they have learned at play, evaluate it, corroborate it with other knowledge, and put it into practice. Encourage employees to have fun when solving problems; they are more likely to push the boundaries and come up with a genuinely creative solution if they do. What kind of invention would Wile E. Coyote, who seems to have an inexhaustible supply of ideas for catching the Roadrunner in those cartoons, create in this situation? How might the Three Stooges approach this problem? What would Kramer of *Seinfeld* suggest? What would a six-year-old do? The idea is to look at a problem or situation from different perspectives.

ENTREPRENEURIAL PROFILE: Johnson Bailey: Man Candles While brainstorming ideas for an entrepreneurship class they were taking, Johnson Bailey jokingly suggested to some friends the idea of "man-scented" candles. The more Bailey thought about his silly idea, the more he was intrigued by it. He noted the success of companies selling candles aimed at women and "realized there weren't any interesting, unique gifts for guys," he says. In 2009, Bailey began working from his home with a chemist to create the first "man candle," which emitted the scent of a leather football. He went on to develop seven other scents and convinced the owner of a local Hallmark store to stock some of his Man Candles. Bailey's unusual candles were a hit, and within one month more than 100 retail stores were selling them. Bailey, who quit his full-time job to focus on his company, produces candles in 23 scents, ranging from bacon and pizza to golf course and hunter's refuge. In 2011, Bailey established a Facebook page for Man Candles, and sales took off.[25] ■

6. *Becoming overly specialized.* Defining a problem as one of "marketing" or "production" or some other area of specialty limits the ability to see how it might be related to other issues. Creative thinkers tend to be "explorers," searching for ideas outside their areas of specialty. The idea for the roll-on deodorant stick came from the ballpoint pen. The famous Mr. Potato Head toy was invented by a father sitting with his family at the dinner table who noted how much fun his children had playing with their food. Velcro was invented by a man who, while hiking one day to take a break from work, had to stop to peel sticky cockleburs from his clothing. As he picked them off, he noticed how their hooked spines caught on and held tightly to the cloth. When he resumed his hike, he began to think about the possibilities of using a similar design to fasten objects together. Thus was born Velcro!

ENTREPRENEURIAL PROFILE: Jessica Smith: Casttoo When Jessica Smith tried to jump a curb on her bicycle, she ended up with a broken wrist. The 21-year-old art student painted a beautiful floral design on her cast, and when she returned to the doctor to have it removed, "he said that if someone would produce art like that for casts, he'd buy them," she recalls. The comment inspired Smith, who transformed her artwork into the first generation of Casttoos, a special adhesive film with brightly colored designs that, when applied to a cast and heated for 10 seconds with a hair dryer, melts into the plaster cast. Smith's simple idea led her to launch the Casttoo Web site, where she has sold tens of thousands of her brightly colored decals. "At any given time, 10 percent of the population is healing from a broken bone," she says. Casttoo recently partnered with global giant 3M and is negotiating the rights to sports and cartoon characters. Designs range from zebra stripes and Egyptian motifs to soccer balls and floral patterns, all of which are consistent with Smith's "Happy Healing" philosophy.[26] ■

7. *Avoiding ambiguity.* Ambiguity can be a powerful creative stimulus; it encourages us to "think something different." Being excessively detailed in an imaginative situation tends to stifle creativity. Ambiguity, however, requires us to consider at least two different, often contradictory notions at the same time, which is a direct channel to creativity. Ambiguous situations force us to stretch our minds beyond their normal boundaries and to consider creative options we might otherwise ignore. Although ambiguity is not a desired element when entrepreneurs are evaluating and implementing ideas, it is a valuable tool when they are searching for creative ideas and solutions. Entrepreneurs are famous for asking a question and then going beyond the first answer to explore other possible answers. The result is that they often find business opportunities by creating ambiguous situations.

8. *Fearing looking foolish.* Creative thinking is no place for conformity! New ideas rarely are born in a conforming environment. People tend toward conformity because they don't want to look foolish. The fool's job is to whack at the habits and rules that keep us thinking in the same old ways. In that sense, entrepreneurs are top-notch "fools." They are constantly questioning and challenging accepted ways of doing things and the assumptions that go with them. The noted entrepreneurship theorist Joseph Schumpeter wrote that entrepreneurs perform a vital function—"creative destruction"—in which they rethink conventional

assumptions and discard those that are no longer useful. According to Schumpeter, "The function of entrepreneurs is to reform or revolutionize the pattern of production by exploiting an invention or, more generally, an untried technological possibility for producing a new commodity or producing an old one in a new way, by opening up a new source of supply of materials or a new outlet for products, by reorganizing an industry or so on."[27] In short, entrepreneurs look at old ways of doing things and ask, "Is there a better way?" By destroying the old, they create the new.

ENTREPRENEURIAL PROFILE: Mike Cheiky: Transonic Combustion Mike Cheiky, a physicist and serial entrepreneur, took a new look at an old technology: fuel injectors. Cheiky's company, Transonic Combustion, has created a fuel injector that can increase the fuel efficiency of a standard car by as much as 33 percent by pressurizing and heating gasoline to a supercritical state (part liquid and part gas) before injecting it into the engine's cylinders. When the superheated fuel enters the engine, it mixes with air quickly and combusts without a spark, allowing it to burn more efficiently than the liquid droplets that standard injectors produce. Cheiky's injector also produces fewer exhaust emissions. Transonic Combustion is working with major automakers who plan to introduce models with the new injection systems in their 2014 models.[28] ∎

9. *Fearing mistakes and failure.* Creative people realize that trying something new often leads to failure; however, they do not see failure as an end. It represents a learning experience on the way to success. As you learned in Chapter 1, failure is an important part of the creative process; it signals entrepreneurs when to change their course of action. Entrepreneurship is all about the opportunity to fail! Many entrepreneurs failed numerous times before finally succeeding. Despite their initial setbacks, they were able to set aside the fear of failure and keep trying.

ENTREPRENEURIAL PROFILE: Arianna Huffington: Huffington Post Arianna Huffington, author of a dozen books and founder of the news and blog Web site Huffington Post, says, "I love talking about my failures more than my successes. Think of failure as a stepping-stone to success. I was rejected by 35 publishers before getting to yes." The highly successful Huffington Post, which Huffington launched in 2005, attracts more than 35 million unique visitors per month, more than the Web sites of any major newspaper in the United States.[29] ∎

Associated Press

The key is to see failure for what it really is: a chance to learn how to succeed. Entrepreneurs who willingly risk failure and learn from it when it occurs have the best chance of succeeding at whatever they try. Charles F. Kettering, a famous inventor (he invented the lighting and ignition systems in automobiles, among other things), explains, "You fail because your ideas aren't right, but you should learn to fail intelligently. When you fail, find out *why* you failed and each time it will bring you nearer to the goal."[30] Successful entrepreneurs equate failure with innovation rather than with defeat.

Thanks to technology, the cost of failed attempts at innovation has never been lower. Entrepreneurs and companies can test new ideas at speeds and costs that were unimaginable only a few years ago. Building prototypes, getting them into potential customers' hands, and getting useful feedback on them has never been easier and less expensive. Entrepreneurs use the Internet and social media to determine whether customers are interested in purchasing their product and service innovations.

10. *Believing that "I'm not creative."* Some people limit themselves because they believe that creativity belongs only to the Einsteins, Beethovens, and da Vincis of the world. Unfortunately, this belief often becomes a self-fulfilling prophecy. A person who believes that he or she is not creative will, in all likelihood, behave that way and will make that belief come true. Some people who are considered geniuses, visionaries, and inventors actually are no smarter and have no more innate creative ability than the average person; however, they have learned how to think creatively and are persistent enough to keep trying until they succeed.

Successful entrepreneurs recognize that "I'm not creative" is merely an excuse for inaction. *Everyone* has within him or her the potential to be creative; not everyone will tap that potential, however. Successful entrepreneurs find a way to unleash their creative powers on problems and opportunities.

TABLE 2.1 Questions to Spur the Imagination

We learn at an early age to pursue answers to questions. Creative people, however, understand that *good questions* are extremely valuable in the quest for creativity. Some of the greatest breakthroughs in history came as a result of creative people asking thought-provoking questions. Bill Bowerman, contemplating a design for the soles of running shoes over a breakfast of waffles, asked, "What would happen if I poured rubber into my waffle iron?" He did, and that's how Nike shoes came to be. (Bowerman's rubber-coated waffle iron is on display in the Nike Town superstore and museum in Chicago.) Albert Einstein, creator of the theory of relativity, asked, "What would a light wave look like to someone keeping pace with it?"

To jump-start creativity, Steve Gillman suggests writing a short list of adjectives, such as light, cheap, fast, big, short, small, fun, and others and use them to ask what-if questions. What if this product could be lighter? What if this process could be faster? What if this service could be cheaper?

The following questions can help spur your imagination:

1. Is there a new way to do it?
2. Can you borrow or adapt it?
3. Can you give it a new twist?
4. Do you merely need more of the same?
5. Less of the same?
6. Is there a substitute?
7. Can you rearrange the parts?
8. What if you do just the opposite?
9. Can you combine ideas?
10. Are customers using your product or service in ways you never expected or intended?
11. Which customers are you not serving? What changes to your product or service are necessary to reach them?
12. Can you put it to other uses?
13. What else could we make from this?
14. Are there other markets for it?
15. Can you reverse it?
16. Can you rearrange it?
17. Can you put it to another use?
18. What idea seems impossible but if, executed, would revolutionize your business?

Automaker BMW recently challenged its design division to disregard accepted conventions and existing processes as it developed new models. The process, which the company calls GINA ("geometry and functions in N [infinite] adaptations"), encouraged designers to ask questions, such as the ones listed here, that led to a shape-shifting car that has no rigid body panels. Wrapped in a spandex-like fabric, hydraulic and electronic controls change the shape of the car at different speeds.

For instance, at highway speeds, rocker panels morph to provide less drag from airflow, and a seamless spoiler rises in the rear. At lower speeds, the grill widens to allow more airflow to cool the engine. Headlights hide under fabric that opens like eyelids only when needed. Although BMW has no plans to produce the prototype as a commercial vehicle, the innovative materials and creative concepts from GINA will find their way into the design of future models.

Associated Press

Sources: Based on Chuck Frey, "How to Develop a Powerful Arsenal of Creative Questions," *Innovation Tools*, March 1, 2011, http://www.innovationtools.com/weblog/innovationblog-detail.asp?ArticleID=1570; David Lidsky, "Brain Calisthenics," *Fast Company*, December 2004, p. 95; Thea Singer, Christopher Caggiano, Ilan Mochari, and Tahl Raz, "If You Come, They Will Build It," *Inc.*, August 2002, p. 70; Creativity Web, "Question Summary," http://www.ozemail.com.au/~caveman/Creative/Techniques/osb_quest.html; *Bits & Pieces*, February 1990, p. 20; *Bits & Pieces*, April 29, 1993; "Creativity Quiz," *In Business*, November/December 1991, p. 18; Doug Hall, *Jump Start Your Brain* (New York: Warner Books, 1995), pp. 86–87; Christine Canabou, "Imagine That," *Fast Company*, January 2001, p. 56; Steve Gillman, "Step Out of Business Mode to Solve Problems," *Regan's Manager's eBulletin*, May 22, 2008, p. 1; and Tim McKeough, "The Shape-Shifting Car," *Fast Company*, November 2008, p. 84.

By avoiding these 10 mental locks, entrepreneurs can unleash their own creativity and the creativity of those around them as well. Successful entrepreneurs are willing to take some risks, explore new ideas, play a little, ask "What if?," and learn to appreciate ambiguity. By doing so, they develop the skills, attitudes, and motivation that make them much more creative—one of the keys to entrepreneurial success. Table 2.1 lists some questions designed to spur imagination.

How to Enhance Creativity

Enhancing Organizational Creativity

LO5

Understand how entrepreneurs can enhance the creativity of their employees as well as their own creativity.

Creativity doesn't just happen in organizations; entrepreneurs must establish an environment in which creativity can flourish—for themselves and for their workers. "Everyone has a creative spark, but many factors can inhibit its ignition," says one writer. "Part of an [entrepreneur's] role is to see the spark in his or her people, encourage its ignition, and champion its success."[31] New ideas are fragile creations, but the right company culture can encourage people to develop and cultivate them. Ensuring that workers have the freedom and the incentive to be creative is one of the best ways to achieve innovation. Entrepreneurs can stimulate their own creativity and encourage it among workers by following these suggestions, which are designed to create a culture of innovation.

INCLUDE CREATIVITY AS A CORE COMPANY VALUE Innovative companies do not take a passive approach to creativity; they are proactive in their search for new ideas. One of the best ways to set a creative tone throughout an organization begins with the company's mission statement. Entrepreneurs should incorporate creativity and innovation into their companies' mission statements and affirm their commitment to them in internal communications. Innovation allows a company to shape, transform, and create its future, and the natural place to define that future is in the mission statement. If creativity and innovation are vital to a company's success (and they usually are!), they also should be a natural part of the performance appraisal process.

Innovation can be a particularly powerful competitive weapon in industries that are resistant to change and are populated by companies that cling to the same old ways of doing business. Even small companies that are willing to innovate can have a significant impact on entire industries by shaking up the status quo with their creative approaches. The result often is growing market share and impressive profits for the innovator.

HIRE FOR CREATIVITY Research published in the *Sloan Management Review* concludes that the most effective way for companies to achieve continuous innovation over the long term is by hiring and cultivating talented people.[32] Often the most creative people also tend to be somewhat different, even eccentric. Two researchers call these employees "the odd clever people every organization needs" because they use their creativity to create disproportionate amounts of value for their companies.[33]

ESTABLISH AN ORGANIZATIONAL STRUCTURE THAT NOURISHES CREATIVITY John Kao, an economist whose nickname is "Mr. Creativity," says that innovative companies are structured like spaghetti rather than a traditional pyramid. In a spaghetti-style organization, employees are encouraged to mix and mingle constantly so that creative ideas flow freely throughout the company.[34] At innovative companies, managers create organizational structures and cultures that emphasize the importance of creativity. Managers at Dunkin' Donuts, with 9,235 coffee and donut outlets worldwide, recognize that innovation is the key to the 60-year-old company's success. A few years ago, they created the Dunkin' Brands Innovation Team, a group of 18 bakery specialists, and assigned them the task of developing new products for the company's menu. Although many product ideas never make it out of the test kitchen, the Innovation Team launches about 20 new product ideas each year. One of its most successful additions was the bagel twist, which took the team 10 months to perfect and comes in a variety of flavors.[35]

EMBRACE DIVERSITY One of the best ways to cultivate a culture of creativity is to hire a diverse workforce. When people solve problems or come up with ideas, they do so within the framework of their own experience. Hiring people from different backgrounds, cultural experiences, hobbies, and interests provides a company with crucial raw materials needed for creativity. Smart entrepreneurs enhance organizational creativity by hiring beyond their own comfort zones.

Focusing the talent and creativity of a diverse group of employees on a problem or challenge is one of the best ways to generate creative solutions. Research by Harvard Business School professor Karim Lakhani concludes that the experiences, viewpoints, and thought processes of diverse groups of people are powerful tools for solving problems creatively. "It's very counterintuitive," says Lakhani, "but not only did the odds of a [problem] solver's success actually increase in fields outside his expertise, but also the further a challenge was from his specialty, the greater was the likelihood of success."[36] The lesson for entrepreneurs: to increase the odds of a successful creative solution to a problem, involve in the process people whose background and experience lies *outside* the particular problem area. One manager says, "They create a little grit to stimulate the oyster to produce a pearl."[37]

EXPECT CREATIVITY Employees tend to rise—or fall—to the level of expectations that entrepreneurs have of them. One of the best ways to communicate the expectation of creativity is to encourage them to be creative.

West Paw Design

ENTREPRENEURIAL PROFILE: West Paw Design West Paw Design, a company based in Bozeman, Montana, that produces eco-friendly pet toys, sponsors a creativity contest in which its 36 employees, from president to seamstresses, form small teams to develop prototypes of new product ideas. The winning team receives the coveted Golden Hairball Award, a statue reminiscent of the Oscar but with one of the company's cat toys perched atop its head. Employees develop ideas and sketches, scrounge through bins of discarded materials, and assemble prototypes in less than two hours. The entire staff votes on a winner by secret ballot, and in addition to the Golden Hairball Award, the winning team members receive $100 gift cards. The winning team in a recent contest was comprised of a sales representative, a seamstress, and a shipping department worker. Their idea: the Eco Bed, a stuffed dog bed made completely from recycled materials. West Paw included the bed in its product line, and it became an instant hit among customers.[38] ■

EXPECT AND TOLERATE FAILURE Creative ideas will produce failures as well as successes. People who never fail are not being creative. Creativity requires taking chances, and managers must remove employees' fear of failure. The surest way to quash creativity throughout an organization is to punish employees who try something new and fail. Google allows employees to spend up to 20 percent of their time working on "pet projects" that they find exciting and believe have potential. In addition, Google provides seed capital for its employees' most promising ideas. The company credits its policy with creating some of its most successful product innovations, including Gmail, its Web-based e-mail service.[39]

INCORPORATE FUN INTO THE WORK ENVIRONMENT Smart entrepreneurs know that work should be fun, and although they expect employees to work hard, they create a company culture that allows employees to have fun. "If you want creative workers, give them enough time to play," says actor John Cleese. At Radio Flyer, the Chicago-based company that makes the classic little red wagon for children, employees routinely participate in fun activities at work that include karaoke, tricycle races, pumpkin-carving contests, a Hollywood Squares game, and others. CEO Robert Pasin intentionally has made fun events a part of the company's culture. "There's method to the madness," says the company's "chief wagon officer," pointing out that the company's success depends on creative employees who are motivated and engaged in their work.[40]

ENCOURAGE CURIOSITY Entrepreneurs and their employees constantly should ask what-if questions and to take a "maybe-we-could" attitude. Challenging standing assumptions about how something should be done ("We've always done it that way.") is an excellent springboard for creativity. Doing so allows people to break out of assumptions that limit creativity. Supporting employees' extracurricular activities also can spur creativity on the job. For instance, M. P. Muller, founder of Door Number 3, a branding agency, paid for a comedy improvisation class for the company's art director, believing that it would enhance the director's creative talents.[41]

Encouraging employees to "think big" also helps. "Incremental innovation is not a winner's game," says creativity expert John Kao. "The opportunity these days is to become a disruptive inventor," striving for major changes that can revolutionize an entire industry and give the company creating it a significant competitive advantage.[42]

DESIGN A WORK SPACE THAT ENCOURAGES CREATIVITY The physical environment in which people work has an impact on their level of creativity. The cubicles made so famous in the Dilbert cartoon strip can suck creativity right out of a work space. Transforming a typical office space—even one with cubicles—into a haven of creativity does not have to be difficult or expensive. Covering bland walls with funny posters, photographs, murals, or other artwork; adding splashes of color; and incorporating live plants enliven a work space and enhance creativity. Designs that foster employee interaction, especially informal interaction, enhance an organization's creative power.

Because creativity is at the heart of their jobs, employees at Davison Design and Development, a product design company, work in a setting that more closely resembles an amusement park than an office complex. CEO George Davison designed the office, known as Inventionland™, to get employees out of their offices, to interact with one another, and to be inspired by a fun, whimsical environment. The 60,000-square-foot space resembles an amusement park and includes a pirate ship where employees design toys and games for clients and a Think-tank Treehouse for hardware designers. Davison calls Inventionland™ "the world's most innovative workplace" and says that the unusual design has helped the company grow by 10 percent in just 15 months.[43] Even though creating their own version of Inventionland™ may not be practical for every business, entrepreneurs can still stimulate creativity by starting meetings with some type of short, fun exercise designed to encourage participants to think creatively.

VIEW PROBLEMS AS OPPORTUNITIES Every problem offers the opportunity for innovation. One of the best ways to channel a company's innovative energy productively is to address questions that focus employees' attention on customers' problems and how to solve them.

ENTREPRENEURIAL PROFILE: Jessica Scorpio: Getaround Jessica Scorpio, a graduate student at Singularity University, was part of a student team whose assignment was to create a company that would have a positive effect on a billion people over the next 10 years. "The transportation industry hasn't really changed much in the last 50 years, and we thought it was ripe for some innovation," she says. Basic research showed the team that the traditional model of auto ownership is very inefficient; the typical car sits idle 92 percent of the time. In a brainstorming session, the team came up with the idea of person-to-person car sharing and began developing a prototype. Within a month, they had created a geo-locating device that sits inside a car and communicates with nearby customers' smart phones to give them access to the car for a fee. The company, Getaround, sells the device for $100 to car owners, who register their cars on the company's network and set rental fees and schedules. (Owners use Getaround's rating system, which is similar to eBay's ratings of vendors, to decide which customers they will rent to and which they won't.) Renters simply go to Getaround's Web site or use the Getaround smart phone app to search for available cars nearby. Once a car owner approves, the renter locates the car and unlocks it using his or her phone. Scorpio's team estimates that Getaround's convenient car-sharing model reduces driving by 40 to 44 percent. The start-up company recently won the $50,000 Tech-Crunch Disrupt competition, where it gained exposure to angel investors, venture capitalists, and the media.[44] ■

PROVIDE CREATIVITY TRAINING Almost everyone has the capacity to be creative, but developing that capacity requires training. One writer claims, "What separates the average person from Edison, Picasso, or even Shakespeare isn't creative capacity—it's the ability to tap that capacity by encouraging creative impulses and then acting upon them."[45] Training accomplished through books, seminars, workshops, and professional meetings can help everyone learn to tap their creative capacity.

PROVIDE SUPPORT Entrepreneurs must give employees the tools and the resources they need to be creative. Entrepreneurs should remember that creativity often requires nonwork phases, and giving employees time to "daydream" is an important part of the creative process. The creativity that employees display when they know that managers value innovation can be amazing—and profitable. These **intrapreneurs**, entrepreneurs who operate within the framework of an existing business, sometimes can transform a company's future or advance its competitive edge. Jim Lynch, an electrical engineer at iRobot, a leading maker of robotic devices including the Roomba vacuum cleaner, was cleaning the gutters on his house one day and thought, "This is the perfect job for a robot because it fits our company's three criteria: dumb, dirty, and dangerous." Lynch began tinkering and built a gutter-cleaning robot using a spaghetti ladle and an electric screwdriver. At the company's "Idea Bake-Off," an event at which employees have 10 minutes to pitch a new product idea, Lynch's idea received solid support and became an official project. Fellow employees volunteered to work on Lynch's team, and within one year, iRobot introduced the Looj, the world's first gutter-cleaning robot![46]

DEVELOP A PROCEDURE FOR CAPTURING IDEAS Small companies that are outstanding innovators do not earn that mantle by accident; they have a process in place to solicit and then collect new ideas. When workers come up with creative ideas, however, not every organization is prepared to capture them. The unfortunate result is that ideas that might have vaulted a company ahead of its competition or made people's lives better simply evaporate. Without a structured approach for collecting of employees' creative concepts, a business leaves its future to chance. Clever entrepreneurs establish processes within their companies that are designed to harvest the results of employees' creativity. Marissa Mayer, a top manager at Google, frequently holds informal "office hours" like a college professor for employees who want to pitch new ideas. At one session, Mayer learned about one employees' pet project—a search engine for his own computer. Mayer assembled a team to work with the employee and provided the resources they needed, and in just two months, the team had created Google Desktop.[47]

TALK WITH CUSTOMERS—OR, BETTER YET, INTERACT WITH THEM Innovative companies take the time to get feedback about how customers use the companies' products or services, listening for new ideas. The voice of the customer can be an important source of creative ideas, and the Internet allows entrepreneurs to hear their customers' voices quickly and inexpensively. Some companies observe their customers actually using their products or services to glean ideas that may lead to improvements and new features. Other companies go farther, forging alliances with customers to come up with creative ideas and develop new products based on them. Cambridge Fine Foods, a small maker of private-label frozen foods, has added nearly 50 new items to its product line, and 70 percent of them have been the result of collaborations with its customers. The process has been so successful that Cambridge now sends its employees on inspiration-seeking adventures to grocery stores and food shows across the United States, Europe, and Canada with employees from its customers.[48]

MONITOR EMERGING TRENDS AND IDENTIFY WAYS YOUR COMPANY CAN CAPITALIZE ON THEM Taco Bell, the quick-service chain of Mexican restaurants, invests resources in monitoring demographic and social trends that influence customers' dining habits. Two trends that the company recently identified are the demand for healthier menus and customers' focus on value-priced meals. To capitalize on these trends, Taco Bell introduced a fresher, lighter, and healthier Fresco product line and is developing a "home replacement menu" that offers food in large containers that customers take home to share with their families. The company normally creates about 200 new product ideas each year before winnowing them down to about 20 products to introduce into test markets. Those that succeed in the test markets are rolled out nationwide. "Fail to innovate at your own risk," says Taco Bell's chief marketing office, David Ovens.[49]

LOOK FOR USES FOR YOUR COMPANY'S PRODUCTS OR SERVICES IN OTHER MARKETS Focusing on the "traditional" uses of a product or service limits creativity—and a company's sales. Entrepreneurs can boost sales by finding new applications, often in unexpected places, for their products and services.

ENTREPRENEURIAL PROFILE: Neil Wadhawan and Raj Raheja: Heartwood Studios In 2002, Neil Wadhawan and Raj Raheja launched Heartwood Studios, a company that produced three-dimensional renderings and animations of buildings and products for architects and designers. Their business was successful, but a brainstorming session helped the entrepreneurs to realize that their company's three-dimensional renderings had applications in other industries as well. Today Heartwood Studios has clients in the defense and aerospace industries as well as in the fields of entertainment and sports. In fact, the company creates animations for use on the giant screens in sports arenas for the Dallas Cowboys and the New Jersey Nets.[50] ■

REWARD CREATIVITY Entrepreneurs can encourage creativity by rewarding it when it occurs. Financial rewards can be effective motivators of creative behavior, but nonmonetary rewards, such as praise, recognition, and celebration, usually offer more powerful incentives for creativity.

ENTREPRENEURIAL PROFILE: Digital Communications Corporation Digital Communications Corporation, a small company that develops advanced wireless technologies, recognizes employees who develop patentable inventions with stock options, cash awards, and honors at an Inventors' Dinner. The reward system works; within two years after implementing it, the number of patent applications that Digital Communications filed increased by a factor of five![51] ■

MODEL CREATIVE BEHAVIOR Creativity is "caught" as much as it is "taught." Companies that excel at innovation find that the passion for creativity starts at the top. Entrepreneurs who set examples of creative behavior, taking chances, and challenging the status quo soon find their employees doing the same.

ENTREPRENEURIAL PROFILE: Mark Constantine: Lush Cosmetics At Lush Cosmetics, a fast-growing maker of soaps, shampoos, lotions, and moisturizers, founder Mark Constantine understands that a constant stream of innovative new products is one key to his company's success. That's why he holds annual "Mafia meetings," at which Constantine and his staff mark one-third of the company's products for elimination. Although dropping one-third of Lush's product line every year is risky and means that the product development team must come up with at least 100 new products annually, it gives team members incredible freedom and fearlessness to dream. CEO Constantine himself works on new product development for Lush, and most of his ideas, like those of other team members, never make it into finished products. By modeling creative behavior, Constantine encourages creativity among his staff. [52] ■

Enhancing Individual Creativity

Just as entrepreneurs can cultivate an environment of creativity in their organizations by using the techniques described above, they can enhance their own creativity by using the following techniques.

ALLOW YOURSELF TO BE CREATIVE As we have seen, one of the biggest obstacles to creativity occurs when a person believes that he or she is not creative. Giving yourself the permission to be creative is the first step toward establishing a pattern of creative thinking. Refuse to give in to the temptation to ignore ideas simply because you fear that someone else may consider them "stupid." When it comes to creativity, there are no stupid ideas!

FORGET THE "RULES" Creative individuals take a cue from Captain Jack Sparrow in the Pirates of the Caribbean series of movies. When faced with a difficult (sometimes impossible) situation, Sparrow (played by Johnny Depp) usually operates outside the rules and, as a result, comes up with innovative solutions. "[Sparrow] creates new degrees of freedom that enable him to act in ways that someone encumbered by the rules cannot," says one writer. "In that space outside the rules are some pretty interesting solutions."[53]

West Paw Design

GIVE YOUR MIND FRESH INPUT EVERY DAY To be creative, your mind needs stimulation. Do something different each day—listen to a new radio station, take a walk through a park or a shopping center, or pick up a magazine you never read.

ENTREPRENEURIAL PROFILE: Doris Raymond: The Way We Wore The Way We Wore, a huge vintage clothing store in Los Angeles started by Doris Raymond in 2004 that stocks garments from the Victorian era to the 1980s, has become a destination for designers from many fashion houses and retailers, ranging from Marc Jacobs to Forever 21, who are looking for inspiration for their clothing collections. Recognizing that meeting customers' demand for fresh designs gives their clothing lines a competitive advantage, many designers are looking to the past for creative ideas, taking note not only of fabrics and patterns but also of the smallest details, such as buttons and the type of stitching used on pockets. These fashion experts have discovered that exposing their minds to "new" designs is a great way to stimulate their own creativity.[54] ■

TRAVEL—AND OBSERVE Visiting other countries (even other states) is a creativity stimulant. Travelers see new concepts and engage in new experiences that can spark creative ideas. Eric Olson and Al Boyce, both beer aficionados from St. Paul, Minnesota, saw their first PedalPub, a unique bar on wheels that seats up to 14 people and, like a bicycle, is powered by pedaling, in Amsterdam, Netherlands. They contacted the PedalPub's inventors, brothers Henk and Zwier van Laar, and now own the rights to sell the van Laars' PedalPubs in North and South America. The PedalPub weighs 2,340 pounds (with no passengers and no beer on board) and has a top speed of six miles per hour with 10 passengers pedaling.[55]

OBSERVE THE PRODUCTS AND SERVICES OF OTHER COMPANIES, ESPECIALLY THOSE IN COMPLETELY DIFFERENT MARKETS Creative entrepreneurs often borrow ideas from companies that are in businesses totally unrelated to their own. One day as Tariq and Kamran Farid were thinking about ways to increase sales at their flower shop, the brothers came up with the creative idea of combining fresh fruits, such as melons, strawberries, pineapples, and others, into artistic, floral-like arrangements. The Farid brothers launched Edible Arrangements in 1999 with $16,000 of their own money, and the business became a hit. Today, Edible Arrangements has nearly 1,150 franchised outlets around the world and generates annual sales of $23.5 million.[56]

RECOGNIZE THE CREATIVE POWER OF MISTAKES AND ACCIDENTS Innovations sometimes are the result of serendipity, finding something while looking for something else, and sometimes they arise as a result of mistakes or accidents. Creative people recognize that even their errors may lead to new ideas, products, and services. Louis Daguerre, a scene painter for the Paris Opera, was fascinated with lighting and in 1822 began conducting experiments with the effect of light on translucent screens. In 1829, Daguerre formed a partnership with Joseph Niecpe, who had invented a primitive version of photography called the heliograph in 1829. (The exposure time for Niecpe's first photograph was a mere eight hours!) The two men worked for years trying to capture photographic images on metal plates treated with silver iodide, but they made little progress before Niecpe died in 1833. One evening in 1835, Daguerre placed one of his treated plates in his chemical cupboard, intending to recoat it for other experiments. When he removed it later, he was surprised to see a photographic image with brilliant highlights. Excited but puzzled by the outcome, Daguerre finally discovered that mercury vapors from a broken thermometer in the cupboard had caused the photographic image to appear on the treated metal plate. Daguerre refined the process, naming it Daguerreotype after himself, and the world of modern photography was born—and an accident played a significant role.[57]

NOTICE WHAT IS MISSING Sometimes entrepreneurs spot viable business opportunities by noticing something, often very practical and simple, that is *missing*. The first step is to determine whether a market for the missing product or service actually exists (perhaps the reason it does not exist is that there is not market potential), which is one of the objectives of building a business plan.

ENTREPRENEURIAL PROFILE: Carla Lenox: Hey Buddy! Vending While living in Miami, Florida, dog lover and fashion model Carla Lenox noticed that when people walked their dogs in the local park, they lacked most of the supplies their pets needed. Thinking about the prevalence of soft-drink vending machines, Lenox came up with the idea for a successful business: vending machines that sell dog supplies. "There was a need for pickup bags, toys, and water," she says. Lenox spent the next several years researching the idea and developing a business plan. In 2005, she received a patent for her doggie vending machine and trademarks for her company logos and launched Hey Buddy! She placed her first Hey Buddy! vending machine—stocked with lots of doggie necessities, such as treats, tennis balls, frisbees, dog sunglasses, water, bowls, and other items—in Bark Park Central in Dallas, Texas, and now has dozens of the machines across the United States.[58] ∎

KEEP A JOURNAL HANDY TO RECORD YOUR THOUGHTS AND IDEAS Creative ideas are too valuable to waste, so always keep a journal nearby to record them as soon as you get them. Leonardo da Vinci was famous for writing down ideas as they struck him. Patrick McNaughton invented the neon blackboards that restaurants use to advertise their specials. In addition to the neon blackboard, McNaughton has invented more than 30 new products, many of which are sold through the company that he and his sister, Jamie, own. McNaughton credits much of his creative success to the fact that he writes down every idea he gets and keeps it in a special folder. "There's no such thing as a crazy idea," he insists.[59]

LISTEN TO OTHER PEOPLE No rule of creativity says that an idea has to be your own! Sometimes the best business ideas come from someone else, but entrepreneurs are the ones to act on them.

ENTREPRENEURIAL PROFILE: Cameron Roelofson: Splash Mobile Car Wash Cameron Roelofson, owner of Splash Mobile Car Wash in Concord, Ontario, washes 2,500 tractor-trailer trucks per week during warm months, but sales in his highly seasonal business fall to nothing during the frigid winters. On one cold winter day, Roelofson was talking with an acquaintance who asked if he would use his mobile truck-washing equipment to put water into an outdoor skating rink. He agreed and quickly realized the potential for a business that would offset seasonality in sales in his truck-washing business. Roelofson began advertising, and sales took off. For $1,000 to $2,000, Splash builds a frame with a reusable liner and then fills it with water. Three days later, frozen solid in Ontario's winter weather, the rink is ready for skating or hockey. In the spring, Splash returns to disassemble the rink and store it until the next winter.[60] ∎

LISTEN TO CUSTOMERS Some of the best ideas for new products and services or new applications of an existing product or service come from a company's customers. Entrepreneurs who take the time to listen to their customers often receive ideas that they may never have come up with on their own. Medtronic, a maker of a variety of medical devices, has created many innovative products and improvements to its existing products by getting feedback from its physician customers. The company has embraced a variety of social networking tools to generate ideas about specific products and problems from employees and from customers and inventors around the globe.[61]

WATCH A MOVIE Great business ideas come from the strangest places, even the movies. As a child, Stanley Yang was fascinated by sci-fi movies such as *Star Wars*. That fascination led him to become an engineer so that he could transform his ideas into reality. Yang's company, NeuroSky,

has developed headsets that allow people to control video games with their minds using biosensor technology, a concept used by an advanced alien race in the movie *Battle Los Angeles*. "Movies may spark an idea," says Yang, who still dreams of building a functional light saber.

TALK TO A CHILD As we grow older, we learn to conform to society's expectations about many things, including creative solutions to problems. Children place very few limitations on their thinking; as a result, their creativity is practically boundless. (Remember all the games you and your friends invented when you were young?)

Courtesy of Pumponator Inc.

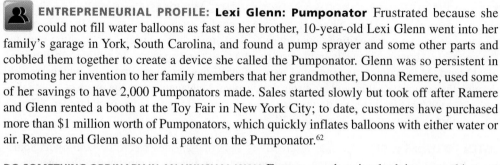 **ENTREPRENEURIAL PROFILE: Lexi Glenn: Pumponator** Frustrated because she could not fill water balloons as fast as her brother, 10-year-old Lexi Glenn went into her family's garage in York, South Carolina, and found a pump sprayer and some other parts and cobbled them together to create a device she called the Pumponator. Glenn was so persistent in promoting her invention to her family members that her grandmother, Donna Remere, used some of her savings to have 2,000 Pumponators made. Sales started slowly but took off after Ramere and Glenn rented a booth at the Toy Fair in New York City; to date, customers have purchased more than $1 million worth of Pumponators, which quickly inflates balloons with either water or air. Ramere and Glenn also hold a patent on the Pumponator.[62]

DO SOMETHING ORDINARY IN AN UNUSUAL WAY Experts say that simply doing something out of the ordinary can stimulate creativity. To stimulate his own creativity, Scott Jones, an entrepreneur who is known as "the guy who invented voice mail" (and many other items as well), often engages in what other people might consider bizarre behavior—eating without utensils, watching television sitting one foot away from the screen, or taking a shower with his eyes closed. "Anything I normally do, I'll do differently just to see what happens," says Jones.[63]

KEEP A TOY BOX IN YOUR OFFICE Your box might include silly objects, such as wax lips, a yo-yo, a Slinky, fortune cookie sayings, feathers, a top, a compass, or a host of other items. When you are stumped, pick an item at random from the toy box and think about how it relates to your problem.

TAKE NOTE OF YOUR "PAIN POINTS" Do other people experience them as well? Entrepreneurs often create innovations to solve problems they themselves face. Observing "pain points" that result from missing products or services or flaws in existing products or services can be an excellent source of business ideas.

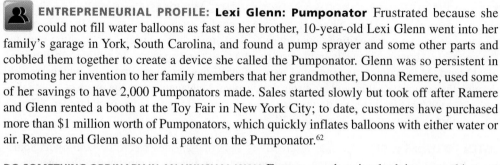 **ENTREPRENEURIAL PROFILE: Ingrid Carney: Ingrid and Isabel** As Ingrid Carney's midsection grew during her first pregnancy, she faced a common problem: she wasn't yet large enough for maternity clothing, but she had "no possibility of buttoning my pants," she recalls. Her solution was to leave her pants unbuttoned and slip a long tank top over them to conceal the gap. Carney began thinking about a better solution and came up with the Bellaband, a wide elastic band that comes in a variety of colors and allows a woman to wear her "regular" clothing far longer into her pregnancy. The band conceals and smoothes the unfastened waistband of pants and skirts and holds the garments in place. Carney launched Ingrid and Isabel (her daughter, who "inspired" the invention) to market the Bellaband, which is sold online, in more than 600 independent maternity boutiques, and in several large department stores. Carney is working to extend her product line and expand into international markets.[64] ∎

DO NOT THROW AWAY SEEMINGLY "BAD" IDEAS Some creative ideas prove to be impractical, too costly, or too silly to work. Creative entrepreneurs, however, do not discard these seemingly bad ideas. Instead, they ask, "What part of this idea can I build on?" and "What could I change about this idea to make it work?" They realize that seemingly bad ideas can be the nucleus of a really good idea. Spencer Williams, president of West Paw Design, the company that encourages creativity with its creativity contest featuring the Golden Hairball Award, says that many of the great ideas for new products come from ideas that don't win the contest. The company's R&D team meets after each contest to review *all* the ideas that employees submit. "We look for one piece of a new idea," he says.[65]

READ BOOKS ON STIMULATING CREATIVITY OR TAKE A CLASS ON CREATIVITY Creative thinking is a technique that anyone can learn. Understanding and applying the principles of creativity can improve dramatically the ability to develop new and innovative ideas.

TAKE SOME TIME OFF Relaxation is vital to the creative process. Getting away from a problem gives the mind time to reflect on it. It is often during this time, while the subconscious works on a problem, that the mind generates many creative solutions. One study reports that 35 percent of entrepreneurs say that they come up with their best ideas during downtime, when they are away from work.[66] One creativity expert claims that fishing is the ideal activity for stimulating creativity. "Your brain is on high alert in case a fish is around," he says, "but your brain is completely relaxed. This combination is the time when you have the 'Aha!' moment."[67]

BE PERSISTENT Entrepreneurs know that one secret to success is persistence and a "don't-quit" attitude. Twelve publishers rejected J. K. Rowling's manuscript about the adventures of a boy wizard and his friends, which she started writing at age 25 when she was a single mother trying to raise her children on welfare, before Bloomsbury, a small London publishing house, agreed to publish 1,000 copies of *Harry Potter and the Philosopher's Stone*. Rowling's seven-part Harry Potter book series went on to sell more than 450 million copies worldwide, making Rowling the first billionaire author.[68]

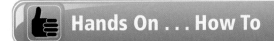

Hands On . . . How To

Be a Successful Innovator

Creativity and innovation traditionally have played an important part in entrepreneurial success. Today, their role has become an even more vital component as businesses face increasing pressure to produce innovations to remain competitive. "Not so long ago," says one writer, "we could find success in life by simply copying the success of others, by learning what others already knew and applying it. But those days are fading. The kind of unique challenges that were once taken on by only a few brave souls with the courage to cross oceans are now a routine part of life."

Entrepreneurs are among the brave souls who challenge existing ideas, norms, values, and business practices and often produce valuable breakthrough products that make them and their companies terrific success stories. What lessons can we learn from successful entrepreneurs about innovation?

Recognize That "Innovation" Is Not Necessarily Synonymous with "Invention"

Some of the most successful entrepreneurs in history actually did not invent the products that made them famous. Henry Ford, founder of Ford Motor Company, said, "I invented nothing new. I simply assembled into a car the discoveries of other men behind whom were centuries of work." Of course, Ford did make innovations in the auto assembly process, creating in 1913 the first mass-assembly process that made cars affordable for the average person. Similarly, Steve Job's Apple Inc. did not invent the MP3 player, but Jobs's innovation was to recognize that people would pay to download music over the Internet, allowing them to create their own customized music libraries. In doing so, he

revolutionized the music industry. Successful entrepreneurs often find new ways to connect existing technologies to create value.

Find the Intersection of "Problem" and "Solution"

Some entrepreneurs launch businesses with a focus on marketing their products or services to a particular audience but fail to ask whether their products and services actually solve a real problem that customers face. "If you're not solving a problem, the world won't care," explains Ben Kaufman, founder of Quirky, a social product development company that serves aspiring inventors. Successful innovators often spot a "pain point" in their own lives and realize that other people face the same problem as well. Romy Taormina and Carla Falcone came up with the idea for Psi (pronounced "sigh") Bands when they bonded over morning sickness during their pregnancies. They wanted relief from morning sickness without taking drugs and discovered the power of an acupressure point on the wrist that alleviates nausea. Taormina and Falcone created an adjustable, waterproof, affordable band that stimulates that acupressure point and reduces feelings of nausea for expectant mothers, people suffering from motion sickness, or patients recovering from anesthesia. The FDA has approved the use of Psi Bands, and the company now sells its products through several drug store chains and the television shopping network QVC.

Entrepreneurs often spot "pain points" by noting the following:

- Complaints they hear from other people

- The inconvenience of buying a product or service

(continued)

Hands On . . . How To (continued)

- A fundamental flaw in an existing product or service

- A product or service that can make life easier

- A product or service that can add to one's well-being (such as the Psi Band)

- A simpler way to access a product or service

Realize That Innovation Typically Is the Result of an Iterative Feedback Cycle

Innovations often come about when entrepreneurs come up with an idea, test it, discover what works (and what doesn't work), and then modify their idea based on this feedback. This cycle of developing ideas, testing them, and refining them is an essential part of the creative process. Thomas Edison, recipient of a record 1,093 patents, including the patents for the phonograph and the lightbulb, said, "The real measure of success is the number of experiments that can be crowded into 24 hours."

Beware of Faulty Assumptions

One of the most dangerous assumptions that innovative entrepreneurs can make is that customers are as excited about their innovations as they themselves are. Like Edison, successful innovators see the pathway to entrepreneurship as a series of experiments. One of the most valuable experiments that an entrepreneur can undertake is to get feedback from potential customers. Confirmation of an idea tells an entrepreneur that he or she is on the right track; conversely, lukewarm or negative customer feedback suggests that he or she drop the idea and move to another, more promising one. Andrew Hargadon, director of the Center for Entrepreneurship at the University of California, Davis, recalls a student entrepreneur who had developed a novel pathology device. Part of her feedback cycle included talking with surgeons, whose response was overwhelmingly positive and gave her the confidence to pursue commercializing the device. Her conversations with the surgeons also produced several suggestions for improvement that she had not thought of.

Innovators, says one writer, are "figure-outers." When faced with problems and opportunities, they figure out how to deal with them successfully and in the process create innovations.

Sources: Based on Andrew B. Hargadon, "7 Ways to Make Students More Entrepreneurial," *Chronicle of Higher Education*, March 28, 2010, http://chronicle.com/article/Teaching-Matters-7-Ways-to/64841; Jeff Cornwall, "The Entrepreneurship Educator," May 2010, p. 1; Donna Fenn, "Will Your New Product Be a Hit or a Flop? Answer These 5 Questions to Find Out," *BNET*, January 20, 2011, http://www.bnet.com/blog/entrepreneurs/will-your-new-product-be-a-hit-or-a-flop-answer-these-5-questions-to-find-out/1571; Dennis Stauffer, "The Best Figure-Outers Win," *Insight Fusion*, June 13, 2011, http://www.insightfusion.com/blog/index.php/.../the-best-figure-outers-win; and "Romy Taormina and Carla Falcone Give Nausea Sufferers a 'Psi' of Relief," National Association of Women Business Owners, http://nawbo.org/content_6847.cfm.

LO6

Describe the steps in the creative process.

The Creative Process

Although creative ideas may appear to strike as suddenly as a bolt of lightning, they are actually the result of the creative process, which involves seven steps:

1. Preparation

2. Investigation

3. Transformation

4. Incubation

5. Illumination

6. Verification

7. Implementation

Step 1. Preparation

This step involves getting the mind ready for creative thinking. Preparation might include a formal education, on-the-job training, work experience, and taking advantage of other learning opportunities. This training provides a foundation on which to build creativity and innovation. As one writer explains, "Creativity favors the prepared mind."[69] For example, Dr. Hamel Navia, a scientist at tiny Vertex Pharmaceuticals, was working on a promising new drug to fight the AIDS virus. His preparation included earning an advanced degree in the field of medicine and learning to use computers to create three-dimensional images of the protein molecules he was studying.[70] How can you prepare your mind for creative thinking?

- Adopt the attitude of a lifelong student. Realize that educating yourself is a never-ending process. Look at every situation you encounter as an opportunity to learn.

ENTREPRENEURIAL PROFILE: Tony Brennan: Sharklet Technologies Tony Brennan, a materials science and engineering professor, was searching for a way to keep barnacles from clinging to ships' hulls. He began studying sharkskin, which is known for its ability to resist microbes, and discovered the key at a microscopic level: the diamond-shaped pattern of tiny tooth-like outcroppings that prevent microbes from sticking. Brennan's research led him to start Sharklet Technologies, a company in Aurora, Colorado, that makes a sharkskin-inspired, micropatterned fabric called SafeTouch that resists the growth of bacteria and can be applied to almost any high-touch surface. Sharklet is selling SafeTouch to hospitals, labs, research centers, and owners of public spaces that are prone to high concentrations of bacteria.[71] ■

- Read—a lot—and not just in your field of expertise. Many innovations come from blending ideas and concepts from different fields in science, engineering, business, and the arts. Reading books, magazines, and papers covering a variety of subject matter is a great way to stimulate your creativity.

- Clip articles of interest to you and create a file for them. Over time, you will build a customized encyclopedia of information from which to draw ideas and inspiration.

- Take time to discuss your ideas with other people, including those who know little about it as well as experts in the field. Sometimes, the apparently simple questions that an "unknowledgeable" person asks lead to new discoveries and to new approaches to an old problem. Don Medoff breathed creativity into his Tucson, Arizona–based supplier of windows and doors by bringing in as consultants college students from the nearby University of Arizona. Medoff and his managers briefed teams of students on several of the company's stickiest problems and asked them for ideas on how to solve them. The student teams created new packaging ideas for several products, developed new television commercials, and made suggestions for updating the company's Web site. Medoff, who implemented most of the students' ideas, says that their input was "invaluable" and is working with the university on other projects for students to tackle.[72]

- Join professional or trade associations and attend their meetings. There you have the chance to interact with others who have similar interests. Learning how other people have solved a particular problem may give you fresh insight into solving it.

- Develop listening skills. It's amazing what you can learn if you take the time to listen to other people—especially those who are older and have more experience. Try to learn something from everyone you meet.

- Eliminate creative distractions. Interruptions from telephone calls, e-mails, and visitors can crush creativity. Allowing employees to escape to a quiet, interruption-free environment enhances their ability to be creative.

Step 2. Investigation

This step requires one to develop a solid understanding of the problem, situation, or decision at hand. To create new ideas and concepts in a particular field, an individual first must study the problem and understand its basic components. Creative thinking comes about when people make careful observations of the world around them and then investigate the way things work (or fail to work). For example, Dr. Navia and another scientist at Vertex had spent several years conducting research on viruses and on a protein that blocks a virus enzyme called protease. His exploration of the various ways to block this enzyme paved the way for his discovery.

ENTREPRENEURIAL PROFILE: Christopher Leamon and Endocyte After earning his PhD in chemistry, Christopher Leamon began researching targeted anticancer therapy using molecules that tumors absorb as "Trojan horses" to deliver drugs that are lethal to them. Initially, Leamon had focused on the vitamin biotin, but after nine months of research and hard work, "it was a total failure," he says. One morning while sitting at the breakfast table with his wife, Leamon, a longtime cereal lover, was reading the ingredients on the nutrition panel of his box of Kellogg's Frosted Flakes. One of the items, folic acid, caught his attention. Leamon dashed off to the library and found a research paper on how folic acid enters a human cell. "I knew this was it," he recalls. Before long, Leamon had developed a technique for attaching cancer drugs to folic acid so that they would be absorbed and enable cells to fight the disease in much the same way they battle infections. Leamon has licensed the promising therapy to a company called Endocyte, which plans to have drugs on the market within a few years. "There are lots of 'Eureka' moments in the lab," says Leamon. "None as great as the one with the folic acid though. That breakfast redefined my career and my life."[73] ■

Step 3. Transformation

convergent thinking
the ability to see similarities and the connections among various data and events.

Transformation involves viewing the similarities and the differences among the information collected. This phase requires two types of thinking: convergent and divergent. **Convergent thinking** is the ability to see the *similarities* and the connections among various and often diverse data and events. "So much of innovation comes from connecting things where other people don't make connections," says Mark Rice, professor of technology entrepreneurship at Olin College.[74]

ENTREPRENEURIAL PROFILE: Kate Szilagyi: Tempaper Kate Szilagyi, a former set decorator in the film industry and window designer for Saks Fifth Avenue, knew all too well how difficult replacing traditional wallpaper is. Working with her nieces, Jennifer and Julia Biancella, Szilagyi combined the concepts of traditional wallpaper and Post-It notes to develop wallpaper that uses a temporary adhesive (similar to the one used on Post-It notes). The resulting wallpaper, which they call Tempaper, acts like a giant sticker and is easily removable and restickable. Installation involves peeling off a backing and sticking it on the wall. The entrepreneurs sell Tempaper through their New York City–based company, Lolliprops, for $75 to $85 for a 33-foot roll.[75] ■

divergent thinking
the ability to see among various data and events.

Divergent thinking is the ability to see the *differences* among various data and events. While developing his AIDS-fighting drug, Dr. Navia studied the work of other scientists whose attempts at developing an enzyme-blocking drug had failed. He was able to see the similarities and the differences in his research and theirs and to build on their successes while avoiding their failures.

How can you increase your ability to transform the information collected into a purposeful idea?

- Evaluate the parts of the situation several times, trying to grasp the "big picture." Getting bogged down in the details of a situation too early in the creative process can diminish creativity. Look for patterns that emerge.

- Rearrange the elements of the situation. By looking at the components of an issue in a different order or from a different perspective, you may be able to see the similarities and the differences among them more readily. Rearranging them also may help uncover a familiar pattern that had been masked by an unfamiliar structure. Engineers at Windtronics, a company in Muskegon, Michigan, rearranged the elements of a traditional power-generating wind turbine, moving them from the center to the outside of the blades. As a result, the blades of Windtronics turbines turn faster, operate more quietly and efficiently, and can generate electricity at wind speeds as low as two miles per hour, compared to six to eight miles per hour for traditional turbines. At just six feet in diameter, Windtronics turbines are suitable for industrial, commercial, and residential use. "We've turned traditional wind turbines inside out," says CEO Reg Adams.[76]

- Try using synectics (a term derived from the Greek words for "to bring together" and "diversity"), taking two seemingly nonsensical ideas and combining them. For instance, why not launch a bookstore with no physical storefront and no books—an accurate description of what Jeff Bezos did when he came up with the idea for Amazon.com.[77]

- Before locking into one particular approach to a situation, remember that several approaches might be successful. If one approach produces a dead end, don't hesitate to jump quickly to another. Considering several approaches to a problem or opportunity simultaneously would be like rolling a bowling ball down each of several lanes in quick succession.

The more balls you roll down the lanes, the greater is the probability of hitting at least one strike. Resist the temptation to make snap judgments on how to tackle a problem or opportunity. The first approach may not be the best one.

Step 4. Incubation

The subconscious needs time to reflect on the information collected. To an observer, this phase of the creative process would be quite boring; it looks as though nothing is happening! In fact, during this phase, it may appear that the creative person is *loafing*. Incubation occurs while the individual is away from the problem, often engaging in some totally unrelated activity. Dr. Navia's creative powers were working at a subconscious level even when he was away from his work, not even thinking about his research on AIDS-fighting drugs.

How can you enhance the incubation phase of the creative process, letting ideas marinate in your mind?

- Walk away from the situation. Time away from a problem is vital to enhancing creativity. A study by Wilson Brill, an expert on creativity, of how 350 great ideas became successful products shows that two-thirds of the ideas came to people while they were *away* from work—in the shower, in their cars, in bed, on a walk, and in other nonwork situations.[78] Doing something totally unrelated to the problem gives your subconscious mind the chance to work on the problem or opportunity. David Baker, a 13-year-old middle school student from Massachusetts, came up with the idea for a pen-sized projection system while sitting in church. Baker, who is fascinated with engineering, earned patent number 7,535,436 for his "light beam delivery system" and has three more patents related to his invention pending. Baker currently is working on a three-dimensional digital printer that produces prototypes of plastic parts.[79]

- Take the time to daydream. Although it may *look* as if you're doing nothing, daydreaming is an important part of the creative process. That's when your mind is most free from self-imposed restrictions on creativity. Research shows a connection between daydreaming and creativity; people who daydream are better at generating new ideas.[80] Feel free to let your mind wander, and it may just stumble onto a creative solution.

- Relax—and play—regularly. Perhaps the worst thing you can do for creativity is to work on a problem or opportunity constantly. Soon enough, fatigue walks in, and creativity walks out! Great ideas often are incubated on the golf course, on the basketball court, on a hiking trail, or in the hammock.

    ENTREPRENEURIAL PROFILE: Aaron Lemieux: Tremont Electric Aaron Lemieux was carrying a backpack while hiking the 1,500-mile Appalachian Trail when the idea for his business struck. Lemieux, trained as a mechanical and biomedical engineer, grew tired of purchasing disposable batteries along the way to power his portable devices and began to think about ways to capture the wasted kinetic energy generated by the movement of his backpack. Lemieux's hiking experience led him to launch Tremont Electric, a company that produces the nPower Personal Energy Generator (PEG), a small, lightweight electrical generator that produces enough energy to power personal electronic devices by simply harvesting kinetic energy from normal human movement, such as walking.[81] ■

- Dream about the problem or opportunity. "Dreams have been responsible for two Nobel prizes, the invention of a couple of major drugs, other scientific discoveries, several important political events, and innumerable novels, films, and works of visual art," says Harvard Medical School psychologist Dierdre Barrett.[82] Although you may not be able to dream on command, thinking about an issue just before you drift off to sleep can be an effective way to encourage your mind to work on it while you sleep, a process called lucid dreaming. Barret's research suggests that about 50 percent of people can focus their dreams by contemplating a particular problem before they go to sleep, in essence, "seeding" the subconscious to influence their dreams.[83] The design for Dennis Hong's latest robot, the HyDRAS, came to him in a dream. "In dreams, I see lines and colors that float around," he says. "Wacky, weird ideas come out of it." The HyDRAS is a snake-like robot that can climb just about anything, which enables it to perform tasks that would be dangerous to humans, such as inspecting towers, bridges, and oil and gas pipelines.[84]

● Work on the problem or opportunity in a different environment—somewhere other than the office. Take your work outside on a beautiful fall day or sit on a bench in a mall. The change of scenery will likely stimulate your creativity.

Step 5. Illumination

This phase of the creative process occurs at some point during the incubation stage when a spontaneous breakthrough causes "the lightbulb to go on." It may take place after five minutes—or five years. In the illumination stage, all the previous stages come together to produce the "Eureka factor"—the creation of the innovative idea. In one study of 200 scientists, 80 percent said that at least once a solution to a problem had "just popped into their heads"—usually when they were away from the problem.[85] For Dr. Navia, the illumination stage occurred one day while he was reading a scientific journal. As he read, Dr. Navia says that he was struck with a "hallucination" of a novel way to block protease.

Although the creative process itself may last for months or even years, the suddenness with which the illumination step occurs can be deceiving, making the process appear to occur much faster than it actually does. One night, Kent Murphy, an electrical engineer, began dreaming about what it would be like to be a photon of light. "I was riding a ray of light moving through the fiber," he recalls about his dream. Murphy, who holds 30 patents, used the insight from his dream to invent a fiber-optic gauge that monitors on a real-time basis the structural wear in airplanes.[86]

Step 6. Verification

For entrepreneurs, validating an idea as realistic and useful may include conducting experiments, running simulations, test-marketing a product or service, establishing small-scale pilot programs, building prototypes, and many other activities designed to verify that the new idea will work and is practical to implement. The goal is to subject the innovative idea to the test of cold, hard reality. At this phase, appropriate questions to ask include the following:

● Is it *really* a better solution to a particular problem or opportunity? Sometimes an idea that appears to have a bright future in the lab or on paper dims considerably when put to the test of reality.

● Will it work?

● Is there a need for it?

● If so, what is the best application of this idea in the marketplace?

● Does this product or service idea fit into our core competencies?

● How much will it cost to produce or to provide?

● Can we sell it at a reasonable price that will produce adequate sales, profit, and return on investment for our business?

Ramtron International Corporation, a maker of memory chips, uses a "product justification form" to collect information from the idea generator as well as from other departments in the company so that it can verify the potential of each idea.[87] To test the value of his new drug formulation, Dr. Navia used powerful computers at Vertex Pharmaceuticals to build three-dimensional Tinkertoy-like models of the HIV virus and then simulated his new drug's ability to block the protease enzyme. Subsequent testing of the drug verified its safety. "I was convinced that I had an insight that no one else had," he recalls.[88]

Step 7. Implementation

The focus of this step is to transform the idea into reality. Plenty of people come up with creative ideas for promising new products or services, but most never take them beyond the idea stage. What sets entrepreneurs apart is that they *act* on their ideas. An entrepreneur's philosophy is "Ready, aim, fire," not "Ready, aim, aim, aim, aim." Innowattech, a company based in Ra'anana, Israel, has developed a variety of piezoelectric (PE) crystals that possess the ability to transform vibrations, motion, and temperature changes into clean energy. Like miniature generators, the pressure-sensitive ceramic crystals give off small electrical charges when "squeezed, squashed, bent, or slapped," says Markys Cain, a materials scientist. In a recent test, Innowattech placed PE generators two inches beneath a small section of Israel's busy Highway 4, where passing cars compressed the road, activated the tiny generators, and produced energy. The company estimates that placing the PE crystals under a one-half-mile stretch of highway would generate enough energy to supply 250 homes. Innowattech also has developed crystals for collecting clean energy from railways, airport runways, and pedestrian walkways. Pavegen Systems, a London-based company, has developed a similar technology for pedestrian walkways that captures the kinetic energy from passersby. Installed on a busy thoroughfare, the company's energy-absorbing pads (which are made from recycled material) can generate enough energy to power the area's lighting and signs.[89] The key to both companies' success is their ability to take a creative idea for a useful new product and turn it into a reality. As one creativity expert explains, "Becoming more creative is really just a matter of paying attention to that endless flow of ideas you generate, and learning to capture and act upon the new that's within you."[90]

For Dr. Navia and Vertex Pharmaceuticals, the implementation phase required testing the drug's ability to fight the deadly virus in humans. If it proved to be effective, Vertex would complete the process by bringing the drug to market. In this final phase of testing, Navia was so certain that he was on the verge of a major breakthrough in fighting AIDS that he couldn't sleep at night. Unfortunately, the final critical series of tests proved that Dr. Navia's flash of creativity was, as he now says, "completely, totally, and absolutely incorrect." Although his intuition proved to be wrong this time, Dr. Navia's research into fighting AIDS continues. Much of the current work at Vertex is based on Dr. Navia's original idea. Although it proved to be incorrect, his idea has served a valuable purpose: generating new ideas. "We are now applying a powerful technology in HIV research that wasn't used before, one inspired by a hunch," he says.[91]

Techniques for Improving the Creative Process

LO7

Discuss techniques for improving the creative process.

Teams of people working together usually can generate more and more creative ideas. Five techniques that are especially useful for improving the quality of creative ideas from teams are brainstorming, mind mapping, force-field analysis, TRIZ, and rapid prototyping.

Brainstorming

Brainstorming is a process in which a small group of people interact with very little structure with the goal of producing a large *quantity* of novel and imaginative ideas. The goal is to create an open, uninhibited atmosphere that allows members of the group to "freewheel" ideas. Participants should suggest any ideas that come to *mind without evaluating or criticizing them*. As group members interact, each idea sparks the thinking of others, and the spawning of ideas becomes contagious. The free-flowing energy generated by the team becomes the genesis of a multitude of ideas, some of which may be impractical; however, those impractical ideas may lead to one idea that results in a breakthrough product or service for a company. For a brainstorming session to be successful, entrepreneurs should follow these guidelines:

brainstorming
a process in which a small group of people interact with very little structure with the goal of producing a large quantity of novel and imaginative ideas.

- Keep the group small—just five to eight members. Amazon founder Jeff Bezos uses the "two-pizza rule"—if a brainstorming group can eat two pizzas, it's too big.[92]

- Make the group as diverse as possible. Include people with different backgrounds, disciplines, and perspectives. At Joe Design Inc., every employee in the small firm takes part in brainstorming sessions. "We bring in everybody from the bookkeeper to the office manager because they see things completely differently than we do," says cofounder Joe Raia.[93]

- Encourage participants to engage in some type of aerobic exercise before the session. One study found that people who exercise—walking, bicycling, swimming, or running—before brainstorming sessions were more creative than those who did not exercise.[94]

- Company rank and department affiliation are irrelevant. Every member of the brainstorming team is on equal ground.

- Give the group a well-defined problem. Stating the problem in the form of a "why," "how," or "what" question often helps.

- Rather than waste precious group meeting time getting participants up to speed, provide everyone involved in the session with relevant background material about the problem to be solved. Invite participants to submit at least three ideas by e-mail before the brainstorming session takes place. This gets people's minds focused on the issue.

- Limit the session to 40 to 60 minutes. Beyond that, participants grow weary, and creativity flags because brainstorming is an intense activity.

- Take a field trip. Visit the scene of the problem, if possible. Research shows that brainstorming teams that go "on-site" actually come up with more and better ideas.[95]

- Appoint someone (preferably not a brainstorming participant) the job of recorder. The recorder should write every idea on a flip chart or board so that everyone can see it.

- Use a seating pattern that encourages communication and interaction (e.g., circular or U-shaped arrangements).

- Throw logic out the window. The best brainstorming sessions are playful and anything but logical.

- Encourage *all* ideas from the team, even wild and extreme ones. Discourage participants from editing their ideas. Not only can ideas that initially seem crazy get the group's creative juices flowing, but they also can spread creativity like wildfire. In addition, the group often can polish some of these wild ideas into practical, creative solutions!

- Establish a goal of *quantity* of ideas over *quality* of ideas. There will be plenty of time later to evaluate the ideas generated. At Ideo Inc., a Silicon Valley design firm, brainstorming teams shoot for at least 150 ideas in a 30- to 45-minute session.[96] When chemist Linus Pauling received his second Nobel Prize, someone asked him how he came up with so many great ideas. Pauling replied simply, "I come up with lots of ideas."[97]

- *Forbid* evaluation or criticism of any idea during the brainstorming session. No idea is a bad idea. Criticism slams the brakes on the creative process instantly!

- Encourage participants to use "idea hitchhiking," building new ideas on those already suggested. Often, some of the best solutions are those that are piggybacked on others.

- Dare to imagine the unreasonable. Creative ideas often arise when people suspend conventional thinking to consider far-fetched solutions.

ENTREPRENEURIAL PROFILE: John Nottingham: Nottingham-Spirk At Nottingham-Spirk, an industrial design firm whose success depends on the creativity of its people, employees routinely use brainstorming to come up with new product ideas and designs. The focus of these sessions is to generate a large quantity of ideas, "from mild to wild," says co-founder John Nottingham, rather than to emphasize the quality of the ideas. By the end of the session, the walls are covered with pieces of paper containing scribbles, sketches, and notes, representing 100 or more ideas. Only after the brainstorming session do employees begin to focus on the quality of the ideas generated. In these meetings, employees judge each idea using a simple scale. Each person can display one of three cards: "Who Cares?," "Nice," and "Wow!" (All participants display their cards simultaneously.) A consensus of "Who Cares?" cards means that the group discards the idea, but a strong showing of "Wow!" cards means that the idea moves forward for refinement. A vote of "Nice" usually means that the idea goes back for more brainstorming, hopefully transforming it into a "Wow!" idea. An idea for a Christmas tree stand that uses a swivel joint and a locking pedal initially received a "Nice" rating from the group. The idea's champion kept tinkering with it, ultimately adding a self-regulating automatic watering device and other features before returning to the group. In its second pass, the idea went from "Nice" to "Wow!" Since 2002, the SwivelStraight tree stand has sold 1 million units.[98] ∎

Mind Mapping

Another useful tool for jump-starting creativity is **mind mapping**, an extension of brainstorming. One strength of mind mapping is that it reflects the way the brain actually works. Rather than throwing out ideas in a linear fashion, the brain jumps from one idea to another. In many creative sessions, ideas are rushing out so fast that many are lost if a person attempts to shove them into a linear outline. Creativity suffers. Mind mapping is a graphical technique that encourages thinking on both sides of the brain, visually displays the various relationships among ideas, and improves the ability to view a problem from many sides.

mind mapping
a graphical technique that encourages thinking on both sides of the brain, visually displays the various relationships among ideas, and improves the ability to view a problem from many sides.

The mind-mapping process works this way:

- Start by writing down or sketching a picture symbolizing the problem or area of focus in the center of a large blank page. Tony Buzan, originator of the mind-mapping technique, suggests using ledger paper or covering an entire wall with butcher paper to establish a wide-open attitude toward creativity.

- Write down *every* idea that comes into your mind, connecting each idea to the central picture or words with a line. Use key words and symbols to record ideas in shorthand. Work as quickly as possible for no more than 20 minutes, doing your best to capture the tide of ideas that flows from your brain. Just as in brainstorming, do not judge the quality of your ideas; just get them onto the paper. Build new ideas on the backs of existing ones. If you see a connection between a new idea and one already on the paper, connect them with a line. If not, simply connect the idea to the center symbol. You will organize your ideas later in the process.

- When the flow of ideas slows to a trickle, stop! Don't try to force creativity.

- Allow your mind to rest for a few minutes and then begin to integrate the ideas on the page into a mind map. Use colored pens and markers to connect ideas with similar themes or to group ideas into related clusters. As you organize your thoughts, look for new connections among your ideas. Sometimes the brain needs time to process the ideas in a mind map. (Recall the incubation stage of the creative process.) Walking away from the mind map and the problem for a few minutes or a few hours may lead to several new ideas or to new relationships among ideas. One entrepreneur created the format for his company's business plan with a mind map rather than with a traditional linear outline. When he finished, he not only knew what he should include in his plan but also had a clear picture of the order in which to sequence the elements.

Force-Field Analysis

Force-field analysis is a useful technique for evaluating the forces that support and oppose a proposed change. It allows entrepreneurs to weigh both the advantages and the disadvantages of a particular decision and work to maximize the variables that support it and minimize those that work against it. The process, which, like brainstorming, works well with a group, begins by making three columns and listing the problem to be addressed in the center column. In the column on the left, the group should list driving forces, those that support the issue and move it forward. In the column on the right, the group should list the restraining forces, those that hold back the company from implementing the idea. The specific forces that the group may come up with are almost limitless, but some of the factors the team should consider include people, values, costs, trends, traditions, politics, costs, revenues, environmental impact, regulations, and attitudes.

Once the group has identified a reasonable number of driving and restraining forces (4 to 10 is typical), the next task is to assign a numerical value that reflects the strength of that particular force. For the driving forces column, scores range from 1 (weak) to 4 (strong), and in the restraining forces column, scores range from -1 (weak) to -4 (strong). Adding the scores for the driving forces column and the restraining forces column shows which set of forces dominates the issue. The higher the total score, the more feasible is the idea. If the decision is a "go," the group can focus on ideas to create new driving forces, strengthen existing driving forces, and minimize the impact of restraining forces.

FIGURE 2.3

Sample Force-Field Analysis

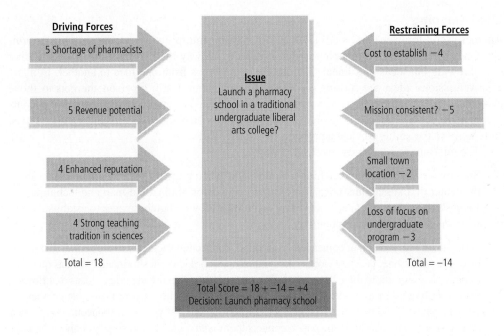

Force-field analysis produces many benefits, particularly when it is combined with other creativity enhancing techniques. It helps entrepreneurs judge the practicality of a new idea, identify resources the company can use to bring the idea to market, recognize obstacles that the company must overcome to implement the idea, and suggest ways to conquer those obstacles.

Figure 2.3 shows a sample force-field analysis for a small liberal arts college that is considering an entrepreneurial venture, launching a pharmacy school.

TRIZ

Developed in 1946 by Genrich Altshuller, a 22-year-old naval officer in the former Soviet Union, TRIZ (pronounced "trees") is a systematic approach designed to help solve any technical problem, whatever its source. The name is derived from the acronym for the Russian phrase that translates as "theory of inventive problem solving." Unlike brainstorming and mind mapping, which are right-brain activities, TRIZ is a left-brain, scientific, step-by-step process that is based on the study of hundreds of the most innovative patents across the globe. Altshuller claimed that these innovations followed a particular set of patterns. Unlocking the principles behind those patterns allows one not only to solve seemingly insurmountable problems but also to predict where the next challenges would arise.

Altshuller and his colleagues developed 40 principles underlying these innovative patents and then developed the "TRIZ contradiction matrix," a tool that combines these principles to solve a problem. They recognized that innovations come about when someone is able to overcome the inherent contradictions in a process. For instance, in the packaging industry, a contradiction exists between the effectiveness of childproof safety caps for medicine containers and making those containers easy for authorized users to open. Manufacturers of mattresses face the contradiction of making mattresses that are both hard and soft. Too often, companies rely on a very unimaginative solution to contradictions such as these; they compromise. Rather than settle for a mediocre compromise, the TRIZ contradiction matrix is designed to *resolve* these conflicts using the 40 principles that Altshuller developed. One axis of the matrix displays the characteristic of the process to be improved, and the other axis displays the conflicting characteristic that is becoming worse.

For example, suppose that a candy maker wants to make syrup-filled, bottle-shaped chocolates by molding the chocolate bottles and then pouring syrup into the mold. To speed production of the finished product to meet demand, the business owner tries heating the syrup to allow for faster pouring, but the heated syrup melts the molded chocolate bottles and distorts their shape (the contradiction; see Figure 2.4). Using the TRIZ contradiction matrix, the candy maker recognizes the problem as a conflict between speed and shape. Speed is the characteristic to be improved, and shape is the characteristic that is getting worse. The principles that the matrix suggests for solving

	Characteristic that is getting worse					
Characteristic to be improved	**Volume of stationary object**	**Speed**	**Force**	**Stress or pressure**	**Shape**	**Stability of the object**
Volume of stationary object	—	*	Taking out Mechanical vibration Thermal expansion	Intermediary Parameter changes	Nested doll Taking out Parameter changes	Discarding and recovering Mechanics substitution Parameter changes Composite materials
Speed	*	—	The other way around Mechanics substitution Dynamics Periodic action	Universality Mechanical vibration Strong oxidants Composite materials	Dynamics Discarding and recovering Mechanical vibration Parameter changes	Mechanics substitution Homogeneity Segmentation Mechanical vibration
Force	Taking out Phase transitions Mechanical vibration Thermal expansion	The other way round Mechanics substitution Dynamics Equipotentiality	—	Mechanical vibration Skipping Beforehand cushioning	Preliminary action Parameter changes Composite materials Discarding and recovering	Parameter changes Preliminary action Skipping
Stress or pressure	Parameter changes Intermediary	Universality Parameter changes Phase transitions	Phase transitions Parameter changes Skipping	—	Parameter changes Asymmetry Dynamics Preliminary action	Parameter changes Homogeneity Taking out Composite materials
Shape	Nested doll Taking out Parameter changes	Parameter changes Discarding and recovering Mechanical vibration	Parameter changes Preliminary action Thermal expansion Composite materials	Discarding and recovering Dynamics Preliminary action Spheroidality and curvature	—	Homogeneity Segmentation Mechanical vibration Asymmetry

FIGURE 2.4

TRIZ Contradiction Matrix

Source: TRIZ 40, http://www.triz40.com/aff_Matrix.htm.

this problem include (1) changing the dynamics of the object or the environment (e.g., making a rigid part flexible), (2) discarding or recovering parts of an object (e.g., dissolving a protective case when it is no longer needed), (3) causing an object to vibrate or oscillate (e.g., transforming a standard knife into an electric knife by introducing oscillating blades), and (4) changing the properties of the object (e.g., freezing the chocolate syrup and then molding the bottles around the syrup).

Choosing principle 4, the candy maker decides to change the properties of the chocolate syrup by adding a compound that causes it to solidify when exposed to air, making it easier and faster to coat with chocolate. Once enclosed inside the chocolate, the syrup once again becomes a liquid. Problem solved![99]

Rapid Prototyping

Generating creative ideas is a critical step in the process of taking an idea for a product or a service successfully to the market. However, recall that many (perhaps most) ideas that entrepreneurs come up with fail. Inventor and serial entrepreneur Scott Jones says that his kids still enjoy teasing him about one of his offbeat ideas that flopped: a pair of microturbines embedded in the soles of shoes that would propel the wearer forward. (Jones abandoned the idea after seeing a similar concept fail flamboyantly in the movie *Jackass*.)[100] Rapid prototyping plays an important part in the creative process because it serves as a way to screen ideas that are not practical or just won't work so that entrepreneurs can focus their creative energy on other ideas. The premise behind **rapid prototyping** is that transforming an idea into an actual model points out flaws in the original idea and leads to improvements in its design. "If a picture is worth a thousand words, a prototype is worth ten thousand," says Steve Vassallo of Ideo Inc.[101]

The three principles of rapid prototyping are the three Rs: rough, rapid, and right. Models do not have to be perfect; in fact, in the early phases of developing an idea, perfecting a model usually is a waste of time. The key is to make the model good enough to determine what works and what does not. Doing so allows an entrepreneur to develop prototypes rapidly, moving closer to a successful design with each iteration. The final R, right, means building lots of small models that focus on solving particular problems with an idea. "You're not trying to build a complete model," says Vassallo. "You're just focusing on a small section of it."[102]

rapid prototyping
the process of creating a model of an idea, enabling an entrepreneur to discover flaws in the idea and to make improvements in the design.

Intellectual Property: Protecting Your Ideas

LO8
Describe the protection of intellectual property through patents, trademarks, and copyrights.

Once entrepreneurs come up with innovative ideas for a product or service that has market potential, their immediate concern should be to protect it from unauthorized use. The U.S. Chamber of Commerce estimates that intellectual property theft and piracy and counterfeiting of goods cost businesses $250 billion a year.[103] The World Trade Organization estimates that between 5 and 7 percent of all goods traded globally are counterfeit.[104] To protect their businesses, entrepreneurs must understand how to put intellectual property—patents, trademarks, and copyrights—to work for them.

Patents

patent
a grant from the federal government's Patent and Trademark Office to the inventor of a product, giving the exclusive right to make, use, or sell the invention in this country for 20 years from the date of filing the patent application.

A **patent** is a grant from the U.S. Patent and Trademark Office (PTO) to the inventor of a product, giving the exclusive right to make, use, or sell the invention in this country for 20 years from the date of filing the patent application. The purpose of giving an inventor a 20-year monopoly over a product is to stimulate creativity and innovation. After 20 years, the patent expires and cannot be renewed. Most patents are granted for new product inventions (called *utility patents*), but *design patents*, extending for 14 years beyond the date the patent is issued, are given to inventors who make new, original, and ornamental changes in the design of existing products that enhance their sales. Inventors who develop a new plant can obtain a *plant patent*, provided that they can reproduce the plant asexually (e.g., by grafting or crossbreeding rather than planting seeds). To be patented, a device must be new (but not necessarily better!), not obvious to a person of ordinary skill or knowledge in the related field, and useful. A device *cannot* be patented if it has been publicized in print anywhere in the world or if it has been used or offered for sale in this country prior to the date of the patent application. A U.S. patent is granted only to the true inventor, not a person who discovers another's invention, and is effective *only* in the United States and its territories. (Congress recently passed legislation that changed the "first to invent" rule formerly in place to "first to file," which means that a patent goes to the first person to *file* a patent application.) Inventors who want to sell their inventions abroad must file for patents in each country in which they plan to do business. Once a product is patented, no one can copy or sell it without getting a license from its creator. A patent does not give one the right to make, use, or sell an invention but rather the right to exclude others from making, using, or selling it.

Although inventors are never assured of getting a patent, they can enhance their chances by following the basic steps suggested by the PTO. Before beginning the often lengthy and involved procedure, inventors should obtain professional assistance from a patent practitioner—a patent attorney or a patent agent—who is registered with the PTO. Only those attorneys and agents who are officially registered may represent an inventor seeking a patent. A list of registered attorneys and agents is available at the PTO's Web site. Approximately 98 percent of all inventors rely on these patent experts to steer them through the convoluted process. Legal fees for filing a patent application range from $4,000 to $25,000, depending on the complexity of the product.

THE PATENT PROCESS Since George Washington signed the first patent law in 1790, the PTO (www.uspto.gov) has issued patents on everything imaginable (and some unimaginable items, too), including mouse traps (of course!), Robert Fulton's steamboat, animals (genetically engineered mice),

Thomas Edison's lightbulb, golf tees (764 different patents), games, and various fishing devices. The J. M. Smucker Company even holds a patent issued in 1999 on a "sealed, crustless sandwich," a peanut butter and jelly sandwich it markets very successfully under the name "Uncrustables."[105] The PTO also has issued patents on business processes—methods of doing business—including Amazon.com's controversial patent on its "1-Click" technology, which allows users to store their customer information in a file and then recall it with one mouse click at checkout. To date, the PTO has issued nearly 9 million patents, and it receives more than 520,000 new applications each year (see Figure 2.5)![106] To receive a patent, an inventor must follow these steps:

Establish the invention's novelty. An invention is not patentable if it is known or has been used in the United States or has been described in a printed publication in this or a foreign country.

Document the device. To protect their patent claims, inventors should be able to verify the date on which they first conceived the idea for their inventions. Inventors should document a device by keeping dated records (including drawings) of their progress on the invention and by having knowledgeable friends witness these records.

Search existing patents. To verify that the invention truly is new, not obvious, and useful, an inventor must conduct a search of existing patents on similar products. The purpose of the search is to determine whether the inventor has a chance of getting a patent. Most inventors hire professionals trained in conducting patent searches to perform the research. Inventors themselves can conduct an online search of all patents granted by the PTO since 1976 from the office's Web site. An online search of these patents does not include sketches; however, subscribers to Delphion's Research Intellectual Property Network can access patents, including sketches, as far back as 1971, at www.delphion.com.

Study search results. Once the patent search is finished, inventors must study the results to determine their chances of getting a patent. To be patentable, a device must be sufficiently different from what has been used or described before and must not be obvious to a person having ordinary skill in the area of technology related to the invention.

Complete a patent application. If an inventor decides to seek a patent, he or she must file an application describing the invention with the PTO. The patent application must include specific *claims*, which describe the invention, what it does, and how it works and any drawings that are necessary to support the claims. The typical patent application runs 20 to 40 pages although some, especially those for biotech or high-tech products, are tens of thousands of pages long.

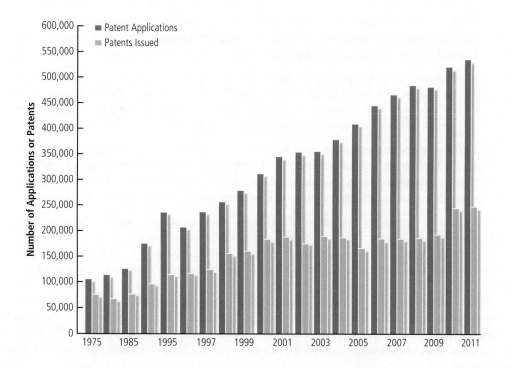

FIGURE 2.5

Patent Applications and Patents Issued

Source: U.S. Patent and Trademark Office, 2012.

FIGURE 2.6

A Sample (and Unusual) Patent

United States Patent [19]

Holmes

[11] **4,320,756**

[45] **Mar. 23, 1982**

[54] **FRESH-AIR BREATHING DEVICE AND METHOD**

[76] Inventor: **William O. Holmes,** 1331 Old Country Rd., Belmont, Calif. 94402

[21] Appl. No.: **237,869**

[22] Filed: **Feb. 25, 1981**

[51] Int. Cl.³ A62B 7/10; A62B 7/12
[52] U.S. Cl. **128/206.12;** 128/207.14; 128/207.12; 128/200.24
[58] Field of Search 128/200.24, 201.11, 128/205.25, 205.12, 205.27, 205.28, 205.29, 206.12, 206.15, 206.21, 206.28, 207.12, 207.14

[56] **References Cited**

U.S. PATENT DOCUMENTS

276,699	5/1883	McIntosh	128/206.12
409,428	8/1889	Richet	128/206.12
1,007,644	10/1911	Cocke	128/207.12
1,423,923	7/1922	Eckert, Jr.	128/201.11
2,577,606	12/1951	Conley	128/205.29

FOREIGN PATENT DOCUMENTS

1473382	3/1967	France	128/201.11
949141	9/1956	Fed. Rep. of Germany	128/207.12

Primary Examiner—Henry J. Recla
Attorney, Agent, or Firm—Phillips, Moore, Weissenberger, Lempio & Majestic

[57] **ABSTRACT**

The recent rash of fires in high-rise hotels and deaths occasioned thereby has given rise to the need for a breathing device and method for supplying a hotel guest and/or fireman with fresh air until he can be rescued. The device and method of this invention provide for the insertion of a breathing tube through the water trap of a toilet to expose an open end thereof to fresh air from a vent pipe connected to a sewer line of the toilet, to enable the user to breathe fresh air through the tube.

4 Claims, 5 Drawing Figures

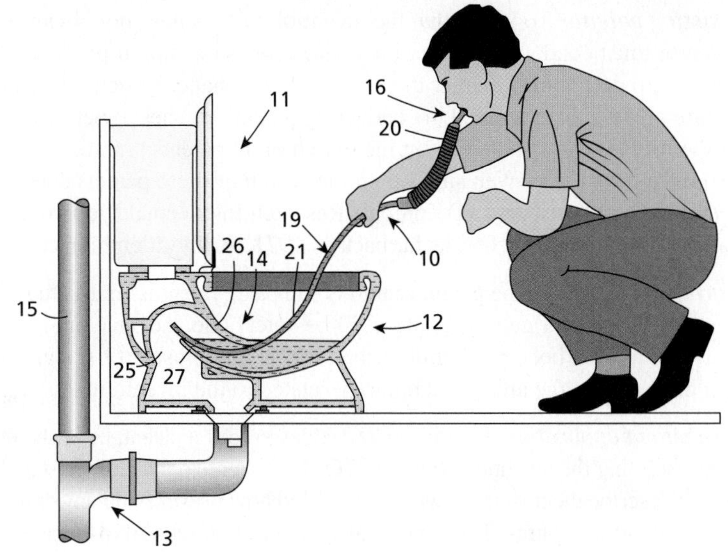

The longest patent application to date is one for a gene patent that was 6 million pages long![107] Most inventors hire patent attorneys or agents to help them complete their patent applications. Figure 2.6 shows a portion of the application for a rather unusual patent.

Inventors also can file a provisional application for a patent for a small fee. Filing for a provisional patent does not require the inventor to file any claims but does give him or her the right to use the phrase "patent pending" on the device. After filing for a provisional patent, an inventor has one year to file a standard patent application.

File the patent application. Before the PTO will issue a patent, one of its examiners studies the application to determine whether the invention warrants a patent. Approval of a patent takes on average 33.9 months from the date of filing.[108] If the PTO rejects the application, the inventor can amend his or her application and resubmit it to the PTO.

Defending a patent against "copycat producers" can be expensive and time consuming but often is necessary to protect an entrepreneur's interest. Patent holders file about 150,000 infringement suits per year, and the median time for a patent infringement case to get to court is 2.5 years. The median cost of a patent infringement lawsuit when the amount in dispute is between $1 million and $25 million is about $2.65 million if the case goes to trial (about 95 percent of patent infringement lawsuits are settled out of court), but the odds of winning are in the patent holder's favor. About two-thirds of patent holders win their infringement suits, and since 1995, the median award is $5.23 million, which is most often based on the royalties lost to the infringer.[109] Recently, managers at Canada Goose, a company started in 1957 in Toronto, Canada, that manufactures

"After fire and the wheel, it was only
logical to invent the patent attorney."

Source: © Chris Wildt/www.CartoonStock.com

high-quality, down-insulated vests and coats that are designed to protect people who wear the company's products from the mind-numbing cold of Antarctica or the gale-force winds on the North Sea, discovered knockoffs of its products that look like the real items but contain no down insulation at all. Instead, the counterfeit garments, which are made in China using child labor, are filled with unsanitary, bacteria-laden materials that offer no protection against the elements. Halting sales of counterfeit Canada Goose items is proving difficult, however.[110] With its global reach and speedy convenience, the Internet compounds the problem of counterfeit sales, especially among brand-name products such as shoes, consumer electronics, handbags, apparel, watches, computers, and others. Most counterfeit goods originate in China, Hong Kong, Taiwan, and India.

TRADEMARKS A **trademark** is any distinctive word, phrase, symbol, design, name, logo, slogan, or trade dress that a company uses to identify the origin of a product or to distinguish it from other goods on the market. (A **service mark** is the same as a trademark except that it identifies and distinguishes the source of a service rather than a product.) A trademark serves as a company's "signature" in the marketplace. A trademark can be more than just a company's logo, slogan, or brand name; it can also include symbols, shapes, colors, smells, or sounds. For instance, Coca-Cola holds a trademark on the shape of its bottle. NBC owns a "sound mark," the auditory equivalent of a trademark, on its three-toned chime, and MGM has similar protection on the roar of the lion (whose name is Leo) that appears at the beginning of its movies.[111]

ENTREPRENEURIAL PROFILE: Bay Quackers: Ride the Ducks John E. Scannell, founder of Bay Quackers, a San Francisco tour company that features amphibious vehicles (known as duck boats), provides his customers with duck bill–shaped kazoos so that they can "quack" at people they pass. A competing company, Ride the Ducks, filed a sound mark infringement lawsuit against Bay Quackers, asking the court to order Bay Quackers to stop using the kazoos. "If you blew their [kazoo] and blew ours, you wouldn't hear any difference," says the chief marketing manager for Ride the Ducks, who claims that the company owns a sound mark on the quack made by its Wacky Quacker kazoos. "[The quack that the kazoos make] is a very important part of our product." To be valid, a sound mark must be "inherently distinctive" and recognizable. U.S. District Court judge Maxine Chesney rejected Ride the Ducks's claim and dismissed the lawsuit, the same outcome that occurred when Ride the Ducks sued a competitor in Philadelphia over the same issue in 2005.[112] ■

trademark
any distinctive word, phrase, symbol, design, name, logo, slogan, or trade dress that a company uses to identify the origin of a product or to distinguish it from other goods on the market.

service mark
offers the same protection as a trademark but identifies and distinguishes the source of a service rather than a product.

trade dress
the unique combination of elements that a company uses to create a product's image and to promote it.

Components of a product's identity such as these are part of its **trade dress**, the unique combination of elements that a company uses to create a product's image and to promote it. For instance, a Mexican restaurant chain's particular decor, color schemes, design, and overall "look and feel" would be its trade dress. To be eligible for trademark protection, trade dress must be inherently unique and distinctive to a company, and another company's use of that trade dress must be likely to confuse customers.

There are 1.65 million trademarks registered and in active use in the United States (see Figure 2.7). Federal law permits a company to register a trademark, which prevents other companies from employing a similar mark to identify their goods. Before 1989, a business could not reserve a trademark in advance of use. Today, the first party who either uses a trademark in commerce or files an application with the PTO has the ultimate right to register that trademark. Unlike patents and copyrights, which are issued for limited amounts of time, trademarks last indefinitely as long as the holder continues to use it. (Five years after a trademark's registration date, the entrepreneur must file an affidavit of use with the PTO.) However, a trademark cannot keep competitors from producing the same product or selling it under a different name. It merely prevents others from using the same or confusingly similar trademark for the same or similar products.

Many business owners are confused by the use of the symbols ™ and ®. Anyone who claims the right to a particular trademark (or service mark) can use the ™ (or ˢᴹ) symbols without having to register the mark with the PTO. The claim to that trademark or service mark may or may not be valid, however. Only those businesses that have registered their marks with the PTO can use the ® symbol. Entrepreneurs do not have to register trademarks or service marks to establish their rights to those marks; however, registering a mark with the PTO does give entrepreneurs greater power to protect their marks. Filing an application to register a trademark or service mark costs from $275 to $375 and is relatively easy, but it does require a search of existing names.

An entrepreneur may lose the exclusive right to a trademark if it loses its unique character and becomes a generic name. Aspirin, escalator, thermos, brassiere, super glue, yo-yo, and cellophane all were once enforceable trademarks that have become common words in the English language. These generic terms can no longer be licensed as trademarks.

FIGURE 2.7

Trademark Applications and Trademarks and Renewals Issued

Source: US Patent and Trademark Office, 2012.

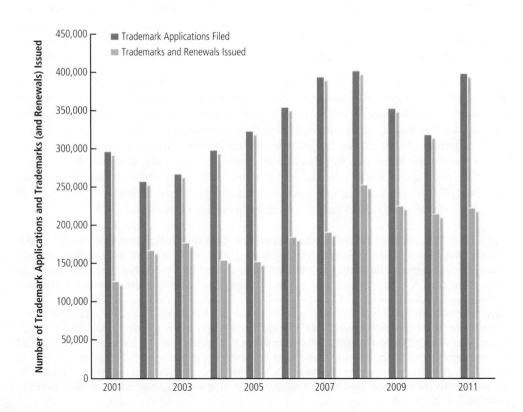

Hands On . . . How To

Protect Your Company's Intellectual Property

For as long as she could remember, Joi Sumpton, a flight attendant for a major airline, aspired to be an inventor. She came up with many ideas for new products, but none of them "ever felt right," she says. Then, while attending story time with her small children at a bookstore, Sumpton took her children to the restroom, where she and other parents lifted their children and held them against the counter so they could wash their hands. Many of them cried because they did not like being pressed against the wet, sharp edge of the countertop so they could reach the sink. That's when the idea hit Sumpton: why are restrooms equipped with diaper-changing tables but nothing to help children reach the sink? She quickly came up with the basic design of a foldable step stool that would fit neatly underneath the sink.

Sumpton excitedly told her husband about her idea, and he began searching the U.S. PTO Web site but found nothing about restroom step stools. A few weeks later, a fellow flight attendant mentioned that her husband was a patent attorney, and Sumpton told her friend about her idea. Before she knew it, Sumpton was sitting in the patent attorney's office, listening to his explanation of the patent process.

Sumpton knew that the next step was to build a prototype device. An Internet search led her to an article that mentioned a product design engineer, John Evans, in Atlanta, Georgia. "The day I met Evans is the day that changed my life forever," says Sumpton. "He took my idea and original design and transformed it into a work of art" that she named the Step 'n Wash. Evans had the experience to tweak Sumpton's original design to make it safer and easier and less expensive to manufacture. Over the course of the next three years, they manufactured prototypes to test Step 'n Wash's functionality and strength, each time improving its design and eliminating dangerous "pinch points" where children might be injured.

When the final design was complete, Sumpton discovered that selling her product was more difficult than she had anticipated, so she gave away Step 'n Washes to several zoos and aquariums. "Almost immediately, I started getting positive feedback," she says. Sales began to grow after she rented a booth at the International Amusement Parks Expo, where her small company took orders from amusement parks across the United States, Canada, Mexico, and Europe. Today, the Step 'n Wash is in more than 500 locations, and Sumpton has her company's sights set on the 5 million public restrooms in the United States.

Joi Sumpton received a utility patent for the Step 'n Wash in 2010, five years after coming up with the idea. She took the proper steps to protect her intellectual property. What lessons can entrepreneurs learn from Sumpton's experience about protecting their intellectual property?

1. ***Recognize that intellectual property, the rights that result when a person uses his or her knowledge and creativity to produce something of value, can be a business's most valuable asset, even for small companies.*** Often intellectual property is the source of a

company's competitive advantage. Experts estimate that in the United States alone, 30 to 40 percent of all gains in productivity over the course of the twentieth century originated with intellectual property. In his book *The Rise of the Creative Class*, Richard Florida says that in 1900, only 10 percent of the U.S. population belonged to the "creative class"; by 2000, that number had grown to 30.1 percent.

2. ***Know the difference in the protection offered by patents, trademarks, and copyrights.*** Each tool protects a particular type of intellectual property. Make sure that you know which one you need to protect your business and its intellectual property.

3. ***Understand the basics of patent, trademark, and copyright protection.*** By understanding the features of each of these shields for intellectual property, you can protect your rights for at least 14 years, often longer.

4. ***Use the appropriate method to file for protection of your intellectual property and do so promptly.*** The processes of filing for a patent, a trademark, and a copyright are different; make sure you know which tool is right for you and how to get maximum protection for your intellectual property. You may be able to apply for more than one type of protection. For instance, an entrepreneur may be able to trademark a company logo and, if it is a form of artistic expression, copyright it as well.

5. ***Use qualified, experienced intellectual property attorneys to gain the proper protection.*** The time to involve attorneys in protecting the product of your knowledge and creativity is *before* you have to bring them in to take action against someone who has stolen your intellectual property. Filing for patents, trademarks, and copyrights can be intimidating if you have never done it before, and doing it incorrectly may mean that you have no protection at all. Attorneys, consultants, examiners, and other professionals specialize in the various types of intellectual property protection. Use their expertise! They can refer you to patent draftspeople (who create the sketches required for a patent application), design engineers, manufacturers, and others.

6. ***Build a prototype.*** As Sumpton discovered, building a prototype (or most likely several rounds of prototypes) allows you to improve the design of your product. Prototypes allow inventors to discover the features of their inventions that actually work and those that have to be redesigned.

7. ***If you do business globally, register your company's patents, trademarks, and copyrights in the countries in which you do business.*** Although enforcing intellectual property laws in some countries can be difficult, the chances that you will be successful rise significantly if you have registered your IP with the proper offices in those nations.

(continued)

Hands On . . . How To *(continued)*

8. ***Protect your rights vigorously.*** If you discover that someone is using your intellectual property without permission, pursue your rights vigorously. Recognize that the costs of taking legal action, especially in foreign lands, may outweigh the benefits, at least in the short run. Entrepreneurs must decide whether pursuing costly legal action to protect their intellectual property rights will yield long-term benefits.

Sources: Based on Joi Sumpton, "Flight Attendant Becomes Woman Inventor," Fox Business, December 26, 2010, http://www.foxbusiness.com/personal-finance/2010/12/26/flight-attendant-woman-inventor; David Hirschmann, "Intellectual Property Theft: Big Problem, Real Solutions, *The ChamberPost*, March 2008, http://www.chamberpost.com/2008/03/intellectual-pr.html; Merrill Matthews Jr. and Tom Giovanetti, "Why Intellectual Property Is Important," *Ideas*, Institute for Policy Innovation, July 8, 2002, p. 1; and Nichole L. Torres, "Getting Intellectual," *Entrepreneur*, December 2007, p. 110.

Copyrights

copyright

an exclusive right that protects the creators of original works of authorship, such as literary, dramatic, musical, and artistic works.

A **copyright** is an exclusive right that protects the creators of original works of authorship, such as literary, dramatic, musical, and artistic works (e.g., art, sculptures, literature, software, music, videos, video games, choreography, motion pictures, recordings, and others). The internationally recognized symbol © denotes a copyrighted work. A copyright protects only the form in which an idea is expressed, not the idea itself. A copyright on a creative work comes into existence the moment its creator puts that work into a tangible form. Just as with a trademark, obtaining basic copyright protection does *not* require registering the creative work with the U.S. Copyright Office (www.copyright.gov).

Registering a copyright does give creators greater protection over their work, however. Copyright applications must be filed with the Copyright Office in the Library of Congress for a fee of $35 to $65 per application (plus recording fees). A valid copyright on a work lasts for the life of the creator plus 70 years after his or her death. When a copyright expires, the work becomes public property and can be used by anyone free of charge.

Because they are so easy to duplicate, computer software programs, CDs, and DVDs are among the most often pirated items by copyright infringers. The Business Software Alliance estimates that the global software industry loses $58.8 billion each year to pirates who illegally copy programs.[113] The motion picture industry loses billions of dollars annually to those who forge counterfeit movies and sell them. Immigration and Customs Enforcement officials recently disabled nine Web sites that were selling downloads of pirated movies, in some cases just hours after the films premiered in theaters.[114]

Table 2.2 provides a summary of the characteristics of patents, trademarks, and copyrights.

TABLE 2.2 Characteristics of Patents, Trademarks, and Copyrights

Protection	What It Protects	Who Is Eligible	Length of Protection	Approximate Cost
Utility Patent	Exclusive right to make, use, and sell an invention	First person to file for a patent	20 years	$4,000 to $25,000, depending on complexity
Design Patent	New, original changes in the design of existing products that enhance their sales	First person to file for a patent	14 years	$4,000 to $25,000, depending on complexity
Trademark	Any distinctive word, phrase, symbol, design, name, logo, slogan, or trade dress that a company uses to identify the origin of a product or to distinguish it from other goods on the market	Entity currently using the mark in commerce or one who intends to use it within six months	Renewable between fifth and sixth years and every 10 years afterward	$1,000 to $2,500
Service mark	Same protection as a trademark except that it identifies and distinguishes the source of a service rather than a product	Entity currently using the mark in commerce or one who intends to use it within six months	Renewable between fifth and sixth years and every 10 years afterward	$1,000 to $2,500
Copyright	Original works of authorship, such as literary, dramatic, musical, and artistic works	Author or creator	Life of the author or creator plus 70 years	$140 to $200

Protecting Intellectual Property

Acquiring the protection of patents, trademarks, and copyrights is useless unless an entrepreneur takes action to protect those rights in the marketplace. Unfortunately, not every businessperson respects others' rights of ownership to products, processes, names, and works, and some infringe on those rights with impunity. In other cases, the infringing behavior simply is the result of a lack of knowledge about others' rights of ownership. After acquiring the proper legal protection through patents, copyrights, or trademarks, entrepreneurs must monitor the market (and the Internet in particular) for unauthorized copycat users. If an entrepreneur has a valid patent, trademark, or copyright, stopping an infringer usually requires nothing more than a stern "cease-and-desist" letter from an attorney. Often, offenders don't want to get into expensive legal battles and agree to stop their illegal behavior. If that tactic fails, the entrepreneur may have no choice but to bring an infringement lawsuit, most of which end up being settled out of court.

The primary weapon an entrepreneur has to protect patents, trademarks, and copyrights is the legal system. The major problem with relying on the legal system to enforce ownership rights, however, is the cost and time of infringement lawsuits, which can quickly exceed the budget of most small businesses and occupy huge blocks of managers' time. Lawsuits always involve costs. Before pursuing what could become an expensive and drawn-out legal battle, an entrepreneur must consider the following issues:

- Can the opponent afford to pay if you win?

- Do you expect to get enough from the suit to cover the costs of hiring an attorney and preparing a case?

- Can you afford the loss of time, money, and privacy from the ensuing lawsuit?

Chapter Summary by Learning Objective

1. Explain the differences among creativity, innovation, and entrepreneurship.

- The entrepreneur's "secret" for creating value in the marketplace is applying creativity and innovation to solve problems and to exploit opportunities that people face every day. Creativity is the ability to develop new ideas and to discover new ways of looking at problems and opportunities. Innovation is the ability to apply creative solutions to those problems and opportunities to enhance or to enrich people's lives. Entrepreneurship is the result of a disciplined, systematic process of applying creativity and innovation to needs and opportunities in the marketplace.

2. Describe why creativity and innovation are such an integral part of entrepreneurship.

- Entrepreneurs must always be on guard against paradigms—preconceived ideas of what the world is, what it should be like, and how it should operate—because they are logjams to creativity. Successful entrepreneurs often go beyond conventional wisdom as they ask, "Why not?"

- Success—even survival—in this fiercely competitive, global environment requires entrepreneurs to tap their creativity (and that of their employees) constantly.

3. Understand how the two hemispheres of the human brain function and what role they play in creativity.

- For years, people assumed that creativity was an inherent trait. Today, however, we know better. Research shows that almost anyone can learn to be creative. The left hemisphere of the brain controls language, logic, and symbols, processing information in a step-by-step fashion. The right hemisphere handles emotional, intuitive, and spatial functions, processing information intuitively. The right side of the brain is the source of creativity and innovation. People can learn to control which side of the brain is dominant in a given situation.

4. Explain the 10 "mental locks" that limit individual creativity.

The number of potential barriers to creativity is limitless, but entrepreneurs commonly face 10 "mental locks" on creativity: Searching for the one "right" answer, focusing on "being logical," blindly following the rules, constantly being practical, viewing play as frivolous, becoming overly specialized, avoiding ambiguity, fearing looking foolish, fearing mistakes and failure, and believing that "I'm not creative."

5. **Understand how entrepreneurs can enhance the creativity of their employees as well as their own creativity.**

   - Entrepreneurs can stimulate creativity in their companies by expecting creativity, expecting and tolerating failure, encouraging curiosity, viewing problems as challenges, providing creativity training, providing support, rewarding creativity, and modeling creativity.

   - Entrepreneurs can enhance their own creativity by using the following techniques: allowing themselves to be creative, giving their minds fresh input every day, keeping a journal handy to record their thoughts and ideas, reading books on stimulating creativity or taking a class on creativity, and taking some time off to relax.

6. **Describe the steps in the creative process.**

   - The creative process consists of seven steps: Step 1, preparation, involves getting the mind ready for creative thinking; step 2, investigation, requires the individual to develop a solid understanding of the problem or decision; step 3, transformation, involves viewing the similarities and the differences among the information collected; step 4, incubation, allows the subconscious mind to reflect on the information collected; step 5, illumination, occurs at some point during the incubation stage when a spontaneous breakthrough causes "the lightbulb to go on"; step 6, verification, involves validating the idea as accurate and useful; and step 7, implementation, involves transforming the idea into a business reality.

7. **Discuss techniques for improving the creative process.**

   - Five techniques are especially useful for improving the creative process:

     - Brainstorming is a process in which a small group of people interact with very little structure with the goal of producing a large *quantity* of novel and imaginative ideas.

     - Mind mapping is a graphical technique that encourages thinking on both sides of the brain, visually displays the various relationships among ideas, and improves the ability to view a problem from many sides.

     - Force field analysis allows entrepreneurs to weigh both the advantages and the disadvantages of a particular decision and work to maximize the variables that support it and minimize those that work against it.

     - TRIZ is a systematic approach designed to help solve any technical problem, whatever its source. Unlike brainstorming and mind mapping, which are right-brain activities, TRIZ is a left-brain, scientific, step-by-step process that is based on the study of hundreds of the most innovative patents across the globe.

     - Rapid prototyping is based on the premise that transforming an idea into an actual model will point out flaws in the original idea and will lead to improvements in its design.

8. **Describe the protection of intellectual property through patents, trademarks, and copyrights.**

   - A patent is a grant from the federal government that gives an inventor exclusive rights to an invention for 20 years.

   - A trademark is any distinctive word, symbol, or trade dress that a company uses to identify its product and to distinguish it from other goods. It serves as a company's "signature" in the marketplace.

   - A copyright protects original works of authorship. It covers only the form in which an idea is expressed and not the idea itself and lasts for 70 years beyond the creator's death.

Discussion Questions

1. Explain the differences among creativity, innovation, and entrepreneurship.
2. How are creativity, innovation, and entrepreneurship related?
3. Why are creativity and innovation so important to the survival and success of a business?
4. One entrepreneur claims, "Creativity unrelated to a business plan has no value." What does he mean? Do you agree?
5. Can creativity be taught or is it an inherent trait? Explain.
6. How does the human brain function? What operations does each hemisphere specialize in? Which hemisphere is the "seat" of creativity?
7. Briefly outline the 10 "mental locks" that can limit individual creativity. Give an example of a situation in which you subjected yourself to one of these mental locks.
8. What can entrepreneurs do to stimulate their own creativity and to encourage it among workers?
9. Explain the steps of the creative process. What can an entrepreneur do to enhance each step?
10. Explain the differences among a patent, a trademark, and a copyright. What form of intellectual property does each protect?

Business Plan Pro™

The creative process can help you to develop your business concept and add dimension to an existing business venture. The process of creating your business plan enables you to refine and test your creative ideas.

Business Plan Exercises

Select one of the creative processes mentioned in this chapter. You may want to consider mind mapping, TRIZ, or brainstorming if you are in a group. Apply this technique to your business concept. If your business idea is in the embryonic stage, use this exercise to bring focus to the business. If you have a solid grasp on your business concept, use one of these creative techniques to address a specific business challenge or to explore a potential opportunity for your business.

On the Web

Identify at least three key words or phrases that you associate with your business concept. For example, if your business is a specialty retail and online store selling wakeboards, you may consider the terms "wakeboards," "water sports," and "boards." Enter terms relevant to your business in your favorite search engine and see what information appears.

1. What companies advertise under those terms?
2. What are the top three listings?
3. How is your business unique from those businesses listed, including the fact that your business may offer a local presence?
4. What other attributes set your business apart from what you see on the Web? Make note of anything that you learned or observed from what you saw online.

In the Software

Open *Business Plan Pro*™ and the business plan you began in Chapter 1. If this exercise has changed any of your initial concepts or produced an entirely different business concept, think about why the exercise led you down a different path. If that venture is different, select the option to create a new business plan and work through the wizards as you did before. You can print the outline created based on those responses by clicking on the Preview icon or going to File, Print, and then Print Preview.

Sample Plans

Open the Sample Plan Browser in *Business Plan Pro*™; it will be helpful to have an Internet connection when you do. Enter one or more of the search terms you selected in the exercise in the search window of the Sample Plan Browser. Do any sample plans appear based on the term you entered? If so, review those plans. Will one of those plans be a potential resource for you as create your business plan? Remember, the sample plan does not have to be identical to your business concept to be useful.

Building Your Business Plan

Open your business plan and go to the section titled "Product and Service Description." You can do that by clicking on the Plan Outline icon at the top of your screen or clicking on View and selecting Outline from the drop-down menu. Within that section, begin to describe the products or services your business will offer. Notice that you have the option to view that section of a sample plan by clicking on "Examples" in the upper right-hand section of the screen. Now, go to the "Market Needs" section of the plan. Make a few notes here regarding the needs that your products and services satisfy. We will revisit these sections, so just make comments that will help you develop your thoughts as you progress through the chapters.

Beyond the Classroom . . .

1. Your dinner guests are to arrive in five minutes, and you've just discovered that you forgot to chill the wine!! Wanting to maintain your reputation as the perfect host/hostess, you must tackle this problem with maximum creativity. What could you do? Generate as many solutions as you can in five minutes working alone. Then work with two or three students in a small group to brainstorm the problem.
2. Work with a group of your classmates to think of as many alternative uses for the commercial lubricant WD-40 as you can. Remember to think *fluidly* (generating a quantity of ideas) and *flexibly* (generating unconventional ideas).
3. A Facebook group of more than 25,000 people is trying to convince Cadbury, the venerable British confectioner (now owed by Kraft Foods), to produce a giant chocolate Cadbury Crème Egg that contains a filling made from fondant that resembles the yolk and white of a real egg. (Currently, giant Cadbury chocolate eggs, which are about the size of an ostrich egg, are hollow, a great disappointment to fans of the company's smaller chocolate eggs that are filled with creamy white and yolk-colored fondant.) A Cadbury spokesman says that "creating a [chocolate] shell that is strong enough to contain the sheer weight of the fondant is technically challenging." Use the creativity-enhancing techniques described in this

chapter to develop potential solutions that would allow Cadbury to manufacture a giant Crème Egg.

4. A major maker of breakfast cereals was about to introduce a new multigrain cereal. Its principal selling point is that it features "three great tastes" in every bowl: corn, rice, and wheat. Because a cereal's name is an integral part of its marketing campaign, the company hired a very costly consulting firm to come up with the right name for the new product. The consulting firm tackled the job using "a combination of structural linguistics and personal creativity." One year and many dollars later, the consulting firm gave its recommendation. Take 20 minutes to list names that you think would be appropriate for this cereal. Make brief notes about why you think each name is appropriate. Your professor may choose to prepare a list of names from all the members of your class and may take a vote to determine the "winner."

5. Every quarter, Inventables, a creative design company in Chicago, sends its clients a package called a DesignAid that contains 20 items, each with "unexpected properties," as a way to stimulate innovation and ideas for new products or services. One Inventables' recent DesignAid package included the following items:

- Translucent concrete—concrete that contains thin layers of fiber optics, which create semitransparent stripes in the concrete.
- Sound-recording paper—A piece of cardboard-like paper that records and plays sounds with the help of ultrathin electronics embedded in the page.
- Impact-absorbing silicon—Silicon that, despite being only one inch thick, absorbs impact, including microvibrations. If you drop an egg on it, the egg won't break.
- Wireless battery-free speakers—Solar-powered speakers receive sound via infrared waves rather than radio frequencies and are capable of producing directional sound. In other words, only the person at whom the speakers are aimed can hear the sound coming from them.

Select one of these items and work with a small group of your classmates to brainstorm as many alternative uses for the item as you can in 15 minutes. Remember to abide by the rules of brainstorming!

6. Each hemisphere of the brain processes information differently, and one hemisphere tends to dominate the other. Consider the following lists of words and decide which one best describes the way you make decisions and solve problems:

Metaphor	Logic
Dream	Reason
Humor	Precision
Ambiguity	Consistency
Play	Work
Approximate	Exact
Fantasy	Reality
Paradox	Direct
Diffused	Focused
Hunch	Analysis
General	Specific
Child	Adult

If you chose the list on the left, you tend to engage in "soft" thinking, which suggests a right-brain orientation, If you chose the list on the right, you tend to engage in "hard" thinking, which suggests a left-brain orientation. Creativity relies on both soft and hard thinking. Each plays an important role in the creative process but at different phases.

A. Identify which type of thinking—soft or hard— would be most useful in each of the seven stages of the creative process.

B. List five things you can do to develop your thinking skills in the area (soft or hard) that least describes your decision making style.

7. Interview at least two entrepreneurs about their experiences as business owners. Where did their business ideas originate? How important are creativity and innovation to their success? How do they encourage an environment of creativity in their businesses?

Endnotes

1. *2011 Global R&D Funding Forecast*, Battelle *R&D Magazine*, December 2010, p. 3.
2. Small Serial Innovators: The Small Firm Contribution to Technical Change, CHI Research, U.S. Small Business Administration Office of Advocacy, No. 225, February 27, 2003, http://www.sba.gov/advo/research/rs225.pdf.
3. "Innovation Quotes," Think Exist, http://thinkexist.com/ quotations/innovation.
4. "IBM 2010 Global CEO Survey: Creativity Selected as Most Crucial Factor for Future Success," IBM, May 18, 2010, http://www-03.ibm.com/press/us/en/pressrelease/31670.wss.
5. Warren Bennis, "Cultivating Creative Collaboration," *Industry Week*, August 18, 1997, p. 86.
6. Christopher Steiner, "Beefed Up," *Forbes*, June 7, 2010, pp. 42–44; "Slim Jims Plus Red Bull = ?" *Inc.*, May 2011, p. 8.
7. Roger von Oech, *A Whack on the Side of the Head* (New York: Warner Books, 1990), p. 108.
8. Anna Vander Broek, "Self-Healing Concrete," *Forbes*, November 2, 2009, pp. 46–48; "New Bridges Made of Bendable Concrete," Live Science, May 6, 2005, http:// www.livescience.com/244-bridges-bendable-concrete .html.
9. Michael Maiello, "They Almost Changed the World," *Forbes*, December 23, 2002, p. 217.
10. Peter Carbonara, "30 Great Small Business Ideas," *Your Company*, August/September 1998, pp. 32–58.

11. Charlie Farrell, "A Penny for Your Thoughts," *Business & Economic Review*, October–December 2006, p. 25.

12. David H. Freedman, "Freeing Your Inner Think Tank, *Inc.*, May 2005, pp. 65–66.

13. Robert Fulghum, "Time to Sacrifice the Queen," *Reader's Digest*, August 1993, pp. 136–138.

14. Carla Goodman, "Sparking Your Imagination," *Entrepreneur*, September 1997, p. 32.

15. Carla Goodman, "Sparking Your Imagination," *Entrepreneur*, September 1997, p. 32.

16. Chuck Salter, "Failure Doesn't Suck," *Fast Company*, May 2007, p. 44; James Dyson, "Cleaning Up in His Industry," *Fortune*, January 22, 2007, p. 33.

17. Kasey Wehrun, "Twice Blessed," *Inc.*, April 2011, p. 120; Stephen Miller, "Helicopter Designer and Guitar Hero," *Wall Street Journal*, February 2, 2011, p. A6.

18. Betty Edwards, *Drawing on the Right Side of the Brain* (Los Angeles: J. P. Tarcher, 1979), p. 32.

19. Roger von Oech, *A Whack on the Side of the Head* (New York: Warner Books, 1990), pp. 21–167; "Obstacles to Creativity," Creativity Web, http://www.ozemail.com.au/~caveman/Creative/Basics/obstacles.htm.

20. Erin Zagursky, "Professor Discusses America's Creativity Crisis in *Newsweek*," William and Mary News and Events, July 14, 2010, http://www.wm.edu/news/stories/2010/professor-discusses-americas-creativity-crisis-in-newsweek-123.php; Po Bronson and Ashley Merryman, "The Creativity Crisis," *Newsweek*, July 10, 2010, http://www.newsweek.com/2010/07/10/the-creativity-crisis.html.

21. "Innovation: Companies on the Cutting Edge," *Inc.*, December 2010/January 2011, pp. 52–53; "Lyric Semiconductor Named in Technology Review's 2011 TR50 List of the World's Most Innovative Companies," Lyric Semiconductor, February 22, 2011, http://www.lyricsemiconductor.com/news.htm.

22. J. J. McCorvey, "Bending the Rules," *Inc.*, March 2011, pp. 40–41; Brittany Sauser, "Commercializing Stretchable Silicon Electronics," *Technology Review*, May 5, 2011, http://www.technologyreview.com/video/?vid=702; "About mc10," mc10, http://mc10inc.com/pages/co_overview.php.

23. Karen Axelton, "Imagine That," *Entrepreneur*, April 1998, p. 96; "Thomas Edison Biography," http://edison-ford-estate.com/ed_bio.htm.

24. Chuck Salter, "Failure Doesn't Suck," *Fast Company*, May 2007, p. 44.

25. Katy Finneran, "How Small Businesses Can Use Social Media for Branding," *Fox Business*, May 20, 2011, http://smallbusiness.foxbusiness.com/technology-web/2011/05/20/small-businesses-use-social-media-branding; Nour Habib, "'Man Candles' a Success," *Broken Arrow Ledger*, May 13, 2011, http://baledger.com/news/man-candles-a-success/article_7df6d568-7bf4-11e0-8f2b-001cc4c002e0.html.

26. Jason Daley, "If It's Broke, Decorate It," *Entrepreneur*, July 2009, p. 17; "About Casttoo," Casttoo, http://www.casttoo.com/Casttoo.com/About_Casttoo.html.

27. Joseph Schumpeter, "The Creative Response in Economic History," *Journal of Economic History*, November 1947, pp. 149–159.

28. Christine Lagorio, "Taking Aim at Gas Guzzlers," *Inc.*, June 2010, pp. 46–47; "Top Technology Stories of 2010," *Automotive Engineering*, December 7, 2010, p. 18.

29. Laurie McCabe, "Seven Daily Inspirations from Dell's Women Entrepreneur Network Event," *Laurie McCabe's Blog*, June 10, 2011, http://lauriemccabe.wordpress.com/2011/06/10/seven-daily-inspirations-from-dell%E2%80%99s-women-entrepreneur-network-event; Daniel McGinn, "How I Did It: Arianna Huffington," *Inc.*, February 1, 2010, http://www.inc.com/magazine/20100201/how-i-did-it-arianna-huffington.html; Jay Yarow, "Huffington Post Traffic Zooms Past the New York Times," *Business Insider*, June 9, 2011, http://www.businessinsider.com/chart-of-the-day-huffpo-nyt-unique-visitors-2011-6?utm_source=twbutton&utm_medium=social&utm_term=&utm_content=&utm_campaign=sai.

30. *Bits & Pieces*, January 1994, p. 6.

31. "Harnessing Your Team's Creativity," *BNET*, June 7, 2007, http://www.bnet.com/2403-13059_23-52990.html.

32. Frank T. Rothaermel and Andrew M. Hess, "Innovation Strategies Combined," *Sloan Management Review* 51, no. 3 (Spring 2010): 13–15.

33. Rob Goffee and Gareth Jones, "The Odd Clever People Every Organization Needs," *Forbes*, August 13, 2009, http://www.forbes.com/2009/08/13/clever-employees-talent-leadership-managing-recruiting.html.

34. Carol Tice, "Fueling Change," *Entrepreneur*, November 2007, p. 47.

35. Beth Kowitt, "Dunkin' Brands' Kitchen Crew," *Fortune*, May 24, 2010, pp. 72–74.

36. Anya Kamenetz, "The Power of the Prize," *Fast Company*, May 2008, pp. 43–45.

37. John Bessant, Kathrin Möslein, and Bettina Von Stamm, "In Search of Innovation," *Wall Street Journal*, June 22, 2009, p. R4.

38. Nadine Heintz, "Employee Creativity Unleashed," *Inc.*, June 2009, pp. 101–102.

39. John Bessant, Kathrin Möslein, and Bettina Von Stamm, "In Search of Innovation," *Wall Street Journal*, June 22, 2009, p. R4.

40. Matthew Carmichael, "Best Places to Work No. 1: Radio Flyer," *Crain's Chicago Business*, March 29, 2010, http://www.radioflyer.com/skin/frontend/blank/radioflyer/docs/media/crains_best_il.pdf; Amelia Forczak, "Rolling Down the Path toward Success," *HR Solutions eNews*, http://www.hrsolutionsinc.com/enews_1010/RadioFlyer_1010.html.

41. Sara Wilson, "5 Ways to Spur Employee Creativity," *Entrepreneur*, March 2009, p. 20.

42. Carol Tice, "Fueling Change," *Entrepreneur*, November 2007, p. 47.

43. J. Michael Krivyanski, "Creative Genius," *Entrepreneur*, January 2008, p. 79.

44. Joel Holland, "Reinventing the Wheels," *Entrepreneur*, September 2010, p. 82; "Getaround Connects Car Owners and Renters with P2P Marketplace," *Business Insider*, June 7, 2011, http://www.businessinsider.com/getaround-connects-car-owners-and-renters-with-p2p-marketplace-2011-6.

45. Robert Epstein, "How to Get a Great Idea," *Reader's Digest*, December 1992, p. 102.

46. Georgia Flight, "How They Did It: Seven Intrapraneur Success Stories," *BNET*, April 18, 2007, http://www.bnet.com/2403-13070_23-196890.html.

47. Brian Libby, "How to Nurture New Ideas," *BNET*, June 7, 2007, http://www.bnet.com/2403-13068_23-68479.html.

48. "Leigh Buchanan, "The Start of a Beautiful Friendship: Partnering with Your Customers on R&D," *Inc.*, March 2008, pp. 37–38.

49. Patrick Seitz, "Using a Double Dose of Product Creativity," *Investor's Business Daily*, June 12, 2009, http://www.investors.com/NewsAndAnalysis/Article/479404/200906121817/Using-A-Double-Dose-Of-Product-Creativity.aspx.

50. Nichole L. Torres, "Industrial Revolution," *Entrepreneur*, November 2007, pp. 142–143.

51. Thea Singer and Lea Buchanan, "Who? What? Where? Why? When? How?," *Inc.*, August 2002, pp. 63–70.

52. Lucas Conley, "Rise and Repeat," *Fast Company*, July 2005, pp. 76–77.

53. Mike Figliuolo, "How to Innovate Like Captain Jack Sparrow," *Thought Leaders*, April 25, 2011, http://www.thoughtleadersllc.com/2011/04/how-to-innovate-like-captain-jack-sparrow.

54. Stephanie Kang, "Fashion Secret: Why Big Designers Haunt Vintage Shops," *Wall Street Journal*, April 2, 2007, pp. A1, A10.

55. Leslie Brenner, "The PedalPub," *Entrepreneur*, December 2010, p. 94; Frank Jossi, "A Better PedalPub? City Cycle Touts High-Tech Features," *Finance and Commerce*, July 5, 2011, http://finance-commerce.com/2011/07/a-better-pedal-pub-city-cycle-touts-high-tech-features.

56. Nichole L. Torres, "How Sweet It Is," *Entrepreneur*, May 2008, p. 82; "About Us," Edible Arrangements, http://www.ediblearrangements.com/about/about.aspx.

57. "Louis-Jacque Mande Daguerre," The Robinson Library, http://www.robinsonlibrary.com/technology/photography/biography/daguerre.htm; Mary Bellis, "Daguerreotype," About, http://www.robinsonlibrary.com/technology/photography/biography/daguerre.htm.

58. Kim Orr, "Vend a Dog a Bone," *Entrepreneur*, April 2007, http://www.entrepreneur.com/magazine/entrepreneur/2007/april/175924.html; "About Us," Hey Buddy! Pet Supply Vending Company, http://www.heybuddyvending.com/about.html.

59. Don Debelak, "Ideas Unlimited," *Business Start-Ups*, May 1999, pp. 57–58.

60. Mark Evans, "Truck Washer Expands into Home Ice Rinks," *Globe and Mail*, December 26, 2010, http://www.theglobeandmail.com/report-on-business/small-business/start/mark-evans/truck-washer-expands-into-home-ice-rinks/article1850030.

61. Emily Singer, "Harvesting Business Ideas from Inside and Out," *Technology Review*, February 23, 2011, http://www.technologyreview.com/business/32426.

62. Anna Lee, "Impromptu Invention Balloons Into Business," *Greenville News*, November 21, 2010, p. 2B.

63. Julie Sloane, "Inside the Mind of a (Rich) Inventor," *FSB*, November 2007, pp. 90–102.

64. Donna Fenn, "Ten Innovative Mompreneurs and How Their Businesses Were Born: It All Started with a Bump," *BNET*, May 7, 2011, http://www.bnet.com/photos/10-innovative-mompreneurs-and-how-their-businesses-were-born/6229260?seq=1&tag=mantle_skin;content.

65. Nadine Heintz, "Employee Creativity Unleashed," *Inc.*, June 2009, pp. 101–102.

66. Rosa Alphonso, "Small Business Optimism Is on an Upswing, according to the OPEN from American Express Small Business Monitor," American Express, May 24, 2007, http://home3.americanexpress.com/corp/pc/2007/monitor.asp.

67. Geoff Williams, "Innovative Model," *Entrepreneur*, September 2002, p. 66.

68. Diana Lodderhose and Marc Graser, "J. K. Rowling Unveils 'Pottermore,'" *Variety*, June 23, 2011, http://www.variety.com/article/VR1118039008?refcatid=1009.

69. Roy Rowan, "Those Hunches Are More Than Blind Faith," *Fortune*, April 23, 1979, p. 112.

70. Michael Waldholz, "A Hallucination Inspires a Vision for AIDS Drug," *Wall Street Journal*, September 29, 1993, pp. B1, B5.

71. Jess McCuan, "A New Way to Fight Germs," *Inc.*, November 2009, pp. 48–49.

72. Max Chafkin, "Student Teachers: Looking for New Ideas? Hire Some College Kids," *Inc.*, October 2006, pp. 44–46.

73. Siri Schubert, "Folate Is Gr-r-reat!," *Business 2.0*, November 2004, p. 72.

74. Josh Dean, "Saul's House of Cool Ideas," *Inc.*, February 2010, p. 71.

75. Shivani Vora, "Wallpaper That's Temporary," *Inc.*, November 2010, p. 124.

76. Nicole Marie Richardson, "The Answer Is Blowing in the (Very Gentle) Wind," *Inc.*, October 2009, pp. 38–39.

77. Nick D'Alto, "Think Big," *Business Start-Ups*, January 2000, pp. 61–65.

78. Brian Nadel, "The Art of Innovation: Advertising Insert," *Fortune*, December 13, 2004, pp. S1–S22.

79. "Lead, Kindly Light," *The Ledlie Letter*, June 2009, p. 1; John Dodge, "Patent Awarded to 13-Year-Old for Pen Projector," *Smart Planet*, June 2, 2009, http://www.smartplanet.com/blog/thinking-tech/patent-awarded-to-13-year-old-for-pen-projector/228.

80. Jonah Lehrer, "Bother Me, I'm Thinking," *Wall Street Journal*, February 19, 2011, http://online.wsj.com/article/SB10001424052748703584804576144192132144506.html.

81. Sarah Kessler, "Walk, Talk, Ride, Recharge," *Inc.*, May 2010, p. 26; "About Us," nPower PEG, http://www.npowerpeg.com/index.php/our-story.

82. "What Are Dreams?," *Nova*, PBS, June 29, 2011, http://www.pbs.org/wgbh/nova/body/what-are-dreams.html.

83. Thea Singer, "Your Brain on Innovation," *Inc.*, September 2002, pp. 86–88.

84. "The Snakebot," *Inc.*, March 2009, pp. 42–43.

85. Paul Bagne, "When to Follow a Hunch," *Reader's Digest*, May 1994, p. 77.

86. Susan Hansen, "The Action Hero," *Inc.*, September 2002, pp. 82–84.

87. Thea Singer and Lea Buchanan, "Who? What? Where? Why? When? How?," *Inc.*, August 2002, p. 66.

88. Michael Waldholz, "A Hallucination Inspires a Vision for AIDS Drug," *Wall Street Journal*, September 29, 1993, pp. B1, B5.

89. Theunis Bates, "Supertiny Power Plants," *Fast Company*, June 2010, p. 38; "Technology," Innowattech, http://www.innowattech.co.il/technology.aspx; Diane Pham, "Pavegen: Energy-Generating Pavement Hits the Streets," *Inhabitat*, October 28, 2009, http://inhabitat.com/energy-generating-pavement.

90. Epstein, "How to Get a Great Idea," p. 104.

91. Michael Waldholz, "A Hallucination Inspires a Vision for AIDS Drug," *Wall Street Journal*, September 29, 1993, pp. B1, B5.

92. Bridget Finn, "Brainstorming for Better Brainstorming," *Business 2.0*, April 2005, pp. 109–114.

93. Chun, "Theory of Creativity," *Entrepreneur*, pp. 130–131.

94. Amantha Imber, "Finding Inspiration on the Treadmill," *Get to the Point: Small Business* (Marketing Profs), May 12, 2008, pp. 1–2.

95. Bridget Finn, "Brainstorming for Better Brainstorming," *Business 2.0*, April 2005, pp. 109–114.

96. Ed Brown, "A Day at Innovation U," *Fortune*, April 12, 1999, pp. 163–165.

97. The Hall of Science and Exploration, "Academy of Achievement: Linus Pauling, PhD," http://www.achievement.org/autodoc/page/pau0pro-1.

98. Anne Fisher, "Ideas Made Here," *Fortune*, June 11, 2007, pp. 35–41.

99. Andy Raskin, "A Higher Plane of Problem-Solving," *Business 2.0*, June 2003, pp. 54–56; "TRIZ 40," Triz 40 Principles, http://www.triz40.com/aff_Principles.htm.

100. Sloane, "Inside the Mind of a (Rich) Inventor," *FSB*, November 2007, pp. 90–102.

101. Ed Brown, "A Day at Innovation U," *Fortune*, April 12, 1999, p. 165.

102. Ed Brown, "A Day at Innovation U," *Fortune*, April 12, 1999, p. 165.

103. StopFakes.gov/smallbusiness, U.S. Patent and Trademark Office, http://www.uspto.gov/smallbusiness.

104. "Get Real: The Truth about Counterfeiting," International Anticounterfeiting Coalition, http://www.iacc.org/counterfeiting/counterfeiting.php.

105. Sara Schaefer Muñoz, "Patent No. 6,004,596: Peanut Butter and Jelly Sandwich," *Wall Street Journal*, April 5, 2005, pp. B1, B9; Malia Rulon, "Smucker Can't Patent PBJ, Court Says," *Greenville News*, April 9, 2005, pp. 18A, 21A.

106. "U.S. Patent Statistics," U.S. Patent and Trademark Office, http://www.uspto.gov/web/offices/ac/ido/oeip/taf/us_stat.pdf.

107. Michael S. Malone, "The Smother of Invention," *Forbes ASAP*, June 24, 2002, pp. 32–40.

108. "Data Visualization Center," U.S. Patent and Trademark Office, http://www.uspto.gov/dashboards/patents/main.dashxml.

109. Chris Barry, Alex Johnston, Ronen Arad, David Stainback, Landan Ansell, and Mike Arnold, *2010 Patent Litigation Study: The Continued Evolution of Patent Damages Law*, PriceWaterhouseCoopers, 2010; "AIPLA Study,"

Intellectual Property Insurance Services Corporation, http://www.patentinsurance.com/iprisk/aipla-survey.

110. Loren Berlein, "Cheap Knockoffs and Counterfeits Can Be Hazardous to Your Health," *Daily Finance*, June 17, 2011, http://www.dailyfinance.com/2011/06/17/cheap-knockoffs-and-counterfeits-can-be-hazardous-to-your-health.

111. Michael B. Sapherstein, "The Registrability of the Harley-Davidson Roar: A Multimedia Analysis," http://www.bc.edu/bc_org/avp/law/st_org/iptf/articles/content/1998101101.html; Tomima Edmark, "How Much Is Too Much?" *Entrepreneur*, February 1998, pp. 93–95.

112. Leslie A. Gordon, "Quackers!" *American Bar Association Journal*, September 1, 2009, http://www.abajournal.com/magazine/article/quackers; Jess McKinley, "A Quacking Kazoo Sets Off a Squabble," *New York Times*, June 3, 2009, http://www.nytimes.com/2009/06/03/us/03quack.html; "Ride the Ducks vs. Bay Quackers," *Justia Dockets and Filings*, April 28, 2010, http://docs.justia.com/cases/federal/district-courts/california/candce/3:2009cv02195/215055/28.

113. *Eighth Annual BSA Software 2010 Piracy Study*, Business Software Alliance, May 2011, p. 1.

114. Ryan Nakashima, "Movie Piracy Websites Seized in Widespread Raids by Feds," *Huffington Post*, June 30, 2010, http://www.huffingtonpost.com/2010/06/30/movie-piracy-websites-sei_n_631192.html.

3

Designing a Competitive Business Model and Building a Solid Strategic Plan

Learning Objectives

On completion of this chapter, you will be able to:

1. Understand the importance of strategic management to a small business.

2. Explain why and how a small business must create a competitive advantage in the market.

3. Develop a strategic plan for a business using the nine steps in the strategic planning process.

4. Discuss the characteristics of three basic strategies—low cost, differentiation, and focus—and know when and how to employ them.

5. Understand the importance of controls, such as the balanced scorecard, in the planning process.

Success depends on adapting more quickly than your competitors do. It's like the movie title, The Quick and the Dead. *Those really are the only two options anymore.*

—Steve Tobak

Strategy without tactics is the slowest route to victory. Tactics without strategy is the noise before the defeat.

—General Sun Tzu

Few activities in the life of a business are as vital—or as overlooked—as that of developing a strategy for success. Too often, entrepreneurs brimming with optimism and enthusiasm launch businesses destined for failure because their founders never stop to define a workable strategy that sets them apart from their competition. Because they tend to be people of action, entrepreneurs often find the process of developing a strategy dull and unnecessary. Their tendency is to start a business, try several approaches, and see what works. Without a comprehensive strategy, however, these entrepreneurs have as much chance of building a successful business as a defense contractor attempting to build a jet fighter without blueprints. Companies without clear strategies may achieve some success in the short run, but as soon as competitive conditions stiffen or an unanticipated threat arises, they usually "hit the wall" and fold. Without a basis for differentiating itself from a pack of similar competitors, the best a company can hope for is mediocrity in the marketplace.

In today's global competitive environment, any business, large or small, that is not thinking and acting strategically is extremely vulnerable. Every business is exposed to the forces of a rapidly changing competitive environment, and in the future small business executives can expect even greater change and uncertainty. From sweeping political changes around the planet and rapid technology advances to more intense competition and newly emerging global markets, the business environment has become more turbulent and challenging to business owners. Although this market turbulence creates many challenges for small businesses, it also creates opportunities for those companies that have in place strategies to capitalize on them. Historically important, entrepreneurs' willingness to adapt, to create change, to experiment with new business models, and to break traditional rules has become more important than ever. "It's not the strongest or the most intelligent [companies that] survive," says American Express CEO Ken Chenault, "but those most adaptive to change."[1]

LO1

Understand the importance of strategic management to a small business.

ENTREPRENEURIAL PROFILE: Charles Kittredge: Crane & Company One of the keys to success for Crane & Company, a family-owned business headquartered in Dalton, Massachusetts, has been its ability to adapt quickly to shifting trends and changing market conditions since its founding in 1800. Crane was the largest maker of paper shirt collars during that wave of fashion in the 1800s, and from the mid-1800s to 1990 the company's largest source of revenue was high-quality stationery made from cotton rather than cheaper wood pulp. Used by U.S. presidents and international heads of state, Crane stationery still has a reputation of stellar quality. However, e-mail, social networking, and the Internet have driven the demand for quality stationery to historically low levels, and CEO Charles Kittredge once again reinvented the company, producing the paper used to print U.S. currency. "We make 100% of U.S. currency paper," he says. "We print currency for other countries as well." Kittredge says that the company's move into the international market was a significant strategic step. "We bought a paper mill and printing plant in Sweden, upgraded it, and now we do all of our papermaking and printing for Europe there." Currently, the driver of Crane's revenue growth is developing technology, such as demetalized thread and micro-optic film, to incorporate into currency paper to combat counterfeiters. Currency paper generates 80 percent of Crane's revenue, but Kittredge has not abandoned traditional stationery. His goal is to transform Crane stationery "from a paper-based business to a personal communication business," he says.[2] ■

Perhaps the biggest change that entrepreneurs face is unfolding now: the shift in the world's economy from a base of *financial to intellectual* capital. "Knowledge is no longer just a factor of production," says futurist Alvin Toffler. "It is the *critical* factor of production."[3] Today, a company's intellectual capital is likely to be the source of its competitive advantage in the marketplace. **Intellectual capital** is comprised of three components:[4]

1. *Human capital* consists of the talents, creativity, skills, and abilities of a company's workforce and shows up in the innovative strategies, plans, and processes that the people in an organization develop and then passionately pursue.

2. *Structural capital* is the accumulated knowledge and experience that a company possesses. It can take many forms, including processes, software, patents, copyrights, and, perhaps most important, the knowledge and experience of the people in a company.

3. *Customer capital* is the established customer base, positive reputation, ongoing relationships, and goodwill that a company builds up over time with its customers.

intellectual capital
a key source of a company's competitive advantage that is comprised of (1) human capital, (2) structural capital, and (3) customer capital.

Increasingly, entrepreneurs are recognizing that the capital stored in these three areas forms the foundation of their ability to compete effectively and that they must manage this intangible capital base carefully. Every business uses all three components in its strategy, but the emphasis they place on each one varies.

ENTREPRENEURIAL PROFILE: Whole Foods Whole Foods, a highly successful retailer of natural and organic foods with more than 270 stores in North America and the United Kingdom, emphasizes human capital in its strategy for achieving a competitive advantage in the marketplace. The company subjects all job applicants to a thorough screening process, carefully selecting only those who demonstrate a passion for what lies at the heart of its competitive edge: a love of food and dedication to customer service. Unlike most of its competitors in the supermarket industry, Whole Foods invests heavily in training its workers (called Team Members inside the company) so that they can demonstrate and explain to customers the features and the benefits of the company's natural foods. In addition, managers recognize that food preferences vary from one region of a nation to another, and they give Team Members at the local level a great deal of autonomy in the selection of foods they stock. The company recognizes the role that Team Members play in the company's success, and its employee-friendly policies have landed it on *Fortune's* "100 Best Companies to Work For" list consistently. Even though its cost structure is not the lowest in the industry, the company is growing rapidly because owners know that its loyal customers do not shop there searching for the lowest prices.[5] ∎

This knowledge shift is creating as much change in the world's business systems as the Industrial Revolution did in the agriculture-based economies of the 1800s. The knowledge revolution threatens the existence of those companies that are not prepared for it, but it is spawning tremendous opportunities for those entrepreneurs who are equipped with the strategies to exploit these opportunities. Management legend Jack Welch, who masterfully guided General Electric for many years, says, "Intellectual capital is what it's all about. Releasing the ideas of people is what we've got to do if we are going to win."[6] However, in practice, releasing people's ideas is much more difficult than it appears. The key is to encourage employees to generate a large volume of ideas, recognizing that only a few (the best) will survive. According to Gary Hamel, author of *Inside the Revolution*, "If you want to find a few ideas with the power to enthrall customers, foil competitors, and thrill investors, you must first generate hundreds and potentially thousands of unconventional strategic ideas. Put simply, you have to crush a lot of rock to find a diamond."[7] In other words, small companies must use the creativity-stimulating techniques discussed in Chapter 2 as one source of competitive advantage over their rivals.

The rules of the competitive game of business are constantly changing. To be successful, entrepreneurs can no longer do things in the way they've always done them. Fortunately, successful entrepreneurs have at their disposal a powerful weapon to cope with a hostile, ever-changing environment: the process of strategic management. **Strategic management** involves developing a game plan to guide a company as it strives to accomplish its vision, mission, goals, and objectives and to keep it from straying off its desired course. The idea is to give an entrepreneur a blueprint for matching the company's strengths and weaknesses to the opportunities and threats in the environment.

strategic management
the process of developing a game plan to guide a company as it strives to accomplish its vision, mission, goals, and objectives and to keep it from straying off course.

Building a Competitive Advantage

LO2

Explain why and how a small business must create a competitive advantage in the market.

The goal of developing a strategic plan is to create for the small company a **competitive advantage**—the combination of factors that sets a small business apart from its competitors and gives it a unique position in the market that is superior to its rivals. It is the differentiating factor that makes customers want to buy from your business rather than from your competitors. From a strategic perspective, the key to business success is to develop a sustainable competitive advantage, one that is durable, creates value for customers, and is difficult for competitors to duplicate. For example, Whole Foods competes successfully with giant chains such as Wal-Mart and Kroger not on price but by emphasizing superior customer service, higher-quality products, a more extensive inventory of local and organic products, and a commitment to fair-trade suppliers. Its stores are well organized, attractive, and entertaining. Asked to describe his recently opened Whole Foods store, team leader Matthew Mell says, "It's a Disney World for foodies."[8]

competitive advantage
the combination of factors that sets a small business apart from its competitors and gives it a unique position in the market that is superior to its competition.

Companies that fail to define their competitive advantage fall into "me-too" strategies that never set them apart from their competitors and do not allow them to become market leaders or to achieve above-average profits.

Entrepreneurs should examine five aspects of their businesses to define their companies' competitive advantages:

1. *Products they sell.* What is unique about the products the company sells? Do they save customers time or money? Are they more reliable and more dependable than those that competitors sell? Do they save energy, protect the environment, or provide more convenience for customers? By identifying the unique customer benefits of their companies' products, entrepreneurs can differentiate their businesses. Peter D'Amato has built a successful business, California Carnivores, that specializes in selling carnivorous plants, such as the Venus flytrap and the hairy sundew, to customers anywhere in the United States from his 11,000-square-foot nursery located in Sebastopol, California. California Carnivores sells more than 1,000 varieties of carnivorous plants, and D'Amato is constantly breeding new varieties and importing exotic ones from foreign locations. "Carnivorous plants are very bizarre; many of them are almost animal-like in their appearance," he says. "Growing them is more like having pets than having plants."[9]

2. *Service they provide.* Many entrepreneurs find that the service they provide their customers is an excellent way to differentiate their companies. Because they are small, friendly, and close to their customers, small businesses are able to provide customer service that is superior to that which their larger competitors can provide. What services does the company provide (or which ones can it provide) to deliver added value and a superior shopping experience for customers?

3. *Pricing they offer.* As we will see later in this chapter, some small businesses differentiate themselves using price. Price can be a powerful point of differentiation; offering the lowest price gives some customers a great incentive to buy. However, offering the lowest price is not always the best way to create a unique image. Small companies that do not offer the lowest prices must emphasize the value that their products offer.

4. *Way they sell.* Customers today expect to be able to conduct business when they want to, meaning that companies that offer extended hours—even 24-hour service seven days a week (perhaps via the Internet)—have the basis for an important competitive advantage. Zoots, a small chain of dry-cleaning stores in the Northeast, offers customers extended hours seven days a week and allows a secure 24-hour pickup and drop-off service. The company also offers a home pickup and delivery service that customers can book online and an environmentally friendly cleaning process, all of which maximize customers' convenience and set the company apart from its competition.[10]

5. *Values to which they are committed.* The most successful companies exist for reasons that involve far more than merely making money. The entrepreneurs behind these companies understand that one way to connect with customers and establish a competitive edge is to manage their companies from a values-based perspective and operate them in an ethical and socially responsible fashion. In other words, they recognize that there is no inherent conflict between earning a profit and creating good for society and the environment.

Building a competitive advantage alone is not enough; the key to success over time is building a *sustainable* competitive advantage. In the long run, a company gains a sustainable competitive advantage through its ability to develop a set of core competencies that enable it to serve its selected target customers better than its rivals. **Core competencies** are a unique set of capabilities that a company develops in key areas, such as superior quality, customer service, innovation, team building, flexibility, responsiveness, and others, that allow it to vault past competitors. As the phrase suggests, they are central to a company's ability to compete successfully and are usually the result of important skills and lessons that a business has learned over time.

Typically, a company develops core competencies in no more than five or six (often fewer) areas. These core competencies become the nucleus of a company's competitive advantage and are usually quite enduring over time. Markets, customers, and competitors may change, but a

core competencies
a unique set of capabilities that a company develops in key operational areas that allow it to vault past competitors.

FIGURE 3.1
Building a Sustainable Competitive Advantage

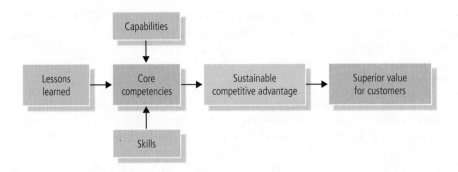

company's core competencies are more durable, forming the building blocks for everything a company does. To be effective strategically, these competencies should be difficult for competitors to duplicate, and they must provide customers with an important perceived benefit. Small companies' core competencies often have to do with the advantages of their size—such as agility, speed, closeness to their customers, superior service, or the ability to innovate. According to Scott Cook, founder of Intuit, agility is what matters most. "Agile firms will win," he says. "Rigid firms will disappear."[11] Smart entrepreneurs use their companies' size to their advantage, recognizing that it allows them to do things that their larger rivals cannot. The key to success is building the company's strategy on its core competencies and concentrating them on providing superior service and value for its target customers (see Figure 3.1).

Successful small companies are able to build strategies that exploit all the competitive advantages that their size gives them by doing the following:

- Responding quickly to customers' needs

- Providing personalized customer service

- Remaining flexible and willing to change

- Constantly searching for new, emerging market segments

- Building and defending small market niches

- Erecting "switching costs," the costs a customer incurs by switching to a competitor's product or service, through personal service and loyalty

- Remaining entrepreneurial and willing to take risks and act with lightning speed

- Constantly innovating

ENTREPRENEURIAL PROFILE: Michael Gordon and Vaughn Lazar: Pizza Fusion When Michael Gordon and Vaughn Lazar decided to start a business in 2006, the two college buddies decided that it would be different, would make a difference in people's lives, and would reflect their belief that social responsibility is just as important as profitability. After numerous brainstorming sessions, Gordon and Lazar came up with the idea for Pizza Fusion, a company that serves delicious, gourmet pizza in its purest form, with no artificial additives, growth hormones, pesticides, preservatives, and trans fats. Pizza Fusion's menu, which also includes sandwiches, salads, desserts, beer, and wine, is 75 percent organic and includes gluten-free, vegetarian, and vegan offerings. The company also reflects its founders' focus on sustainability. Pizza Fusion delivers pizzas in company-owned hybrid vehicles, offsets 100 percent of its energy consumption by buying renewable wind-energy certificates, recycling, and building LEED-certified restaurants. The company, whose motto is "Saving the earth one pizza at a time," has 13 locations in six states and two outlets in Saudi Arabia and is growing rapidly.[12] ■

As Pizza Fusion's success proves, no business can (or should) be everything to everyone. In fact, one of the biggest pitfalls many entrepreneurs stumble into is failing to differentiate their companies from the crowd of competitors. Entrepreneurs often face the challenge of setting their companies apart from their larger, more powerful competitors (who can easily outspend them) by

using their creativity and the special abilities their businesses offer customers. Developing core competencies does *not* necessarily require a company to spend a great deal of money. It does, however, require an entrepreneur to use creativity, imagination, and vision to identify those things that it does best and that are most important to its target customers. Businesses have an infinite number of ways to create a competitive edge, but building a strategy around a company's core competencies allows it to gain a sustainable competitive advantage based on what it does best.

Strategic management enhances a small company's effectiveness, but entrepreneurs first must have a process designed to meet their needs and their business's special characteristics. It is a mistake to attempt to apply a big business's strategic development techniques to a small business because a small business is not merely "a little big business." Because of their size and their particular characteristics—small resource base, flexible managerial style, informal organizational structure, and adaptability to change—small businesses need a different approach to the strategic management process. The strategic management procedure for a small business should include the following features:

- Use a relatively short planning horizon—two years or less for most small companies.

- Be informal and not overly structured; a shirt-sleeve approach is ideal.

- Encourage the participation of employees and outside parties to improve the reliability and creativity of the resulting plan.

- Do not begin with setting objectives because extensive objective setting early on may interfere with the creative process of strategic management.

- Maintain flexibility; competitive conditions change too rapidly for any plan to be considered permanent.

- Focus on strategic *thinking*, not just planning, by linking long-range goals to day-to-day operations.

- Be an ongoing process because businesses and the competitive environment in which they operate constantly change.

The Strategic Management Process

Strategic management is a continuous process that consists of nine steps:

Step 1. Develop a clear vision and translate it into a meaningful mission statement vision.

Step 2. Assess the company's strengths and weaknesses.

Step 3. Scan the environment for significant opportunities and threats facing the business.

Step 4. Identify the key factors for success in the business.

Step 5. Analyze the competition.

Step 6. Create company goals and objectives.

Step 7. Formulate strategic options and select the appropriate strategies.

Step 8. Translate strategic plans into action plans.

Step 9. Establish accurate controls.

Step 1. Develop a Clear Vision and Translate It into a Meaningful Mission Statement Vision

Throughout history, the greatest political and business leaders have been visionaries. Whether the vision is as grand as Martin Luther King Jr.'s "I have a dream" speech or as simple as Ray Kroc's devotion to quality, service, cleanliness, and value at McDonald's, the purpose is the same: to focus everyone's attention on the same target and to inspire them to reach it. The vision is future oriented and touches everyone associated with the company, such as employees, investors, lenders, customers, and the community. It is an expression of what an entrepreneur stands for and believes in. Highly successful entrepreneurs are able to communicate their vision and their enthusiasm about that vision to those around them.

A vision is the result of an entrepreneur's dream of something successful that does not exist yet and the ability to paint a compelling picture of that dream for everyone to see. It answers the question, "Where are we going?" Ari Weinzweig started a small deli, Zingerman's Delicatessen, in Ann Arbor, Michigan, in 1982. Since then, his company has grown into Zingerman's Community of Businesses, eight highly successful businesses with 500 employees and $27 million in sales. "We wouldn't be where we are without visioning," says Weinzweig. A clearly defined vision, which Weinzweig calls "the cathedral everyone is coming to work every day to construct," helps a company in four ways:[13]

1. *Vision provides direction.* Entrepreneurs who spell out the vision for their company focus everyone's attention on the future and determine the path the business will take to get there.

2. *Vision determines decisions.* The vision influences the decisions, no matter how big or how small, that owners, managers, and employees make every day in a business. This influence can be positive or negative, depending on how well defined the vision is.

3. *Vision inspires people.* A clear vision excites and ignites people to action. People want to work for a company that sets its sights high.

4. *Vision allows for perseverance in the face of adversity.* Young companies, their founders, and their employees often face many hardships from a multitude of sources. Having a vision that serves as a company's "guiding star" enables people to overcome imposing obstacles.

Vision is based on an entrepreneur's values. Explaining how an entrepreneur's values are the nucleus around which a company grows, author and consultant Ken Blanchard says, "Winning companies first emphasize values—the beliefs that you, as the business owner, have about your employees, customers, quality, ethics, integrity, social responsibility, growth, stability, innovation, and flexibility. Managing by values—not by profits—is a powerful process."[14] Successful entrepreneurs build their businesses around a set of three to six core values that might range from respect for the individual and innovation to creating satisfied customers and making the world a better place. Indeed, truly visionary entrepreneurs see their companies' primary purpose as more than just "making money." One writer explains, "Almost all workers are making decisions, not just filling out weekly sales reports or tightening screws. They will do what they think is best. If you want them to do as the company thinks best too, then you must [see to it that] they have an inner gyroscope aligned with the corporate compass."[15] That gyroscope's alignment depends on the entrepreneur's values and how well he or she transmits them throughout the company. Table 3.1 offers useful tips for creating a vision for your company.

The best way to put values into action is to create a written mission statement that communicates those values to everyone the company touches.

TABLE 3.1 Creating a Vision for Your Company

Ari Wienzweig, founder of Zingerman's Community of Businesses, emphasizes the importance of creating a vision to achieve entrepreneurial success. A vision is a picture of what success will look like in a business at a particular time in the future. "The power that comes out of visioning is huge," he says. "Effective visioning allows us to move toward the future we want, not just react to a present-day reality we don't like."

How does an entrepreneur start the visioning process? First, select the time frame, ideally 3 to 10 years out. The next step is to write the first draft of your vision, remembering to shoot for something *great*, even those things that other people have told you repeatedly were unachievable. As you proceed, write as if your vision already has happened. The following questions will help you get started:

1. How big is your business?
2. What has your business achieved that you are most proud of?
   a. Relative rank in your industry
   b. Financial success
   c. Product or service quality
   d. Contribution to the community
   e. Awards and recognitions
3. What are your most important product lines or services?
4. What products or services do you refuse to offer?
5. What is a customer's shopping experience like at your business? What makes that experience different from your competition?
6. Who are your customers? How did you find them?
7. If you asked your customers to list the three most noteworthy characteristics of your business, what would they be?
8. How do you describe your management style?
9. What kind of people do you hire as employees and managers?
10. What kind of relationship do you have with your employees? What do they say about their jobs?
11. What do you do every day when you go to work? How many hours a week do you work?
12. How does the community view your business?
13. What do suppliers say about your business?
14. What do industry experts say about your business?

You will probably write several drafts of your vision before sharing it with others, especially with the people who will be involved in making it a reality. Ask for their feedback and input but remember that it's *your* vision. When people ask (and they inevitably will), "How will we achieve that?," remember that vision is about the "what"; strategy, the "how," comes later.

Source: Ari Weinzweig, "Step into the Future," *Inc.*, February 2011, pp. 85–91.

MISSION The **mission statement** addresses another basic question of any business venture: "What business are we in?" Establishing the purpose of the business in writing must come first in order to give the company a sense of direction. "If you don't reduce [your company's purpose] to paper, it just doesn't stick," says the owner of an architecture firm. "Reducing it to paper really forces you to think about what you are doing."[16] As an enduring declaration of a company's purpose, a mission statement is the mechanism for making it clear to everyone the company touches "why we are here" and "where we are going."

mission statement
an enduring declaration of a company's purpose that addresses the first question of any business venture: What business am I in?

ENTREPRENEURIAL PROFILE: Truett Cathy: Chick-Fil-A Truett Cathy, founder of the highly successful restaurant chain Chick-Fil-A, recalls a time when his business was struggling because of intensifying competition from big hamburger chains. The company, with 200 outlets at the time, was struggling to keep operating costs under control as inflation threatened to push them higher. Cathy scheduled an executive retreat at a lake outside of Atlanta where managers could relax and talk about their concerns and ideas for the company. His oldest son, Dan, then director of operations, asked, "Why are we in business? Why are we here?" Cathy was about to tell his son that this retreat was no time to dwell on philosophical issues because there were bigger problems to solve. "Then," recalls Cathy, "I realized he was serious. His question both challenged and inspired us." In the ensuing brainstorming session, the group defined values that became Chick-Fil-A's mission statement: "To glorify God by being faithful stewards of all that is entrusted to our care. To have a positive influence on all who come in contact with Chick-Fil-A." With their purpose clearly defined, the management team went on to lead the company in a growth spurt in which sales climbed 30 percent a year. Today, the company has more than 1,500 restaurants in 39 states and the District of Columbia (none of which are open on Sundays) and generates annual sales of more than $3.5 billion.[17] ∎

Without a concise, meaningful mission statement, a small business risks wandering aimlessly in the marketplace, with no idea of where to go or how to get there. A great mission statement sets the tone for the entire company and focuses its attention in the right direction.

ELEMENTS OF A MISSION STATEMENT A sound mission statement need not be lengthy to be effective. In fact, shorter usually is better. Three key issues entrepreneurs and their employees should address as they develop a mission statement for their businesses follow:

- The *purpose* of the company: What are we in business to accomplish?

- The *business* we are in: How are we going to accomplish that purpose?

- The *values* of the company: What principles and beliefs form the foundation of the way we do business?

ENTREPRENEURIAL PROFILE: Eric Ryan and Adam Lowry: Method At Method, a San Francisco–based company that makes a line of all natural, nontoxic household and personal cleaning products and sells them in attractive bottles that were created by designer Karim Rashid, cofounders Eric Ryan and Adam Lowry identify five core values that support their unique small company's mission: collaboration, innovation, care, "what would McGyver do?," and keeping Method weird. Ryan and Lowry's vision is to build a company that creates a better cleaning experience for their customers by providing safe, environmentally friendly products in cleverly designed packages, constantly engaging in product innovation, and creating a fun work environment for employees.[18] ∎

A company's mission statement may be the most essential and basic communications that it puts forward. It should inspire and motivate employees by communicating the company's overarching values. If the people on the plant, shop, retail, or warehouse floor don't know what a company's mission is, then, for all practical purposes, it does not have one! The mission statement expresses a company's character, identity, and scope of operations, but writing it is only half the battle, at best. The most difficult and important part is *living* that mission every day. *That's* how employees decide what really matters. To be effective, a mission statement must become a natural part of the organization, embodied in the minds, habits, attitudes, and decisions of everyone in the company every day. In other words, a good mission statement is translated into positive performance within an organization. One business writer claims, "If what you say about your firm's values and mission isn't true, you're in worse trouble than if you'd never articulated it in the first place."[19] Five years after founding Field Trip Factory Inc., a business that organizes life skill educational field trips for students, Susan Singer saw the need to update the company's mission statement. At a company retreat, she and her employees decided that their existing mission statement no longer reflected what the company actually stood for and did. A brainstorming session yielded a new mission statement that Singer says is helping her company improve its bottom line. "It became so clear what we do vs. what we want to be," she says.[20]

A well-used mission statement serves as a strategic compass for a small company, guiding both managers and employees as they make decisions in the face of uncertainty. Some companies use short, one- or two-sentence mission statements that are easy to remember and understand, and others create longer mission statements with multiple components. Consider the following examples:

- Google, the world's leading search engine, says that its mission "is to organize the world's information and make it universally accessible and useful."[21]

- The Elephant Sanctuary, which operates on 2,700 acres in Hohenwald, Tennessee, has a simple and inspiring mission: "A natural habitat refuge where sick, old, and needy elephants can once again walk the earth in peace and dignity."[22]

- Pizza Fusion's mission "is to uphold the highest level of integrity in all we do, from the quality and origin of our food to our care for the health of our customers and the environment."[23]

- The mission of Great Harvest Bread Company, which Pete and Laura Wakeman cofounded in Great Falls, Montana, in 1976, conveys both the fun personality of the company and the values that are important to its founders: "Be loose and have fun. Bake phenomenal bread. Run fast to help customers. Create strong and exciting bakeries. And give generously to others."[24]

A company may have a powerful competitive advantage, but it is wasted unless (1) the owner has communicated that advantage to workers, who, in turn, work hard to communicate it to customers and potential customers and (2) customers recommend the company to their friends because they understand the benefits they are getting from it that they cannot get elsewhere. *That's* the real power of a mission statement. Table 3.2 offers some useful tips on writing a mission statement.

Step 2. Assess the Company's Strengths and Weaknesses

Having defined the vision he or she has for her company and translated that vision into a meaningful mission statement, an entrepreneur can turn his or her attention to assessing company strengths and weaknesses. Building a successful competitive strategy requires a business to magnify its strengths and overcome or compensate for its weaknesses. **Strengths** are positive internal factors that a company can draw on to accomplish its mission, goals, and objectives. They might include special skills or knowledge, a superior proprietary product or process, a positive public image, an experienced sales force, an established base of loyal customers, and many other factors. For instance, 1366 Technologies, a company in Lexington, Massachusetts, has developed a revolutionary process called the Direct Wafer method for producing the silicon wafers inside most solar panels. The process represents a major strength for the small company because it reduces wafer manufacturing cost 60 percent and reduces the time required to make a wafer from more than two days to just seconds.[25] **Weaknesses** are negative internal factors that inhibit a company's ability to accomplish its mission, goals, and objectives. Lack of capital, a shortage of skilled workers, the inability to master technology, and an inferior location are examples of weaknesses.

Identifying strengths and weaknesses helps owners understand their businesses as they exist (or that, for start-ups, will exist). An organization's strengths should originate in the core competencies that are essential to gaining an edge in each of the market segments in which the firm competes. The key to building a successful strategy is using the company's underlying strengths as its foundation and matching those strengths against competitors' weaknesses.

One technique for taking this strategic inventory is to prepare a "balance sheet" of the company's strengths and weaknesses (see Table 3.3). The left side should reflect important skills, knowledge, or resources that contribute to the firm's success. The right side should record honestly any limitations that detract from the company's ability to compete. This balance sheet should analyze all key performance areas of the business—human resources, finance, production, marketing, product development, organization, and others. This analysis should give owners a realistic perspective of their businesses, pointing out foundations on which they can build future strengths and obstacles that they must remove for the business to progress. This exercise can help entrepreneurs determine the best way to move from their current position to a desired one.

Step 3. Scan the Environment for Significant Opportunities and Threats Facing the Business

OPPORTUNITIES Once entrepreneurs have taken an internal inventory of company strengths and weaknesses, they must turn to the external environment to identify any opportunities and threats that might have a significant impact on the business. **Opportunities** are positive external options that a firm can exploit to accomplish its mission, goals, and objectives. The number of potential opportunities is limitless; therefore, entrepreneurs should analyze only those that are most significant to the business (probably two or three at most). The key is to focus on the most promising opportunities that fit most closely with the company's strengths and core competencies. That

strengths
positive internal factors that a company can use to accomplish its mission, goals, and objectives.

weaknesses
negative internal factors that inhibit the accomplishment of a company's mission, goals, and objectives.

opportunities
positive external options that a firm can exploit to accomplish its mission, goals, and objectives.

TABLE 3.2 Tips for Writing a Powerful Mission Statement

A mission statement is a useful tool for getting everyone fired up and heading in the same direction, but writing one is not as easy as it may first appear. Here are some tips for writing a powerful mission statement:

- *Keep it short.* The best mission statements are just a few sentences long. If they are short, people tend to remember them better.

- *Keep it simple.* Avoid using fancy jargon just to impress outsiders, such as customers or suppliers. The first and most important use of a mission statement is inside a company.

- *Know what makes your company different.* Your competitors are trying to reach the same customers that you are. A mission statement should address what is unique about your company and what sets it apart from the competition.

- *Take a broad view but not too broad.* If it is too specific, a mission statement can limit a company's potential. Similarly, a mission statement is too broad if it applies to any company in the industry. When asked what business his company was in, Rob Carter, a top manager at FedEx, did not mention shipping packages quickly; instead, his response was, "We're in the business of engineering time."

- *Get everyone involved.* If the boss writes the company mission statement, who is going to criticize it? Although the entrepreneur has to be the driving force behind the mission statement, everyone in the company needs the opportunity to have a voice in creating it. Expect to write several drafts before you arrive at a finished product.

- *Keep it current.* Mission statements can get stale over time. As business and competitive conditions change, so should your mission statement. Make a habit of evaluating your mission periodically so that it stays fresh.

- *Make sure your mission statement reflects the values and beliefs you hold dear.* They are the foundation on which your company is built.

- *Make sure your mission includes values that are worthy of your employees' best efforts.* One entrepreneur says that a mission statement should "send a message to employees, suppliers, and customers as to what the purpose of the company is aside from just making profits."

- *Make sure your statement reflects a concern for the future.* Business owners can get so focused on the present that they forget about the future. A mission statement should be the first link to the company's future.

- *Keep the tone of the statement positive and upbeat.* No one wants to work for a business with a pessimistic outlook of the world.

- *Use your mission statement to lay an ethical foundation for your company.* This is the ideal time to let employees know what your company stands for—and what it won't stand for.

- *Look at other companies' mission statements to generate ideas for your own.* Two books, *Say It and Live It: The 50 Corporate Mission Statements That Hit the Mark* (Currency/Doubleday) and *Mission Statements: A Guide to the Corporate and Nonprofit Sectors* (Garland Publishing), are useful resources. Internet searches also produce useful examples of mission statements.

- *Make sure that your mission statement is appropriate for your company's culture.* Although you should look at other companies' missions, do not make the mistake of trying to copy them. Your company's mission is unique to you and your company.

- *Revise it when necessary.* No business is static, which means that your company's mission statement should change as your company changes. Work with a team of your employees on a regular basis to review and revise your company's mission statement.

- *Use it.* Don't go to all of the trouble of writing a mission statement just to let it collect dust. Post it on bulletin boards, print it on buttons and business cards, or stuff it into employees' pay envelopes. Talk about your mission often and use it to develop your company's strategic plan. That's what it's for!

Sources: Adapted from "Ten Tips for Writing a Mission Statement," AllBusiness, http://www.allbusiness.com/marketing/advertising-copywriting/12185-1.html; Ken Blanchard, "The New Bottom Line," *Entrepreneur*, February 1998, pp. 127–131; Alan Farnham, Brushing Up Your Vision Thing," *Fortune*, May 1, 1995, p. 129; Sharon Nelton, "Put Your Purpose in Writing," *Nation's Business*, February 1994, pp. 61–64; and Jacquelyn Lynn, "Single-Minded," *Entrepreneur*, January 1996, p. 97.

TABLE 3.3 Identifying Company Strengths and Weaknesses

Strengths (Positive Internal Factors)	Weaknesses (Negative Internal Factors)

requires entrepreneurs to say "no" to opportunities, even promising ones, that do not fit their companies' strategic vision.

When identifying opportunities, an entrepreneur must pay close attention to new potential markets. Are competitors overlooking a niche in the market? Is there a better way to reach customers? Can we develop new products that offer customers better value? What opportunities are trends in the industry creating?

ENTREPRENEURIAL PROFILE: Michael Henderson: SmartTruck Rapidly rising fuel prices have created problems for many businesses but have produced a significant opportunity for others, including SmartTruck, a small company based in Greenville, South Carolina, that manufactures six-piece kits that attach to tractor trailers to make them more aerodynamic and fuel efficient. Michael Henderson, founder of SmartTruck, spent 32 years as an engineer with the Boeing Company before studying the trucking industry and discovering that very few trucking companies were reducing their fleets' fuel consumption by utilizing aerodynamic principles that are common in the airline industry. He also saw that a tough new fuel-efficiency requirement was about to take effect in California, something that would increase demand for an aerodynamic product for the trucking industry. Henderson used one of the world's fastest supercomputers at the Oak Ridge National Laboratory to perfect the design of the company's aerodynamic kit, which improves a typical truck's fuel efficiency by 10 percent. Already, trucking companies have outfitted thousands of their trailers with SmartTruck's aerodynamic kits, and Henderson says that the company's sales are increasing rapidly.[26] ∎

As SmartTruck's experience illustrates, opportunities arise as a result of factors that are beyond entrepreneurs' control. Constantly scanning for those opportunities that best match their companies' strengths and core competences and pouncing on them ahead of competitors is the key to success.

Threats are negative external forces that inhibit a company's ability to achieve its mission, goals, and objectives. Threats to the business can take a variety of forms, such as new competitors entering the local market, a government mandate regulating a business activity, an economic recession, rising interest rates, mounting energy prices, technology advances making a company's product obsolete, and many others. For instance, video on demand and digital downloading of movies, when coupled with large-screen, high-definition television sets and home theater sound systems, pose a threat to movie theaters because many people prefer to sit in the comfort of their own homes to watch movies rather than go to a theater. In fact, in 1946, the average person in the United States went to the movies 28 times per year; today, the average person goes to a movie theater only 3.9 times per year! Competition for people's time from the Internet, social networking sites, YouTube, and video games also cut into sales of movie tickets. As a result, several small theater chains, including Muvico, Cinema de Lux, CineBistro, and others, are changing their strategies to encourage movie fans to return to the big screen. These chains have added in-theater dining; some offer midrange movie fare, such as pizza, hamburgers,

threats
negative external forces that inhibit a company's ability to achieve its mission, goals, and objectives.

You Be the Consultant

The Best Little Pizza Chain No One Ever Heard Of

Jack Butorac had retired from a 35-year career at Fuddruckers and Chi-Chi's when he found a sleepy little pizza chain, Marco's Pizza, that had incredible potential. Although he "knew nothing about pizza," Butorac knew the restaurant business extremely well and had a record of success expanding restaurants into the national market. Pasquale "Pat" Giammarco, who founded Marco's Pizza in 1978 in Toledo, Ohio, sold the first Marco's Pizza franchise in 1979, but the chain had grown slowly to just over 100 stores by 2004.

Butorac approached Giammarco with a buyout proposal: Butorac would purchase majority ownership of the company and set up a franchising operation that would allow Marco's Pizza to become a national brand. Giammarco accepted the deal, and Butorac recruited industry veterans with restaurant and franchising experience from Domino's Pizza, Yum! Brands, Papa John's, Wendy's, and others to manage every aspect of the company, from branding and purchasing to market analysis and franchise sales. Butorac recognized that Marco's Pizza had a reputation for delicious pizzas made with high-quality ingredients and a system of consistent operations throughout the chain. They also knew that Marco's Pizza lacked brand recognition. "[Giammarco] is a pizza guy . . . a smart guy," says Butorac, "but he didn't brand Marco's. He didn't distinguish it. He didn't emphasize its strengths. As I went from store to store, I found that the product was the same quality everywhere. What [was lacking] was how to brand it and differentiate it from other brands out there." Butorac and his team identified several factors that set Marco's Pizza apart from the competition, including pizza dough made fresh daily in every store, a sauce made from an old family recipe, and a special blend of three cheeses.

Butorac knew that the challenges facing the management team would test all of their knowledge and experience. Many analysts consider the $30-billion-a-year pizza market to be saturated; competition from strong national chains such as Pizza Hut, Domino's, and Papa John's and independent local operators is intense; and franchising as a whole is sluggish. "The pizza category is mature," says a restaurant industry analyst. "It is tough to expand into new markets. [Marco's Pizza] has to be able to educate the consumer that they offer a better pizza." Other challenges include slow industry growth rates, rapidly rising costs of ingredients, and a growing national concern over obesity. Still, Butorac was convinced that Marco's was the best little pizza chain no one had ever heard of. He and his team had to get the word out.

Butorac's first step was to raise $20 million in private equity funding to help prospective franchisees buy into the franchise system and existing franchisees to expand their operations. He also established an equipment leasing division to help franchisees acquire or upgrade equipment or build entire new stores, which cost about $250,000 and generate average annual sales of more than $700,000. Butorac and his team came up with a new slogan, "Ah!thentic Italian Pizza," to communicate the quality and freshness of their pizzas' ingredients.

The changes that Butorac and his management team have implemented are beginning to work; Marco's Pizza's current store count is 241, and the company is one of the fastest-growing pizza chains in the United States. Most of the stores are located in the Midwest and Southeast, but Butorac is planning to expand into California and other western states. "We're going to start an advertising fund with franchisees and collectively advertise the Marco's message," he says. "We want the franchisees to be successful." Standardization and systemization are crucial elements in the company's recipe for growth. "A mushroom is a mushroom? No, it isn't," he says, explaining that Marco's Pizza established a food supply division when maintaining quality and consistency became a challenge in some new stores. "We've had a lot of fun, but there are lots of challenges and opportunities on the horizon," says Butorac.

1. Visit Marco's Pizza's Web site at www.marcos.com to learn more about the company. Work with a team of your classmates to identify the company's strengths and weaknesses.

2. What opportunities and threats does Marco's Pizza face?

3. Identify Marco's Pizza's major competitors. What are their strengths and weaknesses?

4. Write a short memo (two pages maximum) to Jack Butorac and his management team describing your strategic recommendations for helping Marco's Pizza gain a competitive advantage in the pizza market.

Sources: Based on Deborah L. Cohen, "Fledgling Pizza Chain Eyes Larger Slice of the Pie," *Reuters*, June 1, 2011, http://www.reuters.com/article/2011/06/01/us-column-cohen-pizza-idUSTRE7504WO20110601, and Valerie Killifer, "CEO Q&A: Jack Butorac of Marco's Pizza," *Pizza Marketplace*, January 11, 2011, http://www.pizzamarketplace.com/article/178714/CEO-Q-A-Jack-Butorac-of-Marco-s-Pizza.

---

chicken Caesar salads, and nachos; and others offer upscale dinners, such as limoncello-tossed shrimp and duck quesadillas served by waitstaff. Approximately 350 theaters out of the 5,750 cinemas in the United States now offer full-service restaurants, but the number is growing fast. "These theaters are the future of movie-going," says industry veteran Jeffrey Katzenberg. In addition, the new theaters offer customers amenities such as online seat reservations, valet parking, full bars, stadium seating with plush reclining leather chairs with extra legroom, digital systems that provide crisp images, interactive game rooms for children, and child care services. "We're competing with a million things for people's time," says Jeremy Welman, chief operating officer of CineBistro Theaters. "We have to give them an experience that's worth going out to."[27]

Many small businesses face a threat from larger rivals who offer lower prices because of their high-volume purchasing power, huge advertising budgets, and megastores that attract customers for miles around. However, small businesses with the proper strategies in place do *not* have to fold in the face of intense competition. The accompanying "Hands On . . . How To" feature explains that, with the proper strategy, small companies can not only survive but also thrive in the shadow of larger, more powerful rivals.

Opportunities and threats are products of the interactions of forces, trends, and events outside the direct control of the business. These external forces have direct impact on the behavior of the markets in which the business operates, the behavior of competitors, and the behavior of customers. The number of potential threats facing a business is huge, but entrepreneurs should focus on the three or four most significant threats confronting their companies. Table 3.4 provides a

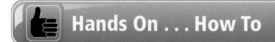

Hands On . . . How To

Beat the Big Guys

It's the news that sends shivers down the spines of small business owners everywhere: Wal-Mart (or any other "big-box" retailer) is coming to town. "How can my small business compete against the largest retailer in the world?" they wonder. "Can my business survive?"

Although no business owner welcomes a threat of this magnitude from a giant competitor with greater buying power, more name recognition, and a reputation for driving small companies out of business, it is no reason to fold up the tent and go home. Smart entrepreneurs know that, by formulating and executing the proper strategy, they can not only survive in the face of larger competitors but also *thrive* in their presence.

Rule 1. Don't Play Their Game

A fundamental concept in strategy is to avoid matching your company's weaknesses against a competitor's strengths. For instance, because Wal-Mart buys in such huge volume from its suppliers, it can extract the lowest prices from them. Small companies purchasing from those same suppliers cannot; therefore, it makes little sense for small companies to try to compete with Wal-Mart and other giant retailers on price. Unless your small company has another more significant cost advantage, competing on the basis of price is a recipe for disaster. Entrepreneurs who compete successfully emphasize features that giant discounters cannot provide—extensive product knowledge, better selection, superior customer service, a hassle-free buying experience, higher quality, and others. "Not everyone wants the lowest quality at the lowest price," says one expert.

Rule 2. Emphasize the Unique Aspects of Your Company and How They Benefit Your Customers

When Brian Kelly, owner of City Beans, a coffee shop with two stores in northern New Jersey, learned that Starbucks was opening

a location in the same building that housed one of his shops, he knew that he had to take action to save his business. Because Kelly purchased coffee beans from a local coffee roaster who made deliveries within 24 hours of roasting, he realized that the coffee City Beans sold was much fresher than Starbucks coffee. Kelly began a "served-fresh-daily" promotion that gave customers an important benefit and provided City Beans with a competitive advantage. He also reenergized his company's loyalty card program (buy 11 cups of coffee and get one free), which provided him with important information about his customers, including their e-mail addresses. Kelly, whose stores also serve a selection of sandwiches, salads, and soups, began e-mailing customers in the loyalty program about daily lunch and coffee specials, and sales increased.

Rule 3. Hit 'em Where They Ain't

Big companies usually aim at big markets and often ignore small but profitable niche markets, which are ideal targets for small companies. When Home Depot moved into town, the owner of a small nursery began changing his company's product mix, emphasizing selections of unusual plants that were quite different from the inexpensive but rather typical plants that its big-box rival sold. In addition, he added a section in his store dedicated to all-natural, organic gardening. Free weekend "workshops" that taught customers how to build different types of gardens brought in existing customers more often and attracted new ones. Two years after Home Depot opened, the small nursery was generating record sales that were higher than they were before its big-box competitor appeared!

Rule 4. Hire the Best—and Train Them

Small companies usually cannot afford to pay the highest wages in an area; however, because their companies are small, entrepreneurs

(continued)

Hands On . . . How To (continued)

have the opportunity to create a work environment in which employees can thrive. For instance, one small company attracts and retains quality workers by allowing them to use flexible work schedules that make it easier for them to manage their busy lives. The owner also invests heavily in training workers so that they can move up the organization—and the pay scale—faster. The training pays off, however, in the form of greater productivity, lower turnover, increased customer satisfaction, and higher sales per employee. Paying attention to seemingly small details, such as more communication, frequent recognition for jobs well done, less bureaucracy, and flexible benefits, enables small companies to build a loyal, motivated workforce that can outperform those at larger companies.

Rule 5. Bring Back What the Big Boys Have Eliminated

Many companies in the supermarket industry have taken a beating as discount mass retailers have expanded their superstore concepts into more markets across the United States. Yet many small supermarket chains have thrived by taking a completely different strategic approach, building small stores that allow shoppers to make their purchases quickly and conveniently. A Wal-Mart supercenter, for instance, adds about 40,000 grocery items to the already mind-boggling 116,000 items in its outlets. Customers have a wide selection of products at low prices, but many have grown weary of the time they have to invest to navigate these cavernous stores just to find the items they need. That's exactly what small grocers such as Save-a-Lot are counting on. Going back to the days of the old corner grocer, the St. Louis–based chain keeps its 1,250 stores small—operated by no more than 25 employees—and sells no more than 1,250 grocery items in each one. To keep its costs and prices low, Save-a-Lot carefully selects neighborhood locations and emphasizes private-label items. (In fact, private-label items make up 75 percent of the company's inventory.)

Rule 6. Use the Cost Advantages of the Internet to Gain an Edge

While in college, Andy Dunn and Brian Spaly noted that men's pants often are either too tight to be comfortable or too baggy to look good and decided to create a line of pants that are both comfortable and fit properly. They raised capital from their college friends to launch their online business, Bonobos, and used the power and low cost of the Internet to compete with established industry giants, such as J. Crew. By avoiding the huge costs of physical stores, they could offer a wider range of styles, sizes, and colors than a traditional retail store could stock. They also rely on low-cost social media to market Bonobos to their target customers, primarily college-age men and recent graduates. Taking a cue from online shoe retailer Zappos, Bonobos offers free shipping anywhere in the United States and a lenient return policy. Storing customers' measurements in a database makes reordering a snap for returning customers. Sales at the up-and-coming clothier are approaching $15 million annually and are growing fast.

Rule 7. Be *Great* at Something Customers Value, Such as Service and Personal Attention

Do not make the mistake of choosing a "middle-of-the-road" strategy where, one writer says, there "are yellow lines, dead armadillos, and once-great companies that are slowly going out of business." Successful small companies differentiate themselves from their larger, more powerful rivals by emphasizing superior, friendly, personal service, something their size makes them uniquely capable of doing. Successful small companies also treat their customers like VIPs. Many small business owners know their customers by name, something that large companies cannot achieve. One of the best ways to determine exactly how to provide superior service and personal attention is to identify your top five customers and periodically ask them, "How can we serve you better?"

Rule 8. Get Involved in the Community

Entrepreneurs can make their small companies stand out from the crowd by supporting events in their local communities. A big budget is not a prerequisite. For instance, every year, Tony Dempsey, owner of Dempsey's Pizza, in Clinton, South Carolina, sponsors a youth baseball team, which involves purchasing T-shirts for the kids (which are emblazoned with Dempsey's Pizza's name) and hosting a pizza party for the team at the end of the season. The goodwill generated by his support of this community activity allows Dempsey to be successful even though several large pizza chains compete in the same market.

1. Why do many small businesses fail when a big discount retailer such as Wal-Mart enters their market?

2. Work with a team of your classmates to identify a local small business that competes with a bigger competitor. Which of these strategies has the small company employed to become a stronger competitor? What other strategies would you recommend to the owner of this business?

3. Based on your work in question 2, develop a one-page report summarizing your strategic suggestions.

Sources: Based on Chad Brooks, "10 Ways You Can Beat Wal-Mart," Business News Daily, April 20, 2011, http://www.businessnewsdaily.com/walmart-small-stores-1201; Norm Brodsky, "How Independents Can Hold Their Ground," *Inc.*, August 2007, pp. 65–66; Thomas M. Box, Kent Byus, Chris Fogliasso, and Warren D. Miller, "Hardball and OODA Loops: Strategy for Small Firms," *Proceedings of the Academy of Strategic Management* 6, no. 1 (2007): 5–10; Matthew Maier, "How to Beat Wal-Mart," *Business 2.0*, May 2005, pp. 108–114; Rhonda Abrams, "Small Businesses Can Compete with the Big Guys," *Business*, September 26, 2004, p. 8; Ann Zimmerman, "Behind the Dollar-Store Boom: A Nation of Bargain Hunters," *Wall Street Journal*, December 13, 2004, pp. A1, A10; Barry Cotton and Jean-Charles Cachon, "Resisting the Giants: Small Retail Entrepreneurs against Mega-Retailers—An Empirical Study," paper presented at the International Council for Small Business 2005 World Conference, June 2005; Amy Merrick, Gary McWilliams, Ellen Byron, and Kortney Stringer, "Targeting Wal-Mart," *Wall Street Journal*, December 1, 2004, pp. B1, B2; William C. Taylor, "The Fallacy of the 'Middle of the Road' Strategy," *BNET*, February 23, 2011, http://www.bnet.com/blog/innovator/the-fallacy-of-the-8220middle-of-the-road-8221-strategy/195; and Jessica Shambora, "David vs. Goliath," *Fortune*, November 15, 2010, p. 55.

TABLE 3.4 Identifying and Managing Threats

Every business faces threats, but entrepreneurs cannot afford to be paranoid or paralyzed by fear when it comes to dealing with them. At the same time, they cannot ignore threats that have the potential to destroy their businesses. The most productive approach to dealing with threats is to identify those that would have the most severe impact on a small company and those that have the highest probability of occurrence.

Research by Greg Hackett, president of management think tank MergerShop, has identified 12 major sources of risk that can wreak havoc on a company's future. The following table helps entrepreneurs determine the threats on which they should focus their attention.

Source	Specific Threat	Severity (1 = Low, 10 = High)	Probability of Occurrence (0 to 1)	Threat Rating (Severity × Probability, Maximum = 10)
1. Channels of distribution				
2. Competition				
3. Demographic changes				
4. Globalization				
5. Innovation				
6. Waning customer or supplier loyalty				
7. Offshoring or outsourcing				
8. Stage in product life cycle				
9. Government regulation				
10. Influence of special interest groups				
11. Influence of stakeholders				
12. Changes in technology				

Once entrepreneurs have identified specific threats facing their companies in the 12 areas (not necessarily all 12), they rate the severity of the impact of each one on their company on a 1–10 scale. Then they assign probabilities (between 0 and 1) to each threat. To calculate the threat rating, entrepreneurs simply multiply the severity of each threat by its probability (maximum threat rating is 10.). The higher a threat's rating, the more attention it demands. Typically, one or two threats stand out above all the others, and those are the ones on which entrepreneurs should focus.

Source: Adapted from Edward Teach, "Apocalypse Soon," *CFO*, September 2005, pp. 31–32.

simple analytical tool to help entrepreneurs identify the threats that pose the greatest danger to their companies.

The interactions of strengths, weaknesses, opportunities, and threats can be the most revealing aspects of using a SWOT analysis as part of a strategic plan. This analysis also requires entrepreneurs to take an objective look at their businesses and the environment in which they operate, as they address many issues fundamental to their companies' success in the future.

Step 4. Identify the Key Factors for Success in the Business

KEY SUCCESS FACTORS Every business is characterized by controllable variables that determine the relative success of market participants. By focusing efforts to maximize their companies' performance on these key success factors, entrepreneurs can achieve dramatic market advantages over their competitors. Companies that understand these key success factors tend to be leaders of the pack, whereas those that fail to recognize them become also-rans.

Key success factors (KSFs) (also called key performance indicators) come in a variety of patterns, depending on the industry. Simply stated, they are the factors that determine a company's ability to compete successfully in an industry. Every company in an industry must understand the KSFs that drive the industry; otherwise, they are likely to become industry also-rans like the horses trailing the pack in the Kentucky Derby. Many of these sources of competitive advantages are based on cost factors, such as manufacturing cost per unit, distribution cost per unit,

key success factors
the factors that determine a company's ability to compete successfully in an industry.

or development cost per unit. Some are less tangible and less obvious but are just as important, such as superior product quality, solid relationships with dependable suppliers, superior customer service, a highly trained and knowledgeable sales force, prime store locations, readily available customer credit, and many others. For example, one restaurant owner identified the following KSFs:

- Experience in the industry

- Sufficient start-up capital

- Tight cost control (labor costs, 15 to 18 percent of sales, and food costs, 35 to 40 percent of sales)

- Accurate sales forecasting, which minimizes wasted food

- Proper inventory control

- Meticulous cash management

- Choosing locations that maximize customer convenience

- Cleanliness

- High food quality

- Friendly and attentive service from a well-trained waitstaff

- Consistency in quality and service over time

- Speed, particularly at lunch, when the restaurant attracts business people who must dine quickly and get back to work

- A clear definition of the restaurant's distinctive concept—its food, decor, service, and ambiance

These controllable variables determine the ability of any restaurant in his market segment to compete. Restaurants lacking these KSFs are not likely to survive, but those that build their strategies with these factors in mind will prosper. However, before entrepreneurs can build a strategy around the industry's KSFs, they must identify them. Table 3.5 presents a form to help owners identify the most important success factors in the industry and their implications for their companies.

Identifying the KSFs in an industry allows entrepreneurs to determine where they should focus their companies' resources strategically. It is unlikely that a company, even a large one, can

TABLE 3.5 Identifying Key Success Factors

List the specific skills, characteristics, and core competences that your business must possess if it is to be successful in its market segment.

Key Success Factor	How Your Company Rates . . .
1	Low 1 2 3 4 5 6 7 8 9 10 High
2	Low 1 2 3 4 5 6 7 8 9 10 High
3	Low 1 2 3 4 5 6 7 8 9 10 High
4	Low 1 2 3 4 5 6 7 8 9 10 High
5	Low 1 2 3 4 5 6 7 8 9 10 High

Conclusions:

excel on every KSF it identifies. Therefore, as they begin to develop their strategies, successful entrepreneurs focus on surpassing their rivals on one or two KSFs to build a sustainable competitive edge. As a result, KSFs become the cornerstones of a company's strategy. The last recession took a heavy toll on the casual dining sector of the restaurant industry, forcing many restaurants to refocus their attention on the KSFs in their respective market segments. At Chili's and Cracker Barrel, managers targeted lunch customers by making changes designed to reduce food preparation and service times. Recognizing that shaving even a few minutes from a lunch visit makes a huge difference for the lunch crowd, managers simplified lunch menus, streamlined their service procedures, retrained waitstaff, and redesigned their kitchen layouts for maximum efficiency.[28]

In the hotly competitive gourmet burger segment of the industry, entrepreneurs behind chains such as Five Guys Burgers and Fries, Blazing Onion Burger Company, and In-N-Out are emphasizing KSFs to fuel their growth: high-quality burgers made from fresh ingredients, clean restaurants, superior service, menus that offer plenty of choices and customization, and prices that offer good value. Because customers wait 10 minutes and pay anywhere from $5 to more than $10 for a burger at fast-growing chains such as these, managers make sure that customers understand that "this is not a typical fast-food burger joint." At Five Guys, which was founded in 1986 by CEO Jerry Murrell, his wife, and three sons, customers enjoy French fries that are hand cut daily and burgers made from fresh beef. Five Guys, now with more than 750 locations, is the fastest-growing restaurant chain in the United States. The Blazing Onion Burger Company, a small chain based in Mill Creek, Washington, offers customers 25 gourmet burgers made from fresh beef as well as a turkey burger, a veggie burger, a meatloaf burger, and an assortment of homemade desserts. Service at Blazing Onion, founded by David Jones in 2007, is paramount. Each table has a "Service Alert" card that resembles a stop sign; when customers post it, "we'll be there in 30 seconds," says Jones, who plans to open a new location every 10 months and recently began franchising.[29]

Step 5. Analyze the Competition

Ask most small business owners to identify the greatest challenge their companies face, and the most common response is *competition*. One study of small business owners by the National Federation of Independent Businesses reports that small business owners believe that they operate in a highly competitive environment and that the level of competition is increasing.[30] The Internet and e-commerce have increased the ferocity and the scope of the competition that entrepreneurs

FIGURE 3.2

Small Business Success Index

Source: Based on the State of Small Business Report: June 2010 Survey of Small Business Success, July 2010, Network Solution and Robert H. Smith School of Business, University of Maryland.

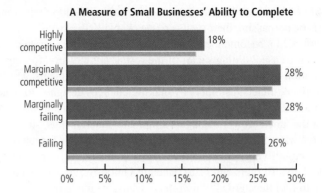

A Measure of Small Businesses' Ability to Complete

face and have forced many business owners to change completely the ways in which they do business. Figure 3.2 shows the results of a recent study of the small business sector's competitive health as measured by the Small Business Success Index, a composite of 28 measures of small business's ability to compete.

ENTREPRENEURIAL PROFILE: Mike and Donna Barsky: Texas Star Pharmacy Mike and Donna Barsky, owners of Texas Star Pharmacy in Plano, Texas, face intense competition from several outlets of large drugstore chains. Mike says, "People ask us, 'How do you compete with the large chain stores in town?'" Like martial arts experts waging battle against a larger opponent, the Barskys simply use their size and flexibility to their advantage and their competitors' size and lack of agility against them. Donna, the company's senior pharmacist, is a gifted communicator and has been interviewed about complex medical topics by local and national media more than 60 times, giving Texas Star Pharmacy great exposure. As flu season approaches, the pharmacy offers flu shots at local churches. Pharmacists know many of their customers by name (Texas Star Pharmacy's mission says, in part, "we treat our patients as part of our family"), and they offer one-on-one drug compatibility counseling for every patient. Texas Star offers customers a full line of medical products, from cotton balls to wheelchairs and a home delivery service for its customers' convenience. The Barskys also reach their customers with timely blogs, podcasts, and YouTube videos, which help them maximize their marketing budget. The Barsky's strategy has been so effective that, despite the presence of larger rivals, the pharmacy's sales have increased steadily, and they are making plans to open a second location.[31] ∎

Keeping tabs on rivals' movements through competitive intelligence programs is a vital strategic activity. "Business is like any battlefield. If you want to win the war, you have to know who you're up against," says one small business consultant.[32] Unfortunately, most businesses are not very good at competitive intelligence; 97 percent of U.S. businesses do not systematically track the progress of their key competitors.[33] A study of business executives around the world by McKinsey and Company reports that just 23 percent of their companies discovered a major competitive innovation by a competitor in time to be able to plan a response before the innovation hit the market.[34] The primary goals of a competitive intelligence program include the following:

● Avoiding surprises from existing competitors' new strategies and tactics

● Identifying potential new competitors

● Improving reaction time to competitors' actions

● Anticipating rivals' next strategic moves

COMPETITOR ANALYSIS Sizing up the competition gives a business owner a realistic view of the market and his or her company's position in it. Yet not every competitor warrants the same level of attention in the strategic plan. *Direct competitors* offer the same products and services, and customers often compare prices, features, and deals from these competitors as they shop. *Significant competitors* offer some of the same products and services. Although their product or service lines may be somewhat different, there is competition with them in several key areas.

Indirect competitors offer the same or similar products or services only in a small number of areas, and their target customers seldom overlap yours. Entrepreneurs should monitor closely the actions of their direct competitors, maintain a solid grasp of where their significant competitors are heading, and spend only minimal resources tracking their indirect competitors.

Collecting competitive intelligence enables entrepreneurs to update their knowledge of top competitors by answering the following questions:

- Who are your primary competitors? Where are they located?

- What distinctive competencies have they developed?

- How do their cost structures compare to yours? Their financial resources?

- How do they market their products and services?

- What do customers say about them? How do customers describe their products or services, their way of doing business, and the additional services they might supply?

- What are their key strategies?

- What are their strengths? How can your company counteract them?

- What are their major weaknesses? How can your company capitalize on them?

- Are new competitors entering the business?

According to the Society of Competitive Intelligence, 95 percent of the competitive intelligence information is available from public sources that anyone can access—if they know how.[35] Gathering competitive intelligence does not require entrepreneurs to engage in activities that are unethical, illegal, or unsavory (such as dumpster diving). One expert says that competitive intelligence involves "taking information from the public domain, adding it to what you know about your company and your industry, and looking for patterns."[36] By collecting many nuggets of information about their competitors, entrepreneurs can assemble the pieces to make reliable inferences about their rivals' overall strategies. Entrepreneurs can use the following low-cost competitive intelligence methods to collect information about their rivals:

- Read industry trade publications for announcements and news stories about competitors.

- Ask questions of customers and suppliers about what they hear competitors may be doing. In many cases, this information is easy to gather because some people love to gossip.

- Regularly debrief employees, especially sales representatives and purchasing agents. Experts estimate that 70 to 90 percent of the competitive information a company needs already resides with employees who collect it in their routine dealings with suppliers, customers, and other industry contacts.[37]

- Attend trade shows and collect competitors' sales literature.

- Monitor social media for insights into your direct competitors.

- Watch for employment ads and job postings from competitors; knowing what types of workers they are hiring can tell you a great deal about their future plans.

- Conduct patent searches (see Chapter 2) for patents that competitors have filed. This gives important clues about new products they are developing.

- Environmental Protection Agency reports can provide important information about the factories of manufacturing companies, including the amounts and the kinds of emissions released. A private group, Environmental Protection, also reports emissions for specific factories.[38]

- Learn about the kinds and amounts of equipment and raw materials that competitors are importing by studying the *Journal of Commerce Port Import Export Reporting Service (PIERS)* database. These clues can alert an entrepreneur to new products that a competitor is about to launch.

- If appropriate, buy competitors' products and assess their quality and features. Benchmark their products against yours. The owner of a mail-order gourmet brownie business periodically places orders from her primary rivals and compares their packaging, pricing, service, and quality to her own.[39]

- Obtain credit reports on each of your major competitors to evaluate their financial condition. For less than $200, Dun & Bradstreet and other research firms provide detailed credit reports of competitors that can be helpful in a strategic analysis.

- Publicly held companies must file periodic reports with the Securities and Exchange Commission, including quarterly 10-Q and annual 10-K reports. Information on publicly held companies is available at the Securities and Exchange Commission Web site (www.sec.gov).

- Investigate Uniform Commercial Code reports. Banks file these with the state whenever they make loans to businesses. These reports often include the amount of the loan and what it is for.

- Check out the resources of your local library, including articles, computerized databases, and online searches. Press releases, which often announce important company news, can be an important source of competitive intelligence. Many companies supply press releases through the PR Newswire. For local competitors, review back issues of the area newspaper for articles on and advertisements by competitors.

- Visit competitors' Web sites periodically to see what news is contained there. The Web enables small companies to uncover valuable competitive information at little or no cost. (Refer to our Web site at www.pearsonhighered.com/scarborough for hundreds of useful small business Web sites.)

- Visit competing businesses periodically to observe their operations. Tom Stemberg, CEO of Staples, a chain of office supply superstores, says, "I've never visited a store where I didn't learn something."[40]

- Don't resort to unethical or illegal practices.

competitive profile matrix

a tool that allows a business owner to evaluate their companies against major competitors using the key success factors for that market.

Entrepreneurs can use the results of their competitive intelligence efforts to construct a competitive profile matrix for its most important competitors. A **competitive profile matrix** allows owners to evaluate their firms against the major competitor using the KSFs for that market segment. The first step is to list the KSFs identified in step 4 of the strategic planning process (refer to Table 3.6) and to attach weights to them reflecting their relative importance. (For simplicity, the weights in this matrix sum add up to 1.00.) In this example, notice that product quality is weighted twice as heavily (twice as important) as price competitiveness.

The next step is to identify the company's major competitors and to rate each one (and your company) on each of the KSFs:

If Factor Is a . . .	Rating Is . . .
Major weakness	1
Minor weakness	2
Minor strength	3
Major strength	4

Once the rating is completed, the owner simply multiplies the weight by the rating for each factor to get a weighted score and then adds up each competitor's weighted scores to get a total weighted score. Table 3.6 shows a sample competitive profile matrix for a small company. The results show which company is strongest, which is weakest, and which of the KSFs each one is best and worst at meeting. By carefully studying and interpreting the results, an entrepreneur can begin to envision the ideal strategy for building a competitive edge in his or her corner of the market. Notice that the small company profiled in Table 3.6 should emphasize the competitive advantages it holds over its rivals in quality and perception of value in its business strategy.

TABLE 3.6 Sample Competitive Profile Matrix

Key Success Factors (from Step 4)	Weight	Your Business		Competitor 1		Competitor 2	
		Rating	Weighted Score	Rating	Weighted Score	Rating	Weighted Score
Quality	0.25	4	1.00	2	0.50	2	0.50
Customer retention	0.20	3	0.60	3	0.60	3	0.60
Location	0.15	4	0.60	3	0.45	4	0.60
Perception of value	0.20	4	0.80	2	0.40	3	0.60
Cost control	0.20	3	0.60	1	0.20	4	0.80
Total	1.00		**3.60**		**2.15**		**3.10**

Step 6. Create Company Goals and Objectives

Before entrepreneurs can build a comprehensive set of strategies, they must first establish business goals and objectives, which give them targets to aim for and provide a basis for evaluating their companies' performance. Without them, it is impossible to know where a business is going or how well it is performing. The following conversation between Alice and the Cheshire Cat, taken from Lewis Carroll's *Alice in Wonderland*, illustrates the importance of creating meaningful goals and objectives as part of the strategic management process:[41]

> "Would you tell me please, which way I ought to go from here?" asked Alice.
> "That depends a good deal on where you want to get to," said the Cat.
> "I don't much care where . . . ," said Alice.
> "Then it doesn't matter which way you go," said the Cat.

A small business that "doesn't much care where" it wants to go (i.e., one that has no goals and objectives) will find that "it really doesn't matter which way" it chooses to go (i.e., its strategy is irrelevant).

GOALS Goals are the broad, long-range attributes that a business seeks to accomplish; they tend to be general and sometimes even abstract. Goals are not intended to be specific enough for a manager to act on but simply state the general level of accomplishment sought. Do you want to boost your market share? Does your cash balance need strengthening? Would you like to enter a new market or increase sales in a current one? Do you want to develop new products or services? Researchers Jim Collins and Jerry Porras studied a large group of businesses for their book *Good to Great* and determined that one of the factors that set apart successful companies from unsuccessful ones was the formulation of very ambitious, clear, and inspiring long-term goals. Collins and Porras called them BHAGs ("Big Hairy Audacious Goals," pronounced "bee-hags") and say that their main benefit is to inspire and focus a company on important actions that are consistent with its overall mission.[42] Figure 3.3 shows that effective BHAGs originate at the intersection of a company's mission, vision, and values; its distinctive competencies; and its KSFs. Addressing these broad issues will help entrepreneurs to focus on the next phase—developing specific, realistic objectives.

goals
the broad, long-range attributes a business seeks to accomplish; they tend to be general and sometimes even abstract.

OBJECTIVES Objectives are more specific targets of performance. Common objectives concern profitability, productivity, growth, efficiency, sales, financial resources, physical facilities, organizational structure, employee welfare, and social responsibility. Because some of these objectives might conflict with one another, it is important to establish priorities. Which objectives are most important? Which are least important? Arranging objectives in a hierarchy according to their priority can help an entrepreneur resolve conflicts when they arise. Well-written objectives have the following characteristics:

objectives
more specific targets of performance, commonly addressing areas such as profitability, productivity, growth, and other key aspects of a business.

> *They are specific.* Objectives should be quantifiable and precise. For example, "to achieve a healthy growth in sales" is not a meaningful objective; however, "to increase retail sales

FIGURE 3.3

**What Makes an
Effective BHAG?**

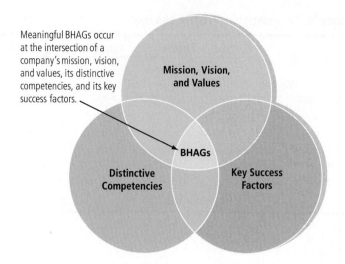

Meaningful BHAGs occur at the intersection of a company's mission, vision, and values, its distinctive competencies, and its key success factors.

Mission, Vision, and Values

BHAGs

Distinctive Competencies

Key Success Factors

by 12 percent and wholesale by 10 percent in the next fiscal year" is precise and spells out exactly what management wants to accomplish.

They are measurable. Managers should be able to plot the organization's progress toward its objectives; this requires a well-defined reference point from which to start and a scale for measuring progress.

They are assignable. Unless an entrepreneur assigns responsibility for an objective to an individual, it is unlikely that the company will ever achieve it. Creating objectives without giving someone responsibility for accomplishing it is futile. Accountability is the key.

They are realistic yet challenging. Objectives must be within the reach of the organization, or motivation will disappear. In any case, managerial expectations must remain high. In other words, the more challenging an objective is (within realistic limits), the higher the performance will be. Set objectives that will challenge your business and its employees.

They are timely. Objectives must specify not only what is to be accomplished but also when it is to be accomplished. A time frame for achievement is important.

They are written down. Setting objectives does not have to be complex; in fact, an entrepreneur should keep the number of objectives relatively small (from 5 to 10). Writing down objectives makes them more concrete and makes it easy to communicate them to everyone in the company.

The strategic planning process works best when managers and employees work together to set goals and objectives. Developing a plan is top management's responsibility, but executing it falls to managers and employees; therefore, encouraging them to participate broadens the plan's perspective and increases the motivation to make the plan work. Unfortunately, only 7 percent of employees understand their company's strategies and what is expected of them to accomplish the company's goals.[43] A recent study by SuccessFactors reports that companies that set goals, align them with their companies' overall strategy, and measure employees' performance against those goals using multiple benchmarks financially outperform companies that do not. SuccessFactors cites three primary benefits of an effective goal-setting process: (1) increased profitability, (2) faster execution of company strategy, and (3) reduced employee turnover.[44]

Step 7. Formulate Strategic Options and Select the Appropriate Strategies

By this point in the strategic management process, entrepreneurs should have a clear picture of what their businesses do best and what their competitive advantages are. They also should understand their firms' weaknesses and limitations as well as those of their competitors. The next step is to evaluate strategic options and then prepare a game plan designed to achieve the stated mission, goals, and objectives.

Ethics and Entrepreneurship

Cascade Engineering's Triple Bottom Line

Fred Keller started Cascade Engineering, a plastics manufacturer based in Grand Rapids, Michigan, in 1973 as a plastic injection molding company with six employees. Today, Cascade Engineering has 1,000 employees, 500 of whom work in 14 locations worldwide and the remaining 500 in Grand Rapids. Keller's company is now a diversified manufacturer with $250 million in annual sales, 15 business units, and a product line that ranges from wind turbines for residential use and trash cans to auto parts and affordable water filters for the developing world. Perhaps more important are the awards and certifications that Cascade Engineering has won, including ISO (quality), LEED (environmentally friendly), and B Corporation. Achieving these is no small task, especially for a manufacturing company, but the most challenging may be the B (which stands for "benefit") corporation certification. To become a B corporation, a company must undergo a rigorous assessment, documentation, and audit process on more than 170 measures of environmental stewardship, employee pay and benefits, and contributions to society and the local community.

"To become B corporations, businesses must care as much about society and the environment as they do about profits," says one writer. Becoming a B corporation (at no insignificant expense) was a natural step for Keller, who manages Cascade Engineering with one basic question in mind: "What good can we do?" In fact, Keller carries a well-used card in his wallet that contains a quotation from eighteenth-century theologian and social reformer John Wesley that says,

Do all the good you can

By all the means you can

In all the ways you can

In all the places you can

At all the times you can

To all the people you can

As long as ever you can.

Keller practices that philosophy through his company. Unlike many manufacturers, Kelly sees most regulation as a helpful guideline, standards that he strives not merely to meet but also to exceed. He believes that proper regulations (not excessive ones) serve as blueprints for improvement, a vital component of the *kaizen* philosophy

of continuous improvement that he and his employees practice every day. For instance, without prompting from the Environmental Protection Agency, Keller voluntarily reduced Cascade Engineering's emissions by 20 percent over a recent five-year period. Keller says that, in addition to being the right thing to do, going beyond regulations usually saves his company money. For instance, Cascade's recent waste reduction program slashed the company's landfill cost from more than $250,000 in 2002 to less than $10,000 today. By achieving LEED Platinum status (the highest green-building standard), Cascade's headquarters uses 22 percent less energy than a comparably sized non-LEED building.

Cascade's certifications also have allowed the company to differentiate itself from competitors and have opened the doors to doing business with new customers, including home improvement retail giant Lowe's. Over the last decade, Keller has focused his company on helping its customers become less dependent on oil and to generate zero waste. That effort led Cascade to open a new division called Triple Quest, which is now headed by Keller's youngest daughter, Christina, and manufactures the Hydraid BioSand Water Filter, a low-cost water purification system designed to give people in developing nations affordable access to clean water. Cascade is testing a microfranchising model to distribute the filter in Honduras.

Keller believes that operating with a triple bottom line— producing profits as well as social and environmental value ("profits, people, and planet")—builds social capital and is the only way to run a business. In short, he recognizes that companies are accountable beyond their walls and balance sheets. A program that Keller started a few years ago focuses on helping welfare recipients win jobs; 40 former welfare recipients now work at Cascade, saving the state of Michigan about $500,000 a year in benefits payments. "We want to make an impact on this world," says Keller, "to do something positive."

1. Is Keller's view that reasonable regulations are blueprints for improvement unusual, especially among manufacturing companies?

2. Use the Internet to research the concept of the triple bottom line. Prepare a one-page summary of the concept.

3. What benefits does Cascade Engineering reap by measuring results using the triple bottom line?

Source: Based on Adam Bluestein, "Regulate Me. Please," *Inc.*, May 2011, pp. 72–79.

STRATEGY A **strategy** is a road map of the actions an entrepreneur draws up to accomplish a company's mission, goals, and objectives. In other words, the mission, goals, and objectives spell out the ends, and the strategy defines the means for reaching them. A strategy is the master plan that covers all the major parts of the organization and ties them together into a unified whole. The plan must be action oriented; it should breathe life into the entire planning process. An entrepreneur must build a sound strategy based on the preceding steps that uses the company's core

strategy
a road map of the actions an entrepreneur draws up to fulfill a company's mission, goals, and objectives.

competencies and strengths as the springboard to success. Joseph Picken and Gregory Dess, authors of *Mission Critical: The 7 Strategic Traps That Derail Even the Smartest Companies*, write, "A flawed strategy—no matter how brilliant the leadership, no matter how effective the implementation—is doomed to fail. A sound strategy, implemented without error, wins every time."[45]

ENTREPRENEURIAL PROFILE: Devon Rifkin: Great American Hanger Company When Devon Rifkin was 23, he left his job as a stockbroker in New York and returned to Miami to help his father's struggling store fixture and display business. He noticed that many of the retailers who shopped there purchased wooden clothes hangers for their homes. Research revealed that there was almost no competition in the high-quality hanger market, and Rifkin borrowed $30,000 and launched the Great American Hanger Company (GAHC) from his apartment. He flew to Asia to learn about hangers and to find reliable suppliers of quality products and sold $25,000 of them in his first three months in business. Rifkin's strategy is to specialize in selling high-quality wooden, metal, and plastic hangers to hotels, cruise ships, individuals, and retailers such as Prada and Sean Jean. Rifkin's customer list also includes celebrities such as Jennifer Lopez (who has purchased more than 10,000 hangers, many of them customized, from the GAHC), National Basketball Association player Dwayne Wade (whose hangers feature his name, jersey number and championship logo), and the Sultan of Brunei (who once ordered $25,000 worth of lacquered walnut hangers emblazoned with his royal monogram). By dominating an obscure niche market, Rifkin says that his company, which now generates more than $10 million in annual sales, "can definitely become a $100 million company."[46] ∎

A successful strategy is comprehensive and well integrated, focusing on establishing the KSFs that the entrepreneur identified in step 4. For instance, if maximum shelf space is a KSF for a small manufacturer's product, the strategy must identify techniques for gaining more in-store shelf space (e.g., offering higher margins to distributors and brokers than competitors do, assisting retailers with in-store displays, or redesigning a wider, more attractive package).

THREE STRATEGIC OPTIONS Obviously, the number of strategies from which the small business owner can choose is infinite. When all the glitter is stripped away, however, three basic strategies remain. In his classic book *Competitive Strategy*, Michael Porter defines these strategies: (1) cost leadership, (2) differentiation, and (3) focus (see Figure 3.4).[47]

COST LEADERSHIP A company pursuing a **cost leadership strategy** strives to be the lowest-cost producer relative to its competitors in the industry. Many companies attempt to compete by offering low prices, but low costs are a prerequisite for success. Low-cost leaders have a competitive advantage in reaching buyers whose primary purchase criterion is price, and they have the power to set the industry's price floor. This strategy works well when buyers are sensitive to price changes, when competing firms sell the same commodity products and compete on the basis of price, and when companies can benefit from economies of scale. Not only is a low-cost leader in the best position to defend itself in a price war, but it also can use its power to attack competitors with the lowest price in the industry.

There are many ways to build a low-cost strategy, but the most successful cost leaders know where they have cost advantages over their competitors, and they use these as the foundation for their strategies. Successful cost leaders often find low-cost suppliers (or use a vertical integration strategy to produce their own products), eliminate the inefficiencies in their channels of distribution, use the Internet to cut costs, and operate more efficiently than their competitors. They are committed to squeezing every unnecessary cost out of their operations.

LO4

Discuss the characteristics of three basic strategies—low cost, differentiation, and focus—and know when and how to employ them.

cost leadership strategy

a strategy in which a company strives to be the low-cost producer relative to its competitors in the industry.

FIGURE 3.4

Three Strategic Options

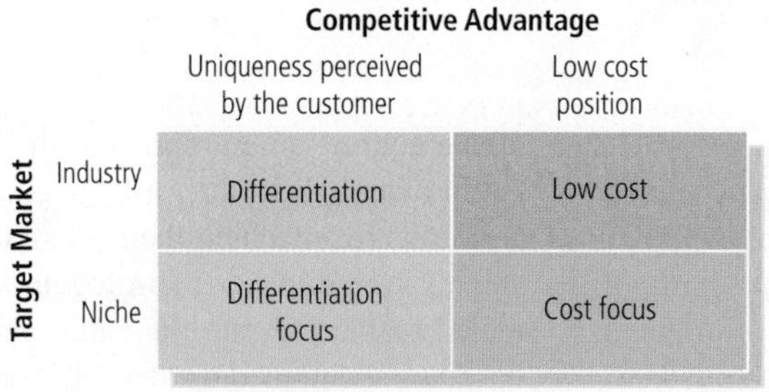

ENTREPRENEURIAL PROFILE: Ralph Ward and Bud Williams: WinCo Foods In 1967, Ralph Ward and Bud Williams started a discount warehouse grocery store in Boise, Idaho, called Waremart. In 1999, the company changed its name to WinCo Foods (an abbreviation of "Winning Company"), but its low-cost strategy remains the same. WinCo operates 79 stores in six western states (Washington, Idaho, California, Nevada, Oregon, and Utah), most of which are located in small cities, where land costs are low. At 90,000 square feet, the typical WinCo store, which is open 24 hours a day, is larger than the typical grocery store, and its interior is intentionally spartan. As part of its low-cost strategy, WinCo does not use baggers; customers bag their own groceries. "It's not fancy by any means," admits one of the company's top managers. "It's just a large supermarket. What we really focus on is low pricing. We strive to be the supermarket price leader in every market where we operate." Stores sell both brand-name and private-label products, offer more than 600 bulk-food items, and include a full-service bakery. Because it is employee owned, WinCo is a nonunion company, another feature that gives it a cost advantage. Rather than incur the cost of building its own stores, WinCo often leases locations abandoned by other retailers but only after conducting a thorough analysis of the area's market potential and competition. WinCo's low-cost strategy has been very successful; the company employs more than 14,000 workers and generates annual sales of nearly $5 billion.[48] ■

Of course, there are dangers in following a cost leadership strategy. Sometimes a company focuses exclusively on lower manufacturing costs, without considering the impact of purchasing, distribution, or overhead costs. Another danger is incorrectly identifying the company's true cost drivers. Although their approach to managing is characterized by frugality, companies that understand cost leadership are willing to invest in those activities that drive costs out of doing business, whether it is technology, preventive maintenance, or some other factor. In addition, over time, competitors may erode a company's cost advantage by finding ways to lower their own costs. Finally, a firm may pursue a low-cost leadership strategy so zealously that, in its drive to push costs downward, it eliminates product or service features that customers consider to be essential.

Under the right conditions, a cost leadership strategy executed properly can be an incredibly powerful strategic weapon. Small discount retailers that live in the shadows of Wal-Mart and thrive even when the economy slows succeed by relentlessly pursuing low-cost strategies. Small chains, such as Fred's, Dollar General, Family Dollar, and 99 Cents Only, cater to low- and middle-income customers who live in inner cities or rural areas. They offer inexpensive products such as food, health and beauty products, cleaning supplies, clothing, and seasonal merchandise, and many of the items they stock are closeout buys (purchases made as low as 10 cents on the dollar) on brand-name merchandise. These companies also strive to keep their overhead costs as low as possible. For instance, 99 Cents Only, whose name describes its merchandising strategy, is housed in a no-frills warehouse in an older section of City of Commerce, California.[49] By keeping their costs low, these retailers offer customers prices that are within 1 to 2 percent of those at Wal-Mart, even though they do not benefit from the quantity discounts that the low-cost giant does.[50] The success of these stores proves that companies pursuing a cost leadership strategy must emphasize cost containment in *every* decision, from where to locate the company headquarters to which items to stock.

DIFFERENTIATION A company following a **differentiation strategy** seeks to build customer loyalty by selling goods or services that provide unique attributes and that customers perceive to be superior to competing products. That, in turn, enables the business to command higher prices for its products or services than competitors. There are many ways to create a differentiation strategy, but the key is to be unique at something that is important to the customer. In other words, a business strives to be better than its competitors at something that customers value.

differentiation strategy
a strategy in which a company seeks to build customer loyalty by positioning its goods or services in a unique or different fashion.

ENTREPRENEURIAL PROFILE: Charlotte Dellal: Charlotte Olympia Charlotte Dellal inherited her mother's love of fashion and old movies and draws inspiration for her collections of designer shoes from film characters. "I always reference the 1940s," she says. "It's an era I love and am inspired by—and an era rich in accessories." Dellal's company, Charlotte Olympia, is based in London and has one retail store in the city's Tony Mayfair district, but upscale retailers such as Bergdorf Goodman in New York and Selfridges in London carry her shoes, which start at $500 and sell for as much as $1,300. To create a line of shoes, Dellal, who is 29 years old and studied at the London College of Fashion, starts with a "pinup," a photo of a glamorous, ornately dressed woman (often from a film from the 1940s), to give her creations character and context. She based a recent fall line on Arlena Stuart Marshall, a character from a film based on the 1941 Agatha Christie novel *Evil under the Sun*, and a recent spring line she called "Blame It on Rio" modeled after Carmen Miranda, a 1940s movie star famous for wearing fruit-laden hats. Because of their unique flair and retro style, Dellal's shoes have attracted the attention of major fashion designers and celebrities such as Emma Watson (Hermione Granger in the Harry Potter films), Cheryl Cole, Sarah Jessica Parker, Blake Lively, and others.[51] ∎

If a small company can improve a product's (or service's) performance, reduce the customer's cost and risk of purchasing it, or provide intangible benefits that customers value (such as status, prestige, exclusivity, a sense of safety, or others), it has the potential to be a successful differentiator. Companies that execute a differentiation strategy successfully can charge premium prices for their products and services, increase their market share, and reap the benefits of customer loyalty and retention. To be successful, a business must make its product or service truly different, at least in the eyes of its customers.

ENTREPRENEURIAL PROFILE: Yngve Bergqvist: Ice Hotel Entrepreneur Yngve Bergqvist has no trouble setting his hotel in Jukkasjärvi, Sweden, apart from others. Located 125 miles above the Arctic Circle, the aptly named Ice Hotel offers travelers a unique experience. *Everything* in the hotel—walls, beds, night tables, chairs, cinema, glasses, and bar—is made from 30,000 tons of snow and 10,000 tons of crystal-clear ice harvested from the Torne River! Each of the 60 rooms is unique, designed by a different artist from around the world. Guests sleep in insulated sleeping bags on ice beds covered with thin mattresses and plenty of reindeer blankets. Because temperatures inside the hotel typically hover at five degrees below zero (centigrade), guests cannot take their luggage to their ice rooms; it will freeze! Amenities include an ice bar, an ice chapel, an ice cinema, and an ice art exhibition. The 30,000-square-foot Ice Hotel is open from December through April (it melts in the spring), but during its brief existence, it will accommodate some 5,000 guests at rates ranging from $200 to $500 per night! Countless rock groups, including Van Halen, have shot music videos at the Ice Hotel. "It's not about comfort," says co-owner Arne Bergh. "It's a journey, an adventure."[52] ∎

Although few businesses are innately as unique as the Ice Hotel, the goal for a company pursuing a differentiation strategy is to create that kind of uniqueness in the minds of its customers. The key to a successful differentiation strategy is to build it on a core competence, something a small company is uniquely good at doing in comparison to its competitors. Common bases for differentiation include superior customer service, special product features, complete product lines, instantaneous parts availability, absolute product reliability, supreme product quality, and extensive product knowledge. To be successful, a differentiation strategy must create the perception of value in the customer's eyes. No customer purchases a good or service that fails to produce its perceived value, no matter how real that value may be. One business consultant advises, "Make sure you tell your customers and prospects what it is about your business that makes you different. Make sure that difference is on the form of a true benefit to the customer."[53]

ENTREPRENEURIAL PROFILE: Robert Deluce: Porter Airlines Robert Deluce differentiates his airline by offering travelers a meaningful benefit: a simpler, more convenient flying experience. In 2005, Deluce purchased the run-down terminal at Toronto's Billy Bishop Toronto City Airport and launched Porter Airlines, a small airline that flies to eight Canadian cities and four cities in the United States. Deluce recently completed the 150,000-square-foot first phase of a total renovation of the airport's terminal that eventually will house two passenger lounges and 10 aircraft gates for Porter Airlines. Deluce's strategy is to offer passengers a better flying experience than they get at Pearson International Airport, which accommodates the major airlines and is 17 miles northwest of the city. Porter Airlines has become a popular choice, especially for business travelers, because it reduces passengers' total travel time. The terminal is conveniently located downtown and is designed to allow passengers to check in and move through security quickly. Passengers also appreciate Porter Airlines' complimentary wine, beer, snacks, newspapers, and WiFi in its lounge; free in-flight meals and drinks; and leather seats that offer more legroom than traditional economy-class seats. A free shuttle bus runs between the airport and downtown hotels. Deluce's philosophy, flying in old-fashioned style, is working; Porter Airlines carries 1.3 million passengers per year, a 383 percent increase since 2007.[54] ∎

Small companies encounter risks when pursuing a differentiation strategy. One danger is trying to differentiate a product or service on the basis of something that does not boost its performance or lower its cost to customers. Another pitfall is trying to differentiate on the basis of something that customers do not see as important. Business owners also must consider how long they can sustain a product's or service's differentiation; changing customer tastes may make the basis for differentiation temporary. Imitations and "knockoffs" from competitors also pose a threat to a successful differentiation strategy. For instance, entrepreneurs have built an ice hotel in Finland to compete with the original ice hotel in Sweden. Designers of high-priced original clothing see much cheaper knockoff products on the market shortly after their designs hit the market. Another pitfall is overdifferentiating and charging so much that the company prices its products out of the market. The final risk is focusing only on the physical characteristics of a product or service and ignoring important psychological factors, such as status, prestige, and image, which can be powerful sources of differentiation.

FOCUS A **focus strategy** recognizes that not all markets are homogeneous. In fact, in any given market, there are many different customer segments, each having different needs, wants, and characteristics. The principal idea of a focus strategy is to select one (or more) segment(s); identify customers' special needs, wants, and interests; and provide them with goods or services designed to excel in meeting these needs, wants, and interests. By focusing on small market niches, focus strategies build on *differences* among market segments. Because they are small, flexible, and attentive to their customers' particular needs, small companies can be successful in niches that are too narrow for their larger competitors to enter profitably. These companies focus on a narrow segment of the overall market and set themselves apart either by becoming cost leaders in the segment or by differentiating themselves from competitors.

Focus strategies will become more prevalent among small businesses in the future as industries increasingly become dumbbell shaped, with a few large companies dominating one end, a relatively small number of midsize businesses in the middle, and a large number of small businesses operating at the other end. A study by Intuit and the Institute for the Future on the small business environment in 2018, *The Intuit Future of Small Business Report*, cites increasingly fragmented markets, customers who demand products and services that are tailored to their specific needs, and advancements that give small companies affordable access to increasingly sophisticated technology as key factors that will make narrow markets increasingly suitable for small businesses to thrive. The report concludes that "there will be increasing opportunities for small businesses to flourish in niches left untouched by global giants."[55]

In fact, serving specific target segments or niches rather than the attempting to reach the total market is the essence of a focus strategy, making it ideally suited to small businesses, which often lack the resources to reach the overall market. Their goal is to serve their narrow target markets more effectively and efficiently than competitors that pound away at the broad market. Common bases for building a focus strategy include zeroing in on a small geographic area, targeting a group of customers with similar needs or interests (e.g., left-handed people), specializing in a specific product or service (e.g., Batteries Plus, a store that sells and services every kind of battery imaginable), or selling specialized knowledge (e.g., restoring valuable and priceless works of art).

focus strategy
a strategy in which a company selects one or more market segments; identifies customers' special needs, wants, and interests; and approaches them with a good or service designed to excel in meeting those needs, wants, and interests.

ENTREPRENEURIAL PROFILE: Mark and Jennifer Bitterman: The Meadow While Mark Bitterman was enjoying a gourmet meal in France, he discovered the joy of artisan salts, an experience that led him and his wife Jennifer to launch The Meadow, an artisan salt shop, in Portland, Oregon. Most people view salt as a simple seasoning, but The Meadow caters to "foodies" who can appreciate the subtle and intricate flavors of the nearly 200 varieties of salt available in the shop. The Bittermans can explain the history and properties of each of the salts they sell, ranging from cherry-smoked sea salt from Japan to volcanic black salt from India. The Meadows even sells a chocolate salt! The company's Web site includes an eclectic blend of recipes for dishes, such as soft scrambled eggs with truffle salt and spinach shiitake gratin with Maine coast sea salt, and a link to a blog, The Salt News. In addition to the line of artisanal salt they carry, the Bittermans sell everything

Pete Perry

related to salt—from salt mills and salt bowls to salt sets (including a set of six salts for popcorn lovers) and books about salt. The Bittermans don't advertise, but they invest a great deal in marketing and promoting their business to their upscale target customers by sponsoring salt tastings at their shops, offering cooking classes, and hosting private parties. Their Portland store has been so successful that the couple opened a second location in New York City, just a few blocks from where Mark grew up.[56] ■

Because of their size and agility, small companies are particularly well suited for serving niche markets. The most successful focusers build a competitive edge by concentrating on specific market niches and serving them better than competitors—even powerful giants—can. "They can establish close, personal, one-on-one bonds with customers that large companies can't match," says Norm Brodsky, a highly successful serial entrepreneur. "Small companies also can outmaneuver giants. That's especially important if they're competing against a chain with a cookie-cutter approach to managing its stores." Brodsky says that with the right focus strategy, entrepreneurs "can do things that [large companies] won't be able to respond to for months, if ever."[57]

A focus strategy depends on creating value for customers either by being the lowest-cost producer or by differentiating the product or service in a unique fashion but doing it in a narrow target segment. To be worth targeting, a niche must be large enough to be profitable, reachable with marketing media, and capable of sustaining a business over time (i.e., not a passing fad). Many small companies operate quite successfully in small yet profitable, niches.

Vicki Thompson

 **ENTREPRENEURIAL PROFILE: Alicia and Chris Allen: Historical Emporium** Alicia and Chris Allen were working at large technology companies in Silicon Valley but wanted to spend more time with their family. The couple drew their entrepreneurial inspiration from Chris's father, who owns a small company that makes clothing and accessories for Civil War reenactors, and launched an e-commerce company, Historical Emporium, to sell historically authentic reproductions of period clothing and accessories. The company focuses on two eras: Victorian England and the Old West. "We tapped a niche market," explains Alicia. Historical Emporium stocks 1,100 items and recently began offering entire outfits, including a saloon keeper and a stagecoach driver for men and a schoolteacher and saloon maid for women. The company's customers include Disney World and the New York Metropolitan Opera as well as theater companies, historic societies, museums, and individuals who want to dress up for special events and parties. International sales (Australia and Canada are the company's largest foreign markets) have helped push Historical Emporium's sales to $2.4 million.[58] ■

Courtesy of Sew What?

Market niches do not have to be glamorous to be profitable. Megan Duckett left Australia at age 19 and began working as a stage electrician for a variety of stage productions but quickly mastered sewing because the skill so often is in demand backstage. Before long, Duckett was sewing stage backdrops and theatrical curtains, leading her to launch Sew What? Inc. in 1996. Today, Sew What? specializes in custom-sewn backdrops, drapes, and curtains for the entertainment and special events industries. The 40-employee company is based in Rancho Dominguez, California, and has created fabric sets and drapes for high schools as well as stars such as Carrie Underwood, Maroon 5, Lady Gaga, Rod Stewart, and many others. To operate her business efficiently, Duckett relies on technology, including a customized system for pricing jobs and a video-conferencing system that allows her to show prospective clients detailed photos of fabrics. Sales at Sew What? have surpassed $4.6 million per year.[59]

Although it can be a highly profitable strategy, pursuing a focus strategy is not without risks. Companies sometimes struggle to capture a large enough share of a small market to be profitable. If a small company is successful in a niche, there is also the danger of larger competitors entering the market and eroding it. Entrepreneurs following this strategy often face a constant struggle to keep costs down; the small volume of business that some niches support pushes production costs upward, making a company vulnerable to lower-cost competitors as their prices spiral higher. Sometimes a company with a successful niche strategy gets distracted by its success and tries to branch out into other areas. As it drifts farther away from its core strategy, it loses its competitive

✓ You Be the Consultant

Strategies Etched in Chocolate

In his book *Break from the Pack*, Oren Harari explains how business owners can escape the problems of the "Copycat Economy, where everyone has access to the same resources and talent, where the Web is the great equalizer, and where the market's twin foundations are imitation and commoditization." He argues that too many businesses are stuck in the pack with "me-too" products and services that customers see as commodities. The danger of being stuck in the pack (or relying on a "middle-of-the-road strategy") is becoming what entrepreneur Terry Brock calls "disgustingly generic." What can small companies, which often lack the resources that large companies have, do to break from the pack strategically? Consider the lessons we can learn from the following small businesses.

Mr. Chocolate

After working as a master pastry chef at New York City's prestigious Le Cirque restaurant, Jacques Torres opened Jacques

© Randy Duchaine / Alamy

Torres Chocolate with two partners. The entrepreneurs invested $150,000 of their savings into transforming an old warehouse in Brooklyn into a wholesale chocolate business, performing much of the work themselves to save money. The location included enough space for a small 400-square-foot retail storefront, and soon Torres was selling chocolate delicacies to passersby. As investors redeveloped the neighborhood, sales increased, reaching $1 million in 2003. Late in 2004, Torres leased 8,000 square feet of industrial space in the trendy SoHo district and opened his flagship store and factory that features a complete "bean-to-bar" operation that starts with raw cacao beans, roasts and grinds them, and transforms them into delectable chocolate delicacies. The retail store, shaped like a giant cacao pod, is encased in glass and surrounded by a working chocolate factory, allowing customers to watch workers transform raw cacao beans into chocolate-covered pretzels, bonbons, crunch puffs, and other tasty bites. The focal point of the operation is a coating conveyor belt, reminiscent of the one that appears in Torres's favorite episode of *I Love Lucy* in which Lucy and Ethel land jobs in a chocolate factory and comedic mayhem ensues. A statue of Quetzlcoatl, the Aztec cacao god, greets customers at the entrance.

Torres actually purchases most of the chocolate he uses to make his chocolate masterpieces ("It costs me less to buy chocolate than to make it," he says), but he understands the power of his highly visible factory as a marketing tool. Torres, who hosts television shows on PBS and the Food Network and is the dean of pastry arts at the French Culinary Institute in Manhattan, has branded himself as "Mr. Chocolate." With his on-site chocolate factory, signature chocolate blend, and delicious, unique creations, Torres has set his business apart from the competition, creating a chocolate nirvana. Prices reflect the products' superior quality and upscale image; luxury gift sets start at $72, and 10-piece boxes sell for $20. Many customers see chocolate as an affordable indulgence and pay $6 for a bag of chocolate-covered Cheerios. Despite the ability to command premium prices, Torres faces rapidly rising prices for ingredients. Cocoa prices recently hit a 30-year high.

Torres is not complaining, however. The company, with six stores in New York City and one in New Jersey, generates sales that now top $10 million per year, and Torres is working at a job he loves. "Making chocolate is a way of life, not a profession," he says.

Xan Confections

Kerry Johnson Anthony also is in the chocolate business, but her company, Xan Confections, based in Irvine, California, relies on a different strategy than Jacques Torres Chocolate. Xan recently introduced its CocoXan line of products, which are aimed squarely at women. Xan's CocoPreggers (tagline: "A happy mom equals a healthy baby") chocolate confections contain folic acid,

(continued)

You Be the Consultant *(continued)*

which prevents birth defects, and DHA, an omega-3 fatty acid that enhances brain development. Anthony says that her company's chocolates are not intended to replace an expectant mom's healthy diet or prenatal vitamins, but they can eliminate the guilt that some mothers-to-be experience when they give in to a chocolate craving. In addition to its CocoPreggers line, Xan also has introduced chocolates with heart-healthy (CocoHeart) and brain-boosting (CocoBrain) properties. CocoBrain chocolates are popular with mothers who are looking for a snack for their children. "'Healthy' doesn't have to be boring or medicinal," says Albert. Xan Confections also sells CocoPMS, chocolate truffles infused with a proprietary blend of antioxidant-rich chasteberry and bilberry, herbs that have been used for centuries because of their anti-inflammatory properties that help fight the symptoms of premenstrual syndrome.

1. Which of the strategies discussed in this chapter are these companies using? Explain.

2. What competitive advantages does the successful execution of their strategies produce for these businesses?

3. What are the risks associated with these companies' strategies?

Sources: Based on Nicole Perlroth, "Sweet Talker," *Forbes*, July 13, 2009, pp. 54–57; Christine Dugas, "'Mr. Chocolate' Is Hands-On Businessman," *USA Today*, July 11, 2010, http://www.usatoday.com/money/companies/management/entre/2010-07-12-torres12_ST_N.htm; Joel Rose, "Rising Cocoa Prices May Leave Chocolate Fans Bitter," *NPR*, February 21, 2011, http://www.npr.org/2011/02/21/133865745/rising-cocoa-prices-may-leave-chocolate-fans-bitter; Courtney Perkes, "O.C. Company Makes Chocolate for Pregnant Women," *Orange County Register*, February 22, 2011, http://healthyliving.ocregister.com/2011/02/23/can-chocolate-really-claim-to-be-healthy/29647; and Kimberly J. Decker, "Candy Bars You Can Feel Good About," *Food Product Design*, June 23, 2011, http://www.foodproductdesign.com/articles/2011/06/candy-bars-you-can-feel-good-about.aspx.

edge and runs the risk of confusing or alienating its customers. Muddying its image with customers puts a company in danger of losing its identity.

Step 8. Translate Strategic Plans into Action Plans

No strategic plan is complete until it is put into action; planning a company's strategy and implementing it go hand in hand. Entrepreneurs must convert strategic plans into operating plans that guide their companies on a daily basis and become a visible, active part of the business. No small business can benefit from a strategic plan sitting on a shelf collecting dust. Unfortunately, failure to implement a strategy effectively is a common problem. In a survey conducted by Marakon Associates and the Economist Intelligence Unit, senior executives reported that their companies had achieved only 63 percent of the results expected in their strategic plans.[60] The lesson is that even sound strategies, unless properly implemented, will fail.

EXECUTING THE STRATEGY "Strategy and execution complement each other," says Steve Tobak, an experienced entrepreneur and management consultant. "Neither one works without the other." Research by Mark Huselid, Brian Becker, and Richard Beatty shows that proper execution of a company's strategy accounts for 85 percent of a company's financial performance.[61] Implementing a strategy successfully requires both a process that fits a company's culture and the right people committed to making that process work. Getting the right people in place starts with the selection process but includes every other aspect of the human resources function—from job design and training to motivational methods and compensation. To make their strategic plans workable, entrepreneurs should divide them into projects, carefully defining each one by the following:

Purpose. What is the project designed to accomplish?

Scope. Which areas of the company will be involved in the project?

Contribution. How does the project relate to other projects and to the overall strategic plan.

Resource requirements. What human and financial resources are needed to complete the project successfully?

Timing. Which schedules and deadlines will ensure project completion?

Once entrepreneurs assign priorities to projects, they can begin to implement the strategic plan. Involving employees and delegating adequate authority to them is essential because these projects affect them most directly. If an organization's people have been involved in the strategic management process to this point, they will have a better grasp of the steps they must take to achieve the organization's goals as well as their own professional goals. Early involvement of the workforce in the strategic management process is a luxury that larger businesses cannot achieve. Commitment to reaching the company's objectives is a powerful force, but involvement is a prerequisite for achieving total employee commitment. The greater the level of involvement of those who will implement a company's strategy (often those at the lower levels of an organization) in the process of creating the strategy (often the realm of those at the top of an organization), the more likely the strategy is to be successful. Without a team of committed, dedicated employees, a company's strategy, no matter how precisely planned, usually fails.

Step 9. Establish Accurate Controls

So far, the planning process has created company objectives and has developed a strategy for reaching them, but rarely, if ever, will the company's actual performance match stated objectives. Entrepreneurs quickly realize the need to control actual results that deviate from plans.

CONTROLLING THE STRATEGY Planning without control has little operational value; therefore, a sound planning program requires a practical control process. The plans and objectives created in the strategic planning process become the standards against which actual performance is measured. It is important for everyone in the organization to understand—and to be involved in—the planning and controlling process. Unless entrepreneurs measure progress against the goals and objectives established in step 6, their companies make little progress toward accomplishing them.

Controlling plans and projects and keeping them on schedule means that an entrepreneur must identify and track key performance indicators. The source of these indicators is the operating data from the company's normal business activity; they are the guideposts for detecting deviations from established standards. Financial, production, sales, inventory, quality, customer service and satisfaction, and other operating records are primary sources of data managers can use to control activities. For example, on a customer service project, performance indicators might include the number of customer complaints, the number of orders returned, the percentage of on-time shipments, and a measure of order accuracy.

The most commonly used indicators of a company's performance are financial measures; however, judging a company's performance solely on the basis of financial measures can lead to strategic myopia. To judge the effectiveness of their strategies, many companies are developing **balanced scorecards**, a set of multidimensional measurements that are unique to a company and that incorporate both financial and operational measures to give managers a quick yet comprehensive picture of the company's overall performance. One writer says that a balanced scorecard

> is a sophisticated business model that helps a company understand what's really driving its success. It acts a bit like the control panel on a spaceship—the business equivalent of a flight speedometer, odometer, and temperature gauge all rolled into one. It keeps track of many things, including financial progress and softer measurements—everything from customer satisfaction to return on investment—that need to be managed to reach the final destination: profitable growth.[62]

Rather than sticking solely to the traditional financial measures of a company's performance, the balanced scorecard gives managers a comprehensive view from *both* a financial and an operational perspective. The premise behind such a scorecard is that relying on any single measure of company performance is dangerous. Just as a pilot in command of a jet cannot fly safely by focusing on a single instrument, an entrepreneur cannot manage a company by concentrating on a single measurement. The complexity of managing a business demands that an entrepreneur be able to see performance measures in several areas simultaneously. "Knowing whether an enterprise is viable or not doesn't mean looking at just the bottom line," says one manager.[63] Scoreboards that combine relevant results from all aspects of the operation allow everyone in the organization to see how their job performance connects to a company's mission, goals, and objectives.

When creating balanced scorecards for their companies, entrepreneurs should create meaningful measures for each mission-related objective they established in step 6. If used properly, a balanced scorecard serves as a call to action. When a key indicator is out of control, everyone

LO5

Understand the importance of controls, such as the balanced scorecard, in the planning process.

balanced scorecards
a set of multidimensional measurements that are unique to a company and that incorporate both financial and operational measures to give managers a quick yet comprehensive picture of a company's overall performance.

in the company knows it and can work together to do something about it quickly. The keys to using scorecards successfully are making sure that the measures included are important to the company's success and that each one tells a different story.

ENTREPRENEURIAL PROFILE: Alex Phinn: Griff Paper and Film Alex Phinn, president of Griff Paper and Film, a maker of protective films, silicone-coated liners, and specialty labeling materials, looks over his company's balanced scorecard with his morning cup of coffee. Rather than use one of the many balanced scorecard software packages available, Phinn designed his own scorecard. His one-page report includes operating data such as new orders received, the number of quotations submitted to potential customers (both measures of future sales), the number of customer complaints, employee absentee rates (both quality indicators), and financial data, such as daily accounts receivables, accounts payables, and cash balances. Phinn's easy-to-use scorecard gives him and his employees the ability to spot problem areas and positive trends in the company quickly.[64] ∎

Ideally, a balanced scorecard looks at a business from five important perspectives (see Figure 3.5).[65]

CUSTOMER PERSPECTIVE How do customers see us? Customers judge companies by at least four standards: time (how long it takes the company to deliver a good or service), quality (how well a company's product or service performs in terms of reliability, durability, and accuracy),

FIGURE 3.5

The Balanced Scorecard Links Performance Measures

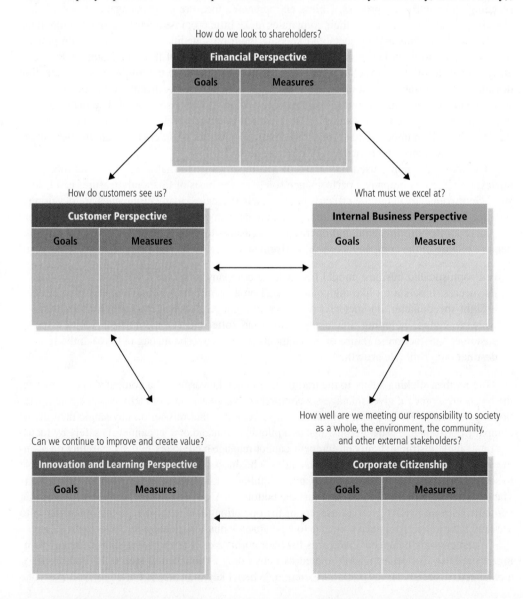

performance (the extent to which a good or service performs as expected), and service (how well a company meets or exceeds customers' expectations of value). Because customer-related goals are external, managers must translate them into measures of what the company must do to meet customers' expectations.

INTERNAL BUSINESS PERSPECTIVE At what must we excel? The internal factors on which managers should focus are those that have the greatest impact on customer satisfaction and retention and on company effectiveness and efficiency. Developing goals and measures for factors such as quality, cycle time, productivity, cost control, and others that employees directly influence is essential.

INNOVATION AND LEARNING PERSPECTIVE Can we continue to improve and create value? This view of a company recognizes that the targets required for success are never static; they are constantly changing. If a company wants to continue its pattern of success, it cannot stand still; it must continuously innovate and improve. Employee training and development are essential ingredients of this component. A company's ability to innovate, learn, and improve determines its future. These goals and measures emphasize the importance of continuous improvement in customer satisfaction and internal business operations.

FINANCIAL PERSPECTIVE How do we look to shareholders? The most traditional performance measures, financial standards tell how much the company's overall strategy and its execution are contributing to its bottom line. These measures focus on such factors as profitability, growth, and shareholder value. On balanced scorecards, companies often break their financial goals into three categories: survival, success, and growth.

CORPORATE CITIZENSHIP How well are we meeting our responsibility to society as a whole, the environment, the community, and other external stakeholders? Even small companies must recognize that they must be good business citizens.

ENTREPRENEURIAL PROFILE: Tesco's Corporate Steering Wheel Tesco is a Cheshunt, Hertfordshire, U.K.-based chain of nearly 5,400 food and general merchandise stores that operates in 14 markets in Europe, Asia, and North America and is recognized as one of the most successful grocery chains in the world. The company recently developed a balanced scorecard called the Tesco Corporate Steering Wheel (see Figure 3.6) to implement and control its seven-part strategy. At the heart of the wheel is Tesco's philosophy, "Every little helps." Surrounding this are two customer-focused values statements that drive the way the company does business. The next ring shows 20 areas in which Tesco has developed specific objectives (e.g., "earn lifetime loyalty") that are separated into the five perspectives described earlier (customer, community, operations, people, and finance). The Wheel works; Tesco's sales increased 31 percent, and its profit increased 36 percent in just a three-year period.[66] ∎

Although the balanced scorecard is a vital tool that helps managers keep their companies on track, it is also an important tool for changing behavior in an organization and for keeping everyone focused on what really matters. Used properly, balanced scorecards allow managers to see how actions in each of the five dimensions of performance influence actions in the others. As competitive conditions and results change, managers can use the balanced scorecard to make corrections in plans, policies, strategies, and objectives to get performance back on track. A practical control system is also economical to operate. Most small businesses have no need for a sophisticated, expensive control system. The system should be so practical that it becomes a natural part of the management process.

Conclusion

The strategic planning process does *not* end with the nine steps outlined here; it is an ongoing procedure that entrepreneurs must repeat. With each round, managers and employees gain experience, and the steps become easier. The planning process described here is designed to be simple. No small business should be burdened with an elaborate, detailed formal planning process that it cannot easily use. Some planning processes require excessive amounts of time to operate and generate a sea of paperwork. Entrepreneurs need neither.

FIGURE 3.6

Tesco's Corporate Steering Wheel, an Application of the Balanced Score Card

Source: Delivering Success: How Tesco Is Managing, Measuring, and Maximizing Its Performance, Advanced Performance Institute, June 23, 2009, p. 4.

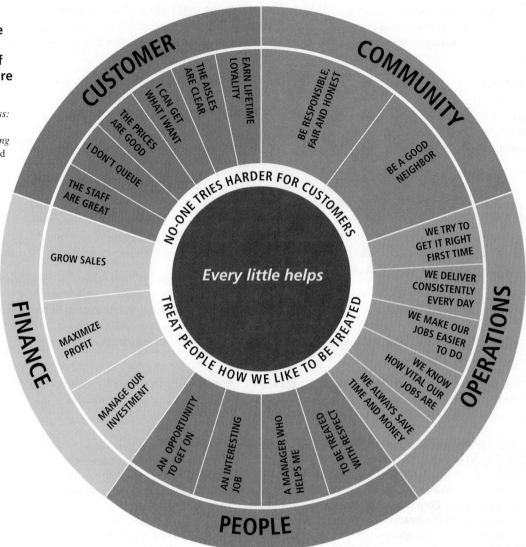

What does this strategic planning process lead to? It teaches business owners a degree of discipline that is important to business survival. It helps them learn about their businesses, their core competencies, their competitors, and, most important, their customers. Although strategic planning cannot guarantee success, it does dramatically increase a small company's chances of survival in a hostile business environment.

Chapter Summary by Learning Objective

1. Understand the importance of strategic management to a small business.

Companies without clear strategies may achieve some success in the short run, but as soon as a competitive threat arises, they often fail.

2. Explain why and how a small business must create a competitive advantage in the market.

The goal of developing a strategic plan is to create for the small company a competitive advantage—the combination of factors that sets the small business apart from its competitors and gives it a unique position in the market. Every small firm must establish a plan for creating a unique image in the minds of its potential customers. A company builds a competitive edge on its core competencies, which are a unique set of capabilities that a company develops in key operational areas, such as quality, service, innovation, team building, flexibility, responsiveness, and others, that allow it to vault past competitors. They are what the company does best and are the focal point of the strategy. This step must identify target market segments and determine how to position the firm in those markets. Entrepreneurs must identify some way to differentiate their companies from competitors.

3. Develop a strategic plan for a business using the nine steps in the strategic planning process.

Small businesses need a strategic planning process designed to suit their particular needs. It should be relatively short, be informal and not structured, encourage the participation of employees, and not begin with extensive objective setting. Linking the purposeful action of strategic planning to an entrepreneur's little ideas can produce results that shape the future.

Step 1. Develop a clear vision and translate it into a meaningful mission statement. Highly successful entrepreneurs are able to communicate their vision to those around them. The firm's mission statement answers the first question of any venture: What business am I in? The mission statement sets the tone for the entire company.

Step 2. Assess the company's strengths and weaknesses. Strengths are positive internal factors; weaknesses are negative internal factors.

Step 3. Scan the environment for significant opportunities and threats facing the business. Opportunities are positive external options; threats are negative external forces.

Step 4. Identify the key factors for success in the business. In every business, key factors determine the success of the firms in it, so they must be an integral part of a company's strategy. KSFs are relationships between a controllable variable and a critical factor influencing the firm's ability to compete in the market.

Step 5. Analyze the competition. Business owners should know their competitors almost as well as they know their own. A competitive profile matrix is a helpful tool for analyzing competitors' strengths and weaknesses.

Step 6. Create company goals and objectives. Goals are the broad, long-range attributes that the firm

seeks to accomplish. Objectives are quantifiable and more precise; they should be specific, measurable, assignable, realistic, timely, and written down. The process works best when managers and employees are actively involved.

Step 7. Formulate strategic options and select the appropriate strategies. A strategy is the game plan the firm plans to use to achieve its objectives and mission. It must center on establishing for the firm the KSFs identified earlier.

Step 8. Translate strategic plans into action plans. No strategic plan is complete until the owner puts it into action.

Step 9. Establish accurate controls. Actual performance rarely, if ever, matches plans exactly. Operating data from the business assembled into a comprehensive scorecard serves as an important guidepost for determining how effective a company's strategy is. This information is especially helpful when plotting future strategies.

The strategic planning process does not end with these nine steps; rather, it is an ongoing process that an entrepreneur will repeat.

4. Discuss the characteristics of three basic strategies: low cost, differentiation, and focus and know when and how to employ them.

Three basic strategic options are cost leadership, differentiation, and focus. A company pursuing a cost leadership strategy strives to be the lowest-cost producer relative to its competitors in the industry. A company following a differentiation strategy seeks to build customer loyalty by positioning its goods or services in a unique or different fashion. In other words, the firm strives to be better than its competitors at something that customers value. A focus strategy recognizes that not all markets are homogeneous. The principal idea of this strategy is to select one (or more) segment(s); identify customers' special needs, wants, and interests; and approach them with a good or service designed to excel in meeting these needs, wants, and interests. Focus strategies build on *differences* among market segments.

5. Understand the importance of controls, such as the balanced scorecard, in the planning process.

Just as a pilot in command of a jet cannot fly safely by focusing on a single instrument, an entrepreneur cannot manage a company by concentrating on a single measurement. The balanced scorecard is a set of measurements unique to a company that includes both financial and operational measures and gives managers a quick yet comprehensive picture of the company's total performance.

Discussion Questions

1. Why is strategic planning important to a small company?
2. What is a competitive advantage? Why is it important for a small business to establish one?
3. What are the steps in the strategic management process?
4. One business writer says, "The test of a mission statement is what you do with it after you put it in place." What does she mean? Do you agree? Explain.
5. "Our customers don't just like our ice cream," write Ben Cohen and Jerry Greenfield, cofounders of Ben and Jerry's Homemade Inc. "They like what our company stands for. They like how doing business with us makes them feel." What do they mean?
6. What are strengths, weaknesses, opportunities, and threats? Give an example of each.
7. When the Detroit Symphony Orchestra (DSO) went on strike recently for four months over pay cuts, all the orchestra's performances were canceled. The strike adversely affected many restaurants near the Max M. Fisher Music Center, where the DSO performs in downtown Detroit, that cater to the orchestra's audience. Dave Zainea, owner of the Majestic Café, says that his restaurant's revenues were "down almost 25 percent. That's about $100,000, all attributable to the strike." What steps can restaurant owners who face threats such as the strike take to minimize the impact on their businesses?

8. Explain the characteristics of effective objectives. Why is setting objectives important?
9. What are business strategies?
10. Describe the three basic strategies available to small companies. Under what conditions is each most successful?
11. "It's better to be a company with a great strategy in a crummy business than to be a company with a crummy strategy in a great business," says one business expert. Do you agree? Explain.
12. Explain how a company can gain a competitive advantage using each of the three strategies described in this chapter: cost leadership, differentiation, and focus. Give an example of a company that is using each strategy.
13. How is the controlling process related to the planning process?
14. What is a balanced scorecard? What value does it offer entrepreneurs who are evaluating the success of their current strategies?

Business Plan Pro™ We are now going to think about your business plan from a strategic perspective. This involves describing your business objectives, drafting your mission statement, identifying "keys to success," conducting a SWOT analysis, and making initial comments about your strategy and your competitive advantage.

Business Plan Exercises

Have you taken the time to create a vision for your business? If not, use the process described in Table 3.1 that Ari Wienzweig, founder of Zingerman's Community of Businesses, relied on to create the vision for his company. Select a time horizon 3 to 10 years from now and answer the questions that Table 3.1 poses to create your vision.

On the Web

Visit www.pearsonhighered.com/scarborough, click on the Companion Site link, and go to the Business Plan Resources tab. Scroll down to find the Standard Industry Classification (SIC) codes heading to identify the SIC code associated with your industry. Next, review the information associated with the Competitor Analysis section. This information may provide insight about your industry competitors on a global, national, or possibly local basis.

In the Software

Open your business plan in *Business Plan Pro™*. You are now going to add text to the strategic areas mentioned in this chapter. Don't worry about perfecting this information. Simply capture your thoughts and ideas so that you can revisit these topics, add detail, and make certain that the sections are congruent with your entire plan.

Sample Plans

Review the following sections, as they appear, in the sample plans that you identified earlier:

Mission Statement

Objectives

SWOT Analysis

Keys to Success

Competition, Buying Patterns, and Main Competitors

Value Proposition

Competitive Edge

Strategy and Implementation Summary

Note the information captured in these sections of the plans. Some areas may be in a narrative style, and others may contain only bullet points. As you look at each plan, determine if it provides the needed information under each topic.

Building Your Business Plan

Here are some tips you may want to consider as you tackle each of these sections:

Mission Statement

The mission statement establishes the fundamental goals for the quality of the business offering. The mission statement represents the opportunity to answer the questions, "What business are you in?" and "Why does your business exist?" This may include the value you offer and the role customers, employees, and owners play in providing and benefiting from that value. A mission statement is a critical element in defining your business and communicating this definition to key stakeholders, including investors, partners, employees, and customers.

Objectives

Each objective should be specific, quantifiable, and measurable. Setting measurable objectives will enable you to track your progress and measure your results.

SWOT Analysis

What are the internal strengths and weaknesses of your business? What are the external opportunities and threats? List the strengths and weaknesses and assess what insight this offers about your business. How can you leverage your strengths to take advantage of the opportunities ahead? How can you further develop or minimize the areas of weaknesses?

Keys to Success

Virtually every business has critical aspects that make the difference between success and failure. These may be brief bullet-point comments that capture those key elements that will make a difference in realizing your mission and accomplishing your stated objectives.

Competition, Buying Patterns, and Main Competitors

Discuss your ideal position in the market. Think about specific kinds of features and benefits your business offers and how that is unique compared to what is available to your market today. Why do people buy your products and services instead of those your competitors offer? Discuss your primary competitors' strengths and weaknesses. Consider their service offering, pricing, reputation, management, financial position, brand awareness, business development, technology, and any other factors that may be important. What market segments do they occupy? What strategy do they appear to pursue? How much of a competitive threat do they present?

Value Proposition

A value proposition is a clear and concise statement that describes the tangible value-based result a customer receives from using your product or service. How effectively does your value proposition communicate and fulfill your promise to your customers or clients?

Your Competitive Edge

A competitive edge builds on your value proposition and capture the unique value—in whatever terms the customer defines that value—that your business offers. Your competitive edge may result from a product, customer service, method of distribution, pricing, or promotional methods. It describes how your business is uniquely different from all others in a sustainable manner.

Strategy and Implementation

Make initial comments that capture your strategies for the business. This strategic game plan provides the focus required to realize your venture's objectives and mission. Based on your initial strategic analysis, which of the three business strategies—low cost, differentiation, or focus—will you use to give your company a competitive advantage? How will this strategy capitalize on your company's strengths and appeal to your customers' need? You will later build on this information as you formulate action plans to bring the strategy section of your plan to life.

Capture your ideas in each of these sections and continually review this information. If it does not add value to your business plan, there is no need to include this information.

Beyond the Classroom . . .

1. Contact the owner of a small business that competes directly with an industry giant (such as Home Depot, Wal-Mart, Barnes & Noble, or others). What does the owner see as his or her competitive advantage? How does the business communicate this advantage to its customers? What competitive strategy is the owner using? How successful is it? What changes would you suggest the owner make?

2. In his book *The HP Way*, Dave Packard, cofounder of Hewlett-Packard, describes the seven commitments of the HP Way:
   - Profit—the ultimate source of corporate strength.
   - Customers—constant improvement in the value of the products and services the company offers them.
   - Field of interest—seeking new opportunities but limiting them to complementary products and services based on company core competencies.
   - Growth—a measure of strength and a requirement for survival.
   - Employees—provide opportunities for advancement, share in their success, and offer job security based on performance.
   - Organization—foster individual motivation, initiative, and creativity by giving employees the freedom to work toward established goals and objectives.

- Citizenship—contribute in a positive way toward the community and society at large.

In what ways do these values help HP define its vision? Its competitive edge? How important is it for entrepreneurs to define a system of values to guide their companies?

3. Contact a local entrepreneur and help him or her devise a balanced scorecard for his or her company. What goals did you and the owner establish in each of the four perspectives? What measures did you use to judge progress toward those goals?

4. Use the strategic tools provided in this chapter to help a local small business owner discover his or her firm's strengths, weaknesses, opportunities, and threats; identify the relevant KSFs; and analyze its competitors. Help the owner devise a strategy for success for his or her business.

5. Choose an entrepreneur in your community and interview him or her. Does the company have a strategic plan? A mission statement? Why or why not? What does the owner consider the company's strengths and weaknesses to be? What opportunities and threats does the owner perceive? What image is the owner trying to create for the business? Has the effort been successful? (Do you agree?) Which of the generic competitive strategies is the company following? Who are the company's primary competitors? How does the owner rate his or her chances for success in the future (use a low [1] to high [10] scale). Compare your evaluation with other classmates. What, if any, generalizations can you draw from the interview?

Endnotes

1. "AmEx's Ken Chenault Talks about Leadership, Integrity, and the Credit Card Business," *Leadership and Change*, Knowledge @Wharton, http://knowledge@wharton.upenn.edu/index/cfm?fa=printArticle&ID=1179.
2. Sara Pepitone, "A 210-Year-Old Company's High-Tech Plans," *CNN Money*, August 9, 2010, http://money.cnn.com/2010/08/09/smallbusiness/cranes/index.htm.
3. Alvin Toffler, "Shocking Truths about the Future," *Journal of Business Strategy*, July/August 1996, p. 6.
4. Thomas A. Stewart, "You Think Your Company's So Smart? Prove It," *Fortune*, April 30, 2001, p. 188.
5. Matthew Boyle, "John Mackey," *Fortune*, July 23, 2007, pp. 72–76; Jeffrey Pfeffer, "Dare to Be Different," *Business 2.0*, September 2004, p. 58; "Company Facts," Whole Foods Market, http://www.wholefoodsmarket.com/company/facts.html.
6. Thomas A. Stewart, "Intellectual Capital: Ten Years Later, How Far We've Come," *Fortune*, May 28, 2001, p. 188.
7. Gary Hamel, "Innovation's New Math," *Fortune*, July 9, 2001, p. 130.
8. Gail Appleson, "Whole Foods Prepares to Open Town and Country Store," *St. Louis Today*, June 20, 2008, http://www.stltoday.com/stltoday/business/stories.nsf/story/6636B1111341CBE38625746E000A730E?OpenDocument; Matthew Boyle, "John Mackey," *Fortune*, July 23, 2007, pp. 72–76.
9. Kara Ohngren, "Stay Hungry," *Entrepreneur*, June 2010, p. 19.
10. "Who Are We?," Zoots, http://www.zoots.com/aboutWhoWeAre.aspx.
11. "A Conversation with Scott Cook," *Inc.*, September 2007, p. 215.
12. "Company Overview," Pizza Fusion, http://www.pizzafusion.com/our-story/company-overview.aspx.
13. Ari Weinzweig, "Step into the Future," *Inc.*, February 2011, pp. 85–91.
14. Ken Blanchard, "The New Bottom Line," *Entrepreneur*, February 1998, p. 127.
15. Thomas A. Stewart, "Why Values Statements Don't Work," *Fortune*, June 10, 1996, p. 137.
16. Michael Barrier, "Back from the Brink," *Nation's Business*, September 1995, p. 21.
17. William Cooper, "Chick-Fil-A CEO, S. Truett Cathy," *ChristiaNet News*, http://christiannews.christianet

.com/1097585115.htm; Richard Schneider, "Chain Reaction," *Guideposts*, April 2003, pp. 18–19; Chick-Fil-A, http://www.chickfila.com/Company.asp; "Chick-Fil-A Founder Truett Cathy's Grandson to Open Chain's Newest Stand-Alone Restaurant in Durham January 10," *Reuters*, January 9, 2008, http://www.reuters.com/article/pressRelease/idUS130426+09-Jan-2008+MW20080109.
18. "The Secret to Innovation at Method," Method, http://peopleagainstdirty.typepad.com/people_against_dirty.
19. Spragins, "Unmasking Your Motivations," p. 86.
20. Chris Penttila, "Missed Mission," *Entrepreneur*, May 2002, pp. 73–74.
21. "Our Philosophy," Google, http://www.google.com/corporate/tenthings.html.
22. "Our Mission," The Elephant Sanctuary, http://www.elephants.com/mission.php.
23. "Mission Statement," Pizza Fusion, http://www.pizzafusion.com/our-story/company-overview.aspx.
24. "Our Story," Great Harvest Bread Company: Duluth, http://getfreshbread.com/ourStory.htm.
25. Christine, Lagorio, "Let There Be Light," *Inc.*, October 2010, pp. 42–43.
26. Rudolph Bell, "Greening the Big Rigs," *Greenville News*, February 20, 2011, pp. 1E, 3E.
27. "Lauren A. E. Shuker, "Double Feature: Dinner and a Movie," *Wall Street Journal*, January 5, 2011, pp. D1–D2; Peggy Edersheim Kalb, "A Movie Theater as Comfy as Our Sofa," *Wall Street Journal*, April 24, 2008, p. D2; Andy Serwer, Corey Hajim, and Susan M. Kaufman, "Movie Theaters: Extreme Makeover," *Fortune*, May 23, 2006, http://money.cnn.com/2006/05/19/magazines/fortune/theater_futureof_fortune/index.htm; Paul Donsky, "New Theaters to Offer One-Stop Dinner and a Movie," *Access Atlanta*, April 25, 2008, http://www.accessatlanta.com/movies/content/movies/stories/2008/04/25/movie_0426.html?cxntlid=homepage_tab_newstab.
28. Jason Daley, "Waiter, Bring Me a Fresh Idea," *Entrepreneur*, March 2010, pp. 89–95.
29. Sharon Bernstein, "Will Five Guys Take Over In-N-Out?," *Los Angeles Times*, April 8, 2011, http://articles.latimes.com/2011/apr/08/business/la-fi-five-guys-20110408; Rob

Sachs, "High-End Burger Joints Raise the Stakes," *National Public Radio*, April 21, 2011, http://www.npr .org/2011/04/21/135569985/high-end-burger-joints-raise-the-stakes; Judy Kneiszel, "Blazing Onion," *QSR Magazine*, October 22, 2010, http://www.qsrmagazine.com/new-concepts/ blazing-onion.

30. William J. Dennis Jr., *National Small Business Poll: Competition* (Washington, DC: National Federation of Independent Businesses, 2003), vol. 3, issue 8, p. 1.

31. Jeff Brady, "What Small Businesses Can Learn from Judo," Brady Media Group, January 2011, http://www.bradymediagroup.com/2011/01/ what-small-businesses-can-learn-from-judo.

32. Carolyn Z. Lawrence, "Know Your Competition," *Business Start-Ups*, April 1997, p. 51.

33. Beth Kwon, "Toolbox: Staying Competitive," *FSB*, December 2002/January 2003, p. 89.

34. Kevin Coyne and John Horne, "How Companies Respond to Competitors: A McKinsey Global Survey," *McKinsey Quarterly*, May 2008, http://www.mckinseyquarterly.com/ How_companies_respond_to_competitors_2146.

35. Kirsten Osound, "Secret Agent Plan," *Entrepreneur*, June 2005, p. 98.

36. Brian Caulfield, "Know Your Enemy," *Business 2.0*, June 2004, pp. 89–90.

37. Shari Caudron, "I Spy, You Spy," *Industry Week*, October 3, 1994, p. 36.

38. Stephen D. Solomon, "Spies Like You," *FSB*, June 2001, pp. 76–82.

39. Lawrence, "Know Your Competition," pp. 51–56.

40. Stephanie Gruner, "Spies Like Us," *Inc.*, August 1998, p. 45.

41. Lewis Carroll, *Alice in Wonderland* (Mount Vernon, NY: Peter Pauper Press, 1937), pp. 78–79.

42. Rhonda Abrams, "Set Sights on One Big New Goal for '05," *Business*, October 10, 2004, p. 7; Mark Henricks, "In the BHAG," *Entrepreneur*, August 1999, pp. 65–67.

43. Robert S. Kaplan and David P. Norton, *The Strategy-Focused Organization* (Cambridge, MA Harvard Business School Press, 2001), p. 234.

44. "SuccessFactors Research Publishes New Study—Proves That Companies Investing in Business Execution Software Achieve Higher Shareholder Returns," SuccessFactors, June 1, 2011, http://www.successfactors.com/press-releases/1569395; "The Incredible Power of Company Goal Alignment," SuccessFactors, http://www.successfactors.com/ articles/corporate-goal-alignment.

45. Joseph C. Picken and Gregory Dess, "The Seven Traps of Strategic Planning," *Inc.*, November 1996, p. 99.

46. Devon Rifkin, "Hang Time," *FSB*, April 2007, pp. 47–48; "Devon Rifkin," Inc. 500 Conference and Awards Ceremony, http://www.globalexec.com/inc500/speakers .php?lname=Rifkin; "The Inc. 500: The Great American Hanger Company," *Inc.*, http://www.inc.com/inc5000/2007/ company-profile.html?id=2006498; Linda Trischitta, "Celebs All about Style, Right Down to the Hangers," *South Florida Sun-Sentinal Daily Press*, March 10, 2008, http://www.daily-press.com/topic/sfl-flbhangers0310sbmar10,0,2755949.story.

47. Michael E. Porter, *Competitive Strategy* (New York: Free Press, 1980), chap. 2.

48. Garin Groff, "WinCo Grocery Chain Plans Arizona Expansion," *East Valley Tribune*, January 23, 2011, http://www .eastvalleytribune.com/business/article_e5682ae0-25b8-11e0-96e0-001cc4c03286.html; Tony Biasotti, "WinCo Foods Gets OK to Open in Ventura," *Ventura County Star*, June 14, 2011, http://www.vcstar.com/news/2011/jun/14/winco-foods-gets-ok-to-open-in-ventura; "About," WinCo Foods, http://www .wincofoods.com/about.

49. Ann Zimmerman, "Behind the Dollar-Store Boom: A Nation of Nargain Hunters," *Wall Street Journal*, December 13, 2004, pp. A1, A10; Brendan Coffey, "Every Penny Counts," *Forbes*, September 30, 2002, pp. 68–70; Amber McDowell, "Discount Retailers Prosper amid Economic Instability," *Greenville News Business*, December 23, 2002, pp. 6, 13.

50. Ann Zimmerman, "Dollar General Lays Bet on Opening New Stores," *Wall Street Journal*, May 14, 2010, p. B8.

51. Cecile Rohwedder, "The '40s Footwear Fashionista," *Wall Street Journal*, February 12–13, 2011, p. C11; Suzy Menkes, "Brazil, Film Noir, and Shoes 'To Die For,'" *New York Times*, February 23, 2011, http://www.nytimes.com/2011/02/24/ fashion/24iht-rolympia24.html?_r=3&ref=fashion.

52. Celia Farber, "Anice Hotel," *Inc.*, June 2002, pp. 88–90; Shelly Branch, "Havin' an Ice Team," *Fortune*, March 1, 1999, pp. 277–278; Eleena De Lisser, "The Hot New Travel Spot Is Freezing Cold," *Wall Street Journal*, October 16, 2002, pp. D1, D4; Ice Hotel, http://www.icehotel.com.

53. Debra Phillips, "Leaders of the Pack," *Entrepreneur*, September 1996, p. 127.

54. Susan Carey, "Tiny Airline Flies Circles around Its Rivals," *Wall Street Journal*, March 17, 2010, p. B8.

55. "Intuit Study: Next-Gen Artisans Fuel New Entrepreneurial Economy," Intuit and Institute for the Future, February 13, 2008, http://www.intuit.com/about_intuit/press_room/press_ release/2008/0213.jsp, p. 1.

56. Anthony Trento, "Birds of Play," *FSB*, April 2008, pp. 44–45; "Feather Designer Tickles Fancy of Celebrities, Broadway," *MCLA Beacon*, September 27, 2007, http://media.www .mclabeacon.com/media/storage/paper802/news/2007/09/27/ Entertainment/Feather.Designer.Tickles.Fancy.Of.Celebrities .Broadway-2994435.shtml.

57. Norm Brodsky, "How Independents Can Hold On," *Inc.*, August 2007, p. 66.

58. Darren Dahl, "Rags and Riches," *Inc.*, April 2011, p. 24; Lizette Wilson Chapman, "Historical Emporium Is Dressed for Success in Period Styles," *San Jose Business Journal*, October 17, 2010, http://www.bizjournals.com/sanjose/ stories/2010/10/18/focus7.html.

59. Michele Pepe-Warren, "Drape Company Makes Technology Fabric of Its Existence," *Information Week*, July 27, 2010, http://www.informationweek.com/blog/smb/229201005; Lia Timson, "Sew What? Founder and CEO Megan Duckett Went to the U.S. Chasing Bright Lights and Ended Up on Curtain Call," *Sydney Morning Herald*, June 28, 2010, http:// www.sewwhatinc.com/news100628b.php.

60. "Three Reasons Why Good Strategies Fail: Execution, Execution . . . ," *Strategic Management*, Knowldege @Wharton, University of Pennsylvania, http://knowledge. wharton.edu/index.cfm?fa=printArticle&ID=1252.

61. Mark Huselid, Brian Becker, and Richard Beatty, *The Workforce Scorecard: Managing Human Capital to Execute Strategy* (Cambridge, MA: Harvard Business School Press, 2005), p. 17.

62. Joel Kurtzman, "Is Your Company Off Course? Now You Can Find Out Why," *Fortune*, February 17, 1997, p. 128.

63. Michelle Bitoun, "Show Them the Data," *Trustee*, September 2002, p. 35.

64. Gene Marks, "The Key to Better Management: A Balanced Scorecard," *Forbes*, April 29, 2008, http://www.forbes. com/2008/04/29/small-business-management-ent-mange-cx_gm_0429genemarksmetric.html.

65. Robert S. Kaplan and David P. Norton, "The Balanced Scorecard—Measures That Drive Performance," *Harvard Business Review*, January–February 1992, pp. 71–79.

66. *Delivering Success: How Tesco Is Managing, Measuring, and Maximizing Its Performance*, Advanced Performance Institute, June 23, 2009, pp. 3–5.

4

Conducting a Feasibility Analysis and Crafting a Winning Business Plan

Learning Objectives

On completion of this chapter, you will be able to:

1. Discuss the steps involved in subjecting a business idea to a feasibility analysis.

2. Explain why every entrepreneur should create a business.

3. Describe the elements of a solid business plan.

4. Explain the "five Cs of credit" and why they are important to potential lenders and investors reading business plans.

5. Describe the keys to making an effective business plan presentation.

Planning without action is futile. Action without planning is fatal.

—Anonymous

It's not the plan that's important; it's the planning.

—Graeme Edwards

For many entrepreneurs, the easiest part of launching a business is coming up with an idea for a new business concept or approach. As you learned in Chapter 2, entrepreneurs do not lack creativity and are responsible for some of the world's most important innovations. Business success, however, requires much more than just a great new idea. Once entrepreneurs develop an idea for a business, the next step is to define the business model they will create and subject it to a feasibility analysis to determine whether they can transform the idea into a viable business. A **business model** defines the process a company will use to generate sales and a profit. A business model is comprised of the following seven components:[1]

1. *A definition of your target customers and how your company will reach them.* Customers are the essential ingredient in any business model. Without them, a company is doomed to failure. Potential customers are not waiting for you to develop the next greatest product or service so that they can hand over their money to you. You must find them and reach them; that takes time and costs money.

2. *The customer value proposition your company offers.* The best business models offer simple customer value propositions. Zygna, the company that created Farmville, Mafia Wars, and Café World, provides free social games for Web users to play. Athenahealth, founded in 1997 by two physicians, Jonathan Bush and Todd Park, provides a Web-based system that helps physicians manage their practices more efficiently and get higher reimbursements from insurance companies. Your business model must define the value that your company offers customers.

3. *Point of differentiation.* As you learned in Chapter 3, a company needs a competitive advantage to be successful. Some businesses achieve that by offering the lowest prices, others focus on serving market niches better than their competitors, and still others find a meaningful way to differentiate themselves in their customers' eyes. Your business model must define what makes your company's product or service unique.

4. *Pricing.* Establishing proper prices is vital because price is a key determinant of a company's revenue and profitability. Entrepreneurs must know how much it costs to provide a product or service and consider how much competitors are charging for similar items. Will customers pay the prices you expect to charge? Even if a company gives away its products (as some Web-based companies do), eventually it must find a way to generate revenue. Although Zygna provides its games for free, the company sells virtual goods (for real money) to customers so that they can advance to higher levels in its games.

5. *Selling process.* Almost everything entrepreneurs do once they come up with a business idea involves selling. Customers rarely buy anything without someone selling it to them. Your business model should define your sales strategy and process.

6. *Distribution system.* How will you get your product or service into your customers' hands? Will you use a direct sales force, distributors or other middlemen, the Internet, or some other mechanism? Delivering goods costs money, and your business model must reflect that cost.

7. *Customer support.* Customer relationships do not end when you make a sale; that is when they begin. Your business model must define how you will provide customer support and service, including answering questions about products' or services' use, resolving problems with defects, and receiving feedback that helps you improve your products and services.

A **feasibility analysis** is the process of determining whether an entrepreneur's idea and business model form a viable foundation for creating a successful business. Its purpose is to determine whether a business idea and model are worth pursuing. If the idea and model pass the feasibility analysis, the entrepreneur's next step is to build a solid business plan for capitalizing on them. If the idea or model fails to pass muster, the entrepreneur either revises it or drops it and moves on to the next opportunity. He or she has not wasted valuable time, money, energy, and other resources creating a full-blown business plan or, worse, launching a business that is destined to fail because it is based on a flawed concept. One aspiring entrepreneur wanted to

business model
defines the process a company will use to generate sales and a profit.

feasibility analysis
the process of determining whether an entrepreneur's idea is a viable foundation for creating a successful business.

start a business that created custom scrapbooks until a feasibility study revealed that she would earn far below the minimum wage on her investment of time.[2] Although it is impossible for a feasibility study to guarantee an idea's success, conducting a study reduces the likelihood that entrepreneurs will waste their time pursuing fruitless business ventures.

A feasibility study is *not* the same as a business plan; both play important but separate roles in the start-up process. A feasibility study answers the question, "Should we proceed with this business idea?" Its role is to serve as a filter, screening out ideas that lack the potential for building a successful business, *before* an entrepreneur commits the necessary resources to building a business plan. A feasibility study is primarily an *investigative* tool. It is designed to give an entrepreneur a picture of the market, sales, and profit potential of a particular business idea. Will a ski resort located here attract enough customers to be successful? Will customers in this community support a sandwich shop with a retro rock-and-roll theme? Can we build the product at a reasonable cost and sell it at a price that customers are willing and able to pay? Does this entrepreneurial team have the ability to implement the idea successfully?

A business plan, on the other hand, is a planning tool for transforming an idea into reality. It builds on the foundation of the feasibility study but provides a more comprehensive analysis than a feasibility study. It functions primarily as a planning tool, taking an idea that has passed the feasibility analysis and describing how to turn it into a successful business. Its primary goals are to guide entrepreneurs as they launch and operate their businesses and to help them acquire the financing needed to launch.

Feasibility studies are particularly useful when entrepreneurs have generated multiple ideas for business concepts and must winnow their options down to the "best choice." They enable entrepreneurs to explore quickly the practicality of each of several potential paths for transforming an idea into a successful business venture. Sometimes the result of a feasibility study is the realization that an idea simply won't produce a viable business—no matter how it is organized. In other cases, a study shows an entrepreneur that the business idea is a sound one but that it must be organized in a different fashion to be profitable.

LO1

Discuss the steps involved in subjecting a business idea to a feasibility analysis.

Conducting a Feasibility Analysis

A feasibility analysis consists of three interrelated components: an industry and market feasibility analysis, a product or service feasibility analysis, and a financial feasibility analysis (see Figure 4.1).

Industry and Market Feasibility Analysis

When evaluating the feasibility of a business idea, entrepreneurs find a basic analysis of the industry and targeted market segments a good starting point. The focus in this phase is twofold: (1) to determine how attractive an industry is overall as a "home" for a new business and (2) to identify possible niches a small business can occupy profitably.

FIGURE 4.1

Elements of a Feasibility Analysis

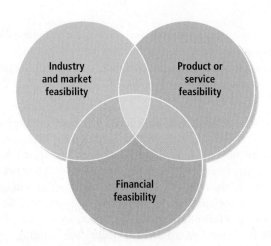

The first step in assessing industry attractiveness is to paint a picture of the industry with broad strokes, assessing it from a "macro" level. Answering the following questions will help:

- How large is the industry?

- How fast is it growing?

- Is the industry as a whole profitable?

- Is the industry characterized by high profit margins or razor-thin margins?

- How essential are its products or services to customers?

- What trends are shaping the industry's future?

- What threats does the industry face?

- What opportunities does the industry face?

- How crowded is the industry?

- How intense is the level of competition in the industry?

- Is the industry young, mature, or somewhere in between?

Addressing these questions helps entrepreneurs determine whether sufficient demand for their products and services exists.

Battered by the convenience of online movie downloads from Netflix, inexpensive rentals from more than 27,000 locations of Redbox DVD kiosks, and online entertainment options such as YouTube and Facebook, video rental stores are fading away. Video rental stores became part of the landscape in the 1980s as growing numbers of households acquired the technology to play videos. Sales at video rental stores have declined 56 percent to $3.56 billion since their peak in 2001, and industry leaders such as Movie Gallery and Blockbuster have filed for bankruptcy protection. Independent stores also are struggling to survive. Alan Sklar, owner of Alan's Alley Video in Manhattan's Chelsea neighborhood since 1988, has seen his company's sales decline and wonders how much longer he will be able to stay in business.[3]

A useful tool for analyzing an industry's attractiveness is the **five-forces model** developed by Michael Porter of the Harvard Business School (see Figure 4.2).[4] Five forces interact with

five-forces model
a model that recognizes the power of five forces—rivalry among competing firms, bargaining power of suppliers, bargaining power of buyers, threat of new entrants, and threat of substitute products or services—on an industry.

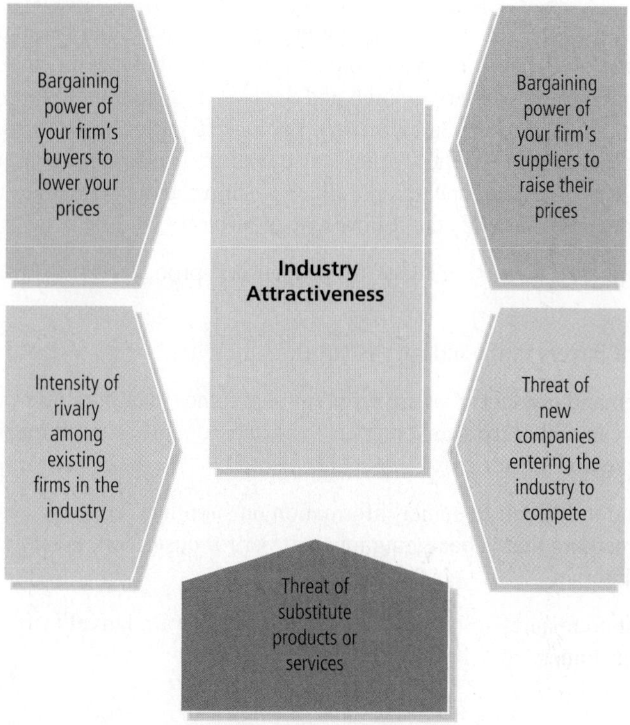

FIGURE 4.2
Five-Forces Model

Source: Adapted from Michael E. Porter, "How Competitive Forces Shape Strategy," *Harvard Business Review* 57, no. 2 (March–April 1979): 137–145.

one another to determine the setting in which companies compete and hence the attractiveness of the industry: (1) the rivalry among the companies competing in the industry, (2) the bargaining power of suppliers to the industry, (3) the bargaining power of buyers, (4) the threat of new entrants to the industry, and (5) the threat of substitute products or services.

RIVALRY AMONG COMPANIES COMPETING IN THE INDUSTRY The strongest of the five forces in most industries is the rivalry that exists among the businesses competing in a particular market. Much like the horses running in the Kentucky Derby, businesses in a market are jockeying for position in an attempt to gain a competitive advantage. When a company creates an innovation or develops a unique strategy that transforms the market, competing companies must adapt or run the risk of being forced out of business. This force makes markets a dynamic and highly competitive place. Generally, an industry is more attractive when the following conditions exist:

- The number of competitors is large or, at the other extreme, quite small (fewer than five).

- Competitors are not similar in size or capability.

- The industry is growing at a fast pace.

- The opportunity to sell a differentiated product or service exists.

BARGAINING POWER OF SUPPLIERS TO THE INDUSTRY The greater the leverage that suppliers of key raw materials or components have, the less attractive is the industry. For instance, because they supply the chips that serve as the "brains" of PCs and because those chips make up a sizable portion of the cost of a computer, chip makers such as Intel and Advanced Micro Devices (AMD) exert a great deal of power over computer manufacturers such as Dell, Hewlett-Packard, and Gateway. Generally, an industry is more attractive when the following conditions exist:

- Many suppliers sell a commodity product to the companies in it.

- Substitute products are available for the items suppliers provide.

- Companies in the industry find it easy to switch from one supplier to another or to substitute products (i.e., "switching costs" are low).

- The items that suppliers provide the industry account for a relatively small portion of the cost of the industry's finished products.

BARGAINING POWER OF BUYERS Just as suppliers to an industry can be a source of pressure, buyers also have the potential to exert significant power over businesses, making it less attractive. When the number of customers is small and the cost of switching to competitors' products is low, buyers' influence on companies is high. Famous for offering its customers low prices, Wal-Mart, the largest company in the world, is also well known for applying relentless pressure to its 21,000 suppliers for price concessions, which it almost always manages to get.[5] Generally, an industry is more attractive when the following conditions exist:

- Industry customers' "switching costs" to competitors' products or to substitutes are relatively high.

- The number of buyers in the industry is large.

- Customers demand products that are differentiated rather than purchase commodity products that they can obtain from any supplier (and subsequently can pit one company against another to drive down price).

- Customers find it difficult to gather information on suppliers' costs, prices, and product features—something that is becoming much easier for customers in many industries to do by using the Internet.

- The items that companies sell to the industry account for a relatively small portion of the cost of their customers' finished products.

THREAT OF NEW ENTRANTS TO THE INDUSTRY New entrants to an industry can erode existing companies' market share and profits. The larger the pool of potential new entrants to an industry, the greater is the threat to existing companies in it. This is particularly true in industries where the barriers to entry, such as capital requirements, specialized knowledge, access to distribution channels, and others are low. Generally, an industry is more attractive to new entrants when the following conditions exist:

- The advantages of economies of scale are absent. Economies of scale exist when companies in an industry achieve low average costs by producing huge volumes of items (e.g., computer chips).

- Capital requirements to enter the industry are low.

- Cost advantages are not related to company size.

- Buyers are not extremely brand loyal, making it easier for new entrants to the industry to draw customers away from existing businesses.

- Governments, through their regulatory and international trade policies, do not restrict new companies from entering the industry.

THREAT OF SUBSTITUTE PRODUCTS OR SERVICES Substitute products or services can turn an entire industry on its head. For instance, many makers of glass bottles have closed their doors in recent years as their customers—from soft-drink bottlers to ketchup makers—have switched to plastic containers, which are lighter, less expensive to ship, and less likely to break. Printed newspapers have seen their readership rates decline as new generations of potential readers turn to online sources of news that are constantly updated. Substitute products also impose an implicit price ceiling for existing products and services. Generally, an industry is more attractive when the following conditions exist:

- Quality substitute products are not readily available.

- The prices of substitute products are not significantly lower than those of the industry's products.

- Buyers' cost of switching to substitute products is high.

After surveying the power these five forces exert on an industry, entrepreneurs can evaluate the potential for their companies to generate reasonable sales and profits in a particular industry. In other words, they can answer the question, "Is this industry a good home for my business?" Table 4.1 provides a matrix that allows entrepreneurs to assign quantitative scores to the five forces influencing industry attractiveness. Note that the lower the score for an industry, the more attractive it is.

Entrepreneurs can shield their companies from some of the negative impact of these five forces by focusing on profitable niches. As you learned in Chapter 3, many small businesses prosper by sticking to niches in a market that are too small to attract the attention of large competitors. The key question that entrepreneurs address here is, "Can we identify a niche that is large enough to produce a profit, or can we position our company uniquely in the market to differentiate it from the competition in a meaningful way?" Entrepreneurs who have designed successful focus or differentiation strategies for their companies can use them to their advantage.

Questions that entrepreneurs should address in this portion of the feasibility analysis include the following:

- Which niche in the market will we occupy?

- How large is this market segment, and how fast is it growing?

- What is the basis for differentiating our product or service from competitors?

- Do we have a superior business model that will be difficult for competitors to reproduce?

TABLE 4.1 Five-Forces Matrix

Assign a value to rate the importance of each of the five forces to the industry on a 1 (not important) to 5 (very important) scale. Then assign a value to reflect the threat that each force poses as a threat to the industry.

Multiply the importance rating in column 2 by the threat rating in column 3 to produce a weighted score.

Add the weighted scores in column 3 to get a total weighted score. This score measures the industry's attractiveness. The matrix is a useful tool for comparing the attractiveness of different industries.

Minimum score = 5 (very attractive)
Maximum score = 125 (very unattractive)

Force	Importance (1 to 5) (1 = Not Important, 5 = Very Important)	Threat to Industry (1 to 5) (1 = Low, 3 = Medium, 5 = High)	Weighted Score Col 2 × Col 3
Rivalry among companies competing in the industry	5	3	15
Bargaining power of suppliers in the industry	2	2	4
Bargaining power of buyers	2	4	8
Threat of new entrants to the industry	3	4	12
Threat of substitute products or services	4	3	12
Total			51

Park It! Guides

business prototyping
a process in which entrepreneurs test their business models on a small scale before committing serious resources to launch a business that might not work.

ENTREPRENEURIAL PROFILE: Margot Tohn: Park It! Guides In 2006, Margot Tohn decided to launch a business in an unusual niche: selling guides to New York City's parking lots and garages. She drew inspiration from the popular Zagat restaurant guides and launched Park It! Guides, a business that sells printed guides to New York City's 1,100 parking lots and garages. "I couldn't believe that a city as big and wonderful as New York City still had parking as a major issue for residents and visitors," says Tohn. "I set out to make parking easier and painless for everyone." She spent 18 months driving city streets, creating detailed maps of every parking lot and garage, and assembling useful data about each one. Tohn soon discovered that the cost of printing and distributing the guides was prohibitive and quickly adapted her business model. She created a Web site, http://parkitnyc.com, where guests complete a request form and receive a link with special discounts from more than 600 parking lots and garages. Her company earns a referral fee from each new customer that a lot or garage attracts. Because the operating cost of her new business model is so low (less than $500 per month), Tohn's company became profitable very quickly. She is taking her niche strategy to other major cities, including Boston, Chicago, Los Angeles, Washington, and Philadelphia.[6] ∎

One technique for gauging the quality of a company's business model involves **business prototyping**, in which entrepreneurs test their business models on a small scale before committing serious resources to launch a business that might not work. Business prototyping recognizes that every business idea is a hypothesis that needs to be tested before an entrepreneur takes it to full scale. If the test supports the hypothesis and its accompanying assumptions, it is time to launch a company. If the prototype flops, the entrepreneur scraps the business idea with only minimal losses and turns to the next idea.

Travis Anderson/The Chef Shack

ENTREPRENEURIAL PROFILE: Nicolette Mall and Lisa Carlson: Chef Shack Nicolette Mall and Lisa Carlson, both experienced chefs, knew that they wanted to operate their own food truck in Minneapolis, Minnesota. However, before investing in a food truck, which can cost between $50,000 and $100,000, Mall and Carlson set up a booth at a farmer's market in downtown Minneapolis to test their concept and their menu. For one year, they operated their booth, listened to their customers, and observed the items customers purchased most frequently (and perhaps as important, the items they did not purchase) before they invested in a food truck called the Chef Shack. Today, their mobile restaurant is profitable, debt free, and so successful that it allows them to travel the world during Minnesota's frigid winters.[7] ■

The Internet makes business prototyping practical, fast, and easy. Entrepreneurs can test their ideas by selling their products on established sites such as eBay or by setting up their own Web sites to gauge customers' response. Sometimes business prototyping means that the companies that entrepreneurs end up with bear little resemblance to the businesses that their founders originally envisioned.

 ENTREPRENEURIAL PROFILE: Caterina Fake and Stewart Butterfield: Flickr In 2002, Caterina Fake and Stewart Butterfield launched an online multiplayer social game called Game Neverending. The game had a loyal fan base, but their company had no revenue-generating business model. Fake and Butterfield abandoned it, raised $250,000 from family members and friends, and created an instant-messaging service with game-like features that also allowed users to manage their photographs. Customer feedback led the entrepreneurs to drop the instant-messaging feature and focus on the photo management aspect of their Web site, Flickr. When tagging came along a year later, Flickr, based in Vancouver, British Columbia, provided users with an easy way to organize photos using key words and soon became one of the top photo-sharing sites. Fake credits business prototyping with the company's ultimate success. Originally, "we weren't planning to build a photo-sharing site," she says. Yet business prototyping led the entrepreneurs to do just that, and within one year of launching Flickr, Fake and Butterfield sold the company to Yahoo! for $35 million.[8] ■

Product or Service Feasibility Analysis

Once entrepreneurs discover that sufficient market potential for their product or service idea actually exists, they sometimes rush in with their exuberant enthusiasm ready to launch a business without actually considering whether they can actually produce the product or provide the service at a reasonable cost. A **product or service feasibility analysis** determines the degree to which a product or service idea appeals to potential customers and identifies the resources necessary to produce the product or provide the service. This portion of the feasibility analysis addresses two questions:

- Are customers willing to purchase our goods and services?

- Can we provide the product or service to customers at a profit?

product or service feasibility analysis
an analysis that determines the degree to which a product or service idea appeals to potential customers and indentifies the resources necessary to produce the product or provide the service.

✓ **You Be the Consultant**

Does Your Business Model GEL?

Don Debelak, author of *Business Models Made Easy*, has developed a **GEL** analysis for evaluating business models: **G**reat Customers, **E**asy Sales, and **L**ong Life.

- Four factors make for Great Customers:

  1. **Number of customers.** There should be a sufficient number of customers to allow a business to reach its break-even point.
  2. **Easy to find.** A company should not have to saturate the market or "beat the bushes," both of which are expensive, to reach potential customers.
  3. **Spending patterns.** A company's customers are willing to spend freely on its products or services.
  4. **Ongoing sales support.** Ideally, a company does not have to spend large sums of money for ongoing sales support of its product or service.

Businesses that sell organic food and beverages, a market that is growing at 15 to 20 percent a year, have access to Great Customers because they score high on all four factors.

- Three factors determine whether a business model will have Easy Sales, which Debelak says is the most important GEL factor:

  1. **Importance to potential customers.** Unless customers perceive a company's product as important to them, they are not likely to make buying it a priority. This is where having a clear and compelling competitive advantage makes a difference.
  2. **Customers are easy and inexpensive to acquire.** A business that finds customers easy and inexpensive to acquire usually can reach them in many ways, including retail stores, Web sites, catalogs, home shopping networks, and others.

(continued)

You Be the Consultant *(continued)*

3. **Product or service requires minimal promotional activity.** Like ongoing sales support, promotional activities can require a great deal of effort and money. However, if customers are easy to find (see GEL factor number 1), a business should not have to spend disproportionate sums of money to advertise and promote its product or service.

Many companies in the pet care business have the advantage of Easy Sales because 63 percent of households in the United States (that's 71.1 million households) have pets, and 80 percent of pet owners consider themselves to be "pet parents" who are willing to spend freely across multiple channels to indulge their four-legged "children."

- Five factors influence a company's capacity for Long Life:

  1. **Initial investment required.** The lower the initial investment required to enter a business, the more attractive it is because the risk is lower.
  2. **Cost of staying in business.** Two of the major costs of staying in business are fighting off competitors and investing in technology or product updates to maintain market share.
  3. **Profit margins.** The most important factor in a company's staying power is its profit margins because high profit margins can make up for deficiencies in other GEL factors. The higher the profit margins a business model generates, the more attractive it is.
  4. **Potential for cross selling.** Acquiring a new customer costs seven to nine times as much as selling to an existing one; therefore, a business model that provides the opportunity to sell other products or services to existing customers yields a big advantage.
  5. **Ongoing product costs.** Ongoing product costs, such as providing follow-up sales support or keeping customers informed about changes to a product or service, reduce profits and make a business model less attractive.

Debelak says that a business start-up that does not score high on the GEL factors is likely to struggle to get established and to succeed. Try your hand at applying the model by evaluating the following actual business ideas using the GEL approach. (You may want to establish a 1 [low] to 5 [high] scoring system for each factor to make your analysis more quantifiable.) When you are done, compare your answers to those of some of your classmates. Be prepared to justify the reasoning behind your scores.

Smackages

Rosilyn Rayborn is the founder of Smackages, a Web site that allows women to subscribe and receive free makeup samples sent to their homes from cosmetic companies. "Smackages is like an online makeup counter," says Rayborn, who points out that her company eliminates the hassles of shopping for makeup in stores:

pushy salespeople working on commissions, unsanitary samples, and unflattering fluorescent lighting. Rayborn forecasts sales of $360,000 in the company's first full year of operation. "Cosmetic companies will pay us to distribute samples," she says, "because sampling is the most effective way to get consumers to buy new products." Cawley landed a $20,000 equity investment from the Capital Factory, a business incubator in Austin, Texas, that serves as home to her company. She already has 1,000 subscribers and is seeking $1 million in capital so that she can hire a sales team, license a skin color-matching tool that helps women select the right makeup shades, and add features to the site that allow users to post reviews on Facebook.

ERT Systems

John Ellis, a 25-year veteran firefighter, worked with Dennis Carmichael, owner of an information technology company, and Tony Mazzola, an experienced software developer, to launch ERT Systems, a company that used radio-frequency identification (RFID) tags to track firefighters' locations during a fire. "Fire commanders need to know where their squad members are at all times in case of an emergency, such as a structural collapse during a fire," says Ellis. However, most fire departments use rudimentary systems such as plastic ID cards or whiteboards to make head counts. "Our easily deployable system, OnSite ERT, locates firefighters in real time," he says. The RFID tags that firefighters wear transmit signals to the commander's laptop, which displays the identity and exact location of each firefighter. "Our system also can be used by other emergency personnel, such as SWAT teams," says Ellis. ERT Systems' product is in 40 fire stations, and the company generates $450,000 in annual sales. The price of a system ranges from $20,000 to $50,000, depending on the size of the fire station, and the founders say that the average sales cycle is a lengthy nine months. They are seeking $750,000 in financing to develop the second generation of the OnSite ERT and to sell to more fire departments.

1. Use Debelak's GEL analysis to evaluate the quality of Smackages's and ERT Systems's business models. (You may have to do more research to evaluate each company more accurately.)

2. Based on your analysis in question 1, would you invest in these businesses? Explain.

3. What steps could the founders of these businesses take to improve the quality of their business models?

Sources: Adapted from Nichole L. Torres, "Does It GEL?," *Entrepreneur*, February 2007, p. 93; Don Debelak, "Having a Hard Time Getting Your Product Launched? Maybe It's Your Business Model," *Inventor Help*, 2008, http://dondebelak.net/index.php?page=Online_Article_77; Don Debelak, "GEL Factors—Part 1: Great Customers, '*Inventor Help*, 2008, http://dondebelak.net/index.php?page=Online_Article_78; Don Debelak, "GEL Factors—Part 2: Easy Sales, '*Inventor Help*, 2008, http://dondebelak.net/index.php?page=Online_Article_81; Don Debelak, "Does Your Business Have Staying Power? GEL Factors—Part 3: Long Life," *Inventor Help*, 2008, http://dondebelak.net/index.php?page=Online_Article_84; Issie Lapowsky, "Smackages Lets Women Sample Makeup Online," *Inc.*, March 2011, pp. 100–101; and April Joyner, "ERT Systems Helps Keep Tabs on Firefighters," *Inc.*, December 2009/January 2010, pp. 122–123.

To answer these questions, entrepreneurs need feedback from potential customers. Getting that feedback might involve in primary research such as customer surveys and focus groups, gathering secondary customer research, building prototypes, and conducting in-home trials.

Conducting **primary research** involves collecting data firsthand and analyzing it; **secondary research** involves gathering data that have already been compiled and that are available, often at a very reasonable cost or sometimes even free. In both types of research, gathering both quantitative and qualitative information is important to drawing accurate conclusions about a product's or service's market potential. Primary research techniques are discussed in the following section.

CUSTOMER SURVEYS AND QUESTIONNAIRES Keep surveys short. Word your questions carefully so that you do not bias the results and use a simple ranking system (e.g., a 1-to-5 scale, with 1 representing "definitely would not buy" and 5 representing "definitely would buy"). Test your survey for problems on a small number of people before putting it to use. Web surveys using Survey Monkey and other online tools are inexpensive, are easy to conduct, and provide feedback fast.

Entrepreneur Hugh Crean suggests putting business ideas to the "$20 Starbucks Test" to get honest feedback about their feasibility from people: Walk up to a random person in the nearest Starbucks and tell him or her that you are worried about your brother, who is about to put his life savings into a business idea that you think is totally crazy. Offer to buy the person a cup of coffee to tell you what he or she honestly thinks about the idea. Then pitch your business idea, making note of each person's support or objections. Repeat until you have spent the $20. "If you are talking about a brother who's not there, people will be more candid about shooting down [the idea]," says Crean.[9]

FOCUS GROUPS A **focus group** involves enlisting a small number of potential customers (usually 8 to 12) to give you feedback on specific issues about your product or service (or the business idea itself). Listen carefully for what focus group members like and don't like about your product or service as they tell you what is on their minds. The founders of one small snack food company that produced apple chips conducted several focus groups to gauge customers' acceptance of the product and to guide many key business decisions, ranging from the product's name to its packaging. Once again, consider creating virtual focus groups on the Web; one small bicycle retailer conducts 10 online focus groups each year at virtually no cost and gains valuable marketing information from them. Feedback from online customers is fast, convenient, and real time.

Secondary research, which is usually less expensive to collect than primary data, includes the following sources.

TRADE ASSOCIATIONS AND BUSINESS DIRECTORIES To locate a trade association, use *Business Information Sources* (University of California Press) or the *Encyclopedia of Associations* or the *World Directory of Trade and Business Associations* (Gale Research). To find suppliers, use the *Thomas Register of American Manufacturers* (Thomas Publishing Company) or *Standard & Poor's Register of Corporations, Executives, and Industries* (Standard & Poor's Corporation). *The American Wholesalers and Distributors Directory* (Gale Research) includes details on more than 18,000 wholesalers and distributors.

DIRECT MAIL LISTS You can rent mailing lists for practically any type of business. The *Standard Rates and Data Service (SRDS) Directory of Mailing Lists* (Standard Rates and Data), which includes more than 60,000 lists for rent, is a good place to start looking.

DEMOGRAPHIC DATA To learn more about the demographic characteristics of customers in general, use the *Statistical Abstract of the United States* (Government Printing Office). Profiles of more specific regions are available in the *State and Metropolitan Data Book* (Government Printing Office). The *Sourcebook of ZIP Code Demographics* (ESRI, Inc.) provides detailed breakdowns of the population in every ZIP code in the country. *Sales and Marketing Management's Survey of Buying Power* (Nielsen Business Media) contains comprehensive statistics, rankings, and projections on consumer, retail, and industrial purchasing, including its popular buying power index.

primary research
information that an entrepreneur collects firsthand and analyzes.

secondary research
information that has already been compiled and is available for use, often at a very reasonable cost or sometimes even free.

focus group
a market research technique that involves enlisting a small number of potential customers (usually 8 to 12) to give an entrepreneur feedback on specific issues about a product or service (or the business idea itself).

CENSUS DATA The Bureau of the Census publishes a wide variety of reports that summarize the wealth of data found in its census database, which is available at most libraries and at the Census Bureau's Web site (www.census.gov). Located on the Census Bureau's Web site, the American Factfinder allows entrepreneurs to collect important demographic data ranging from income levels and educational attainment to age and home value for every county and most towns and cities in the United States.

MARKET RESEARCH Someone may already have compiled the market research you need. MarketResearch.com lists more than 160,000 research reports from more than 600 sources that are available for purchase. Other sources of market research include Experian Consumer Research (formerly Simmons Market Research Bureau Inc.), which covers more than 8,000 product categories, and the *A. C. Neilsen Retail Index* (A. C. Neilsen Company).

ARTICLES Magazine and journal articles pertinent to your business are a great source of information. Use the *Reader's Guide to Periodical Literature*, the *Business Periodicals Index* (similar to the *Reader's Guide* but focuses on business periodicals), and *Ulrich's Guide to International Periodicals* to locate the ones you need.

LOCAL DATA Your state department of commerce and your local chamber of commerce will very likely have useful data on the local market of interest to you. Call to find out what is available.

INTERNET Most entrepreneurs are astounded at the marketing information that is available on the Internet. Using one of the search engines, you can gain access to a world of information—literally!

Prototypes

One of the most effective ways to gauge the viability of a product is to build a prototype of it. A **prototype** is an original, functional model of a new product that entrepreneurs can put into the hands of potential customers so that they can see it, test it, and use it. Prototypes usually point out potential problems in a product's design, giving inventors the opportunity to fix them even before they put the prototype into customers' hands. The feedback that customers give entrepreneurs based on prototypes often leads to design improvements and new features, some of which the entrepreneurs might never have discovered on their own. Every entrepreneur can benefit from getting prototypes into customers' hands, gathering feedback and suggestions for improvement, and incorporating them into creating a better product.

prototype
an original, functional model of a new product that entrepreneurs can put into the hands of potential customers so that they can see it, test it, and use it.

ENTREPRENEURIAL PROFILE: Joi Sumpton: Step 'n Wash Joi Sumpton, who invented the Step 'n Wash, a foldable step that gives children easy access to sinks in public restrooms (refer to Chapter 2), spent three years creating prototypes of her product and getting feedback from potential customers. "We tweaked the design several times," she says, "and each time we had to make a new prototype and test everything again." Sumpton thought the design was final with her "last" prototype and began production only to discover a "pinch-point" where a child could be injured that required another prototype that ultimately became the Step 'n Wash. The prototypes played a vital role in helping Sumpton prove that her product was safe, functional, and marketable.[10] ■

Existing companies can benefit from creating prototypes as well.

ENTREPRENEURIAL PROFILE: Ava DeMarco and Robert Brandegee: Little Earth Productions Ava DeMarco and Robert Brandegee, founders of Little Earth Productions, a company that makes distinctive fashion accessories such as belts, handbags, and wallets from recycled bottle caps, license plates, tires, and hubcaps, use prototypes to determine which new products sell best. "When we first started out, we designed new products two weeks before a trade show and hoped people would buy them," says DeMarco. Today, the company creates a small number of prototypes, places them in half a dozen or so retail stores, and tests customers' responses to them. "The feedback lets us know if we're on the right track with a new product before we invest time and money," explains DeMarco.[11] ■

In-Home Trials

One technique that reveals some of the most insightful information into how customers actually use a product or service is also the most challenging to coordinate: in-home trials. An

in-home trial involves sending researchers into customers' homes to observe them as they use the company's product or service.

ENTREPRENEURIAL PROFILE: Scott Cook: Intuit Intuit, the software company that produces popular programs such as Quicken, QuickBooks, and TurboTax, was one of the first companies to adopt in-home trials as part of its product development process in 1989. In the company's follow-me-home program, software engineers would hang around a retail store, waiting for customers to buy an Intuit product. They would then ask to go into customers' homes, where they watch how customers install and use the software and listen to their suggestions in a natural setting. Intuit has adapted the program to its call centers, where customers call with questions about Intuit software. Software managers and product engineers periodically sit at call center employees' desks, looking for ways to improve the employees' ability to serve customers more effectively. The company also combs through blogs and Intuit online communities, looking for comments and feedback about its software products. The process works; the latest version of Quicken included 121 customer-recommended improvements.[12] ∎

Financial Feasibility Analysis

The final component of a feasibility analysis involves assessing the financial feasibility of a proposed business venture. At this stage of the process, a broad financial analysis is sufficient. If the business concept passes the overall feasibility analysis, an entrepreneur should conduct a more thorough financial analysis when creating a full-blown business plan. The major elements to be included in a financial feasibility analysis include the initial capital requirement, estimated earnings, and the resulting return on investment.

CAPITAL REQUIREMENTS Just as a Boy Scout needs fuel to start a fire, an entrepreneur needs capital to start a business. Some businesses require large amounts of capital, but others do not. Typically, service businesses require less capital to launch than do manufacturing or retail businesses. Start-up companies often need capital to purchase equipment, buildings, technology, and other tangible assets as well as to hire and train employees, promote their products and services, and establish a presence in the market. A good feasibility analysis provides an estimate of the amount of start-up capital an entrepreneur needs to get the business up and running. You will learn more about finding sources of business funding, both debt and equity, in Chapter 14.

ESTIMATED EARNINGS In addition to producing an estimate of the start-up company's capital requirements, an entrepreneur also should forecast the earning potential of the proposed business. Industry trade associations and publications such as the *RMA Annual Statement Studies* offer guidelines on preparing sales and earnings estimates. From these, entrepreneurs can estimate the financial results they and their investors can expect to see from the business venture.

RETURN ON INVESTMENT The final aspect of the financial feasibility analysis combines the estimated earnings and the capital requirements to determine the rate of return the venture is expected to produce. One simple measure is the rate of return on the capital invested, which is calculated by dividing the estimated earnings the business yields by the amount of capital invested in the business. Although financial estimates at the feasibility analysis stage typically are rough, they are an important part of the entrepreneur's ultimate "go/no-go" decision about the business ventures. A venture must produce an attractive rate of return relative to the level of risk it requires. This risk–return trade-off means that the higher the level of risk a prospective business involves, the higher the rate of return it must provide to the entrepreneur and investors. Why would an entrepreneur take on all the risks of starting and running a business that produces a mere 1 or 2 percent rate of return when he or she could earn about as much in a risk-free investment at a financial institution? You will learn more about developing detailed financial forecasts for a business start-up in Chapter 12.

Wise entrepreneurs take the time to subject their ideas to a feasibility analysis like the one described here, whatever outcome it produces. If the study suggests that transforming the idea into a viable business is not feasible, the entrepreneur can move on to the next idea, confident that he or she has not wasted valuable resources launching a business destined to fail. If the analysis shows that the idea has real potential as a profitable business, the entrepreneur can pursue it, using the information gathered during the feasibility analysis as the foundation for building a sound business plan. We now turn our attention to that process.

LO2

Explain why every entrepreneur should create a business plan as well as the benefits of developing a plan.

Why Develop a Business Plan?

Any entrepreneur who is in business or is about to launch a business needs a well-conceived and factually based business plan to increase the likelihood of success. For decades, research has proven that companies that engage in business planning outperform those that do not (see Figure 4.3). A recent study by the Small Business Administration reports that entrepreneurs who write business plans early on are two-and-a-half times more likely to actually start their businesses than those who do not.[13] Unfortunately, many entrepreneurs never take the time to develop plans for their businesses, and the implications of the lack of planning are all too evident in the high failure rates that small companies experience.

business plan
a written summary of an entrepreneur's proposed business venture, its operational and financial details, its marketing opportunities and strategy, and its managers' skills and abilities.

A **business plan** is a written summary of an entrepreneur's proposed business venture, its operational and financial details, its marketing opportunities and strategy, and its managers' skills and abilities. There is no substitute for a well-prepared business plan, and there are no shortcuts to creating one. The plan serves as an entrepreneur's road map on the journey toward building a successful business. As a small company's guidebook, a business plan describes the direction the company is taking, what its goals are, where it wants to be, and how it's going to get there. The plan is written proof that an entrepreneur has performed the necessary research, has studied the business opportunity adequately, and is prepared to capitalize on it with a sound business model. One business planning expert says that a business plan is "a written description of your business's future."[14] In short, a business plan is an entrepreneur's best insurance against launching a business destined to fail or mismanaging a potentially successful company.

A business plan serves two essential functions. First and most important, it guides an entrepreneur by charting the company's future course of action and devising a strategy for success. The plan provides a battery of tools—a mission statement, goals, objectives, market analysis, budgets, financial forecasts, target markets, and strategies—to help entrepreneurs lead a company successfully. It gives managers and employees a sense of direction, but only if everyone is involved in creating, updating, or altering it. As more team members become committed to making the plan work, the plan takes on special meaning. It gives everyone targets to shoot for, and it provides a yardstick for measuring actual performance against those targets, especially in the crucial and chaotic start-up phase. Creating a plan also forces entrepreneurs to subject their ideas to the test of reality. Can this business idea actually produce a profit?

The second function of the business plan is to attract lenders and investors. Too often, small business owners approach potential lenders and investors without having prepared to sell themselves and their business concept. Simply scribbling a few rough figures on a notepad to support a loan application is not enough. Applying for loans or attempting to attract investors without a solid business plan rarely attracts needed capital. Rather, the best way to secure the necessary capital is to prepare a sound business plan, enabling an entrepreneur to communicate to potential

FIGURE 4.3
The Benefits of Creating a Business Plan

Source: Palo Alto Software, 2010.

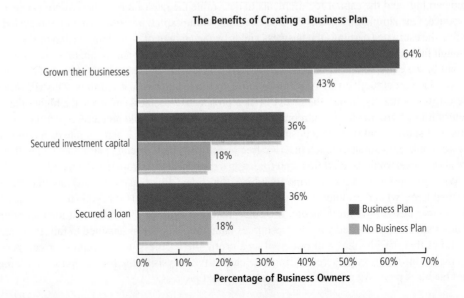

lenders and investors the potential that the business opportunity offers. Entrepreneurs must pay attention to details because they are germane to their sales presentations to potential lenders and investors. The quality of the firm's business plan weighs heavily in the decision to lend or invest funds. It is also potential lenders' and investors' first impression of the company and its managers. Therefore, the finished product should be highly polished and professional in both form and content.

A business plan must prove to potential lenders and investors that the company will be able to repay loans and produce an attractive rate of return. When writing their plans, entrepreneurs who attract capital from lenders and investors must realize that they are stewards of other people's money. If their businesses fail, entrepreneurs lose everything, and their lenders and investors stand to lose all of the money they have put into the company. The goal is to use lenders' and investors' money wisely and return it to them with an attractive yield.

Building a plan forces a potential entrepreneur to look at his or her business idea in the harsh light of reality. It also requires the entrepreneur to assess the venture's chances of success objectively. A well-assembled plan helps prove to outsiders that a business idea can be successful. To get external financing, an entrepreneur's plan must pass three tests with potential lenders and investors: (1) the reality test, (2) the competitive test, and (3) the value test. The first two tests have both an external and an internal component:

REALITY TEST The external component of the reality test revolves around proving that a market for the product or service really does exist. It focuses on industry attractiveness, market niches, potential customers, market size, degree of competition, and similar factors. Entrepreneurs who pass this part of the reality test prove in the marketing portion of their business plan that there is strong demand for their business idea.

The internal component of the reality test focuses on the product or service itself. Can the company *really* build it for the cost estimates in the business plan? Is it truly different from what competitors are already selling? Does it offer customers something of value?

COMPETITIVE TEST The external part of the competitive test evaluates the company's position relative to its key competitors. How do the company's strengths and weaknesses match up with those of the competition? Do these reactions threaten the new company's success and survival?

The internal competitive test focuses on management's ability to create a company that has an edge over existing rivals. To pass this part of the competitive test, a plan must prove the quality, skill, and experience of the venture's management team. What other resources does the company have that can give it a competitive edge in the market?

VALUE TEST To convince lenders and investors to put their money into the venture, a business plan must prove to them that it offers a high probability of repayment or an attractive rate of return. Entrepreneurs usually see their businesses as good investments because they consider the intangibles of owning a business—gaining control over their own destinies, freedom to do what they enjoy, and others; lenders and investors, however, look at a venture in colder terms: dollar-for-dollar returns. A plan must convince lenders and investors that they will earn an attractive return on their money.

The same business basics that investors have employed for decades to evaluate the financial potential of a new venture are still valid today, although during the dot-com craze in the late 1990s, many entrepreneurs and investors lost sight of the importance of practical, profitable business models. The collapse of many of those dot-com companies at the beginning of the twenty-first century proved that unrealistic "smoke-and-mirror" assumptions are no substitute for sound business basics. "Those businesses had full tech staffs and fat marketing budgets," says one business writer, "but a lot of them went belly up because their business plans were no better than the Titanic's plans for dealing with icebergs."[15]

A new venture must have both a long-term strategic vision and a practical focus on operations. In their business plans, entrepreneurs must be able to communicate clearly an understanding of the following:

- Cost of raw materials and supplies
- Unit labor costs

- Market-determined selling prices and gross profit margins
- Break-even point for their businesses[16]

ENTREPRENEURIAL PROFILE: Mike Gaber: Saxon Motorcycles After retiring as chief financial officer from Pulte Homes, Mike Gaber launched Saxon Motorcycles, a builder of semicustom motorcycles, with two former colleagues. Given his business background, Gaber understood the importance of creating a business plan. Writing the plan revealed key insights into competitors' strengths and weaknesses and pricing strategies as well as Saxon's cost structure and break-even point. The plan also helped Gaber and his cofounders to build an efficient, highly productive business. "We introduced process efficiency, controls, and inventory management," says Gaber. "All of the things we learned in homebuilding come into play."[17] ∎

Sometimes the greatest service a business plan provides an entrepreneur is the realization that "it just won't work." The time to find out that a potential business idea won't succeed is in the planning stages *before* an entrepreneur commits significant resources to a venture. In other cases, it reveals important problems to overcome before launching a company.

The real value in preparing a business plan is not so much in the plan itself as it is in the *process* that an entrepreneur goes through to create the plan. Although the finished product is useful, the process of building a plan requires an entrepreneur to subject his or her idea to an objective, critical evaluation. What an entrepreneur learns about his or her company, its target market, its financial requirements, and other factors can be essential to making the start-up a success. "It helped us to think about the company from different angles—product, marketing, sales, financials," says Alex Schultz after presenting the plan for George Guest, the Boston-based retailer of high-end luggage and travel accessories that he cofounded.[18] This process allows the entrepreneur to replace "I think" with "I know" and to make mistakes on paper, something that is much cheaper than making them in reality. Simply put, building a business plan reduces the risk and uncertainty in launching a company by teaching the entrepreneur to do it the right way! Scott Shane, who has conducted studies on entrepreneurs' use of business plans, says,

> The data show that writing business plans increases the odds that a venture will undertake other organizational activities and product development as well as continue in business. Completing a business plan also increases the pace of initiating product development, obtaining inputs, starting marketing, talking to customers, and asking for external funds.[19]

A business plan should reflect the fire and passion an entrepreneur has for the venture; therefore, entrepreneurs should not allow others to prepare the business plan for them because outsiders cannot understand the business concept or envision the proposed company as well as they can. The entrepreneur is the driving force behind the business idea and is the one who can best convey the vision and the enthusiasm he or she has for transforming that idea into a successful business. In addition, because the entrepreneur will make the presentation to potential lenders and investors, he or she must understand every detail of the business plan. Otherwise, an entrepreneur cannot present it convincingly, and in most cases the financial institution or investor will reject it. Investors want to know that an entrepreneur has realistically evaluated the risk involved in the new venture and has a strategy for addressing it. They also want to see proof that a business will be profitable and produce a reasonable return on their investment.

Perhaps the best way to understand the need for a business plan is to recognize the validity of the "two-thirds rule," which says that only two-thirds of the entrepreneurs with a sound and viable new business venture idea will find financial backing. Those who do find financial backing will get only two-thirds of what they initially requested, and it will take them two-thirds longer to get the financing than they anticipated.[20] The most effective strategy for avoiding the two-thirds rule is to build a business plan!

<table>
<tr><td>**LO3**</td></tr>
<tr><td>Describe the elements of a
solid business plan.</td></tr>
</table>

The Elements of a Business Plan

Smart entrepreneurs recognize that every business plan is unique and must be tailor-made. They avoid the off-the-shelf, "cookie-cutter" approach that produces look-alike plans. The elements of a business plan may be standard, but the way entrepreneurs tell their stories should be unique and

✓ You Be the Consultant

Battle of the Plans

In 1984, two MBA students at the University of Texas thought that an experience to teach entrepreneurship in the same comprehensive way that "moot court" competitions taught law would be a good idea. They approached some of their professors and soon launched Moot Corp., the country's first business plan competition in which students competed not only for pride but also for start-up capital to launch their businesses. Known as the Super Bowl of business plan competitions, the Global Moot Court business plan competition now hosts top teams from other qualifying competitions as they compete for cash prizes and in-kind services. In 1989, the Massachusetts Institute of Technology (MIT) started the MIT $10K (now $100K) Entrepreneurship Competition, and many other colleges and universities have followed suit with business plan competitions of their own. "In the 1980s and even in the 1990s, putting on a competition like this was a radical concept," says Randy Swangard, director of the New Venture Championship, a business plan competition started in 1991 at Lundquist College.

Today, hundreds of colleges, universities, and other organizations across the United States sponsor business plan competitions. About 85 colleges and universities sponsor major competitions in which the prizes start in the tens of thousands

Associated Press

of dollars, and it is not uncommon for winners of these competitions to attract serious venture capital from judges. "I have been amazed at the quality of the plans and the companies coming out of these competitions," says Steve Kaplan of the University of Chicago. The largest and richest business plan competition is the Rice Business Plan Competition, hosted by Rice University's Rice Alliance for Technology and Entrepreneurship. The competition began in 2001 with nine teams competing for $10,000 in prize money. Today, 42 teams from across the globe compete in six categories for a share of more than $1.1 million in cash and prizes. The competition's grand prize is worth nearly $650,000, including $500,000 in equity investments, $121,000 in business services, and $20,000 in cash. Rice University officials say that 38 percent of the 354 teams that have participated in the competition have actually launched their companies and are still in business, have raised more than $337 million in financing, and employ more than 600 people.

The cofounders of BiologicsMD, Michael Thomas, Robyn Goforth, Misty Stevens, and Paul Mlaker, found their business opportunity when they discovered that researchers at the University of Arkansas had developed a drug that treats osteoporosis with an annual injection (rather than the less effective, daily injections that other treatments require) and reverses the effects of the disease by stimulating the growth of new, stronger bone. The drug, called OsteoFlor, also helps heal bone fractures quickly. The student entrepreneurs created a business plan, launched BiologicsMD to commercialize the new treatment, and began entering business plan competitions across the United States. In just one year, the team won $102,500 in cash, $150,000 in business services, and $300,000 in investments in six business plan competitions and placed first in both the Rice Business Plan Competition and the Global Moot Corp. competition. BiologicsMD has since raised $2.3 million from the Department of Defense and another $500,000 from private sources and is now working OsteoFlor through drug trials mandated by the Food and Drug Administration. Team members say that once OsteoFlor is on the market, they intend to scour the world to identify other lifesaving breakthroughs that may be languishing in university research labs.

Faculty and students alike find the idea of business plan competitions appealing because they provide an all-encompassing educational experience. As they prepare their plans, students learn a comprehensive set of business skills, ranging from conducting industry and market research and assembling a new venture team to developing realistic financial forecasts and writing mission statements. They also learn valuable skills as they present their plans to panels of judges that often include successful entrepreneurs, bankers, venture capitalists, and other business heavy hitters. "If you want to launch an entrepreneurship program at your business school," advises Gary Cadenhead, director of Moot Corp., "it makes sense to start a business plan competition because students learn topics such as intellectual property and trademarks, venture capital, and guerrilla marketing." Two valuable lessons that often come from business plan competitions are that it takes more than

(continued)

You Be the Consultant (continued)

just a good idea to build a successful business venture and that building a business is hard work.

Competition winners say that start-up capital is just one of the many benefits they receive. The feedback from the judges, the recognition and credibility they earn as winners, and the contacts they make with potential partners, private investors, and venture capitalists may be worth more in the long run. Many entrepreneurs also cite the benefits of the discipline that writing a business plan requires. Angela Keaveny, founder of Rowdydow BBQ, which makes seasoned, ready-to-cook pork, failed to place two years in a row in the City Treasurer's Business Plan Competition in Chicago but says that the process and the experience were priceless. She credits the plan she prepared for the competition with keeping her on track to generate sales of $250,000 and attracting capital from private investors to get her product into supermarkets.

Much like the runners-up on *American Idol*, teams that don't win the competition usually reap significant benefits. Since placing second in a recent Rice Business Plan Competition, the cofounders of Rebellion Photonics, a company that developed hyperspectral imaging technology that allows users to determine an object's chemical composition in real time, have used the contacts and publicity from the competition to raise more than $1 million, which allowed them to bring their product to market. The team, which operates the business in a five-bedroom house near Rice University, is now seeking $10 million to introduce its second product, a camera capable of detecting gas leaks that are invisible to the naked eye.

According to one business writer, "Business plan competitions remind would-be entrepreneurs that success requires a solid business plan even more than a bountiful bank balance. Once students have truly learned that business basic, they're not only better prepared to play the entrepreneurial game, they're more likely to end up as winners."

1. If your school does not already have a business plan competition, work with a team of your classmates in a brainstorming session to develop ideas for creating one. What would you offer as a prize? How would you finance the competition? Whom would you invite to judge it? How would you structure the competition?

2. Use the Internet to research business plan competitions at other colleges and universities across the nation. Using the competitions at these schools as benchmarks and the ideas you generated in the previous question, develop a format for a business plan competition at your school.

3. Assume that you are a member of a team of entrepreneurial students competing in a prestigious business plan competition. Outline your team's strategy for winning the competition.

Sources: Based on Josh Hyatt, "Battle of the Business Plans," *Fortune*, May 24, 2010, pp. 35–42; "Rice University Business Plan Competition Awards $1.3 Million in Cash and Prizes," *Rice Alliance*, April 18, 2011, http://www.alliance.rice.edu/alliance/NewsBot.asp?MODE=VIEW&ID=128; Anne VanderMey, "What Happens to Biz Plan Competition Winners?," *CNNMoney*, May 27, 2011, http://money.cnn.com/galleries/2011/smallbusiness/1104/gallery.rice_business_plan_competition_past_winners.fortune/index.html; Lora Kolodny, "Company with Osteoporosis Treatment Wins the 'Super Bowl,'" *New York Times*, May 10, 2010, http://boss.blogs.nytimes.com/2010/05/10/company-with-osteoporosis-treatment-wins-the-super-bowl; Emily Maltby, "And the Prize Goes to . . . a Different Company," *Wall Street Journal*, June 10, 2010, p. B4; Alina Dizik, "Where Big Ideas Win Big Bucks," *Business Week*, November 13, 2007, http://www.businessweek.com/bschools/content/nov2007/bs20071113_247178.htm?chan=search; Alison Damast, "How to Win a B-School Competition," *Business Week*, May 30, 2007, http://www.businessweek.com/bschools/content/may2007/bs20070530_800860.htm; Kelly K. Spors, "Business Plan Contests Become 'American Idol Meets Trump,'" *Wall Street Journal*, December 11, 2007, pp. B1, B4; Amy Haimerl, "Killer Start-Ups," *FSB*, November 2007, pp. 75–80; Zak Stambor, "Venture Prone," *University of Chicago Magazine* 100, no. 4 (March/April 2008), http://magazine.uchicago.edu/0834/features/venture.shtml; and "Eight Great Business Plans, but Only One Is the Winner," Knowledge@Wharton, May 5, 2005, http://knowledge.wharton.upenn.edu/index.cfm?fa=printArticle&ID=1190.

reflect their enthusiasm for the new venture. If this is a first attempt at writing a business plan, it may be very helpful to seek the advice of individuals with experience in this process. Accountants, business professors, attorneys, and consultants with Small Business Development Centers can be excellent sources of advice in creating and refining a plan. (For a list of Small Business Development Center locations, see the Small Business Administration's Web SBDC Web page at www.sba.gov/SBDC.) Entrepreneurs also can use business planning software available from several companies to create their plans. Some of the most popular programs include Business Plan Pro* (Palo Alto Software), BizPlan Builder (Jian Tools), PlanMaker (Power Solutions for Business), and Plan Write (Business Resources Software). These planning packages help entrepreneurs organize the material they have researched and gathered, and they provide helpful tips on plan writing and templates for creating financial statements. These planning packages produce professional-looking business plans, but entrepreneurs who use them face one drawback: the plans they produce often look the same, as if they came from the same mold. That can be a turnoff for professional investors, who see hundreds of business plans each year.

Initially, the prospect of writing a business plan may appear to be overwhelming. Many entrepreneurs would rather launch their companies and "see what happens" than invest the necessary time and energy defining and researching their target markets, defining their strategies, and mapping out their finances. After all, building a plan is hard work! However, it is hard work

---

*Business Plan Pro is available at a nominal cost with this textbook.

that pays many dividends—not all of them immediately apparent. Entrepreneurs who invest their time and energy building plans are better prepared to face the hostile environment in which their companies will compete than those who do not. Earlier, we said that a business plan is like a road map that guides an entrepreneur on the journey to building a successful business. If you were making a journey to a particular destination through unfamiliar, harsh, and dangerous territory, would you rather ride with someone equipped with a road map and a trip itinerary or with someone who didn't believe in road maps or in planning trips, destinations, and layovers? Although building a business plan does not *guarantee* success, it *does* raise an entrepreneur's chances of succeeding in business.

A business plan typically ranges from 20 to 40 pages in length. Shorter plans usually are too sketchy to be of any value, and those much longer than this run the risk of never getting used or read! This section explains the most common elements of a business plan. However, entrepreneurs must recognize that, like every business venture, every business plan is unique. An entrepreneur should view the following elements as a starting point for building a plan and should modify them as needed to better tell the story of his or her new venture.

Title Page and Table of Contents

A business plan is a professional document and should contain a title page with the company's name, logo, and address as well as the names and contact information of the company founders. Many entrepreneurs also include the copy number of the plan and the date on which it was issued on the title page. Business plan readers appreciate a table of contents that includes page numbers so that they can locate the particular sections of the plan in which they are most interested.

Executive Summary

To summarize the presentation to each potential financial institution or investors, an entrepreneur should write an executive summary. It should be concise—a maximum of two pages—and should summarize all of the relevant points of the business venture. The executive summary is a synopsis of the entire plan, capturing its essence in a capsulized form. It should briefly describe the following:

- Customer's "pain point" and why it is significant
- Company's target market(s) and the benefits that its products or services will provide customers
- Company's business model and the basis for its competitive edge
- Qualifications of the founding team and key employees
- Key financial highlights (e.g., sales and earnings projections, capital required, rates of return on the investment, and when any loans will be repaid)

The executive summary is a written version of what is known as the "elevator pitch." Imagine yourself on an elevator with a potential lender or investor. Only the two of you are on the elevator, and you have that person's undivided attention for the duration of the ride, but the building is not very tall! To convince the investor that your business is a great investment, you must boil your message down to its essence—key points that you can communicate in just a matter of one or two minutes: what your company does, why it matters, and what sets it apart. An elevator pitch must answer the natural question that anyone who reads or hears it asks: "So what?" The following five-part framework helps entrepreneurs develop a meaningful elevator pitch:

1. *Context.* What does your company do in easy-to-understand words?
2. *Benefit.* What benefit or advantage does your company offer customers?
3. *Target customers.* For whom does your company provide the benefit?
4. *Point of differentiation.* How is your company different from other companies that provide similar products, services, or solutions?
5. *Clincher.* Can you leave the listener or reader with a memorable, bottom-line sound bite about your company?[21]

Dave Yewman, co-owner of Elevator Speech, a company that helps executives hone their elevator pitches, shows a video to his clients that features what he says is "the worst elevator speech ever." When asked what his e-commerce consulting company did, the founder replied, "We've asked our clients to reconceptualize their business. We've reconceptualized what it is to be in the service business." When asked once again to explain what his company did *in English*, the CEO replied, "We provide services to companies that help them win." A third attempt produced no better results: "We radically transform businesses to invent and reinvent them."[22]

An entrepreneur must make sure that the company's elevator pitch is fine-tuned and on target because an executive summary *must* capture the reader's attention. If it misses the mark, the chances of the remainder of the plan being read are minimal. "If you can't tell it, you can't sell it," says Nell Merlino, CEO of Count Me In for Women's Economic Independence, which sponsors an elevator pitch competition for women business owners.[23] A well-developed, coherent summary introducing the financial proposal establishes a favorable first impression of the entrepreneur and the business and can go a long way toward obtaining financing. Although the executive summary is the first part of the business plan, it should be the last section written.

Vision and Mission Statement

As you learned in Chapter 3, a mission statement expresses in words an entrepreneur's vision for what his or her company is and what it is to become. It is the broadest expression of a company's purpose and defines the direction in which it will move. It anchors a company in reality and serves as the thesis statement for the entire business plan. Every good plan captures an entrepreneur's passion and vision for the business, and the mission statement is the ideal place to express them.

Company History

The owner of an existing small business who is creating a business plan should prepare a brief history of the operation, highlighting the significant financial and operational events in the company's life. This section should describe when and why the company was formed, how it has evolved over time, and what the owner envisions for the future. It should highlight the successful accomplishment of past objectives, such as developing prototypes, earning patents, achieving market-share targets, or securing long-term customer contracts. This section also should describe the company's current image in the marketplace.

Business and Industry Profile

To acquaint lenders and investors with the industry in which a company competes, an entrepreneur should describe it in the business plan. This section should provide the reader with an overview of the industry or market segment in which the new venture will operate. Industry data such as market size, growth trends, and the relative economic and competitive strength of the major firms in the industry all set the stage for a better understanding of the viability of the new product or service. Strategic issues such as ease of market entry and exit, the ability to achieve economies of scale or scope, and the existence of cyclical or seasonal economic trends further help readers evaluate the new venture. This part of the plan also should describe significant industry trends and key success factors as well as an overall outlook for its future. Information about the evolution of the industry helps the reader comprehend its competitive dynamics.

goals
broad, long-range statements of what a company plans to achieve in the future that guide its overall direction.

objectives
short-term specific performance targets that are attainable, measurable, and controllable.

Goals and Objectives

This section should contain a statement of the company's general business goals and then work down to a narrower definition of its immediate objectives. Together, they should spell out what the business plans to accomplish, how and when it plans to do so, and who will do it. **Goals** are broad, long-range statements of what a company plans to achieve in the future that guide its overall direction. In other words, they address the question, "What do I want my company to look like in three to five years?"

Objectives, on the other hand, are short-term, specific performance targets that are attainable, measurable, and controllable. Every objective should reflect some general business goal and should include a technique for measuring progress toward its accomplishment. To be meaningful, an objective must have a time frame for achievement. Both goals and objectives should relate to the company's basic mission (see Figure 4.4).

FIGURE 4.4

Mission, Goals, and Objectives

Business Strategy

Another important part of a business plan is the owner's view of the strategy needed to meet—and beat—the competition. In the previous section, the entrepreneur defined *where* to take the business by establishing goals and objectives. This section addresses the question of *how* to get there—business strategy. Here an entrepreneur must explain how he or she plans to gain a competitive edge in the market and what sets the business apart from the competition, commenting on how he or she plans to achieve business goals and objectives in the face of competition and identifying the image that the business will try to project. An important theme in this section is what makes the company unique in the eyes of its customers. One of the quickest routes to business failure is trying to sell "me-too" products or services that offer customers nothing new, better, or different from existing products or services.

The strategy section of the business plan should outline the methods the company can use to satisfy the key success factors required to thrive in the industry. If, for example, a strong, well-trained sales force is considered critical to success, the owner must devise a plan of action for assembling one. The foundation for this part of the business plan comes from the material in Chapter 3.

Description of the Company's Product or Service

An entrepreneur should describe the company's overall product line, giving an overview of how customers use its goods or services. Drawings, diagrams, and illustrations may be required if the product is highly technical. It is best to write product and service descriptions in a jargon-free style so that laypeople can understand them. A statement of a product's position in the product life cycle might also be helpful. An entrepreneur should include a summary of any patents, trademarks, or copyrights protecting the product or service from infringement by competitors. Finally, it is helpful to provide an honest comparison of the company's product or service with those of competitors, citing specific advantages or improvements that make his or her goods or services unique and indicating plans for creating the next generation of goods and services that will evolve from the present product line.

The emphasis of this section should be on defining the unique characteristics of the company's products or services and the *benefits* customers get by purchasing them rather than on just a "nuts-and-bolts" description of the *features* of those products or services. A **feature** is a descriptive fact about a product or service ("An ergonomically designed, more comfortable handle"). A **benefit** is what a customer gains from the product or service feature ("Fewer problems with carpal tunnel syndrome and increased productivity"). Advertising legend Leo Burnett once said, "Don't tell the people how good you make the goods; tell them how good your goods make them." This part of the plan must describe how a business will transform tangible product or service *features* into important but often intangible customer *benefits*—for example, lower energy bills, faster access to the Internet, less time writing checks to pay monthly bills, greater flexibility in building floating structures, shorter time required to learn a foreign language, or others. Remember that customers buy benefits, *not* product or service features.

feature
a descriptive fact about a product or service.

benefit
what a customer gains from the product or service.

ENTREPRENEURIAL PROFILE: Lynn Jurich and Edward Fenster: Sunrun While enrolled at the Stanford Graduate School of Business, Lynn Jurich and Edward Fenster developed the business model for Sunrun. The company owns, insures, monitors, and maintains the solar panels on a home owner's roof (costing about $40,000 to purchase and install), while families pay a low rate for clean energy. The plan required a significant amount of capital to purchase and install the panels on customers' homes. Jurich, who had worked at venture capital firm Summit Partners, understood the importance of selling benefits rather than features, and Sunrun's business model offered significant benefits. "It's a win-win-win," says Jurich. When Sunrun installs solar panels on homes for nominal or no cost, the owners sign 20-year agreements to purchase solar-generated electricity at fixed rates that are 10 to 15 percent lower than their current rates. (If customers sell their houses, their contracts are transferable to the next owner.) Sunrun reaps the benefit of predictable long-term revenues and costs, and the environment is cleaner because home owners are using a clean energy source. By pitching the benefits that their business model offers, Jurich and Fenster have landed more than 20,000 customers in 10 states. They also used their business plan to raise capital to support the purchase of over $1 billion in solar systems.[24] ■

Marketing Strategy

One crucial concern of entrepreneurs and the potential lenders and investors who finance their companies is whether there is a real market for the proposed good or service. Every entrepreneur must therefore describe the company's target market and its characteristics. Defining the target market and its potential is one of the most important—and most challenging—parts of building a business plan. Creating a successful business depends on an entrepreneur's ability to attract real customers who are willing and able to spend real money to buy its products or services. Perhaps the worst marketing error an entrepreneur can commit is failing to define his or her target market and trying to make his or her business "everything to everybody." Small companies usually are much more successful focusing on a specific market niche where they can excel at meeting customers' special needs or wants.

One technique for identifying potential target markets is to list all of the features that your company's product or service provides and then translate those features into a list of benefits (refer to the previous section). The next step is to develop a list of the types of people who need or could use those benefits. Be creative and let your mind roam free. Once you have identified potential target markets, you can begin to research them to narrow the list down to the most promising one or two. Those are the markets your company should pursue.

One growing and evolving target market for small businesses is the U.S. Hispanic market, which is the second largest in the world, behind only Mexico. With 50.5 million people, the Hispanic market makes up 15.1 percent of the total U.S. population and is expected to grow to 64 million by 2015 and have purchasing power that exceeds $1.3 trillion.[25] "If you want your company to grow, you had better market to Latinos or you are missing the boat," says Hispanic marketing expert Chiqui Cartagena.[26]

Pizza Patrón Inc.

ENTREPRENEURIAL PROFILE: Antonio Swad: Pizza Patrón In 1986, Antonio Swad started Pizza Patrón ("Pizza Boss" in Spanish) in Dallas, Texas, and differentiated his brand by targeting an untapped segment of the pizza market: Hispanic customers. In addition to traditional pizzas, Swad's menu includes toppings such as chorizo, a spicy sausage that originated in Mexico, and side items such as lime-and-pepper chicken wings, cheese sticks called QuesoStix, and churros, a fried dough dessert with a caramel filling. Pizza Patrón also runs limited-time offers of Hispanic dishes such as caramel candies made with goat's milk and pecans. Pizza Patrón's sales have grown in step with the Hispanic population in the United States, and in 2007 the company solidified its position as the number one Latin pizza brand when it began accepting Mexican pesos in all of its stores. Traditionally, Pizza Patrón opened its stores in neighborhoods in which at least 50 percent of the population was Hispanic and ran almost all of its ads in Spanish-language media. Responding to a changing Hispanic customer base that is now younger and more bicultural, Swad has begun producing more ads in English, opening stores in locations with as little as 30 percent Hispanic residents, and expanding into states in which the Hispanic population is growing fast, such as North Carolina, Michigan, and Oregon. "These are Hispanics born in the U.S. who have one foot in each culture," says Andrew Gamm, the company's brand director. Pizza Patrón now operates more than 100 restaurants in seven southwestern states and generates more than $40 million in annual sales.[27] ■

Defining a company's target market involves using the techniques described in more detail in Chapter 6, but a business plan should address the following questions:

● Who are my target customers (age, gender, income level, and other demographic characteristics)?

● Where do they live, work, and shop?

- How many potential customers are in my company's trading area?

- Why do they buy? What needs and wants drive their purchase decisions?

- What can my business do to meet those needs and wants better than my competitors?

- Knowing my customers needs, wants, and habits, what should be the basis for differentiating my business in their minds?

Proving that a profitable market exists involves two steps: documenting market claims and showing customer interest.

Documenting Market Claims

Too many business plans rely on vague generalizations such as, "This market is so huge that if we get just 1 percent of it, we will break even in eight months." Statements such as this are not backed by facts and usually reflect an entrepreneur's unbridled optimism. In most cases, they are also unrealistic, and potential lenders and investors quickly dismiss them. Market share determination is not obtained by "shoot-from-the-hip" generalizations; on the contrary, sophisticated investors expect to see research that supports the claims an entrepreneur makes about the market potential of a product or service.

Providing facts about the sales potential of a product or service requires market research. Results of market surveys, customer questionnaires, and demographic studies lend credibility to an entrepreneur's frequently optimistic sales projections. (You will learn more about market research techniques and resources in Chapter 8.)

ENTREPRENEURIAL PROFILE: James Poss: Seahorse Power In his business plan, James Poss, founder of Seahorse Power, a company that makes solar-powered trash compactors, identified the primary target customer as resorts and amusement parks and included market research on them. Today, Poss admits that the plan was off "by a long shot"; in realty, the company's major customers turned out to be cities and municipal governments. "We were out there selling a boxy-looking, ugly machine for close to two years," he says. "I could have shown [potential customers] a picture and said, 'Would you buy this?' and saved myself a lot of money." Although Seahorse Power now generates sales of more than $3 million, Poss learned a valuable lesson about "actually getting out in the field and talking to people."[28] ■

Showing Customer Interest

As important as providing convincing market research is, proving that a significant group of target customers actually need or want a company's good or service and are willing to pay for it is even more so. Two of the most reliable techniques involve building a working prototype of a product so that customers can see how it works and producing a small number of products so that customers can actually use them. An entrepreneur might offer a prototype or an actual product to several potential customers to get written testimonials and evaluations to show potential investors.

ENTREPRENEURIAL PROFILE: Nate Alder: Klymit That's the approach that Nate Alder took for his company, Klymit, which makes a temperature-adjustable jacket for snow skiers. Alder, a scuba diver, knew that divers used inert gases such as argon as insulation in dry suits during cold-water dives and thought that the same concept could keep skiers comfortable on the slopes. "It's inconvenient to wear bulky layers for the summit just to peel them off at the base, where it is 30 degrees warmer," he says. Alder, a student at Brigham Young University, created a prototype jacket that contains a series of airtight chambers and a lipstick case–sized cartridge of pressurized argon. At cold temperatures, the wearer turns a knob to fill the chambers with argon, which has properties that seal in heat and block out cold. Turning the valve the other way releases the harmless gas, cooling the skier. A cartridge, which sells for $15, lasts for 10 days on the slopes. Before approaching potential lenders and investors, Alder used the prototype to acquire letters of intent from three top sports companies that want to license the technology for use in their products. "Like Velcro, [Klymit] is a simple solution to a big problem," says Alder.[29] ■

Another way to get useful feedback is to sell the product to several customers at a discount. This proves that potential customers for the product do exist and allows for demonstrations of the product in operation. Getting a product into customers' hands early in the process also is an excellent way to get valuable feedback that can lead to significant design improvements and increased sales down the road.

One of the goals of the marketing strategy section of the business plan is to lay the foundation for the financial forecasts that come later in the plan. A start-up company's financial forecasts must be based on more than just wishful thinking. As much as possible, they should be built on research and facts. Many entrepreneurs build financial models for their potential business by applying information collected from trade or professional associations, local chambers of commerce, articles in magazines and newspapers, market studies conducted by themselves or others, government agencies, and, of course, the Internet. With the availability of this volume of information, the sales, cost, and net income projections in a business plan should be a great deal more accurate than sketchy estimates scribbled on the backs of napkins.

This section of the business plan also should address the following topics:

Advertising. Once entrepreneurs define their companies' target markets, they can design promotion and advertising campaigns to reach those customers most effectively and efficiently. Which media are most effective in reaching the target market? How much will the promotional campaign cost? How can the company utilize publicity?

Market size and trends. How large is the potential market? Is it growing or shrinking? Why? Are the customer's needs changing? Are sales seasonal? Is demand tied to another product or service?

Location. For many businesses, choosing the right location is a key success factor. For retailers, wholesalers, and service companies, the best location usually is one that is most convenient for their target customers. By combining census data and other market research with digital mapping software, entrepreneurs can select sites with the greatest concentrations of their customers and the least interference from competitors. Which specific sites put the company in the path of its target customers? Do zoning regulations restrict the use of the site? For manufacturers, the location issue often centers on finding a site near its key raw materials or near its major customers. Using demographic reports and market research to screen potential sites takes the guesswork out of choosing the ideal location for a business.

Pricing. What does the product or service cost to produce or deliver? What is the company's overall pricing strategy? What image is the company trying to create in the market? Is the pricing strategy consistent with the company's desired image? Will it produce a profit? How does the price compare to those of similar products or services? Are customers willing to pay it? What price tiers exist in the market? How sensitive are customers to price changes? Will the business sell to customers on credit? Will it accept credit cards?

Distribution. A company's distribution strategy defines how it will get its products or services into customers' hands. Retail stores with physical locations count on customers walking in and taking the goods they purchase with them, but other types of businesses must create a viable, efficient distribution strategy. Will your company be solely Internet based? Will you hire a sales force to make calls on customers? Will you sell to retailers or value-added resellers who are responsible for distributing your product or service? Will you use independent sales representatives?

Photo Courtesy Stella & Dot

ENTREPRENEURIAL PROFILE: Jessica DiLullo Herrin: Stella & Dot *Jessica DiLullo Herrin, founder of Stella & Dot, a San Francisco–based company that sells boutique-style jewelry and accessories, relies on the Internet and in-home trunk shows led by more than 10,000 independent sales representatives (called "stylists" inside the company) for distribution. After launching one successful business, WeddingChannel, at 24, Herrin became a mother and wanted to use a distribution system for her second company that would allow her and other mothers to generate income for their families while retaining flexibility in their schedules and balance in their lives. Stella & Dot recently made* Inc. *magazine's list of the 500 fastest-growing companies and generates sales of more than $100 million annually.*[30] ∎

Competitor Analysis

An entrepreneur should discuss the new venture's competition. Failing to assess competitors realistically makes entrepreneurs appear to be poorly prepared, naive, or dishonest, especially to potential lenders and investors. An analysis of each significant competitor should be presented. Entrepreneurs who believe that they have no competitors are only fooling themselves and are raising a huge red flag to potential lenders and investors. Gathering information on competitors' market shares, products, and strategies is usually not difficult. Trade associations, customers, industry journals, marketing representatives, and sales literature are valuable sources of data. This section of the plan should focus on demonstrating that the entrepreneur's company has an advantage over its competitors. Who are the company's key competitors? What are their strengths and weaknesses? What are their strategies? What images do they have in the marketplace? How successful are they? What distinguishes the entrepreneur's product or service from others already on the market, and how will these differences produce a competitive edge? This section of the plan should demonstrate that the company's strategy is customer focused.

ENTREPRENEURIAL PROFILE: Shelly Gardner-Alley: Paper Mojo Frustrated with her job as a Web site designer, Shelly Gardner-Alley decided to launch an e-commerce business with her husband. The couple did not have a particular product in mind, but they invested considerable time in researching markets that would be most suitable for e-commerce and that would allow them to differentiate their business from the competition. They finally settled on an online business selling high-end, decorative paper from all over the world—ranging from silk paper from Japan to translucent vellum from France—at prices ranging from $2 to $16 per sheet. Before launching their business, Paper Mojo, one of their first tasks was to study their competition. Gardner-Alley discovered that most companies lacked extensive product lines, and she decided to use that as one differentiating point for her business. As a former Web site designer, Gardner-Alley also noted that the few companies that did have broad product lines suffered from poorly designed Web sites that made shopping a chore for customers. A well-designed Web site that would be easy to navigate became another basis for differentiating her company from the competition. Paper Mojo's sales took off after Gardner-Alley submitted the site to search engine Yahoo!, which featured the new business in a newsletter. Gardner-Alley's extensive research and the decision to base her business model on outperforming the competition in ways that directly benefit customers are paying off.[31] ■

Description of the Management Team

The most important factor in the success of a business venture is the quality of its management, and lenders and investors weigh heavily the ability and experience of the company's managers in their financing decisions. Thus, a plan should describe the qualifications of business officers, key directors, and any person with at least 20 percent ownership in the company. Remember that lenders and investors prefer experienced managers. A management team with industry experience and a proven record of success goes a long way in adding credibility to the new venture.

ENTREPRENEURIAL PROFILE: Eric Lagier, Harry Vangberg, and Nikolaj Nielsen: Momolane Eric Lagier, a former manager at Skype, attended a Startup Weekend event in Copenhagen, Denmark, where he pitched an idea for a company that would allow customers to consolidate their online presence from sites such as Facebook, YouTube, Twitter, Flickr, and others into an interactive time line that tells their social life stories. During the Startup Weekend, Lagier met Harry Vangberg, cofounder of FirmaFon ApS, a telecommunications company, and Nikolaj Nielsen, a software engineer and developer, and the three decided to launch a company, Memolane, based on Lagier's idea. Recognizing the importance of a solid team, the three cofounders added designer Aubrey Johnson, Cody Lindley, "a JavaScript McGyver," and former journalist Meghan Krane to their start-up team. "The team is the key to success," says Lagier. "Invest your time in finding the right cofounders and team members." After building a prototype Web site, the founders of Memolane landed $2 million in venture capital funding.[32] ■

Résumés in a plan should summarize each key person's education, work history (emphasizing managerial responsibilities and duties), and relevant business experience. Entrepreneurs should not hide previous business failures. Failing in business no longer has a terrible stigma attached to it. In fact, many investors are suspicious of entrepreneurs who have never experienced a business failure.

When considering investing in a business, lenders and investors look for the experience, talent, and integrity of the people who will breathe life into the plan. This portion of the plan should show that the company has the right people organized in the right fashion for success. One experienced private investor advises entrepreneurs to remember the following:

- Ideas and products don't succeed; people do. Show the strength of your management team. A top-notch management team with a variety of proven skills is crucial.

- Show the strength of key employees and how you will retain them. Most small companies cannot pay salaries that match those at large businesses, but stock options and other incentives can improve employee retention.

- A board of directors or advisers consisting of industry experts lends credibility and can enhance the value of the management team.[33]

Plan of Operation

To complete the description of the business, the owner should construct an organizational chart that identifies the business's key jobs and the qualifications of the people occupying them. Assembling a management team with the right stuff is difficult, but keeping it together until the company is established may be harder. Therefore, the entrepreneur should describe briefly incentives he or she offers to encourage important officers to remain with the company. Employment contracts, shares of ownership, and benefits are commonly used to keep and motivate key employees.

Finally, a description of the form of ownership (partnership, joint venture, S corporation, or limited liability company) and of any leases, contracts, and other relevant agreements pertaining to the business is helpful. (You will learn more about this topic in Chapter 5.)

Pro Forma (Projected) Financial Statements

One of the most important sections of the business plan is an outline of the proposed company's financial statements—the "dollars and cents" of the proposed venture. In fact, one survey found that 74 percent of bankers say that financial documentation is the most important aspect of a business plan for entrepreneurs seeking loans.[34] For an existing business, lenders and investors use past financial statements to judge the health of the company and its ability to repay loans or generate adequate returns; therefore, an owner should supply copies of the firm's financial statements from the past three years. Ideally, these statements should be audited by a certified public accountant because most financial institutions prefer that extra reliability, although a financial review of the statements by an accountant may be acceptable.

Whether assembling a plan for an existing business or for a start-up, an entrepreneur should carefully prepare monthly projected financial statements for the operation for the next year (and for two more years by quarter) using past operating data, published statistics, and research to derive three sets of forecasts of the income statement, balance sheet, cash forecast (always!), and a schedule of planned capital expenditures. (You will learn more about creating projected financial statements in Chapter 12 and about cash forecasts in Chapter 13.) The forecasts should cover pessimistic, most likely, and optimistic conditions to reflect the uncertainty of the future.

It is essential that all three sets of forecasts be realistic, and this often gives entrepreneurs problems because they are quite optimistic. A recent study of start-up companies in Germany over a five-year time period reports that entrepreneurs' financial estimates are rather inaccurate. Their forecasted revenues were 388 percent higher on average than their actual revenues, and they also overestimated their expenses by an average of 211 percent. The entrepreneurs' plans overestimated their actual profits by 136 percent, although their estimates of first-year profits were consistently too low.[35] The study shows why many potential lenders and investors discount entrepreneurs' financial projections as they analyze their business plans. In addition to projected income statements, balance sheets, and cash flow forecasts, an entrepreneur should perform a break-even analysis. The study of German start-up companies shows that the typical company expects to break even after three years.

It is also important to include a statement of the *assumptions* on which these financial projections are based. Potential lenders and investors want to know how an entrepreneur derived forecasts for sales, cost of goods sold, operating expenses, accounts receivable, collections, accounts payable, inventory, taxes, and other items. Spelling out realistic assumptions gives a plan more credibility and reduces the tendency to include overly optimistic estimates of sales growth and profit margins. Greg Martin, a partner in the venture capital company Redpoint Ventures, says, "I have problems with start-ups making unrealistic assumptions—how much money they need or how quickly they can ramp up revenue. Those can really kill a deal for me."[36]

In addition to providing valuable information to potential lenders and investors, projected financial statements help entrepreneurs run their businesses more effectively and more efficiently after the start-up. They establish important targets for financial performance and make it easier for an entrepreneur to maintain control over routine expenses and capital expenditures.

The Loan or Investment Proposal

The loan or investment proposal section of the business plan should state the purpose of the financing, the amount requested, and the plans for repayment or, in the case of investors, an attractive exit strategy. When describing the purpose of the loan or investment, an entrepreneur must specify the planned use of the funds. General requests for funds using terms such as "for modernization," "working capital," or "expansion" are unlikely to win approval. Instead, entrepreneurs should use more detailed descriptions such as "to modernize production facilities by purchasing five new, more efficient looms that will boost productivity by 12 percent" or "to rebuild merchandise inventory for fall sales peak, beginning in early summer." Entrepreneurs should state the precise amount requested and include relevant backup data, such as vendor estimates of costs or past production levels. Entrepreneurs should not hesitate to request the amount of money needed but should not inflate the amount anticipating the financial officer to "talk them down." Remember that lenders and investors are normally very familiar with industry cost structures.

Another important element of the loan or investment proposal is the repayment schedule and exit strategy. A lender's main consideration in granting a loan is the reassurance that the applicant will repay, whereas an investor's major concern is earning a satisfactory rate of return. Financial projections must reflect a company's ability to repay loans and produce adequate returns. Without this proof, a request for funding stands little chance of being approved. It is necessary for the entrepreneur to produce tangible evidence showing the ability to repay loans or to generate attractive returns. "Plan an exit for the investor," advises the owner of a financial consulting company. "Generally, the equity investor's objective with early stage funding is to earn a 30% to 50% annual return over the life of the investment. To enhance the investor's

interest in your enterprise, show how they can 'cash out' perhaps through a public offering or acquisition."[37]

Finally, an entrepreneur should have a timetable for implementing the proposed plan. He or she should present a schedule showing the estimated start-up date for the project and noting any significant milestones along the way. Entrepreneurs tend to be optimistic, so document how and why the timetable of events is realistic.

It is beneficial to include an evaluation of the risks of a new venture. Evaluating risk in a business plan requires an entrepreneur to walk a fine line, however. Dwelling too much on everything that can go wrong discourages potential lenders and investors from financing the venture. Ignoring the project's risks makes those who evaluate the plan tend to believe an entrepreneur to be either naive, dishonest, or unprepared. The best strategy is to identify the most significant risks the venture faces and then to describe the plans the entrepreneur has developed to avoid them altogether or to overcome the negative outcome if the event does occur.

There is a difference between a *working* business plan—the one the entrepreneur is using to guide his or her business—and the *presentation* business plan—the one he or she is using to attract capital. Although coffee rings and penciled-in changes in a working plan don't matter (in fact, they're a good sign that the entrepreneur is actually using the plan), they have no place in a plan going to someone outside the company. A plan is usually the tool that an entrepreneur uses to make a first impression on potential lenders and investors. To make sure that the impression is a favorable one, an entrepreneur should follow these tips:

- Realize that first impressions are crucial. Make sure the plan has an attractive (not necessarily expensive) cover.

- Make sure the plan is free of spelling and grammatical errors and "typos." It is a professional document and should look like one.

- Make it visually appealing. Use color charts, figures, and diagrams to illustrate key points. Don't get carried away, however, and end up with a "comic book" plan.

- Include a table of contents with page numbers to allow readers to navigate the plan easily. Reviewers should be able to look through a plan and quickly locate the sections they want to see.

- Make it interesting. Boring plans seldom get read.

- A plan must prove that the business will make money. In one survey of lenders, investors, and financial advisers, 81 percent said that, first and foremost, a plan should prove that a venture will earn a profit.[38] Start-ups do not necessarily have to be profitable immediately, but sooner or later (preferably sooner) they must make money.

- Use computer spreadsheets to generate financial forecasts. They allow entrepreneurs to perform valuable "what-if" (sensitivity) analysis in just seconds.

- *Always* include cash flow projections. Entrepreneurs sometimes focus excessively on their proposed venture's profit forecasts and ignore cash flow projections. Although profitability is important, lenders and investors are much more interested in cash flow because they know that's where the money to pay them back or to cash them out comes from.

- The ideal plan is "crisp," long enough to say what it should but not so long that it is a chore to read.

- Remember the importance of the executive summary. It must feature the highlights of your plan for investors who will not wade through the detail of the full-blown plan.

- Tell the truth. Absolute honesty is always critical when preparing a business plan.

The accompanying "Hands On . . . How To" feature describes how to create a plan for and launch a lean start-up.

Hands On . . . How To

Launch a Lean Start-Up

The traditional approach to starting a business is develop an idea for a product or service, build a business plan around the idea, and launch the company, hoping to attract a sufficient number of customers to make the business successful. Eric Ries, who worked with serial entrepreneur Steve Blank to create a Lean Startup methodology, which has its roots in the software industry, says that the traditional approach is wasteful, inefficient, and ineffective. Ries sees a business start-up as an experiment designed not to answer the question "*Can* we build this business?" but rather to answer the question "*Should* we build this business?" Blank says that a start-up company is "a temporary organization used to search for a scalable and repeatable business model." He goes on to say that "your job at this stage is to test and learn as much as you can. Once you've learned that many of your assumptions are wrong, your job is to leverage that insight into building the product or service that your customers really want. You could say at this stage, it's your job to fail. And fail again. And the faster you do it, the better."

The Lean Startup process traces its roots to the "lean" concepts from the Toyota Production System, which focuses on avoiding wasted time, effort, and money. Rather than build a business model or full-featured product in secrecy and then launch it with great fanfare, a lean start-up launches a "minimum viable product" (MVP), one that includes just enough features to get meaningful feedback from customers. In a customer-focused, iterative process, entrepreneurs observe customers' purchasing behavior and use the feedback they get from the MVP to revise and improve the original product or business model before going back to the market to get more feedback from customers. The idea is to get to market much faster with a product or business model whose features reflect just what customers want and to reduce the probability of wasting time incorporating features that customers don't want. "Lean start-ups don't try to scale up the business until they have a solution that matches the problem, a product-market fit," says Tom Eisenman, a professor of entrepreneurial management at Harvard University. "After you have that solution, then you can step on the gas pedal."

Drew Houston and Arash Ferdowsi, the cofounders of cloud storage company Dropbox, used the Lean Startup process when they launched their company. They announced a bare-bones version of their storage service on the Web site, Hacker News, with the goal of collecting feedback from early users about the features they preferred and which ones they did not use. Houston and Ferdowsi incorporated customers' input into each successive version of their storage software, a process that took just 15 months. In that time, Dropbox's user base grew from 100,000 users to more than 4 million users. Today, more than 25 million people around the world store more than 200 million files each day with Dropbox, which they can access from any computer, tablet, or smart phone.

Sometimes the Lean Startup process leads to a business model or product that is quite different from the one that the entrepreneur originally envisioned. Ries and Blank call this kind of business model or product shift a pivot after the basketball maneuver in which a player keeps one foot planted while changing direction with the other foot. In a start-up, a pivot occurs when the entrepreneur moves the company in a new direction based on customer responses while still keeping it grounded in the original business. In reality, successful entrepreneurs are quite skilled at making pivots and always have been; they introduce an idea, observe how customers respond, and determine whether the business is viable. This requires an adjustment in some component of the business model or needs a pivot. "Through pivots, we can build companies where the failure of the initial idea isn't the failure of the company," says Ries.

Steve DeKorte and Rich and Meg Collins started their business, Stylous, with the idea that users would be able to search the company's Web site visually for clothing listed on other Web sites without the clutter of product descriptions and other text. When shoppers click on an item, Stylous directs them to the retailer's site so that they can complete the purchase, and Stylous collects a commission on the sale. Eight months after the site's launch, sales were dismal, and Stylous was headed for a cash crisis and extinction. The cofounders decided that it was time for a pivot and began meeting with users to get feedback on the site's features. They learned that most shoppers were looking for brand-name items that were on sale. The cofounders reworked their business model, creating Twitter accounts to announce limited-time sales on designer brands. Every time a shopper clicks on the link in a tweet and purchases the item, Stylous earns a commission. One day after Stylous launched its first 10 Twitter accounts, its sales increased 10-fold! The company now has more than 80,000 followers in its 160 Twitter accounts.

A lean start-up process demands a different type of business planning process that has the following characteristics:

Keep the plan simple. A plan for a lean start-up should not contain frills. Stick to the basics. Until you figure out a business model or product to which customers respond favorably, the plan is almost solely for internal use.

Keep the plan fluid. Like your business model or product, your plan is constantly changing, sometimes dramatically, based on the feedback you get from customers.

Keep your planning flexible and agile. Remember that a basic premise of a lean start-up is *speed*, and that requires flexibility and agility. Don't get bogged down in a complex process.

Remember that the planning process is a cycle. A good plan really never ends. Smart entrepreneurs plan, implement, and revise—and then repeat the process.

Sources: Based on Jason Del Ray, "A Change of Direction," *Inc.*, February 2011, pp. 100–104; Tim Berry, "Business Planning for the 'Lean Startup,'" *Entrepreneur*, September 22, 2010, http://www.entrepreneur.com/article/217343; Lindsay Blakely, "There Are 387 Million Ways to Fail: Do You Know How to Fail Well?," *BNET*, October 25, 2010, http://www.bnet.com/blog/smb/there-are-387-million-ways-to-fail-do-you-know-how-to-fail-well/2608; Carmen Nobel, "Teaching a 'Lean Startup' Strategy," *Harvard Business School Working Knowledge*, April 11, 2011, http://hbswk.hbs.edu/item/6659.html; and Joe McKendrick, "'Lean Startup' Movement Seeks to Inject New Vigor into Economy," *Smart Planet*, June 15, 2011, http://www.smartplanet.com/blog/business-brains/-8216lean-startup-movement-seeks-to-inject-new-vigor-into-economy/16449.

What Lenders and Investors Look for in a Business Plan

Banks usually are not a new venture's sole source of capital because a bank's return is limited by the interest rate it negotiates, but its risk could be the entire amount of the loan if the new business fails. Once a business is operational and has established a financial track record, however, banks become a regular source of financing. For this reason, the small business owner needs to be aware of the criteria that lenders and investors use when evaluating the creditworthiness of entrepreneurs seeking financing. Lenders and investors refer to these criteria as the **five Cs of credit**: capital, capacity, collateral, character, and conditions.

Capital

A small business must have a stable capital base before any lender is willing to grant a loan. Otherwise, the lender would be making, in effect, a capital investment in the business. Most banks refuse to make loans that are capital investments because the potential for return on the investment is limited strictly to the interest on the loan, and the potential loss would probably exceed the reward. In fact, the most common reasons that banks give for rejecting small business loan applications are undercapitalization or too much debt. Lenders expect a small company to have an equity base of investment by the owner(s) to support the venture during times of financial strain, which are common during the start-up and growth phases of a business. Lenders and investors see capital as a risk-sharing strategy with entrepreneurs.

Capacity

A synonym for capacity is cash flow. Lenders and investors must be convinced of a company's ability to meet its regular financial obligations and to repay loans, and that takes cash. In Chapter 12, you will learn that more small businesses fail from lack of cash than from lack of profit. It is possible for a company to earn a profit and run out of cash—that is, to be technically bankrupt. Lenders expect small businesses to pass the test of liquidity, especially for short-term loans. Potential lenders and investors examine closely a small company's cash flow position to decide whether it has the capacity necessary to survive until it can sustain itself.

Collateral

Collateral includes any assets an entrepreneur pledges to a lender as security for repayment of a loan. If the company defaults on the loan, the lender has the right to sell the collateral and use the proceeds to satisfy the loan. Typically, banks make very few unsecured loans (those not backed by collateral) to business start-ups. Bankers view the entrepreneurs' willingness to pledge collateral (personal or business assets) as an indication of their dedication to making the venture a success.

Character

Before extending a loan to or making an investment in a small business, lenders and investors must be satisfied with an entrepreneur's character. The evaluation of character frequently is based on intangible factors, such as honesty, integrity, competence, polish, determination, intelligence, and ability. Although the qualities judged are abstract, this evaluation plays a critical role in the decision to put money into a business.

Lenders and investors know that most small businesses fail because of incompetent management, and they try to avoid extending loans to high-risk entrepreneurs. A solid business plan and a polished presentation by the entrepreneur can go far in convincing the banker of the entrepreneur's capability.

Conditions

The conditions surrounding a funding request also affect an entrepreneur's chances of receiving financing. Lenders and investors consider factors relating to a business's operation, such as potential growth in the market, competition, location, strengths, weaknesses, opportunities, and threats. Again, the best way to provide this relevant information is in a business plan. Another important condition influencing the banker's decision is the shape of the overall economy, including interest rate levels, inflation rate, and demand for money. Although these factors are beyond an entrepreneur's control, they still are an important component in a banker's decision.

The higher a small business scores on these five Cs, the greater its chance will be of receiving a loan.

Table 4.2 describes 12 mistakes that entrepreneurs often make in their business plans.

TABLE 4.2 Don't Make These Business Plan Mistakes

According to venture capitalists and business planning experts, the following 12 critical mistakes are the ones that entrepreneurs most often commit in their business plans.

Mistake 1: Failure to explain the business opportunity clearly. Too many entrepreneurs fail to explain why their business ideas make sense and why their business models will be successful. This is one reason that a concise, meaningful elevator pitch that tells a compelling story is so important.

Mistake 2: Trying to be everything to everybody. Business strategy is all about focusing on what your business does best (and better than the competition). Entrepreneurs who try to do everything usually find themselves doing nothing very well. Stay focused.

Mistake 3: Falling into the "Chinese soda" trap. "If just 1 percent of the people in China, buy our soda, we will be successful." Big market numbers make it easy to hide behind, but they just are not realistic for small companies, especially start-ups. Build your forecasts on real market data, backed up by demographics, customer testimonials, and results of business prototyping, focus groups, and customer trials. Rather than aim for a small piece of a giant market, shoot for a large piece of a small market that you actually can reach.

Mistake 4: Unrealistic financial projections. Entrepreneurs tend to be optimistic, sometimes overly so, and it shows up in the form of unrealistic financial projections. Make sure that your forecasts are *realistic* by comparing them to industry averages and verifying them with people who have experience in the industry.

Mistake 5: Forgetting the importance of cash flow. Entrepreneurs intuitively understand the importance of forecasting their companies' profits, but they often forget that cash flow is just as important. Profits are important, but cash is what keeps a company alive and growing. Always include a realistic cash flow forecast.

Mistake 6: Overly simplistic assumptions. Some business plans gloss over complex areas that are vital to business success. For instance, if a reliable supply chain is a key to your company's success, make sure that your plan includes a strategy for assembling one.

Mistake 7: Weak competitor analysis. One sure path to having your business plan rejected is to say, "We have no competition." Experienced business people know better! Other entrepreneurs run into problems when they underestimate their competitors' strengths. Take the time to identify your primary competitors and to learn about what makes them successful and where their weaknesses lie.

Mistake 8: Failure to describe the company's competitive advantage. A business plan must explain the way in which a company will set itself apart from the competition. What factors will give your business an edge in attracting and retaining customers?

Mistake 9: Counting on a low-price strategy for success. Pricing is an important part of a company's strategy because it is the strongest signal of its relative position in the marketplace. It also influences a company's profitability. Inspired by the success of Wal-Mart and other discount retailers, many entrepreneurs make the mistake of pursuing a low-cost strategy when they lack the resources to execute one successfully. Your prices must reflect the quality, value, and convenience that you provide your customers.

Mistake 10: A sloppy plan that contains errors. A business plan is a reflection of its creator. A plan that is filled with errors and mistakes sends up warning signals to potential lenders and investors. Make sure your document is polished and professional.

Mistake 11: Exaggerating the qualifications of the management team. Venture capitalists invest in management, and they investigate thoroughly the backgrounds of the managers in the start-up companies in which they are considering investing. A business plan should highlight the management team's experience and accomplishments but should not overstate them. Few mistakes will destroy a deal faster.

Mistake 12: A plan that is incomplete. Venture capitalists tend to trash business plans that are missing key sections or that have insufficient financial data. Although every entrepreneur should tell the story of his or her business in a unique fashion, every plan should include the basic elements described in this chapter.

Source: Based on "Don't Make These Mistakes in Your Business Plans," The Capital Connection, 2008, http:// www.capital-connection.com/vcsurvey.html.

LO5

Describe the keys to making an effective business plan presentation.

Making the Business Plan Presentation

Lenders and investors are favorably impressed by entrepreneurs who are informed and prepared when requesting a loan or investment. When attempting to secure funds from professional venture capitalist or private investors, the written business plan almost always precedes the opportunity to meet "face-to-face." Typically, an entrepreneur's time for presenting his or her business opportunity will be limited. (When presenting a plan to a venture capital forum, the allotted time is usually no more than 15 to 20 minutes, and at some forums, the time limit is a mere five or six minutes.) When the opportunity arises, an entrepreneur must be well prepared. It is important to rehearse, rehearse, and rehearse some more. It is a mistake to begin by leading the audience into a long-winded explanation about the technology on which the product or service is based. Within minutes, most of the audience will be lost, and so is any chance the entrepreneur has of obtaining the necessary financing for his or her new venture. Entrepreneur-turned-venture-capitalist Guy Kawasaki is famous for his 10/20/30 rule: a business plan presentation should have 10 slides, last no more than 20 minutes, and contain no font smaller than 30 points.

Some helpful tips for making a business plan presentation to potential lenders and investors include the following:

- Demonstrate enthusiasm about the venture but don't be overemotional.

- Know your audience thoroughly and work to establish a rapport with them.

- "Hook" investors quickly with an up-front explanation of the new venture, its opportunities, and the anticipated benefits to them.

- Hit the highlights; specific questions will bring out the details later. Don't get caught up in too much detail in early meetings with lenders and investors.

- Keep your presentation simple by limiting it to the two or three (no more) major points you must get across to your audience.

- Avoid the use of technical terms that will likely be above most of the audience. Do at least one rehearsal before someone who has no special technical training. Tell him or her to stop you anytime he or she does not understand what you are talking about. When this occurs (and it likely will), rewrite that portion of your presentation.

- Use visual aids because they make it easier for people to follow your presentation, but do not make the visual aids the "star" of the presentation. They should merely support and enhance your message.

- Close by reinforcing the nature of the opportunity. Be sure you have sold the benefits the investors will realize when the business is a success.

- Be prepared for questions. In many cases, there is seldom time for a long question-and-answer session, but interested investors may want to get you aside to discuss the details of the plan.

- Follow up with every investor to whom you make a presentation. Don't sit back and wait; be proactive. They have what you need—investment capital. Demonstrate that you have confidence in your plan and have the initiative necessary to run a business successfully.

Conclusion

Although there is no guarantee of success when launching a business, the best way to protect against failure is to create a business plan. A good plan serves as an entrepreneurial strategic compass that keeps a business on course as it travels into an uncertain future. Will the business that an entrepreneur actually creates look exactly like the company described in the business plan? Of course not. One experienced entrepreneur who has created several business plans for the companies that he has launched says, "A start-up business plan is a piece of good fiction filled with great ideas."[39] The *real* value in preparing a business plan is not so much in the finished document itself but in the *process* the entrepreneur goes through to create it, a process in which he or she learns how to compete successfully in the marketplace. In addition, a solid plan is essential to raising the capital needed to start a business; lenders and investors demand it.

Business Plan Format

Although every company's business plan will be unique, reflecting its individual circumstances, certain elements are universal. The following outline summarizes these components:

I. Executive Summary (not to exceed two pages)
   A. Company name, address, and phone number
   B. Name(s), addresses, and phone number(s) of all key people
   C. Brief description of the business, its products and services, and the customer problems they solve
   D. Brief overview of the market for your products and services
   E. Brief overview of your company's competitive advantage
   F. Brief description of the managerial and technical experience of key people
   G. Brief statement of the financial request and how the money will be used
   H. Charts or tables showing highlights of financial forecasts

II. Vision and Mission Statement
   A. Entrepreneur's vision for the company
   B. "What business are we in?"
   C. Values and principles on which the business stands
   D. What makes the business unique? What is the source of its competitive advantage?

III. Company History (for existing businesses only)
   A. Company founding
   B. Financial and operational highlights
   C. Significant achievements

IV. Business and Industry Profile
   A. Industry analysis
      1. Industry background and overview
      2. Significant trends
      3. Growth rate
      4. Key success factors in the industry
   B. Outlook for the future stage of growth (start-up, growth, maturity)
   C. Company goals and objectives
      1. Operational
      2. Financial
      3. Other

V. Business Strategy
   A. Desired image and position in market
   B. SWOT analysis
      1. Strengths
      2. Weaknesses
      3. Opportunities
      4. Threats
   C. Competitive strategy
      1. Cost leadership
      2. Differentiation
      3. Focus

VI. Company Products and Services
   A. Description
      1. Product or service features
      2. Customer benefits

3. Warranties and guarantees

4. Uniqueness

B. Patent or trademark protection

C. Description of production process (if applicable)

    1. Raw materials

    2. Costs

    3. Key suppliers

D. Future product or service offerings

VII. Marketing Strategy

    A. Target market

       1. Complete demographic profile

       2. Other significant customer characteristics

    B. Customers' motivation to buy

    C. Market size and trends

       1. How large is the market?

       2. Is it growing or shrinking? How fast?

    D. Advertising and promotion

       1. Media used—reader, viewer, listener profiles

       2. Media costs

       3. Frequency of usage

       4. Plans for generating publicity

    E. Pricing

       1. Cost structure

          a. Fixed

          b. Variable

       2. Desired image in market

       3. Comparison against competitors' prices

    F. Distribution strategy

       1. Channels of distribution used

       2. Sales techniques and incentives

VIII. Location and Layout

    A. Location

       1. Demographic analysis of location versus target customer profile

       2. Traffic count

       3. Lease/rental rates

       4. Labor needs and supply

       5. Wage rates

    B. Layout

       1. Size requirements

       2. Americans with Disabilities Act compliance

       3. Ergonomic issues

       4. Floor plan (suitable for an appendix)

IX. Competitor Analysis

    A. Existing competitors

       1. Who are they? (create a competitive profile matrix)

       2. Strengths

       3. Weaknesses

    B. Potential competitors (companies that might enter the market)

       1. Who are they?

       2. Impact on your business if they enter

X. Description of Management Team

    A. Key managers and employees

       1. Their backgrounds

       2. Experience, skills, and know-how they bring to the company

    B. Résumés of key managers and employees (suitable for an appendix)

XI. Plan of Operation
    A. Form of ownership chosen and reasoning
    B. Company structure (organization chart)
    C. Decision making authority
    D. Compensation and benefits packages

XII. Financial Forecasts (suitable for an appendix)
    A. Financial statements
        1. Income statement
        2. Balance sheet
        3. Cash flow statement
    B. Break-even analysis
    C. Ratio analysis with comparison to industry standards (most applicable to existing businesses)

XIII. Loan or Investment Proposal
    A. Amount requested
    B. Purpose and uses of funds
    C. Repayment or "cash out" schedule (exit strategy)
    D. Timetable for implementing plan and launching the business

XIV. Appendices (supporting documentation, including market research, financial statements, organization charts, résumés, and other items)

Chapter Summary by Chapter Objective

1. Discuss the steps involved in subjecting a business idea to a feasibility analysis.

- A feasibility analysis consists of three interrelated components: an industry and market feasibility analysis, a product or service feasibility analysis, and a financial feasibility analysis. The goal of the feasibility analysis is to determine whether an entrepreneur's idea is a viable foundation for creating a successful business.

2. Explain why every entrepreneur should create a business plan as well as the benefits of developing a plan.

- A business plan serves two essential functions. First and most important, it guides the company's operations by charting its future course and devising a strategy for following it. The second function of the business plan is to attract lenders and investors. Applying for loans or attempting to attract investors without a solid business plan rarely attracts needed capital.

- Preparing a sound business plan clearly requires time and effort, but the benefits greatly exceed the costs. Building the plan forces a potential entrepreneur to look at his or her business idea in the harsh light of reality. It also requires the owner to assess the venture's chances of success more objectively. A well-assembled plan helps prove to outsiders that a business idea can be successful.

- The *real* value in preparing a business plan is not so much in the plan itself as it is in the process the entrepreneur goes through to create the plan. Although the finished product is useful, the process of building a plan requires an entrepreneur to subject his or her idea to an objective, critical evaluation. What the entrepreneur learns about his or her company, its target market, its financial requirements, and other factors can be essential to making the venture a success.

3. Describe the elements of a solid business plan.

- Although a business plan should be unique and tailor-made to suit the particular needs of a small company, it should cover these basic elements: an executive summary, a mission statement, a company history, a business and industry profile, a description of the company's business strategy, a profile of its products or services, a statement explaining its marketing strategy, a competitor analysis, owners' and officers' résumés, a plan of operation, financial data, and the loan or investment proposal.

4. Explain the "five Cs of credit" and why they are important to potential lenders and investors reading business plans.

- Small business owners need to be aware of the criteria bankers use in evaluating the creditworthiness of loan applicants—the five Cs of credit: capital, capacity, collateral, character, and conditions.

- Capital—Lenders expect small businesses to have an equity base of investment by the owner(s) that will help support the venture during times of financial strain.
- Capacity—A synonym for "capacity" is "cash flow." The bank must be convinced of the firm's ability to meet its regular financial obligations and to repay the bank loan, and that takes cash.
- Collateral—Collateral includes any assets the owner pledges to the bank as security for repayment of the loan.
- Character—Before approving a loan to a small business, the banker must be satisfied with the owner's character.
- Conditions—The conditions (interest rates, the health of the nation's economy, industry growth

rates, and so no) surrounding a loan request also affect the owner's chance of receiving funds.

5. Understand the keys to making an effective business plan presentation.

- Lenders and investors are favorably impressed by entrepreneurs who are informed and prepared when requesting a loan or investment.
- Tips include the following: demonstrate enthusiasm about the venture but don't be overemotional; "hook" investors quickly with an up-front explanation of the new venture, its opportunities, and the anticipated benefits to them; use visual aids; hit the highlights of your venture; don't get caught up in too much detail in early meetings with lenders and investors; avoid the use of technological terms that will likely be above most of the audience; rehearse your presentation before giving it; close by reinforcing the nature of the opportunity; and be prepared for questions.

Discussion Questions

1. Explain the steps involved in conducting a feasibility analysis.
2. Why should an entrepreneur develop a business plan?
3. Describe the major components of a business plan.
4. How can an entrepreneur seeking funds to launch a business convince potential lenders and investors that a market for the product or service really does exist?
5. How would you prepare to make a formal presentation of your business plan to a venture capital forum?
6. What are the five Cs of credit? How does a potential lender use them to evaluate a loan request?

This chapter discusses the importance of testing your business concept. Does the idea represent a viable business concept? A comprehensive business plan can help answer this question.

Business Plan Exercises

The following exercises will assist you in validating your business concept. You will also begin to work through the situation analysis part of your plan to better understand your market. Be objective as you work through these exercises. Rely on your ability to gather information and make realistic assessments and projections.

On the Web

Go to www.pearsonhighered.com/scarborough to the Business Plan Resource tab. If you have not done this yet, find the Standard Industry Classification (SIC) code associated with your industry. You will find a link in the SIC code information that will connect you to a resource. Explore the information and links that are available to you on that site

to learn more about the size of the industry and its growth, trends, and issues. Based on the industry you have selected and the associated SIC code, apply Porter's five-forces model. Consider the five forces—the bargaining power of buyers, the power of suppliers, the threat of new entrants, the threat of substitute products, and the level of rivalry. You will find additional information on Porter's five-forces model in the Strategy section of this same site. Look for information on the Web that may assist you with this analysis. Based on this information, how attractive do you consider this industry? How would you assess the opportunity this industry presents? Does this information encourage you to become involved in this industry, or does it highlight significant challenges?

In the Software

Your text may include Business Feasibility Analysis Pro. This software steps you through assessing the feasibility of your business concept. It addresses the overall feasibility of your product or service, helps you to conduct an industry assessment, reviews your management skills, and takes you through a preliminary financial analysis. The software provides initial "feedback" based on your input of four components of the feasibility analysis with a numeric assessment. You can then export this information directly into *Business Plan Pro™*. *Business Plan Pro™* will also help assess the feasibility of your business concept in the areas of product, service, market organization, and financial feasibility. For example, you can enter the initial capital requirements for the business in the start-up and expenses section. Combined with a sales forecast, the software calculates your return on investment. If you have these estimates available, enter those into your plan. Next, refer to the Profit and Loss statement. At what point, if any, does that statement indicate that your venture will begin generating a profit based on those forecasts and expenses. In what year does that occur? Do you find that amount of time acceptable? If you are seeking investors, will they find that time frame acceptable? Is the return on investment promising, and does this venture merit taking on the associated level of risk? We will talk more about these sections of your plan as you progress through the chapters.

Sample Plans

Review the start-up sample plans called InteliChild.com and Corporate Fitness.

1. What was the total amount of the start-up investment for each of these plans?

2. What is the break-even point?

3. What is the total profit that was projected in the year after the business reaches its break-even point?

4. Based on the break-even point, which of these ventures do you find most attractive?

5. Based on the profit projections by year 3, which plan appears to offer the greatest financial potential?

6. How does the scale and potential of these two opportunities compare to those in your plan?

Building Your Business Plan

Review the information in the Market Analysis section. Continue to build the information in this section based on the outline. You will find information to help project your expenses in the Sales Strategy section. Enter numbers directly in the table itself or use the wizard that pops up to assist you. Manipulate the graph to build that forecast based on a visual growth curve or enter the actual data. If your business is a start-up venture, your expenses will include those figures along with your on-going expense projections. Don't worry about the accuracy of your projections. Get some numbers entered into the software; you can change those numbers at any time. Look at the Profit and Loss statement. Are your forecasts realistic? At what point in time will your business begin making a profit? As you build your plan, check to see that the outline and structure of your plan are a good fit to tell your story. Although the outline in *Business Plan Pro™* is not identical to the outline presented in the chapter, by right-clicking on the outline, you can move, add, and delete any topic you choose to modify the plan you create.

Beyond the Classroom . . .

1. Many business plan experts say that the executive summary, the written statement of the company's "elevator pitch," may be the most important part of a business plan. Do you agree? Work with a local entrepreneur, preferably one who is searching for start-up or growth capital, and use the following recipe to create a meaningful elevator pitch for his or her business: "[Your company name] helps [your company's target customers] to [the benefit your company provides]. Unlike other companies that provide similar solutions, [your company name] [point of differentiation, which answers the 'so what?' question]."[40]

2. Go to you YouTube and watch the elevator pitch for a company that recently won one of the major business plan competitions, such as the Rice Business Plan Competition or MIT's $100K Business Plan Contest. How does the pitch score on the five-part framework described in this chapter: context, benefit, target customers, point of differentiation, and clincher? What lessons can you learn from watching this elevator pitch?

3. Contact a local entrepreneur who recently launched a business. Did he or she prepare a business plan before starting the company? Why or why not? If the entrepreneur did not create a plan, is he or she considering doing so now? If the entrepreneur did create a plan, what benefits did he or she gain from the process? How long did it take to complete the plan? How did he or she put the plan to use during the start-up phase? Does he or she intend to keep the business plan updated? What advice does he or she have to offer another entrepreneur about to begin writing a business plan?

4. Interview a local banker who has experience in making loans to small businesses. Ask him or her the following questions:

   a. How important is a well-prepared business plan?

   b. How important is a smooth presentation?

   c. How does the banker evaluate the owner's character?

   d. How heavily does the bank weigh the five Cs of credit?

e. What percentage of small business owners are well prepared to request a bank loan?

f. What are the most common reasons the bank rejects small business loan applications?

5. Interview a small business owner who has requested a bank loan or an equity investment from external sources. Ask him or her these questions:

a. Did you prepare a written business plan before approaching the financial officer?

b. If the answer is "yes" to part a, did you have outside or professional help in preparing it?

c. How many times have your requests for additional funds been rejected? What reasons were given for the rejection?

Endnotes

1. Vivek Wadhwa, "What Exactly Is a Business Model?," *Tech Crunch*, Janaury 8, 2011, http://techcrunch.com/2011/01/08/business-models-and-teenage-sex; Tom Taulli, "Three Steps to a Sound Business Model," *Bloomberg Business Week*, February 27, 2009, http://www.businessweek.com/smallbiz/content/feb2009/sb20090226_798877.htm.

2. Kelly K. Spors, "Do Start-Ups Really Need Formal Business Plans?," *Wall Street Journal*, January 9, 2007, p. B9.

3. Jessica E. Vascellaro and Sam Schechner, "Slow Fade-Out for Video Stores," *Wall Street Journal*, September 30, 2010, p. A6; Brad Bauer, "Movie Rentals: Local Store's Closing Signals End of Entertainment Era," *Marietta Times*, May 25, 2010, http://www.mariettatimes.com/page/content.detail/id/522133.html.

4. Michael E. Porter, "How Competitive Forces Shape Strategy," *Harvard Business Review*, Volume 57, No. 2, March-April 1979, pp. 137–145.

5. Charles Fishman, "The Wal-Mart You Don't Know," *Fast Company*, December 2003, http://www.fastcompany.com/magazine/77/walmart.html.

6. Jason Meyers, "A Parking Business Gets Stuck in Park," *Entrepreneur*, May 2010, p. 120; "About Us," Park It! Guides, http://parkitnyc.com/about.html.

7. Don Debelak, "Join Hands," *Entrepreneur*, September 2005, pp. 138–140.

8. Lindsay Blakely, "Go Ahead, Write a Killer Business Plan. Just Be Willing to Tear It Up," *BNET*, May 18, 2010, http://www.bnet.com/article/go-ahead-write-a-killer-business-plan-just-be-willing-to-tear-it-up/424819.

9. Pascal-Emmanual Gobry, "Want to Test Your Idea? Try the $20 Starbucks Test," *Business Insider*, December 24, 2010, http://www.businessinsider.com/want-to-test-your-startup-idea-try-the-20-starbucks-test-2010-12.

10. Joi Sumpton, "Flight Attendant Becomes Woman Inventor," *Fox Business*, December 26, 2010, http://www.foxbusiness.com/personal-finance/2010/12/26/flight-attendant-woman-inventor.

11. Carla Goodman, "Can You Get There from Here?," *Entrepreneur*, December 1996, http://www.entrepreneur.com/article/0,4621,226677,00.html; "About Little Earth," Little Earth Productions, Inc., http://www.littlearth.com/pages05/about.shtml.

12. Jena McGregor, "The Art of Service: Intuit," *Fast Company*, October 2005, p. 53; Michael S. Hopkins, "America's 25 Most Fascinating Entrepreneurs: Scott Cook, Intuit," *Inc.*, April 2004, http://www.inc.com/magazine/20040401/25cook.html; "How Intuit Found Fame and Fortune and Beat Out Microsoft," *Knowledge@Wharton*, November 5, 2003, http://knowledge.wharton.upenn.edu/index.cfm?fa=viewArticle&id=869.

13. Mark Henricks, "Do You Really Need a Business Plan?," *Entrepreneur*, December 2008, pp. 93–95; Kelly Spors, "Advance Planning Pays Off for Start-Ups," *Wall Street Journal*,

February 9, 2009, http://blogs.wsj.com/independentstreet/2009/02/09/advance-planning-pays-off-for-start-ups.

14. Karen E. Klein, "Building a Better Business Plan," *Business Week*, September 12, 2006, http://www.businessweek.com/smallbiz/content/sep2006/sb20060912_981004.htm.

15. James Maguire, "Starting Your Own E-Business: Part 1," *Small Business Computing*, October 3, 2005, www.smallbusinesscomputing.com/emarketing/article.pho/35553126.

16. David Newton, "Model Behavior," *Entrepreneur*, March 2002, pp. 68–71.

17. Kate O'Sullivan, "Easy Rider," *CFO*, November 2005, p. 108.

18. Adam Bluestein, "How's My Pitch?," *Inc.*, February 2011, p. 95.

19. Scott A. Shane, *The Illusions of Entrepreneurship* (New Haven, CT: Yale University Press, 2008), p. 74.

20. Steve Marshall Cohen, "Money Rules," *Business Start-Ups*, July 1995, p. 31.

21. Bill Reichert, "Part II: A Framework for Building Your Wow Statement," *Open Forum*, November 1, 2010, http://www.openforum.com/idea-hub/topics/the-world/article/part-ii-a-framework-for-building-your-wow-statement-bob-reichert.

22. Alison Stein Wellner, "You Know What Your Company Does: Can You Explain It in 30 Seconds?," *Inc.*, July 2007, pp. 92–97.

23. Emily Maltby, "Three Minutes to a Million," *Wall Street Journal*, June 17, 2010, http://online.wsj.com/article/SB10001424052748704198004573311222146718844.html.

24. Jennifer Wang, "Just Brilliant," *Entrepreneur*, April 2010, p. 74; Leigh Buchanan, "Say Yes to Solar," *Inc.*, December 1, 2010, http://www.inc.com/magazine/20101201/say-yes-to-solar.html; Jessica Shambora, "Most Powerful Women Entrepreneurs: Lynn Jurich," *CNNMoney*, December 18, 2009, http://money.cnn.com/galleries/2009/fortune/0912/gallery.most_powerful_women_entrepreneurs.fortune/7.html.

25. Conor Dougherty, "Minority Report," *Wall Street Journal*, May 28–29, 2011, p. A11; Shannon Bryant, "Hispanic Buying Power Expected to Reach $1.3 Billion in 2015," Marketing Forecast, January 17, 2011, http://www.marketingforecast.com/archives/9461.

26. Sharon McLoone, "Booming Hispanic Market Opens Business Opportunities," *Washington Post*, June 27, 2008, http://blog.washingtonpost.com/small-business/2008/06/booming_hispanic_market_opens.html.

27. Julie Jargon, "Pizza Chain Seeks Slice of Bicultural Pie," *Wall Street Journal*, December 29, 2010, http://online.wsj.com/article/SB10001424052970204204004576049952412468360.html?mod=dist_smartbrief; "Two Years in Development, Pizza Patrón Debuts New Chorizo," Pizza Patrón, June 29, 2011, http://www.pizzapatron.com/news/blog.

28. Kerry Miller, "How to Write a Winning Business Plan," *Business Week*, December 3, 2007, http://www.businessweek.com/smallbiz/content/dec2007/sb2007123_109728.htm.

29. Andriana Gardella, "Tickets, Anyone?" *FSB*, May 2008, pp. 61–67.

30. Tamara Schweitzer and Jessica DiLullo Herrin, "Why I Push So Hard," *Inc.*, September 2010, pp. 151–152.

31. James Maguire, "Veteran E-Commerce Designer Finds Her Mojo," *Small Business Computing*, April 22, 2005, http://www.ecommerce-guide.com/article.php/3499766; James Maguire, "Starting Your Own E-Business: Part 1," *Small Business Computing*, October 3, 2005, http://www.smallbusinesscomputing.com/emarketing/article.pho/35553126.

32. John Kincaid, "Internet Time Machine," *Tech Crunch*, November 5, 2010, http://techcrunch.com/2010/11/05/memolane-tell-your-stories-with-an-internet-time-machine; "For Startup Weekend Alumni, Memolane, Success Is All about the Team," *Startup Weekend*, January 15, 2011, http://startupweekend.org/2011/01/15/for-startup-weekend-alum-memolane-success-is-all-about-the-team; Jason Kincaid, "Memolane Raises $2 Million to Become Your "Digital Memory,'" *Tech Crunch*, September 13, 2010, http://techcrunch.com/2010/09/13/memolane-raises-2-million-to-become-your-digital-memory.

33. Conversation with Charles Burke, CEO, Burke Financial Associates.

34. "Raising Money," *Entrepreneur*, July 2005, p. 58.

35. Kimberly Weisul, "Entrepreneurs Are Worse at Financial Projections Than You Think," *BNET*, May 16, 2011, http://www.bnet.com/blog/business-research/entrepreneurs-are-worse-at-financial-projections-than-you-think/1535; Christopher F. Mokwa and Soenke Sievers, *Blurry Prospects of Venture-Backed Start-ups: Biases in Multi-Year Management Forecasts and the Bright Side of Milestone Contracting*, Social Science Research Network, January 10, 2011.

36. Michael V. Copeland, "How to Make Your Business Plan the Perfect Pitch," *Business 2.0*, September 2005, p. 88.

37. Conversation with Charles Burke, CEO, Burke Financial Associates.

38. Karen Axelton, "Good Plan, Stan," *Business Start-Ups*, March 200, p. 17.

39. Vivek Wadhwa, "Before You Write a Business Plan," *Business Week*, January 7, 2008, http://www.businessweek.com/smallbiz/content/jan2008/sb2008017_119570.htm?chan=smallbiz_special+report+--+the+abcs+of+business+plans_the+abcs+of+business+plans.

40. Jocelyn Broder, "4 Tips for Creating an Intriguing Elevator Speech," *Ragan*, March 1, 2011, http://www.ragan.com/Main/Articles/4_tips_for_creating_an_intriguing_elevator_speech_42730.aspx.

5

Forms of Business Ownership

Learning Objectives

On completion of this chapter, you will be able to:

1. Explain the advantages and the disadvantages of the three major forms of ownership: the sole proprietorship, the partnership, and the corporation.

2. Discuss the advantages and disadvantages of the S corporation, the limited liability company, the professional corporation, and the joint venture.

A friendship founded on business is a good deal better than a business founded on friendship.

—John D. Rockefeller

Over a long distance, you learn about the strength of your horse; over a long time, you learn about the character of your friend.

—Chinese proverb

Once an entrepreneur makes the decision to launch a business, one of the first issues he or she faces is choosing a form of ownership. Too often, entrepreneurs invest insufficient time and effort evaluating the impact that the various forms of ownership will have on them and on their businesses. They simply select a form of ownership by default or choose the form that appears to be most popular at the time. Choosing a form of ownership is important because it is a decision that has far-reaching effects for both the entrepreneur and the business. Although the decision is not irreversible, changing from one ownership form to another can be difficult, time consuming, complicated, and expensive. In many instances, switching an existing business from one form of ownership to another can trigger onerous tax consequences for the owners. Therefore, it is important for entrepreneurs to get it right the first time.

There is no one "best" form of ownership. The form of ownership that is best for one entrepreneur may not be suitable at all for another. Choosing the "right" form of ownership means that entrepreneurs must understand the characteristics of each form and how well those characteristics match their business and personal circumstances. Only then can an entrepreneur make an informed decision about a form of ownership. "Choose a structure that gives you the protection you need but with as few rules as possible," advises one attorney. "Entrepreneurs should move up the complexity chain only when it is necessary because each step up means more requirements and more paperwork."[1] The following are some of the most important issues entrepreneurs should consider when they are evaluating the various forms of ownership:

Tax considerations. The amount of net income an entrepreneur expects the business to generate and the tax bill the owner must pay are important factors when choosing a form of ownership. The graduated tax rates that apply to each form of ownership, the government's constant tinkering with the tax code, and the year-to-year fluctuations in a company's income make some forms of ownership more attractive than others.

Liability exposure. Certain forms of ownership offer business owners greater protection from personal liability that might result from financial problems, faulty products, lawsuits, and a host of other difficulties. Entrepreneurs must decide the extent to which they are willing to assume personal responsibility for their companies' financial obligations. Two entrepreneurs who started a company with a portable climbing wall formed a limited liability company to limit their personal liability exposure because of the high-risk nature of their business.

Start-up and future capital requirements. Forms of ownership differ in their ability to raise start-up capital. Depending on how much capital an entrepreneur needs and where he or she plans to get it, some forms are superior to others. In addition, as a business grows, so does its appetite for capital, and some forms of ownership make it easier to attract external growth capital than others.

Control. By choosing certain forms of ownership, an entrepreneur automatically gives up some control over the company. Entrepreneurs must decide early on how much control they are willing to sacrifice in exchange for help from other people to build a successful business.

Managerial ability. Entrepreneurs must assess their skills and abilities to manage a business effectively. If they lack ability or experience in key areas, they may need to choose a form of ownership that allows them to bring in other owners who can provide the necessary skills for the company to succeed.

Business goals. How big and how profitable an entrepreneur plans for the business to become influences the form of ownership chosen. Businesses often switch forms of ownership as they grow, but moving from some formats to others can be extremely complex and expensive.

Management succession plans. When choosing a form of ownership, business owners must look ahead to the day when they will pass their companies on to the next generation or to a buyer. Some forms of ownership make this transition much easier than others.

Cost of formation. Some forms of ownership are much more costly and involved to create. Entrepreneurs must weigh carefully the benefits and the costs of the particular form they choose.

When it comes to organizing their businesses, entrepreneurs have a wide choice of forms of ownership, including a sole proprietorship, a general partnership, a limited partnership, a corporation, an S corporation, and a limited liability company. Figure 5.1 provides a breakdown of these

FIGURE 5.1

Forms of Business
Ownership. (A) Percent-
age of Businesses;
(B) Percentage of Sales;
(C) Percentage of Net
Income

Source: Based on data from
Sources of Income, Internal
Revenue Service.

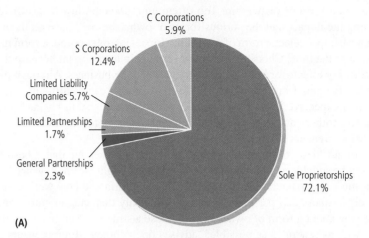

Percentage of Businesses

C Corporations 5.9%

S Corporations 12.4%

Limited Liability Companies 5.7%

Limited Partnerships 1.7%

General Partnerships 2.3%

Sole Proprietorships 72.1%

(A)

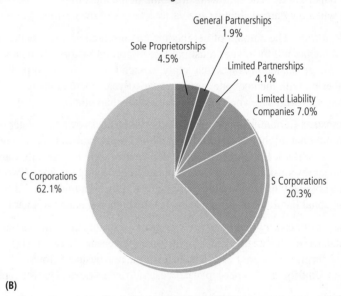

Percentage of Sales

General Partnerships 1.9%

Sole Proprietorships 4.5%

Limited Partnerships 4.1%

Limited Liability Companies 7.0%

S Corporations 20.3%

C Corporations 62.1%

(B)

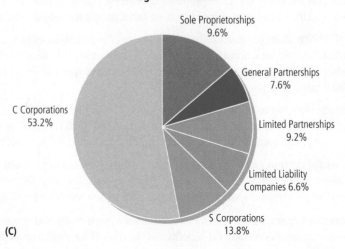

Percentage of Net Income

Sole Proprietorships 9.6%

General Partnerships 7.6%

Limited Partnerships 9.2%

Limited Liability Companies 6.6%

S Corporations 13.8%

C Corporations 53.2%

(C)

forms of ownership. Notice that sole proprietorships account for the greatest percentage of businesses but that corporations generate the largest portion of business sales. This chapter discusses the key features of these various forms of ownership, beginning with the three most basic forms (from simplest to most complex): the sole proprietorship, the partnership, and the corporation.

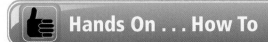

Hands On . . . How To

Come Up with the Perfect Moniker for Your Business

© Pictorial Press Ltd / Alamy

Lady Gaga is known for her outlandish outfits and makeup, but, given those, would she still sell out concerts if she performed under the name Stefani Joanne Angelina Germanotta (her real name)? Perhaps. But Lady Gaga's stage name is an important part of her persona and her marketing success. Similarly, choosing the right name for a company can enhance its success by creating the proper image and telling customers what it does. A good business name should do the following:

- Reinforce the company's brand positioning. A good name communicates to potential customers something about the brand's personality. For example, Twitter conjures up images of a flock of birds twittering in a tree or excitement over some event ("all atwitter"), both of which reinforce the company's purpose: allowing users to share short bursts of information about their lives.

- Resonate with the company's target audience. The founders of Rent-A-Wreck, a car rental company started in Los Angeles in 1968 that rents only used cars, selected a name that appealed to its target customers: people who are looking for lower auto rental rates than those offered by industry leaders, whose fleets include only the latest models.

- Suggest to customers what your company does. YouTube, the online video-sharing Web site, is a catchy name because it incorporates the slang term for television ("tube") and makes it clear to users that the videos are all about them.

- Be clever and differentiate your company from its competitors. Many waxing salons take an upscale salon approach, but the name that Jen Eichhorn selected for her edgy, unique business sends a clear signal that it is not a typical waxing salon: Screamin Peach. "I wanted to go for the gusto," says Eichhorn, who says her business more closely resembles a tattoo parlor than a salon.

- Be short, fun, attention getting, and memorable. Not only is Google fun to say, but it is also quite memorable. Naming experts say that a great name has "emotional hang time," a football metaphor to describe a name that stays in your mind.

- Be easy to spell and pronounce. This is especially important for companies that operate solely online because their names often serve as the URLs for their Web sites. "Wikipedia" works, but "Eefoof," a failed video-sharing site, did not.

- Grow with your business. When choosing a name, it is a good idea to keep an eye on the future. Many entrepreneurs select names for their businesses that can be limiting as their companies grow beyond their existing product lines, geographic areas, and target markets. As Popeyes Chicken and Biscuits expanded its menu, the company changed its name to Popeyes Louisiana Kitchen.

Choosing a memorable name can be one of the most fun—and most challenging—aspects of starting a business. It also is an extremely important task because it has long-term implications, is the single most visible attribute of a company, and has the capacity to either engage or repel customers. The business name is the first connection that many customers will have with a company, and it should create an appropriate image in their minds. "A name is a cornerstone for branding," says the president of one small design firm specializing in branding. If done properly, a company's name will portray the business's personality, will stand out in a crowd, and will stick in the minds of consumers. Large companies may spend hundreds of thousands of dollars in their

(continued)

Hands On . . . How To *(continued)*

search for just the right name. Although entrepreneurs don't have the resources to enable them to spend that kind of money finding the ideal name, they can use the following process to come up with the perfect name for their businesses:

1. Decide on the image you want your company to project to customers, suppliers, bankers, the press, the community, and others. Do you want to create an air of sophistication, the suggestion of a bargain, a sense of adventure, the implication of trustworthiness and dependability, or a spirit of fun and whimsy? The right name can go a long way toward communicating the right image for a company.

2. Make a list of your competitors' business names. The idea is *not* to borrow from their ideas but to try to come up with a name that is unique. Do you notice any trends among competitors' names? What are the similarities? What are the differences?

3. Work with a group of the most creative people you know to brainstorm (refer to Chapter 2 for details on the brainstorming process) potential names for your business. One entrepreneur called on 10 customers and 10 vendors to help him come up with a business name. Don't worry about quality at this point; the goal is to generate a large quantity of names. The idea is to come up with at least 100 potential names. Having a dictionary, a thesaurus, a rhyming dictionary, and samples (or graphics) of your company's products and services help to stimulate creativity. Consider names from unrelated sources that might be meaningful. "If you want to name a clothing line, think of names of hip places, like London nightclubs," says Alexandra Watkins, owner of Eat My Words, a name consulting company. "If it's a new energy drink, look up the names of race horses."

4. After allowing them to percolate for a few days, evaluate the names generated in the brainstorming session. Narrow the list of choices to 10 or so names with the greatest potential. Print each name in large font on a single page and look at them. Which ones are visually appealing? Which ones lend themselves to being paired with a clever logo?

5. Reassemble your creative group, present each name you have printed, and discuss its merits and challenges. Having a designated person to record the group's comments helps. The group may come to a consensus on a preferred name; if not, you can use a round-by-round voting process to move the group toward a consensus.

6. Conduct a search at the U.S. Patent and Trademark Office Web site (www.uspto.gov) to see whether the leading names on your list are already registered trademarks for existing businesses. Remember, however, that the same name can be registered as a trademark as long as the product, service, or company's business does not overlap.

7. Make your choice. Including input from others is useful when selecting a business name, but the final choice is yours.

8. Register your company name with the U.S. Patent and Trademark Office. Doing so gives you maximum protection from

others using the name you worked so hard to create. Diane Dassow thought she had the ideal name for her personal history and memoir service business in Lombard, Illinois: Bridging Generations. However, Dassow soon discovered a funeral home in Pennsylvania that was using that name. She checked with the U.S. Patent and Trademark Office and learned that the funeral home had already registered "Bridging Generations." She changed the name of her company to Binding Legacies and registered it as a trademark to protect her business.

Other helpful tips for creating the ideal business name include the following:

- Look at your name from your potential customer's perspective. Do customers need reassurance (Gentle Dentistry), or do they prefer a bit of humor (Barking Lot Dog Grooming)? Other options include using a name that conveys an image to your customers that expresses your business strategy, such as Tires Now, Quality Muffler, or Pay-Less Auto Detailing.

- Decide the most appropriate quality of your business that you want to convey and incorporate it into your business name. Avoid sending a mixed or inappropriate message. Avoid business names that might leave potential customers confused about what your business does. Remember that the company name will be displayed on all of your advertising, packaging, and printed materials.

- Conduct a name search to make sure that no one else in your jurisdiction has already claimed the name. This can be particularly challenging for companies that intend to use their names as the URLs for their Web sites because so many names already are registered.

There are millions of names in the marketplace. Coming up with the one that is just right for your business can help greatly in creating a brand image for your business. Choosing a name that is distinctive, memorable, and positive can go a long way toward helping you achieve success in your business venture. Naming experts at Landor, an international branding firm, say that a name "acts as the primary handle for a brand; it's a recall and recognition device, it communicates desired attributes or specific benefits, and, through time and consistent use, it becomes a valuable asset and intellectual property." What's in a name? Everything!

Sources: Based on Denise Lee Yohn, "How to Name Your Concept (and Do It Right)," *QSR*, March 10, 2011, http://www.qsrmagazine.com/denise-lee-yohn/how-name-your-concept-and-do-it-right; Emily Maltby, "And Now, the Tricky Part: Naming Your Business," *Wall Street Journal*, http://online.wsj.com/article/SB10001424052748704103904575336942902327092.html; Laurel Sutton, "10 Best and Worst Internet Company Names of the Decade," *Marketing Profs*, December 29, 2009, http://www.marketingprofs.com/articles/2009/3278/10-best-and-worst-internet-company-names-of-the-decade; Charlie Szold, "Rent-A-Wreck Trades in Its Beat-Up Car Rental Image," *USA Today*, July 21, 2010, http://www.usatoday.com/money/autos/2010-07-21-rentawreck21_ST_N.htm; Ivy Hughes, "Wax Artistic," *Entrepreneur*, March 22, 2011, http://www.entrepreneur.com/article/219356; Scott Trimble, "18 Strategies and Tools for Naming Your Business or Product," *Marketing Profs*, January 24, 2008, https://www.marketingprofs.com/login/join.asp?adref=rdblk&source=%2F8%2Fhow%2Dto%2Dname%2Dproducts%2Dcompanies%2Dtrimble%2Easp; Alex Frankel, "The New Science of Naming," *Business 2.0*, December 2004, pp. 53–55; Jeff Wuorio, "'Oedipus Wrecks' and Other Business Names to Avoid," *bCentral*, www.bCentral.com/articles/wuorio/153.asp; and Suzanne Barlyn, "Name That Firm," *Wall Street Journal*, March 17, 2008, p. R7.

The Sole Proprietorship

The simplest and most popular form of ownership remains the **sole proprietorship**. The sole proprietorship, as its name implies, is a business owned and managed by one individual. Sole proprietorships make up about 72 percent of all businesses in the United States.

LO1A

Explain the advantages and disadvantages of the sole proprietorship.

sole proprietorship
a business owned and managed by one individual; the business and the owner are one and the same in the eyes of the law.

The Advantages of a Proprietorship

SIMPLE TO CREATE One of the most attractive features of a proprietorship is how fast and simple it is to begin. If an entrepreneur wants to operate a business under his or her own name (e.g., Strossner's Bakery), he or she simply obtains the necessary licenses from state, county, and/or local governments and begins operation. Entrepreneurs who operate a business under a trade name usually must file a certificate of trade name (or fictitious business name statement) with the secretary of state. Filing this statement notifies the public of the identity of the person behind the business. For most entrepreneurs, it is possible to start a proprietorship in a single day.

LEAST COSTLY FORM OF OWNERSHIP TO BEGIN In addition to being easy to begin, the proprietorship is generally the least expensive form of ownership to establish. There is no need to create and file legal documents that are recommended for partnerships and required for corporations. An entrepreneur simply goes to the city or county government, states the nature of the business he or she will start, and purchases the necessary business licenses. Businesses with employees (including sole proprietorships) must obtain from the Internal Revenue Service (IRS) (at no charge) an employer identification number, a nine-digit number that serves as the equivalent of a business Social Security number. In addition, companies that have employees may be required to register with the state labor department that administers the unemployment insurance and the workers' compensation programs. Businesses that sell goods or services must obtain a state sales tax license from the state tax office that allows them to collect sales tax from their customers and pass it on to the state department of revenue.

PROFIT INCENTIVE One major advantage of proprietorships is that once owners pay all of their companies' expenses, they can keep the remaining profits (less taxes, of course). The profit incentive is a powerful one, and profits represent an excellent way of "keeping score" in the game of the business. Sole proprietors report the net income of their businesses on Schedule C of IRS Form 1040, and the amount is taxed at the entrepreneur's personal tax rate. Because they are self-employed, sole proprietors' income from their business activities also is subject to the self-employment tax, which currently stands at 15.3 percent (an amount equal to the 7.65 percent employers pay plus the 7.65 percent employees contribute toward the Social Security and Medicare programs) of the proprietor's income. A ceiling on the Social Security portion of the self-employment tax does apply.

TOTAL DECISION-MAKING AUTHORITY Because the sole proprietor is in total control of operations, he or she can respond quickly to changes, which is an asset in a rapidly shifting market. The freedom to set the company's course of action is a major motivational force. For those who thrive on the enjoyment of seeking new opportunities in business, the freedom of fast, flexible decision making is vital. Many sole proprietors thrive on the feeling of control they have over their personal financial futures and the recognition they earn as the owners of their businesses.

NO SPECIAL LEGAL RESTRICTIONS The proprietorship is the least-regulated form of business ownership. In a time when government regulation seems never ending, this feature has much merit.

EASY TO DISCONTINUE If an entrepreneur decides to discontinue operations, he or she can terminate the business quickly even though he or she will still be personally liable for any outstanding debts and obligations that the business cannot pay.

mangostock/Shutterstock

The Disadvantages of a Proprietorship

Entrepreneurs considering the sole proprietorship as a form of ownership also must be aware of its disadvantages.

unlimited personal liability

a situation in which the sole proprietor is personally liable for all of the business's debts.

UNLIMITED PERSONAL LIABILITY Probably the greatest disadvantage of a sole proprietorship is the **unlimited personal liability** of the owner, meaning that the sole proprietor is personally liable for all of the business's debts. In a proprietorship, the owner *is* the business. He or she owns all of the business's assets, and if the business fails, creditors can force the sale of these assets to cover its debts. If unpaid business debts remain, creditors can also force the sale of the proprietor's *personal* assets to recover payment. In short, the *company's* debts are the *owner's* debts. Laws vary from one state to another, but most states require creditors to leave the failed business owner a minimum amount of equity in a home, a car, and some personal items. The reality is that failure of a business can ruin a sole proprietor financially.

ENTREPRENEURIAL PROFILE: Ann Siegle: Tria Marketing and Design Ann Siegle started a home-based marketing and design firm, Tria Marketing and Design, as a sole proprietorship. As her business grew, Siegle moved the business out of her home and hired employees. Siegle realized that a sole proprietorship put all of her personal assets at risk and converted her company into an S corporation to gain the benefit of limited personal liability that a corporation offers while retaining the tax advantages of a sole proprietorship.[2] ∎

LIMITED SKILLS AND CAPABILITIES A sole proprietor has total decision-making authority, but that does not mean that he or she has the range of skills that running a successful business requires. Each of us has areas in which our education, training, and work experiences have taught us a great deal, yet there are other areas in which our decision-making ability is weak. Many business failures occur because owners lack the skills, knowledge, and experience in areas that are vital to business success. Owners tend to push aside problems they don't understand or don't feel comfortable with in favor of those they can solve more easily. Unfortunately, the problems they set aside seldom solve themselves. By the time an owner decides to ask for help in addressing these problems, it may be too late to save the company.

FEELINGS OF ISOLATION Running a business alone allows an entrepreneur maximum flexibility, but it also creates feelings of isolation; there is no one else to turn to for help when solving problems or getting feedback on a new idea. Most sole proprietors admit that there are times when they feel the pressure of being alone and fully and completely responsible for every major business decision.

LIMITED ACCESS TO CAPITAL If a business is to grow and expand, a sole proprietor often needs additional financial resources. However, many proprietors have already put all of the resources they have into their businesses and have used their personal assets as collateral to acquire loans, making it difficult to borrow additional funds. A sole proprietorship is limited to whatever capital the owner can contribute and whatever money he or she can borrow. In short, proprietors find it difficult to raise additional money and maintain sole ownership. Most banks and other lending institutions have well-defined formulas for determining borrowers' eligibility. Unfortunately, many sole proprietors cannot meet those borrowing requirements, especially in the early days of business.

LACK OF CONTINUITY OF THE BUSINESS Lack of continuity is inherent in a sole proprietorship. If the proprietor dies, retires, or becomes incapacitated, the business automatically terminates. Unless a family member or employee can take over (which means that person is now a sole proprietor), the business will disappear. Because people look for secure employment and an opportunity for advancement, proprietorships often have trouble recruiting and retaining good employees. If no one is willing to step in to run the business in the founder's absence, creditors can petition the courts to liquidate the assets of the dissolved business to pay outstanding debts.

Some entrepreneurs find that forming partnerships is one way to overcome the disadvantages of the sole proprietorship. For instance, when one person lacks specific managerial skills or has insufficient access to needed capital, he or she can compensate for these weaknesses by forming a partnership with someone with complementary management skills or money to invest. In fact, businesses that have multiple owners (not necessarily partners) are more likely to be larger and to survive longer than sole proprietorships.[3] "In business, the chance that you can find one person with all of the skills needed, especially for a start-up, is almost zero," says Barry Nalebuff, a professor at Yale University who teamed up with former student Seth Goldman to launch beverage company Honest Tea.[4]

The Partnership

A **partnership** is an association of two or more people who co-own a business for the purpose of making a profit. In a partnership, the co-owners (partners) share the business's assets, liabilities, and profits according to the terms of a previously established partnership agreement (if one exists).

The law does not require a partnership agreement (also known as the articles of partnership), but it is wise to work with an attorney to develop one that spells out the exact status and responsibility of each partner. All too often, the parties think they know what they are agreeing to only to find later that no real meeting of the minds took place. A **partnership agreement** is a document that states in writing the terms under which the partners agree to operate the partnership and that protects each partner's interest in the business. Every partnership should be based on a written agreement. "When two entrepreneurial personalities are combined, there is a tremendous amount of strength and energy, but it must be focused in the same direction, or it will tear the relationship apart," explains one business writer. "A good partnership agreement will guide you through the good times, provide you with a method for handling problems, and serve as the infrastructure for a successful operation."[5]

ENTREPRENEURIAL PROFILE: Ken Clansky After several years of running his own business that specialized in creating government databases, Ken Clansky decided to enter into a partnership with the owner of a company whose services complemented those Clansky's business offered. The two agreed to be equal partners in the combined venture, but they neglected to create a partnership agreement. They soon discovered that their business goals and their managerial styles differed significantly, and conflicts surfaced. In retrospect, "We were both trying to run the show," says Clansky, who left the partnership and made a career change. "A business partnership is much more complex than it seems," he says.[6] ■

When no partnership agreement exists, the Revised Uniform Partnership Act governs a partnership. If a partnership agreement contains gaps in its coverage, the act will fill them. However, its provisions may not be as favorable as a specific agreement hammered out among the partners. Creating a partnership agreement is not necessarily costly. In most cases, the partners can discuss their preferences for each of the provisions in advance. Once they have reached an agreement, an attorney can draft the formal document. Bankers often want to see a copy of a partnership agreement before lending money to a partnership. Perhaps the most important feature of the partnership agreement is that it resolves potential sources of conflict that, if not addressed in advance, could later result in partnership battles and the dissolution of an otherwise successful business. Spelling out details—especially sticky ones such as profit splits, contributions, workloads, decision making authority, dispute resolution, dissolution, and others—in a written agreement at outset helps to avoid damaging tension in a partnership that could lead to a business "divorce." Business divorces, like marital ones, are almost always costly and unpleasant for everyone involved.

Generally, a partnership agreement can include any terms the partners want (unless they are illegal). The standard partnership agreement will likely include the following:

1. *Name of the partnership.*

2. *Purpose of the business.* What is the reason the business was brought into being?

3. *Location of the business.*

LO1B

Explain the advantages and disadvantages of the partnership.

partnership
an association of two or more people who co-own a business for the purpose of making a profit.

partnership agreement
a document that states in writing the terms under which the partners agree to operate the partnership and that protects each partner's interest in the business.

4. *Duration of the partnership.* How long will the partnership last?

5. *Names of the partners and their legal addresses.*

6. *Contributions of each partner to the business* at the creation of the partnership and later. This includes each partner's investment in the business. In some situations, a partner may contribute assets that are not likely to appear on a balance sheet. Experience, sales contacts, or a good reputation in the community may be reasons for asking a person to join in partnership.

7. Agreement on *how the profits or losses will be distributed.*

8. Procedure for *expansion through the addition of new partners.*

9. *Agreement on the distribution of assets if the partners voluntarily dissolve the partnership.*

10. *Sale of partnership interest.* The articles of partnership should include terms defining how a partner can sell his or her interest in the business.

11. *Salaries, draws, and expense accounts for the partners.* How much money will each partner draw from the business? Under what circumstances? How often?

12. *Absence or disability of one of the partners.* If a partner is absent or disabled for an extended period of time, should the partnership continue? Will the absent or disabled partner receive the same share of profits that he or she did prior to the absence or disability? Should the absent or disabled partner be held responsible for debts incurred while unable to participate?

13. *Dissolution of the partnership.* Under what circumstances will the partnership dissolve? How will the assets of the business be valued for dissolution?

14. *Alterations or modifications of the partnership agreement.* No document is written to last forever. Partnership agreements should contain provisions for alterations or modifications.

THE REVISED UNIFORM PARTNERSHIP ACT The Revised Uniform Partnership Act (RUPA) codifies the body of law dealing with partnerships in the United States. Under the RUPA, the three key elements of any partnership are common ownership interest in a business, sharing the business's profits and losses, and the right to participate in managing the operation of the partnership. Under the act, each partner has the *right* to do the following:

1. Participate in the management and operations of the business

2. Share in any profits the business might earn from operations

3. Receive interest on loans made to the business

4. Be compensated for expenses incurred in the name of the partnership

5. Receive their original capital contributions if the partnership terminates

6. Have access to the business's books and records

7. Receive a formal accounting of the partnership's business affairs

The RUPA also sets forth the partners' general obligations. Each partner is *obligated* to do the following:

1. Share in any losses sustained by the business

2. Work for the partnership without salary

3. Submit differences that may arise in the conduct of the business to majority vote or arbitration

4. Give the other partners complete information about all business affairs

5. Give a formal accounting of the partnership's business affairs

6. Live up to a fiduciary responsibility of the partnership and place the interest of the partnership above his or her personal interests

David Gage, a partnership mediator, suggests that partners also create a "partnership charter," a document that "serves as a guide for running the business and dealing with one another." Whereas a partnership agreement addresses the legal and business issues of running a business, a partnership charter covers the interpersonal aspects of the partners' relationships and serves as a helpful tool for managing the complexity of partnership relations.[7] Even with a partnership charter and a partnership agreement, a partnership must have two more essential elements above all others: mutual trust and respect. Any partnership missing these elements is destined to fail.

The Advantages of the Partnership

EASY TO ESTABLISH Like the proprietorship, the partnership is easy and inexpensive to establish. The owner must obtain the necessary business licenses and submit a minimal number of forms. In most states, partners must file a Certificate for Conducting Business as Partners if the business is run under a trade name.

COMPLEMENTARY SKILLS In a sole proprietorship, the owner must wear lots of different hats, and not all of them will fit well. In successful partnerships, the parties' skills and abilities usually complement one another, strengthening the company's managerial foundation. For years, entrepreneur Norm Brodsky, founder of CitiStorage, a successful document storage company in New York City, thought that partnerships were a recipe for disaster in business—until he had the chance to work with Sam Kaplan. Over time, Brodsky saw how Kaplan's values and philosophies were similar to his own and that Kaplan's strengths were skills that he lacked. The two became business partners, and with their combined skills, CitiStorage went on to achieve record levels of success. "Alone I might be right six or seven times out of ten," says Brodsky. "With Sam, I can be right nine times out of ten. That's a big advantage."[8]

DIVISION OF PROFITS There are no restrictions on how partners distribute the company's profits as long as they are consistent with the partnership agreement and do not violate the rights of any partner. The partnership agreement should articulate each partner's contribution to the business and his or her share of the profits. If the partners fail to create an agreement, the RUPA says that the partners share equally in the partnership's profits, even if their original capital contributions were unequal.

LARGER POOL OF CAPITAL The partnership form of ownership can significantly broaden the pool of capital available to a business. Each partner's asset base enhances the business's pool of capital and improves its ability to borrow needed funds; together, partners' personal assets support greater borrowing capacity.

ABILITY TO ATTRACT LIMITED PARTNERS When partners share in owning, operating, and managing a business, they are **general partners**. General partners have unlimited liability for the partnership's debts and usually take an active role in managing the business. Every partnership must have at least one general partner, although there is no limit on the number of general partners a business can have.

　　Limited partners are financial investors in a partnership, cannot participate in the day-to-day management of a company, and have limited liability for the partnership's debts. If the business fails, they lose only what they have invested in it and no more. A limited partnership can attract investors by offering them limited liability and the potential to realize a substantial return on their investments if the business is successful. Many individuals find it very profitable to invest in high-potential small businesses but only if they avoid the disadvantages of unlimited liability while doing so. If limited partners are "materially and actively" engaged in a business (defined as spending more than 500 hours per year in the company) or if they hold themselves out as general partners, they will be treated as general partners and will lose their limited liability protection. Two types of limited partners are silent partners and dormant partners. **Silent partners** are not active in a business but generally are known to be members of the partnership. **Dormant partners** are neither active nor generally known to be associated with the business.

general partners
partners who share in owning, operating, and managing a business and who have unlimited personal liability for the partnership's debts.

limited partners
partners who make financial investments in a partnership, who do not take an active role in managing a business, and whose liability for the partnership's debts is limited to the amount they have invested.

ENTREPRENEURIAL PROFILE: Pascal Rigo and Thomas Lefort: La Boulange Pascal Rigo spent years working for bakeries in his native Bordeaux, France, and in Paris before moving to San Francisco, California, in 1999 to open La Boulange, a bakery and café that sells a wide variety of fresh-baked delicacies to both wholesale and retail customers. In 2003, Rigo partnered with Thomas Lefort, whose business acumen helped the company bakery expand to 13 locations in the Bay area. In 2006, Rigo and Lefort brought in a silent partner whose investment provided the company with a sufficient capital base to fund its future growth.[9] ∎

We will discuss limited partnerships in the next section of this chapter.

MINIMAL GOVERNMENT REGULATION Like the sole proprietorship, partnerships are not burdened with excessive red tape.

FLEXIBILITY Although not as flexible as sole ownership, a partnership can generally react quickly to changing market conditions because the partners can respond quickly and creatively to new opportunities. In large partnerships, however, getting partners' approval can slow a company's strategic actions. Unless the partnership agreement states otherwise, each partner has a single vote in the management of the company no matter how large his or her contribution to the partnership is.

TAXATION A partnership itself is not subject to federal taxation. It serves as a conduit for the profit or losses it earns or incurs; its net income or loss is passed through to the partners as personal income, and the partners pay income tax on their distributive shares at their individual tax rates. The partnership files an informational return, Form 1065, with the IRS that reports its net income for the tax year and the percentages of the business that each partner owns. The partnership provides each partner with a Schedule K-1 that shows his or her share of partnership's net income (or loss). Partners must pay taxes on their respective shares of the partnership's net income, even if none of that income actually is distributed to them. A partnership, like a sole proprietorship, avoids the "double-taxation" disadvantage associated with the corporate form of ownership.

The Disadvantages of the Partnership

Before entering into a partnership, every entrepreneur should double-check the decision to be sure that the prospective business partner will add value to the business. A partnership is like a business marriage, and before entering into one, an entrepreneur should be aware of the disadvantages.

UNLIMITED LIABILITY OF AT LEAST ONE PARTNER At least one member of every partnership must be a general partner. The general partner has unlimited personal liability for any debts that remain after the partnerships assets are exhausted. In addition, general partners' liability is *joint and several*, which means that creditors can hold all general partners equally responsible for the partnership's debts or can collect the entire debt from just one partner.

ENTREPRENEURIAL PROFILE: AmyLynn Keimach and Kenneth Tran: Border7 Studios AmyLynn Keimach and Kenneth Tran operate their Simi Valley, California–based Web-services firm, Border7 Studios, as a general partnership. Even though they recognize the liability risks that choosing to operate as a partnership, Keimach and Tran, who started the company after they were laid off from their jobs without severance pay, say that they cannot yet afford to form an S corporation, their desired form of ownership. "If any of our clients sue our company, they could take everything my partner and I own," says Keimach. "It's scary."[10] ∎

CAPITAL ACCUMULATION Although the partnership form of ownership is superior to the proprietorship in its ability to attract capital, it is generally not as effective as the corporate form of ownership, which can raise capital by selling shares of ownership to outside investors.

DIFFICULTY IN DISPOSING OF PARTNERSHIP INTEREST Most partnership agreements restrict how partners can dispose of their shares of the business. Usually, an agreement requires a partner to sell his or her interest to the remaining partner(s). Even if the original agreement contains such a requirement and clearly delineates how the value of each partner's ownership will be determined, there is no guarantee that the other partner(s) will have the financial resources to buy the seller's interest. When the money is not available to purchase a partner's interest, the other partner(s) may be forced to either accept a new partner or dissolve the partnership, distribute the remaining assets, and begin again. Under prior versions of the RUPA, when a partner withdrew from a partnership (an act called disassociation), the partnership automatically dissolved, requiring the remaining partners to form a new partnership. Current provisions of the RUPA, however, do not require dissolution and allow the remaining partners to continue to operate the business without the disassociated partner through a continuation agreement. The disassociated partner no longer has the authority to represent the business or to take part in managing it.

A similar problem arises when a partner dies. The deceased partner's interest in the partnership passes to his or her heirs, in which case the partnership is dissolved and the heirs receive the value of the deceased partner's share of the business. However, the partnership agreement may provide for the partnership to continue to operate with the remaining partner(s) purchasing the deceased partner's share of the business from his or her estate. To ensure that sufficient funds are available to purchase a deceased partner's interest in the business, the partnership should purchase life insurance policies on all partners and use the proceeds to purchase the deceased partner's share of the business for the surviving partner(s).

POTENTIAL FOR PERSONALITY AND AUTHORITY CONFLICTS Being in a partnership is much like being in a marriage. Making sure that partners' work habits, goals, ethics, and general business philosophy are compatible is an important step in avoiding a nasty business divorce. Engaging in serious discussions with potential partners before launching a business together is a valuable and revealing exercise. A better way to "test-drive" a potential partnership is to work with a prospective partner on a joint project to get a sense of how compatible your work styles, business philosophies, and personalities really

iofoto/Shutterstock

are. That project might be a small business venture or working together to create a business plan for the proposed partnership. The idea is to work together before committing to a partnership to determine how compatible the potential partners' values, goals, personalities, views, and ethics are.

ENTREPRENEURIAL PROFILE: Rocco DiSpirito and Jeffrey Chodorow: Rocco's 22nd Street Celebrity chef Rocco DiSpirito ended up in a lawsuit over ownership and management issues with his business partners concerning the operation of the New York City restaurant they owned. Jeffrey Chodorow and several partners invested $3 million to open Rocco's 22nd Street, but a nasty dispute led to the demise of the once promising partnership. At one point, Chodorow filed a lawsuit against DiSpirito, who countersued Chodorow. Just before the restaurants closed, Chodorow asked a New York court to ban DiSpirito from the Rocco's 22nd Street restaurant.[11] ■

No matter how compatible partners are, friction among them is inevitable. The key is to have a mechanism such as a partnership agreement and open lines of communication for managing conflict. The demise of many partnerships can be traced to interpersonal conflicts and the lack of a process to resolve those conflicts.

PARTNERS ARE BOUND BY THE LAW OF AGENCY Each partner is an agent for the business and can legally bind the partnership and, hence, the other partners to contracts—even without the remaining partners' knowledge or consent. Because of this agency power, all partners must exercise good faith and reasonable care when performing their responsibilities. For example, if a partner signs a three-year lease for a business jet, a move that only worsens the small company's cash flow struggles, the partnership is legally bound by the agreement even though the remaining partners may not be in favor of the decision.

Some partnerships survive a lifetime, while others struggle because they suffer from many of the problems described here. Conflicts between or among partners can force an otherwise thriving business to close. Too many partners never put into place a mutually agreed-on method of conflict resolution such as a partnership agreement. Without such a mechanism, disagreements can escalate to the point where the partnership is dissolved and the business ceases to operate.

Limited Partnerships

A **limited partnership** is composed of at least one general partner and at least one limited partner. In a limited partnership, the general partner is treated, under the law, the same as in a general partnership. Limited partners are treated as investors in the business venture, and they have limited liability for the partnership's debts. They can lose only the amount they have invested in the business. Because of this advantage, limited partnerships own many professional sports teams, including the Miami Heat, Chicago Bulls, and Minnesota Timberwolves of the National Basketball Association (NBA).

Most states have ratified the Revised Uniform Limited Partnership Act. Forming a limited partnership requires its founders to file a Certificate of Limited Partnership with the secretary of state's office. A limited partnership must include "limited partnership," "L.P.," or "LP" in its business name. Although the requirements vary from one state to another, the Certificate of Limited Partnership typically includes the following information:

- The name of the limited partnership
- The general character of its business
- The address of the office of the firm's agent authorized to receive summonses or other legal notices
- The name and business address of each partner, specifying which ones are general partners and which are limited partners
- The amount of cash contributions actually made and agreed to be made in the future, by each partner
- A description of the value of noncash contributions made or to be made by each partner
- The times at which additional contributions are to be made by any of the partners
- Whether and under what conditions a limited partner has the right to grant limited partner status to an assignee of his or her interest in the partnership
- If agreed on, the time or the circumstances when a partner may withdraw from the firm (unlike the withdrawal of a general partner, the withdrawal of a limited partner does *not* automatically dissolve a limited partnership)
- If agreed on, the amount of or the method of determining the funds to be received by a withdrawing partner
- Any right of a partner to receive distributions of cash or other property from the firm and the times and circumstances for such distributions
- The time or circumstances when the limited partnership is to be dissolved
- The rights of the remaining general partners to continue the business after withdrawal of a general partner
- Any other matters the partners want to include

Every limited partnership must have at least one general partner, but there is no limit to the number of general or limited partners allowed. The general partner has the same rights and duties as under a general partnership: the right to make decisions for the business, to act as an agent for the partnership, to use the property of the partnership for normal business, and to share in the business's profits. The limited partner does not have the right to engage actively in managing the business. In fact, limited partners who take an active part in managing the business (more than 500 hours per year) forfeit their limited liability status and are treated just like general partners. Limited partners can, however, make management suggestions to the general partners, inspect the business, and make copies of business records. A limited partner is, of course, entitled to a share of

✓ You Be the Consultant

Making a Partnership Work

College Hunks Hauling Junk. www.CollegeHunksHaulingJunk.com Effortless
Entrepreneur: Work Smart, Play Hard www.EffortlessEntrepreneur.com

Structured properly, a partnership can be very successful and quite rewarding for its founders. Nick Friedman and Omar Soliman met in the tenth grade and became best friends. In his senior year at the University of Miami in Coral Gables, Florida, Soliman enrolled in an entrepreneurship class where he created a business plan for College Hunks Hauling Junk, the moving and junk-hauling company that he and Friedman operated during their summer breaks from college. He submitted his plan to the Leigh Rothschild Entrepreneurship Competition, where it won first prize and $10,000. After graduating from Pomona College, Friedman accepted a job at a Washington, D.C., consulting firm but quickly became disenchanted with his corporate career. At age 22, he and Soliman decided to launch College Hunks Hauling Junk and became the youngest franchisors in the United States.

Today their company, which recycles 50 percent of the material they process, has grown into a $3.5 million junk removal business with 35 franchisees and has been featured in the *Inc.* 500 list of fastest-growing small companies and on *Shark Tank*. Friedman and Soliman are best friends, something that has strengthened their business partnership and made their company a success. However, that is not always the outcome when best friends go into business together. Friedman and Soliman offer the following lessons for making a business partnership work:

- ***Make certain that you have a common vision before you start.*** "The key to our partnership is that our vision and values have been in perfect alignment," says Friedman. Before they officially launched College Hunks Hauling Junk, each of them wrote separately about where they expected their business to be in five years. "We were amazed that our visions were very much in alignment," says Friedman. "We both talked about franchising, being a media success, creating a household brand, and being a popular employer of young adults and college students." Friedman goes on to say that "Omar and I have disagreements, but we never disagree on what direction the company is going in and what our mission and values are."

- ***The ideal partner is one whose skills, experience, talents, and abilities complement yours rather than mirror them.*** As their company has grown, Friedman and Soliman have developed distinctive roles that support one another. "Omar is the big picture guy," explains Friedman. "I'm more of a nuts-and-bolts guy. I figure out how we're going to get there."

- ***Create a partnership agreement—always.*** No matter how strong a friendship is, partners should create a partnership agreement. Discussing and then putting in writing how partners will handle sensitive issues, such as financing, daily decision making, handling deadlocks in decisions, compensation, withdrawing from the partnership, and many others, not only helps resolve disputes down the road but also allows the partners to avoid disputes.

- ***Create an advisory board.*** Friedman and Soliman are equal owners of College Hunks Hauling Junk. What happens when they disagree on an important decision? In the early stages of the business, they simply "duked it out." (Friedman laughingly concedes that actual punches have been involved on occasion.) Today, the business partners consult with the advisory board they created that includes professors, executives from large companies, and other entrepreneurs who can offer valuable insight.

In other cases, forming a partnership can be the beginning of an extended nightmare. Three entrepreneurs formed a partnership to sell male enhancement products but never created a partnership agreement. The partner who controlled the company's finances and operations distributed more than $11 million to himself from the partnership but less than $1 million to his partners. The two partners became suspicious and demanded a full accounting of the partnership's records. The managing partner refused, prompting the two partners to file an arbitration claim against him. During the arbitration hearing, the managing partner claimed that because there was no partnership agreement, no partnership existed. The two partners argued that the parties' original intent was to create a partnership and that they should receive equal shares of the partnership's profits. A panel of arbitrators agreed with the two partners and ordered the managing partner to pay them $4.5 million. Of course, the business did not survive the dispute.

Avoiding ugly and costly business divorces that too often bring an end to businesses requires an ongoing and active effort. Experts suggest that partners follow these guidelines to keep their partnerships going strong:

- Ask yourself, "Do I really need a partner?" You should take on a partner only if doing so is essential to your company's success. A potential partner should bring to the business skills, contacts, financing, knowledge, or something else that you don't have.

(continued)

You Be the Consultant (continued)

- Take a close look at what you're getting. How well do you really know your potential partner? One of the best ways to test your compatibility is to work on small projects together before you decide to go into business with one another. Doing so allows you to judge how compatible your management styles, business philosophies, and values are.

- Invest in the relationship, not just the deal making. Partners must constantly work to strengthen their relationships. You cannot delegate or ignore this role; otherwise, the partnership is destined to fail.

- Respect your differences but expect to work out conflicts. When potential sources of conflict exist, address them immediately. Festering wounds seldom heal themselves.

- Divide business responsibilities and duties according to each partner's skills, interests, and abilities.

- Be prepared to change. Be open to new opportunities and share with your partners what you see. Partnerships must evolve to survive.

- Help your partners to succeed. Work hard to see that every partner plays a role in the business that affords him or her the opportunity to be successful.

- Make sure your partners are people you admire, respect, and enjoy being around.

Brothers Kai and Charles Huang shared a room when they were growing up and, like many brothers, had their share of arguments and scuffles. Years later, the brothers launched RedOctane, the company that created the hit video game *Guitar Hero*, which has generated more than $1 billion in sales. Kai and Charles admit that their partnership dynamic resembles the relationship they had growing up. "We get into disagreements," says Kai, "and sometimes we just start yelling at each other. We're totally comfortable with that." Even though they sometimes fight, the Huangs have a strong bond, making them better business partners. "There's an implicit trust that we've built up over 30-some-odd years," says Charles. "We walked into business knowing how each other thinks and what the other is likely to do. We trust each other."

1. Research relationships between partners and add at least three guidelines to those listed here.

2. Develop a list of the behaviors that are almost certain to destroy a partnership.

3. Suppose that two of your friends are about to launch a business together with nothing but a handshake. "We've been best friends since grammar school," they say. What advice would you give them?

Sources: Based on Donna Fenn, "Advice from College Hunks: How to Start a Company with Your Best Friend," *BNET*, September 7, 2010, http://www.bnet.com/blog/entrepreneurs/advice-from-college-hunks-how-to-start-a-company-with-your-best-friend/1213; Laura Petrecca, "A Partner Can Give Your Business Shelter or a Storm," *USA Today*, October 9, 2009, http://www.usatoday.com/money/smallbusiness/startup/week4-partnerships.htm; Patricia Laya, "This Guy Quit His Consulting Job to Haul People's Junk, and Is Making Millions," *Business Insider*, August 8, 2011, http://www.businessinsider.com/business-tips-nick-friedman-college-hunks-hauling-junk-08-2011?op=1; and "$4.5 Million Judgment for Aiken Schenk Clients in Partnership Dispute," Aiken Schenk Hawkins, and Ricciardi, 2011, http://www.ashrlaw.com/news/oral-partnership.htm.

---

the business's profits as specified in the Certificate of Limited Partnership. The primary disadvantage of limited partnerships is the complexity and the cost of establishing and maintaining them.

ENTREPRENEURIAL PROFILE: Wolfgang Puck and Barbara Lazaroff: Food Company Wolfgang Puck, the Austrian-born chef who has won national acclaim for his unique food combinations such as scrambled egg pizza with smoked salmon and banana chocolate chip soufflé, and his wife Barbara Lazaroff operate three dozen upscale restaurants across the United States. The largest division of their business, the Food Company, is a corporation, but Puck and Lazaroff rely on limited partnerships to operate the restaurants in their Fine Dining Group. For instance, each of the company's various Spago's (Beverly Hills, Palo Alto, Maui, and Las Vegas) has a distinct collection of owners, as do the other restaurants in the group, such as Postrio and Chinois.[12] ∎

Limited Liability Partnerships

limited liability partnership (LLP)
a special type of limited partnership in which *all* partners, who in many states must be professionals, are limited partners.

Many states now recognize **limited liability partnerships (LLPs)**, in which *all* partners in a business are limited partners, giving them the advantage of limited liability for the debts of the partnership. Most states restrict LLPs to certain types of professionals, such as attorneys, physicians, dentists, accountants, and others. However, many states restrict the limited liability advantage of LLPs to the results of actions taken by other partners. For instance, if an LLP sells a defective product that injures a customer, the injured customer could sue the business *and* the partners as individuals. The partners' unlimited personal liability exposure means that their personal assets would be at risk.

Just as with any limited partnership, the partners must file a Certificate of Limited Partnership in the state in which the partnership will conduct business, and the partnership must identify itself as an LLP to those with whom it does business. In addition, like every partnership, an LLP does not pay taxes; its income is passed through to the limited partners, who pay taxes on their shares of the company's income.

"SURE IT'S A PARTNERSHIP, ELWOOD, BUT IT'S A LIMITED PARTNERSHIP, AND' YOU'RE THE ONE WHO'S LIMITED".

© S. Harris/www.CartoonStock.com

Corporations

The corporation is the most complex of the three major forms of business ownership. It is a separate entity apart from its owners and may engage in business, make contracts, sue and be sued, own property, and pay taxes. The Supreme Court has defined the **corporation** as "an artificial being, invisible, intangible, and existing only in contemplation of the law."[13] Because the life of the corporation is independent of its owners, the shareholders can sell their interests in the business without affecting its continuation.

Corporations (also known as "C corporations") are creations of the states. When a corporation is founded, it accepts the regulations and restrictions of the state in which it is incorporated and any other state in which it chooses to do business. A corporation doing business in the state in which it is incorporated is a **domestic corporation**. When a corporation conducts business in another state, that state considers it to be a **foreign corporation**. A corporation that is formed in another country but does business in the United States is called an **alien corporation**.

Corporations have the power to raise large amounts of capital by selling shares of ownership to outside investors, but many corporations have only a handful of shareholders. A **closely held corporation** has shares that are controlled by a relatively small number of people, often family members, relatives, friends, or employees. Its stock is not traded on any stock exchange but instead is passed from one generation to the next. Most small corporations are closely held. A **publicly held corporation** has a large number of shareholders, and its stock usually is traded on one of the large stock exchanges.

In general, a corporation must report annually its financial operations to its home state's secretary of state. These financial reports become public record. If a corporation's stock is sold in more than one state, the corporation must comply with federal regulations governing the sale of corporate securities. There are substantially more reporting requirements for a corporation than for the other forms of ownership.

How to Incorporate

Most states allow entrepreneurs to incorporate without the assistance of an attorney. Some states even provide incorporation kits to help in the incorporation process. More entrepreneurs are using Web sites such as MyCorporation, BizFilings, and LegalZoom to create corporations because they can incorporate for as little as $100.

LO1C

Explain the advantages and the disadvantages of the corporation.

corporation
a separate legal entity apart from its owners that receives the right to exist from the state in which it is incorporated.

domestic corporation
a corporation doing business in the state in which it is incorporated.

foreign corporation
a corporation doing business in a state other than the one in which it is incorporated.

alien corporation
a corporation formed in another country but doing business in the United States.

closely held corporation
a corporation whose shares are controlled by a relatively small number of people, often family members, relatives, friends, or employees.

publicly held corporation
a corporation that has a large number of shareholders and whose stock usually is traded on one of the large stock exchanges.

Elaine's Toffee Company

ENTREPRENEURIAL PROFILE: Janet Long: Elaine's Toffee Company Janet Long used her mother's secret recipe to make 70 pounds of toffee for a holiday fund-raiser at her children's school. She sold all of the toffee and, after the event, received numerous requests to purchase more. That Christmas, Long, her sisters, and her father decided to launch Elaine's Toffee Company, named in memory of her mother. They decided that their family business would be an S corporation and used LegalZoom to incorporate. "We wanted to make sure there was a definitive line between the business and our personal finances," says Long. Elaine's Toffee has come a long way since the school fund-raiser and sells its delectable treats in several major retail outlets and at the company's Web site.[14] ■

Although it is cheaper for entrepreneurs to complete the incorporation process themselves, it is not always the best idea. In some states, the application process is complex, and the required forms are confusing. The price for filing incorrectly can be high. If an entrepreneur completes the incorporation process improperly, it is generally invalid.

Once entrepreneurs decide to form a corporation, they must choose a state in which to incorporate. If the business will operate within a single state, it is most logical to incorporate in that state. States differ—sometimes dramatically—in the requirements they place on the corporations they charter and how they treat the corporations created within their borders. They also differ in the tax rates they impose on corporations, the restrictions they place on their activities, the capital they require for a company to incorporate, and the fees or organization taxes they charge to incorporate. Some states, such as Delaware, Vermont, and Nevada, offer low incorporation fees, favorable laws concerning the sale of securities, low taxes, and minimal legal requirements, and many *Fortune* 500 corporations are chartered in these states. However, for most entrepreneurs, incorporating in the state from which they intend to operate the business usually is best because they are not likely to reap any real benefits by incorporating out of state.

To create a corporation, every state requires a Certificate of Incorporation or charter to be filed with the secretary of state. The following information is generally required to be in the Certificate of Incorporation:

The corporation's name. The corporation must choose a name that is not so similar to that of another company in that state that it causes confusion or lends itself to deception. It must also include a term such as "corporation," "incorporated," "company," or "limited" to notify the public that they are dealing with a corporation.

The corporation's statement of purpose. The incorporators must state in general terms the intended nature of the business. The purpose must, of course, be lawful. An illustration might be "to engage in the sale of office furniture and fixtures." The purpose should be broad enough to allow for some expansion in the activities of the business as it develops.

The corporation's time horizon. Most corporations are formed with no specific termination date; they are formed "for perpetuity." However, it is possible to incorporate for a specific duration, for example, 50 years.

Names and addresses of the incorporators. The incorporators must be identified in the articles of incorporation and are liable under the law to attest that all information in the articles of incorporation is correct. Some states require one or more of the incorporators to reside in the state in which the corporation is being created.

Place of business. The street and mailing addresses of the corporation's principal office must be listed. For a domestic corporation, this address must be in the state in which incorporation takes place.

Capital stock authorization. The articles of incorporation must include the amount and class (or type) of capital stock the corporation wants to be authorized to issue. This is *not* the number of shares it must issue; a corporation can issue any number of shares up to the total number authorized. This section must also define the different classification of stock and any special rights, preferences, or limits each class has.

Capital required at the time of incorporation. Some states require a newly formed corporation to deposit in a bank a specific percentage of the stock's par value prior to incorporating.

Provisions for preemptive rights, if any, that are granted to stockholders. If a corporation later issues more shares of the stock it is authorized to issue, its original investors' shares of ownership would be diluted. To prevent this dilution, some corporations grant **preemptive rights** to shareholders, which give them the ability to purchase enough shares to maintain their original percentage of ownership in the company.

Restrictions on transferring shares. Many closely held corporations—those owned by a few shareholders, often family members—require shareholders interested in selling their stock to offer it first to the corporation. (Shares the corporation itself owns are called **treasury stock**.) To maintain control over their ownership, many closely held corporations exercise this right, known as the **right of first refusal**.

Names and addresses of the officers and directors of the corporation.

Rules under which the corporation will operate. **Bylaws** are the rules and regulations the officers and directors establish for the corporation's internal management and operation.

Once the secretary of state of the incorporating state has approved a request for incorporation and the corporation pays its fees, the approved articles of incorporation become its charter. With the charter in hand, the next order of business is to hold an organizational meeting for the stockholders to formally elect directors who in turn will appoint the corporate officers.

The Advantages of the Corporation

LIMITED LIABILITY OF STOCKHOLDERS Because it is a separate legal entity, a corporation allows investors to limit their liability to the total amount of their investment in the business. In other words, creditors of the corporation cannot lay claim to shareholders' personal assets to satisfy the company's unpaid debts. The legal protection of personal assets from business creditors is of critical concern to many potential investors. John Gazzola, founder of Toyopolis, a company that sells toys, games, and collectibles online, chose the corporate form of ownership because of his desire to limit his personal liability and for "peace of mind."[15]

This shield of limited liability may not be impenetrable, however. Because start-up companies are so risky, lenders and other creditors often require the founders of corporations to personally guarantee loans made to the business. Experts estimate that 95 percent of small business owners have to sign personal guarantees to get the debt financing they need. By making these guarantees, owners are putting their personal assets at risk (just as in a proprietorship) despite choosing the corporate form of ownership.

The corporate form of ownership also does not protect its owners from being held personally liable for fraudulent or illegal acts. Court decisions have extended the personal liability of the owners of small corporations beyond the financial guarantees that banks and other lenders require, "piercing the corporate veil" much more than ever before. Courts increasingly are holding entrepreneurs *personally* liable for environmental, pension, and legal claims against their corporations. Courts will pierce the corporate veil and hold entrepreneurs liable for the company's debts and obligations if the owners deliberately commit criminal or negligent acts when handling corporate business. Courts ignore the limited liability shield the corporate form of ownership provides when an entrepreneur does the following:

1. Uses corporate assets for personal reasons or commingles them with his or her personal assets

2. Fails to act in a responsible manner and creates an unwarranted level of financial risk for the stockholders

3. Makes financial misrepresentations, such as operating with more than one set of books

4. Takes actions in the name of the corporation that were not authorized by the board of directors

preemptive rights
the rights of a corporation's original investors to purchase enough shares of future stock issues to maintain their original percentage of ownership in the company.

treasury stock
the shares of its own stock that a corporation owns.

right of first refusal
a provision requiring shareholders who want to sell their stock to offer it first to the corporation.

bylaws
the rules and regulations the officers and directors establish for a corporation's internal management and operation.

TABLE 5.1 Avoiding Legal Tangles in a Corporation

Steps that entrepreneurs should take to avoid legal problems if they own a corporation include the following:

- *Identify the company as a corporation by using "Inc." or "Corporation" in the business name.* This alerts all who do business with a company that it is a corporation.

- *File all reports and pay all necessary fees required by the state in a timely manner.* Most states require corporations to file reports with the secretary of state on an annual basis. Failing to do so will jeopardize the validity of your corporation and will open the door for personal liability problems for its shareholders.

- *Hold annual meetings to elect officers and directors.* In a closely held corporation, the officers elected may *be* the shareholders, but that does not matter. Corporations formed by an individual are not required to hold meetings, but the sole shareholder must file a written consent form.

- *Keep minutes of every meeting of the officers and directors, even if it takes place in the living room of the founders.* It is a good idea to elect a secretary who is responsible for recording the minutes.

- *Make sure that the corporation's board of directors makes all major decisions.* Problems arise in closely held corporations when one owner makes key decisions alone without consulting the elected board.

- *Make it clear that the business is a corporation by having all officers sign contracts, loan agreements, purchase orders, and other legal documents in the corporation's name rather than their own names.* Failing to designate their status as agents of the corporation can result in the officers being held personally liable for agreements they think they are signing on the corporation's behalf.

- *Keep corporate assets and the personal assets of the owner's separate.* Few things make courts more willing to hold shareholder's personally liable for a corporation's debts than commingling corporate and personal assets. In some closely held corporations, owners have been known to use corporate assets to pay their personal expenses (or vice versa) or to mix their personal funds with corporate funds into a single bank account. Protect the corporation's identity by keeping it completely separate from the owner's personal identities.

Source: U.S. Small Business Administration, 2010.

private placement
a fund-raising tool in which a company sells shares of its stock to a limited number of private investors.

initial public offering (IPO)
a fund-raising tool in which a company sells shares of its stock to the public.

Liability problems associated with piercing the corporate veil almost always originate from actions and decisions that fail to maintain the integrity of a corporation. The most common cause of these problems, especially in closely held corporations, is corporate owners and officers failing to keep their personal funds and assets separate from those of the corporation. Table 5.1 offers some useful suggestions for avoiding legal tangles in a corporation.

ABILITY TO ATTRACT CAPITAL Because of the limited liability they offer their investors, corporations have proved to be the most effective form of ownership for accumulating large amounts of capital. Limited only by the number of shares authorized in its charter (which can be amended), a corporation can raise money to begin business and expand by selling shares of its stock to investors. A corporation can sell its stock to a limited number of private investors in a **private placement** or to the public through an **initial public offering (IPO)**.

ENTREPRENEURIAL PROFILE: Reid Hoffman: LinkedIn LinkedIn, the professional social networking Web site with more than 100 million members, recently sold 7.84 million shares of stock in an IPO, raising more than $350 million in capital to finance the company's growth. On the day the company went public, the value of the shares held by LinkedIn founder Reid Hoffman, the company's largest shareholder, was $1.8 billion.[16] ■

You will learn more about IPOs in Chapter 14.

ABILITY TO CONTINUE INDEFINITELY Unless a corporation fails to pay its taxes or is limited to a specific length of life by its charter, it can continue indefinitely. The corporation's existence does not depend on the fate of any single individual. Unlike a proprietorship or partnership in which the death of a founder ends the business, a corporation lives beyond the lives of those who gave it life. This perpetual life gives rise to the next major advantage—transferable ownership.

TRANSFERABLE OWNERSHIP Unlike an investment in a partnership, shares of ownership in a corporation are easily transferable. If stockholders want to liquidate their shares of ownership in a corporation, they can sell their shares to someone else. Millions of shares of stock representing ownership in companies are traded daily on the world's stock exchanges. Shareholders can also transfer their stock through inheritance to a new generation of owners. During all of these transfers of ownership, the corporation continues to conduct business as usual. The market for stock of closely held corporations, which often are held by company founders, family members, or employees, is limited, and this can make transfer of ownership difficult.

The Disadvantages of the Corporation

COST AND TIME INVOLVED IN THE INCORPORATION PROCESS Corporations can be costly and time consuming to establish and to maintain. The owners are giving birth to an artificial legal entity, and the gestation period can be prolonged, especially for a novice. Many entrepreneurs hire attorneys to handle the incorporation process, but in most states entrepreneurs can complete all of the required forms, most of which are online, themselves. However, entrepreneurs must exercise great caution when incorporating without the help of an attorney. Incorporating a business requires a variety of fees that are not applicable to proprietorships or partnerships. The average cost to create a corporation is around $1,000, but, depending on the complexity of the organization, fees can range from $500 to $5,000. In addition, a corporation must have a board of directors, and the board must conduct an annual meeting and maintain written records of that meeting even if the entity is a single-shareholder corporation.

DOUBLE TAXATION Because a corporation is a separate legal entity, it must pay taxes on its net income at the federal level, in most states, and to some local governments as well. Before stockholders receive a penny of its net income as dividends, a corporation must pay taxes at the *corporate* tax rate, a graduated tax on corporate profits. Then, stockholders must pay taxes on the dividends they receive from these same profits at their *individual* tax rates. Thus, a corporation's profits are taxed twice. This **double taxation** is a distinct disadvantage of the corporate form of ownership. Table 5.2 shows a comparison of the tax bill for a small company organized as a C corporation and as an S corporation (or a limited liability company).

double taxation
a disadvantage of the corporate form of ownership in which a corporation's profits are taxed twice: at the corporate rate and at the individual rate (on the portion of profits distributed as dividends).

POTENTIAL FOR DIMINISHED MANAGERIAL INCENTIVES As corporations grow, they often require additional managerial expertise beyond that which the founder can provide. Because they often have most of their personal wealth tied up in their companies, entrepreneurs have an intense interest in making them a success and are willing to make sacrifices for them. Professional managers the entrepreneur brings in to help run the business as it grows do not always have the same degree of loyalty to the company. As a result, the business may falter without the founder's energy, attention, and devotion. One way to minimize this potential problem is to link managers' (and even employees') compensation to the company's financial performance through a profit-sharing or bonus plan. Corporations can also stimulate managers' and employees' incentive on the job by creating an employee stock ownership plan (ESOP) in which managers and employees become part or whole owners in the company.

LEGAL REQUIREMENTS AND REGULATORY RED TAPE Corporations are subject to more legal, reporting, and financial requirements than other forms of ownership. Corporate officers must meet more stringent requirements for recording and reporting management decisions and actions. They must also hold annual meetings and consult the board of directors about major decisions that are beyond day-to-day operations. Managers may be required to submit some major decisions to the stockholders for approval. Corporations that are publicly held must file quarterly (10-Q) and annual (10-K) reports with the Securities and Exchange Commission. These reports are available to the public, and anyone, including competitors, can access them.

POTENTIAL LOSS OF CONTROL BY THE FOUNDER(S) When entrepreneurs sell shares of ownership in their companies, they relinquish some control. Especially when they need large capital infusions for start-up or growth, entrepreneurs may have to give up *significant* amounts of control, so much, in fact, that the founder becomes a minority shareholder. Losing majority ownership—and therefore control—in a company leaves the founder in a precarious position. He or she no longer has the power to determine the company's direction; "outsiders" do. In some cases, founders' shares have been so diluted that majority shareholders actually vote them out of their jobs!

ENTREPRENEURIAL PROFILE: Steve Jobs and Steve Wozniak: Apple In 1985, John Sculley, then CEO of Apple, forced Steve Jobs, who cofounded the business with Steve Wozniak, out of the company in a high-level power struggle. Jobs and Wozniak founded Apple Computer as a partnership in Jobs's parents' garage in 1976 with each owning 50 percent of the company. The

TABLE 5.2 Tax Rate Comparison: C Corporation and S Corporation or Limited Liability Company

The form of ownership that an entrepreneur chooses has many important business implications, not the least of which is the amount of taxes the business or entrepreneur must pay. A recent study by the Small Business Administration's Office of Advocacy reports that, on average, taxes consume 19.8 percent of the typical small company's net income. The study also shows the average effective tax rate (the actual amount of taxes paid by a company as a percentage of its net income) for small businesses under each form of ownership:

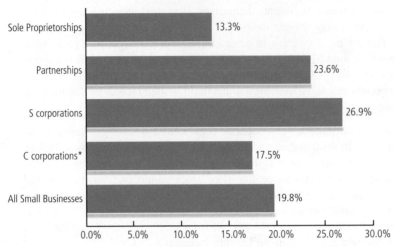

Average Tax Rate by Form of Ownership

Form of Ownership	Average Tax Rate
Sole Proprietorships	13.3%
Partnerships	23.6%
S corporations	26.9%
C corporations*	17.5%
All Small Businesses	19.8%

*Not directly comparable because taxes on salaries and dividends are not reflected.

Source: U.S. Small Business Administration, 2010.

Although these averages are revealing, entrepreneurs must consider the tax bills that their particular companies incur under the various forms of ownership. For example, S corporations do not pay taxes on their net income. Instead, that income passes through to the owners, who pay taxes on it at their individual tax rates. C corporations, on the other hand, pay a corporate tax on their net income. If the C corporation pays out some or all of that net income as dividends to shareholders, the dividends are taxed a second time at the shareholders' individual tax rates. Therefore, the tax obligations for an owner of an S corporation may be considerably lower than that of a C corporation.

The following example illustrates the effect of these tax rate differentials. This somewhat simplified example assumes that a small company generates a net income of $500,000 and that all after-tax income is distributed to the owner.

	C Corporation	S Corporation or LLC
Corporate or limited liability company net income	$500,000	$500,000
Maximum corporate tax	39%	0%
Corporate tax	**$170,000**	**0**
After-tax income	$330,000	$500,000
Maximum shareholder tax rate	33%	35%
Shareholder tax	**$49,500***	**$175,000****
Total tax paid	**$219,500**	**$175,000**

(Corporate tax plus shareholder tax)

Total tax savings by choosing an S corporation or limited liability company = $44,500

*Using the marginal 15% tax rate on dividends: $330,000 × 15% = $49,500.

**Using the marginal 35% tax rate on ordinary income: $500,000 × 35% = $175,000.

entrepreneurs incorporated their business in 1977, and as the company grew, so did its capital needs. They sold shares of Apple to other investors, and in 1980, Apple made an IPO, selling 4.6 million shares of stock at $14 per share and generating more than $644 million in capital for the company. Over time, Jobs's percentage of ownership has been diluted to less than 1 percent of the company's outstanding stock. Jobs later returned as Apple's CEO (drawing an annual salary of just $1); when Jobs died, the value of his Apple stock was more than $2 billion![17] ■

Other Forms of Ownership

LO2

Discuss the advantages and disadvantages of the S corporation, the limited liability company, the professional corporation, and the joint venture.

In addition to the sole proprietorship, the partnership, and the corporation, entrepreneurs can choose from other forms of ownership, including the S corporation, the limited liability company, the professional corporation, and the joint venture.

The S Corporation

In 1954, the IRS Code created the Subchapter S corporation. In recent years, the IRS has shortened the title to "S corporation" and has made some modifications in its qualifications. An **S corporation** is a distinction that is made only for federal income tax purposes and is, in terms of its legal characteristics, no different from any other corporation. A corporation seeking S status must meet the following criteria:

S corporation
a corporation that retains the legal characteristics of a regular (C) corporation but has the advantage of being taxed as a partnership if it meets certain criteria.

1. It must be a domestic (U.S.) corporation.

2. It cannot have a nonresident alien as a shareholder.

3. It can issue only one class of common stock, meaning that all shares must carry the same rights (e.g., the right to dividends or liquidation rights). The exception is voting rights, which may differ. In other words, an S corporation can issue voting and nonvoting common stock.

4. It must limit its shareholders to individuals, estates, and certain trusts, although tax-exempt creations such as ESOPs and pension plans can be shareholders.

5. It cannot have more than 100 shareholders (increased from 75), which is an important benefit for family businesses making the transition from one generation of owners to another. Members of one family are treated as a single shareholder.

6. Less than 25 percent of the corporation's gross revenues during three successive tax years must be from passive sources.

If a corporation meets the criteria of an S corporation, its shareholders must elect to be treated as one. An S corporation election may be filed at any time during the 12 months that precede the taxable year for which the election is to be effective. (The corporation must have been eligible for S status for the entire year.) To make the election of S status effective for the current tax year, entrepreneurs must file Form 2553 with the IRS within the first 75 days of the corporation's fiscal year. *All* shareholders must consent to have the corporation treated as an S corporation. Jennifer Chu launched Chu Shu, a company that makes odor-absorbing liners for women's shoes, after she was laid off from her investment banking job. Chu incorporated her business and intended to transform it into an S corporation but missed the filing deadline the first year, causing her to forgo several thousands of dollars in tax savings.[18]

THE ADVANTAGES OF AN S CORPORATION An S corporation retains all of the advantages of a regular corporation, such as continuity of existence, transferability of ownership, and limited personal liability for its owners. The most notable provision of the S corporation is that it serves as a conduit for its net income, passing all of its profits or losses through to the individual shareholders, meaning that its income is taxed only once at the individual tax rate. Thus, electing S corporation status avoids a primary disadvantage of the regular (or C) corporation—double taxation. In essence, the tax treatment of an S corporation is exactly like that of a partnership. The corporation files an informational return (1120-S) with the IRS and provides its shareholders with Schedule K-1, which reports their proportionate shares of the company's profits. The shareholders report their portions of the S corporation's earnings on their individual income tax returns (Form 1040) and pay taxes on those profits at the individual tax rates (even if they never take the money out of the business). This tax treatment can cause problems for individual share-holders, however. If an S corporation earns a profit but managers choose to plow that income back into the business in the form of retained earnings to fuel its growth and expansion, share-holders still must pay taxes on their share of the company's net income. In that case, shareholders will end up paying taxes on "phantom income" they never actually received.

Another advantage that the S corporation offers is avoiding the tax that C corporations pay on assets that have appreciated in value and are sold. S corporations' earnings also are not subject to the self-employment tax that sole proprietors and general partners must pay; however, they are responsible for payroll taxes (for Social Security and Medicare) on the wages and salaries that the S corporation pays its employees. Therefore, owners of S corporations must be sure that the salaries they draw are reasonable; salaries that are too low or too high draw scrutiny from the IRS.

Before 1998, if an entrepreneur owned separate but affiliated companies, he or she had to maintain each one as a distinct S corporation with its own accounting records and tax return. Under current law, business owners can set up all of these affiliated companies as qualified S corporation subsidiaries ("Q subs") under the umbrella of a single company, each with its own separate legal identity, and still file a single tax return for the parent company. For entrepreneurs with several lines of businesses, this change means greatly simplified tax filing. Owners also can use losses from one subsidiary company to offset profits from another to minimize their tax bills.

DISADVANTAGES OF AN S CORPORATION When the Tax Reform Act of 1986 restructured indi-vidual and corporate tax rates, many business owners switched to S corporations to lower their tax bills. For the first time since Congress enacted the federal income tax in 1913, the maximum individual rate was lower than the maximum corporate rate. Although Congress has realigned the tax structure several times since then, marginal tax rates for corporations with net incomes be-tween $75,000 and $335,000 currently are higher than the marginal tax rates for individuals with similar earnings, making S corporations attractive. Although tax implications should not be the sole criterion when choosing a form of ownership, entrepreneurs must consider them. Entrepre-neurs who are considering both C corporation and S corporation status must review the impact of the decision on their companies, including the impact of the C corporation's double taxation penalty on the portion of its net income distributed as dividends.

WHEN IS AN S CORPORATION A WISE CHOICE? Choosing S corporation status is usually beneficial to start-up companies anticipating net losses because their founders can use the loss to offset other in-come, thus lowering their tax bills. At the other extreme, founders who expect their companies to earn more than $100,000 in net income consistently should consider S corporation status. Companies that plan to reinvest most of their earnings to finance growth also find S corporations favorable. Small busi-ness owners who intend to sell their companies in the near future will prefer S over C status because the taxable gains on the sale of an S corporation are generally lower than those of a C corporation.

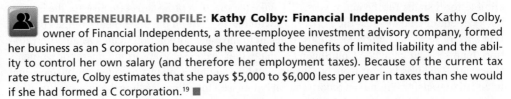

ENTREPRENEURIAL PROFILE: Kathy Colby: Financial Independents Kathy Colby, owner of Financial Independents, a three-employee investment advisory company, formed her business as an S corporation because she wanted the benefits of limited liability and the abil-ity to control her own salary (and therefore her employment taxes). Because of the current tax rate structure, Colby estimates that she pays $5,000 to $6,000 less per year in taxes than she would if she had formed a C corporation.[19] ∎

Financial Independents

Small companies with the following characteristics are *not* likely to benefit from S corpora-tion status:

- Highly profitable personal service companies with large numbers of shareholders, in which most of the profits are passed on to shareholders as compensation or retirement benefits

- Shareholders who pay marginal tax rates that are higher than the marginal tax rates that C corporations pay

- Fast-growing companies that must retain most of their earnings to finance growth and capi-tal spending

- Corporations in which the cost of employee benefits exceeds the tax savings that S status produces

The Limited Liability Company

The **limited liability company (LLC)**, like an S corporation, is a cross between a partnership and a corporation. Like S corporations, LLCs offer their owners limited personal liability for the debts of the business, providing a significant advantage over sole proprietorships and partnerships. LLCs, however, are not subject to many of the restrictions currently imposed on S corporations and offer more flexibility than S corporations. For example, S corporations cannot have more than 100 shareholders, and none of these can be foreigners or corporations. S corporations are also limited to only one class of stock. LLCs eliminate those restrictions. Although an LLC can have just one owner, most have multiple owners (called "members"). LLCs offer their owners limited liability without imposing any requirements on their characteristics or any ceiling on their numbers. LLC members can include non-U.S. citizens, partnerships, and corporations. Unlike a limited partnership, which prohibits limited partners from participating in the day-to-day management of the business, an LLC does not restrict its members' ability to become involved in managing the company.

In addition to offering its members the advantage of limited liability, LLCs also avoid the double taxation imposed on C corporations. Like an S corporation, an LLC does not pay income taxes; its income flows through to the members, who are responsible for paying income taxes on their shares of the LLC's net income. Because they are not subject to the many restrictions imposed on other forms of ownership, LLCs offer entrepreneurs another significant advantage: flexibility. An LLC permits its members to divide income (and thus tax liability) as they see fit, including allocations that differ from their percentages of ownership. Like an S corporation, the members' shares of an LLC's earnings are not subject to the self-employment tax. However, the managing member's share of the LLC's earnings is subject to the self-employment tax (15.3 percent) just as a sole proprietor's or a general partner's earned income is.

These advantages make the LLC an ideal form of ownership for many small companies across many industries—retail, wholesale, manufacturing, real estate, or service. Because it offers the tax advantage of a partnership, the legal protection of a corporation, and maximum operating flexibility, the LLC is the fastest-growing form of business ownership. Mark Cuban, billionaire owner of the NBA's Dallas Mavericks, recently created an LLC, Radical Football LLC, a company whose mission is to fund the creation of a playoff system that will crown a real champion in major college football. The current collegiate football postseason consists of 35 bowl games in which many of the teams that compete are determined by computerized formulas. Cuban says that he started the LLC so that "the last two teams playing are the best two teams."[20]

Creating an LLC is much like creating a corporation. Forming an LLC requires an entrepreneur to create two documents: the articles of organization (which must be filed with the secretary of state) and the operating agreement. The LLC's **articles of organization**, similar to the corporation's articles of incorporation, actually creates the LLC by establishing its name and address, its method of management (board managed or member managed), its duration, and the names and addresses of each organizer. In most states, the company's name must contain the words "limited liability company," "limited company," or the letters "L.L.C." or "L.C." Unlike a corporation, an LLC does not have perpetual life; in most states, an LLC's charter may not exceed 30 years. However, the same factors that would cause a partnership to dissolve would also cause the dissolution of an LLC before its charter expires.

Once the members form an LLC, they must adopt an operating agreement. The **operating agreement**, similar to a corporation's bylaws, outlines the provisions that govern the way the LLC will conduct business, such as members' capital contributions to the LLC; members' rights, roles, and responsibilities; the admission or withdrawal of members; distributions from the business; and how the LLC will be managed. To ensure that their LLCs are classified as a partnership for tax purposes, entrepreneurs must draft the operating agreement carefully. The operating agreement must create an LLC that has more characteristics of a partnership than of a corporation to maintain this favorable tax treatment.

Despite their universal appeal to entrepreneurs, LLCs suffer some disadvantages. They can be expensive to create, often costing between $1,500 and $5,000. Some states also impose annual fees on LLCs. Unlike corporations, which can operate "for perpetuity," LLCs have limited life spans. Entrepreneurs who want to provide attractive benefits to themselves and their employees will not find this form of ownership appealing because

limited liability company (LLC)
a relatively new form of ownership that, like an S corporation, is a cross between a partnership and a corporation; it is not subject to many of the restrictions imposed on S corporations.

articles of organization
the document that creates an LLC by its name, its method of management, its duration, and other details.

operating agreement
the document that establishes for an LLC the provisions governing the way it will conduct business.

the cost of those benefits is not tax deductible in an LLC. Because there is no stock involved, this form of ownership also is not suitable for companies whose owners plan to raise money through an IPO or who want to use stock options or an ESOP as incentives for employees.

 ENTREPRENEURIAL PROFILE: Richard Burke: Trek Bicycle Trek Bicycle, the company that became famous for making the carbon fiber bicycles that have accounted for an unprecedented seven victories in the Tour de France, switched to an S corporation so that it could create an employee stock ownership plan. Selecting S status, says founder Richard Burke, "has been good for my family; everyone owns 3 percent to 4 percent. It's been good for the ESOP, which holds about 25 percent of the company's stock. We tie a lot of direct and indirect compensation to company performance. If you're making money, you ought to share it."[21] ■

Although an LLC may be ideally suited for an entrepreneur launching a new company, it may pose problems for business owners considering converting an existing business to an LLC. Switching to an LLC from a general partnership, a limited partnership, or a sole proprietorship to bring in new owners is usually not a problem. However, owners of corporations and S corporations could incur large tax obligations if they converted their companies to LLCs.

The Professional Corporation

Professional corporations are designed to offer professionals—lawyers, doctors, dentists, accountants, and others—the advantages of the corporate form of ownership. They are ideally suited for professionals, who must always be concerned about malpractice lawsuits, because they offer limited liability. For example, if three doctors formed a professional corporation, none of them would be liable for the others' malpractice. (Of course, each would be liable for his or her own actions.) Creating a professional corporation is no different

You Be the Consultant

Which Form Is Best?

Watoma Kinsey and her daughter Katrina are about to launch a business that specializes in children's parties. Their target audience is upscale families who want to throw unique, memorable parties to celebrate special occasions for their children between the ages of 5 and 15. The Kinseys have leased a large building and have renovated it to include many features designed to appeal to kids, including special gym equipment, a skating rink, an obstacle course, a mock-up of a pirate ship, a ball crawl, and even a movable haunted house. They can offer simple birthday parties (cake and ice cream included) or special theme parties as elaborate as the customer wants. Their company will provide magicians, clowns, comedians, jugglers, tumblers, and a variety of other entertainers.

Watoma and Katrina each have invested $45,000 to get the business ready to launch. Based on the quality of their business plan and their preparation, the Kinseys have negotiated a $40,000 bank loan. Because both have families and own their own homes, the Kinseys want to minimize their exposure to potential legal and financial problems. A significant portion of their start-up costs went to purchase a liability insurance policy to cover the Kinseys in case a child is injured at a party. If their business plan is accurate, the Kinseys will earn a small profit in their first

year (about $1,500) and a more attractive profit of $16,000 in their second year of operation. Within five years, they expect their company to generate as much as $50,000 in profits. The Kinseys have agreed to split the profits—and the workload—equally.

If the business is as successful as they think it will be, the Kinseys eventually want to franchise their company. That, however, is part of their long-range plan. For now, they want to perfect their business system and prove that it can be profitable before they try to duplicate it in the form of franchises.

As they move closer to the launch date for their business, the Kinseys are reviewing the different forms of ownership. They know that their decision has long-term implications for themselves and for their business, but they aren't sure which form of ownership is best for them.

1. Which form(s) of ownership would you recommend to the Kinseys? Explain.

2. Which form(s) of ownership would you recommend the Kinseys *avoid*? Explain.

3. What factors should the Kinseys consider as they evaluate the various forms of ownership?

from creating a regular corporation. Professional corporations are often identified by the abbreviations P.C. (professional corporation), P.A. (professional association), or S.C. (service corporation). A professional corporation has the following additional limitations beyond the standard corporation:

- All shares of stock of the corporation must be owned and held by individuals licensed in the profession of the corporation.

- At least one of the incorporators must be licensed in the profession.

- At least one director and one officer must be licensed in the profession.

- The articles of incorporation, in addition to all other requirements, must designate the personal services to be provided by the corporation.

- The professional corporation must obtain from the appropriate licensing board a certification that declares the shares of stock are owned by individuals who are duly licensed in the profession.

The Joint Venture

A joint venture is very much like a partnership, except that it is formed for a specific purpose. For instance, suppose that you own a 500-acre tract of land 60 miles from Chicago that has been cleared and is normally used in agricultural production. You have a friend who has solid contacts among major musical groups and would like to put on a concert. You expect prices for your agricultural products to be low this summer, and you and your friend form a joint venture for the specific purpose of staging a three-day concert. Your contribution will be the exclusive use of the land for one month, and your friend will provide all the performers as well as technicians, facilities, and equipment. All costs will be paid out of receipts, and the profits will be split with you receiving 20 percent for the use of your land. When the concert is over, the facilities are removed, and the accounting for all costs is completed, you and your friend split the profits 20-80, and the joint venture terminates.

In any endeavor in which neither party can effectively achieve the purpose alone, a joint venture is a common choice. The "partners" form a new joint venture for each new project they undertake. The income derived from a joint venture is taxed as if it arose from a partnership.

Table 5.3 provides a summary of the key features of the major forms of ownership discussed in this chapter.

TABLE 5.3 Characteristics of the Major Forms of Ownership

Characteristic	Sole Proprietorship	General Partnership	Limited Partnership	C Corporation	S Corporation	LLC
Definition	A for-profit business owned and operated by one person	A for-profit business jointly owned and operated by two or more people	One general partner and one or more partners with limited liability and no rights of management	An artificial legal entity separate from its owners and formed under state and federal laws	An artificial legal entity that is structured like a C corporation but taxed by the federal government like a partnership	A business entity that provides limited liability like a corporation but is taxed like a partnership; owners are referred to as members
Ease of formation	Easiest form of business to set up; if necessary, acquire licenses and permits, register fictitious name, and obtain taxpayer identification	Easy to set up and operate; a written partnership agreement is highly recommended; must acquire an employer ID number; if necessary, register fictitious name	File a Certificate of Limited Partnership with the secretary of state; name must show that business is a limited partnership; must have written agreement and must keep certain records	File articles of incorporation and other required reports with the secretary of state; prepare bylaws and follow corporate formalities	Must meet all criteria to file as an S corporation; must file timely election with the IRS (within two and a half months of first taxable year	File articles of organization with the secretary of state; adopt operating agreement and file necessary reports with secretary of state; the name must show that it is an LLC
Owner's personal liability	Unlimited	Unlimited for general partners; limited for limited partners	Limited	Limited	Limited	Limited
Number of owners	One	Two or more	At least one general partner and any number of limited partners	Any number	Maximum of 100 with restrictions as to who they are	One (a few states require two or more)
Tax liability	Single tax: personal tax rate	Single tax: partners pay on their proportional shares at their individual rate	Same as general partnership	Double tax: corporation pays tax, and shareholders pay tax on dividends distributed	Single tax: owners pay on their proportional shares at individual rate	Single tax: members pay on their proportional shares at individual rate
Current maximum tax rate	35%	35%	35%	39% corporate plus 35% individual	35%	35%
Transferability of ownership	Fully transferable through sale or transfer of company assets	May require consent of all partners	Same as general partnership	Fully transferable	Transferable (but transfer may affect S status)	Usually requires consent of all members
Continuity of the business	Ends on death or insanity of proprietor or on termination by proprietor	Dissolves on death, insanity, or retirement of a general partner (business may continue)	Same as general partnership	Perpetual life	Perpetual life	Perpetual life
Cost of formation	Low	Moderate	Moderate	High	High	High
Liquidity of the owner's investment in the business	Poor to average	Poor to average	Poor to average	High	High	High
Ability to raise capital	Low	Moderate	Moderate to high	Very high	High	High
Formation procedure	No special steps required other than buying necessary licenses	No written partnership agreement required (but highly advisable)	Must comply with state laws regarding limited partnership	Must meet formal requirements specified by state law	Must follow same procedures as C corporation, then elect S status with IRS	Must meet formal requirements specified by state law

Chapter Summary by Learning Objective

1-A. Explain the advantages and the disadvantages of the sole proprietorship.

- A sole proprietorship is a business owned and managed by one individual and is the most popular form of ownership.

- Sole proprietorships offer these *advantages*: They are simple to create, they are the least costly form to begin, the owner has total decision-making authority, there are no special legal restrictions, and they are easy to discontinue.

- They also suffer from these *disadvantages*: unlimited personal liability of owner, limited managerial skills and capabilities, limited access to capital, and lack of continuity.

1-B. Explain the advantages and the disadvantages of the partnership.

- A partnership is an association of two or more people who co-own a business for the purpose of making a profit. Partnerships offer these *advantages*: ease of establishing, complementary skills of partners, division of profits, larger pool of capital available, ability to attract limited partners, little government regulation flexibility, and tax advantages.

- Partnerships suffer from these *disadvantages*: unlimited liability of at least one partner, difficulty in disposing of partnership, interest lack of continuity, potential for personality and authority conflicts, and partners bound by the law of agency.

1-C. Explain the advantages and the disadvantages of the corporation.

- A corporation, the most complex of the three basic forms of ownership, is a separate legal entity. To form a corporation, an entrepreneur must file the articles of incorporation with the state in which the company will incorporate. Corporations offer these *advantages*: limited liability of stockholders, ability to attract capital, ability to continue indefinitely, and transferable ownership.

- Corporations suffer from these *disadvantages*: cost and time involved in incorporating, double taxation, potential for diminished managerial incentives, legal requirements and regulatory red tape, and potential loss of control by the founder(s).

2. Discuss the advantages and the disadvantages of the S corporation, the LLC, the professional corporation, and the joint venture.

- Entrepreneurs can also choose from several other forms of ownership, including S corporations, and LLCs. An S corporation offers its owners limited liability protection but avoids the double taxation of C corporations.

- An LLC, like an S corporation, is a cross between a partnership and a corporation yet operates without the restrictions imposed on an S corporation. To create an LLC, an entrepreneur must file the articles of organization with the secretary of state and create an operating agreement.

- A professional corporation offers professionals the benefits of the corporate form of ownership.

- A joint venture is like a partnership, except that it is formed for a specific purpose.

Discussion Questions

1. What factors should an entrepreneur consider before choosing a form of ownership?
2. Why are sole proprietorships so popular as a form of ownership?
3. How does personal conflict affect partnerships?
4. What issues should the articles of partnership address? Why are the articles important to a successful partnership?
5. Can one partner commit another to a business deal without the other's consent? Why?
6. What issues should the Certificate of Incorporation cover?
7. How does an S corporation differ from a regular corporation?
8. What role do limited partners play in a partnership? What happens if a limited partner takes an active role in managing the business?
9. What advantages does an LLC offer over an S corporation? A partnership?
10. How is an LLC created? What criteria must an LLC meet to avoid double taxation?
11. Briefly outline the advantages and disadvantages of the major forms of ownership.

Business Plan Pro™

Selecting the form of ownership is an important decision. This chapter discusses how this decision affects the number of business owners, tax obligations, the time and cost to form the entity, the ability to raise capital, and options for transferring ownership.

Business Plan Exercises

The Company Ownership section in the business plan is where you will discuss the form of business ownership and how it will impact other areas, including the management and finance sections.

On the Web

Go to www.pearsonhighered.com/scarborough and review the business entity links for Chapter 5. This provides additional information and resources to assist with selecting the optimal form of business. Search for the term "business entity" in your favorite search engine and note the resources and information it generates.

Sample Plans

Go to the Sample Plan Browser in *Business Plan Pro™* and look at these three business plans: Calico Computer Consulting is a sole proprietorship, Lansing Aviation is an LLC, and Southeast Health Plans, Inc., is a corporation. After reviewing the executive summaries of each of these plans, answer these questions:

- Why might the owners select this form of ownership?
- What are the advantages and disadvantages each of these business entities offer the business owners?
- Why are these choices a good match for the business relating to the ease of starting, liability, control, ability to raise capital, and transfer of ownership?

In the Software

Go to the section of *Business Plan Pro™* called Company Ownership. Look at the comparison matrix of the Characteristics of Major Forms of Ownership, Table 5.3, on page 190, and consider the ramifications of your choice.

- If a sole proprietorship or a partnership issued, you may be personally liable. Is the nature of your business one that may present this type of risk? Is this an appropriate business entity based on that potential outcome?
- Once your business becomes profitable, what are the potential tax ramifications compared to your current situation?
- What is your ideal situation regarding the long-term ownership of the business, and what are the possible choices based on that preference?
- How much should you budget for legal fees and other expenditures to form the business?
- How much time do you estimate you will need to invest to establish this business entity?
- If you need to raise capital, how much money will the venture require? Is this form of ownership optimal for accomplishing that objective?

As you review the instructions provided within *Business Plan Pro™*, refer to Table 5.3 to help you select the form of ownership that is best for you and your venture.

Building Your Business Plan

Review the work that you have completed on your business plan to date. Does your chosen form of ownership fit the vision and the scope of the business? Will this choice of business entity offer the type of protection and flexibility you desire for your business? You may also want to include comments in your plan regarding changing factors that may require you to reexamine your form of ownership in the future.

Beyond the Classroom . . .

1. Interview four local small business owners. What form of ownership did each choose? Why? Prepare a brief report summarizing your findings and explain the advantages and disadvantages those owners face because of their choices. Do you think that these business owners have chosen the form of ownership that is best for their particular situations? Explain.

2. Invite entrepreneurs who operate as partners to your classroom. Do they have a written partnership agreement? Are their skills complementary? How do they divide responsibility for running their company? How do they handle decision making? What do they do when disputes and disagreements arise?

Endnotes

1. Virginia Munger Kahn, "Room to Grow," *Business Week*, September 3, 2007, http://www.businessweek.com/magazine/content/07_36/b4048436.htm?chan=search.

2. Nina Kaufman, "Five Reasons to Incorporate," *Women Entrepreneur*, January 5, 2011, www.womenentrepreneur.com/article/2025.html.

3. *State of Small Business Report: Wave 2 of the Small Business Success Index*, Network Solutions, August 2009, p. 2; Laura Petrecca, "A Partner Can Give Your Business Shelter or a Storm," *USA Today*, October 9, 2009, http://www.usatoday.com/money/smallbusiness/startup/week4-partnerships.htm.

4. Laura Petrecca, "A Partner Can Give Your Business Shelter or a Storm," *USA Today*, October 9, 2009, http://www.usatoday.com/money/smallbusiness/startup/week4-partnerships.htm.

5. Jacquelyn Lynn, "Partnership Procedures," *Business Start-Ups*, June 1996, p. 73.

6. Amy Joyce, "Getting It Together," *Washington Post*, June 12, 2005, http://www.washingtonpost.com/wp-dyn/content/article/2005/06/10/AR2005061001353.html.

7. Amy Joyce, "Getting It Together," *Washington Post*, June 12, 2005, http://www.washingtonpost.com/wp-dyn/content/article/2005/06/10/AR2005061001353.html.

8. Norm Brodsky, "Sam and Me," *Inc.*, June 2006, p. 67.

9. Judy Kneiszel, "La Boulange," *QSR Magazine*, September 16, 2010, http://www.qsrmagazine.com/new-concepts/la-boulange.

10. Sarah E. Needleman, "Setting Up a Business Structure," *Wall Street Journal*, September 26, 2010, http://online.wsj.com/article/SB10001424052748703905604575514562263291610.html.

11. Laura Petrecca, "A Partner Can Give Your Business Shelter or a Storm," *USA Today*, October 9, 2009, http://www.usatoday.com/money/smallbusiness/startup/week4-partnerships.htm.

12. Michael Barrier, "Someone's in the Kitchen with Wolfgang," *Success*, September 2000, pp. 28–33; "Company Info," Wolfgang Puck, http://www.wolfgangpuck.com/company.

13. Chief Justice John Marshall, cited by Henry R. Cheeseman, *Contemporary Business and Online Commerce Law*, 6th ed. (Upper Saddle River, NJ: Pearson, 2008), p. 750.

14. Reiko Joseph, "The Sweet Taste of Success," LegalZoom, November 2008, http://www.legalzoom.com/business-management/success-stories/sweet-taste-success.

15. Virginia Munger Kahn, "Room to Grow," *Business Week*, September 3, 2007, http://www.businessweek.com/magazine/content/07_36/b4048436.htm?chan=search.

16. Nathan Olivares-Giles, "LinkedIn Values Itself at About $3 Billion before IPO", *Los Angeles Times*, May 9, 2011, http://latimesblogs.latimes.com/technology/2011/05/linkedin-value-3-billion.html; Todd Wasserman, "Linked In Founder Worth $1.8 Billion as Stock Climbs," *Mashable*, May 19, 2011, http://mashable.com/2011/05/19/linkedin-founder-ipo.

17. John C. Ogg, "Steve Jobs: $1 Salary, $630 Million Gain in Stock in 2010," *WallSt24/7*, January 11, 2011, http://247wallst.com/2011/01/07/steve-jobs-1-salary-620-million-stock-gain-in-2010-aapl; "The History of Apple Computer Inc.," Apple Museum, http://www.theapplemuseum.com/index.php?id=53; *Definitive Proxy Statement*, February 23, 2011, U.S. Securities and Exchange Commission, http://www.sec.gov/Archives/edgar/data/320193/000119312511003231/ddef14a.htm.

18. Sarah E. Needleman, "Setting Up a Business Structure," *Wall Street Journal*, September 26, 2010, http://online.wsj.com/article/SB100014240527487039056045755145622632916 10.html.

19. Virginia Munger Kahn, "Room to Grow," *Business Week*, September 3, 2007, http://www.businessweek.com/magazine/content/07_36/b4048436.htm?chan=search.

20. Tom MacMahon, "Mark Cuban Registers Radical Football," *ESPN*, February 22, 2011, http://sports.espn.go.com/dallas/ncf/news/story?id=6136815; Brent Schrotenboer, "Cuban Starts Business for College Football Playoff," *SignOnSanDiego*, February 17, 2011, http://www.signonsandiego.com/news/2011/feb/17/cuban-starts-business-college-football-playoff.

21. Richard Burke, "How I Did It: Pulling Away from the Pack," *Inc.*, July 2005, pp. 110–112.

© alejandro dans/Fotolia

6

Franchising and the Entrepreneur

Learning Objectives

On completion of this chapter, you will be able to:

1. Describe the three types of franchising: trade name, product distribution, and pure.

2. Explain the benefits and the drawbacks of buying a franchise.

3. Understand the laws covering franchise purchases.

4. Discuss the *right* way to buy a franchise.

5. Outline the major trends shaping franchising.

A man who carries a cat by the tail learns something he can learn in no other way.

—Mark Twain

Where else [but franchising] can we find a job creator, an economic growth stimulator, and a personal wealth creator that gives [people] the opportunity to realize their dreams and financial security for their families beyond their wildest expectations?

—Don DeBolt

Michelle Kendall began working at age 17 as a hostess at De Dutch Pannekoek House, a British Columbia, Canada–based restaurant franchise that specializes in breakfast, brunch, and lunch with a European flair. She worked hard and soon became a general manager for one of the company's restaurants. Then at age 24, Kendall became De Dutch's youngest franchisee, opening an outlet in South Surrey, British Columbia, with the help of investments from family members, friends, and the franchisor to pay the total cost of opening a De Dutch franchise, about $400,000. Kendall says that her frontline experience with the company has helped her achieve success as a franchisee. In her outlet's first year, sales were 20 percent higher than her forecasts and costs were below budget. "De Dutch is a proven business model that works well," says Kendall, who, in addition to working on a degree in business, spends time every day in her restaurant and admits that she is "picky about the food and the presentation."[1]

Western Investor www.WesternInvestor.com

Like Kendall's restaurant, most franchised outlets are small, but as a whole, they have a significant impact on the global economy. In the United States alone, more than 3,000 franchisors operate more than 825,000 franchise outlets, and more are opening constantly both in the United States and around the world. Franchises generate nearly 17 percent of total annual sales in the United States and employ nearly one in eight workers in the United States in more than 300 industries. The total economic impact of franchising on the U.S. economy is an impressive $2.1 trillion.[2] Much of the popularity of franchising stems from its ability to offer those who lack business experience the chance to own and operate a business with a high probability of success. This booming industry has moved far beyond the traditional boundaries of fast food and hotels into fields as diverse as automotive air bag replacement, used clothing, mold detection, and pet sitting. Even the famous Naked Cowboy (Robert Burck), who plays his guitar in his underwear in New York City's Times Square, has a franchisee, the Naked Cowgirl (Louisa Holmlund), who also strolls through Times Square with her guitar wearing a miniskirt, a cowboy hat, and not much else.[3]

In **franchising**, semi-independent business owners (franchisees) pay fees and royalties to a parent company (franchisor) in return for the right to become identified with its trademark, to sell its products or services, and often to use its business format and system. Franchisees do not establish their own autonomous businesses; instead, they buy a "success package" from the franchisor, who shows them how to use it. Franchisees, unlike independent business owners, don't have the freedom to change the way they run their businesses—for example, shifting advertising strategies or adjusting product lines—but they do have access to a formula for success that the franchisor has worked out. "As a franchisee, your role is to operate," says franchising expert Mark Spriggs. "You have to be willing to follow the rules."[4] Fundamentally, when they buy their franchises, franchisees are purchasing a successful business model. Many successful franchisors claim that neglecting to follow the formula is one of the chief reasons that some franchisees fail. "If you are overly entrepreneurial and you want to invent you own wheel, or if you are not comfortable with following a system, don't go down [the franchise] path," says Don DeBolt, former head of the International Franchise Association.[5]

franchising
a system of distribution in which semi-independent business owners (franchisees) pay fees and royalties to a parent company (franchisor) in return for the right to become identified with its trademark, to sell its products or services, and often to use its business format and system.

ENTREPRENEURIAL PROFILE: Schlachter's Maaco Auto Painting and Bodyworks Anita Schlachter, co-owner of a highly successful Maaco (automotive services) franchise with her husband and her son, is convinced that the system the franchisor taught them is the key to their company's progress and growth to date. The Schlachters follow the franchisor's plan, using it as a road map to success. "If you listen to what your franchisor says and follow its policies and procedures, you'll be successful," she says. "Those who think they know more [than the franchisor] should not go into franchising."[6] ■

Franchising is built on an ongoing relationship between a franchisor and a franchisee. The franchisor provides valuable services, such as a proven business system, training and support, name recognition, and many other forms of assistance; in return, the franchisee pays an initial

FIGURE 6.1

The Franchising Relationship

Source: From *Economic Impact of Franchised Businesses: A Study for the International Franchise Association Educational Foundation.* Copyright © 2004 by the International Franchise Association. Reprinted with permission.

Element	The Franchisor	The Franchisee
Site selection	Oversees and approves; may choose site.	Chooses site with franchisor's approval.
Design	Provides prototype design.	Pays for and implements design.
Employees	Makes general recommendations and training suggestions.	Hires, manages, and fires employees.
Products and services	Determines product or service line.	Modifies only with franchisor's approval.
Prices	Recommends prices.	Sets final prices.
Purchasing	Establishes quality standards; provides list of approved suppliers; may require franchisees to purchase from the franchisor.	Must meet quality standards; must purchase only from approved suppliers; must purchase from supplier if required.
Advertising	Develops and coordinates national ad campaign; may require minimum level of spending on local advertising.	Pays for national ad campaign; complies with local advertising requirements; gets franchisor approval on local ads.
Quality control	Sets quality standards and enforces them with inspections; trains franchisees.	Maintains quality standards; trains employees to implement quality systems.
Support	Provides support through an established business system.	Operates business on a day-to-day basis with franchisor's support.

LO1

Describe the three types of franchising: trade name, product distribution, and pure.

trade-name franchising

a system of franchising in which a franchisee purchases the right to use the franchisor's trade name without distributing particular products under the franchisor's name.

product distribution franchising

a system of franchising in which a franchisor licenses a franchisee to sell its products under the franchisor's brand name and trademark through a selective, limited distribution network.

pure franchising

a system of franchising in which a franchisor sells a franchisee a complete business format and system.

franchise fee as well as an ongoing percentage of his or her outlet's sales to the franchisor as a royalty and agrees to operate the outlet according to the franchisor's terms. Because franchisors develop the business systems that their franchisees use and direct their distribution methods, they maintain substantial control over their franchisees. Yet this standardization lies at the core of franchising's success as a method of distribution (see Figure 6.1).

Types of Franchising

There are three basic types of franchising: trade-name franchising, product distribution franchising, and pure franchising. **Trade-name franchising** involves a brand name, such as True Value Hardware or Western Auto. Here, the franchisee purchases the right to use the franchisor's trade name without distributing particular products exclusively under the franchisor's name. **Product distribution franchising** involves a franchisor licensing a franchisee to sell specific products under the franchisor's brand name and trademark through a selective, limited distribution network. This system is commonly used to market automobiles (Chevrolet, Lexus, Ford), gasoline products (ExxonMobil, Sunoco, Texaco), soft drinks (Pepsi Cola, Coca-Cola), appliances, cosmetics, and other products. These two methods of franchising allow franchisees to acquire some of the parent company's identity.

Pure franchising (also called comprehensive or business format franchising) involves providing the franchisee with a complete business format, including a license for a trade name, the products or services to be sold, the store layout, the methods of operation, a marketing plan, a quality control process, a two-way communications system, and the necessary business support services. In short, the franchisee purchases the right to use all of the elements of a fully integrated business operation. Business format franchising is the most common and the fastest

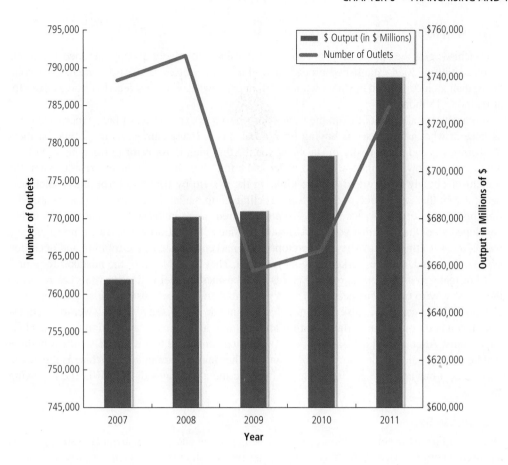

FIGURE 6.2

Number of Business Format Franchises

Source: Franchise Business Economic Outlook: 2011, International Franchise Association and PriceWaterhouseCoopers, p.3.

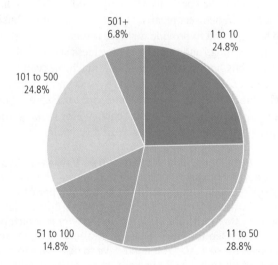

FIGURE 6.3

Number of Franchised Outlets

Source: FRANdata, 2007.

growing of the three types of franchising and accounts for 85.1 percent of all franchise outlets in the United States (see Figure 6.2).[7] It is common among fast-food restaurants, hotels, business service firms, car rental agencies, educational institutions, beauty aid retailers, and many other types of businesses.

Figure 6.3 shows a breakdown of the number of outlets franchisors operate; note that 25 percent of franchise systems have no more than 10 outlets, another indicator of the franchising industry's fast growth.

The Benefits of Buying a Franchise

A franchisee gets the opportunity to own a small business relatively quickly and, because of the identification with an established product and brand name, often reaches the break-even point faster than an independent business would. Still, most new franchise outlets don't break even for at least 6 to 18 months.

Franchisees also benefit from the franchisor's business experience. In fact, experience is the essence of what a franchisee is buying from a franchisor. Many entrepreneurs go into business by themselves and make costly mistakes. Given the thin margin for error in the typical start-up, a new business owner cannot afford to make many mistakes. In a franchising arrangement, the franchisor already has worked out the kinks in the system by trial and error, and franchisees benefit from that experience. A franchisor has climbed up the learning curve and can share with franchisees the secrets of success they have discovered in the industry. "A great franchisor has developed all of the tools that you need to start a business," says Lori Kiser-Block, president of a franchise consulting firm. "They've developed the marketing system, the training and operation system, the brand, and the marketing tools you need. They've made all of the mistakes for you."[8]

For many first-time entrepreneurs, access to a business model with a proven track record is the safest way to own a business. Still, every potential franchisee must consider one important question: "What can a franchise do for me that I cannot do for myself?" The answer to this question depends on one's particular situation and requires a systematic evaluation of a franchise opportunity. After careful deliberation, one person may conclude that a franchise offers nothing that he or she could not do independently, and another may decide that a franchise is the key to success as a business owner. Franchisees often cite the advantages discussed in the following sections.

A Business System

One of the biggest benefits of buying a franchise is gaining access to a business system that has a proven record of success. In many cases, the business system that a franchisor provides allows franchisees to get their businesses up and running faster than if they had tried to launch them on their own. Fran Lubin, who left the corporate office of Goddard School, an early education franchise, to become a Goddard franchisee, recalls, "I understood that the business was mine to run. Goddard was there to help me and to provide multiple resources and a proven system, but it was up to me to take all of those things and to make my business successful."[9]

Using the franchisor's business system as a guide, franchisees can be successful even though they may have little or no experience in the industry. "Assuming a person is financially qualified," says Jerry Perch, director of franchise development for Express Oil Change, "we are not looking for a mechanic or someone to work on cars. We're looking for someone who, with proper training, can manage a million-dollar business."[10]

ENTREPRENEURIAL PROFILE: Brent Burger: True Value Hardware Brent Burger was a franchisee for yogurt franchise TCBY before joining the company as an executive. When Burger began visiting TCBY stores, he was surprised at the number of franchisees who were not following the company's business formula. A few years later, Burger decided to make a switch and become a franchisee in the hardware business, an industry in which he had no prior experience. Now a successful franchisee for True Value Hardware, Burger advises other franchisees to stick to the franchisor's plan for success. "You don't have to be a slave to it or drink the Kool-Aid," he says. "Just open yourself up to it. Lay down your arms and work with the franchisor as a true partner."[11] ■

Management Training and Support

Franchisors want to give their franchisees a greater chance for success than independent businesses and offer management training programs to franchisees prior to opening a new outlet. Many franchisors, especially well-established ones, also provide follow-up training and consulting services. This service is vital because most franchisors do not require franchisees to have experience in the business. These programs teach franchisees the details they need to know for day-to-day operations as well as the nuances of running their businesses successfully. Because Jerry Heath's neighbor was the president of Hungry Howie's Pizza, it was only natural for Heath to become one of the company's franchisees, particularly after he spent a year managing a Hungry Howie's outlet. With financial backing from his father, Heath, just 23 years old, moved from Detroit to Jenison, Michigan, to open his own pizza franchise. "[The franchisor] offered quite a bit of support," recalls Heath. "If I had a question or problem, I'd call them and they would help me out."[12]

Training programs often involve both classroom and on-site instruction to teach franchisees the basic operations of the business. Before beginning operations, McDonald's franchisees spend 14 days in Illinois at Hamburger University, where they learn everything from how to clean equipment correctly to the essential elements of managing a business with high community visibility and great profit potential. They also work in a simulated store where instructors grade their performances. Ben & Jerry's Homemade franchisees spend eight days studying at Scoop University at the company's headquarters in Burlington, Vermont.

To ensure franchisees' continued success, many franchisors supplement their start-up training programs with ongoing instruction and support. For instance, Ben & Jerry's sends regional trainers to new franchisees' locations for additional training before they open their Scoop Shops. Once they are up and running, franchisees also benefit from ongoing training programs from Ben & Jerry's field-based support team.[13] Franchisors offer these training programs because they realize that their ultimate success depends on the franchisee's success.

Brand-Name Appeal

A franchisee purchases the right to use a nationally known and advertised brand name for a product or service. Thus, the franchisee has the advantage of identifying his business with a widely recognized trademark, which provides a great deal of drawing power, particularly for franchisees of established systems. Customers recognize the identifying trademark, the standard symbols, the store design, and the products of an established franchise. Because of the franchise's name recognition, franchisees who have just opened their outlets often discover a ready supply of customers ready to purchase their products or services. Entrepreneurs who launch independent businesses may have to work for years and spend many thousands of dollars in advertising to build a customer base of equivalent size. "One of the reasons I bought an AAMCO [transmission repair] franchise was its name recognition," says Stephen Rogers, who owns a franchise in Lockport, New York.[14]

One of the basic tenets of franchising is cloning the franchisor's success. For example, nearly everyone recognizes the golden arches of McDonald's or the pigtailed little girl on the Wendy's sign (founder Dave Thomas named the company after his daughter) and the standard products and quality offered at each. A customer can be confident that the quality and content of a meal at a Fort Lauderdale McDonald's will be consistent with a meal at a San Francisco McDonald's. However, franchisees must be equally aware that negative actions by the franchisor or other franchisees can undermine the value of the brand name and have a negative impact on other stores in the chain. For instance, one of the worst cases of food poisoning ever recorded in the United States hit Washington when customers of a fast-food franchise ate contaminated food at several of its outlets. More than 600 people were treated at local hospitals for *E. coli* poisoning, and three children died after eating the undercooked, contaminated beef served at the stores. This tragic event not only required the company to pay millions of dollars in legal settlements but also led to a drop in sales throughout the entire chain of restaurants for a period of time. Fortunately, the company has since rebounded from the crisis and now is one of the industry leaders in food safety procedures.

Standardized Quality of Goods and Services

Because a franchisee purchases a license to sell the franchisor's product or service and the privilege of using the associated brand name, the quality of the goods or service sold determines the franchisor's reputation. Building a sound reputation in business is not achieved quickly, although destroying a good reputation takes no time at all. If some franchisees were allowed to operate at substandard levels, the image of the entire chain would suffer irreparable damage; therefore, franchisors normally demand compliance with uniform standards of quality and service throughout the entire chain. In many cases, the franchisor conducts periodic inspections of local facilities to assist in maintaining acceptable levels of performance.

ENTREPRENEURIAL PROFILE: John Schnatter: Papa John's John Schnatter, founder of Papa John's, a fast-growing pizza franchise with more than 3,500 outlets in every state and 29 global markets, makes personal visits to some of his franchisees' stores four or five times each week to make sure they are performing up to the company's high quality standards. Franchisees say that Schnatter, known for his attention to detail, often checks pizzas for air bubbles in the crust or tomato sauce for freshness. "Pizza is Schnatter's life, and he takes it very seriously," says one industry analyst.[15] ■

Maintaining quality is so important that most franchisors retain the right to terminate the franchise contract and to repurchase the outlet if the franchisee fails to comply with established standards.

National Advertising Programs

An effective advertising program is essential to the success of every franchise operation. Marketing a brand-name product or service across a wide geographic area requires a far-reaching advertising campaign. A regional or national advertising program benefits all franchisees, and most franchisors have one. In fact, one study reports that 79 percent of franchisors require franchisees to contribute to a national advertising fund (the average amount is 2 percent of sales).[16] Typically, these advertising campaigns are organized and controlled by the franchisor, but franchisees actually pay for the campaigns. In fact, they are financed by each franchisee's contribution of a percentage of monthly sales, usually 1 to 5 percent, or a flat monthly fee. For example, franchisees at Subway, the sandwich chain with more than 37,000 restaurants in 100 countries, pay 4.5 percent of weekly gross sales to the company's national advertising program. These funds are pooled and used for a cooperative advertising program; doing so has more impact than if the franchisees spent the same amount of money separately.

Many franchisors also require franchisees to spend a minimum amount on local advertising. In fact, 41 percent of franchisors require their franchisees to invest in local advertising (once again, the average amount is 2 percent of sales).[17] To supplement their national advertising efforts, both Wendy's and Burger King require franchisees to spend at least 3 percent of gross sales on local advertising. Some franchisors assist each franchisee in designing and producing its local ads. Many companies help franchisees create promotional plans and provide press releases and advertisements for grand openings.

Financial Assistance

Purchasing a franchise can be just as expensive (if not more so) than launching an independent business, and the recent upheaval in the financial markets has made many lenders hesitant to fund business start-ups, including franchises. A recent survey by the International Franchise Association reports that 87 percent of franchisors say that lack of available credit has either moderately or significantly affected their ability to expand.[18] Another study estimates that the funding gap between the capital that franchises need to grow and the capital that lenders actually provide is between 20 and 23 percent per year for the last several years.[19]

ENTREPRENEURIAL PROFILE: Don McFee: Ductz After being laid off from three management positions in 13 years, Don McFee decided that he was ready to control his own destiny by owning a business. After weighing his options, McFee decided that, for him, purchasing a franchise was the best route to entrepreneurship and committed to purchasing a Ductz air duct–cleaning franchise. He approached six banks with his business plan and requested the $100,000 he needed to purchase the necessary equipment and pay franchising fees. "The banks wouldn't even look at me," he says. "They kept saying, 'You have great credit, but we don't want to take a chance on a start-up business.'" McFee ended up using his retirement account to purchase the Ductz franchise, which he now operates with his wife and two sons.[20] ■

Although franchisees typically invest a significant amount of their own money in their businesses, most need additional financing. In some cases, the franchisor will provide at least some of that additional financing. A basic principle of franchising is to use franchisees' money to grow their businesses, but some franchisors realize that because start-up costs have reached breathtakingly high levels, they must provide financial help for franchisees. In fact, a study by FRANdata, a franchising research company, reports that 20 percent of franchisors offer direct financing to their franchisees.[21] However, the credit crunch has caused a growing number of franchisors to provide financial assistance to franchisees. "Helping franchisees access financing wasn't a franchisor function a couple of years ago," says Shelly Sun, founder and CEO of BrightStar Franchising LLC, which provides in-home care service for senior citizens and children. "Now it's job number one."[22]

Small franchise systems are more likely to provide direct financial assistance to franchisees than are larger, more established franchisors. Traditionally, franchisors rarely make loans to enable franchisees to pay the initial franchise fee. However, once a franchisor locates a suitable prospective franchisee, it may offer the qualified candidate direct financial assistance in specific areas, such as purchasing equipment, inventory, or even the franchise fee.

In most instances, financial assistance from franchisors takes a form other than direct loans, leases, or short-term credit. Franchisors usually are willing to assist qualified franchisees in establishing relationships with banks, nonbank lenders, and other sources of financing. The support and connections from the franchisor enhance a franchisee's credit standing because lenders recognize the lower failure rate among established franchises. For instance, BrightStar recently hired a lending specialist to establish relationships with lenders to whom it refers franchisees in search of financing. Before hiring the specialist, fewer than 10 percent of BrightStar franchisees received loans; today, the percentage has increased to 75 percent.[23] Other franchisors are reducing fees, cutting royalties, and extending credit to help franchisees open outlets.

The Small Business Administration (SBA) has created a program called the Franchise Registry that is designed to provide financing for franchisees through its loan guarantee programs (more on these in Chapter 13). The Franchise Registry streamlines the loan application process for franchisees who pass the screening tests at franchises that are members of the Registry. Franchisors submit their franchise agreements and other documents to the Registry for preapproval by the SBA, which expedites the loan application process for prospective franchisees. Nearly 1,500 franchises ranging from AAMCO Transmissions (automotive repair) to Zaxby's (fast-food chicken restaurants) participate in the Franchise Registry program. Approximately 6.3 percent of all SBA loan guarantees go to franchisees, and the amount typically ranges from $250,000 to $500,000.[24] Franchisees who are interested in the Franchise Registry program should visit its Web site at www.franchiseregistry.com.

Proven Products, Processes, and Business Formats

As we have seen, franchisees essentially purchase a franchisor's experience in the form of a business system. A franchise owner does not have to build the business from scratch. Instead of being forced to rely solely on personal ability to establish business processes and attract a clientele, a franchisee can depend on the methods and techniques of an established business. At Papa John's, researchers are constantly looking for ways to improve their pizza and their franchisees' operations. Recent improvements include a simple system for making sauce measurements more precise and an oven calibration process to ensure more even heating throughout franchisees' pizza ovens, thereby producing more consistent pizzas.[25] These standardized procedures and operations greatly enhance the franchisee's chances of success and avoid the most inefficient type of learning—trial and error. In addition, franchisees do not have to struggle for recognition in the local marketplace as much as independent owners do.

ENTREPRENEURIAL PROFILE: Steven Taylor and Chris Smith: Moe's Southwest Grill Steven Taylor, just 29 years old and with little business experience, realized that the best way for him to realize his goal of owning a business was to purchase a franchise. "I knew the power behind [franchising]," he says. Taylor began investigating franchise options, focusing on Subway and Moe's Southwest Grill, a quick-service Mexican restaurant that he frequented. One of the Subway franchisees whom Taylor interviewed, a man who owned 45 outlets, was so impressed with Taylor's ambition and enthusiasm that he agreed to help finance the initial cost of a franchise. Within a year, Taylor and business partner Chris Smith had opened their first Moe's Southwest Grill in Columbia, South Carolina, and have since added four more locations. Their stores have won numerous company awards, but Taylor and Smith credit following the franchisor's system for their success. They rely on a battery of tools ranging from activity checklists, time-and-temperature logs, and food and labor cost calculators to make sure their stores run smoothly and efficiently. "In the same way the franchisor gave us a system to run, we, in turn, create systems that we expect the managers to run," says Taylor. "As long as they're running the systems, we're running an A-plus store."[26] ■

Centralized Buying Power

A significant advantage a franchisee has over an independent small business owner is participation in the franchisor's centralized, volume buying power. If franchisors sell goods and supplies to franchisees (not all do), they may pass on to franchisees cost savings from quantity discounts that they earn by buying in volume. Tom Curdes, owner of two Weed Man franchises in Toledo, Ohio, cites the lawn care franchisor's buying power as a major advantage. "The national buying power and the negotiations [with vendors] they do behind the scenes . . . I couldn't do that myself," says Curdes, whose franchises generate $750,000 in sales and employ 25 people.[27]

Site Selection and Territorial Protection

A proper location is critical to the success of any small business, and franchises are no exception. In fact, franchise experts consider the three most important factors in franchising to be *location*, *location*, and *location*. For instance, one franchise of the Rainforest Café, a restaurant chain with a jungle theme and an in-store "retail village," located in the Mall at the Source in Westbury, New York, closed because the customer base in the location did not match the company's target audience. The successful stores in the chain tend to count on visitors to popular tourist destinations, something that Westbury lacked.[28]

Sometimes, entrepreneurs discover that becoming affiliated with a franchisor is the best way to get into prime locations. Many franchisors conduct an extensive location analysis for each new outlet, including researching traffic patterns, zoning ordinances, accessibility, and population density. McDonald's, for example, is well known for its ability to obtain prime locations in high-traffic areas. Although choosing a location usually is the franchisee's responsibility, some franchisors control the site selection process. Stephen Rogers decided to leave a family business to purchase an AAMCO transmission service franchise and relied on the franchisor to select a location for his service center because of the company's experience in selecting prime locations for their outlets. (AAMCO has been selling franchises since 1963.)[29] Even when the franchisee makes the location decision, the franchisor reserves the right to approve the final site. Choosing a suitable location requires a thorough location analysis, including studies of traffic patterns, zoning ordinances, accessibility, population density, and demographics. You will learn more about the location decision in Chapter 14.

Some franchisors offer franchisees territorial protection, which gives existing franchisees the right to exclusive distribution of brand-name goods or services within a particular geographic area. A clause establishing such a protective zone that bars other outlets from the same franchise gives franchisees significant protection and security. The size of a franchisee's territory varies from industry to industry. For example, one national fast-food restaurant agrees not to license another franchisee within a mile and a half of existing locations. An ice cream franchisor defines its franchisees' territories on the basis of ZIP code designations. The purpose of territorial protection is to prevent an invasion of the existing franchisee's territory and the accompanying dilution of sales. One study of successful franchises reports that the failure rate for franchisees is lower in systems that offer exclusive territories than in those that do not.[30]

As existing markets have become increasingly saturated with franchise outlets, the placement of new outlets has become a source of friction between franchisors and franchisees. Existing franchisees complain that franchisors are encroaching on their territories by granting new franchises so close to them that their sales are diluted. Before signing a franchise contract, every prospective franchisee must know exactly what kind of territorial protection, if any, the franchisor guarantees. Why invest years building a successful franchise in a particular location only to have the franchisor allow another franchisee to open nearby, siphoning off sales of your existing outlet?

Greater Chance for Success

Investing in a franchise is not risk free. Since 2000, an average of 258 new franchises have entered the market each year, but not all of them survive. A study by The Coleman Report shows

You Be the Consultant

Would You Buy This Franchise?

Although opening a franchise is not a "sure thing," franchising's immense popularity is due, in part, to the support, experience, and training that franchisors provide their franchisees. Many would-be entrepreneurs believe that franchising reduces their risk of failure and see it as the key to their success. Large, established franchises have systems in place that have been replicated thousands of times and allow franchisees to follow a formula for success that the franchisor has worked out over many years. Many small franchisors don't have the benefit of learning from the mistakes of setting up thousands of outlets to fine-tune their business systems. Some of these small franchises have the potential to become tomorrow's franchise giants; others will fall by the wayside.

Monster Mini Golf

After Christina Vitagliano sold the auction house that she co-owned with another entrepreneur, she and her husband Patrick, who owned a theatrical production company, were left with a lease on the old mill that had housed the auction business in Danielson, Connecticut. They sat around their kitchen table one evening, thinking of ways to use the property, and came up with the idea of an indoor miniature golf course with a haunted house theme. They laid out a course, installed black lights, built papier-mâché monsters, and opened the doors to Monster Mini Golf. Customers loved it, often waiting in long lines to bank shots off of Frankenstein's feet. The Vitaglianos opened a second location near Providence, Rhode Island, and soon began to receive calls from customers who wanted to purchase franchises. Today, Monster Mini Golf has 26 franchises in 12 states. "Every course is custom-designed," says Christina. "All of the art is hand-painted. Franchisees [tell us] which monsters they like, and we give them a choice of animatronics. I'll research the town and get a history on the course; we turn it into a monster version. Our construction company, Twisted Toy Box, does the construction." For a total cost that ranges from $336,000 to $404,500, including the $30,000 initial franchise fee, franchisees get the use of the Monster Mini Golf name, management training (four weeks) and support, site selection assistance, marketing and public relations services, and proprietary, custom designs for their miniature golf courses. "Because we have years of experience with the concept, we know what works and works great, and . . . what doesn't," say the Vitaglianos. "We know what is safe and what isn't. These are things that you should not find out through trial-and-error. In addition to buying a proven system and name, you are buying the founders' experience and expertise and a quality concept."

Chocolate Martini Bar

Bill Panzica launched the Chocolate Martini Bar in Buffalo, New York, in 2006. The restaurant is popular with chic, upscale urbanites and stays open late to serve an eclectic mix of entrees (ranging from a turkey berry sandwich to a chocolate bar baguette),

martinis (including a chocolate cream pie martini and the Megatini, a 35-ounce martini for $69.95), and desserts (including a Belgian chocolate pyramid, Snickerbocher mud mousse, and a variety of ice cream flavors). After visiting Panzica's packed restaurant, copreneurs Joe Novak and Tammy Gunya-Novak and their partner Dominec Fanelli purchased the first Chocolate Martini Bar franchise and opened their outlet in their hometown of Cleveland. "Where else can you get a sundae at 1 in the morning?" laughs Tammy. "We liked this concept so much that if Bill were going to franchise, we wanted to be the first. We thought about doing something similar ourselves, but why gamble? With the franchise, we get proven recipes. The trial-and-error of coming up with a menu would have been more expensive and taken more time. We were novices, but we knew Bill would guide us through."

Originally, Panzica brought the Novaks to Buffalo for training, "but it wasn't very effective," says Tammy. Panzica, who developed a 300-page training manual that "covers every aspect of the business, from how the food is plated to how to answer the phone," agreed. He took his entire staff to the Novak's franchise in Cleveland and taught them how to run the business on site. "When we left, I felt we did every single thing we could do to train them," he says.

Purchasing a Chocolate Martini Bar franchise costs between $252,000 and $502,000, depending on the location, which the franchisor says must be a high-traffic area, such as a hotel (where both the original Chocolate Martini Bar and the franchise are located), entertainment district, or tourist area. Franchisees also pay

(continued)

You Be the Consultant *(continued)*

a royalty of 4 percent of sales and contribute 1 percent of sales to an advertising fund. Despite the costs, the Novaks wanted the security of a franchise rather than experiencing the uncertainty of an independent start-up. They also believe that the Chocolate Martini Bar's menu offers good value; only a few items are priced at more than $10.

1. What are the advantages and the disadvantages of purchasing an outlet from a small franchise system such as the ones described here?

2. Suppose that one of your friends is considering purchasing one of the franchises described here and asks your opinion. What advice would you offer him or her?

Source: Based on "Golf Scream," *Entrepreneur*, October 2010, p. 146, and "First Bite," *Entrepreneur*, April 2010, p. 110.

---

that the failure rate of franchisees in various franchise systems over a recent 10-year period averaged 17 percent but ranged from 0 to 82 percent, depending on the chain.[31] Despite the fact that franchising offers no guarantees of success, experts contend that franchising is less risky than building a business from the ground up. The tradition of success for franchises is attributed to the broad range of services, assistance, guidelines, and the comprehensive business system that the franchisor provides. Statistics regarding the success of a given franchise must be interpreted carefully, however. For example, sometimes when a franchise is in danger of failing, the franchisor often repurchases or relocates the outlet and does not report it as a failure.* As a result, some franchisors boast of never experiencing a failure.

A recent study of franchises reports that the success rate of franchisees is higher when a franchise system does the following:

● Requires franchisees to have prior industry experience

● Requires franchisees to actively manage their stores (no "absentee" owners)

● Has built a strong brand name

● Offers training programs designed to improve franchisees' knowledge and skills[32]

The risk involved in purchasing a franchise is two pronged: success—or failure—depends on the franchisee's managerial skills and motivation and on the franchisor's business experience, system, and support. Many franchisees are convinced that franchising has been the key to their success in business. Their success is proof of the common sentiment that franchising offers the opportunity to be in business *for* yourself but not *by* yourself. "[Franchising is] the perfect combination of having an independently owned and operated office, but with support," says Olivier Hecht, who left his corporate job to open a Handyman Matters home repair franchise.[33]

LO2B

Explain the drawbacks of buying a franchise.

The Drawbacks of Buying a Franchise

The benefits of buying a franchise can mean the difference between success and failure for some entrepreneurs. Prospective franchisees must understand the disadvantages of franchising before choosing this method of doing business. Perhaps the biggest drawback of franchising is that a franchisee must sacrifice some freedom to the franchisor. Other disadvantages are discussed in the following sections.

Franchise Fees and Ongoing Royalties

Virtually every franchisor imposes some type of fees and demands a share of franchisees' sales revenue in return for the use of the franchisor's name, products or services, and business system. The fees and the initial capital requirements vary among the different franchisors. The total

---

*As long as an outlet's doors never close, most franchisors do not count it as a failure even if the outlet has struggled for survival and has been through a series of owners who have tried unsuccessfully to turn around its performance.

investment required for a franchise varies from around $1,000 for some home-based service franchises to $6.5 million or more for hotel and motel franchises. For example, Jazzercise, an aerobics exercise franchise, requires a capital investment that ranges from just $2,980 to $76,500, and Subway, the sandwich and salad chain, estimates that the total cost of opening a franchise ranges from $84,800 for a kiosk location to $258,800 for a traditional restaurant. Culver's, a fast-growing regional chain that sells sandwiches (including the delicious ButterBurger®), salads, dinners, and frozen custard, requires an investment of $1,363,500 to $3,189,500, depending on land acquisition and building construction costs.

Start-up costs for franchises often include a variety of fees. Most franchises impose an initial franchise fee for the right to use the company name. The average up-front fee that franchisors charge is $25,147.[34] Subway's franchise fee is $15,000, but Culver's charges a franchise fee of $55,000. Other franchise start-up costs might include a location analysis, site purchase and preparation, construction, signs, fixtures, equipment, management assistance, and training. Some franchise fees include these costs, but others do not. Before signing any contract, a prospective franchisee should determine the total cost of a franchise, something that every franchisor is required to disclose in item 7 of its Franchise Disclosure Document (see the section "Franchising and the Law" later in this chapter).

Franchisors also impose continuing royalty fees as revenue-sharing devices. The royalty usually involves a percentage of gross sales with a required minimum, or a flat fee levied on the franchise. (In fact, 82 percent of franchisors charge a royalty based on a percentage of franchisees' sales.[35]) Royalty fees range from 1 to 11 percent, and the average royalty rate is 6.7 percent.[36] The Atlanta Bread Company charges franchisees a royalty of 5 percent of gross sales, which is payable weekly, and Subway charges a royalty of 8 percent of weekly gross sales. These ongoing royalties increase a franchisee's overhead expenses significantly. Because the franchisor's royalties and fees (the total fees the average franchisor collects amount to 8.4 percent of a franchisee's sales) are calculated as a percentage of a franchisee's sales, the franchisor gets paid—even if the franchisee fails to earn a profit.[37] Sometimes, unprepared franchisees discover (too late) that a franchisor's royalties and fees are the equivalent of the normal profit margin for a business. To avoid this problem, prospective franchisees should determine exactly how much fees will be and then weigh the benefits of the services and benefits the fees cover. One of the best ways to do this is to itemize what you are getting for your money and then determine whether the cost is worth the benefits provided. Be sure to get the details on all expenses—the amount, the timing of payments, and financing arrangements; find out which items, if any, are included in the initial franchise fee and which ones are "extra."

Strict Adherence to Standardized Operations

Although franchisees own their businesses, they do not have the autonomy that independent owners have. To protect its image, a franchisor requires that franchisees maintain certain operating standards. In fact, conformity is standard operating procedure in franchising. The franchisor controls layout and the color schemes that its franchisees use in their stores, the products they sell, the personnel and operating policies they use, and many other aspects of running the business. At McDonald's, franchisees must operate their businesses by the franchise manual, which specifies nearly every detail of running a franchise—including how many hamburger patties per pound of beef (10), how long to toast a bun (17 seconds), and how much sanitizer to use when cleaning the milkshake machine (one packet for 2.5 gallons of water).

If a franchise constantly fails to meet the minimum standards established for the business, the franchisor may terminate its license. Many franchisors determine compliance with standards with periodic inspections and secret shoppers. Secret shoppers work for a survey company and, although they look like any other customer, are trained to observe and then later record on a checklist a franchise's performance on key standards, such as cleanliness, speed of service, employees' appearances and attitudes, and others. At Five Guys Burgers and Fries, founder Jerry Murrell uses secret shoppers to ensure that franchisees comply with the company's strict quality and service standards. "We have two third-party audits in each store every week," he says. "One is a secret shopper—folks who pretend they're customers and rate crews on bathroom cleanliness, courtesy, and food preparation. Then we have safety audits."[38] At times, strict adherence to franchise standards may become a burden to some franchisees.

Restrictions on Purchasing

In the interest of maintaining quality standards, franchisors may require franchisees to purchase products, special equipment, or other items from the franchisor or from a list of "approved" suppliers. For example, KFC requires that franchisees use only seasonings blended by a particular company because a poor image could result from franchisees using inferior products to cut costs. Under some conditions, these purchase arrangements may be challenged in court as a violation of antitrust laws, but generally franchisors have a legal right to ensure that franchisees maintain acceptable quality standards. Franchisees of one ice cream franchise have complained that their profit margins suffer because the franchisor requires them to purchase costly ingredients from a single supplier.[39]

For many years, franchisors could legally set the prices they charge for the products they sell to franchisees but could not control the retail prices franchisees charge for products. However, a 1997 Supreme Court decision opened the door for franchisors to establish maximum prices that franchisees can charge. Many franchisors do not impose maximum prices, choosing instead to provide franchisees with suggested prices, but some do establish price limits. For instance, Burger King requires franchisees to charge no more than $1 for items on its Value Menu. Franchisees filed a lawsuit against the franchisor, claiming that Burger King did not have the right to dictate maximum prices under the franchise agreement. Franchisees argued that being forced to sell a double cheeseburger for $1 caused them to lose more than 10 cents per sandwich. A federal court judge ruled that the franchisor did have the right to set maximum prices for the products its franchisees sell. In response to franchisees' concerns, Burger King removed the double cheeseburger from the Value Menu, allowing franchisees to raise its price to $1.19, and replaced it with the BK Dollar Double, a sandwich that has two beef patties but only one slice of cheese.[40]

Limited Product Line

In most cases, the franchise agreement stipulates that the franchisee can sell only those products approved by the franchisor. Unless they are willing to risk the cancellation of their licenses, franchisees must avoid selling any unapproved products through the franchise. A franchise may be required to carry an unpopular product or be prevented from introducing a desirable one by the franchise agreement. A franchisee's freedom to adapt a product line to local market conditions is restricted. However, some franchisors actively solicit innovations and product suggestions from their franchisees. In fact, some of McDonald's most successful products came not from the corporate kitchen but from franchisees such as Jim Delligatti, who invented the legendary Big Mac in 1967. In 1968, McDonald's put the sandwich on franchisees' menus, where its original price was 49 cents. Today, McDonald's sells 560 million Big Macs each year—an average of more than 17 sandwiches per second![41] Subway's wildly successful "$5 Footlong" idea did not come from corporate headquarters but originated with Miami franchisee Stuart Frankel.[42]

ENTREPRENEURIAL PROFILE: Diana Tavary: Curves Some franchisees of Curves, a chain of exercise outlets that offer a 30-minute workout aimed at busy women, claim that the company ignored their requests to update its exercise format to help them retain members and attract new ones. Diana Tavary walked away from her Curves franchise after 10 years because the company failed to adapt to new exercise trends. "They didn't allow you to offer anything but the 30-minute circuit," she says. Tom Garmon, a business broker in the fitness industry, agrees. "They're so constrained by their present model that they don't appear to be open to feedback from their franchisees," he says. Franchisees say that they have lost business to rival gyms that allow customers to exercise at any time without supervision because the company does not allow that practice. Curves, which started franchising in 1995, currently has 4,000 franchised outlets, about half the number it had at its peak in 2005.[43] ■

Contract Terms and Renewal

Because they are written by the franchisor's attorneys, franchise contracts always are written in favor of the franchisor. Some franchisors are willing to negotiate the terms of their contracts, but many of the well-established franchisors are not because they know that they don't have to. The franchise contract is extremely important because it governs the franchisor–franchisee relationship over its life, which may last as long as 20 years. In fact, the average length of a franchise contract is 10.3 years. [44] Yet one study conducted by the Federal Trade Commission found that 40 percent of new franchisees signed their contracts without reading them![45]

Franchisees also should understand the terms and conditions under which they may renew their franchise contracts at the expiration of the original agreement. In most cases, franchisees are required to pay a renewal fee and to repair any deficiencies in their outlets or to modernize and upgrade them. One study by the International Franchise Association and FRANdata reports that the renewal rate of franchise agreements is 94 percent.[46]

Unsatisfactory Training Programs

A major benefit of purchasing a franchise is the training that the franchisor provides franchisees so that they are able to run successful operations. The quality of franchise training programs can vary dramatically, however. "Many franchisees think they will get a lot of training but find out it's a one-week crash course," says Marko Grunhagen, a franchising expert at Southern Illinois University.[47] Before signing on with a franchise, it is wise to find out the details of the training program the franchisor provides to avoid unpleasant surprises.

Market Saturation

Franchisees in fast-growing systems reap the benefits of the franchisor's expanding reach, but they also may encounter the downside of a franchisor's aggressive growth strategy: market saturation. As the owners of many fast-food, sandwich shops, and yogurt and ice cream franchises have discovered, market saturation is a very real danger. Subway, for example, which started franchising in 1974, has grown from just 166 outlets in 1981 to more than 37,000 outlets today![48] Any franchise growing that rapidly runs the risk of having outlets so close together that they cannibalize sales from one another. Franchisees of one fast-growing ice cream chain claim that the franchisor's rapid expansion has resulted in oversaturation in some markets, causing them to struggle to reach their break-even points. Some franchisees saw their sales drop precipitously and were forced to close their outlets.

Although some franchisors offer franchisees territorial protection, others do not. Territorial encroachment, competition from within the franchise, has become a hotly contested issue in franchising as growth-seeking franchisors have exhausted most of the prime locations and are now setting up new franchises in close proximity to existing ones. In some areas of the country, franchisees are upset, claiming that their markets are oversaturated and that their sales are suffering.

Less Freedom

When franchisees sign a contract, they agree to sell the franchisor's product or service by following its prescribed formula. This feature of franchising is the source of the system's success, but it also gives many franchisees the feeling that they are reporting to a "boss." Franchisors want to ensure franchisees' success, and most monitor their franchisees' performances closely to make sure that franchisees follow the system's specifications. "Everything you do in a franchise will be dictated [by the franchisor] from the moment you turn the key in the door in the morning," warns Eric Karp, a Boston attorney who teaches franchising at Babson College.[49]

Strict uniformity is the rule rather than the exception. For example, a group of franchisees filed a lawsuit against Burger King, claiming that the company had no right to require them to open their stores as early as 6 a.m. and to stay open as late as 2 a.m., but the court dismissed their argument, ruling that the franchise contract, which authorized the extended hours, is unambiguous and enforceable.[50] "There is no independence," says one writer. "Successful franchisees are happy prisoners."[51] As a result, highly independent, "go-my-own-way" entrepreneurs often are frustrated with the basic "go-by-the-rules" philosophy of franchising. Table 6.1 describes 10 myths of franchising.

Franchising and the Law

The franchising boom spearheaded by McDonald's and others in the late 1950s brought with it many prime investment opportunities. However, the explosion of legitimate franchises also ushered in with it numerous fly-by-night franchisors who defrauded their franchisees. By the 1970s, franchising was rife with fraudulent practitioners. David Kaufman, a renowned franchise expert with more than 30 years of experience, says, "In the late 1960s and 1970s, the words

LO3

Understand the laws covering franchise purchases.

TABLE 6.1 10 Myths of Franchising

Myth #1. Franchising is the safest way to go into business because franchises never fail. Although the failure rate for franchises is lower than that of independent businesses, there are no guarantees of success. Franchises can—and do—fail. Potential franchisees must exercise the same degree of caution in judging the risk of a franchise as they would any other business.

Myth #2. I'll be able to open my franchise for less money than the franchisor estimates. Launching a business, including a franchise, normally takes more money and more time than entrepreneurs estimate. Be prepared. One franchisee of a retail computer store advises, "If a franchisor tells you you'll need $100,000 to get started, you better have $150,000."

Myth #3. The bigger the franchise organization, the more successful I'll be. Bigger is not always better in the franchise business. Some of the largest franchise operations are struggling to maintain their growth rates because the best locations are already taken and their markets have become saturated. Market saturation is a significant problem for many large franchises, and smaller franchises are accounting for much of the growth in the industry. Early franchisees in new franchise systems often can negotiate better deals and receive more individual attention from the franchisor than those who purchase units in well-established systems.

Myth #4. I'll use 80 percent of the franchisor's business system, but I'll improve on it by substituting my experience and know-how. When franchisees buy a franchise, they are buying, in essence, the franchisor's experience and knowledge. Why pay all of that money to a franchisor if you aren't willing to use their system? When franchisors screen potential franchisees, they look for people who are willing to fit into their systems rather than fiercely independent entrepreneurs. "[Franchisors] have spent years building the company," says Jeff Elgin, founder of FranChoice, a franchise referral consulting firm. "They don't want someone who will come in and try to innovate because that produces chaos." Ideally, franchisors look for franchisees who exhibit a balance between the freewheeling entrepreneurial spirit and a system-focused approach.

Myth #5. All franchises are basically the same. Each franchise has its own unique personality, requirements, procedures, and culture. Naturally, some will suit you better than others. Avoid the tendency to select the franchise that offers the lowest cost. If the franchise does not fit your needs, it is not a bargain, no matter how inexpensive it is. Ask the franchisor and existing franchisees lots of questions to determine how well you will fit into the system. One of the best ways to get a feel for a franchise's personality is to work in a unit for a time.

Myth #6. I don't have to be a hands-on manager. I can be an absentee owner and still be very successful. Most franchisors shy away from absentee owners, and some simply do not allow them in their systems at all. They know that franchise success requires lots of hands-on attention, and the franchise owner is the best person to provide that.

Myth #7. Anyone can be a satisfied, successful franchise owner. With more than 3,000 franchises available, the odds of finding a franchise that appeals to your tastes are high. However, not everyone is cut out to be a franchisee. "If a person is highly entrepreneurial, he or she should not even consider a franchise investment," says Kevin Murphy, a franchise attorney. Those "free spirits" who insist on doing things their way most likely will be miserable in a franchise.

Myth #8. Franchising is the cheapest way to get into business for yourself. Although bargains do exist in franchising, the price tag for buying into some well-established systems is breathtaking, sometimes running more than $1 million. Franchisors look for candidates who are on solid financial footing.

Myth #9. The franchisor will solve my business problems for me; after all, that's why I pay an ongoing royalty. Although franchisors offer franchisees start-up and ongoing training programs, they will not run their franchisees' businesses for them. As a franchisee, your job is to take the formula that the franchisor has developed and make it work in your location. Expect to solve many of your own problems.

Myth #10. Once I open my franchise, I'll be able to run things the way I want to. Franchisees are not free to run their businesses as they see fit. Every franchisee signs a contract that requires him or her to run the business according to the franchisor's requirements. Franchisees who violate the terms of that agreement run the risk of having their franchise relationship terminated.

Sources: Based on Mark Henricks, "Finding the Perfect Fit: How Franchisers Select Franchisees," Advertising Insert, *Inc.*, February 2011, p. 110; April Y. Pennington, "The Right Stuff," *Entrepreneur B.Y.O.B.*, September 2004, pp. 90–100; Andrew A. Caffey, "There's More to a Franchise Than Meets the Eye," *Entrepreneur*, May 1998, http://www.entrepreneur.com/article/0,4621,228443,00.html; Andrew A. Caffey, "Myth vs. Reality," *Entrepreneur*, October 1998, http://www.entrepreneur.com/mag/article/0,1539,229435,00.html; Chieh Chieng, "Do You Want to Know a Secret?" *Entrepreneur*, January 1999, pp. 174–178; "Ten Most Common Mistakes Made by Franchise Buyers," Franchise Doctor, http://www.franchisedoc.com/mistakes.html; and Devlin Smith, "The Sure Thing," *Entrepreneur B.Y.O.B.*, May 2004, p. 100.

'franchise' and 'fraud' had almost become synonymous."[52] Thousands of people lost millions of dollars to criminals and unscrupulous operators who sold flawed business concepts and phantom franchises to unsuspecting investors. In an effort to control the rampant fraud in the industry and the potential for deception inherent in a franchise relationship, California in 1971 enacted the first Franchise Investment Law. The law (and those of 14 other states that passed similar laws) required franchisors to register a Uniform Franchise Offering Circular (UFOC) and deliver a copy to prospective franchisees before any offer or sale of a franchise. In October 1979, the Federal Trade Commission (FTC) adopted similar legislation at the national level that established full disclosure guidelines for any company selling franchises and was designed to give potential franchisees the information they needed to protect themselves from unscrupulous franchisors.

In 2008, the FTC replaced the UFOC with a similar document, the **Uniform Franchise Disclosure Document (UFDD)**, which requires all franchisors to disclose detailed information on their operations at least 14 days before a franchisee signs a contract or pays any money. The UFDD applies to all franchisors, even those in the 35 states that lack franchise disclosure laws. The purpose of the regulation is to assist potential franchisees' investigations of a franchise deal and to introduce consistency into the franchisor's disclosure statements. The FTC also established a "plain English" requirement for the UFDD that prohibits legal and technical jargon and makes a document easy to read and understand. The FTC's philosophy is not so much to prosecute abusers as to provide information to prospective franchisees and help them to make intelligent decisions. Although the FTC requires each franchisor to provide a potential franchisee with this information, it does not verify its accuracy. Prospective franchisees should use this document only as a starting point for their investigations.

Uniform Franchise Disclosure Document (UFDD)
a document that every franchisor is required by law to give prospective franchisees before any offer or sale of a franchise; it outlines 23 important pieces of information.

The Trade Regulation Rule requires a franchisor to include 23 major topics in its disclosure statement:

1. Information identifying the franchisor and its affiliates and describing the franchisor's business experience and the franchises being sold.

2. Information identifying and describing the business experience of each of the franchisor's officers, directors, and managers responsible for the franchise program.

3. A description of the lawsuits in which the franchisor and its officers, directors, and managers have been involved. Although most franchisors will have been involved in some type of litigation, an excessive number of lawsuits, particularly if they relate to the same problem, is alarming. Another red flag is an excessive number of lawsuits brought against the franchisor by franchisees. "The history of the litigation will tell you the future of your relationship [with the franchisor]," says the founder of a maid-service franchise.[53]

4. Information about any bankruptcies in which the franchisor and its officers, directors, and managers have been involved.

5. Information about the initial franchise fee and other payments required to obtain the franchise, the intended use of the fees, and the conditions under which the fees are refundable.

6. A table that describes all of the other fees that franchisees are required to make after start-up, including royalties, service fees, training fees, lease payments, advertising or marketing charges, and others. The table also must include the due dates for the fees.

7. A table that shows the components of a franchisee's total initial investment. The categories included are preopening expenses, the initial franchise fee, training expenses, equipment, opening inventory, initial advertising fee, signs, real estate (purchased or leased), equipment, opening inventory, security deposits, business licenses, initial advertising fees, and other expenses, such as working capital and legal and accounting fees. These estimates, usually stated as a range, give prospective franchisees an idea of how much their total start-up costs will be. Franchising expert Don Schadle says that for a typical franchisee, the total cost to open a franchise is $150,000; only 5 percent of franchisees invest more than $500,000.[54]

8. Information about quality requirements of goods, services, equipment, supplies, inventory, and other items used in the franchise and where franchisees may purchase them, including required purchases from the franchisor.

9. A cross-reference table that shows the location in the UFDD and in the franchise contract of the description of the franchisee's obligations under the franchise contract.

10. A description of any financial assistance available from the franchisor in the purchase of the franchise. Although many franchisors do not offer direct financial assistance to franchisees, they may have special arrangements with lenders who help franchisees find financing.

11. A description of all obligations the franchisor must fulfill in helping a franchisee prepare to open and operate a unit, including site selection, advertising, computer systems, pricing, training, (a table describing the length and type of training is required), and other forms of assistance provided to franchisees. This usually is the longest section of the UFDD.

12. A description of any territorial protection that the franchise receives and a statement as to whether the franchisor may locate a company-owned store or other franchised outlet in that territory. The franchisor must specify whether it offers exclusive or nonexclusive territories. Given the controversy in many franchises over market saturation, franchisees should pay close attention to this section.

13. All relevant information about the franchisor's trademarks, service marks, trade names, logos, and commercial symbols, including where they are registered. Prospective franchisees should look for a strong trademark or service mark that is registered with the U.S. Patent and Trademark Office.

14. Similar information on any patents, copyrights, and proprietary processes that the franchisor owns and the rights that franchisees have to use them.

15. A description of the extent to which franchisees must participate personally in the operation of the franchise. Many franchisors look for "hands-on" franchisees and discourage or even prohibit "absentee owners."

16. A description of any restrictions on the goods or services that franchises are permitted to sell and with whom franchisees may deal. The agreement usually restricts franchisees to selling only those items that the franchisor has approved.

17. A table that describes the conditions under which the franchise may be repurchased or refused renewal by the franchisor, transferred to a third party by the franchisee, and terminated or modified by either party. This section also addresses the method established for resolving disputes between franchisees and the franchisor.

18. A description of the involvement of celebrities and public figures in the franchise.

19. A complete statement of the basis for any earnings claims made to the franchisee, including the percentage of existing franchises that have actually achieved the results that are claimed. Franchisors that make earnings claims must include them in the UFDD, and the claims must "have a reasonable basis" at the time they are made. However, franchisors are *not* required to make any earnings claims at all; in fact, 81.7 percent of franchisors do not, primarily because of liability concerns about committing such numbers to writing.[55]

20. A table that displays systemwide statistical information about the expansion or the contraction of the franchise over the last three years. This section also includes the current number of franchises, the number of franchises projected for the future and the states in which they are to be sold, the number of franchises terminated, the number of agreements the franchisor has not renewed, the number of franchises that have been sold to new owners, the number of outlets the franchisor has repurchased, and a list of the names and addresses (organized by state) of other franchisees in the system and of those who have left the system within the last year. Contacting some of the franchisees who have left the system can alert would-be franchisees to potential problems with the franchise.

21. The franchisor's audited financial statements.

22. A copy of all franchise and other contracts (leases, purchase agreements, and others) that the franchisee will be required to sign.

23. A standardized, detachable receipt to prove that the prospective franchisee received a copy of the UFDD. The FTC now allows franchisors to provide the UFDD to prospective franchisees electronically.

The typical UFDD is from 100 to 200 pages long, but every potential franchisee should read and understand it. Unfortunately, many do not, often resulting in unpleasant surprises for franchisees. The information contained in the UFDD neither fully protects a potential franchise from deception nor guarantees success. The UFDD does, however, provide enough information to begin a thorough investigation of the franchisor and the franchise deal, and prospective franchisees should use it to their advantage.

The *Right* Way to Buy a Franchise

The UFDD is a powerful tool designed to help would-be franchisees select the franchise that is right for them and to avoid being duped by dishonest franchisors. The best defenses a prospective entrepreneur has against unscrupulous franchisors are preparation, common sense, and patience. By asking the right questions and resisting the urge to rush into an investment decision, potential franchisees can avoid being taken by unscrupulous operators.

Not every franchise "horror story" is the result of dishonest franchisors. More often than not, the problems that arise in franchising have more to do with franchisees who buy legitimate franchises without proper research and analysis. They end up in businesses that they don't enjoy and that they are not well suited to operate. How can you avoid this mistake? The steps discussed in the following sections will help you to make the right choice.

"Here's your lemonade and here's some descriptive literature about my franchising opportunities ."

© a. bacall/www.CartoonStock.com

Evaluate Yourself

Before looking at any franchise, entrepreneurs should study their own traits, goals, experience, likes, dislikes, risk orientation, income requirements, time and family commitments, and other characteristics. Knowing how much you can invest in a franchise is important, but it is not the only factor to consider. "You not only have to understand simple things such as what kind of investment you're willing to make, but also what kind of risks you are willing to take, how hard you want to work, how many hours you want to work, and what kind of environment you want to work in," advises Lori Kiser-Block, head of franchise consulting service FranChoice.[56] Will you be comfortable working in a structured environment? In what region of the country or world do you want to live and work? What is your ideal job description? Do you want to sell a product or a service? What hours do you expect to work? Do you want to work with people, or do you prefer to work alone? Knowing what you enjoy doing (and what you *don't* want to do) will help you to narrow your search. Which franchises are a good match for your strengths, weaknesses, interests, and professional experience? The goal is to find the franchise that is right—for *you*!

LO4

Discuss the *right* way to buy a franchise.

ENTREPRENEURIAL PROFILE: Todd and Bambi Stringham: Signs by Tomorrow
After spending 15 years in the corporate world, Todd and Bambi Stringham grew disillusioned and decided to make a career change. After evaluating their experience, strengths, and finances, they decided to make their dream of owning a business a reality by buying a franchise. The Stringhams spent months reviewing the features of more than 30 franchisors that matched their profile of what they were looking for in a franchise before settling on Signs by Tomorrow, a Maryland-based company with nearly 200 outlets that makes a variety of signs, primarily for businesses. They wanted a franchisor that would support their operation with a solid business system and that would allow them to use their own creativity. "I have always wanted to own my own business," says Todd. "After a lot of research, we found that Signs by Tomorrow had the business model and support system we were looking for."[57] ■

TABLE 6.2 Are You Franchisee Material?

Not everyone is cut out to be a franchisee. What characteristics do successful franchise owners have?

- *Commitment.* Like all entrepreneurs, successful franchisees must be committed to making their businesses successful. For franchisees, that means learning how the franchisor's system works and how to apply it in their individual markets.

- *Learning attitude.* Franchisees must exhibit a learning attitude and be willing to learn from the franchisor, other franchisees, and other experts. "Franchisors are not necessarily looking for experts in their industry," says one franchise consultant, "but for individuals with a great work ethic, broad business knowledge, and a willingness to follow a proven system."

- *Willingness to work with others.* Franchising success requires a willingness to work with the franchisor in a close, mutually beneficial relationship.

- *Patience.* Franchisees must understand that franchising is *not* a ticket to overnight success; success often requires years of hard work.

- *Positive attitude.* Franchisors look for franchisees who have a positive outlook and are focused on success.

- *General business skills.* Although franchisors usually do not require franchisees to have years of experience in the particular industry in which they operate, they do look for people who have general business experience. Sound leadership and communication skills are important in every industry.

- *Leadership ability.* Getting a franchise up and running successfully requires every ounce of leadership ability that a franchisee has.

- *Coachability.* In addition to being successful leaders, franchisees also must be good followers. Franchisors say that their most successful franchisees are coachable and are willing to learn from the experience of others. Reaping the advantages of the franchisor's experience is one of the primary benefits of franchising, and franchisees should take advantage of it. "Be prepared to listen to others who have blazed the path for you," says John Hewitt, founder of the Jackson Hewitt Tax Service franchise.

- *Perseverance.* Successful franchisees are dedicated to making their franchises successful and work hard to get the job done.

- *Solid people skills.* Whatever field they enter, successful franchisees require good people skills because they will be managing employees and working with customers.

- *Adequate capital.* Franchisors look for franchisees who have adequate financial resources to launch their businesses and to keep them going until they can generate enough cash flow to support themselves.

- *Compatible values.* Successful franchisees have value systems that are compatible with those of the franchisor.

- *Willingness to follow the system.* Some people enter the world of franchising because they have an entrepreneurial streak, which could be a mistake. Although creativity and a fresh approach are valuable assets in any business, franchising boils down to following the system that the franchisor has established. Why pay a franchisor for the benefit of experience if you are not willing to put that experience to work for yourself?

Sources: Based on Jerry Chautin, "Tips to Help Succeed at Owning a Franchise," *Herald Tribune,* September 27, 2010, http://www.heraldtribune.com/article/20100927/COLUMNIST/9271021; Jeff Elgin, "Are You Franchisee Material?," *Entrepreneur,* April 4, 2005, http://www.entrepreneur.com/franchises/buyingafranchise/franchisecolumnistjeffelgin/article76896.html; Kim Ellis, "Key Characteristics of Successful Franchise Owners," *Bison,* July 1, 2007, http://www.bison.com/articles_investigationellis_07012007; Jennifer Openshaw, "Five Keys to Success as a Franchise Owner," *AOL Small Business,* October 8, 2007, http://smallbusiness.aol.com/article/_a/five-keys-to-success-as-a-franchise/2007101217280999000; and Sara Wilson, "Show Me the Way," *Entrepreneur,* September 2006, p. 120.

Table 6.2 is designed to help prospective franchisees to evaluate their potential as successful franchisees.

Research Your Market

Before shopping for a franchise, research the market in the area you plan to serve. How fast is the overall area growing? In which areas is that growth occurring fastest? How many competitors already operate in the area? How strong is the competition? Investing some time to develop a profile of the customers in your target area is essential; otherwise, you will be flying blind. Who are your potential customers? How many of them are in your proposed trading area? What are their characteristics? What are their income and education levels? What kinds of products and services do they buy? What gaps exist in the market? These gaps represent potential franchise opportunities for you. Market research also should confirm that a franchise is not merely a fad that will quickly fade. Steering clear of fads and into long-term trends is one way to sustain the success of a franchise. Before Papa John's Pizza allows franchisees to open a franchise, the company requires them to spend six months to a year evaluating the market potential of the local area. "We don't just move into an area and open up 200 stores," says one manager. "We do it one store at a time."[58]

Consider Your Franchise Options

Small business magazines (and their Web sites), such as *Entrepreneur*, *Inc.*, and others, devote at least one issue to franchising in which they often list hundreds of franchises. These guides can help you to find a suitable franchise within your price range. The Internet is another valuable tool for gathering information on franchises. The Web sites of organizations such as the International Franchise Association, the American Association of Franchisees and Dealers, the Canadian Franchise Association, and others offer valuable resources and advice for prospective franchisees. In addition, many cities host franchise trade shows throughout the year where hundreds of franchisors gather to sell their franchises. Attending one of these franchise showcases is a convenient, efficient way to collect information about a variety of available opportunities.

Many franchisors offer prospective franchisees visits to corporate headquarters where they have the opportunity to learn more about the franchise, the people who manage it, and its products and services. Known as "Discovery Days," these visits are an excellent way for prospective franchisees to peek behind the curtain of a franchise operation and for franchisors to size up potential franchisees.

ENTREPRENEURIAL PROFILE: Bob and Kathy Summers: Spring-Green Lawn Care Bob and Kathy Summers traveled nearly 900 miles to the corporate headquarters of Spring-Green Lawn Care, a franchise they were considering purchasing. They met with a top executive who explained the sales that franchisees typically generate in their first year of operation, had lunch with the office staff, and saw firsthand the equipment they would purchase for their business. Their visit convinced them that Spring-Green was the right franchise for them.[59] ∎

Some franchisors use technology to allow prospective franchisees to make virtual visits to the company's headquarters, watch online videos, and talk with executives in videoconferences.

Get a Copy of the Franchisor's UFDD

Once you narrow down your franchise choices, you should contact each franchise (at least two in the industry that you have selected) and get a copy of its UFDD. Then read it! This document is an important tool in your search for the right franchise, and you should make the most of it. When evaluating a franchise opportunity, what should a potential franchisee look for? Although there is never a guarantee of success, the following characteristics make a franchise stand out:

- *A unique concept or marketing approach.* "Me-too" franchises are no more successful than me-too independent businesses. Pizza franchisor Papa John's has achieved an impressive growth rate by emphasizing the quality of its ingredients, while Domino's is known for its fast delivery.

- *Profitability.* A franchisor should have a track record of profitability, and so should its franchisees. If a franchisor is not profitable, its franchisees are not likely to be either. Franchisees who follow the business format should expect to earn a reasonable rate of return.

- *A registered trademark.* Name recognition is difficult to achieve without a well-known and protected trademark.

- *A business system that works.* A franchisor should have in place a system that is efficient and is well documented in its manuals.

- *A solid training program.* One of the most valuable components of a franchise system is the training that it offers franchisees. The system should be relatively easy to teach.

- *Affordability.* A franchisee should not have to take on an excessive amount of debt to purchase a franchise. Being forced to borrow too much money to open a franchise outlet can doom a business from the outset. Respectable franchisors verify prospective franchisees' financial qualifications as part of the screening process rather than hand out franchises to anyone who has the money to buy one.

- *A positive relationship with franchisees.* The most successful franchises are those that see their franchisees as partners—and treat them accordingly.

The UFDD covers the 23 items discussed in the previous section and includes a copy of the company's franchise agreement and any contracts accompanying it. Although the law requires a UFDD to be written in plain English rather than "legalese," it is best to have an attorney experienced in franchising review the UFDD and discuss its provisions with you. Watch for clauses that give the franchisor absolute control and discretion. The franchise contract summarizes the details that will govern the franchisor–franchisee relationship over its life. It outlines *exactly* the rights and the obligations of each party and sets the guidelines that govern the franchise relationship. Because franchise contracts typically are long term (50 percent run for 15 years or more), it is extremely important for prospective franchisees to understand their terms *before* they sign them.

One of the most revealing items in the UFDD is the **franchisee turnover rate**, the rate at which franchisees leave the system. If the turnover rate is less than 5 percent, the franchise is probably sound. However, a double-digit franchise turnover rate is cause for concern, and one approaching 20 percent is a sign of serious underlying problems in a franchise. Satisfied franchisees are not inclined to leave a successful system.

Item 3, the description of the lawsuits in which the franchise has been involved, provides valuable insight into the franchisor–franchisee relationship. Although franchise lawsuits are not uncommon, an unusual number of lawsuits relating to the same issue should alert a potential franchisee to problems. For instance, a judge recently upheld a settlement concerning four class-action lawsuits filed by more than 8,000 current or former franchisees against Quiznos Subs. The lawsuits involved complaints concerning the franchisor's supply chain and food costs, marketing and advertising funds, and fees and royalties on territories that franchisees purchased but in which they never opened restaurants. Although Quiznos paid $206 million to the franchisees, the settlement involved no admission of wrongdoing on the franchisor's part.[60]

Another important aspect of investigating a potential franchise is judging how well you fit into the company culture. Unfortunately, the UFDD isn't much help here. The best way to determine this is to actually work for a unit for a time (even if it's without pay). Doing so not only gives prospective franchisees valuable insight into the company culture but also enables them to determine how much they enjoy the daily activities involved in operating the franchise. "Many people don't do enough research, digging into what a company is about, what they believe in, what they're trying to accomplish, and whether they will fit into the culture," says Kevin Hogan, a consultant who works with the Whattaburger franchise.[61]

franchisee turnover rate
the rate at which franchisees leave a franchise system.

Talk to Existing Franchisees

One of the best ways to evaluate the reputation of a franchisor is visit several franchise owners who have been in business at least one year and interview them about the positive and the negative features of the agreement and whether the franchisor delivered what was promised. Were their start-up costs consistent with the franchisor's estimates in item 7 of the UFDD? Do they get the support the franchisor promised them? Was the training the franchisor provided helpful? How long did it take to reach the break-even point? Have they incurred any unexpected expenses? What risks are involved in purchasing a franchise? Has the franchise met their expectations concerning sales, profitability, and return on investment? What is involved in operating the franchise on a typical day? How many hours do they work in a typical week? What do they like best (and least) about their work? Knowing what they know now, would

TABLE 6.3 Questions to Ask Existing Franchisees

One of the most revealing exercises for entrepreneurs who are evaluating potential franchises is to visit and interview franchisees who already are operating outlets for a franchise. This is the chance to get the "inside scoop" from people who know best how a particular franchise system works. Following are some questions to ask:

1. Are you happy with your relationship with the franchisor? Explain.
2. How much control does the franchisor exercise over you and the way you run your franchise?
3. What did it actually cost you to get your franchise running? How close was the actual amount to the amount the franchisor told you it would cost?
4. Is your franchise profitable? How long did it take for your franchise to break even? How much does your franchise earn? Are the earnings consistent with your expectations?
5. Did the franchisor estimate accurately the amount of working capital necessary to sustain your business until it began generating positive cash flow?
6. What is the training program like? Were you pleased with the training you received from the franchisor? Did the training prepare you adequately for operating your franchise successfully?
7. Did you encounter any unexpected franchise fees or hidden costs? If so, what were they?
8. Are you pleased with the size of your territory? Is it large enough for you to reach your sales and profitability goals? What kind of territorial protection does the franchisor offer?
9. What restrictions do you face on the products and services that you can sell? Are you required to purchase from approved suppliers? Are their prices reasonable?
10. Does the franchisor advertise as much as it said it would? Is the advertising effective in producing sales?
11. What kind of education and business experience do you have? How important have they been to your success in the franchise?
12. Given what you know now, would you purchase this franchise again?

Sources: Adapted from Sara Wilson, "Final Answer," *Entrepreneur*, December 2007, pp. 122–126, and "Ten Questions to Ask Other Franchisees in the Franchise Chain," *AllBusiness*, 2006, http://www.allbusiness.com/buying-exiting-businesses/franchising-franchises/2188-1.html.

they buy the franchise again? When you are on-site, note the volume of customer traffic and the average transaction size. Are they large enough for an outlet to be profitable? How well managed are the franchises you visit? Michael Whalen, who left a management position with a large office supply chain after 20 years to purchase a Huntington Learning Center franchise, says that the most helpful part of his franchise evaluation process "was meeting with current franchise owners."[62] Table 6.3 offers a list of questions prospective franchisees should ask existing franchisees.

Interviewing past franchisees, particularly those whose outlets failed, getting their perspectives on the franchisor–franchisee relationship is also helpful. (Their contact information is available in the UFDD.) Why did they leave the system? If their franchises were unsuccessful, what were the causes? Franchisees in some companies have formed associations that can provide prospective franchisees with valuable information. Sometimes prospective franchisees go to work in existing franchises to determine whether owning an outlet is the right career choice.

ENTREPRENEURIAL PROFILE: Reynolds Corea: BrightStar After Reynolds Corea was laid off from his executive position at a large consulting firm, he decided that buying a franchise was the best way to realize his entrepreneurial dreams. He went to work at $10 per hour at a local Chick-Fil-A restaurant, serving chicken sandwiches, mopping floors, and closing the store "to get a better feel for the business." After nine months, Corea decided that owning a restaurant franchise was not for him and worked with a franchise consultant to find a franchise that better suited his interests, goals, and skills. Corea ultimately chose to purchase a franchise from BrightStar, an in-home care service for senior citizens and children. Corea tapped his retirement accounts for the franchise fee and start-up costs, which totaled about $200,000. Corea's franchise is off to a solid start, with two full-time employees and 10 part-time caregivers and plans to hire more.[63] ■

Ask the Franchisor Some Tough Questions

Take the time to ask the franchisor questions about the company and its relationship with its franchisees. As a franchisee, you will be in this relationship a long time, and you need to know as much about it as you possibly can beforehand. What is the franchisor's philosophy concerning the relationship? Is there a franchise association made up of franchisees who consult and work with the franchisor's management team? What is the company culture like? How much input do franchisees have into the system? What are the franchise's future expansion plans? How will they affect your franchise? Are you entitled to an exclusive territory? Under what circumstances can either party terminate the franchise agreement? What happens if you decide to sell your franchise in the future? Under what circumstances would you not be entitled to renew the agreement? What kind of earnings can you expect? (If the franchisor made no earnings claims in item 19 of the UFOC, why not?) Does the franchisor have a well-formulated strategic plan? How many franchisees own multiple outlets? (A significant percentage of multiunit franchisees is a good sign that a franchise's brand name and business system are strong.) Has the franchisor terminated any franchisee's contracts? If so, why? Have any franchisees failed? If so, why? How are disputes between the franchisor and franchisees settled?

Make Your Choice

The first lesson in franchising is, "Do your homework *before* you get out your checkbook." Robyn Vescovi left behind a 25-year career as an executive in the financial industry to become a Tasti D-Lite franchisee in Boynton Beach, Florida. Before making the career switch, Vescovi spent a year studying her franchise options before making Tasti D-Lite her final choice. "Franchising seemed right for me," she says. "I learned about the board. I knew what the product could do, and I knew who was behind it."[64] Once you have done your research, you can make an informed choice about which franchise is right for you. Then it is time to put together a solid business plan that will serve as your road map to success in the franchise you have selected. The plan is also a valuable tool to use as you arrange the financing for your franchise.

Appendix A at the end of this chapter offers a checklist of questions a potential franchisee should ask before entering into any franchise agreement.

LO5

Outline the major trends shaping franchising.

Trends Shaping Franchising

Franchising has experienced three major growth waves since its beginning. The first wave occurred in the early 1970s when fast-food restaurants used the concept to grow rapidly. The fast-food industry was one of the first to discover the power of franchising, but other businesses soon took notice and adapted the franchising concept to their industries. The second wave took place in the mid-1980s as the U.S. economy shifted heavily toward the service sector. Franchises followed suit, springing up in every service business. A third wave began in the early 1990s and continues today. It is characterized by new low-cost franchises that focus on specific market niches. In the wake of major corporate downsizing and the burgeoning costs of traditional franchises, these new franchises allow would-be entrepreneurs to get into proven businesses faster and at reasonable costs. These companies feature start-up costs in the range of $2,000 to $250,000 and span a variety of industries—from leak detection in homes and auto detailing to day care and tile glazing.

Other significant trends affecting franchising are discussed in the following sections.

Changing Face of Franchisees

Franchisees today are a more diverse group than in the past. The U.S. Census Bureau reports that minorities own about 20 percent of all franchises, and women own 25 percent of them.[65] To encourage diversity among their franchisees, some franchisors have established programs that offer special deals and financing opportunities to members of minority groups. Focus Brands, a company that operates several franchises, including Cinnabon, Carvel, Moe's Southwest Grill, and Schlotsky's, has a Growth Through Diversity program that gives minority franchisees discounts on the initial franchise fee and operating fees. Focus Brands also is a member of MinorityFran, a program sponsored by the International Franchise Association that has the goal of recruiting minority franchisees.[66]

Hands On . . . How To

Select the Ideal Franchise—*For You*!

When Aaron Miller was a student at the University of Vermont, he wrote a business plan for a sports bar as part of an entrepreneurship class that he was taking. More than 15 years later, Miller, a former Olympic and professional ice hockey player, and Martti Matheson, close friends since their college days, transformed that business plan into reality when they opened their first Buffalo Wild Wings Grill and Bar franchise in Burlington, Vermont. What lessons can prospective franchisee can learn from Miller and Matheson's experience and that of other franchisees?

Lesson 1. Don't be in a rush; start with a self-evaluation to determine whether franchising is right for you. Finding the right franchise can take months—sometimes years. The first step to finding the right franchise is not screening potential franchisees; it is to consider whether franchising is the proper route for you. For would-be entrepreneurs who are independent and have definite ideas about how they want their businesses to operate, franchising is not the path they should follow to get into business. Miller and Matheson considered launching their own independent sports bar but after evaluating their lack of experience in the restaurant business decided to "go with an established model," says Matheson. "So many people come and go in the restaurant business. With a franchise, you have constant support on menu items, on how the kitchen works, on advertising."

Lesson 2. Make sure that you understand both the advantages and the disadvantages of franchising before making a commitment. The best franchisors offer their franchisees a recipe for success and the support to help them make it work. However, they require that franchisees pay them for the recipe with up-front fees and ongoing royalties and then stick to the recipe as they operate their businesses. "With a private business," says Matheson, "You make every decision. [A franchise] can be frustrating because in some places, your hands are tied. You have to stick with the menu, the look and feel, the architectural design." For Matheson and Miller, the advantages outweighed the disadvantages. "For the benefits they provide, I'd give them 5 percent [of sales, the royalty] any day," says Matheson. "Their average franchise restaurant has almost $3 million in sales a year. It would take us a long time to get there without them."

Lesson 3. Review the UFDD with the help of an experienced attorney. The UFDD is an extremely valuable resource for anyone who is considering purchasing a franchise. Poring over the document alone can be frustrating, however, because it covers so much. "The typical UFDD is enormously complex because it is so multifaceted," says Eric Karp, an attorney who teaches franchising courses at Babson College. Karp says that some franchisees are so overwhelmed by the size of the UFDD that they make the mistake of not reading it at all.

Lesson 4. Use the UFDD to screen potential franchises and don't be shy about asking lots of questions. Rob Parsons worked as the franchise development director for Popeyes Louisiana Kitchen for six years before he decided to switch sides and become one of the company's franchisees. "Something a franchisee said kept ringing in my head," he recalls. "He said, 'You did all the work. Why are you letting me reap all the benefits?" Parsons, who has experienced the UFDD from both the franchisor's and the franchisee's perspective, says that the UFDD can be extremely useful to prospective franchisees. "The UFDD has a list of all of the franchisees in a system," says Parsons. "That's a huge resource." Use the list to contact current and past franchisees to discover what it's really like to operate an outlet in the franchisor's system. If they were making the decision today, would they still purchase the franchise?

Lesson 5. Make sure that you can afford the franchise without getting in over your head. Some franchises cost millions of dollars; others require only a few thousand dollars. Because the financial crisis made getting credit more difficult, many franchisors have raised the requirements that franchisees must meet to qualify for consideration. Before the financial crisis, Firehouse Subs allowed franchisees to make a down payment of 10 to 20 percent of the total cost; today, the franchisor *requires* a down payment of at least 30 percent because lenders will not consider less financially qualified candidates. The credit crunch has required franchisors to get more creative when it comes to helping franchisees finance the purchase of their outlets. Marco's Pizza, which operates nearly 250 restaurants, offers qualified franchisees personal guarantee insurance that repays a bank 70 percent of a franchisee's loan in case the franchisee cannot repay the loan. Marco's also has assembled a group of private investors to create a $5 million private equity fund that will invest up to $100,000 in each Marco's restaurant. In addition, Marco's has established a leasing program that finances the $250,000 cost of opening one of its pizza outlets. When Remi Tessler approached a bank for a loan to open a Marco's Pizza franchise in Warner Robbins, Georgia, the bank told him that it could finance only the cost of the equipment for just five years, despite his stellar credit score. "I was shocked," says Tessler, who then turned to his franchisor for financing assistance. Tessler made a down payment of $62,500 and used Marco's leasing program to finance the remaining $187,500, which he will repay over eight years.

Lesson 6. Visit your top franchise candidates. After narrowing the list of potential franchises to your top choices, go visit them. Most franchisors sponsor Discovery Days events in which they host potential franchisees at their headquarters. Be observant and, once again, ask lots of questions. Ted

(continued)

Hands On . . . How To *(continued)*

Dowell says that his visit to the operations center of TSS Photography, a franchise that specializes in taking photographs of sports, school, and special events, convinced him to become a franchisee. "They walked us through the production side, and it was working like a machine," he says. "I realized why they have such a high success rate and why they always ship the right products at the right time. If I hadn't seen that, I'm not sure I would have joined the franchise." In addition, recognize that franchisors use these on-site visits to evaluate prospective franchisees.

Lesson 7. Realize that no business, not even a franchise, runs itself. Some new franchisees believe that they can be absentee owners because the business system they purchase from the franchisor will allow their franchises to operate by themselves. It's just not true. "Some people think that running a franchise won't be a lot of work," says Matt Haller of the International Franchise Association. "They think that all they have to do is pay the franchise fee and then sit back and watch the money roll in." Although the franchisor provides franchisees with a formula for success, franchisees must implement the formula and make it work. "In franchising, like anything else, hard work pays off," says Haller.

Sources: Based on Melissa Pasanen, "Chain Restaurant Model Works for Many Vermont Entrepreneurs," *Burlington Free Press*, June 7, 2010, http://www.burlingtonfreepress.com/article/20100607/NEWS01; Dianne Molvig, "Buying a Franchise: Potential and Precautions," Educational Employees Credit Union, January 10, 2011, http://hffo.cuna.org/11270/article/3171/html; Anne Fisher, "Risk Reward," *FSB*, December 2005/January 2006, pp. 45–61; Julie Bennett, "The Road to Discovery," *Entrepreneur*, February 2011, pp. 83–87; Kermit Patterson, "Tight Credit Is Turning Franchisors into Lenders," *New York Times*, June 9, 2010, http://www.nytimes.com/2010/06/10/business/smallbusiness/10sbiz.html; Jason Daley, "The Cross Over," *Entrepreneur*, March 2011, pp. 101–105; and Emily Maltby, "Want to Buy a Franchise: The Requirements Went Up," *Wall Street Journal*, November 15, 2010, p. R9.

ENTREPRENEURIAL PROFILE: Isaac Green: McDonald's Isaac Green, an African American owner of eight McDonald's restaurants in Maryland, started working as a crew member at McDonald's in high school and later was promoted to general manager of a store. In 2001, Green bought his first McDonald's franchise, tapping his retirement savings to make the purchase. His restaurants now employ 450 people and generate $21 million in annual sales. "In what other industry can you start out as a crew member making $2.95 an hour and later become a franchise owner managing a $5.7 million payroll?" he asks. Green's goal is to own 30 McDonald's restaurants within the next five years. "As a franchise owner," says Green, "you have to follow the playbook, but you can also change the plays; you can localize them for each community."[67] ∎

Modern franchisees also are better educated, are more sophisticated, have more business acumen, and are more financially secure than those of just 20 years ago. People of all ages and backgrounds are choosing franchising as a way to get into business for themselves. A survey by Franchise Business Review reports that 13 percent of franchisees are between the ages of 18 and 34.[68] Franchising also is attracting skilled, experienced businesspeople who are opening franchises in their second careers and whose goal is to own multiple outlets that cover entire states or regions. Many of them are former corporate managers—either corporate castoffs or corporate dropouts—looking for a new start on a more meaningful and rewarding career. They have the financial resources, management skills and experience, and motivation to operate their franchises successfully. "[Former executives] have financial discipline, understand business cycles and growth curves, and know how to work within a system," says David Omholt, owner of a franchise brokerage company.[69]

International Opportunities

One of the major trends in franchising is the internationalization of American franchise systems. Increasingly, franchising is becoming a major export industry for the United States, where franchises are focusing on international markets to boost sales and profits as the domestic market becomes saturated. A survey by the International Franchise Association reports that 52 percent of U.S.-based franchisors have an international presence, and more domestic franchisors are looking to expand abroad.[70] Yum! Brands, the parent company of Taco Bell, KFC, and Pizza Hut, earns 65 percent of its profits from international franchises and forecasts that the percentage will grow to 75 percent by 2015. McDonald's, which had restaurants in

28 countries in 1980, now operates nearly 14,000 outlets in 116 nations outside the United States; international locations account for 66 percent of the company's sales.[71] Europe is the primary market for U.S. franchisors, with Pacific Rim countries, Canada, and South America following, but China and India are becoming franchising hot spots. These markets are attracting franchisors because they are growing rapidly and offer rising personal incomes, strong demand for consumer goods, growing service economies, and spreading urbanization. Yum! Brands was an early entry into China, opening its first KFC store there in 1987. Today, the company has 3,000 KFC locations in 650 Chinese cities and opens one store in China on average every 18 hours. The company launched its first Pizza Hut in China in 1990, and the brand, which is regarded by Chinese customers as an upscale, trendy restaurant (often requiring reservations), now holds the top position in the pizza market in China.[72] McDonald's, which opened its first outlet in China in 1990, also sees the country as a prime growth market and recently built its first Hamburger University training center in Shanghai to support its expansion in China.[73]

As they venture into foreign markets, franchisors have learned that adaptation is one key to success. Although a franchise's overall business format may not change in foreign markets, some of the details of operating its local outlets must. For instance, fast-food chains in other countries often must make adjustments to their menus to please locals' palates. In Japan, McDonald's (known as "Makudonarudo") outlets sell teriyaki burgers, rice burgers, and katsu burgers (cheese wrapped in a roast pork cutlet topped with katsu sauce and shredded cabbage) in addition to their traditional American fare. McDonald's has eliminated beef and pork from its menu and has substituted mutton for beef in its burgers in India, where it sells sandwiches such as the Maharaja Mac (two specially seasoned chicken patties with locally flavored condiments), the McAloo (a patty made from potatoes, peas, and special spices), and the McSpicy Paneer (a spicy cottage cheese patty made from buffalo milk topped with a tandoori sauce).[74] In India, Pizza Hut restaurants offer customers a selection of beer and wine.[75] In China, KFC quickly learned that residents were not interested in coleslaw, so the company dropped the item from its menu and added local delicacies, such as the Dragon Twister (a chicken wrap soaked in a spicy Peking duck sauce), congee (rice porridge), bamboo shoots, and soy milk.[76]

As China's economy continues to grow and its capital markets expand, increasing numbers of franchisors are opening locations there. In China, Subway, known as Sai Bei Wei (which translates as "tastes better than others" in Mandarin), learned the importance of patience in building a franchise presence in challenging international markets. When the company opened its first outlet in China, managers had to print signs explaining how to order a sandwich. Sales of tuna salad were dismal because residents, accustomed to seeing their fish whole, did not believe that the salad was made from fish at all. In addition, because Chinese diners do not like to touch their food, many of them held their sandwiches vertically, peeled the paper wrapper away gradually, and ate the contents as they would eat a banana![77] McDonald's faced similar challenges in India, where customers were puzzled by placing their orders at a counter and had no understanding of the golden arches; the company's signs read "McDonald's Family Restaurant" so that customers would know that it was a restaurant.[78]

Smaller, Nontraditional Locations

As the high cost of building full-scale locations continues to climb, more franchisors are searching out nontraditional locations in which to build smaller, less expensive outlets. Based on the principle of **intercept marketing**, the idea is to put a franchise's products or services directly in the paths of potential customers, wherever that may be. Locations within locations have become popular. Franchises are putting scaled-down outlets on college campuses; in high school cafeterias, sports arenas, churches, hospitals, museums, zoos; and on airline flights. Subway has more than 8,000 franchises in nontraditional locations that range from airports and military bases to college campuses and convenience stores. The company has restaurants located in a Goodwill store in Greenville, South Carolina, and inside the True Bethel Baptist Church in Buffalo, New York. Perhaps Subway's most unusual location was a temporary restaurant that served only

intercept marketing
the principle of putting a franchise's products or services directly in the paths of potential customers, wherever they may be.

Russia: A Rising Star for Franchisors

As franchisors have found wringing impressive growth rates from a franchise-saturated domestic market increasingly difficult, they have begun to export their franchises to international markets, including those with developing economies. Indeed, franchising is ideally suited for developing economies because it allows people with limited business experience and financial resources to become part of an established business. China and India, with combined populations of 2.4 billion people with rising incomes, are drawing franchisors from across the globe. Russia also is becoming the target of many franchises, particularly quick-service restaurant franchises, because of its size, growth potential, and relative scarcity of fast-food outlets. "There's a growing middle class in Russia, strong movement toward American brands, and a relative lack of competition," says Nigel Travis, CEO of Dunkin' Brands, the parent company of Dunkin' Donuts.

Currently, more than 450 franchisors operate 8,500 franchised outlets in Russia. McDonald's was the fast-food pioneer in Russia, opening its first outlet in Moscow's Pushkin Square in 1990. McDonald's executives endured 14 years of negotiations with the Communist Party, which was in control at the time, before opening the outlet. With a seating capacity of 700, it was the largest McDonald's in the world, but hungry Muscovites, who saw the franchise's hamburgers and fries as delicacies, often stood in lines to make their purchases. "It was like going to a major premier," says one Moscow resident who waited for hours in subzero temperatures to buy her first Big Mac the day McDonald's opened. "When guests came to visit, taking them to McDonald's was just as important as showing them around the Kremlin." The appearance of the golden arches in Russia gave people there more than just another dining option. "McDonald's was not so much a fast-food chain but rather a symbol of freedom—a symbol of Western values coming to Russia," says Viktor Loshak, editor of *Ogonyok Magazine*. McDonald's Moscow restaurant is still the busiest in the chain of 33,000 global outlets.

Other quick-service restaurant franchises are flocking to Russia, where 32 percent of all restaurants are part of chains. Burger King, Subway, Wendy's, Carl's Jr., Cinnabon, Dunkin' Donuts, and many others have followed in front-runner McDonald's footsteps. Subway has 240 restaurants in Russia, its second-fastest-growing market, but plans to expand the number to 2,500 by 2020. Like McDonald's, Subway's leading store in sales is an outlet in Russia, one located on the busy Nevsky Prospekt, St. Petersburg's bustling main street, just minutes from the city's famous Winter Palace. Prices at Russian fast-food outlets are higher than in the United States. The average check in Russia is $8.92, compared to $6.50 in the United States.

Franchisors' path to the Russian market has not always been smooth. Subway spent eight years in a legal wrangle over its St. Petersburg outlet, its first in Russia. Subway's partner in the franchise seized the store, and there were allegations of mafia involvement. After the case worked its way through an arbitration tribunal, a St. Petersburg city court, and the Russian Supreme Court, Subway prevailed, and the courts restored ownership of the restaurant to the company. Inadequate protection of intellectual property in Russia also is a problem. Papa John's recently settled out of court with a competing business owner who named his independent restaurant Papa John's. As part of the settlement, the owner changed the name of his restaurant to Papa's Place. In 1999, Dunkin' Donuts

Alexander Nemenov/AFP/Getty Images/Newscom

pulled out of Russia after three years of losses, complicated by a rogue franchisee who was selling unauthorized products, including liquor and meat pies, in addition to the company's coffee and doughnuts. Fighting endemic corruption is a constant battle for Western companies doing business in Russia, and franchises are no exception. American companies must comply with the Foreign Corrupt Practices Act, under which executives can be prosecuted if their companies engage in corruption in foreign countries.

Christopher Wynne left a position in the U.S. National Nuclear Security Administration to become a Papa John's franchisee in Russia. Wynne says that setting up a Papa John's store in Moscow costs about $400,000 and that the stores reach their break-even point very quickly, usually within just three months. "There is so much opportunity here," says Wynne, who owns 25 Papa John's outlets and plans to open many more. Moscow, a city of nearly 13 million people, has only 300 pizza restaurants, compared to Manhattan, which has 4,000 pizza places to serve its 1.6 million residents. For Papa John's, average sales per restaurant are the highest in Russia than in any of the other 34 countries where the company's stores are located. The most popular item on Papa John's menu among its Russian customers is a localized dish: a pizza topped with chicken, blue cheese, celery, and Tabasco sauce. Nigel Travis of Dunkin' Donuts says that the most popular items in its Russian outlets include "scalded cream and a very nice raspberry jam as a pastry filling."

1. What steps should U.S.-based franchisors take when establishing outlets in foreign countries?

2. Describe the opportunities and the challenges franchisors face when entering emerging markets such as Russia.

3. Use the Web as a resource to develop a list of at least five suggestions that will help new franchisors looking to establish outlets in Russia.

Sources: Based on Andrew E. Kramer, "Russia Becomes a Magnet for U.S. Fast Food Chains," *New York Times*, August 3, 2011, http://www.nytimes.com/2011/08/04/business/global/russia-becomes-a-magnet-for-american-fast-food-chains.html?pagewanted=all; Kevin Helliker, "Dunkin' Donuts Returns to Russia," *Wall Street Journal*, April 27, 2010, p. B10; Howard Amos, "Subway Takes Advantage of Franchising to Expand Reach," *Moscow Times*, August 4, 2011, http://www.themoscowtimes.com/mobile/article/441576.html; "Franchising in Russia," *World Franchise Associates*, February 11, 2011, http://www.worldfranchiseassociates.com/franchise-news-article.php?nid=870; and "McDonald's Celebrates 20 Tasty Years in Moscow," *World Focus*, March 4, 2010, http://worldfocus.org/blog/2010/03/04/mcdonalds-celebrates-20-tasty-years-in-moscow/9955.

AP Photo/Mark Lennihan

the construction workers building the skyscraper at 1 World Trade Center in New York City. As work progressed on the 105-story building, a hydraulic lift elevated the restaurant, which was housed inside 36 shipping containers welded together.[79]

Many franchisees have discovered that smaller outlets in nontraditional locations generate nearly the same sales volume as full-size outlets at just a fraction of the cost! Locations that emphasize convenience by being close to their customers will be a key to continued franchise growth in the market. To reach customers online, Dunkin' Donuts recently "opened" virtual locations in the Sims Social Facebook game in an effort "to reach out to young adults who are spending more time in the digital world," says a Dunkin' Donuts spokesperson.[80]

Conversion Franchising

The recent trend toward **conversion franchising**, in which owners of independent businesses become franchisees to gain the advantage of name recognition, will continue. One study reports that 72 percent of franchisors in North America use conversion franchising as a growth strategy.[81] In a franchise conversion, the franchisor gets immediate entry into new markets and experienced operators; franchisees get increased visibility and often a big sales boost. It is not unusual for entrepreneurs who convert their independent stores into franchises to experience an increase of 20 percent or more in sales because of the instant name recognition the franchise offers.

conversion franchising
a franchising trend in which owners of independent businesses become franchisees to gain the advantage of name recognition.

ENTREPRENEURIAL PROFILE: John Andikian: 7-Eleven John Andikian opened a convenience store in Tustin, California, in 2004 and named it Andy's Market in memory of his father. He sold typical convenience store fare, including his own version of the Slurpee, the Andy Freeze. After 18 months in business, Andy's Market still had not reached its break-even point, and Andikian was running out of cash and time. The problem: "Nobody knew what Andy's Market was," he says. To save his business, Andikian decided to convert it into a 7-Eleven franchise, paying a $20,000 franchise fee and $100,000 for inventory and remodeling costs. The transformation required only 48 hours, and Andikian noticed the dramatic difference that adding the franchisor's well-known name made almost immediately. "As soon as they put the 7-Eleven sign outside, my sales doubled," he says. "I was doing about $70,000 a month in sales; now I'm doing about $160,000."[82] ■

Multiple-Unit Franchising

Twenty-five years ago, the typical franchisee operated a single outlet. The current generation of franchisees, however, strives to operate multiple franchise units. According to the International Franchise Association, 19.8 percent of franchisees are multiple-unit owners, a number that is expected to continue to grow over the next several years. Multi-unit franchisees own 52.6 percent of all franchise units.

Jeff Clark

Although the typical multiple-unit franchise owns 4.5 outlets, it is no longer unusual for a single franchisee to own 25, 75, or even 100 units.[83]

ENTREPRENEURIAL PROFILE: Ulysses Bridgeman: Wendy's and Chili's After Ulysses "Junior" Bridgeman retired from a 12-year career with the National Basketball Association's Milwaukee Bucks, he invested in several Wendy's restaurants. Today, Bridgeman is the owner of 161 Wendy's and 121 Chili's restaurants that generate more than $500 million in annual sales.[84] ■

Franchisors are finding that multiple-unit franchising is an efficient way to do business. For a franchisor, the time and cost of managing 10 franchisees each owning 12 outlets are much less than managing 120 franchisees each owning one outlet. A multiple-unit strategy also accelerates a franchise's growth rate. Not only is multiple-unit franchising an efficient way to expand quickly, but it also is effective for franchisors who are targeting foreign markets, where having a local representative who knows the territory is essential.

The popularity of multiple-unit franchising has paralleled the trend toward increasingly experienced, sophisticated franchisees who set high performance goals that a single outlet cannot meet. For franchisees, multiple-unit franchising offers the opportunity for rapid growth without leaving the safety net of the franchise. In addition, franchisees may be able to get fast-growing companies for a bargain when franchisors offer discounts off their standard fees for buyers who purchase multiple units.

Although operating multiple units offers advantages for both franchisors and franchisees, there are dangers. Operating multiple units requires franchisors to focus more carefully on selecting the right franchisees—those who are capable of handling the additional requirements of multiple units. The impact of selecting the wrong franchise owners is magnified when they operate multiple units and can create huge headaches for the entire chain. Franchisees must be aware of the dangers of losing their focus and becoming distracted if they take on too many units. In addition, operating multiple units means more complexity because the number of business problems that franchisees face also is multiplied.

Area Development and Master Franchising

area development
a method of franchising in which a franchisee earns the exclusive right to open multiple units in a specific territory within a specified time.

Driving the trend toward multiple-unit franchising are area development and master franchising. Under an **area development** franchise, a franchisee earns the exclusive right to open multiple outlets in a specific area within a specified time. Launched in 1987 in New York City, Tasti D-Lite, the retail chain of frozen low-calorie desserts, has benefited from celebrity buzz, a loyal customer base, and publicity from television shows such as *30 Rock*, *The Apprentice*, and others. The company did not begin franchising until 2008, and to accelerate its growth, it turned to area development agreements. Jim Amos, Tasti D-Lite's CEO, recently announced area development agreements for 65 new franchise locations in three U.S. markets: Dallas, Texas, Las Vegas, Nevada, and Washington, D.C. In Dallas, area developer Francisco Gomez-Palacio, who emigrated to the United States in 1998 and founded the telephone company Latino Communications, will open at least 25 outlets within 10 years.[85]

master franchise
a method of franchising that gives a franchisee the right to create a semi-independent organization in a particular territory to recruit, sell, and support other franchisees.

A **master franchise** (or subfranchise) gives a franchisee the right to create a semi-independent organization in a particular territory to recruit, develop, and support other franchisees. A master franchisee buys the right to develop subfranchises within a territory or sometimes an entire country, takes over many of the duties and responsibilities of the franchisor, and typically earns a portion of the franchise fees and royalties from its subfranchises. Like multiple-unit franchising, area development and master franchising "turbocharge" a franchisor's growth. Many franchisors use master franchising to open outlets in international markets because the master franchisees understand local laws and the nuances of selling in local markets. Edible Arrangements, a company that sells fresh-fruit "bouquets" that resemble floral arrangements, recently signed master franchise agreements to develop territories in several countries, including China, India, and Italy. In China, the company partnered with brothers Jack Wang and Zhigang Liu, owners of Top Chef, a company that grows and processes cherries for bakeries in China, to supervise the opening of 40 stores within five years. Since founding Edible Arrangements in 1999, Tariq and Kamran Farid's have grown the franchise to nearly 1,100 locations in 13 countries.[86]

Cobranding

Some franchisors also are discovering new ways to reach customers by teaming up with other franchisors selling complementary products or services. A growing number of companies are **cobranding** outlets—combining two or more distinct franchises under one roof. This "buddy-system" approach works best when the two franchise ideas are compatible and appeal to similar customers. For example, Yum! Brands, whose stable of franchises includes Taco Bell, KFC, Pizza Hut, A&W, and Long John Silver, is building hundreds of combination outlets, a concept that has proved to be highly successful. About 15 percent of the company's restaurants involve multibranding, with two or more concepts in the same location. "We find customers prefer a double-branded concept to a single brand six to one," says Yum! Brands CEO David Novak.[87]

Properly planned, cobranded franchises can magnify many times over the sales and profits of individual, self-standing outlets. Many quick-service franchises, such as McDonald's, Taco Bell, Subway, and Quiznos, have added locations inside gasoline stations and convenience stores. Owners of these multibranded franchises usually see sales and profits increase. John Shambo, who replaced the deli inside his Exxon gasoline station and convenience store with a Quiznos sandwich franchise, says that in just one year, food sales quadrupled and overall sales increased by 15 percent. Quiznos officials say that its convenience store locations generate twice the sales per square foot as its stand-alone outlets.[88]

cobranding
a method of franchising in which two or more franchises team up to sell complementary products or services under one roof.

Serving Dual-Career Couples and Aging Baby Boomers

Now that dual-career couples have become the norm, the market for franchises offering convenience and time-saving devices is booming. Customers are willing to pay for products and services that will save them time or trouble, and franchises are ready to provide them. The Maids, a home cleaning company founded by Daniel Bishop in 1979, began franchising in 1981 and now has nearly 1,100 franchisees across the United States. The Maids has become one of the fastest-growing franchises in the country by targeting the nation's 35 million busy dual-career couples whose hectic schedules demand that they hire cleaning services for their homes.[89] Other areas in which franchising is experiencing rapid growth include home delivery of meals, continuing education and training (especially computer and business training), leisure activities (such as hobbies, health spas, and travel-related activities), products and services aimed at home-based businesses, and health care.

A number of franchises are aiming at one of the nation's largest population segments: aging baby boomers. About 40.2 million people, 12.4 percent of the U.S. population, are 65 or older, and by 2030 that number is expected to reach 72 million. A survey by the American Association of Retired Persons shows that 90 percent of senior citizens want to remain in their homes as they age, creating a great business opportunity for franchises such as Comfort Keepers, Home Helpers, Home Watch, and Home Instead, franchises that provide in-home non–health care services to senior citizens.

ENTREPRENEURIAL PROFILE: Lisa and Eric Wiedemann: Home Instead Senior Care Lisa and Eric Wiedemann purchased a Home Instead Senior Care franchise not only because they saw it as an ideal path to owning their own business but also because it was "a labor of love." Lisa, an occupational therapist and long-distance caregiver for her elderly mother, and Eric, a psychologist, enjoy the challenge of coordinating care for their clients, training their 80 employees, and marketing their business with the franchisor's support.[90] ■

Conclusion

Franchising has proved its viability in the U.S. economy and has become a key part of the small business sector because it offers many would-be entrepreneurs the opportunity to own and operate a business with a greater chance for success. Despite its impressive growth rate to date, the franchising industry still has a great deal of room to grow. "Franchising is really small business at its best," says Don DeBolt, president of the International Franchise Association.[91]

Chapter Summary by Learning Objective

1. Describe the three types of franchising: trade name, product distribution, and pure.

- Trade-name franchising involves a franchisee purchasing the right to become affiliated with a franchisor's trade name without distributing its products exclusively.

- Product distribution franchising involves licensing a franchisee to sell products or services under the franchisor's brand name through a selective, limited distribution network.

- Pure franchising involves a selling a franchisee a complete business format.

2. Explain the benefits and the drawbacks of buying a franchise.

- Franchises offer many benefits: management training and support, brand-name appeal, standardized quality of goods and services, national advertising programs, financial assistance, proven products and business formats, centralized buying power, territorial protection, and a greater chance of success.

- Franchising also suffers from certain drawbacks: franchise fees and profit sharing, strict adherence to standardized operations, restrictions on purchasing, limited product lines, unsatisfactory training programs, market saturation, and less freedom.

3. Explain the laws covering franchise purchases.

The FTC requires all franchisors to disclose detailed information on their operations in a UFDD at the first personal meeting or at least 14 days before a franchise contract is signed or before any money is paid. The FTC rule covers *all* franchisors. The UFDD requires franchisors to provide information on 23 topics in their disclosure statements. The UFDD is an extremely helpful tool for prospective franchisees.

4. Discuss the *right* way to buy a franchise.

The following steps will help you make the right franchise choice: evaluate yourself, research your market, consider your franchise options, get a copy of the franchisor's UFOC, talk to existing franchisees, ask the franchisor some tough questions, and make your choice.

5. Outline the major trends shaping franchising.

Key trends shaping franchising today include the changing face of franchisees; international franchise opportunities; smaller, nontraditional locations; conversion franchising; multiple-unit franchising; master franchising; and cobranding (or combination franchising).

Discussion Questions

1. What is franchising?
2. Describe the three types of franchising and give an example of each.
3. Discuss the advantages and the disadvantages of franchising for the franchisee.
4. Why might an independent entrepreneur be dissatisfied with a franchising arrangement?
5. Fran Lubbs, who after a five-year stint left the corporate office of Goddard School, an early education franchise, to become a franchisee, says, "Follow the system. It's one of the reasons you bought the franchise. Don't try to change it, break it, or fix it." Do you agree with her? Explain.
6. What steps should a potential franchisee take before investing in a franchise?
7. Two franchising experts recently debated the issue of whether new college graduates should consider franchising as a pathway to entrepreneurship. Jeff Elgin said that recent college graduates are not ready to be franchise owners. "First, most recent college graduates don't have the financial resources to fund a franchise start-up. Second, many lack the life experience and the motivation to

run a business effectively and stick with it when times get tough. Jennifer Kushell says that franchising is the perfect career choice for many recent college graduates, and she cites several reasons: (1) the support system that franchising provides is ideal for young entrepreneurs, (2) young people have grown up with franchising and understand it well, (3) many college graduates already have launched businesses of their own, and (4) they think big. Which view do you think is correct? Explain.
8. What is the function of the UFDD? Outline the protection the UFDD gives prospective franchisees.
9. Describe the current trends in franchising.
10. One franchisee says, "Franchising is helpful because it gives you somebody [the franchisor] to get you going, nurture you, and shove you along a little. But, the franchisor won't make you successful. That depends on what you bring to the business, how hard you are prepared to work, and how committed you are to finding the right franchise for you." Do you agree? Explain.
11. Robyn Vescovi, a former financial executive who recently became a Tasti D-Lite franchisee,

offers the following advice to first-time franchisees:

Do your homework:

- Research the brand (long- and short-term business model)
- Know the team behind this brand and understand their vision for that product/business. Know them as franchise experts and their proven successes.

- Know yourself and your limits. This will help you determine the right business (i.e., new and innovative franchise or well-established franchise).
- Be involved! Don't expect that things "will just happen." You have your own business, but you are part of something bigger, and it is in your best interest to participate in whatever you can in support of that brand/product. Don't be an "absentee franchisee."

Do you agree? Explain. What other advice can you offer first-time franchisees?

Business Plan Pro™

Most franchises will require you to submit a business plan with the application process. In many cases, the franchisor will specify what the business plan should include and may even require you follow an established business plan outline. If you are planning to purchase a franchise, investigate all of the application requirements.

Business Plan Exercises

Submitting a business plan is often a major milestone in the franchise application process. The business plan is another assessment of your ability to become a successful franchisee.

On the Web

Go to www.pearsonhighered.com/scarborough and click on the Chapter 6 tab. Review the online franchise resources and find the link "The World Franchise Directory." Click on that link and enter the first letter of a familiar franchise, the letter "S," for example. The number of franchise systems that will appear, many of them with an international presence, is staggering. If you plan to purchase a franchise, visit the franchise system's Web site and request information. In most cases, the franchise will expect you to respond to a set of initial questions before you receive detailed franchise information. As you proceed through the process, note the specific questions regarding your sources of capital. Your access to capital will be a major qualification in determining whether you are "franchise worthy" in addition to other criteria.

Sample Plans

Find the Tennis Master Pro Shops, Inc., plan in *Business Plan Pro's*™ sample plan browser. Read the Executive Summary, Objectives, Mission, and Keys to Success and note the information about franchising. Review the sales forecast and note the projected revenue sources.

In the Software

If you plan to own a franchise with specific business plan requirements, modify the outline in *Business Plan Pro*™ to match the franchise's recommendation. To view the outline in the left-hand navigation, click on the Plan Outline icon or go to the "View" menu and click on "Outline." Then right-click on each topic that you need to change, move, or delete to meet the franchise's requirement. You may move topics up or down the outline with the corresponding arrows. To change topics from headings to subheadings, you "demote" the topic. When you "promote" a topic, you move a subheading to the left to a more dominant position.

Building Your Business Plan

Continue building your franchise business plan based on that outline. Determine the expectations regarding the content and structure of the franchise business plan. Inquire whether the franchisor has a recommended outline, an example plan, or an actual business plan from another franchisee that is available for review. Use the information and verbiage that is familiar to the franchise system whenever possible. Your plan may be one of dozens received that week, and you want the plan to demonstrate your knowledge, competence, and credibility. Your franchise business plan can be a sales tool to position you as an informed, attractive, and capable future franchise owner.

Beyond the Classroom . . .

1. Visit a local franchise operation. Is it a trade name, product distribution, or pure franchise? To what extent did the franchisee investigate before investing? What assistance does the franchisor provide? How does the franchisee feel about the franchise contract he or she signed? What would he or she do differently now?

2. Use the Internet to locate several franchises that interest you. Contact the franchisors and ask for their franchise packages. Write a report comparing their treatment of the topics covered by the Trade Regulation Rule. Analyze the terms of their franchise contracts. What are the major differences? Are some terms more favorable than others? If you were about to invest in this franchise, which terms would you want to change?

3. Ask a local franchisee to approach his or her regional franchise representative about leading a class discussion on franchising.

Endnotes

1. Kevin O'Brien, "24-Year-Old Manager Began as a Hostess and Credits an Emphasis on Service for First-Year Success," *Western Investor*, April 2011, http://westerninvestor.com/index.php/news/55-features/373-youngest-franchisee-sets-sales-pace-.

2. Laura Fenwick, "Franchises Aren't Running on Empty," *Franchising World*, July 2011, pp. 68–70; Julie Bennett, "By the Numbers," *Entrepreneur*, January 2011, p. 114; Joseph Picard, "Census Offers Franchise Data," September 14, 2010, *International Business Times*, September 14, 2010, http://www.ibtimes.com/articles/62257/20100914/census-franchise-business.htm; *Franchise Business Economic Outlook: 2011*, International Franchise Association and PriceWaterhouseCoopers, January 3, 2011, p. 3.

3. Jason Daley, "The Unlikeliest Franchisee," *Entrepreneur*, October 2010, p. 160.

4. Alex Robinson, "Lenders Hesitating to Back New Franchises," *Star Tribune*, August 26, 2009, http://www.startribune.com/business/53990777.html.

5. Megan Barnett, "Size Up a Ready-Made Business," *U.S. News & World Report*, August 2, 2004, p. 70.

6. Chieh Chieng, "Do You Want to Know a Secret?," *Entrepreneur*, January 1999, p. 174–178.

7. *Economic Impact of Franchised Businesses, Volume 2: Executive Summary and Highlights* (Washington, DC: International Franchise Association and PriceWaterhouseCoopers, 2007), pp. 10, 15.

8. Melana Yanos, "Franchise Opportunities for Young People," *NuWire Investor*, May 13, 2008, http://www.nuwireinvestor.com/articles/franchise-opportunities-for-young-people-51561.aspx.

9. Jason Daley, "The Cross Over," *Entrepreneur*, March 2011, pp.101–105.

10. Mark Henricks, "Finding the Perfect Fit: How Franchisers Select Franchisees," Advertising Insert, *Inc.*, February 2011, p. 113.

11. Jason Daley, "The Cross Over," *Entrepreneur*, March 2011, pp. 101–105.

12. Sara Wilson, "Early to Rise," *Entrepreneur*, August 2008, pp. 90–94.

13. "FAQ," Ben & Jerry's Homemade, Inc., http://www.benjerry.com/scoop_shops/franchise_info/faqs.cfm.

14. Michele Deluca, "Franchise Owners Pay Price for Success," *Tonawanda News*, April 28, 2008, http://www.tonawanda-news.com/business/gnnbusiness_story_119141835.html.

15. "Papa John's Receives Highest Customer Satisfaction Rating for Ninth Consecutive Year," *Reuters*, May 20, 2008, http://www.reuters.com/article/pressRelease/idUS139161+20-May-2008+BW20080520; Anne Field, "Piping Hot Performance," *Success*, March 1999, pp. 76–80.

16. *The Profile of Franchising 2006* (Washington, DC: International Franchise Association, 2007), p. 67.

17. *The Profile of Franchising 2006* (Washington, DC: International Franchise Association, 2007), p. 67.

18. Alisa Harrison and Matthew Haller, "Franchise Businesses Poised for Stronger Growth in 2011," International Franchise Association, January 12, 2011, http://www.franchise.org/Franchise-Industry-News-Detail.aspx?id=53160.

19. *Small Business Lending Matrix and Analysis: The Impact of the Credit Crisis on the Franchise Sector*, International Franchise Association Educational Foundation and FRANdata, March 2011, p. 5.

20. Alex Robinson, "Lenders Hesitating to Back New Franchises," *Star Tribune*, August 26, 2009, http://www.startribune.com/business/53990777.html.

21. *The Profile of Franchising 2006* (Washington, DC: International Franchise Association, 2007), p. 70.

22. Sarah E. Needleman, "Franchisers Focus on Loans," *Wall Street Journal*, August 4, 2011, p. B13.

23. Sarah E. Needleman, "Franchisers Focus on Loans," *Wall Street Journal*, August 4, 2011, p. B13.

24. Darrell Johnson and John Reynolds, "A Study of Franchise Loan Performance in the SBA Guaranty Programs," *Franchising World*, September 2007, pp. 53–56; Richard Gibson, "How to Finance a Franchise," *Wall Street Journal*, March 17, 2008, p. R8.

25. Brenna Fisher, "Corner Office: Papa John's John Schnatter Is Building a Better Pizza Empire," *Success*, 2011, http://www.successmagazine.com/papa-johns-john-schnatter/PARAMS/article/947.

26. Sara Wilson, "Early to Rise," *Entrepreneur*, August 2008, pp. 90–94.

27. Sheena Harrison, "Franchises Get Head Start on Starting Businesses," *Toledo Blade*, September 23, 2010, http://www.toledoblade.com/local/2010/09/23/Franchises-get-head-start-on-starting-businesses.html.

28. Tara Siegel Bernard, "The More the Merrier," *Wall Street Journal*, December 15, 2004, p. R6.

29. Michele Deluca, "Franchise Owners Pay Price for Success," *Tonawanda News*, April 28, 2008, http://www.tonawanda-news.com/business/gnnbusiness_story_119141835.html.

30. Steven C. Michael and James G. Combs, "Entrepreneurial Failure: The Case of Franchisees," *Journal of Small Business Management* 46, no. 1 (January 2008): 75–90.

31. "Clark Howard: How to Pick a Winning Franchise," WSBTV, June 14, 2010, http://www.wsbtv.com/money/23894120/detail.html.

32. Steven C. Michael and James G. Combs, "Entrepreneurial Failure: The Case of Franchisees," *Journal of Small Business Management* 46, no. 1 (January 2008): 75–90.

33. Iris Taylor, "Franchises Can Be Freedom from Corporate America," *WSLS*, July 9, 2008, http://www.wsls.com/sls/business/consumer/article/franchises_can_be_freedom_from_corporate_america/13747.

34. *The Profile of Franchising 2006* (Washington, DC: International Franchise Association, 2007), p. 62.

35. *The Profile of Franchising* (Washington, DC: FRANdata and the IFA Educational Foundation, 2000), p. 123.

36. *The Profile of Franchising 2006* (Washington, DC: International Franchise Association, 2007), p. 66.

37. *The Profile of Franchising 2006* (Washington, DC: International Franchise Association, 2007), p. 68.

38. Jerry Murrell and Liz Welch, "How I Did It: Five Guys Burgers and Fries," *Inc.*, April 2010, p. 80.

39. Wendy Bounds, "Cold Stone Case Study: Three Warnings for Franchise Buyers," *Wall Street Journal*, June 16, 2008, http://blogs.wsj.com/independentstreet/2008/06/16/cold-stone-case-study-three-warnings-for-franchise-buyers.

40. Richard Gibson, "Burger King Franchisees Can't Have It Their Way," *Wall Street Journal*, January 21, 2010, http://online.wsj.com/article/SB10001424052748704320104575014941842011972.html; Elaine Walker, "BK Franchisees Lose Pricing War," *Miami Herald*, November 23, 2010, http://www.miamiherald.com/2010/11/23/1939144/bk-franchisees-lose-pricing-war.html; Elaine Walker, "Burger King, Franchisees Clash over $1 Burger Deal," *Miami Herald*, February 3, 2010, http://www.miamiherald.com/2010/02/03/1459724/burger-king-franchisees-clash.html; Elaine Walker, "BK to Switch Out $1 Double Cheeseburger," *Nation's Restaurant*

News, February 17, 2010, http://www.nrn.com/article/bk-switch-out-1-double-cheeseburger.

41. "Super-Size What? The Big Mac Turns 40," *USA Today*, August 24, 2007, http://www.usatoday.com/news/nation/2007-08-24-big-mac-at-40_N.htm.

42. Matthew Boyle, "The Accidental Hero," *Bloomberg Business Week*, November 5, 2009, http://www.businessweek.com/magazine/content/09_46/b4155058815908.htm.

43. Richard Gibson, "In Search of More Muscle," *Wall Street Journal*, August 22, 2011, http://online.wsj.com/article/SB10001424052702303365804576432062058517684.html; Richard Gibson, "Curves Closes Clubs as Stamina Runs Out," *Wall Street Journal*, July 7, 2010, p. B1.

44. *The Profile of Franchising* (Washington, DC: FRANdata and the IFA Educational Foundation, 2000), p. 116.

45. Jeannie Ralston, "Before You Bet Your Buns," *Venture*, March 1988, p. 57.

46. *The Profile of Franchising 2006* (Washington, DC: International Franchise Association, 2007), p. 73.

47. Richard Gibson, "Franchise Fever," *Wall Street Journal*, December 15, 2003, p. R1.

48. Kelly K. Spors, "Not So Fast," *Wall Street Journal*, September 19, 2005, p. R11; Joshua Kurlantzick, "Serving Up Success," *Entrepreneur*, November 2003, http://www.entrepreneur.com/article/print/0,2361,311429,00.html; "Subway Restaurant News," Subway, http://www.subway.com/subwayroot/index.aspx.

49. Anne Fisher, "Risk Reward," *FSB*, December 2005/January 2006, p. 58.

50. "Burger King Late-Night Hours Suit Dismissed," *QSR Online*, November 11, 2008, http://www.qsrweb.com/article/101069/Burger-King-franchisees-late-night-hours-suit-dismissed.

51. Gregory Matusky, "What Every Business Can Learn from Franchising," *Inc.*, January 1994, p. 90.

52. David J. Kaufman, "What a Ride!," *Entrepreneur*, May 2007, p. 111.

53. Elaine Pofeldt, "Success Franchisee Satisfaction Survey," *Success*, April 1999, p. 59.

54. Laurie Kulikowski, "How to Spot a Hot Franchise," *The Street*, June 7, 2011, http://www.thestreet.com/story/11144060/1/how-to-spot-a-hot-franchise.html.

55. *The Profile of Franchising 2006* (Washington, DC: International Franchise Association, 2007), p. 77.

56. Douglas MacMillan, "Finding the Perfect Franchise Fit," *Business Week*, July 31, 2006, http://www.businessweek.com/smallbiz/content/jul2006/sb20060728_328561.htm?chan=top+news_top+news.

57. Hilary Maynard, "Sign of the Times," *Business Examiner*, March 17, 2008, http://exchange.franchoice.com/Documents/News/Business%20Examiner%203.17.2008.pdf.

58. Anne Field, "Piping Hot Performance," *Success*, March 1999, pp. 76–80.

59. Julie Bennett, "The Road to Discovery," *Entrepreneur*, February 2011, pp. 83–87.

60. Alan J. Liddle, "Judge Upholds Settlement in Quiznos Class Action," *Nation's Restaurant News*, August 16, 2010, http://www.nrn.com/article/judge-upholds-settlement-quiznos-class-action.

61. April Y. Pennington, "Would You Like a Franchise with That?," *Entrepreneur*, January 2005, pp. 120–127.

62. Paula Schleis, "Franchise Freedom," *Ohio.com*, December 17, 2007, http://www.ohio.com/business/12555331.html?page=all&c=y.

63. Angus Loten, "Finding the Right Franchise," *Smart Money*, June 2, 2011, http://www.smartmoney.com/small-business/small-business/finding-the-right-franchise-1306952100853.

64. Jason Daley, "Exile from Wall Street," *Entrepreneur*, November 2010, pp. 112–119.

65. "Businesses Recruit Minority Franchisees to Improve Innovation," Einbinder and Dunn, LLP, July 25, 2011, http://www.franchiselawyerblog.com/blog/2011/07/businesses-recruit-minority-franchisees-to-improve-innovation.shtml.

66. Sara Wilson, "Running Start," *Entrepreneur*, January 2008, pp. 144–150.

67. Lindsey Robbins, "Franchise Owner Green Works Way Up to Become Fast-Food Magnate," *The Gazette*, May 27, 2011, http://ww2.gazette.net/stories/05272011/businew193722_32533.php.

68. Jacy Cochran, "Generation Y: Make Way for the Fresh Faces of Franchising," *AllBusiness*, January 1, 2007, http://www.allbusiness.com/retail-trade/3969190-1.html.

69. Julie Bennett, "Corporate Experience Can Boost the Bottom Line," *Wall Street Journal*, October 7, 2010, p. D4.

70. David J. Kaufman, "What a Ride!," *Entrepreneur*, May 2007, pp. 108–113.

71. Jason Daley, "No Boundaries," *Entrepreneur*, May 2011, pp. 99–103; *McDonald's Corporation 2010 Annual Report*, p. 14.

72. Jack Perkowski, "Pizza Anyone?" *Forbes*, November 29, 2010, http://www.forbes.com/sites/jack-perkowski/2010/11/29/pizza-anyone; William Mellor, "Local Menu, Managers Are KFC's Secret in China," *Washington Post*, February 12, 2011, http://www.washingtonpost.com/wp-dyn/content/article/2011/02/12/AR2011021202412.html.

73. Esther Fung, "McDonald's Sets Plans for China," *Wall Street Journal*, March 31, 2010, p. B12.

74. Kushan Mitra, "Paneer Burger for the Indian Palate," *Business Today*, June 4, 2011, http://businesstoday.intoday.in/story/-paneer-burger-mcspicy-paneer-mccurry-pan/1/15778.html; Dhawal Shah, "India: A Market for the Masses," *Franchising World*, June 2008, http://www.franchise.org/Franchise-News-Detail.aspx?id=40638.

75. "Beer and Pizza Together Again," *Pizza Marketplace*, August 22, 2011, http://www.pizzamarketplace.com/article/183577/Beer-and-pizza-together-again.

76. William Mellor, "Local Menu, Managers Are KFC's Secret in China," *Washington Post*, February 12, 2011, http://www.washingtonpost.com/wp-dyn/content/article/2011/02/12/AR2011021202412.html; Carlyle Adler, "How China Eats a Sandwich," *Fortune*, March 21, 2005, pp. 210[B]–210[D].

77. *Franchising Industry in China* (Washington, DC: Stat-USA, U.S. Foreign Commercial Service, 2004), http://www.buyusainfo.net/docs/x_5566195.pdf.

78. Bret Thorn, "McDonald's: Lessons Learned from India," *Nation's Restaurant News*, April 11, 2011, http://www.nrn.com/article/mcdonald%E2%80%99s-lessons-learned-india.

79. Alan J. Liddle, "10 Non-Traditional Subway Restaurants," *Nation's Restaurant News*, July 26, 2011, http://www.nrn.com/article/10-non-traditional-subway-restaurants; Geoff Williams, "Subway Opens First Gravity-Defying Restaurant at the Freedom Tower," Daily Finance, January 4, 2010, http://www.dailyfinance.com/2010/01/04/subway-opens-first-restaurant-at-the-freedom-tower-restaurant.

80. Stuart Elliott, "Dunkin Donuts Opens Shop in Sims' Universe," *New York Times*, August 18, 2011, http://mediadecoder.blogs.nytimes.com/2011/08/18/dunkin-donuts-opens-shop-in-sims-universe.

81. Richard C. Hoffman and John F. Preble, "Convert to Compete: Competitive Advantage through Conversion Financing," *Journal of Small Business Management* 41, no. 2 (April 2003): 127–140.

82. Tracy Stapp, "Losing the Dream But Saving the Store," *Entrepreneur*, August 2010, pp. 91–96.

83. Carol Tice, "Running the Numbers," *Entrepreneur*, July 2009, pp. 87–95.

84. Ellen Florian, "Where Are They Now?," *Fortune*, November 15, 2010, p. 153.

85. "Tasti D-Lite Franchise Inks Three Area Development Agreements for More Than 60 Locations across the Country," *Franchising.com*, August 17, 2010, http://www.franchising .com/news/20100817_tasti_dlite_franchise_inks_three_area_ development_.html.

86. "Edible Arrangements Signs Master Franchise Agreement in China," *PR Newswire*, August 2, 2011, http://www.prnewswire .com/news-releases/edible-arrangements-signs-master- franchisee-agreement-in-china-126575783.html.

87. Julia Boorstin, "Yum Isn't Chicken of China—or Atkins," *Fortune*, March 8, 2004, p. 50.

88. Julie Jargon, "Quiznos Carves Out a Broader Niche," *Wall Street Journal*, March 1, 2010, p. B5.

89. "Why The Maids," The Maids, http://www.themaidsfranchise .com/why-maids.php.

90. Samantha Maziarz Christmann, "Franchising Widens Appeal," *Buffalo News*, May 31, 2010, http://www.buffalonews.com/ incoming/article51321.ece; Raymund Flandez, "A Look at High-Performing Franchises," *Wall Street Journal*, February 12, 2008, p. B5; Lindsay Holloway, James Park, Nichole L. Torres, and Sara Wilson, "This Just In . . ." *Entrepreneur*, January 2008, pp. 100–110.

91. April Y. Pennington, "An American Icon," *Entrepreneur*, January 2005, http://www.entrepreneur.com/magazine/ entrepreneur/2005/january/74992.html.

Appendix A. A Franchise Evaluation Checklist

Yourself

1. Are you qualified to operate a franchise successfully? Do you have adequate drive, skills, experience, education, patience, and financial capacity? Are you prepared to work hard?

2. Are you willing to sacrifice some autonomy in operating a business to own a franchise?

3. Can you tolerate the financial risk? Would business failure wipe you out financially?

4. Can you juggle multiple tasks simultaneously and prioritize various projects so that you can accomplish those that are most important?

5. Are you genuinely interested in the product or service you will be selling? Do you enjoy this kind of business? Do you like to sell?

6. Do you enjoy working with and managing people? Are you a "team player"?

7. Will the business generate enough profit to suit you?

8. Has the franchisor investigated your background thoroughly enough to decide whether you are qualified to operate the franchise?

9. What can this franchisor do for you that you cannot do for yourself?

The Franchisor and the Franchise

1. Is the potential market for the product or service adequate to support your franchise? Will the prices you charge be in line with the market?

2. Is the market's population growing, remaining static, or shrinking? Is the demand for your product or service growing, remaining static, or shrinking?

3. Is the product or service safe and reputable?

4. Is the product or service a passing "fad," or is it a durable business idea?

5. What will the competition, direct or indirect, be in your sales territory? Do any other franchisees operate in this general area?

6. Is the franchise international, national, regional, or local in scope? Does it involve full- or part-time involvement?

7. How many years has the franchisor been in operation? Does it have a sound reputation for honest dealings with franchisees?

8. How many franchise outlets now exist? How many will there be a year from now? How many outlets are company owned?

9. How many franchises have failed? Why?

10. How many franchisees have left the system within the past year? What were their reasons for leaving?

11. What service and assistance will the franchisor provide? What kind of training program does the franchisor offer? How long does it last? What topics does it cover? Does the franchisor offer ongoing assistance and training?

12. Will the franchise perform a location analysis to help you find a suitable site? If so, is there an extra charge for doing so?

13. Will the franchisor offer you exclusive distribution rights for the length of the agreement, or may it sell to other franchises in this area?

14. What facilities and equipment are required for the franchise? Who pays for construction? Is there a lease agreement?

15. What is the total cost of the franchise? What are the initial capital requirements? Will the franchisor provide financial assistance? Of what nature? What is the interest rate? Is the franchisor financially sound enough to fulfill all its promises?

16. How much is the franchise fee? Exactly what does it cover? Are there any ongoing royalties? What additional fees are there?

17. Does the franchisor provide an estimate of expenses and income? Are they reasonable for your particular area? Are they sufficiently documented?

18. How risky is the franchise opportunity? Is the return on the investment consistent with the risks?

19. Does the franchisor offer a written contract that covers all the details of the agreement? Have your attorney and your accountant studied its terms and approved it? Do you understand the implications of the contract?

20. What is the length of the franchise agreement? Under what circumstances can it be terminated? If you terminate the contract, what are the costs to you? What are the terms and costs of renewal?

21. Are you allowed to sell your franchise to a third party? Does the franchisor reserve the right to approve the buyer?

22. Is there a national advertising program? How is it financed? What media are used? What help is provided for local advertising?

23. Once you open for business, *exactly* what support will the franchisor offer you?

24. How does the franchise handle complaints from and disputes with franchisees? How well has the system worked?

The Franchisees

1. Are you pleased with your investment in this franchise?

2. Has the franchisor lived up to its promises?

3. What was your greatest disappointment after getting into this business?

4. How effective was the training you received in helping you run the franchise?

5. What are your biggest challenges and problems?

6. What is your franchise's cash flow like?

7. How much money are you making on your investment?

8. What do you like most about being a franchisee? Least?

9. Is there a franchisee advisory council that represents franchisees?

10. Knowing what you know now, would you buy this franchise again?

7

Buying an Existing Business

Learning Objectives

On completion of this chapter, you will be able to:

1. Understand the advantages and disadvantages of buying an existing business.

2. Define the steps involved in the *right* way to buy a business.

3. Explain the process of evaluating an existing business.

4. Describe the various techniques for determining the value of a business.

5. Understand the seller's side of the buyout decision and how to structure the deal.

6. Understand how the negotiation process works and identify the factors that affect it.

It is far better to buy a wonderful company at a fair price than a fair company at a wonderful price.

—**Warren Buffett**

In business, you don't get what you deserve; you get what you negotiate.

—**Chester L. Karrass**

Mark Shelstad, a portfolio manager in Chicago, was concerned about the impact of the financial crisis on the long-term prospects of his career and decided to become his own boss. Rather than start a company, however, Shelstad decided to purchase an existing business. "I wanted to get up and running quickly due to my age," says Shelstad, who is in his mid-50s. "I didn't have a creative idea worthy of starting a business from scratch." Shelstad researched potential companies for months and worked with a business broker before he purchased a 23-year-old lending-fraud investigation company that he renamed Armitage Investigative Services. He used his savings and a five-year loan from the seller to buy the company, which sold for more than $1 million.[1]

Rather than launch their own businesses or purchase a franchise, some entrepreneurs opt for a more direct route to business ownership: they buy an existing business. In fact, in a typical year, between 500,000 and 1 million small businesses are bought and sold. Over the next 10 years, a wave of retiring entrepreneurial baby boomers whose family members are not interested in running a business means that as many as 70 percent of small companies in the United States will hang "for sale" signs in their windows.[2] Some of those companies represent a terrific opportunity to young entrepreneurs who would rather buy an ongoing business than start one from scratch. Because of the lingering effects of a severe recession and a crisis in the financial markets, prices for existing businesses have been suppressed. At BizBuySell, an online marketplace for small companies that are for sale, the median asking price is $175,000, but the median actual closing price of a sale is $155,000.[3]

Each circumstance is unique, but the process of evaluating a potential business acquisition is not. The due diligence process that involves analyzing and evaluating an existing business for possible purchase is no less time consuming than developing a comprehensive business plan for a start-up. Done correctly, this due diligence process reveals both the negative and the positive aspects of an existing business. Glossing over or skipping altogether the due diligence process is a mistake because a business that looks good on the surface may have serious flaws hidden at its core. Investigating a business to discover its real condition and value requires time, dedication, and, as the name implies, diligence, but the process is worthwhile because it can prevent an entrepreneur from purchasing a business destined for failure.

When considering purchasing a business, the first rule is, "Do not rush into a deal." Taking shortcuts when investigating a potential business acquisition almost always leads to nasty—and expensive—surprises. Prospective buyers must be sure that they discover the answers to the following fundamental questions:

- Is the right type of business for sale in a market in which you want to operate?

- What experience do you have in this particular business and the industry in which it operates? How critical to your ultimate success is experience in the business?

- What is the company's potential for success?

- What changes will you have to make—and how extensive will they be—to realize the business's full potential?

- What price and payment method are reasonable for you and acceptable to the seller?

- Is the seller willing to finance part of the purchase price?

- Will the company generate sufficient cash to pay for itself and leave you with a suitable rate of return on your investment?

- Should you be starting a business and building it from the ground up rather than buying an existing one?

Figure 7.1 shows a profile of the four major categories of buyers and their characteristics that business brokers have identified.

Buying an Existing Business

The Advantages of Buying an Existing Business

Over the next decade, entrepreneurs looking to buy existing businesses will have ample opportunities to consider. Those who purchase an existing business may reap the benefits discussed in the following sections.

LO1A

Understand the advantages of buying an existing business.

FIGURE 7.1

Types of Business Buyers

Source: From "Meet the Buyers" by Darren Dahl, from INC. MAGAZINE, April 1, 2008, pp. 98–99. Copyright © 2008 by Inc. Magazine. Reprinted with permission.

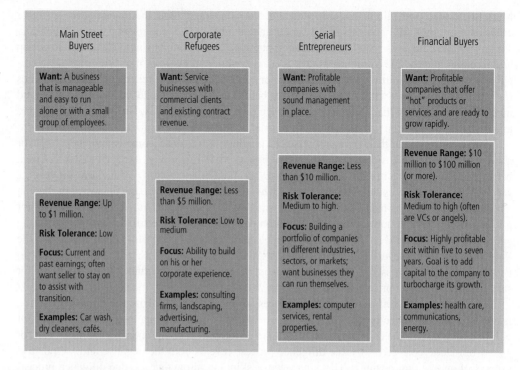

Main Street Buyers	Corporate Refugees	Serial Entrepreneurs	Financial Buyers
Want: A business that is manageable and easy to run alone or with a small group of employees.	**Want:** Service businesses with commercial clients and existing contract revenue.	**Want:** Profitable companies with sound management in place.	**Want:** Profitable companies that offer "hot" products or services and are ready to grow rapidly.
Revenue Range: Up to $1 million.	**Revenue Range:** Less than $5 million.	**Revenue Range:** Less than $10 million.	**Revenue Range:** $10 million to $100 million (or more).
Risk Tolerance: Low	**Risk Tolerance:** Low to medium	**Risk Tolerance:** Medium to high.	**Risk Tolerance:** Medium to high (often are VCs or angels).
Focus: Current and past earnings; often want seller to stay on to assist with transition.	**Focus:** Ability to build on his or her corporate experience.	**Focus:** Building a portfolio of companies in different industries, sectors, or markets; want businesses they can run themselves.	**Focus:** Highly profitable exit within five to seven years. Goal is to add capital to the company to turbocharge its growth.
Examples: Car wash, dry cleaners, cafés.	**Examples:** consulting firms, landscaping, advertising, manufacturing.	**Examples:** computer services, rental properties.	**Examples:** health care, communications, energy.

SUCCESSFUL EXISTING BUSINESSES OFTEN CONTINUE TO BE SUCCESSFUL Purchasing a thriving business at a reasonable price increases the likelihood of success. Although buying an existing business brings with it certain risks, it tends to be less risky than starting a company from scratch. The previous management team already has established a customer base, built supplier relationships, and set up a business system. The customer base inherited in a business purchase can carry an entrepreneur while he or she learns how to build on the company's success. The new owner's objective is to make modifications that attract new customers without alienating the company's existing customers. "You're not just buying a company," says the owner of a business brokerage firm. "You're buying a history of relationships."[4]

SUPERIOR LOCATION When the location of the business is critical to its success (as is often the case in retailing), purchasing a business that is already in the right place may be the best choice. Opening in a second-choice location and hoping to draw customers usually proves fruitless.

EMPLOYEES AND SUPPLIERS ARE IN PLACE An existing business already has experienced employees who can help the new owner through the transition phase. Experienced employees enable a company to continue to earn money while a new owner learns the business. Many new owners find soliciting ideas from employees about methods for increasing sales or reducing costs to be valuable. In many cases, the previous owner may not have involved employees in this fashion and never gained the advantages found in their wisdom and experience. Few people know a job better than the people who perform it every day.

In addition, an existing business has an established set of suppliers with a history of business dealings. Those vendors can continue to supply the business while the new owner investigates the products and services of other suppliers.

INSTALLED EQUIPMENT WITH KNOWN PRODUCTION CAPACITY Acquiring and installing new equipment exerts a tremendous strain on a fledgling company's financial resources. A buyer of an existing business can determine the condition of the plant and equipment and its capacity before making the purchase. In many cases, entrepreneurs can purchase physical facilities and equipment at prices significantly below their replacement costs.

INVENTORY IN PLACE The proper amount of inventory is essential to both controlling costs and generating adequate sales volume. Carrying too little inventory means that a business will not have the quantity and variety of products to satisfy customer demand, and holding too much inventory ties up excessive capital unnecessarily, thereby increasing costs, reducing profitability, and putting a strain on cash flow. Owners of successful established businesses have learned the proper balance between these extremes.

TRADE CREDIT IS ESTABLISHED Previous owners have established trade credit relationships with vendors that can benefit the new owner. The business's proven track record gives the new owner leverage in negotiating favorable trade credit terms.

THE TURNKEY BUSINESS Starting a company can be a daunting, time-consuming task, and buying an existing business is one of the fastest pathways to entrepreneurship. When things go well, purchasing an existing business saves the time and energy required to plan and launch a new business. The buyer gets a business that is already generating cash and perhaps profits as well. The day the entrepreneur takes over the ongoing business is the day revenues begin.

THE NEW OWNER CAN USE THE EXPERIENCE OF THE PREVIOUS OWNER In many business sales, the agreement calls for the seller to spend time with a new owner during the transition period, giving the new manager the time to become acclimated to the business and to learn about the keys to success. Previous owners also can be extremely helpful in unmasking the unwritten rules of business in the area, critically important intangibles such as how to keep customers happy and whom one can trust. Hiring the previous owner as a consultant for at least several months can be a valuable investment and increase the probability that the business will continue to be successful.

EASIER ACCESS TO FINANCING Attracting financing to purchase an existing business often is easier than finding the money to launch a company from scratch. Many existing businesses already have established relationships with lenders, which may open the door to financing through traditional sources such as banks. As we will see later in this chapter, many business buyers also have access to another important source of financing: the seller.

HIGH VALUE Some existing businesses are real bargains. If the current owner must sell quickly, he or she may have set a bargain price for the company that is below its actual worth. Special skills or training that are required to operate the business limits the number of potential buyers; therefore, the more specialized the business is, the greater the likelihood is that a buyer will find a bargain. If the owner wants a substantial down payment or the entire selling price in cash, there may be few qualified buyers, but those who do qualify may be able to negotiate a good deal.

Disadvantages of Buying an Existing Business

CASH REQUIREMENTS One of the most significant challenges to buying a business is acquiring the necessary funds for the initial purchase price. "[Because] the business concept, customer base, brands, and other fundamental work have already been done, the financial costs of acquiring an existing business is usually greater then starting one from nothing," observes the Small Business Administration.[5]

LO1B

Understand the disadvantages of buying an existing business.

THE BUSINESS IS LOSING MONEY A business may be for sale because it is struggling and the owner wants out. In these situations, a prospective buyer must be wary. Business owners sometimes attempt to disguise the facts and employ creative accounting techniques to make the company's financial picture appear much brighter than it really is. Few business sellers honestly state "It's losing money" as the reason for putting their companies up for sale. If there is one area of business where the maxim "let the buyer beware" still prevails, it is in the purchase of an existing business. Any buyer unprepared to do a thorough analysis of a business may be stuck with a real money loser. One expert says that entrepreneurs who purchase troubled companies in hopes of turning them around face an 85 percent failure rate.[6]

Although buying a money-losing business is risky, it is not necessarily taboo. If a company is poorly managed or suffering from neglect, a new owner may be able to turn it around. However, a prospective buyer who does not have well-defined plan for improving a struggling business should *not* consider buying it!

ENTREPRENEURIAL PROFILE: Chuck and Alan Bush: Fuzzy's Taco Shop Former restaurateur Chuck Bush was enjoying a meal at Fuzzy's Taco Shop in Fort Worth, Texas, and observing the restaurant's operating system in action. He saw the potential of the restaurant

Jake Dean/Dallas Business Journal

but realized that it suffered from a sloppy operating system. "There was no control," he says. "I asked, 'How many shrimp in that dish?' and one guy said, "'Six.' Another said, 'This many' and grabbed a big handful." Chuck and his father, Alan, an accountant, put together a group of investors to buy the money-losing restaurant for $80,000. They also assumed $10,000 in liabilities and invested another $15,000 for working capital. Chuck became the on-site manager, and his first step was to close the restaurant for four days, power wash every surface, repaint and redecorate the interior, and retrain the staff. He transcribed all of the recipes, which existed only in one cook's head, and assembled them into a notebook to ensure consistency and cost control. "The food was simple and good, and the price was right," says Chuck, describing why Fuzzy's attracted his attention in the first place. "It just needed some fine-tuning, and the store needed to be cleaned up." The changes the Bushes made were successful. "We made money the first year," says Chuck. They soon opened a second location in Forth Worth and began fielding inquiries about franchises. Today, 75 Fuzzy's operate across Texas and in 10 other states.[7] ■

Like Fuzzy's, unprofitable businesses often result from at least one of the following problems:

- High inventory levels
- Excessively high wage and salary expenses due to excess pay or inefficient use of personnel
- Excessively high compensation for the owner
- Inadequate accounts-receivable collection efforts
- Excessively high rental or lease rates
- High-priced maintenance costs or service contracts
- Poor location or too many locations for the business to support
- Inefficient equipment
- Intense competition from rivals
- Prices that are too low
- Low profit margins
- Losses due to employee theft, shoplifting, and fraud

Like Chuck Bush, a potential buyer usually can trace the causes of a company's lack of profitability by analyzing a company and its financial statements. The question is, Can the new owner take steps to resolve the problems and return the company to profitability?

PAYING FOR ILL WILL Just as sound business dealings can create goodwill, improper business behavior or unethical practices can create ill will. A business may look great on the surface, but customers, suppliers, creditors, or employees may have negative feelings about their dealings with it. Too many business buyers discover—after the sale—that they have inherited undisclosed credit problems, poor supplier relationships, soon-to-expire leases, lawsuits, mismanaged customer relationships, building code violations, and other problems created by the previous owner. Vital business relationships may have begun to deteriorate, but their long-term effects may not yet be reflected in the company's financial statements. Ill will can permeate a business for years. The only way to avoid these problems is to investigate a prospective purchase target thoroughly *before* moving forward in the negotiation process.

EMPLOYEES INHERITED WITH THE BUSINESS MAY NOT BE SUITABLE Previous managers may have kept marginal employees because they were close friends or because they started with the company. A new owner, therefore, may have to make some very unpopular termination decisions. For this reason, employees often do not welcome a new owner because they feel threatened by change. Some employees may not be able to adapt to the new owner's management style, and a culture clash may result. If the due diligence efforts reveal that existing employees are a significant cause of the problems a business faces, the new owner will have no choice but to terminate them and hire new ones.

UNSATISFACTORY LOCATION What was once an ideal location may have become obsolete as market and demographic trends change. Large shopping malls, new competitors, or highway reroutings can spell disaster for small retail shops. Prospective buyers should always evaluate the existing market in the area surrounding an existing business as well as its potential for expansion. Buyers must remember that they are buying the future of a business, not its past. If business success is closely linked to a good location, acquiring a business in a declining area or where demographic trends are moving downward is not a good idea. The value of the business can erode faster than the neighborhood surrounding it.

OBSOLETE OR INEFFICIENT EQUIPMENT AND FACILITIES Potential buyers sometimes neglect to have an expert evaluate a company's facilities and equipment before they purchase it. Only later do they discover that the equipment is obsolete and inefficient and that the business is suffering losses from excessively high operating costs. Modernizing equipment and facilities is seldom inexpensive.

THE CHALLENGE OF IMPLEMENTING CHANGE It is easier to plan for change than it is to implement it. Methods, policies, and procedures the previous owner used in a business may have established precedents that a new owner finds difficult to modify. Employees and customers may resist changes to established procedures.

OBSOLETE INVENTORY Inventory is valuable only if it is salable. Smart buyers know better than to trust the inventory valuation on a firm's balance sheet. Some of it may actually appreciate in value in periods of rapid inflation, but inventory is more likely to depreciate. A prospective buyer must judge inventory by its market value, *not* by its book value.

WORTHLESS ACCOUNTS RECEIVABLE MAY BE WORTH LESS THAN FACE VALUE Like inventory, accounts receivable rarely are worth their face value. Prospective buyers should age a company's accounts receivable (a breakdown of accounts 30, 60, 90, and 120 days old and beyond) to determine their collectibility. The older the receivables are, the less likely they are to be collected, and, consequently, the lower their value is. Table 7.1 shows a simple but effective method of evaluating accounts receivable once they have been aged, using the estimated probabilities of collecting the accounts.

THE BUSINESS MAY BE OVERPRICED Each year, many people purchase businesses at prices far in excess of their value, which can impair the companies' ability to earn a profit and generate a positive cash flow. If a buyer accurately values a business' accounts receivable, inventories, and other assets, he or she will be in a better position to negotiate a price that will allow the business

TABLE 7.1 Valuing Accounts Receivable

A prospective buyer asked the current owner of a business about the value of her accounts receivable. The owner's business records showed $101,000 in accounts receivable. However, when the prospective buyer aged them and then multiplied the resulting totals by his estimated probabilities of collection, he discovered their *real* value.

Age of Accounts (Days)	Amount	Probability of Collection	Value (Amount × Probability of Collection)
0–30	$40,000	95%	$38,000
31–60	$25,000	88%	$22,000
61–90	$14,000	70%	$9,800
91–120	$10,000	40%	$4,000
121–150	$7,000	25%	$1,750
151+	$5,000	10%	$500
Total	$101,000		$76,050

Note: Had he blindly accepted the "book value" of these accounts receivable, this prospective buyer would have overpaid by nearly $25,000 for them!

The Saga of Selling My Business: Part 1

Norm Brodsky is a serial entrepreneur who owns three businesses—a records storage company, a document destruction business, and a trucking company—and all of them are successful. Over the years, Brodsky has received many offers from people interested in buying his companies, but he had refused them all. Now at age 60, Brodsky has received an offer that got his attention, one that is "by far the best I've ever gotten," he says. "It has always been my belief that I would ultimately sell my company. You'd think I'd be thrilled, but the prospect of selling a business raises a whole range of emotional issues. When you've been in business as long as I have, the company becomes part of your identity, even your personality. You're no longer quite sure where the business ends and you begin. I feel a certain anxiety at the thought of separating from the business. What will be left of me if I no longer own it?"

Following is a chronicle of the ups and downs that Brodsky experienced as he considered selling his company when faced with "an offer that might be the best I'll ever get, the opportunity of a lifetime." His story offers valuable lessons to both business sellers and business buyers.

"Selling your business is especially difficult if, like me, you're not sure you're ready to sell, you're enjoying your life as it is, you don't have the slightest interest in retiring, and you don't know what you'll do after the sale." Several years ago, when people asked Brodsky about selling his companies, he told them that he had "a number" in mind, one that was considerably higher than the company was worth at the time. As his company grew, however, Brodsky realized that its value was approaching his number. Cintas, a large company that wanted to get into the documents storage business, contacted Brodsky and expressed interest in buying his business. Brodsky quoted a price that was one-third higher than his original "number," and to his surprise, "the Cintas people didn't blink," which meant that he had a big decision to make: to sell or not. "I agonized over it," says Brodsky. "Finally, I told the Cintas people that we just weren't ready to sell."

Brodsky had put aside the idea of selling his company until he met venture capitalist Chris Debbas of CD Ventures in Berwyn, Pennsylvania, at an industry trade conference the next year. During the course of a conversation, Debbas said, "I think it's time for us to buy your company. What's it going to take?"

Brodsky laughed and then told Debbas, "We'll do it as a multiple of EBITDA (earnings before interest, taxes, depreciation, and amortization), but there's one thing: I won't negotiate. I'll give you the multiple, but I won't discuss it. If you're interested in buying us under those conditions, I'll talk to you. If you're not, you'll still be my friend."

Like the representative from Cintas, Debbas didn't blink at Brodsky's terms. "Can you get me some financials?" he asked.

"Of course," replied Brodsky. "You'll just have to sign a confidentiality agreement."

"No problem," said Debbas.

As fast as that, Brodsky's company was back on the market. "CD Ventures would buy our records storage, document-shredding, and deliver businesses for a lot more money than we had ever been offered before," he says. "One thing I can be pretty sure of: I will never get a deal like this again. Therein lies the paradox: the less interest you have in doing a deal, the more likely you are to get one you'll find difficult to refuse."

As Brodsky and Debbas began working on a potential deal, Brodsky began having second thoughts about selling his business. "Part of the problem is not knowing what I'll do if I sell the business," he says. "I certainly won't retire. What's going to happen to me when I sell my business? The frightening part is going from a somebody to a former somebody. In a way, I really want to do the sale, and in a way, I really don't. I am about as conflicted as a person can be."

1. Is the deal that Brodsky and CD Ventures are working on typical of most business sales? Is it common for buyers and sellers to determine the value of a company by using a multiple of earnings? What are the advantages and the disadvantages of using this approach?

2. Brodsky says, "Therein lies the paradox: The less interest you have in doing a deal, the more likely you are to get one you'll find difficult to refuse." What does he mean? Do you agree?

3. Brodsky also says, "One thing I can be pretty sure of: I will never get a deal like this again." How does that mind-set affect an entrepreneur's decision to sell his or her company?

4. Is it typical for a business owner to ask a prospective buyer to sign a confidentiality agreement before opening up his or her business to the buyer? Explain.

Source: Adapted from "The Offer: Part One" by Norm Brodsky, from INC. MAGAZINE, November 1, 2006; "The Offer: Part Two" by Norm Brodsky, from INC. MAGAZINE, December 1, 2006; and "The Offer: Part Three" by Norm Brodsky, from INC. MAGAZINE, January 1, 2007. Copyright © 2006, 2007 by Inc. Magazine. Reprinted with permission., pp. 67–68.

to be profitable. Making payments on a business that was overpriced is a millstone around the new owner's neck, making it difficult to keep the business afloat.

Although most buyers do not realize it, the price they pay for a company typically is not as crucial to its continued success as the terms on which they make the purchase. Of course, wise business buyers will try to negotiate a fair and reasonable price, but they are often equally interested in the more specific terms of the deal. For instance, how much cash they must pay out and when, how much of the price the seller is willing to finance and for how long, the interest rate at which the deal is financed, and other such terms can make or break a deal. A buyer's primary concern is making sure that the terms of the deal do not endanger the company's future financial health and that they preserve the company's cash flow.

The Steps in Acquiring a Business

Buying an existing business can be risky if approached haphazardly. Kevin Mulvaney, a professor of entrepreneurship at Babson College and a consultant to business sellers, says that 50 to 75 percent of all business sales that are initiated fall through.[8] To avoid blowing a deal or making costly mistakes, an entrepreneur-to-be should follow these seven steps:

1. Conduct a self-inventory, objectively analyzing skills, abilities, and personal interests to determine the type(s) of business that offer the best fit.

2. Develop a list of the criteria that define the "ideal business" for you.

3. Prepare a list of potential candidates that meet your criteria.

4. Thoroughly investigate the potential acquisition targets that meet your criteria. This *due diligence process* involves practical steps, such as analyzing financial statements and making certain that the facilities are structurally sound. The goal is to minimize the pitfalls and problems that arise when buying any business.

5. Explore various financing options for buying the business.

6. Negotiate a reasonable deal with the existing owner.

7. Ensure a smooth transition of ownership.

Analyze Your Skills, Abilities, and Interests

The first step in buying a business is *not* searching out potential acquisition candidates. Every entrepreneur who is considering buying a business should begin by conducting a self-audit to determine the ideal business for him or her. The primary focus is to identify the type of business that *you* will be happiest and most successful owning. Consider, for example, the following questions:

- What business activities do you enjoy most? Least? Why?

- Which industries or markets offer the greatest potential for growth?

- Which industries interest you most? Least? Why?

- What kind of business would you enjoy running?

- What kinds of businesses do you want to *avoid*?

- What do you expect to get out of the business?

- How much time, energy, and money can you put into the business?

- What business skills and experience do you have? Which ones do you lack?

- How easily can you transfer your skills and experience to other types of businesses? In what kinds of businesses would that transfer be easiest?

- How much risk are you willing to take?

- Are you willing and able to turn around a struggling business?

- What size company do you want to buy?

- Is there a particular geographic location you desire?

Answering these and other questions beforehand allows you to develop a list of criteria a company must meet to become a purchase candidate. Addressing these issues early in the process will also save a great deal of time, trouble, and confusion as you wade through a multitude of business opportunities. The better you know yourself and your skills, competencies, and interests, the more likely you will be to find and manage a successful business.

LO2

Define the steps involved in the *right* way to buy a business.

Develop a List of Criteria

Based on the answers to the self-inventory questions, the next step is to develop a list of criteria that a potential business acquisition must meet. Investigating every business that you find for sale is a waste of time. The goal is to identify the characteristics of the "ideal business" for you so that you can focus on the most viable candidates as you wade through a multitude of business opportunities. These criteria will provide specific parameters against which you can evaluate potential acquisition candidates.

Prepare a List of Potential Candidates

Once you know what your goals are for acquiring a business, you can begin your search. Do *not* limit yourself to only those businesses that are advertised as being "for sale." In fact, the **hidden market** of companies that might be for sale but are not advertised as such is one of the richest sources of top-quality businesses. Many businesses that can be purchased are not publicly advertised but are available either through the owners themselves or through business brokers and other professionals. Although they maintain a low profile, these hidden businesses represent some of the most attractive purchase targets a prospective buyer may find.

ENTREPRENEURIAL PROFILE: Art and Alan McCraw: B. W. Burdette and Sons When brothers Art and Allan McCraw, two enterprising college graduates, returned to their hometown, they approached the owners of B. W. Burdette and Sons, a local hardware store that had been founded by the current owners' father 80 years earlier about buying the business. The company was not listed for sale, but because the McCraws were familiar with the business, they knew that the current owners might be interested in selling. After several months of due diligence and negotiations, the young entrepreneurs closed the deal. They have since expanded the business to include two more locations, expanded its market reach, and increased its profitability many times over. ∎

How can you tap into this hidden market of potential acquisitions? Typical sources include the following:

- The Internet, where several sites such as Bizbuysell.com, Bizquest, and others, include listings of business brokers and companies for sale

- Business brokers—to locate a broker near you, visit the Web site for the International Business Brokers Association at www.ibba.org

- Professionals who provide business services, such as bankers, accountants, attorneys, investment bankers, and others

- Industry contacts—suppliers, distributors, customers, insurance brokers, and others

- Networking—social and business contact with friends and relatives

- Knocking on the doors of businesses you would like to buy (even if they're not advertised as being "for sale")

- Trade associations

- Newspapers and trade journals listing businesses for sale

The more opportunities an entrepreneur has to find and evaluate potential acquisitions, the greater the likelihood of finding a match that meets his or her criteria.

Investigate and Evaluate Potential Companies: The Due Diligence Process

Finding the right company requires patience. Although some buyers find a company after only a few months of looking, the typical search takes much longer, sometimes as much as two or three years. Once you have a list of prospective candidates, it is time to do your homework. The next step is to investigate the candidates in more detail:

- What are the company's strengths? Weaknesses?

- Is the company profitable? What is its overall financial condition?

- What is its cash flow cycle? How much cash will the company generate?

- Who are its major competitors?

- How large is the customer base? Is it growing or shrinking?

- Are the current employees suitable? Will they stay?

- What is the physical condition of the business, its equipment, and its inventory?

- What new skills must you learn to be able to manage this business successfully?

Determining the answers to these and other questions addressed in this chapter allow a prospective buyer to develop a list of the most attractive prospects and to prioritize them in descending order of attractiveness. This process also makes the task of valuing the business much easier. The next section of this chapter explains the due diligence process in more detail.

Explore Financing Options

Placing a value on an existing business (a topic you will learn more about later in this chapter) represents a major hurdle for many would-be entrepreneurs. The next challenging task in closing a successful deal is financing the purchase. According to a recent survey of business brokers by BizBuySell, an online marketplace for businesses that are for sale, the principal cause of business sales failing to close is lack of available financing.[9] Although financing the purchase of an existing business usually is easier than financing a new one, some traditional lenders shy away from deals involving the purchase of an existing business, especially in the wake of the financial crisis. Those that are willing to finance business purchases normally lend only a portion of the value of the assets, and buyers often find themselves searching for alternative sources of funds. Fortunately, most business buyers have access to a ready source of financing: the seller. Seller financing often is more flexible, faster, easier to obtain than loans from traditional lenders—and currently an essential part of most deals. "With the tightening of the credit markets, our brokers have made it very clear to our clients [business sellers] that they're going to have to take the place of the bank," says one senior business broker.[10]

Once a seller finds a suitable buyer, he or she typically will agree to finance anywhere from 25 to 80 percent of the purchase price. Dan Steppe, a serial entrepreneur who leads the University of Houston's Center for Entrepreneurship, tells his college students, "You will soon be talking to a 67-year-old guy who is a bit tired of what he's doing, who's already talked to his son and his daughter, and the family options don't exist. The seller will enable the buyer to buy his company fairly inexpensively. You can buy a $10 million company for $2 million and the seller will finance the other $8 million."[11]

Usually, a deal is structured so that the buyer makes a sizable down payment to the seller, who then finances a note for the balance. The buyer makes regular principal and interest payments over 5 to 10 years—perhaps with a larger balloon payment at the end—until the note is paid off. The terms and conditions of the loan are a vital concern to both buyer and seller. They cannot be so burdensome that they threaten the company's continued existence; that is, the buyer must be able to make the payments to the seller out of the company's cash flow. At the same time, the deal must give the seller the financial security he or she is seeking from the sale. Defining reasonable terms is the result of the negotiation process between the buyer and the seller.

ENTREPRENEURIAL PROFILE: Donna Merelli: Ocean Liquors After Donna Merelli lost her job as an officer-manager at a mill that closed, she worked with a business broker to purchase Ocean Liquors, LLC, in Boca Raton, Florida, for $325,000, $50,000 less than the seller's asking price. As part of the negotiations, Merelli convinced the seller to finance $100,000 of the purchase price, an amount she will repay at 7 percent interest within five years, and used her savings to pay the balance. Merelli also invested $26,000 in remodeling and upgrading the store with a new wine cooler.[12] ∎

Negotiate a Reasonable Deal with the Owner

The buyer must sit down with the seller to negotiate the actual selling price for the business and, more important, the terms of the deal. The final deal the buyer strikes depends, in large part, on his or her negotiating skills. The first "rule" of negotiating a deal is to avoid confusing price with value.

Value is what the business is actually worth; *price* is what the buyer agrees to pay. In a business sale, the party who is the better negotiator usually comes out on top. Buyers seek to do the following:

- Get the business at the lowest possible price.

- Negotiate favorable payment terms, preferably over time.

- Get assurances that they are buying the business they think that they are getting.

- Avoid putting the seller in a position to open a competing business.

- Minimize the amount of cash paid up front.

Sellers are looking to do the following:

- Get the highest price possible for the business.

- Sever all responsibility for the company's liabilities.

- Avoid unreasonable contract terms that might limit his or her future opportunities.

- Maximize the cash they get from the deal.

- Minimize the tax burden from the sale.

- Make sure the buyer will be able to make all future payments.

One factor that makes the process of negotiating the purchase of a business challenging is that many business founders overestimate the value of their companies because of all of the "sweat equity" they have poured into their businesses over the years. Indeed, the second most common reason that business brokers say causes business purchases from closing is the seller's unwillingness to lower the asking price.[13] One entrepreneur recalls a negotiation that he was involved in for the potential purchase of a rival's business. The company had $4 million in sales but had incurred losses of more than $1 million in the previous two years, owed more than $2.5 million in unpaid bills, and had no machinery that was less than 30 years old. Much to the prospective buyer's amazement, the owner was asking $4 million for the business![14]

Ensure a Smooth Transition

Once the parties strike a deal, the challenge of making a smooth transition immediately arises. No matter how well planned the sale is, there are *always* surprises. For instance, the new owner may have ideas for changing the business—sometimes radically—that cause a great deal of stress and anxiety among employees and the previous owner. Charged with such emotion and uncertainty, the transition phase is always difficult and frustrating—and sometimes painful. To avoid a bumpy transition, a business buyer should do the following:

- Concentrate on communicating with employees. Business sales are fraught with uncertainty and anxiety, and employees need reassurance.

- Be honest with employees. Avoid telling them only what they want to hear. Share with the employees your vision for the business in the hope of generating a heightened level of motivation and support.

- Listen to employees. They have firsthand knowledge of the business and its strengths and weaknesses and usually can offer valuable suggestions for improving it.

- Consider asking the seller to serve as a consultant until the transition is complete. The previous owner can be a valuable resource, especially to an inexperienced buyer.

LO3

Explain the process of evaluating an existing business.

Evaluating an Existing Business: The Due Diligence Process

When evaluating an existing business, a buyer can quickly feel overwhelmed by the tremendous number and complexity of the issues involved. Therefore, a smart buyer will assemble a team of specialists to help investigate a potential business opportunity. This team is usually composed of a banker, an accountant familiar with the particular industry, an attorney, and perhaps a small business consultant or a business broker. The cost of assembling a team can range from $3,000 to $20,000, but most buyers agree that using a team significantly lowers the likelihood of making a bad purchase. Because the expense of making a bad purchase is many times the cost of a team of experts, most buyers see it as a wise investment. It is important for a buyer to trust the members of the business evaluation team. With this team assembled, the potential buyer is ready to explore the business opportunity by examining five critical areas.

1. *Motivation.* Why does the owner want to sell?

2. *Asset valuation.* What is the physical condition of the business?

3. *Market potential.* What is the potential for the company's products or services?

4. *Legal issues.* What legal aspects of the business represent known or hidden risks?

5. *Financial condition.* Is the business financially sound?

Evaluating these five areas of a business occurs in a process called **due diligence**, which involves reviewing, investigating, and analyzing the relevant details about the top acquisition candidates to determine which one best meets a buyer's purchase criteria. "There are so many ugly stories," explains Robert Strang, president of Strang Hayes Consulting, a firm that specializes in helping prospective buyers through the due diligence process. For one of its clients, Strang Hayes discovered that the CEO of a company that one of its clients was considering purchasing had hidden five sexual harassment lawsuits that had been filed against him. Another search revealed that the business another buyer was considering purchasing had been banned from doing business in Florida, which was a major market for the prospective buyer.[15] The message is clear: buyers who neglect to perform thorough due diligence do so at their own peril.

due diligence
the process of reviewing, investigating, and analyzing the relevant details about the top acquisition candidates to determine which one best meets a buyer's purchase criteria.

"When you asked if I'd 'like a little company' I didn't expect you to start trying to sell me your dry-cleaning business!"

© Fry/www.CartoonStock.com

Motivation

Why does the owner want to sell? Every prospective business buyer should investigate the *real* reason the business owner wants to sell. Common reasons for selling a business include planned retirement, personal reasons such as health or the desire for a new interest in life, reducing the risk of having most of their personal assets tied up in their businesses, the inability to make enough money from the business, and looming changes in the business environment that will have an adverse impact on the company. Many owners tell buyers that they have become bored or burned out and want to move on to other business ventures, but is that really the case?

Smart business buyers know that the biggest and most unpleasant surprises can crop up outside the company's financial records and may never appear on the spreadsheets designed to analyze a company's financial position. For instance, a business owner might be looking to sell his or her business because a powerful new competitor is about to move into the market, a major highway rerouting will cause customer traffic to evaporate, the lease agreement on the ideal location is about to expire, or the primary customer base is declining. Every prospective buyer should investigate thoroughly any reason a seller gives for wanting to sell a business.

Businesses do not last forever, and smart entrepreneurs know when the time has come to sell. Some owners consider their behavior ethical only if they do not make false or misleading statements. Buyers should not expect to get a full disclosure of the whole story behind the reasons for a business being offered for sale. In most business sales, the buyer bears the responsibility of determining whether the business is a good value. The best way to do that is to get out into the local community, talk to people, and ask a lot of questions. Visiting local business owners may reveal general patterns about the area and its overall vitality. The local chamber of commerce also may have useful information. Suppliers, customers, and even competitors may be able to shed light on why a business is up for sale. By combining this information with an analysis of the company's financial records, a potential buyer should be able to develop a clear picture of the business and its real value.

Asset Valuation

A prospective buyer should evaluate the business's assets to determine their value. Are the assets really useful, or are they obsolete? Will they require replacement soon? Do machinery and equipment operate efficiently? Are the company's assets reasonably priced?

A potential buyer should check the condition of both the equipment and the building. It may be necessary to hire a professional to evaluate the major components of the building—its structure and its plumbing; its electrical, heating, and cooling systems; and other elements. Unexpected renovations are rarely inexpensive or simple and can punch a gaping hole in a buyer's financial plans.

How fresh is the company's inventory? Is it consistent with the image that the new owner wants to project? How much of it would the buyer have to sell at a loss? Determining the value of the company's inventory and other assets may require an independent appraisal because sellers often price them above their actual value. These items typically make up the largest portion of a business's value, and a potential buyer should not accept the seller's asking price blindly. Remember that *book value is not the same as market value*. Usually, a buyer can purchase equipment and fixtures at substantially lower prices than book value. Value is determined in the marketplace, not on a balance sheet.

Other important factors that the potential buyer should investigate include the following:

Accounts receivable. If the sale includes accounts receivable, the buyer should check their quality before purchasing them. How creditworthy are the accounts? What portion of them is past due? How likely are you to be able to collect them? By aging the accounts receivable, a buyer can judge their quality and determine their value (see Table 7.1).

Lease arrangements. Is the lease included in the sale? When does it expire? What restrictions does it have on renovation or expansion? The buyer should determine *beforehand* what restrictions the landlord has placed on the lease and negotiate any change prior to purchasing the business.

Business records. Accurate business records can be a valuable source of information and can tell a prospective buyer a lot about the company's pattern of success (or lack of it).

Typically, buyers should expect to see financial statements documenting revenues and net income, operating budgets, and cash flow statements for at least five years. Sales and earnings forecasts from the seller for at least three years also can be helpful when trying to determine the value of a business. Unfortunately, many business owners are sloppy record keepers. Consequently, a potential buyer and his or her team may have to reconstruct some critical records. It is important to verify as much information about the business as possible. For instance, does the owner have customer mailing lists? These lists can be a valuable marketing tool for a new business owner. Has the owner created an operations manual outlining the company's policies and procedures?

Intangible assets. Does the sale include any intangible assets, such as trademarks, patents, copyrights, or goodwill? How long do patents have left to run? Is the trademark threatened by lawsuits for infringement? Does the company have registered logos or slogans that are unique or widely recognized? Determining the value of such intangibles is much more difficult than computing the value of the tangible assets, yet intangible assets can be a significant part of a company's real value.

Location and appearance. The location and the overall appearance of a business are important factors for a prospective buyer to consider. What had been an outstanding location in the past may be totally unacceptable today. Even if the building and equipment are in good condition and are fairly priced, the business may be located in a declining area. Are the other businesses that operate in the surrounding area compatible with the image the buyer wants the company to project?

Market Potential

What is the potential for the company's products or services? No one wants to buy a business with a shrinking customer base. A thorough market analysis helps a buyer to develop his or her own sales forecast for an existing business (in addition to the one he or she should ask the seller to prepare). This research will reveal important trends in the business's sales and customer base. Two important aspects of a market analysis include learning about customers and competitors.

CUSTOMER CHARACTERISTICS AND COMPOSITION Before purchasing an existing business, a buyer should analyze both existing and potential customers. Discovering why customers buy from the business and developing a profile of the company's existing customer base can help the buyer identify a company's strengths and weaknesses and discover how to market more effectively to them. A potential buyer should determine the answers to the following questions:

- Who are the company's target customers? Is the customer base growing or shrinking?

- How is the composition of the customers in the local market changing?

- What do customers want the business to do for them? What needs are they satisfying when they make a purchase?

- How often do customers buy? Do they buy in seasonal patterns?

- How loyal are present customers?

- Why do some potential customers *not* buy from the business?

- How easily can the company attract new customers?

- Do the company's customers come from a large geographic area, or do they live near the business?

Analyzing the answers to these questions can help a potential buyer create and implement a more powerful marketing plan.

COMPETITOR ANALYSIS A potential buyer must identify the company's direct competitors, those businesses in the immediate area that sell the same or similar products or services. The potential profitability and survival of the business may depend on the behavior of these competitors. Important factors to consider are the number of competitors and the intensity of the competition.

How many competitors have opened in recent years? How many have closed in the last five years? What caused them to fail? Has the market already reached the saturation point? Being a latecomer in an already saturated market is not the pathway to long-term success. When evaluating the competitive environment, a prospective buyer should address other questions:

- What are the characteristics that have led to the success of the company's most direct competitors?

- How do competitors' sales volumes compare with those of the business the entrepreneur is considering?

- What unique services do competitors offer?

- How well organized and coordinated are competitors' marketing efforts?

- How strong are competitors' reputations?

- What are their strengths and weaknesses?

- If you purchase this business, how can you gain market share in this competitive environment?

Legal Issues

What legal aspects of the business represent known or hidden risks? Business buyers face several legal pitfalls as they negotiate the final deal. The biggest potential legal traps include liens, contract assignments, covenants not to compete, and ongoing legal liabilities.

lien
a creditor's claim against an asset.

LIENS The key legal issue in the sale of any asset is typically the proper transfer of good title from seller to buyer. However, because most business sales involve a collection of assorted assets, the transfer of a good title can be complex. Some business assets may have **liens** (creditors' claims) against them, and unless the lien is satisfied before the sale, the buyer must assume it and is financially responsible for it. One way to reduce this potential problem is to include a clause in the sales contract stating that any liability not shown on the balance sheet at the time of sale remains the responsibility of the seller. A prospective buyer should have an attorney thoroughly investigate all of the assets for sale and their lien status before buying any business.

CONTRACT ASSIGNMENTS Buyers must investigate the rights and the obligations they would assume under existing contracts with suppliers, customers, employees, lessors, and others. To continue the smooth operation of the business, the buyer must assume the rights of the seller under many existing contracts. Assuming these rights and obligations requires the seller to assign existing contracts to the new owner. For example, the current owner may have four years left on a 10-year lease that he or she will assign to the buyer (if the lease allows assignments). To protect his or her interest, the buyer (who is the assignee) should notify the other party involved in the contract of the assignment. In the previous example, the business buyer should notify the landlord promptly of the lease assignment from the previous owner.

due-on-sale clause
a loan contract provision that prohibits a seller from assigning a loan arrangement to the buyer. Instead, the buyer is required to finance the remaining loan balance at prevailing interest rates.

Generally, the seller can assign any contractual right to the buyer, unless the contract specifically prohibits the assignment or the contract is personal in nature. For instance, loan contracts sometimes prohibit assignments with **due-on-sale clauses**. These clauses require the buyer to pay the full amount of the remaining loan balance or to finance the balance at prevailing interest rates. Thus, the buyer cannot assume the seller's loan (which may be at a lower interest rate than the prevailing rate on a loan). In addition, a seller usually cannot assign his or her credit arrangements with suppliers to the buyer because they are based on the seller's business reputation and are personal in nature. If contracts such as these are crucial to the business operation and cannot be assigned, the buyer must renegotiate new contracts. A prospective buyer also should evaluate the terms of any other unique contracts the seller has, including exclusive agent or distributor contracts, real estate leases, financing and loan arrangements, and union contracts.

covenant not to compete (restrictive covenant or noncompete agreement)
an agreement between a buyer and a seller in which the seller agrees not to compete with the buyer within a specific time and geographic area.

COVENANTS NOT TO COMPETE One of the most important and most often overlooked legal considerations for a prospective buyer is negotiating a **covenant not to compete (restrictive covenant or noncompete agreement)** with the seller. Under a restrictive covenant, the seller agrees not to open a new, competing business within a specific time period and geographic area of the existing one. (The covenant should be negotiated with the *owner*, not with the corporation, because if the corporation signs the agreement, the owner may not be bound by it.) Although some states place limitations on the enforceability of restrictive covenants, business buyers should insist on the seller signing one. Without this protection, a buyer may find his or her new business eroding beneath his or her feet.

To be enforceable, a restrictive covenant must be reasonable in geographic scope and in duration, must protect a legitimate business interest (such as a company's goodwill), and must be tied to a contract for the sale of an existing business (i.e., no "free-standing" restrictive covenants that restrain trade). The sales contract also should establish the portion of the total purchase price allocated to restrictive covenant. An early case concerning the enforceability of a restrictive covenant took place over the sale of a blacksmith shop in Little Otter Creek, West Virginia, in 1916.

ENTREPRENEURIAL PROFILE: James Boggs vs. Silas Friend James Boggs and Silas Friend entered into a contract in which Friend sold to Boggs his thriving blacksmith business, the land on which it sat, the building and all of the tools in it, and goodwill for $375. As part of the deal, Friend agreed to a restrictive covenant that said that he "would not engage in the blacksmith business in the vicinity or neighborhood where said blacksmith shop was located, or at any other place so near thereto as to constitute a rival business, or detract from the patronage which would naturally or likely go to the shop and business so purchased by plaintiff from him." However, within two months, Friend had opened a rival blacksmith shop within 400 yards of the shop that Boggs had purchased and was attracting many of his former customers. Boggs filed a lawsuit to enforce the restrictive covenant. A circuit court dismissed his complaint, but on appeal the Supreme Court of West Virginia reversed the lower court's decision, enforced the restrictive covenant, and issued an injunction that prevented Friend from competing with Boggs in the blacksmith business "within such limits about the place as the business there located would naturally embrace.[16] ■

ONGOING LEGAL LIABILITIES Finally, a potential buyer must look for any potential legal liabilities the purchase might expose. These typically arise from three sources:

Physical premises. A buyer must examine the physical premises for safety. Are employees at risk because of asbestos or some other hazardous material? If the business is a manufacturing operation, does it meet Occupational Safety and Health Administration and other regulatory agency requirements? One entrepreneur who purchased a retail business located in a building that once housed a gasoline service station was quite surprised when the Environmental Protection Agency informed him that he would have to pay for cleaning up the results of an old, leaking gas tank that still sat beneath the property. Even though he had no part in running the old gas station and did not know the leaking tank was there, he was responsible for the cost of the cleanup! Removing the tank and cleaning up the site cost him several thousand dollars that he had not budgeted.

Product liability claims. The buyer must consider whether existing products contain defects that could result in **product liability lawsuits**, which claim that a company is liable for damages and injuries caused by the products or services they make or sell. Existing lawsuits might be an omen of more to follow. In addition, the buyer must explore products that the company has discontinued because he or she might be liable for them if they prove to be defective. The final bargain between the parties should require the seller to guarantee that the company is not involved in any product liability lawsuits.

product liability lawsuits
lawsuits that claim that a company is liable for damages and injuries caused by the products it makes or sells.

Labor relations. What is the relationship between management to employees? Does a union contract exist? The time to discover sour management–labor relations is before the purchase, not after.

The presence of legal liabilities such as these does necessarily eliminate a business from consideration. Insurance coverage can shift such risks from the potential buyer, but the buyer should check to see whether the insurance will cover lawsuits resulting from actions predating the purchase.

Financial Condition

Is the business financially sound? A prospective buyer must analyze the financial records of a target business to determine its financial health, and hiring an accountant to help usually is a good idea. Accounting systems and methods vary tremendously from one type of business to another and can be quite confusing to a novice. Some business sellers know all of the tricks to make profits appear higher than they actually are. For the buyer, the most dependable financial records are audited statements, those prepared by a certified public accounting firm in accordance with generally accepted accounting principles.

ENTREPRENEURIAL PROFILE: Charles Carroll: Integrated Biometric Technology When Charles Carroll decided to sell his business, Integrated Biometric Technology (IBT), a company that allows employers to conduct criminal background checks in just minutes, he attracted more attention from potential buyers by switching to audited financial statements from reviewed statements. Meeting the more stringent standards increased his accounting costs from $10,000 to $35,000, but Carroll received offers that were higher than he expected from multiple prospects. Ultimately, he sold IBT to a larger company, Viisage, for $35 million in cash, $25 million in Viisage stock, and the prospect of a $10 million earn-out if IBT hits specific performance targets.[17] ■

Unlike IBT, audited records do not exist in many small companies that are for sale. In some cases, a potential buyer has to hire an accountant to construct reliable financial statements because the owner's accounting and record keeping are so sloppy.

When evaluating the financial status of any business prospect, buyers must remember that any investment in a company should produce a reasonable salary for themselves, an attractive return on the money they invest, and enough to cover the amount they must borrow to make the purchase. Otherwise, it makes no sense to purchase the business. Buyers also must remember that they are purchasing the future profit potential of an existing business. To evaluate the firm's profit potential, they should review past sales, operating expenses, and profits as well as the assets used to generate those profits. They must compare current balance sheets, income statements, and statements of cash flow with previous ones and then develop a set of projected statements for the next two to three years. Sales tax records, income tax returns, and financial statements are valuable sources of information.

Trends in earnings also are important. Are profits consistent over the years, or are they erratic? Is this pattern typical in the industry, or is it a result of unique circumstances or poor management? Can the business survive with serious fluctuations in revenues, costs, and profits? If these fluctuations are the result of poor management, can a new owner turn the business around? Some of the financial records that a potential buyer should examine are discussed in the following sections.

INCOME STATEMENTS AND BALANCE SHEETS FOR THE PAST THREE TO FIVE YEARS It is important to review data from several years because creative accounting techniques can distort financial data in any single year. Even though buyers are purchasing the future profits of a business, they must remember that many businesses intentionally keep net income low to minimize the owners' tax bills. Low earnings should prompt a buyer to investigate their causes.

INCOME TAX RETURNS FOR THE PAST THREE TO FIVE YEARS Comparing basic financial statements with tax returns can reveal discrepancies of which the buyer should be aware. Some small business owners engage in **skimming** from their businesses—taking money from sales without reporting it as income. Owners who skim will claim that their businesses are more profitable than their tax returns show. Although such underreporting is illegal and unethical, it is surprisingly common. Buyers should *not* pay for undocumented, "phantom" earnings that a seller claims exist. In fact, buyers should consider whether they want to buy a business from someone who admits to doing business unethically.

skimming
taking money from sales without reporting it as income.

OWNER'S COMPENSATION (AND THAT OF RELATIVES) The owner's compensation is especially important in small companies; and the smaller the company is, the more important it will be. Although many companies do not pay their owners what they are worth, others compensate their owners lavishly. The buyer must consider the impact of benefits—company cars, insurance contracts, country club memberships, and the like. It is important to adjust the company's income statements for the salary and benefits that the seller has paid himself or herself and others.

CASH FLOW Most buyers understand the importance of evaluating a company's profitability, but fewer recognize the necessity of analyzing its cash flow. They assume that if earnings are adequate, there will be sufficient cash to pay all of the bills and to fund an attractive salary for themselves. *That is not necessarily the case!* Before agreeing to a deal, prospective buyers should sit down with an accountant and convert the target company's financial statements into a cash flow forecast. This forecast not only must take into account existing debts and obligations but also any modifications the buyer would make in the business, including necessary capital expenditures. It must also reflect the repayment of any financing the buyer arranges to purchase the company, whether it is through the seller or a traditional lender. Will the company generate enough cash to be self-supporting? How much cash will it generate for you?

A potential buyer should walk away from a deal—no matter how good it may appear on the surface—if the present owner refuses to disclose the company's financial records—or any other operating information the buyer needs to make an informed decision. If that is the case, says Marc Kramer, author of *Small Business Turnaround*, "don't walk—run—away."[18]

Buying an existing business is a process filled with potential missteps along the way. The expression "Let the buyer beware" should be the prospective buyer's mantra throughout the entire process. However, by following the due diligence procedure described in this section, buyers can lower dramatically the probability of getting "burned" with a business that does not suit their personalities or one that is in on the verge of failure. Figure 7.2 illustrates the sequence of events leading up to a successful negotiation with a seller.

| 1. Identify and approach candidate | 2. Sign nondisclosure statement | 3. Sign letter of intent | 4. Buyer's due diligence investigation | 5. Draft the purchase agreement | 6. Close the final deal | 7. Begin the transition |

Negotiations

1. Approach the candidate. If a business is advertised for sale, the proper approach is through the channel defined in the ad. Sometimes buyers will contact business brokers to help them locate potential target companies. If you have targeted a company in the "hidden market," an introduction from a banker, accountant, or lawyer often is the best approach. During this phase, the seller checks out the buyer's qualifications, and the buyer begins to judge the quality of the company.

2. Sign a nondisclosure document. If the buyer and the seller are satisfied with the results of their preliminary research, they are ready to begin serious negotiations. Throughout the negotiation process, the seller expects the buyer to maintain strict confidentiality of all of the records, documents, and information he or she receives during the investigation and negotiation process. The nondisclosure document is a legally binding contract that ensures the secrecy of the parties' negotiations.

3. Sign a letter of intent. Before a buyer makes a legal offer to buy the company, he or she typically will ask the seller to sign a letter of intent. The letter of intent is a nonbinding document that says that the buyer and the seller have reached a sufficient "meeting of the minds" to justify the time and expense of negotiating a final agreement. The letter should state clearly that it is nonbinding, giving either party the right to walk away from the deal. It should also contain a clause calling for "good faith negotiations" between the parties. A typical letter of intent addresses terms such as price, payment terms, categories of assets to be sold, and a deadline for closing the final deal.

4. Buyer's due diligence. While negotiations are continuing, the buyer is busy studying the business and evaluating its strengths and weaknesses. In short, the buyer must "do his or her homework" to make sure that the business is a good value.

5. Draft the purchase agreement. The purchase agreement spells out the parties' final deal. It sets forth all of the details of the agreement and is the final product of the negotiation process.

6. Close the final deal. Once the parties have drafted the purchase agreement, all that remains to making the deal "official" is the closing. Both buyer and seller sign the necessary documents to make the sale final. The buyer delivers the required money, and the seller turns the company over to the buyer.

7. Begin the transition. For the buyer, the real challenge now begins: making the transition to a successful business owner!

FIGURE 7.2

The Acquisition Process

Source: Sources: Adapted from *Buying and Selling: A Company Handbook*, Price Waterhouse, (New York: 1993) pp. 38–42; Charles F. Claeys, "The Intent to Buy," *Small Business Reports*, May 1994, pp. 44–47.

✓ You Be the Consultant

The Saga of Selling My Business: Part 2

Once Norm Brodsky and Chris Debbas decided to explore the possibility of Debbas's company, CD Ventures, purchasing Brodsky's business, they embarked on the due diligence process in which the potential buyer investigates the quality of the company, its financial performance, its relationships with customers, and a million other details. "What would you think about having a team of outside accountants, lawyers, and operations people descend on your business to go through your records, question your employees, dissect everything you do, and judge how good your company is and how truthful you really are?" says Brodsky, describing the due diligence process.

On the financial front, Brodsky knew that his company was ready for due diligence. Several years before, he had begun having an accounting firm provide audited financial statements for CitiStorage. The move had increased the company's accounting expenses significantly, but Sam Kaplan, Brodsky's partner in the business, had convinced him that doing so would make raising capital or selling the business much easier. He was right. "The audited statements made the financial part of the due diligence process a walk in the park," says Brodsky. The goal was to adjust the company's income statement to reflect the revenues and expenses that CD Ventures could expect, thus arriving at an earnings value on which both parties could agree. (Recall that the deal was to apply Brodsky's multiplier to the company's earnings; therefore, coming up with the right number was a major part of the deal.)

Throughout the process, everyone at CitiStorage followed what Brodsky calls a "warts-and-all" policy, refusing to hide the company's problems and giving the due diligence team full access to the records they wanted. "In this kind of transaction, you should tell people on the other side everything that is bad, that might be bad, or has a one-in-a-million chance of going bad," he says.

In the end, CD Ventures settled on an earnings value that was $600,000 less than the one that Brodsky had come up with—not a huge gap considering the size of the deal. "When we got together to discuss our different numbers, I told [Debbas] that he should just accept mine," says Brodsky. "For every dollar that your accountants find, I'm going to find a dollar fifty the other way. You might as well just go with our number." Debbas refused, but eventually, he and Brodsky were able to agree on an earnings value for CitiStorage.

While the CD Ventures team was completing its due diligence, Brodsky had time to reflect on what it meant to sell the company that he had launched 16 years before and nurtured into a successful business. "Once I put my emotions aside, I realized it was now or never," he says. "The decision wasn't about selling to this particular group or even about getting the right price. It came down to whether I was ever going to sell." Brodsky knew that his company was financially sound and well managed and that the document storage industry was "hot," with many players looking to buy businesses in that sector. "If I'm ever going to sell [my company], now is the time," he says. For Brodsky, two issues dominated the decision: he wanted to the right price for the company, and he wanted his employees to be treated well by the buyer.

Brodsky set a deadline for closing the sale of his business, but it passed with no deal done. As time dragged on, he began to wonder whether CD Ventures and Nova Records Management, the company they planned to fold CitiStorage into, were still interested in doing a deal. The deal makers assured Brodsky that they were committed to buying his business. Then Debbas called and told Brodsky that the "equity guys" (the people who were providing the equity capital to purchase CitiStorage) had backed out.

"What now?" Brodsky asked.

Debbas told him about "plan B," in which investment banker Goldman Sachs would provide all of the financing to complete the deal. After hearing the details, Brodsky agreed that it was a better plan, but it also meant more delays in closing the sale of the business. In a conference call, members of the Nova Records Management board expressed their commitment to completing the purchase of CitiStorage but brought up three issues that had to be resolved. One of them involved changes to the leases on the land where CitiStorage was located. Brodsky was confident that the outside parties would approve the changes but was concerned about the time required to secure approval. "It will take three months at least," he says, "but I won't wait that long."

The delays were creating another problem. CitiStorage was having its best year ever, meaning that its value had gone up. Yet the sales price that Brodsky had agreed to was based on the previous year's earnings. "It would be very tough for me to sell my company for substantially less than it is worth," says Brodsky.

In an attempt to move the process forward, Brodsky called a meeting with key members from Nova's board and attorneys for both sides with the goal of putting on the table unresolved issues. The group discussed four matters ranging from the company's 401(k) program to the lease agreements and was able to resolve them all. "When can you have this done?" Brodsky asked the attorneys. After some discussion, the parties agreed that the closing would take place on April 5. A year had passed since Brodsky had talked with Debbas about selling his company. "I don't know whether I'm more amazed at how far we've come or how long it's taken," says Brodsky. "I just hope the suspense is over soon and I can finally start focusing on the future."

1. Why is it important for business buyers to be thorough when conducting their due diligence of a company they are considering purchasing?

2. Brodsky followed a warts-and-all policy with CD Ventures and Nova Records Management during due diligence. How typical is his approach among business sellers? Explain your reasoning.

3. Often, deals such as the one Brodsky is involved in fall through at the end and are never completed. Do you see any potential deal breakers in the sale of CitiStorage?

Source: Adapted from Norm Brodsky, "The Offer, Part Four," *Inc.*, February 2007, pp. 63–65; Norm Brodsky, "It's All About Trust," *Inc.*, March 2007, pp. 116–119; Norm Brodsky, "The Offer, Part Six," *Inc.*, April 2007, pp. 67–68; and Norm Brodsky, "The Offer: Part Seven," *Inc.*, May 2007, pp. 73–74.

Methods for Determining the Value of a Business

LO4

Describe the various techniques for determining the value of a business.

Business valuation is partly an art and partly a science. Part of what makes establishing a reasonable price for a privately held business so difficult is the wide variety of factors that influence its value: the nature of the business itself; its position in the market or industry; the outlook for the market or industry; the company's financial status; its earning capacity; any intangible assets it may own (e.g., patents, trademarks, or copyrights); the value of other, similar companies; and many other factors. The median selling price of a private company is $150,000 according to the BizComps database compiled by Business Valuation Resources, a company that tracks sales of private company (see Figure 7.3).[19] However, some businesses sell for much more. In 1999, Jeffrey Price, Ashok Singhal, and Robert Rogers started 3Par, a data storage company that was among the first to offer customers the convenience of cloud storage, in Fremont, California, with a simple mission: to make storage solutions simple and efficient. Eleven years after starting the company, Price and Singhal (Rogers had left the company by then) sold it to Hewlett-Packard for $2.35 billion, netting the founders and their early investors handsome payouts![20]

Computing the value of the company's tangible assets normally poses no major problem, but assigning a price to the intangibles, such as goodwill, almost always creates controversy. **Goodwill** represents the difference in the value of an established business and one that has not yet built a solid reputation for itself. A buyer is willing to pay extra only for those intangible assets that produce additional income. A seller, however, believes that goodwill is a measure of the hard work, sacrifice, and long hours invested in building the business, something for which he or she expects to be paid—often quite handsomely.

goodwill
the difference in the value of an established business and one that has not yet built a solid reputation for itself.

Potential buyers also must recognize the role that the seller's ego can play in the business valuation process. Norm Brodsky, who recently sold his successful document storage business to a larger company, explains,

> As a group, we [entrepreneurs] tend to have fairly large egos, which isn't entirely bad. You need one to make a business grow. . . . But our egos can get us into trouble when it comes to putting a dollar value on something we've created. We generally take the highest valuation we've heard for a company somewhat like ours—and multiply it.[21]

So how can the buyer and the seller arrive at a fair price? There are few hard-and-fast rules in establishing the value of a business, but the following guidelines are helpful:

- The wisest approach is to compute a company's value using several techniques and then to choose the one that makes the most sense.

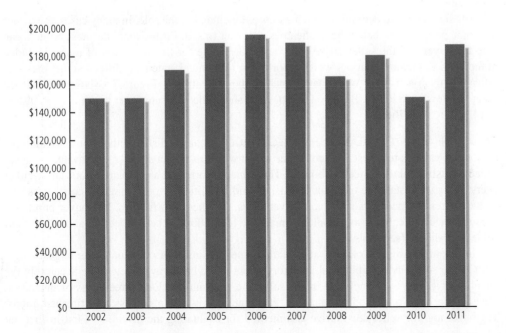

FIGURE 7.3

Median Sales Price of Private Companies

Source: Based on *Deal Review*, BizComps/BVR, Spring 2012, p. 2.

- The deal must be financially feasible for both parties. The seller must be satisfied with the price received for the business, but the buyer cannot pay an excessively high price that would require heavy borrowing that strains the company's cash flow from the outset.

- The potential buyer must have access to the business records.

- Valuations should be based on facts, not fiction.

- No surprise is the best surprise. Both parties should commit to dealing with one another honestly and in good faith.

The main reason that buyers purchase existing businesses is to get their future earning potential. The second most common reason is to obtain an established asset base; it is much easier to buy assets than to build them. Although some valuation methods take these goals into consideration, many business sellers and buyers simplify the process by relying on rules of thumb that use multiples of a company's net earnings or sales to estimate the value of a business. Although the multipliers vary by industry, most small companies sell for 2 to 12 times their earnings before interest and taxes (EBIT), with an average selling price of between 6 and 7 times EBIT. For instance, a study by Business Valuation Resources of 3,666 business sales over a recent three-year period shows that the median selling price of a lawn and garden service is 2.93 times EBIT, the median price of a grocery store is 6.00 times EBIT, and the median price of business consulting service is 11.39 times EBIT.[22] Factors that increase the value of the multiplier include proprietary products and patents; a strong, diversified customer base; above-average growth rate; a strong, balanced management team; and dominant market share. Factors that decrease the value of the multiplier include generic, "me-too" products; dependence on a single customer or a small group of customers for a significant portion of sales; reliance on the skills of a single manager (e.g., the founder); declining market share; and dependence on a single product for generating sales.[23]

The next section describes three basic techniques and several variations on them for determining the value of a hypothetical business, Bowler Avionics.

Balance Sheet Techniques: Net Worth = Assets − Liabilities

BALANCE SHEET TECHNIQUE The **balance sheet technique** is a commonly used methods of evaluating a business, although it is not highly recommended because it oversimplifies the valuation process. This method computes the company's net worth or owner's equity (net worth = total assets − total liabilities) and uses this figure as the value. The problem with this technique is that it fails to recognize reality: most small businesses have market values that exceed their reported book values.

balance sheet technique
a method of valuing a business on the basis of the value of the company's net worth (net worth = total assets − total liabilities).

The first step is to determine which assets are included in the sale. In many cases, the owner has some personal assets that he or she does not want to sell. Professional business brokers can help the buyer and the seller arrive at a reasonable value for the collection of assets included in the deal. Remember that net worth reported on a financial statement differs, sometimes significantly, from actual net worth determined in the marketplace. Figure 7.4 shows the balance sheet for Bowler Avionics. Based on this balance sheet, the company's net worth is $266,091 − $114,325 = $151,766.

VARIATION: ADJUSTED BALANCE SHEET TECHNIQUE A more realistic method for determining a company's value is to adjust the book value of net worth to reflect *actual* market value—the so-called **adjusted balance sheet technique**. The values reported on a company's books may either overstate or understate the true value of assets and liabilities. Typical assets in a business sale include notes and accounts receivable, inventories, supplies, and fixtures. If a buyer purchases accounts receivable, he or she should estimate the likelihood of their collection and adjust their value accordingly (see Table 7.1).

adjusted balance sheet technique
a method of valuing a business on the basis of the *market value* of the company's net worth (net worth = total assets − total liabilities).

In manufacturing, wholesale, and retail businesses, inventory is usually the largest single asset in the sale. Taking a physical inventory count is the best way to determine accurately the quantity of goods to be included in the sale. The sale may include three types of inventory, each having its own method of valuation: raw materials, work in process, and finished goods. The buyer and the seller must arrive at a method for evaluating the inventory. First-in-first-out

FIGURE 7.4

**Balance Sheets—
Bowler Avionics**

**Bowler Avionics
Balance Sheet
June 30, 20XX**

Assets

Current Assets:		
Cash	$ 11,655	
Accounts Receivable	15,876	
Inventory	56,523	
Supplies	8,574	
Prepaid Insurance	5,587	
Total Current Assets		$ 98,215
Fixed Assets:		
Land	$ 24,000	
Buildings	$ 141,000	
Less Accumulated Depreciation	51,500	89,500
Office Equipment	$ 12,760	
Less Accumulated Depreciation	7,159	5,601
Factory Equipment	$ 59,085	
Less Accumulated Depreciation	27,850	31,235
Trucks and Autos	$ 28,730	
Less Accumulated Depreciation	11,190	17,540
Total Fixed Assets		$ 167,876
Total Assets		$ 266,091

Liabilities

Current Liabilities:		
Accounts Payable	$ 19,497	
Mortgage Payable (current portion)	5,215	
Salaries Payable	3,671	
Note Payable	10,000	
Total Current Liabilities		$ 38,383
Long-Term Liabilities:		
Mortgage Payable	$ 54,542	
Note Payable	21,400	
Total Long-Term Liabilities		$ 75,942
Total Liabilities		$ 114,325

Owners' Equity

Owners' Equity		$ 151,766
Total Liabilities and Owners' Equity		$ 266,091

(FIFO), last-in-first-out (LIFO), and average costing are three frequently used techniques, but the most common methods use the cost of last purchase and the replacement value of the inventory. Before accepting any inventory value, the buyer should evaluate the condition of the goods. One young couple purchased a lumberyard without sufficiently examining the inventory. After completing the sale, they discovered that most of the lumber in a warehouse that they had neglected to inspect was warped and was of little value as building material. The bargain price they paid for the business turned out not to be the good deal they had expected.

To avoid problems, some buyers insist on having a knowledgeable representative on an inventory team to count the inventory and check its condition. Nearly every sale involves merchandise that cannot be sold, but by taking this precaution, a buyer minimizes the chance of being stuck with worthless inventory. Fixed assets transferred in a sale include land, buildings, equipment, and fixtures. Business owners frequently carry real estate and buildings at values well below their actual market value. Equipment and fixtures, depending on their condition and usefulness, may increase or decrease the true value of the business. Appraisals of these assets on insurance policies are helpful guidelines for establishing market value. In addition, business brokers can be useful in determining the current market value of fixed assets. Some brokers use an estimate of what it would cost to replace a company's physical assets (less a reasonable allowance for depreciation) to determine their value. For Bowler Avionics, the adjusted net worth is $274,638 − $114,325 = $160,313 (see the adjusted balance sheet in Figure 7.5), indicating that some of the entries in its books did not accurately reflect true market value.

FIGURE 7.5

Balance Sheet—Bowler Avionics, Adjusted to Reflect Market Value

Bowler Avionics
Adjusted Balance Sheet
June 30, 20XX

Assets

Current Assets:			
Cash		$ 11,655	
Accounts Receivable		10,051	
Inventory		39,261	
Supplies		7,492	
Prepaid Insurance		5,587	
Total Current Assets			$ 74,046
Fixed Assets:			
Land		$ 36,900	
Buildings	$ 177,000		
Less Accumulated Depreciation	51,500	125,500	
Office Equipment	$ 11,645		
Less Accumulated Depreciation	7,159	4,486	
Factory Equipment	$ 50,196		
Less Accumulated Depreciation	27,850	22,346	
Trucks and Autos	$ 22,550		
Less Accumulated Depreciation	11,190	11,360	
Total Fixed Assets			$ 200,592
Total Assets			$ 274,638

Liabilities

Current Liabilities:			
Accounts Payable		$ 19,497	
Mortgage Payable (current portion)		5,215	
Salaries Payable		3,671	
Note Payable		10,000	
Total Current Liabilities			$ 38,383
Long-Term Liabilities:			
Mortgage Payable		$ 54,542	
Note Payable		21,400	
Total Long-Term Liabilities			$ 75,942
Total Liabilities			$ 114,325

Owners' Equity

Owners' Equity			$ 160,313
Total Liabilities and Owners' Equity			$ 274,638

Business valuations based on balance sheet methods suffer one major drawback: they do not consider the future earning potential of the business. These techniques value assets at current prices and do not consider them as tools for creating future earnings. The next method for computing the value of a business is based on its expected future earnings.

Earnings Approach

The buyer of an existing business is essentially purchasing its future income. The **earnings approach** focuses on the future income potential of a business and assumes that a company's value depends on its ability to generate consistent earnings over time. In other words, the earnings approach recognizes that assets derive their *real* value from the income they produce in the future. There are three variations of the earnings approach.

VARIATION 1: EXCESS EARNINGS METHOD This method combines both the value of a business's existing assets (minus its liabilities) and an estimate of its future earnings potential to determine its selling price. One advantage of this technique is that it offers an estimate of goodwill. Goodwill is an intangible asset that often creates problems in a business sale. In fact, the most common method of valuing a business is to compute its tangible net worth and then to add an often arbitrary adjustment for goodwill. In essence, goodwill is the difference between an established, successful business and one that has yet to prove itself. It is based on a company's reputation and its ability to attract customers. A buyer should not accept blindly the seller's arbitrary adjustment for goodwill because it is likely to be inflated. The *real* value of a company's goodwill lies in its financial value to the buyer, not in its emotional value to the seller.

The excess earnings method provides a consistent and realistic approach for determining the value of goodwill. It measures goodwill by the amount of profit that a business earns above that of the average firm in the same industry (its "extra earning power"). It also assumes that the owner is entitled to a reasonable return on the company's adjusted tangible net worth.

Step 1. *Compute adjusted tangible net worth.* Using the adjusted balance sheet method of valuation, the buyer should compute the company's adjusted tangible net worth. Total tangible assets (adjusted for market value) minus total liabilities yields adjusted tangible net worth. In the Bowler Avionics example, adjusted tangible net worth is $274,638 − $114,325 = $160,313 (see Figure 7.5).

Step 2. *Calculate the opportunity costs of investing in the business.* Opportunity cost represents the cost of forgoing a choice. If a buyer chooses to purchase the assets of a business, he or she cannot invest that money elsewhere. Therefore, the opportunity cost of the purchase would be the amount that the buyer could earn by investing the same amount *in a similar risk investment.*

There are three components in the rate of return used to value a business: (1) the basic, risk-free return; (2) an inflation premium; and (3) the risk allowance for investing in the particular business. The basic, risk-free return and the inflation premium are reflected in investments such as U.S. Treasury bonds. To determine the appropriate rate of return for investing in a business, a buyer must add to this base rate a factor reflecting the risk of purchasing the company. The greater the risk, the higher will be the rate of return. A normal-risk business typically translates into a rate of return in the 20 to 25 percent range. Because Bowler Avionics is a normal-risk business, we will use a rate of return of 22 percent, which means that the opportunity cost of an investment in it is $160,313 × 22% = $35,269.

The second part of the buyer's opportunity cost is the salary that he or she could earn working for someone else. For the Bowler Avionics example, if the buyer purchases the business, he or she must forgo a modest $35,000 salary that he or she could earn working elsewhere. Adding these amounts together yields a total opportunity cost of $70,269.

Step 3. *Project net earnings.* The buyer must estimate the company's net earnings for the upcoming year before subtracting the owner's salary. Averages can

earnings approach
a method of valuing a business that recognizes that a buyer is purchasing the future income (earnings) potential of a business.

opportunity cost
the cost of the next best alternative choice; the cost of giving up one alternative to get another.

be misleading; therefore, the buyer must be sure to investigate the trend of net earnings. Have they risen steadily over the last five years, dropped significantly, remained relatively constant, or fluctuated wildly? As you learned earlier in this chapter, past income statements provide useful guidelines for estimating earnings. However, business sellers often "recast" their companies' earnings to create a more realistic picture of them because their goal is to minimize their tax bills by keeping earnings low. One experienced business broker suggests using the following process for recasting a small company's earnings:[24]

- Add back any direct payments to the owner(s), including salary and bonuses.
- Add a reasonable salary for a manager to take the owner's place.
- Add all other expenses the company pays for the owner(s), such as auto leases, insurance, memberships, retirement benefits, profit sharing, and others.
- Add the cost of any leases the company has with the owner or his or her family members.
- Add any extraordinary expenses, such as the costs of hiring a business broker to sell the company, an accounting firm to audit the company's financial statements, and others.

In the Bowler Avionics example, the prospective buyer and his accountant project net earnings for the upcoming year to be $75,000.

Step 4. *Compute extra earning power.* A company's extra earning power is the difference between forecasted earnings (step 3) and total opportunity costs (step 2). Many small businesses that are for sale do not have extra earning power (i.e., excess earnings), and they show marginal or no profits. The extra earning power of Bowler Avionics is $75,000 - $70,269 = $4,731.

Step 5. *Estimate the value of intangibles.* The owner can use the business's extra earning power to estimate the value of its intangible assets—that is, its goodwill. Multiplying the extra earning power by a years-of-profit figure yields an estimate of the intangible assets' value. The years-of-profit figure for a normal-risk business ranges from three to four. A very high risk business may have a years-of-profit figure of just one, whereas a well-established firm might warrant a years-of-profit figure of seven.

Rating the company on a scale of 1 (low) to 7 (high) on the following factors allows an entrepreneur to calculate a reasonable years-of-profit figure to use to estimate the value of the intangibles:[25]

	Score						
Factor	1	2	3	4	5	6	7
1. Risk	More risky						Less risky
2. Degree of competition	Intense competition						Few competitors
3. Industry attractiveness	Fading						Attractive
4. Barriers to entry	Low						High
5. Growth potential	Low						High
6. Owner's reason for selling	Poor performance						Retiring
7. Age of business	Young						10+ years old
8. Current owner's tenure	Short						10+ years
9. Profitability	Below average						Above average
10. Location	Problematic						Desirable
11. Customer base	Limited and shrinking						Diverse and growing
12. Image and reputation	Poor						Stellar

To calculate the years-of-profit figure, the entrepreneur adds the score for each factor and divides by the number of factors (12). For Bowler Avionics, the scores are as follows:

Risk	4
Degree of competition	3
Industry attractiveness	4
Barriers to entry	3
Growth potential	4
Owner's reason for selling	6
Age of business	6
Owner's tenure	6
Profitability	4
Location	4
Customer base	4
Image and reputation	5
Total	53

Thus, for Bowler Avionics, the years of profit figure is 53 ÷ 12 = 4.4. Therefore, the estimated value of company's intangible assets is $4,731 × 4.4 = $20,896.

Step 6. *Determine the value of the business.* To determine the value of the business, the buyer simply adds together the adjusted tangible net worth (step 1) and the value of the intangibles (step 5). Using this method, we find that the value of Bowler Avionics is $160,313 + $20,896 = $181,209.

The buyer and the seller should consider the tax implications of including in the purchase the value of goodwill and the value of a covenant not to compete. Because the *buyer* can amortize both the cost of goodwill and a restrictive covenant over 15 years, the tax treatment of either would be the same for him or her. However, the *seller* would prefer to have the amount of the purchase price in excess of the value of the assets allocated to goodwill, which is a capital asset. The gain on the capital asset would be taxed at lower capital gains rates (which Congress raised from 15 to 20 percent in 2013). If that same amount were allocated to a restrictive covenant (which is negotiated with the seller personally, not with the business), the seller must treat it as ordinary income, which would be taxed at regular rates that currently are higher than the capital gains rates.

VARIATION 2: CAPITALIZED EARNINGS APPROACH A variation of the earnings approach capitalizes expected net earnings to determine the value of a business. As you learned earlier in this chapter, buyers should prepare their own projected income statements and should ask the seller to prepare them also. Many appraisers use a five-year weighted average of past sales (with the greatest weights assigned to the most recent years) to estimate sales for the upcoming year.

Once again, a buyer must evaluate the risk of purchasing the business to determine the appropriate rate of return on the investment. The greater the perceived risk, the higher the return that the buyer requires. Risk determination is always somewhat subjective, but it is necessary for proper evaluation.

The **capitalized earnings approach** divides estimated net earnings (*after* subtracting the owner's reasonable salary) by the rate of return that reflects the risk level. For Bowler Avionics, the capitalized value (assuming a reasonable salary of $35,000) is

$$\frac{\text{Net earnings (after deducting owner's salary)}}{\text{Rate of return}} = \frac{\$75,000 - \$35,000}{22\%} = \$181,818$$

capitalized earnings approach
a method of valuing a business that divides estimated earnings by the rate of return the buyer could earn on a similar risk investment.

Companies with lower risk factors are more valuable (a 10 percent rate of return would yield a value of $400,000 for Bowler Avionics) than are those with higher risk factors (a 50 percent rate of return would yield a value of $80,000). Most normal-risk businesses use a rate-of-return factor ranging from 20 to 25 percent. The lowest risk factor that most buyers are willing to accept for a business is around 15 percent.

VARIATION 3: DISCOUNTED FUTURE EARNINGS APPROACH This variation of the earnings approach assumes that a dollar earned in the future is worth less than that same dollar today. Therefore, using this approach, the buyer estimates the company's net income for several years into the future and then discounts these future earnings back to their present value. The resulting present value is an estimate of the company's worth because it reflects the company's future earning potential stated in today's dollars.

The reduced value of future dollars represents the cost of the buyers' giving up the opportunity to earn a reasonable rate of return by receiving income in the future instead of today, a concept known as the time value of money. To illustrate the importance of the time value of money, consider two $1 million sweepstake winners. Rob wins $1 million in a sweepstakes, but he receives it in $50,000 installments over 20 years. If Rob invested every installment at 6 percent interest, he would have accumulated $1,839,280 at the end of 20 years. Lisa wins $1 million in another sweepstakes, but she collects her winnings in one lump sum. If Lisa invested her $1 million today at 6 percent, she would have accumulated $3,207,135 at the end of 20 years. The difference in their wealth is the result of the time value of money.

discounted future earnings approach
a method of valuing a business that forecasts a company's earnings several years into the future and then discounts them back to their present value.

DISCOUNTED FUTURE EARNINGS APPROACH The **discounted future earnings approach** includes five steps:

Step 1. *Project future earnings for five years into the future.* One way is to assume that earnings will grow by a constant amount over the next five years. Perhaps a better method is to develop three forecasts—an optimistic, a pessimistic, and a most likely—for each year and then find a weighted average using the following formula, which weights the most likely forecast four times as heavily as either the optimistic or pessimistic forecasts:

$$(\text{Optimistic earnings forecast for year } i + \text{Most likely earnings} \\ \text{forecast for year } i \times 4 + \text{Pessimistic earnings forecast for year } i) \div 6$$

For Bowler Avionics, the buyer's forecasts are as follows:

Year	Pessimistic	Most Likely	Optimistic	Weighted Average
XXX1	62,000	74,000	82,000	73,333
XXX2	68,000	80,000	88,000	79,333
XXX3	75,000	88,000	95,000	87,000
XXX4	82,000	96,000	102,000	94,667
XXX5	90,000	105,000	110,000	103,333

Buyers must remember that the farther into the future they forecast, the less reliable their estimates will be.

Step 2. *Discount these future earnings at the appropriate present value rate.* The rate that the buyer selects should reflect the rate he or she could earn on a similar risk investment. Because Bowler Avionics is a normal-risk business, the buyer chooses a present value rate of 22 percent.

Year	Income Forecast (Weighted Average)	Present Value Factor (at 22%)*	Net Present Value
XXX1	73,333	0.8197	60,109
XXX2	79,333	0.6719	53,301
XXX3	87,000	0.5507	47,912
XXX4	94,667	0.4514	42,732
XXX5	103,333	0.3700	38,233
		Total	242,287

*The appropriate present value factor can be found by looking in published present value tables, by using modern calculators or computers, or by solving this formula:

$$\text{Present value factor} = \frac{1}{(1 + k)^t}$$

where k = rate of return
t = year ($t = 1, 2, 3 \ldots n$)

Step 3. *Estimate the income stream beyond five years.* One technique suggests multiplying the fifth-year income by 1 ÷ rate of return. For Bowler Avionics, the estimate is

$$\text{Income beyond year 5 } \$103,333 \times \frac{1}{25\%} = \$469,697$$

Step 4. *Discount the income estimate beyond five years using the present value factor for the sixth year.* For Bowler Avionics,

$$\text{Present value of income beyond year 5} = \$469,697 \times 0.3033 = \$142,449$$

Step 5. *Compute the total value of the business.* Add the present value of the company's estimated earnings for years 1 through 5 (step 2) and the present value of its earnings from year 6 on (step 4):

$$\text{Total value} = \$242,287 + \$142,449 = \$384,736$$

The primary advantage of this technique is that it evaluates a business solely on its future earning potential, but its reliability depends on making forecasts of future earnings and on choosing a realistic present value rate. In other words, a company's present value is tied to its future performance, which is not always easy to project. The discounted cash flow technique is especially well suited for valuing service businesses (whose asset bases are often very thin) and for companies experiencing high growth rates.

Market Approach

The **market approach** (or price/earnings approach) uses the price/earnings (P/E) ratios of similar businesses listed on a stock exchange to establish the value of a company. A buyer must use businesses in the same industry whose stocks are publicly traded to get a meaningful comparison. A company's P/E ratio is the price of one share of its common stock in the market divided by its earnings per share (after deducting preferred stock dividends). To get a representative P/E ratio, a buyer should average the P/Es of as many similar businesses as possible. However, because a private company's stock lacks the liquidity of a public company's stock, its estimated P/E ratio typically is discounted by 35 to 75 percent.

To compute the company's value, the buyer multiplies the average P/E ratio by the private company's estimated earnings. For example, suppose that the buyer found four companies that are comparable to Bowler Avionics but whose stock is publicly traded. Their P/E ratios are the following:

market approach
a method of valuing a business that uses the price/earnings (P/E) ratio of similar, publicly held companies to determine value.

Company 1	4.5
Company 2	5.3
Company 3	5.0
Company 4	4.8
Average P/E ratio	4.90

Applying a 40 percent "private company" discount to the average public company P/E ratio produces an estimated private company P/E ratio of 2.94 (4.90 × 40%). Therefore, the estimated value of Bowler Avionics using this method is $220,500:

$$\text{Value} = \text{Private company estimated P/E ratio} \times \text{Estimated net earnings}$$
$$= 2.94 \times \$75,000 = \$220,500$$

The biggest advantage of the market approach is its simplicity. However, this method does have several disadvantages, including the following:

Necessary comparisons between publicly traded and privately owned companies. Because the stock of privately owned companies is not as liquid as that of publicly held companies, the P/E ratio used is often subjective and lower than that of publicly held companies.

Unrepresentative earnings estimates. A private company's net earnings may not realistically reflect its true earning potential. To minimize taxes, owners usually attempt to keep earnings low and rely on benefits and bonuses to make up the difference.

Finding similar companies for comparison. Often, it is extremely difficult for a buyer to find comparable publicly held companies when estimating the appropriate P/E ratio.

Applying the after-tax earnings of a private company to determine its value. If a prospective buyer is using an after-tax P/E ratio from a public company, he or she also must use the after-tax earnings from the private company.

Despite its drawbacks, the market approach is useful as a general guideline to establishing a company's value.

Which of these methods is best for determining the value of a small business? Simply stated, there is no single best method. Valuing a business is partly an art and partly a science. Use of these techniques will yield a range of values. Buyers should look for values that cluster together and then use their best judgment to determine a reasonable offering price. For Bowler Avionics, a value of $180,000 to $220,000 appears to be reasonable, but if the future earnings forecasts are reliable, the business is worth as much as $385,000.

 You Be the Consultant

The Saga of Selling My Business: Part 3

As Norm Brodsky was preparing for the April 5 closing on the sale of his company CitiStorage, a deal he had been negotiating for the last year, a snag popped up and threatened to undo the entire project. Frank, a member of board of directors of Nova Records Management, the company into which CitiStorage would be folded, wanted to cut the sale price by $2.5 million based on a complex calculation that he had developed concerning the land leases that the CitiStorage held. Brodsky was furious. "Two-and-a-half-million dollars is a relatively small amount, less than 3 percent of the total deal," he says. "We had an understanding, however, that the price was set and we weren't going to reopen the issue." Brodsky told Frank that he refused to negotiate because the price had already been established and that the four other members of Nova's board were in favor of closing the deal at that price. Then Frank dropped a bomb on the deal: "Those votes are meaningless. I have veto power."

Brodsky was stunned and immediately called Debbas. "You might have told me before now. I've been negotiating with the wrong guy."

A few telephone calls to other entrepreneurs who had sold their companies to Nova revealed that this was a common tactic that Frank used to buy companies at reduced prices. "He'd drag out the negotiations and then come up with new demands at the end when the other party had committed so much time and money to the sale that it had no choice but to go along," says Brodsky. "I had a choice. I could give in to Frank's demands, or I could call off the sale." For Brodsky, it boiled down to trust, and apparently he could not trust Nova.

Brodsky insisted that Frank give up his veto power on the deal or there would be no deal. "This deal is off as long as he insists on retaining his veto," he told Debbas.

Brodsky blamed himself. "I hadn't known about [Frank's veto power], but I should have," he says. I had clearly failed in my due diligence. I would have known if I had asked enough questions in the beginning. Shame on me for not doing it." Brodsky called meetings, first with his managers and then with all of his employees, to tell them that the sale of CitiStorage had fallen through. None of them was shocked or upset. It was April 5, the target date for closing the deal.

You Be the Consultant (continued)

Word spread quickly across the industry that CitiStorage's deal with Nova had failed, and almost immediately, Brodsky began receiving calls from others interested in buying the company. "We began to feel besieged," he says, as the trickle of calls turned into a torrent. Once again, Brodsky and his partner were faced with a decision: what to do with the company. They decided that it was time to sell CitiStorage and that two factors were paramount in any deal: CitiStorage employees and company culture would not be at risk, and they would work only with private equity firms that had the resources to finance a deal themselves.

Brodsky and his partner locked themselves in a room and came up with five criteria for screening potential buyers, one of whom was Allied Capital, a private equity company founded in 1958 from which CitiStorage had received financing six times over the last 35 years. "Over that time, we had formed strong bonds with Allied Capital's people," says Brodsky. When they ranked the top six prospects on the five criteria, Allied capital came out on top. "Why didn't we think to approach Allied much sooner?" Brodsky wondered.

Brodsky and Allied Capital representatives signed a letter of intent, and Allied began its due diligence process. The process moved much faster than it had during negotiations with Nova. "At every step, I couldn't help noticing the enormous difference between negotiating with Allied and negotiating with Nova," says Brodsky. "I can sum up that difference in one word: trust. With Allied, we had it to begin with, and it got stronger as we went along. With Nova, there had never been any trust, and any hints that it might have been developing were an illusion."

On December 21, after four months of due diligence and negotiations, Brodsky signed a deal to sell CitiStorage to Allied Capital that included Brodsky's staying on for a time with the company as a consultant. "Allied Capital clearly wanted us to wind up with a deal we felt good about," he says. "Looking back, we could thank our lucky stars that the Nova deal hadn't happened. My fiasco wasn't such a fiasco after all. It opened my eyes to possibilities I had never considered."

Brodsky admits that selling his company has required him to make some big adjustments, something he is still in the process of doing. "On December 21, I no longer had a job at CitiStorage," he says. "My wife, Elaine, and I are still shareholders. I still have my office. I'm still getting paid, but the money is a consulting fee, not a salary. My work for CitiStorage doesn't get my juices flowing the way starting a business does. There's a bit of a hole in my life at the moment, and I don't know yet how I'm going to fill it. While I loved chasing the rainbow, I have to say that I have mixed feelings about having caught it."

1. How important is the ability to trust the other party in a business sale? Why?

2. One negotiating expert advises, "Never try to extract the last drop of blood in a negotiation. Do not leave the other person feeling as if they have been cheated." Did Nova violate this negotiating principle? If so, what repercussions did doing so have on the final deal?

3. What emotional issues do entrepreneurs face after they sell the companies they founded? What advice would you give Brodsky about filling the hole in his life after selling his company?

Source: Adapted from Norm Brodsky, "The Offer, Part Eight," *Inc.*, June 2007, pp. 61–64; Norm Brodsky, "The Offer: Part Nine," *Inc.*, July 2007, pp. 59–61; Norm Brodsky, "The Offer, Part Ten," *Inc.*, April 2008, pp. 65–68; and Norm Brodsky, "The Offer: Part Eleven," *Inc.*, May 2008, pp. 73–74.

Understanding the Seller's Side

LO5
Understand the seller's side of the buyout decision and how to structure the deal.

For entrepreneurs, few events are more anticipated—and more emotional—than selling their businesses. Selling their companies often produces vast personal wealth and a completely new lifestyle, and this newly gained wealth offers freedom and the opportunity to catch up on all the things the owners missed out on while building their businesses. Yet many entrepreneurs who sell out experience a tremendous void in their lives, a "postsale separation anxiety" that results from having their lives revolve around the businesses they created and nurtured for so many years. Will Schroter, a serial entrepreneur and CEO of Go Big Network, explains:

> Selling your company is a lot like selling your kid. This is something that you've created, nurtured since inception and watched grow up into something beautiful. Now someone else has come along and taken that little baby away from you, and they're not going to give it back. The hardest thing about selling your company is realizing that it's not yours. The big decisions are ultimately made by someone else.[26]

For many business owners, their companies were the focal point of their lives and were an essential part of their identities. When they sell their companies, a primary concern for many entrepreneurs is preserving the reputation, culture, and principles on which they built and operated the company. Will the new owner display the same values in managing the business? Can the company founder cope with the inevitable changes the new owner will make to the business? Some entrepreneurs regret their decision to sell their companies and become "boomerang" business owners, buying back their companies.

ENTREPRENEURIAL PROFILE: Garret Camp and Geoff Smith: StumbleUpon While writing their theses on information discovery as students at the University of Calgary, Garret Camp and Geoff Smith developed the idea for a discovery engine Web site that allows users to find and share interesting Web sites that they otherwise would have missed. Camp and Smith operated the business, StumbleUpon, part-time while they worked on their graduate degrees. When Camp graduated in 2006, he moved to San Francisco, where he raised $1.2 million in capital to fuel the company's growth from a "who's who" group of Silicon Valley investors. Within a year, Camp and Smith sold StumbleUpon to eBay for $75 million, but the promising young company quickly began to struggle under the mantle of corporate hierarchy. Less than two years later, Camp assembled a team of investors to buy back the company he had founded, paying a reported $29 million for it. Once again the company's CEO, Camp quickly tripled StumbleUpon's revenues and increased its user base to more than 15 million.[27] ■

Some business brokers differentiate between *financial buyers* and *strategic buyers*. Financial buyers, usually individuals, see buying a business as a way to generate income for themselves and their families. They look for businesses in which they can make an initial down payment and finance the remaining 50 to 80 percent of the purchase price. Because they often borrow the money to purchase a business, their primary concern is the company's ability to generate profits and positive cash flow in the future. Strategic buyers, often other businesses or even competitors, view buying a company as part of a larger picture, a piece in a strategic puzzle that gives them an advantage, such as access to a new, fast-growing market; a unique product; or a new technological innovation. They are looking for companies that fit strategically with their existing business. "Financial buyers typically will pay a lower price because they have a 'fire sale' mentality," says Andy Agrawal, a partner in an investment banking firm. "You need to find strategic buyers and paint a picture for them," he advises. "Show the strategic buyer how one plus one equals three."[28]

ENTREPRENEURIAL PROFILE: Catherine, David, and Geoff Cook: myYearbook In 2005, Catherine Cook, a 15-year-old freshman at Montgomery High School in Skillman, New Jersey, and her 16-year-old brother David were looking through their school's printed yearbook and thought that an online yearbook that allowed young people to meet and interact with others would be much more useful. Over dinner one evening, they told their older brother, Geoff, who had just graduated from Harvard and sold a company that he had founded, about their idea. Geoff saw the potential and began helping his siblings launch myYearbook, which became one of the most trafficked social networking sites. The Cooks raised $17 million in financing to fuel their company's growth, attracted 20 million users, and generated 1.2 billion monthly page views and $24 million in annual revenue. Six years after starting myYearbook, the Cooks sold it to a strategic buyer, social network company Quepasa, which changed the company's name to MeetMe, for $100 million.[29] ■

Selling a business involves developing a plan that maximizes the value of the business. Before selling his or her business, an entrepreneur must ask himself or herself some important questions: Do you want to walk away from the business completely, or do you plan to stay on after the sale? If you decide to stay on, how involved do you want to be in running the company? How much can you realistically expect to get for the business? Is this amount of money sufficient to maintain your desired lifestyle? Rather than sell the business to an outsider, should you be transferring ownership to your children or to your employees? Who are the professionals— business brokers, accountants, attorneys, and tax advisers—you will need to help you close the sale successfully? How do you expect the buyer to pay for the company? Are you willing to finance at least some of the purchase price? Sellers who have answered these fundamental questions are prepared to move forward with the sale of their companies.

Structuring the Deal

Next to picking the right buyer, planning the structure of the deal is one of the most important decisions a seller can make. Entrepreneurs who sell their companies without considering the tax implications of the deal may wind up paying the Internal Revenue Service as much as 70 percent of the proceeds in the form of capital gains and other taxes! A skilled tax adviser or financial planner can help business sellers to legally minimize the bite that various taxes take out of the proceeds of the sale. When it comes to exit strategies, entrepreneurs have the following options available to them.

Exit Strategies

STRAIGHT BUSINESS SALE A straight business sale often is best for those entrepreneurs who want to step down and turn over the reins of the company to someone else right away.

Andrea Artz/laif/Redux

ENTREPRENEURIAL PROFILE: Alyssa Torey: Magnolia Bakery In 1996, Alyssa Torey cofounded the Magnolia Bakery with Jennifer Appel (who left the company in 2000 to open the Buttercup Bake Shop) in New York's West Village, and the bakery soon became famous for its homemade cupcakes. After being featured on the popular television shows *Sex and the City* and *Saturday Night Live*, Magnolia Bakery became a hot spot not only for New Yorkers but also for tourists. In 2007, Torey sold the bakery to friend Steven Abrams, a restaurateur and construction company owner, for a fraction of its value so that she could spend time writing more cookbooks. "She could have sold it for 10 times what I gave her," Abrams says incredulously.[30] ∎

A study of small business sales in 60 categories found that 94 percent were asset sales; the remaining 6 percent involved the sale of stock. About 22 percent were for cash, and 75 percent included a down payment with a note carried by the seller. The remaining 3 percent relied on a note from the seller with no down payment. When the deal included a down payment, it averaged 33 percent of the purchase price. Only 40 percent of the business sales studied included covenants not to compete. Although cash only deals are not viable for most business buyers, they typically produce a discount of 10 to 15 percent of the asking price.[31] Typically, a deal is structured so that the buyer makes a down payment to the seller, who then finances a note for the balance. The buyer makes regular principal and interest payments over time—perhaps with a larger balloon payment at the end—until the note is paid off.

Although selling a business outright is often the safest exit path for an entrepreneur, it is usually the most expensive. Sellers who want cash and take the money up front may face a significant tax burden. They must pay a capital gains tax on the sale price less their investments in the company. Nor is a straight sale an attractive exit strategy for those who want to stay on with the company or for those who want to surrender control of the company gradually rather than all at once.

SALE OF A CONTROLLING INTEREST Some business owners sell a majority interest in their companies to investors, competitors, suppliers, or large companies; retain a portion of the ownership themselves; and agree to stay on after the sale as managers or consultants. This strategy gives buyers more confidence in the acquisition if they know the current owner is willing to stay involved in managing the company that he or she founded. Increasing a buyer's confidence with a management agreement is important because 65 percent of all mergers and acquisitions fail.[32] Mitchell Schlimer, founder of the Let's Talk Business Network, a support community for entrepreneurs, says that about 90 percent of small business owners who sell their companies to larger businesses remain with the acquiring company—at least for a little while. "They often don't stay long," says Schlimer, "because entrepreneurs are not good soldiers."[33]

Although this exit strategy sounds like the ideal solution for entrepreneurs who are seeking more free time without stepping away entirely from the companies they built, it does not always prove to be. Accustomed to being in control, making the key decisions, and calling all the shots, entrepreneurs who sell out with an agreement to stay on often have great difficulty relinquishing control of the company to the new owner, especially when the new owner takes the company in a new direction. The situation is particularly grueling when the new owner makes decisions that jeopardize the company's future, forcing the founder to stand by and watch the business spiral slowly downward.

ENTREPRENEURIAL PROFILE: Mike and Anthony Medico: E+M Advertising In 2006, Mike Medico and his son, Anthony, sold the company, E+M Advertising, that Mike had started in 1980 in New York City to a larger company that focused on digital display ads for $4 million in cash and stock. The plan was for E+M to retain its corporate structure and operate as a unit of the larger company. Both men agreed to stay on in executive positions, and E+M continued to grow under their leadership. When the acquiring company ran into a cash crisis and was teetering on the verge of bankruptcy, however, the Medicos decided to buy back their business. They were able to purchase E+M for less than $1 million but in a risky move agreed to take on $8 million of the company's debt. The Medicos closed a secondary office in Los Angeles, reduced staff, and cut expenses where they could. Within 18 months, the company, now called E+M Media Driven Marketing, was debt free and profitable. "Buying back our company gave us the opportunity to reinvent ourselves," says Anthony.[34] ∎

earn-out

an exit strategy in which an entrepreneur can increase his or her payout by staying on and making sure that the company hits specific performance targets.

A variation of this strategy is an **earn-out**, in which an entrepreneur can increase his or her payout by staying on and making sure that the company hits specific performance targets usually cast over several years. Properly structured, earn-outs give sellers an incentive to make sure their companies continue to be successful and prevent buyers from overpaying for a business. ·

ENTREPRENEURIAL PROFILE: Lane Merrifield, Dave Krysko, and Lance Priebe: Club Penguin When Lane Merrifield, Dave Krysko, and Lance Priebe, cofounders of Club Penguin, a virtual world aimed at children, sold the company to the Walt Disney Company, the three entrepreneurs became Disney executives and continued to manage the business. The deal included a $350 million up-front payment and an earn-out of another $350 million if the company achieved earnings targets over three years. Although Club Penguin did increase Disney's revenues, it missed the three-year earn-out target.[35] ■

FORM A FAMILY LIMITED PARTNERSHIP Entrepreneurs also can transfer their businesses to their children but still maintain control over them by forming a family limited partnership. The entrepreneur takes the role of the general partner, and the children become limited partners in the business. The general partner keeps just 1 percent of the company, but the partnership agreement gives him or her total control over the business. The children own 99 percent of the company but have little or no say over how to run the business. Until the founder decides to step down and turn over the reins of the company to the next generation, he or she continues to run the business and, with proper planning, can set up significant tax savings when the ultimate transfer of power takes place.

RESTRUCTURE THE COMPANY Another way for business owners to cash out gradually is to replace the existing corporation with a new one formed with other investors. The owner essentially is performing a leveraged buyout of his or her own company. For example, assume that you own a company worth $15 million. You form a new corporation with $12 million borrowed from a bank and $3 million in equity: $1.5 million of your own equity and $1.5 million in equity from an investor who wants you to stay on with the business. The new company buys your company for $15 million. You net $13.5 in cash ($15 million minus your $1.5 million equity investment) and still own 50 percent of the new leveraged business (see Figure 7.6).[36]

SELL TO AN INTERNATIONAL BUYER In an increasingly global marketplace, small U.S. businesses have become attractive buyout targets for foreign companies. Companies from Canada and Great Britain lead the world in acquiring U.S. companies, but companies in China and India are moving up the list as they look for inexpensive ways to enter U.S. markets. It is not unusual in today's global economy to find companies based in other countries with substantial financial resources that are looking to acquire small businesses in the United States. In many instances, foreign companies buy U.S.-based companies to gain access to a lucrative, growing market. They look for a team of capable managers whom they typically retain for a given time period. They also want companies that are profitable, stable, and growing. Selling to foreign buyers can have disadvantages, however. They typically purchase 100 percent of a company, thereby making the founder merely an employee. Relationships with foreign owners also can be difficult to manage because of cultural and philosophical differences.

FIGURE 7.6

Restructuring a Business for Sale

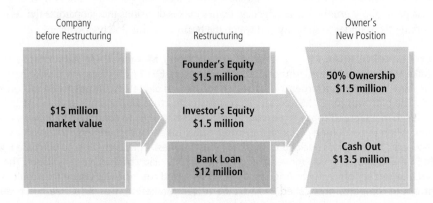

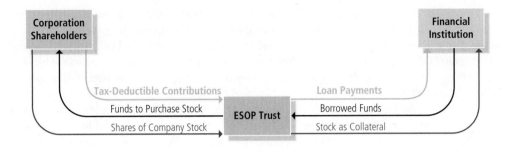

FIGURE 7.7

A Typical Employee Stock Ownership Plan (ESOP)

Source: From "Sharing Ownership with Employees" by Corey Rosen, from *Small Business Reports*, December 1990. Copyright © 1990 by Corey Rosen, National Center for Employee Ownership. Reprinted with permission.

ESTABLISH AN EMPLOYEE STOCK OWNERSHIP PLAN Some owners who want to sell their businesses but keep them intact cash out by selling to their employees through an **employee stock ownership plan (ESOP)**. An ESOP is a form of employee benefit plan in which a trust that is created for employees purchases their employer's stock. Here's how an ESOP works. The company transfers shares of its stock to the ESOP trust, and the trust uses the stock as collateral to borrow enough money to purchase the shares from the company. The company guarantees payment of the loan principal and interest and makes tax-deductible contributions to the trust to repay the loan (see Figure 7.7). As the company repays the loan, it distributes the stock to employees' accounts using a predetermined formula. Because of their flexibility, ESOPs permit owners to transfer all or part of a company to employees as gradually or as quickly as they want.

To use an ESOP successfully, a small business should have annual sales of at least $1 million, be profitable (with pretax profits exceeding $100,000), and have a payroll of at least $500,000 a year. Generally, companies with fewer than 15 to 20 employees do not find ESOPs beneficial because the cost to set up an ESOP is $50,000 to $60,000. The ESOP Association, an industry trade association, reports that the typical annual sales for its members range from $20 million to $50 million.[37] For companies that prepare properly, ESOPs offer significant financial and managerial benefits. Owners get tax benefits as well as great flexibility in determining their retirement schedules. An ESOP allows all parties involved to benefit, and the transfer of ownership can be timed to meet the entrepreneur's personal and financial goals.

employee stock ownership plan (ESOP)
an employee benefit plan in which a trust created for employees purchases stock in their employers' company.

ENTREPRENEURIAL PROFILE: Bob and Charlee Moore and John Wagner: Bob's Red Mill Natural Foods In 1978, long before people knew about the health benefits of whole-grain products, Bob Moore and his wife, Charlee, salvaged an abandoned 125-year-old flour mill and launched Bob's Red Mill Natural Foods, a company in Portland, Oregon, that produces a variety of products, including grain and flour to hot cereal and baking mixes. In 1993, Moore brought in John Wagner as chief financial officer and co-owner, and the two soon launched a profit-sharing plan for their employees. As Moore passed the normal retirement age, employees began to wonder about the future, especially if Moore and Wagner decided to sell the company to a larger business. Moore and Wagner decided not to sell Bob's Red Mill Natural Foods to a large company; instead, they decided to transfer ownership of the company through the ESOP to the 200 people whom they considered to be instrumental in its success. "It's been my dream all along to turn this company over to the employees, and to make that dream a reality is very, very special to me," says Moore, who announced the plan on his eighty-first birthday. "We could have positioned the company to sell it, but we just felt that the people in this company deserve to have it. They have made it what it is."[38] ∎

Bob's Red Mill Natural Foods

Negotiating the Deal

On the surface, the negotiation process appears to be strictly adversarial. Although each party may be trying to accomplish objectives that are at odds with those of the opposing party, the negotiation process does not have to turn into a nasty battle of wits with overtones of "If you win,

LO6

Understand how the negotiation process works and identify the factors that affect it.

then I lose." The negotiation process will go much more smoothly and much faster if both parties work to establish a cooperative relationship based on honesty and trust from the outset. A successful deal requires both parties to examine and articulate their respective positions while trying to understand the other party's position. Recognizing that neither of them will benefit without a deal, both parties must work to achieve their objectives while making certain concessions to keep the negotiations alive.

To avoid a stalled deal, a buyer should go into the negotiation with a list of objectives ranked in order of priority. Once he or she has developed a list of priorities, it is useful to develop what he or she perceives to be the seller's list of priorities. That requires learning as much as possible about the seller. Knowing which terms are most important (and which are least important) to him or her and to the seller enables a buyer to make concessions without "giving away the farm" and without getting bogged down in "nitpicking," which often leads to a stalemate. If, for instance, the seller insists on a term that the buyer cannot agree to, he or she can explain why and then offer to give up something in exchange. The buyer also should identify the one concrete objective that sits at the top of that list, the one thing that he or she absolutely must come away from the negotiations with. The final stage of preparing for the actual negotiation is to study his or her list and the one that he or she has developed based on his or her perceptions of the seller to determine where the two mesh and where they conflict. The key to a successful negotiation is to use this analysis to look for areas of mutual benefit and to use them as the foundation for the negotiation. The accompanying "Hands On: How To . . ." feature offers tips to help entrepreneurs become more effective negotiators.

wavebreakmedia ltd/Shutterstock

Hands On . . . How To

Become a Successful Negotiator

Buying or selling a business always involves a negotiation, and so do many other business activities, whether an entrepreneur is dealing with a bank, a customer, or a vendor. "Everyone negotiates something every day," says Roger Fisher and William Ury in their book *Getting to Yes*. "All of us negotiate many times a day." That's why negotiating skills are among the most important skills that entrepreneurs can learn. How can you become a more successful negotiator? The following advice will help.

1. ***Prepare.*** Good negotiators know that the formula for a successful negotiation is 90 percent preparation and 10 percent bargaining. What you do—or don't do—*before* the actual negotiation ever begins is a primary determinant of how successful your negotiation will be. The key is to learn as much as possible about the party with whom you will be negotiating, the issues that are most important to him or her, and his or her likely positions on those issues. Leo Riley, president of his own training and consulting firm, says, "Knowledge of their hobbies, families, dietary habits, religious beliefs, and [other traits] can be used as ice breakers or to avoid making embarrassing mistakes."

    Your preparation for a negotiation also should include a statement of the outcome you desire from the negotiation. "Write down exactly what your goals are and then edit this description furiously until it is laser-focused and precise," advises John Patrick Nolan, a negotiation specialist. You also should write down what you think your *counterpart's* goals from the negotiation are. This encourages you to look at the negotiation from a different perspective and can be a valuable and revealing exercise.

2. ***Remember the difference between a "position" and an "interest."*** The outcome a person wants from a negotiation is his or her position. What is much more important, however, is his or her interest, the reason behind the position that he or she hopes to achieve. Focusing strictly on their positions usually leads two parties into a win–lose mentality in a negotiation in which they try to pound one another into submission. When the parties involved in a negotiation focus on their *interests* rather than on their *positions*, however, they usually discover that there are several different solutions that both will consider acceptable and reasonable.

    The parable of the orange provides an excellent lesson on the difference between the two. Two parties each want an orange, but there is only one orange. After much intense negotiating, the two agree to cut the orange in half. As it turns out, however, one party wanted only the rind of the orange to make cookies, and the other party wanted the orange to make orange juice. If the parties involved in the negotiation had focused on their interests and taken a problem-solving approach, both could have gotten exactly what they wanted from the negotiation!

3. ***Develop the right mind-set.*** Inexperienced negotiators see a negotiation as a zero-sum, win–lose game. "If you win, then I lose." Entrepreneurs who want or need to maintain ongoing relationships with the other party (e.g., buying a business from the company founder, whom you want to convince to stay on through a transition period to help you learn the business) must see negotiations in a different light. Their goal is to work toward a mutually beneficial agreement that both parties consider to be fair and reasonable.

    Successful negotiations almost always involve compromise on both sides, meaning that *neither* party gets *everything* that he or she wanted. "Sometimes the best deal you are going to get won't leave you jumping with joy," says Mike Staver, a negotiation consultant. In other words, successful negotiators see a negotiation not just as deal making but also as problem solving.

4. ***Always leave yourself an escape hatch.*** In any negotiation, you should be prepared to walk away without making a deal. Doing so, however, requires you to define what negotiation experts call a best alternative to a negotiated agreement (BATNA), which is the next best alternative to a negotiated outcome. You cannot determine whether a negotiated agreement is suitable unless you know what your alternatives are, and one alternative (although not always the best one) is to walk away from the negotiation without an agreement—your BATNA. One writer explains, "You may never need [your BATNA], but just knowing it's in your back pocket gives you peace of mind. Without one, you can become anxious, appear desperate, and settle for a less-than-ideal solution."

    Having a BATNA increases your power in a negotiation, but you should use that power judiciously. Do not use your BATNA as a threat to coerce an agreement. In addition, don't kill the deal just because you can. Instead, use your BATNA as the baseline against which you measure your negotiated alternatives.

5. ***Keep your emotions in check.*** Negotiations can become emotionally charged, especially if those involved allow their egos to enter into the process. It is always best to abide by the golden rule of negotiating: treat others the way you want to be treated in the negotiation. Be fair but firm. If the other party forgets the golden rule of negotiating, remember that you can always walk away from the negotiation and fall back on your BATNA.

6. ***Don't fall into the "rules" trap.*** Successful negotiations involve give-and-take by both parties. While negotiating a

(continued)

Hands On . . . How To *(continued)*

deal, one entrepreneur struck through several provisions in a contract that he was not willing to meet. Somewhat surprised, the other party said, "You're not allowed to make changes to our contracts like that." "Oh, really?" replied the entrepreneur, who explained that he did not feel compelled to comply with the other party's "rules." "If you cannot agree to the changes that I am suggesting," he said, "let's talk about them so that we can work out terms that will be satisfactory to both of us, but please refrain from telling me that I don't have permission to make changes to a contract that I believe are necessary."

7. ***Sometimes it's best to remain silent.*** A common mistake many people make in the negotiation process is talking too much. Not only does remaining silent allow you to listen to the other party, but it also encourages the other party to make the first offer. Some people are disconcerted by prolonged periods of silence and begin talking, only to erode the strength of their negotiation base.

Source: Based on "How to Negotiate Effectively," *Inc. Guidebook*, vol. 2, no. 7, pp. 1–4; "My Best Negotiation Tips," *Paul's Tips*, June 11, 2006, http://www.paulstips.com/brainbox/pt/home.nsf/link/10062006-My-eight-best-negotiation-tips; Rhonda Abrams, "Know What You Need Before Starting to Negotiate Deal," *Greenville News Business*, May 29, 2005, p. 8; "Negotiating to Resolve Conflict," Fed Ex Small Business Center, January 22, 2003, http://www.mysmallbizcenter.com/rawdoc.asp?docID=7169&temp=6378; Scott Smith, "Negotiate from Strength," *Success*, July/August 2000, pp. 74–75; Susan St. John, "Five Steps to Better Negotiating," *E-Merging Business*, Fall–Winter 2000, pp. 212–214; and Rob Walker, "Take It or Leave It: The *Only* Guide to Negotiating You Will *Ever* Need, *Inc.*, August 2003, pp. 75–82.

Chapter Summary by Learning Objective

1. Understand the advantages and disadvantages of buying an existing business.

The *advantages* of buying an existing business include the following: a successful business may continue to be successful, the business may already have the best location, employees and suppliers are already established, equipment is installed and its productive capacity known, inventory is in place and trade credit established, the owner hits the ground running, the buyer can use the expertise of the previous owner, and the business may be a bargain.

The disadvantages of buying an existing business include the following: an existing business may be for sale because it is deteriorating, the previous owner may have created ill will, employees inherited with the business may not be suitable, its location may have become unsuitable, equipment and facilities may be obsolete, change and innovation are hard to implement, inventory may be outdated, accounts receivable may be worth less than face value, and the business may be overpriced.

2. Define the steps involved in the *right* way to buy a business.

Buying a business can be a treacherous experience unless the buyer is well prepared. The right way to buy a business is to analyze your skills, abilities, and interests to determine the ideal business for you; prepare a list of potential candidates, including those that might be in the "hidden market"; investigate and evaluate candidate businesses and evaluate the best one; explore financing options before you actually need the money; and, finally, ensure a smooth transition.

3. Explain the process of evaluating an existing business.

Rushing into a deal can be the biggest mistake a business buyer can make. Before closing a deal, every business buyer should investigate five critical areas: (1) Why does the owner want to sell? Look for the *real* reason. (2) Determine the physical condition of the business. Consider both the building and its location. (3) Conduct a thorough analysis of the market for your products or services. Who are the present and potential customers? Conduct an equally thorough analysis of competitors, both direct and indirect. How do they operate and why do customers prefer them? (4) Consider all of the legal aspects that might constrain the expansion and growth of the business: Did you comply with the provisions of a bulk transfer? Negotiate a restrictive covenant? Consider ongoing legal liabilities? (5) Analyze the financial condition of the business, looking at financial statements, income tax returns, and especially cash flow.

4. Describe the various techniques for determining the value of a business.

Placing a value on a business is partly an art and partly a science. There is no single "best" method for determining the value of a business. The following techniques (with several variations) are useful: the balance sheet technique (adjusted balance sheet technique), the earnings approach (excess earnings method, capitalized earnings approach, and discounted future savings approach), and the market approach.

5. Understand the seller's side of the buyout decision and how to structure the deal.

Selling a business takes time, patience, and preparation to locate a suitable buyer, strike a deal, and make the transition. Sellers must always structure the deal with tax consequences in mind. Common exit strategies include a straight business sale, a business sale with an agreement for the founder to stay on, forming a family limited partnership, selling a controlling interest in the business, restructuring the company, selling to an international buyer, using a two-step sale, and establishing an ESOP.

6. Understand how the negotiation process works and identify the factors that affect it.

The first rule of negotiating is to never confuse price with value. In a business sale, the party who is the better negotiator usually comes out on top. Before beginning negotiations, a buyer should identify the factors that are affecting the negotiations and then develop a negotiating strategy. The best deals are the result of a cooperative relationship between the parties based on trust.

Discussion Questions

1. What advantages can an entrepreneur who buys a business gain over one who starts a business "from scratch"?
2. How would you go about determining the value of the assets of a business if you were unfamiliar with them?
3. Why do so many entrepreneurs run into trouble when they buy an existing business? Outline the steps involved in the *right* way to buy a business.
4. When evaluating an existing business that is for sale, what areas should an entrepreneur consider? Briefly summarize the key elements of each area.
5. What is goodwill? How should a buyer evaluate a business's goodwill?
6. What is a restrictive covenant? Is it fair to ask the seller of a restaurant located in a small town to sign a restrictive covenant for one year covering a 20-square-mile area? Explain.
7. How much negative information can you expect the seller to give you about the business? How can a prospective buyer find out such information?
8. Why is it so difficult for buyers and sellers to agree on a price for a business?
9. Which method of valuing a business is best? Why? What advice would you offer someone who is negotiating to buy a business about determining its value?
10. Outline the different exit strategy options available to a seller.
11. What tips would you offer someone about to enter into negotiations to buy a business?
12. One entrepreneur who recently purchased a business advises buyers to expect some surprises in the deal no matter how well prepared they may be. He says that potential buyers must build some "wiggle room" into their plans to buy a company. What steps can a buyer take to ensure that he or she has sufficient wiggle room?

Business Plan Pro™

This chapter addresses the process of acquiring an existing business. If this is your situation, determine whether the company has a business plan. If so, how recent is that plan? Does it accurately represent the current state of the organization? Do you have access to other historical information, including the financial statements (profit and loss statements), balance sheet, and cash flow statements? These documents may be a valuable resource to help you to evaluate the business you may purchase.

Business Plan Exercises

A business plan can act as an effective investigative tool to evaluate the attractiveness of acquiring an existing business.

On the Web

If the business has a Web site, review the site. Assess the "online personality" of the business and gather as much information as you can about the business. Does it match what you have learned about the business through the owner and other documents you have reviewed? Do a search for the business name and the owners' names on the Web. Note what you find and determine whether this information correlates with information from other sources.

Sample Plans

Review the executive summaries of these ongoing business plans through the Sample Plan Browser in *Business Plan Pro™*:

- Machine Tooling
- Take Five Sports Bar
- Web Solutions, Inc.

Scan the table of contents and find the section of the plan with information on the company's past performance. What might this historical information tell you about the future of the venture? Which of these businesses would you expect to present the greatest profit potential based on their past performance? Which business represents the greatest risk based on these same criteria? How might this impact its purchase price?

In the Software

If the company that you are considering to acquire has a business plan, enter information into *Business Plan Pro*™. Begin by selecting the "Existing" business plan option in the opening window. Go the Company Summary section and include the results of the due diligence process. The financial statements of the business, including the balance sheet, profit and loss, and cash flow statements for the last three years, will be valuable historical data. This will set a baseline for you as you enter sales and expense scenarios into this plan. This process may help you to better assess the business's future earning potential and its current value.

Building Your Business Plan

One of advantages of using *Business Plan Pro*™ is the ease of creating different financial scenarios for your business. This can be an excellent way to explore multiple "what-if" scenarios. Once your business is up and running, updating the plan is a quick and easy process. This will be an efficient way to keep your plan current and, by dating each of these files, offer an excellent historical perspective of your business.

Beyond the Classroom . . .

1. Ask several new owners who purchased existing businesses the following questions:

    a. How did you determine the value of the business?

    b. How close was the price paid for the business to the value assessed prior to purchase?

    c. What percentage of the accounts receivable was collectible?

    d. How accurate were their projections concerning customers (especially sales volume and number of customers)?

2. Visit a business broker and ask him or her how he or she brings a buyer and seller together. What does he or she do to facilitate the sale? What methods does he or she use to determine the value of a business?

3. Invite an attorney to speak to your class about the legal aspects of buying a business. How does he or she recommend that a business buyer protect himself or herself legally in a business purchase?

Endnotes

1. Sarah E. Needleman, "Buying an Established Business," *Wall Street Journal*, July 31, 2011, http://online.wsj.com/article/SB10001424053111904800304576478790019087086.html.
2. Darren Dahl, "A Tough Sell," *Inc.*, November 2010, pp. 108–113.
3. "BizBuySell.com Reports Improving Business-for-Sale Conditions," BizBuySell, January 4, 2012, http://www.bizbuysell.com/news/article079.html.
4. Jenna Schnuer, "See You on the Other Side," *Entrepreneur*, May 2011, p. 18.
5. "Buying a Business," Small Business Administration, http://www.sba.gov/smallbusinessplanner/start/buyabusiness/SERV_SBP_S_BUYB.html.
6. Jennifer Wang, "Good Buy," *Entrepreneur*, March 2011, p. 22.
7. Barry Shlachter, "How Fuzzy's Taco Shop Build a Restaurant Empire," *Star-Telegram*, July 29, 2011, http://www.star-telegram.com/2011/07/29/3257185/how-fuzzys-taco-shop-built-an.html.
8. Justin Martin," The Time to Sell Is Now!," *FSB*, September 2006, pp. 28–43.
9. "Nation's Business Brokers Remain Discouraged by Funding Availability for Small Business Transactions," *PR Web*, August 16, 2011, http://www.prweb.com/releases/2011/8/prweb8725008.htm.
10. Sarah Needleman, "Sales of Small Firms Are Up," *Wall Street Journal*, July 14, 2011, p. B8.
11. Elaine Appleton Grant, "How to Buy a Small Business without Getting Taken," *U.S. News and World Report*," February 26, 2008, http://www.usnews.com/articles/business/small-business-entrepreneurs/2008/02/26/how-to-buy-a-small-business-without-getting-taken.html.
12. Sarah Needleman, "Sales of Small Firms Are Up," *Wall Street Journal*, July 14, 2011, p. B8.
13. "Survey of Nation's Business Brokers Reveals That 2011 Likely to Be a Stronger Year for Selling a Business," BizBuySell, February 22, 2011, http://www.bizbuysell.com/news/article073.html.
14. Kevin Kelly, "Look Under the Hood," *FSB*, October 2004, p. 35.
15. Luisa Kroll, "Gotcha: Pushing the Limits of Due Diligence," *Forbes*, October 30, 2000, pp. 186–187.
16. *Boggs v. Friend*, 77 W.Va. 531, S.E. 873, 1916 W.Va. LEXIS 188.
17. Justin Martin, "The Time to Sell Is Now!" *FSB*, September 2006, pp. 28–43.
18. Nicole L. Torres, "Fixer Upper," *Entrepreneur*, November 2001, p. 126.
19. *Deal Review*, BizComps/BVR, July 2011, p. 2.
20. Scott Austin and Scott Denne, "3Par Founders Reap Windfall," *Wall Street Journal*, September 3, 2010, http://online.wsj.com/article/SB1000142405274870420680455746773084958966 8.html.

21. Norm Brodsky, "What's Your Business Really Worth?," *Inc.*, April 2005, p. 55.

22. Darren Dahl, "The Most Valuable Companies in America," *Inc.*, April 2008, pp. 97–105.

23. James Laabs, ""What Is Your Company Worth?," *The Business Sale Center*, http://www.businesssalecenter.com/new_page_3.htm.

24. James Laabs, "Recasting: A Key to Building Value for the Seller," *The Business Sale Center*, http://www.businesssalecenter.com/new_page_3.htm.

25. *Business Planning Tools: Buying and Selling a Small Business*, MasterCard Worldwide, http://www.mastercard.com/us/business/en/smallbiz/businessplanning/businessplanning.html, p. 11.

26. Will Schroter, "Selling Company to Another Entails Entrepreneur's Hardest, Best Move," *Washington Business Journal*, June 25, 2007, http://washington.bizjournals.com/extraedge/consultants/go_big/2007/06/25/column6.html?market=washington.

27. Joel Holland, "Sorry, But No Sale," *Entrepreneur*, October 2010, p. 122; Joshua Brustein, "StumbleUpon Gets More Specific," *New York Times*, August 17, 2011, http://bits.blogs.nytimes.com/2011/08/17/stumbleupon-gets-more-specific.

28. David Worrell, "Go for the Gold," *Entrepreneur*, October 2004, p. 70.

29. Alyson Shontell, "This 21-Year-Old Just Sold Her Start-Up for $100 Million," *Business Insider*, July 20, 2011, http://www.businessinsider.com/myyearbook-acquired-by-quepasa-for-100-million-2011-7; "Quepasa and MyYearbook Announce Merger Agreement," MyYearbook, July 20, 2011, http://www.myyearbook.com/press/release38.

30. "Jennifer Fermino, "A Fair $hake & Bake," *New York Post*, January 4, 2007, http://www.nypost.com/seven/01042007/news/regionalnews/a_fair_hake__bake_regionalnews_jennifer_fermino.htm; Lee McGrath, "Off the Menu," *New York*

Times, January 3, 2007, http://www.nytimes.com/2007/01/03/dining/03off.html?scp=1&sq=Magnolia+Bakery+Abrams&st=nyt.

31. Ryan McCarthy, "A Buyer's Market," *Inc.*, June 2009, p. 85.

32. Jenna Schnuer, "Blended Families," *Entrepreneur*, April 2011, p. 22.

33. Abby Ellin, "After Selling the Company, Remorse," *New York Times*, July 10, 2008, http://www.nytimes.com/2008/07/10/business/smallbusiness/10sbiz.html?partner=rssnyt&emc=rss.

34. Emily Maltby, "Sell the Store, Then Buy It Back," *Wall Street Journal*, November 11, 2010, p. B6; Kathryn Hawkins and Anthony Medico, "We Sold Our Company, Then Bought It Back," *BNET*, January 26, 2011, http://www.bnet.com/blog/smb/why-we-sold-our-company-then-bought-it-back/3469?tag=mantle_skin;content.

35. "The Walt Disney Company Acquires Club Penguin," Club Penguin, August 1, 2007, http://www.clubpenguin.com/company/news/070801-the-walt-disney-company.htm; David Kaplan, "Disney's Club Penguin Misses Profit Targets—No $350 Million Earnout," *Paid Content*, May 13, 2010, http://paidcontent.org/article/419-disneys-club-penguin-misses-profit-targets-no-350-million-earnout.

36. Peter Collins, "Cashing Out and Maintaining Control," *Small Business Reports*, December 1989, p. 28.

37. "ESOP Fact Sheet," ESOP Association, http://www.esopassociation.org/media/media_factsheet.asp.

38. Karen E. Klein, "ESOPs on the Rise among Small Businesses," *Bloomberg Business Week*, March 26, 2010, http://www.businessweek.com/smallbiz/content/mar2010/sb20100325_591132.htm; Nancy Mann Jackson, "ESOP Plans Let Owners Cash Out and Employees Cash In," *CNNMoney*, June 17, 2010, http://money.cnn.com/2010/06/03/smallbusiness/esop_plans/index.htm.

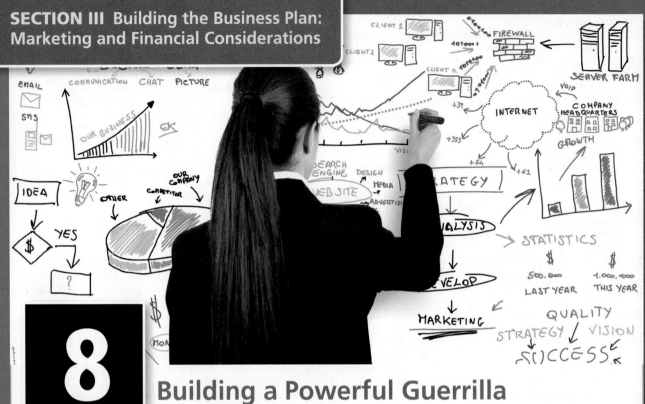

© alphaspirit/Fotolia

8

Building a Powerful Guerrilla Marketing Plan

Learning Objectives

On completion of this chapter, you will be able to:

1. Describe the principles of building a guerrilla marketing plan, and explain the benefits of preparing one.

2. Explain how small businesses can pinpoint their target markets.

3. Discuss the role of market research in building a guerrilla marketing plan and outline the market research process.

4. Describe how a small business can build a competitive edge in the marketplace using guerrilla marketing strategies.

The key to excellent marketing is to make your message about the buyer and not about your own rhetoric.

—Chris Brogan

The customer isn't always right, but he's still the customer.

—Steve Tobak

As you learned in Chapter 4, creating a solid business plan improves an entrepreneur's odds of building a successful company. A business plan is a valuable document that defines *what* an entrepreneur plans to accomplish in both quantitative and qualitative terms and *how* he or she plans to accomplish it. The plan consolidates many of the topics we have discussed in preceding chapters with those in this section to produce a concise statement of how an entrepreneur plans to achieve success in the marketplace. This section focuses on building two major components of every business plan: the marketing plan and the financial plan.

Too often, business plans describe in great detail what the entrepreneur intends to accomplish (e.g., "the financials") and pay little, if any, attention to the strategies to achieve those targets. Too often, entrepreneurs squander enormous effort pulling together capital, people, and other resources to sell their products and services because they fail to determine what it will take to attract and keep a profitable customer base. Sometimes they fail to determine whether a profitable customer base even exists! To be effective, a solid business plan must contain both a financial plan *and* a marketing plan. Like the financial plan, an effective marketing plan projects numbers and analyzes them but from a different perspective. Rather than focus on cash flow, net income, and owner's equity, a marketing plan concentrates on the *customer*.

This chapter is devoted to creating an effective marketing plan, which is a subset of a total business plan. Before producing reams of computer-generated spreadsheets of financial projections, an entrepreneur must determine what to sell, to whom and how, and on what terms and at what price and how to get the product or service to the customer. In short, a marketing plan identifies a company's target customers and describes how that business will attract and keep them. Its primary focus is cultivating and maintaining a competitive edge for a small business. Table 8.1 explains how to build a seven-sentence guerrilla marketing strategy.

Building a Guerrilla Marketing Plan

Marketing is the process of creating and delivering desired goods and services to customers and involves all of the activities associated with winning and retaining loyal customers. The "secret" to successful marketing is to understand what your target customers' needs, demands, and wants are before your competitors can; offer them the products and services that will satisfy those needs, demands, and wants; and provide customer service, convenience, and value so that they will keep coming back.

The marketing function cuts across the entire company, affecting every aspect of its operation—from finance and production to hiring and purchasing—as well as the company's ultimate success. As competition for customers becomes more intense, entrepreneurs must understand the importance of developing creative marketing strategies; their success and survival depend on it. Traditional marketing techniques emphasize pushing messages out to potential customers. However, modern technology gives consumers the ability to filter and block many of these messages, limiting the effectiveness of "push" techniques. Successful entrepreneurs recognize that modern marketing strategies also must include techniques such as social media and cause marketing that pull customers into their companies' sphere of influence. The good news is that many of these "pull" strategies are relatively inexpensive and, when infused with a healthy dose of creativity, are extremely effective.

Although they may be small and cannot match their larger rivals' marketing budgets, entrepreneurial companies are not powerless when it comes to developing effective marketing strategies. By using **guerrilla marketing strategies**—unconventional, low-cost, creative techniques—small companies can wring as much or more "bang" from their marketing bucks. For instance, facing the power of discount giants such as Wal-Mart, Target, and "category killer" superstores such as Best Buy and Home Depot that are determined to increase their market shares, small retail shops are turning to guerrilla marketing tactics to attract new customers and to keep existing ones. J. Conrad Levinson, a guerrilla marketing guru, says that guerrilla marketing is all about maximizing the efficiency of a small company's marketing budget.

An effective guerrilla marketing campaign does *not* require an entrepreneur to spend large amounts of money, but it does demand creativity, ingenuity, and an understanding of customers' buying habits. Levinson estimates that guerrilla marketers spend between 4 percent and 8 percent

LO1

Describe the principles of building a guerrilla marketing plan, and explain the benefits of preparing one.

marketing
the process of creating and delivering desired goods and services to customers; involves all of the activities associated with winning and retaining loyal customers.

guerrilla marketing strategies
unconventional, low-cost, creative marketing strategies designed to give small companies an edge over their larger, richer, more powerful rivals.

TABLE 8.1 A Seven-Sentence Guerrilla Marketing Strategy

Building a successful guerrilla marketing plan does not have to be complex. Guerrilla marketing expert J. Conrad Levinson says that entrepreneurs can create a guerrilla marketing plan with just seven sentences:

1. *What is the purpose of your marketing?* In other words, what action do you want customers or prospective customers to take as a result of your marketing efforts? Should they visit your store? Go to your company's Web site? Call a toll-free number for more information?

2. *What primary benefit can you offer customers?* In other words, what is your company's competitive advantage, and what does it do for customers? Guerrilla marketers express their companies' competitive advantage as a solution to a customer's problem, which is easier to market than just a positive benefit. Successful guerrilla marketing requires an entrepreneur to have a clear understanding of a company's unique selling proposition, a key customer benefit of a product or service that sets it apart from its competition.

3. *Who is your target market?* At whom are you aiming your marketing efforts? Answering this question often requires some basic research about your target customers, their characteristics, their habits, and their preferences. Guerrilla marketers know that broadcasting is old school; they realize that narrowcasting—focusing their marketing efforts on those people who are most interested in and are likely to purchase their goods and services—is much more efficient and effective. Most small companies have more than one target market; be sure to identify all of them.

4. *Which marketing tools will you use to reach your target audience?* This list should include only those tools that your company understands, knows how to use effectively, and can afford. The good news is that marketing tools do not have to be costly to be effective. In fact, guerrilla marketers are experts at using low-cost methods to market their companies.

5. *What is your company's niche in the marketplace?* In other words, how do you intend to position your company against your competition? Guerrilla marketers understand that their markets are crowded with competitors, some of them much larger with gigantic marketing budgets that dwarf their own, and that finding a profitable niche to occupy can be highly profitable. Recall from Chapter 3 that many successful entrepreneurs position their companies in profitable niches. One insurance agent markets his agency as one that "specializes in serving the needs of small businesses." Conrad Levinson is the recognized expert in guerrilla marketing. SweetskinZ, launched in 1999, is a company that specializes in high-quality bicycle tires that feature full-color graphics and patterns that are also reflective. The key is to carve out a position that allows your company to differentiate itself from all of its competitors.

6. *What is your company's identity in the marketplace?* A company's identity is a reflection of its personality, its DNA. Small companies often have an advantage over large businesses when it comes to communicating their identities because of the interesting, unique stories behind their creation and the enthusiasm and passion of their founders. Customers enjoy doing business with small companies that have a clear, meaningful, and compelling identity in the marketplace. Southwest Airlines built its business by attracting customers who were drawn to its fun-loving, somewhat irreverent culture and its reputation for taking care of its customers.

7. *How much money will you spend on your marketing; in other words, what is your marketing budget?* Entrepreneurs should decide how much they intend to invest in their marketing efforts, an amount that they usually express as a percentage of sales. The average company in the United States devotes 4 percent of its sales revenue to marketing. Small companies should allocate a portion of their budget to marketing; after all, it drives sales. The good news is that many of the guerrilla marketing techniques that small companies can use (and that are described in this chapter) are either low cost or no cost. When allocating their budgets, guerrilla marketers recognize the importance of putting their money where they will get the greatest "bang."

Answering these seven questions will give you an outline of your company's marketing plan. *Implementing* a guerrilla marketing plan boils down to two essentials:

1. Having a thorough understanding of your target market, including what customers want and expect from your company and its products and services.

2. Identifying the obstacles that stand in your way of satisfying customers (competitors, barriers to entry, processes, outside influences, budgets, knowledge, and others) and eliminating them.

Sources: Adapted from Jay Conrad Levinson and Jeannie Levinson, "Here's the Plan," *Entrepreneur*, February 2008, pp. 92–97; and Alan Lautenslager, "Write a Creative Marketing Plan in Seven Sentences," *Entrepreneur*, April 24, 2006, http://www.entrepreneur.com/marketing/marketingideas/guerrillamarketingcolumnistallautenslager/article159486.html.

of sales on marketing, but they put their money into clever, creative marketing efforts that reach their target customers and raise the profile of their products, services, and companies.[1]

ENTREPRENEURIAL PROFILE: Roxanne Pettipas and Buddy: Class Art Productions Inc. In 1997, Roxanne Pettipas crafted a unique body harness for her beloved dog, Buddy, to replace the traditional dog collar that exerted undue pressure and stress on his neck, spine, and throat when the enthusiastic Dachshund pulled on his leash during walks. Pettipas recognized that a growing number of people were treating their pets like children and, in 2001, launched a business, Class Art Productions Inc., from her Toronto, Canada, home to manufacture and market the high-quality leather harness, which she named the Buddy Belt in honor of her dog. "The timing was great for the Buddy Belt," says Pettipas. "In Canada, the pet industry was worth $3 billion annually, and in the United States, it's worth $34 billion annually." Her challenge was to make customers and distributors aware of the benefits of the hand-crafted harness that her company offered. "I decided to tell our story from Buddy's perspective and have him promote the product since he's the one wearing the belt," says Pettipas. It proved to be one of the smartest guerrilla marketing moves she made. Pettipas and Buddy attended the PET Expo in Toronto and attracted the attention of many vendors, and within two years, Pettipas had moved the business out of her home and into a factory to handle the growing volume of orders. The company's Web site features measuring tips to ensure proper sizing for dogs that weigh from 2 to more than 100 pounds, testimonials from satisfied customers, and, of course, photos of Buddy and his friends. One of the biggest marketing events for Pettipas and Buddy is Woofstock, the largest outdoor festival for dogs in North America, drawing more than 300,000 people and their dogs every year. Buddy also has his own Facebook page, where other dogs often send him messages and owners post glowing reviews of the product. Pettipas also uses Buddy's Facebook page to engage fans in product development and marketing, asking them for input on new styles and colors. Buddy Belt's guerrilla marketing campaign has "created a real buzz around Buddy and given him more of a presence," says Pettipas. Fans have posted videos on YouTube promoting the Buddy Belt. Buddy, now an Internet celebrity, has enabled the company to establish an emotional connection with its customers and to expand beyond its North American market into nine countries in Europe and Asia.[2] ∎

Buddy Belts

A sound guerrilla marketing plan reflects a company's understanding of its customers and acknowledges that satisfying them is the foundation of every business. It recognizes that the customer is the central player in the cast of every business venture. According to marketing expert Ted Levitt, the primary purpose of a business is not to earn a profit; instead, it is "to create and keep a customer. The rest, given reasonable good sense, will take care of itself."[3] Every area of the business must practice putting the customer first in planning and actions.

A guerrilla marketing plan should accomplish three objectives:

1. It should pinpoint the specific target markets the small company will serve.

2. It should determine customer needs and wants through market research.

3. It should analyze the firm's competitive advantages and build a guerrilla marketing strategy around them.

The rest of this chapter focuses on these three objectives of the small company's marketing plan.

Pinpointing the Target Market

One of the first steps in building a guerrilla marketing plan is to identify a small company's **target market**—the specific group of customers at whom the company aims its goods or services. The more a business knows about its local markets and its customers and their buying habits and preferences, the more precisely it can focus its marketing efforts on the group(s) of customers who are most likely to buy its products or services. Most marketing experts contend that the greatest marketing mistake small businesses make is failing to define clearly the target market they serve. These entrepreneurs develop new products that do not sell because they are not targeted at a specific audience's needs, they broadcast ads that attempt to reach everyone and

LO2

Explain how small businesses can pinpoint their target markets.

target market
the specific group of customers at whom a company aims its goods or services.

end up reaching no one, they spend precious time and money trying to reach customers who are not the most profitable, and many of the customers they attract leave because they do not know what the company stands for. Why, then, do so many small companies make this mistake? Because it is easy and does not require market research or a marketing plan! Smart entrepreneurs know that they do not have the luxury of wasting resources; they must follow a more focused, laser-like approach to marketing. "The real investment is in the time and sweat spent understanding the needs of your customers and coming up with creative ways of communicating your value proposition," says Conrad Levinson. "Broadening your search isn't as important as aiming your message at the right people."[4]

To be customer driven, an effective marketing strategy must be based on a clear, comprehensive understanding of a company's target customers and their needs. A customer-driven marketing strategy is a powerful weapon for any company that lacks the financial and physical resources of its competitors. Customers respond when companies take the time to learn about their unique needs and offer products and services designed to satisfy them.

ENTREPRENEURIAL PROFILE: Levi Strauss At Levi Strauss, the famous maker of jeans founded in 1873 by a German immigrant who named the company after himself, products for men account for 73 percent of sales. Levi's saw a market opportunity in women's jeans and spent 18 months interviewing and studying the body scans of more than 60,000 women in 13 countries. The result is a line of jeans called Curve ID that is based on women's shapes rather than traditional sizes and comes in four fits: a slight curve, a demi curve, a bold curve, and a supreme curve. "Our research showed that 96 percent of women around the world fall into four distinct body shapes," says Mary Alderete, the company's vice president of women's global marketing. "Our goal is to engage women online with our interactive, custom-fit experience that will match them with their perfect Levi's Curve ID fit." Customers use a proprietary configuration tool in a digital fitting room to discover their Curve ID, which means they can avoid the hassle of going to a store and trying on multiple pairs of jeans to find the right fit. The company also scored a marketing coup for the Curve ID line with a YouTube video called Rear View Girls that received 4 million views in just a few days.[5] ■

Most successful businesses have well-defined portraits of the customers they are seeking to attract. From market research, they know their customers' income levels, lifestyles, buying patterns, likes and dislikes, and even their psychological profiles—why they buy. These companies offer prices that are appropriate to their target customers' buying power, product lines that appeal to their tastes, and service they expect. The payoff comes in the form of higher sales, profits, and customer loyalty. For entrepreneurs, pinpointing target customers has become more important than ever before as markets in the United States have become increasingly fragmented and diverse. Mass marketing techniques no longer reach customers the way they did 30 years ago because of the splintering of the population and the influence exerted on the nation's purchasing patterns by what were once minority groups such as Hispanic, Asian, and African Americans (see Figure 8.1). Peter Francese, marketing consultant and author of the research report *2010 America*, says that "the average American" no longer exists.[6] The United States is a multicultural nation in which no race or ethnicity comprises a majority in its two most populous states, California and Texas. In addition, racial and ethnic minorities accounted for 92 percent of the population growth in the United States between 2000 and 2010.[7] By 2025, multiculturalism will explode, baby boomers' spending will be in decline, the most economically disadvantaged market segments will expand, and household spending will grow at a slow pace, all of which will create a very different world for marketers.[8]

When companies follow a customer-driven marketing strategy, they ensure that their target customers permeate the entire business—from the merchandise sold and the music played on the sound system to the location, layout, and decor of the store. These entrepreneurs have an advantage over their larger rivals because the buying experience they create resonates with their target customers, and that's why they prosper.

ENTREPRENEURIAL PROFILE: Megan and Mike Tamte: Hot Mama Megan Tamte came up with the idea for her company, Hot Mama, a boutique store aimed at new mothers, shortly after the birth of her first baby. Her first post-baby shopping trip was a disaster that left her walking away from stores frustrated, empty handed, and "feeling frumpy." In 2004, Megan

Courtesy of Hot Mama

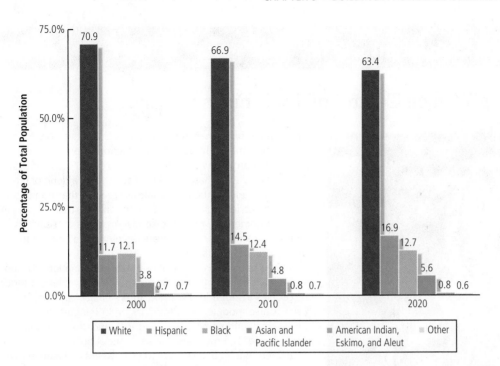

FIGURE 8.1

U.S. Population by Race

Source: Based on data from the U.S. Census Bureau, 2011.

and her husband, Mike, opened the first Hot Mama store in Edina, Minnesota, tailoring everything about it to their target customers, whom Megan understands extremely well. Each of the company's 30 locations includes a centrally located kids area equipped with toys, books, games, and movies to keep little ones entertained while moms shop. Store employees, also known as stylists, double as babysitters; it is not uncommon to see one carrying a toddler as she takes garments to a customer in a fitting room. The goal is to give customers at least 15 minutes of uninterrupted shopping time. The strategy works; most customers shop for at least an hour. Hot Mama carries more than 200 brands, including Splendid, Michael Stars, Hudson, and Joe's Jeans, all aimed at mothers who want a classic, contemporary style rather than a sweat pants, soccer mom look. Tamte also uses customer service to set her stores apart. As new employees, stylists go through detailed certification programs on denim and fitting various body types. "Our stylists can outfit any woman, aged 25 to 65, the minute she walks through the door," says Hot Mama president, Kimberly Ritzer, "but they also build personal relationships to find a style that makes her feel comfortable. It's like shopping with a girlfriend." The Tamte's marketing strategy has proved to be very successful. The company's sales recently hit $33 million, and the Tamtes plan to have 100 stores by 2015.[9] ■

Determining Customer Needs and Wants through Market Research

The changing nature of the U.S. population is a potent force altering the landscape of business. Shifting patterns in age, income, education, race, and other population characteristics (which are the subject of **demographics**) have a major impact on companies, their customers, and the way companies do business with those customers. Businesses that ignore demographic trends and fail to adjust their strategies accordingly run the risk of becoming competitively obsolete. Entrepreneurs who stay in tune with demographic, social, and economic trends are able to spot growing and emerging market opportunities.

LO3

Discuss the role of market research in building a guerrilla marketing plan and outline the market research process.

demographics

the study of important population characteristics, such as age, income, education, race, and others.

ENTREPRENEURIAL PROFILE: Bertrand Sosa: Mango Money Center Bertrand Sosa, founder of Mpower Ventures, spotted an opportunity in the $106 billion nonbank financial services industry, which consists of check-cashing services, payday loan companies, and pawn shops and is often characterized by high fees and predatory practices. In fact, nearly 26 percent of

✔ You Be the Consultant

Learnvest: Giving Women Control of Their Financial Lives

Joe Corrigan/Stringer/Getty Images

After graduating from an Ivy League university without having taken a personal finance course and working for a time at Morgan Stanley, Alexa von Tobel realized that she had no idea how to manage her own money. She talked with other women and discovered a common theme: "I don't know where to start" when it comes to investing, avoiding excessive debt, and planning for retirement. Von Tobel took a leave of absence from her course work at the Harvard Business School and started Learnvest, a financial literacy and planning Web site aimed at women under the age of 40. Her goal is to help women take control of their financial lives by creating a site designed specifically for them that is easy and convenient to use, personalized, and reasonably priced. "We don't want to be a pretty site with information," says von Tobel. "We want to change behaviors. Having command of your finances is a huge aspect of taking command of your life."

Learnvest is the equivalent of a financial fitness center that allows women to purchase a day pass or year-round access. The key to a financial literacy and planning site that women would feel comfortable with and use, von Tobel realized, is to incorporate elements from products and services that women already know and like—for example, the glossy aesthetics of *Glamour* or the point-tracking system of Weight Watchers. Learnvest's centerpiece is "My Money Center," which consolidates subscribers' financial transactions from checking and savings accounts, credit and debit cards, investment accounts, and others into a single, easy-to-use location. The center automatically organizes a user's financial transactions into color-coded folders using an automated filing system that also helps her set

up a simple budget. A financial inbox that drives My Money Center automatically pulls in transactions from a user's accounts and organizes them much like an e-mail inbox. If a customer makes a purchase at Whole Foods using a debit or credit card, the financial inbox automatically records that transaction in the "groceries" folder. A budgeting tool asks users to plug in her take-home pay, identify essential expenses and savings or investment amounts, and allocate the remaining amount to the other account folders.

The site contains plenty of useful free information, but subscribers have access to Learnvest's financial curriculum, a series of courses at three levels: basic, intermediate, and advanced. Each course module takes from 15 to 30 minutes, and topics range from budgeting basics and insurance to investing and tax planning. Learnvest also offers financial boot camps, highly structured courses that last two to three weeks and require users to complete one task each day. The boot camps, which cover topics such as investing in stocks and getting a mortgage, are organized to take a large, potentially overwhelming task and break it down into smaller, simple steps, which is "something that women respond to," says von Tobel. Learnvest also offers customers the equivalent of a personal trainer with its "Ask an Expert" feature. For prices that range from $4.99 to $139.99, depending on the subscription period, subscribers can e-mail their questions to Learnvest certified financial planners, who follow up with customers after every individual question-and-answer session. Learnvest also is developing a Baby Bootcamp designed to meet the financial needs of expectant mothers and a product that targets mothers with young children to help them save money to pay for college.

Von Tobel, who started Learnvest when she was just 25, has raised $5 million in venture capital to support the growth of her business, which averages 350,000 visits per month. "Women are the ones who manage household budgets," she says, "and no one is speaking directly to that audience. I just want to go after one niche and own it."

1. Visit the company's Web site at www.learnvest.com to learn more about the business, the services it offers, and its culture. Work with a team of your classmates to develop a list of guerrilla marketing techniques that the company can use to promote its services and its brand.

2. What steps can von Tobel take to enhance the Learnvest brand and build customer recognition of it? Refer to Figure 8.4 (connection between branding and a unique selling proposition) and use the table below to do the following:
   a. List threshold, performance, and excitement attributes for Learnvest.
   b. Identify "proof points," reasons for customers to believe in the brand, that support each of the attributes you list.
   c. Use the attributes and their proof points to develop a unique selling proposition for Learnvest.

You Be the Consultant *(continued)*

Threshold Attributes	Performance Attributes	Excitement Attributes
Threshold Proof Points	Performance Proof Points	Excitement Proof Points
Unique selling proposition:		

Sources: Based on Dan Macsai, "A Source of Their Own," *Fast Company*, October 2010, p. 64; Tara Siegel Bernard, "Learnvest: A Money-Management Site for Women," *New York Times*, August 9, 2011, http://bucks.blogs.nytimes.com/2011/08/09/learnvest-a-money-management-site-for-women; Kim-Mai Cutler, "A Female VC-Founder Match Made in Heaven as Accel Backs Learnvest," *Venture Beat*, April 1, 2010, http://venturebeat.com/2010/04/01/learnvest-accel-raises; Alyson Shontell, "Women Finance Site Learnvest Is Launching New Products for Moms," *Business Insider*, August 30, 2011, http://www.businessinsider.com/learnvest-newsletter-for-moms-2011-8; and Bianca Bosker, "Learnvest CEO Alexa von Tobel: What Women Do That Holds Them Back," *Huffington Post*, July 23, 2011, http://www.huffingtonpost.com/2011/07/23/learnvest-ceo-alexa-von-tobel_n_907454.html.

U.S. households, about 30 million, are either "unbanked or underbanked" and rely on alternative financial service companies for check cashing and loans. Serving mainly low- and moderate-income households that have no banking relationship, these alternative financial service companies collect more than $8 billion annually in fees. Seeking to build long-term relationships with "unbanked and underbanked" customers, Sosa launched the Mango Money Center, which charges customers a one-time $10 fee that allows them to cash as many checks as they want by putting the money onto debit cards. More sophisticated services, such as international money transfers and electronic bill payments, cost extra, but in an effort to promote transparency and trust, Sosa uses colorful wall banners to display clearly its simple fees, which are significantly lower than traditional alternative finance companies. Unlike the neon signs, metal cages, and bulletproof glass that characterize so many businesses that serve this market, the Mango Money Center uses a clean look, open spaces, and bright colors. "Money coaches" clad in bright orange T-shirts assist customers who have questions or need help. The Mango Money Center also offers online and mobile access to its financial services and prepaid credit cards.[10] ■

A demographic trend is like a train; a business owner must find out early on where it's going and decide whether to get on board. Waiting until the train is roaring down the tracks and gaining speed means it's too late to get on board. However, by checking the schedule early and planning ahead, an entrepreneur may find himself or herself at the train's controls wearing the engineer's hat! Similarly, small companies that spot demographic trends early and act on them can gain a distinctive edge in the market. An entrepreneur's goal is to make sure that his or her company's marketing plan is on track with the most significant trends that are shaping the industry. Trend tracking not only keeps a company on the pathway to success but also helps it avoid losing its focus by pursuing opportunities that are out of favor.

Trends are powerful forces and can be an entrepreneur's greatest friend or greatest foe. For entrepreneurs who are observant and position their companies to intercept them, trends can be to their companies what the perfect wave is to a surfer. For entrepreneurs who ignore them or discount their importance, trends can leave their companies stranded like a boat stuck in the mud at low tide.

The Value of Market Research

By performing some basic market research, small business owners can detect key demographic and market trends. Indeed, *every* business can benefit from a better understanding of its market, customers, and competitors. "Market information is just as much a business asset and just as important as your inventory or the machine you have in the back room," says one marketing consultant.[11] **Market research** is the vehicle for gathering the information that serves as the foundation for the marketing plan. It involves systematically collecting, analyzing, and interpreting data

market research
the vehicle for gathering the information that serves as the foundation for the marketing plan; it involves systematically collecting, analyzing, and interpreting data pertaining to a company's market, customers, and competitors.

pertaining to a company's market, customers, and competitors. The objective of market research is to learn how to improve the level of satisfaction for existing customers and to find ways to attract new customers.

Small companies cannot afford to make marketing mistakes because there is little margin for error when funds are scarce and budgets are tight. Small businesses simply cannot afford to miss their target markets, and market research can help them zero in on the bull's-eye. Market research does *not* have to be time consuming, complex, or expensive to be useful. By applying the same type of creativity to market research that they display when creating their businesses, entrepreneurs can perform effective market research "on the cheap."

Felix Clay/eyevine/Redux

ENTREPRENEURIAL PROFILE: Richard Reed, Adam Balon, and Jon Wright: Innocent Drinks Cambridge graduates Richard Reed, Adam Balon, and Jon Wright were hesitant to dive into entrepreneurship even though they had spent six months testing their smoothie recipes on approving friends when they decided to conduct some inexpensive market research. The reluctant entrepreneurs purchased £500 worth of fresh fruit and used it to make smoothies that they sold at a small music festival in London. They put up a big sign that said, "Do you think we should give up our jobs to make these smoothies?" and put out a bin marked "yes" and another marked "no" and asked people to vote by putting the empty smoothie container in the appropriate bin. "By the end of the weekend, the 'yes' bin was so full we went in the next day and resigned," recalls Reed. Today, Innocent Drinks, which makes all-natural, healthy smoothies, thickies (yogurt-based drinks), and juices, employs 275 people and sells its fruity concoctions in more than 10,000 retail outlets around the world.[12] ■

Established companies also can conduct market research on the cheap. Ron Shaich, founder of Panera Bread, a chain of bakery cafés with 1,185 locations in 40 states, still visits stores regularly, where he works the cash registers and serves customers so that he can listen to their ideas and concerns.[13] Hands-on market research techniques such as these allow entrepreneurs to get past the barriers that consumers often put up and to uncover their true preferences and hidden thoughts.

Many entrepreneurs are discovering the power, the speed, the convenience, and the low cost of conducting market research over the Internet. Online surveys, customer opinion polls, and other research projects are easy to conduct, cost virtually nothing, and help companies to connect with their customers. With online surveys, businesses can get real-time feedback from customers, often using surveys they have designed themselves. Web sites such as Survey Monkey and Zoomerang allow entrepreneurs to conduct low-cost (sometimes free) online surveys of existing or prospective customers. Many companies are using social media sites such as Facebook and Twitter as market research tools. "In the past companies would hire market research firms to understand their [target customers]," says Mike Hudack, CEO of Blip.tv, a New York City–based video Web site. "We use Twitter to get the fastest, most honest research any company ever heard—good, bad, and ugly—and it doesn't cost a cent." Using Twitter, Hudack monitors everything other Twitterers say about Blip.tv and gets feedback on new ideas that the company is considering.[14]

ENTREPRENEURIAL PROFILE: Houlihan's Restaurants To solicit meaningful feedback, Houlihan's Restaurants, a restaurant chain based in Leawood, Kansas, with 94 franchised locations, created its own social networking site, HQ, to which it invited a select group of 10,500 customers called "Houlifans" from its database of more than 600,000 customers to join. Through the site, managers share ideas with customers about restaurant redesigns, menu additions, recipes, ingredients, and other "insider information." The feedback customers provide has helped transform the chain and has allowed it reconnect with its target customers. Customer input guided the company through the introduction of its small-plate menu—tapas-style dishes such as flat-bread pizza and chicken fajitas—allowing it to make changes on the fly. The informal market research paid off; Houlihan's small-plate menu accounts for 26 percent of item sales and has boosted the company's profits.[15] ∎

Faith Popcorn, a marketing consultant, encourages small business owners to be their own "trend-tracking sleuths." Merely by observing their customers' attitudes and actions, small business owners can shift their product lines and services to meet changing tastes in the market. To spot significant trends, Popcorn suggests the following:[16]

- Read as many current publications as possible, especially ones you normally would not read.

- Watch the top 10 television shows because they are indicators of consumers' attitudes and values and what they're going to be buying.

- See the top 10 movies. They also influence consumer behavior, from language to fashions. In 1936, after Hollywood star Clark Gable took off his shirt in *It Happened One Night* and revealed a bare chest, undershirt sales soon took a dive. After Will Smith and Tommy Lee Jones donned Ray-Ban sunglasses in *Men in Black*, sales of the sunglasses tripled![17]

- Talk to at least 150 customers a year. Make a conscious effort to spend time with some of your target customers, preferably in an informal setting, to find out what they are thinking. Start by asking them two important questions: "Will you buy from us again?" and "Will you recommend us to your friends?"

- Talk with the 10 smartest people you know. They can offer valuable insights and fresh perspectives that you may not have considered.

- Listen to your children. ("They can be tremendous guides for you," says Popcorn.)

Next, entrepreneurs should make a list of the major trends they spot and should briefly describe how well their products or services match these trends. Companies whose products or services are diverging from major social, demographic, and economic trends rather than converging with them must change their course or else run the risk of failing because their markets can evaporate before their eyes. How can entrepreneurs find the right match among trends, their products or services, and the appropriate target markets? Market research!

How to Conduct Market Research

The goal of market research is to reduce the risks associated with making business decisions. It can replace misinformation and assumptions with facts. Opinion and hearsay are not viable foundations on which to build a solid marketing strategy. Successful market research consists of four steps: define the problem, collect the data, analyze and interpret the data, and draw conclusions.

Step 1.   ***Define the objective.*** The first—and most crucial—step in market research is to define the research objective clearly and concisely. A common error at this stage is to confuse a symptom with the true problem. For example, dwindling sales is not a problem; it is a symptom. To get to the heart of the matter, entrepreneurs must list all the possible factors that could have caused it. Do we face new competition? Are our sales representatives impolite or unknowledgeable? Have customer tastes changed? Is our product line too narrow? Do customers have trouble finding what they want? Is our Web site giving customers what they want? Is it easy to navigate?

Step 2.   ***Collect the data.*** The marketing approach that dominates today is **individualized (one-to-one) marketing**, which involves gathering data on individual customers and then developing a marketing program designed specifically to appeal to their needs, tastes, and preferences. In a society in which people feel so isolated and interactions are so impersonal, one-to-one marketing gives a business a competitive edge. Companies following this approach know their customers, understand how to give them the value they want, and, perhaps most important, know how to make them feel special and important. The idea is to treat each customer as an individual, and the goal is to transform a company's best and most profitable customers into loyal, lifetime customers.

individualized (one-to-one) marketing
a system based on gathering data on individual customers and developing a marketing program designed to appeal specifically to their needs, tastes, and preferences.

Individualized marketing requires business owners to gather and assimilate detailed information about their customers. Fortunately, owners of even the smallest companies now have access to affordable technology that creates and manages computerized databases, allowing them to develop close, one-to-one relationships with their customers. Much like gold nuggets waiting to be discovered, significant amounts of valuable information about customers and their buying habits are hidden *inside* many small businesses, tucked away in computerized databases. For most business owners, collecting useful information about their customers and potential new products and markets is simply a matter of sorting and organizing data that are already floating around somewhere in their companies. One marketing research expert explains the situation this way:[18]

> You know a lot about your customers. You know who they are, where they live, what their buying habits are. And if you're like most companies, you've done absolutely nothing with that pile of market intelligence. It just sits there, earning you no money and creating zero shareholder value.

The key is to mine the data that most companies have at their disposal and turn them into useful information that allows the company to "court" its customers with special products, services, ads, and offers that appeal most to them. How can entrepreneurs gather valuable market and customer information? Two basic methods are available: conducting *primary research*, data you collect and analyze yourself, and gathering *secondary research* (data that have already been compiled and that are available, often at a very reasonable cost or even free). Primary research techniques include the following:

- *Customer surveys and questionnaires.* Keep them short. Word your questions carefully so that you do not bias the results and use a simple ranking system (e.g., a 1-to-5 scale, with 1 representing "unacceptable" and 5 representing "excellent"). Test your survey for problems on a small number of people before putting it to use. Online surveys are inexpensive, are easy to conduct, and provide feedback fast. Mimi's Café, a full-service restaurant with a New Orleans decor and 145 locations in 24 states, periodically sends short e-mail surveys to members of its eClub to solicit their views on new menu items and other topics.

- *Focus groups.* Enlist a small number of customers to give you feedback on specific issues in your business—quality, convenience, hours of operation, service, and so on. Listen carefully for new marketing opportunities as customers or potential customers tell you what is on their minds. Once again, consider using the Internet; one small bicycle company conducts 10 online focus groups each year at virtually no cost and gains valuable marketing information from them.

- *Social media conversations and monitoring.* With social media, companies have the opportunity to engage in direct conversations with their customers. In addition, monitoring social media for comments about a business and its products or services can provide useful feedback from customers. Many companies use the Google Alerts feature of the leading search engine to track and receive e-mail updates whenever someone writes about their brands online. Most social networking sites, including Facebook and Twitter, offer search features that allow users to track what people are saying about a company and its products or services. Culver's, a quick-service restaurant chain with more than 400 locations in 18 states, not only actively uses social media to solicit feedback from customers about new products and promotions but also constantly monitors Facebook and Twitter posts for mentions of its brand and products.[19]

- *Test market.* One of the best ways to gauge customer response to a new product or service is to set up a test market. Wendy's, one of the last major quick-service restaurants to enter the fast-growing breakfast market, recently ran tests of a breakfast menu at locations in Pittsburgh, Kansas City, and Phoenix. Based on the test, Wendy's estimates that breakfast could contribute as much as $150,000 in additional sales at each of its restaurants.[20]

- *Daily transactions.* Sift as much data as possible from existing company records and daily transactions—customer warranty cards, personal checks, frequent-buyer clubs, credit applications, and others.

- *Other ideas.* Set up a suggestion system (for customers and employees) and use it. Establish a customer advisory panel to determine how well your company is meeting needs. Talk with suppliers about trends they have spotted in the industry. Contact customers who have not bought anything in long time and find out why. Contact people who are not customers and find out why. Teach employees to be good listeners and then ask them what they hear.

Secondary research, which is usually less expensive to collect than primary data, includes the following sources:

- *Business directories.* To locate a trade association, use *Business Information Sources* (University of California Press) or the *Encyclopedia of Associations* (Gale Research). To find suppliers, use the *Thomas Register of American Manufacturers* (Thomas Publishing Company) or *Standard & Poor's Register of Corporations, Executives, and Industries* (Standard & Poor's Corporation). *The American Wholesalers and Distributors Directory* includes details on more than 18,000 wholesalers and distributors.

- *Direct mail lists.* You can buy mailing lists for practically any type of business. The *Standard Rates and Data Service Directory of Mailing Lists* (Standard Rates and Data) is a good place to start looking.

- *Demographic data.* To learn more about the demographic characteristics of customers in general, use the *Statistical Abstract of the United States* (Government Printing Office). Profiles of more specific regions are available in the *State and Metropolitan Data Book* (Government Printing Office). The *Sourcebook of ZIP Code Demographics* (CACI, Inc.) provides detailed breakdowns of the population in every ZIP code in the country. *Sales and Marketing Management's Survey of Buying Power* (Bill Communications) has statistics on consumer, retail, and industrial buying.

- *Census data.* The Bureau of the Census publishes a wide variety of reports that summarize the wealth of data found in its census database, which is available at most libraries and at the Census Bureau's Web site (www.census.gov).

- *Forecasts.* The *U.S. Global Outlook* tracks the growth of 200 industries and gives a five-year forecast for each one. Many government agencies, including the U.S. Department of Commerce, offer forecasts on everything from interest rates to the number of housing starts. A government librarian can help you find what you need.

- *Market research.* Someone may already have compiled the market research you need. The *FINDex Worldwide Directory of Market Research Reports, Studies, and Surveys* (Cambridge Information Group) lists more than 10,600 studies available for purchase. Other directories of business research include the *Simmons Study of Media and Markets* (Simmons Market Research Bureau Inc.) and the *A. C. Nielsen Retail Index* (A. C. Nielsen Company).

- *Articles.* Magazine and journal articles pertinent to your business are a great source of information. Use the *Reader's Guide to Periodical Literature*, the *Business Periodicals Index* (similar to the *Reader's Guide* but focusing on business periodicals), and *Ulrich's Guide to International Periodicals* to locate the ones you need.

- *Local data.* Your state department of commerce and your local chamber of commerce will very likely have useful data on the local market of interest to you. Call to find out what is available.

- *The Internet.* Most entrepreneurs are astounded at the marketing information that is available on the Internet. Using one of the search engines, you can gain access to a world of information—literally!

Thanks to advances in computer hardware and software, data mining, once available only to large companies with vast computer power and large market research budgets, is now possible for even very small businesses. **Data mining** is a process in which computer software that uses statistical analysis, database technology, and artificial intelligence finds hidden patterns, trends, and connections in data so that business owners can make better marketing decisions and predictions about customers' behavior. By finding relationships among the many components of a data set, identifying clusters of customers with similar buying habits, and predicting customers' buying patterns, data mining gives entrepreneurs incredible marketing power.

data mining
a process in which computer software that uses statistical analysis, database technology, and artificial intelligence finds hidden patterns, trends, and connections in data so that business owners can make better marketing decisions and predictions about customers' behavior.

Step 3. *Analyze and interpret the data.* The results of market research alone do not provide a solution to the problem; business owners must interpret them. What do the data tell you? Is there a common thread running through the responses? Do the results suggest any changes needed in the way the business operates? Are there new opportunities the entrepreneur can take advantage of? There are no hard-and-fast rules for interpreting market research results; entrepreneurs must use judgment and common sense to determine what the results of their research mean.

Step 4. *Draw conclusions and act.* The market research process is not complete until the business owner acts on the information collected. In many cases, the conclusion is obvious once a small business owner interprets the results of the market research. Based on an understanding of what the facts really mean, the owner must then decide how to use the information in the business. For example, the owner of a small ladies' clothing boutique discovered from a survey that her customers preferred evening shopping hours over early morning hours. She made the schedule adjustment, and sales began to climb.

LO4

Describe how a small business can build a competitive edge in the marketplace using guerrilla marketing strategies.

Plotting a Guerrilla Marketing Strategy: How to Build a Competitive Edge

To be successful guerrilla marketers, entrepreneurs must be as innovative in creating their marketing strategies as they are in developing new product and service ideas. Table 8.2 describes several low-cost, creative, and highly effective guerrilla marketing tactics small businesses have used to outperform their larger rivals.

Guerrilla Marketing Principles

The following 14 principles can help business owners create powerful, effective guerrilla marketing strategies.

FIND A NICHE AND FILL IT As you learned in Chapter 3, many successful small companies choose their niches carefully and defend them fiercely rather than compete head-to-head with larger rivals. A focus (niche) strategy allows a small company to maximize the advantages of its size and to compete effectively even in industries dominated by giants by serving its target customers better than its competitors. Focusing on niches that are too small to be attractive to large companies is a common recipe for success among thriving small companies. "Finding unserved niches is an excellent way to begin 'whupping' the big guys, if not in their own back yard, at least on the same street," says one marketing expert.[21]

ENTREPRENEURIAL PROFILE: Doug Schattinger: Pioneer Athletics Pioneer Athletics, based in Cleveland, Ohio, specializes in manufacturing the field paint used to mark athletic fields. Founded in 1905 by Otto Wehe, the company originally sold house paint and chicken feed before finding its niche with Bright Stripe paint, which is designed to stick to natural grass and synthetic turf without flaking or rubbing off on uniforms. Doug Schattinger, Wehe's great-grandnephew, now runs the 120-employee company, whose paint is used on nearly 25,000 athletic fields across the United States, including the turf at Heinz Field, the home of the Pittsburgh Steelers.[22] ∎

Niche markets, such as the one Pioneer Athletics is targeting, are ideally suited for small businesses. "If a small business follows the principles of targeting, segmenting, and differentiating, it doesn't have to collapse to larger companies," says marketing expert Phil Kotler.[23]

TABLE 8.2 Guerrilla Marketing Tactics

- Help organize and sponsor a service- or community-oriented project.
- Sponsor offbeat, memorable events. Build a giant banana split or rent a theater for a morning and invite kids for a free viewing.
- Always be on the lookout for new niches to enter. Try to develop multiple niches.
- Offer to speak about your business, industry, product, or service to local organizations.
- Launch a loyalty program that gives customers a reason to return. Be sure to provide loyalty program members with benefits, such as special offers, discounts, shopping previews, and others.
- Reward existing customers for referring new customers to your company. When customers refer business to Choice Translating, a language translation company in Charlotte, North Carolina, they receive a special gift.
- Sell at every opportunity. One brewery includes a minicatalog advertising T-shirts and mugs in every six-pack it sells. Orders for catalog items are climbing fast.
- Develop a sales "script" that asks customers a series of questions to hone in on what they are looking for and what will lead them to the conclusion that your product or service is *it*!
- Sell gift certificates. They really boost your cash flow.
- Create samples of your product and give them to customers. You'll increase sales later.
- Offer a 100%, money-back, no-hassles guarantee. By removing the customer's risk of buying, you increase your product's attractiveness.
- Create a frequent-buyer program. Remember how valuable existing customers are. Work hard to keep the customers you have! One coffee shop kept its customers coming back with a punch-card promotion that gave a free pound of coffee after a customer purchased nine pounds.
- Clip articles that feature your business and send reprints to customers and potential customers. Keep reminding them of who you are and why you're valuable to them.
- Test how well your ads "pull" with coded coupons that customers bring in. Focus your ad expenditures on those media that produce the best results for you.
- Create "tip sheets" to pass out to customers and potential customers (e.g., landscape tips on lawn maintenance).
- Find ways to make your product or service irresistible to your customers. One furniture company e-mails photos of big-ticket items customers are considering, and sales closing rates have climbed 25 percent.
- Create an award for your community (e.g., a landscape company presented a "best yard" award each season).
- Create a big event of your own: "January is Customer Appreciation Month. Buy one suit and get a second one at 50 percent off."
- Conduct a contest in the community (e.g., a photographer sponsored a juried photo contest for different age groups). One restaurant that targeted the business crowd for lunch encouraged customers to leave their business cards (which gave the restaurateur the ability to e-mail them daily lunch specials) to enter a drawing for a free $50 iTunes gift card.
- Collect testimonials from satisfied customers and use them in ads, brochures, and so on. Testimonials are one of the most effective forms of advertising!
- Purchase customized postage stamps that feature your company's logo (see PhotoStamps at http://photo.stamps.com) and use them on business correspondence.
- Get a former journalist to help you write a story "pitch" for local media.
- Show an interest in your customers' needs. If you spot a seminar that would be of interest to them, tell them! Become a valuable resource for them.
- Find unique ways to thank customers (especially first-time buyers) for their business (e.g., a note, a lunch, a gift basket, and so on).
- Give loyal customers a "freebie" occasionally. You might be surprised at how long they will remember it.
- Create a newsletter that features your customers or clients and their businesses (e.g., a photo of a client using your product in his or her business).
- Cooperate with other businesses selling complementary products and services in marketing efforts and campaigns, a process called fusion marketing. Share mailing lists and advertising time or space or work together on a special promotion.
- Use major competitors' coupons against them. The owner of an independent sandwich shop routinely pulled business from a nearby national chain by advertising that he would accept its coupons.
- Market your company's uniqueness. Many customers enjoy buying from small companies that are different and unique. The owners of the only tea plantation in the United States used that fact to their advantage in establishing a customer base.

Sources: Adapted from Mickey Meece, "How to Keep Momentum Going for Customers and Employees," *New York Times*, January 3, 2008, http://www.nytimes.com/2008/01/03/business/smallbusiness/03tips.html; Jay Conrad Levinson, "Attention Getters," *Entrepreneur*, March 1998, p. 88; Lynn Beresford, Janean Chun, Cynthia E. Griffin, Heather Page, and Debra Phillips, "Marketing 101," *Entrepreneur*, May 1996, pp. 104–114; Guen Sublette, "Marketing 101," *Entrepreneur*, May 1995, pp. 86–98; Denise Osburn, "Bringing Them Back for More," *Nation's Business*, August 1995, p. 31R; Jay Conrad Levinson, "Survival Tactics," *Entrepreneur*, March 1996, p. 84; Tom Stein, "Outselling the Giants," *Success*, May 1996, pp. 38–41; and Gwen Moran, "Get Noticed," *Entrepreneur*, October 2008, pp. 58–61.

publicity
any commercial news covered by the media that boosts sales but for which a small company does not pay.

USE THE POWER OF PUBLICITY **Publicity** is any commercial news covered by the media that boosts sales but for which a small company does not pay. Publicity has power; because it is from an unbiased source, a news feature about a company or a product that appears in a newspaper or magazine has more impact on people's buying decisions than an advertisement does. Exposure in any medium raises a company's visibility and boosts sales, and, best of all, publicity is free! It does require some creativity and effort, however.

The following tactics can help entrepreneurs stimulate publicity for their companies:

Write an article that will interest your customers or potential customers. One investment advisor writes a monthly column for the local newspaper on timely topics such as "Retirement Planning," "Minimizing Your Tax Bill," and "How to Pay for College." Not only do the articles help build her credibility as an expert, but they also have attracted new customers to her business.

Sponsor an event designed to attract attention. In 1982, Bob Bisbee, owner of a small fuel dock and fishing store in Newport Beach, California, created a fishing tournament, Bisbee's Black and Blue Tournament (the focus was on black marlin and blue marlin), in an attempt to boost sales for his business. Before long, the event was picked up by major media outlets. The public relations strategy was so successful that the fishing tournament, now one of the world's richest and best-known fishing events, has replaced Bisbee's original business![24]

Involve celebrities "on the cheap." Few small businesses can afford to hire celebrities as spokespersons for their companies. Some companies have discovered other ways to get celebrities to promote their products, however. For instance, when Karen Neuburger, owner of Karen Neuburger's Sleepwear, learned that Oprah Winfrey is a "pajama connoisseur," she sent the talk show host a pair of her pajamas. The move paid off; Neuburger appeared on Oprah's popular television show on three separate occasions, each one resulting in an increase in sales for her company.[25]

Contact local television and radio stations and offer to be interviewed. Many local news or talk shows are looking for guests to talk about topics of interest to their audiences (especially in January and February). Even local shows can reach new customers.

Publish a newsletter. With a personal computer and desktop publishing software, any entrepreneur can publish a professional-looking newsletter. Freelancers can offer design and editing advice. Use the newsletter to reach present and potential customers.

Contact local business and civic organizations and offer to speak to them. A powerful, informative presentation can win new business. (Be sure your public speaking skills are up to par first! If not, consider joining Toastmasters.)

Offer or sponsor a seminar. Teaching people about a subject you know a great deal about builds confidence and goodwill among potential customers. The owner of a landscaping service and nursery offers a short course in landscape architecture and always sees sales climb afterward!

Write news releases and fax or e-mail them to the media. The key to having a news release picked up and printed is finding a unique angle on your business or industry that would interest an editor. Keep it short, simple, and interesting. E-mail press releases should be shorter than printed ones—typically four or five paragraphs rather than one or two pages—and they should include a link to the company's Web site.

Volunteer to serve on community and industry boards and committees. You can make your town a better place to live and work and raise your company's visibility at the same time.

Sponsor a community project or support a nonprofit organization or charity. Not only will you be giving something back to the community, but you will also gain recognition, goodwill, and, perhaps, customers for your business. The key is to partner with charities that match the company's values and mission, whether that involves rescuing homeless pets or providing back-to-school supplies for underprivileged kids. Kim Gordon, owner of a marketing consulting business in the Florida Keys, recently sponsored an *American Idol*–style fashion show and luncheon featuring local male celebrities as models. The sold-out show raised money for a local shelter for abused women and children and spotlighted Gordon's firm as the lead sponsor.[26]

Promote a cause. According to the Cone Cause Evolution and Environmental Survey, 79 percent of customers (and 88 percent of the Millennial generation) say that, other things being equal, they are likely to switch from one brand to another if the other brand is associated with a good cause.[27] By engaging in cause marketing, entrepreneurs can support a worthy cause that is important to them and generate publicity and goodwill for their companies at the same time. The key is choosing a cause that is important to your customers. One marketing expert offers the following formula for selecting the right cause: mission statement + personal passion + customer demographics = ideal cause.[28]

ENTREPRENEURIAL PROFILE: Jonathan Fornaci: Straw Hat Pizza Every year, Straw Hat Pizza, a small chain of pizza restaurants based in San Leandro, California, raises money to support Share Our Strengths' "No Kid Hungry Campaign," a national effort to end childhood hunger. "Straw Hat Pizza has served children and families for more than 50 years, and 'No Kid Hungry' has always been our fund-raising focus," says Jonathan Fornaci, the company's president. The company also is known for providing free team pizza parties for the children who play on youth athletic teams in the communities it serves.[29] ■

DON'T JUST SELL; ENTERTAIN Numerous surveys have shown that consumers are bored with shopping and that they are less inclined to spend their scarce leisure time shopping than ever before. Winning customers today requires more than low prices and wide merchandise selection; increasingly, businesses are adopting strategies based on **entertailing**, the notion of drawing customers into a store by creating a kaleidoscope of sights, sounds, smells, and activities, all designed to entertain—and, of course, sell (think Disney). The primary goal of entertailing is to catch customers' attention and engage them in some kind of entertaining experience so that they shop longer and buy more goods or services. Entertailing involves "making [shopping] more fun, more educational, more interactive," says one retail consultant.[30] For instance, at the Corvallis, Washington, location of the Book Bin, a small chain of bookstores, customers can read books as they sip lattes and relax on a comfortable couch with the store cat, Tess, lounging nearby as they wait for a lecture and book signing by the author or a live music concert.[31]

Research supports the benefits of entertailing's hands-on, interactive, educational, approach to selling; one study found that, when making a purchase, 34 percent of consumers are driven more by emotional factors, such as fun and excitement, than by logical factors, such as price and convenience.[32] Entertailing's goal, of course, is not only to entertain customers but also to boost sales.

entertailing
a marketing concept designed to draw customers into a store by creating a kaleidoscope of sights, sounds, smells, and activities, all designed to entertain—and, of course, sell.

ENTREPRENEURIAL PROFILE: The LEGO Store The LEGO Store in Troy, Michigan, engages customers with an effective entertailing strategy. At the entrance, an eight-foot-tall Buzz Light Year, made entirely of LEGOs by children under the supervision of a LEGO Master Builder during the shop's grand opening, greets visitors. The store stocks more than 4 million LEGO bricks, many of which are featured on the back wall in a colorful Pick a Brick display that allows customers to select LEGO bricks of various sizes, colors, and shapes. The store also offers a living room area in which children (and adults) can play with LEGOs and test their engineering and building skills. "Children and their families are able to experience the creativity and imagination that goes into LEGO building," says Skip Kodak, the company's vice president. Another way that the store engages customers is through its LEGO Educational Center, where young people can take classes in building LEGO projects while improving their problem-solving, math, engineering, and robotic skills and stimulating their creativity. LEGO also interacts with customers through its LEGO Club and its Web site, where children can watch videos, download plans for LEGO building projects, and ask questions of Max, the company's mascot.[33] ■

Successful entertailers rely on the following principles:

- *Sponsor events that will attract your target customers.* One goal of entertailing is to get potential customers into the store. An upscale men's clothing store could offer a workshop on personal finance and investing or how to pull off "business casual" dress appropriately.

- *Transform an offbeat holiday into an entertailing event.* Did you know that October 28 is National Chocolate Day or that October 18 is National Chocolate Cupcake Day? Almost every day of the year is designated as a "holiday" to celebrate something unusual, such as National Eat Ice Cream for Breakfast Day, which takes place on the first Saturday in February. Pick one and create a special event around it.

● *Give customers the opportunity to interact with your products.* One golf store has an indoor putting green where customers can try out new putters before buying them. A sporting goods retailer has a 20-foot rock wall that allows climbing enthusiasts to test climbing gear.

● *Use technology creatively.* One golf retailer has invested in a golf course simulator that allows customers to "play" some of the world's most famous courses. A landscape architect uses computer software that allows him to landscape digital photographs of his customers' homes so that they can see exactly how different designs look.

● *Remember that the ultimate goal is to sell.* No matter which entertailing techniques you decide to use, remember to design them with the goal of increasing sales.[34]

Table 8.3 describes seven principles that retailers can use to transform their businesses into destination stores that draw customers like magnets.

STRIVE TO BE UNIQUE One of the most effective guerrilla marketing tactics is to create an image of uniqueness for your business. As you learned in Chapter 3, entrepreneurs can achieve a unique place in the market in a variety of ways, including through the products and services they offer, the marketing and promotional campaigns they use, the store layouts they design, and the business strategies they employ. The goal is to stand out from the crowd; few things are as uninspiring to customers as a "me-too" business that offers nothing unique.

ENTREPRENEURIAL PROFILE: Brad Anderson and Mike LaVecchia: Grain Surfboards In the 1950s, surfboard makers substituted lighter and cheaper polyurethane foam for wood to make the core of their boards. Some modern manufacturers also use expanded polystyrene coated with an epoxy resin to create a highly durable, extremely lightweight board that floats higher in the water and is easier to paddle. Grain Surfboards, founded by Brad Anderson and Mike LaVecchia in LaVecchia's basement just minutes from the ocean in York Beach, Maine, has set itself apart from its larger competitors by returning to wood to make its boards. Combining his love of surfing with his passion for traditional wooden boat building, LaVecchia developed a construction method that uses just one-third of the wood that traditional methods required. Board builders at Grain rely mostly on hand tools and a sustainable building process that uses local cedar constructed around an internal mahogany frame. "Our wooden boards are sustainable and strong, but have all of the benefits of modern design," says LaVecchia. Grain surfboards not only are beautiful, but they also are extremely durable. Anderson calls them "lifetime boards." "Surf one of our boards for years, and it will still look like it did the day you got it," he says.[35] ■

BUILD A COMMUNITY WITH CUSTOMERS Some of the most successful companies interact with their customers regularly, intentionally, and purposefully to create meaningful, lasting relationships with them. Ducati, an Italian company that makes stylish, high-performance motorcycles, has shifted its marketing strategy from reliance on advertising in traditional media to building a community with customers by sponsoring rallies, races, parties, and shows. Ducati has benefited in two ways from this guerrilla marketing strategy: feedback from customers has led to better quality and more popular features in its motorcycles, and fan enthusiasm has raised the company's visibility.[36]

Company Web sites and social media also are important tools for building a community with customers. MAC, a popular cosmetics company, entertains customers with its "Cute Pinball" game on Facebook that features the characters in the company's upcoming cosmetics collections. Jaeger-LeCoultre, a maker of premium watches, invites customers to join its online community, where they receive invitations to special events, participate in discussions with company managers and other customers, and play a creative watchmaking game. On its Facebook page, the company invites visitors to create a piece of virtual artwork using one of its classic Reverso watches.[37]

CONNECT WITH CUSTOMERS ON AN EMOTIONAL LEVEL Closely linked to building a community with customers is the strategy of creating an emotional attachment with them. Companies that establish a deeper relationship with their customers than one based merely on making a sale have the capacity to be exceptional guerrilla marketers. These businesses win because customers

TABLE 8.3 Seven Principles That Make Your Shop Pop

Pamela Danziger, president of the marketing consulting firm Unity Marketing, offers seven principles that can transform any store into a shop that "pops."

1. *Offer high levels of customer involvement and interaction.* When customers have the opportunity to interact with a product, they spend more time in the store, which increases the probability that they will buy something. That's the guiding principle behind Barnes & Noble's decision to incorporate chairs and couches as well as coffee and snack bars into its bookstores.

2. *Evoke shoppers' curiosity to explore with a unique displays, store layout, and selection of merchandise.* One jewelry store captured the attention of passersby with a window display that featured not only unique pieces of jewelry but also a collection of interesting fossils, crystals, geodes, and unusual rock formations. The display increased the number of walk-in shoppers and sales.

3. *Exude a contagious air of excitement, energy, and "electricity."* Apple Stores generate an astonishing volume of sales per square foot by creating an energized atmosphere. The decor is modern and minimalist so that products stand out. iPads located next to every product on display provide interactive product, service, and support information and allow shoppers to summon a salesperson in a flash. Shoppers who have questions or technical problems can ask a highly trained expert at the Genius Bar. Employees periodically offer free classes on using Apple products.

4. *Create a synergistic convergence of atmosphere, store design, and merchandise that results in a special place for customers.* The goal is to create a "paradox environment," one that offers customers displays and products that they expect but that also surprises them with something that is unique and unusual, even bizarre. To promote a new loyalty card program called Sprize with the tagline "Turning shopping on its head," a Gap store in London surprised shoppers by displaying 32 mannequins suspended from the ceiling upside down and arranged for three cars and a hot dog stand parked in front of the store to be flipped on their tops.

5. *Provide an authentic values-driven experience.* Godfrey's Welcome to Dogdom, a pet boutique located in Mohnton, Pennsylvania, sees the world from a dog's point of view and stocks a full line of dog-related products, ranging from essentials such as specialty foods, health-related products, and pet care items to luxuries such as hand-cast stone sculptures, cast bronze statues, dog apparel, and healthy fresh-baked dog biscuits in a multitude of flavors. Customers can book their pets for a doggie play group or schedule family time with their pets at one of the store's play parks. Special events such as a Valentine's Day Whine and Dine Brunch, a Pooch Smooch Easter photography session, and a Howl-o-ween Pawrade and Pawty keep customers and their beloved pets coming back to Godfrey's.

6. *A price-value model that customers understand and support.* The Great Recession has made shoppers value conscious, but that does not mean that discounting is the best way to attract customers. Businesses that show customers the value their products provide create a good value proposition without having to resort to price cuts. "Our focus is on solutions to our customers' problems and issues with their dogs and is not based on commodity price and product selling," says Barb Emmett of Godfrey's Welcome to Dogdom.

7. *A friendly store that is welcoming, friendly, and gives customers a reason to return.* In some stores, salespeople act as if they are doing customers a favor by waiting on them. Stores that pop take the opposite approach, welcoming customers and treating them as if they are important (because they are!). At an Arby's franchise in Camp Hill, Pennsylvania, 89-year-old Pearl Weaver greets customers with waving pom-poms, a big smile, and a happy "Welcome to Arby's." The store's manager, Christian Stakes, says that not a week goes by without "Miz Pearl," as customers affectionately call her, being mentioned in online and in-store customer satisfaction surveys. "If she's off for a week, people ask about her," he says.

The goal is to create a store with "soul" that engages customers on many different levels; that creates a fun, festive atmosphere; and that has a mission that goes far beyond merely selling products.

Sources: Based on Paula Holewa, "Does Your Shop Pop?," *JCK*, January 13, 2011, http://www.jckonline.com/blogs/retail-details/2011/01/13/does-your-shop-pop; Kerry Bodine, "Apple Store 2.0: Why Customer Experience Leaders Should Care," *Forbes*, May 26, 2011, http://www.forbes.com/sites/forrester/2011/05/26/apple-store-2-0-why-customer-experience-leaders-should-care; Pam Danziger, "A Shop That Pops: How Godfrey's, a Pet Boutique, Creates the Ultimate Customer Experience," Unity Marketing, Shops That Pop, http://www.shopsthatpop.com/cms/Home_Page/White_Papers_Articles.php; Pam Danziger, "Does Your Shop Pop?," Unity Marketing, Shops That Pop, http://www.shopsthatpop.com/cms/Home_Page/White_Papers_Articles.php; Glen Stansberry, "10 Examples of Shockingly-Excellent Customer Service," *American Express OPEN Forum*, May 4, 2010, http://www.openforum.com/idea-hub/topics/managing/article/10-examples-of-shockingly-excellent-customer-service-1; and Lara Brenckle, "Camp Hill Woman, 89, Hands Out Cheers with Sandwiches at Fast-Food Restaurant," *PennLive*, August 10, 2009, http://www.pennlive.com/midstate/index.ssf/2009/08/camp_hill_woman_89_hands_out_c.html.

receive an emotional boost every time they buy these companies' products or services. They connect with their customers emotionally by providing captivating products, supporting causes that are important to their customer base, taking exceptional care of their customers, surpassing customers' expectations in quality and service, or making doing business with them a fun and enjoyable experience. "Shoppers don't love a store because they love the merchandise it carries," says Pamela Danziger, a consumer insights expert. "They love a store because it touches them personally and emotionally."[38] Building and nurturing an ongoing relationship with customers establishes a relationship of trust, a vital component of every marketing effort. The Cone Cause Evolution and Environmental Survey reports that 69 percent of Americans consider a company's business practices when making purchase decisions.[39]

The goal is not only to create lifelong, loyal customers but also to transform customers into passionate brand advocates, people who promote a company's products or services to friends, family members, and others. Although many companies manufacture tablet PCs, few have achieved the iconic status of Apple's iPad, which allows customers to perform a variety of tasks, ranging from word processing and downloading e-books and music to accessing the Internet and making face-to-face video calls. Its sleek, lightweight, touch-screen design resonates with customers because it reflects the way they want to use a tablet PC and evokes an image of "cool." The result of this emotional connection with customers: sales of 25 million units in a little more than a year and a base of loyal fans who happily promote the company to their friends—at no cost.

One important aspect of connecting with customers is defining the company's **unique selling proposition (USP)**, a key customer benefit of a product or service that sets it apart from its competition. To be effective, a USP must actually *be* unique—something the competition does not (or cannot) provide—as well as compelling enough to encourage customers to buy. Unfortunately, many business owners never define their companies' USP, and the result is an uninspiring me-too message that cries out "buy from us" without offering customers any compelling reason to do so.

A successful USP answers the critical question that every customer asks: "What's in it for me?" A USP should express in no more than 10 words what a business can do for its customers. Can your product or service save your customers time or money, make their lives easier or more convenient, improve their self-esteem, or make them feel better? If so, you have the foundation for building a USP. For instance, the owner of a quaint New England bed-and-breakfast came up with a four-word USP that captures the essence of the escape her business offers guests from their busy lives: "Delicious beds, delicious breakfasts." Shmuel Gniwisch, CEO of Ice.com, an online jewelry store, expresses his company's USP quite simply: "We are a candy store for women."[40] Department store Target's USP is "Expect more. Pay less." Naomi Dunford, founder of IttyBiz, a marketing consulting firm that helps small companies with no more than five employees create guerrilla marketing strategies, says that her company's USP is "Marketing for businesses without marketing departments."[41]

The best way to identify a meaningful USP that connects a company to its target customers is to describe the primary benefit(s) its product or service offers customers and then to list other, secondary benefits it provides. A business is unlikely to have more than three primary benefits, which should be unique and able to set it apart. When describing the top benefits the company offers its customers, entrepreneurs must look beyond just the physical characteristics of the product or service. Sometimes the most powerful USP emphasizes the *intangible, psychological, and emotional* benefits a product or service offers customers—for example, safety, "coolness," security, acceptance, status, and others. The goal is to use the USP to enable a company to stand out in customers' minds.

It is also important to develop a brief list of the facts that support your company's USP, such as 24-hour service, a fully trained staff, awards won, and so on. By focusing the message on these top benefits and the facts supporting them, business owners can communicate their USPs to their target audiences in meaningful, attention-getting ways. Building a firm's marketing message around its core USP spells out for customers the specific benefit they get if they buy that product or service and why they should do business with your company rather than with the competition. Finally, once a small company begins communicating its USP to customers, it has to fulfill the promise! Nothing erodes a company's credibility as quickly as promising customers a benefit and then failing to deliver on that promise.

Many small companies are finding common ground with their customers on an issue that is becoming increasingly important to many people: the environment. Small companies selling everything from jeans to toothpicks are emphasizing their "green" products and are making an emotional connection with their customers in the process. Companies must be truthful, however, or their marketing pitches can backfire and damage their reputations. Consumers are becoming

unique selling proposition (USP)
a key customer benefit of a product or service that sets it apart from the competition; it answers the critical question every customer asks: "What's in it for me?"

more vigilant in their search for companies that are guilty of "greenwashing," touting unsubstantiated or misleading claims about the environmental friendliness of their products. Customers feel good about doing business with companies that manufacture products according to green principles, support environmental causes, donate a portion of their pretax earnings to philanthropic organizations, and operate with a clear sense of fulfilling their social responsibility.

CREATE AN IDENTITY FOR YOUR BUSINESS THROUGH BRANDING One of the most effective ways for entrepreneurs to differentiate their businesses from the competition is to create a unique identity for it through **branding**. Although they may not have the resources to build a brand name as well known as Coca-Cola (Coca-Cola's brand is estimated to be worth more than $70 billion), entrepreneurs can be successful in building a brand identity for their companies on a smaller scale in the markets they serve. A large budget is not a prerequisite for building a strong brand, but creating one does take a concerted, well-coordinated effort that connects every touch point a company has with its customers with the company's desired image. A strong brand evokes the company's story in customers' minds. "Every element that you use to interact with the customer is part of your brand and your story," says Seth Godin, entrepreneur and author of numerous marketing books. "If you build your brand right, you won't need to allocate more funds for marketing."[42]

> **branding**
> communicating a company's unique selling proposition (USP) to its target customers in a consistent and integrated manner.

Branding involves communicating a company's unique selling proposition to its target customers in a consistent and integrated manner. A brand is a company's "face" in the marketplace, and it is built on a company's promise of providing quality goods or services to satisfy multiple customer needs. A brand sends an important message to customers; it signals that the benefits a company offers (which may be intangible) are worth more than those its competitors can offer. "Branding is what sets you apart; it's a natural magnet [for customers]," says Mary van de Wiel, CEO of a brand consulting firm.[43] Companies that build brands successfully benefit from increased customer loyalty, the ability to command higher prices, greater visibility, and increased name recognition. Small companies that attempt to lure customers with discounts or constant sales often dilute their brands and cheapen them in the customers' eyes. "A brand is the most valuable piece of real estate in the world," says one marketing expert, "[It is] a corner of the customer's mind."[44] Figure 8.2 on page 290 shows the connection between a company's brand and its unique selling proposition.

ENTREPRENEURIAL PROFILE: David Oreck: Oreck Corporation David Oreck, founder of the vacuum cleaner manufacturer that bears his name, has spent 45 years building his company's brand by emphasizing the power, durability, and light weight of its vacuum cleaners. "We don't sell the cheapest product on the market," says Oreck, acknowledging that Oreck vacuum cleaners sell at prices that are 33 percent higher than many competitors' models. "But price is only one component of value. Customers want value. If they have confidence in your brand, they'll pay a premium for it."[45] ∎

EMBRACE SOCIAL MARKETING Although social networking sites such as Facebook and Twitter are better known for their personal applications, they also have significant potential as marketing tools. Fifty-nine percent of Internet users participate in at least one social networking site, a significant increase from just 34 percent in 2008.[46] Businesses recognize that many of their current and potential customers use social networking sites and are reaching out to them with social marketing efforts. Forty-four percent of entrepreneurs use social media to connect with existing and potential customers, and Facebook, with more than 900 million active users, is the most popular tool (see Figure 8.3).[47]

Social networking sites are an ideal guerrilla marketing tool because they allow entrepreneurs to market their companies effectively and at little or no cost. One recent survey reports that 88 percent of marketers say that their social media marketing efforts have generated greater exposure for their companies and many other benefits (see Figure 8.4).[48] Small companies use a variety of social networking tools to market their companies, but three of the most popular are Facebook, LinkedIn, and Twitter:

Facebook. People spend nearly 12 *billion* hours per month on Facebook, the world's largest social network. Creating a Facebook business page is not the same as creating a personal profile page, however. On Facebook, an entrepreneur should create a Welcome page

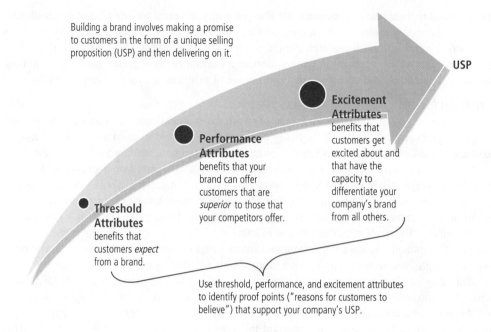

FIGURE 8.2

The Connection between Branding and a USP

Source: Adapted from Brand-Savvy, Highlands Ranch, Colorado.

Building a brand involves making a promise to customers in the form of a unique selling proposition (USP) and then delivering on it.

USP

Excitement Attributes benefits that customers get excited about and that have the capacity to differentiate your company's brand from all others.

Performance Attributes benefits that your brand can offer customers that are *superior* to those that your competitors offer.

Threshold Attributes benefits that customers *expect* from a brand.

Use threshold, performance, and excitement attributes to identify proof points ("reasons for customers to believe") that support your company's USP.

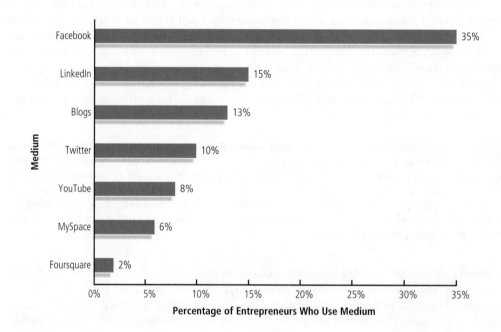

FIGURE 8.3

Social Media That Entrepreneurs Use as Marketing Tools

Source: American Express OPEN Small Business Monitor, Spring 2011.

Facebook 35%
LinkedIn 15%
Blogs 13%
Twitter 10%
YouTube 8%
MySpace 6%
Foursquare 2%

Medium

Percentage of Entrepreneurs Who Use Medium

that is designed to create interest in the company's products or services and that encourages visitors to "like" the business. Businesses can generate likes (formerly Fans) by posting the Facebook URL on in-store signs, business cards, shopping bags, and anything else customers are likely to see. E-mail and "refer-a-friend" campaigns and links to Facebook from a company's Web site and blog also increase the number of likes the company receives. One key to using Facebook successfully as a marketing tool is to keep a company's page fresh, just like the merchandise displays in a physical store. Adding photographs, announcements of upcoming events, polls and surveys, and games and contests or promoting a cause the company supports are excellent ways to create buzz and keep fans coming back.

You Be the Consultant

The Social Sauce Experiment

Big Papa's BBQ, a restaurant in Denver, Colorado, co-owned by Bill Cossoff and Frank Alfonso, made some of the best barbecue in town but, like many small companies, lacked a comprehensive marketing plan (although it spent $40,000 a year on advertising) and had no social media presence at all. *Entrepreneur* magazine challenged Denver-based marketing firm LeeReedy/Xylem Digital to take Big Papa's BBQ from social zero to social hero in just 60 days. Their goal was to employ social media to improve Big Papa's name recognition, increase sales by 50 percent, and increase profits during one of the restaurant's slowest seasons: winter. The marketing firm would plan and implement the restaurant's social media strategy for the first 30 days of the experiment before turning the reins over to Cossoff and Alfonso. How did the experiment go?

Results would be easy to measure; at the beginning of the contest, Big Papa's had no real brand and no social media presence. LeeReedy/Xylem decided to use four social media–based guerrilla marketing strategies to get Big Papa's BBQ into the big leagues of local barbecue:

- Pop-up events during which Big Papa's would give away barbecue at local hot spots and promote the event on social media.

- An exclusive "Super-Secret Supper Society" made up of fans and followers who would meet for dinners of ribs and beer.

- A "Win Big Papa" contest in which Alfonso would host a catered party for the winner.

- A rib "throwdown" contest that would challenge other barbecue restaurants in the area to a taste test.

Pop-Up Events

The first guerrilla marketing tactic was a pop-up rib giveaway that Big Papa's hosted in the parking lot of *Westword*, a local weekly alternative newspaper. Staffers from LeeReedy/Xylem began tweeting to *Westword* employees about free ribs in the parking lot at lunch. In turn, the *Westword* employees began retweeting, and by the time that Alfonso had finished cooking a smoker full of ribs, 75 people had showed up in 38-degree temperatures for a free lunch. All the hungry donors had to do was provide their e-mail addresses, which became the foundation of a database of potential customers that Big Papa's could build. Other pop-up events in Denver's funky LoDo district, a University of Denver hockey game, and a holiday lighting celebration after Thanksgiving generated more buzz and a growing database of potential customers.

Super-Secret Supper Society

Big Papa's Super-Secret Supper Society also proved to be a big hit with fans and followers. By listening to Twitter conversations about barbecue, LeeReedy/Xylem was able to identify potential society members. To be eligible for membership, however, people had to sign up as e-mail subscribers on Facebook. Employees in both restaurant locations promoted the supper society with hand-drawn signs, calling it "an exclusive evening of beers and bones." In January, Big Papa's selected 50 winners and invited them to a swanky barbecue dinner, including beer from New Belgium Brewing Company, at its Littleton, Colorado, location. "It was a home run," says Cossoff proudly, noting that several society members were taking pictures of the event and posting them to Facebook and tweeting about their free dinners.

"Throwdown" Challenge

The "throwdown" promotion, in which Big Papa's used Facebook and Twitter to challenge competing barbecue restaurants to a taste test, produced mixed results. Owners of many competing barbecue restaurants never saw the "throwdown" challenge, and of those who did, almost none responded.

The Transition

Halfway through the Social Sauce Experiment, LeeReedy/Xylem transferred ownership of the social media marketing effort to Big Papa's. Initially, the crew had difficulty deciding who would take control of the day-to-day management of the company's social media presence, and the job ultimately fell to Maureen Cossoff, Bill's wife. Originality quickly became an issue. Rather than listening to what people were talking about in social media and responding, the company began regurgitating some of the same tweets and Facebook posts that had been successful for LeeReedy/Xylem weeks before. "The switchover took a lot more effort than anyone suspected it would," says Nick Williams of LeeReedy/Xylem.

Results

Despite some challenges, Big Papa's BBQ considers the Social Sauce Experiment a success. The company's e-mail open and click-through rates were 35 and 14 percent, respectively (compared to industry average rates of 26 and 3.4 percent). In addition, the social media efforts enticed an average of 725 new customers each week to eat at Big Papa's, generating a sales increase of 22 percent. "We were able to turn one of our slowest times of the year into a moneymaker," says Alfonso. "You can't ask for more than that."

Big Papa's staff plans to continue the most successful parts of the social media experiment, including the pop-up events and the Secret Society. They also are making plans to conduct a "Name the Sauce" competition and to tap into the network of local food bloggers using social media. "It's all about the marketing mix," says Cossoff. "What this project has taught us is that social networking must be part of that mix and that it's not nearly as difficult to manage as we once thought."

(continued)

You Be the Consultant *(continued)*

1. Identify at least three lessons that entrepreneurs can learn from the Social Sauce Experiment.

2. Work with a team of your classmates to create your own Social Sauce Experiment. Select a local business that has no social media presence and develop a plan to boost its visibility, sales, and profits with a social media strategy.

3. Identify at least three guerrilla marketing strategies discussed in this chapter that Big Papa's BBQ can use to increase its visibility, sales, and profits. Explain how the company should implement each one.

Sources: Based on Matt Villano, "The Secret Sauce Project," *Entrepreneur*, January 2011, pp. 70–72; "Think Social Media Won't Help Your Business? Think Again . . . ," National Puerto Rican Chamber of Commerce, January 19, 2011, http://nprchamber.org/blog/2011/01/19/think-social-media-wont-help-your-business-think-again; and Matt Villano, "The Secret Sauce," *Entrepreneur*, April 2011, pp. 96–99.

FIGURE 8.4

Benefits of Social Media Marketing

Source: 2011 *Social Media Marketing Report,* Social Media Examiner, p. 16.

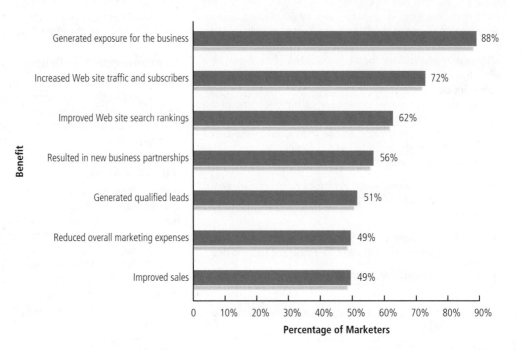

Entrepreneurs must invest time in their social media marketing effort; nearly 58 percent of marketers spend at least six hours a week on social media marketing.[49]

Frazer Harrison/Getty Images for Stella Cafe

ENTREPRENEURIAL PROFILE: Tim League: Alamo Draft House Cinema Tim League, founder of the Alamo Draft House Cinema, an 11-theater chain based in Austin, Texas, uses social media marketing as the centerpiece of his company's guerrilla marketing strategy. League was an early adopter of social media marketing, using e-mail marketing shortly after starting the business in 1997 and building the company's first Web site himself. Today, League relies on a blog, Twitter, and Facebook to engage customers; create a community; and encourage movie buffs to attend special events, such as a Tough Guy Cinema series, a Hecklevision showcase, and a Quote-Along showing. "We've developed a unique fan base, and our patrons are very knowledgeable of movies," says League, who links Alamo's online community with real-time events. "All of our special events are hosted by members of our programming staff, and we hang out with the audience when the movie ends." League says that Facebook "works well because it expands the scope and reach of Alamo Drafthouse's ongoing dialogue with its patrons. Facebook isn't a one-way means of communication. You have to monitor comments, respond, and engage your customers. It's a way of telegraphing that you're listening and that you care."[50] ■

LinkedIn. To use LinkedIn as a marketing tool, entrepreneurs should create a personal profile that focuses on their role as owner of a business, send invitations to people with whom they have connections, join (or form) groups that are of interest to customers, and use Answers to demonstrate their expertise. They also should create a link to their company's Web sites, blog, and Twitter feed. Entrepreneurs also can post upcoming events at their businesses and conduct polls among other LinkedIn users.

Twitter. Twitter users send more than 1 billion tweets per week, and 42 percent of users look to Twitter for information about the products and services that they buy.[51] Twitter, a microblogging (no more than 140 characters) service, is ideal for interacting with customers or potential customers, promoting daily specials and upcoming events, and driving traffic to a company's Web site or blog. Whole Foods, the upscale grocery chain, interacts with 1.9 million Twitter followers by responding to customer service requests and links to recipes on its Web site and news stories about natural food. Clothing retailer Old Navy sends Tweets and text messages telling customers about upcoming specials and "secret sales," such as a camisole normally priced at $8.50 on sale for $2.[52] Twitter also is a useful tool for monitoring a company's customer service performance, something that companies are discovering is essential to preserving the quality of their brands. A recent poll from RightNow and Harris Interactive reports that 85 percent of customers who posted a negative shopping experience with a company and were subsequently contacted by that company ultimately took an action online that benefited the business (such as changing their negative review to a positive one).[53] The following tips help entrepreneurs use Twitter successfully as a guerrilla marketing tool:

- Connect with others as a person, not as a brand. Twitter users want to talk with people, not companies.
- Engage in conversations. Twitter is a two-way communication tool, not an outlet for sending one-way messages, such as press releases and marketing copy.
- Give people a reason to follow you. Reveal the "inside story" of your company, ask customers for feedback, or offer special deals to followers.
- Link Twitter to your company's Web site. Refer followers to your company's Web site, blog, or a video about your company and its products or services.[54]

Start a Blog A Web log ("blog") is a frequently updated online journal that contains a writer's ideas on a multitude of topics and links to related sites. A recent survey by eMarketer reports that 39 percent of companies now use blogs as part of their marketing strategies.[55] Business blogging can be an effective part of a guerrilla marketing strategy, enabling small businesses to communicate with large numbers of potential customers very economically. In fact, 57 percent of companies that publish blogs say that they have acquired a customer through their blogs, and 62 percent rated their blogs as either "important" or "critical" to their companies' success.[56] Common platforms for creating blogs include WordPress, Blogger, Tumblr, Posterous, and SquareSpace.

Blogs are a popular guerrilla marketing tool because they work. eMarketer estimates that nearly 134 million people in the United States, 56.5 percent of U.S. Internet users, read blogs.[57] Blogs that attract the attention of existing and potential customers boost a company's visibility and its sales. Companies post their blogs, promote them on their Web sites and in other social media, and then watch as the viral nature of the Internet takes over with visitors posting comments and telling their friends about the blog. Many small companies allow customers to contribute to their blogs, offering the potential for one of the most valuable marketing tools: unsolicited endorsements from satisfied users. Blogging's informal dialogue is an ideal match for small companies whose culture and style also are casual. Linked to a company's other social media marketing efforts (such as Facebook, LinkedIn, and Twitter), a blog can serve as its social media hub. "A business blog is where you create your point of distinction in the marketplace and demonstrate your expertise in building credibility and trust," says Denise Wakeman, founder of The Blog Squad.[58]

Blogs can serve many business purposes, including keeping customers updated on new products, enhancing customer service, and promoting the company. If monitored regularly, blogs also can give entrepreneurs keen insight into their customers' viewpoints and preferences. One business writer says that blogs are "like a never-ending focus group."[59] Creating a blog is not risk free, however. Companies must be prepared to deal with negative feedback from some visitors.

The following tips can help entrepreneurs implement a successful blogging strategy:

- *Be honest, balanced, and interesting when writing a blog.* High-pressure sales pitches do not work in the blogger's world. Telling an interesting "inside story" about the company, its products or services, or some aspect of the business attracts readers.

- *Post blog entries consistently so that readers have a reason to return.*

- *Ask customers for feedback.* Blogs are powerful tools for collecting real-time market research inexpensively.

- *Strive to cultivate the image of an expert or a trusted friend on a topic that is important to your customers.* In his blog, the owner of a company that installs water gardens posts tips for maintaining a healthy water garden and answers questions that his readers post.

- *Use services such as Google Alerts that scan the Web for a company's name and send e-mail alerts when it finds posts about a company.* Entrepreneurs must monitor the online "buzz" about their companies; if they discover negative comments, they can address the issues in their blogs. Web analyst and author Pete Blackshaw says, "About 60 percent of Americans are putting content on the Web, and it can affect how your product or service is perceived in the marketplace."[60]

- *Promote the blog via social media and e-mail.*[61]

ENTREPRENEURIAL PROFILE: Matt Buchan and Alex Garcia: Emerson Salon Matt Buchan and Alex Garcia decided to purchase a struggling hair salon in downtown Seattle, Washington, believing that they could turn it around with an incisive social marketing strategy centered on a company blog. Frequent blog posts feature stories about customers' new hairstyles as well as those of celebrities and useful tips on hair care and on how customers can achieve the newest look. A button on the Emerson Salon Web site allows customers to book an appointment and post it automatically to Facebook and Twitter. Since launching their social media marketing strategy, traffic to the salon's Web site has more than tripled, and 75 percent of Emerson Salon's bookings originate from the company blog, Facebook, or Twitter. "It's rare for even a walk-in customer not to have read our blog or seen our Tweets," says Buchan.[62] ■

Create Online Videos Video hosting sites such as YouTube give creative entrepreneurs the opportunity to promote their businesses at no cost by creating videos that feature their company's products and services in action. Unlike television ads, uploading a video to YouTube costs nothing, and in some cases, the videos reach millions of potential customers. Watching online videos is pervasive; YouTube reports that visitors view 3 billion videos per day.[63] The Pew Internet and American Life Project reports that 69 percent of Internet users have watched videos online.[64]

To market their companies successfully using online videos, entrepreneurs should do the following:

- *Think "edutainment."* Some of the most successful online videos combine both educational content and entertainment.

ENTREPRENEURIAL PROFILE: Terrence Kelleman: Dynomighty Design Terrence Kellemen, founder of Dynomighty Design, created a one-minute video showing a unique magnetic bracelet that his company designed and posted it on YouTube. In just three months, the video generated 2.7 million views and $130,000 in sales. "Video allows you to tell a more in-depth story about your product," explains Kelleman, who says that 50 percent of the traffic to the company's Web site comes from YouTube. "It gets our customers involved and engaged and gives them a much deeper understanding of our product than a still photograph. The video changed my company overnight. Now, every time we release a new product, we do a video related to that release."[65] ■

- *Be funny.* A common denominator among many successful online videos is humor. For businesses, the key is to link the humor in the video to the company's product or service and its customer benefits. Tom Dickson, CEO of Blendtec, a maker of commercial blenders in Orem, Utah, created a series of videos called "Will It Blend?" that have catapulted his company into the spotlight. In the short videos, Dickson, outfitted in a white lab coat and safety goggles, has blended a multitude of objects including lightbulbs, marbles, a golf club—even an iPad! At the end of the videos appears the tagline "Yes, it blends." The videos have drawn more than 60 million downloads, and Blendtec's sales have increased 700 percent, from $5 million to $40 million.[66]

- *Post videos on multiple social media sites.* Potential customers are more likely to see a video and share it with others when a company makes it available through multiple social media sites, such as Facebook and Twitter.

- *Involve your customers.* Some small businesses have delegated the task of creating videos that promote their companies to their customers. Doing so not only allows them to sidestep the cost and technical issues of creating videos (create a contest!) but also engages their customers and connects them with the company in unique ways.

- *Keep it short.* For a video to produce maximum benefit, it should be between one and three minutes long.

Host a Special Event Another effective guerrilla marketing strategy is to host a special event that reinforces the company's brand in customers' minds. Princess Jenkins, owner of Brownstone, a New York City clothing and accessories boutique that targets women 40 and older, rented a ballroom next to her store and sponsored a spring fashion show to which she issued special invitations to her top 200 clients. Sales from the show were "incredible," says Jenkins. She also participated in a fair spotlighting small businesses during Harlem Week and held another fashion show in November to promote her fashions in the all-important Christmas season. Jenkins says the events helped Brownstone increase sales by 10 percent—even in the face of a recession.

DEDICATION TO SERVICE AND CUSTOMER SATISFACTION Many businesses have lost sight of the most important component of every business: the customer. Entrepreneurs must realize that everything in the business—even the business itself—depends on creating a satisfied customer. The rewards for providing excellent customer service are great, and the penalties for failing to do so are severe. A recent survey by Harris Interactive reports that 55 percent of consumers have become customers of a company just because of the company's reputation for providing outstanding customer service. The study also revealed that 85 percent of customers are willing to pay extra (as much as 25 percent more) for products that are accompanied by excellent customer service.[67] Conversely, another Harris Poll reports that 80 percent of customers say that they will never return to a business after a negative customer service experience.[68]

Lost sales are only the beginning of a company's woes, however. Unhappy customers are likely to tell their poor service stories to family members and friends. The Harris Interactive survey also shows that 79 percent of customers who have negative customer service experiences tell others about them.[69] This negative word of mouth has a detrimental effect on the offending company. A study by the Jay H. Baker Retailing Initiative at the University of Pennsylvania reports that 48 percent of shoppers say that they will not patronize stores where they know that other customers have had bad service experiences.[70] Most of these customers never complain; in fact, for every complaint that a company receives, there are 17 other complaints that go unspoken.[71] These disgruntled customers exact revenge over their poor treatment, however. These days, a company that provides poor service may find itself being panned on Yelp, Twitter, Facebook, a YouTube video, a blog, or a Web site. A recent study by Cone reports that 89 percent of consumers find online product reviews trustworthy and that 80 percent of shoppers have changed their minds about a purchase on the basis of negative information found online.[72]

Smart companies are rediscovering that unexpected, innovative, customized service can be a powerful marketing weapon. Perhaps the most effective marketing tool is satisfied customers who become passionate brand evangelists for a company. Providing incomparable service—not necessarily low prices—is one of the most effective ways to attract and maintain a growing customer base. Successful businesses recognize that superior customer service is only an intermediate step toward the goal of customer *satisfaction*. The best companies seek to go beyond customer satisfaction, striving for *customer astonishment*! One way to achieve customer

Hands On . . . How To

Make Social Media Work for Your Business

Social media, such as Facebook, Twitter, LinkedIn, YouTube, and others, can be a vital and productive component of a company's guerrilla marketing strategy. Because the typical customer sees more than 20,000 advertising and sales messages each week, small businesses' marketing efforts, particularly their social media marketing efforts, must be well planned, consistent, and focused. Otherwise, they will become lost in a sea of ads, posts, tweets, and blogs.

The first key to a successful social media marketing strategy is understanding your customers and knowing where they are in the social media universe and what they expect from you. Entrepreneurs can use the following tips and success stories to develop a social media marketing strategy that works for their businesses:

Use social media to level the playing field. One of the greatest advantages of using social media is its low cost, which means that large companies have no more of a marketing advantage than small businesses. "We've never been able to compete with larger casual dining restaurants that own the airwaves," says Jen Gulvik, vice president of marketing for Houlihan's Restaurants, a small restaurant chain based in Leawood, Kansas. "We can't outshout them with our marketing budget, but it's still essentially free to play in social media. We can be in this space and do as well, if not better, than our larger competitors."

Build your brand—and your customer base—with social media. Einstein Bros. Bagels, a bagel, sandwich, and coffee chain with nearly 450 locations across the United States, had amassed 4,700 Facebook fans before launching a social media–based bagel giveaway during the fall. Customers responded and within one week, the number of fans had increased to 300,000. When Einstein Bros. repeated the promotion on Facebook the following spring, its fan base jumped to more than 600,000! "We're not a national advertiser," says James O'Reilly, the company's chief concept officer. "We decided to make social media a pillar of our marketing efforts. It's a whole new channel for businesses to engage their customers in a two-way dialogue." Today, Einstein Bros. boasts nearly 700,000 Facebook fans who ask about new products and upcoming promotions, post photos of themselves (and their pets) enjoying an Einstein Bros. bagel, and respond to questions the company posts on its Wall ("Which bagel and shmear combination do you crave most—sweet or savory?").

Remember that no matter what media you use to promote your business, no one really cares what you do; potential customers care only about what you can do for them. One of the greatest advantages for small businesses that use social media is its ability to naturally showcase their uniqueness, their informal culture, and their staff's passion for what they do. Once prospects understand the value that a company's products or services hold for them, selling to them becomes much easier. Use social media to showcase the results that your company can create for customers.

Be creative in your social media promotions. Using a creative Facebook campaign, California Tortilla, a 26-unit restaurant chain in Rockville, Maryland, increased the number of Facebook fans by 50 percent and generated a 10 percent increase in same-store sales—and spent less than $700. The company offered a free order of chips and queso to its Facebook fans but promised to upgrade the offer to a free taco if its fan base reached 13,000 people. The viral nature of social media took over, and California Tortilla ended up with more than 16,000 likes. "The people who got involved were super-passionate fans," says marketing director Stacey Kane. "Based on customer engagement, it was a win."

Listen before you talk. Success with social media marketing requires a different approach than traditional advertising, which relies primarily on one-way communication, telling your audience about your business and its products and services. Social media marketing requires that businesses *listen* before they engage their audience in a two-way conversation. Mari Luangrath, owner of Foiled Cupcakes, an upscale cupcake bakery in Chicago, has no physical storefront for her business yet manages to sell 1,000 dozen cupcakes each month at an average price of $38 per dozen. Luangrath says that she developed 94 percent of her customers using social media marketing tools, especially Twitter. Her strategy is to identify online conversations about food, baking, and cupcakes that she and her employees can join naturally and build trust by providing useful content and comments. "I'm very comfortable with traditional marketing," says Luangrath, "but I don't want to market to everybody. I want to find people who want to hear what I have to say and then, at the end of the engagement, purchase my product." Luangrath also has joined groups of Chicago administrative professionals—the people who plan office parties and events—on LinkedIn and posts useful articles for them. "You want to engage people, get feedback, and start a conversation. Then you can say, 'Why don't we drop some cupcakes by and show you what we can do?'"

Use social media to reward loyal customers, fans, followers, and promoters of your brand. Jordan Zweigoron, founder and "chief psycho" of Psycho Donuts, a doughnut shop in Campbell, California, that sells uniquely flavored doughnuts served by employees wearing nurse uniforms, uses Fanminder, a mobile marketing service that allows businesses to send text messages containing special offers and promotions to customers who opt in. The company also uses Twitter to reward its loyal customers, but Zweigoron says that Psycho Donuts's Fanminder offers generate a response that is three to four times greater than its Twitter promotions.

Use online video to show off your products and services. Television advertisers have known for decades that video is the ideal way to show people how a product or service works. Social media sites such as YouTube give even the

Hands On . . . How To *(continued)*

smallest businesses the opportunity to show their products and services in action at minimal cost. BBQ Guys, a store in Baton Rouge, Louisiana, that sells everything related to barbecuing, began posting videos featuring its grills on YouTube in 2006. The videos were so successful that the company recruited a local chef to host them. BBQ Guys has posted more than 400 videos on YouTube that have more than 1.4 million views. A visitor who watches a video is twice as likely to make a purchase as one who does not. "We see the videos almost like a TV commercial," says Troy Olson, the company's digital advertising manager. "We're planting our brand name."

Give customers a reason to tune in to your business. Create a destination by posting fresh content and promoting upcoming specials, sales, and events. Resist the tendency to let the hectic nature of your schedule drive out the time necessary to make social marketing work for your business. To make social media marketing pay off, entrepreneurs must make social media marketing a regular part of their work schedules.

Use social media to encourage your customers to talk—and then listen. Social media are ideal for engaging customers in two-way conversations. Beachbody, a Santa Monica, California–based maker of fitness videos, realized that many of the online conversations in which its employees participated originated from faith-based sites. It was a market niche that the company had never considered until

its employees began listening to potential customers' conversations. The company introduced Body Gospel, a series of workouts set to contemporary Christian music that have been successful.

Use analytics to measure your company's social media results. Entrepreneurs should measure the results of their social media marketing efforts so that they know which ones work best. Social media marketing efforts are always evolving, and entrepreneurs need useful feedback on their results. Many tools are available to measure success, but many of the standards that fit traditional advertising media, such as sales leads, sales, Web site traffic, customer engagement and retention, and profits, apply to social media.

Sources: Based on Heidi Cohen, "How to Jump into the Social Media Pool without Drowning," *SmartBlogs*, May 10, 2011, http://smartblogs.com/socialmedia/2011/05/10/how-to-jump-into-the-social-media-pool-without-drowning; Courtney Jeffries, "How 3 Brands Generate Buzz by Employing Social Technologies," *Social Media Club*, August 24, 2011, http://socialmediaclub.org/blogs/from-the-clubhouse/social-business-snapshot-how-3-brands-generate-buzz-employing-social-techno; Jason Ankeny, "Social Climbers," *Entrepreneur*, January 2011, pp. 116–123; Lisa Nicole Bell, "3 Rules for Selling in the New Economy," *Reuters*, January 10, 2011, http://blogs.reuters.com/small-business/2011/01/10/3-rules-for-selling-in-the-new-economy; Mark Brandau, "California Tortilla: Lessons Learned from Facebook Promo," *Nation's Restaurant News*, March 30, 2011, http://www.nrn.com/article/california-tortilla-lessons-learned-facebook-promo; Brian Quinton, "Baking, Listening, and Selling," *Entrepreneur*, February 2011, pp. 60–61; Jason Ankeny, "Crazy for Mobile Deals," *Entrepreneur*, October 2010, pp. 40–41; Kermit Pattison, "Online Video Offers Low-Cost Marketing for Your Company," *New York Times*, March 16, 2011, http://www.nytimes.com/2011/03/17/business/smallbusiness/17sbiz.html; and April Joyner, "Social Networking: Who's Talking About You?," *Inc.*, September 2010, pp. 63–64.

---

astonishment is to "underpromise and overdeliver." "When you do exactly what you said you would do, you end up with satisfied customers," explains one business writer. "But when you give them something more than they expect—faster service, extra help, more options, early delivery, and so on—you end up with the loyal, raving fans you need to propel your business into the stratosphere."[73] Smart entrepreneurs create reasonable expectations among their customers and then exceed them, knowing that those customers will generate positive "buzz" for the companies, which is more valuable and more effective than the most expensive advertising campaign.

Certainly the least expensive—and the most effective—way to achieve customer satisfaction is through friendly, personal service. Numerous surveys of customers in a wide diversity of industries—from manufacturing and services to banking and high tech—conclude that the most important element of service is "the personal touch." Calling customers by name; making attentive, friendly contact; and truly caring about their needs and wants is much more essential than any other factor—even convenience, quality, and speed! In our society, business transactions have become so automated that the typical customer is starved for personal attention. Genuine customer service requires that a business bridge that service gap, treat each customer as an individual, and transform "high-tech" applications into a "high-touch" attitude.

How can a company achieve stellar customer service and satisfaction?

Listen to customers. The best companies constantly listen to their customers and respond to what they hear! This allows them to keep up with customers' changing needs and expectations. The best way to find out what customers really want and value is to ask them. Businesses rely on a number of techniques, including surveys, focus groups, telephone interviews, comment cards, suggestion boxes, toll-free hotlines, and regular one-on-one conversations (perhaps the best technique). The Internet is another useful tool for getting feedback from customers; many companies solicit complaints, suggestions, and ideas through their Web sites.

Keeping customer feedback in its proper perspective is important, however. Although listening to customers does produce valuable feedback for business owners in many areas, it is *not* a substitute for an innovative company culture, solid market research, and a well-devised marketing plan. Companies that rely solely on their customers to guide their marketing efforts often find themselves lagging the competition. Customers rarely have the foresight to anticipate market trends and do not always have a clear view of how new products or services could satisfy their needs.

Define superior service. Based on what customers say, managers and employees must decide exactly what "superior service" means in the company. Such a statement should (1) be a strong statement of intent, (2) differentiate the company from others, and (3) have value to customers. Deluxe Corporation, a printer of personal checks, defines superior service quite simply: "Forty-eight hour turnaround; zero defects."[74]

Set standards and measure performance. To be able to deliver on its promise of superior service, a business must establish specific standards and measure overall performance against them. Satisfied customers should exhibit at least one of three behaviors: loyalty (increased customer retention rate), increased purchases (rising sales and sales per customer), and resistance to rivals' attempts to lure them away with lower prices (market share and price tolerance).[75] Companies must track their performance on these and other service standards and reward employees accordingly.

Examine your company's service cycle. What steps must a customer go through to purchase your product or service? Business owners often are surprised at the complexity that has seeped into their customer service systems as they have evolved over time. One of the most effective techniques is to work with employees to flowchart each component in the company's service cycle, including *everything* a customer has to do to buy your product or service. The goal is to look for steps, policies, and procedures that are unnecessary, redundant, or unreasonable and then to eliminate them.

See customer complaints as a mechanism for improving customer service. Smart entrepreneurs see customer complaints as an important tool for improving their businesses and as a bridge to long-term customer relationships. Linda Stanfield, who owns three plumbing businesses with her husband in Phoenix, Arizona, makes a "happy call" to every customer once the job is completed. "I want to know as soon as possible if a customer has concerns," she says. "If we do get a complaint, I'll take steps to investigate the situation and address the problem. I'm always willing to refund customers' money if they're unhappy, even in cases where we've done nothing wrong. Other plumbers ask me how we can afford to take that approach. My answer to them is, 'How can you afford not to?' Even though it costs us money to make refunds, I can't say it hurts our business. Making sure that our customers walk away happy is good for our bottom line. We now receive more than 2,000 referrals a year from satisfied customers."[76]

When you create a negative customer experience, apologize and fix it—fast. No customer service system is perfect, and companies can recover from creating a negative customer experience. A recent survey shows that 92 percent of customers say that would return to a company after a negative customer experience if the company offered an apology, a discount, or proof that its customer service would be better.[77]

Hire the right employees. A company's customer service process is important, but the key ingredient in the superior service equation is the *people* who make it work. There is no substitute for friendly, courteous sales and service representatives, and hiring them requires a sound selection process. Business owners must always be on the lookout for employees who emanate a customer service attitude and are empathetic, flexible, articulate, creative, and able to think for themselves. "You can teach people skills, but you can't teach personality," says Michael Hess, founder of Skooba Design, a company that makes bags for laptop computers.[78]

Train employees to deliver superior service. Successful businesses train *every* employee who deals directly with customers; they don't leave customer service to chance. Superior service companies devote 1 to 5 percent of their employees' work hours to training, concentrating on how to meet, greet, and serve customers. Leading catalog companies such as Lands' End and L. L. Bean spend *many* hours training the employees who handle telephone orders before they deal with their first customer.

Empower employees to offer superior service. One of the most important variables that determines whether employees deliver superior service is the degree to which they perceive they have permission to do so. The goal is to push decision making down the organization to the employees who have contact with customers. This includes giving them the latitude to circumvent "company policy" if it means improving customer satisfaction. Michael Hess, founder of Skooba Designs, the company that makes laptop bags, gives his employees the freedom to do whatever it takes to make customers happy. "No company has ever gone broke taking care of its customers," he says.[79] If frontline workers don't have this power to solve disgruntled customers' problems, they fear being punished for overstepping their boundaries become frustrated, and the superior service cycle breaks down. To be empowered, employees need knowledge and information, adequate resources, and managerial support.

Treat employees with respect and show them how valuable they are. Satisfied employees tend to create satisfied customers. "There's a definite proven connection between employee happiness and customer happiness," says JoAnna Brandi, a customer service consultant. In fact, one study reports that a 1 percent change in employee morale results in a 2 percent change in customer satisfaction.[80]

ENTREPRENEURIAL PROFILE: Don Slivensky: MicroTek Computer Labs Don Slivensky, CEO of MicroTek Computer Labs, a computer training company, understands the connection well and works hard to keep his employees happy. In the past, Slivensky has paid for employees' honeymoons, provided down payments for employees to purchase homes, and sent $500 gift cards to workers expecting babies. "If people are happy," he says, "they enjoy taking care of customers.[81] ■

Use technology to provide improved service. The role of technology is not to create a rigid bureaucracy but to free employees from routine clerical tasks, giving them more time and better tools to serve customers more effectively. Ideally, technology gives workers the information they need to help their customers and the time to serve them.

To use technology effectively, entrepreneurs must ask, "What is the best technology for our strategy?" This question leads to four key service issues: (1) "What is our primary service strategy?" (i.e., "What do we want customers to think of when they hear our name?"), (2) "What barriers are preventing our company from fully implementing this strategy now?," (3) "What, if anything, can technology do to overcome these barriers," and (4) "What is our strategy for encouraging our customers to adopt the new technology?"[82]

Reward superior service. What gets rewarded gets done. Companies that want employees to provide stellar service must offer rewards for doing so. A study by the National Science Foundation concluded that when pay is linked to performance, employees' motivation and productivity climb by as much as 63 percent.[83]

Get top managers' support. The drive toward superior customer service will fall far short of its target unless top managers support it fully. Success requires more than just a verbal commitment; it calls for managers' involvement and dedication to making service a core company value. Achieving customer satisfaction must become ingrained in the strategic planning process and work its way into every nook and cranny of the organization. Once it does, employees will be able to provide stellar customer service with or without a checklist of "dos and don'ts."

Give customers an unexpected surprise. In Louisiana, locals call it a lagniappe ("lan-yap"), a small gift that a merchant gives to a customer. The surprise does not have to be expensive to be effective. For instance, when a customer makes a sizeable purchase at Wilson Creek Outfitters, a fly-fishing shop in Morganton, North Carolina, the owner includes a dozen flies in the order for free. The cost of the lagniappe is minimal, but the goodwill and loyalty it garners is significant.

View customer service as an investment, not an expense. The companies that lead the way when it comes to retaining their customers view the money they spend on customer service as an investment rather than an expense. One of the most effective ways for entrepreneurs to learn this lesson is to calculate the cost of poor customer service to their companies. Once they calculate it, the cost of lost customers due to poor service is so astonishing to most business owners that they quickly become customer service zealots. For instance, the owner of a small restaurant calculated that if every day he lost to poor service just one customer who spent just $5 per week, his business was losing $94,900 in revenue per year! The restaurateur immediately changed his approach to customer service.

RETAIN EXISTING CUSTOMERS Loyal, long-term customers are the bedrock of every business. High customer retention rates translate into superior financial performance. Earning customers' loyalty requires businesses to take customer focus and service to unprecedented levels, and that means building long-term relationships with customers. Research shows that customers who are satisfied with a company's products and customer service are more likely to be repeat customers and are less sensitive to price increases.[84]

Many studies also show that high levels of customer retention result in above-average profits and superior growth in market share.[85] Powell's Books, a Portland, Oregon, landmark known as the "City of Books" for its 68,000-square-foot store and huge inventory, has built a solid base of loyal customers in its 40-plus year history, enabling the company to compete successfully against industry giants Amazon and Barnes & Noble. Powell's Books has hosted several weddings for customers who met there, and one customer's ashes are interred (at his request) in one of the columns that is made to look like a stack of books at the northwest entrance to the store. Now *that's* customer loyalty![86]

Because about 20 percent of a typical company's customers account for about 80 percent of its sales, focusing resources on keeping the best (and most profitable) customers is a better investment than chasing "fair-weather" customers who will defect to any better deal that comes along. Suppose that a company increases its customer base by 20 percent each year but retains only 85 percent of its existing customers. Its effective growth rate is just 5 percent per year [20% − (100% − 85%) = 5%]. If this same company can raise its customer retention rate to 95 percent, its net growth rate *triples* to 15 percent [20% − (100% − 5%) = 15%].[87]

Although winning new customers keeps a company growing, keeping existing ones is essential to success. Dunnhumby, a global customer loyalty consulting firm, reports that a company must land 12 to 20 new customers to offset the impact of one lost loyal customer.[88] Research shows that repeat customers spend 67 percent more than new customers. In addition, attracting a new customer actually costs the typical business *seven to nine times* as much as keeping an existing one.[89] Therefore, small business owners would be better off asking "How can we improve customer value and service to encourage our existing customers to do more business with us?" than "How can we increase our market share by 10 percent?" One way that companies can entice current customers to keep coming back is with a loyalty program, which many companies' are linking to their social media presence.

ENTREPRENEURIAL PROFILE: Tasti D-Lite When customers of Tasti D-Lite, the New York City–based yogurt company, make a purchase with their TreatCards (loyalty cards), they can automatically post news of the transaction on their Facebook, Twitter, and Foursquare accounts. The loyalty program awards a point toward free treats for every dollar that customers spend at Tasti D-Lite and for each social media message they send out. Incorporating the social media angle has been successful; not only does the company benefit from increased online exposure, but customers who use it spend 36 percent more than those who use only the traditional loyalty card.[90] ■

You Be the Consultant

A Company with Soul

In 1974, Bill Crutchfield was living in his mother's house and working as the general manager of a forklift company after an unsuccessful stint in Hollywood, where he tried to sell a screenplay he wrote to a movie studio. He took $1,000 that he had saved and started a mail-order car stereo company after trying in vain to find a stereo that he could install himself in an old Porsche that he was restoring for resale. Of course, Crutchfield needed far more than $1,000 to start an electronics catalog company and was able to convince a local banker to extend a $25,000 line of credit to the new company, which he named Crutchfield after himself.

Crutchfield kept his job at the forklift company and ran his business as a one-man operation. "I'd leave my job at five o'clock, race down to the post office to pick up the few orders that came in, race home and pack them in my mother's basement, write a personal thank-you letter, and drive them to UPS to make sure they got out the same day," he recalls. Unfortunately, only seven months into the venture, Crutchfield was incurring a loss and was about to run out of cash. As a last-ditch effort, he sent a one-page questionnaire to everyone who had ordered a catalog, asking customers what the company could do better and noncustomers why they had not placed an order. Crutchfield says that the responses he received not only saved his company but still guide its customer service philosophy to this day. The problem was not with the catalog's products, brands, or prices; instead, customers were intimidated at the idea of installing a car stereo on their own.

That feedback inspired Crutchfield to redesign his catalog (after all, it was the 1970s, long before the Internet) into a more polished product that included easy-to-follow articles on car stereo installation techniques, step-by-step photographs, and customer testimonials. The redesigned catalog worked, and sales increased dramatically in just a few months. That simple survey taught Crutchfield the importance of listening and responding to his customers, a lesson that has stuck with him for 40 years. Crutchfield's product line has expanded to include more than 9,500 high-end audiovisual products ranging from flat-screen televisions to cameras and speaker systems. In the company's research department (yes, a retailer that manufactures no products has a research department), employees are busy dissecting the products that Crutchfield sells so that they can share the details of their features and designs with the members of the sales, call center, and technical support teams. "We take [products] apart to see what's going on inside," says Phil Jones, the head of Crutchfield's technical support department.

Digging into the details of every product the company sells is a vital component in the company's customer service equation, but Crutchfield takes a broad view of customer service. "A lot of companies get into trouble because they think customer service is just how you deal with back-end complaints," he says. "Customer service is everything you do. It's all about putting yourself in the customer's shoes." Toward that end,

Crutchfield has developed detailed car stereo installation guides for more than 16,100 vehicles, many of which contain how-to photos of the technical crew as they remove a factory radio and install one from the Crutchfield catalog. "Customers are going to ask, 'Will it fit in my car?'" says Crutchfield. "The only way to know is to do what we do: take the car apart and check it." To enhance customers' experience, Crutchfield also makes a significant investment in training its 500 employees. In addition to the extensive training that technical support workers receive, sales advisers spend 13 weeks of classroom and hands-on installation training before they begin fielding customers' calls.

Crutchfield's focus on his customers pays off. The company generates $250 million in annual sales, is debt free, and has never experienced a layoff in its history. It has earned a five-star rating from Yelp and is the only retailer to win BizRate's Circle of Excellence award for 11 consecutive years. In 2007, Bill Crutchfield was inducted into the Consumer Electronics Hall of Fame, where he joined the ranks of notables such as Steve Jobs and Thomas Edison.

Crutchfield's passion for taking care of customers has never subsided even as the company grows. He recently penned a set of core values—including exceeding customers' expectations, passionately pursuing continuous improvement, and treating employees with respect—that he explains to every employee in face-to-face meetings. Those core values are a significant part of the company's hiring process, in which managers look for candidates who demonstrate an attitude of service. "You can train [people] on the tech stuff, but you can't train somebody to enjoy helping other people," says Crutchfield.

Although Internet sales now account for 70 percent of sales, catalogs remain an important part of the business; Crutchfield mails more than 30 million of them each year. Crutchfield does not compete with low prices. "We're never going to be a Wal-Mart or Amazon," he says. "You can go on the Internet and find hundreds of retailers who sell product for less than we do, but you're not going to find a retailer who provides the level of service that we provide. People have the assurance that if they call us, there will be a highly trained, nice person on the other end of the phone who can truly help them. That's very important. Crutchfield is a business you need to run with soul."

1. What impact has Crutchfield's strategy of providing superior customer service had on the company's success? In what ways does the company communicate its superior service strategy to customers?

2. Crutchfield makes it clear that his company does not compete with its rivals using low prices. What lessons can other small businesses learn from Crutchfield about the relationship between prices and customer service?

Source: Based on Kasey Wehrum, "Learning, and Relearning, to Listen," *Inc.*, March 2011, pp. 64–68.

customer experience management
the process of systematically creating the optimum experience for customers every time they interact with the company.

The most successful small businesses have developed a customer focus and have instilled a customer satisfaction attitude *throughout* the company. They understand that winning customers for life requires practicing **customer experience management**, systematically creating the optimum experience for their customers every time they interact with the company. Companies with world-class customer experience management attitudes set themselves apart by paying attention to "little things," such as responding to questions or complaints promptly, remembering a customer's unique product or service preferences, or sending a customer a copy of an article of interest to him or her. Small companies cannot always be leaders in creating product or technology innovations. However, because their size allows them to have more personal contact with their customers than large companies, small companies can develop *experience* innovations that keep customers coming back and create a competitive advantage. Taking care of every small interaction a company has with its customers over time adds up to a positive service experience and can create a strong bond with them. For example, after Dr. Peter Polack, an ophthalmologist in Ocala, Florida, performs corrective LASIK surgery on his patients, he sends each one a $25 gift certificate to Barnes & Noble with a card that says, "Enjoy your new eyesight!" The unexpected surprise reinforces customers' positive service experience with the doctor's practice and enhances its brand awareness.[91] Jacqui Pini, co-owner of Museum Way Pearls, an online retailer of pearls based in Boston, Massachusetts, focuses on making customers' experiences with the company memorable. "We send a handwritten thank-you note along with a coupon for everything from free overnight shipping or a percentage off of a particular item or an entire purchase."[92] The goal is to create a total customer experience that is so positive that customers keep coming back and tell their friends about it.

How do these companies manage their customer relationships and stay focused so intently on their customers? They constantly ask customers four basic questions and then act on what they hear:

1. What are we doing right?

2. How can we do that even better?

3. What have we done wrong?

4. What can we do in the future?

Table 8.4 offers some basic strategies for developing and retaining loyal customers.

DEVOTION TO QUALITY In this intensely competitive global business environment, quality goods and services are a prerequisite for success. According to one marketing axiom, the worst of all marketing catastrophes is to have great advertising and a poor-quality product. Customers have come to expect and demand quality goods and services, and those businesses that provide them consistently have a distinct competitive advantage. Today, quality is more than just a slogan posted on the company bulletin board; world-class companies treat quality as a strategic objective— an integral part of a company's strategy and culture. This philosophy is called **total quality management (TQM)**—quality not just in the product or service itself but also in *every* aspect of the business and its relationship with the customer and *continuous improvement* in the quality delivered to customers.

total quality management (TQM)
the philosophy of producing a high-quality product or service and achieving quality in every aspect of the business and its relationship with the customer; the focus is on continuous improvement in the quality delivered to customers.

Companies on the cutting edge of the quality movement are developing new ways to measure quality. Manufacturers were the first to apply TQM techniques, but retail, wholesale, and service organizations have seen the benefits of becoming champions of quality. They are tracking customer complaints, contacting "lost" customers, and finding new ways to track the cost of quality and their return on quality (ROQ). ROQ recognizes that, although any improvement in quality may improve a company's competitive ability, only those improvements that produce a reasonable rate of return are worthwhile. In essence, ROQ requires managers to ensure that the quality improvements they implement will more than pay for themselves.

The key to developing a successful TQM philosophy is seeing the world from the customer's point of view. In other words, quality must reflect the needs and wants of the customer. How do customers define quality? According to one survey, Americans rank the quality of a product in this order: reliability (average time between failures), durability (how long it lasts), ease of use, a known or trusted brand name, and, last, low price.[93] When buying services, customers look for

TABLE 8.4 Strategies for Developing and Retaining Loyal Customers

- Identify your best customers and give them incentives to return. Focus resources on the 20 percent of customers who account for 80 percent of sales.

- When you create a dissatisfied customer, fix the problem *fast*. One study found that, given the chance to complain, 95 percent of customers will buy again *if* a business handles their complaints promptly and effectively. The worst way to handle a complaint is to ignore it, to pass it off to a subordinate, or to let a lot of time slip by before dealing with it. Shortly after luxury car maker Lexus introduced the new ES 350 model, managers discovered that about 700 cars had a small transmission problem that was the result of a factory error. Lexus contacted the affected owners and asked them to take their cars to their local dealers, where they received brand new Lexus 350s—no questions asked. Surveys of these customers that were conducted later showed that they were *more* loyal to Lexus than buyers whose cars did not have the problem in the first place.

- Make sure your business system makes it easy for customers to buy from you. Eliminate unnecessary procedures that challenge customers' patience.

- *Encourage* customer complaints. You can't fix something if you don't know it's broken. Find out what solution the customer wants and try to come as close to that as possible. Smart companies learn from customer complaints and use the feedback to make improvements in their products, services, and processes.

- Contact lost customers to find out why they left. You may uncover a problem you never knew existed.

- Ask employees for feedback on improving customer service. A study by Technical Assistance Research Programs, a customer service research firm, found that frontline service workers can predict nearly 90 percent of the cases that produce customer complaints. Emphasize that *everyone* is part of the customer satisfaction team.

- Get total commitment to superior customer service from top managers—and allocate resources appropriately.

- Allow managers to wait on customers occasionally. It's a great dose of reality. Ron Shaich, founder of Panera Bread, a chain of bakery cafés with 1,185 locations in 40 states, still visits stores regularly, working the cash registers and serving customers so that he can listen to their ideas and concerns.

- Carefully select and train *everyone* who will deal with customers. Never let rude employees work with customers.

- Develop a service theme that communicates your attitude toward customers. Customers want to feel they are getting something special.

- Empower employees to do whatever it takes to satisfy customers. At Ritz-Carlton hotels, employees are authorized to spend up to $2,000 to resolve a customer's complaint. At Zappos, the online shoe retailer, members of the Customer Loyalty Team are authorized to spend as much time as necessary on the phone with customers and to assist with anything customers need, even those that are unrelated to Zappos.

- Reward employees "caught" providing exceptional service to customers.

- Get in the habit of calling customers by name. It's one of the most meaningful ways of connecting with your customers.

- *Remember*: Customers pay the bills; without them, you have no business. Special treatment wins customers and keeps them coming back.

Sources: Based on Kasey Wehrum, "How May We Help You?" *Inc.*, March 2011, p. 63; Brandi Stewart, "Able Baker," *FSB*, December 2007/January 2008, pp. 53–58; Jerry Fisher, "The Secret's Out," *Entrepreneur*, May 1998, pp. 1112–1119; Laura M. Litvan, "Increasing Revenue with Repeat Sales," *Nation's Business*, January 1996, pp. 36–37; "Encourage Customers to Complain," *Small Business Reports*, June 1990, p. 7; Dave Zielinski, "Improving Service Doesn't Require a Big Investment;" *Small Business Reports*, February 1991, p. 20; John H. Sheridan, "Out of the Isolation Booth," *Industry Week*, June 19, 1989, pp. 18–19; Lin Grensing-Pophal, "At Your Service," *Business Start-Ups*, May 1995, pp. 72–74; and Bill Taylor, "Lessons from Lexus: Why It Pays to Do the Right Thing," Mavericks at Work, December 12, 2007, http://www.mavericksatwork.com/?p=102.

similar characteristics: tangibles (equipment, facilities, and people), reliability (doing what you say you will do), responsiveness (promptness in helping customers and in solving problems), and assurance and empathy (conveying a caring attitude). For example, the owner of a very successful pest control company offers his customers a unique, unconditional guarantee: if the company fails to eliminate all insect and rodent breeding and nesting areas on a client's premises, it will refund the customer's last 12 monthly payments and will pay for one year's service by another exterminator. The company has had to honor its guarantee only once in 17 years.

Companies that excel at providing quality products and services discover tangible benefits in the form of increased sales, more repeat customers, higher customer retention, and lower costs. Small businesses that have succeeded in building a reputation for top-quality products and services rely on the following guidelines to "get it right the first time":

- Build quality into the process; don't rely on inspection to obtain quality.

- Foster teamwork and dismantle the barriers that divide disparate departments.

- Establish long-term ties with select suppliers; don't award contracts on low price alone.

- Provide managers and employees the training needed to participate fully in the quality improvement program.

- Empower workers at all levels of the organization; give them authority and responsibility for making decisions that determine quality.

- Get managers' commitment to the quality philosophy. Otherwise, the program is doomed. Describing his leadership role in his company's TQM philosophy, one CEO says, "People look to see if you just talk about it or actually do it."[94]

- Rethink the processes the company uses to get its products or services to its customers.

- Be willing to make changes in processes wherever they may be necessary.

- Reward employees for quality work. Ideally, workers' compensation is linked clearly and directly to key measures of quality and customer satisfaction.

- Develop a company-wide strategy for constant improvement of product and service quality.

- Back up the company's quality pledge with a guarantee. Jim and Suzanne Faustlin, owners of The Maids Home Service franchise in Tucson, Arizona, have built a successful business by emphasizing the quality of their cleaning services. Their maids clean floors "the old-fashioned way"—on their hands and knees—and the company offers a quality guarantee: 100 percent satisfaction, or the customer receives a reclean at no charge.[95]

ATTENTION TO CONVENIENCE Ask customers what they want from the businesses they deal with, and one of the most common responses is "convenience." In this busy, fast-paced world of dual-career couples and lengthy commutes to and from work, customers increasingly are looking for convenience. Several studies have found that customers rank easy access to goods and services at the top of their purchase criteria. Unfortunately, too few businesses deliver adequate levels of convenience, and they fail to attract and retain customers. One print and framing shop, for instance, alienated many potential customers with its abbreviated business hours—nine to five daily, except for Wednesday afternoons, Saturdays, and Sundays, when the shop was closed! Other companies make it a chore to do business with them. In an effort to defend themselves against unscrupulous customers, these businesses have created elaborate procedures for exchanges, refunds, writing checks, and other basic transactions. One researcher claims, "What they're doing is treating the 98% of honest customers like crooks to catch the 2% who are crooks."[96]

Successful companies go out of their way to make sure that it is easy for customers to do business with them. To provide their customers with more a more convenient way to order, some restaurants are replacing printed menus with iPads. Stacked: Food Well Built, a southern California restaurant chain that offers 61 options just for a burger, uses iPads on every table that allow customers to drag and drop ingredients with the touch of a finger to create the perfect burger, pizza, or salad. Customers also pay their bills without having to flag a waiter. "The iPad controls when they order and when they pay," says cofounder Paul Monteko. "Those are two of the most frustrating things in the dining experience."[97] At Do, an upscale pizza restaurant in Atlanta, Georgia, that uses a similar concept, customers not only order and pay for their meals using the iPads on their tables but also can control the music they listen to and alert the valet that they are ready for their cars.[98]

Other restaurants are taking their food to customers in food trucks rather than waiting for customers to come to their brick-and-mortar locations. Copreneurs Erik Cho and Brook Howell launched Frysmith, a food truck in Los Angeles, California, that offers a menu of French fries topped with unique and eclectic items such as kimchi, shawarma-marinated steak, and tamatillo-tamarind chicken. Cho and Howell keep their growing base of fans informed of the truck's location and menu with regular updates on Facebook, Twitter, and the company's Web site. "We're inundated with requests to show up at events," says Cho.[99]

Service companies are focusing on convenience as well. In Las Vegas, a couple can pull up into the Tunnel of Vows at the famous Little White Chapel, and an ordained minister at the drive-through window will marry them! Business has been so brisk that the owner of the chapel recently expanded the tunnel to include "a romantic ceiling with cherubs and starlights."[100]

How can entrepreneurs boost the convenience level of their businesses? By conducting a "convenience audit" from the customer's point of view to get an idea of its ETDBW ("Easy-to-Do-Business-With") index:

- Is your business located near your customers? Does it provide easy access?

- Are your business hours suitable to your customers? Should you be open evenings and weekends to serve them better?

- Would customers appreciate pickup and delivery service? To enhance customer convenience, nearly 25 percent of takeout restaurants, especially pizza and sandwich shops, give customers the option of ordering online and have discovered that customer satisfaction, order accuracy, and speed increase.[101]

- Are your employees trained to handle business transactions quickly, efficiently, and politely? Waiting while rude, poorly trained employees fumble through routine transactions destroys customer goodwill.

- Do your employees treat customers with courtesy?

- Does your company provide a sufficient number of checkout stations so that shoppers do not have to stand in long lines to pay for their purchases? Does your company make it easy for customers to make purchases with debit or credit cards?

- Are you using technology to enhance customers' shopping experience? At Stop & Shop and Giant supermarkets in the Northeast, customers can pick up a smart phone–like device called Scan It that allows them to scan and bag their own groceries as they roam the stores' aisles. The device shows a running total of their purchases and periodically provides electronic coupons based on customers' purchases. Shoppers are happy because Scan It eliminates long waits at the checkout counter, and the supermarkets are happy because Scan It shoppers spend 10 percent more on average.[102]

- Does your company offer "extras" that make customers' lives easier? With a phone call to Hoyt Hanvey Jewelers, a small gift store in Clinton, South Carolina, customers in need of a special gift simply tell how much they want to spend, and the owner takes care of the rest—selecting the gift, wrapping it, and shipping it. All customers have to do is pay the invoice when it arrives in the mail.

- Can you "bundle" some of your existing products or services to make it easier for customers to use them? Whether it involves gardening tools or a spa treatment, assembling products and services into ready-made, all-in-one kits appeals to busy customers and can boost sales.

- Can you adapt existing products to make them more convenient for customers? When J. M. Smucker Company began test-marketing a premade, frozen peanut butter and jelly sandwich, CEO Tim Smucker was amazed at the results. The sandwiches, called Uncrustables, generated $20 million in sales, and Smucker now sells them nationwide.[103]

● Does your company handle telephone calls quickly and efficiently? Long waits "on hold," transfers from one office to another, and too many rings before answering signal to customers that they are not important. Jerre Stead, CEO of Ingram Micro Inc., a distributor of computer products, expects every telephone call to the company to be answered within three seconds![104]

CONCENTRATION ON INNOVATION Innovation is the key to future success. Markets change too quickly and competitors move too fast for a small company to stand still and remain competitive. Because they cannot outspend their larger rivals, small companies often turn to superior innovation as the way to gain a competitive edge. "Never stop innovating or taking risks," says Michael Dell, founder of Dell Computer. "Keep raising the bar, not just for the industry but for yourself."[105]

Thanks to their organizational and managerial flexibility, small businesses often can detect and act on new opportunities faster than large companies. Innovation is one of the hallmarks of entrepreneurs, and it shows up in the new products, unique techniques, and unusual marketing approaches they introduce. Despite their limited resources, small businesses frequently are leaders in innovation. There is much more to innovation than spending megadollars on research and development. "It takes money to fund a business," says one small business adviser, "but it's continuous creativity that keeps the venture running smoothly and profitably."[106] How do small businesses manage to maintain their leadership role in innovating new products and services? They use their size to their advantage, maintaining their speed and flexibility much like a martial arts expert does against a larger opponent. Their closeness to their customers enables them to read subtle shifts in the market and to anticipate trends as they unfold. Their ability to concentrate their efforts and attention in one area also gives small businesses an edge in innovation. One venture capitalist explains, "Small companies have an advantage: a dedicated management team totally focused on a new product or market."[107]

ENTREPRENEURIAL PROFILE: Thomas Davis and Franco Harris: SilverSport While exercising at a YMCA in Pittsburgh, Pennsylvania, Thomas Davis watched people move their sweaty towels from one station to the next and came up with the idea for an antibacterial gym towel. Davis convinced his friend, National Football League Hall of Famer Franco Harris, to work with him to build a business around his idea. They discovered that most antibacterial towels on the market were chemically treated and decided to pursue natural options to set their product apart from the competition. They decided to apply silver, which is naturally bacteria resistant, to bamboo fabric, which is softer and more odor resistant than cotton or nylon. They found manufacturers in South Carolina to produce the towels and apply nanosilver particles to them. Their company, SilverSport, has sold more than 50,000 Silver Towels and introduced several other new products, including an antimicrobial yoga mat.[108] ■

EMPHASIS ON SPEED Technology, particularly the Internet, has changed the pace of business so dramatically that speed has become a major competitive weapon. Today's customers expect businesses to serve them at the speed of light! Providing a quality product at a reasonable price once was sufficient to keep customers happy, but that is not enough for modern customers who can find dozens of comparable products with a just few mouse clicks. Customers become disgruntled when companies fail to show respect for their busy schedules and corresponding lack of time. At world-class companies, speed reigns. They recognize that reducing the time it takes to develop, design, manufacture, and deliver a product reduces costs, increases quality, improves customer satisfaction, and boosts market share. A study by McKinsey and Company found that high-tech products that come to market on budget but six months late earn 33 percent less profit over five years. Bringing the product out on time but 50 percent over budget cuts profits just 4 percent![109] Service companies also know that they must build speed into their business systems if they are to satisfy their impatient, time-pressured customers. Business is moving so rapidly that companies must "accomplish in 90 days what traditionally took a year," says one entrepreneur.[110]

This philosophy of speed is based on **time compression management (TCM)**, which involves three principles: (1) speeding new products to market, (2) shortening customer response time in manufacturing and delivery, and (3) reducing the administrative time required to fill an order. Studies show plenty of room for improvement; most businesses waste 85 to 99 percent of the time it takes to produce products or services without ever realizing it![111] Victory in this

time compression management (TCM)
a marketing strategy that relies on three principles: (1) speeding products to market, (2) shortening customer response time in manufacturing and delivery, and (3) reducing the administrative time required to fill an order.

© Scott Hilburn/www.CartoonStock.com

time-obsessed economy goes to the company that can deliver goods and services the fastest, not necessarily those that are the biggest and most powerful. Businesses that can satisfy their customers' insatiable appetites for speed have a distinct advantage. McDonald's, the company that put the "fast" in fast food, designs the operation of its restaurants and the selection of its menu items around speed. "We don't put something on the menu until it can be produced at the speed of McDonald's," says CEO James Skinner. The company's Angus Snack Wrap, for example, is designed to take no more than 40 seconds to prepare. "Seconds always matter," says Executive Vice President Jeff Stratton. "Seconds beget volume." In the interest of speed, McDonald's recently upgraded to new cash registers that allow employees to be 50 percent more efficient at processing orders. "Our focus is execution," says Stratton. "We serve 60 million customers a day around the globe. That's a big responsibility."[112]

Although speeding up the manufacturing process is a common goal, companies using TCM have learned that manufacturing takes only 5 to 10 percent of the total time between an order and getting the product into the customer's hands. The rest is consumed by clerical and administrative tasks. "The primary opportunity for TCM lies in its application to the administrative process," says one manager. Companies relying on TCM to help them turn speed into a competitive edge should do the following:

- *"Reengineer" the entire process rather than attempt to do the same things in the same way—only faster.* Peter Schultz, founder of Symyx, a small technology company in Santa Clara, California, applied the principles of rapid drug development used in the pharmaceutical industry to the field of materials science and changed the way new chemical compounds are created. Symyx's technology allows its employees to test small amounts of chemicals and metals in parallel—up to 1,000 combinations per day—to create new materials. Processes that not so long ago required two years of intense work now produce marketable results in less time. "If you have speed advantage, you win," explains a manager at Dow Chemical Company, one of Symyx's customers.[113]

- *Create cross-functional teams of workers and give them the power to attack and solve problems.* In world-class companies, product teams include engineers, manufacturing workers, salespeople, quality experts—even customers.

- *Set aggressive goals for time reduction and stick to the schedule.* Some companies using TCM have been able to reduce cycle time from several weeks to just a few hours!

- *Rethink your supply chain.* Can you electronically link with your suppliers or your customers to speed up orders and deliveries?

- *Instill speed in the culture.* At Domino's Pizza, kitchen workers watch videos of the fastest pizza makers in the country.

- *Use technology to find shortcuts wherever possible.* Properly integrated into a company's strategy for speed, technology can restructure a company's operating timetable. Rather than build costly, time-consuming prototypes, many time-sensitive businesses use computer-aided design and computer-assisted manufacturing to speed product design and testing.

- *Put the Internet to work.* Perhaps nothing symbolizes speed better than the Internet, and companies that harness its lightning-fast power can become leaders in TCM.

Conclusion

Small companies lack the marketing budgets of their larger rivals, but that does not condemn them to the world of second-class marketers and its resulting anonymity. By using clever, innovative guerrilla marketing strategies such as the ones described in this chapter, entrepreneurs can put their companies in the spotlight and create a special connection with their customers.

Chapter Summary by Learning Objective

1. Describe the principles of building a guerrilla marketing plan, and explain the benefits of preparing one.

A major part of the entrepreneur's business plan is the marketing plan, which focuses on a company's target customers and how best to satisfy their needs and wants. A solid marketing plan should do the following:

- Determine customer needs and wants through market research.
- Pinpoint the specific target markets the company will serve.
- Analyze the firm's competitive advantages and build a guerrilla marketing strategy around them.

2. Explain how small businesses can pinpoint their target markets.

Sound market research helps the owner pinpoint his or her target market. The most successful businesses have well-defined portraits of the customers they are seeking to attract.

3. Discuss the role of market research in building a guerrilla marketing plan and outline the market research process.

Market research is the vehicle for gathering the information that serves as the foundation of the marketing plan. Good research does *not* have to be complex and expensive to be useful. The steps in conducting market research include the following:

- Defining the objective: "What do you want to know?"
- Collecting the data from either primary or secondary sources.
- Analyzing and interpreting the data.
- Drawing conclusions and acting on them.

4. Describe how a small business can build a competitive edge in the marketplace using guerrilla marketing strategies.

When plotting a marketing strategy, owners must strive to achieve a competitive advantage—some way to make their companies different from and better than the competition. Successful small businesses rely on 14 sources to develop a competitive edge:

- Find a niche and fill it.
- Use the power of publicity.
- Don't just sell—entertain.
- Strive to be unique.
- Build a community with customers.
- Connect with the customer on an emotional level.
- Create an identity for your business through branding.

- Embrace social marketing.
- Be dedicated to service and customer satisfaction.
- Retain existing customers.
- Be devoted to quality.

- Pay attention to convenience.
- Concentrate on innovation.
- Emphasize speed.

Discussion Questions

1. Define the marketing plan. What lies at its center?
2. What objectives should a marketing plan accomplish?
3. How can market research benefit a small business owner? List some possible sources of market information.
4. Does market research have to be expensive and sophisticated to be valuable? Explain.
5. Describe several trends that are driving markets today and their impact on small businesses.
6. Why is it important for small business owners to define their target markets as part of their marketing strategies?
7. What is a competitive advantage? Why is it important for a small business owner to create a plan for establishing one?
8. Describe how a small business owner could use the following sources for a competitive advantage:
   - Find a niche and fill it.
   - Use the power of publicity.
   - Don't just sell—entertain.
   - Strive to be unique.
   - Build a community with customers.
   - Connect with the customer on an emotional level.
   - Create an identity for your business through branding.
   - Embrace social marketing.
   - Be dedicated to service and customer satisfaction.
   - Retain existing customers.
   - Be devoted to quality.
   - Pay attention to convenience.
   - Concentrate on innovation.
   - Emphasize speed.

9. One manager says, "When a company provides great service, its reputation benefits from a stronger emotional connection with its customers, as well as from increased confidence that it will stand behind its products." Do you agree? Explain. If so, describe a positive service experience you have had with a company and your impressions of that business. What are the implications of a company providing poor customer service? Once again, describe a negative service experience you have had with a company and your impressions of that business. How likely are you to do business with that company again?
10. First, consumer behavior expert and retail consultant Paco Underhill says, "A [retail] store is a 3-D brand. Everything that's there has to be there for a reason." Do you agree? Explain. Second, find two retail stores in the local area—one that offers a good example of a 3-D brand and one that does not. Prepare a one-page summary explaining you reasoning for selecting these two stores.
11. With a 70 percent customer retention rate (average for most U.S. firms, according to the American Management Association), every $1 million of sales will grow to more than $4 million in 10 years. If you retain 80 percent of your customers, the $1 million will grow to a little over $6 million. If you can keep 90 percent of your customers, that $1 million will grow to more than $9.5 million. What can the typical small business do to increase its customer retention rate?

Business Plan Pro™   The marketing plan section of the business plan will tell the story of the "4 Ps" as it supports the mission and objectives of the business.

On the Web

The Internet is an efficient tool for conducting market research. The Web can help you determine which form of market research is going to work best for your plan. Your market research should provide specific information about your target market and the key factors that influence their buying decisions. Market research is often associated with elaborate processes conducted by third parties that demand a tremendous amount of time and money. However, casual and efficient market research can be valuable. Your business plan will benefit from even the most elementary market research, and, if it does not provide new information, that research will validate what you already know. Your investment in market research may be based on the quality, cost, or the amount of time to acquire the information. Make that determination based on the value you will receive versus the time and other resources you need to invest to gain access to that information.

The Internet can help you identify relevant industry associations. Assess the information that is on the association's

Web site. Does the association have publications available? What benefits do they provide to their members? What does it cost to join the association? Industry associations may be a valuable source of market research.

Excellent data are also available through U.S. government resources on the Web in the following areas:

- Small Business Administration: www.sba.gov
- Small Business Development Center: www.sba.gov/sbdc
- U.S. Census Bureau: www.census.gov
- U.S. Department of Commerce: www.trade.gov
- U.S. Chamber of Commerce: www.uschamber.com

For example, the information through the U.S. Census Bureau at www.census.gov provides a menu of available demographic reports that include reports on various manufacturing industries, county-specific economic surveys, business patterns for a specific ZIP code, and others. Additional online information is available through educational resources on community college, college, and university Web sites.

Private market research sources are plentiful on the Web. Although most provide this information for a fee, many sites offer preliminary information at no cost. One example is geocluster data called PRIZM, an acronym for "Potential Rating Index by Zip Markets." This information, available through Claritas Inc., offers descriptions of consumers by ZIP code and 62 distinct lifestyle groups based on education, affluence, family life cycle, urbanization, mobility, race, and ethnicity. You can look up PRIZM information by going to www.claritas.com/MyBestSegments and clicking on the "Zip Code Look-Up" tab at the top. Enter your ZIP code into the search window for your results. This information may be very useful—available at no cost.

The Web can also be helpful in finding publications that focus on your geographic area. Reviewing online magazine, newspaper, and other publications may be an efficient way to search for related articles and other information. Many industry-specific magazines publish statistical editions and market reviews at regular intervals. Search the indexes to identify published information that might help the marketing section of your business plan. You may find an index listing for an article that forecasts your industry or addresses industry economics or trends. You can also contact their editorial departments for additional information.

Sample Plans

Review the marketing sections of a sample plan that you found to be helpful. Note the information regarding market segmentation, the target market, the industry, and the competitors. Notice the use of tables and graphics in these sections that illustrate this marketing information. This type of marketing information is essential to establish a solid understanding of the market your business will serve. It will establish a basis for developing and validating your marketing strategy.

In the Software

With this information in mind, review each of the following sections in your business plan:

Your company. Does this section capture a viable marketing focus? Does this section place the necessary emphasis on valuing the customer relationship? Add to and edit your work to reflect this critical perspective.

What you are selling. Make certain that this section presents what you are selling to your customers. It must concisely communicate to your customers the value they will realize from choosing to do business with you and the benefits of your products and services.

Service summary. Think about the unique nature of the services your business provides. How will your services offer greater benefit than those of your competitors? How will your services be superior and provide meaningful value to your customers in a way that will enhance their loyalty? Address these questions in this section of your plan.

Your market. Add new information that you have gleaned from your marketing research to describe your market in as much detail as possible.

Target market segment. Review the concepts in "Pinpointing the Target Market" on pages 273 to 275. Use those concepts to help you to develop a clear picture of your target customers. Consider writing a profile of those customers. You may want to incorporate these profiles into this section to describe your target market segment.

Competition. A thorough discussion and analysis of each of the current and potential competitor is critical. There is no substitute for this depth of analysis. The business plan must demonstrate that you have evaluated this critical factor and can identify, in realistic and practical terms, how your business will successfully compete. Demonstrate your knowledge of why customers make purchasing decisions and how your proposed venture can gain their business. Be honest and objective as you describe your competitors' strengths and weaknesses. Discuss the customer appeal, pricing strategies, advertising campaigns, and the products and services that competitors offer.

Competitive edge. What unique attributes does your business offer that provide real or perceived benefits for your customers? Make sure that you capture those thoughts in this section. Be as detailed as possible and specifically explain your strategies for creating this advantage. Incorporate material from your marketing and sales plan that will show how these strategic advantages will support your sales forecast.

The sales forecast. Is the sales forecast realistic? Is the cost of goods sold amount accurate? Go to the narrative section of the sales forecast and explain the numbers in the sales forecast. Include any assumptions on which you have developed your sales forecast. Explain why your sales volume will change over time. Include any key events that may affect your sales and how and why they will influence the sales forecast. Developing financial forecasts using published statistics from sources such as RMA Annual Statement Studies (www. rmahq.org), market research, industry studies, and other sources lends credibility to you plan. Once again, you will find information and links at www.prenhall/ scarborough.com that may be helpful.

Marketing plan summary. A marketing strategy should present a clear link to generate sales revenue. Be sure to include an explanation of all assumptions on which your analysis rests. Your company's pricing, product distribution, and promotion plans combined should produce a unified marketing strategy.

Building Your Business Plan

Continue to build your business plan with the new information you have acquired. Step back to assess whether you have a solid understanding of your market and whether your business plan effectively communicates that knowledge.

Beyond the Classroom . . .

1. Interview the owner of a local restaurant about its marketing strategy. From how large a geographic region does the restaurant draw its clientele? What is the company's target market? What is the demographic profile of the company's target customers? Does the restaurant have a competitive edge?

2. Visit the Web site for the Small Business Administration's page on marketing at http://www.sba.gov/ category/navigation-structure/starting-managing-business/managing-business/running-business/ marketin.

   Interview a local business owner, using the resources there as a guide. What sources for developing a competitive edge did you find? What weaknesses do you see? How do you recommend overcoming them? What recommendations can you make to help the owner make better use of its marketing techniques?

What guerrilla marketing strategies can you suggest to enhance current marketing efforts?

3. Contact two local small business owners and ask them about their marketing strategies. What guerrilla marketing strategies do the companies use? How have they achieved a competitive edge? How do the businesses compare?

4. Select three local businesses (one large and two small) and play the role of "mystery shopper." How easy was it to do business with each company? How would you rate their service, quality, and convenience? Were sales people helpful and friendly? Did they handle transactions professionally and courteously? How would rate the business's appearance? How would you describe each company's competitive advantage? What future do you predict for each company? Prepare a brief report for your class on your findings and conclusions.

Endnotes

1. Scott Reeves, "How to Swing with Guerrilla Marketing," *Forbes*, June 8, 2006, http://www.forbes.com/ entrepreneurs/2006/06/08/entrepreneurs-marketing-harley-davidson-cx_sr_0608askanexpert.html.
2. Mia Wedbury, "Lessons Learned from Buddy, the Doggie CEO," *Globe and Mail*, June 10, 2010, http://www .theglobeandmail.com/report-on-business/small-business/ sb-tools/sb-columnists/lessons-learned-from-buddy-the-doggie-ceo/article1598965; "Paul Brent, "Buddy's Many Friends Help Boost Belt Sales," *The Star*, November 9, 2010, http://www.thestar.com/business/smallbusiness/ article/887886--buddy-s-many-friends-help-boost-belt-sales.
3. Howard Dana Shaw, "Customer Care Checklist," *In Business*, September/October, 1987, p. 28.
4. Scott Reeves, "How to Swing with Guerrilla Marketing," *Forbes*, June 8, 2006, http://www.forbes.com/entrepreneurs/2006/06/08/entrepreneurs-marketing-harley-davidson-cx_sr_0608askanexpert.html.
5. Adam Tschorn, "Levi's New Jeans Throw Some Women Curves," *Greenville News*, August 23, 2010, p. 1C; "Levi's Attempt at Mass Customization," *Tree House Logic*, November 4, 2010, http://blog.treehouselogic.com/2010/11/04/ levis-second-attempt-at-mass-customization; "Levi's Rear View Girls Video Viral Campaign," *Good Marketing Bad Marketing*, February 25, 2011, http://goodmarketingbadmarketing .com/2011/02/levis-rear-view-girls-viral-video-campaign.
6. Karen Talavera, "Do You Really Know Your Customers? Marketing to a Rapidly Diversifying Population," *Marketing*

Profs, May 17, 2011, http://www.marketingprofs.com/articles/2011/5057/do-you-really-know-your-customers-marketing-to-a-rapidly-diversifying-population.

7. "Minorities Represent 91% of Total U.S. Growth," *Marketing Charts*, March 28, 2011, http://www.marketingcharts.com/uncategorized/hispanics-represent-16-of-us-population-16759.

8. "Nielsen: Marketing 'Gravy Train' to Derail by 2020," Marketing Charts, July 30, 2009, http://www.marketingcharts.com/topics/behavioral-marketing/nielsen-marketer-gravy-train-will-derail-by-2020-9978.

9. Stephanie Schomer, "Mum's the Word," *Fast Company*, February 2011, pp. 40–41.

10. Dan Macsai, "America's First Unbanked Bank," *Fast Company*, July/August 2010, p. 44; *FDIC National Survey of Unbanked and Underbanked Households: Executive Summary*, Federal Deposit Insurance Corporation, Washington, DC, 2009, p. 4.

11. Roberta Maynard, "New Directions in Marketing" *Nation's Business*, July 1995, p. 26.

12. "Our Story," Innocent Drinks, http://www.innocentdrinks.co.uk/us/?Page=our_story.

13. Brandi Stewart, "Able Baker," *FSB*, December 2007/January 2008, pp. 53–58.

14. Jefferson Graham, "Twitter and Twitterers: Running Full Speed Ahead to Keep Up," *E-Commerce Times*, July 29, 2008, http://www.technewsworld.com/story/63943.html.

15. Jason Ankeny, "Social Climbers," *Entrepreneur*, January 2011, pp. 116–123; Ben Paynter, "Social Network Rockets Houlihan Restaurants' Profits," *Fast Company*, March 1, 2010, http://www.fastcompany.com/magazine/143/next-tech-happy-hour.html.

16. Nancy L. Croft, "Smart Selling," *Nation's Business*, March 1988, pp. 51–52.

17. Al Cole, "Cinematic Chic," *Modern Maturity*, March–April 1998, p. 24.

18. Larry Selden and Geoffrey Colvin, "A Measure of Success," *Business 2.0*, November 2001, p. 59.

19. Alicia Kelso, "Social Media Monitoring Becoming a Necessity," *Pizza Marketplace*, September 6, 2011, http://www.pizzamarketplace.com/article/184188/Social-media-monitoring-becoming-a-necessity.

20. Jeremiah McWilliams, "Wendy's Sees Opportunity in the A.M.," *Atlanta Journal Constitution*, September 21, 2010, http://www.ajc.com/business/wendys-sees-opportunity-in-618248.html.

21. Paul Hughes, "Service Savvy," *Business Start-Ups*, January 1996, p. 48.

22. Kasey Wehrum, "Behind the Scenes," *Inc.*, November 2010, pp. 26–27.

23. Roberta Maynard, "Rich Niches," *Nation's Business,* November 1993, pp. 39–42.

24. Eilene Zimmerman, "Big Marlin, Big Money," *FSB*, October 2006, pp. 104–110.

25. Debra Phillips, "Fast Track," *Entrepreneur*, April 1999, p. 42.

26. Kim T. Gordon, "How to Start a Cause Marketing Campaign," *Entrepreneur*, January 19, 2011, http://www.entrepreneur.com/article/217935.

27. *Past. Present. Future: The 25th Anniversary of Cause Marketing* (Boston: Cone LLC), 2010, p. 11.

28. Peggy Linial, "Small Business and Cause Related Marketing: Getting Started," Cause Marketing Forum, http://www.cause-marketingforum.com/framemain.asp?ID=189.

29. "Straw Hat Pizza Joins No Kid Hungry Cause," *Pizza Marketplace*, September 8, 2011, http://www.pizzamarketplace.com/article/184281/Straw-Hat-Pizza-joins-No-Kid-Hungry-cause.

30. Dale D. Buss, "Entertailing," *Nation's Business*, December 1997, p. 18.

31. Marty Schultz, "Welcome to Entertailing," *Albany Biz Center*, http://www.bizcenter.org/Article/105/959/1103; Book Bin, "About Us: Corvallis," http://www.bookbin.com.

32. Dale D. Buss, "Entertailing," *Nation's Business*, December 1997, pp. 12–18.

33. Terry Oarka, "Shops That Pop," *C and G News*, September 29, 2010, http://www.candgnews.com/Homepage-Articles/2010/9-29-10/Troy-Somerset-new-stores.asp.

34. Marty Schultz, "Welcome to Entertailing," *Albany Biz Center*, http://www.bizcenter.org/Article/105/959/1103.

35. Stephanie Schomer, "The Perfect (Wooden) Board, *Fast Company*, June 2011, p. 65; Patrick Rizzo, "U.S. Surfboard Makers Thrive in Choppy Waters," MSNBC, August 5, 2010, http://www.msnbc.msn.com/id/38472495/ns/business-us_business/t/us-surfboard-makers-thrive-choppy-waters/#.TnH__uz5muI.

36. Barry Libert, "Seven Principles for Social Success and the Companies Already Getting Them Right," *Marketing Profs*, April 6, 2011, http://www.marketingprofs.com/articles/2011/4765/seven-principles-for-social-success-and-the-companies-already-getting-them-right.

37. David Rogers, "How Savvy Brands Use Facebook," *BNET*, June 15, 2011, http://www.bnet.com/blog/digital-marketing/how-savvy-brands-use-facebook/204.

38. "Pam Dinziger: Build a New Retailing Model," *Rough and Polished*, July 21, 2009, http://www.rough-polished.com/en/expertise/27985.html.

39. *2007 Cone Cause Marketing and Environmental Survey* (Boston: Cone LLC), http://www.coneinc.com/files/2007ConeSurveyReport.pdf, p. 12.

40. James Maguire, "Business Remains Hot at Ice.com," *e-Commerce Guide*," May 23, 2005, http://www.e-commerceguide.com/solutions/advertising /article.php/3507011; Lin Grensing-Pophal, "Who Are You?," *Business Start-Ups*, September 1997, pp. 38–44.

41. Corbett Barr, "10 Examples of Killer USPs on the Web," *Think Traffic*, August 4, 2010, http://thinktraffic.net/10-examples-of-killer-unique-selling-propositions-on-the-web.

42. Maureen Farrell, "How to Market Your New Idea," *Forbes*, December 21, 2007, http://www.forbes.com/entrepreneurs/2007/12/21/marketing-branding-identity-ent-cx_mf_1221brand.html.

43. Jason Ankeny, "Building a Brand on a Budget," *Entrepreneur*, May 2010, p. 50.

44. "Marketing Definitions: Brand," BuildingBrands Inc., http://www.buildingbrands.com/definitions/02_brand_definition.shtml.

45. Fawn Fitter, "Selling Clean Machines," *FSB*, July/August 2008, pp. 104–108.

46. "Social Networking Sites and Our Lives," Pew Internet and American Life Project, June 16, 2011, http://www.pewinternet.org/Reports/2011/Technology-and-social-networks/Summary.aspx.

47. "The Small Business Priorities: Growth, Hiring, and Cash Flow," American Express OPEN Small Business Monitor, Spring 2011, http://www.openforum.com/idea-hub/topics/marketing/article/the-small-business-priorities-growth-hiring-and-cash-flow.

48. "9 in 10 Marketers Use Social Media," *Marketing Charts*, April 6, 2011, http://www.marketingcharts.com/direct/9-in-10-marketers-use-social-media-16879.

49. *2011 Social Media Marketing Industry Report*, Social Media Examiner, p. 13.

50. Jason Arkeny, "How Small Companies Are Marketing through Facebook," *Entrepreneur*, June 2011, http://www.entrepreneur.com/article/219643.

51. "#Numbers," Twitter, March 14, 2011, http://blog.twitter .com/2011/03/numbers.html; Kristin Piombino, "Infographic: Is Twitter a Waste of Our Time?," Ragan, http:// www.ragan.com/SocialMedia/Articles/Infographic_Is_ Twitter_a_waste_of_our_time__43217.aspx.

52. Elizabeth Holmes, "Why Pay Full Price?," *Wall Street Journal*, May 5, 2011, pp. D1, D6.

53. "Social Media Creates Advocates," *Marketing Charts*, March 8, 2011, http://www.marketingcharts.com/direct/ social-media-creates-brand-advocates-16503.

54. Robert Gourley, "Twitter 101: Seven Tips for Effective Marketing," *Marketing Profs*, June 15, 2010, http://www.marketingprofs.com/articles/2010/3704/ twitter-101-seven-tips-for-effective-marketing.

55. "Is Blogging a Mainstream Media Channel?," *eMarketer*, September 23, 2010, http://www.emarketer.com/ PressRelease.aspx?R=1007945.

56. *The 2011 State of Inbound Marketing*, HubSpot, February 2011, pp. 10, 14.

57. "The Continued Rise of Blogging," *eMarketer*, September 23, 2010, http://www.emarketer.com/%28S%28hyezjifgz1sz wkmqcfycpl55%29%29/Article.aspx?R=1007941.

58. Janie Pettit, "10 Business-Building Tips from 5 Successful Entrepreneurs," *Smart Track Small Business Big Results*, April 26, 2010, http://smallbusiness-bigresults.com/blog/ 10-business-building-tips-from-5-successful-entrepreneurs.

59. John Nardini, "Create a Blog to Boost Your Business," *Entrepreneur*, September 27, 2005, http://www.entrepreneur.com/ article/0,4621,323598,00.html; Amanda C. Kooser, "Who Let the Blogs Out?," *Entrepreneur*, October 2002, http:// www.entrepreneur.com/article/0,4621,303129,00.html.

60. John J. Curran, "What Are They Saying about You?" *FSB*, July/August 2008, p. 63.

61. Guy Kawasaki, "Blog-A-Thon," *Entrepreneur*, February 2008, p. 44.

62. Jean Chatzky, "Entrepreneur Friday: Emerson Salon," *Jean Chatzky*, 2010, http://www.jeanchatzky.com/homepage/ entrepreneur-friday-emerson-salon.

63. Russell Working, "Brands Use YouTube to Create StoryTelling Presence," Ragan, June 15, 2011, http://www.ragan.com/ Main/Articles/Brands_use_YouTube_to_create_a_ storytelling_presen_43130.aspx.

64. "The State of Online Video," Pew Research Center, June 3, 2010, http://www.pewinternet.org/Reports/2010/State-of- Online-Video.aspx.

65. Greg Jarboe, "Dynomighty YouTube Video Marketing Case Study," YouTube, March 30, 2010, http://www.youtube.com/ watch?v=gRzQlMAhstA&feature=youtu.be.

66. Leigh Buchanan, Max Chafkin, and Ryan McCarthy, "Get Ready for Your Close-Up," *Inc.*, February 2008, p. 88; Raymund Flandez, "Lights! Camera! Sales!," *Wall Street Journal*, November 26, 2007, pp. R1, R3.

67. "Consumers Pay More for Great Experience," *Marketing Charts*, October 19, 2010, http://www.marketingcharts.com/ direct/consumers-pay-more-for-great-experience-14657.

68. "Debbie Kelly, "Poor Customer Service Paralyzes U.S. Companies," *CRM Daily*, February 8, 2008, www.crm-daily.com/ story.xhtml?story_id=103001XXU5EQ.

69. "Consumers Pay More for Great Experience," *Marketing Charts*, October 19, 2010, http://www.marketingcharts.com/ direct/consumers-pay-more-for-great-experience-14657.

70. Cathryn Creno, "Retailers Use Customer Satisfaction to Create Loyalty," *Arizona Republic*, December 15, 2007, http://www .azcentral.com/business/articles/1215biz-threestores1216.html.

71. "Beware of Dissatisfied Customers: They Like to Blab," *Knowledge @ Wharton*, March 8, 2006, http://knowledge .wharton.upenn.edu/article.cfm?articleid=1422.

72. *2011 Online Trend Tracker*, Cone, August 30, 2011, p. 1.

73. Mike Michalowicz, "How to Turn Customers into Loyal, Raving Fans," *Wall Street Journal*, July 15, 2011, http:// online.wsj.com/article/SB10001424052702304203304576447 8 23427183788.html.

74. Ron Zemke and Dick Schaaf, "The Service Edge," *Small Business Reports*, July 1990, pp. 57–60.

75. Thomas A. Stewart, "After All You've Done for Your Customers, Why Are They Still NOT HAPPY?," *Fortune*, December 11, 1995, pp. 178–182.

76. Linda Stanfield and Kathryn Hawkins, "Why Customer Complaints Are the Best Business Tools," BNET, April 5, 2011, http://www.bnet.com/blog/smb/ why-customer-complaints-are-the-best-business- tools/4214.

77. "Consumers Pay More for Great Experience," *Marketing Charts*, October 19, 2010, http://www.marketingcharts.com/ direct/consumers-pay-more-for-great-experience-14657.

78. Michael Hess, "I Turn Disgruntled Customers into Loyal Fans," *BNET*, May 12, 2010, http://www.bnet.com/blog/ customer-relationship/i-turn-disgruntled-customers-into- loyal-fans/103.

79. Michael Hess, "I Turn Disgruntled Customers into Loyal Fans," *BNET*, May 12, 2010, http://www.bnet.com/blog/ customer-relationship/i-turn-disgruntled-customers-into- loyal-fans/103.

80. Brian Lee, "The 3 Cornerstones of Cultural Change," *CEO's Kickstart Retreat*, September 2005, pp. 1–5.

81. Anne Fisher, "A Happy Staff Equals Happy Customers," *Fortune*, July 12, 2004, p. 52.

82. Leonard L. Berry, "Customer Service Solutions," *Success*, July/August 1995, pp. 90–95.

83. Ron Zemke and Dick Schaaf, "The Service Edge," *Small Business Reports*, July 1990, p. 60.

84. Charles Gerena, "Hey, A Little Service Here?" *Region Focus*, Summer 2004, p. 52.

85. Adam Stone, "Retaining Customers Requires Constant Contact," *Small Business Computing*, January 11, 2005, http://www.smallbusinesscomputing.com/biztools/print .pho/3457221; Rahul Jacob, "Why Some Customers Are More Equal Than Others," *Fortune*, September 19, 1994, pp. 215–224.

86. Susan Hauser, "Out of Print? Not Walter Powell," *Wall Street Journal*, January 24, 2002, p. A16.

87. William A. Sherden, "The Tools of Retention," *Small Business Reports*, November 1994, pp. 43–47.

88. Elizabeth Holmes, "Why Pay Full Price?," *Wall Street Journal*, May 5, 2011, pp. D1, D6.

89. Richard Stone, "Retaining Customers Requires Constant Contact," *Small Business Computing*, January 11, 2005, http://www.smallbusinesscomputing.com/biztools/print .pho/3457221.

90. Matt Wilson, "At Tasti D-Lite, Social Media Rewards Program Yields Loyalty," *Ragan's HR Communication*, November 9, 2010, http://www.hrcommunication.com/Main/ Articles/At_Tasti_DLite_social_media_rewards_program_ yields_3258.aspx.

91. "How Can You Give Customers a Little Thrill?," *Marketing-Profs: Get to the Point*, April 30, 2008, p. 1.

92. Jennifer Lawler, "Rewarding the Repeaters," *Entrepreneur*, January 2010, p. 72.

93. Faye Rice, "How to Deal with Tougher Customers," *Fortune*, December 3, 1990, pp. 39–40.

94. Rahul Jacob, "TQM: More Than a Dying Fad," *Fortune*, October 18, 1993, p. 67.

95. Lee Allen, "From the World of Computers to the Bucket Brigade," *Inside Tucson Business*, January 3, 2008, http://

www.azbiz.com/articles/2008/01/03/news/profiles/doc477d887f83d2e289092759.txt.

96. Dave Zielinski, "Improving Service Doesn't Require a Big Investment," *Small Business Reports*, February 1991, p. 20.

97. Tamara Chuang, "iPads Replacing Restaurant Menus," *Sign On San Diego*, August 27, 2011, http://www.signonsandiego.com/news/2011/aug/27/pass-the-ipad-please; Bruce Horovitz, "iPads Replacing Restaurant Menus, Staff," *USA Today*, February 16, 2011, http://www.usatoday.com/money/industries/food/2011-02-16-ipadcafe16_ST_N.htm.

98. Mike Bastoli, "Restaurant Replaces Menu and More with iPad," *Cult of Mac*, August 6, 2011, http://www.cultofmac.com/107929/restaurant-replaces-menus-and-more-with-ipad.

99. Maura Ewing, "5 Startup Tips from 5 Successful Food Truck Entrepreneurs," BNET, http://www.bnet.com/photos/startup-tips-from-5-successful-food-truck-entrepreneurs/6235454?seq=5&tag=mantle_skin;content.

100. A Little White Wedding Chapel, http://www.alittlewhitechapel.com/html/tunnel_of_love.html.

101. Sheryl E. Kimes, *The Current State of Online Food Ordering in the U.S. Restaurant Industry*, Cornell University Center for Hospitality Research, vol. 11, no. 17, September 2011, pp. 6–16.

102. Ann Zimmerman, "Check Out the Future of Shopping," *Wall Street Journal*, May 18, 2011, pp. D1–D2.

103. Emily Nelson, "Marketers Push Individual Portions and Families Bite," *Wall Street Journal*, July 23, 2002, pp. A1, A6.

104. Lucy McCauley, "Measure What Matters," *Fast Company*, May 1999, p. 100.

105. Michael Dell, "Thrive in a Sick Economy," *Business 2.0*, December 2002/January 2003, p. 88.

106. Bob Weinstein, "Bright Ideas," *Business Start-Ups*, August 1995, p. 57.

107. Alan Deutschman, "America's Fastest Risers," *Fortune*, October 7, 1991, p. 58.

108. Lindsey Silberman, "Big Idea: An AntiMicrobial Gym Towel," *Inc.*, May 2011, p. 56.

109. Desiree De Meyer, "Get to Market Faster," *Smart Business*, October 2001, pp. 62–65; Brian Dumaine, "How Managers Can Succeed through Speed," *Fortune*, February 13, 1989, pp. 54–59.

110. Geoff Williams, "Speed Freaks," Entrepreneur, September 1999, p. 120.

111. Mark Henricks, "Time Is Money," *Entrepreneur*, February 1993, p. 44.

112. John Berman, "McDonald's Kitchen Lab Puts New Products to Test," *ABC News*, August 20, 2010, http://abcnews.go.com/Nightline/mcdonalds-tests-recipes-taste-speed/story?id=11444997; "Speed Key to McDonald's Success: CEO Skinner," *CNBC*, May 13, 2010, http://www.cnbc.com/id/37129588/Speed_Key_to_McDonald_s_Success_CEO_Skinner.

113. Zina Moukheiber, "The World's Fastest Chemicals," *Forbes*, October 17, 2005, p. 63.

9

E-Commerce and the Entrepreneur

Learning Objectives

On completion of this chapter, you will be able to:

1. Understand the factors an entrepreneur should consider before launching into e-commerce.
2. Explain the 10 myths of e-commerce and how to avoid falling victim to them.
3. Explain the basic strategies entrepreneurs should follow to achieve success in their e-commerce efforts.
4. Learn the techniques of designing a killer Web site.
5. Explain how companies track the results from their Web sites.
6. Describe how e-businesses ensure the privacy and security of the information they collect and store from the Web.

The Internet remains a place where you can start with nothing and soon challenge the gods.

—Mark DiMassimo

Give a person a fish, and you feed him for a day. Teach that person to use the Internet, and he won't bother you for weeks.

—Anonymous

E-commerce has created a new way of doing business, one that is connecting producers, sellers, and customers via technology in ways that have never been possible before. The result is a new set of companies built on business models that are turning traditional methods of commerce and industry on their heads. Companies that ignore the impact of the Internet on their markets run the risk of becoming as relevant to customers as a rotary-dial telephone. The most successful companies are embracing the Internet not only as merely another advertising medium or marketing tool but also as a mechanism for transforming their companies and changing *everything* about the way they do business. As these companies discover new, innovative ways to use the Internet, computers, and communications technology to connect with their suppliers and to serve their customers better, they are creating a new industrial order. In short, e-commerce has launched a revolution. Just as in previous revolutions in the business world, some old established players are being ousted, and new leaders are emerging. The winners are discovering new business opportunities, improved ways of designing work, and better ways of organizing and operating their businesses. Yet one lesson that entrepreneurs engaged in e-commerce have learned is that business basics still apply; companies engaged in e-commerce still have to take care of their customers and earn a profit to stay in business. Making a Web-based business succeed requires entrepreneurs to strike a balance, creating an e-commerce strategy that capitalizes on the strengths of the Internet while meeting customers' expectations of convenience and service.

In the world of e-commerce, new business models recognize the power that the Internet gives customers, whether they buy online or offline. In 2014, online sales and Internet activity will account for or influence 53 percent of total retail sales, or more than $1.65 trillion, in the United States.[1] Pricing, for example, has become more transparent than ever before because of the Internet. The Internet's global reach means that entrepreneurs can no longer be content to take into account only local competitors when setting their prices. With a few mouse clicks, customers can compare the prices of the same or similar products and services from companies across the globe. In the new wired and connected economy, the balance of power is shifting to customers, and new business models recognize this fact. Whatever products they may sell—from books and digital cameras to cars and flowers—retailers are dealing with customers who are more informed and aware of the price and feature comparisons of the items for which they are shopping. A study by the Pew Internet and American Life Project reports that 58 percent of Americans research products and services online before buying them, up from 35 percent in 2000.[2] These informed shoppers are taking price out of the buying equation, causing retailers to emphasize other factors, such as service or convenience, to build long-term relationships. The connection between online and offline business runs both ways. As a result of offline exposure to a company's ads, shoppers are likely to conduct online Web searches of the products and services they see advertised. In addition, customers share their opinions about products and their shopping experience with companies; nearly one-fourth of Americans say that they have posted online reviews of products they purchase.[3] These trends point to the need for retailers to market their products and services by taking a multichannel selling approach that includes the Internet as one option.

In the fast-paced world of e-commerce, size doesn't matter as much as speed and flexibility. One of the Internet's greatest strengths is its ability to provide companies with instantaneous customer feedback, giving them the opportunity to learn and to make necessary adjustments. Businesses, whatever their size, that are willing to experiment with different approaches to reaching customers and are quick to learn and adapt will grow and prosper; those that cannot will fall by the wayside. E-commerce is transforming the way businesses in almost every industry operate. One of the most significant changes has occurred in the video rental business. Launched in 1985, Blockbuster first transformed the video rental industry, which was characterized by small, independent stores with limited inventories of videos, by opening rental stores stocked with a huge selection of 8,000 videos. Ultimately, the company grew to more than 8,000 stores, but in 1997, Reed Hastings, after paying a $40 late fee on *Apollo 13*, launched Netflix, a company that initially mailed videos (no more late fees) from regional warehouses that customers rented online from its extensive library of more than 11,000 video titles. By 2003, Netflix had more than 1 million subscribers and in 2006 lived up to its name and began offering movies that subscribers could download over the Internet. With the Internet bandwidth and technology in place to realize his original strategy for Netflix, Hastings now calls his business "a streaming company that also offers DVD-by-mail." Netflix has more than 25 million subscribers worldwide and has spun off

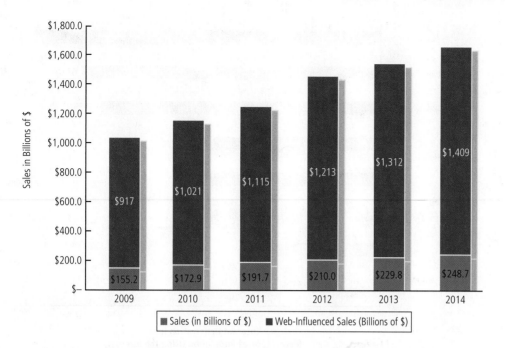

FIGURE 9.1

Online and Web-Influenced Retail Sales in the United States

Source: Forrester Research, 2010.

its movie-rental-by-mail business into a separate division. In the meantime, Blockbuster struggled to compete, shuttered hundreds of stores, and declared bankruptcy before Dish Network bought the company in 2011 for $320 million. Dish Network quickly introduced the Blockbuster Movie Pass, a service that gives Dish Network subscribers instant Internet access to more than 100,000 movie, television, and video game titles.[4]

A Nielsen study of global e-commerce trends reports that 84 percent of the world's online population has used the Internet to make a purchase, up from 40 percent in 2006. The items purchased most often online globally are books, clothing/accessories/shoes, airline tickets, electronic equipment, and hotels.[5] However, companies can—and do—sell practically anything over the Web, from antiques and pharmaceuticals to groceries and drug-free urine. Forrester Research estimates that 8 percent of total retail sales in the United States will occur online in 2014, totaling nearly $249 billion (see Figure 9.1).[6]

Companies of all sizes are busy establishing a presence on the Internet because that's where their customers are. The number of Internet users worldwide now stands at more than 2.1 billion, up from 147 million in 1998 (see Figure 9.2).[7] Consumers have adopted the Internet much more quickly than any other major innovations in the past. It reached 50 percent penetration in the United States in just seven years compared to 30 years for the computer, 40 years for electricity, and more than 100 years for steam power.[8]

Factors to Consider before Launching into E-Commerce

LO1

Understand the factors an entrepreneur should consider before launching into e-commerce.

The first e-commerce transaction took place on August 11, 1994, when NetMarket, a small company founded by recent college graduate Daniel Kohn, sold a CD by Sting, *Ten Summoner's Tales*, to a student at Swarthmore College for $12.48 plus shipping.[9] From these humble beginnings grew a distribution channel that now accounts for $235 billion in annual retail sales. Despite the many benefits the Internet offers, however, not every small business owner is ready to embrace e-commerce. According to a survey by Ad-ology, 64 percent of small business owners in the United States have Web sites, double the percentage that were operating online in 1997.[10] However, another survey by Newtek Business Services reports that 65 percent of small business owners do not actually engage in e-commerce because their Web sites cannot accept payments.[11] Why are owners of small companies hesitant to embrace the Web as a business tool? For many entrepreneurs, the key barrier is not knowing where or how to start an e-commerce effort, while

FIGURE 9.2

Internet Penetration Rate

Source: "Internet Usage Statistics: The Internet Big Picture," Internet World Stats 2012, www .internetworldstats.com/stats .htm.

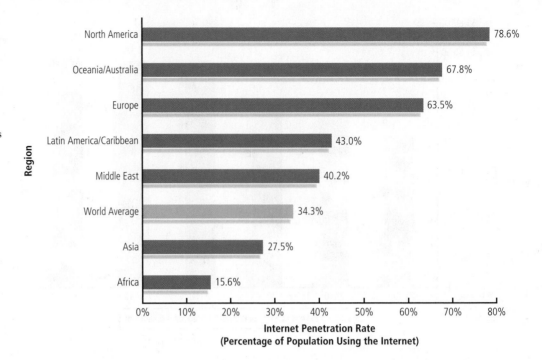

for others cost and time concerns are major issues. Other roadblocks include the fear that customers will not use the Web site and the problems associated with ensuring online security.

No matter how small their companies are, entrepreneurs must realize that establishing a presence on the Internet is no longer an option. A recent survey reports that 59 percent of global customers prefer online shopping over shopping in brick-and-mortar stores.[12] The message is clear: entrepreneurs who ignore the strategic implications of establishing a Web presence for their companies are putting their businesses at risk. "Any company that wants to make it in the years ahead must make the technology and the processes of the Internet part of its core competence," says one experienced venture capitalist.[13] However, before launching an e-commerce effort, business owners should consider the following important issues:

- The way in which a company exploits the Internet's interconnectivity and the opportunities it creates to transform relationships with its suppliers and vendors, its customers, and other external stakeholders are crucial to its success.

- Success requires a company to develop a plan for integrating the Internet into its overall strategy. The plan should address issues such as Web site design and maintenance, creating and managing a brand name, marketing and promotional strategies, sales, and customer service.

- Developing deep, lasting relationships with customers takes on even greater importance on the Internet. Attracting online customers costs money, and companies must be able to retain their online customers to make their Web sites profitable. That means that online companies must give their customers good reasons to keep coming back.

- Creating a meaningful presence on the Internet requires an ongoing investment of resources—time, money, energy, and talent. Establishing an attractive Web site brimming with catchy photographs and descriptions of products is only the beginning.

- Measuring the success of its Internet-based sales effort is essential if a company is to remain relevant to customers whose tastes, needs, and preferences are always changing.

Doing business on the Internet takes more time and energy than many entrepreneurs expect. Answering the following questions will help entrepreneurs make sure they are ready to do business on the Web and avoid unpleasant surprises in their e-commerce efforts:

- What exactly do you expect a Web site to do for your company? Will it provide information only, reach new customers, increase sales to existing customers, improve communication with customers, enhance customer service, or reduce your company's cost of operation? Will customers be able to place orders from the site (true e-commerce), or must they call your company to buy?

- How much can you afford to invest in an e-commerce effort?

- What rate of return do you expect to earn on that investment?

- How long can you afford to wait for that return?

- How well suited are your products and services for selling on the Web?

- How will the "back office" of your Web site work? Will your site be tied into your company's inventory control system?

- How will you handle order fulfillment? Can your fulfillment system handle the increase in volume you are expecting from online sales?

- What impact, if any, will your Web site have on your company's traditional channels of distribution?

- What mechanism will your site use to ensure secure customer transactions?

- How will your company handle customer service for the site? What provisions will you make for returned items?

- How do you plan to promote the site to draw traffic to it?

- What information will you collect from the visitors to your site? How will you use it? Will you tell visitors how you intend to use this information?

- Have you developed a privacy policy? Have you posted that policy on your company's Web site for customers?

- Have you tested your site with real, live customers to make sure that it is easy to navigate and easy to order from?

- How will you measure the success of your company's Web site? What objectives have you set for the site?

Ten Myths of E-Commerce

LO2

Explain the 10 myths of e-commerce and how to avoid falling victim to them.

Although many entrepreneurs have made their fortunes through e-commerce, setting up shop on the Internet is no guarantee of success. Scores of entrepreneurs have plunged unprepared into the world of e-commerce only to discover that there is more to it than merely setting up a Web site and waiting for orders to start pouring in. Make sure that you do not fall victim to one of the following e-commerce myths.

Myth 1. If I Launch a Site, Customers Will Flock to It

Some entrepreneurs think that once they set up their Web sites, their expenses end there. Not true! Without promotional support, no Web site will draw enough traffic to support a business. With more than 255 million Web sites in existence and 21 million added each year, getting a site noticed in the crowd has become increasingly difficult.[14] Listing a site with popular search engines does not guarantee that online customers will find your company's Web site. Just like traditional retail stores seeking to attract customers, virtual companies have discovered that drawing sufficient traffic to a Web site requires constant promotion—and lots of it! Setting up a Web site and then failing to drive customers to it with adequate promotional support is like setting up a physical store in a back alley; you may be in business, but nobody knows you're there!

Entrepreneurs with both physical and virtual stores must promote their Web sites at every opportunity by printing their Uniform Resource Locators (URLs; a company's address on the Internet) on everything related to their physical stores—on signs, in print and broadcast ads, on shopping bags, on merchandise labels, and anywhere else their customers will see. Quick-response (QR) codes allow smart phone users to go directly to a Web site's relevant page without

© ZUMA Wire Service / Alamy

having to type in a long URL. Entrepreneurs can use social media such as Facebook and You-Tube to drive traffic to their Web sites and purchase ads on high-traffic sites such as Google (Google Adsense) and Facebook, both of which allow companies to establish maximum expenditures based on the number of people who click on their ads. Using these tools, companies can aim their ads at specific target customers by location, age, and interests.

ENTREPRENEURIAL PROFILE: Chris Meyer: CM Photographics CM Photographics, a photography studio founded by Chris Meyer in Minneapolis, Minnesota, uses Facebook Ads to target women between the ages of 24 and 30 in the local area whose Facebook profiles indicate that they are engaged. In one year, Meyer spent just $600 on ads that directed potential customers to the studio's Web site and generated $40,000 in additional revenue for his business.[15] ■

Virtual shop owners also should consider buying ads in traditional advertising media as well as using banner ads, banner exchange programs, and cross-marketing arrangements with companies selling complementary products on their own Web sites. The keys to promoting a Web site are *networking*—building relationships with other companies, customers, trade associations, online directories, and other Web sites that your company's customers visit—and *interacting* with existing and potential customers online through social media outlets.

As more Internet users gain online access from mobile devices, entrepreneurs are making their Web sites easily accessible from smart phones, tablets, and other devices by creating mobile versions of their sites. Digital analytics firm comScore reports that more than more than 82 million people in the United States own smart phones and that 50 million own iPads that give them mobile access to the Internet.[16] These mobile device owners are using them to locate stores, research products they want to buy, conduct price comparisons, and search for discount coupons. A recent study by inMobi reports that 73 million people shop from their mobile devices and that annual shopping sales volume from mobile devices (known as m-commerce) is $9 billion.[17] The projected growth rate in the use of mobile Internet devices is phenomenal; by 2015, 788 million people globally will be mobile-only Internet users, and m-commerce sales will grow to $119 billion.[18]

The bottom line is that small businesses must adapt their Web sites to accommodate these mobile customers by making them compatible with mobile devices. Unfortunately, only 7 percent of small businesses have developed mobile Web sites.[19] Companies that have not are missing the opportunity to sell to countless numbers of customers each day. To create Web sites that are compatible with mobile devices, entrepreneurs simply register for one in the same way that they

rangizzz/Shutterstock.com

register for any other Web site. Although many mobile devices now display standard Web sites with no trouble, others do not. To handle these devices, entrepreneurs should optimize their mobile sites so that they appear appropriately on smaller screens and require easier navigation. That typically requires stripping a site down to its basics, minimizing graphics, eradicating clutter, simplifying navigation by making buttons larger and increasing the space between links, and eliminating Flash and Javascript.[20] Once a mobile Web site is completed, an entrepreneur should test it on multiple mobile devices (borrow them from friends) to make sure that it functions properly.

Another aspect of mobile marketing involves the use of QR codes, those Rorschach-looking tags that, when scanned, take smart phone users to a specific Web site where they can learn more about the product and its features, read reviews, watch a video about it, and even check on its availability. Zabar's, a retailer of gourmet specialty foods and upscale kitchen equipment located in New York City's Upper West Side, displays QR codes on its in-store signage. Doing so not only increases sales in the store but also reminds customers that they can shop at Zabar's Web site at any time of the day.[21] Retailers such as Zabar's that use cross-channel methods that blend both point-of-sale and online shopping experiences will continue to be the most successful as growing numbers of shoppers acquire smart phones and other mobile devices.

Myth 2. Online Customers Are Easy to Please

Customers who shop online today tend to be experienced Internet users whose expectations of their online shopping experiences are high and continue to rise. Experienced online shoppers tend to be unforgiving, quickly clicking to another site if their shopping experience is subpar or they cannot find the products and information they want. Because Web shoppers are becoming more discriminating, companies are finding that they must improve their Web sites to attract and keep their customers.

To be successful online marketers, small companies must create Web sites with the features that appeal to experienced Web shoppers, such as simple navigation, customer reviews, rock-solid security, and quick access to product information, videos, and blogs. Many small businesses outsource most (sometimes all) of the activities associated with conducting business online to companies that specialize in e-commerce services. These companies prefer to focus on their core competencies—product design, marketing, extending a brand, manufacturing, and others—and hire other companies whose core competencies reside in e-commerce to handle Web site design, hosting, order processing, and order fulfillment ("pick, pack, and ship"). Rather than make constant investments in technology that may not produce a reasonable return, these small companies preserve their capital and their energy and focus them on the aspects of business that they do best. Other entrepreneurs prefer to keep the design and operation of their Web sites in-house.

Companies that decide to operate their own e-commerce businesses quickly learn that setting up a site is only the first investment required. Sooner or later, companies encounter follow-up investments, including updating the Web site, automating or expanding their supply chain to meet customer demand, integrating their inventory control system into the Web site, and increasing customer service capacity. When it comes to e-commerce, the lesson for entrepreneurs is this: focus your efforts on the core competencies that your company has developed, whether they reside in "traditional" business practices or online, and outsource all of the other aspects of doing business online to companies that have the expertise to make your e-commerce business successful.

Myth 3. Making Money on the Web Is Easy

Promoters who hawk "get-rich-quick" schemes on the Internet lure many entrepreneurs with the promise that making money online is easy. It isn't. Doing business online can be very profitable, but making money online requires an up-front investment of time, money, and energy. Success online also requires a sound business strategy that is aimed at the appropriate target audience and that an entrepreneur must implement effectively and efficiently—in other words, the same elements that are required for success *offline*. Many entrepreneurs are earning healthy profits from their Web-based businesses, but doing so takes hard work!

As thousands of new sites spring up every day, getting a company's site noticed requires more effort and marketing muscle than ever before. Attracting customers to a Web site is really no different from attracting customers to a brick-and-mortar store; entrepreneurs must define their target customers, devise a marketing plan to reach them, and offer them good value and superior customer service to keep them coming back. Successful e-tailers have discovered that promoting their Web sites via social media and providing comprehensive FAQ (frequently asked questions) pages, e-mail order confirmations and shipment notices, and highly visible telephone and e-mail contact information followed by quick responses enhance their reputations for online customer service.

"We're in a dying industry, and you're just sitting there! Well, I'm going to do something about it—I'm starting a Web site."

You Be the Consultant

Selling on the Go

Just when many entrepreneurs are beginning to get a handle on designing Web sites for their companies that allow them to capitalize on the opportunities of e-commerce, another fast-growing technology emerges, one that demands just as much attention to detail to attract customers: m-commerce. M-commerce allows shoppers with a wireless mobile device, such as a smart phone, or a tablet PC, such as an iPad, to make purchases while they are on the go. The m-commerce revolution is well under way. In 2010, U.S. consumers spent more than $3.4 billion on mobile shopping, an increase from $1.2 billion in 2009, and experts estimate that m-commerce will generate sales of $119 billion, 8 percent of all e-commerce sales, by 2015. Almost half of smart phone users in the United States either have used their devices for mobile shopping or plan to do so in the near future.

Darren Baldwin, e-commerce manager at Dungarees.net, a company based in Columbia, Missouri, that sells denim and canvas work wear and accessories, decided to get his company on the leading edge of the m-commerce trend. Baldwin worked with m-commerce technology provider CardinalCommerce Corporation to build a mobile version of the Dungarees Web site in 2009. Initially, just 1 percent of the traffic to the company's e-commerce site originated from mobile devices; within one year, the volume had increased to 4 percent. Currently, 8 percent of the company's online customers (and growing) use mobile devices to shop at Dungarees.net.

Richard Sexton, founder of Carolina Rustica, a Concord, North Carolina–based retailer that specializes in handcrafted iron and wood furniture, also sees the potential of m-commerce. According to Sexton, whose company went online in 2000, 85 to 90 percent of his company's sales originate on the Web, making m-commerce a natural extension of his company's strategy. Although selling bedroom suites and dining room tables to people using smart phones and iPads may seem strange to some, Sexton says that it is essential to his company's future. "People are doing everything on their smart phones, including shopping," he says.

As rich as the opportunity that m-commerce offers, it also poses significant challenges because mobile shoppers must view companies' sites on the smaller screens of their mobile devices—often just three or four inches on a smart phone and 10 inches on an iPad. "You've got to rethink your entire page layout for mobile because of the tiny screens," says David Gould, CEO of mShopper, a company that provides mobile commerce platforms. "The context also is a challenge; you're trying to reach a user who is on the go and whose needs are different." How can a small company maximize its impact on such small screens? The following tips will help:

- **Simplify.** Do *not* attempt to use your company's existing Web site as its m-commerce site; the space simply isn't there, and your conversion rate will suffer. Use the analytics from your existing Web site to determine what most customers look for on your site and translate that content into your m-commerce site. Eliminate every element of your site that will be cumbersome to download on a mobile device: large graphics, Flash components, animation, videos, and others. Your mobile Web site may offer fewer products than your regular Web site. Remember that in m-commerce, less is definitely more.

- **Create a clean layout and easy navigation.** On small screens, every square millimeter is important, and a company's site must make the most of every one. Clean, easy-to-follow layouts and simple navigation are essential for m-commerce success, especially on the home page. Avoid using too many levels of subpages and be sure to give customers an easy way back to the home page from any page in the site. Larger fonts actually work better because most shoppers are on the move, holding the smart phone or tablet in their hands.

- **Benchmark successful m-commerce companies.** View other companies that are experiencing success with m-commerce, even those in other industries, and take note of the concepts, designs, and features that you can incorporate into your own site. Google, Amazon, and eBay provide excellent examples.

- **Consider a professional m-commerce checkout service.** Many customers are even more hesitant to send their credit card information over a wireless device in public than they are to send it from a computer. Incorporating a reliable checkout service that allows customers to store their checkout data can increase a company's conversion rate.

- **Test your m-commerce site.** Once your m-commerce site is up and running, test it on the "big three" mobile devices: iPhone, Android, and Blackberry.

- **Realize that it's a never-ending race.** Just as a company's regular Web site is never finished, an m-commerce site is an ongoing work. The key is using analytics to discover what is working—and what is not—and constantly revising and improving the site.

With the right approach to m-commerce, small companies can tap into their customers' mobile wallets via the devices that many people never leave at home: their smart phones and tablet computers.

1. Use the Web to research mistakes that small business owners typically make when designing m-commerce sites for their companies. Write a one-page summary of the most common mistakes you discover.

2. Go online to research other tips for creating an m-commerce site that works. Write a brief description of three design techniques.

3. Visit the mobile Web sites for Dungarees.net and Carolina Rustica and note the design elements that they employ. What recommendations can you make for improving their sites?

Source: Based on Mark Simpson, "Feng Shui for Mobile Marketers: Best Practices for Creating a Harmonious Mobile Environment," *Marketing Profs*, August 15, 2011, http://www.marketingprofs.com/articles/2011/5686/feng-shui-for-mobile-marketers-best-practices-for-creating-a-harmonious-mobile-environment; Eddie Davis, "How to Create a Mobile-Friendly Shopping Web Site," *Entrepreneur*, August 25, 2010, http://www.entrepreneur.com/article/217255; Jason Ankeny, "The New Smart Money," *Entrepreneur*, February 22, 2011, http://www.entrepreneur.com/article/218100; Bill Siwicki, "Dungarees.net Targets the 8% of Consumers Shopping on Its Site on Smartphones," *Internet Retailer*, September 15, 2011, http://www.internetretailer.com/2011/09/15/dungareesnet-targets-8-consumers-shopping-phones; and Jason Ankeny, "Setting Sale on Smartphones," *Entrepreneur*, December 2010, p. 44.

Myth 4. Privacy Is Not an Important Issue on the Web

The Internet allows companies to gain access to almost unbelievable amounts of information about their customers' online behavior. Tracking tools monitor customers' behavior while they are on a site, giving Internet-based businesses the information they need to make their Web sites more customer friendly. Many sites also offer visitors "freebies" in exchange for information about themselves. Companies then use this information to learn more about their target customers and how to market to them more effectively. Concern over privacy and the proper use of this information has become the topic of debate by many interested parties, including government agencies, consumer watchdog groups, and customers themselves. A recent study by Harris Interactive and TRUSTe reports that 94 percent of consumers believe that online privacy is important.[22]

Businesses that collect information from their online customers have the responsibility for keeping it secure. Shoppers' privacy concerns are a limiting factor on e-commerce. The Pew Internet and American Life Project reports that if Internet users had more confidence in revealing their credit card numbers and other personal information online, the percentage of online buyers would increase from 66 to 73 percent.[23]

Companies that collect information from their online customers must safeguard their customers' privacy, protect the information they collect from unauthorized use, and use it responsibly. That means that businesses should post a privacy policy on their Web sites, explaining to customers how they intend to use the information they collect. Then they must be sure to follow it! One of the surest ways to alienate online customers is to abuse the information collected from them by selling it to third parties or by spamming customers with unwanted solicitations. BBBOnline offers a useful resource center (http://www.bbbonline.org/UnderstandingPrivacy/ PMRC) that is designed to help small business owners who want to establish or upgrade their Web site's privacy policies.

Many customers don't trust Web sites, especially those of companies they don't know. A recent survey by PayPal and comScore reports that 21 percent of online shoppers have abandoned their shopping carts because of security issues. Therefore, a key component of a successful e-commerce effort, especially for small companies that tend to be less well known, is building trust among customers. Posting security icons from TRUSTe, Norton (formerly Verisign), McAfee, WhiteHat, Thawte, and other certification services assures customers that a site meets security standards. Another way that businesses can build trust is to create meaningful privacy policies, post them on their Web sites, and then adhere to them. According to John Briggs, director of e-commerce for the Yahoo Network, customers "need to trust the brand they are buying and believe that their online purchases will be safe transactions. They need to feel comfortable that [their] personal data will not be sold and that they won't get spammed by giving their e-mail address. They need to know about shipping costs, product availability, and return policies up front."[24] Privacy *does* matter on the Web, and businesses that respect and protect their customers' privacy win their customers' trust. Trust is the foundation on which the long-term customer relationships that are so crucial to Web success are built.

Myth 5. "Strategy? I Don't Need a Strategy to Sell on the Web! Just Give Me a Web Site, and the Rest Will Take Care of Itself"

Building a successful e-business is no different than building a successful brick-and-mortar business, and that requires a well-thought-out strategy. Building a strategy means that an entrepreneur must first develop a clear definition of the company's target audience and a thorough understanding of those customers' needs, wants, likes, and dislikes. To be successful, a Web site must be appealing to the customers it seeks to attract just as a traditional store's design and decor must draw foot traffic. If a Web site is to become the foundation for a successful e-business, an entrepreneur must create it with the target audience in mind.

Recall from Chapter 3 that one goal of developing a strategy is to set a business apart from its competition. The same is true for creating a strategy for conducting business online. It is just as important, if not more important, for an online business to differentiate itself from the competition if it is to be successful. Unlike customers in a retail store, who must exert the effort to go to a competitor's store if they cannot find what they want, online customers only have to make a mouse click or two to go to a rival Web site. Therefore, competition online is fierce, and to succeed, a company must have a sound strategy.

ENTREPRENEURIAL PROFILE: Jim Threadgill: Easy to Grow Bulbs With years of experience in the flower bulb industry, Jim Threadgill decided in 2004 to launch his own business, Easy to Grow Bulbs, that specializes in selling bulbs that grow best in warm climates such as southern California. "The largest bulb companies focus on cool-weather Dutch bulbs, plants best suited to the North and upper Midwest," says Threadgill. Initially targeting only local customers, Threadgill saw the potential for his Oceanside, California, company to sell online to customers anywhere in the world who loved to garden and lived in warm climates. In 2005, the company launched its initial Web site and watched sales increase. Easy to Grow Bulbs has systematically and intentionally built a reputation for providing high-quality bulbs, superior customer service, and fast shipping that has resulted in a growing base of loyal, repeat customers. Threadgill has assembled a team of five employees who have experience in the bulb industry and are passionate gardeners. He also has developed a network of both local and global suppliers who provide the company with top-quality bulbs. "We've tested hundreds of varieties and know from experience which ones are the winners," says Threadgill. The Easy to Grow Bulbs Web site includes "Boost Your Success" articles, "How To" videos that offer customers useful guidelines for planting and growing beautiful bulbs, and tips on arranging flowers from their gardens. It also allows shoppers to enter their ZIP codes to determine which growing zone they live in and to search for bulbs that grow best in that zone. Easy to Grow Bulb's thoughtful strategic blend of quality products, outstanding customer service, and helpful information has made the company an e-commerce success story.[25] ■

Easy to Grow Bulbs

Myth 6. The Most Important Part of Any E-Commerce Effort Is Technology

Although understanding the technology of e-commerce is an important part of the formula for success, it is *not* the most crucial ingredient. What matters most is the ability to understand the underlying business and to develop a workable business model that offers customers something of value at a reasonable price while producing a reasonable return for the company. The entrepreneurs who are proving to be most successful in e-commerce are those who know how their industries work inside and out and then build an e-business around their expertise. They know that they can hire Web designers, database experts, and fulfillment companies to manage the technical aspects of their businesses but that nothing can substitute for a solid understanding of their industry, their target market, and the strategy needed to pull the various parts together. The key is seeing the Web for what it really is: a way to transform the way they do business by serving their customers more efficiently and effectively through another channel that offers maximum convenience.

The foundation of e-commerce success is the knowledge that a company's owners, managers, and employees have built over time about their industry, what it takes to succeed in that industry, and how to serve their customers to which they then apply the technology of the Internet.

ENTREPRENEURIAL PROFILE: Mike Shearwood: Aurora Fashions Aurora Fashions, a British company that sells women's clothing brands that include Karen Millen, Oasis, and Warehouse, uses Internet technology to make the shopping experience more convenient for its customers. In the three largest cities in which the company has brick-and-mortar stores (London, Glasgow, and Birmingham), it offers online shoppers delivery of their orders within 90 minutes. Rather than rely on a central distribution hub, the company uses couriers coordinated by Internet start-up Shutl to pick up customer orders from its stores and deliver them to customers. CEO Mike Shearwood says the service is a natural extension of Aurora's existing "reserve-and-collect" program, which allows customers to place orders online and pick them up in the location of their choice. "We are able to leverage our stores to offer our customers faster response times," he says.[26] ■

Unfortunately, many entrepreneurs tackle e-commerce by focusing on technology first and then determining how that technology fits their business idea. "If you start with technology, you're likely to going to buy a solution in search of a problem," says Kip Martin, program director of META Group's Electronic Business Strategies. Instead, he suggests, "Start with the business and ask yourself what you want to happen and how you'll measure it. *Then* ask how the technology will help you achieve your goals. Remember: Business first, technology second."[27]

Myth 7. Customer Service Is Not as Important Online as It Is in a Traditional Retail Store

Many Web sites treat customer service as an afterthought, and it shows. The average conversion rate for e-commerce sites is just 3.2 percent.[28] In other words, out of 1,000 visitors to the typical company's Web site, only 32 of them actually make a purchase! Sites that are slow to load, difficult to navigate, suffer from complicated checkout systems, or confuse shoppers turn customers away, and many of them never return. The fact is that customer service is just as important (if not more so) on the Web as it is in traditional brick-and-mortar stores. As shoppers become more accustomed to shopping online, they have higher expectations of the sites on which they shop. One recent study by Harris Interactive reports that more 22 percent of online shoppers said that they expect higher levels of customer service than they do in offline, traditional stores.[29]

There is plenty of room for improvement in customer service on the Web. Shoppers' unmet expectations of superior customer service translate into a high shopping cart abandonment rate. According to e-commerce research company Forrester Research, 75 percent of Web shoppers who fill their online shopping carts abandon them without checking out.[30] Figure 9.3 shows the leading causes of shopping cart abandonment. When customers do abandon their shopping carts, companies can close a significant percentage of those "lost" sales by sending prompt follow-up e-mails designed to convince the customer to complete the purchase. On average, nearly 21 percent of shoppers who abandon their carts and receive a follow-up e-mail from the company return to complete their purchases, spending 55 percent more than shoppers who completed their purchases without abandoning their carts.[31]

In an attempt to improve the level of service they offer, many sites provide e-mail links to encourage customer interaction. Unfortunately, when responding to e-mail takes a very low priority at some e-businesses, customers take it as a clear sign of poor service. The lesson for e-commerce entrepreneurs is simple: Devote time, energy, and money to developing an effective system for providing superior customer service. Those who do will build a sizable base of loyal customers who will keep coming back.

Perhaps the most significant actions online companies can take to bolster their customer service efforts are to create a clean, intuitive Web site; hire a well-trained customer response team; offer a simple return process; provide an easy order-tracking process so that customers can check the status of their orders at any time; and offer the opportunity to chat live with a customer service representative. Live chat serves as a cyberspace version of a call center, where representatives answer customers' questions that go beyond the scope of the typical FAQ section. Even small companies that lack the manpower to staff a live chat center can still provide customer-responsive chat options on their Web sites by using virtual chat agents. Loaded onto a company's site, these virtual employees can step in at the appropriate time to interact with one customer or millions of customers, answering their questions or giving them the extra nudge they need—an offer of free shipping or a discount or details on how buyers can create customized assortments of nuts, for example—to close the deal.

FIGURE 9.3

Reasons for Abandoning Online Shopping Carts

Source: Forrester Research, 2011.

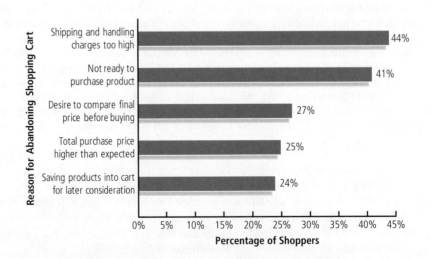

Myth 8. Flashy Web Sites Are Better Than Simple Ones

Businesses that fall into this trap pour significant amounts of money into designing flashy Web sites with all of the "bells and whistles." The logic is that to stand out online, a site really has to sparkle. That logic leads to a "more-is-better" mentality when designing a site. On the Web, however, "more" does *not* necessarily equate to "better." The most effective sites are simple, intuitive, and efficient and allow shoppers to find what they are looking for quickly. Although fancy graphics, photographs, videos, playful music, and spinning icons attract attention, they also can be distracting and slow to download. The time required to download a Web site is one of the most important determinants of its sales effectiveness. In fact, slow download time is the leading reason that Web users abandon sites. To online customers, whose expectations concerning online speed continue to escalate, a good online shopping experience is a fast, uncomplicated one. Successful e-tailers set their sights on meeting the two-second rule: if a Web site does not download within two seconds, users are likely to abandon it. Proper content, formatting, and design are important ingredients in determining a site's performance. Smart e-tailers frequently test their sites' performance on performance, speed, and reliability measures in different browsers using a variety of online tools such as Dotcom-Monitor and others.

ENTREPRENEURIAL PROFILE: Jason Marrone: Jelly Belly Candy Company Jelly Belly Candy Company, a company that sells jelly beans in a multitude of flavors, recently redesigned its Web site to follow a simpler, "minimalistic approach," says e-commerce director Jason Marrone. "We needed less clutter and more focus on the product." The company also upgraded the site's navigation and search capabilities, giving shoppers the ability to search for jelly beans by color, taste, package type, or occasion. Filters for price, color, and container size allow them to narrow their choices further. "People can find what they want more easily now," says Marrone. "It's making a difference." Since the redesign, Jelly Belly's conversion rate has increased 38 percent, and its average order value has gone up by 15 percent.[32] ∎

Myth 9. It's What's Up Front That Counts

Designing an attractive, efficient Web site and driving traffic to it are important to building a successful e-business. However, designing the back office, the systems that take over once customers place their orders on a Web site, is just as important as designing the site itself. If the behind-the-scenes support is not in place or cannot handle the traffic from the Web site, a company's entire e-commerce effort will come crashing down. The potentially large number of orders that a Web site can generate can overwhelm a small company that has failed to establish the infrastructure needed to support the site. Although e-commerce can lower many costs of doing business, it still requires a basic infrastructure in the channel of distribution to process orders, maintain inventory, fill orders, and handle customer service. "The companies with warehouses, supply-chain management, and solid customer service are going to be the ones that survive," says Daryl Plummer, head of the Gartner Group's Internet and new media division.[33]

To customers, a business is only as good as its last order. Web-based entrepreneurs often discover that the greatest challenge their businesses face is not necessarily attracting customers on the Web but creating a viable order fulfillment strategy. Order fulfillment involves everything required to get goods from a warehouse into a customer's hands and includes order processing, warehousing, picking and packing, shipping, and billing.

Some entrepreneurs choose to handle order fulfillment in-house with their own employees, but others find it more economical to hire specialized fulfillment houses to handle these functions. Virtual order fulfillment (or drop shipping) suits many small e-tailers perfectly. When a customer orders a product from its Web site, the company forwards the order to a wholesaler or distributor who then ships the product to the customer with the online merchant's label on it. This strategy allows a small business to avoid the cost and the risk of carrying inventory. Danny Wong and Fan Bi, cofounders of Blank Label, an online retailer of custom-made men's shirts, found a manufacturer in Shanghai, China, that was willing to build shirts to the specifications (fabric, size, collar style, cuff type, button color, and more) that shoppers identify on the Blank Label Web site and drop ship them directly to customers. Their fulfillment strategy minimizes the risk that the entrepreneurs, both in their early twenties, incur and has enabled their company to become one of the fastest-growing online companies in the United States.[34]

Although e-tailers who use virtual order fulfillment avoid the major investments in inventory and the problems associated with managing it, they lose control over delivery times and service quality. In addition, finding a fulfillment house willing to handle a relatively small volume of orders at a reasonable price can be difficult for some small businesses. Some businesses use a combination of virtual order fulfillment, distribution centers, and store pickup to process customers' orders. Bon-Ton, a family of seven chains of retail department stores, including Boston Store, Carson Pirie Scott, Herberger's, and others, recently integrated its order management and warehouse management systems so that it can fill customers' orders by drop shipping directly from manufacturers or shipping from one of its three distribution centers or any of its retail stores. Customers appreciate the convenience, and the company's online sales have experienced double-digit growth.[35]

Myth 10. It's Too Late to Get into E-Commerce

A common myth, especially among small companies, is that those businesses that have not yet moved into e-commerce have missed a golden opportunity. E-commerce is still in its childhood. Companies are still figuring out how to succeed on the Internet, learning which techniques work and which ones don't. For every e-commerce site that exists, a trio of others has failed. An abundance of business opportunities exists for those entrepreneurs insightful enough to spot them and clever enough to capitalize on them.

One fact of e-commerce that has emerged is the importance of speed. Companies doing business on the Web have discovered that those who reach customers first often have a significant advantage over their slower rivals. "The lesson of the Web is not how the big eat the small, but how the fast eat the slow," says a manager at a venture capital firm specializing in Web-based companies.[36]

Succumbing to this myth often leads entrepreneurs to make a fundamental mistake once they finally decide to go online: they believe they have to have a "perfect" site before they can launch it. Few businesses get their sites "right" the first time. In fact, the most successful e-commerce sites are constantly changing, analyzing customers' behavior, removing what does not work, and adding new features to see what does. Successful Web sites are much like a well-designed flower garden, constantly growing and improving yet changing to reflect the climate of each season. Their creators worry less about creating the perfect site at the outset than about getting a site online and then fixing it, tweaking it, and updating it to meet changing customer demands. "The person trying to create the perfect [online] store will fail," says Gerry Goldsholle, founder of two Web sites aimed at small companies. "Part of the Internet process is 'try it, learn from it, and fix it.'"[37]

LO3

Explain the basic strategies entrepreneurs should follow to achieve success in their e-commerce efforts.

Strategies for E-Success

People now spend more time online than ever before. The average American spends as much time on the Internet as he or she does watching television, and young people below age 30 spend more time online than watching television.[38] However, converting these Internet users into online customers requires a business to do more than merely set up a Web site and wait for the hits to start rolling up. Building sufficient volume for a site takes energy, time, money, creativity, and, perhaps most important, a well-defined strategy.

Although the Web is a unique medium for creating a company, launching an e-business is not much different from launching a traditional offline company. The basic drivers of a successful business remain in place on the Internet as well as on Main Street. To be successful, both offline and online companies require solid planning and a well-formulated strategy that emphasizes customer service. The goals of e-commerce are no different from traditional offline businesses—to increase sales, improve efficiency, and boost profits by serving customers better. How a company integrates the Internet into its overall business strategy determines how successful it will be. Following are some guidelines for building a successful e-commerce strategy for a small company.

FOCUS ON A NICHE IN THE MARKET Rather than try to compete head-to-head with the dominant players on the Web who have the resources and the recognition to squash smaller competitors, many entrepreneurs find success serving market niches. Smaller companies' limited resources usually are better spent focusing on niche markets than trying to be everything to everyone (recall

You Be the Consultant

Complete Fulfillment

Brett Teper and Rich Williams came up with a design for a better cat litter box and launched a company, ModProducts LLC, and a Web site to sell the product. They contracted with a manufacturer in Taiwan to produce the ModKat to their specifications, but the New York City–based entrepreneurs encountered a logistical problem: storing and shipping the bulky product to their customers. Warehouse space in New York City is expensive, and coordinating shipments of goods around the world is a daunting task, especially for people who have no experience. Teper and Williams decided to outsource the distribution of the ModKat to a fulfillment company, Shipwire, which performs the logistics function for small and medium-size companies that lack the budgets or the expertise to handle it themselves. With Shipwire, Teper and Williams never actually handle the products they sell. The Taiwanese manufacturer ships the ModKats that ModProducts orders to a Shipwire warehouse near Los Angeles, California. When a customer purchases a ModKat from ModProducts's Web site, an employee verifies the order and then forwards it to Shipwire. Shipwire packs the order at its warehouse and ships it directly to the customer (drop shipping) within 24 hours. Shipwire's service "allows us to run the business without really thinking about fulfillment and logistics," says Teper.

Fulfillment companies such as Shipwire, Webgistix, Fulfillment by Amazon, and others have become popular among small online companies whose founders lack knowledge and experience in logistics or who simply don't want the hassle of storing, packing, and shipping goods to customers. In many cases, fulfillment companies, especially those with strategically located warehouses, can ship goods to customers faster than a small company can on its own. Shipwire, based in Palo Alto, California, has warehouses in California, Illinois, Canada, and Great Britain, allowing the company to ship products quickly almost anywhere in the world. Fulfillment businesses typically charge companies a fee to store products (one company charges 45 cents per cubic foot per month) and per-item fees to pack and ship products.

Perhaps the biggest disadvantage to entrepreneurs who use fulfillment companies is the loss of control over the quality and speed of delivery. That's why selecting the right fulfillment company is essential to success. ModProducts has encountered a few problems with orders from big-box retailers, whose ordering software did not mesh well with Shipwire's logistics software. ModProducts also has experienced some order errors, but Teper says that Shipwire was able to work out all of the problems satisfactorily. Shipwire charges ModProducts $10 to ship a ModKat to locations in California and $15 to locations across the country. Teper admits that having ModProducts ship the litter boxes would be slightly cheaper but says that this would require renting a warehouse and staffing it.

Although fulfillment companies work best for some small businesses, others, such as Power Equipment Direct, a company

Courtesy of ModProducts

in Bolingbrook, Illinois, that sells lawn mowers, snowblowers, electric generators, and other equipment, choose to handle logistics in-house. CEO John Hoch says that Power Equipment Direct, now with Web sales of nearly $50 million annually, saw sales increase 71 percent in one year after the company created five new niche e-commerce sites that specialize in log splitters, chain saws, water pumps, sump pumps, and mowers. The company also revamped its search engine optimization strategy and links each one of its nine niche Web sites to the other. Its Facebook page, now with 8,000 likes, has attracted customers to its Web sites as well. Hoch also has added a storefront to its warehouse, which fills all of the company's online orders. Keeping the order fulfillment process in-house allows Power Equipment Direct to control the quality, accuracy, and speed of its deliveries to ensure top-quality customer service.

1. What logistical challenges do small Web-based companies face in filling customers' orders?

2. What factors should entrepreneurs consider when they must decide how to handle order fulfillment?

3. Contact the owner of a local company that does business online. How does the owner handle order fulfillment? What factors drove the decision?

Source: Based on Stu Woo, "Fulfilling Work: The Shippers," *Wall Street Journal*, June 23, 2011, p. B6, and Paul Demery, "Power Equipment E-Retailer Picks Up the Pace," *Internet Retailer*, September 14, 2011, http://www.internetretailer.com/2011/09/14/power-equipment-e-retailer-picks-pace.

the discussion of the focus strategy in Chapter 3). The idea is to concentrate on serving a small corner of the market that the giants have overlooked. Niches exist in every industry and can be highly profitable given the right strategy for serving them. A niche can be defined in many ways, including by geography, customer profile, product, product usage, and many others.

Because of its pervasive reach and ability to tap large numbers of customers with a common interest, the Web provides an ideal mechanism for implementing a focus strategy.

ENTREPRENEURIAL PROFILE: Chris Miller and William Hale: Christmas Lights Etc. Chris Miller and William Hale focus on a niche market with their business, Christmas Lights Etc., a company that specializes in high-quality Christmas lights, prelit artificial Christmas trees (that range from less than $200 for a four-and-a-half-foot tree to more than $77,000 for a 50-foot leviathan) and wreaths, and other Christmas decorations. Launched in 2000 with just $4,000 in personal savings, the Internet-based company, which operates from a 40,000-square-foot warehouse in Alpharetta, Georgia, generates $5.8 million in annual sales. Christmas Lights Etc.'s customer list includes thousands of residential home owners and a long list of commercial accounts, including Walt Disney Company, Six Flags, Lucky Brand Jeans, Seaworld, and many others. The company recently sold its largest tree ever, a giant 60-foot prelit Fraser fir, to a theme park.[39] ■

DEVELOP A COMMUNITY On the Web, competitors are just a mouse click away. To attract customers and keep them coming back, companies have discovered the need to offer more than just quality products and excellent customer service. Many seek to develop a community of customers with similar interests, the nucleus of which is their Web site. Others include features on their Web sites that allow visitors to share content easily with the people in their social networks. These entrepreneurs intentionally build a social component into their Web sites, with the goal of increasing customers' loyalty by giving them the ability to interact with other like-minded visitors or with experts to discuss and learn more about topics about which they are passionate.

Customer polls ("What is your favorite sports drink?"), contests, product ratings and reviews, videos, games, company blogs, guest books, and message boards are powerful tools for building a community of visitors online because they give visitors the opportunity to interact and have conversations about products, services, activities, and topics that interest them. The most successful companies are those that seamlessly blend their Web sites with their social media presence and use one to support the other. Engaging customers through social media such as Facebook, Twitter, and YouTube helps companies build a loyal following of fans who are passionate about its products or services and share news about the company with their friends. (According to a recent Nielsen survey, 53 percent of active adult social networkers follow at least one brand.[40]) Internet users frequent sites of companies that embrace the social aspects of the Internet and give them the opportunity to interact as part of a community with other customers and with company employees. Companies that successfully create a community online turn mere customers into loyal fans who keep coming back and, better yet, invite others to join them.

ATTRACT VISITORS BY GIVING AWAY "FREEBIES" One of the most important words on the Internet is "free." Many successful e-merchants have discovered the ability to attract visitors to their sites by giving away something free and then selling them something else. One e-commerce consultant calls this cycle of giving something away and then selling something "the rhythm of the Web."[41] The "freebie" must be something customers value, but it does *not* have to be expensive, nor does it have to be a product. In fact, one of the most common giveaways on the Web is *information.* (After all, that's what most people on the Web are after!) Creating a free online or e-mail newsletter with links to your company's site, of course, and to others of interest is one of the most effective ways of driving potential customers to a site. Meaningful content presented in a clear, professional fashion is a must. Experts advise keeping online newsletters short—no more than about 600 words.

ENTREPRENEURIAL PROFILE: Amanda Zink and Randi Karmin: Salty Paw Amanda Zink and Randi Karmin saw the need for a pet day care center, spa, and accessory boutique where they lived in New York City's Seaport District, and in 2006, the friends opened Salty Paw, which targets both local residents and tourists who are passionate about their pets. "We cater to animal lovers who want to care for and shop for their pets in a warm, inviting atmosphere," says

Courtesy of The Salty Paw

Karmin. To attract customers to their store and their Web site, Zink and Karmin send a monthly e-mail newsletter filled with useful information for pet owners, coupons, and, of course, promotions about the unique new products they sell. "E-mail marketing is the most cost-effective, most successful, way to build and strengthen our relationships with our customers," says Karmin. "We've been successful building strong and powerful relationships with our customers despite very tight budgets." E-mail marketing is "the number one way of communicating with a lot of people at one time and getting across messages about sales and specials and, most important, to promote our events," which range from fund-raisers for a local animal society to a "Puppy Prom." The e-mail newsletter's open rate is an impressive 27.4 percent, and Karmin appreciates the ability to segment their mailing list and target specific groups of customers with individual messages that are most meaningful to them based on their purchasing patterns. "I credit our e-mail marketing campaign with much of the success that we've had to date," says Karmin.[42] ∎

MAKE CREATIVE USE OF E-MAIL BUT AVOID BECOMING A "SPAMMER" E-mail is still the backbone of online marketing, especially for small businesses. A recent survey by Pittney Bowes reports that 68 percent of small business owners say that e-mail marketing is their most common marketing tool.[43] Used properly and creatively, e-mail can be an effective, low-cost way to build traffic on a Web site. According to Forrester Research, the average **click-through rate** (the percentage of recipients who open an e-mail and click the link to the company's Web site) for e-mail marketing is 11 percent, and the average conversion rate for e-mails is 4 percent, which is higher than the average conversion rate of 3.2 percent for Web sites as a whole.[44] Another survey reports that retailers rank e-mail as having the highest return on investment of their marketing methods, including paid search, affiliate marketing, and Facebook marketing.[45] Unfortunately, spam, those unsolicited and universally despised e-mail messages (which rank below postal "junk mail" and telemarketing calls as the worst form of junk advertising), limits the effectiveness of companies' e-mail legitimate marketing efforts. Spam is a persistent problem for online marketers; Internet security firm Symantec reports that 77 percent of e-mails sent are spam.[46] Companies must comply with the CAN-SPAM Act, a law passed in 2003 that regulates commercial e-mail and sets standards for commercial e-mail messages. (The penalties can be as much as $16,000 per e-mail for companies that violate the law.)

To avoid having their marketing messages become part of that electronic clutter, companies rely on permission e-mails, collecting customers' and visitors' e-mail addresses (and their permission to send them e-mail messages) when they register on a site to receive a freebie. The most

click-through rate
the percentage of recipients who open an e-mail and click through to the company's Web site.

successful online retailers post e-mail opt-in messages prominently throughout their Web sites and on their Facebook pages as well. When customers sign up to receive permission e-mails, a company should send them "welcome" e-mails immediately. One-third of retailers do not despite research showing that welcome e-mails can generate as much as six times the revenue that standard broadcast e-mails do.[47] To be successful at collecting a sufficient number of e-mail addresses, a company must make clear to customers that they will receive messages that are meaningful to them and that the company will not sell e-mail addresses to others (which should be part of its posted privacy policy). Once a business has a customer's permission to send information in additional e-mail messages, it has a meaningful marketing opportunity to create a long-term customer relationship and to build customer loyalty.

Just as with a newsletter, an e-mail's content should offer something of value to recipients. Customers welcome well-constructed permission e-mail that directs them to a company's site for information or special deals. The typical company sends its customers 64 e-mails per year, an average of slightly more than one e-mail a week.[48]

MAKE SURE YOUR WEB SITE SAYS "CREDIBILITY" Online shoppers are wary, and with the prevalence of online fraud, they have every right to be. In essence, many shoppers simply do not trust Web sites. Unless a company can build visitors' trust in its Web site, selling to them is virtually impossible. Visitors begin to evaluate the credibility of a site as soon as they arrive. Does the site look professional? Are there misspelled words and typographical errors? If the site provides information, does it note the sources of that information? If so, are those sources legitimate? Are they trustworthy? Is the presentation of the information fair and objective, or is it biased? Are there dead links on the site? Does the company have its privacy and merchandise return policies posted in a prominent place?

One of the simplest ways to establish credibility with customers is to use brand names they know and trust. Whether a company sells nationally recognized brands or its own well-known private brand, using those names on its site creates a sense of legitimacy. People buy brand names they trust, and online companies can use that to their advantage. Businesses selling lesser-known brands should use customer testimonials and endorsements (with their permission, of course) about a product or service.

An effective way to build customer confidence is by joining an online seal program such as TRUSTe or BBBOnline. The online equivalent of the Underwriter Laboratories stamp or the Good Housekeeping Seal of Approval, these seals mean that a company meets certain standards concerning the privacy of customers' information and the resolution of customer complaints. Home and Away, a small art gallery in Kennebunkport, Maine, started by former corporate finance officer Dave Shultz and his wife Ann that specializes in Inuit and Native American art, has won the BBBOnline reliability seal of approval and displays it prominently on its Web site. Providing a street address, an e-mail address, and a toll-free telephone number also sends a subtle message to shoppers that a legitimate business is behind a Web site.

Another effective technique is to include an "about us" page on the Web site so that customers can read about the company's "story"—its founders, how they started the business, the challenges they have overcome, and other details. Customers enjoy supporting small businesses with which they feel a connection, and this is a perfect opportunity for a small company to establish that connection. Many small companies include photographs of their brick-and-mortar stores and of their employees to combat the Web's anonymity and to give shoppers the feeling that they are supporting a friendly small business. One small online retailer includes on his Web site short anecdotes about his dog, Cody, the official company mascot and Cody's "views" on featured products. The response to the technique has been so strong that Cody has become a celebrity among the company's customers and even has her own e-mail account. Table 9.1 offers 12 guidelines for building the credibility of a Web site.

MAKE THE MOST OF THE WEB'S GLOBAL REACH Despite the Web's reputation as an international marketplace, many Web entrepreneurs fail to utilize fully its global reach. Nearly 2.1 billion people around the world use the Internet, and 87 percent of them live outside North America![49] In addition, more than 73 percent of Web users throughout the world speak a language other than English.[50] Limiting a global market to only a small portion of its potential by ignoring foreign customers makes little sense. E-companies wanting to draw significant sales from foreign

TABLE 9.1 Twelve Guidelines for Building the Credibility of a Web Site

Guideline	Tips
1. Allow visitors to verify easily the accuracy of the information on your site.	Include references, which you should cite, from credible third parties to support the information that you present on your site.
2. Show that there are real people behind your site.	List a physical address for your business and post photographs of your store or office or the people who work there. Photos allow shoppers to put faces with the names of the people with whom they are dealing.
3. Emphasize the skills, experience, and knowledge of the people in your company.	Tell visitors about the experts you have on your team, their credentials, and their accomplishments. Is your company or your employees associated with a well-known, respected national organization? If so, mention it and provide a link to its Web site.
4. Show that honest, trustworthy people stand behind your site.	In addition to posting photographs of the owner and employees, include brief biographical sketches that might include "fun" facts about each person, their hobbies, and links to blogs that they create. Erik Leamon, owner of The Ride, a full-service bicycle store in Conway, Arkansas, markets the charm of his business on The Ride's Web site, which profiles the company's five employees, including Pokey, the shop dog, who serves as the shop's unofficial customer service representative.
5. Make it easy for customers to contact you.	One of the simplest ways to enhance your site's credibility is to include contact information in a highly visible location. Be sure to include a physical address, a telephone number, and e-mail addresses. Always respond promptly to customer communications.
6. Make sure your site has a professional look.	Online shoppers evaluate the quality of a Web site by its appearance within the first few seconds of arriving. Pay careful attention to layout, navigation, search tools, images, grammar, spelling, and other seemingly "minor" details because they *do* make a difference. A professional site does not have to look "corporate" to be professional, however. It should reflect your company's unique personality.
7. Make your site easy to use—and useful.	Sites that are easy for customers to use and that are useful to them score high on credibility. Resist the temptation to dazzle visitors with all of the coolest features; instead, focus on keeping your site simple and user friendly. Visitors perceive sites that combine useful information with a purchasing opportunity as more credible than those that merely try to sell them something.
8. Update your site regularly.	Visitors rate sites that show that they have been updated or reviewed recently higher than those that contain outdated or obsolete information.
9. Prominently display your company's privacy policy.	Visitors perceive sites that display a meaningful privacy policy—and follow it—as more credible than those that do not.
10. Be vigilant for errors of all types, no matter how insignificant they may seem.	Typographical errors, misspellings, grammatical mistakes, broken links, and other problems cause a site to lose credibility in customers' eyes. Details matter!
11. Post the seals of approval your company has won.	Seals of approval from third parties such as the Better Business Bureau, TRUSTe, WebTrust, and others give shoppers confidence that an online company is reputable and trustworthy.
12. Make sure customers know that their online transactions are secure.	To conduct business effectively online, companies must ensure that customers' credit card transactions are secure. Online retailers typically use Secure Sockets Layer technology that is verified as secure by a third party such as VeriSign. Be sure to post the secure seal prominently on your Web site.

Sources: Based on J. Walker, "Instilling Credibility into Your Web Site," GNC Web Creations, 2011, http://www.gnc-web-creations.com/website-credibility.htm; B. J. Fogg, "Stanford Guides for Web Credibility: A Research Summary from the Stanford Persuasive Technology Lab, Stanford University, May 2002, http://www.webcredibility.org/guidelines; and "The Ride: Your Full Service Bicycle Store," http://therideonline.net/index.php?option=com_frontpage&Itemid=1.

markets must design their sites with these foreign customers in mind. A common mechanism is to include several "language buttons" on the opening page of a site that take customers to pages in the language of their choice. Experienced e-commerce companies have learned that offering a localized page for every country or region they target pays off in increased sales. Doing so allows entrepreneurs to adapt the terminology they use on their sites and in their search engines to local dialects. For instance, an e-commerce company based in the United States might think it is selling diapers, but its customers in Australia and the United Kingdom are looking for "nappies."

Virtual companies trying to establish a foothold in foreign markets by setting up Web sites dedicated to them run the same risk that actual companies do: offending international visitors by using the business conventions and standards the companies are accustomed to using in the United States. Business practices, even those used online, that are acceptable, even expected, in the United States may be taboo in other countries. Color schemes can be important, too. Selecting the "wrong" colors and symbols on a site targeting people in a particular country can hurt sales and offend visitors. For example, in the United States and Asia, the "thumbs-up" gesture indicates a positive result, but in Europe and Latin America, it is an obscene gesture! A little research into the subtleties of a target country's culture and business practices can save a great deal of embarrassment and money. Creating secure, simple, and reliable payment methods for foreign customers also will boost sales.

When translating the content of their Web sites into other languages, entrepreneurs must use extreme caution. This is *not* the time to pull out their notes from an introductory Spanish course and begin their own translations. Hiring professional translation and localization services to convert a company's Web content into other languages minimizes the likelihood of a company unintentionally offending foreign customers.

PROMOTE YOUR WEB SITE ONLINE AND OFFLINE E-commerce entrepreneurs must use every means available—both online and offline—to promote their Web sites and to drive traffic to them. In addition to using traditional online techniques, such as registering with search engines, using pay-per-click techniques, and creating blogs, Web entrepreneurs must promote their sites offline as well. Ads in other media, such as direct mail or newspapers, that mention a site's URL will bring customers to it. It is also a good idea to put the company's Web address on *everything* a company publishes, from its advertisements and letterhead to shopping bags, business cards, and even employees' uniforms! The techniques for generating publicity for an offline business described in Chapter 8 can be just as effective for online businesses needing to make their domain names better known without breaking their budgets. A passive approach to generating Web site traffic is a recipe for failure; entrepreneurs who are as innovative at promoting their e-businesses as they are at creating them can attract impressive numbers of visitors to their sites.

USE THE TOOLS OF ENTERPRISE 2.0 TO ATTRACT AND RETAIN CUSTOMERS The social aspects of the Internet that are evident in sites such as Facebook, Twitter, LinkedIn, and YouTube have become key components of companies' e-commerce efforts. Known as Enterprise 2.0, these interactive sales techniques recognize that shoppers, especially young ones, expect to take a proactive role in their shopping experience by writing (and reading) product reviews, asking questions, reading and writing blogs, watching and creating videos, posting comments, and engaging in other interactive behavior. According to the Pew Internet and American Life Project, 65 percent of online adults participate in social networks, a significant increase from just 8 percent in 2005. The highest level of participation in social media is among adults under 30.[51] In addition, 71 percent of adult Internet users watch online videos, 10 percent publish blogs, and 48 percent have posted online reviews of products and services.[52] Shoppers perceive online reviews as credible, and the reviews influence buying behavior. Eighty percent of consumers say that they have changed their minds about a purchase based solely on negative reviews they found online.[53]

Small businesses are responding to the opportunity to connect with their customers online by adding the following social components to their e-commerce strategies:

mashup
a Web site or an application that combines content from multiple sources.

Really Simple Syndication (RSS)
an application that allows subscribers to aggregate content from their favorite Web sites into a single feed that is delivered automatically whenever the content is updated.

- *Mashups.* A **mashup** is a Web site or an application that combines content from multiple sources into a single Web service. For example, Twitzu is a mashup that allows users to manage invitations and responses to events. They invite their Twitter followers to an event—the grand opening of a new location, for example—and then receive responses from guests on Twitter.

- *Really Simple Syndication.* **Really Simple Syndication (RSS)** is an application that allows subscribers to aggregate content from their favorite Web sites into a single feed that is delivered automatically whenever the content is updated. RSS is ideal for companies whose customers are information junkies. "[RSS] is a must-have for any company Web site or blog because it allows people to track current news via their RSS feeds," says Louis Columbus, an expert on using social media.[54]

- *Social networking.* Many small businesses drive traffic to their Web sites from their Facebook pages, Twitter posts, and LinkedIn accounts. They use their Web sites as a "hub" supported by the "spokes" of social media.

> **ENTREPRENEURIAL PROFILE: Paddy Johnson, Willie Calvert, Jim Morrison, and Bob Morrison: Windsor and Eton Brewery** The cofounders of the Windsor and Eton Brewry, located within site of Windsor Castle in Windsor, England, integrated social networking into their business strategy from the outset. The company's Facebook page is designed to engage customers and create a sense of community among them. The company promotes its latest brews, special events such as "meet-the-brewer" nights, and contests, including "name-the-new-beer" competitions. In just one year, Windsor and Eton Brewery has attracted more than 2,600 fans who have helped drive the company's sales.[55] ∎

Businesses also have discovered that encouraging customers to post their favorite products to their Facebook pages or sending tweets about them increases sales.

- *Wikis.* A **wiki** is a dynamic collection of Web pages that allows users to add to or edit their content. The most popular wiki is Wikipedia, the user-created online encyclopedia for which users provide the content. Some companies use wikis to encourage customers to participate in the design of their products, a process called cocreation.

- *Widgets.* Another tool that small companies use to attract attention on the Web is **widgets** (also known as gadgets), low-cost applications that appear like small television screens on Web sites, blogs, or computer desktops and perform specific functions. Entrepreneurs can create their own widgets or purchase them from developers and customize them, adding their own names, brands, and logos. Customers and visitors can download the widget to their desktops or, perhaps, post it to their own blogs or Facebook pages, where other Web users see it and the social nature of the Web exposes the company to thousands of potential customers. A popular widget not only drives customers to a site but also can improve a company's ranking on major search engines. "It's a great way to continually remind people that you exist," says Ivan Pope, CEO of widget developer Snipperoo.[56] Papa John's, which has sold more than $2 billion worth of pizza online, developed a widget that allows customers to order a pizza from almost anywhere, including a Facebook page, a YouTube video, a Google search, or a smart phone.[57]

wiki
a dynamic collection of Web pages that allows users to add to or edit their content.

widget
a low-cost application that appears like a small television screen on a Web site, a blog, or a computer desktop and performs a specific function.

DEVELOP AN EFFECTIVE SEARCH ENGINE OPTIMIZATION STRATEGY Because of the popularity of search engines among Internet shoppers, Web search strategies have become an essential part of online companies' promotion strategies. With more than 275 million Web sites (and growing), it is no surprise that online shoppers' first stop usually is a search engine. Ninety-three percent of shoppers rely on search engines to help them find the products and services they want to purchase.[58] Smart entrepreneurs are devoting more of their marketing budgets to search engine listings that are focused on landing their Web sites at or near the top of the most popular search engines. For a company engaged in e-commerce, a well-defined search marketing strategy is a vital part of its overall marketing strategy.

One of the biggest challenges facing e-commerce entrepreneurs is maintaining the effectiveness of their search engine marketing strategies. Because the most popular search engines are constantly updating and refining their algorithms—the secretive formulas and methodology search engines use to find and rank the results of Web searches—entrepreneurs also must evaluate and constantly refine their search strategies. After Google, the leading search engine, changed its algorithms recently, many businesses that had ranked highly in searches found that their listings fell sharply down the search engine results page.

> **ENTREPRENEURIAL PROFILE: Mitchell Lieberman: One Way Furniture** Mitchell Lieberman, CEO of One Way Furniture, an online furniture retailer in Melville, New York, saw his company's sales decline 64 percent after the changes pushed the business's Google ranking far down the results page. "Traffic fell off a cliff," says Lieberman, who discovered that the

source of the problem was the standardized product descriptions his Web site used for the 30,000 products its sells. Many companies sell the same manufacturers' products and use the same product descriptions, a practice that the new Google algorithm punishes. Lieberman hired freelance writers to develop original, more detailed descriptions and made changes that allow pages to load faster. Although One Way Furniture's traffic and sales have not fully recovered, the company's Google ranking is improving.[59] ■

A company's Web search strategy must incorporate the two basic types of search engine results: natural or organic listings and paid or sponsored listings. Although shoppers more often click on organic listings (70 percent vs. 30 percent for paid listings), research shows that shoppers are more likely to purchase from a particular Web site that ranks high both in organic and paid listings.[60]

Natural (organic) listings arise as a result of "spiders," powerful programs that search engines use to crawl around the Web and analyze sites for key words, links, and other data. Based on what they find, spiders use complex algorithms to index Web sites so that a search engine can display a listing of relevant Web sites when a person enters a key word in the engine to start a search. Some search engines use people-powered searches rather than spider-powered ones to assemble their indexes. With natural listings, an entrepreneur's goal is to get his or her Web site displayed at or near the top of the list of search results. **Search engine optimization (SEO)** involves managing the content, key words, titles, tags, features, and design of a Web site so that it appears at or near the top of Internet search results. The reason that SEO is so important is that iProspect reports that 68 percent of search engine users click on a link to a site that appears on the first page of the search results.[61] "The difference between being seen on page one and page two of search results can mean thousands, even millions, of dollars for a business in revenue," says Martin Falle, CEO of SEO Research, a search engine marketing company.[62] Unfortunately, only 27 percent of small businesses have a search engine optimization strategy.[63] A useful resource for entrepreneurs is SEO Book, a search engine optimization site (www.seobook.com) that offers both free tools and more than 100 training modules on a variety of SEO topics for a fee.

Companies can use the following tips to improve their search placement results:

- Conduct brainstorming sessions to develop a list of key words and phrases that searchers are likely to use when using a search engine to locate a company's products and services and then use those words and phrases on your Web pages. Usually, simple terms are better than industry jargon.

- Use Google's AdWords Keyword Tool to determine how many monthly searches users conduct globally and locally for a key word or phrase. More specific, lower-volume key words and phrases usually produce higher search rankings because they provide potential customers the more focused results they are seeking.

- Use these key words in the title tags (metatags, which are limited to 140 characters) and headlines of your Web pages. Some search engines are geared to pick them up. For best results, you should focus each page of your site on one specific key word or phrase that should appear in the page's title. Placing key words in these critical locations can be tedious, but it produces better search results for the companies that take the time to do it.

- Create the content of each Web page with your customers in mind. Each page should contain between 500 and 1,500 words that are relevant to the key word used in the title tag. Organize the text into well-structured paragraphs and include photographs (that have file names that match the key word of that page) and videos.

- Visit competitors' sites for key word ideas but avoid using the exact phrases. Simply right-clicking on a competitor's Web page and choosing "View Source" will display the key words used in the metatags on the site.

- Consider using less obvious key words and brand names. For instance, rather than using simply "bicycles," a small bicycle retailer should consider key words such as "racing bikes" or "LeMond" to draw customers.

natural (organic) listings
search engine listings that are the result of "spiders," powerful programs that crawl around the Web and analyze sites for key words, links, and other data.

search engine optimization (SEO)
the process of managing the content, key words, titles, tags, features, and design of a Web site so that it appears at or near the top of Internet search results.

- Ask customers which words and phrases they use when searching for the products and services the company sells.

- Use data analysis tools to review Web logs to find the words and phrases (and the search engines) that brought visitors to the company's Web site.

- Check blogs and bulletin boards related to the company's products and services for potential key terms.

- Don't forget about misspellings; people often misspell the words they type into search engines. Include them in your list.

- Hire services such as Wordtracker that monitor and analyze Web users' search engine tendencies.

- Block irrelevant results with "negative key words," those that are excluded in a search.

- Include links to other relevant Web sites and land links to your Web site on high-profile Web sites. Search engines rank sites that have external links to high-volume sites higher than those that do not.

- Start a blog. Well-written blogs not only draw potential customers to your site but also tend to attract links from other Web sites. Blogs also allow entrepreneurs to use key words strategically and frequently, moving their sites up in search result rankings.

- Post videos on your site. In addition to uploading them to video sites such as YouTube, companies can wait for organic listings to appear, or they can submit their videos to search engines for listing. Forrester Research estimates that a properly submitted video is 50 times more likely to achieve a first-page listing on Google than any text-based page.[64]

Because organic listings can take months to materialize, many e-commerce companies rely on paid listings, giving them an immediate presence in search engines. **Paid (sponsored) listings** are short text advertisements with links to the sponsoring company's Web site that appear on the results pages of a search engine when a user types in a key word or phrase. Entrepreneurs use paid search listings to accomplish what natural listings cannot. Fortunately, just five search engines—Google, Yahoo!, Microsoft Bing, AOL, and Ask.com,—account for 99 percent of the searches conducted in the United States.[65] Google, the most popular search engine with 65 percent of all searches, displays paid listings as "sponsored links" at the top and down the side of each results page, and Yahoo! shows "sponsored results" at the top and the bottom of its results pages. Advertisers bid on key words to determine their placement on a search engine's results page. On Google, an ad's placement in search results is a function of the ad's relevance (determined by a quality score of 1 to 10 that Google assigns) and the advertiser's bid on the key word. The ad that gets the most prominent placement (at the top) of the search engine's results page when a user types in that key word on the search engine is the one with the highest combination of quality score and bid price. An advertiser pays only when a shopper clicks through to its Web site from the search engine. For this reason, paid listings also are called pay-for-placement, pay-per-click, and pay-for-performance ads. On Google's Adwords program, the minimum key word bid is five cents, but some words can cost $75 or more!* Internet marketing firm Hochman Consultants estimates that the cost per click on Google Adwords is $1.24, up from 38 cents in 2005.[66] Although paid listings can be expensive, they allow advertisers to evaluate their effectiveness using the statistical reports the search engine generates. Pay-per-click advertisers can control costs by geotargeting their ads, having them appear only in certain areas, and by setting a spending limit per day.

Using generic terms results in large numbers of searches but often produces very small conversion rates and very little in sales; normally, entrepreneurs get better results bidding on more precise, lower-volume key words. Rather than competing with much larger companies for 5 or

paid (sponsored) listings
short advertisements with links to the sponsoring company's Web site that appear on the results page of a search engine when the user types in a key word or phrase.

---

* An online merchant's cost per sale = cost per click ÷ merchant's conversion rate. For example, a merchant with a 1 percent conversion rate who submits a key word bid of 10 cents per click is paying $10 per sale ($0.10 ÷ 0.01 = $10).

FIGURE 9.4

Number of Target Pay-Per-Click Key Words

Source: MarketingSherpa, 2010.

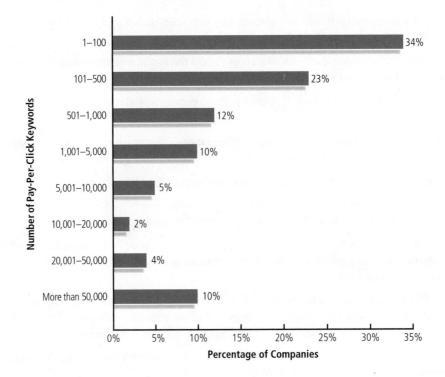

10 common key words, a more effective strategy is to bid on 200 less popular, more specific key words (see Figure 9.4).

> **ENTREPRENEURIAL PROFILE: Jake Sharpless: Gemvara** Jake Sharpless, marketing specialist at online jeweler Gemvara, a company founded by Babson College student Matt Lauzon, has had success focusing on less expensive, specific words and phrases that he refers to as "long-tail" phrases because they are not as popular (or expensive) as more common terms. For instance, rather than bidding on the common term "jewelry," Sharpless bids on specific words such as "necklaces," "ruby necklaces," or "fire opal wedding rings." "By using long-tail terms, you're going to match better with customers and pay less for the terms," he says. Sharpless also bids on common misspellings of key words and blocks irrelevant results with negative key words.[67] ∎

click fraud

a situation that occurs when a company pays for clicks that are generated by someone with no interest in or intent to purchase its products or services.

One problem facing companies that rely on paid listings to generate Web traffic is **click fraud**, which occurs when a company pays for clicks that are generated by someone with no interest in or intent to purchase a product or service. "Clickbots," programs that can generate thousands of phony clicks on a Web site, are a common source of click fraud. Experts estimate that the pay-per-click fraud rate is between 18 and 20 percent.[68] Web analytics software can help online merchants detect click fraud, which can be quite costly. Large numbers of visitors who leave within seconds of arriving at a site, computer IP addresses that appear from all over the world, and pay-per-click costs that rise without any corresponding increase in sales are clues that a company is a victim of click fraud.

LO4

Learn the techniques of designing a killer Web site.

Designing a Killer Web Site

The primary reason that customers buy online is *convenience*. Yet many businesses make their online shopping experiences grueling with lengthy registration and checkout procedures and unnavigable Web sites that are poorly organized and confusing to shoppers. Setting up a shop online has never been easier, but creating a Web site that drives sales requires time and commitment. To be successful, entrepreneurs must pay careful attention to the look, feel, efficiency, and navigability of their Web sites and the impression their sites create with shoppers. A site's look

✓ You Be the Consultant

A Total Makeover

In 2008, Scott Brown started Marbles: The Brain Store, a company that sells games that improve memory and critical thinking skills, from a small kiosk in a mall in Chicago. Catering primarily to tourists, the company grew quickly, and Brown invested $100,000 to open a full-size store in downtown Chicago and $5,000 to launch a Web site (www.marblesthebrainstore.com), which Brown maintained himself. After customers returned to their homes, the only way they could make more purchases from Marbles: The Brain Store was through the Web site, but the site was confusing and difficult to navigate. As a result, the Web site produced a low conversion rate and accounted for less than 1 percent of the company's sales.

By the end of 2009, Marbles: The Brain Store had opened three more stores and was generating a profit of $150,000. Brown saw more opportunities to expand but faced a choice: add another store or engage in a major overhaul of the Web site. The company could not afford to do both. "Opening another store seemed like a natural choice," says Brown. "Our existing stores had more business than they could handle, but opening another store could get us only so far. Our downtown store had maxed out at about $1 million in annual revenue. Adding another store would at best double that, and we were aiming higher."

Brown knew that the company needed a new Web site, but he wasn't sure that the timing was right. "Before we spent gobs of money on a Web site, we wanted to learn what works and what doesn't work in the store," he says. Performing a major overhaul of the Marbles: The Brain Store's Web site also provided several opportunities and challenges. "A Web site would give us access to markets anywhere in the world," says Brown, "and it's a lot cheaper to maintain a Web site than to pay rent and maintenance costs for a physical store." Brown began interviewing professional Web design companies and learned that transforming the Web site into a prolific sales generator would cost between $125,000 and $150,000 and would take several months to complete.

Brown realized that what set Marbles: The Brain Store apart from its competition was the in-store experience. The company is known for its stellar customer service. Well-trained salespeople, known as Brain Coaches, spend time with customers and explain how to use the games and products they sell and how each game improves a particular brain function. Translating the in-store experience to the Web site would be crucial to its success, but doing so would be expensive and time consuming.

Brown decided that revamping the Web site would produce better results for Marbles: The Brain Store than adding another store. Rather than using the old stock product photos from manufacturers from the original Web site, Brown opted for professional photos of the company's product line. The new site also featured fresh descriptions of each product and a design that was clean and easy to navigate. Tabs on the home page allow customers to browse easily for games in different product categories, such as memory, coordination, word skills, and visual perception. Another page features "Brain Coach Recommendations." A new "smart filter" gives shoppers the ability to quickly search for items by type (games, puzzles, software, and others), price, age, number of players, and function (critical thinking, math skills, dyslexia, visual perception, creativity, concentration, and others). A blog features both fun and informative articles about new additions to the product line and maintaining brain health.

The Web site redesign cost $130,000 and took six months, but Marbles: The Brain Store began to see a difference almost immediately. Traffic to the site has increased from 9,000 unique visitors per month to 50,000 unique visitors per month. Before the redesign, the Web site accounted for just 1 percent of the company's sales. Today, it accounts for 10 percent of total sales, even though the company's revenue doubled in that same time period. In addition, the site has generated enough earnings to enable Brown to add more store locations. The company plans to open 33 stores in the Midwest and on the East Coast. Brown says that within a couple of years, he expects the Web site to account for 30 percent of Marbles: The Brain Store's sales.

1. One expert observes, "Most small businesses have Web sites, but many have not dedicated the resources necessary to make them viable." Do you agree? Explain.

2. What lessons can other entrepreneurs learn about creating a robust, sales-generating Web site from Scott Brown's experience?

3. What advice would you offer a friend who is about to launch an online retail business and plans to build and maintain the Web site him- or herself?

Sources: Based on Monica Ginsburg, "If your Small Business Web Site Isn't Designed to Sell, What Good Is It Doing You?," *Chicago Business*, April 11, 2011, http://www.chicagobusiness.com/article/20110409/ISSUE02; and Scott Brown, "Why I Blew $130,000 on a New Web Site," *CBS Moneywatch*, March 30, 2011, http://www.cbsnews.com/8301-505143_162-40244121/why-i-blew-130000-on-a-new-website/?tag=bnetdomain.

---

and design determine a visitor's first impression of the company. "Your Web site isn't 'about' your company," says one writer. "It's an extension of your company. If it's unprofessional, you're unprofessional. If it's cluttered, you're cluttered. If it's hard to work with, you're hard to work with. By contrast, if it's well put together, smart, and easy to use, so is your company."[69]

Web users are not a patient lot. They sit before their computers, their fingers poised on their mouse buttons, daring any Web site to delay them with files that take too long to load.

FIGURE 9.5

Factors That Web Shoppers Say Are Most Important When Deciding Whether to Buy from a Web Site

Source: Revolutionizing Web Site Design: The New Rules of Usability, Oneupweb, Traverse City, Michigan: 2010, p. 11.

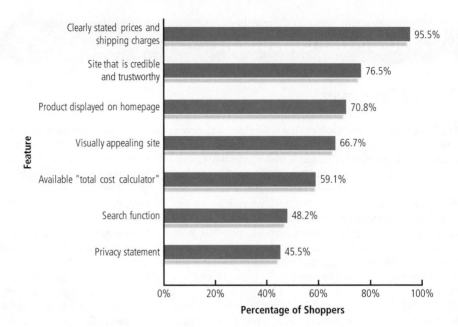

Slow-loading sites or sites that don't deliver on their promises will cause a Web user to move on faster than a bolt of lightning can strike. How can entrepreneurs design Web sites that capture and hold potential customers' attention long enough to make a sale? What can they do to keep customers coming back on a regular basis? There is no surefire formula for stopping online customers in their tracks, but the following suggestions will help:

START WITH YOUR TARGET CUSTOMER Before launching into the design of their Web sites, entrepreneurs must develop a clear picture of their target customers. Only then will they be ready to design a site that will appeal to their customers. The goal is create a design in which customers see themselves when they visit. Creating a site with which customers find a comfortable fit requires a careful blend of market research, sales know-how, and aesthetics. The challenge for a business on the Web is to create the same image, style, and ambiance in its online presence as in its offline stores. For example, a Web site that sells discount baby clothing will have an entirely different look and feel than one that sells upscale outdoor gear.

GIVE CUSTOMERS WHAT THEY WANT Although Web shoppers are price conscious, they rank fast, reliable delivery as the most important criteria in their purchase decisions. Studies show that online shoppers also look for a large selection of merchandise available to them immediately. Remember that the essence of the selling on the Web is providing *convenience* to customers. Sites that allow customers to choose from a wide selection of products, find what they are looking for quickly and easily, and pay for it conveniently and securely keep them coming back. Clear images of products with alternative views that allow customers to zoom in for detail, rotate them 360 degrees, and see color changes increase sales. Product descriptions should be simple, detailed, and jargon free. Figure 9.5 shows the factors that online shoppers say are most important when they are deciding whether to buy from a Web site.

SELECT AN INTUITIVE DOMAIN NAME Decide on a domain name that is consistent with the image you want to create for your company and register it. Entrepreneurs should never underestimate the power of the right domain name or URL. It not only tells online shoppers where to find a company but also should suggest something about the company and what it does. Even the casual Internet shopper could guess that the "toys.com" name belongs to a company selling children's toys. (It does; it belongs to eToys Inc., which also owns "etoys.com," "e-toys.com," and several other variations of its name.) Entrepreneurs must recognize that a domain name is part of the brand they are creating and should create the proper image for the company.

The ideal domain name should be as follows:

- *Short.* Short names are easy for people to remember, so the shorter a company's URL is, the more likely it is that potential customers will recall it.

- *Memorable.* Not every short domain name is necessarily memorable. Some business owners use their companies' initials as their domain name (e.g., www.sbfo.com for Stanley Brothers Furniture Outlet). The problem with using initials for a domain name is that customers rarely associate the two, making a company virtually invisible on the Web.

- *Indicative of a company's business or business name.* Perhaps the best domain name for a company is one that customers can guess easily if they know the company's name. For instance, mail order catalog company J.Crew's URL is www.jcrew.com, and New Pig, a maker of absorbent materials for a variety of industrial applications, uses www.newpig .com as its domain name. (The company carries this concept over to its toll-free number, which is 1-800-HOT-HOGS.)

- *Easy to spell.* Even though a company's domain name may be easy to spell, it is usually wise to buy several variations of the correct spelling simply because some customers are not likely to be good spellers!

Just because entrepreneurs come up with the perfect URL for their companies' Web sites does not necessarily mean that they can use them. With more than 202 million registered domain names (88 million of which are ".com"s), finding a relevant, unregistered domain name can be a challenge.[70] Domain names are given on a first-come, first-serve basis. Before business owners can use a domain name, they must ensure that someone else has not already taken it. The simplest way to do that is to go to a domain name registration service such as Network Solutions' (www.networksolutions.com), Netnames (www.netnames.com), or Go Daddy (www.godaddy .com) to conduct a name search.

Once entrepreneurs find an unused name that is suitable, they should register it (plus any variations of it)—and the sooner, the better! Registering is quite easy: simply use one of the registration services cited previously to fill out a form and pay the necessary fees. The next step is to register the domain name with the U.S. Patent and Trademark Office (USPTO) at a cost of $275. The office's Web site (www.uspto.gov) not only allows users to register a trademark online but also offers useful information on trademarks and the protection they offer.

MAKE YOUR WEB SITE EASY TO NAVIGATE Research shows that the leading factor in convincing online shoppers to make a purchase from a Web site is its ease of navigation. The starting point for evaluating a site's navigability is to conduct a user test. Find several willing shoppers, sit them down in front of a computer, and watch them as they cruise through the company's Web site to make a purchase. It is one of the best ways to get meaningful, immediate feedback on the navigability of a site. Watching these test customers as they navigate the site also is useful. Where do they pause? Do they get lost in the site? Are they confused by the choices the site gives them? Is the checkout process too complex? Are the navigation buttons from one page of the site to another clearly marked, and do they make sense? (One popular Web site critic says that sites with vague navigation tools are guilty of "mystery meat navigation.") Web analytics tools (more about these later in this chapter) also offer insight into how long visitors spend on a company's Web site, where they abandon the site, how they arrived, and much other valuable feedback for improving the navigability of a site.

Because many visitors do not start from a Web site's home page, the starting point for easy navigability involves creating the right **landing pages**, the pages on which visitors land after they click on a sponsored link in a search engine, e-mail ad, or online ad. Ideally, a landing page should have the same marketing message as the link that led to it; otherwise, customers are likely to abandon the site immediately (an occurrence that is measured by a site's "bounce rate," the percentage of visits in which customers leave a site from the landing page). A good landing page also allows customers to search or to dig deeper into the company's Web site to the products or services that they are seeking.

Successful Web sites recognize that shoppers employ different strategies to make a purchase. Some shoppers want to use a search tool, others want to browse through product categories, and still others prefer a company to make product recommendations. Effective sites accommodate all three strategies in their design. Two important Web site design features that online companies

landing pages
the pages on which visitors land after they click on a sponsored link in a search engine, e-mail ad, or online ad.

often get wrong involve the mechanisms by which customers locate products and then get information about them:

Locating products. Customers won't buy what they cannot find! Products should be easy for customers to find, no matter how many pages a Web site includes. Too often, online companies do a poor job of product categorization, listing their product lines in ways that may make sense to them but that befuddle the typical shopper. User tests can be extremely helpful in revealing product categorization problems. After Supercircuits, a company that sells business and personal security equipment, redesigned its landing pages for security cameras using easy-to-understand product categories, its bounce rate declined 20 percent.[71]

In addition to establishing simple product categories that reflect the way customers actually shop (e.g., including categories such as business dress, business casual, sportswear, outerwear, formal wear, shoes, and accessories for a clothing store), another simple solution is to use an internal search tool. An easy-to-use internal search tool can pay for itself many times over in increased sales and higher conversion rates. To make the search feature useful, it should appear in the same place on every page in the site (usually the top right). An internal search tool reveals extremely useful information about which items shoppers are looking for and how they search for them, information that online merchants can use in their key word strategies for paid listings. Rather than building their own internal search engines, many online companies use Google's Site Search, which can cost as little as $100 a year, to power customer searches on their sites.

ENTREPRENEURIAL PROFILE: ToolHawker Managers at ToolHawker, a distributor of power and hand tools, safety equipment, and supplies to automotive repair professionals, knew that they were losing sales online because the company's antiquated search system was slow and sometimes provided useless results to customers shopping among its product line of more than 6,000 items. "We want buyers to find what they are looking for—and fast—or they'll look elsewhere," says software engineer Sean Mayo. After creating an internal search engine using Google Site Search, ToolHawker saw its sales increase and the average number of page views per visit go up by 25 percent.[72] ∎

Getting product information. Once a site is designed to enable shoppers to find products easily, the next task online merchants face is to provide enough product information to convince shoppers to buy. One survey reports that 72 percent of online shoppers say that they have abandoned a Web site in favor of a competitor's site (even if the competitor's prices were higher) if they encounter incomplete product information.[73] Unlike at brick-and-mortar stores, customers cannot pick up an item, try it on, or engage a salesperson in a face-to-face conversation about its features and merits. Online merchants must walk a fine line because providing too little information may fail to answer the questions customers have, causing them to abandon their shopping carts. On the other hand, providing too much information can overwhelm customers who aren't willing to wade through reams of text just to find the answer to some basic questions. The solution is to provide basic product information in easy-to-understand terms (always including a picture of the item) and a link to more detailed information (which should be only one click away) that customers can click to if they choose.

OFFER SUGGESTIONS FOR RELATED PRODUCTS Many online merchants increase sales with the help of "searchandising" techniques, which combine internal searches with merchandising techniques that are designed to cross sell. For example, a customer who enters the words "French cuff shirt" into a company's search tool might see a link to the company's selection of cufflinks and ties in addition to all of the French cuff shirts that appear. Amazon.com is famous for the success of its searchandising techniques, including its "customers who bought this item also bought . . ." product suggestions.

ADD WISH LIST CAPABILITY Giving customers the ability to create wish lists of products and services they want and then connecting other people to those lists, often using social media, not only boosts a company's sales but also increases its online visibility.

CREATE A GIFT IDEA CENTER Online retailers have discovered that one of the most successful tools for improving their conversion rates is to offer a gift idea center. A gift idea center is a section of a

Web site that includes a variety of gift ideas that shoppers can browse through for ideas based on price, gender, or category. Gift centers can provide a huge boost for e-tailers, particularly around holidays, because they offer creative suggestions for shoppers looking for the perfect gift.

PROVIDE CUSTOMER RATINGS AND REVIEWS Customer ratings and reviews have become extremely important to online shoppers. The Global Consumer Shopping Habits Survey reports that 90 percent of online shoppers read reviews from other shoppers and that 83 percent say that the reviews influence whether they actually make a purchase.[74] Allowing customers to post product reviews and ratings enhances a site's credibility and leads to increased sales.

USE ONLINE VIDEOS A study by the Pew Internet and American Life Project reports that 69 percent of online adults have either watched or downloaded a video.[75] Adding video to a Web site not only can increase customer traffic but also can increase its conversion rate, and this explains why 73 percent of online retailers feature video on their product pages.[76] Smart online marketers include more than mere product videos on their Web sites, creating instead videos that offer viewers (i.e., potential customers) something of value—a virtual factory tour that shows the company's dedication to quality, customer testimonials about the company's service, or informational videos that teach customers something.

ENTREPRENEURIAL PROFILE: Lizanne Falsetto: Thinkthin Lizanne Falsetto, founder of Thinkthin, a company that sells low- and no-sugar, gluten-free, high-protein snack bars, produces a weekly cooking show called Lizanne Naturally. Although the videos sell Thinkthin products only indirectly, they emphasize the company's dedication to wholesome, natural ingredients that support health and wellness and establish Falsetto as an expert in the field. Links that allow users to download the videos' recipes take viewers to relevant Thinkthin product Web pages.[77] ∎

Posting a video on YouTube, the most popular video Web site, that includes a link to the company's site also drives traffic to a company's site. YouTube's Insight tools offer business owners analytics tools that give them the ability to determine how effective the videos they post are at reaching potential customers. These tools show entrepreneurs how many times their videos have been viewed over a period of time, how popular their videos are compared to other YouTube videos, how viewers discovered their videos, and basic demographic profiles of their viewers.

ESTABLISH THE APPROPRIATE CALL TO ACTION ON EACH PAGE Every page of a Web site should have a purpose, steering customers to take a specific action—place an order, review the company's services, request a consultation, read customer testimonials, and more. Make sure that the call to action on every page is highly visible and appropriate.

BUILD LOYALTY BY GIVING ONLINE CUSTOMERS A REASON TO RETURN TO YOUR WEB SITE Just as with brick-and-mortar retailers, e-tailers that constantly have to incur the expense of attracting new customers find it difficult to remain profitable because of the extra cost required to acquire customers. One of the most effective ways to encourage customers to return to a site is to establish an incentive program that rewards them for repeat purchases. "Frequent-buyer" programs that offer discounts or points toward future purchases, giveaways such as T-shirts emblazoned with a company's logo, or special services are common components of incentive programs. Incentive programs that are properly designed with a company's target customer in mind really work.

ESTABLISH HYPERLINKS WITH OTHER BUSINESSES, PREFERABLY THOSE SELLING PRODUCTS OR SERVICES THAT COMPLEMENT YOURS Listing the Web addresses of complementary businesses on a company's site and having them list its address on their sites offers customers more value and can bring traffic to your site that you otherwise would have missed. For instance, the owner of a site selling upscale kitchen gadgets should consider a cross-listing arrangement with sites that feature gourmet recipes, wines, and kitchen appliances.

INCLUDE AN E-MAIL OPTION AND A TELEPHONE NUMBER IN YOUR SITE Customers appreciate the opportunity to communicate with your company, and your Web site should give them many options for doing so. When you include e-mail access on your site, be sure to respond to it promptly. Nothing alienates customers faster than a company that is slow to respond or that fails to respond to their e-mail messages. Also be sure to include a toll-free telephone number for customers who prefer to call with their questions. Unfortunately, many companies either fail to include their telephone numbers on their sites or bury them so deeply within the site's pages that customers never find them.

GIVE SHOPPERS THE ABILITY TO TRACK THEIR ORDERS ONLINE Many customers who order items online want to track the progress of their orders. One of the most effective ways to keep a customer happy is to send an e-mail confirmation that your company received the order and another e-mail notification when you ship the order. The shipment notice should include the shipper's tracking number and instructions on how to track the order from the shipper's site. Order and shipping confirmations instill confidence in even the most Web-wary shoppers.

OFFER WEB SHOPPERS A SPECIAL ALL THEIR OWN Give Web customers a special deal that you don't offer in any other advertising piece. Change your specials often (weekly, if possible) and use clever "teasers" to draw attention to the offer. Regular special offers available only on the Web give customers an incentive to keep visiting a company's site.

FOLLOW A SIMPLE DESIGN Catchy graphics and photographs are important to snaring customers, but designers must choose them carefully. Designs that are overly complex take a long time to download, and customers are likely to move on before they appear.

Following are some specific design tips:

- Avoid clutter, especially on your site's home page. The best designs are simple and elegant with a balance of both text and graphics. A minimalist approach usually works best.

- Avoid huge graphic headers that must download first, prohibiting customers from seeing anything else on your site as they wait (or, more likely, *don't* wait). Use graphics judiciously so that the site loads quickly. Many studies show that customers abandon Web sites that load slowly. For impatient online shoppers, faster is better.

- Include a menu bar at the top of the page that makes it easy for customers to find their way around the site.

- Make the site easy to navigate by including navigation buttons at the bottom of pages that enable customers to return to the top of the page or to the menu bar. This avoids what one expert calls the "pogo effect," when visitors bounce from page to page in a Web site looking for what they need. Without navigation buttons or a site map page, a company runs the risk of customers getting lost in its site and leaving. An online merchant never knows which page a customer will land on; therefore, it is important for each page to provide a consistent look; relevant, concise content; and easy navigation.

- Regularly look for broken links on your site and purge them.

- Incorporate meaningful content in the site that is useful to visitors, well organized, easy to read, and current. The content should be consistent with the message a company sends in the other advertising media it uses. Although a Web site should be designed to sell, providing useful, current information attracts visitors, keeps them coming back, and establishes a company's reputation as an expert in the field.

- Include a "frequently asked questions" (FAQ) section. Adding this section to a page can reduce dramatically the number of telephone calls and e-mails customer service representatives must handle. FAQ sections typically span a wide range of issues—from how to place an order to how to return merchandise—and cover whatever topics customers most often want to know about.

- Be sure to post prominently privacy and return policies as well as product guarantees the company offers.

- If your site is heavy on content, say, 100 or more pages, or has more than 100 products for sale, include a search tool that allows visitors to find the product or information they want. Smaller, simpler sites can get by without a search tool if they are organized properly.

- Avoid fancy typefaces and small fonts because they are too hard to read. Limit font and color choices to two or three to avoid a circus look.

- Be vigilant for misspelled words, typographical errors, and formatting mistakes; they destroy a site's credibility.

- Avoid using small fonts on "busy" backgrounds; no one will read them!

- Use contrasting colors of text and graphics. For instance, blue text on a green background is nearly impossible to read.

- Be careful with frames. Using frames that are so thick that they crowd out text makes for a poor design.

- Test your site on different Web browsers and on different-size monitors. A Web site may look exactly the way it was designed to look on one Web browser and be a garbled mess on another. Sites designed to display correctly on large monitors may not view well on small ones.

- Use your Web site to collect information from visitors but don't tie up visitors immediately with a tedious registration process. Most will simply leave the site, never to return. Allow new customers to complete purchases without registering but give them the option of saving their customer information for easy ordering in the future. Be sure to make the registration process short. Offers for a free e-mail newsletter or a contest giveaway can give visitors enough incentive to register with a site.

- Avoid automated music that plays continuously and cannot be cut off.

- Make sure the overall look of the page is appealing. "When a site is poorly designed, lacks information, or cannot support customer needs, that [company's] reputation is seriously jeopardized," says one expert.[78]

- Remember that simpler usually is better.

CREATE A FAST, SIMPLE CHECKOUT PROCESS One surefire way to destroy an online company's conversion rate is to impose a lengthy, convoluted checkout process that requires customers to wade through pages of forms to fill out just to complete a purchase. When faced with a lengthy checkout process, customers simply abandon a site and make their purchases elsewhere. The fewer the steps required for customers to check out, the more successful is a site at generating sales. A progress indicator that shows customers where they are in the checkout process also can help.

Entrepreneurs must make sure that their sites' display a prominent "click to add to cart" button in the same place on every page to ensure that customers know how to make their purchases. Once customers put items into a shopping cart, they should be able to see a complete list and photographs of the products they have selected and should be able to access more information about them with one click. The cart should allow customers to change product quantities (and, believe it or not, to remove items from the cart) without having to go back to a product page. Every cart should have a "return to shopping" link in it as well.

PROVIDE CUSTOMERS MULTIPLE PAYMENT OPTIONS Because some customers are skittish about using their credit cards online, online merchants should offer the option to pay by PayPal, Google Checkout, or other payment service.

ASSURE CUSTOMERS THAT THEIR ONLINE TRANSACTIONS ARE SECURE If you are serious about doing business on the Web, make sure that your site includes the proper security software and encryption devices. The average amount of an online order is $147, and missing a sale because your site lacks proper security makes no sense![79] Web-savvy customers are not willing to divulge their credit card information on sites that are not secure.

ESTABLISH REASONABLE SHIPPING AND HANDLING CHARGES AND POST THEM UP FRONT The number one reason that shoppers do not buy more goods online is high shipping costs. A closely related gripe among online shoppers is that some e-tailers reveal their shipping and handling charges too late in the checkout process. Responsible online merchants keep shipping and handling charges reasonable and display them early on in the buying process to avoid customer "cart shock." Merchants have discovered that free shipping (often with a minimum purchase amount) is a powerful tool for boosting online sales because more shoppers have come to expect it. However, because shipping costs have risen quickly in recent years, online merchants must balance the need to convert browsers into buyers with free or low-cost shipping and keeping costs under control. L. L. Bean, the online and catalog retailer of outdoor clothing and gear, offers free shipping on all orders to its customers, tangible evidence of the company's commitment to superior customer service. "We tested free shipping offers with no minimum purchase for several months, and the customer response was overwhelming," says CEO Chris McCormick. L. L. Bean is one of just seven companies in Internet Retailer's Top 100 online retailers that offers free shipping.[80]

CONFIRM TRANSACTIONS When customers complete their orders, a Web site should display a confirmation page. In addition, order confirmation e-mails, which a company can generate automatically, let customers know that the company received the online order and can be an important first line of defense against online fraud. If a customer claims not to have placed the order, the company can cancel it and report the credit card information as suspicious. Confirmation e-mails can contain ads or coupons for future purchases, but they should be short.

KEEP YOUR SITE UPDATED A good Web site is never done. Customers want to see something new when they visit stores, and they expect the same when they visit virtual stores as well. Unfortunately, only 19 percent of small businesses with Web sites update them at least once a week.[81] Entrepreneurs must be diligent about deleting links that have disappeared and keeping the information on their sites current. One sure way to run off customers on the Web is to continue to advertise your company's "Christmas Special" in August! Fresh information and new specials keep customers coming back. Smart entrepreneurs are always looking for new ways to engage their customers with interesting, relevant content.

TEST YOUR SITE OFTEN Smart e-commerce entrepreneurs check their sites frequently to make sure they are running smoothly and not causing customers unexpected problems. A good rule of thumb is to check your site at least monthly—or weekly if its content changes frequently.

RELY ON ANALYTICS TO IMPROVE YOUR SITE Web analytics (see the following section) provide a host of useful information ranging from the key words that shoppers use to find your site and how long they stay on it to the number of visitors and their locations. The best way to increase a site's conversion rate is to use analytics to determine which techniques work best and integrate them throughout the site.

CONSIDER HIRING A PROFESSIONAL TO DESIGN YOUR SITE Pros can do it a lot faster and better than you can. However, don't give designers free rein to do whatever they want to with your site. Make sure it meets your criteria for an effective site that can sell.

Entrepreneurs must remember that on the Internet, every company, no matter how big or small it is, has the same screen size for its site. What matters most is not the size of your company but how you put that screen size to use. Figure 9.6 illustrates the purchase funnel and ways that companies can improve customers' online shopping experience.

FIGURE 9.6

The Purchase Funnel

Source: From "Improving the Online Shopping Experience, Part 1: Getting Customers to Your Products," by Lyndon Cerejo, from *Smashing Magazine,* September 15, 2011. Copyright © Smashing Magazine. Reprinted with permission. http://media. smashingmagazine.com/wp-content/uploads/2011/08/purchase-funnel-and-ways-to-improve-online-experience.jpg

The Purchase Funnel & Ways to Improve the Online Shopping Experience

Browse

Shop

Buy

1. Promote Online Presence
2. Create Customer Confidence
3. Enhance Product Findability
4. Enable Customer Decision Making
5. Reduce Shopping Cart Abandonment
6. Keep Registration Short & Optional
7. Streamline Checkout

Tracking Web Results

LO5

Explain how companies track the results from their Web sites.

Web sites offer entrepreneurs a treasure trove of valuable information about how well their sites are performing—if they take the time to analyze it. **Web analytics**, tools that measure a Web site's ability to attract customers, generate sales, and keep customers coming back, help entrepreneurs to know what works—and what doesn't—on their sites. Online companies that use Web analytics have an advantage over those that do not. Unfortunately, only 21 percent of small businesses use Web analytics to track traffic patterns on their sites and to strategically refashion them to improve their sites' performance.[82] Owners who use analytics review the data collected from their customers' Web site activity, analyze them, make adjustments to their Web sites, and then start the monitoring process over again to see whether the changes improve the site's performance. In other words, Web analytics give entrepreneurs the ability to apply the principles of continuous improvement to their sites. In addition, the changes these e-business owners make are based on facts (the data from the Web analytics) rather than on mere guesses about how customers interact with a site. There are many Web analytics software packages, but effective ones offer the following types of information:

Web analytics

tools that measure a Web site's ability to attract customers, generate sales, and keep customers coming back.

- *Commerce metrics.* These are basic analytics, such as sales revenue generated, number of items sold, which products are selling best (and which are not), and others.

- *Visitor segmentation measurements.* These measurements provide entrepreneurs with valuable information about online shoppers and customers, including whether they are return customers or new customers, how they arrived at the site (e.g., via a search engine or a pay-per-click ad), which search terms they used (if they used a search engine), and others.

- *Content reports.* This information tells entrepreneurs which products customers are looking for and which pages they view most often (and least often), how they navigate through the site, how long they stay, which pages they are on when they exit, and more. Using this information, an entrepreneur can get an idea of how effective the site's design is.

- *Process measurements.* These metrics help entrepreneurs to understand how their Web sites attract visitors and convert them into customers. Does the checkout process work smoothly? How often do shoppers abandon their carts? At what point in the process do they abandon them? These measures can lead to higher conversion rates for an online business.

Other common measures of Web site performance include the following:

- The **cost per acquistion** is the cost that a company incurs to generate each purchase (or customer registration):

  Cost per acquisition = Total cost of acquiring a new customer ÷ Number of new customers

  For example, if a company purchases an advertisement in an e-magazine for $200 and it yields 15 new customers, then the cost of acquistion is $200 ÷ 15 = $13.33.

cost per acquisition

measures the cost that a company incurs to generate each purchase (or customer registration).

- The **bounce rate** is the percentage of visitors to a company's Web site who view a single page and leave without viewing other pages. A high bounce rate indicates that a company's Web site lacks credibility or suitable content to attract customers' attention or suffers from some other malady. The bounce rate is calculated as follows:

  Bounce rate = Number of single-page viewers ÷ Total number of visitors

bounce rate

measures the percentage of visitors to a company's Web site who view a single page and leave without viewing other pages.

- The **cart abandonment rate** is the percentage of shoppers who place at least one item in a shopping cart but never complete the transaction:

  Cart abandonment rate = 1 − (Number of customers who complete a transaction ÷ Number of shoppers who place at least one item in a shopping cart)

  If 500 shoppers place at least one item in a shopping cart but only 175 of them complete their transactions, the company's cart abandonment rate is 1 − (175 ÷ 500) = 65 percent.

cart abandonment rate

measures the percentage of shoppers who place at least one item in a shopping cart but never complete the transaction.

- The **conversion (browse-to-buy) rate** is the proportion of visitors to a site who actually make a purchase. It is one of the most important measures of Web success and is calculated as follows:

  Conversion rate = Number of customers who make a purchase ÷ Number of visitors to the site

conversion (browse-to-buy) rate

measures the proportion of visitors to a site who actually make a purchase.

Although conversion rates vary dramatically across industries, the average conversion rate is 3.2 percent.[83] In other words, out of every 1,000 people who visit a Web site, about 32 of them actually make a purchase. Only 25 percent of companies are satisfied with their conversion rates.[84]

LO6

Describe how e-businesses ensure the privacy and security of the information they collect and store from the Web.

Ensuring Web Privacy and Security

Privacy

The Web's ability to track customers' every move naturally raises concerns over the privacy of the information companies collect. Concerns about privacy and security are two of the greatest obstacles to the growth of e-commerce. E-commerce gives businesses access to tremendous volumes of information about their customers, creating a responsibility to protect that information and to use it wisely. To make sure they are using the information they collect from visitors to their Web sites legally and ethically, companies should take the following steps:

Take an inventory of the customer data collected. The first step to ensuring proper data handling is to assess exactly the type of data the company is collecting and storing. How are you collecting them? Why are you collecting them? How are you using them? Do visitors know how you are using the data? Do you need to get their permission to use them in this way? Do you use all of the data you are collecting?

privacy policy

a statement explaining the nature of the information a company collects online, what it does with that information, and the recourse that customers have if they believe the company is misusing the information.

Develop a company privacy policy for the information you collect. A **privacy policy** is a statement explaining the nature of the information a company collects online, what it does with that information, and the recourse that customers have if they believe the company is misusing the information. Every online company should have a privacy policy, but many do not. A survey by TRUSTe, a provider of Internet privacy services, reports that 56 percent of small businesses' Web sites have no privacy policy.[85] Several online privacy firms, such as TRUSTe (www.truste.org), BBBOnline (www.bbbonline.com), and BetterWeb (www.betterweb.com) offer Web "seal programs," the equivalent of the Good Housekeeping seal of privacy approval. To earn a privacy seal of approval, a company must adopt a privacy policy, implement it, and monitor its effectiveness. Many of these privacy sites also provide online policy wizards, which are automated questionnaires that help e-business owners create comprehensive privacy statements.

Post your company's privacy policy prominently on your Web site and follow it. Creating a privacy policy is not sufficient; posting it in a prominent place on the Web site (it should be accessible from *every* page on the Web site) and then abiding by it make a policy meaningful. One of the worst mistakes a company can make is to publish its privacy policy online and then to fail to follow it. Not only is this unethical, but it also can lead to serious damage awards if customers take legal action against the company.

Security

For online merchants, the result of shoppers' privacy and security concerns is lost sales. In fact, shoppers cite security concerns as the primary reason they are hesitant to shop online.[86] Every company doing business on the Internet faces two conflicting goals: (1) to establish a presence on the Web so that customers from across the globe can have access to its site and (2) to maintain a high level of security so that the business, its site, and the information it collects is safe from hackers and intruders intent on doing harm. Companies have a number of safeguards available to them, but hackers with enough time, talent, and determination usually can beat even the most sophisticated safety measures. If hackers manage to break into a system, they can do irreparable damage, stealing programs and sensitive customer data, modifying or deleting valuable information, changing the look and content of sites, or crashing sites altogether. The damage a company experiences from security breaches can be devastating. A survey by the Identity Theft Center reports that 73 percent of customers say they would stop shopping at a Web site from which their personal information had been stolen.[87]

Hackers and intruders, whose attacks are growing increasingly sophisticated, have begun targeting small companies, which have limited budgets, few (if any) technical experts on staff,

Increase Your Web Site's Conversion Rate

An online company's conversion rate is the percentage of visitors to the site who actually make a purchase. Conversion rates vary from one online industry to another, but the average conversion rate is about 3.2 percent. That means that for every 1,000 visitors to a company's site, 32 of them actually make a purchase. For many small companies that are less visible online, conversion rates hover between 1 and 2 percent. What steps can entrepreneurs take to increase their conversion rates? Try the following tips:

- **Start with your company's unique selling proposition.** Just as in a brick-and-mortar store, converting online visitors into customers begins with a company's unique selling proposition (refer to Chapter 8). Every page of a company's Web site, from the home page and individual product pages to the blog or video pages, should ooze its unique selling proposition. Design your Web site with the question that every customer asks: "What's in it for me?"

- **Build a call to action into every page.** Every page should drive customers to take a particular action, perhaps registering for a newsletter or blog updates, downloading a free white paper, liking your company on Facebook, or completing a purchase. Remember that if you don't ask customers to take a particular action, they won't. A call to action has four components:

  - **The call.** This is the request to the user to take a particular action.

  - **The action.** This is the specific action you want the user to take.

  - **The outcome.** This is what happens when the user takes the requested action.

  - **The design.** This is how your site visually represents the call to action to the user.

One Web page designer suggests printing several different types of pages from your Web site, taping them to a wall, and viewing them from a distance of six feet. Can you see a clear and identifiable call to action on each page? If not, it's time for a redesign.

- **Keep your site clean, simple, and focused.** A common mistake among online companies, especially those that have been around a while, is that their sites have mushroomed over time into a hodgepodge of pages that create a convoluted, spaghetti-like structure for visitors. Sites with too many messages and too many interaction points confuse customers and destroy conversion rates.

- **Give customers exactly what they want.** Fan Bi, cofounder of Blank Label, an online company that sells custom men's shirts, discovered that the company's core customers wanted the ability to zoom in to see the texture of shirt fabrics and to see what a finished shirt looks like. Blank Label added a zoom feature and three-dimensional photos of its shirts and saw its conversion rate increase 25 percent in just one month. E-tailers are learning that great photographs and videos that show a product in use are excellent selling tools. Ceilume, a maker of decorative ceiling tiles, uses videos on its Web site and on YouTube to show customers how its products are different from competing products and how easy they are to install. Ed Davis, president of the $5 million company, which is based in Grafton, California, credits the videos, which have been viewed more than 500,000 times, helping the company increase its sales by 15 percent.

- **Use landing pages effectively.** A landing page is any stand-alone page to which a customer arrives, often from an online ad or search engine. Every landing page should connect directly to the source that brought the visitor there. If a customer clicks on a search engine listing for a camouflage flashlight, the landing page should display a camouflage flashlight with easy instructions for purchasing it. This also is the time to cross sell, listing in a sidebar products under the heading "Customers who bought this also bought . . ."

- **Design for balance, rhythm, emphasis, and unity.** *Balance* is determined by the size, shape, color intensity, and line thickness of an object. Think of your design as a teeter-totter. A lighter element can balance a heavier element by being farther away from the center. Color and texture also can balance an asymmetrical design. *Rhythm* involves repetition. Repeating similar elements throughout a Web site in a consistent manner or changing the size, position, or form of the same elements creates a unified design that allows the brain to absorb easily. *Emphasis* provides the focal point for a Web page, and designers can achieve it by using larger fonts, bold print, angled text, bright or contrasting colors, photographs, and other design tools. Web sites with the highest conversion rates emphasize the call to action on every page. *Unity* allows all of the elements on a Web page to look as though they fit together. A site that achieves balance, rhythm, and emphasis has a head start on achieving unity. Using the same fonts, heading styles, colors, and shapes creates unity.

- **Use analytics to test and optimize.** The key to a successful Web site is continuous improvement, which requires entrepreneurs to have access to meaningful information about their sites' performance from analytics and conducting tests to see what works and what doesn't. Analytics give entrepreneurs ideas about how to improve their sites (and conversion rates), and tests confirm or refute those ideas. The simplest tests involve driving traffic randomly to two Web pages with only one element that is different (the headline, graphic, call to action, and so on) and monitoring the results to see which one produces a higher conversion rate.

Sources: Based on Oli Gardner, "Clicking Me Softly: A Five-Day Crash Course in Conversion (Day 2), *Marketing Profs*, February 22, 2011, http://www.marketingprofs.com/articles/2011/4494/clicking-me-softly-a-five-day-crash-course-in-conversion-day-2; Oli Gardner, "Clicking Me Softly: A Five-Day Crash Course in Conversion (Day 3), *Marketing Profs*, February 23, 2011, http://www.marketingprofs.com/articles/2011/4501/clicking-me-softly-a-five-day-crash-course-in-conversion-day-3; Oli Gardner, "Clicking Me Softly: A Five-Day Crash Course in Conversion (Day 4), *Marketing Profs*, February 24, 2011, http://www.marketingprofs.com/articles/2011/4512/clicking-me-softly-a-five-day-crash-course-in-conversion-day-4; Oli Gardner, "Clicking Me Softly: A Five-Day Crash Course in Conversion (Day 5), *Marketing Profs*, February 25, 2011, http://www.marketingprofs.com/articles/2011/4521/clicking-me-softly-a-five-day-crash-course-in-conversion-day-5; Guillermo Cedillo, "Principles of Design," *Web Magazine*, November 2010, pp. 42–43; Stefany Moore, "Blank Label's Redesign Boosts Its Conversion Rate 30%," *Internet Retailer*, September 22, 2011, http://www.internetretailer.com/2011/09/22/blank-labels-redesign-boosts-its-conversion-rate-30; and Kermit Pattison, "Online Video Offers Low-Cost Marketing for Your Company," *Wall Street Journal*, March 16, 2011, http://www.nytimes.com/2011/03/17/business/smallbusiness/17sbiz.html.

and, as a result, less secure systems. Hackers in Ukraine recently hacked into more than 8 million Web pages, most of them from small companies, and set them to take control of the computers of unsuspecting visitors to the sites.[88] Every company, no matter how small, is a potential target. The U.S. Secret Service and the forensic analysis unit of Verizon Communications report that 63 percent of the successful cyberattacks they investigate occur in small companies with fewer than 100 employees.[89] The costs associated with a security breach include not only the actual cost of the lost data and the lawsuits that inevitably result from customers but also the long-term impact of the lost trust that customers have for a business whose security has been breached. Yet a survey by Newtek Business Services reports that 73 percent of small businesses have not had a third party test their Web sites for security.[90]

To minimize the likelihood of invasion by hackers, e-companies rely on several tools, including virus detection software, intrusion detection software, and firewalls. At the most basic level of protection is **virus detection software**, which scans computer drives for viruses, nasty programs written by devious hackers and designed to harm computers and the information they contain. The severity of viruses ranges widely, from relatively harmless programs that put humorous messages on a user's screen to those that erase a computer's hard drive or cause the entire system to crash. Because hackers are *always* writing new viruses to attack computer systems, entrepreneurs must keep their virus detection software up to date and must run it often. An attack by one virus can bring a company's entire e-commerce platform to a screeching halt in no time!

Intrusion detection software is essential for any company doing business on the Web. These packages constantly monitor the activity on a company's network server and sound an alert if they detect someone breaking into the company's computer system or if they detect unusual network activity. Intrusion detection software not only can detect attempts by unauthorized users to break into a computer system while they are happening but also can trace the hacker's location. Most packages also have the ability to preserve a record of the attempted break-in that will stand up in court so that companies can take legal action against cyberintruders. Web security companies such as McAfee provide software such as ScanAlert that scans a small business's Web site daily to certify that it is "Hacker Safe." Online companies using the software are able to post a certification mark signifying that their sites are protected from unauthorized access.

A **firewall** is a combination of hardware and software operating between the Internet and a company's computer network that allows employees to have access to the Internet but keeps unauthorized users from entering a company's network and the programs and data it contains. Establishing a firewall is essential to operating a company on the Web, but entrepreneurs must make sure that their firewalls are set up properly. Otherwise, they are useless! Even with all of these security measures in place, it is best for a company to run its Web site on a separate server from the network that runs the business. If hackers break into the site, they still do not have access to the company's sensitive data and programs.

In e-commerce, just as in traditional retailing, sales do not matter unless a company gets paid! On the Web, customers demand transactions that they can complete with ease and convenience, and the simplest way to allow customers to pay for e-commerce transactions is with credit cards. From a Web customer's perspective, however, one of the most important security issues is the security of his or her credit card information. To ensure the security of their customers' credit card information, online retailers typically use **Secure Sockets Layer (SSL) technology** to encrypt customers' transaction information as it travels across the Internet. By using secure shopping cart features from storefront-building services or Internet service providers, even the smallest e-commerce stores can offer their customers secure on-line transactions.

Processing credit card transactions requires a company to obtain an Internet merchant account from a bank or financial intermediary. Setup fees for an Internet merchant account typically range from $500 to $1,000, but companies also pay monthly access and statement fees of between $40 and $80 plus a transaction fee of 10 to 60 cents per transaction. Once an online company has a merchant account, it can accept credit cards from online customers.

Online credit card transactions also pose a risk for merchants; online fraud cost companies an estimated $2.7 billion a year, nearly 1 percent of their annual revenues (see Figure 9.7).[91] The most common problem is **charge-backs**, online transactions that customers dispute. Unlike credit card transactions in a retail store, those made online ("card-not-present" transactions) involve no signatures, and Internet merchants incur the loss when a customer disputes an online

---

virus detection software

programs that scan computer drives for viruses, or nasty programs written by devious hackers and designed to harm computers and the information they contain.

intrusion detection software

programs that constantly monitor the activity on a company's network server and sound an alert if they detect someone breaking into the system or if they detect unusual network activity.

firewall

a combination of hardware and software that allows employees to have access to the Internet but keeps unauthorized users from entering a company's network and the programs and data it contains.

Secure Sockets Layer (SSL) technology

an encryption device that secures customers' transaction information as it travels across the Internet.

charge-backs

online transactions that customers dispute.

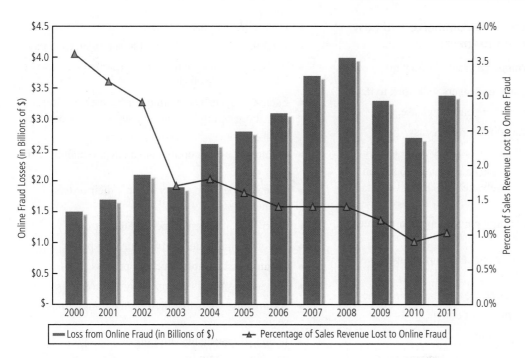

FIGURE 9.7

Losses to Online Fraud

Source: Online Fraud Report: Thirteenth Annual Edition, Cybersource Corporation, Mountain View, California: 2012, p. 4.

credit card transaction. One way to prevent fraud is to ask customers for their card verification value (CVV or CVV2), the three-digit number above the signature panel on the back of the credit card, as well as their card number and expiration date. Online merchants also can subscribe to a real-time credit card processing service that authorizes credit card transactions, but the fees can be high. Sending confirmation e-mails that include the customer's shipping information after receiving an order also reduced the likelihood of a charge-back. In addition, using a shipper that provides the ability to track shipments enables online merchants to prove that the customer actually received the merchandise can help minimize the threat of payment fraud.

Chapter Summary by Learning Objective

E-commerce is creating a new economy, one that is connecting producers, sellers, and customers via technology in ways that have never been possible before. In this fast-paced world of e-commerce, size no longer matters as much as speed and flexibility do. The Internet is creating a new industrial order, and companies that fail to adapt to it will soon become extinct.

1. Understand the factors an entrepreneur should consider before launching into e-commerce.

Before launching an e-commerce effort, business owners should consider the following important issues:

- How a company exploits the Web's interconnectivity and the opportunities it creates to transform relationships with its suppliers and vendors, its customers, and other external stakeholders is crucial to its success.

- Web success requires a company to develop a plan for integrating the Web into its overall strategy. The plan should address issues such as site design and maintenance, creating and managing a brand name, marketing and promotional strategies, sales, and customer service.

- Developing deep, lasting relationships with customers takes on even greater importance on the Web. Attracting customers on the Web costs money, and companies must be able to retain their online customers to make their Web sites profitable.

- Creating a meaningful presence on the Web requires an ongoing investment of resources—time, money, energy, and talent. Establishing an attractive Web site brimming with catchy photographs of products is only the beginning.

- Measuring the success of its Web-based sales effort is essential to remaining relevant to customers whose tastes, needs, and preferences are always changing.

2. Explain the 10 myths of e-commerce and how to avoid falling victim to them.

The 10 myths of e-commerce are the following:

Myth 1. If I launch a site, customers will flock to it.

Myth 2. Online customers are easy to please.

Myth 3. Making money on the Web is easy.

Myth 4. Privacy is not an important issue on the Web.

Myth 5. "Strategy? I don't need a strategy to sell on the Web! Just give me a Web site, and the rest will take care of itself."

Myth 6. The most important part of any e-commerce effort is technology.

Myth 7. Customer service is not as important online as it is in a traditional retail store.

Myth 8. Flashy Web sites are better than simple ones.

Myth 9. It's what's up front that counts.

Myth 10. It's too late to get into e-commerce.

3. Explain the basic strategies entrepreneurs should follow to achieve success in their e-commerce efforts.

Following are some guidelines for building a successful Web strategy for a small e-company:

- Focus on a niche in the market.
- Develop a community of online customers.
- Attract visitors by giving away "freebies."
- Make creative use of e-mail but avoid becoming a "spammer."
- Make sure that your Web site says "credibility."
- Make the most of the Web's global reach.
- Promote your Web site online and offline.
- Use the tools of Enterprise 2.0 to attract and retain customers.
- Develop an effective search engine optimization strategy.

4. Learn the techniques of designing a killer Web site.

There is no surefire formula for stopping Web shoppers in their tracks, but the following suggestions will help:

- Understand your target customer.
- Give customers want they want.
- Select a domain name that is consistent with the image you want to create for your company and register it.
- Make your Web site easy to navigate.
- Offer suggestions for related products.
- Add wish list capability.
- Create a gift idea center.
- Provide customer ratings and reviews.

- Use online videos.
- Establish the appropriate call to action on each page.
- Build loyalty by giving online customers a reason to return to your Web site.
- Establish hyperlinks with other businesses, preferably those selling products or services that complement yours.
- Include an e-mail option and a telephone number in your site.
- Give shoppers the ability to track their orders online.
- Offer Web shoppers a special all their own.
- Follow a simple design for your Web page.
- Create a fast, simple checkout process.
- Provide customers multiple payment options.
- Assure customers that their online transactions are secure.
- Establish reasonable shipping and handling charges and post them up front.
- Confirm transactions.
- Keep your site updated.
- Test your site often.
- Rely on analytics to improve your site.
- Consider hiring a professional to design your site.

5. Explain how companies track the results from their Web sites.

One option for tracking Web activity is through log-analysis software. Server logs record every page, graphic, audio clip, or photograph that visitors to a site access, and log-analysis software analyzes these logs and generates reports describing how visitors behave when they get to a site. Key metrics for measuring the effectiveness of a site's performance include the cost per acquisition, and the bounce rate, the cart abandonment rate, and the conversion rate.

6. Describe how e-businesses ensure the privacy and security of the information they collect and store from the Web.

To make sure that they are using the information they collect from visitors to their Web sites legally and ethically, companies should take the following steps:

- Take an inventory of the customer data collected.
- Develop a company privacy policy for the information collected.
- Post the company's privacy policy prominently on the Web site and follow it.

To ensure the security of the information they collect and store from Web transactions, companies should rely on virus and intrusion detection software and firewalls to ward off attacks from hackers.

Discussion Questions

1. In what ways have the Internet and e-commerce changed the ways companies do business?
2. Discuss the factors entrepreneurs should consider before launching an e-commerce site.
3. What are the 10 myths of e-commerce? What can an entrepreneur do to avoid them?
4. Most shoppers turn to search engines to find the products and services they want to purchase online. Very few shoppers look beyond the first page of the search engine results. Suppose that your company, which once ranked on the first results page, has slipped to a spot many pages down and that sales are declining. What steps can you take to remedy this problem?
5. What strategic advice would you offer an entrepreneur about to start an e-company?
6. What design characteristics make for a successful Web page?
7. Explain the characteristics of an ideal domain name. Give an example of a company with a good domain name and an example of a company with a poor domain name.
8. Describe common metrics that e-companies use to track the effectiveness of their Web sites. What advantages does each offer?
9. What steps should e-businesses take to ensure the privacy of the information they collect and store from the Web?
10. What techniques can e-companies use to protect their banks of information and their customers' transaction data from hackers?
11. What challenges does evaluating the effectiveness of a Web site pose for online entrepreneurs?

Business Plan Pro™

One question in the *Business Plan Pro™* wizard relates to your business Web site. Think about the presence that you would like your business to have on the Web. Will your Web site be an "information-only" site, or do you plan to have an online store? As you look through the list of the 10 myths mentioned in this chapter, ask yourself whether you have fallen prey to any of these myths.

Business Plan Exercises

Creating an effective Web presence may be a critical piece of business planning and your overall strategy.

On the Web

If you plan to host an information-only Web site, visit sites that accomplish that goal. Note the layout and navigation of the site and how it presents this information. If you plan to have a dynamic online store, visit sites that do that best. What aspects of the site make it simple and efficient for new and returning buyers? Next, select three Web sites that you find to have attractive parallels with the look and feel of your future Web site. These sites may be from entirely different industries but possess appealing attributes you want to incorporate into your Web site. Identify those qualities and explore how your site might also benefit from those attributes.

Sample Plans

Find the PrintingSoutions.com sample plan in *Business Plan Pro™*. Review the Executive Summary and then go to the Web Plan Summary in section 6.0. The Web will play a critical role in this online business. What role will the Web play in yours?

In the Software

Open your business plan in *Business Plan Pro™* and go to the Web Summary section. If you have changed your mind about having a Web site, click on View and Wizard and change that decision. The outline of your business plan will then reflect that change and bring the Web Summary section into your outline. Read the instructions within the software and click on the sample plan link in the upper right-hand section of the instructions. If beneficial, add content to this section. These questions may help you to consider the following:

- Do you have a URL registered for your business? If not, how will you begin that process to secure and register that Web address?
- Describe your target market's expected use of the Web site.
- List the objectives you hope to realize through the site.
- Is the site going to have an online store? If so, explore how to implement credit card and other online payment options.
- Who will design and launch the site? Will you or someone in your organization do this work, or will you outsource that work?
- How will you measure, track, and assess the performance of your site? How often that will occur?
- Are you going to incorporate Web analytics tools and resources that may help you to measure your Web site's performance?
- Does your business plan demonstrate that you have planned and budgeted for your Web site on the basis of the required resources to design, launch, and maintain your site?

Building Your Business Plan

Step back and review what you have captured in your plan to date. With these additions, does your plan continue to tell a consistent and coherent story about your business? Review and edit other sections that interact with the additions to the Web section. Some of those sections may include areas that relate to marketing promotions, communications, expenses, and revenues.

Beyond the Classroom . . .

1. Work with a team of your classmates to come up with an Internet business you would be interested in launching. Come up with several suitable domain names for your hypothetical e-company. Once you have chosen a few names, go to a domain name registration service, such as Network Solutions's Internic at www.networksolutions.com or Netnames at www.netnames.com, to conduct a name search. How many of the names your team came up with were already registered to someone? If an entrepreneur's top choice for a domain name is already registered to someone else, what options does he or she have?

2. Select several online companies with which you are familiar and visit their Web sites. What percentage of them have privacy policies posted on their sites? How comprehensive are these policies? What percentage of the sites you visited belonged to a privacy watchdog agency such as TRUSTe or BBBOnline? How important is a posted privacy policy for e-companies? Explain.

3. Visit three e-commerce sites on the Web and evaluate them on the basis of the Web site design principles described in this chapter. How well do they measure up? What suggestions can you offer for improving the design of each site? If you were a customer trying to make a purchase from each site, how would you respond to the design?

Endnotes

1. Erick Schonfeld, "Forecast: Online Retail Sales Will Grow to $250 Billion by 2014," *Seeking Alpha*, March 8, 2010, http://seekingalpha.com/article/192498-forecast-online-retail-sales-will-grow-to-250-billion-by-2014.

2. Jim Jansen, "Online Product Research," Pew Internet and American Life Project, September 29, 2010, http://www.pewinternet.org/Reports/2010/Online-Product-Research.aspx.

3. Jim Jansen, "Online Product Research," Pew Internet and American Life Project, September 29, 2010, http://www.pewinternet.org/Reports/2010/Online-Product-Research.aspx.

4. Scott Cendrowski, "Bytes Beat Bricks," *Fortune*, July 4, 2011, p. 13; "Blockbuster Movie Pass to Compete for Netflix Customers," *CNET*, September 23, 2011, http://news.cnet.com/1606-2_3-50112049.html; Don Reisinger, "Netflix Grabs 20 Percent of Peak Time U.S. Traffic," *CNET*, October 22, 2010, http://news.cnet.com/8301-13506_3-20020434-17.html; "Company Profile," Netflix, http://ir.netflix.com/#.

5. *Global Trends in Online Shopping: A Nielsen Global Consumer Report*, Nielsen Company, June 2010, pp. 2–3.

6. Erick Schonfeld, "Forecast: Online Retail Sales Will Grow to $250 Billion by 2014," *Seeking Alpha*, March 8, 2010, http://seekingalpha.com/article/192498-forecast-online-retail-sales-will-grow-to-250-billion-by-2014.

7. "Internet Usage Statistics," Internet World Stats, http://www.internetworldstats.com/stats.htm.

8. Jerry Useem, "Our 10 Principles of the New Economy, Slightly Revised," *Business 2.0*, August/September 2001, p. 85.

9. Susan Kuchinskas, "Where Are We Now? A Decade of E-Commerce," E-Commerce Guide, http://www.ecommerce-guide.com/news/trends/article.php/3426371.

10. Michelle O'Brien, "U.S. Small Businesses Plan to Spend More on Online, Video and Mobile Marketing in 2011, January 10, 2011, http://www.marketingforecast.com/archives/9290.

11. Seventy-Nine Percent of Small Business Owners Say They Don't Use Traffic Tracking Tools," *PR Web*, April 26, 2011, http://www.prnewswire.com/news-releases/april-2011-small-business-market-sentiment-survey-shows-small-businesses-underutilize-e-commerce-120695554.html.

12. *2011 Global Consumer Shopping Habits Survey*, Channel Advisor, p. 3.

13. "e or Be Eaten," *Fortune*, November 8, 1999, p. 87.

14. "Internet 2010 in Numbers," Pingdom, January 12, 2011, http://royal.pingdom.com/2011/01/12/internet-2010-in-numbers.

15. "Case Studies: Reach the Right People at the Right Time," Facebook, http://www.facebook.com/advertising.

16. "comScore Reports July 2011 U.S. Mobile Subscriber Share," *comScore*, August 30, 2011, http://www.comscore.com/Press_Events/Press_Releases/2011/8/comScore_Reports_July_2011_U.S._Mobile_Subscriber_Market_Share.

17. "Mobile Shopping on the Rise, Sales Volume to Reach US$9 Billion in 2011," inMobi, August 23, 2011, http://www.inmobi.com/company-news/2011/08/23/mobile-shopping-on-the-rise-sales-volume-to-reach-us9bil-in-2011.

18. *Cisco Visual Networking Index: Global Mobile Data Traffic Forecast Update, 2010–2015*, Cisco Systems, February 1, 2011, pp. 2–3; "M-Commerce to Hit $119 Billion in 2015," *Marketing Charts*, July 11, 2011, http://www.marketingcharts.com/direct/m-commerce-to-hit-119b-in-15-18553/bitwizards-mobile-commerce-and-shopping-trends-2015-jul11gif.

19. *The State of Small Business Report: January 2011 Survey of Small Business Success*, Network Solutions and the University of Maryland's Robert A. Smith School of Business, February 9, 2011, p. 24.

20. Cameron Chapman, "Mobile Web Design: Tips and Best Practices," *Noupe*, February 9, 2010, http://www.noupe.com/how-tos/mobile-web-design-tips-and-best-practices.html.

21. *Quick Response Codes in a Multi-Channel World*, Demandware Inc., 2011, p. 8.

22. *2011 Consumer Research Results: Privacy and Online Behavioral Advertising*, TRUSTe Research and Harris Interactive, July 25, 2011, p. 11.

23. John B. Horrigan, *Online Shopping*, Pew Internet and American Life Project, February 13, 2008, p. ii.

24. "Survival of the Fastest," *Inc. Technology*, No. 4, 1999, p. 57.

25. "About Us," Easy to Grow Bulbs, http://www.easytogrowbulbs.com/t-about.aspx.
26. Claer Barrett, "Aurora Fashions Speeds Up Web Delivery," *Financial Times*, May 23, 2011, http://www.ft.com/intl/cms/s/0/efb52086-856a-11e0-ae32-00144feabdc0.html#axzz1a6zfawZd.
27. Steve Bennett and Stacey Miller, "The E-Commerce Plunge," *Small Business Computing*, February 2000, p. 50.
28. Sucharita Mulpuru, "Five Retail E-Commerce Trends to Watch in 2011," Forrester Research, January 31, 2011, p. 3.
29. Kenneth Corbin, "Study Cites Flaw in E-tail Experience," *E-Commerce Guide*, September 19, 2008, http://www.ecommerce-guide.com/news/news/article.php/3772771.
30. "Shopping Cart Abandonment Rate Tops 75%," SeeWhy, August 2, 2011, http://seewhy.com/blog/2011/08/02/shopping-cart-abandonment-rate-tops-75.
31. "Shopping Cart Abandonment E-mails Generate $17.90 per E-mail," SeeWhy, June 22, 2011, http://seewhy.com/blog/2011/06/22/shopping-cart-abandonment-emails-generate-17-90-per-email.
32. Stafany Moore, "JellyBelly.com's Redesign Boosts Conversion and Average Ticket," *Internet Retailer*, September 27, 2011, http://www.internetretailer.com/2011/09/27/jellybelly-coms-redesign-boosts-conversion-and-average-ticket.
33. Fred Vogelstein, "A Cold Bath for Dot-Com Fever," *U.S. News & World Report*, September 13, 1999, p. 37.
34. Stefany Moore, "Youngsters Make It to the Big Time in E-Retailing," *Internet Retailer*, August 4, 2011, http://www.internetretailer.com/2011/08/04/youngsters-make-it-big-time-e-retailing.
35. Paul Demery, "Bon-Ton Rolls into Holidays on New E-Commerce Wheels," *Internet Retailer*, December 7, 2010, http://www.internetretailer.com/2010/12/07/bon-ton-rolls-holidays-new-e-commerce-wheels.
36. Bronwyn Fryer and Lee Smith, ".Com or Bust," *FSB*, December 1999/January 2000, p. 41.
37. Dana Dratch, "These E-Gardening Tips Will Help Your Web Site Grow from Sprout to Giant," *Bankrate.com*, February 29, 2000, http://www.bankrate.com/brm/news/biz/Ecommerce/20000117.asp.
38. Brian Morrissey, "Forrester: Time Spent on Internet Is Equal to TV," *Ad Week*, December 13, 2010, http://www.adweek.com/news/technology/forrester-time-spent-internet-equal-tv-104018.
39. "Hot 500: Christmas Lights Etc.," *2007 Entrepreneur Hot 500*, http://www.entrepreneur.com/Hot500/Details/274.html; "About Us," Christmas Lights Etc., http://www.christmaslightsetc.com/AboutUs.asp.
40. *State of the Media: The Social Media Report*, Nielsen, Quarter 3, 2011, p. 2.
41. Ralph F. Wilson, "The Five Mutable Laws of Web Marketing," *Web Marketing Today*, April 1, 1999, http://www.wilsonweb.com/wmta/basic-principles.htm, pp. 1–7.
42. "Going to the Dogs," Constant Contact, http://www.constantcontact.com/email-marketing/customer-examples/salty-paw.jsp.
43. Thad Rueter, "Small Business Owners Say E-mail Works Better Than Social Media," *Internet Retailer*, June 2, 2011, http://www.internetretailer.com/2011/06/02/small-business-owners-say-e-mail-works-better-social-media.
44. "Facebook Won't Become E-Commerce Force, Analyst Says," *Wall Street Journal,* April 7, 2011, http://blogs.wsj.com/digits/2011/04/07/facebook-wont-become-e-commerce-force-analyst-says.
45. Lyndon Cerejo, "Improving the Online Shopping Experience, Part 1: Getting Customers to Your Products, *Smashing Magazine*, September 2011, http://uxdesign.smashingmagazine.com/2011/09/15/improving-the-online-shopping-experience-part-1-getting-customers-to-your-products.
46. Nicole Henderson, "Symantec Report Finds Spam Accounts for 73 Percent of June E-Mail," *Web Host Industry Review*, June 28, 2011, http://www.thewhir.com/web-hosting-news/062811_Symantec_Report_Finds_Spam_Accounts_for_73_Percent_of_June_Email.
47. Sara Rand, "Three Best Practices for E-Mail, Derived from the Top Retailers," National Retail Federation, September 14, 2011, http://blog.shop.org/2011/09/14/three-best-practices-for-email-of-the-top-retailers.
48. Tamara Gielen, "State of Retailing Online 2007," *B2B E-mail Marketing*, September 27, 2007, http://www.b2bemailmarketing.com/2007/09/state-of-retail.html.
49. "World Internet Usage and Population Statistics," *Internet World Stats*, 2010, http://www.internetworldstats.com/stats.htm.
50. "The Top Ten Languages Used in the Internet," *Internet World Stats*, 2010, http://www.internetworldstats.com/stats7.htm.
51. Mary Madden and Kathryn Zickuhr, "65% of Online Adults Use Social Networking Sites," *Pew Internet and American Life Project*, August 26, 2011, http://www.pewinternet.org/Reports/2011/Social-Networking-Sites/Report/Part-1.aspx.
52. "ChannelAdvisor Online Shopper Survey: Customer Reviews, Facebook 'Likes' More Important Than Ever in Purchase Decision Making," *iStockAnalyst*, October 3, 2011, http://www.istockanalyst.com/business/news/5451478/channeladvisor-online-shopper-survey-customer-reviews-facebook-likes-more-important-than-ever-in-purchase-decision-making; "71% of Online Adults Now Use Video Sharing Sites," Pew Internet and American Life Project, July 26, 2011, http://pewresearch.org/pubs/2070/online-video-sharing-sites-you-tube-vimeo; "Social Media and Young Adults," February 3, 2010, Pew Internet and American Life Project, http://www.pewinternet.org/Reports/2010/Social-Media-and-Young-Adults/Summary-of-Findings.aspx.
53. Kelly Faville, "Game Changer: Cone Survey Finds Four Out of Five Consumers Reverse Purchase Decisions Based on Negative Online Reviews," Cone Communications, August 30, 2011, http://www.coneinc.com/negative-reviews-online-reverse-purchase-decisions.
54. Louis Columbus, "Is Social Networking and Asset or a Liability for Your Company?" *CRM Buyer*, September 2, 2008, http://www.crmbuyer.com/story/64352.html.
55. Jane Brocklebank, "A Facebook Success Story for Small Business," Facebook, December 15, 2010, http://www.facebook.com/note.php?note_id=475502725874; "About Us," Windsor and Eton Brewery," http://www.webrew.co.uk/aboutus.html.
56. Dan Briody, "Puppy Power," *Inc.*, November 2007, pp. 55–56.
57. Evan Schuman, "Pizza Hut, Papa John's to Merge E-Commerce with Social Networks," *Storefront Back Talk*, October 19, 2008, http://www.storefrontbacktalk.com/story/101908pizzahut.
58. *From Intent to In-Store: Search's Role in the New Retail Shopper Profile*, GroupM Search and Compete, October 2011, p. 2.
59. Sarah E. Needleman, "Sites Retool for Google Effect," *Wall Street Journal*, April 21, 2011, p. B4; Allison Enright, "An E-Tailer Digs Out from a Google Update," *Internet Retailer*, May 16, 2011, http://www.internetretailer.com/2011/05/16/e-retailer-digs-out-google-update.
60. Jason Prescott, "How to Optimize Your Site for Google in 2010," *iMedia Connection*, March 23, 2010, http://www.imediaconnection.com/content/26275.asp.

61. *iProspect Blended Search Results Study*, iProspect, April 2008, p. 13.
62. James A. Martin, "Search Engine Optimization: SEO Tips for Small Business," *Small Business Computing*, September 29, 2009, http://www.smallbusinesscomputing.com/buyersguide/article.php/3841381/Search-Engine-Optimization-SEO-Tips-for-Small-Business.htm.
63. *The State of Small Business Report: January 2011 Survey of Small Business Success*, Network Solutions and the University of Maryland's Robert H. Smith School of Business, February 2011, p. 3.
64. Nate Elliot, "The Easiest Way to a First-Page Ranking on Google," *Forrester Blogs*, January 8, 2009, http://blogs.forrester.com/interactive_marketing/2009/01/the-easiest-way.html.
65. "Top Search Engines for 2010," SEO Consultants Directory, July 2, 2010, http://www.seoconsultants.com/search-engines.
66. "The Historical Cost of Pay-Per-Click (PPC) Advertising," Hochman and Associates, 2011, http://www.hochmanconsultants.com/articles/je-hochman-benchmark.shtml.
67. Bill Briggs, "IRCE 2011 Report: A Retailer's Size Poses No Restrictions for Search Marketing," *Internet Retailer*, June 16, 2011, http://www.internetretailer.com/2011/06/16/irce-2011-report-size-poses-no-restrictions-paid-search.
68. Barry Schwartz, "Report: Click Fraud Drops to 19.1% in Q4 2010," *Search Engine Land*, January 26, 2011, http://searchengineland.com/click-fraud-q42010-62471.
69. Steve McKee, "Make Your Web Site Work for You," *Business Week*, June 2008, http://www.businessweek.com/smallbiz/content/jun2008/sb2008069_643453.htm.
70. "Internet 2010 in Numbers," *Royal Pingdom*, January 12, 2011, http://royal.pingdom.com/2011/01/12/internet-2010-in-numbers.
71. "Reduce Bounce Rate by Making a Landing Page More Like a Landing Page," SmileyCat, April 11, 2011, http://www.smileycat.com/miaow/archives/002455.php.
72. "ToolHawker Increased Average Customer Page Views Per Visit by 25 Percent with Google Site Search," Google Site Search Case Study, http://www.google.com/sitesearch.
73. Michelle Magna, "Creating Content That Turns Browsers into Buyers," *E-Commerce Guide*, April 24, 2008, http://www.ecommerce-guide.com/solutions/design/article.php/3742836.
74. "Facebook 'Likes' More Important Than Ever in Purchase Decision-Making," *IT Analysis*, October 4, 2011, http://www.it-analysis.com/channels/online/news_release.php?rel=27417.
75. "The State of Online Video," Pew Internet and American Life Project, June 3, 2010, http://pewinternet.org/Press-Releases/2010/State-of-Online-Video.aspx.
76. Jeremy Scott, "Video Marketing Advice for Retailers: Product Videos Aren't Enough Anymore," *ReelSEO*, October 3, 2011, http://www.reelseo.com/video-marketing-advice-for-retailers.
77. Jeremy Scott, "Video Marketing Advice for Retailers: Product Videos Aren't Enough Anymore," *ReelSEO*, October 3, 2011, http://www.reelseo.com/video-marketing-advice-for-retailers.
78. Stavraka, "There's No Stopping E-Business. Are You Ready?," *Forbes*, December 13, 1999, Special Advertising Section.
79. Allison Enright, "E-Tailers Book an 18% Revenue Increase for Q3," *Internet Retailer*, October 20, 2011, http://www.internetretailer.com/2011/10/20/e-retailers-book-18-revenue-increase-q3.
80. Don Davis, "LLBean.com Will No Longer Charge Shipping Fees," *Internet Retailer*, March 24, 2011, http://www.internetretailer.com/2011/03/24/llbeancom-will-no-longer-charge-shipping-fees.
81. *The State of Small Business Report: January 2011 Survey of Small Business Success*, Network Solutions and the University of Maryland's Robert H. Smith School of Business, February 2011, p. 16.
82. Teresa Novellino, "Small Business Chintzes Out on Ecommerce," *Portfolio*, May 2, 2011, http://www.portfolio.com/views/blogs/resources/2011/05/02/survey-finds-small-businesses-not-maximizing-websites-or-ecommerce.
83. Sucharita Mulpuru, "Five Retail E-Commerce Trends to Watch in 2011," Forrester Research, January 31, 2011, p. 3.
84. "Satisfaction with Online Conversion Rates Falls," *Marketing Charts*, November 1, 2011, http://www.marketingcharts.com/direct/satisfaction-with-online-conversion-rates-falls-19847/?utm_campaign=rssfeed&utm_source=mc&utm_medium=textlink.
85. Courtney Rubin, "Why You Should Make Privacy a Priority," *Inc.*, March 12, 2010, http://www.inc.com/news/articles/2010/03/making-privacy-a-priority.html.
86. *RSA 2010 Global Online Consumer Security Survey*, RSA Security Inc., p. 12.
87. *First Annual Identity Theft Resource Center Consumer Internet Transaction Concerns Survey*, Identity Theft Resource Center, June 14, 2010, p. 3.
88. Byron Acohido, "Millions of Web Pages Are Hacker Landmines," *USA Today*, August 12, 2011, http://www.usatoday.com/money/industries/technology/2011-08-11-mass-website-hacking_n.htm.
89. Geoffrey A. Fowler, "Hackers Shift Attacks to Small Firms," *Wall Street Journal*, July 21, 2011, http://online.wsj.com/article/SB10001424052702304567604576454173706460768.html.
90. "Three-Quarters of U.S. Small Firms Have Not Tested Web Site Cybersecurity," Infosecurity, September 27, 2011, http://www.infosecurity-magazine.com/view/20980/threequarters-of-us-small-firms-have-not-tested-website-cybersecurity.
91. *Online Fraud Report*, 12th ed. (Mountain View, CA: Cybersource, 2010), p. 4.

10

Pricing Strategies

Learning Objectives

On completion of this chapter, you will be able to:

1. Discuss the relationships among pricing, image, competition, and value.
2. Describe effective pricing techniques for introducing new products or services and for existing ones.
3. Explain the pricing methods and strategies for retailers, manufacturers, and service firms.
4. Describe the impact of credit on pricing.

'We'll give it all away for free and figure out how to make money later' isn't much of business model.

—Jason Fried

The price is what you pay; the value is what you receive.

—Anonymous

Setting prices is a business decision governed by both art and science—with a measure of instinct thrown in for good measure. Setting prices for their products and services requires entrepreneurs to balance a multitude of complex forces, many of them working in opposite directions. Entrepreneurs must determine prices for their goods and services that will draw customers and produce a profit. Unfortunately, many small business owners set prices without enough information about their cost of operations and their customers. Price is an important factor in building long-term relationships with customers, and haphazard pricing techniques can confuse and alienate customers and endanger a small company's profitability. Research shows that proper pricing strategies have far greater impact on a company's profits than corresponding reductions in fixed or variable costs.[1] For instance, when a company that earns a 10 percent net profit margin raises its prices by one percent, its profits increase by 10 percent (assuming that its unit sales remain the same).

Another complicating factor is a holdover from the last recession: customers are more price sensitive and are using technology such as smart phones and tablet PCs with price comparison apps to shop for the best deals—often right in the middle of a store's aisles. In a recent survey by Deloitte, one in four smart phone owners use their phones to shop; 59 percent of these mobile shoppers use their phones to compare product prices, and 41 percent use them to download coupons.[2] The result is a new age of price transparency that retailers have never before experienced (see Figure 10.1).

Setting prices is not only one of the toughest decisions small business owners face but also one of the most important. Setting prices too high drives customers away and destroys a company's sales. Establishing prices that are too low, a common tendency among first-time entrepreneurs, robs a business of its ability to generate a profit, creates the impression among customers that the company's products and services are of inferior quality, and threatens its long-term success. Improper pricing has destroyed countless businesses whose owners mistakenly thought that their prices were high enough to generate a profit when, in fact, they were not.

ENTREPRENEURIAL PROFILE: Jeff Trott: Timeless Message After working with a consultant, Jeff Trott, founder of Timeless Message, a company that sells bottles with greeting messages inside them, raised its prices from an average of $30 per bottle to $60 per bottle. The company had underestimated both its costs and the market value of its products. The price increase resulted in a brief sales dip, but, according to Trott, "We started making a profit for the first time in four years. It was like we had been shipping a ten-dollar bill out the door with each order."[3] ∎

Pricing decisions cut across every aspect of a small company, influencing everything from its marketing and sales efforts to its operations and strategy. Price is the monetary value of a product or service in the marketplace; it is a measure of what the customer must give up to obtain various goods and services. Price also is a signal of a product's or service's value to an individual, and different customers assign different values to the same goods and services. From an entrepreneur's viewpoint, price must be compatible with customers' perceptions of value. "Pricing is not just a math problem," says one business writer. "It's a psychology test."[4] The psychology of pricing is an art much more than it is a science. It focuses on creating value in the customer's mind but recognizes that value is what the customer perceives it to be. Customers often look to

FIGURE 10.1

Business Challenges That Drive Pricing Decisions

Source: Optimizing Price in a Transparent World: Benchmark Report, Retail Systems Research, April 2011, p.5.

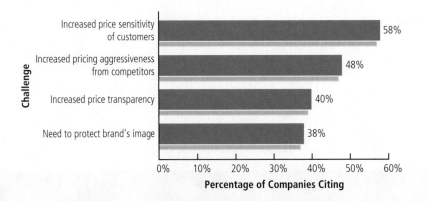

Blondie © 2010 King Features Syndicate, Inc. World Rights reserved.

a product's or service's price for clues about value. Consider the following examples, which illustrate the sometimes puzzling connection between price and perceived value:

- In the ultrapremium segment of the watch industry, companies such as Greubel Forsey, Grönefield Timepieces, Roger Dubuis, and A. Lange and Söhne blend Old World craftsmanship, engineering, and artistry to create some of the most extravagant timepieces in the world. Prices for these chronographs start at $100,000, but many of these highly crafted masterpieces sell for $400,000 to $500,000. Franck Muller's Aeternitas Mega 4, which is the most complex watch in the world with 1,483 moving parts and a 1,000-year calendar, sells for an incredible $2.7 million! To some people, owning one of these watches is a hallmark of financial success, even though some of them are no more accurate at keeping time than an inexpensive quartz-driven Timex.[5]

- E. S. Kluft and Company, based in Rancho Cucamonga, California, has manufactured upscale mattresses since 1946, and its top models sell for more than some new cars. CEO Earl Kluft started working in the sewing room of the family business at age 14 and recently introduced the Sublime mattress, handcrafted with mohair, cashmere, New Zealand wool, organic cotton, silk, and natural latex to create a "cradling" effect—and priced at $44,000.[6]

- At DB Bistro Moderne in New York City, chef Daniel Boulud serves an ultragourmet Double Truffle Burger that sells for $125. An outer layer of ground sirloin surrounds a thick blend of foie gras, boneless short ribs braised in red wine, and root vegetables. Topped with shaved black truffles and nestled on a homemade poppy seed and parmesan bun, the exotic burger is served with fries (of course!).[7]

As you can see, setting higher prices sometimes can *increase* the appeal of a product or service ("If you charge more, you must be worth it"). Value for these products is found not solely in their superior technical performance but also in their scarcity and uniqueness and the resulting image they create for the buyer. Although entrepreneurs must recognize the shallow depth of the market for ultraluxury items such as these, the ego-satisfying ownership of limited-edition watches, pens, cars, jewelry, and other items is the psychological force supporting a premium price strategy.

Three Potent Forces: Image, Competition, and Value

LO1

Discuss the relationships among pricing, image, competition, and value.

Because pricing decisions have such a pervasive influence on all aspects of a small company, one of the most important considerations for entrepreneurs is to take a strategic rather than a piecemeal approach to pricing their companies' products and services. Research by the University of Pennsylvania's Wharton School shows that companies that take a strategic approach to pricing and monitor its results can raise their sales revenue between 1 and 8 percent. After analyzing its existing pricing techniques using price management software, New York City drugstore chain Duane Reade discovered that parents of newborns are less price sensitive than are parents of toddlers. Managers decided to make diaper pricing a function of the child's age, cutting prices to meet those of competitors on toddlers' diapers and raising them on diapers for newborns. A year later, the company's new pricing strategy had produced a 27 percent increase in its baby care revenue.[8]

You Be the Consultant

The Benefits of Premium Pricing

The 20-person staff at 37signals, a Chicago-based software company, ran into the same problem every time they collaborated on a software development project: sharing sketches of ideas required multiple steps (drawing, scanning, uploading, and sharing) that slowed the process, limited productivity, and inhibited creativity. To remedy their problem, the software team developed an easy-to-use app for tablet computers such as the iPad that allows users to draw sketches on the screen with their fingers and share the drawings with others instantly via e-mail or other communications software. The beauty of the software, which the company calls Draft, is its simplicity. There are no shape tools, text tools, brushes, textures, or color fills. Draft mimics a person drawing sketches on a piece of paper. "No Sharpie, no paper, no scanner, no waste, no extra steps," says Jason Fried, cofounder of 37signals. "Just draw, tap, done."

The software team was so pleased with Draft that they decided other people would like to use it as well and decided to sell it on Apple's App Store. "If you search the App store, you'll find dozens of similar drawing apps," says Fried. "You'll also find a mix of prices. From free to $9.99, there's a product and a price to satisfy nearly everyone." Most drawing apps range between "free" and $4.99.

Only 20 strong, the staff at 37signals devotes most of its time on the company's four primary software products, and Fried wanted to make sure that the time they invested in Draft would pay off. "We're a rare company in the Web-based software business," says Fried. "We actually charge for things. We provide our software like a restaurant provides its food, a cabby provides transportation, and a clothing store offers a shirt—in exchange for money."

Fried takes a different view of creating a customer base than most business owners. "Most companies seem to want as many customers as they can get," says Fried. "At 37signals, we don't want lots of customers. We want lots of the *right* customers. Our goal is to maximize profits, not market share. We also want to maximize happiness—for our customers and for ourselves. When we set out to put a price tag on Draft, we decided not to pay attention to what the other drawing apps sell for. We didn't look to compete on price."

Fried and his team knew that most apps sell for 99 cents but had no intentions of joining what he calls "a race to the bottom." Instead, they took a fresh approach to selling their software. They wanted to use price to *reduce* the number of customers who purchased Draft rather than to increase it. "That's right," says Fried, "we wanted *fewer* customers to buy Draft. With a price tag of a buck or two, we could have easily sold 10,000 copies of the software. On the surface, that sounds great but not when you think about the resources required to serve 10,000 customers. A good number of those 10,000 people are going to need help. Some are going to complain. Some will ask a lot of questions." Fried says that providing customer service is part of being in the software business and that 37signals works really hard at it. He also points out that its four principal products sell for $24 to $149 per month. "At those prices, we can afford to provide excellent service. Could we provide excellent service for many thousands of additional customers paying a one-time price of $1.99? Would that reduce our ability to serve our $24-a-month or our $149-a-month customers? We believe it would."

The team decided to price the Draft app at $9.99, well above the prices of most competing drawing apps. "Instead of going for a land grab," says Fried, "we created a small island. We've sold nearly 2,000 copies of Draft. That's about $20,000 in revenue. We are much happier with $20,000 in revenue from 2,000 customers than $20,000 in revenue from 10,000 or 20,000 customers. Given our current resources and team, we can happily serve 2,000 Draft customers, plus all of our other customers."

1. Do you find Fried's philosophy of using pricing to create fewer customers rather than more customers to be unique? Do you agree with him? Explain.

2. Why do so many entrepreneurs, especially first-time entrepreneurs, fall victim to the mistake of pricing their goods and services too low?

Source: Jason Fried, "Go Ahead, Raise Your Prices," *Inc.*, November 2010, pp. 44–45.

A company's pricing strategy is a major determinant of its image in the marketplace, is influenced by the pricing strategies of its competitors, and is an important element in the value that customers perceive its products or services provide.

Price Conveys Image

A company's pricing policies communicate important information about its overall image to customers. "Pricing tells a story," says Per Sjofors, a pricing consultant. For example, the prices charged by a posh men's clothing shop reflect a completely different image from those charged by a factory outlet store.[9] Customers look at prices to determine the type of store they are dealing with. High prices frequently convey the idea of quality, prestige, and uniqueness to customers. "People bring a whole set of equations with them when they make a purchase, and one of the values for most people is that high price equals quality," says Rob Docters, a pricing expert.[10]

Accordingly, when developing a marketing approach to pricing, entrepreneurs must establish prices that are compatible with what customers expect and are willing to pay. Too often, entrepreneurs *underprice* their goods and services, believing that low prices are the only way they can achieve a competitive advantage.

ENTREPRENEURIAL PROFILE: Chris Carmon: Carmon Group Chris Carmon, cofounder of the Carmon Group, a Cleveland, Ohio, recruiting firm, estimates that over the first three years that he was in business, he missed out on $1 million in revenue by establishing prices that were too low for the fast, highly specialized search services that he provides his clients. Carmon's original pricing strategy, which was simply to match what other recruiting company's charged (25 percent of an employee's first year's salary), failed to reflect the extra value he offered by taking on difficult or fast-track searches. Today, Carmon sets prices for searches based on the client's demands. He recently found a veteran bridge designer for a company and charged 35 percent of the first year's salary. Carmon says that the 24-employee company's new pricing strategy has increased both sales and profits.[11] ■

Like Chris Carmon, many entrepreneurs make the common pricing mistake of failing to recognize the extra value, convenience, service, and quality they give their customers—all things that many customers are willing to pay for. These companies fall into the trap of trying to compete solely on the basis of price when they lack the sales volume—and, hence, the lower cost structures—of their larger rivals. It is a recipe for failure. "People want quality," says one merchant selling upscale goods at upscale prices. "They want value. But if you lower prices, they think that you are lowering the value and lowering the quality."[12] It is a dangerous cycle that can destroy a business. A study of businesses in multiple industries by Rafi Mohammed, author of *The Art of Pricing*, found that those companies that raised prices by 1 percent saw their profits increase 11 percent. Those that raised their prices by 10 percent realized profit increases of 100 percent![13] The study does not imply that businesses have free rein to raise prices to any level, but it does suggest that many companies can raise their prices enough to improve their financial results significantly as long as they convince customers that their products or services offer superior value.

A key ingredient to setting prices properly is to understand a company's target market: the customer groups at which the small company is aiming its goods or services. Rather than ask "How much should I charge for my product or service?" entrepreneurs should ask "How much are my target customers willing to pay?" Target market, business image, and pricing strategy are closely related.

ENTREPRENEURIAL PROFILE: Rob Dickinson: Singer Vehicle Design Rob Dickinson's company, Singer Vehicle Design, is aimed squarely at members of the baby-boom generation who now can afford that dream car from their youth. The company specializes in rebuilding classic Porsches using the latest parts and technology, including carbon fiber body parts, modern suspension and disc brake systems, and air-cooled engines from a maker of Formula One race cars. A number of replica car makers appeal to buyers with a wide range of models, from coupes from the 1930s to muscle cars from the 1960s, across a wide range of prices. Singer Vehicle Design targets affluent baby boomers who are willing to spend $190,000 to $300,000 on a modern version of a classic Porsche. "It's restored, done with authenticity, and updated with as much new wisdom as we have access to," says Dickinson.[14] ■

Competition and Prices

Small businesses face competition from local, foreign, and online businesses. A recent global survey reports that 74 percent of retailers say that they operate "within an extremely price competitive environment."[15] When setting prices, entrepreneurs should take into account their competitors' prices, but they should *not* automatically match or beat them. However, unless a small company can differentiate itself by creating a distinctive image in customers' minds or by offering superior service, quality, design, convenience, or speed, it must match its competitors' prices or risk losing sales. Before matching any competitor's prices, however, small business owners should consider a rival's motives. A competitor may establish its price structure on the basis of a unique set of criteria and a totally different strategy. Blindly matching competitors' prices can lead a company to financial ruin, and companies that set their prices this way typically do so because they perceive themselves in a position of strategic weakness. Recall from Chapter 3 that companies that execute a successful differentiation strategy can charge prices higher than those of their competitors.

The similarity of competitors' goods and services also influences a company's pricing policies. Entrepreneurs must monitor competitors' prices on products that are identical to or that are close substitutes for those they sell and then strive to keep their prices in line with them. For example, the local sandwich shop should consider the hamburger restaurant, the taco shop, and the roast beef shop as competitors because they all serve fast foods. Although none of them offers the identical menu of the sandwich shop, they are all competing for the same quick-meal dollar. Because competitors' prices can have a dramatic impact on a small company's prices, entrepreneurs should make it a habit to monitor their rivals' prices, especially on identical items.

 ENTREPRENEURIAL PROFILE: Anthony Shurman: Yosha Enterprises When Anthony Shurman launched Yosha Enterprises in 2002, a company that markets liquid breath mints, he established a price of $1.99 for a 36-mint package. Later, in response to competitors' prices, he lowered the price to $1.79 and then to $1.69 per pack. Momints contained more mints than any of the competing brands, but customers failed to recognize that benefit and based their purchase decisions on the package price. When Shurman recently rolled out Momints at a regional chain of grocery stores, he cut the size of the pack to the industry standard 28 mints and set a price of 99 cents. "Our sales went up 350 percent," he says. Yosha generates $3 million in annual revenue, and Shurman believes that he can sell even more mints at the lower 99-cent price.[16] ■

Generally, entrepreneurs should avoid head-to-head price competition with other firms that can more easily achieve lower prices through lower cost structures. For instance, most locally owned drugstores cannot compete with the prices of large national drug chains that buy in large quantities and negotiate significant discounts. However, many local drugstores operate successfully by using nonprice competition; these stores offer more personalized service, free delivery, credit sales, and other extras that the chains have eliminated. Nonprice competition can be an effective strategy for a small business in the face of larger, more powerful companies because experimenting with price changes can be dangerous for small companies. Price changes cause fluctuations in sales volume that a small company may not be able to tolerate. In addition, frequent price changes may muddle a company's image and damage customer relations.

Attempting to undercut competitors' prices may lead to a price war, one of the deadliest games a small business can play. Price wars can eradicate companies' profit margins and scar an entire industry for years. "Many entrepreneurs cut prices to the point of unprofitability just to compete," says one business writer. "In doing so, they open the door to catastrophe. Less revenue often translates into lower quality, poorer service, sloppier salesmanship, weaker customer loyalty, and financial disaster."[17] Price wars usually begin when one competitor thinks that he or she can achieve higher volume instantaneously by lowering prices. Rather than sticking to their strategic guns, competitors believe they must follow suit. In an attempt to regain market share lost to smaller rivals over time, Tesco, Great Britain's largest grocery chain started by Jack Cohen in 1919 in a market stall in London's East End, recently launched a price war, indicating a seismic shift in the company's strategy, which previously focused on price promotions on selected items and discounts for loyalty card holders. The company's "big price drop" initiative reduced prices by as much as 30 percent on 3,000 items, mostly Tesco's private label products. Richard Brasher, Tesco's CEO, says that the move to "everyday low prices" resonates with customers who say they are weary of constantly fluctuating prices and the need to canvass multiple stores for the best prices. With the announcement, stock prices of every company in the United Kingdom's grocery business plunged as analysts predicted a crash in supermarket profits. "They all have a gun to each other's head," says one industry analyst.[18]

Entrepreneurs usually overestimate the power of price cuts. In reality, sales volume rarely increases enough to offset the lower profit margins of a lower price. A business with a 25 percent gross profit margin that cuts its price by 10 percent would have to *triple* its sales volume just to break even.

ENTREPRENEURIAL PROFILE: Steve Richardson: Stave Puzzles When a severe recession caused sales during the crucial holiday season to slow, Steve Richardson, owner of

Stave Puzzles, a Norwich, Connecticut–based maker of hand-crafted wooden jigsaw puzzles, resorted to heavy price cuts to stimulate sales. Looking back, Richardson says the 15 percent discount ran contrary to the company's reputation for superior quality and service and was not successful in generating enough traffic to offset the price cuts. "We were so scared" by the economy "that we were throwing things against the wall to see whatever worked," he says. Richardson believes that Staves could have earned a profit for the year had he held prices steady or even raised them. "I have to get a grip on pricing," he says with determination. "I have to right this ship."[19] ∎

As Steve Richardson learned, a company may cut its prices so severely that it is impossible to achieve the volume necessary to offset the lower profit margins. Discounts also threaten to cheapen a company's image for providing quality products and services. Even when price cuts work, their effects often are temporary. Customers lured by the lowest price usually exhibit very little loyalty to a business. Rather than join in a price war by cutting prices, entrepreneurs can adjust their product and service offerings to appeal to different market segments: lower-priced items that use less expensive materials and offer fewer extras for price-sensitive customers and higher-quality, premium products for those who care less about price and more about quality and service. The lesson: the best way to survive a price war is to stay out of it by emphasizing the unique features, benefits, and value your company offers its customers!

Focus on Value

Ultimately, the "right" price for a product or service depends on one factor: the value that it provides for a customer. There are two aspects of value, however. Entrepreneurs may recognize the *objective* value of their products and services, which is the price that customers would be willing to pay if they understood perfectly the benefits that a product or service delivers for them. Unfortunately, few if any customers can see a product's or a service's true objective value; instead, they see only its *perceived* value, which determines the price they are willing to pay for it. Research into purchasing decisions has revealed a fundamental problem that adds to the complexity of a business owner's pricing decision: people faced with pricing decisions often act irrationally. In one classic study, researchers asked shoppers if they would travel an additional 20 minutes to save $5 on a calculator that costs $15; most said they would. When asked the same question about a $125 jacket, most of the shoppers said no, even though they would be saving the exact same amount of money! "People make [purchasing] decisions piecemeal, influenced by the context of the choice," says Richard Thaler, who won a Nobel Prize for his work in behavioral economics.[20]

CBS via Getty Images

"Value" does not necessarily equate to low price, however. Businesses that underprice their products and services or run special discount price promotions may be short-circuiting the value proposition they are trying to build and communicate to their customers. "Charging too little is more dangerous than charging too much," says veteran entrepreneur Norm Brodsky, owner of CitiStorage, a document storage company in New York City. "If you set your prices too high, you can always reduce them. If you undercharge, you develop the wrong kind of reputation."[21]

ENTREPRENEURIAL PROFILE: Lyn and Jenny Gaylord: Lyn Gaylord Accessories
In 1992, Lyn Gaylord and her daughter Jenny launched Lyn Gaylord Accessories, a small company that sells belts with sterling silver buckles that feature unique designs of horses, dogs, butterflies, and other characters that are drawn from the European antiques that have fascinated the Gaylords for years. At one point when the company's sales were slipping, Gaylord cut the prices of her unique belts and buckles to less than $100 because she thought she had to match rivals' prices. Sales continued to fall, and Gaylord realized her mistake. "I priced too cheaply," she says, "and people weren't sure my belts were special." With silver prices skyrocketing, Gaylord raised her prices by 75 percent to an average price of $350, and the company's sales and profits increased. "Price doesn't matter if customers want what they can't get elsewhere," Gaylord says.[22] ∎

Customers may respond to price cuts, but companies that rely on them to boost sales risk undermining the perceived value of their products and services. In addition, once customers grow accustomed to buying products and services during special promotions, the habit can be difficult to break. They simply wait for the next sale. The results are extreme swings in sales and diminished value of the brand.

One of the most important determinants of customers' response to a price is whether they perceive the price to be a fair exchange for the value they receive from the product or service. The good news is that, through marketing and other efforts, companies can influence customers' perception of value. "Determine what your offering is worth and use your pricing strategy to set customers' value perceptions accordingly," advises on marketing expert.[23] Because price is one part of a product's or a service's features, it is another way a company can communicate value to its customers.

For most shoppers, three reference points define a fair price: the price they have paid for the product or service in the past, the prices competitors charge for the same or similar product or service, and the costs a company incurs to provide the product or service. The price that customers have paid in the past for an item serves as a baseline reference point, but people often forget that inflation causes a company's costs to rise from year to year. Therefore, it is important for business owners to remind customers periodically that they must raise prices to offset the increased cost of doing business. "Over time, costs always go up," says Norm Brodsky, owner of a successful document storage company. "I'd rather raise prices a little every year or with every new contract than be forced to demand a big increase down the road."[24] In the face of rising food costs and a sluggish economy, McDonald's, the largest restaurant chain in the world, has relied on small, consistent price increases to maintain its profit margins without alienating customers.[25]

As we have seen already, companies often find it necessary to match competitors' prices on the same or similar items unless they can establish a distinctive image in customers' minds. One of the most successful strategies for companies facing direct competition is to differentiate their products or services by adding value for customers and then charging for it. For instance, a company might offer faster delivery, a longer product warranty, extra service, or something else that adds value to an item for its customers and allows the business to charge a higher price.

Perhaps the least understood of the three reference points is a company's cost structure. Customers often underestimate the costs businesses incur to provide products and services, whether it is a simple cotton T-shirt on a shelf in a beachfront shop or a lifesaving drug that may have cost hundreds of millions of dollars and many years to develop. For instance, in a study on pricing conducted by the University of Pennsylvania's Wharton School, shoppers estimated the average grocery store's net profit margin to be 27 percent when, in reality, it is less than 2 percent.[26] Customers forget that business owners must make or buy the products they sell, market them, pay their employees, and cover a host of other operating expenses, ranging from health care to legal fees.

Skillet Street Food

ENTREPRENEURIAL PROFILE: Joshua Henderson: Skillet Street Food Joshua Henderson was a pioneer in the gourmet food truck industry when he launched Skillet Street Food in Seattle, Washington, from a converted Airstream trailer. "There was no model to follow," he recalls. "We had to figure out how to price things, what our trailer should look like, how large our menu was—pure trial and error." Getting Skillet's prices right took some time, but Henderson eventually found a sweet spot below the prices of brick-and-mortar restaurants but high enough to cover food costs and generate sustainable profit margins. For instance, the original price of Skillet's popular burger and poutine (hand-cut fries covered in cheese and gravy) was $15, but "when we raised it to $17, we saw an effect on the bottom line," says Henderson. "It put our cost of goods sold in line and put our profit margin where it should be for a restaurant." Skillet Street Food now generates $2 million in annual sales.[27] ∎

Entrepreneurs often find themselves squeezed by rising operating and raw material costs but are hesitant to raise prices because they fear losing customers. Businesses facing rapidly rising costs in their businesses should consider the following strategies:

- *Communicate with customers.* Let your customers know why you have to raise prices. Danny O'Neill, owner of The Roasterie, a wholesale coffee business that sells to upscale restaurants, coffeehouses, and supermarkets, operates in a market in which the cost of raw material and supplies can fluctuate wildly because of forces beyond his control. When coffee prices nearly doubled in just three months, O'Neill was able to pass along the rising costs of his company's raw material to customers without losing a single one. He sent his customers a six-page letter and copies of newspaper articles about the increases in coffee prices. The approach gave the Roasterie credibility and helped show customers that the necessary price increases were beyond his control.[28]

- *Rather than raise the price of the good or service, include a surcharge.* Price increases tend to be permanent, but if higher costs are the result of a particular event (e.g., a hurricane that disrupted the nation's ability to process oil and resulted in rapidly rising fuel costs), a company can include a temporary surcharge. If the pressure on its costs subsides, the company can eliminate the surcharge. When fuel prices began climbing rapidly, Mark Bergland, owner of Washington Floral Service, a flower wholesaler in Tacoma, Washington, added to each customer's order a surcharge tied to the average diesel fuel price.[29]

- *Eliminate customer discounts, coupons, and "freebies."* Eliminating discounts, coupons, and other freebies is an invisible way of raising prices that can add significantly to a small company's profit margin. One bookstore chain restructured its generous discount program because it had begun to cut too deeply into the company's profitability. Loyal customers still earn discounts (as do loyal customers at its competitors), but the discounts are smaller and expire faster.[30]

- *Offer products in smaller sizes or quantities.* As food costs soared, many restaurants introduced "small plates," reduced-portion items that enabled them to keep their prices in check. In the quick-service sector, miniburgers billed as "fun food" and offered in bundles became a popular item on many menus.

● *Focus on improving efficiency everywhere in the company.* Although raw materials costs may be beyond a business owner's control, other costs within the company are not. One way to cope with the effects of a rapid increase in costs is to find ways to cut costs and to improve efficiency in other areas. These improvements may not totally offset higher raw materials costs, but they can dampen their impact. Rather than raise prices, the owners of Jen-Mor Florists, a family-run flower shop in Dover, Delaware, decided to cut the number of deliveries to the edge of their territory to just one per day to reduce the company's delivery expenses.[31]

● *Emphasize the value your company provides to customers.* Unless a company reminds them, customers can forget the benefits and value its products offer. "If you provide great value to your customers, a little price increase isn't going to scare them away," says Elizabeth Gordon, a small business consultant.

● *Raise prices incrementally and consistently rather than rely on large periodic increases.* Companies that do so are less likely to experience resistance due to customers' sticker shock.

● *Shift to less expensive raw materials if possible.* Some small businesses combat rising raw materials cost by adding new products that cost less to their lines. When seafood and beef prices increased, many restaurants revamped their menus to include dishes with less expensive ingredients, such as chicken. McDonald's, for example, added new chicken-based sandwich, salad, and nugget selections to its menu to shore up profit margins.[32]

● *Anticipate rising materials costs and try to lock in prices early.* It pays to keep tabs on raw materials prices and be able to predict cycles of inflation. Entrepreneurs who can anticipate rising prices may be able to make purchases early or lock in long-term contracts before prices take off. Starbucks uses this strategy successfully to lock in coffee bean prices with suppliers, thus insulating the company from the risk of price increases that slammed many of its competitors when coffee bean prices hit a 13-year high.[33]

● *Consider absorbing cost increases.* When Norm Brodsky, owner of the document storage company mentioned earlier, saw his competitors add a fuel surcharge to their customers' bills to offset steep increases in gas prices, he decided *not* to add a fuel surcharge. Then he used the pricing decision to attract new accounts, telling them, "We have found other ways besides a surcharge to deal with the problem. When we say the price [of our contract] is fixed for five years, we mean it, and you can count on it." Brodsky also used the fuel surcharge issue to build loyalty among his existing customers, something he is certain will pay off in the future.[34]

● *Modify the product or service to lower its cost.* Taco Bell introduced the first "value menu" in 1988 with items priced at just 59 cents, and Wendy's, Burger King, McDonald's, and other quick-service restaurants soon followed suit. Price-sensitive customers responded, and value menu items now account for a significant part of restaurants' sales. However, rapidly rising food and energy costs have squeezed or eliminated franchisees' profits on these items, forcing chains to modify the items by eliminating a slice of cheese (which saves six cents) or shaving two ounces of beef from the patty to maintain the $1 price.[35] Companies using this strategy must exercise caution, taking care not to reduce the quality of their products and services so much that they damage their reputations.

● *Differentiate your company and its products and services from the competition.* Many retailers and restaurants struggle to wean customers off of the discounts they offered during a lingering recession and fragile economic recovery.

ENTREPRENEURIAL PROFILE: Clarence Otis: Darden Restaurants Clarence Otis, CEO of Darden Restaurants, which owns Red Lobster, Olive Garden, and other restaurants, resisted resorting to deep price cuts to stimulate sales, choosing instead to add a line of moderately priced seafood dishes to its menu and to differentiate its restaurants from competitors. For instance, at Red Lobster, Otis introduced wood-fired grill and a daily fresh fish menu and remodeled restaurants to include warm wood paneling, cozy booths, and nautical decor and artwork that resemble a classic Bar Harbor lobster house, a move that analysts say should generate sales increases in the future. "We're a very strong brand, and we wanted to make sure that we didn't reduce [the value of our brand] to the point where price was the primary attribute that we reinforced in people's minds," says Otis.[36] ∎

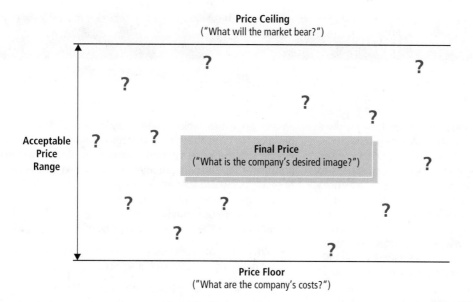

FIGURE 10.2

What Determines Price?

Setting prices with an emphasis on value is more important than trying to choose the ideal price for a product. In fact, for most products, there is an acceptable price range, not a single ideal price. This price range is the area between the price ceiling defined by customers in the market and the price floor established by the company's cost structure. An entrepreneur's goal is to position the company's prices within this acceptable price range. The final price that business owners set depends on the desired image they want to create for the business in their customers' minds—discount, middle of the road, or prestige (see Figure 10.2).

Pricing Strategies and Tactics

LO2

Describe effective pricing techniques for introducing new products or services and for existing ones.

There is no limit to the number of variations in pricing strategies and tactics. This wide variety of options is exactly what allows entrepreneurs to be so creative. This section examines some of the more commonly used tactics. Pricing always plays a critical role in a firm's overall strategy; pricing policies must be compatible with a company's total marketing plan and the image it intends to create in the marketplace.

Introducing a New Product

Most entrepreneurs approach setting the price of a new product with a great deal of apprehension because they have no precedent on which to base their decisions. If the new product's price is excessively high, it is in danger of failing because of low sales volume. However, if its price is too low, the product's sales revenue might not cover costs. In addition, the company runs the risk of establishing the product's value at a low level. Management consulting firm McKinsey and Company claims that 80 to 90 percent of the pricing problems on new products are the result of companies setting prices that are too low.[37] When pricing any new product, the owner should try to satisfy three objectives:

1. *Get the product accepted.* No matter how unusual a product is, its price must be acceptable to a company's potential customers. The acceptable price range for a new product depends, in part, on the product's position:

   • **Revolutionary products** are so new and unique that they transform existing markets. The acceptable price range for revolutionary products tends to be rather wide, but the businesses introducing them must be prepared to make an investment in educating customers about them.

   • **Evolutionary products** offer upgrades and enhancements to existing products. The acceptable price range for evolutionary products is not as wide as it is for revolutionary products. Companies that introduce evolutionary products with many new features at prices that are too low may initiate a price war.

revolutionary products products that are so new and unique that they transform existing markets.

evolutionary products products that offer upgrades and enhancements to existing products.

Is the Price Right?

To increase sales of a particular product or service, business owners often resort to lowering its price. After all, doing so is consistent with the law of demand, which says that as price decreases, quantity demanded increases. However, there are exceptions to every rule, including the law of demand. A product's or a service's price tag says a great deal about it. Shoppers often have difficulty judging the quality of the goods and services they purchase and look to their prices for clues. Mike Faith, CEO of Headsets .com, an online company that sells a variety of wireless, Bluetooth, and corded headsets, involuntarily conducted an interesting pricing study a few years ago when a computer error caused all of the company's products to be listed at cost rather than their normal retail prices for an entire weekend. Headset sales did not soar despite the price decrease. "It was a big lesson for us," says Faith, who discovered that the prices his company charges are less important to his target customers than the stellar customer service it offers. "Every call we get is answered by a human being within four rings," he says, "and our sales reps are well trained and know a lot about the headsets." Since the incident, Faith has raised prices only once, by 8 percent, and saw the company's sales *increase* by 8 percent.

The prices that entrepreneurs set for the products and services they sell are a significant factor in the image they create for their companies in their customers' minds, whether that image is one of a discount store or one of an upscale, exclusive shop. The following entrepreneurs are faced with pricing decisions that will influence the image and ultimately the success of their companies:

Nomie Baby

Katie Danzinger, founder of Nomie Baby in New York City, sells removable, washable covers for infant and child car seats. When Danzinger, a first-time entrepreneur, launched her company, she looked at the cost of materials and manufacturing and set her prices slightly above those costs at $34 per cover. "I just looked at what I thought would be my biggest costs," she says. "I hadn't taken into account the cost of shipping, storage, designing and printing marketing materials, packaging, and liability insurance. These ended up much more significant than I expected." Danzinger fell victim to a common mistake—setting prices for her products that were too low to cover their total costs—and now she faces the unnerving possibility that raising prices will send her customers fleeing.

Kriser's Pet Supplies

Jeff Kalish is cofounder of this start-up chain of pet supplies and dog grooming services in Chicago and has plans to expand the business rapidly. Dog grooming services are a key part of the company's sales equation because they drive customer traffic to the company's three stores. In an attempt to generate more customer traffic, Kriser's Pet Supplies set its dog grooming prices at an average of $46, which is noticeably lower than those of other pet groomers. Feedback from potential customers makes Kalish wonder whether Kriser's pricing strategy is creating the wrong impression of the chain in customers' eyes. "When they heard our price, people would start asking questions," says Kalish. "Did we do full service? Were our groomers experienced?"

What steps can entrepreneurs take when it comes to setting the right prices? The following tips will help:

- Know your costs, including the direct and the indirect costs, of providing your product or service.

- Don't set your price below your costs. "We lose money on every unit we sell, but we make up for it in volume" is a business philosophy that never works.

- Price increases are easier to accomplish when a company faces fewer competitors. The more intense the competition, the more difficult it is to raise prices.

- If you need to raise prices shortly after launching your business, try to soften the blow by bundling products and services to create more value for customers.

- Assign someone in your company to track competitors' prices regularly (at least monthly) and to present the results on a timely basis.

- Do not simply follow your competitors' pricing strategies.

- Base your pricing on the value that your product or service offers customers. Remember that sometimes the most valuable components of a product or service are intangible.

- Define the image you want to create for your business and use your pricing strategy to communicate that image to your customers and to position your company in the market.

1. Why do many entrepreneurs underprice their goods and services, especially when they first get into business? Discuss the connection between the prices a company establishes for its goods and services and the image it creates for the company.

2. What advice on pricing can you offer Katie Danzinger and Jeff Kalish? Work with a group of your classmates to brainstorm various pricing strategies and the impact that they might have on these companies. How should they implement your pricing suggestions?

Sources: Based on Eilene Zimmerman, "Real-Life Lessons in the Delicate Art of Setting Prices," *New York Times*, April 20, 2011, http://www.nytimes.com/2011/04/21/business/smallbusiness/21sbiz.html?_r=1&pagewanted=print; Stephanie Clifford, "How Low Can You Go?," *Inc.*, August 2007, pp. 42–43; and Bridget McCrea, "When Is the Price Right? Effective Pricing Is Crucial to Remain Competitive and Move Product," *Black Enterprise*, July 2004, pp. 78–79.

- **Me-too products**, as the name suggests, offer the same basic features as existing products on the market. The acceptable price range for these products is quite narrow, and many companies introducing them find themselves left with me-too pricing strategies that are the same or similar to those of their competitors.

me-too products
products that offer the same basic features as existing products on the market.

2. *Maintain market share as competition grows.* If a new product is successful, competitors will enter the market, and the small company must work to expand or at least maintain its market share. Continuously reappraising the product's price in conjunction with special advertising and promotion techniques helps to retain a satisfactory market share.

3. *Earn a profit.* A small business must establish a price for a new product that is higher than its cost. Entrepreneurs should not introduce a new product at a price below cost because it is much easier to lower a price than to increase it once the product is on the market. Pricing their products too low is a common and often fatal mistake for new businesses; entrepreneurs are tempted to underprice their products and services when they enter a new market to ensure their acceptance or to gain market share quickly. Doing so, however, sets customers' value expectations at low levels as well, and that can be a difficult perception to overcome. Steve McKee, president of McKee Wallwork Cleveland Advertising, an advertising agency that targets small companies, says, "It can be odd to feel good about losing customers because of price, but if you're not, you may be backing yourself into a low-margin corner. Don't kid yourself; other than Wal-Mart, very few companies can sustain a low-price position."[38]

Entrepreneurs have three basic strategies to choose from when establishing a new product's price: penetration, skimming, and life cycle pricing.

PENETRATION If a small business introduces a product into a highly competitive market in which a large number of similar products are competing for acceptance, the product must penetrate the market to be successful. To gain quick acceptance and extensive distribution in the mass market, some entrepreneurs introduce the product at a low price. They set the price just above total unit cost to develop a wedge in the market and quickly achieve a high volume of sales. When Amazon introduced its Kindle Fire tablet, the retailer set the price at $199, but analysts say that tablet actually cost $201.70 to make ($185.60 for the components and $16.10 for a contract manufacturer to assemble them). Industry experts say that Amazon priced the Kindle Fire to undercut the popular iPad2, which started at $499, with the goal of generating a profit on the sale of books and movies for the Fire—and eventually on the tablet itself as the cost of the chips that serve as the device's "brain" declined. Within six months of its introduction, the cost of the Kindle Fire's components had declined to $153, and Amazon was earning a profit on each unit sold.[39]

A penetration pricing strategy is ideal for introducing relatively low-priced goods into a market where no elite segment and little opportunity for differentiation exists. The introduction is usually accompanied by heavy advertising and promotional techniques, special sales, and discounts. This strategy works best when customers' "switching costs" (the cost of switching to a lower-priced competitor's product) is high (e.g., video game consoles). Entrepreneurs must recognize that penetration pricing is a long-range strategy; until customers accept the product, profits are likely to be small.

A danger of a penetration pricing strategy is that it attracts customers who know no brand loyalty. Companies that garner customers by offering low introductory prices run the risk of losing their customer bases if they raise their prices or a competitor undercuts their prices. If the strategy works and the product achieves mass-market penetration, sales volume increases, and the company earns adequate profits. The objectives of the penetration strategy are to break into the market quickly, generate a high sales volume as soon as possible, and build market share. Many consumer products, such as soap, shampoo, and lightbulbs, are introduced with penetration pricing strategies.

ENTREPRENEURIAL PROFILE: Ido Leffler: Yes to Carrots In 2006, Ido Leffler, founder of Yes To Inc, a company that markets a line of skin and hair care products made from carrots, tomatoes, cucumbers, and blueberries introduced the all-natural beauty products at very affordable prices. "Our pricing is based on what we call a guilt-free pricing model," says Leffler.

Source: Yes To Inc.

"We don't think you will feel guilty buying a moisturizer or shampoo that retails from $8.99 to $19.99. We also look at our competitors, and we try to be a better value than them." Yes to Carrots, which started with 6 products in just 16 stores, now has more than 80 products that are sold in nearly 28,000 stores in 29 countries.[40] ■

SKIMMING A skimming pricing strategy often is used when a company introduces a new product into a market with little or no competition or to establish the company and its products or services as unique and superior to those of its competitors. Sometimes a business employs this tactic when introducing a product into a competitive market that contains an elite group that is able to pay a higher price. Here an entrepreneur uses a higher-than-normal price in an effort to quickly recover the initial developmental and promotional costs of the product. The idea is to set a price well above the total unit cost and to promote the product heavily to appeal to the segment of the market that is not sensitive to price. This pricing tactic often reinforces the unique, prestigious image of a business and portrays the product as high quality. Another advantage of this technique is that entrepreneurs can correct pricing mistakes quickly and easily. If a product's price proves to be too low under a penetration strategy, raising the price can be very difficult. If a company using a skimming strategy sets a price too high to generate sufficient volume, it can always lower the price. Successful skimming strategies require a company to differentiate its products or services from those of the competition, justifying the above-average price.

ENTREPRENEURIAL PROFILE: **Jeff Lubell: True Religion** True Religion, one of several Los Angeles–based makers of jeans, focuses on a small but profitable segment of the denim market: premium jeans that sell at retail for $225 to $665. Only about 1 percent of the jeans sold in the United States cost more than $50, but price is not the primary concern of customers in this ultrapremium segment of the market, whom Jeff Lubell, founder and CEO of True Religion, calls "jeaners." Premium denim brands such as True Religion, whose jeans are recognized for their stylish pocket embroidery, generate profit margins that are two to three times those of less expensive, traditional jeans or private-label brands. True Religion, which sells about 4 million units of clothing each year, recently introduced its Phantom jeans, which have a small American flag hand embroidered on the waistband and a ghost-like image of the company's logo on the pocket (hence the name "Phantom") and sell for $310 to $375.[41] ■

LIFE CYCLE PRICING A variation of the skimming price strategy is called life cycle pricing. Using this technique, a small company introduces a product at a high price. Then technological advances enable the firm to lower its costs quickly and to reduce the product's price before its competition can. By beating other businesses in a price decline, the small company discourages competitors and gradually, over time, becomes a high-volume producer. High-definition television sets are a prime example of a product introduced at a high price that quickly cascaded downward as companies forged important technological advances and took advantage of economies of scale. When high-definition televisions were first introduced in 1999, they sold for $19,000; today, they are priced at $300 or less.

Life cycle pricing is a strategy that assumes that competition will emerge over time. Even if no competition arises, however, companies almost always lower the product's price to attract a larger segment of the market. Nonetheless, the initial high price contributes to a rapid return of start-up costs and generates a pool of funds to finance expansion and technological advances.

Pricing Established Goods and Services

Each of the following pricing tactics or techniques can become part of the toolbox of pricing tactics entrepreneurs can use to set prices of established goods and services.

ODD PRICING Many small business managers use the technique known as **odd pricing**. These managers prefer to establish prices that end in odd numbers, such as 5, 7, or 9 because they believe that merchandise selling for $12.69 appears to be much cheaper than the item priced at $13.00. Psychological techniques such as odd pricing are designed to appeal to certain customer interests, but research on their effectiveness is mixed. Some studies show no benefits from using odd pricing, but others have concluded that the technique can produce significant increases in sales. Omitting the "$" symbol from prices may help, too. Researchers

odd pricing
a pricing technique that sets prices that end in odd numbers to create the psychological impression of low prices.

at Cornell University have discovered that restaurants that list menu prices without the "$" symbol achieved $5.55 more in sales on average than those whose menu prices were written in script or included a "$" symbol.[42]

PRICE LINING **Price lining** is a technique that greatly simplifies the pricing decision by pricing different products in a product line at different price points, depending on their quality, features, and cost. Under this system, entrepreneurs stock merchandise in several different price ranges, or price lines. Each category of merchandise contains items that are similar in appearance but that differ in quality, cost, performance, or other features. Many lined products appear in sets of three—good, better, and best—at prices designed to satisfy different market segment needs and incomes. Apple uses price lining in its iTunes store, selling songs for 69 cents, 99 cents, or $1.29, depending on the artist's popularity. Price lining can boost a store's sales because it makes goods available to a wide range of shoppers, simplifies the purchase decision for customers, and allows them to keep their purchases within their budgets.

DYNAMIC PRICING For many businesses, the pricing decision has become more challenging because the Internet gives customers access to real-time pricing information of almost any item ranging from cars to computers. Increasingly, customers are using the Internet to find the lowest prices available. To maintain their profitability, companies have responded with **dynamic (customized) pricing**, in which they set different prices on the same products and services for different customers using the information they have collected about their customers. Rather than sell their products at fixed prices, companies using dynamic pricing rely on fluid prices that may change based on supply and demand and on which customer is buying or when a customer makes a purchase. For instance, a first-time customer making a purchase at an online store may pay a higher price for an item than a regular customer who shops there frequently pays for the same item.

Dynamic pricing is not a new concept. The standard practice in ancient bazaars involved merchants and customers haggling until they came to a mutually agreeable price, meaning that different customers paid different prices for the same goods. Although the modern version of dynamic pricing often involves sophisticated market research or the Internet, the goal is the same: to charge the right customer the right price at the right time. For example, travelers can use Priceline and similar Web sites to purchase last-minute airline tickets at significant discounts, such as a round-trip ticket from New York to Los Angeles for just $250 rather than for the full-fare price of $750. Travelers benefit from lower prices, and the airlines are able to generate revenue from seats that otherwise would have gone unsold.

LEADER PRICING **Leader pricing** is a technique in which a retailer marks down the customary price (i.e., the price consumers are accustomed to paying) of a popular item in an attempt to attract more customers. The company earns a much smaller profit on each unit because the markup is lower, but purchases of other merchandise by customers seeking the leader item often boost sales and profits. In other words, the incidental purchases that consumers make when shopping for the leader item boost sales revenue enough to offset a lower profit margin on the leader. Grocery stores frequently use leader pricing. For instance, during the holiday season, stores often use turkeys as a price leader, knowing that they will earn higher margins on the other items that shoppers purchase with their turkeys. Many discount warehouses, such as Costco, and supermarket chains, such as Albertsons, Kroger, and Ingles, sell gasoline as a price leader to encourage customers to make more frequent visits to their retail stores.[43]

GEOGRAPHIC PRICING Small businesses whose pricing decisions are greatly affected by the costs of shipping merchandise to customers across a wide range of geographic regions frequently employ one of the geographic pricing techniques. For these companies, freight expenses make up a substantial portion of the cost of doing business and may cut deeply into already narrow profit margins. One type of geographic pricing is **zone pricing**, in which a company sells its merchandise at different prices to customers located in different territories. For example, a manufacturer might sell at one price to customers east of the Mississippi and at another to those west of the Mississippi. A company must be able to show a legitimate basis (e.g., differences in selling or transportation costs) for the price discrimination or else risk violating Section 2 of the Clayton Act.

price lining
a technique that greatly simplifies the pricing function by pricing different products in a product line at different price points, depending on their quality, features, and cost.

dynamic (customized) pricing
a technique in which a company sets different prices for the same products and services for different customers using the information they have collected about their customers.

leader pricing
a technique that involves marking down the normal price of a popular item in an attempt to attract more customers who make incidental purchases of other items at regular prices.

zone pricing
a technique that involves setting different prices for customers located in different territories because of different transportation costs.

Ethics and Entrepreneurship

The Ethics of Dynamic Pricing

In *Casablanca*, the classic romance drama film from 1942, Ilse, the character played by Ingrid Bergman, is looking at a set of lace napkins in a shopping bazaar when she mentions that she is a friend of Rick, the film's lead character played by Humphrey Bogart. The merchant quickly replaces the original 700-franc price tag with one bearing a 100-franc price. "For special friends of Rick's, we have special discounts," he explains to Ilse. The message was clear: different prices apply to different customers.

Companies now have access to more data on their customers than at any other point in business history, and many of these businesses use that information to serve their customers better, providing them with the goods and services they need just when they need them. One offshoot of this wealth of information is dynamic or customized pricing, a system in which companies charge different prices for the same products and services for different customers using the information they have collected about their customers. The principle is the same as that in *Casablanca*: different prices apply to different customers. Movie theaters have used a simple version of dynamic pricing for years. Buy a ticket for an afternoon showing, traditionally a slower time for sales of movie tickets, and you get a lower price. Airlines have used dynamic pricing for years as well, but their systems are much more complex. (When asked about the pricing strategies of airlines, the CEO of a major airline company said, only half jokingly, "I don't understand airline pricing either!") Business travelers who fly on short notice on weekdays typically pay higher prices than those who book in advance and travel over weekends. The axiom about no two people on the same flight paying the same price for their seats has an element of truth to it.

Online game store Indie Royale offers bundles of its games using a dynamic pricing system. The company allows customers to purchase a bundle of four games normally valued at $40 for any price over $1.99. However, the more people buy at the lowest price, the faster the price rises. Customers who purchase the games at prices above the "going price" cause prices to decrease anywhere from a few cents to several dollars.

The practice of dynamic pricing has created controversy, however. Is it ethical for companies to charge different customers different prices for the same goods and services? A study by the Annenberg Public Policy Center of the University of Pennsylvania reports that 87 percent of people surveyed say that customized pricing is *not* an acceptable business practice. However, empirical evidence shows that customized pricing benefits not only the companies using it but also customers. For instance, a study by the Texas Department of Insurance reports that a credit-based dynamic pricing approach in the insurance industry has *reduced* premiums for 70 percent of customers. Managers at Allstate Insurance, one of the leading users of dynamic pricing, say that they have been able to use their massive databases of customer information to understand the actual risk levels potential customers represent and to price their insurance products more appropriately. "Now we can offer coverage to many more people and at far more competitive

prices," explains Fred Cripe, vice president for product operations. However, 40 states now have laws in place to limit the use of credit-based pricing for insurance premiums on the grounds that doing so discriminates against people with bad credit.

Dynamic pricing has stood successfully against several legal challenges. Denise Katzman filed a class-action lawsuit against retailer Victoria's Secret when she discovered that a catalog that she received offered higher prices than a nearly identical catalog the company sent to a male coworker. She alleged that the company had engaged in illegal price discrimination by charging different prices for identical items to different categories of customers. Because Victoria's Secret had sent the catalogs through the U.S. mail, Katzman claimed that the company's discriminatory pricing structure constituted mail fraud. U.S. District Court Judge Robert W. Sweet upheld the validity of Victoria's Secret's dynamic pricing policies, ruling that "offering different discounts to different catalogue customers does not constitute mail fraud under any reading of the law." On appeal, the U.S. Court of Appeals for the Second Circuit upheld Judge Sweet's decision. This case suggests that businesses can charge different customers different prices as long as the price differences are based on reasonable business practices, such as rewarding loyal customers, and do not discriminate against customers for race, gender, national origin, or some other illegal reason.

Dynamic pricing has emerged as a marketing strategy out of necessity. Entrepreneurs say that the Internet has lowered the transaction costs of doing business and moves business along at such a fast pace that the fixed pricing strategies of the past no longer work. To keep up with fluid, fast-changing markets, companies must change their prices quickly. They must be able to adapt the prices they charge their customers on a real-time basis and to charge higher prices to those customers who cost their companies more to serve.

1. Work with a team of your classmates to define the ethical issues involved in dynamic pricing.

2. What are the advantages and the disadvantages of dynamic pricing to the companies that use it? To the customers of the companies that use it?

3. According to an old proverb, "The value of a thing is what it will bring." Do you agree? Explain. Should companies be allowed to engage in dynamic pricing?

4. If you owned your own business and had the information required to engage in dynamic pricing, would you do so? Explain.

Sources: Based on Mark Brown, "Indie Royale Bundle Starts a Price War between the Stingy and the Wealthy," Wired, October 26, 2011, http://www.wired.co.uk/news/archive/2011-10/26/indie-royale-bundle; Robert M. Weiss and Ajay K. Mehrotra, "Online Dynamic Pricing: Efficiency, Equity, and the Future of E-Commerce," *Virginia Journal of Law and Technology* 6, no. 2 (Summer 2001): 7; Matthew Maier, "Finding Riches in a Mine of Credit Data," *Business 2.0*, October 2005, pp. 72–74; and Peter Coffee, "More 'Dynamic Pricing' Is on the Way," *eWeek*, September 2002, http://www.eweek.com/article2/0,1759,1011178,00.asp.

Another variation of geographic pricing is uniform **delivered pricing**, a technique in which a firm charges all of its customers the same price regardless of their location, even though the cost of selling or transporting merchandise varies. The firm calculates the proper freight charges for each region and combines them into a uniform fee. The result is that local customers subsidize the company's charges for shipping merchandise to distant customers.

A final variation of geographic pricing is **F.O.B. factory**, in which the small company sells its merchandise to customers on the condition that they pay all shipping costs. In this way, the company can set a uniform price for its product and let each customer cover the freight costs.

DISCOUNTS Many small business managers use **discounts (markdowns)**—reductions from normal list prices—to move stale, outdated, damaged, or slow-moving merchandise. A seasonal discount is a price reduction designed to encourage shoppers to purchase merchandise before an upcoming season. For instance, many retail clothiers offer special sales on winter coats in midsummer. Many retailers also offer after-Christmas discounts to make room for their spring merchandise. Some firms grant purchase discounts to special groups of customers, such as senior citizens or students, to establish a faithful clientele and to generate repeat business.

As tempting as discounts are to businesses when sales are slow, they carry risks. Companies that frequently resort to discounts may ruin their reputation for superior quality and service, thereby diluting the value of their brand and image in the marketplace. Frequent discounting sends customers the message that a company's regular prices are too high and that they should wait for the next sale to make a purchase. As many retailers and restaurants learned from the last recession, weaning customers off of discounts can be difficult; the climb back to "normal" pricing can be long and arduous. One less visible way for companies to offer discounts is to enroll customers in a loyalty program that entitles them to "free" benefits and earned discounts. Loyalty programs, such as those at supermarkets, pet stores, and bookstores, not only encourage shoppers to return but also provide businesses with meaningful data on customers' buying habits, allowing them to decipher meaningful patterns and trends. Belk, a family-owned chain of department stores with more than 300 locations in 16 southern states, offers rewards to customers who make purchases on the store-branded credit card. For every $400 customers spend, they receive $10 in Belk Reward Dollars they can use for future purchases. Researchers at Southern Methodist University have determined the effectiveness of another tool that companies can use to avoid diluting customers' perceptions of their products and services: the time-limited discount ("$150 regular price; $120 sale price *for three days only*").[44]

delivered pricing
a technique in which a company charges all customers the same price regardless of their locations and different transportation costs.

F.O.B. factory
a pricing method in which a company sells merchandise to customers on the condition that they pay all shipping costs.

discounts (markdowns)
reductions from normal list prices.

magicinfoto/Shutterstock

You Be the Consultant

A Good Deal—Or Not?

Rachel Brown, owner of Need A Cake, a small bakery in Woodley, England, wanted to increase sales of specialty cupcakes and decided to run a discount coupon on the daily deal site Groupon. Brown, who has owned Need A Cake for 25 years, offered customers a dozen cupcakes for just £6.50, a 75 percent discount off of the regular £26 price, and expected a few dozen orders to come in. Instead, Brown received a tidal wave of orders that overwhelmed the small bakery and almost cost her the entire business. More than 8,500 orders poured in, and Brown had to ramp up production and hire 25 temporary employees at a cost of£12,500 to turn out 102,000 cupcakes a month, a significant increase from the usual 100 cupcakes a month. After paying Groupon a fee that amounted to 62 percent of the discounted price, Need A Cake generated only £2.50 per order—not even enough to cover the cost of making the cupcakes. The deal turned out not to be a good one for Brown and her bakery, wiping out her profits for the entire year. "Without doubt, it's the worst ever business decision I have made," says Brown. "It's been an absolute nightmare."

When sales are slow, business owners are tempted to reduce prices to get customers in the front door and move merchandise, and daily deal sites such as Groupon, LivingSocial, and others that offer shoppers coupons that yield significant discounts at local businesses are ready to promote the deal (Think social media meets coupons). To promote a small company's special, Groupon, which claims that it has more than 60 million subscribers, collects at least 50 percent of the discounted price (which is usually at least 50 percent of an item's normal price) for each coupon it sells, meaning that business owners have to be extremely careful concerning the deals and discounts they offer. As Brown learned, daily deal sites have the power to drive significant volumes of traffic to a business, but making a profit on the increased volume can be a challenge. A study by the Jesse H. Jones Graduate School of Business at Rice University reports that one-third of businesses lose money on Groupon discount deals. In addition, 40 percent of companies that have conducted deals with Groupon say that they will not conduct another social coupon promotion. Given the nature of daily discount sites such as Groupon, the customers that companies attract with the discount coupons tend to be bargain shoppers and deal seekers who are looking for low prices. "Groupon offers can be great for small businesses, but business owners need to be very careful when they sign up to work with sites like this," says Chris Moriarity of the Chartered Institute of Marketing.

"Our life changed after Groupon," says Michele Casadei Massari, owner of Piccolo Café, a restaurant with two locations in Manhattan. "We would do it again." Massari recently posted a limited time Groupon offer for a $14 meal at 50 percent off and sold 1,142 coupons in just 24 hours. "You don't make money on the deal," he admits, "but in the end we broke even because people spend more than the coupon amount. They've been ordering about double the $14 amount." In addition, Piccolo Café benefits in the long run because 80 percent of Groupon customers "come back without a coupon," says Massari. In fact, creating repeat customers is a common goal among business that use daily deal sites to offer discounts.

What steps can business owners take to ensure that they reap the benefits of promotions on Groupon and other daily deal sites and avoid the pitfalls?

- ***Emphasize customer service.*** The best way to create repeat customers is to provide them with excellent service and make sure that their first experience with your company is a positive one.

- ***Be ready for a surge in business.*** Groupon offers can create significant increases in the volume of business for companies in a short period of time. Make sure that you have the staff, cash, and raw materials ready to handle it. "If people come in the door and get frustrated by long lines, it's a total backfire," says Brendan Shapiro, owner of outdoor store Potomac River Running and a regular Groupon user.

- ***Limit your promotion.*** To avoid nasty surprises, smart Groupon users place time and quantity limits and blackout dates on their offers.

- ***Run specials on overstocked merchandise or underutilized services.*** A Groupon special can be a useful tool for selling slow-moving merchandise.

- ***Know your costs and the revenue that each coupon will generate.*** The typical Groupon sale generates only 25 percent of the normal revenue that a company earns, and this makes earning a profit challenging. Two-thirds of companies make money on their Groupon offers; your goal is to be one of them.

- ***View your Groupon offer as a marketing expense.*** Heather Speizman, owner of Bottles and Brushes, an art studio in Mount Pleasant, South Carolina, offered a $15 Groupon for an art class normally priced at $35 to generate buzz about a new location she was opening in nearby Summerville. The promotion worked, generating lots of buzz for her new store. "It was a great experiment in social media at its best," she says.

- ***Track the results.*** The only way to determine whether a Groupon deal was successful is to monitor the results it produces. How many coupons did customers purchase? How many did they redeem? What is the average sale for customers who used the coupons? What proportion of them bought additional products or services? How many of them become repeat customers?

You Be the Consultant (*continued*)

1. Use the Internet to find examples of companies that have experienced great success with and great failure with Groupon. What lessons can you draw from them?

2. Work with a group of your classmates to brainstorm local businesses that could benefit from an offer on a daily deal site such as Groupon. What deal do you suggest the business offer?

Sources: Based on Tim Donnelly, "How Groupon Can Boost Your Company's Exposure," *Inc.*, January 24, 2011, http://www.inc.com/guides/201101/how-groupon-works-for-small-businesses.html; Deborah Arthurs, "My Groupon Nightmare! Baker Who Sells 100 Cakes a Month Is Forced to Make 102,000 after Bargain Hunters Flock to Her 75% Off Web Deal," *Mail Online*, November 21, 2011, http://www.dailymail.co.uk/femail/article-2064208/Groupon-baker-nearly-ruined-bargain-hunters-flock-75-web-deal.html; Courtney Rubin, "Study: One-Third of Businesses Don't Profit from Groupon Deal," *Inc.*, October 2010, http://www.inc.com/topic/utpal%20dholakia; Glenn Collins, "Wise for Some Restaurants, Coupons Are a Drain for Others," *New York Times*, April 12, 2011, http://www.nytimes.com/2011/04/13/dining/13discounts.html?pagewanted=all; Geoff Williams, "How to Avoid a Groupon Disaster," *AOL Small Business*, December 2, 2010, http://smallbusiness.aol.com/2010/12/02/how-to-avoid-a-groupon-disaster; Carla Dewing, "Will Groupon Really Boost Your Local Business?," *Social Media Examiner*, June 2, 2011, http://www.socialmediaexaminer.com/will-groupon-really-boost-your-local-business; Susan Payton, "What's Wrong with Groupon (and How to Succeed Anyway)," *Small Business Trends*, April 22, 2011, http://smallbiztrends.com/2011/04/whats-wrong-with-groupon.html; and Kevin Eklund, "Small Business Owner Success Tips for Using Daily Deal Sites Like Groupon," *ToMuse*, 2010, http://tomuse.com/daily-deal-sites-groupon-tips-small-business-owners.

Multiple unit pricing is a promotional technique that offers customers discounts if they purchase in quantity. Many products, especially those with relatively low unit value, are sold using multiple pricing. For example, instead of selling an item for 50 cents, a small company might offer five for $2.

multiple unit pricing
a technique offering customers discounts if they purchase in quantity.

BUNDLING Many small businesses have discovered the marketing benefits of **bundling**, grouping together several products or services or both into a package that offers customers extra value at a special price. Bundling is another way for companies to offer customers discounts without damaging their reputations. As more consumers embrace e-books, publishers are using a bundling price strategy to generate sales and to promote up-and-coming authors. RosettaBooks LLC recently offered a bundled price of $9.99 for two books by science-fiction writer Richard Matheson that the publisher normally prices at $8.99 each. "By bundling titles at a discount, we're raising their visibility and making them more price attractive," says CEO Arthur Klebanoff.[45] Fast-food outlets often bundle items into "meal deals" that customers can purchase at lower prices than if they bought the items separately. Even upscale restaurants use bundled pricing; at New York City's Tony Per Se, diners can choose between two nine-course prix fixe chef's tasting menus for $295 per person.

bundling
grouping together several products or services or both into a package that offers customers extra value at a special price.

OPTIONAL-PRODUCT PRICING **Optional-product pricing** involves selling the base product for one price but selling the options or accessories for it at a much higher markup. Automobiles are often sold at a base price with each option priced separately. In some cases, the car is sold with some of the options "bundled" together, as explained previously.

optional-product pricing
a technique that involves selling the base product for one price but selling the options or accessories for it at a much higher markup.

ENTREPRENEURIAL PROFILE: Amish Backyard Structures Amish Backyard Structures, a small company in tiny Oxford, Pennsylvania, that makes children's playhouses, sheds, barns, gazebos, and lawn furniture, uses an optional-product pricing strategy. The company's playhouses are handcrafted from top-quality materials, range in size from 6 by 8 feet to 10 by 20 feet, and come in designs that resemble Cape Cod cottages and Victorian mansions. Parents can choose to customize their children's playhouses with a variety of options that include heart-shaped windows, chimneys, porch swings, fully finished interiors, and playhouse furniture, including wooden sink and stove combinations and refrigerators. ∎

CAPTIVE-PRODUCT PRICING **Captive-product pricing** is a pricing strategy in which the base product is not functional without the appropriate accessory. King Gillette, the founder of Gillette, taught the business world that the real money is not in selling the razor (the product) but in selling the blades (the accessory)! Manufacturers of electronic games also rely on captive-product pricing, earning lower margins on the game consoles and substantially higher margins on the game cartridges they sell.

captive-product pricing
a technique that involves selling a product for a low price and charging a higher price for the accessories that accompany it.

BY-PRODUCT PRICING **By-product pricing** is a technique in which the revenues from the sale of by-products allow a company to be more competitive in its pricing of the main product. For years, sawmills saw the bark from the trees they processed as a nuisance, something they had to discard.

by-product pricing
a technique in which a company uses the revenues from the sale of by-products to be more competitive in pricing the main product.

Now it is packaged and sold to gardeners who use the bark chips for ground cover. Zoos across the globe offer one of the most creative examples of by-product pricing, packaging once worthless exotic animal droppings and marketing it as fertilizer under the clever name "Zoo Doo."

SUGGESTED RETAIL PRICES Many manufacturers print suggested retail prices on their products or include them on invoices or in wholesale catalogs. Small business owners frequently follow these suggested retail prices because this eliminates the need to make a pricing decision. Nonetheless, following prices established by a distant manufacturer may create problems for a small company. For example, a men's clothing store may try to create a high-quality, exclusive image through a prestige pricing policy, but manufacturers may suggest prices that are incompatible with the company's image. Another danger of accepting the manufacturer's suggested price is that it does not take into consideration a small company's cost structure or competitive situation. A recent U.S. Supreme Court decision overturned a nearly 100-year-old ruling and allows manufacturers to set and enforce minimum prices that retailers can charge for the manufacturer's products as long as doing so does not reduce competition. Several states and some members of Congress are considering passing new antitrust laws in an attempt to preempt the court's decision.

FOLLOW-THE-LEADER PRICING Some small companies make no effort to be price leaders in their immediate geographic areas and simply follow the prices that their competitors establish. Entrepreneurs should monitor their competitors' pricing policies and individual prices by reviewing their advertisements or by hiring part-time or full-time comparison shoppers. However, some retailers use this information to establish me-too pricing policies, which eradicate any opportunity to create a special price image for their businesses. Although many retailers must match competitors' prices on identical items, maintaining a follow-the-leader pricing policy may not be healthy for a small business because it robs the company of the opportunity to create a distinctive image in its customers' eyes.

The underlying forces that dictate how a business prices its goods or services vary across industries. The next three sections investigate pricing techniques used in retailing, manufacturing, and service businesses.

Pricing Strategies and Methods for Retailers

LO3A

Explain the pricing methods and strategies for retailers.

As customers have become more price conscious, retailers have changed their pricing strategies to emphasize value. This value–price relationship allows for a wide variety of highly creative pricing and marketing practices. As discussed previously, delivering high levels of recognized value in products and services is one key to retail customer loyalty.

Markup

The basic premise of a successful business operation is selling a good or service for more than it costs to produce or provide. The difference between the cost of a product or service and its selling price is called **markup (or markon)**. Markup can be expressed in dollars or as a percentage of either cost or selling price:

markup (markon)
the difference between the cost of a product or service and its selling price.

$$\text{Dollar markup} = \text{Retail price} - \text{Cost of the merchandise}$$

$$\text{Percentage (of retail price) markup} = \frac{\text{Dollar markup}}{\text{Retail price}}$$

$$\text{Percentage (of cost) markup} = \frac{\text{Dollar markup}}{\text{Cost of unit}}$$

For example, if a shirt costs $14, and a retailer plans to sell it for $30, the markup would be as follows:

$$\text{Dollar markup} = \$30 - \$14 = \$16$$

$$\text{Percentage (of retail price) markup} = \frac{\$16}{\$30} = 53.3\%$$

$$\text{Percentage (of cost) markup} = \frac{\$16}{\$14} = 114.3\%$$

Component	Kohl's Jeans	True Religion's Phantom Jeans
Denim fabric – 3.25 yards	$ 4.75	$ 31.05
Trim – buttons, rivets, zipper, labels, and tags	$ 0.80	$ 3.32
Labor – cutting, sewing, marking, and grading	$ 0.66	$ 11.65
Other expenses, including shipping and tariffs, if applicable*	$ 2.72	$ .70
Wash/Finish (Makes jeans look broken in)	$ 0.58	$ 11.00
Manufacturer's profit	$ 1.42	$ 9.34
Total Cost	**$10.93**	**$ 67.06**
Final Selling Price	**$22.00**	**$310.00**
Dollar Markup = Price − Cost	**$11.07**	**$242.94**
Percentage (of cost) markup	**101.3%**	**362.0%**

FIGURE 10.3

Costs and Markup on True Religion's Phantom Jeans

Sources: Based on Jacob Goldstein, "Global Poverty and the Cost of a Pair of Jeans," *National Public Radio*, March 3, 2010; "Anatomy of Exploitation," Institute for Global Labour and Human Rights, July 25, 2007; Christina Binkley, "How Can Jeans Cost $300?" *Wall Street Journal*, July 7, 2011, pp. D1–D2.

*Tariff depends on country in which jeans are manufactured

The cost of merchandise used in computing markup includes not only the wholesale price of the merchandise but also any other costs (e.g., selling or transportation charges) that the retailer incurs and a profit minus any discounts (quantity, cash) that the wholesaler offers. Markups vary across industries, but in the fashion clothing business, a markup (of cost) of about 140 percent is common. However, some brands command much higher markups. For instance, True Religion's Phantom jeans generate an impressive 362 percent markup of cost (see Figure 10.3).

Once entrepreneurs create a financial plan, including sales estimates and anticipated expenses, they can compute their companies' initial markup. The initial markup is the *average* markup required on all merchandise to cover the cost of the items, all incidental expenses, and a reasonable profit:

$$\text{Initial dollar markup} = \frac{\text{Operating expenses + Reductions + Profit}}{\text{Net sales + Reductions}}$$

where operating expenses include the cost of doing business, such as rent, utilities, and depreciation, and reductions include employee and customer discounts, markdowns, special sales, and the cost of stock-outs.

For example, if a small retailer forecasts sales of $980,000, operating expenses of $544,000, and $24,000 in reductions and he or she establishes a target profit of $58,000, the initial markup (of retail price) percentage is calculated as follows:

$$\text{Initial markup percentage} = \frac{544,000 + 24,000 + 58,000}{980,000 + 24,000} = 62\%$$

Any item in the store that carries a markup (of retail price) of at least 62 percent covers costs and meets the owner's profit objective. Any item that has a markup of less than 62 percent reduces the company's net income.

Once an entrepreneur determines the initial percentage markup, he or she can compute the appropriate retail price using the following formula:

$$\text{Retail Price} = \frac{\text{Dollar cost}}{(1 - \text{Percentage of retail price markup})}$$

For instance, applying the 62 percent markup to an item that cost the retailer $17.00 gives the following result:

$$\text{Retail price} = \frac{\$17.00}{(1 - .62)} = \$44.74$$

The owner establishes a retail price of $44.74 for this item using a 62 percent (of retail price) markup.

FIGURE 10.4

The Mathematics of Markups and Markdowns

The Sale Rack Shuffle

Have you ever purchased an item of clothing at a significant discount from the sale rack and then wondered if the store actually made any profit on the item? Here is how the markup and mark down process typically works:

1. Clothing company makes dress at a cost of $50.
2. Sells dress to retailer at a wholesale cost of $80.
3. Retailer marks up dress to $200 (60 percent markup (of price).
4. If unsold after eight to twelve weeks, dress is marked down by 25 percent to $150.
5. If dress still does not sell, it is marked down further until it does. Clothing company and retailer negotiate on how to share the cost of the markdown.

Finally, retailers must verify that the retail price they have calculated is consistent with their companies' image. Will it cover costs and generate the desired profit? Is the final price in line with the company's strategy? Is it within an acceptable price range? How does it compare to the prices charged by competitors? And, perhaps most important, are customers willing and able to pay this price? Figure 10.4 explains the mathematics of markups—and markdowns—at the retail level.

Pricing Concepts for Manufacturers

LO3B

Explain the pricing methods and strategies for manufacturers.

cost-plus pricing
a pricing technique in which a manufacturer establishes a price that covers the cost of direct materials, direct labor, factory overhead, selling and administrative costs, and a desired profit margin.

For manufacturers, the pricing decision requires the support of accurate, timely accounting records. The most commonly used pricing technique for manufacturers is **cost-plus pricing**. Using this method, a manufacturer establishes a price that is composed of direct materials, direct labor, factory overhead, selling and administrative costs, plus a desired profit margin. Figure 10.5 illustrates the cost-plus pricing components.

The main advantage of the cost-plus pricing method is its simplicity. Given the proper cost accounting data, computing a product's final selling price is relatively easy. In addition, because they add a profit onto the top of their companies' costs, manufacturers are likely to achieve their desired profit margins. This process, however, does not encourage the manufacturers to use their resources efficiently. Even if the company fails to employ its resources in the most effective manner, it still earns a profit, and thus there is no motivation to conserve resources in the manufacturing process. Finally, because manufacturers' cost structures vary so greatly, cost-plus pricing fails to consider the competition (and market forces) sufficiently. Despite its drawbacks, the cost-plus method of establishing prices remains popular in industries such as construction and printing.

Direct Costing and Pricing

One requisite for a successful pricing policy in manufacturing is a reliable cost accounting system that can generate timely reports to determine the costs of processing raw materials into

FIGURE 10.5

Cost-Plus Pricing Components

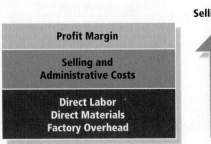

Selling Price

| Profit Margin |
| Selling and Administrative Costs |
| Direct Labor Direct Materials Factory Overhead |

finished goods. The traditional method of product costing is called **absorption costing** because all manufacturing and overhead costs are absorbed into a finished product's total cost. Absorption costing includes direct materials, direct labor, plus a portion of fixed and variable factory overhead in each unit manufactured. Full absorption financial statements are used in published annual reports and in tax reports and are very useful in performing financial analysis. However, full absorption statements are of little help to manufacturers when determining prices or the impact of price changes.

A more useful technique for managerial decision making is **variable (direct) costing**, in which the cost of the products manufactured includes only those costs that vary directly with the quantity produced. In other words, variable costing encompasses direct materials, direct labor, and factory overhead costs that vary with the level of the company's output of finished goods. Factory overhead costs that are fixed (rent, depreciation, and insurance) are *not* included in the costs of finished items. Instead, they are considered to be expenses of the period.

A manufacturer's goal when establishing prices is to discover the combination of selling price and sales volume that covers the variable costs of producing a product and contributes toward covering fixed costs and earning a profit. Full-absorption costing clouds the true relationships among price, volume, and costs by including fixed expenses in unit cost. Direct costing, however, yields a constant unit cost for the product no matter what volume of production. The result is a clearer picture of the relationship among price, volume, and costs.

The starting point for establishing product prices is the direct cost income statement. As Table 10.1 indicates, the direct cost statement yields the same net income as does the full-absorption income statement. The only difference between the two statements is the format. The full-absorption statement allocates costs such as advertising, rent, and utilities according to the activity that caused them, but the direct cost income statement separates expenses into their fixed and variable components. Fixed expenses remain constant regardless of the production level, but variable expenses fluctuate according to production volume.

When variable costs are subtracted from total revenues, the result is the manufacturer's **contribution margin**—the amount remaining that contributes to covering fixed expenses and earning a profit. Expressing this contribution margin as a percentage of total revenue yields the company's contribution percentage. Computing the contribution percentage is a critical step in establishing prices through the direct costing method. This manufacturer's contribution margin percentage is 36.5 percent, which is calculated as follows:

$$\text{Contribution percentage} = 1 - \frac{\text{Variable expenses}}{\text{Revenues}}$$

$$= 1 - \frac{\$502{,}000}{\$790{,}000} = 36.5\%$$

Computing the Break-Even Selling Price

The manufacturer's contribution percentage tells what portion of total revenues remains after covering variable costs to contribute toward meeting fixed expenses and earning a profit. This manufacturer's contribution percentage is 36.5 percent, which means that variable costs absorb 63.5 percent of total revenue. In other words, variable costs make up 63.5 percent ($1.00 - 0.365 = 0.635$) of the product's selling price. Suppose that this manufacturer's variable costs include the following:

Material	$2.08/unit
Direct labor	$4.12/unit
Variable factory overhead	$0.78/unit
Total variable cost	$6.98/unit

The minimum price at which the manufacturer would sell the item for is $6.98. Any price below this would not cover variable costs. To compute the break-even selling price for this product, we find the selling price using the following equation:

$$\text{Break-even selling price} = \frac{\text{Profit} + (\text{Variable cost per unit} \times \text{Quantity produced}) + \text{Total fixed cost}}{\text{Quantity produced}}$$

absorption costing
the traditional method of product costing in which all manufacturing and overhead costs are absorbed into the product's total cost.

variable (direct) costing
a method of product costing that includes in the product's cost only those costs that vary directly with the quantity produced.

contribution margin
the amount left over out of a dollar of sales after variable expenses are paid that contributes to covering fixed expenses and earning a profit.

TABLE 10.1 Full-Absorption versus Direct-Cost Income Statement

Full-Absorption Income Statement

Sales revenue		$790,000
Cost of goods sold		
Materials	250,500	
Direct labor	190,200	
Factory overhead	120,200	560,900
Gross profit		$229,100
Operating expenses		
General and administrative	66,100	
Selling	112,000	
Other	11,000	
Total operating expenses		189,100
Net income (before taxes)		$ 40,000

Direct-Cost Income Statement

Sales revenue (100%)		$790,000
Variable costs		
Materials	250,500	
Direct labor	190,200	
Variable factory overhead	13,200	
Variable selling expenses	48,100	
Total variable costs (63.5%)		502,000
Contribution margin (36.5%)		288,000
Fixed costs		
Fixed factory overhead	107,000	
Fixed selling expenses	63,900	
General and administrative	66,100	
Other fixed expenses	11,000	
Total fixed expenses (31.4%)		248,000
Net income (before taxes) (5.1%)		$ 40,000

To break even, the manufacturer assumes $0 profit. Suppose that his plans are to produce 50,000 units of the product and that fixed costs will be $110,000. The break-even selling price is as follows:

$$\text{Break-even selling price} = \frac{\$0 + (\$6.98 \times 50,000 \text{ units}) + \$110,000}{50,000 \text{ units}}$$

$$= \frac{\$459,000}{50,000 \text{ units}}$$

$$= \$9.18/\text{unit}$$

Thus, $2.20 ($9.18/unit − $6.98/unit) of the $9.18 break-even price contributes to meeting fixed production costs. But suppose the manufacturer wants to earn a $50,000 profit. Then the selling price is calculated as follows:

$$\text{Selling price} = \frac{\$50,000 + (\$6.98/\text{unit} \times 50,000 \text{ units}) + \$110,000}{50,000 \text{ units}}$$

$$= \frac{\$509,000}{50,000 \text{ units}}$$

$$= \$10.18/\text{unit}$$

Now the manufacturer must decide whether customers will purchase 50,000 units at $10.18. If not, he or she must decide either to produce a different, more profitable product or to lower the selling price by lowering either its cost or its profit target. Any price above $9.18 will generate some profit although less than that desired. In the short run, the manufacturer could sell the product for less than $9.18 if competitive factors dictate but *not* below $6.98 because a price below $6.98 would not cover the variable cost of production.

Because the manufacturer's capacity in the short run is fixed, pricing decisions should be aimed at employing these resources most efficiently. The fixed costs of operating the plant cannot be avoided, and the variable costs can be eliminated only if the firm ceases offering the product. Therefore, the selling price must be at least equal to the variable costs (per unit) of making the product. Any price above this amount contributes to covering fixed costs and providing a reasonable profit.

Of course, over the long run, a manufacturer cannot sell below total costs and continue to survive. The final selling price must cover total product cost—both fixed and variable—and generate a reasonable profit.

Hands On... How To

Calculate Your Company's Pocket Price Band

When entrepreneurs make pricing decisions, they usually look at the retail price or the invoice price they charge. Doing so, however, may be misleading if the company offers significant "off-invoice" discounts, such as cash discounts for paying early, quantity discounts for large purchases, special promotional discounts, and others. These invoice leakages mean that a business is getting less—sometimes far less—than the retail or invoice price listed. In some cases, a company's pocket price, the price it receives for a product or a service after deducting all discounts and purchase incentives, is far below the listed retail or invoice price. The impact of these discounts can be significant. Research by the consulting firm McKinsey and Company shows that a decrease of 1 percent in a typical company's average prices will reduce its operating profits by 8 percent if all other factors remain constant.

How are discounts affecting your business? To find out, you must estimate your company's pocket price waterfall and its pocket price band. The pocket price waterfall starts with a company's invoice or retail price on the far left of the diagram and then shows how much every discount or incentive the company offers its customers reduces that price. In the example in Figure 1, this small manufacturer offers a cash discount for early payment that shaves 2.0 percent off of the retail price, a 3.5 percent discount for companies whose purchases exceed a particular volume, a cooperative advertising program (in which it splits the cost of advertising its products with retailers) that amounts to 4.4 percent, and periodic promotional discounts to move products that average 10.8 percent. Other discounts the company offered customers further reduced its pocket price. In the end, the company's average pocket price is 77.2 percent of the listed invoice price (see Figure 1).

Not every customer qualifies for every discount, however. The type and the amount of the discount vary from one customer to another; the pocket prices they pay can vary a good deal. Therefore, it is important to estimate the width of the company's pocket price band, which shows the percentage of sales that each pocket price (shown as a percentage of the listed invoice or retail price) accounts for (see Figure 2). In this

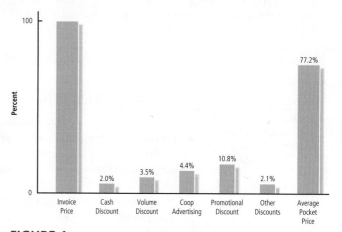

FIGURE 1

example, pocket prices that are 90 percent or more of the company's invoice price account for just 28.3 percent of its total revenue. Conversely, pocket prices that are 80 percent or less of its invoice price make up 46.2 percent of its total revenue. The final step in the process is to identify the individual customers that make up each segment of the company's pocket price band. When one manufacturer analyzed its pocket price band, managers discovered that sales to 20 percent of its customers had slipped below its break-even point, causing the company to lose money on sales to those customers. To restore profitability, managers raised prices selectively and lowered their costs by reducing the frequency of deliveries and encouraging customers to place orders online.

A wide pocket price band is not necessarily bad. It simply shows that some customers generate much higher pocket prices than others. When a band is wide, small changes in its shape can produce big results for a company. If an entrepreneur can increase sales at the upper end of the band while reducing or

(continued)

Hands On... How To (continued)

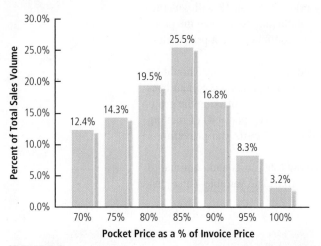

FIGURE 2

When one lighting company calculated its pocket price band, managers were surprised at its width. Once managers realized how big a dent discounts were putting in its revenues and profits, they worked with the sales force to realign the company's discount structure. Some of the company's smallest accounts had been getting the largest discounts despite their small volume of purchases. Managers also focused on boosting sales to those accounts that were producing the highest pocket prices. These changes resulted in the company's average pocket price rising by 3.8 percent and its profits climbing 51 percent!

Discounts tend to work their way into a company's pricing structure gradually over time, often one transaction at a time, especially if an entrepreneur gives sales representatives latitude to negotiate prices with customers. Few companies make the effort to track these discounts, and, as a result, few companies realize the impact that discounts have on their profitability. By monitoring their companies' pocket price waterfall and the resulting pocket price band, entrepreneurs can improve significantly the revenue and the profits they generate.

even dropping altogether those at the lower end of the band, the company's revenues and profits will climb. If a company's price band is narrow, an entrepreneur has less room to maneuver prices, changing the shape of the band is more difficult, and any changes the entrepreneur can make tend to have less impact on the company's sales and revenues.

Sources: Michael V. Marn, Eric V. Roegner, and Craig C. Zawada, "The Power of Pricing," *McKinsey Quarterly,* no. 1, 2003, http://www.mckinseyquarterly.com; and Cheri N. Eyink, Michael V. Marn, and Stephen C. Moss, "Pricing in an Inflationary Downturn," *McKinsey Quarterly,* September 2008, http://www.mckinseyquarterly .com/Pricing_in_a_downturn_2189.

LO3C

Explain the pricing methods and strategies for service firms.

Pricing Strategies and Methods for Service Firms

Service businesses must establish their prices on the basis of the materials used to provide the service, the labor employed, an allowance for overhead, and a profit. As in a manufacturing operation, a service business must have a reliable, accurate accounting system to keep a tally of the total costs of providing the service. Most service firms base their prices on an hourly rate, usually the actual number of hours required to perform the service. Some companies, however, base their fees on a standard number of hours, determined by the average number of hours needed to perform the service. For most firms, labor and materials make up the largest portion of the cost of the service. To establish a reasonable, profitable price for service, small business owners must know the cost of materials, direct labor, and overhead for each unit of service they provide. Using these basic cost data and a desired profit margin, an owner of a small service firm can determine the appropriate price for the service.

Consider a simple example for pricing a common service—computer repair. Ned's Computer Repair Shop uses the direct costing method to prepare an income statement for exercising managerial control (see Table 10.2).

Ned estimates that he and his employees spent about 9,250 hours in the actual production of computer repair service. Therefore, total cost per productive hour for Ned's Computer Repair Shop comes to the following:

$$\frac{\$104,000 + \$68,000}{9,250 \text{ hours}} = \$18.59/\text{hour}$$

Now Ned must add in an amount for his desired profit. He expects a net operating profit of 18 percent on sales. To compute the final price, he uses the following equation:

$$\text{Price Total cost per hour} = \text{productive hour} \div (1 - \text{net profit target as \% of sales})$$

$$= \$18.59 \div (1 - .18)$$

$$= \$22.68/\text{hour}$$

TABLE 10.2 Direct-Cost Income Statement, Ned's Computer Repair Shop

Sales revenue		$199,000
Variable expenses		
Labor	52,000	
Materials	40,500	
Variable factory overhead	11,500	
Total variable expenses		104,000
Fixed expenses		
Rent	2,500	
Salaries	38,500	
Fixed overhead	27,000	
Total fixed expenses		68,000
Net income		$ 27,000

A price of $22.68 per hour will cover Ned's costs and generate the desired profit. Smart service shop owners compute their cost per production hour at regular intervals throughout the year. Rapidly rising labor costs and material prices dictate that an entrepreneur calculate the company's price per hour even more frequently. As in the case of the retailer and the manufacturer, Ned must evaluate the pricing policies of competitors and decide whether his price is consistent with his company's image.

Of course, the price of $22.68 per hour assumes that each job requires the same amount of materials. If this is not a valid assumption, Ned must recalculate the price per hour *without* including the cost of materials:

$$\text{Cost per productive hour} = \frac{\$172,000 - \$40,500}{9,250 \text{ hours}}$$

$$= \$14.22/\text{hour}$$

Adding in the desired 18 percent net operating profit on sales gives the following:

$$\text{Price per hour} = \$14.22/\text{hour} \div (1.00 - 0.18)$$

$$= \$17.34/\text{hour}$$

Under these conditions, Ned would charge $17.34 per hour plus the actual cost of materials used and any markup on the cost of material. A repair job that takes four hours to complete would have the following price:

Cost of service (4 hours × $17.34/hour)	$ 69.36
Cost of materials	$ 41.00
Markup on materials (60%)	$ 24.60
Total price	$134.96

Because services are intangible, their pricing offers more flexibility than do tangible products. One danger that entrepreneurs face is pricing their services too low because prospective customers' perceptions of a service are heavily influenced by its price. In other words, establishing a low price for a service may actually harm a service company's sales. For service companies in particular, the right price reflects both the company's cost of providing the service and the customers' perceived value of the service.

The Impact of Credit on Pricing

LO4

Describe the impact of credit on pricing.

Consumers crave convenience when they shop, and one of the most common conveniences they demand is the ability to purchase goods and services on credit. Small businesses that fail to offer credit to their customers lose sales to competitors who do. However, companies that sell on credit incur additional expenses for offering this convenience. Small companies have three options for selling to customers on credit: credit cards, installment credit, and trade credit.

Credit Cards

Consumers in the United States hold 1.4 billion credit cards; in fact, the average credit card holder in the United States has 7.7 cards. Shoppers use credit cards to make 20 billion transactions a year that account for $2.4 trillion worth of goods and services annually—more than $76,000 in sales per second. The average shopper uses a credit card 119 times per year and charges on average $88 in goods and services.[46] The message is clear: customers expect to make purchases with credit cards, and small companies that fail to accept credit cards run the risk of losing sales to competitors who do. Research shows that customers who use credit cards make purchases that are 112 percent higher than if they had used cash.[47] In addition, surveys show that customers rate businesses offering credit options higher on key performance measures such as reputation, reliability, and service.[48] In short, accepting credit cards broadens a small company's customer base and closes sales that it would normally lose if customers had to pay in cash.

Companies that accept credit cards incur additional expenses for offering this convenience, however. Businesses must pay to use the system, typically 1 to 6 percent of the total credit card charge, which they must factor into the prices of their products or services. They also pay a transaction fee of 5 to 25 cents per charge. (The average fee is 10 cents per transaction.) Given customer expectations, small businesses cannot afford to drop major cards, even when credit card companies raise the fees that merchants must pay. Fees operate on a multistep process (see Figure 10.6). On a typical $100 credit card purchase that a customer makes, the bank that issued the customer's card receives $1.80, an amount that consists of a 1.70 percent processing fee called the **interchange fee**, the fee that banks collect from retailers whenever customers use a credit or a debit card to pay for a purchase, and a 10-cent flat transaction fee. The retailer's bank, called the processing bank, receives a processing fee of 0.4 percent of the purchase amount (or 40 cents in this example), leaving the retailer with $97.80. Before it can accept credit cards, a business must obtain merchant status from either a bank or an independent sales organization.

Credit card processing fees, commonly known as "swipe fees," cost merchants $50 billion per year, and small businesses typically pay higher credit card processing fees than their larger

interchange fee
the fee that banks collect from retailers whenever customers use a credit or a debit card to pay for a purchase.

FIGURE 10.6

How a Typical Credit Card Transaction Works

Source: Adapted from "Credit Cards," United States Government Accounting Office, September 2006, 99. 73–74.

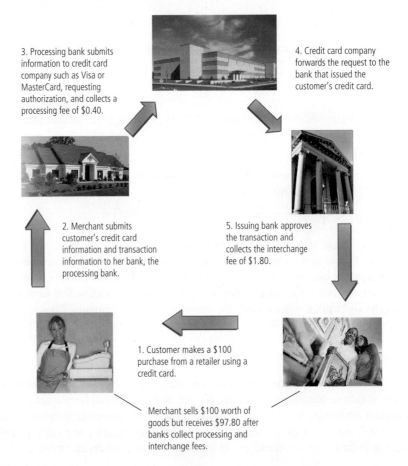

3. Processing bank submits information to credit card company such as Visa or MasterCard, requesting authorization, and collects a processing fee of $0.40.

4. Credit card company forwards the request to the bank that issued the customer's credit card.

2. Merchant submits customer's credit card information and transaction information to her bank, the processing bank.

5. Issuing bank approves the transaction and collects the interchange fee of $1.80.

1. Customer makes a $100 purchase from a retailer using a credit card.

Merchant sells $100 worth of goods but receives $97.80 after banks collect processing and interchange fees.

counterparts.[49] These fees, especially on small purchases, can wipe out any profit the company might have earned. To minimize the fees associated with credit card transactions, some entrepreneurs offer customers incentives to pay with cash.

ENTREPRENEURIAL PROFILE: Doug Hendrick: Steamer's Café Doug Hendrick, owner of Steamer's Café, a small restaurant in Clinton, South Carolina, conducts a monthly drawing for a $20 gift card for customers who pay with cash rather than with credit cards. Hendrick says that fees absorb 3 percent of every credit card purchase. "Multiply that by thousands of customers and divide it by a thin profit margin, and it's a huge chunk," he says.[50] ■

E-COMMERCE AND CREDIT CARDS When it comes to online business transactions, the most common method of payment is the credit card. Internet merchants are constantly challenged by the need to provide secure methods for safe, secure online transactions. As you learned in Chapter 9, many shoppers are suspicious of online transactions for reasons of security and privacy. Therefore, online merchants must ensure their customers' privacy and the security of their credit card transactions by using encryption software.

Online merchants also face another obstacle: credit card fraud. Because they lack the face-to-face contact with their customers, online merchants face special challenges to avoid credit card fraud. Identity and credit card theft results in customers denying the authenticity of certain purchases and disputing the charges that appear on their bills. Unless merchants are vigilant, they will end up shouldering most of the burden for these charge-backs. About 0.9 percent of online credit card transactions are fraudulent, costing merchants $2.7 billion a year![51] Because small companies are less likely than large businesses to use high-tech online fraud detection tools, they are more likely to be victims of e-commerce fraud. The following steps can help online merchants reduce the probability that they will become victims of credit card fraud:

- Use an address verification system to compare every customer's billing information on the order form with the billing information in the bank or credit card company's records.

- Require customers to provide the CVV2 number from the back of the credit card. Although crooks can get access to this number, it can help screen out some fraudulent orders.

- Check customers' Internet protocol (IP) addresses. If an order contains a billing address in California but the IP address from which the order is placed is in China, chances are that the order is fraudulent.

- Monitor activity on the Web site with the help of a Web analytics software package. There are many packages available, and analyzing log files can help online entrepreneurs pinpoint the sources of fraud.

- Verify large orders. Large orders are a cause for celebration but only if they are legitimate. Check the authenticity of large orders, especially if the order is from a first-time customer.

- Post notices on the Web site that your company uses antifraud technology to screen orders. These notices make legitimate customers feel more confident about placing their orders and crooks trying to commit fraud tentative about running their scams.

- Contact the credit card company or the bank that issued the card. If you suspect that an order may be fraudulent, contact the company *before* processing it. Taking this step could save a company thousands of dollars in losses.[52]

DEBIT CARDS Consumers in the United States carry more than 530 million debit cards that act as electronic checks, automatically deducting the purchase amount immediately from a customer's checking account. Shoppers conduct nearly 53 billion debit card transactions, totaling $2.1 trillion each year.[53] In 2003, for the first time in history, shoppers used credit and debit cards more often than cash or checks to make retail purchases.[54] As customers' use of debit cards continues to grow, more small businesses are equipping their stores to handle debit card transactions. The equipment is easy to install and to set up, and the cost to the company is negligible. The payoff can be big, however, in the form of increased sales, improved cash flow, and decreased losses from bad checks. In addition, interchange fees on debit cards are lower than those on credit cards.

Installment Credit

Small companies that sell big-ticket consumer durables—such as major appliances, cars, and boats—frequently rely on installment credit to support their sales efforts. Because very few customers can purchase such items in a single lump-sum payment, small businesses finance them over an extended time. The time horizon may range from just a few months up to 30 or more years. Most companies require customers to make an initial down payment for the merchandise and then finance the balance for the life of the loan. The customer repays the loan principal plus interest on the loan. One advantage of installment loans for a small business is that the owner retains a security interest as collateral on the loan. If a customer defaults on the loan, the owner still holds the title to the merchandise. Because installment credit absorbs a small company's cash, many rely on financial institutions, such as banks and credit unions, to provide installment credit. When a company has the financial strength to "carry its own paper," the interest income from the installment loan contract often yields more than the initial profit on the sale of the product. For some businesses, such as furniture stores, this traditionally has been a major source of income.

Trade Credit

Companies that sell small-ticket items frequently offer their customers trade credit—that is, they create customer charge accounts. The typical small business bills its credit customers each month. To speed collections, some offer cash discounts if customers pay their balances early; others impose penalties on late payers. Before deciding to use trade credit as a competitive weapon, business owners must make sure that their companies' cash position is strong enough to support the additional pressure.

LAYAWAY Although technically not a form of credit, layaway plans, like trade credit, enable customers to purchase goods over time. In the typical layaway plan, a customer selects an item, pays a deposit on it, and makes regular payments on the item until it is paid in full. Unlike trade credit, the retailer keeps the item until the customer has finished paying. Most stores establish minimum payments and maximum payoff dates, and some charge a service fee. Created during the Great Depression as a way to help shoppers purchase goods, layaway has become popular once again, especially around the holiday season, as stubborn unemployment and slow economic growth have posed challenges for shoppers.

ENTREPRENEURIAL PROFILE: Marlana Williams: The Everyday Gourmet Marlana Walters, owner of The Everyday Gourmet, a kitchen and household accessory store with two locations in Mississippi, recently introduced a layaway plan for the holiday season on popular big-ticket items that cost at least $300. "I saw people's reluctance to purchase some of our more expensive items, and I understand that people need a little more time to pay for what they need," she says. "If layaway helps people get the gift they really want to give and not put them in a bind, why not go for it?" she asks. The Everyday Gourmet has a simple layaway plan: Divide the item's price into four equal payments, the last of which must be paid by the week of December 20. "The whole point of layaway is making it easy for the customer," says Williams.[55] ■

Chapter Summary by Learning Objective

1. Discuss the relationships among pricing, image, competition, and value.

- Pricing decisions cut across every aspect of a small company, influencing everything from its marketing and sales efforts to its operations and strategy. A company's pricing strategy is a major determinant of its image in the marketplace, is influenced by the pricing strategies of its competitors, and is an important element in the value that customers perceive its products or services provide.

- Ultimately, the "right" price for a product or service depends on one factor: the value that it provides for a customer. For most shoppers, three reference points define a fair price: the price they have paid for the product or service in the past, the prices competitors charge for the same or similar product or service, and the costs a company incurs to provide the product or service.

2. **Describe effective pricing techniques for introducing new products or services and for existing ones.**

- Pricing a new product is often difficult for business owners but it should accomplish three objectives: getting the product accepted, maintaining market share as the competition grows, and earning a profit. Generally, there are three major pricing strategies used to introduce new products into the market: penetration, skimming, and life cycle.

- Pricing techniques for existing products and services include odd pricing, price lining, dynamic pricing, leader pricing, geographic pricing, discounts, multiple unit pricing, bundling, optional product pricing, captive product pricing, by-product pricing, suggested retail pricing, and follow-the-leader pricing.

3. **Explain the pricing methods and strategies for retailers, manufacturers, and service firms.**

- Pricing for the retailer means pricing to move merchandise. Markup is the difference between the cost of a product or service and its selling price. Most retailers compute their markup as a percentage of retail price.

- A manufacturer's pricing decision depends on the support of accurate cost accounting records. The most common technique is cost-plus pricing, in which the manufacturer charges a price that covers the cost of producing a product plus a reasonable profit. Every manufacturer should calculate a product's break-even price, the price that produces neither a profit nor a loss.

- Service firms often suffer from the effects of vague, unfounded pricing procedures and frequently charge the going rate without any idea of their costs. A service firm must set a price on the basis of the cost of materials used, labor involved, overhead, and a profit. The proper price reflects the total cost of providing a unit of service.

4. **Describe the impact of credit on pricing.**

- Offering consumer credit enhances a small company's reputation and increases the probability, speed, and magnitude of customers' purchases. Small firms offer three types of consumer credit: credit cards, installment credit, and trade credit (charge accounts).

Discussion Questions

1. How does pricing affect a small firm's image?
2. What competitive factors must the small firm consider when establishing prices?
3. Describe the strategies a small business could use in setting the price of a new product. What objectives should the strategy seek to achieve?
4. Define the following pricing techniques: odd pricing, price lining, leader pricing, geographical pricing, and discounts.
5. Why do many small businesses use the manufacturer's suggested retail price? What are the disadvantages of this technique?
6. What is a markup? How is it used to determine individual price?
7. What is a markup? How is the markup for a product calculated?
8. What is cost-plus pricing? Why do so many manufacturers use it? What are the disadvantages of using it?
9. Explain the difference between full-absorption costing and direct costing. How does absorption costing help a manufacturer determine a reasonable price?
10. Explain the technique for a small service firm setting an hourly price.
11. What benefits does a small business get by offering customers credit? What costs does it incur?

Business Plan Pro™ Setting the price of your products and services and understanding your break-even point are important elements of your business plan. Resources and information in *Business Plan Pro*™ may help you to gain a perspective regarding the impact that pricing will have on your business.

Business Plan Exercises

Business Plan Pro™ will guide you through the steps of documenting your fixed cost, variable cost, and an average price. Once you enter this information, the software automatically creates a break-even chart for your plan.

Sample Plans

Review the break-even information in your favorite sample plans. Note how the plans use the fixed and variable costs with an average price to determine the break-even point. Look at the break-even graph and find the break-even point for each sample plan.

On the Web

Perform competitive pricing research on the Web. Search for products and services that are similar to what you are offering. Confirm that you are making parallel comparisons of these products. For example, are you considering the entire price, which may include shipping, handling, complementary products, and other attributes that will influence the final price to the customer? Do you consider these businesses to be direct competitors? If not, why? What does this information tell you about your price point? Does your price coincide with your business strategy?

In the Software

Open your business plan and locate the Break-Even Analysis section under the Financial Plan. Follow the instructions and enter the information that will enable to you to determine your break-even point. This will require you to have estimated figures for your fixed costs, variable costs, and price. Once you have entered that information, look at the break-even point shown in units and revenue. Based on what you find, is this break-even point realistic? How many months will it take to reach the break-even point? Is this time period acceptable? Now, increase your price by 10 percent. What does this do to your break-even point? You may want to experiment with your break-even point by entering different price points and costs to see the impact that price will have on the break-even point when you will begin making a profit.

Building Your Business Plan

Go to the Sales Forecast table under the Sales Strategy section. You may use the wizard or enter information directly into the worksheet. If you have not done so yet, enter your pricing information in that section. Work through the table and estimate your direct unit costs. The instructions and examples will assist you through the process.

Beyond the Classroom . . .

1. Apple Inc. dominates the market for media players with its line of iPods, which currently includes the Shuffle, the Nano, the Classic, and the Touch. Because the company constantly introduces new models and features, it also adjusts prices on these popular players. Use the Web to research the history of the iPod and write a brief summary of Apple's pricing strategy on its popular media player. Which products compete with the iPod? How do the prices of similar models compare to the iPod? Is Apple able to command a premium for its brand? If so, what factors allow the company to do so?

2. Interview a successful small retailer and ask the following questions: Do they seek a specific image through their prices? What type of outlet would you consider the retailer to be? What role do competitors play in the business owner's pricing? Does the retailer use specific pricing techniques, such as odd pricing, price lining, leader pricing, and geographic pricing? How are discounts calculated? What markup percentage does the firm use? How are prices derived? What are their cost structures?

3. Select an industry that has several competing small firms in your area. Contact these firms and compare their approaches to determining prices. Do prices on identical or similar items differ? Why?

Endnotes

1. Amy Cortese, "The Power of Optimal Pricing," *Business* 2.0, September 2002, pp. 68–70.
2. Han Li, "Shopping by Smartphone This Holiday Season," *Los Angeles Times*, November 5, 2011, http://articles.latimes.com/2011/nov/05/business/la-fi-cover-holiday-kickoff-20111106.
3. Ron Stodghill, "The Shipping News," *FSB*, December 2005/January 2006, p. 80.
4. Howard Scott, "The Tricky Art of Raising Prices," *Nation's Business*, February 1999, p. 32.
5. "Minute Repeaters," *Forbes Life*, September 9, 2011, p. 31; "World's Most Complicated Wristwatch: Franck Muller Aeternitas Mega 4," Professional Watches, January 11, 2010, http://professionalwatches.com/2010/01/worlds_most_complicated_wristw.html; Jonathon Keats, "Spring Ahead," *Forbes Life*, March 10, 2008, pp. 84–91; Jack Forster, "It's About Time," *Forbes Life*, September 15, 2008, pp. 120–125.
6. Anjali Athavaley, "What Makes a Mattress Cost $33,000?," *Wall Street Journal*, June 16, 2010, pp. D1-D2; Geoff Williams, "The Business of Sleep: Sublime Mattress," CNNMoney, April 7, 2011, http://money.cnn.com/galleries/2011/smallbusiness/1103/gallery.business_of_sleep/3.html.
7. Lauren Torrisi, "Top Five Most Expensive Burgers," *Good Morning America*, May 30, 2012, http://abcnews.go.com/GMA/top-expensive-burgers/story?id=16460055#3.
8. "The Price Is Right, but Maybe It's Not, and How Do You Know?," *Knowledge @ Wharton*, October 3, 2007, http://knowledge.wharton.upenn.edu/article.cfm?articleid=1813; Victoria Murphy Barret, "What the Market Will Bear," *Forbes*, July 3, 2006, http://www.forbes.com/business/forbes/2006/0703/069.html.
9. Stephanie Clifford, "How Low Can You Go?," *Inc.*, August 2007, p. 42.
10. Geoff Williams, "Name Your Price," *Entrepreneur*, September 2005, p. 112.
11. Justin Martin, "Gentlemen (and Ladies), Raise Your Prices!," *FSB*, October 2007, pp. 26–30.
12. William Echilkson, "The Return of Luxury," *Fortune*, October 17, 1994, p. 18.
13. Mark Henricks, "Stop on a Dime," *Entrepreneur*, January 2006, p. 27.
14. Joseph B. White, "Dream Cars You Coveted in High School, but Brand New," *Wall Street Journal*, July 27, 2011, pp. D1, D2.

15. Nikki Baird and Paula Rosenblum, *Optimizing Price in a Transparent World: Benchmark Report*, Retail Systems Research, April 2011, p. 7.

16. Geoff Williams, "Name Your Price," *Entrepreneur*, September 2005, pp. 108–115.

17. Gayle Sato Stodder, "Paying the Price," *Entrepreneur*, October 1994, p. 54.

18. Zoe Wood, "Tesco Declares War on Rivals with £500m Price Cutting Offensive," *The Guardian*, September 22, 2011, http://www.guardian.co.uk/business/2011/sep/22/tesco-price-cut-war; Zoe Wood, "Tesco's Price War Threat Sends Supermarket Shares Plunging," *The Guardian*, September 21, 2011, http://www.guardian.co.uk/business/2011/sep/21/tesco-price-war-threatens-supermarkets.

19. Emily Maltby, "In Season of Big Discounts, Small Shops Suffer," *Wall Street Journal*, November 24, 2010, http://online.wsj.com/article/SB100014240527487042439045756307926948452292.html.

20. Alison Stein Wellner, "Boost Your Bottom Line by Taking the Guesswork Out of Pricing," *Inc.*, June 2005, p. 78.

21. Norm Brodsky, "Street Smarts," *Inc.*, September 2010, p. 34.

22. Justin Martin, "Gentlemen (and Ladies), Raise Your Prices!," *FSB*, October 2007, pp. 26–30.

23. Denise Lee Yohn, "The Price Is Complicated," *QSR Magazine*, November 12, 2010, http://www.qsrmagazine.com/denise-lee-yohn/price-complicated.

24. Norm Brodsky, "Dealing with Cost Hikes," Inc., August 2005, p. 49.

25. Sarah E. Lockyer, "McDonald's Outlines Pricing Strategy," *Nation's Restaurant News*, April 21, 2011, http://www.nrn.com/article/mcdonalds-outlines-pricing-strategy.

26. "Pricing and Fairness: Do Your Customers Assume You Are Gouging Them?," Knowledge @ *Wharton*, September 11, 2002, http://knowledge.wharton.upenn.edu/article.cfm?articleid=622#.

27. Megan Duckett, "Startup Tips from 5 Successful Food Truck Entrepreneurs," *CBS Moneywatch*, May 20, 2011, http://www.cbsnews.com/8334-505143_162-57235454/startup-tips-from-5-successful-food-truck-entrepreneurs/?pageNum=5.

28. Rick Bruns, "Tips for Coping with Rising Costs of Key Commodities," *Fast Company*, December 1997, pp. 27–30.

29. "Fuel Surcharge Information," Washington Floral Service, http://www.washingtonfloral.com/index.php/About-Us/fuel-surcharge.html.

30. Jeffrey A. Trachtenberg, "Borders Slashes Buyer Rewards, Cuts Discounts," *Wall Street Journal*, March 28, 2007, pp. D1, D4.

31. "Gas Prices Could Affect the Price of Pizzas, Flowers," *Greenville News*, April 29, 2006, p. 3A.

32. Sarah E. Lockyer, "McDonald's Outlines Pricing Strategy," *Nation's Restaurant News*, April 21, 2011, http://www.nrn.com/article/mcdonalds-outlines-pricing-strategy.

33. Julie Jargon, "Coffee Talk: Starbucks Chief on Prices, McDonald's Rivalry," *Wall Street Journal*, March 7, 2011, p. B6.

34. Norm Brodsky, "Dealing with Cost Hikes," *Inc.*, August 2005, p. 49.

35. Sam Oches, "The Value Equation," *QSR Magazine*, February 2010, http://www.qsrmagazine.com/competition/value-equation?microsite=9342;microsite=9342; Blair Chancey, "Wendy's Counters McDonald's Struggling $1 Menu," *QSR Magazine*, September 2, 2008, http://www.qsrmagazine.com/news/wendys-counters-mcdonalds-struggling-1-menu.

36. Paul Ziobro, "Restaurants Struggle," *Wall Street Journal*, June 22, 2010, p. B8; Paul Frumkin, "Red Lobster Looking to Lower Price Points," *Nation's Restaurant News*, November 11, 2010, http://www.nrn.com/article/red-lobster-looking-lower-price-points; Allison Linn, "Restaurant Chain Sees Bets Pay Off," *MSNBC*, February 25, 2010, http://www.msnbc.msn.com/id/35486250/ns/business-success_in_hard_times/t/restaurant-chain-sees-bets-pay/#.

37. Michael V. Marn, Eric V. Roegner, and Craig C. Zawada, "Pricing New Products," *McKinsey Quarterly*, no. 3, 2003, p. 1.

38. Steve McKee, "Low Prices Are Not Always Your Friend," *Business Week*, April 2008, http://www.businessweek.com/smallbiz/content/apr2008/sb20080414_027855.htm.

39. Peter Svenson, "Research Firm: Amazon Sells Its Kindle Fire Tablet at a Loss," *Greenville News*, November 19, 2011, p. 7A; Tony Smith, "Amazon Kindle Fire: $199 to Buy, $202 to Make," *Reg Hardware*, November 21, 2011, http://www.reghardware.com/2011/11/21/amazon_teardown_reveals_manufacturing_cost_higher_than_sale_price; Cromwell Schubarth, "Google's $199 Nexus 7 Costs $184 to Make," *Silicon Valley/San Jose Business Journal*, July 5, 2012, http://www.bizjournals.com/sanjose/news/2012/07/05/googles-199-nexus-7-costs-184-to-make.html.

40. "Q & A: The Natural," *Inc.*, November 2010, p. 14; Ronnie Cohen, "Marin Businessman Turns Carrots into Cash," *JWeekly*, October 28, 2010, http://www.jweekly.com/article/full/59717/marin-businessman-turns-carrots-into-cash.

41. Christina Binkley, "How Can Jeans Cost $300?," *Wall Street Journal*, July 7, 2011, pp. D1–D2.

42. Sarah Schmidt, "Diners Spend More if Menu Avoids $ Sign," *Edmonton Journal*, August 14, 2008, http://www.canada.com/edmontonjournal/news/business/story.html?id=73e86808-da12-4430-acfc-6d64bc3b8efc.

43. Amy Feldman, "The Tiger in Costco's Tank," *Fast Company*, July/August 2007, pp. 38–40.

44. "On Sale Now, but Time's a' Wastin'," *Marketing Profs*, April 9, 2008, http://www.marketingprofs.com/short-articles/311/on-sale-now-but-times-a-wastin.

45. Jeffrey A. Trachtenberg, "Sellers of E-Books Bundling Titles to Promote Authors, New and Old," *Wall Street Journal*, February 11, 2011, p. B6.

46. Richard Barrington, "2011 Credit Card Facts and Statistics: Free Infographic Report," Index Credit Cards, January 20, 2011, http://www.indexcreditcards.com/finance/creditcardstatistics/2011-report-on-credit-card-usage-facts-statistics.html.

47. "Credit Counseling Statistics," Consumer Credit Counseling Service, http://creditcounselingbiz.com/credit_counseling_statistics.htm.

48. "Top 10 Reasons to Start Accepting Credit Cards Today," *100 Best Merchant Accounts*, http://www.100best-merchant-accounts.com/articles1.html.

49. Testimony of Doug Kanto, counsel, Merchant Payments Coalition, before the U.S. House of Representatives Financial Services Subcommittee on Financial Institutions and Consumer Credit, hearing on "Understanding the Federal Reserve's Proposed Rule on Interchange Fees: Implications and Consequences of the Durbin Amendment," February 17, 2011, p. 6.

50. Dana Dratch, "Merchants May Require Up to $10 Minimum Credit Card Purchase," CreditCards.com, August 22, 2011, http://www.creditcards.com/credit-card-news/credit-card-minimum-payment-purchases-law-1282.php.

51. *2011 Online Fraud Report*, 12th ed., Cybersource Corporation, 2011, p. 4.

52. Michael Bloch, "Preventing Credit Card Chargebacks-Anti-Fraud Strategies," Taming the Beast, http://www.tamingthebeast.net/articles2/card-fraud-strategies.htm.

53. *Statistical Abstract of the United States 2012*, U.S. Census Bureau, p. 740.

54. Robin Sidel, "Banks, Customers Adapt to Paperless Check Processing," *Wall Street Journal*, October 28, 2004, pp. B1, B3.

55. Cassandra Mickens, "Leading Retailers Return to Layaway," *Greenville News*, November 20, 2011, pp. 1E, 3E.

11

Creating a Successful Financial Plan

Learning Objectives

On completion of this chapter, you will be able to:

1. Understand the importance of preparing a financial plan.
2. Describe how to prepare the basic financial statements and use them to manage a small business.
3. Create projected (pro forma) financial statements.
4. Understand the basic financial statements through ratio analysis.
5. Explain how to interpret financial ratios.
6. Conduct a break-even analysis for a small company.

Without knowing where you financially are at all times, you are destined to fail.

—Dean Austin

With knowledge of finance comes a better ability to manage it.

—William Hettinger

Fashioning a well-designed financial plan as part of a comprehensive business plan is one of the most important steps to launching a new business venture. Entrepreneurs who fail to develop workable strategies for earning a profit from the outset eventually suffer the ultimate business penalty: failure. In addition, potential lenders and investors demand a realistic financial plan before putting their money into a start-up company. More important, a financial plan is a vital tool that helps entrepreneurs to manage their businesses more effectively, steering their way around the pitfalls that cause failures. Proper **financial management** requires putting in place a system that provides entrepreneurs with relevant financial information in an easy-to-read format on a timely basis; it allows entrepreneurs to know not only *how* their businesses are doing financially but also *why* their companies are performing that way. The information in a small company's financial records is one resource to which competitors have no access. Smart entrepreneurs recognize this and put their companies' numbers to work for them so that they can make their businesses more successful. "Salted away in your accounting records are financial alerts, ways to trim costs, and tips on where profit is hiding," explains one business writer.[1]

Unfortunately, failure to collect and analyze basic financial data is a common mistake among entrepreneurs. A recent survey by Sage North America reports that 23 percent of small business owners lack sufficient financial literacy to identify the cost that has the greatest impact on their companies.[2] Both research and anecdotal evidence suggest that a significant percentage of entrepreneurs run their companies without any kind of financial plan and never analyze their companies' financial statements as part of the decision-making process. Bill Hettinger, business consultant and author of *Finance without Fear*, estimates that 75 percent of business owners do not understand or fail to focus on the financial details of their companies.[3] To reach profit objectives, entrepreneurs must be aware of their companies' overall financial position and the changes in financial status that occur over time. Most accounting experts advise entrepreneurs to use one of the popular computerized small business accounting programs such as Quickbooks, Peachtree Accounting, and others to manage routine record-keeping tasks. Working with an accountant to set up the system at the outset and then having an employee or a bookkeeping service enter the transactions is most efficient for most businesses. These programs make preparing reports, analyzing a company's financial statements, and summarizing data a snap. Studies show that business owners who use accounting software are more likely to be financially literate than those who do not.[4]

This chapter focuses on some practical tools that help entrepreneurs to develop a workable financial plan, keep them aware of their company's financial plan, and enable them to plan for profit. They can use these tools to help them anticipate changes and plot an appropriate profit strategy to meet them head-on. These profit-planning techniques are not difficult to master, nor are they overly time consuming. We will discuss the techniques involved in preparing projected (pro forma) financial statements, conducting ratio analysis, and performing break-even analysis.

Basic Financial Statements

Before we begin building projected financial statements, it would be helpful to review the basic financial reports that measure a company's financial position: the balance sheet, the income statement, and the statement of cash flows. The level of financial sophistication among small business owners may not be high, but the extent of financial reporting among small businesses is. Most small businesses regularly produce summary financial information, almost all of it in the form of these traditional financial statements.

The Balance Sheet

Like a digital camera, the **balance sheet** takes a "snapshot" of a business's financial position, providing owners with an estimate of its worth on a given date. Its two major sections show the assets the business owns and the claims that creditors and owners have against those assets. The balance sheet is usually prepared on the last day of the month. Figure 11.1 shows the balance sheet for Sam's Appliance Shop for the year ended December 31, 201X.

The balance sheet is built on the fundamental accounting equation: Assets = Liabilities + Owner's equity. Any increase or decrease on one side of the equation must be offset by an increase or decrease on the other side, hence the name *balance sheet*. It provides a baseline from

LO1

Understand the importance of preparing a financial plan.

financial management
a process that provides entrepreneurs with relevant financial information in an easy-to-read format on a timely basis; it allows entrepreneurs to know not only how their businesses are doing financially but also why they are performing that way.

LO2

Describe how to prepare the basic financial statements and use them to manage a small business.

balance sheet
a financial statement that provides a snapshot of a business's financial position, estimating its worth on a given date; it is built on the fundamental accounting equation:
Assets = Liabilities + Owner's equity.

FIGURE 11.1

Balance Sheet, Sam's Appliance Shop

Assets		
Current Assets		
Cash		$49,855
Accounts Receivable	$179,225	
Less Allowance for Doubtful Accounts	$6,000	$173,225
Inventory		$455,455
Prepaid Expenses		$8,450
Total Current Assets		$686,985
Fixed Assets		
Land		$59,150
Buildings	$74,650	
Less Accumulated Depreciation	$7,050	$67,600
Equipment	$22,375	
Less Accumulated Depreciation	$1,250	$21,125
Furniture and Fixtures	$10,295	
Less Accumulated Depreciation	$1,000	$9,295
Total Fixed Assets		$157,170
Intangibles (Goodwill)		$3,500
Total Assets		$847,655
Liabilities		
Current Liabilities		
Accounts Payable		$152,580
Notes Payable		$83,920
Accrued Wages/Salaries Payable		$38,150
Accrued Interest Payable		$42,380
Accrued Taxes Payable		$50,820
Total Current Liabilities		$367,850
Long-Term Liabilities		
Mortgage		$127,150
Note Payable		$85,000
Total Long-Term Liabilities		$212,150
Owner's Equity		
Sam Lloyd, Capital		$267,655
Total Liabilities and Owner's Equity		$847,655

current assets

assets such as cash and other items to be converted into cash within one year or within the company's normal operating cycle.

fixed assets

assets acquired for long-term use in a business.

liabilities

creditors' claims against a company's assets.

current liabilities

those debts that must be paid within one year or within the normal operating cycle of a company.

which to measure future changes in assets, liabilities, and equity. The first section of the balance sheet lists the company's assets (valued at cost, not actual market value) and shows the total value of everything the business owns. **Current assets** consist of cash and items to be converted into cash within one year or within the normal operating cycle of the company, whichever is longer, such as accounts receivable and inventory, and **fixed assets** are those acquired for long-term use in the business. Intangible assets include items such as goodwill, copyrights, and patents that, although valuable, are not tangible.

The second section shows the business's **liabilities**—the creditors' claims against the company's assets. **Current liabilities** are those debts that must be paid within one year or within the normal operating cycle of the company, whichever is longer, and **long-term liabilities** are those that come due after one year. This section of the balance sheet also shows the **owner's equity**, the value of the owner's investment in the business. It is the balancing factor on the balance sheet, representing all of the owner's capital contributions to the business plus all accumulated (or retained) earnings not distributed to the owner(s).

The Income Statement

The **income statement** (also called the profit-and-loss statement) compares expenses against revenue over a certain period of time to show the firm's net income (or loss). Like a digital video recorder, the income statement is a "moving picture" of a company's profitability over time. The annual income statement reports the bottom line of the business over the fiscal or calendar year. Figure 11.2 shows the income statement for Sam's Appliance Shop for the year ended December 31, 201X.

To calculate net income or loss, an entrepreneur records sales revenues for the year, which includes all income that flows into the business from sales of goods and services. Income from other sources (rent, investments, and interest) also must be included in the revenue section of the income statement. To determine net sales revenue, owners subtract the value of returned items and refunds from gross revenue. **Cost of goods sold** represents the total cost, including shipping, of the merchandise sold during the accounting period. Manufacturers, wholesalers, and retailers calculate cost of goods sold by adding purchases to beginning inventory and subtracting ending inventory. Service-providing companies typically have no cost of goods sold because they do not carry inventory.

Subtracting the cost of goods sold from net sales revenue results in a company's gross profit. Allowing the cost of goods sold to get out of control whittles away a company's gross profit and

long-term liabilities liabilities that come due after one year.

owner's equity the value of the owner's investment in the business.

income statement a financial statement that represents a moving picture of a business, comparing its expenses against its revenue over a period of time to show its net income (or loss).

Net Sales Revenue		$1,870,841
Credit Sales	$1,309,589	
Cash Sales	$561,252	
Cost of Goods Sold		
Beginning Inventory, 1/1/xx	$805,745	
+ Purchases	$939,827	
Goods Available for Sale	$1,745,572	
– Ending Inventory, 12/31/xx	$455,455	
Cost of Goods Sold		$1,290,117
Gross Profit		$580,724
Operating Expenses		
Advertising	$139,670	
Insurance	$46,125	
Depreciation		
Building	$18,700	
Equipment	$9,000	
Salaries	$224,500	
Travel	$4,000	
Entertainment	$2,500	
Total Operating Expenses		$444,495
General Expenses		
Utilities	$5,300	
Telephone	$2,500	
Postage	$1,200	
Payroll Taxes	$25,000	
Total General Expenses		$34,000
Other Expenses		
Interest Expense	$39,850	
Bad Check Expense	$1,750	
Total Other Expenses		$41,600
Total Expenses		$520,095
Net Income		$60,629

FIGURE 11.2

Income Statement, Sam's Appliance Shop

cost of goods sold
the total cost, including shipping, of the merchandise sold during the accounting period.

gross profit margin
gross profit divided by net sales revenue.

threatens its ability to generate positive net income because a company must pay all of its operating expenses out of its gross profit. Dividing gross profit by net sales revenue produces the **gross profit margin**, a ratio that every small business owner should watch closely. If a company's gross profit margin slips too low, it is likely that it will operate at a loss (negative net income). A business that operates at a gross profit margin of 50 percent must generate $2 in sales for every $1 of operating expenses just to break even. However, a company with a 10 percent gross profit margin must generate $10 in sales for every $1 of operating expenses to reach its break-even point.

Many business owners whose companies are losing money mistakenly believe that the problem is inadequate sales volume; therefore, they focus on pumping up sales at any cost. In many cases, however, the losses their companies are incurring are the result of an inadequate gross profit margin, and pumping up sales only deepens their losses! Repairing a poor gross profit margin requires a company to raise prices, cut manufacturing or purchasing costs, refuse orders with low profit margins, "fire" unprofitable customers (see Figure 11.3), or add new products with more attractive profit margins. *Increasing sales will not resolve the problem.* Monitoring the gross profit margin over time and comparing it to those of other companies in the same industry are important steps to maintaining a company's long-term profitability.

FIGURE 11.3

Customer Profitability Map

Source: Based on Gwen Moran, "Six Weeks to a Better Bottom Line," Entrepreneur, January 2010, pp. 47-51; "Retaining and Divesting Customers: An Exploratory Study of Right Customers, `At-Risk' Right Customers, and Wrong Customers," Kashing Woo and Henry K. Y. Fock, Journal of Services Marketing, Vol. 18, Issue 2/3, 2004, pp. 187-197.

A classic study reports that 20 percent of the typical company's customers are unprofitable. Many business owners who take the time to analyze their customer bases are surprised to discover that some of the customers they thought were profitable actually are costing their companies money. The solution: Raise prices or fees, or "fire" the unprofitable customers. The following customer profitability map helps entrepreneurs identify which of their customers are best – and worst – for their businesses.

Methodology: Select your biggest customers and assign each one a "resonance score" from 1 (difficult) to 10 (easy) that reflects how easy they are to serve. Then calculate the profit margin (profit as a percentage of sales) your company makes from each customer. Plot each customer's score on the map as a circle. The size of the circle should be proportionate to the percentage of the company's total sales for which the customer accounts. The result is a map that shows how your company's customers fall into each of the 4 quadrants.

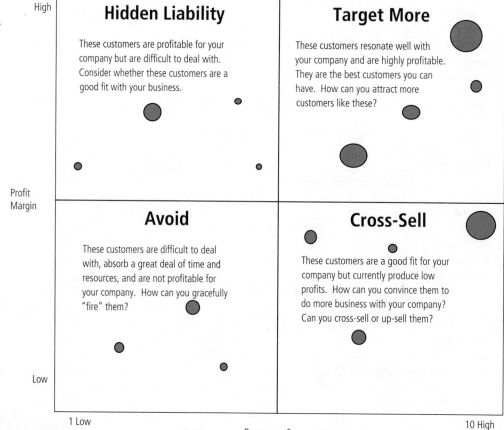

High

Hidden Liability

These customers are profitable for your company but are difficult to deal with. Consider whether these customers are a good fit with your business.

Target More

These customers resonate well with your company and are highly profitable. They are the best customers you can have. How can you attract more customers like these?

Profit
Margin

Avoid

These customers are difficult to deal with, absorb a great deal of time and resources, and are not profitable for your company. How can you gracefully "fire" them?

Cross-Sell

These customers are a good fit for your company but currently produce low profits. How can you convince them to do more business with your company? Can you cross-sell or up-sell them?

Low

1 Low   10 High

Resonance Score

ENTREPRENEURIAL PROFILE: Debra Brede: D. K. Brede Investment Management Debra Brede, owner of D. K. Brede Investment Management in Needham, Massachusetts, once had a client with a million-dollar account who was demanding and required many hours of her and her staff's time. For 20 years, Brede accommodated the client's whims because Brede assumed that the account was highly profitable for her company. Only after Brede spent two months analyzing her company's accounts did she discover that although the client's account balance was sizable, it generated very little in fees and was actually costing her company money. "I was shocked," says Brede, who informed the client that she would have to charge for the additional time that maintaining the client's account required. The client became furious, and Brede suggested that she take her business elsewhere. Once the client left, the company's profits increased 25 percent, and Brede found more time to recruit new clients.[5] ■

Operating expenses include those costs that contribute directly to the manufacturing and distribution of goods. General expenses are indirect costs incurred in operating the business. "Other expenses" is a catchall category covering all other expenses that don't fit into the other two categories. Subtracting total expenses from total revenue gives the company's net income (or loss) for the accounting period. Reducing expenses increases a company's net income, and even small reductions in expenses can add up to big savings.

operating expenses
those costs that contribute directly to the manufacture and distribution of goods.

ENTREPRENEURIAL PROFILE: Wesley Hutchen: Oak Environmental Wesley Hutchen, owner of Oak Environmental, an environmental remediation rental company based in Calgary, Alberta, switched from tracking its equipment by hand to an automated bar-code system that dramatically increased the accuracy of the company's rental records. Although implementing the new system required three months, error rates fell from 20 percent to less than 2 percent, and employees cut in half the time spent tracking equipment. According to Hutchen, the automated system saves $50,000 a year in costs and allows the company to generate $36,000 more per year in equipment rental revenue.[6] ■

"We're showing a profit, compliments of Photoshop."

From *The Wall Street Journal*, permission Cartoon Features Syndicate

Comparing a company's current income statement to those of prior accounting periods often reveals valuable information about key trends and a company's progress toward its financial goals. "Numbers run companies," says Norm Brodsky, serial entrepreneur and owner of CitiStorage, a successful storage company based in New York City. "It's your responsibility as an owner to know and understand not only the income statement but also the balance sheet of your business. You ignore them at your peril."[7]

The Statement of Cash Flows

The **statement of cash flows** show the changes in a company's working capital from the beginning of the accounting period by listing both the sources of funds and the uses of those funds. Many small businesses never need to prepare such a statement; instead, they rely on a cash budget, a less formal managerial tool that you will learn about in Chapter 12 that tracks the flow of cash into and out of a company over time. Sometimes, however, creditors, lenders, investors, or business buyers may require this information.

statement of cash flows
a financial statement showing the changes in a company's working capital from the beginning of the year by listing both the sources and the uses of those funds.

To prepare the statement, owners must assemble the balance sheet and the income statement summarizing the present year's operations. They begin with the company's net income for the period (from the income statement). Then they add the sources of the company's funds—borrowed funds, owner contributions, decreases in accounts receivable, increases in accounts payable, decreases in inventory, depreciation, and any others. Depreciation is listed as a source of funds because it is a noncash expense that has already been deducted as a cost of doing business. Because the owner has already paid for the item being depreciated, however, its depreciation is a source of funds. Next the owner subtracts the uses of these funds—plant and equipment purchases, dividends to owners, repayment of debt, increases in accounts receivable, decreases in accounts payable, increases in inventory, and so on. The difference between the total sources and the total uses is the increase or decrease in working capital. By investigating the changes in their companies' working capital and the reasons for them, owners can create a more practical financial action plan for the future of the enterprise.

These financial statements are more than just complex documents used only by accountants and financial officers. When used in conjunction with the analytical tools described in the following sections, they can help entrepreneurs to map a firm's financial future and actively plan for profit. Mere preparation of these statements is not enough, however; owners and employees must *understand and use* the information contained in them to make the business more effective and efficient.

LO3

Create projected (pro forma) financial statements.

Creating Projected Financial Statements

Creating projected financial statements helps entrepreneurs to transform their business goals into reality. These projected financial statements answer questions such as the following: What profit can the business expect to earn? If the owner's profit objective is *x* dollars, what sales level must the company achieve? What fixed and variable expenses can the owner expect at that level of sales? The answers to these and other questions are critical in formulating a functional financial plan for the small business.

This section focuses on creating projected income statements and balance sheets for a small start-up. These projected (or pro forma) statements are a crucial component of every business plan because they estimate the profitability and the overall financial condition of a company in the future. They are an integral part of convincing potential lenders and investors to provide the financing needed to get the company off the ground (the topic of Chapter 13). In addition, because these statements project a company's financial position through the end of the forecasted period, they help entrepreneurs to plan the route to improved financial strength and healthy business growth. To be useful, however, these forecasts must be *realistic*! "A business plan is not complete until it contains a set of financial projections that are not only inspiring but also logical and defensible," says one business writer.[8]

Because an established business has a history of operating data from which to construct projected financial statements, the task is not nearly as difficult as it is for a start-up company. When creating pro forma financial statements for a business start-up, entrepreneurs typically rely on published statistics that summarize the operation of similar-size companies in the same industry. These statistics are available from a number of sources (described later), but this section draws on information found in the *Annual Statement Studies*, a compilation of financial data collected from 250,000 companies across more than 760 industries organized by Standard Industrial Classification (SIC) Code and North American Industry Classification System (NAICS) published by the Risk Management Association (RMA). Because conditions and markets change so rapidly, entrepreneurs developing financial forecasts for start-ups should focus on creating projections for two years into the future. Investors want to see that entrepreneurs have realistic expectations about their companies' income and expenses and when they expect to start earning a profit.

Projected Financial Statements for a Small Business

One of the most important tasks confronting the entrepreneur launching a new enterprise is to determine the amount of funding required to begin operation as well as the amount required to keep the company going until it begins to generate positive cash flow. The amount of money needed to begin a business depends on the type of operation, its location, inventory requirements, sales volume, and many other factors. Every new firm must have enough capital to cover all start-up costs, including funds to rent or buy plant, equipment, and tools, and to pay for advertising, wages, licenses, utilities, and other expenses. In addition, an entrepreneur must maintain a reserve of capital to carry the company until it begins to generate positive cash flow. Too often, entrepreneurs are overly optimistic in their financial plans and fail to recognize that expenses initially exceed income (and cash outflow exceeds cash inflow) for most small firms. This period of net losses (and negative cash flow) is normal and may last from just a few months to several years. During this time, entrepreneurs must be able to pay the company's regular bills, meet payroll, purchase inventory, take advantage of cash discounts, pay the company's regular bills, grant customers credit, and meet their personal financial obligations.

THE PROJECTED INCOME STATEMENT When creating a projected income statement, the first step is to create a sales forecast. An entrepreneur has two options: to develop a sales forecast and work down or to set a profit target and work up. Developing a realistic sales forecast for a business start-up is not always easy, but with creativity and research it is possible. Talking with owners of existing businesses in the industry (outside of the local trading area, of course) can provide meaningful insight into the sales levels a company can expect to generate during its early years. For a reasonable fee, entrepreneurs can access published aggregated financial statistics that industry trade associations collect on the companies in their industries. Other organizations, such as the Risk Management Association and Dun & Bradstreet, publish useful financial information for a wide range of industries. Internet searches and trips to the local library will produce the necessary information. Interviews with potential customers and test-marketing an actual product or service also can reveal the number of customers a company can expect to attract. One method for checking the accuracy of a sales estimate is to calculate the revenue other companies in the same industry generate per employee and compare it to your own projected revenue per employee. A value that is out of line with industry standards is not likely to be realistic.

Many entrepreneurs prefer the second method of creating a projected income statement, targeting a profit figure and then "working up" to determine the sales level they must achieve to reach it. Of course, it is important to compare this sales target against the results of the marketing plan to determine whether it is realistic. Once an entrepreneur determines a reasonable profit target, the next step is to estimate the expenses the business will incur to generate that profit.

The profit a small company produces must be large enough to provide a reasonable return on time the owners spend operating the business and a return on their investment in the business. Entrepreneurs who earn less in their own businesses than they could earn working for someone else must weigh carefully the advantages and disadvantages of choosing the path of entrepreneurship. Why be exposed to all of the risks, sacrifices, and hard work of beginning and operating a small business if the rewards are less than those of remaining in the secure employment of another? Although there are many nonfinancial benefits of owning a business, the net income a company generates should be at least as much as an entrepreneur could earn by working for someone else.

An adequate profit must also include a reasonable return on the owner's total investment in the business. (The owner's total investment is the amount contributed to the company plus any retained earnings from previous years that were funneled back into the business.) In other words, an entrepreneur's target income is the sum of a reasonable salary for the time spent running the business and a normal return on the amount invested in the company. Determining this amount is the first step in creating the projected income statement.

An entrepreneur then must translate this target profit into a net sales figure for the forecasted period. To calculate net sales from a target profit, the entrepreneur can use published industry statistics. Suppose an entrepreneur wants to launch a small retail flower shop and has determined that his target net income is $30,000. Statistics gathered from RMA's *Annual Statement Studies* show that the typical flower shop's net profit margin (Net profit ÷ Net sales) is 7.2 percent. Using this information, he can compute the sales level required to produce a net profit of $30,000:

$$\text{Net profit margin} = \frac{\text{Net income}}{\text{Sales (annual)}}$$

Solving for net sales produces the following result:

$$\text{Net sales} = \frac{\$30,000}{0.072}$$

$$= \$416,667$$

Now the entrepreneur knows that to make a net profit of $30,000 (before taxes), he or she must achieve annual sales of $416,667. To complete the projected income statement, the owner simply applies the appropriate statistics from the *Annual Statement Studies* to the annual sales figure. Because the statistics for each income statement item are expressed as percentages of net sales, the entrepreneur merely multiplies the proper percentage by the annual sales figure to obtain the desired value. For example, cost of goods sold usually makes up 46.6 percent of net sales for the typical small flower shop; therefore, the owner of this new flower shop expects his cost of goods sold to be the following:

$$\text{Cost of goods sold} = \$416,667 \times 0.466 = \$194,167$$

The flower shop's complete projected income statement is shown as follows:

Net sales	(100%)	$416,667
–Cost of goods sold	(46.6%)	$194,167
Gross profit margin	(53.4%)	$222,500
–Operating expenses	(46.2%)	$192,500
Net profit (before taxes)	(7.2%)	$30,000

At this point, the business appears to be a viable venture. But remember that this income statement represents a sales *goal* that the owner may not be able to reach. The next step is to determine whether this required sales volume is reasonable. One useful technique is to break down the required annual sales volume into *daily* sales figures. Assuming that the shop will be open six days per week for 52 weeks (312 days), we see that the owner must average $1,335 per day in sales:

$$\text{Average daily sales} = \frac{\$416,667}{312 \text{ days}} = \$1,335/\text{day}$$

This calculation gives the owner a better perspective of the sales required to yield an annual profit of $30,000.

To determine whether the profit expected from the business will meet or exceed the target income, the entrepreneur also should use this same process to create income statements that are built on pessimistic, most likely, and optimistic sales estimates. The previous analysis shows an entrepreneur the sales level needed to reach a desired profit. But what happens if sales are lower? Higher? Making these projections requires a reliable sales forecast using the market research techniques described in Chapter 6.

Suppose, for example, that after conducting research on the industry, a marketing survey of local customers, and talking with owners of flower shops in other markets, the prospective entrepreneur projects annual sales for the proposed business's first year of operation to be only $395,000. The entrepreneur can take this sales estimate and develop a projected income statement:

Net sales	(100%)	$395,000
–Cost of goods sold	(46.6%)	$184,070
Gross profit margin	(53.4%)	$210,930
–Operating expenses	(46.2%)	$182,490
Net profit (before taxes)	(7.2%)	$28,440

Based on sales of $395,000, this entrepreneur can expect a net income (before taxes) of $28,440. If this amount is acceptable as a return on the investment of time and money in the business, the entrepreneur should proceed with his or her planning.

At this stage in developing the financial plan, the owner should create a more detailed picture of the venture's expected operating expenses. In addition to gathering information from industry trade associations about typical operating expenses, an entrepreneur can contact potential vendors, suppliers, and providers to get estimates of the expenses he or she can expect to incur in his or her area of operation. One entrepreneur who was preparing a business plan for the launch of an upscale women's clothing store contacted local utility companies, insurance agencies, radio and television stations, newspapers, and other vendors to get estimates of her utility, insurance, advertising, and other expenses.

To ensure that they have not overlooked any business expenses in preparing the business plan, entrepreneurs should list all of the expenses they will incur and have an accountant review the list. Sometimes in their estimates of expenses, entrepreneurs neglect to include salaries for themselves, immediately raising a "red flag" among lenders and investors. Without drawing a salary, how will an entrepreneur pay his or her own bills? At the other extreme, lenders and investors frown on exorbitantly high salaries for owners of business start-ups. Typically, salaries are not the best use of cash in a start-up; one guideline is to draw a salary that is about 25 to 30 percent below the market rate for a similar position (and to make adjustments from there if conditions warrant). In addition, as the company grows, executive salaries should be among the *last* expenses to be increased. Reinvesting the extra money in the company accelerates its growth rate.

THE PROJECTED BALANCE SHEET In addition to projecting a start-up's net profit or loss, an entrepreneur must develop a pro forma balance sheet outlining the fledgling firm's assets and liabilities. Most entrepreneurs' primary concern is profitability because, on the surface, the importance of a business's assets is less obvious. In many cases, small companies begin their lives on weak financial footing because entrepreneurs fail to determine their firms' total asset requirements. To prevent this major oversight, entrepreneurs should prepare a projected balance sheet listing every asset their businesses will need and all the claims against these assets.

ASSETS Cash is one of the most useful assets the business owns; it is highly liquid and can quickly be converted into other tangible assets. But how much cash should a small business have at its inception? Obviously, there is no single dollar figure that fits the needs of every small firm. One practical rule of thumb, however, suggests that a company's cash balance should cover its operating expenses (less depreciation, a noncash expense) for at least one inventory turnover period. Using this guideline, we can calculate the cash balance for the small flower shop as follows:

Operating expenses = \$182,490 (from projected income statement)

Less depreciation (1.9% of annual sales*) of \$7,505 (a noncash expense)

Equals: cash expenses (annual) = \$174,985

Annual inventory turnover ratio* = 13.6 times per year

$$\text{Cash requirement} = \frac{\text{Cash expenses}}{\text{Average inventory turnover}}$$

$$= \frac{\$174,985}{13.6}$$

$$= \$12,867$$

*From Risk Management Association, *Annual Statement Studies*.

Notice the inverse relationship between the small firm's average turnover ratio and its cash requirement. The higher the number of inventory turns a company generates, the lower its cash requirement. For instance, if this florist could turn its inventory 17 times per year, its cash requirement would be \$174,985 ÷ 17 = \$10,293.

Another decision facing the entrepreneur is how much inventory the business should carry. A rough estimate of the inventory requirement can be calculated from the information found on the projected income statement and from published statistics:

Cost of goods sold = \$184,070 (from projected income statement)

$$\text{Average inventory turnover} = \frac{\text{Cost of goods sold}}{\text{Average inventory level}} = 13.6 \text{ times/year}$$

Rearranging the equation to solve for inventory level produces the following:

$$\text{Average inventory level} = \frac{\$184,070}{13.6 \text{ times/year}}$$

Average inventory level = \$13,535

The entrepreneur also includes \$1,800 in miscellaneous current assets. The estimate of fixed assets is as follows:

Fixtures (including refrigeration units)	\$54,500
Office equipment	5,250
Computers/cash register	5,125
Signs	7,200
Miscellaneous	1,500
Total	\$73,575

LIABILITIES To complete the projected balance sheet, the owner must record all of the small firm's liabilities, the claims against its assets. The flower shop owner was able to finance 50 percent of

FIGURE 11.4

Projected Balance Sheet for a Small Flower Shop

Assets		Liabilities	
Current Assets		**Current Liabilities**	
Cash	$ 12,867	Accounts Payable	$ 34,018
Inventory	13,535	Note Payable	3,750
Miscellaneous	1,800		
Total Current Assets	$ 28,202	Total Current Liabilities	$ 37,768
Fixed Assets		**Long-Term Liabilities**	
Fixtures	$ 54,500	Note Payable	$ 25,000
Office Equipment	5,250		
Computer/Cash Register	5,125	Total Liabilities	$ 62,768
Signs	7,200		
Miscellaneous	1,500		
Total Fixed Assets	$ 73,575	**Owner's Equity**	$ 39,009
Total Assets	$101,777	**Total Liabilities and Owner's Equity**	$101,777

the inventory and fixtures ($34,018) through suppliers and has a short-term note payable in the amount of $3,750. The only other major claim against the firm's assets is a note payable to the entrepreneur' father-in-law for $25,000. The difference between the company's assets ($101,777) and its total liabilities ($62,768) represents the owner's investment in the business (owner's equity) of $39,009.

The final step is to compile all of these items into a projected balance sheet, as shown in Figure 11.4.

LO4

Understand the basic financial statements through ratio analysis.

Ratio Analysis

Would you be willing to drive a car on an extended trip without being able to see the dashboard displays showing fuel level, engine temperature, oil pressure, battery status, or the speed at which you were traveling? Not many people would! Yet many small business owners run their companies exactly that way. They never take the time to check the vital signs of their businesses using their "financial dashboards." The result: their companies develop engine trouble, fail, and leave them stranded along the road to successful entrepreneurship. To avoid becoming a failure statistic, entrepreneurs must understand the numbers that drive their businesses. Norm Brodsky, a successful serial entrepreneur, explains:

> To be successful in any business, you need to develop a feel for the numbers. You need to get a sense of the relationships between them, see the connections, figure out which ones are critical and have to be monitored. Why? Because these numbers run businesses. They tell you how you can make the most money in the least time and with the least effort. You can give it all away if you want to, but first you have to earn it, and the numbers can tell you how to do that as efficiently as possible, provided you understand their language. When the numbers change, those changes can be significant. They may herald new competition arriving or indicate a shift in your customers' preferences or reflect unseen problems with your products or services. But you'll see [the reasons for the changes]—and be able to respond quickly—only if you get into the habit early on of looking for them and trying to understand what they mean.[9]

Smart entrepreneurs know that once they have their businesses up and running with the help of a solid financial plan, the next step is to keep their companies moving in the right direction with the help of proper financial controls. Establishing these controls—and using them consistently— is one of the keys to keeping a business vibrant and healthy. A sound system of financial controls serves as an early warning device for underlying problems that could destroy a young business. According to one writer,

A company's financial accounting and reporting systems will provide signals, through comparative analysis, of impending trouble, such as:

- Decreasing sales and falling profit margins.
- Increasing corporate overheads.
- Growing inventories and accounts receivable.

These are all signals of declining cash flows from operations, the lifeblood of every business. As cash flows decrease, the squeeze begins:

- Payments to vendors become slower.
- Maintenance on production equipment lags.
- Raw material shortages appear.
- Equipment breakdowns occur.

All of these begin to have a negative impact on productivity. Now the downward spiral has begun in earnest. The key is hearing and focusing on the signals.[10]

What are these signals, and how does an entrepreneur go about hearing and focusing on them? One extremely helpful tool is ratio analysis. **Ratio analysis**, a method of expressing the relationships between any two elements on financial statements, provides a convenient technique for performing financial analysis. When analyzed properly, ratios serve as barometers of a company's financial health. "You owe it to yourself to understand each ratio and what it means to your business," says one accountant. "Ratios point out potential trouble areas so you can correct them before they multiply."[11] Ratio analysis allows entrepreneurs to determine whether their companies are carrying excessive inventory, experiencing heavy operating expenses, overextending credit, taking on too much debt, and managing to pay their bills on time and to answer other questions relating to the efficient and effective operation of the overall business. Unfortunately, few business owners actually compute financial ratios and use them to manage their businesses.

Smart business owners use financial ratio analysis to identify problems in their businesses while they are still problems and not business threatening crises. Tracking these ratios over time permits an owner to spot a variety of red flags that are indications of these problem areas. This is critical to business success because business owners cannot solve problems they do not know exist! Business owners also can use ratio analysis to increase the likelihood of obtaining loans. By analyzing their financial statements with ratios, business owners can anticipate potential problems and identify important strengths in advance. Lenders and investors *do* use ratios to analyze the financial statements of companies looking for financing, comparing them against industry averages and looking for trends over time.

How many ratios should an entrepreneur monitor to maintain adequate financial control over a business? The number of ratios that an owner could calculate is limited only by the number of accounts on a firm's financial statements. However, tracking too many ratios only creates confusion and saps the meaning from an entrepreneur's financial analysis. The secret to successful ratio analysis is *simplicity*, focusing on just enough ratios to provide a clear picture of a company's financial standing.

Twelve Key Ratios

In keeping with the idea of simplicity, we will describe 12 key ratios that enable most business owners to monitor their companies' financial positions without becoming bogged down in financial details. This section presents explanations of these ratios and examples based on the balance sheet and the income statement for Sam's Appliance Shop shown in Figure 11.1 and Figure 11.2. We will group them into four categories: liquidity ratios, leverage ratios, operating ratios, and profitability ratios.

LIQUIDITY RATIOS **Liquidity ratios** tell whether a small business will be able to meet its short-term financial obligations as they come due. These ratios forewarn a business owner of impending cash flow problems. A small company with solid liquidity not only is able to pay its bills on time but also has enough cash to take advantage of attractive business opportunities as they arise. Liquidity ratios measure a company's ability to convert its assets to cash quickly and without a

ratio analysis
a method of expressing the relationship between any two accounting elements that allows business owners to analyze their companies' financial performances.

liquidity ratios
tell whether a small business will be able to meet its short-term financial obligations as they come due.

loss of value to pay its short-term liabilities. The primary measures of liquidity are the current ratio and the quick ratio.

1. Current Ratio. The **current ratio** measures a small firm's solvency by indicating its ability to pay current liabilities (debts) from current assets. It is calculated in the following manner:

$$\text{Current ratio} = \frac{\text{Current assets}}{\text{Current liabilities}}$$
$$= \frac{\$686,985}{\$367,850}$$
$$= 1.87:1$$

Sam's Appliance Shop has $1.87 in current assets for every $1 it has in current liabilities.

Current assets are those that an owner expects to convert into cash in the ordinary business cycle and normally include cash, notes/accounts receivable, inventory, and any other short-term marketable securities. Current liabilities are those short-term obligations that come due within one year and include notes/accounts payable, taxes payable, and accruals.

The current ratio is sometimes called the *working capital ratio* and is the most commonly used measure of short-term solvency. Typically, financial analysts suggest that a small business maintain a current ratio of at least 2:1 (i.e., $2 of current assets for every $1 of current liabilities) to maintain a comfortable cushion of working capital. Generally, the higher a company's current ratio, the stronger its financial position; however, a high current ratio does not guarantee that a company is using its assets in the most profitable manner. For example, a business may have an abundance of accounts receivable (many of which may not even be collectible) or may be over-investing in inventory.

With its current ratio of 1.87, Sam's Appliance Shop could liquidate its current assets at 53.5 percent ($1 \div 1.87 = 53.5\%$) of its book value and still manage to pay its current creditors in full.

2. Quick Ratio. The current ratio sometimes can be misleading because it does not reflect the *quality* of a company's current assets. As we have already seen, a company with a large number of past-due receivables and stale inventory could boast an impressive current ratio and still be on the verge of financial collapse. The **quick ratio** (sometimes called the acid test ratio) is a more conservative measure of a company's liquidity because it shows the extent to which its most liquid assets cover its current liabilities. This ratio includes only a company's "quick assets"—those assets that a company can convert into cash immediately if needed—and excludes the most illiquid asset of all, inventory. It is calculated as follows:

$$\text{Quick ratio} = \frac{\text{Quick assets}}{\text{Current liabilities}}$$
$$= \frac{\$\,686,985 - \$455,455}{\$367,850}$$
$$= 0.63:1$$

Sam's Appliance Shop has 63 cents in quick assets for every $1 of current liabilities.

The quick ratio is a more rigorous test of a company's liquidity. It measures a company's capacity to pay its current debts if all sales income ceased immediately. Generally, a quick ratio of 1:1 is considered satisfactory. A ratio of less than 1:1 indicates that the small firm is dependent on inventory and on future sales to satisfy short-term debt. A quick ratio of greater than 1:1 indicates a greater degree of financial security.

LEVERAGE RATIOS **Leverage ratios** measure the financing supplied by a firm's owners against that supplied by its creditors; they are a gauge of the depth of a company's debt. These ratios show the extent to which an entrepreneur relies on debt capital (rather than equity capital) to finance the business. They also provide a measure of the degree of financial risk in a company. Generally, small businesses with low leverage ratios are less affected by economic downturns, but the returns for these firms are lower during economic booms. Conversely, small companies with high leverage ratios are more vulnerable to economic slides because their debt loads demolish cash flow; however, they have greater potential for large profits.

Today, 78 percent of small businesses rely on some type of debt (loans, credit cards, mortgages, trade credit, and others), an increase from 70 percent of small companies in 2006.[12] Debt is a powerful financial tool, but companies must handle it carefully—just as a demolitionist handles dynamite. Like dynamite, too much debt can be deadly. Unfortunately, some companies push their debt loads beyond the safety barrier and threaten their ability to survive. Heavy debt loads can be deadly, particularly when a company's sales or earnings falter.

James Atoa/Newscom

ENTREPRENEURIAL PROFILE: Eva Longoria: Beso Beso, a restaurant in Las Vegas, Nevada, in which actress Eva Longoria is an investor, filed for Chapter 11 bankruptcy (reorganization) after incurring losses of $76,000 per month despite generating monthly revenue of $1.2 million. Operating at a loss put the company in a downward financial spiral and a deepening cash bind as it racked up large amounts of debt in an attempt to survive. At the time of the bankruptcy filing, Beso reported $2.5 million in assets and $5.7 million in liabilities, including $3.6 million in past-due rent to its landlord, CityCenter. A bankruptcy judge approved a plan in which Landry's, a restaurant chain with 30 brands and 300 locations, purchased Beso for $1 million. In a turnaround attempt, Landry's will operate Beso, and Longoria will have an ownership stake in the business and is contractually obligated to make appearances there.[13] ∎

Managed carefully, however, debt can boost a company's performance and improve its productivity.

3. Debt Ratio. A small company's **debt ratio** measures the percentage of total assets financed by its creditors compared to its owners. The debt ratio is calculated as follows:

$$\text{Debt ratio} = \frac{\text{Total debt (or liabilities)}}{\text{Total assets}}$$
$$= \frac{\$367,850 + \$212,150}{\$847,655}$$
$$= 0.68{:}1$$

debt ratio
measures the percentage of total assets financed by a company's creditors compared to its owners.

Creditors have claims of 68 cents against every $1 of assets that Sam's Appliance Shop owns, meaning that creditors have contributed twice as much to the company's asset base as its owners have.

Total debt includes all current liabilities and any outstanding long-term notes and bonds. Total assets represent the sum of the firm's current assets, fixed assets, and intangible assets. A high debt ratio means that creditors provide a large percentage of a company's total financing and, therefore, bear most of its financial risk. Owners generally prefer higher leverage ratios; otherwise, business funds must come either from the owners' personal assets or from taking on new owners, which means giving up more control over the business. In addition, with a greater portion of a firm's assets financed by creditors, the owner is able to generate profits with a smaller personal investment. Creditors, however, typically prefer moderate debt ratios because a lower debt ratio indicates a smaller chance of creditor losses in case of liquidation. To lenders and creditors, high debt ratios mean a higher risk of default.

ENTREPRENEURIAL PROFILE: Sbarro Inc. Sbarro, a franchised chain of more than 1,000 quick-service Italian restaurants operating in 42 countries that began in 1956 as an Italian grocery store in Brooklyn, New York, was hammered by rapidly rising food costs, a global economic downturn, and a decline in traffic at shopping malls, where most of its stores are located. Because of the financial challenges the company faced, its debt climbed, ultimately outweighing its asset base, and the company filed for Chapter 11 bankruptcy (reorganization) protection. At the time of the filing, Sbarro's debt ratio was 1.03:1, $1.03 in debt for every $1 of assets. A bankruptcy court approved the company's reorganization plan, which provided access to $35 million of new capital from a new ownership group and, more important, reduced its debt level by 70 percent. When Sbarro emerged from bankruptcy, its debt ratio was 0.29:1, 29 cents in debt for every $1 of assets.[14] ∎

According to a senior analyst at Dun & Bradstreet's Analytical Services, "If managed properly, debt can be beneficial because it's a great way to have money working for you. You're leveraging your assets, so you're making more money than you're paying out in interest." However, excessive debt can be the downfall of a business. "As we pile up debt on our personal credit cards our lifestyles are squeezed," he says. "The same thing happens to a business. Overpowering debt sinks thousands of businesses each year."[15]

✓ You Be the Consultant

The Perils of Debt: Part 1

Chuck Bidwell, a serial entrepreneur, and Jennifer Guarino, a former handbag designer, agreed that if they ever found the right business to purchase, they would do so together. Over the course of several years, the entrepreneurs passed on many businesses, but when the opportunity arose to purchase J. W. Hulme Company, a St. Paul, Minnesota–based small maker of hunting bags and fishing rod cases, Bidwell and Guarino bought the company for $600,000. Founded in 1905, Hulme made military tents during World War I, canvas awnings in the postwar era, and travel bags for upscale retailers such as Orvis. When Bidwell and Guarino purchased the company, it employed three people who made outdoor gear.

Their vision for Hulme was to ramp up the company's growth rate by focusing on luxury markets with a broader line of products that included briefcases, backpacks, and handbags that they would market through catalogs and a Web site. Doing so, however, would require the entrepreneurs to borrow heavily. Their business plan called for increasing the company's mailing list from just 1,000 customers to more than 10,000 and expanding its product line from just 100 items to 250 products. If their strategy worked, their forecast showed annual sales of $2 million and positive cash flow.

To fund their expansion plans, Bidwell took a $130,000 second mortgage on his house, and he and Guarino presented their business plan to Fizal Kassim, head of Maple Bank in nearby Champlin, Minnesota. Maple Bank granted the entrepreneurs a $70,000 loan and a $200,000 line of credit, the first in a series of ever-larger loans to the small company with big growth plans. Within three years, the plans that Bidwell and Guarino seemed to be coming to fruition; Hulme had increased sales by 89 percent to $1.4 million and earned a profit (before interest, depreciation, and taxes) of $325,000.

Bidwell and Guarino approached another local lender, St. Stephen Bank, for a $700,000 loan that would be guaranteed by the Small Business Administration (SBA). Expecting the loan to be processed quickly, the company hired employees and raw materials and began cranking up production. They also began planning an all-important catalog mailing for the upcoming season. Management changes at St. Stephen Bank delayed the loan for six months, meaning that Bidwell and Guarino had to borrow more money—and fast. They turned to family members, friends, and business associates for loans totaling $500,000, but piecing together that much money took longer than expected, and Hulme missed several important catalog mailing deadlines, handicapping the company's ability to generate sales. By the end of the year, the small company, now laden with debt, had generated only $1.5 million in sales, well below the $2 million target that Bidwell and Guarino had established.

The SBA-backed loan from St. Stephen Bank finally came through, helping the entrepreneurs pay for new equipment, inventory, catalogs, and other expenses associated with their growth plans. Unfortunately, the loans from the banks, friends, and relatives pushed Hulme's debt-to-equity ratio from 2.94:1 to

5.53:1 in just one year. Because lenders prefer to see companies keep this ratio below 3:1, Hulme's creditors began to get nervous. When Bidwell approached Maple Bank for another $250,000 loan to print and mail the next round of catalogs, Kassim explained that a looming credit crisis (which would later sweep through the banking industry) made it difficult for Maple Bank to lend any more money to Hulme. Kassim also expressed concerns that an economic recession could slow demand for the company's upscale product line, which included $500 garment bags and $1,200 leather duffle bags. Kassim also was concerned about the company's building inventory. Kassim told Bidwell that Maple Bank preferred to see inventory levels that were no more than 50 percent of sales, but Hulme's inventory represented 67 percent of sales.

Bidwell and Guarino stopped drawing their modest $40,000 salaries from the company and laid off 6 of their 14 employees. One seamstress who was laid off says, "They had been running out of supplies, like the hardware that goes on the bags, because they didn't have the money." The entrepreneurs went back to Maple Bank and told Kassim that if they could not get a $250,000 loan, they would have to shut down the company, meaning that the bank and all of the company's other creditors would lose all of their money. Meanwhile, Hulme's catalog printer became aware of the company's cash problems and demanded advance payment for the upcoming round of catalogs. Caught in a bind, Bidwell convinced some friends to guarantee a $125,000 loan from Maple Bank. The money allowed Hulme to get its catalogs in customers' hands, although the mailing was more than a month late. The company's sales shrank because it could send out only 175,000 catalogs, down from 600,000 the previous year. "If we'd had the proper financing in place and had been able to mail our catalogs on time, we would have had a very successful year," says Bidwell. Instead, he and Guarino are battling to save their company. Guarino has drained her savings, lost all her credit cards, and constantly fields calls from creditors wondering when—and if—they will be paid. Bidwell lost his house and has been forced to sell his collection of vintage Buicks. The entrepreneurs have had to lay off employees and renegotiate payments with their suppliers as well as with the banks that extended them loans. They know that there is no guarantee that J. W. Hulme will survive.

1. What are the benefits to entrepreneurs who use debt capital (leverage) to finance their companies' growth?

2. What are the risks associated with debt financing?

3. Assume the role of a small business banker. Suppose that Bidwell and Guarino had approached you for a bank loan when they were buying J. W. Hulme. Which financial ratios would you be most interested in? Why? What advice would you offer them?

Source: Based on Julie Jargon, "On Front Lines of Debt Crisis, Luggage Maker Fights for Life," *Wall Street Journal*, January 9, 2009, pp. A1, A8.

4. Debt-to-Net-Worth Ratio. A small company's **debt-to-net-worth (debt-to-equity) ratio** also expresses the relationship between the capital contributions from creditors and those from owners and measures how highly leveraged a company is. This ratio reveals a company's capital structure by comparing what the business "owes" to "what it is worth." It is a measure of a small company's ability to meet both its creditor and owner obligations in case of liquidation. The debt-to-net-worth ratio is calculated as follows:

$$\text{Debt-to-net worth ratio} = \frac{\text{Total debt (or liabilities)}}{\text{Tangible net worth}}$$
$$= \frac{\$367,850 + \$212,150}{\$267,655 - \$3,500}$$
$$= 2.20:1$$

debt-to-net-worth (debt-to-equity) ratio expresses the relationship between the capital contributions from creditors and those from owners and measures how highly leveraged a company is.

Sam's Appliance Shop owes creditors $2.20 for every $1 of equity that Sam owns.

Total debt is the sum of current liabilities and long-term liabilities, and tangible net worth represents the owners' investment in the business (capital + capital stock + earned surplus + retained earnings) less any intangible assets (e.g., goodwill) the firm owns.

The higher this ratio, the more leverage a business is using and the lower the degree of protection afforded creditors if the business should fail. A higher debt-to-net-worth ratio also means that the firm has less capacity to borrow; lenders and creditors see the firm as being "borrowed up." Conversely, a low ratio typically is associated with a higher level of financial security, giving the business greater borrowing potential.

ENTREPRENEURIAL PROFILE: Vicorp Restaurants Inc.: Village Inn and Bakers Square Founded in 1958, Vicorp Restaurants Inc., the parent company of Village Inn and Bakers Square restaurant chains, began incurring losses when sales declined and food and operating costs increased. The company's 250 restaurants were serving 1.1 million eggs each week, but when egg prices tripled over a two-year period, its earnings were squeezed even though the company raised menu prices. Increases in the minimum wage and energy costs pushed the company's operating expenses even higher. Vicorp increased its debt load to cover the higher costs and to remodel its stores, actions that pushed its debt-to-net-worth ratio from 4:1 to 10:1, just months before the company filed for Chapter 11 bankruptcy protection.[16] ∎

As a company's debt-to-net worth ratio approaches 1:1, the creditors' interest in the business approaches that of the owners. If the ratio is greater than 1:1, creditors' claims exceed those of the owners, and the business may be undercapitalized. In other words, the owner has not supplied an adequate amount of capital, forcing the business to be overextended in terms of debt. Lenders become nervous when a company's debt-to-equity ratio reaches 3:1 or more.

5. Times-Interest-Earned Ratio. The **times-interest-earned ratio** is a measure of a small company's ability to make the interest payments on its debt. It tells how many times a company's earnings cover the interest payments on the debt it is carrying. This ratio measures the size of the cushion a company has in covering the interest cost of its debt load. The times-interest-earned ratio is calculated as follows:

times-interest-earned ratio measures a small firm's ability to make the interest payments on its debt.

$$\text{Times interest earned ratio} = \frac{\text{Earnings before interest and taxes (or EBIT)}}{\text{Total interest expense}}$$
$$= \frac{\$60,629 + \$39,850}{\$39,850}$$
$$= 2.52:1$$

Sam's Appliance Shop's earnings are 2.5 times greater than its interest expense.

EBIT is the firm's profit *before* deducting interest expense and taxes; the denominator measures the amount the business paid in interest over the accounting period. A high ratio suggests that a company has little difficulty meeting the interest payments on its loans; creditors see this as a sign of safety for future loans. Conversely, a low ratio is an indication that the company is overextended in its debts; earnings will not be able to cover its debt service if this ratio is less than one. "I look for a [times-interest-earned] ratio of higher than three-to-one," says one financial analyst, "which indicates that management has considerable breathing room to make its debt payments. When the ratio drops below one-to-one, it clearly indicates management is under tremendous pressure to raise cash. The risk of default or bankruptcy is very high."[17] Many creditors look for a times-interest-earned ratio of at least 4:1 to 6:1 before pronouncing a company a good credit risk. Before Vicorp Restaurants Inc., the owner of Village Inn and Bakers Square restaurant chains, filed for bankruptcy, its times-interest-earned ratio had slipped from nearly 3:1 to just 1.85:1.[18]

Although low to moderate levels of debt can boost a company's financial performance, trouble looms on the horizon for businesses whose debt loads are so heavy that they must starve critical operations, research and development, customer service, and other vital areas just to pay interest on the debt. Because their interest payments are so large, highly leveraged companies find that they are restricted when it comes to spending cash, whether on an acquisition, normal operations, or capital spending. Some entrepreneurs are so averse to debt that they run their companies with little or no borrowing, relying instead on their business's cash flow to finance growth.

Courtesy of Zamolution

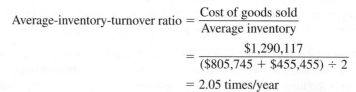

ENTREPRENEURIAL PROFILE: Jim Zamichieli: Zamolution When Jim Zamichieli started his digital marketing company, Zamolution, he invested $20,000 in personal savings rather than borrow start-up capital. "Not taking out a loan absolutely makes me more conservative in my spending," he says. The former corporate executive saw many companies founder when they took on too much debt, something he vows never to do, even though he admits that his company "could grow dramatically with a loan."[19] ∎

operating ratios

help an entrepreneur evaluate a small company's overall performance and indicate how effectively the business employs its resources.

average-inventory-turnover ratio

measures the number of times its average inventory is sold out, or turned over, during an accounting period.

OPERATING RATIOS Operating ratios help an entrepreneur evaluate a small company's overall performance and indicate how effectively the business employs its resources. The more effectively its resources are used, the less capital a small business will require. These five operating ratios are designed to help an entrepreneur spot those areas he or she must improve if his or her business is to remain competitive.

6. Average-Inventory-Turnover Ratio. A small firm's **average-inventory-turnover ratio** measures the number of times its average inventory is sold out, or turned over, during the accounting period. This ratio tells the owner whether an entrepreneur is managing inventory properly. It indicates whether a business's inventory is understocked, overstocked, or obsolete. The average-inventory-turnover ratio is calculated as follows:

$$\text{Average-inventory-turnover ratio} = \frac{\text{Cost of goods sold}}{\text{Average inventory}}$$

$$= \frac{\$1,290,117}{(\$805,745 + \$455,455) \div 2}$$

$$= 2.05 \text{ times/year}$$

HappyAlex/Fotolia

Sam' Appliance Shop turns its inventory about two times a year, or once every 178 days.

Average inventory is the sum of the value of the firm's inventory at the beginning of the accounting period and its value at the end of the accounting period, divided by 2.

This ratio tells an entrepreneur how fast merchandise is moving through the business and helps him or her to balance the company's inventory on the fine line between oversupply and undersupply. To determine the average number of days units remain in inventory, the owner can divide the average-inventory-turnover ratio into the number of days in the accounting period (e.g., 365 days ÷ average-inventory-turnover ratio). The result is called *days' inventory* (or *average age of inventory*).

Auto dealerships often use the average age of inventory as a measure of their performance and consider 50 to 60 days' worth of new cars to be an adequate inventory. Used car dealers' goal is to have 35 to 45 days' worth of used cars in inventory. Slow-turning inventory cannibalizes car

You Be the Consultant

The Perils of Debt: Part 2

J. W. Hulme Company, the Minnesota-based maker of upscale briefcases, travel bags, duffels, and purses, had borrowed so much money to finance its ambitious expansion plans that its debt-to-equity ratio increased from 2.94:1 to 5.53:1 in just one year. Borrowing money to finance growth is an age-old strategy that many companies use, but when debt loads become too heavy or sales falter, a company's problems are magnified. Anticipating that a bank would process their approved loan quickly, J. W. Hulme's co-owners, Chuck Bidwell and Jennifer Guarino, purchased raw materials, hired several employees, and ramped up production. The loan was delayed, and Bidwell and Guarino scrambled to borrow money from their family members and friends. The delay caused them to miss key mailing dates for their catalogs, hurting the company's sales and led to late payments to lenders and vendors.

Dean Vanech, CEO of Olympus Capital Investments, a private equity firm, learned about J. W. Hulme's plight and decided to purchase a 49 percent stake in the struggling but promising company. Olympus Capital's investment and the $794,000 Bidwell invested in the company from the sale of six vintage Buicks allowed J. W. Hulme to cut its debt by 50 percent, to $1 million. The entrepreneurs also converted the loans from family and friends into equity, making those people shareholders in the company. The changes gave Bidwell and Guarino some breathing room, and they rehired several former employees and added four new ones. With Olympus's guidance, they invested in modernizing the business, upgrading its ordering system, and updating its Web site. The entrepreneurs also culled slow-moving products from their line and added new items, including iPad cases, designed to appeal to new groups of customers.

Blogger Michael Williams was so impressed with J. W. Hulme's products that he included them on his "American List" of home-grown brands. Designer Steve Alan, owner of upscale boutiques in New York, California, and Korea, read about J. W. Hulme on Williams's blog and decided to add the company's bags to his stores and to his Web site. "I like things that will last a long time and are timeless," says Alan. "Their products have that quality." Buyers from Barneys New York discovered J. W. Hulme's products at Alan's store in New York City, and soon the upscale retailer was featuring them in its Madison Avenue store and in its catalog. "There's a return to things that exude heritage and quality," says Julie Gilhart, fashion director at Barney's. "It's cool that J. W. Hulme was making canvas tents during the First World War and then hunting accessories."

The publicity, attention, and orders have reinvigorated J. W. Hulme. Bidwell says that the company has sales of $2.6 million, three times its revenue in 2009, and will generate a profit. Just as important, the entrepreneurs have worked their way out from under a burdensome debt load that was threatening their company's future. "What I didn't do was really make it a priority to look beneath the numbers," says a wiser Guarino. "We took the fast track to growth. We were growing 40 percent a year, spending money on new product, new customers, and reengineering." Guarino is optimistic about J. W. Hulme's future and looks forward to the day when she can return to managing its operations rather than scrambling to find financing. "If this works, I'm going to get back to running the business," she says. "I've spent the last year bootstrapping, finding financing. I look so forward to that day because that's what I do best."

1. Why is using ratio analysis to keep track of their companies' financial performances over time so important for entrepreneurs?

2. What lessons concerning the use of debt financing can entrepreneurs learn from J. W. Hulme's experience?

Sources: Based on Julie Jargon, "Restitching a Firm That Nearly Unraveled," *Wall Street Journal*, August 3, 2011, pp. B8; and Beth Ewen, "President Jen Guarino on Trying to Save the Century-Old Luggage Manufacturer and Retailer J. W. Hulme," *Upsize Mag*, April 2009, http://www.upsizemag.com/article.asp?issueID=67&articleID=1219.

---

dealers' profitability because of the interest and other expenses they incur. "The speed of inventory dictates profit," says Joseph Lescota, a retail automotive expert. At luxury new car dealerships, Lescota says that the cost of holding a car in inventory can be as high as $90 per day; at the typical used car dealership, the cost is $21 per day. If a used car dealership sells a car within 20 days, it earns an average gross profit of $2,000. However, if that same car sits on the lot for 80 days before it sells, the average gross profit is just $740 (an occurrence known in the industry as "lot rot.")

ENTREPRENEURIAL PROFILE: Steve Matthews: Matthews Motors Steve Matthews, owner of Matthews Motors in Clayton, North Carolina, focuses on keeping his inventory turnover ratio above the industry average. "We stay on top of inventory," he says. "We look at it once a week to see what needs to go." Matthews typically stocks between 80 and 85 cars on his lot and sells between 45 and 60 per month. For cars that linger on his lot, Matthews provides additional incentives to salespeople, reduces the price, runs Internet specials, or sells it to another dealer at a used car auction.[20] ∎

An above-average inventory turnover indicates that the small business has a healthy, salable, and liquid inventory and a supply of quality merchandise that is supported by sound pricing policies. A below-average inventory turnover suggests an illiquid inventory characterized by obsolescence, over-stocking, stale merchandise, and poor purchasing procedures. Businesses that turn their inventories more rapidly require a smaller inventory investment to produce a particular sales volume. That means that these companies tie up less cash in inventory that idly sits on shelves. For instance, if Sam's could turn its inventory *four* times each year instead of just *two*, the company would require an average inventory of just $322,529 instead of the current level of $630,600 to generate sales of $1,870,841. Increasing the number of inventory turns would free up more than $308,000 in cash currently tied up in excess inventory! Sam's would benefit from improved cash flow and higher profits.

The inventory turnover ratio can be misleading, however. For example, an excessively high ratio could mean that a company does not have enough inventory on hand and may be losing sales because of stock-outs. Similarly, a low ratio could be the result of planned inventory stock-piling to meet seasonal peak demand. Another problem is that the ratio is based on an inventory balance calculated from two days out of the entire accounting period. Thus, inventory fluctuations due to seasonal demand patterns are ignored, and this may bias the resulting ratio. There is no universal, ideal inventory turnover ratio. Financial analysts suggest that a favorable turnover ratio depends on the type of business, its size, its profitability, its method of inventory valuation, and other relevant factors. The most meaningful benchmark for comparison is other companies of similar size in the same industry. For instance, the typical supermarket turns its inventory on average about 15 times a year, but a jewelry store averages just 1.5 to 2 inventory turns a year.

7. Average-Collection-Period Ratio. A small firm's **average-collection-period ratio** (or days sales outstanding [DSO]) tells the average number of days it takes to collect accounts receivable. To compute the average collection period ratio, an entrepreneur must first calculate the company's receivables turnover. Given that Sam's *credit* sales for the year were $1,309,589 (out of the total sales of $1,870,841), the company's receivables turnover ratio is as follows:

average-collection-period ratio
measures the number of days it takes to collect accounts receivable.

$$\text{Receivables turnover ratio} = \frac{\text{Credit sales}}{\text{Accounts receivable}}$$

$$= \frac{\$1,309,589}{\$179,225}$$

$$= 7.31 \text{ times/year}$$

Sam's Appliance Shop turns over its receivables 7.31 times per year. This ratio measures the number of times the firm's accounts receivable turn over during the accounting period. The higher the firm's receivables turnover ratio, the shorter the time lag is between the sale and the cash collection.

Use the following to calculate the firm's average-collection-period ratio:

$$\text{Average-collection-period ratio} = \frac{\text{Days in accounting period}}{\text{Receivables turnover ratio}}$$

$$= \frac{365 \text{ days}}{7.31 \text{ times/year}}$$

$$= 50.0 \text{ days}$$

Sam's Appliance Shop's accounts receivable are outstanding for an average of 50 days. Typically, the higher a firm's average collection period ratio, the greater its chance of incurring bad debt losses. Sales don't count unless a company collects the revenue from them.

One of the most useful applications of the collection period ratio is to compare it to the industry average and to the company's credit terms. This comparison indicates the degree of control a small company exercises over its credit sales and collection techniques. A healthy collection period ratio depends on the industry in which a company operates. For instance, the average collection period for companies that manufacture laboratory instruments is 49 days; for tire retailers, it is just 20 days.[21] Perhaps the most meaningful analysis is comparing the collection period ratio to a company's credit terms. One rule of thumb suggests that a company's collection period ratio should be no more than one-third greater than its credit terms. For example, if a small company's credit terms are net 30 (payment due within 30 days), its average-collection-period ratio should be no more than 40 days (30 + 30 × 1/3). For this company, a ratio greater than 40 days indicates poor collection procedures.

TABLE 11.1 How Lowering Your Average Collection Period Can Save You Money

Too often, entrepreneurs fail to recognize the importance of collecting their accounts receivable on time. After all, collecting accounts is not as glamorous or as much fun as generating sales. Lowering a company's average collection period ratio, however, *can* produce tangible—and often significant— savings. The following formula shows how to convert an improvement in a company's average collection period ratio into dollar savings:

Annual savings

$$= \frac{(\text{Credit sales} \times \text{Annual interest rate} \times \text{Number of days average collection period is lowered})}{365}$$

where
credit sales = company's annual credit sales in dollars,
annual interest rate = the interest rate at which the company borrows money,
and number of days average collection period is lowered = the difference between the
    previous year's average collection period ratio and the current one.

Example

Sam's Appliance Shop's average collection period ratio is 50 days. Suppose that the previous year's average-collection-period ratio was 58 days, an eight-day improvement. The company's credit sales for the most recent year were $1,309,589. If Sam borrows money at 8.75%, this six-day improvement has generated savings for Sam's Appliance Shop of

$$\text{Savings} = \frac{\$1,309,589 \times 8.75\% \times 8 \text{ days}}{365 \text{ days}} = \$2,512$$

By collecting his accounts receivable just eight days faster on average, Sam has saved his business more than $2,512! Of course, if a company's average-collection-period ratio rises, the same calculation will tell the owner how much that change costs.

Source: Adapted from "Days Saved, Thousands Earned," *Inc.*, November 1995, p. 98.

Slow payers represent a great risk to many small businesses. Many entrepreneurs proudly point to rapidly rising sales only to find that they must borrow money to keep their companies going because their credit customers are paying their bills in 45, 60, or even 90 days instead of the desired 30. Slow receivables are a real danger because they usually lead to a cash crisis that threatens a company's survival. Table 11.1 shows how to calculate the savings associated with lowering a company's average-collection-period ratio.

8. Average-Payable-Period Ratio. The converse of the average-collection-period ratio, the **average-payable-period ratio** (or days payables outstanding, DPO) tells the average number of days it takes a company to pay its accounts payable. Like the average collection period, it is measured in days. To compute this ratio, an entrepreneur first calculates the payables turnover ratio. Sam's payables turnover ratio is as follows:

average-payable-period ratio measures the number of days it takes a company to pay its accounts payable.

$$\text{Payables turnover ratio} = \frac{\text{Purchases}}{\text{Accounts payable}}$$

$$= \frac{\$939,827}{\$152,580}$$

$$= 6.16 \text{ times/year}$$

To find the average payable period, use the following computation:

$$\text{Average-payable-period ratio} = \frac{\text{Days in accounting period}}{\text{Payables turnover ratio}}$$

$$= \frac{365 \text{ days}}{6.16 \text{ times per year}}$$

$$= 59.3 \text{ days}$$

Sam's Appliance Shop takes an average of 59 days to pay its accounts with vendors and suppliers.

One of the most meaningful comparisons for this ratio is against the credit terms suppliers offer (or an average of the credit terms offered). If the average payable ratio slips beyond vendors' credit terms, a company probably suffers from a sloppy accounts-payable procedure or from cash shortages, and its credit rating is in danger. An excessively high average-payables-period ratio indicates the presence of a significant amount of past-due accounts payable. Although sound cash management calls for a business owner to keep his or her cash as long as possible, slowing payables too drastically can severely damage the company's credit rating. If this ratio is significantly lower than vendors' credit terms, the company is not using its cash most effectively by paying vendors too quickly.

Comparing a company's average-collection-period ratio (DSO) to its average-payable-period ratio (DPO) gives owners meaningful insight into their companies' cash position. Ideally, the average payable period matches (or exceeds) the time it takes to convert inventory into sales and ultimately into cash. In this case, the company's vendors are financing its inventory and its credit sales. Online retailer Amazon benefits from this situation. On average, the company does not pay its vendors until 127 days after it collects payments from its customers.[22] Subtracting DSO from DPO yields a company's **float**, the net number of days of cash that flow into or out of a company. Sam's Appliance Shop's float is

float
the net number of days of cash flowing into or out of a company; float = days payables outstanding (DPO) – days sales outstanding (DSO).

$$\text{Float} = \text{DPO} - \text{DSO} = 59.3 \text{ days} - 50.0 \text{ days} = 9.3 \text{ days}$$

A positive value for float means that cash will accumulate in a company over time, but a negative number means that the company's cash balance will diminish over time. Multiplying float by the company's average daily sales tells Sam how much the company's cash balance will change over the course of the year as a result of its collection and payable processes:

$$\text{Change in cash position} = \$1,870,841 \div 365 \text{ days} \times 9.3 \text{ days} = \$47,668$$

We will see the impact that these three operating ratios—inventory turnover, accounts receivable, and accounts payable—have on a small company's cash flow in the next chapter.

9. Net-Sales-to-Total-Assets Ratio. A small company's **net-sales-to-total-assets (also called the total-asset-turnover) ratio** is a general measure of its ability to generate sales in relation to its assets. It describes how productively the firm employs its assets to produce sales revenue. The total-assets-turnover ratio is calculated as follows:

net-sales-to-total assets (total asset turnover) ratio
measures a company's ability to generate sales in relation to its asset base.

$$\begin{aligned}
\text{Total-assets-turnover ratio} &= \frac{\text{Net sales}}{\text{Net total assets}} \\
&= \frac{\$1,870,841}{\$847,655} \\
&= 2.21{:}1
\end{aligned}$$

Sam's Appliance Shop is generating $2.21 in sales for every dollar of assets.

The denominator of this ratio, net total assets, is the sum of all of a company's assets (cash, inventory, land, buildings, equipment, tools, and everything it owns) less depreciation. This ratio is meaningful only when compared to that of similar firms in the same industry category. Monitoring it over time is very helpful for maintaining a sufficient asset base as a small business grows. A total-assets-turnover ratio below the industry average indicates that a small company is not generating an adequate sales volume for its asset size.

A recent survey by the National Federation of Independent Businesses reports "poor sales" as the one of the most commonly cited problems among small businesses, ranking just behind perennial top problems "government regulation" and "taxes."[23] If a company's sales fall below its break-even point, it operates at a loss, which is not sustainable.

ENTREPRENEURIAL PROFILE: Real Mex Restaurants Real Mex Restaurants, a company that operates 178 fast-casual Mexican restaurants under four brands, saw its sales decline from $553 million to $478 million in just three years. Rapidly rising food costs also slammed the company, causing it to operate at a loss and straining its cash flow so much that the company missed payments on its debt. Real Mex filed for Chapter 11 bankruptcy protection in an attempt to reorganize and survive.[24] ∎

PROFITABILITY RATIOS **Profitability ratios** indicate how efficiently a small company is being managed. They provide the owner with information about a company's ability to use its resources to generate a profit, its "bottom line."

10. Net-Profit-on-Sales Ratio. The **net-profit-on-sales ratio** (also called the profit-margin-on-sales ratio or the net-profit-margin ratio) measures a company's profit per dollar of sales. This ratio (which is expressed as a percentage) shows the portion of each sales dollar remaining after deducting all expenses. The profit margin on sales is calculated as follows:

$$\text{Net-profit-on-sales ratio} = \frac{\text{Net profit}}{\text{Net sales}}$$

$$= \frac{\$60,629}{\$1,870,841}$$

$$= 3.24\%$$

For every dollar in sales Sam's Appliance Shop generates, Sam keeps 3.24 cents in profit.

A recent study by *Inc.* magazine and Sageworks shows that the average net profit margin for privately held companies normally falls between 5 and 6.5 percent, but this ratio varies from one industry to another. The retail industry typically produces a net-profit-on-sales ratio that falls between 2 and 4 percent, but profit margins in the health care field range between 10 and 16 percent.[25] If a company's profit margin on sales is below the industry average, it may be a sign that its prices are too low, that its costs are excessively high, or both.

ENTREPRENEURIAL PROFILE: Don Fox: Firehouse Subs "The restaurant business is a penny business," says Don Fox, CEO of Firehouse Subs. "We work on relatively thin margins and don't have the luxury of harboring a casual attitude when it comes to controlling costs. We must meticulously control and monitor recipes and portioning and manage labor down to the quarter hour to ensure optimum productivity whenever an employee is on the clock. We must control and minimize waste in all areas—food, paper, utilities, operating supplies—the list is endless." Bill Glover, head chef and owner of Sage American Bistro in Columbus, Ohio, says that rising fuel and food costs are "eating away the bottom line" of his business. "[Profit] margins are already so thin; it's stressful to see costs rise because our business is so vulnerable." Fox, Glover, and other restaurateurs are constantly juggling their menus to keep food costs down and are involving their employees in finding ways to operate more efficiently.[26] ■

Angel Luis Garcia/El Nuevo Dia de Puerto Rico/Newscom

A natural reaction to low profitability ratios is to embark on a cost-cutting effort. Although minimizing costs does improve profitability, entrepreneurs must be judicious in their cost cutting, taking a strategic approach rather than imposing across-the-board cuts. The key is to reduce costs without diminishing customer service and damaging employee morale. Cutting costs in areas that are vital to operating success—such as a retail jeweler eliminating its advertising expenditures or a restaurant reducing the quality of its ingredients—usually hurts a company's ability to compete and can lead to failure. For instance, choosing to lay off workers, a common reaction at many companies facing financial challenges, often backfires. Not only does a company risk losing talented workers and the knowledge they have built up over time, but research also shows that repeated rounds of layoffs destroy the morale and the productivity of the remaining workers.[27]

In other cases, entrepreneurs on cost-cutting vendettas alienate employees and sap worker morale by eliminating nitpicking costs that affect employees adversely and really don't save much money. The owner of one company thought he would save money by eliminating the free coffee the company provided for its workers. Employee productivity took a hit, however, when workers began taking trips several times a day to a nearby coffee shop. "What a wonderful productivity enhancer!" says one former employee sarcastically.[28]

If a company's net-profit-on-sales ratio is excessively low, the owner first should check the gross profit margin (net sales minus cost of goods sold expressed as a percentage of net sales). Of course, a reasonable gross profit margin varies from industry to industry. For instance, a service company may have a gross profit margin of 75 percent, while a manufacturer's may be 35 percent. The key is to know what a reasonable gross profit margin is for your particular business. If this margin slips too low, the company's future is in immediate jeopardy. An inadequate gross profit margin cannot cover all of a company's business expenses and still be able to generate a profit.

Monitoring the net profit margin is especially important for fast-growing companies in which sales are climbing rapidly. Unbridled growth can cause expenses to rise faster than sales, eroding a company's net profit margin. Success can be deceptive: Sales are rising, but profits are shrinking. Ideally, a company reaches a point at which it achieves **operating leverage**, a situation in which increases in operating efficiency mean that expenses as a percentage of sales revenues flatten or even decline. As a result, the company's net profit margin climbs as it grows.

operating leverage
a situation in which increases in operating efficiency mean that expenses as a percentage of sales revenue flatten or even decline.

net-profit-to-assets (return-on-assets) ratio
measures how much profit a company generates for each dollar of assets that it owns.

11. Net-Profit-to-Assets Ratio. The **net-profit-to-assets (return-on-assets) ratio** tells how much profit a company generates for each dollar of assets that it owns. This ratio describes how efficiently a business is putting to work all of the assets it owns to generate a profit. It tells how much net income an entrepreneur is squeezing from each dollar's worth of the company's assets. It is calculated as follows:

$$\text{Net-profit-to-assets ratio} = \frac{\text{Net profit}}{\text{Total assets}}$$
$$= \frac{\$60,629}{\$847,655}$$
$$= 7.15\%$$

Sam's Appliance shop earns a return of 7.15 percent on its asset base. This ratio provides clues about the asset intensity of an industry. Return-on-assets ratios that are below 5 percent are indicative of asset-intense industries that require heavy investments in assets to stay in business (e.g., manufacturing and railroads). Return on assets ratios that exceed 20 percent tend to occur in asset-light industries such as business or personal services—for example, advertising agencies and computer services. A net-profit-to-assets ratio that is below the industry average suggests that a company is not using its assets very efficiently to produce a profit. Another common application of this ratio is to compare it to the company's cost of borrowed capital. Ideally, a company's return-on-assets ratio should exceed the cost of borrowing money to purchase those assets. Companies that experience significant swings in the value of their assets over the course of a year often use an average value of the asset base over the accounting period to get a more realistic estimate of this ratio.

net-profit-to-equity ratio
measures the owners' rate of return on investment.

12. Net-Profit-to-Equity Ratio. The **net-profit-to-equity ratio** (or return on net worth ratio) measures the owners' rate of return on investment (ROI). Because it reports the percentage of the owners' investment in the business that is being returned through profits annually, it is one of the most important indicators of a firm's profitability or a management's efficiency. The net-profit-to-equity ratio is computed as follows:

$$\text{Net-profit-to-equity ratio} = \frac{\text{Net profit}}{\text{Owners' equity (or net worth)}}$$
$$= \frac{\$60,629}{\$267,655}$$
$$= 22.65\%$$

Sam is earning 22.65 percent on the money he has invested in this business.

This ratio compares profits earned during the accounting period with the amount the owner has invested in the business at the time. If this interest rate on the owners' investment is excessively low, some of this capital might be better employed elsewhere. A business should produce a rate of return that exceeds its cost of capital.

LO5

Explain how to interpret financial ratios.

Interpreting Business Ratios

Ratios are useful yardsticks when measuring a small firm's performance and can point out potential problems before they develop into serious crises. But calculating these ratios is not enough to ensure proper financial control. In addition to knowing how to calculate these ratios,

You Be the Consultant

All Is Not Paradise in Eden's Garden: Part 1

Joe and Kaitlin Eden, co-owners of Eden's Garden, a small nursery, lawn, and garden supply business, have just received their

Balance Sheet, Eden's Garden

Assets

Current Assets

Cash		$6,457
Accounts Receivable	$29,152	
Less Allowance for Doubtful Accounts	$3,200	$25,952
Inventory		$88,157
Supplies		$7,514
Prepaid Expenses		$1,856
Total Current Assets		$129,936

Fixed Assets

Land		$59,150
Buildings	$51,027	
Less Accumulated Depreciation	$2,061	$48,966
Autos	$24,671	
Less Accumulated Depreciation	$12,300	$12,371
Equipment	$22,375	
Less Accumulated Depreciation	$1,250	$21,125
Furniture and Fixtures	$10,295	
Less Accumulated Depreciation	$1,000	$9,295
Total Fixed Assets		$150,907
Intangibles (Goodwill)		$0
Total Assets		$280,843

Liabilities

Current Liabilities

Accounts Payable	$54,258
Notes Payable	$20,150
Credit Line Payable	$8,118
Accrued Wages/Salaries Payable	$1,344
Accrued Interest Payable	$1,785
Accrued Taxes Payable	$1,967
Total Current Liabilities	$87,622

Long-Term Liabilities

Mortgage	$72,846
Note Payable	$47,000
Total Long-Term Liabilities	$119,846

Owner's Equity

Sam Lloyd, Capital	$73,375
Total Liabilities and Owner's Equity	$280,843

Income Statement, Eden's Garden

Net Sales Revenue*		$689,247

Cost of Goods Sold

Beginning Inventory, 1/1/xx	$78,271	
+ Purchases	$403,569	
Goods available for Sale	$481,840	
− Ending Inventory, 12,31/xx	$86,157	
Cost of Goods Sold		$395,683
Gross Profit		$293,564

Operating Expenses

Advertising	$22,150	
Insurance	$9,187	
Depreciation		
Building	$26,705	
Autos	$7,895	
Equipment	$11,200	
Salaries	$116,541	
Uniforms	$4,018	
Repairs and Maintenance	$9,097	
Travel	$2,658	
Entertainment	$2,798	
Total Operating Expenses		$212,249

General Expenses

Utilities	$7,987	
Telephone	$2,753	
Professional Fees	$3,000	
Postage	$1,892	
Payroll Taxes	$11,589	
Total General Expenses		$27,221

Other Expenses

Interest Expense	$21,978	
Bad check Expense	$679	
Miscellaneous expense	$1,248	
Total Other Expenses		$23,905
Total Expenses		$263,375
Net Income		$30,189

*Credit sales represented $289,484 of this total.

year-end financial statements from their accountant. At their last meeting with their accountant, Shelley Edison, three months ago, the Edens had mentioned that they seemed to be having trouble paying their bills on time. "Some of our suppliers have threatened to put us on 'credit hold,'" said Joe.

(continued)

You Be the Consultant (continued)

"I think you need to sit down with me very soon and let me show you how to analyze your financial statements so you can see what's happening in your business," Edison told them at that meeting. Unfortunately, that was the beginning of Eden's Garden's busy season, and the Edens were so busy running the company that they never got around to setting a time to meet with Shelley.

"Now that business has slowed down a little, perhaps we should call Shelley and see what she can do to help us understand what our financial statements are trying to tell us," said Kaitlin.

"Right. Before it's too late to do anything about it," said Joe, pulling out the following financial statements.

1. Assume the role of Shelley Edison. Using the financial statements for Eden's Garden, calculate the 12 ratios covered in this chapter.

2. Do you see any ratios that, on the surface, look suspicious? Explain.

---

entrepreneurs must understand how to interpret them and apply them to managing their businesses more effectively and efficiently.

ENTREPRENEURIAL PROFILE: Linda Nespole: Hi-Shear Technology With the help of financial ratios, Linda Nespole, a top manager at Hi-Shear Technology, an aerospace subcontracting company in Torrance, California, noticed the company's performance beginning to slip. Given the signals her analysis revealed, she immediately devised a strategy to restore Hi-Shear's financial position, focusing first on cost-cutting measures. Simply charting the company's major costs led Nespole to discover leaking water pipes and inefficient lighting that were driving up costs unnecessarily. Some basic repairs lowered utility costs significantly, and a new, more efficient lighting system paid for itself in just six months. Nespole's cost-saving attitude took hold throughout the entire company, and soon all 125 employees were finding ways to keep costs down—from switching long-distance carriers to cutting the cost of its 401(k) retirement plan by 30 percent.[29] ∎

Not every business measures its success with the same ratios. In fact, key performance ratios vary dramatically across industries and even within different segments of the same industry. Entrepreneurs must know and understand which ratios are most crucial to their companies' success and focus on monitoring and controlling those. Sometimes business owners develop ratios and measures that are unique to their own operations to help them achieve success. Known as **critical numbers (or key performance indicators [KPIs])**, these indicators measure key financial and operational aspects of a company's performance. When these critical numbers are headed in the right direction, a business is on track to achieve its objectives. Norm Brodsky, owner of a successful document storage and delivery business in New York City, breaks his business into four categories and tracks critical numbers for each one. Every Monday morning, he receives a report comparing the previous week's critical numbers to those of the previous 28 weeks and the same week for the previous three years. "In 30 seconds, I can see what's going on in every part of my delivery business," he says. "I get another sheet for my storage business because I need to track a different set of numbers there, but the idea is the same."[30] Examples of critical numbers at other companies include the following:

critical numbers (key performance indicators [KPIs]) indicators that measure key financial and operational aspects of a company's performance; when these numbers are moving in the right direction, a business is on track to reach its objectives.

- A bank's "happy-to-grumpy" ratio, which measures the level of satisfaction of its employees. Studies show that employees at the bank who score high on this index are more productive and receive higher customer satisfaction ratings.[31]

- Sales per labor hour at a supermarket.

- The number of new boxes put into storage each week in a records storage business. "Tell me how many new boxes came in during [a particular week]," says Norm Brodsky, owner of CitiStorage, the successful records storage company, "and I can tell you our overall sales figure for [that week] within one or two percent of the actual figure."[32]

- Food costs as a percentage of sales for a restaurant. When rapidly rising flour and cheese prices pushed food costs as a percentage of sales from the normal 34 percent to 40 percent at Mark Parry's pizza restaurant, he was forced to raise prices. "We're not set to [earn] a profit when we're [operating] at 40 percent food costs," says Parry.[33] At Dos Caminos, a Mexican restaurant in New York City, chef Ivy Stark's goal is to keep the restaurant's food cost at or below 26 percent of sales. Stark relies on a five-page spreadsheet generated each morning to keep food costs under control.[34]

- The utilization ratio, billable hours as a percentage of total hours worked at an Internet service provider.

- The load factor, the percentage of seats filled with passengers at an airline.[35]

Critical numbers may be different for two companies who compete in the same industry. The key is identifying *your* company's critical numbers, monitoring them, and then driving them in the right direction. That requires communicating the importance of these critical numbers to employees and giving them feedback on how well the business is achieving them. For instance, one California retail chain established the daily customer count and the average sale per customer as its critical numbers. The company organized a monthly contest with prizes and posted charts tracking each store's performance. Soon, employees were working hard to improve their stores' performances over the previous year and to outdo other stores in the chain. The healthy rivalry among stores boosted the company's performance significantly.[36]

Another valuable way to use ratios is to compare them with those of similar businesses in the same industry. By comparing their companies' financial statistics to industry averages, entrepreneurs are able to locate problem areas and maintain adequate financial controls. "Knowing your own numbers is only half the story," says Brian Hamilton, founder of Sageworks, a company that tracks financial data for thousands of private companies. "When you look at how you compare to your peers, you can see where you are strong and what you need to work on."[37]

The principle behind calculating these ratios and comparing them to industry norms is the same as that of most medical tests in the health care profession. Just as a healthy person's blood pressure and cholesterol levels should fall within a range of normal values, so should a financially healthy company's ratios. A company cannot deviate too far from these normal values and remain successful for long. When deviations from "normal" do occur (and they will), a business owner should focus on determining the cause of the deviations. In some cases, deviations are the result of sound business decisions, such as taking on inventory in preparation for the busy season, investing heavily in new technology, and others. In other instances, however, ratios that are out of the normal range for a particular type of business are indicators of what could become serious problems for a company. When comparing a company's critical numbers to industry standards, entrepreneurs should ask the following questions:

- Is there a significant difference in my company's ratio and the industry average?

- If so, is the difference meaningful?

- Is the difference good or bad?

- What are the possible causes of this difference? What is the most likely cause?

- Does this cause require that I take action?

- If so, what action should I take to correct the problem?

When used properly, critical numbers can help owners to identify potential problem areas in their businesses early on—*before* they become crises that threaten their very survival. Several organizations regularly compile and publish operating statistics, including key ratios, that summarize the financial performance of many businesses across a wide range of industries. The local library should subscribe to most of these publications:

Risk Management Association. Founded in 1914, the RMA publishes its *Annual Statement Studies*, showing ratios and other financial data for more than 760 different industrial, wholesale, retail, and service categories that are organized by NAICS and SIC code.

Dun & Bradstreet, Inc. Since 1932, Dun & Bradstreet has published *Industry Norms and Key Business Ratios*, which covers more than 800 business categories. Dun & Bradstreet also publishes Cost of Doing Business, a series of operating ratios compiled from the Statistics of Income reports of the Internal Revenue Service (IRS).

Almanac of Business and Financial Ratios. Published by CCH, this almanac reports comparative financial data and ratios for nearly 200 industries by company size.

Standard & Poor's Industry Surveys. In addition to providing information on financial ratios and comparative financial analysis, these surveys also contain useful details on how the industry operates, current industry trends, key terms in the industry, and others.

Industry Spotlight. Published by Schonfeld & Associates, this publication, which can be customized for any one of 250 industries, contains financial statement data and key ratios gleaned from IRS tax returns. *Industry Spotlight* also provides detailed financial information for both profitable companies and those with losses. Schonfeld & Associates also publishes *IRS Corporate Financial Ratios*, a comprehensive reference book that features 76 financial ratios for more than 250 industries using NAICS codes.

Online Resources. Many companies publish comparative financial resources online. Some require subscriptions, but others are free:

- Bizstats publishes common-size financial statements and ratios for 95 business categories for sole proprietorships, S corporations, and corporations.
- Reuters provides an overview of many industries that includes industry trends and news as well as financial ratios.
- A subscription to Lexis/Nexis allows users to view detailed company profiles, including financial reports and analysis, for publicly held companies.

Industry Associations. Virtually every type of business is represented by a national trade association that publishes detailed financial data compiled from its membership. For example, owners of small supermarkets could contact the National Association of Retail Grocers or check the *Progressive Grocer*, its trade publication, for financial statistics relevant to their operations.

Government Agencies. Several government agencies, including the IRS, the Federal Trade Commission, the Department of Commerce, the Census Bureau, the Department of Agriculture, and the Securities and Exchange Commission, periodically publish reports that provide financial operating data on a variety of industries, although the categories are more general. For instance, the IRS publishes *Statistics of Income*, which includes income statement and balance sheet statistics that are compiled from income tax returns and are arranged by industry, asset size, and annual sales. Every five years (years ending in 2 and 7), the Census Bureau publishes the *Economic Census* (www.census.gov/econ/census), which provides general industry statistics and ratios.

What Do All of These Numbers Mean?

Learning to interpret financial ratios just takes a little practice! This section and Table 11.2 show you how it's done by comparing the ratios from the operating data already computed for Sam's to those taken from the RMA's *Annual Statement Studies*. (The industry median is the ratio falling exactly in the middle when sample elements are arranged in ascending or descending order.) Calculating the variance from the industry median—(company ratio − industry median) ÷ industry median—helps entrepreneurs identify the areas in which the company is out of line with the typical company in the industry.

When comparing ratios for their individual businesses to published statistics, entrepreneurs must remember that the comparison is made against averages. An entrepreneur should strive to achieve ratios that are at least as good as these average figures. The goal should be to manage the business so that its financial performance is above average. As they compare their company's financial performance to those covered in the published statistics, they inevitably will discern differences between them. They should note those items that are substantially out of line from the industry average. However, a ratio that varies from the average does not *necessarily* mean that the small business is in financial jeopardy. Instead of making drastic changes in financial policy, entrepreneurs must explore *why* the figures are out of line.

TABLE 11.2 Ratio Analysis: Sam's Appliance Shop versus the Industry Median

Sam's Appliance Shop	Industry Median	Variance (%)
Liquidity Ratios—Tell whether a small business will be able to meet its maturing obligations as they come due.		
1. Current Ratio = 1.87:1	1.60:1	16.7%
Sam's Appliance Shop falls short of the rule of thumb of 2:1, but its current ratio is above the industry median by a significant amount. Sam's should have no problem meeting its short-term debts as they come due. By this measure, the company's liquidity is solid.		
2. Quick Ratio = 0.63:1	0.50:1	25.9%
Again, Sam's is below the rule of thumb of 1:1, but the company passes this test of liquidity when measured against industry standards. Sam's relies on selling inventory to satisfy short-term debt (as do most appliance shops). If sales slump, the result could be liquidity problems for Sam's.		
Leverage Ratios—Measure the financing supplied by the company's owners against that supplied by its creditors and serve as a gauge of the depth of a company's debt.		
3. Debt Ratio = 0.68:1	0.62:1	10.4%
Creditors provide 68 percent of Sam's total assets, which is above the industry median of 62 percent. Although Sam's does not appear to be overburdened with debt, the company might have difficulty borrowing additional money, especially from conservative lenders.		
4. Debt-to-Net-Worth-Ratio = 2.20:1	2.30:1	−4.5%
Sam's Appliance Shop owes $2.20 to creditors for every $1 the owners have invested in the business (compared to $2.30 in debt to every $1 in equity for the typical business). Although this is not an exorbitant amount of debt by industry standards, many lenders and creditors see Sam's as "borrowed up." Borrowing capacity is somewhat limited because creditors' claims against the business are more than twice those of the owners.		
5. Times-Interest-Earned Ratio = 2.52:1	2.10:1	20.1%
Sam's earnings are high enough to cover the interest payments on its debt by a factor of 2.52, better than the typical firm in the industry, whose earnings cover its interest payments just 2.1 times. Sam's Appliance Shop has a comfortable cushion when meeting its interest payments, although some lenders want to see times-interest-earned ratios of at least 3:1.		
Operating Ratios—Evaluate a company's overall performance and show how effectively it is putting its resources to work.		
6. Average-Inventory-Turnover Ratio = 2.05 times/year	4.4 times/year	−53.5%
Inventory is moving through Sam's at a very slow pace, *half* that of the industry median. The company has a problem with slow-moving items in its inventory and, perhaps, too much inventory. Which items are they, and why are they slow moving? Does Sam need to drop some product lines?		
7. Average-Collection-Period Ratio = 50.0 days	10.5 days	376.3%
Sam's Appliance Shop collects the average accounts receivable after 50 days, compared with the industry median of about 11 days, nearly five times longer. A more meaningful comparison is against Sam's credit terms; if credit terms are net 30 (or anywhere close to that), Sam's has a dangerous collection problem, one that drains cash and profits and demands *immediate* attention!		
8. Average-Payable-Period Ratio = 59.3 days	23.0 days	158.1%
Sam's payables are significantly slower than those of the typical firm in the industry. Stretching payables too far could seriously damage the company's credit rating, causing suppliers to cut off future trade credit. This could be a sign of cash flow problems or a sloppy accounts-payable procedure. This problem, which indicates that the company suffers from cash flow problems, also demands *immediate* attention.		

(continued)

TABLE 11.2 Ratio Analysis: Sam's Appliance Shop versus the Industry Median (*continued*)

Sam's Appliance Shop	Industry Median	Variance (%)
9. Net-Sales-to-Total-Assets Ratio = 2.21:1	3.4:1	−35.1%

   Sam's Appliance Shop is not generating enough sales, given the size of its asset base. This could be the result of a number of factors—improper inventory, inappropriate pricing, poor location, poorly trained sales personnel, and many others. The key is to find the cause—*fast*!

   Profitability Ratios—Measure how efficiently a firm is operating and offer information about its bottom line.

	Industry Median	Variance (%)
10. Net-Profit-on-Sales Ratio = 3.24%	4.3%	−24.6%

   After deducting all expenses, 3.24 cents of each sales dollar remains as profit for Sam's—nearly 25 percent below the industry median. Sam should review his company's gross profit margin and investigate its operating expenses, checking them against industry standards and looking for those that are out of balance.

	Industry Median	Variance (%)
11. Net-Profit-to-Assets Ratio = 7.15%	4.0%	78.8%

   Sam's generates a return of 7.15% for every $1 in assets, which is nearly 79 percent *above* the industry median. Given his asset base, Sam is squeezing an above-average return from his company. This could be an indication that Sam's business is highly profitable; however, given the previous ratio, this is unlikely. It is more likely that Sam's asset base is thinner than the industry average.

	Industry Median	Variance (%)
12. Net-Profit-to-Equity Ratio = 22.65%	16.0%	41.6%

   Sam's Appliance Shop's owners are earning 22.65 percent on the money they have invested in the business. This yield is well above the industry median and, given the previous ratio, is more a result of the owner's relatively low investment in the business than an indication of its superior profitability. Sam is using O.P.M. (other people's money) to generate a profit.

ENTREPRENEURIAL PROFILE: Greg Smith: Petra Group Greg Smith, CEO of Petra Group, a systems integrator with $1.5 million in annual sales, once gave little thought to comparing his company's financial performance against industry standards. Then Petra Group's sales flattened, and Smith's company faced the prospect of losing money for the first time. Smith worked with an accounting firm, using information from the RMA and a nonprofit organization that provides similar studies, to analyze his company's financial position. Comparing his numbers to industry statistics, Smith quickly saw that payroll expenses for his 15-person company were too high to allow the company to generate a profit. He also discovered that Petra Group's debt ratio was too high. To restore his company's financial strength, Smith reduced his staff by two and began relying more on temporary employees and independent contractors. He realigned Petra Group's financing, reducing the company's line of credit from $100,000 to just $35,000. The analysis also revealed several strengths for the company. For instance, the company's average collection period was 36.5 days compared to an industry average of 73 days! Smith continues to use ratio comparisons to make key decisions for his company, and he credits the initial financial analysis with getting his company back on the track to profitability.[38] ■

   In addition to comparing ratios to industry averages, owners should analyze their firms' financial ratios over time. By themselves, these ratios are "snapshots" of a company's financial position at a single instant; however, by examining these trends over time, an entrepreneur can detect gradual shifts that otherwise might go unnoticed until a financial crisis is looming (see Figure 11.5).

LO6

Conduct a break-even analysis for a small company.

break-even point
the level of operation (sales dollars or production quantity) at which a company neither earns a profit nor incurs a loss.

Break-Even Analysis

Another key component of every sound financial plan is a break-even (or cost-volume-profit) analysis. A small company's **break-even point** is the level of operation (typically expressed as sales dollars or production quantity) at which it neither earns a profit nor incurs a loss. At

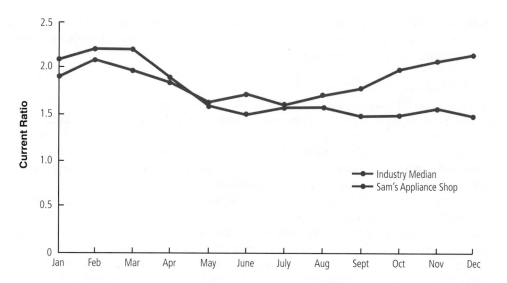

FIGURE 11.5

Trend Analysis of Ratios

this level of activity, sales revenue equals expenses—that is, the firm "breaks even." A business that generates sales that are greater than its break-even point will produce a profit, but one that operates below its break-even point will incur a net loss. By analyzing costs and expenses, an entrepreneur can calculate the minimum level of activity required to keep a company in operation. These techniques can then be refined to project the sales needed to generate the desired profit. Most potential lenders and investors expect entrepreneurs to prepare a break-even analysis to assist them in evaluating the earning potential of the new business. In addition to its being a

You Be the Consultant

All Is Not Paradise in Eden's Garden: Part 2

Remember Joe and Kaitlin Eden, co-owners of Eden's Garden? Assume the role of Shelley Edison, their accountant. Tomorrow, you have scheduled a meeting with them to review their company's financial statements and to make recommendations about how they can improve their company's financial position. Use the following worksheet to summarize the ratios you calculated

Ratio Comparison

Ratio	Eden's Garden	Garden Supply Industry Median*
Liquidity Ratios		
Current ratio		1.4
Quick ratio		0.5
Leverage Ratios		
Debt ratio		0.6
Debt to net worth ratio		1.8
Times interest earned ratio		2.6

Operating Ratios	
Average inventory turnover ratio	5.6
Average collection period ratio	9 days
Average payable period ratio	17 days
Net sales to total assets ratio	3.0
Profitability Ratios	
Net profit on sales ratio	7.5%
Net profit to assets ratio	9.1%
Net profit to equity ratio	15.0%

*Risk Management Association's *Annual Statement Studies*.

earlier in this chapter. Then compare them against the industry averages from the RMA's *Annual Statement Studies*.

1. Analyze the comparisons you have made of Eden's Garden's ratios with those from RMA. What red flags do you see?

2. What might be causing the deviations you have observed?

3. What recommendations can you make to the Edens to improve their company's financial performance in the future?

simple, useful screening device for financial institutions, break-even analysis can also serve as a planning device for entrepreneurs. It can show an entrepreneur just how unprofitable a poorly planned business venture is likely to be.

Calculating the Break-Even Point

An entrepreneur can calculate a company's break-even point by using a simple mathematical formula. To begin the analysis, the entrepreneur must determine fixed costs and variable costs. **Fixed expenses** are those that do not vary with changes in the volume of sales or production (e.g., rent, depreciation expense, insurance, lease or loan payments, and others). **Variable expenses**, on the other hand, vary directly with changes in the volume of sales or production (e.g., raw material costs, sales commissions, hourly wages, and others).

Some expenses cannot be neatly categorized as fixed or variable because they contain elements of both. These semivariable expenses change, although not proportionately, with changes in the level of sales or production (electricity is one example). These costs remain constant up to a particular production or sales volume and then climb as that volume is exceeded. To calculate the break-even point, an entrepreneur must separate these expenses into their fixed and variable components. A number of techniques are available (which are beyond the scope of this text), but a good cost accounting system can provide the desired results.

Here are the steps an entrepreneur must take to compute the break-even point using an example of a typical small business, the Magic Shop:

Step 1. Forecast the expenses the business can expect to incur. With the help of a budget, an entrepreneur can develop estimates of sales revenue, cost of goods sold, and expenses for the upcoming accounting period. The Magic Shop expects net sales of $950,000 in the upcoming year, with a cost of goods sold of $646,000 and total expenses of $236,500.

Step 2. Categorize the expenses estimated in step 1 into fixed expenses and variable expenses. Separate semivariable expenses into their component parts. From the budget, the owner anticipates variable expenses (including the cost of goods sold) of $705,125 and fixed expenses of $177,375.

Step 3. Calculate the ratio of variable expenses to net sales. For the Magic Shop, this percentage is $705,125 ÷ $950,000 = 74 percent. The Magic Shop uses 74 cents out of every sales dollar to cover variable expenses, which leaves 26 cents ($1.00 − 0.74) of each sales dollar as a contribution margin to cover fixed costs and make a profit.

Step 4. Compute the break-even point by inserting this information into the following formula:

$$\text{Break-even sales (\$)} = \frac{\text{Total fixed cost}}{\text{Contribution margin expressed as a percentage of sales}}$$

For the Magic Shop,

$$\text{Break-even sales} = \frac{\$177,375}{0.26}$$
$$= \$682,212$$

Thus, the Magic Shop will break even with sales of $682,212. At this point, sales revenue generated will just cover total fixed and variable expense. The Magic Shop will earn no profit and will incur no loss. We can verify this with the following calculations:

Sales at break-even point	$ 682,212
−Variable expenses (74% of sales)	−504,837
Contribution margin	177,375
− Fixed expenses	−177,375
Net profit (or net loss)	$ 0

fixed expenses
expenses that do not vary with changes in the volume of sales or production.

variable expenses
expenses that vary directly with changes in the volume of sales or production.

Some entrepreneurs find it more meaningful to break down their companies' annual break-even point into a daily sales figure. If the Magic Shop will be open 312 days per year, the average daily sales it must generate just to break even is $682,212 ÷ 312 days = $2,187 per day.

Adding a Profit

What if the Magic Shop's owner wants to do *better* than just break even? The analysis can be adjusted to consider such a possibility. Suppose the owner expects a reasonable profit (before taxes) of $80,000. What level of sales must the Magic Shop achieve to generate this? The entrepreneur can calculate this by treating the desired profit as if it were a fixed cost, modifying the break-even formula to include the desired net income:

$$\text{Sales (\$)} = \frac{\text{Total fixed expenses} + \text{Desired net income}}{\text{Contribution margin expressed as a percentage of sales}}$$

$$= \frac{\$177,375 + \$80\,000}{0.26}$$

$$= \$989,904$$

To achieve a net profit of $80,000 (before taxes), the Magic Shop must generate net sales of $989,904. Once again, if we convert this annual sales volume into a daily sales volume, we get $989,904 ÷ 312 days = $3,173 per day.

Break-Even Point in Units

Some small businesses prefer to express the break-even point in units produced or sold instead of in dollars. Manufacturers often find this approach particularly useful. The following formula computes the break-even point in units:

$$\text{Break-even volume} = \frac{\text{Total fixed costs}}{\text{Sales price per unit} - \text{Variable cost per unit}}$$

For example, suppose that Trilex Manufacturing Company estimates its fixed costs for producing its line of small appliances at $390,000. The variable costs (including materials, direct labor, and factory overhead) amount to $12.10 per unit, and the selling price per unit is $17.50. Trilex computes its contribution margin this way:

$$\text{Contribution margin} = \text{Price per unit} - \text{Variable cost per unit}$$

$$= \$17.50 \text{ per unit} - \$12.10 \text{ per unit}$$

$$= \$5.40 \text{ per unit}$$

So, Trilex's break-even volume is as follows:

$$\text{Break-even volume (units)} = \frac{\text{Total fixed costs}}{\text{Per unit contribution margin}}$$

$$= \frac{\$390,000}{\$5.40 \text{ per unit}}$$

$$= 72,222 \text{ units}$$

To convert this number of units to break-even sales dollars, Trilex simply multiplies it by the selling price per unit:

$$\text{Break-even sales} = 72,222 \text{ units} \times \$17.50 \text{ per unit} = \$1,263,889$$

Trilex could compute the sales required to produce a desired profit by treating the profit as if it were a fixed cost:

$$\text{Sales (units)} = \frac{\text{Total fixed costs} + \text{Desired net income}}{\text{Per unit contribution margin}}$$

For example, if Trilex wanted to earn a $60,000 profit, its required sales would be

$$\text{Sales (units)} = \frac{390,000 + 60,000 = 83,333 \text{ units}}{5.40}$$

which would require 83,333 units × $17.50 per unit = $1,458,328 in sales.

Constructing a Break-Even Chart

The following steps outline the procedure for constructing a graph that visually portrays a company's break-even point (that point where revenues equal expenses):

Step 1. On the horizontal axis, mark a scale measuring sales volume in dollars (or in units sold or some other measure of volume). The break-even chart for the Magic Shop shown in Figure 11.6 uses sales volume in dollars because it applies to all types of businesses, departments, and products.

Step 2. On the vertical axis, mark a scale measuring income and expenses in dollars.

Step 3. Draw a fixed expense line intersecting the vertical axis at the proper dollar level parallel to the horizontal axis. The area between this line and the horizontal axis represents the company's fixed expenses. On the break-even chart for the Magic Shop shown in Figure 11.6, the fixed expense line is drawn horizontally beginning at $177,375 (point A). Because this line is parallel to the horizontal axis, it indicates that fixed expenses remain constant at all levels of activity.

Step 4. Draw a total expense line that slopes upward beginning at the point where the fixed cost line intersects the vertical axis. The precise location of the total expense line is determined by plotting the total cost incurred at a particular sales volume. The total cost for a given sales level is found by using the following formula:

Total expenses = Fixed expenses + Variable expenses expressed as a % of sales × Sales level

Arbitrarily choosing a sales level of $950,000, the Magic Shop's total costs would be as follows:

$$\text{Total expenses} = \$177,375 + (0.74 \times \$950,000)$$

$$= \$880,375$$

Thus, the Magic Shop's total cost is $880,375 at a net sales level of $950,000 (point B). The variable cost line is drawn by connecting points A and B. The area between the total

FIGURE 11.6

Break-Even Chart for the Magic Shop

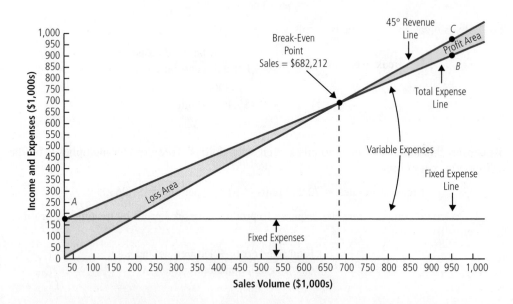

You Be the Consultant

Where Do We Break Even?

Anita Dawson is doing some financial planning for her small gift store. According to her budget for the upcoming year, Anita is expecting sales of $495,000. She estimates that the cost of goods sold will be $337,000 and that other variable expenses will total $42,750. Using the previous year as a guide, Anita anticipates fixed expenses of $78,100.

Anita recalls a meeting she had recently with her accountant, who mentioned that her store already had passed its break-even point eight and a half months into the year. She was pleased but really didn't know how the accountant had come up with that calculation. Now Anita is considering expanding her store into a vacant building next door to her existing location and taking on three new product lines. The company's cost structure would

change, adding another $66,000 to fixed costs and $22,400 to variable expenses. Anita believes the expansion could generate additional sales of $102,000 in the first year.

She wonders what she should do.

1. Calculate Anita's break-even point without the expansion plans. Draw a break-even chart.

2. Compute the break-even point assuming that Anita decide to expand her business.

3. Do you recommend that Anita expand her business? Explain.

---

cost line and the horizontal axis measures the total costs the Magic Shop incurs at various levels of sales. For example, if the Magic Shop's sales are $850,000, its total costs will be $806,375.

Step 5. Beginning at the graph's origin, draw a 45-degree revenue line showing where total sales volume equals total income. For the Magic Shop, point C shows that sales = income = $950,000.

Step 6. Locate the break-even point by finding the intersection of the total expense line and the revenue line. If the Magic Shop operates at a sales volume to the left of the break-even point, it will incur a loss because the expense line is higher than the revenue line over this range. This is shown by the triangular section labeled "Loss Area." On the other hand, if the firm operates at a sales volume to the right of the break-even point, it will earn a profit because the revenue line lies above the expense line over this range. This is shown by the triangular section labeled "Profit Area."

Using Break-Even Analysis

Break-even analysis is a useful planning tool for the potential small business owner, especially when approaching potential lenders and investors for funds. It provides an opportunity for integrated analysis of sales volume, expenses, income, and other relevant factors. Break-even analysis is a simple, preliminary screening device for the entrepreneur faced with the business start-up decision. It is easy to understand and use. With just a few calculations, an entrepreneur can determine the effects of various financial strategies on the business operation. It is a helpful tool for evaluating the impact of changes in investments and expenditures. Greg Smith, for instance, knows that Petra Group's break-even point is $23,000 per week, and he compares sales to that figure every week.[39]

Calculating the break-even point for a start-up business is important because it tells an entrepreneur the minimum volume of sales required to stay in business in the long run.

ENTREPRENEURIAL PROFILE: Albert Poland: Blue Man Albert Poland, a Broadway producer and general manager of the Astor Place Theater, an off-Broadway theater in New York City that has been the home of the famous Blue Man Group for many years, knows that the show must generate ticket sales of $40,000 per week to break even. In addition to performers' salaries, the show's costs include weekly rent, a service package fee that covers the salaries of

© Jeff Moore/ZUMA Press/Alamy

the house and box office staff, and a percentage of the gross weekly box office receipts. The show's break-even point represents sales of about 450 seats per week. The theater's capacity is 300 seats per performance, which means that the show reaches its break-even point by selling out 1.5 of its 9 performances each week. Most of the Blue Man Group performances at the Astor Place Theater are sold out, making it a highly profitable business.[40] ∎

Break-even analysis does have certain limitations. It is too simple to use as a final screening device because it ignores the importance of cash flows. In addition, the accuracy of the analysis depends on the accuracy of the revenue and expense estimates. Finally, the assumptions pertaining to break-even analysis may not be realistic for some businesses. Break-even calculations assume the following: fixed expenses remain constant for all levels of sales volume, variable expenses change in direct proportion to changes in sales volume, and changes in sales volume have no effect on unit sales price. Relaxing these assumptions does not render this tool useless, however. For example, the owner could employ nonlinear break-even analysis to determine a company's break-even point.

Chapter Summary by Learning Objective

1. Understand the importance of preparing a financial plan.

- Launching a successful business requires an entrepreneur to create a solid financial plan. Not only is such a plan an important tool in raising the capital needed to get a company off the ground, but it also is an essential ingredient in managing a growing business.

- Earning a profit does not occur by accident; it takes planning.

2. Describe how to prepare the basic financial statements and use them to manage a small business.

- Entrepreneurs rely on three basic financial statements to understand the financial conditions of their companies:

  1. *The balance sheet*—Built on the accounting equation: Assets = Liabilities + Owner's equity, it provides an estimate of the company's value on a particular date.

2. *The income statement*—This statement compares the firm's revenues against its expenses to determine its net income (or loss). It provides information about the company's bottom line.

3. *The statement of cash flows*—This statement shows the change in the company's working capital over the accounting period by listing the sources and the uses of funds.

3. Create projected (pro forma) financial statements.

- Projected financial statements are a basic component of a sound financial plan. They help the manager plot the company's financial future by setting operating objectives and by analyzing the reasons for variations from targeted results. In addition, the small business in search of start-up funds will need these pro forma statements to present to prospective lenders and investors. They also assist in determining the amount of cash, inventory, fixtures, and other assets the business will need to begin operation.

4. Understand the basic financial statements through ratio analysis.

- The 12 key ratios described in this chapter are divided into four major categories: *liquidity ratios*, which show the small firm's ability to meet its current obligations; *leverage ratios*, which tell how much of the company's financing is provided by owners and how much by creditors; *operating ratios*, which show how effectively the firm uses its

resources; and *profitability ratios*, which disclose the company's profitability.

- Many agencies and organizations regularly publish such statistics. If there is a discrepancy between the small firm's ratios and those of the typical business, the owner should investigate the reason for the difference. A below-average ratio does not necessarily mean that the business is in trouble.

5. Explain how to interpret financial ratios.

- To benefit from ratio analysis, the small company should compare its ratios to those of other companies in the same line of business and look for trends over time.

- When business owners detect deviations in their companies' ratios from industry standards, they should determine the cause of the deviations. In some cases, such deviations are the result of sound business decisions; in other instances, however, ratios that are out of the normal range for a particular type of business are indicators of what could become serious problems for a company.

6. Conduct a break-even analysis for a small company.

- Business owners should know their firm's break-even point, the level of operations at which total revenues equal total costs; it is the point at which companies neither earn a profit nor incur a loss. Although just a simple screening device, break-even analysis is a useful planning and decision-making tool.

Discussion Questions

1. Why is developing a financial plan so important to an entrepreneur about to launch a business?
2. How should a small business manager use the 12 ratios discussed in this chapter?
3. Outline the key points of the 12 ratios discussed in this chapter. What signals does each give a business owner?
4. Describe the method for building a projected income statement and a projected balance sheet for a beginning business.
5. Why are pro forma financial statements important to the financial planning process?
6. How can break-even analysis help an entrepreneur planning to launch a business?

Business Plan Pro™   One of the advantages that *Business Plan Pro*™ offers is the efficient creation of pro forma financial statements, including the balance sheet, profit and loss statement, and cash flow statement. Once you enter the revenues, expenses, and other relevant figures, your financial statements are complete. This can save time and produces a format that bankers and investors recognize and understand. This process also enables you to create "what-if" scenarios applying various revenues and expenses simply by saving versions of your business plan under unique file names.

Business Plan Exercises

Clear and accurate financial statements are an essential part of an effective business plan. These statements are only as good as the information that you provide.

On the Web

Go to www.bplans.com or use the link at www.pearsonhighered .com/scarborough under the Business Plan Resource tab. Find the Finance and Business Calculators tab. Here you will see a collection of online tools including the Break Even Calculator. Open this tool and enter the information it requests, including the average per unit revenue, the average per unit cost, and the estimated monthly fixed costs you anticipate. This tool will calculate your break-even point in units and revenue. Change the data and observe the difference in your break-even point. What does this tell you about the level of risk that you may experience based on the most realistic projections you can make?

Sample Plans

Review a sample plan and note the format and organization of the financial section. Note how the plan presents the break-even information along with the balance sheet, profit and loss statement, and cash flow statement.

In the Software

Provide the month-to-month detail for the first year with annual totals for subsequent years. In addition, note the tables and graphics that appear within the financial plan. Graphics can be excellent communication tools, particularly when you are communicating information about financial trends and relationships.

Building Your Business Plan

Review all information within the Financial Plan section of your business plan. Add any important assumptions to this section. This is a good place to make notes and comments to test or further research any of these assumptions. If you are in the start-up stage, capture the costs that you expect will be incurred to launch your business. The Investment Offering may appear, based on your choice in the Plan Wizard, and this may be a good opportunity to add that information. Review your break-even analysis and the financial statements, including your profit-and-loss, cash flow, and balance sheet statements. What does this tell you about the financial opportunity and health of your business?

This chapter identifies 12 key business ratios. Once you enter your projections, review each ratio and compare them to industry standard ratios. If there are significant differences in these comparisons, determine why those variances exist. Might this tell you something about the reality of your projections, or is this just due to the stage and differences of your business compared to the larger industry? These ratios can be excellent tools for helping question, test, and validate assumptions and projections. Good business planning, solid financial projections, and a thorough analysis of these ratios can help you to launch a more viable business with greater certainty of the outcome.

Beyond the Classroom . . .

1. Ask the owner of a small business to provide your class with copies of his or her company's financial statements (current or past).

   - Using these statements, compute the 12 key ratios described in this chapter.
   - Compare the company's ratios with those of the typical firm in this line of business.
   - Interpret the ratios and make suggestions for operating improvements.

   Prepare a break-even analysis for the owner.
2. Find a publicly held company of interest to you that provides its financial statements on the Web. You can conduct a Web search using the company's name, or you can find lists of companies at the Securities and Exchange Commission's EDGAR database at www.sec .gov/edgar/searchedgar/webusers.htm or visit AnnualReports.com at www.annualreports.com to download the annual report of a company that interests you. Analyze the company's financial statements by calculating the 12 ratios covered in this chapter and compare these ratios to industry averages found in RMA's *Annual Statement Studies* or one of the other financial analysis resources found in your library. Do you spot any problem areas? Strengths? What recommendations can you make to improve the company's financial position? What do you project the company's future to be? Do you recommend investing in the company? Explain.

Endnotes

1. Mike Hogan, "Stay in Touch," *Entrepreneur*, September 2005, pp. 44–46.
2. "Sage Financial Literacy Survey Reveals That Canadian Small Businesses Continue to Struggle to Identify Key Costs, but Are Embracing Technology," Sage North America, October 8, 2011, http://www.sagenorthamerica.com/Accounting/News-room/Details/SNA_Corporate/2011/10/Sage_Financial_Literacy_Survey_Reveals_that_Canadian_Small_Businesses.
3. Karen E. Klein, "Building a Business vs. Making a Living," *Bloomberg Business Week*, June 10, 2011, http://

www.businessweek.com/smallbiz/content/jun2011/ sb20110610_994351.htm.

4. "Sage Financial Literacy Survey Reveals That Canadian Small Businesses Continue to Struggle to Identify Key Costs, but Are Embracing Technology," Sage North America, October 8, 2011, http://www.sagenorthamerica.com/Accounting/ Newsroom/Details/SNA_Corporate/2011/10/Sage_Financial_ Literacy_Survey_Reveals_that_Canadian_Small_Businesses.

5. Amy Barrett, "When, Why, and How to Fire That Customer," *Bloomberg Business Week*, October 29, 2007, http://www .businessweek.com/magazine/content/07_44/b4056431.htm.

6. Gwen Moran, "How I Saved $86,000 per Year," *Entrepreneur*, September 2011, p. 90.

7. Norm Brodsky, "Balance Sheet Blues," *Inc.*, October 2011, p. 34.

8. Paul A. Broni, "Making Your Financials Add Up," *Inc.*, March 2002, http://www.inc.com/articles/2002/03/24019.html.

9. Excerpt from "Follow the Numbers" by Norm Brodsky, from INC. MAGAZINE, January1, 2008, p. 63. Copyright © 2008 by Inc. Magazine. Reprinted with permission.

10. Diedrich Von Soosten, "The Roots of Financial Destruction," *Industry Week*, April 5, 1993, pp. 33–34.

11. Richard Maturi, "Take Your Pulse," *Business Start-Ups*, January 1996, p. 72.

12. *2011 Mid-Year Economic Report*, National Small Business Association, Washington, DC, June 2011, p. 13.

13. Josh Grossberg, "Ay-Yi-Yi! Eva Longoria's Beso Goes Bust," *EOnline*, January 7, 2011, ttp://www.eonline.com/ news/ay-yi-yi_eva_longorias_beso_goes_bust/219438; Steve Green, "Longoria to Own 30 Percent of New Beso Restaurant," *Vegas Inc.*, August 27, 2011, http://www .vegasinc.com/news/2011/aug/27/longoria-own-30-percent- new-beso-restaurant-busine; Ron Rugless, "Landry's Assumes Control of Eva Longoria's Beso Restaurant," *Nation's Restaurant News*, August 18, 2011, http://nrn.com/article/ landrys-assumes-control-eva-longorias-beso-restaurant.

14. Ross Sorkin, "Sbarro Files for Bankruptcy," *New York Times DealBook*, April 4, 2011, http://dealbook.nytimes .com/2011/04/04/sbarro-files-for-bankruptcy; "Disclosure Approved, Sbarro Sets Nov 17 Plan Confirmation," *Business Week*, October 12, 2011, http://news.businessweek.com/ar- ticle.asp?documentKey=1376-LSX6VS07SXKX01 1ONC24EGM2QPQBD1UHSDR36GPV; "Sbarro Officially Emerges from Bankruptcy," *Pizza Marketplace*, November 29, 2011, http://www.pizzamarketplace.com/article/187505/ Sbarro-officially-emerges-from-bankruptcy.

15. Bak, "The Numbers Game," *Entrepreneur*, April 1993, p. 57.

16. Dina Berta, "Village Inn, Bakers Square Parent Files for Bankruptcy," *Nation's Restaurant News*, April 3, 2008, http://www .nrn.com/breakingNews.aspx?id=352348#; Jeffrey McCracken and Janet Adamy, "Restaurants Feel Sting of Surging Costs, Debt," *Wall Street Journal*, April 24, 2008, pp. A1, A10.

17. "Analyzing Creditworthiness," *Inc.*, November 1991, p. 196.

18. Dina Berta, "Village Inn, Bakers Square Parent Files for Bankruptcy," *Nation's Restaurant News*, April 3, 2008, http://www .nrn.com/breakingNews.aspx?id=352348#; Jeffrey McCracken and Janet Adamy, "Restaurants Feel Sting of Surging Costs, Debt," *Wall Street Journal*, April 24, 2008, pp. A1, A10.

19. Catherine Clifford, "Ditching Debt: Business Loan? No Way!" October 17, 2011, http://money.cnn.com/galler- ies/2011/smallbusiness/1110/gallery.debt_free/3.html.

20. Alex Taylor III, "Survival on Dealer's Row," *Fortune*, March 31, 2008, p. 24; Peter Salinas, "Inventory Turn: Moving Metal Quickly Increases Gross," *Dealer Business Journal*, March 2006, http://www.dealerbusinessjournal.com/ articleview.php?id=932-74534.

21. *RMA Annual Statement Studies: Financial Ratio Benchmarks, 2010–2011* (Philadelphia: Risk Management Association, 2011), pp. 670, 926.

22. "Amazon.com," Equity Hive, December 5, 2011, http://www.equityhive.com/Main/Company/Riskview .aspx?s=639&tracking=AboutUs.

23. William Dunkelberg and Holly Wade, *NFIB Small Business Economic Trends,* National Federation of Independent Businesses, September 2012, p. 18.

24. Lisa Jennings, "Real Mex Struggles to Pay Loans," Nation's Restaurant News, May 12, 2011, http://nrn.com/article/ real-mex-stuggles-pay-loans; Jason Cornell, "Real Mex Restaurants Files for Bankruptcy in Delaware, Hoping to Sell Assets under a Section 363 Sale," *Delaware Bankruptcy Litigation*, October 23, 2011, http://delawarebankruptcy .foxrothschild.com/2011/10/articles/bankruptcy-case- summary/real-mex-restaurants-files-for-bankruptcy-in- delaware-hoping-to-sell-assets-under-a-section-363-sale.

25. Darren Dahl, "The Truth about Profits," *Inc.*, October 2009, pp. 91–96.

26. Don Fox, "Share the Wealth," *Fast Casual*, August 1, 2011, http://www.fastcasual.com/blog/6043/Share-the-wealth; Denise Trowbridge, "Fuel Costs Cut into Restaurants' Thin Profit Margins," *Columbus Dispatch*, April 19, 2011, http:// www.dispatch.com/content/stories/business/2011/04/19/ fuel-costs-cut-into-restaurants-thin-profit-margins.html.

27. Jon E. Hilsenrath, "Adventures in Cost Cutting," *Wall Street Journal*, May 10, 2004, pp. R1, R3.

28. Audrey Warren, "The Small Stuff," *Wall Street Journal*, May 10, 2004, p. R9.

29. Ilan Mochari, "A Simple Little System," *Inc.*, October 1999, p. 87.

30. Bo Burlingham, "Inc. Query: Number Crunching," *Inc.*, February 1, 2002, http://www.inc.com/articles/finance/ fin_manage/basic_fin_manage/23857.html.

31. Scott Leibs, "Measuring Up," *CFO*, June 2007, pp. 63–66.

32. Norm Brodsky, "The Magic Number," *Inc.*, September 2003, pp. 43–46.

33. Al Olson, "Pizza and Beer Now Cost an Arm and a Leg," *MSNBC*, February 29, 2008, http://www.msnbc.msn.com/ id/23415510; Richard Breen, "Margins Melt as Cheese Burns Pizza Industry," *GSA Business*, January 24, 2005, pp. 1, 6.

34. Dirk Smillie, "What Recession?," *Forbes*, August 11, 2008, p. 64.

35. John Case, "Critical Numbers in Action," *Inc.*, January 21, 2000, http://www.inc.com/articles/finance/fin_manage/ forecast/15981.html.

36. John Case, "Critical Numbers in Action," *Inc.*, January 21, 2000, http://www.inc.com/articles/finance/fin_manage/ forecast/15981.html.

37. Hannah Clark Steiman, "Quarterly Financial Report: How Do You Stack Up?," Inc., November 2008, p. 105.

38. Ilan Mochari, "Significant Figures," *Inc.*, July 2000, p. 128.

39. Ilan Mochari, "Significant Figures," *Inc.*, July 2000, p. 128.

40. Bruce Lazarus, "Negotiating Theater Licenses-Part 1," *Broadway University*, 2011, http://www.broadwayuniversity .com/pc14.htm.

12

Managing Cash Flow

Learning Objectives

On completion of this chapter, you will be able to:

1. Explain the importance of cash management to a small company's success.

2. Differentiate between cash and profits.

3. Understand the five steps in creating a cash budget.

4. Describe fundamental principles involved in managing the "big three" of cash management: accounts receivable, accounts payable, and inventory.

5. Explain the techniques for avoiding a cash crunch in a small company.

A deficit is what you have when you haven't got as much as when you had nothing.

—Gerald F. Lieberman

There ain't nothing slow about us but our cash flow.

—Chris, owner of a small feed and seed store

Cash—a four-letter word that has become a curse for many small businesses. Lack of this valuable asset has driven countless small companies into bankruptcy. Unfortunately, many more firms will become failure statistics because their owners have neglected the principles of cash management that can spell the difference between success and failure. "Everything is about cash," says entrepreneur-turned-venture-capitalist Guy Kawasaki, "raising it, conserving it, collecting it."[1] Indeed, developing a cash forecast is essential for new businesses because start-up companies usually do not generate positive cash flow right away. A common cause of business failures, especially in start-up and fast-growth companies, is overemphasis on increasing sales with little concern for collecting the receivables those sales generate. "Your sales figures may be great, but it's cash flow that determines whether you can keep the doors open," says one business writer.[2] Another problem is that owners neglect to forecast how much cash their companies will need until they reach the point of generating positive cash flow. The result is always the same: a cash crisis.

As you learned in the previous chapter, controlling the financial aspects of a business using the analysis of basic financial statements with ratios is immensely important; however, by themselves, these techniques are insufficient for achieving business success. Entrepreneurs are prone to focus on their companies' income statements—particularly sales and profits. The income statement, of course, shows only part of a company's financial picture. It is entirely possible for a business to earn a profit and still go out of business by *running out of cash*. In other words, managing a company's total financial performance effectively requires an entrepreneur to look beyond the "bottom line" and focus on what it takes to keep a company going—cash. "If a company isn't producing cash from its ongoing business, all the rest is smoke and mirrors," says Michael Connellan, a successful entrepreneur and former investment banker.[3]

Cash Management

A survey by American Express OPEN Small Business Monitor reports that 57 percent of small business owners say they experience problems managing cash flow.[4] Although cash flow is a common concern for many business owners, the Great Recession and a sluggish recovery have combined to put excess strain on many companies' cash flow. Since 2007, the percentage of small business owners who report that their companies' cash flow is either somewhat or very poor has increased, while the percentage of owners who say that their companies' cash flow is either somewhat or very good has declined (see Figure 12.1). The best way to avoid a potentially business-crushing cash crisis is to use the principles of sound cash management. **Cash management** involves forecasting, collecting, disbursing, investing, and planning for the cash a company needs to operate smoothly. Cash management is a vital task because cash is the most important yet least productive asset that a small

LO1

Explain the importance of cash management to a small company's success.

cash management
the process of forecasting, collecting, disbursing, investing, and planning for the cash a company needs to operate smoothly.

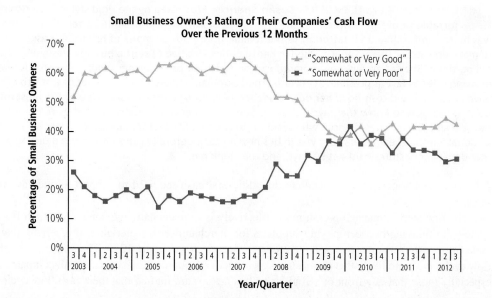

FIGURE 12.1

Small Business Owner's Rating of Their Companies' Cash Flow

Source: Wells Fargo Small Business Index, 3rd Quarter 2012, p.7.

business owns. A business must have enough cash to meet its obligations, or it will be declared bankrupt. Creditors, employees, and lenders expect to be paid on time, and cash is the required medium of exchange. But some companies retain an excessive amount of cash to meet any unexpected circumstances that might arise. These dormant dollars have an income-earning potential that owners are ignoring; investing this cash, even for a short time, can add to a company's earnings. Proper cash management permits owners to adequately meet the cash demands of their businesses, avoid retaining unnecessarily large cash balances, and stretch the profit-generating power of each dollar their companies own.

Although cash flow difficulties afflict companies of all sizes and ages, young companies, especially, are cash sponges, soaking up every available dollar, and always hungry for more. The reason usually is that their cash generating "engines" are not operating at full speed yet and cannot provide enough power to generate the cash necessary to cover rapidly climbing operating expenses. Entrepreneurs must manage cash flow from the day they launch their businesses.

ENTREPRENEURIAL PROFILE: Henry Ford: Ford Motor Company Shortly after he launched his new company on June 16, 1903, entrepreneur Henry Ford ran headlong into a cash crisis that nearly wiped out the Ford Motor Company. Start-up expenses (including $10,000 to the Dodge brothers for engines and other parts and $640 to the Hartford Rubber Works for 64 tires) quickly soaked up Ford's $28,000 in start-up capital that he and 11 associates invested, and by July 10, the company's cash balance had fallen a mere $223.65. Another payroll and more parts orders were just around the corner, and the 25-day-old company was already on the brink of a financial collapse. On July 11, an investor saved the day with a $5,000 contribution. Four days later, the Ford Motor Company sold its first car to Dr. E. Pfennig of Chicago, pushing the company's cash balance to $6,486.44. From this shaky financial beginning grew one of the largest automakers in the world![5] ∎

Managing cash flow is also an acute problem for rapidly growing businesses. In fact, fast-track companies are most likely to suffer cash shortages. Many successful, growing, and profitable businesses fail because they become insolvent; they do not have adequate cash to meet the needs of a growing business with a booming sales volume. If a company's sales are up, its owner also must hire more employees, expand plant capacity, increase the sales force, build inventory, and incur other drains on the firm's cash supply. During rapid growth, cash collections typically fall behind, compounding the problem. Cash flows out of these high-growth companies much faster than it comes in. The head of the National Federation of Independent Businesses says that many small business owners "wake up one day to find that the price of success is no cash on hand. They don't understand that if they're successful, inventory and receivables will increase faster than profits can fund them."[6] The resulting cash crisis may force the owner to lose control of the business or, ultimately, declare bankruptcy and close.

ENTREPRENEURIAL PROFILE: Susan Spencer Frustrated by the rigid styles and uncomfortable fit of tennis dresses in the late 1960s, Susan Spencer designed a tennis dress that was more comfortable and flattering to the female figure. When many of her friends asked her to make dresses for them, Spencer, then in her twenties, decided to start a business designing and selling them. She found a clothing manufacturer and took on a partner whose main focus was growing sales as fast as possible. Spencer learned a valuable and costly lesson about fast growth, payment terms, and cash flow; her business failed when it ran out of cash. "One of the most important things is to know the payment terms your customers are setting, what they're going to pay you and when," says Spencer, who went on to become the first female general manager of a National Football League team. "I was in business 4 years, before I figured this out. I didn't know that department stores paid net 90 days, and that sunk me."[7] ∎

cash flow cycle
the time lag between paying suppliers for merchandise or materials and receiving payment from customers.

Table 12.1 shows how to calculate the additional cash required to support an increase in sales.

The first step in managing cash more effectively is to understand the company's **cash flow cycle**—the time lag between paying suppliers for merchandise or materials and receiving payment from customers after they sell the product or service (see Figure 12.2). The longer this cash flow cycle, the more likely that the business owner will encounter a cash crisis. Small companies, especially those that buy from or sell to larger businesses, are finding that their cash flow cycles

TABLE 12.1 How Much Cash Is Required to Support an Increase in Sales?

Too often, entrepreneurs believe that increasing sales is the ideal solution to a cash crunch, only to discover (often after it is too late) that it takes extra cash to support extra sales. The following worksheet demonstrates how to calculate the amount of additional cash required to support an increase in sales.

To make the calculation, a business owner needs the following information:

- The increase in sales planned ($)
- The time frame for adding new sales (days)
- The company's gross profit margin, gross profit ÷ net sales (%)
- The estimated additional expenses required to generate additional sales ($)
- The company's average collection period (days)

To calculate the amount of additional cash needed, use the following formula:

Extra cash required = [(New sales − Gross profit + Extra overhead) × (Average collection period × 1.20*)] ÷ (Time frame in days for adding new sales)

Consider the following example:

The owner of Ardent Company wants to increase sales by $75,000 over the next year. The company's gross profit margin is 30 percent of sales (so its gross profit on these additional sales would be $75,000 × 30% = $22,500), its average collection period is 47 days, and managers estimate that generating the additional sales will require an increase in expenses of $21,300. To calculate the additional cash that Ardent will need to support this higher level of sales, use the following formula:

Extra cash required = [($75,000 − $22,500 + 21,300) × (47 × 1.2)] ÷ 365 = $11,404

Advent will need $11,404 in extra cash to support the additional sales of $75,000 it plans to bring in over the next year.

---

*The extra 20 percent is added as a cushion.

Source: Adapted from Norm Brodsky, "Paying for Growth: How Much Cash You Need to Carry New Sales," Inc. Online Tools & Apps: Worksheet, http://www.inc.com/tools/details/0,6152,CNT61_HOM1_LOC0_NAVhome_TOL11648,00.html.

are growing longer as large companies have stretched their invoice payment times to suppliers and decreased their invoice collection times from customers to improve their cash flow. A recent study by REL Consultancy shows that large companies, those with more than $5 billion in annual sales, have an average days' sales outstanding (DSO) of 41 days but an average days' payable outstanding (DPO) of 55.8 days (a difference of −14.8 days). The numbers for small companies, those with less than $500 million in annual sales, show the "cash squeeze" that large companies are putting them in: Their DSO is 58.9 days, and their DPO is 40.1 days (a difference of 18.8 days).[8]

Once entrepreneurs understand their companies' cash flow cycle, the next step in effective cash management is to analyze it, looking for ways to reduce its length. For the company whose cash flow is illustrated in Figure 12.2, reducing the cycle from 240 days to, say, 150 days would free up incredible amounts of cash that this company could use to finance growth and dramatically reduce its borrowing costs. What steps do you suggest the owner of this business take to reduce its cash flow cycle?

FIGURE 12.2
The Cash Flow Cycle

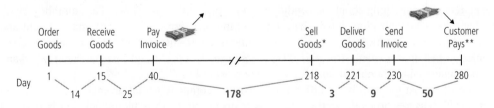

*Based on Average Inventory Turnover:

$$\frac{365 \text{ days}}{2.05 \text{ times/year}} = 178 \text{ days}$$

**Based on Average Collection Period:

$$\frac{365 \text{ days}}{7.31 \text{ times/year}} = 50 \text{ days}$$

© Ralph Hagen/www.CartoonStock.com

Preparing a cash forecast that recognizes this cycle helps to avoid a cash crisis. Understanding the cash flow patterns of a business over the course of a year is essential to creating a successful cash management strategy. Business owners should calculate their cash flow cycles whenever they prepare their financial statements (or at least quarterly). On a *daily* basis, business owners should generate a report showing the following items: total cash on hand, bank balance, a summary of the day's sales, a summary of the day's cash receipts, a summary of the day's cash disbursements, and a summary of accounts-receivable collections. Compiling these reports into monthly summaries provides the foundation for making reliable cash forecasts.

Cash and Profits Are Not the Same

LO2

Differentiate between cash and profits.

When analyzing cash flow, entrepreneurs must understand that cash and profits are not the same. Attempting to discern the status of a small company's cash position by analyzing its profitability is futile; profitability is not necessarily highly correlated with cash flow. "Entrepreneurs think, 'If I'm selling products and I've got revenue, then I'm going to have cash,'" says one small business consultant. "That's not necessarily so."[9] In fact, a company can be growing and earning a profit and still be forced to close its doors because it runs out of cash. For instance, say that a company sells $5,000 of merchandise on credit. The sale shows up as revenue on the income statement, but the company's cash balance does not increase until it actually collects (if it ever collects) the account receivable, which may be months later. An income statement does not tell an entrepreneur anything about the condition of the company's cash flow. "The stumbling block is that a lot of organizations have a hard time getting their arms around cash management and understanding it operationally," says John Cummings, a consultant at KPMG who advises companies on cash management strategies. "They're so used to a profit-and-loss statement world and do not understand the implications of cash flow on operations."[10]

Profit (or net income) is the difference between a company's total revenue and its total expenses. It measures how efficiently a business is operating. Cash is the money that is free and readily available to use in a business. **Cash flow** measures a company's liquidity and its ability to pay its bills and other financial obligations on time by tracking the flow of cash into and out of the business over a period of time. Many small business owners soon discover that profitability does not guarantee liquidity. As important as earning a profit is, no business owner can pay suppliers, creditors, employees, the government, and lenders in profits; that requires *cash*! Many entrepreneurs focus on their company's earnings because they know that a company must earn

cash flow

a method of tracking a company's liquidity and its ability to pay its bills and other financial obligations on time by tracking the flow of cash into and out of the business over a period of time.

FIGURE 12.3
Cash Flow

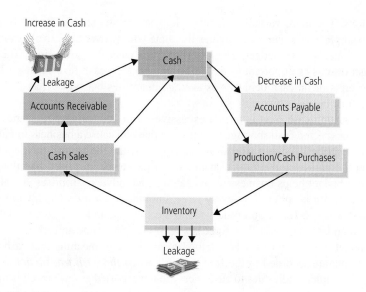

a profit to stay in business. However, adequate cash flow also is essential because it represents the money that flows through a business in a continuous cycle without being tied up in any other asset. "Businesses fail not because they are making or losing money," warns one financial expert, "but because they simply run out of cash."[11]

Figure 12.3 shows the flow of cash through a typical small business. Cash flow is the volume of actual cash that comes into and goes out of the business during an accounting period. Decreases in cash occur when the business purchases, on credit or for cash, goods for inventory or materials for use in production. A business sells the resulting inventory either for cash or on credit. When a company takes in cash or collects payments on accounts receivable, its cash balance increases. Notice that purchases for inventory and production *lead* sales; that is, these bills typically must be paid *before* sales are generated. On the other hand, collection of accounts receivable *lags* behind sales; that is, customers who purchase goods on credit may not pay until the next month (or later).

The Cash Budget

The need for a cash budget arises because in every business the cash flowing in is rarely "in sync" with the cash flowing out of the business. This uneven flow of cash creates periodic cash surpluses and shortages, making it necessary for entrepreneurs to track the flow of cash through their businesses so that they can project realistically the cash available throughout the year. Many entrepreneurs operate their businesses without knowing the pattern of their cash flows, believing that the process is too complex or time consuming. In reality, entrepreneurs simply cannot afford to disregard the process of cash management. They must ensure that their businesses have on hand an adequate but not excessive supply of cash to meet their operating needs. The goal of cash management is to have enough cash available to meet the company's cash needs at a given time.

How much cash is enough? What is suitable for one business may be totally inadequate for another, depending on each firm's size, nature, seasonal pattern of sales, and particular situation. The small business manager should prepare a **cash budget**, which is nothing more than a "cash map" showing the amount and the timing of the cash receipts and the cash disbursements day by day, week by week, or month by month. It is used to predict the amount of cash a company will need to operate smoothly over a specific period of time, and it is a valuable tool in managing a company successfully. A cash budget can illuminate a host of approaching problems, giving entrepreneurs adequate time to handle or, better yet, avoid them. A cash budget reveals important clues about how well a company balances its accounts payable and accounts receivable, controls inventory, finances its growth, and makes use of the cash it has.

Typically, small business owners should prepare a projected monthly cash budget for at least one year into the future and quarterly estimates for another. The forecast must cover all seasonal

LO3

Understand the five steps in creating a cash budget.

cash budget
a "cash map" showing the amount and the timing of cash receipts and cash disbursements on a daily, weekly, or monthly basis.

sales fluctuations. The more variable a firm's sales pattern, the shorter should be its planning horizon. For example, a company whose sales fluctuate widely over a relatively short time frame might require a weekly cash budget. The key is to track cash flow over time. The timing of a company's cash flow is as important as the amounts. "An alert cash flow manager keeps an eye not on cash receipts or on cash demands as average quantities but on cash as a function of the *calendar*," says one business owner.[12]

Creating a written cash plan is not an excessively time-consuming task and can help the owner to avoid unexpected cash shortages, a situation that can cause a business to fail. One financial consultant describes "a client who won't be able to make the payroll this month. His bank agreed to meet the payroll for him—but banks don't like to be surprised like that," he adds.[13] Preparing a cash budget helps business owners avoid such adverse surprises and also lets them know whether they are keeping excessively large amounts of cash on hand. Computer spreadsheets such as Microsoft Excel and others make the job fast and easy to complete and allow entrepreneurs to update their cash flow forecasts with very little time and effort.

A cash budget is based on the cash method of accounting, meaning that cash receipts and cash disbursements are recorded in the forecast *only when the cash transaction is expected to take place*. For example, credit sales to customers are not reported as cash receipts until the company expects to collect the cash from them. Similarly, purchases made on credit are not recorded until the owner expects to pay them. Because depreciation, bad-debt expense, and other noncash items involve no cash transfers, they are omitted entirely from the cash budget.

A cash budget is nothing more than a forecast of the firm's cash inflows and outflows for a specific time period, and it will never be completely accurate. However, it does give an entrepreneur a clear picture of a company's estimated cash balance for the period, pointing out when it may require external cash infusions or when surplus cash balances are available to invest. In addition, by comparing actual cash flows with projections, an owner can revise the forecast so that future cash budgets will be more accurate.

ENTREPRENEURIAL PROFILE: Joseph Popper: Computer Gallery Joseph Popper, CEO of Computer Gallery, knows how deadly running out of cash can be for a small company and does everything he can to make sure his business avoids that trap. Popper uses a spreadsheet to extract key sales, collection, and disbursement totals and to generate the resulting cash balance each day. Even when he is traveling, Popper keeps up with his company's daily cash balance. He has the spreadsheet results e-mailed to him whenever is out of the office. "We've been paranoid about cash from day one," Popper says. But his system keeps accounts receivable in control, ensures that the company's available cash is working hard, and improves his relationship with the company's banker.[14] ∎

Formats for preparing a cash budget vary depending on the pattern of a company's cash flow. Table 12.2 shows a most likely monthly cash budget for a small department store over a six-month period. (Creating pessimistic and optimistic cash forecasts is a snap once the most likely cash budget is in place.) Each monthly column should be divided into two sections— estimated and actual (not shown)—so that each succeeding cash forecast can be updated to reflect actual cash flows. (The Service Corps of Retired Executives provides a handy set of templates, including one for forecasting cash flow, on its Web site at www.score.org/resources/business-plans-financial-statements-template-gallery.)

Comparing forecasted amounts to actual cash flows and learning the causes of any significant discrepancies allows entrepreneurs to improve the accuracy of future cash budgets.

Creating a cash budget requires five basic steps:

1. Determining an adequate minimum cash balance

2. Forecasting sales

3. Forecasting cash receipts

4. Forecasting cash disbursements

5. Estimating the end-of-month cash balance

Step 1: Determining an Adequate Minimum Cash Balance

What is considered an excessive cash balance for one small business may be inadequate for another, even though the two companies are in the same industry. Some suggest that a firm's cash balance should equal at least one-fourth of its current liabilities, but this general rule clearly will not work for all small businesses. The most reliable method of deciding the right minimum cash balance is based on past experience. Past operating records will indicate the cash cushion an entrepreneur needs to cover any unexpected expenses after all normal cash outlays are deducted from the month's cash receipts. For example, past records may indicate that it is desirable to maintain a cash balance equal to five days' sales. Seasonal fluctuations may cause a firm's minimum cash balance to change. For example, the minimum cash balance for a retailer may be greater in June than in December.

TABLE 12.2 Cash Budget for a Small Department Store

Assumptions:

Cash balance on December 31 is $12,000

Minimum cash balance is $10,000

Sales are 75% credit and 25% cash

Credit sales are collected in the following manner:

* 60% collected in the first month after the sale

* 30% collected in the second month after the sale

* 5% collected in the third month after the sale

* 5% are never collected

Sales forecasts are as follows:	Pessimistic	Most Likely	Optimistic
October (actual)	–	$ 300,000	–
November (actual)	–	350,000	–
December (actual)	–	400,000	–
January	120,000	150,000	175,000
February	160,000	200,000	250,000
March	160,000	200,000	250,000
April	250,000	300,000	340,000
May	260,000	315,000	360,000
June	265,000	320,000	375,000

Rent is $3,000 per month

Interest payments of $664 and $817 are due in April and May, respectively.

A tax prepayment of $18,000 is due in March.

A capital addition payment of $130,000 is due in February.

A bank note payment of $7,500 is due in March.

Insurance premiums are $475 per month.

Other expense estimates include:	Purchases	Wages and Salaries	Utilities	Advertising	Miscellaneous
January	$ 140,000	$ 30,000	$ 1,450	$ 1,600	$ 500
February	140,000	38,000	1,400	1,600	500
March	210,000	40,000	1,250	1,500	500
April	185,000	42,000	1,250	2,000	550
May	190,000	44,000	1,250	2,000	550
June	180,000	44,000	1,400	2,200	550

(continued)

TABLE 12.2 Cash Budget—Most Likely Sales Forcast (*continued*)

	Oct	Nov	Dec	Jan	Feb	Mar	Apr	May	Jun
Cash Receipts									
Sales	$ 300,000	$ 350,000	$ 400,000	$ 150,000	$ 200,000	$ 200,000	$ 300,000	$ 315,000	$ 320,000
Credit Sales	225,000	262,500	300,000	112,500	150,000	150,000	225,000	236,250	240,000
Collections									
60%—First month after sale				180,000	67,500	90,000	90,000	135,000	141,750
30%—Second month after sale				78,750	90,000	33,750	45,000	45,000	67,500
5%—Third month after sale				11,250	13,125	15,000	5,625	7,500	7,500
Cash Sales				37,500	50,000	50,000	75,000	78,750	80,000
Other cash receipts				25	35	50	60	60	65
Total Cash Receipts				307,525	220,660	188,800	215,685	266,310	296,815
Cash Disbursements									
Purchases*				140,000	140,000	210,000	185,000	190,000	180,000
Rent				3,000	3,000	3,000	3,000	3,000	3,000
Utilities				1,450	1,400	1,250	1,250	1,250	1,400
Bank Note				–	–	7,500	–	–	–
Tax Prepayment				–	–	18,000	–	–	–
Capital Additions				–	130,000	–	–	–	–
Wages and Salaries				30,000	38,000	40,000	42,000	44,000	44,000
Insurance				475	475	475	475	475	475
Advertising				1,600	1,600	1,500	2,000	2,000	2,200
Interest				–	–	–	664	817	–
Miscellaneous				500	500	500	550	550	550
Total Cash Disbursements				177,025	314,975	282,225	234,939	242,092	231,625
End-of-Month Balance									
Beginning cash balance				12,000	142,500	48,185	10,000	10,000	14,218
+ Cash receipts				307,525	220,660	188,800	215,685	266,310	296,815
– Cash disbursements				177,025	314,975	282,225	234,939	242,092	231,625
Cash (end-of-month)				142,500	48,185	(45,240)	(9,254)	34,218	79,408
Borrowing				–	–	55,240	19,254	–	–
Repayment				–	–	–	–	20,000	54,944
Final Cash Balance				$ 142,500	$ 48,185	$ 10,000	$ 10,000	$ 14,218	$ 24,464
Monthly Surplus/(Deficit)				130,500	(94,315)	(93,425)	(19,254)	24,218	65,190

Step 2: Forecasting Sales

The heart of the cash budget is the sales forecast. It is the central factor in creating an accurate picture of the firm's cash position because sales ultimately are transformed into cash receipts and cash disbursements. For most businesses, sales constitute the major source of the cash flowing into the business. Similarly, sales of merchandise require that cash be used to replenish inventory. As a result, the cash budget is only as accurate as the sales forecast from which it is derived.

For an established business, a sales forecast is based on past sales, but owners must be careful not to be excessively optimistic in projecting sales. Economic swings, increased competition, fluctuations in demand, normal seasonal variations, and other factors can drastically affect sales patterns and, therefore, a company's cash flow. Most businesses, from retailers and hotels to accounting firms and builders, have sales patterns that are "lumpy" and not evenly distributed throughout the year. Lindsey's Bakery, a small bakery in Circleville, Ohio, generates 25 percent of its annual sales during the town's Pumpkin Show, a fall festival started in 1906. To handle the surge in sales, owner Katie Miller adds two shifts to operate the bakery around the clock to make 100,000 pumpkin doughnuts from an old family recipe.[15]

Ed Matthews/Columbus Dispatch

Many small retailers generate most of their sales and as much as one-third of their profits in the months of November and December. For instance, 40 percent of all toy sales take place in the last six weeks of the year, and companies that make fruitcakes typically generate 50 to 90 percent of their sales during the holiday season.[16] The typical wine and spirits shop makes 15 to 18 percent of its total sales volume for the entire year between December 15 and December 31.[17] Companies that sell television sets and recliners see sales surge in the weeks before the Super Bowl, and Super Bowl Sunday is the busiest day of the year for pizza restaurants, producing revenues that are five times that of the typical Sunday.[18] For fireworks companies, the three weeks before July 4 account for the majority of annual sales with another smaller peak occurring before New Year's Eve.[19] Costume makers generate almost all of their sales before Halloween but must invest in the raw materials and the labor to make the costumes in the spring and summer months, when their cash balances are at their lowest.[20] For companies with highly seasonal sales patterns, proper cash management is an essential activity.

Several quantitative techniques that are beyond the scope of this text (linear regression, multiple regression, time-series analysis, and exponential smoothing) are available to owners of existing businesses with an established sales pattern for forecasting sales. These methods enable the small business owner to extrapolate past and present sales trends to arrive at a fairly accurate sales forecast.

The task of forecasting sales for a start-up is more difficult but not impossible. For example, the entrepreneur might conduct research on similar firms and their sales patterns in the first year of operation to come up with a forecast. The local chamber of commerce and trade associations in various industries also collect such information. Publications such as the *Annual Statement Studies* published by the Risk Management Association (RMA), which profiles financial statements for companies of all sizes in hundreds of industries, is also a useful tool. Market research is another source of information that may be used to estimate annual sales for the fledgling firm. Other potential sources that may help to predict sales include census reports, newspapers, radio and television customer profiles, polls and surveys, and local government statistics. Talking with owners of similar businesses (outside the local trading area, of course) can provide entrepreneurs with realistic estimates of start-up sales. Table 12.3 on page 439 provides an example of how one entrepreneur used such marketing information to derive a sales forecast for his first year of operation.

No matter what techniques entrepreneurs employ, they must recognize that even the best sales estimates will be wrong. Many financial analysts suggest that the owner create *three* estimates— an optimistic, a pessimistic, and a most likely sales estimate—and then make a separate cash budget for each forecast (a very simple task with a spreadsheet). This dynamic forecast enables the owner to determine the range within which his or her sales will likely be as the year progresses.

Step 3: Forecasting Cash Receipts

As you learned earlier, sales constitute the primary source of cash receipts. When a company sells goods and services on credit, the cash budget must account for the delay between the sale and the actual collection of the proceeds. Remember that you cannot spend cash you haven't collected yet! For instance, an appliance store might not collect the cash from a refrigerator sold

You Be the Consultant

A Short Season

Bruce Zoldan, CEO of Phantom Fireworks, is monitoring the heavy rush of customer traffic at the Phantom Fireworks outlet in Youngstown, Ohio. In the three-week period leading up to July 4, the small chain of fireworks stores will face a heavy flood of customers pouring through its doors from 7 a.m. until midnight, all of them looking for the ingredients for a brilliant Fourth of July fireworks celebration. During this three-week burst of activity, Phantom Fireworks sells more than 25 million pounds of fireworks, and sales at any one of its 41 stores often reach $400,000 a day. After the peak Independence Day holiday, however, sales at many Phantom stores typically plummet to just $5,000 a day. That's when the real work for Zoldan and his staff begins. "We have 11 months of logistics for one month of sales," he says. Not only does gearing up for a one-month sales blitz require lots of advance planning, but it also demands some clever cash management techniques. Even though sales are concentrated in just one month of the year, Phantom Fireworks expenses continue year-round.

"A seasonal business is infinitely more difficult to manage than most other businesses," says Les Charm, who teaches entrepreneurship at Babson College. How can business owners whose companies face highly seasonal sales patterns manage the uneven cash flow?

- **Be financially disciplined.** Seasonal business owners must establish a realistic budget, stick to it, and avoid the temptation to spend lavishly when cash flow is plentiful. Teevan McManus, owner of the Coronado Surfing Academy in San Diego, failed to heed this advice in his first year of business. "I burned through everything I made in the summer and was living off of my business line of credit before the next season came around," he recalls. "I barely made it to the next June."

- **Manage your time and your employees' time carefully.** During the busy season, employees may be working overtime to serve the rush of customers; during the off-season, a business owner may cut back to 20-hour workweeks or operate with a skeleton crew.

- **Use permanent employees sparingly.** Many owners of seasonal businesses use a small core of permanent employees and then hire part-time workers or student interns during their busy season. Planning for the right number of seasonal employees and recruiting them early ensures that a business will be able to serve its customers properly.

- **Put aside cash in a separate account that you use only for the lean months of your seasonal business.**

- **Maximize your productivity in the off-season.** Use the slow season to conduct market research, perform routine maintenance and repairs, revise your Web site, and stay in touch with customers. Steve Kopelmam's company, HauntedHouse.com, earns all of its $2.6 in annual revenue in a six-week period leading up to Halloween. Starting in

© Monkey Business/Fotolia

You Be the Consultant *(continued)*

November, Kopelman surveys his customers so that he can refine his marketing efforts for the next season and solicit suggestions for improvement. He visits trade shows to look for the latest technology and gadgets to keep his haunted houses fresh and exciting for his customers. Kopelman also negotiates leases on properties for the next season and studies his competition by visiting every haunted house Web site that he can find.

- *Keep inventory at minimal levels during the off-season.* As you will learn in this chapter, holding inventory unnecessarily merely ties up valuable cash uselessly.

- *Offer off-peak discounts.* Doing so may generate some revenue during slow periods.

- *Consider starting a complementary seasonal business.* The weeks leading up to Halloween are the peak season for Sam Fard, owner of Los Angeles–based Roma Costume, a manufacturer of costumes for women. To reduce the highly seasonal nature of his business, Fard added a line of bikinis and lingerie to his company's product mix.

- *Create a cash flow forecast.* Perhaps one of the most important steps that seasonal business owners can take is to develop a forecast of their companies' cash flow. Doing so allows them to spot patterns and trends and to make plans for covering inevitable cash shortages. Make sure that you include a pessimistic or worst-case scenario in your cash forecast.

- *Establish a bank line of credit.* The line of credit should be large enough to cover at least three months' worth of expenses. Use your cash flow forecast to show the banker how and when your company will be able to repay the loan. "[A good cash forecast] shows the banker that you know exactly where the peaks and valleys are and what your cash needs are," says one banker.

1. What impact do highly seasonal sales have on a small company's cash flow?

2. What other advice can you offer owners of seasonal businesses about coping with the effects of their companies' highly irregular sales patterns? About managing cash flow in general?

Sources: Based on Cindy Vanegas, "Creating a Successful Seasonal Business All Year-Round," *Fox Business*, November 16, 2011, http://smallbusiness.foxbusiness.com/marketing-sales/2011/11/16/creating-successful-seasonal-business-all-year-round; Gwendolyn Bounds, "Preparing for the Big Bang," *Wall Street Journal*, June 29, 2004, pp. B1, B7; Rich Mintzer, "Running a Seasonal Business," *Entrepreneur*, March 16, 2007, http://www.entrepreneur.com/management/operations/article175954.html; Sarah Pierce, "Surviving a Seasonal Business," *Entrepreneur*, July 15, 2008, http://www.entrepreneur.com/startingabusiness/businessideas/article195680.html; Dan Kehrer, "10 Steps to Seasonal Success," *Business.com*, May 2006, http://www.business.com/directory/advice/sales-and-marketing/sales/10-steps-to-seasonal-success; and Amy Barrett, "Basics for Seasonal Business Owners," *Business Week*, April 16, 2008, http://www.businessweek.com/magazine/content/08_64/s0804058908582.htm?chan=smallbiz_smallbiz+index+page_best+of+smallbiz+magazine.

TABLE 12.3 Forecasting Sales for a Business Start-Up

Robert Adler wants to open a repair shop for imported cars. The trade association for automotive garages estimates that the owner of an imported car spends an average of $485 per year on repairs and maintenance. The typical garage attracts its clientele from a trading zone (the area from which a business draws its customers) with a 20-mile radius. Census reports show that the families within a 20-mile radius of Robert's proposed location own 84,000 cars, of which 24 percent are imports. Based on a local consultant's market research, Robert believes that he can capture 9.9 percent of the market this year. Robert's estimate of his company's first year's sales are as follows:

Number of cars in trading zone	84,000 autos
× Percent of imports	× 24 %
= Number of imported cars in trading zone	20,160 imports
Number of imports in trading zone	20,160 imports
× Average expenditure on repairs and maintenance	× $485
= Total import repair sales potential	$9,777,600
Total import repair sales potential	$9,777,600
× Estimated share of the market	× 9.9%
= Sales estimate	$967,982

Now Robert Adler can convert this annual sales estimate of $967,982 into monthly sales estimates for use in his company's cash budget.

FIGURE 12.4

**Probability
of Collecting
Accounts
Receivable**

Source: Based on data from
the Commercial Agency
Section, Commercial Law
League of America, 2011.

Probability of Collecting Accounts Receivable

Number of Months Since Account Due Date

in February until April or May, and the cash budget must reflect this delay. To project accurately cash receipts, an entrepreneur must analyze accounts receivable to determine the company's collection pattern. For example, past records may indicate that 20 percent of sales are for cash, 50 percent are paid in the month following the sale, 20 percent are paid two months after the sale, 5 percent are paid after three months, and 5 percent are never collected. In addition to cash and credit sales, a small business may receive cash in a number of forms—interest income, rental income, dividends, and others.

Collecting accounts receivable promptly poses problems for many small companies. Dun & Bradstreet, a financial information services company, reports that currently 5 percent of all business payments are delinquent (more than 90 days past due), a percentage that is significantly higher than the historical average of 2 percent.[21] Figure 12.4 demonstrates the importance of acting promptly once an account becomes past due. Notice how the probability of collecting an outstanding account diminishes the longer the account is delinquent. Table 12.4 illustrates a concept of which many business owners are not aware: the high cost of failing to collect accounts receivable on time.

ENTREPRENEURIAL PROFILE: Ron Box: Joe Money Machinery Ron Box, chief financial officer of Joe Money Machinery, a family-owned reseller of heavy construction equipment in Birmingham, Alabama, has watched as the company's large customers, mainly construction firms and municipal governments, stretch out payment times on their invoices to 60 or more days, a practice that puts pressure on the small company's cash flow. In an attempt to speed up collections, Box recently began offering customers cash discounts for early payments. About 30 percent of Joe Money Machinery's customers have taken advantage of the discounts, "but they don't always do it," says Box. The company also has encouraged customers to pay with corporate credit cards, but that option has had limited success.[22]

**electronic (Automated
Clearing House)
collections**
a bank service that allows
businesses to deduct automatically invoice amounts
from customers' accounts
and deposit them into the
seller's account within
24 hours.

remote deposit
a bank service that allows
businesses to scan customers' checks and deposit
them from anywhere
using a portable scanner, a
computer, and an Internet
connection.

Many banks now offer cash management tools designed to speed up the collection of invoices to small companies that once were reserved only for large businesses. Once set up with a bank, **electronic (Automated Clearing House) collections** automatically deduct invoice amounts from customers' accounts and deposit them into the seller's account within 24 hours. Businesses can use electronic collections for single or periodic transactions, but they are ideal for recurring transactions. **Remote deposit** allows businesses to scan customers' checks and deposit them from anywhere using a portable scanner, a computer, and an Internet connection. Scanned checks create an online, digital deposit that eliminates time-consuming runs to the bank. Banks typically charge a monthly fee and a charge for each scanned check to provide the remote deposit service. Entrepreneurs should compare the benefits and the costs of these services at various banks, which should be able to provide a daily list of transactions to allow entrepreneurs to reconcile payments with their accounts-receivable records.

TABLE 12.4 The High Cost of Slow Payers

Are your customers who purchase on credit paying late? If so, these outstanding accounts receivable represent a significant leak in your company's cash flow. Slow-paying customers, in effect, are borrowing money from your business interest free. One experienced business owner says, "Whether you realize it or not, you're sort of a banker, and you need to start thinking like one . . . to assess the quality of your [customers' accounts]." Slow-paying customers are using your money without paying you interest while you forgo opportunities to place it in interest-earning investments or pay interest on money that you must borrow to replace the missing funds. Exactly how much is poor credit control costing your company? The answer may surprise you.

The first step is to calculate your company's average collection period ratio (see the section "Operating Ratios" in Chapter 9). The second step is to age your accounts receivable to determine how many accounts are current and how many are overdue. The following example shows how to use these numbers to calculate the cost of past-due accounts for a company whose credit terms are "net 30":

Average collection period	65 days
− Credit terms	−30 days
Excess in accounts receivable	35 days
Average daily sales of $21,500* × 35 days	$752,500
× Normal rate of return	× 8%
Annual cost of excess	$60,200

Slow-paying customers are costing this company more than $60,000 a year! If your business is highly seasonal, quarterly or monthly figures may be more meaningful than annual ones.

*Average daily sales = Annual sales ÷ 365 days = $7,847,500 ÷ 365 = $21,500 per day

Source: Adapted from Norm Brodsky, "What Are You, a Bank?," *Inc.*, November 2007, pp. 81–82, and "Financial Control," *Inc.* Reprinted with permission of the publisher.

Step 4: Forecasting Cash Disbursements

Entrepreneurs must have sufficient cash on hand to pay their bills as they come due (see Figure 12.5). Fortunately, most owners of established businesses can easily develop a clear picture of their companies' pattern of cash disbursements. Many cash payments, such as rent, loan repayments, and interest, are fixed amounts due on specified dates; others, such as purchases of goods and services, vary from one month to another. The key factor when

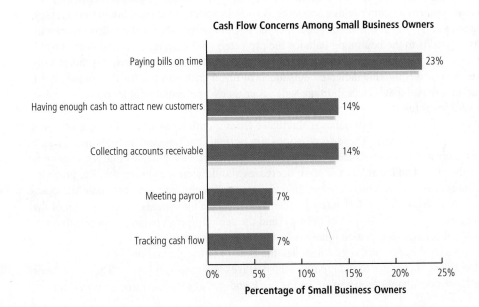

Cash Flow Concerns Among Small Business Owners

Paying bills on time — 23%
Having enough cash to attract new customers — 14%
Collecting accounts receivable — 14%
Meeting payroll — 7%
Tracking cash flow — 7%

0%   5%   10%   15%   20%   25%
Percentage of Small Business Owners

FIGURE 12.5

Cash Flow Concerns among Small Business Owners

Source: American Express OPEN Survey, April 14, 2011.

forecasting disbursements for a cash budget is to record them in *the month in which they will be paid, not when the obligation is incurred*. Of course, the number of cash disbursements varies with each particular business, but the following disbursement categories are common: purchase of inventory or raw materials, wages and salaries, rent, utilities, taxes, loan payments, interest, advertising, fixed-asset purchases, and miscellaneous expenses.

When preparing a cash budget, one of the worst mistakes an entrepreneur's can make is to underestimate cash disbursements, which can result in a cash crisis. To prevent this, wise entrepreneurs cushion their cash disbursement estimates, assuming that they will be higher than expected. This is particularly important for entrepreneurs opening new businesses. In fact, some financial analysts recommend that new owners estimate cash disbursements as best they can and then add another 25 to 50 percent of the total! (Remember Murphy's Law?)

Sometimes business owners have difficulty developing initial forecasts of cash receipts and cash disbursements. One of the most effective techniques for overcoming the "I don't know where to begin" hurdle is to make a *daily* list of the items that generated cash (receipts) and those that consumed it (disbursements).

ENTREPRENEURIAL PROFILE: Susan Bowen: Champion Awards Susan Bowen, CEO of Champion Awards, a $9 million T-shirt screen printer, monitors cash flow by tracking the cash that flows into and out of her company every day. Focusing on keeping the process simple, Bowen sets aside a few minutes each morning to track updates from the previous day on four key numbers:

Accounts receivable:

1. What did we bill yesterday?
2. How much did we actually collect?

Accounts payable:

3. What invoices did we receive yesterday?
4. How much in total did we pay out?

If Bowen observes the wrong trend——more new bills than new sales or more money going out than coming in——she makes immediate adjustments to protect her cash flow. The benefits produced (not the least of which is the peace of mind in knowing that no cash crisis is looming) more than outweigh the 10 minutes she invests in the process every day. "I've tried to balance my books every single day since I started my company in 1970," says Bowen.[23] ■

Step 5: Estimating the End-of-Month Cash Balance

To estimate a company's cash balance for each month, entrepreneurs first must determine the cash balance at the beginning of each month. The beginning cash balance includes cash on hand as well as cash in checking and savings accounts. As development of the cash budget progresses, the cash balance at the *end* of one month becomes the *beginning* balance for the following month. Next, the owner adds to the beginning balance the projected total cash receipts and subtracts the projected total cash disbursements to obtain the end-of-month balance before any borrowing takes place. A positive amount indicates that the firm has a cash surplus for the month, but a negative amount shows that a cash shortage will occur unless the owner is able to collect, raise, or borrow additional funds.

Normally, a company's cash balance fluctuates from month to month, reflecting seasonal sales patterns in the business. These fluctuations are normal, but business owners must watch closely for *trends* in the cash balance over time. A trend of increases indicates that a company is solvent; on the other hand, a pattern of cash decreases should alert the owner that the business is approaching a cash crisis. One easy but effective tracking technique is to calculate the company's monthly cash surplus or deficit (cash receipts − cash disbursements) at the bottom of the cash budget (see Table 12.2). Strings of deficits (and the declining cash balance that results from them) should set off alarms that a company is headed for a cash crisis.

Preparing a cash budget not only illustrates the flow of cash into and out of the small business but also allows the owner to *anticipate* cash shortages and cash surpluses. "Then," explains a small business consultant, "you can go to the bank and get a 'seasonal' line of credit for six months instead of twelve. Right there you can cut your borrowing costs in half."[24] By planning cash needs ahead of time, a small business is able to achieve the following benefits:

- Increase the amount and the speed of cash flowing into the company

- Reduce the amount and the speed of cash flowing out of the company

- Make the most efficient use of available cash

- Take advantage of money-saving opportunities, such as quantity and cash discounts

- Finance seasonal business needs

- Develop a sound borrowing program

- Develop a workable program of debt repayment

- Impress lenders and investors with its ability to plan and repay financing

- Provide funds for expansion

- Plan for investing surplus cash

"Cash flow spells survival for every business," claims one expert. "Manage cash flow effectively, and your business works. If your cash flow is not well managed, then sooner or later your business goes under. It's that simple."[25] Unfortunately, most small business owners forgo these benefits because they fail to track their company's cash flow consistently. Because cash flow problems usually sneak up on a business over time, improper cash management often proves to be a costly—and fatal—mistake. One way to avoid this pitfall is to establish a *daily* report that shows the amount of cash on hand, the cash received, and the cash spent. Some entrepreneurs also monitor the status of the company's accounts-receivable and accounts-payable balances daily.

 You Be the Consultant

In Search of a Cash Flow Forecast

"I'll never make that mistake again," Douglas Martinez said to himself as he got into his car. Martinez had just left a meeting with his banker, who had not been optimistic about the chances of Martinez's plumbing supply company getting the loan it needed. "I should have been better prepared for the meeting," he muttered, knowing that he could be angry only at himself. "That consultant at the Small Business Development Center [SBDC] was right. Bankers' primary concern when making loans is cash flow."

"At least I salvaged the meeting by telling him I wasn't ready to officially apply for a loan yet," Martinez thought. "But I've got a lot of work to do. I've got a week to figure out how to put together a cash budget to supplement my loan application. Maybe that consultant can help me."

When he returned to his office, Martinez gathered up the file folders containing all of his fast-growing company's financial reports and printed his projected revenues and expenses using his computer spreadsheet. Then he called the SBDC consultant he had worked with when he was launching his company and explained the situation. When he arrived at the consultant's office that afternoon, they started organizing the information. Here is what they came up with:

Current cash balance	$8,750
Sales pattern	71% on credit and 29% in cash
Collections of credit sales	68% in the same month as the sale;
	19% in the first month after the sale;
	7% in the second month after the sale;
	6% never collected (bad debts).

(continued)

You Be the Consultant (continued)

Sales forecasts:

	Pessimistic	Most Likely	Optimistic
July (actual)	—	$18,750	—
August (actual)	—	$19,200	—
September (actual)	—	$17, 840	—
October	$15,000	$17,500	$19,750
November	$14,000	$16,500	$18,500
December	$11,200	$13,000	$14,000
January	$9,900	$12,500	$14,900
February	$10,500	$13,800	$15,800
March	$13,500	$17,500	$19,900

Utilities expenses	$800 per month
Rent	$1,200 per month
Truck loan	$317 per month

The company's wages and salaries (including payroll taxes) estimates are the following:

October	$2,050
November	$1,825
December	$1,725
January	$1,725
February	$1,950
March	$2,425

The company pays 63 percent of the sales price for the inventory it purchases, an amount that it actually pays in the following month. (Martinez has negotiated "net 30" credit terms with his suppliers.)

Other expenses include the following:

Insurance premiums	$1,200, payable in August and February
Office supplies	$95 per month
Maintenance	$75 per month
Computer supplies	$75 per month
Advertising	$550 per month
Legal and accounting fees	$250 per month
Miscellaneous expenses	$60 per month

A tax payment of $1,400 is due in December.
Martinez has established a minimum cash balance of $2,000 and can borrow money at an interest rate of 8.75 percent.

"Well, what do you think?" Douglas asked the consultant.

1. Assume the role of the SBDC consultant and help Douglas put together a cash budget for the six months beginning in October.

2. What conclusions can you draw about Douglas's business from this cash budget?

3. What suggestions can you make to help Douglas improve his company's cash flow?

The "Big Three" of Cash Management

LO4

Describe fundamental principles involved in managing the "big three" of cash management: accounts receivable, accounts payable, and inventory.

It is unrealistic for business owners to expect to trace the flow of every dollar through their businesses. However, by concentrating on the three primary causes of cash flow problems, they can dramatically lower the likelihood of experiencing a devastating cash crisis. The "big three" of cash management are accounts receivable, accounts payable, and inventory. These three variables are leading indicators of a company's cash flow. If a company's accounts-receivable balance is increasing, its cash balance may be declining. Similarly, accounts-payable and inventory balances that are increasing faster than sales are signs of mounting pressure on a company's cash flow. A good cash management "recipe" involves accelerating a company's receivables to collect cash as quickly as possible, paying out cash as slowly as possible (without damaging the company's credit rating), and maintaining an optimal level of inventory. The big three of cash management interact to create a company's **cash conversion cycle**, the length of time required to convert inventory and accounts payable into sales and accounts receivable and finally back into cash. A company's cash conversion cycle equals its days' inventory outstanding + days' sales outstanding − days' payable outstanding. Ideally, a company's cash conversion cycle is negative, meaning that it turns over its inventory quickly and collects payments from its customers before it pays its vendors and suppliers. Apple Inc. enjoys the benefits of a cash conversion cycle *negative* 30 days (see Figure 12.6).

cash conversion cycle a measure of the length of time required to convert inventory and accounts payable into sales and accounts receivable and finally back into cash. Equals days' inventory outstanding + days' sales outstanding − days' inventory outstanding.

Accounts Receivable

Selling merchandise and services on credit is a necessary evil for most small businesses. Many customers expect to buy on credit, and business owners extend it to avoid losing customers to competitors. However, selling to customers on credit is expensive; it requires more paperwork, more staff, and more cash to service accounts receivable. In addition, because extending credit is, in essence, lending money, the risk involved is higher. Every business owner who sells on credit encounters customers who pay late or, worst of all, who never pay at all. Software publisher Intuit reports that the average small business chases after $1,500 in past-due accounts receivable per month and incurs $1,900 in bad-debt losses each year, the latter costing them $42 billion in lost revenue annually.[26]

Most small companies operate with very thin cash reserves; therefore, a late payment from a major customer can create a cash crisis. Many business owners speculate that the last recession caused a permanent shift to longer payment terms, especially among large businesses. "There's a power struggle on Main Street," says Sung Won Sohn, a former economist for Wells Fargo. "Big firms force their [payment] terms on suppliers and customers. If you're a small business, you have no bargaining power and have to take what they give you." Point.360, a small provider of video postproduction services, is caught in that struggle. The company's customers, many of whom are major movie studios, now take an average of 66 days to pay invoices; one year earlier, the average was 54 days.[27] A recent survey by the National Federation of Independent Businesses reports that 74 percent of small companies have accounts receivable outstanding for 60 or more days.[28] Slower payments from customers put more pressure on these small companies' cash flow.

ENTREPRENEURIAL PROFILE: David Schier: Jacobus Energy Jacobus Energy, a company founded in 1919 in Milwaukee, Wisconsin, that distributes petroleum, faced the problem of slowing receivables. The company had outgrown its manual system for tracking

*Cash Conversion Cycle = Days' Inventory Outstanding + Days' Sales Outstanding − Days' Payable Outstanding = 6 + 31 − 67 = −30 days

FIGURE 12.6

Apple Inc.'s Cash Conversion Cycle

Source: Based on data from David M. Katz, "Easing the Squeeze," *CFO*, July/August 2011, pp. 44–50.

past-due accounts receivable, and nearly 9 percent of its accounts were more than 30 days past due. Credit manager David Schier switched to an online credit-checking and collection system, and the percentage of 30-plus-day past-due accounts declined to just 3.3 percent. In addition, the company's average collection period ratio decreased from 27.3 days to 20.2 days, greatly improving its cash flow.[29] ∎

Selling on credit is a common practice in business, accounting for about $2 trillion in transactions annually.[30] Experts estimate that 90 percent of industrial and wholesale sales are on credit and that 40 percent of retail sales are on account.[31] Because credit sales are so prevalent, an assertive collection program is essential to managing a company's cash flow. A credit policy that is too lenient can destroy a business's cash flow, attracting nothing but slow-paying or "deadbeat" customers who never pay. On the other hand, a carefully designed policy can be a powerful selling tool, attracting customers and boosting cash flow. Transforming accounts receivable into cash is essential to staying in business; entrepreneurs must remember that a sale does not count until they collect the cash from it!

HOW TO ESTABLISH A CREDIT AND COLLECTION POLICY The first step in establishing a workable credit policy is to screen customers carefully *before* granting them credit. Unfortunately, few small businesses conduct any kind of credit investigation before selling to a new customer. Many entrepreneurs that sell on credit sell to *anyone* who wants to buy; most have no credit-checking procedure.

The first line of defense against bad-debt losses is a detailed credit application. Before selling to any customer on credit, a business owner should have the customer fill out a customized application designed to provide the information needed to judge the potential customer's creditworthiness. At a minimum, this credit profile should include the following information about customers:

- Name, address, tax identification number, and telephone number

- Form of ownership (proprietorship, S corporation, LLC, corporation, and so on) and number of years in business

- Credit references (e.g., other suppliers), including contact names, addresses, and telephone numbers

- Bank and credit card references

After collecting this information, a business owner should use it to check the potential customer's credit references! The savings from lower bad-debt expenses can more than offset the cost of using a credit reporting service. Companies such as Dun & Bradstreet (www.dnb.com), Experian (www.experian.com), Equifax (www.equifax.com), TransUnion (www.transunion.com), and KnowX (www.knowx.com) enable entrepreneurs to gather credit information on potential customers. For entrepreneurs who sell to other business, Dun & Bradstreet offers many useful services, including a Small Business Risk New Account Score, a tool for evaluating the credit risk of new businesses. The National Association of Credit Management (www.nacm.org) is another important source of credit information because it collects information on many small businesses that other reporting services ignore. The cost to check a potential customer's credit at reporting services such as these starts at $119, a small price to pay when a small business is considering selling thousands of dollars worth of goods or services to a new customer. Unfortunately, few small businesses take the time to conduct a credit check.

ENTREPRENEURIAL PROFILE: Ron Phelps: Boulevard Tire Center Ron Phelps, commercial credit manager at Boulevard Tire Center, a tire retailer with 26 locations in Florida, uses an online business credit reporting service called Cortera Pulse to screen new credit customers and to keep tabs on existing ones. Recently, when Pulse alerted Phelps that the Internal Revenue Service had imposed a large federal tax lien on one of its customers, Phelps immediately cut off the small trucking company's credit to avoid the risk of writing off a bad debt. "We decided to make them a cash [only] customer because we were concerned about their ability to pay," he says.[32] ∎

The next step involves establishing a firm written credit policy and letting every customer know in advance the company's credit terms. The credit agreement must be in writing and should specify a customer's credit limit (which usually varies from one customer to another, depending on their credit ratings), any deposits that are required (often stated as a percentage of the purchase price), the terms of any discounts (e.g., a 2 percent discount if the invoice is paid within 10 days), and the number of days before payment is due (immediately, 30 days, 60 days, and so on). A credit agreement should state clearly all the terms the business will enforce if the account goes bad—including interest, late charges, attorney's fees, and others. Failure to specify these terms in the contract means that they *cannot* be added later after problems arise. When will you send invoices? To maximize its cash flow, a small company's credit policies should be as tight as possible and within federal and state credit laws. According to the American Collectors Association, if a business is writing off more than 5 percent of sales as bad debts, the owner should tighten its credit and collection policy.[33]

The third step in an effective credit policy is to send invoices promptly because customers rarely pay *before* they receive their bills. Unfortunately, 20 percent of small business owners admit that they forget to send invoices or follow up on past-due invoices.[34] The sooner a company sends invoices, the sooner its customers will pay them.

ENTREPRENEURIAL PROFILE: Sam Goodner: Catapult Systems Sam Goodner, owner of Catapult Systems, an information technology (IT) consulting firm in Austin, Texas, switched from billing his clients every 30 days to every 15 days when he realized the "terrible cash flow story" that the longer billing cycle created for his company. He continued to extend "net 30" credit terms, and more than 90 percent of the company's clients never complained.[35] ■

Manufacturers and wholesalers should make sure invoices are en route to customers as soon as the shipments go out the door (if not before). Service companies should keep track of billable hours daily or weekly and bill as often as the contract with the client permits. Online or computerized billing makes managing accounts receivable much easier, is less expensive, and produces faster payments than paper invoices.[36] However, only 34 percent of small businesses use these programs.[37] Some businesses use **cycle billing**, in which a company bills a portion of its credit customers each day of the month, to smooth out uneven cash receipts.

cycle billing
a method in which a company bills a portion of its credit customers each day of the month to smooth out uneven cash receipts.

When an account becomes past due, a small business owner must take *immediate* action. The longer an account is past due, the lower is the probability of collecting it. One of the most effective techniques is to have someone in the company who already has a relationship with the customer, perhaps a salesperson or a customer service representative, contact him or her about the past-due account. When contacting a delinquent customer, the goal is to get a commitment to pay the full amount of the bill by a specific date (*not* "soon" or "next week"). Following up the personal contact with an e-mail or a letter that summarizes the verbal commitment also helps. If the customer still refuses to pay the bill, collection experts recommend the following:

- Send a letter from the company's attorney.

- Turn the account over to a collection attorney.

- As a last resort, hire a collection agency. (The Commercial Law League of America (www.clla.org) can provide a list of reputable agencies.)

Although collection agencies and attorneys typically take 25 to 30 percent of any accounts they collect, they are often worth the price. Companies turn over $150 billion annually in past-due debt to collection agencies, which collect about $40 billion for their clients.[38] According to the American Collectors Association, only 5 percent of accounts more than 90 days delinquent will be paid voluntarily.

Business owners must be sure to abide by the provisions of the federal Fair Debt Collection Practices Act, which prohibits any kind of harassment when collecting debts (e.g., telephoning repeatedly, issuing threats of violence, telling third parties about the debt, or using abusive language). The primary rule when collecting past-due accounts is "*Never* lose your cool." Establishing a friendly but firm attitude that treats customers with respect is more likely to produce payment than hostile threats. Table 12.5 outlines 10 collection blunders small business owners typically make and how to avoid them.

TABLE 12.5 Ten Collection Blunders and How to Avoid Them

Business owners often make mistakes when trying to collect the money their customers owe. Checking potential credit customers' credit records and creating a thorough sales contract that spells out exactly what happens if the account becomes past due can help minimize collection problems. Sooner or later, however, even the best system will encounter late payers. What happens then? Business owners should avoid these collection blunders.

Blunder 1: Delaying collection phone calls. Many entrepreneurs waste valuable time and resources sending four or five "past-due" letters to delinquent customers, usually with limited effectiveness.

Instead: Once a bill becomes past due, call the customer within a week to verify that he or she received the bill and that it is accurate. Ask for payment.

Blunder 2: Failing to ask for payment in clear terms. To avoid angering a customer, some entrepreneurs ask meekly, "Do you think you could take care of this bill soon?"

Instead: Firmly but professionally ask for payment (the full amount) by a specific date.

Blunder 3: Sounding desperate. Some entrepreneurs show weakness by saying that they must have payment or they "can't meet payroll" or "can't pay bills." That gives the customer more leverage to negotiate additional discounts or time.

Instead: Ask for payment simply because the invoice is past due—without any other explanation. Don't apologize for your request; it's *your* money.

Blunder 4: Talking tough. Getting nasty with delinquent customers does not make them pay any faster and may be a violation of the Fair Debt Collections Practices Act.

Instead: Remain polite and professional when dealing with past-due customers, even if you think they don't deserve it. *Never* lose your temper. Don't ruin your reputation by being rude.

Blunder 5: Trying to find out the customer's problem. Some entrepreneurs think it is necessary to find out why a delinquent customer has not paid a bill.

Instead: Don't waste time playing private investigator. Focus on the "business at hand," collecting your money.

Blunder 6: Asking customers how much they can pay. When customers claim that they cannot pay the bill in full, inexperienced entrepreneurs ask, "Well, how much can you pay?" They don't realize that they have just turned control of the situation over to the delinquent customer.

Instead: Take charge of negotiations from the outset. Let the customer know that you expect full payment. If you cannot get full payment immediately, suggest a new deadline. Only as a last resort should you offer an extended payment plan.

Blunder 7: Continuing to talk after you get a promise to pay. Some entrepreneurs "blow the deal" by not knowing when to stop talking. They keep interrogating a customer after they have a promise to pay.

Instead: Wrap up the conversation as soon as you have a commitment. Summarize the agreement, thank the customer, and end the conversation on a positive note.

Blunder 8: Calling without being prepared. Some entrepreneurs call customers without knowing exactly which invoices are past due and what amounts are involved. The effort is usually fruitless.

Instead: Have all account details in front of you when you call and be specific in your requests.

Blunder 9: Trusting your memory. Some entrepreneurs think that they can remember previous collection calls, conversations, and agreements.

Instead: Keep accurate records of all calls and conversations. Take notes about each customer contact and resulting agreements.

Blunder 10: Letting your computer control your collection efforts. Inexperienced entrepreneurs tend to think that their computers can manage debt collection for them.

Instead: Recognize that a computer is a valuable tool in collecting accounts but that you are in control. "Past-due" notices from a computer may collect some accounts, but your efforts will produce more results. Getting to know the people who handle the invoices at your customers' businesses can be a major advantage when collecting accounts.

Source: Adapted from "Tips for Collecting Cash," *FSB*, May 2002, p. 72; Janine Latus Musick, "Collecting Payments Due," *Nation's Business*, January 1999, pp. 44–46; Bob Weinstein, "Collect Calls," *Entrepreneur*, August 1995, pp. 66–69; and Elaine Pofeldt, "Collect Calls," *Success*, March 1998, pp. 22–24.

TECHNIQUES FOR ACCELERATING ACCOUNTS RECEIVABLE Small business owners can rely on a variety of other techniques to speed cash inflow from accounts receivable:

- Speed up orders by having customers e-mail or fax them to you.

- Send invoices when goods are shipped—not a day or a week later; consider faxing or e-mailing invoices to reduce in-transit time to a minimum. Most small business accounting software has features that allow users to e-mail the invoices they generate. When Jim Malarney, CEO of Vanguard Services, a company based in Indianapolis, Indiana, that provides contract truck drivers to companies, noticed that the company's collections on its accounts receivable were slowing, he began e-mailing invoices to customers. Malarney also began establishing personal contacts with more people in the companies that Vanguard serves. Vanguard's collection strategy has resulted in the percentage of past-due accounts decreasing from 25 percent to just 8 percent.[39]

- Ensure that all invoices are clear, accurate, and timely. State clearly a description of the goods or services purchased and an account number and make sure that the prices and the language on invoices agree with the price quotations on purchase orders or contracts.

- Include a telephone number and a contact person in your organization in case the customer has a question or a dispute.

- Call the customer a week after sending the invoice to make sure it arrived and to ensure that the customer has no problems with the quality of the product or service.

- Highlight the balance due and the terms of sale (e.g., "net 30") on all invoices. A study by Xerox Corporation found that highlighting with color the "balance due" and "due date" sections of invoices increased the speed of collection by 30 percent.[40]

- Allow customers to use multiple payment methods such as checks, credit cards, PayPal, money, orders, and cash.

- Restrict a customer's credit until past-due bills are paid. Make sure salespeople know which of their customers are behind in their payments.

- Deposit customer checks and credit card receipts *daily*.

- Identify the top 20 percent of your customers (by sales volume), create a separate file system for them, and monitor them closely. Twenty percent of the typical company's customers generate 80 percent of all accounts receivable.

- Ask customers to pay at least a portion of the purchase price up front. To maximize her company's cash flow, Jane Conner, owner of the Whitefish Gymnastics Club, requires her customers to pay for their 10-week exercise classes after the first session.[41]

- Watch for signs that a customer may be about to declare bankruptcy. If that happens, creditors typically collect only a small fraction, if any, of the debt owed.

- If a customer does file for bankruptcy, the bankruptcy court notifies all creditors with a "Notice of Filing" document. If an entrepreneur receives one of these notices, he or she should create a file to track the events surrounding the bankruptcy and take action immediately. To have a valid claim against the debtor's assets, a creditor must file a proof-of-claim form with the bankruptcy court within a specified time, often 90 days. If, after paying the debtor's secured creditors, any assets remain, the court will distribute the proceeds to unsecured creditors who have legitimate proof of claim.

- Consider using a bank's lockbox collection service (located near customers) to reduce mail time on collections. In a **lockbox** arrangement, customers send payments to a post office box that the company's bank maintains. The bank collects payments several times each day and deposits them immediately in the company's account. The procedure sharply reduces processing and clearing times, especially if the lockboxes are located close to the firm's biggest customers' business addresses. The system can be expensive to operate and

lockbox
an arrangement in which customers send payments to a post office box that a company's bank maintains; several times a day, the bank collects payments and deposits them in the company's account.

is most economical for companies with a high volume of large checks (at least 200 checks each month).

- Track the results of the company's collection efforts. Managers and key employees should receive a weekly report on the status of the company's outstanding accounts receivable.

Another strategy that small companies, particularly those selling high-priced items, can use to protect the cash they have tied up in receivables is to couple a security agreement with a financing statement. This strategy falls under Article 9 of the Uniform Commercial Code (UCC), which governs a wide variety of business transactions, including the sale of goods and security interests. A **security agreement** is a contract in which a business selling an asset on credit gets a security interest in that asset (the collateral), protecting its legal rights in case the buyer fails to pay. To get the protection it seeks in the security agreement, the seller must file a financing statement called a UCC-1 form with the proper state or county office (a process the UCC calls "perfection"). The UCC-1 form gives notice to other creditors and to the general public that the seller holds a secured interest in the collateral named in the security agreement. The UCC-1 form must include the name, address, and signature of the buyer; a description of the collateral; and the name and address of the seller. If the buyer declares bankruptcy, the small business that sells the asset is not guaranteed payment, but the filing puts its claim to the asset ahead of those of unsecured creditors. A small company's degree of safety on a large credit sale is much higher with a security agreement and a properly filed financing statement than if it did not file the security agreement.

security agreement
a contract in which a business selling an asset on credit gets a security interest in that asset (the collateral), protecting its legal rights in case the buyer fails to pay.

Accounts Payable

The second element of the big three of cash management is accounts payable. The timing of payables is just as crucial to proper cash management as the timing of receivables, but the objective is exactly the opposite. Entrepreneurs should strive to stretch out payables as long as possible *without damaging their companies' credit rating*. Otherwise, suppliers may begin demanding prepayment or cash-on-delivery (C.O.D.) terms, which severely impair a company's cash flow, or they may stop doing business with it altogether. When Borders, once the second-largest bookstore chain in the United States, ran into cash flow problems, the company stopped making payments to book publishers, many of whom halted shipments to the book retailer. In an attempt to survive, Borders downsized to just 400 stores but ultimately succumbed to its cash flow woes, declared bankruptcy, and closed its doors for good.[42] One cash management consultant says, "Some companies pay too early and wind up forgoing the interest they could have earned on their cash. Others pay too late and either wind up with late penalties or being forced to buy on a C.O.D. basis, which really kills them."[43] It is perfectly acceptable for small business owners to regulate payments to their companies' advantage. Efficient cash managers set up a payment calendar each month that allows them to pay their bills on time and to take advantage of cash discounts for early payment.

ENTREPRENEURIAL PROFILE: Nancy Dunis: Dunis & Associates Nancy Dunis, CEO of Dunis & Associates, a Portland, Oregon, marketing firm, recognizes the importance of controlling accounts payable. "Our payables must be functioning just right to keep our cash flow running smoothly," says Dunis. She has set up a simple five-point accounts-payable system:[44]

1. *Set scheduling goals.* Dunis strives to pay her company's bills 45 days after receiving them and to collect all her receivables within 30 days. Even though "it doesn't always work that way," her goal is to make the most of her cash flow.
2. *Keep paperwork organized.* Dunis dates every invoice she receives and carefully files it according to her payment plan. "This helps us remember when to cut the check," she says, and "it helps us stagger our payments, over days or weeks," significantly improving the company's cash flow.
3. *Prioritize.* Dunis cannot stretch out all of her company's creditors for 45 days; some demand payment sooner. Those suppliers are at the top of the accounts-payable list.
4. *Be consistent.* "Companies want consistent customers," says Dunis. "With a few exceptions," she explains, "most businesses will be happy to accept 45-day payments, so long as they know you'll always pay your full obligation at that point."

Hands On . . . How To

Control Your Company's Accounts Receivable

Dann Battina, CEO of Beltmann Group, a moving company in Roseville, Minnesota, was pleased that his business was on track to match the previous year's sales of $100 million because he knew that the economy was slowing. He also knew that to weather the coming economic storm, his company would require a larger minimum cash balance. The problem he faced, however, involved Beltmann's average collection period ratio, which stood at 61 days. Just 5 percent of the company's customers paid on delivery, which meant that at any given time, approximately $16.7 million in cash was in Battina's customers' accounts rather than in his company's bank account. Battina frequently had to tap Beltmann line of credit to pay his vendors on time, usually within 30 days. "I knew it was time to figure out how to get our hands on more money before the situation became really extreme," he says.

With the help of a financial consultant, Battina began to examine his company's collection and payable procedures and its cash flow. To move customers' furnishings, Beltmann uses 300 independent contractors who submit the job's details to one of the company's 13 nationwide branches. The analysis revealed that 40 percent of the documents were filled out or handled incorrectly, lengthening the company's cash flow cycle. Battina also discovered that the documents followed a convoluted path inside the company, bouncing from one department to another, meaning that sending an invoice to a customer required 10 days. "It was embarrassing how severe the problem was," says Battina.

Bettina redesigned his company's billing and collection procedures and included a quality control checklist that the independent contractors must complete for each job. He also began tracking the time that each branch takes to send invoices. Already the changes have allowed Beltmann to reduce the time required to send invoices to six days, freeing up $1.1 million in cash.

Small businesses report that their customers, particularly large companies, are stretching their accounts payable longer, paying invoices more slowly now than they were just a few years ago. When faced with 30-day credit terms, it is not uncommon for large companies to delay their payments to 45 or even 60 days. The Small Business Network Monitor, a study of small businesses by American Express, confirms the challenge this presents for entrepreneurs. More than half of the small business owners surveyed say their companies experienced cash flow problems, and one of their primary concerns is collecting accounts receivable. The average small business incurs $1,500 in past-due payments from its customers each month.

"If the money is coming in the front door at 100 miles per hour," explains Brian Hamilton, CEO of Sageworks, a financial consulting firm, "and going out the back door at 110 miles per hour, that's not a good thing. Businesses don't fail because they are unprofitable; they fail because they get crushed on the accounts receivable side." What steps can entrepreneurs take to avoid a cash crisis caused by accounts receivable that turn slowly? The following steps can help:

- **Evaluate your company's collection process.** How many people are involved in generating an invoice? (Fewer is better.) Where do bottlenecks in the billing process occur? (Setting a time limit on processing paperwork helps.) What percentage of your company's invoices are erroneous? (The higher the percentage of errors, the slower the company's collections will be.)

- **Increase your company's cash reserves.** Smart business owners keep at least three months' worth of expenses on hand so that they aren't caught cash short if receivables slow down more than expected or if sales suddenly drop.

- **Boost your company's line of credit.** Business owners can increase their lines of credit with their banks, but the key is to do so *before* you need the money. Be prepared to use your company's financial statements to prove to your banker why you need—and deserve—an increased line of credit.

- **Monitor accounts receivable closely.** Some small business owners generate daily summaries of their company's accounts receivable, always on the lookout for disturbing trends. Doing so enables them to spot slow payers who might become nonpayers unless the company takes immediate action.

- **Get to know the people responsible for paying invoices at your biggest customers' or clients' companies.** Collections are easier if you know the right person to call.

- **Take immediate action when an account becomes past due.** Resist the tendency to simply sit back and wait for the customer to pay. If a customer has not paid by the invoice due date, contact him or her immediately and ask for payment.

- **Watch for signs that customers may be about to declare bankruptcy.** When a customer declares bankruptcy, the probability that a company can collect the cash it is owed is miniscule. Terri Oyarzun, founder of Goats R Us, a company that owns a herd of goats that provide fire mitigation services by eating shrubs and brush that could fuel blazes, realized that when Lehman Brothers declared bankruptcy, she would never be able to collect the $53,000 the financial company owed her company. Oyarzun says that she had to postpone purchasing a new truck for the farm and hiring new goat herders.

- **Stick to your credit terms.** Define the credit terms with every client up front. If clients balk when it comes time for payment, remind them that they have a commitment to live up to the terms of the sales contract.

(continued)

Hands On . . . How To (continued)

- **_Raise prices to cover the extra cost of late payments._** If clients refuse to pay on time, determine how much their slower payments cost your company and raise your rates or your prices enough to cover the cost.

- **_Require customers to pay at least part of total price of a contract up front._** Because the jobs that one small film production company performs require the owner to incur some rather sizable expenses before they are completed, he implemented a policy that requires customers to pay one-third of the cost up front, another one-third at mid-project, and the balance on completion.

- **_Offer discounts to encourage early payment._** Cash discounts (such as "2/10, net 30," which means that you offer the client a 2 percent discount if he or she pays within 10 days; otherwise, the full invoice amount is due in 30 days) can reduce a small company's profit margin, but they also provide an incentive for clients to pay early. Remember: More companies fail for lack of cash than for lack of profit.

Sources: Adapted from Shivani Vora, "Need Cash? Try Looking Inward," *Inc.*, May 2008, pp. 43–44; Amy Feldman, "The Cash-Flow Crunch," *Inc.*, December 2005, pp. 50–52; and Michael Corkery and Alex Frangos, "Far Away from Wall Street, a Herd Gets Gored," *Wall Street Journal*, January 24–25, 2009, pp. A1, A12.

---

5. **_Look for warning signs._** Dunis sees her accounts-payable as an early warning system for cash flow problems. "The first indication I get that cash flow is in trouble is when I see I'm getting low on cash and could have trouble paying my bills according to my staggered filing system," she says. ∎

Other signs that a business is heading for cash flow problems include difficulty making payments on loans and incurring penalties for late payment of routine bills.

Business owners should verify all invoices before paying them. Some unscrupulous vendors send out invoices for goods they never shipped or services they never rendered, knowing that many business owners will simply pay the bill without checking its authenticity. Two common scams aimed at small business owners involve bogus operators sending invoices for office supplies or ads in nonexistent printed or online "yellow pages" directories. In some cases, the directories actually do exist, but their distribution is so limited that ads in them are useless. To avoid falling victim to such scams, someone in the company—for instance, the accounts-payable clerk—should have the responsibility of verifying *every* invoice received.

A clever cash manager also negotiates the best possible credit terms with his or her suppliers. Almost all vendors grant their customers trade credit, and small business owners should take advantage of it. However, because trade credit can be so easy to get, entrepreneurs must be careful not to abuse it, putting their businesses in a precarious financial position. Favorable credit terms can make a tremendous difference in a company's cash flow. Table 12.6 shows the same most likely cash budget from Table 12.2 with one exception: instead of purchasing on C.O.D. terms as shown in Table 12.2, the owner has negotiated "net 30" payment terms (Table 12.6). Notice the drastic improvement in the company's cash flow that results from improved credit terms.

If owners do find themselves financially strapped when payment to a vendor is due, they should avoid making empty promises that "the check is in the mail" or sending unsigned checks. Instead, they should discuss the situation honestly with the vendor. Most vendors will work out payment terms for extended credit. One small business owner who was experiencing a cash crisis claims,

> One day things got so bad I just called up a supplier and said, "I need your stuff, but I'm going through a tough period and simply can't pay you right now." They said they wanted to keep me as a customer, and they asked if it was okay to bill me in three months. I was dumbfounded: *They didn't even charge me interest.*[45]

Entrepreneurs also can improve their firms' cash flow by scheduling controllable cash disbursements so that they do not come due at the same time. For example, paying employees every two weeks (or every month) rather than every week reduces administrative costs and gives the business more time to use its cash. Owners of fledgling businesses may be able to conserve cash by hiring part-time employees or by using freelance workers rather than full-time, permanent workers. Scheduling insurance premiums monthly or quarterly rather than annually also can improve cash flows.

TABLE 12.6 Cash Budget-—Most Likely Sales Forecast after Negotiating "Net 30" Trade Credit Terms

Cash Receipts	Oct	Nov	Dec	Jan	Feb	Mar	Apr	May	Jun
Sales	$300,000	$350,000	$400,000	$150,000	$200,000	$200,000	$300,000	$315,000	$320,000
Credit sales	225,000	262,500	300,000	112,500	150,000	150,000	225,000	236,250	240,000
Collections	—	—	—	—	—	—	—	—	—
60%—first month after sale				180,000	67,500	90,000	90,000	135,000	141,750
30%—second month after sale				78,750	90,000	33,750	45,000	45,000	67,500
5%—third month after sale				11,250	13,125	15,000	5,625	7,500	7,500
Cash sales				37,500	50,000	50,000	75,000	78,750	80,000
Other cash receipts	—	—	—	25	35	50	60	60	65
Total Cash Receipts				307,525	220,660	188,800	215,685	266,310	296,815
	—	—	—						
Cash Disbursements									
Purchases*				105,000	140,000	140,000	210,000	185,000	190,000
Rent				3,000	3,000	3,000	3,000	3,000	3,000
Utilities				1,450	1,400	1,250	1,250	1,250	1,400
Banknote				—	—	7,500	—	—	—
Tax prepayment				—	—	18,000	—	—	—
Capital additions				—	130,000	—	—	—	—
Wages and salaries				30,000	38,000	40,000	42,000	44,000	44,000
Insurance				475	475	475	475	475	475
Advertising				1,600	1,600	1,500	2,000	2,000	2,200
Interest				—	—	—	249	—	—
Miscellaneous				500	500	500	550	550	550
Total Cash Disbursements				142,025	314,975	212,225	259,524	236,275	241,625
	—	—	—						
End-of-Month Balance									
Beginning cash balance				12,000	177,500	83,185	59,760	15,921	45,956
+ Cash receipts				307,525	220,660	188,800	215,685	266,310	296,815
− Cash disbursements	—	—	—	142,025	314,975	212,225	259,524	236,275	241,625
Cash (end of month)				177,500	83,185	59,760	15,921	45,956	101,146
Borrowing				—	—	—	—	—	—
Repayment	—	—	—	—	—	—	—	—	—
Final Cash Balance				$177,500	$83,185	$59,760	$15,921	$45,956	$101,146
Monthly Surplus/(Deficit)				165,500	(94,315)	(23,425)	(43,839)	30,035	55,190

* After negotiating "net 30" trade credit terms.

Inventory

Offering customers a wider variety of products is one way a business can outshine its competitors, but product proliferation increases the need for tight inventory control to avoid a cash crisis. The typical grocery store now stocks about 50,000 stock-keeping units, three times as many as it did 20 years ago, and many other types of businesses are following this pattern.[46] Although inventory is the largest investment for many businesses, entrepreneurs often manage it haphazardly, creating a severe strain on their companies' cash flow. As a result, the typical small business has not only too much inventory but also too much of the *wrong* kind of inventory! Because inventory is illiquid, it can quickly siphon off a company's pool of available cash. "Small companies need cash to grow," says one consultant. "They've got to be able to turn [cash] over quickly. That's difficult to do if a lot of money is tied up in excess inventory."[47]

Surplus inventory yields a zero rate of return and unnecessarily ties up a company's cash. "Carrying inventory is expensive," says one small business consultant. "A typical manufacturing company pays 25 percent to 30 percent of the value of the inventory for the cost of borrowed money, warehouse space, materials handling, staff, lift-truck expenses, and fixed costs. This shocks a lot of people. Once they realize it, they look at inventory differently."[48] Marking down items that don't sell keeps inventory lean and allows it to turn over frequently. Even though volume discounts lower inventory costs, large purchases may tie up the company's valuable cash. Wise business owners avoid overbuying inventory, recognizing that excess inventory ties up valuable cash unproductively. In fact, only 20 percent of a typical business's inventory turns over quickly; therefore, owners must watch constantly for stale items.[49] If a small business must pay its suppliers within 30 days of receiving an inventory shipment and the merchandise sits on the shelf for another 30 to 60 days (or more!), the pressure on its cash flow intensifies. Increasing a company's inventory turnover ratio frees surprising amounts of cash. For instance, if a company with $2 million in annual sales that turns its inventory twice each year improves its inventory turnover ratio by just two weeks, it will improve its cash flow by nearly $18,900.

Carrying too little inventory is not the ideal solution to cash flow challenges because companies with excessive "stock-outs" lose sales (and eventually customers if the problem persists). However, carrying too much inventory usually results in slow-moving inventory and a low inventory turnover ratio. Experienced business owners understand the importance of shedding slow-moving inventory during end-of-season sales, even if they must resort to markdowns. Businesses must be "proactive with their markdowns," says a retail merchandising expert. "Cash flow and [inventory] turnover are the name of the game."[50]

Carrying too much inventory increases the chances that a business will run out of cash. An entrepreneur's goal is to minimize the company's investment in inventory without sacrificing sales, selection, and customer satisfaction. "The cash that pays for goods is channeled into inventory," says one business writer, "where its flow is dead-ended until the inventory is sold and the cash is set free again. The cash flow trick is to commit just enough cash to inventory to meet demand."[51] Scheduling inventory deliveries at the latest possible date prevents premature payment of invoices. In addition, given goods of comparable quality and price, an entrepreneur should purchase goods from the fastest supplier to keep inventory levels as low as possible. All of these tactics require entrepreneurs to manage their supply chains carefully and to treat their suppliers as partners in their businesses. Keeping inventory churning rapidly through a small business requires creating a nimble, adaptive supply chain that responds to a company's changing needs.

© brinkstock / Alamy

ENTREPRENEURIAL PROFILE: Zara Zara, a chain of retail stores that sells inexpensive, stylish clothing to young, fashion-conscious people, manages its supply chain so efficiently that its inventory turnover ratio is much higher than the industry average, meaning that the company ties up less cash in inventory than its competition. Zara's fast-fashion approach also keeps customers coming back by keeping stores' inventory fresh, adding new items constantly at a rate that leaves most of its competitors in awe. In fact, Zara can take a garment from design to store shelf in just two to three weeks instead of the five to twelve months that most clothing retailers require. The company tracks the latest fashion trends and manufactures small runs of items, which allows it to avoid being stuck with large quantities of unpopular garments that it must mark down. The result is that Zara's stores, which are located in Europe and the United States, sell 85 percent of their inventory at full price, compared to the industry average of 50 to 70 percent. Zara has created an irresistible image of scarcity that appeals to its faithful customers, who know that when they find something they like, they had better buy it, or it may be gone—for good. The result is a minimal investment in inventory that ties up little cash but yields above-average sales and profits.[52] ■

Business owners also should take advantage of quantity discounts and cash discounts that their suppliers offer. **Quantity discounts** give businesses a price break when they order large quantities of merchandise and supplies and exist in two forms: noncumulative and cumulative. Noncumulative quantity discounts are granted only if a certain volume of merchandise is purchased in a single order. For example, a wholesaler may offer small retailers a 3 percent discount only if they purchase 10 gross of Halloween masks in a single order. Cumulative quantity discounts apply if a company's purchases from a particular vendor exceed a specified quantity or dollar value over a predetermined time period. The time frame varies, but a yearly basis is most common. For example, a manufacturer of appliances may offer a small business a 3 percent discount on subsequent orders if its purchases exceed $10,000 per year.

Cash discounts are offered to customers as an incentive to pay for merchandise promptly. Many vendors grant cash discounts to avoid being used as an interest-free bank by customers who purchase merchandise and then fail to pay by the invoice due date. To encourage prompt payment of invoices, many vendors allow customers to deduct a percentage of the purchase amount if they pay within a specified time. Cash discount terms "2/10, net 30" are common in many industries. These terms mean that the total amount of the invoice is due 30 days, but if the bill is paid within 10 days, the buyer may deduct 2 percent from the total. A discount offering "2/10, EOM" (EOM means "end of month") indicates that the buyer may deduct 2 percent if the bill is paid by the tenth of the month after purchase.

In general, it is sound business practice to take advantage of cash discounts because a company incurs an implicit (opportunity) cost by forgoing a cash discount. By failing to take advantage of the cash discount, an entrepreneur is, in effect, paying an annual interest rate to retain the use of the discounted amount for the remainder of the credit period. For example, suppose the Print Shop receives an invoice for $1,000 from a vendor offering a cash discount of 2/10, net 30. Figure 12.7 illustrates this situation and shows how to compute the cost of forgoing the cash discount. Notice that the cost of forgoing this cash discount is 37.25 percent. Table 12.7 summarizes the cost of forgoing cash discounts with different terms.

Monitoring the big three of cash management helps every business owner to avoid a cash crisis while making the best use of available cash. According to one expert, maximizing cash flow involves "getting money from customers sooner; paying bills at the last moment possible; consolidating money in a single bank account; managing accounts payable, accounts receivable, and inventory more effectively; and squeezing every penny out of your daily business."[53]

quantity discounts
discounts that give businesses a price break when they order large quantities of merchandise and supplies. They exist in two forms: cumulative and noncumulative.

cash discounts
discounts offered to customers as an incentive to pay for merchandise promptly.

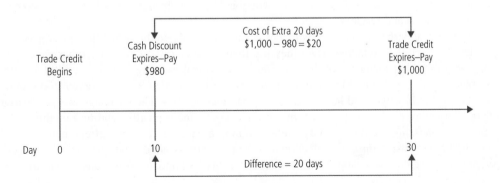

FIGURE 12.7
A Cash Discount

Cost of Extra 20 days
$1,000 − 980 = $20

Trade Credit Begins
Cash Discount Expires—Pay $980
Trade Credit Expires—Pay $1,000

Day   0   10   30

Difference = 20 days

Annual Cost of Foregoing a 2/10, net 30 Cash Discount:

Rate = Interest/Principle × Time

$$\text{Rate} = \frac{\$20}{\$980 \times 20 \text{ days}/365 \text{ days}}$$

Rate = 37.25%

TABLE 12.7 Cost of Forgoing Cash Discounts

Cash Discount Terms	Cost of Forgoing the Cash Discount (Annually)
2/10, net 30	37.25%
2/10, net 40	24.83%
3/10, net 30	56.44%
3/10, net 40	37.63%

LO5

Explain the techniques for avoiding a cash crunch in a small company.

Avoiding the Cash Crunch

Nearly every small business has the potential to improve its cash position with little or no investment. The key is to make an objective evaluation of the company's financial policies, searching for inefficiency in its cash flow. Young firms cannot afford to waste resources, especially one as vital as cash. By utilizing the following techniques, entrepreneurs can get maximum benefit from their companies' pool of available cash.

Barter

bartering

the exchange of goods and services for other goods and services rather than for cash.

Bartering, the exchange of goods and services for other goods and services rather than for cash, is an effective way to conserve cash. An ancient concept, bartering has regained popularity in recent years. Today, more than 500 barter exchanges operate across the United States, and they cater primarily to small- and medium-size businesses looking to conserve cash. More than 350,000 companies—most of them small—engage in more than $8.5 billion worth of barter each year.[54] Every day, entrepreneurs across the nation use bartering to buy much-needed materials, services, equipment, and supplies—*without* using precious cash.

ENTREPRENEURIAL PROFILE: Barrett Ersek: HappyLawn of America Barrett Ersek, a serial entrepreneur and founder of HappyLawn of America, is a member of the Atlantic Barter exchange in Wilmington, Delaware. Ersek recently bartered several old trailers from his business to another exchange member for $5,000 in barter credits, which he applied to another member's $7,500 display booth for trade shows. "This is a great way to conserve cash," says Ersek, whose HappyLawn business's bartering totals $250,000 per year.[55] ■

In addition to conserving cash, companies that use barter also have the opportunity to transform slow-moving inventory into much-needed products and services. Buying goods and services with barter also offers the benefit of a built-in discount. Although a company gets credit for the retail value of the goods or services it offers, the real cost to the company is less and depends on its gross profit margin. For instance, the owner of an Italian restaurant bartered $1,000 worth of meals for some new furniture, but his actual cost of the meals was only $680, given his gross profit margin of 32 percent. Entrepreneurs who join barter exchanges often find new customers for their products and services.

In a typical barter exchange, businesses accumulate trade credits when they offer goods or services through the exchange. Then they use their trade credits to purchase other goods and services from other members of the exchange. The typical exchange charges a $400 to $800 membership fee, a $10 to $15 monthly maintenance fee, and an 8 to 10 percent transaction fee (half from the buyer and half from the seller) on every deal. The exchange acts as a barter "bank," tracking the balance in each member's account and typically sending monthly statements summarizing account activity. Before joining a barter exchange, entrepreneurs should investigate its fee structure, the selection and the prices of its goods and services, and its geographic coverage to make sure the fit is a good one. In addition, all barter transactions are subject to taxes.

Trim Overhead Costs

High overhead expenses can strain a small company's cash supply to the breaking point; simple cost-cutting measures can save big money. Frugal small business owners can trim their overhead in a number of ways.

ASK FOR DISCOUNTS AND "FREEBIES" Entrepreneurs can conserve cash by negotiating discounts on the purchases they make and to making the use of free services whenever possible. For instance, rather than pay a high-priced consultant to assist him with his business plan, one entrepreneur opted instead to use the free services of his local SBDC. The move not only improved the quality of his business plan, enabling him to get the financing he needed to launch his business, but also conserved valuable cash for the start-up.

ENTREPRENEURIAL PROFILE: Sid Jaridly: Original Mr. Cabinet Care Sid Jaridly, CEO of the Original Mr. Cabinet Care, a kitchen remodeling business in Anaheim, California, saw his company's profit margins being squeezed from an industry downturn and approached his top 50 vendors and asked for price reductions of 10 to 15 percent. Nearly 30 of his suppliers agreed to his request for price concessions, a move that saved his company nearly $500,000 in just one year![56] ■

CONDUCT PERIODIC EXPENSE AUDITS Business owners not only should attempt to keep their operating costs low but also should evaluate them periodically to make sure they have not gotten out of line. Comparing current expenses with past levels is helpful, and so is comparing a company's expenses against industry standards. Useful resources for determining typical expenses in an industry include the RMA's *Annual Statement Studies*, Dun & Bradstreet's *Industry Norms and Key Business Ratios*, and Prentice *Hall's Almanac of Business and Industrial Financial Ratios*.

ENTREPRENEURIAL PROFILE: Sam Goodner: Catapult Systems At least twice a year, Sam Goodner, founder of Catapult Systems, an IT consulting firm in Austin, Texas, reviews every invoice his company pays with a member of his accounting staff, looking for ways to reduce the company's expenses. Recently, Goodner replaced a monthly $600 bottled water service with a water filtration system that cost just $600 annually. He also saved $40,000 a year by switching his public relations firm from a retainer to project-based assignments. "There are tens of thousands of dollars a year I can cut, and the company doesn't feel the difference, says Goodner."[57] ■

WHEN PRACTICAL, LEASE INSTEAD OF BUY Businesses spend about $800 billion on equipment annually, and companies acquire about one-third of that equipment through leases.[58] By leasing automobiles, computers, office equipment, machinery, and many other types of assets rather than buying them, entrepreneurs can conserve valuable cash. The value of these assets is not in *owning* them but in *using* them. Leasing is a popular cash management strategy; about 85 percent of companies lease some or all of their equipment.[59] "These companies are long on ideas, short on capital, and in need of flexibility as they grow and change," says Suzanne Jackson of the Equipment Leasing Association of America. "They lease for efficiency and convenience."[60]

ENTREPRENEURIAL PROFILE: Mark Kolodziej: Hudson Bread Mark Kolodziej grew up in Poland, spending most of his afternoons in his father's bakery. In 1994, Kolodziej opened his own bakery, Hudson Bread, in New York City and soon was supplying baguettes, focaccias, and other artisanal breads to some of the city's finest restaurants. Hudson Bread grew, and in 2003, Kolodziej opened a 50,000-square-foot baking facility in North Bergen, New Jersey. Bakery equipment is quite expensive, and to conserve capital, Kolodziej decided to lease rather than buy the equipment his company needed. He used the same strategy in 2008 when Hudson Bread turned to GE Capital to lease the $1.5 million equipment to open a second baking facility outside of Philadelphia.[61] ■

Hudson Bread

Although total lease payments typically are greater than those for a conventional loan, most leases offer 100 percent financing, meaning that the owner avoids the large capital outlays required as down payments on most loans. (Sometimes a lease requires the first and last months' payments to be made up front.) Leasing also protects a business against obsolescence, especially when it comes to equipment such as computer hardware and software, whose technological life is limited to perhaps just two or three years. Furthermore, leasing is an "off-the-balance-sheet" method of financing and requires no collateral. The equipment a company leases does not have to be depreciated because the small business does not actually own it. A lease is considered an operating expense on the income statement, not a liability on the balance sheet. Thus, leasing conserves a company's borrowing capacity. Because lease payments are fixed amounts paid over a particular time period, leasing allows business owners to forecast more accurately their cash flows. Lease agreements also are flexible; entrepreneurs can customize their lease payments to coincide with the seasonal fluctuations in their companies' cash balances. Leasing companies typically allow businesses to stretch payments over a longer time period than do conventional loans. "There are so many ways to tailor a lease agreement to a company's individual equipment and financial needs that you might call it a personalized rental agreement," says the owner of a small construction firm.[62]

Entrepreneurs can choose from two basic types of leases: operating leases and capital leases. At the end of an **operating lease**, a business turns the equipment back over to the leasing company with no further obligation. Businesses often lease computer and telecommunications equipment through operating leases because it becomes obsolete so quickly. At the end of a **capital lease**, a business may exercise an option to purchase the equipment, usually for a nominal sum.

operating lease

a lease at the end of which a company turns the equipment back to the leasing company and has no further obligation.

capital lease

a lease at the end of which a company may exercise an option to purchase the equipment, usually for a nominal sum.

AVOID NONESSENTIAL OUTLAYS By forgoing costly ego indulgences like ostentatious office equipment, first-class travel, and flashy company cars, entrepreneurs can make the most efficient use of a company's cash and put their money where it really counts. Before putting scarce cash into an asset, every business owner should put the decision to the acid test: "What will this purchase add to my company's ability to compete and to become more successful?" The secret to successful cost saving is cutting *nonessential* expenditures. Making across-the-board spending cuts to conserve cash is dangerous because the owner runs the risk of cutting expenditures that drive the business. One common mistake during business slowdowns is cutting marketing and advertising expenditures. Economic slowdowns present a prime opportunity for smart business owners to bring increased attention to their products and services and to gain market share if they hold the line on their marketing and advertising budgets as their competitors cut back. "If the lifeblood of your company is marketing, cut it less," advises one advertising executive. "If it is customer service, that is the last thing you want to cut back on. Cut from areas that are not essential to business growth."[63]

BUY USED OR RECONDITIONED EQUIPMENT, ESPECIALLY IF IT IS "BEHIND-THE-SCENES" MACHINERY One restaurateur saved thousands of dollars in the start-up phase of his business by buying used equipment from a restaurant equipment broker.

HIRE PART-TIME EMPLOYEES AND FREELANCE SPECIALISTS WHENEVER POSSIBLE Hiring part-time workers and freelancers rather than full-time employees saves on the cost of salaries, vacations, and benefits.

ENTREPRENEURIAL PROFILE: Gina Kleinworth: HireBetter Gina Kleinworth, CEO of HireBetter, a business based in Austin, Texas, that helps small and midsize companies find the talent they need, relies on an entirely part-time workforce of 35 employees. Kleinworth keeps her company's payroll costs under control, and her workers appreciate the flexibility in their schedules. "Employees have time to get their work done, and go to the gym, take their kids to the park, or volunteer in their communities," she says.[64] ■

OUTSOURCE One technique that many entrepreneurs use to conserve valuable cash is to outsource certain activities to businesses that specialize in performing them rather than hiring someone to do them in-house (or doing the activities themselves). According to a recent survey by the Human Capital Institute, 90 percent of U.S. companies outsource at least some of their work. On average, companies outsource 27 percent of work, an increase from just 6 percent in 1990.[65] In addition to saving cash, outsourcing enables entrepreneurs to focus on the most important aspects of running their businesses. "Stick to what you are good at and outsource everything else," advises one entrepreneur.[66] Outsourcing is one principle of building a lean start-up.

ENTREPRENEURIAL PROFILE: Danny Wong: Blank Label Danny Wong, cofounder of Blank Label, a maker of custom dress shirts for men, keeps his core team of employees small, just eight people, and outsources about 60 hours of e-mails, live chat, programming, and Web site content creation each week. "It increased the quality of our lives and the quality of our service," he says. "The result, not the process, is what matters."[67] ■

USE E-MAIL RATHER THAN MAIL Whenever appropriate, entrepreneurs should use e-mail rather than mail to correspond with customers, suppliers, and others to reduce postage costs.

USE CREDIT CARDS TO MAKE SMALL PURCHASES Using a credit card to make small purchases from vendors who do not offer credit terms allows entrepreneurs to defer payment for up to 30 days. Entrepreneurs who use this strategy must be disciplined, however, and pay off the entire credit card balance each month. Carrying a credit card balance from month to month exposes an entrepreneur to annual interest rates of 15 to 25 percent—*not* a cash-conserving technique!

Negotiate Fixed Loan Payments to Coincide with Your Company's Cash Flow Cycle

Many banks allow businesses to structure loans so that they can skip specific payments when their cash flow ebbs to its lowest point. Negotiating such terms gives businesses the opportunity to customize their loan repayments to their cash flow cycles.

ENTREPRENEURIAL PROFILE: Ted Zoli: Torrington Industries Ted Zoli, president of Torrington Industries, a construction materials supplier and contracting business, consistently uses "skipped payment loans" in his highly seasonal business. "Every time we buy a piece of construction machinery," he says, "we set it up so that we're making payments for eight or nine months, and then skipping three or four months during the winter."[68] ∎

Establish an Internal Security and Control System

Too many owners encourage employee theft by failing to establish a system of controls. Reconciling the bank statement monthly and requiring approval for checks over a specific amount, say, $1,000, helps to minimize losses. Separating record-keeping and check-writing responsibilities, rather than assigning them to a single employee, offers additional protection against fraud.

Develop a System to Battle Check Fraud

Although the use of checks written in the United States continues to decline, customers still write more than 76 million checks per day.[69] Unfortunately, about 1.7 million of those are bad checks that cost businesses more than $50 million per day.[70] Bad checks and check fraud can wreak havoc on a small company's cash flow. Simple techniques for minimizing losses from bad checks include requesting proper identification (preferably with a photograph) from customers, recording customers' telephone numbers, and training cashiers to watch for forged or counterfeit checks. Perhaps the most effective way to battle bad and fraudulent checks is to subscribe to an electronic check approval service. The service works at the cash register, and approval takes only a minute or less. The fee a small business pays to use the service depends on the volume of checks. For most small companies, charges amount to 1 to 2 percent of the cleared checks' value.

Change Your Shipping Terms

Changing a company's shipping terms from "F.O.B. (free on board) buyer," in which the *seller* pays the cost of freight, to "F.O.B. seller," in which the *buyer* absorbs all shipping costs, improves its cash flow.

Start Selling Gift Cards

Gift cards are a huge business, generating annual sales of $73 billion, and can provide a real boost to a small company's cash flow.[71] Customers pay for the cards up front, but the typical recipient does not redeem the gift card until later, sometimes much later, giving the company the use of the cash during that time. Selling gift cards also increases a company's revenue because studies show that 72 percent of card recipients spend an average of 56 percent more than the value of the card.[72] Unfortunately, only 8 to 10 percent of small and midsize merchants sell gift cards.[73]

ENTREPRENEURIAL PROFILE: Colleen Stone: Inspa Corporation Colleen Stone, owner of Inspa Corporation, a fast-growing Seattle, Washington–based chain of day spas, uses gift cards to stretch her company's cash flow. Gift cards account for 25 percent of her company's sales, and Stone has discovered that many of the gift cards she sells are not redeemed for a year, giving her a source of interest-free cash in the interim. "We plow all that cash flow right back into opening new stores," says Stone.[74] ■

Switch to Zero-Based Budgeting

Zero-based budgeting (ZBB) primarily is a shift in the philosophy of budgeting. Rather than build the current-year budget on *increases* from the previous year's budget, ZBB starts from a budget of zero and evaluates the necessity of every item. "Start with zero and review all expenses, asking yourself whether each one is necessary," says one business consultant.[75]

Be on the Lookout for Shoplifting and Employee Theft

Companies lose billions of dollars each year to shoplifting and employee theft. Although any business can be a victim of shoplifting or employee theft, retailers are particularly vulnerable. Retailers in the United States lose 1.12 percent of their sales, about $26.1 billion, each year to shoplifting and employee theft. Shoplifting is the most common business crime, costing retailers an estimated $11.7 billion each year.[76] Shoplifting takes an especially heavy toll on small businesses because they usually have the weakest lines of defense against shoplifters. If a shoplifter steals just one item that sells for $100 from a small business with an 8 percent net profit margin, the company must sell an additional $1,250 worth of goods to make up for the loss.

Even though shoplifting is more common than employee theft, businesses lose more money each year to employee theft. The Association of Certified Fraud Examiners estimates that companies worldwide lose 5 percent of their annual revenue to fraud by employees. Because small business owners often rely on informal procedures for managing cash (or no procedures at all) and often lack proper control procedures, they are most likely to become victims of employee theft, embezzlement, and fraud by their employees. The median loss suffered by small companies in the United States is $160,000, well above the $105,000 median loss for all U.S. companies. The most common methods employees use to steal from small businesses are fraudulent billing schemes and check tampering. Alarmingly, the typical fraud goes on for 18 months before the owner discovers it, most often after another employee tips off the owner to the theft.[77] Although establishing a totalitarian police state and trusting no one is not conducive to a positive work environment, putting in place adequate financial control systems is essential. Separating among at least two employees key cash management duties, such as writing checks and handling bank statements and conducting regular financial audits, can be effective deterrents to employee theft.

Build a Cash Cushion

Entrepreneurs who have experienced a cash crisis keenly understand the need for every business to build a working capital account as an emergency fund. How much should an entrepreneur put aside? Opinions differ, but most experts say that a small business should put aside enough cash to cover three to six months' worth of expenses—more if conditions warrant.

ENTREPRENEURIAL PROFILE: Carrie Davenport: Century Personnel Carrie Davenport, owner of Century Personnel, a company that specializes in filling jobs in manufacturing, engineering, accounting, and health care, did everything she could to reduce expenses when sales plummeted during a recent recession. She also began putting aside more money into Century Personnel's working capital account, which now has $300,000 more than usual in it. "It's there in case the economy gets bad again so that I'll have enough to keep the business afloat," says Davenport, who in 2005 purchased the business that her father, Deane Shepard, started in 1977. Even after reducing her staff from 36 to 14 in the height of the recession, Davenport was concerned that she had only enough cash tucked aside to cover the company's expenses for a couple of months. "That's an unforgettable experience," she says. That prompted her to build a larger cash cushion for her company's protection by adding consistently to Century Personnel's "rainy-day fund."[78] ■

Invest Surplus Cash

Because of the uneven flow of receipts and disbursements, a company will often temporarily have more cash than it needs—for a week, month, quarter, or even longer. When this happens, most small business owners simply ignore the surplus because they are not sure how soon they will need it. They believe that relatively small amounts of cash sitting around for just a few days or weeks are not worth investing. However, this is not the case. Small business owners who put

✔ You Be the Consultant

Foul Play

Like many business owners, Karin Wilson saw sales slide at Page and Palette Inc., the bookstore in Fairhope, Alabama, that she co-owns with her husband during the last recession. By the time the all-important holiday season arrived, the store was running low on its inventory of books. However, cash flow at Page and Palette was extremely tight, and Wilson was unable to convince her book suppliers to extend the store additional credit. One week before Christmas, Wilson happened to see the company's credit card bill, which indicated the Page and Palette was months behind on its payments and was racking up huge fees and interest expense. She began investigating and soon discovered evidence that the company's bookkeeper, who had a personal account with the same bank, had been using money from the company's account intended to pay publishers for the store's book orders to write checks to herself and to pay her personal credit card bills. Wilson says the former employee also used the money that she embezzled from Page and Palette to pay for membership in a local golf club and for private school tuition for her child.

Wilson was shocked because the bookkeeper was one of her most trusted employees. "Many times I have [business owners] in my office crying because it was their trusted bookkeeper," says Isabel Cumming, an attorney who leads a state white-collar crime division. Wilson estimates that the former employee took about $150,000 over two-and-a-half years and covered the theft by forging reports that made it look as though she had paid the company's vendors and credit card bills. Because the theft left the store in a cash bind, Wilson was unable to order a sufficient inventory of books, ultimately costing the business as much as 20 percent of its annual revenue in lost sales. "She realized quickly how trusting we were," says Wilson.

Since discovering that she was a victim of employee theft, Wilson has changed the way she operates her business. She destroyed the stamp bearing her signature that the former employee used on business checks. Employees no longer have access to the company's credit cards; Wilson now approves every credit card purchase. She also has the company's bank statements sent to her home rather than to the business.

Because small businesses often lack the financial and control procedures that large companies impose, they are disproportionately more likely to be victims of employee theft. One workplace crime prevention expert says that small companies are common targets of employee theft because employees "know their systems, controls, and weaknesses and can bide their time waiting for the right opportunity." Indeed, more than 94 percent of employees who steal have been with their companies for at least five years. One expert cites the following "formula" for employee theft:

Pressure + Rationalization + Opportunity = Employee theft

The only factor in the equation that employers can control is opportunity, which is why entrepreneurs' money is better spent *preventing* employee theft rather than *detecting* it.

A survey by Auditors Inc. reports that 40 percent of small companies are victims of employee theft or embezzlement but that only 2 percent of victimized small companies report the crimes. The median amount stolen among small companies is $160,000, an amount significant enough to threaten the existence of the businesses themselves. In small businesses, the typical fraud goes on for 18 months before the owner discovers it. One-third of the time, an employee tips off the owner to the theft, double the percentage of thefts that are discovered by management review (15.3 percent). Nearly 1 in 10 thefts is discovered by accident.

One accountant says that in most cases the perpetrator is the person one would least expect, "the long-term, very trusted, very valued employee who never committed fraud before." In the United States, employees (46.2 percent) are more likely to steal than are managers (36.7 percent), but thefts by managers cause three times more damage ($150,000) than those by employees ($50,000). Managers' thefts also are more difficult to detect, requiring a median of 18 months to detect, compared to 13 months for those that employees commit. In the United States, 57 percent of the perpetrators are male, 55 percent are between the ages of 31 and 45, and 52 percent have a college or postgraduate degree. The most common "red flags" that lead to detection are employees who are living beyond their means, those who are having financial difficulties, those who are unwilling to share their job duties (for fear of detection), and those who have an unusually close association with a company vendor.

1. Identify the factors that led Page and Palette to become a victim of employee theft and embezzlement. What impact does this crime have on a company's cash flow?

2. Do you agree that small businesses are more likely to be victims of employee theft? Explain.

3. List at least five steps that entrepreneurs should take to prevent their businesses from becoming victims of employee theft and embezzlement.

Sources: Based on Simona Cowell, "Small Businesses Face More Fraud in Downturn," *Wall Street Journal*, February 19, 2009, p. B5; Sarah E. Needleman, "Businesses Say Employee Theft Is Up," *Wall Street Journal*, December 11, 2008, http://online.wsj .com/article/SB122896381748896999.html; Kathleen Johnston Jarboe, "Employee Theft at Small Business High and Hard to Detect," *The Daily Record*, October 14, 2005, http://findarticles.com/p/articles/mi_qn4183/is_20051014/ai_n15712876; John Tate, "Little White Thefts," *Small Business Development Center Business Report*, September 5, 2008, p. 2; "Employee Theft Statistics Infographic," *Infographics Showcase*, March 3, 2010, http://www.infographicsshowcase.com/employee-theft-statistics-infographic; and *Report to the Nations on Occupational Fraud and Abuse: 2010 Global Fraud Study*, Association of Certified Fraud Examiners, 2010.

surplus cash to work *immediately* rather than allowing it to sit idle soon discover that the yield adds up to a significant amount over time. This money can help ease the daily cash crunch during business troughs. "Your goal . . . should be to identify every dollar you don't need to pay today's bills and to keep that money invested to improve your cash flow," explains a consultant.[79]

money market account
an interest-bearing account that allows depositors to write checks without tying up their money for a specific period of time.

zero-balance account (ZBA)
a checking account that never has any funds in it. A company keeps its money in an interest-bearing master account tied to the ZBA; when a check is drawn on the ZBA, the bank withdraws enough money from the master account to cover it.

sweep account
a checking account that automatically sweeps all funds in a company's checking account above a predetermined minimum into an interest-bearing account.

However, when investing surplus cash, an entrepreneur's primary objective should *not* be to earn the highest yield (which usually carries with it high levels of risk); instead, the focus should be on the safety and the liquidity of the investments. Making high-risk investments with a company's cash cushion makes no sense and could jeopardize its future. The need to minimize risk and to have ready access to the cash restricts an entrepreneur's investment options to just a few such as money market accounts, zero-balance accounts, and sweep accounts. A **money market account** is an interest-bearing account offered by a variety of financial institutions ranging from banks to mutual funds. Money market accounts pay interest while allowing depositors to write checks (most have minimum check amounts) without tying their money up for a specific period of time.

A **zero-balance account (ZBA)** is a checking account that technically never has any funds in it but is tied to a master account. The company keeps its money in the master account, where it earns interest, but it writes checks on the ZBA. At the end of the day, the bank pays all of the checks drawn on the ZBA; then it withdraws enough money from the master account to cover them. ZBAs allow a company to keep more cash working during the float period, the time between a check being issued and its being cashed. A **sweep account** automatically "sweeps" all funds in a company's checking account above a predetermined minimum into an interest-bearing account, enabling it to keep otherwise idle cash invested until it is needed to cover checks.

Keep Your Business Plan Current

Before approaching any potential lender or investor, a business owner must prepare a solid business plan. Smart owners keep their plans up to date in case an unexpected cash crisis forces them to seek emergency financing. Revising the plan annually also forces the owner to focus on managing the business more effectively.

 You Be the Consultant

The Challenges of Cash Flow

The founder of a small consulting firm recently received a letter from an important *Fortune* 500 client that the large company would extend its payment terms from 90 days to 120 days, "a fancy legalese version of 'we're going to start paying you later because it's better for us; get used to it,'" she says. While she waits four months for payment, this entrepreneur must meet the payroll for her 20 employees; pay rent, utilities, insurance, and a host of other operating expenses; and purchase new computers and other technology to support the work her staff does for clients. Managing cash flow for her business has become more complex, a situation that many small business owners are facing as large companies stretch their accounts payable and speed up collections of their own accounts receivable.

Drew Davies started M&J Kitchens, a custom cabinet seller, in 1985 and weathered several recessions, some of which caused sales to decline by more than 50 percent. Davies thought that his company had turned the corner in the last economic slowdown because sales were running 42 percent ahead of the previous year. Then, M&J Kitchens's customers began stretching their payments from 30 days to 60 days and eventually 90 days. At the same time, the cabinetmakers who supplied his inventory began requiring deposits on all orders and decreased the credit terms they offered. That combination squeezed the company's cash flow by $60,000 to $120,000 per

month. The final blow came when Davies's bank pulled the plug on the M&J Kitchens's line of credit even though he was current on all loan payments. The bank said that the company's asset base had dropped below the level required in one of the loan's covenants. M&J Kitchens, which once generated annual sales of $4 million and employed 12 people, could not pay its bills and closed its doors. "We were getting squeezed from both sides," says Davies.

Laura Yurs, founder of Earth Images, Inc., an erosion control contractor in Greenwood, Indiana, knew that cash flow was tight. Revenue from state building projects, a significant source of her company's revenue, had all but dried up. In addition, customers for whom the company worked were taking longer to pay their bills. Then came the call from her banker, who had noticed that Earth Images was gradually pushing up to the limit of its line of credit. "I've never gotten a call like that before," says Yurs. "He didn't need to say anything more." Yurs had been relying on the line of credit to pay bills because its cash flow was caught in a squeeze.

Yurs knew that if the bank withdrew her line of credit, her business would not be able to survive. She called on Chris Stump, a project manager at Butler University's Butler Business Accelerator, for help. After Stump reviewed several years of Earth Images's financial data, he met with Yurs and told her that her 14-year-old

You Be the Consultant (continued)

company had serious cash flow problems. If she wanted to save it, she would have to make some significant changes—and quickly.

Every week, Yurs and her staff compiled cash flow statements; prepared reports on the company's accounts receivable, accounts payable, and inventory; and used them to create cash flow forecasts. She also began holding monthly financial meetings with Stump and her management team. She and her staff worked to reduce costs, revamp the company's back office, and make the entire company more efficient. Yurs began focusing on collecting cash more quickly. The accounts-receivable department began sending customers invoices weekly rather than monthly, and when an invoice slipped past the due date, someone made an immediate follow-up telephone call. Yurs also stopped paying invoices from her vendors early and began sending the checks so that they arrived on the invoice due date.

The changes worked. Earth Images ended the year with positive cash flow, and sales are climbing once again, on track to hit $10 million. "They are the poster child for effective cash management," says Stump proudly of Yurs and her employees. "She changed the way her company managed cash in a three- to six-month period."

1. How typical are the cash flow problems that these three companies face? Explain.

2. What advice can you offer business owners about managing their cash flow?

Sources: Based on Terra Terwilliger, "Why America's Small Businesses Are Becoming Like Banks," *Reuters*, November 15, 2010, http://blogs.reuters.com/small-business/2010/11/15/why-america%E2%80%99s-small-businesses-are-becoming-like-banks; John Tozzi, "For Small Business, a Cash Flow Crisis," *Bloomberg Business Week*, March 24, 2011, http://www.businessweek.com/magazine/content/11_14/b4222059377221.htm; and Elizabeth Wasserman, "Cash Is King, Again," *Inside Edge*, September 21, 2010, http://corp.americanexpress.com/gcs/insideedge/articles/cash-is-king-again-elizabeth-wasserman.aspx.

Conclusion

Successful owners run their businesses "lean and mean." Trimming wasteful expenditures, investing surplus funds, and carefully planning and managing the company's cash flow enable them to compete effectively. The simple but effective techniques covered in this chapter can improve every small company's cash position. One business writer says, "In the day-to-day course of running a company, other people's capital flows past an imaginative CEO as opportunity. By looking forward and keeping an analytical eye on your cash account as events unfold (remembering that if there's no real cash there when you need it, you're history), you can generate leverage as surely as if that capital were yours to keep."[80]

Chapter Summary by Learning Objective

1. Explain the importance of cash management to a small company's success.

- Cash is the most important but least productive asset the small business has. An entrepreneur must maintain enough cash to meet the company's normal requirements (plus a reserve for emergencies) without retaining excessively large, unproductive cash balances.

- Without adequate cash, a small business will fail.

2. Differentiate between cash and profits.

- Cash and profits are *not* the same. More businesses fail for lack of cash than for lack of profits.

- Profits, the difference between total revenue and total expenses, are an accounting concept. Cash flow represents the flow of actual cash (the only thing businesses can use to pay bills) through a business in a continuous cycle. A business can be earning a profit and be forced out of business because it runs out of cash.

3. Understand the five steps in creating a cash budget and use them to create a cash budget.

- The cash budgeting procedure outlined in this chapter tracks the flow of cash through the business and enables the owner to project cash surpluses and cash deficits at specific intervals.

- The five steps in creating a cash budget are as follows: determining a minimum cash balance, forecasting sales, forecasting cash receipts, forecasting cash disbursements, and determining the end-of-month cash balance.

4. **Describe fundamental principles involved in managing the "big three" of cash management: accounts receivable, accounts payable, and inventory.**

- Controlling accounts receivable requires business owners to establish clear, firm credit and collection policies and to screen customers *before* granting them credit. Sending invoices promptly and acting on past-due accounts quickly also improve cash flow. The goal is to collect cash from receivables as quickly as possible.

- When managing accounts payable, a manager's goal is to stretch out payables as long a possible without damaging the company's credit rating. Other techniques include verifying invoices before paying them, taking advantage of cash discounts, and negotiating the best possible credit terms.

- Inventory frequently causes cash headaches for small business managers. Excess inventory earns a zero rate of return and ties up a company's cash unnecessarily. Owners must watch for stale merchandise.

5. **Explain the techniques for avoiding a cash crunch in a small company.**

- Trimming overhead costs by bartering; leasing assets rather than buying them, avoiding nonessential outlays, buying used equipment, and hiring part-time employees; negotiating fixed payments to coincide with a company's cash flow cycle; implementing an internal control system boost a firm's cash flow position; developing a system to battle check fraud, selling gift cards; using zero-based budgeting; being on the lookout for shoplifting and employee theft; building a cash cushion; and keeping the business plan current.

- In addition, investing surplus cash maximizes the firm's earning power. The primary criteria for investing surplus cash are security and liquidity.

Discussion Questions

1. Why must entrepreneurs concentrate on effective cash flow management?
2. Explain the difference between cash and profit.
3. Outline the steps involved in developing a cash budget.
4. How can an entrepreneur launching a new business forecast sales?
5. What are the big three of cash management? What effect do they have on a company's cash flow?
6. Outline the basic principles of managing a small firm's receivables, payables, and inventory.
7. How can bartering improve a company's cash position?
8. What steps can entrepreneurs take to conserve the cash within their companies?
9. What should be a small business owner's primary concern when investing surplus cash?

Business Plan Pro™ In addition to being a valuable planning tool, the cash flow statement helps you to assess the future health and potential of your venture. As you learned in this chapter, cash and profits are not the same. There are aspects of cash flow that are nonintuitive, and the cash flow statement provides a realistic view of the availability of cash for the business.

Business Plan Exercises

Review the cash flow statement in your plan, determine what you can learn from that statement, and assess the financial viability and health of your proposed business venture.

On the Web

Go to www.pearsonhighered.com/scarborough and look at the links associated with Chapter 12. These online resources offer additional information regarding the cash flow statement and the role it will play in your business plan.

Sample Plans

Review one or more of the sample plans to get a sense of how the cash flow statement predicts the availability of cash. Find the lowest point of cash flow. This is the point where cash is limited.

In the Software

Review the sales forecast and the expense information. Change any figures that look unrealistic. Review the pro forma profit-and-loss statement. Are you comfortable with the status of those statements? Go to the Financial Statement section and look at your Projected Cash Flow Statement. Do any of these months show a negative cash flow? If this is the case, your projections indicate you do not have an adequate cash cushion. The largest deficit amount indicates the minimum amount of additional cash your business needs. Make sure that your projections are realistic and that you have adequate cash to make it through this negative period by bringing in additional cash. Advanced planning is your best opportunity to avoid business failure by running out of cash. Conversely, if there are months where your projections indicate an excess amount of cash, explore your options to use this cash to its best ability when that time comes.

Save the changes you have made in your plan. Assume that this version of your plan represents your "most likely" outcome based on realistic expense and revenue projections. We are now going to do two "what-if" scenarios. For example, save this same file with the words "worst case" after the file name, or use a file name that will enable you to save all your work from before and create another version of your business plan. This will enable you to make changes in your plan and assess what that does to your cash flow. Reduce revenues by 25 percent. What does that do to your company's cash flow? Then increase expenses by 25 percent. What impact does that have regarding the amount of cash you will need to get through the lowest cash flow months? If you assume that customers will pay in 30 days, increase that to 45 days. What does your cash flow statement look like now? Make pessimistic changes to paint a negative picture and save the plan under the "worst case" file name. Save and close that plan. Next, open your original so that we can start with your "most likely" scenario again. Save your original under a "best case" file name. If you are planning to extend credit, decrease the number of collection days by seven. What does that do to your cash flow? Increase your revenues by 15 percent. Decrease your projected expenses by 15 percent. Working through these scenarios can help you to test and validate your numbers and prepare you for contingencies and options as your plan becomes a reality.

Building Your Business Plan

Review the data that affect your cash flow statement. Are there revisions you need to make based on your pro forma cash flow statement? What are some of the most significant cash demands of your business? Is excessive cash tied up in inventory? Do payroll expenses demand substantial amounts of cash? Are rent or lease expenditures disproportionately high based on your projected revenues? Can you take steps to reduce or better control these expenditures as you build your revenue stream? Once you have answered these questions, determine whether you have adequate cash for your venture, allowing for potential cost overruns or revenues below your projections.

Beyond the Classroom . . .

1. Interview several local small business owners about their cash management policies. Do they know how much cash their businesses have during the month? How do they track their cash flows? Do they use some type of cash budget? If not, ask if you can help the owner develop one. Does the owner invest surplus cash? If so, where?

2. Volunteer to help a small business owner develop a cash budget for his or her company. What patterns do you detect? What recommendations can you make for improving the company's cash management system?

3. Contact the International Reciprocal Trade Association (www.irta.net) and get a list of the barter exchanges in your state. Interview the manager of one of the exchanges and prepare a report on how barter exchanges work and how they benefit small businesses. Ask the manager to refer you to a small business owner who benefits from the barter exchange and interview him or her. How does the owner use the exchange? How much cash has bartering saved? What other benefits has the owner discovered?

4. Use the resources of the Internet to research leasing options for small companies. The Equipment Leasing and Financing Association of America (www.elfaonline.org) is a good place to start. What advantages does leasing offer? Disadvantages? Identify and explain the various types of leases.

5. Contact a local small business owner who sells on credit. Is collecting accounts receivable on time a problem? What steps does the owner take to manage the company's accounts receivable? Do late payers strain the company's cash flow? How does the owner deal with customers who pay late?

6. Conduct an online search for the National Retail Security Survey that the University of Florida Department of Criminology, Law, and Society conducts annually. Summarize the key findings of the survey concerning losses that businesses incur from shoplifting, employee theft, and fraud. What steps can small businesses take to minimize their losses to these problems?

Endnotes

1. Wendy Taylor and Marty Jerome, "Dead Men Talking," *Smart Business*, December 2001/January 2002, p. 19.
2. Ilana DeBare, "Tips for Small Businesses to Survive Recession," *San Francisco Chronicle*, March 23, 2008, http://www.sfgate.com/cgi-bin/article.cgi?f=/c/a/2008/03/22/BUSQVMKH3.DTL.
3. Michael Connellan, "'Show Me the Kwan, Jerry!' Cash Is King," *Seeking Alpha*, December 8, 2011, http://seekingalpha.com/article/312705-show-me-the-kwan-jerry-cash-is-king.
4. "Economic Uncertainty Shaping the New, More Pragmatic Entrepreneur, according to American Express Open Small Business Monitor, *American Express Open*, October 4, 2011, p. 2.
5. Jerry Useem, "The Icon That Almost Wasn't," *Inc: The State of Small Business* 1998, p. 142; "History," Ford Motor Company, http://www.ford.com/en/heritage/history/default.htm.

6. Daniel Kehrer, "Big Ideas for Your Small Business," *Changing Times*, November 1989, p. 58.

7. Howard Greenstein, "A Female Spin on Starting a Business," *Inc.*, February 23, 2011, http://www.inc.com/howard-greenstein/a-female-spin-on-starting-a-business.html; "Susan T. Spencer's 'Briefcase Essentials' for Women in Business," *Knowledge@Wharton*, May 19, 2011, http://knowledge.wharton.upenn.edu/article.cfm?articleid=2782.

8. Serena Ng and Cari Tuna, "Big Firms Are Quick to Collect, Slow to Pay," *Wall Street Journal*, August 31, 2009, pp. A1, A7.

9. Nichole L. Torres, "Got Money?," *Entrepreneur*, March 2009, p. 88.

10. Elizabeth Wasserman, "Cash Is King, Again," *American Express Inside Edge*, September 21, 2010, http://corp.americanexpress.com/gcs/insideedge/articles/cash-is-king-again-elizabeth-wasserman.aspx.

11. Douglas Bartholomew, "4 Common Financial Management Mistakes . . . and How to Avoid Them," *Your Company*, Fall 1991, p. 9.

12. Robert A. Mamis, "Money In, Money Out," *Inc.*, March 1993, p. 98.

13. Bartholomew, "4 Common Financial Management Mistakes … and How to Avoid Them," p. 9.

14. Phaedra Hise, "Paging for Cash Flow," *Inc.*, December 1995, p. 131.

15. Clare Ansberry, "Smashing Event: In This Small Town, Pumpkins Are a Big Deal," *Wall Street Journal*, October 19, 2011, pp. A1, A12.

16. Kortney Stringer, "Neither Anthrax nor the Economy Stops the Fruitcake," *Wall Street Journal*, December 19, 2001, pp. B1, B4; Dirk Smillie, "Signs of Life," *Forbes*, November 11, 2002, p. 160.

17. Gwendolyn Bounds, "Store's Sales Can Rest on a Moment," *Wall Street Journal*, January 3, 2006, p. A.23.

18. Michelle Lock, "Pie-Makers Aim for Pizza Super Bowl Action," *Washington Post*, January 31, 2011, http://www.washingtonpost.com/wp-dyn/content/article/2011/01/31/AR2011013102711.html; Ashwin Verghese, "Rochester-Area Pizza Shops Prepare for Annual Super Bowl Blitz," *Democrat Chronicle*, January 26, 2009, http://www.democratandchronicle.com/article/20090126/NEWS01/901260336.

19. Gwendolyn Bounds, "Preparing for the Big Bang," *Wall Street Journal*, June 29, 2004, pp. B1, B7.

20. Jenny Munro, "Halloween in July," *Business*, July 25, 2004, pp. 1, 6–7.

21. Alix Stuart, "Negotiating with Goliath," *CFO*, May 2011, p. 12.

22. Alix Stuart, "Negotiating with Goliath," *CFO*, May 2011, p. 12.

23. Jill Andresky Fraser, "Monitoring Daily Cash Trends," *Inc.*, October 1992, p. 49.

24. William G. Shepherd Jr., "Internal Financial Strategies," *Venture*, September 1985, p. 66.

25. David H. Bangs, *Financial Troubleshooting: An Action Plan for Money Management in the Small Business* (Dover, NH: Upstart Publishing Company, 1992), p. 61.

26. Sharna Brockett and Brooke Tvedten, "Intuit Billing Manager 'Get Paid Survey' Results," Intuit, 2009 Fact Sheet, p. 1.

27. Serena Ng and Cari Tuna, "Big Firms Are Quick to Collect, Slow to Pay," *Wall Street Journal*, August 31, 2009, pp. A1, A7.

28. William J. Dennis Jr., *Financing Small Business: Small Business and Credit Access*, National Federation of Independent Businesses, January 2011, p. 2.

29. "Jacobus Energy Fuels Up with Cortera," Cortera, December 13, 2011, http://www.cortera.com/customer-success-stories/jacobus-energy.

30. Gwen Moran, "When Money Is Due," *Entrepreneur*, March 2011, p. 69.

31. "Cash Flow/Cash Flow Management," *Small Business Reporter*, no. 9, p. 5.

32. Hannah Seligson, "Learn How to Collect from Slow Payers," *New York Times*, April 6, 2011, http://www.nytimes.com/2011/04/07/business/smallbusiness/07sbiz.html?pagewanted=all.

33. American Collectors Association, http://www.collector.com; Howard Muson, "Collecting Overdue Accounts," *Your Company*, Spring 1993, p. 4.

34. Sharna Brockett and Brooke Tvedten, "Intuit Billing Manager 'Get Paid Survey' Results," Intuit, 2009 Fact Sheet, p. 1.

35. Verne Harnish, "Has Your Bank Turned Its Back on You? Five Ways to Come Up with More Cash and Get Business Going Again," *Fortune*, October 18, 2010, p. 70.

36. Gwen Moran, "Better Billing," *Entrepreneur*, November 2011, p. 76.

37. Sharna Brockett and Brooke Tvedten, "Intuit Billing Manager 'Get Paid Survey' Results," Intuit, 2009 Fact Sheet, p. 1.

38. Wayne Parry, "Debt Collectors: Struggling Economy Brings Ups and Downs for Business," *Huffington Post*, September 21, 2011, http://www.huffingtonpost.com/2011/09/21/debt-collectors-bad-economy_n_973987.html.

39. Simona Covell and Kelly K. Spors, "To Help Collect the Bills, Firms Try the Soft Touch," *Wall Street Journal*, January 22, 2009, pp. B1, B6.

40. Elaine Pofeldt, "Collect Calls," *Success*, March 1998, pp. 22–24.

41. Janine Latis Musick, "Collecting Payments Due," *Nation's Business*, January 1999, pp. 44–46.

42. Jeffrey A. Trachtenberg, "Borders to Try Again to Sway Publishers," *Wall Street Journal*, January 13, 2011, p. B3; "Borders Announces Liquidation, Closing 400 Stores," KTLA, July 18, 2011, http://www.ktla.com/news/landing/ktla-borders-bankrupt,0,2928708.story.

43. Jill Andresky Fraser, "A Confidence Game," *Inc.*, December 1989, p. 178.

44. Jill Andresky Fraser, "How To Get Paid," *Inc.*, March 1992, p. 105.

45. G. Shepherd Jr., "Internal Financial Strategies," *Venture*, September 1985, p. 68.

46. Beth Kowitt, "Inside the Secret World of Trader Joe's," *CNN Money*, August 23, 2010, http://money.cnn.com/2010/08/20/news/companies/inside_trader_joes_full_version.fortune/index.htm; Mark Henricks, "No Long-Term Parking," *Entrepreneur*, January 2002, http://www.entrepreneur.com/article/0,4621,295660.html.

47. Stephanie Barlow, "Frozen Assets," *Entrepreneur*, September 1993, p. 53.

48. Roberta Maynard, "Can You Benefit from Barter?," *Nation's Business*, July 1994, p. 6.

49. "33 Ways to Increase Your Cash Flow and Manage Cash Balances," *The Business Owner*, February 1988, p. 8.

50. R. J. Anderson, "Mark Down and Turn Up," *Inside Outdoor*, no. 9, April 2004, p. 28.

51. Robert A. Mamis, "Money In, Money Out," *Inc.*, March 1993, p. 102.

52. Doug Hardman, Simon Harper, and Ashok Notaney, "Keeping Inventory-and Profits-Off the Discount Rack," Booz, Allen, and Hamilton, http://www.boozallen.com/media/file/Off_the_Discount_Rack.pdf, pp. 1-2; Rachel Tiplady, "Zara: Taking the Lead in Fast-Fashion," *Business Week*, April 4, 2006, http://www.boozallen.com/media/file/Off_the_Discount_Rack.pdf.

53. Jeffrey Lant, "Cash Is King," *Small Business Reports*, May 1991, p. 49.

54. "Reciprocal Trade Statistics," International Reciprocal Trade Administration, December 2011, http://www.irta.com/component/content/article/39.html.

55. Verne Harnish, "Has Your Bank Turned Its Back on You? Five Ways to Come Up with More Cash and Get Business Going Again," *Fortune*, October 18, 2010, p. 70.

56. Raymund Flandez, "Small Businesses Cut Costs by Renegotiation," *Wall Street Journal*, January 20, 2009, http://online.wsj.com/article/SB123241078342495977.html.

57. Verne Harnish, "Has Your Bank Turned Its Back on You? Five Ways to Come Up with More Cash and Get Business Going Again," *Fortune*, October 18, 2010, p. 70.

58. "Leasing Statistics," Beacon Funding, 2011, http://www.beaconfunding.com/vendor_programs/statistics.aspx.

59. "Leasing Statistics," Beacon Funding, 2011, http://www.beaconfunding.com/vendor_programs/statistics.aspx.

60. Jill Amadio, "To Lease or Not to Lease?" *Entrepreneur*, February 1998, p. 133.

61. "Customer Success Story: Hudson Bread," GE Capital, 2010, http://www.hudsonbread.com/media.html.

62. Jack Wynn, "To Use but Not to Own," *Nation's Business*, January 1991, p. 38.

63. Roger Thompson, "Business Copes with the Recession," *Nation's Business*, January 1991, p. 20.

64. "Shifting Full-Time Employees to Part-Time," National Federation of Independent Businesses, http://www.nfib.com/business-resources/business-resources-item?cmsid=55167.

65. Kate Lister, "Freelance Nation," *Entrepreneur*, September 2010, pp. 89–94.

66. Gerry Blackwell, "Don't Hire, Outsource," *Small Business Computing*, July 5, 2005, http://www.smallbusinesscomputing.com/news/article.php/3512451.

67. Emily Maltby, "Overseas Outsourcing Heats Up Again," *CNN Money*, November 11, 2008, http://money.cnn.com/2008/11/10/smallbusiness/outsourcing.smb/index.htm.

68. Bruce G. Posner, "Skipped-Payment Loans," *Inc.*, September 1992, p. 40.

69. *The 2010 Federal Reserve Payments Study*, Federal Reserve System, April 5, 2011, p. 13.

70. "I'll Take 'What Is Check Fraud?' for 500, Alex," First Mariner Bank, November 9, 2011, http://blog.1stmarinerbank.com/tag/bad-checks.

71. Jessica Shambora, "Plastic Presents," *Fortune*, December 6, 2010, p. 33.

72. Jessica Shambora, "Plastic Presents," *Fortune*, December 6, 2010, p. 33.

73. Cyndia Zwahlen, "Firms Putting Gift Cards on Their Own Wish Lists," *Los Angeles Times*, June 7, 2010, http://articles.latimes.com/2010/jun/07/business/la-fi-0607-smallbiz-giftcards-20100607.

74. David Worrell, "It's in the Cards," *Entrepreneur*, April 2005, p. 57.

75. Roger Thompson, "Business Copes with the Recession," *Nation's Business*, January 1991, p. 21.

76. Kathy Grannis, "Retail Losses Hit $41.6 Billion Last Year, according to National Retail Security Survey," National Retail Federation, June 11, 2007, http://www.nrf.com/modules.php?name=News&op=viewlive&sp_id=318.

77. *Report to the Nations on Occupational Fraud and Abuse*, 2010 Global Fraud Study, Association of Certified Fraud Examiners, 2010.

78. Emily Maltby, "Another Season of Horders," *Wall Street Journal*, May 16, 2011, p. R4.

79. Jill Andresky Fraser, "Better Cash Management," *Inc.*, May 1993, p. 42.

80. Robert A. Mamis, "Money In, Money Out," *Inc.*, March 1993, p. 103.

© kentoh/Fotolia

13

Sources of Financing: Equity and Debt

Learning Objectives

On completion of this chapter, you will be able to:

1. Describe the differences between equity capital and debt capital and the advantages and disadvantages of each.

2. Discuss the various sources of equity capital available to entrepreneurs, including personal savings, friends and relatives, crowd funding, angels, partners, venture capital firms, corporate venture capital, public stock offerings, and simplified registrations and exemptions.

3. Describe the process of "going public" as well as its advantages and disadvantages and the various simplified registrations and exemptions from registration that are available to small businesses.

4. Describe the various sources of debt capital and the advantages and disadvantages of each: banks, asset-based lenders, vendors (trade credit), equipment suppliers, commercial finance companies, savings-and-loan associations, stockbrokers, credit

unions, bonds, private placements, Small Business Investment Companies (SBICs) and Small Business Lending Companies (SBLCs).

5. Identify the various federal loan programs aimed at small businesses.

6. Describe the various loan programs available from the Small Business Administration.

7. Explain other methods of financing a business, including factoring, leasing assets, and using credit cards.

People who want to start a business should know that they're going to end up having to use their own money, their existing credit, the equity in their house, or borrow from well-meaning friends and family.

—Margie Mullen, entrepreneur

Capital is a crucial element in the process of creating new ventures, yet raising the money to launch a new business venture has always been a challenge for entrepreneurs. Capital markets rise and fall with the stock market, overall economic conditions, and investors' fortunes. These swells and troughs in the availability of capital make the search for financing look like a wild roller-coaster ride. Entrepreneurs, especially those in less glamorous industries or those just starting out, face difficulty finding outside sources of financing. Many banks shy away from making loans to start-ups, venture capitalists are looking for ever-larger deals, private investors have grown cautious, and making a public stock offering remains a viable option for only a handful of promising companies with good track records and fast-growth futures. The result has been a credit crunch for entrepreneurs looking for small to moderate amounts of start-up capital. Entrepreneurs and business owners who need between $100,000 and $3 million are especially hard hit because of the vacuum that exists at that level of financing.

In the face of this capital crunch, business's need for capital has never been greater. Lenders and investors pump billions of dollars into small businesses every year, yet entrepreneurs are left clamoring for more capital. In a recent survey by the National Federation of Independent Businesses (NFIB), 41 percent of small business owners say that lack of capital is an impediment to the growth of their companies.[1] When searching for the capital to launch their companies, entrepreneurs must remember the following "secrets" to successful financing:

- *Choosing the right sources of capital for a business can be just as important as choosing the right form of ownership or the right location.* It is a decision that will influence a company for a lifetime, and entrepreneurs must weigh their options carefully before committing to a particular funding source. "It is important that companies in need of capital align themselves with sources that best fit their needs," says one financial consultant. "The success of a company often depends on the success of that relationship."[2]

- *The money is out there; the key is knowing where to look.* Entrepreneurs must do their homework *before* they set out to raise money for their ventures. Understanding which sources of funding are best suited for the various stages of a company's growth and then taking the time to learn how those sources work is essential to success.

- *Raising money takes time and effort.* Sometimes entrepreneurs are surprised at the energy and the time required to raise the capital needed to feed their cash-hungry, growing businesses. The process usually includes lots of promising leads, most of which turn out to be dead ends. Meetings with and presentations to lots of potential investors and lenders can crowd out the time needed to manage a growing company. Entrepreneurs also discover that raising capital is an ongoing job. "The fund-raising game is a marathon, not a sprint," says Jerusha Stewart, founder of iSpiritus Soul Spa, a store selling personal growth and well-being products.[3]

- *Creativity counts.* Although some traditional sources of funds now play a lesser role in small business finance than in the past, other sources—from large corporations and customers to international venture capitalists and state or local programs—are taking up the slack. To find the financing their businesses demand, entrepreneurs must use as much creativity in attracting financing as they did in generating the ideas for their products and services. For instance, after striking out with traditional sources of funding, EZConserve, a company that makes software that provides energy management tools for large PC networks, turned to the nonprofit group Northwest Energy Efficiency Alliance and received a sizable grant as well as marketing assistance that fueled its growth.[4]

- *The Internet puts at entrepreneurs' fingertips vast resources of information that can lead to financing; use it.* The Internet often offers entrepreneurs, especially those looking for relatively small amounts of money, the opportunity to discover sources of funds that they otherwise might miss. The Web site created for this book (www.pearsonhighered.com/scarborough) provides links to many useful sites related to raising both start-up and growth capital. The Internet also provides a low-cost convenient way for entrepreneurs to get their business plans into potential investors' hands anywhere in the world.

- *Put social media to work to locate potential investors.* Social media such as Facebook, Twitter, LinkedIn, and others are useful tools for locating potential investors.

ZUMA Press/Newscom

ENTREPRENEURIAL PROFILE: Robbie Vitrano, Jeff Leach, Randy Crochet, and Brock Fillinger: Naked Pizza Although Robbie Vitrano and Jeff Leach, who along with Randy Crochet and Brock Fillinger cofounded Naked Pizza, a pizza chain based in New Orleans, Louisiana, that specializes in all-natural, low-calorie pizzas, do not specifically target potential investors with their messages on Twitter, the entrepreneurs say that their humorous Tweets and online presence have resulted in more than 8,000 investment inquiries in just 18 months. "The intent is more about starting a conversation in which like minds will engage," says Vitrano. "Some of those like minds, it turns out, are investors." About 25 percent of the inquiries have led to actual investments. Managers at Kraft Group, a private equity firm in Foxborough, Massachusetts, learned about Naked Pizza from Vitrano's and Leach's Tweets and ended up making two investments in the growing company, which now has 25 locations around the globe with nearly 500 more in the works.[5] ■

- *Be thoroughly prepared before approaching potential lenders and investors.* In the hunt for capital, tracking down leads is tough enough; don't blow a potential deal by failing to be ready to present your business idea to potential lenders and investors in a clear, concise, convincing way. That, of course, requires a solid business plan and a well-rehearsed elevator pitch—one or two minutes on the nature of your business and the source of its competitive edge to win over potential investors and lenders. "Entrepreneurs who come across with unsubstantiated market assessments, no competitive analysis, and flimsy marketing and sales plans will be the losers in the race to money," says venture capitalist John May.[6]

- *Entrepreneurs cannot overestimate the importance of making sure that the "chemistry" among themselves, their companies, and their funding sources is a good one.* Too many entrepreneurs get into financial deals because they needed the money to keep their businesses growing only to discover that their plans do not match those of their financial partners.

- *Plan an exit strategy.* Although it may seem peculiar for entrepreneurs to plan an exit strategy for investors when they are seeking capital to *start* their businesses, doing so increases their chances of closing a deal. Investors do not put their money into a business with the intent of leaving it there indefinitely. Their goal is to get their money back—along with an attractive return on it. Entrepreneurs who fail to define potential exit strategies for their investors reduce the likelihood of getting the capital their companies need to grow.

Rather than rely primarily on a single source of funds as they have in the past, entrepreneurs must piece together capital from multiple sources, a method known as **layered financing**. They have discovered that raising capital successfully requires them to cast a wide net to capture the financing they need to launch their businesses.

layered financing
the technique of raising capital from multiple sources.

ENTREPRENEURIAL PROFILE: James Reinhart, Chris Homer, and Oliver Lubin: thredUp After graduating from college, James Reinhart, Chris Homer, and Oliver Lubin realized that they wore only 25 percent of their clothes; the rest just took up valuable space in their tiny apartments. The trio of entrepreneurs also discovered that other people faced the same situation. "We thought, 'What if we took everything out of everybody's closet and created this virtual pile in the middle of the floor and then redistributed that pile?'" says Lubin. In 2009, after cobbling together $70,000 of their own money and investments from family members and friends, the entrepreneurs launched thredUp, a San Francisco–based company that provided an online exchange in which members could buy and sell gently used clothing. Within three months, thredUP had 10,000 members, but research convinced the cofounders to refocus their business on children's clothing. To relaunch the site for the children's clothing exchange, the entrepreneurs landed $250,000 from angel investors. The company grew quickly, and within months the founders closed a $1.4 million round of financing from three venture capital firms. They recently secured a second round of venture capital ("Round B" financing) of $7 million to fortify thredUp's customer service as the company grows.[7] ∎

This chapter will guide you through the myriad financing options available to entrepreneurs, focusing on both sources of equity (ownership) and debt (borrowed) financing.

Planning for Capital Needs

LO1

Describe the differences between equity capital and debt capital and the advantages and disadvantages of each.

Becoming a successful entrepreneur requires one to become a skilled fund-raiser, a job that usually requires more time and energy than most business founders realize. In start-up companies, raising capital can easily consume as much as one-half of the entrepreneur's time and can take many months to complete. In addition, many entrepreneurs find it necessary to raise capital constantly to fuel the hefty capital appetites of their young, fast-growing companies. Research by the Kauffman Foundation shows that the average amount of capital that entrepreneurs use to start small businesses in the United States is nearly $80,000.[8] However, these "small" amounts of capital can be most difficult to secure.

capital
any form of wealth employed to produce more wealth.

Capital is any form of wealth employed to produce more wealth. It exists in many forms in a typical business, including cash, inventory, plant, and equipment. Entrepreneurs have access to two different types of capital: equity and debt.

Equity Capital versus Debt Capital

equity capital
capital that represents the personal investment of the owner (or owners) of a company; sometimes called risk capital.

Equity capital represents the personal investment of the owner (or owners) in a business and is sometimes called *risk capital* because these investors assume the primary risk of losing their funds if the business fails.

ENTREPRENEURIAL PROFILE: Vern Raburn: Eclipse Aviation In 1999, Vern Raburn launched Eclipse Aviation Corporation, a company that manufactured small low-cost personal jets with the vision of transforming the air transportation industry. Production and cash flow problems plagued the company, however, and after nine years in business, Eclipse filed for bankruptcy, meaning that investors lost all of the money they had put into the company. In addition to Raburn, Eclipse investors included Microsoft founder Bill Gates (Raburn's former boss), the State of New Mexico (which invested $19 million), and billionaire Alfred Mann (who invested $139 million in the company). As part of the bankruptcy filing, Eclipse's largest stockholder, Luxembourg-based ETIRC Aviation, agreed to acquire the company's remaining assets.[9] ∎

If a venture succeeds, however, founders and investors share in the benefits, which can be quite substantial. The founders of and early investors in Yahoo!, Sun Microsystems, Federal Express, Intel, and Microsoft became multimillionaires when the companies went public and their equity investments finally paid off. Michael Moritz, a partner in the venture capital firm Sequoia

Capital, recalls a meeting in 1999 that took place around a ping-pong table that doubled as a conference table for Sergey Brin and Larry Page, the founders of a start-up company that had developed a search engine called Google. The young company had just changed its name from Backrub and had only 12 employees when Moritz agreed to invest $25 million in exchange for 16 percent of the company's stock. When Google made an initial public offering five years later, Moritz's original investment was worth $3 billion![10]

To entrepreneurs, the primary advantage of equity capital is that it does not have to be repaid like a loan does. Equity investors are entitled to share in the company's earnings (if there are any) and usually to have a voice in the company's future direction. The primary disadvantage of equity capital is that the entrepreneur must give up some—sometimes even *most*—of the ownership in the business to outsiders. Although 50 percent of something is better than 100 percent of nothing, giving up control of a company can be disconcerting and dangerous. Entrepreneurs are most likely to give up significant amounts of equity in their businesses in the start-up phase than in any other. To avoid having to give up control of their companies early on, entrepreneurs should strive to launch their companies with the least amount of money possible.

debt capital

the financing that an entrepreneur borrows and must repay with interest.

Debt capital is the financing that an entrepreneur borrows and must repay with interest. Very few entrepreneurs have adequate personal savings to finance the total start-up costs of a small business; many of them must rely on some form of debt capital to launch their companies. Lenders of capital are more numerous than investors, but small business loans can be just as difficult (if not more difficult) to obtain. Although borrowed capital allows entrepreneurs to maintain complete ownership of their businesses, it must be carried as a liability on the balance sheet as well as be repaid with interest in the future. In addition, because lenders consider small businesses to be greater risks than bigger corporate customers, they require higher interest rates on loans to small companies because of the risk–return trade-off—the higher the risk, the greater the return demanded. Most small firms pay the prime rate—the interest rate banks charge their most creditworthy customers—*plus* a few percentage points. Still, the cost of debt financing often is lower than that of equity financing. Because of the higher risks associated with providing equity capital to small companies, investors demand greater returns than lenders. In addition, unlike equity financing, debt financing does not require entrepreneurs to dilute their ownership interest in their companies. We now turn our attention to eight common sources of equity capital.

Sources of Equity Financing

Personal Savings

LO2

Discuss the various sources of equity capital available to entrepreneurs, including personal savings, friends and relatives, crowd funding, angels, partners, venture capital firms, corporate venture capital, public stock offerings, and simplified registrations and exemptions.

bootstrapping

a process in which entrepreneurs tap their personal savings and use creative, low-cost start-up methods to launch their businesses.

The *first* place entrepreneurs should look for start-up money is in their own pockets. It's the least expensive source of funds available! "The sooner you take outside money, the more ownership in your company you have to surrender," warns one small business expert.[11] Entrepreneurs apparently see the benefits of self-sufficiency; tapping their personal savings and using creative, low-cost start-up methods, a technique known as **bootstrapping**, is one of the most common sources of funds used to start a business. According to a survey by the Federal Reserve, more than 70 percent of U.S. entrepreneurs use personal savings and assets as a primary source of financing for their start-ups.[12] The Kauffman Foundation reports that the average business start-up in the United States requires $78,400 and that the typical entrepreneur provides 35 percent of the initial capital requirement; the remainder comes through a combination of debt and equity financing (see Figure 13.1).[13] Bootstrappers learn quickly to be frugal and stretch the income-generating power of every dollar. "Don't spend money on anything that doesn't have the ability to put money directly back into your business," advises Wayne Mullins, founder of Ugly Mug Marketing.[14]

ENTREPRENEURIAL PROFILE: John Krech: RightOn Inventory After 20 years as an inventory management specialist with 3M, John Krech saw an opportunity to help small businesses to manage their inventories more effectively. During one of his nightly walks along the river, Krech realized that most companies treated their inventory as an expense rather than a profit center. "It was a revelation," he recalls. He began developing proprietary formulas and equations (which he posted on his bedroom wall) that use inventory to maximize companies'

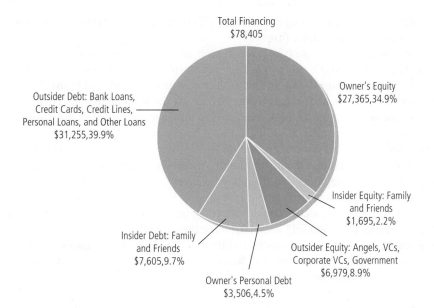

FIGURE 13.1

Sources of Financing for the Typical Start-Up Businesses

Source: Alicia M. Robb and David T. Robinson, *The Kauffman Firm Survey*, Kauffman Foundation, November 2008, p. 10.

Total Financing $78,405

Owner's Equity $27,365,34.9%

Outsider Debt: Bank Loans, Credit Cards, Credit Lines, Personal Loans, and Other Loans $31,255,39.9%

Insider Equity: Family and Friends $1,695,2.2%

Insider Debt: Family and Friends $7,605,9.7%

Outsider Equity: Angels, VCs, Corporate VCs, Government $6,979,8.9%

Owner's Personal Debt $3,506,4.5%

profits and cash flow and transformed them into software, RightOn Inventory, that allows business owners to determine when to order inventory and how much stock to keep on hand. Krech needed $350,000 to launch his company and decided to bootstrap his start-up, emptying his retirement account (despite having to pay a 10 percent penalty), selling his house, and cutting his living expenses by 40 percent. "I'm living for a few years like most people won't so I can live the rest of my life like most people can't," reasons the entrepreneur. RightOn Inventory, which sells for as little as $30 per month, generates $500,000 in sales and is growing rapidly. Krech's decision to bootstrap has paid off; he owns 100 percent of RightOn Inventory and already has received a seven-figure offer for his company but turned it down.[15] ■

Kevin J. Miyazaki/Redux

Lenders and investors *expect* entrepreneurs to put their own money into a business start-up. If an entrepreneur is not willing to risk his or her own money, potential investors are not likely to risk their money in the business either. Furthermore, failing to put up sufficient capital of their own means that entrepreneurs must either borrow an excessive amount of capital or give up a significant portion of ownership to outsiders to fund the business properly. Excessive borrowing in the early days of a business puts intense pressure on its cash flow, and becoming a minority shareholder may dampen a founder's enthusiasm for making a business successful.

Friends and Family Members

Although most entrepreneurs look to their own bank accounts first to finance a business, few have sufficient resources to launch their businesses alone. After emptying their own pockets, where should entrepreneurs should turn for capital? The second place most entrepreneurs look is to friends and family members who might be willing to invest in (or lend to) a business venture. Because of their relationships with the founder, these people are most likely to invest. Often they are more patient than other outside investors and are less meddlesome in a business's affairs (but not always!) than many other types of investors.

ENTREPRENEURIAL PROFILE: Leslie Wexner: Limited Brands In 1963, Leslie Wexner, then in his mid-twenties, borrowed $5,000 from his aunt to open a small women's clothing store, Leslie's Limited, in Columbus, Ohio. His business was successful and grew to become Limited Brands, which owns Victoria's Secret, Pink, Bath & Body Works, Henri Bendel, and other brands. Limited Brands generates sales of nearly $10 billion a year and has made Wexner a billionaire, appearing on the *Forbes* list of the world's richest people.[16] ■

Investments from family and friends are an important source of capital for entrepreneurs, but the amounts invested typically are small, often no more than just a few thousand dollars. In the United States, family members and friends invest an average of $27,715 in a typical small business start-up for an astonishing total of $100 billion per year, far greater than the investments of either angels or venture capital firms![17]

Investments (or loans) from family and friends are an excellent source of seed capital and can get a start-up far enough along to attract money from private investors or venture capital companies. Inherent dangers lurk in family business investments and loans, however. One study reports a default rate of 14 percent on business loans from family and friends compared to a default rate of 1 percent for bank loans.[18] Unrealistic expectations or misunderstood risks have destroyed many friendships and have ruined many family reunions. To avoid problems, an entrepreneur must honestly present the investment opportunity and the nature of the risks involved to avoid alienating friends and family members if the business fails. Smart entrepreneurs treat family members and friends who invest in their companies in the same way they would treat outside investors. Some investments in start-up companies return more than friends and family members ever could have imagined. In 1995, Mike and Jackie Bezos invested $300,000 in their son Jeff's start-up business, Amazon.com. Today, Mike and Jackie own 6 percent of Amazon.com's stock, and their shares are worth billions of dollars![19] The accompanying "Hands On . . . How To" feature offers suggestions for structuring successful family or friendship financing deals.

Crowd Funding

crowd funding
a method of raising capital that taps the power of social networking and allows entrepreneurs to post their elevator pitches and proposed investment terms on specialized Web sites and raise money from ordinary people who invest as little as $100.

Once limited to artists, musicians, and filmmakers looking to finance their creative projects, crowd funding has expanded into the world of entrepreneurship. **Crowd funding** taps the power of social networking and allows entrepreneurs to post their elevator pitches and proposed investment terms on crowd-funding Web sites, such as Profounder, Peerbackers, Kickstarter, or IndieGoGo, and raise money to fund their ventures from ordinary people who invest as little as $100. Normally, the amount of capital these entrepreneurs seek is small, typically less than $10,000, and the "returns" they offer investors are mere tokens, such as discount coupons and free product samples. However, some entrepreneurs have raised significantly more money with crowd funding and offer "real" returns.

ENTREPRENEURIAL PROFILE: Bronson Chang: Uncle Clay's House of Pure Aloha LLC When Bronson Chang, a recent college graduate, joined his uncle's candy shop, Uncle Clay's House of Pure Aloha LLC, in Honolulu, Hawaii, he used crowd funding to finance a much-needed renovation. Chang set up a fund-raising Web page at ProFounder, and 19 friends and family members invested $54,000 in exchange for payments of 2 percent of the shop's revenues over four years. "Raising capital through the community, through a more democratic process, was a perfect match for our business," says Chang, who is now looking to raise another $60,000 via crowd funding.[20] ■

Crowd-funding sites typically charge a fee of about 4 percent to host a funding request, and many proposals fail to attract enough investors to reach their targets. Currently, a proposal before Congress would allow companies to raise up to $2 million in equity financing through crowd funding. The proposal limits investments to $10,000 per year or 10 percent of the investor's annual income, whichever is less.[21]

Angels

private investors (angels)
wealthy individuals, often entrepreneurs themselves, who invest in business start-ups in exchange for equity stakes in the companies.

After dipping into their own pockets and convincing friends and relatives to invest in their business ventures, many entrepreneurs still find themselves short of the seed capital they need. Frequently, the next stop on the road to business financing is private investors. These **private investors (angels)** are wealthy individuals, often entrepreneurs themselves, who invest their own money in business start-ups in exchange for equity stakes in the companies. Angel investors have provided much-needed capital to entrepreneurs for many years. In 1938, when World War I flying ace Eddie Rickenbacker needed money to launch Eastern Airlines, millionaire Laurance Rockefeller provided it.[22] Alexander Graham Bell, inventor of the telephone, used angel capital to start Bell Telephone in 1877. More recently, companies such as Google, Apple, Starbucks, Kinko's, and the Body Shop relied on angel financing in their early years to finance growth.

Hands On . . . How To

Structure Family and Friendship Financing Deals

Tapping family members and friends for start-up capital, whether in the form of equity or debt financing, is a popular method of financing business ideas. In a typical year, some 6 million individuals in the United States invest about $100 billion in entrepreneurial ventures. Unfortunately, not all of these deals work to the satisfaction of both parties. The following suggestions can help entrepreneurs avoid needlessly destroying family relationships and friendships:

- **Choose your financier carefully.** One of the first issues to consider is the impact of the investment on everyone involved. Will it work a hardship on the investor or lender? Is the investor putting up the money because he or she wants to or because he or she feels obligated? Can all parties afford the loan if the business folds? No matter how much capital you may need, accepting more than family members or friends can afford to lose is a recipe for disaster—and perhaps bankruptcy for the investors. Lynn McPhee, who used $250,000 from family members to launch Xuny, a Web-based clothing store, says, "Our basic rule was, if [the investment is] going to strap someone, we won't take it." Remember that relationships often suffer if a business fails and friends and family members lose their money.

- **Keep the arrangement strictly business.** The parties should treat all loans and investments in a business-like manner, no matter how close the friendship or family relationship, to avoid problems down the line. If the transaction is a loan exceeding $10,000, it must carry a rate of interest at least as high as the market rate; otherwise, the Internal Revenue Service may consider the loan a gift and penalize the lender. "[Family] investors should act more like professional, early-stage investors," advises one experienced small business consultant.

- **Prepare a business plan.** Treat friends and family members just as you would angel investors, bankers, venture capitalists, and other professionals by doing your research and preparing a business plan. Before Denis Haber, an attorney in New York, and his brother Larry helped Denis's sons, Jason and Cory, start a real estate brokerage business with a six-figure investment, they insisted that the aspiring entrepreneurs prepare a comprehensive business plan. "We hit the books and a few weeks later had a very polished plan," says Jason, now CEO of Rubicon Property LLC, which has listed $30 million in property so far.

- **Settle the details up front.** Before any money changes hands, both parties must agree on the details of the deal.

How much money is involved? Is it a loan or an investment? How will the investor cash out? How will the loan be paid off? What happens if the business fails?

- **Create a written contract.** Don't make the mistake of closing a financial deal with just a handshake. The probability of misunderstandings skyrockets! Putting an agreement in writing demonstrates the parties' commitment to the deal and minimizes the chances of disputes from faulty memories and misunderstandings.

- **Treat the money as "bridge financing."** Although family and friends can help you launch your business, it is unlikely that they can provide enough capital to sustain it over the long term. Sooner or later, you will need to establish a relationship with other sources of credit if your company is to survive and thrive. Consider money from family and friends as a bridge to take your company to the next level of financing.

- **Develop a payment schedule that suits both the entrepreneur and the lender or investor.** One of the primary benefits of financing from family members and friends is that the repayment or cash-out schedule usually is flexible. Although lenders and investors may want to get their money back as quickly as possible, a rapid repayment or cash-out schedule can jeopardize a fledgling company's survival. Establish a realistic repayment plan that works for the parties without putting excessive strain on your young company's cash flow. "Unlike a bank, [family and friends] can provide 'patient capital' should the business not progress as quickly as planned," says a family business expert.

- **Have an exit plan.** Every deal should define exactly how investors will "cash out" their investments or loans.

Sources: Based on Caron Beesley, "6 Tips for Borrowing Startup Funds from Friends or Family," *SBA Community*, January 3, 2012, http://community.sba.gov/community/blogs/community-blogs/small-business-cents/6-tips-borrowing-startup-funds-friends-or-family; Rosalind Resnick, "For You, Graduate, Some Start-Up Capital," *Wall Street Journal*, June 7, 2011, http://online.wsj.com/article/SB10001424052702304432304576369842747489336.html; Sarah Dougherty, "'Love Money' Seeds Many Budding Ventures," *Financial Post*, January 30, 2008, http://www.financialpost.com/small-business/business-solutions/story.html?id=269859; Paulette Thomas, "It's All Relative," *Wall Street Journal*, November 29, 2004, pp. RR4, R8; Andrea Coombes, "Retirees as Venture Capitalists," *CBS Market-Watch*, November 2, 2003, http://netscape.marketwatch.com/news/story.asp?dist=feed&siteid=netscape&guid={1E1267CD-32A4-4558-9F7E-40E4B7892D01}; Paul Kvinta, "Frogskins, Shekels, Bucks, Moolah, Cash, Simoleans, Dough, Dinero: Everybody Wants It. Your Business Needs It. Here's How to Get It," *Smart Business*, August 2000, pp. 74–89; Alex Markels, "A Little Help from Their Friends," *Wall Street Journal*, May 22, 1995, p. R10; and Heather Chaplin, "Friends and Family," *Your Company*, September 1999, p. 26.

ENTREPRENEURIAL PROFILE: Troy Tolle: Digital Chalk In 2007, Troy Tolle and a partner started Digital Chalk, an Asheville, North Carolina-based company that provides software and payment services for online education businesses, with their own money. A $3 million capital infusion from angel investors has allowed the company to grow rapidly, but Tolle says that Digital Talk could be twice as large if he had access to more capital. "If we had more money, we could reach more customers," he says. Tolle believes that he could get financing from venture capital firms but is hesitant to do so because he does not want to give up a significant share of the ownership in his company. "They want so much for so little," he says.[23] ∎

In many cases, angels invest in businesses for more than purely economic reasons—for example, because they have a personal interest or experience in a particular industry—and they are willing to put money into companies in the earliest stages, long before venture capital firms and institutional investors jump in. Angel financing, the fastest-growing segment of the small business capital market, is ideal for companies that have outgrown the capacity of investments from friends and family but are still too small to attract the interest of venture capital companies. Angel financing is vital to the nation's small business sector because it fills this capital gap in which small companies need investments ranging from $100,000 or less to perhaps $5 million or more. For instance, after raising the money to launch Amazon.com from family and friends, Jeff Bezos turned to angels for capital because venture capital firms were not interested in investing in a business start-up. Bezos attracted $1.2 million from a dozen angels before landing $8 million from venture capital firms a year later.[24]

Angels are a primary source of start-up capital for companies in the start-up stage through the growth stage, and their role in financing small businesses is significant. Research at the University of New Hampshire shows that more than 318,000 angels and angel groups invest $22.5 billion a year in 66,000 small companies, most of them in the start-up phase.[25] In short, angels are one of the largest and most important sources of external equity capital for small businesses. Their investments in young companies nearly match those of professional venture capitalists, providing vital capital to 18 times as many small companies (see Figure 13.2).

FIGURE 13.2
Angel Financing

Source: Center for Venture Financing, Whittemore School of Business, University of New Hampshire, http://www.wsbe.unh.edu/cvr-news.

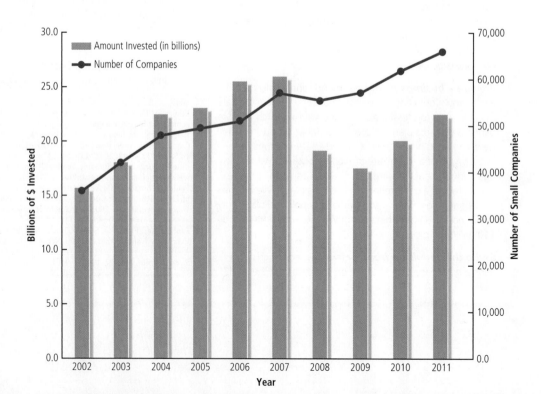

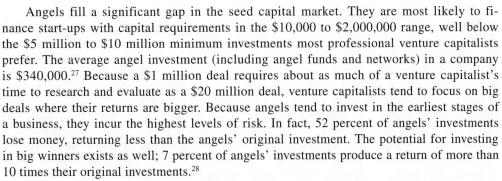

ENTREPRENEURIAL PROFILE: Jules Pieri: Daily Grommet Jules Pieri, an experienced strategic development executive for several national brands, was accustomed to spotting emerging consumer trends and noticed that many innovative products, many of them from small companies, were having difficulty landing retail shelf space. She also observed growing numbers of customers who engaged in social media and wanted to purchase products that represented "something good in the world." Pieri decided to leave the corporate world behind to launch Daily Grommet, a Web site that champions cool, innovative products from entrepreneurs by providing an online storefront and building a large online community. She pitched her idea to two friends, who became Pieri's first angel investors and contributed $150,000 in equity capital to get the business up and running. Since Daily Grommet's inception, Pieri has garnered a total of $5.71 million in investments from other angels, including a recent $3.4 million round of angel financing. Daily Grommet lists more than 400 unique products, ranging from an extreme pogo stick and lanolin-based lip gloss with an LED-illuminated applicator to a Soggy Doggy Super Shammy and do-it-yourself yogurt maker.[26] ∎

Photo by David Lang

Angels fill a significant gap in the seed capital market. They are most likely to finance start-ups with capital requirements in the $10,000 to $2,000,000 range, well below the $5 million to $10 million minimum investments most professional venture capitalists prefer. The average angel investment (including angel funds and networks) in a company is $340,000.[27] Because a $1 million deal requires about as much of a venture capitalist's time to research and evaluate as a $20 million deal, venture capitalists tend to focus on big deals where their returns are bigger. Because angels tend to invest in the earliest stages of a business, they incur the highest levels of risk. In fact, 52 percent of angels' investments lose money, returning less than the angels' original investment. The potential for investing in big winners exists as well; 7 percent of angels' investments produce a return of more than 10 times their original investments.[28]

Lewis Gersh, an experienced angel investor, says that out of 10 companies that an angel invests in, five will fail, two will break even, and two will return two to three times the original investment. Just one company out of 10 will produce a significant return, "which means that every one of them has to have the potential of being a home run," says Gersh. Most angels consider a "home-run" investment to be one that results in a return of 10 to 30 times the original investment in five to seven years, somewhat lower than the returns that venture capital firms expect.[29] Because of the inherent risks in start-up companies, many venture capitalists have shifted their investment portfolios away from start-ups toward more established businesses. That's why angel financing is so important: Angels often finance deals that no venture capitalist will consider.

Angels accept between 10 and 15 percent of the deals pitched to them and invest an average of $50,000 in a company that is at the seed or start-up growth stages.[30] Most angels are seasoned entrepreneurs themselves; on average, angel investors have founded 2.7 companies and have 14.5 years of entrepreneurial experience. They also are well educated; 99 percent have college degrees. Research also shows that 86 percent of angel investors are men (their average age is 57 years) who have been investing in promising small companies for nine years. The typical angel invests in one company per year.[31] The average time required to close an angel financing deal is 67 days.[32] When evaluating a proposal, angels look for a qualified management team and a business with a clearly defined niche, market potential, and a competitive advantage. They also want to see market research that proves the existence of a sizable customer base and a viable exit strategy, the avenue by which they get their investments back, ideally with a handsome return. "It's a good deal only if there's an exit option that offers us the return we want," says one angel investor.[33]

Entrepreneurs in search of capital quickly learn that the real challenge lies in *finding* angels. Most angels have substantial business and financial experience, and many of them are entrepreneurs or former entrepreneurs. Because most angels frown on "cold calls" from entrepreneurs they don't know, locating them boils down to making the right contacts. Networking is the key. Asking friends, attorneys, bankers, stockbrokers, accountants, other business owners, and consultants for suggestions and introductions is a good way to start. "I found my best angels through my accountant," says Doug Steiner, a serial entrepreneur who has started two successful technology companies.[34] Angels almost always invest their money locally, so entrepreneurs should look close to home for them—typically within a 50- to 100-mile radius. In fact, 7 out of 10 angels invest in companies that are within 50 miles of their homes or offices.[35] Angels also look for businesses they know something about, and most expect to invest their knowledge, experience, and energy as well as their money in a company. In fact, the advice and the network of contacts that angels bring to a deal can sometimes be as valuable as their money!

Angel investing has become more organized and professional than it was 20 years ago, with investors pooling their resources to form angel networks and angel capital funds, dubbed "superangels," that operate like miniature versions of professional venture capital firms and draw on investors' skills, experience, and contacts to help the start-ups in which they invest to succeed. "If you land one angel investor," says entrepreneur Doug Steiner, "chances are you'll end up with a gaggle. These men (and occasionally women) usually travel in packs."[36] Today 340 angel capital networks operate in cities of all sizes across the United States (up from just 10 in 1996). Angel networks make the task of locating angels much easier for entrepreneurs in search of capital.

ENTREPRENEURIAL PROFILE: Evan Solida: Cerevellum Inc. Evan Solida came up with the idea for a digital bicycle mirror, a small screen attached to a tiny camera on the rear of the bicycle that gives cyclists a view of what is behind them without having to take their eyes off of the road, after being struck by a car while riding his bicycle. The device, which Solida named Hindsight 35, also acts as a cyclometer and a "black box" for bicycles, and its LED lights serve as a taillight. He applied for a patent, created a modest Web site, and quit his job as a designer for a kayak maker to launch Cerevellum Inc. in Easley, South Carolina. A year later, the money that Solida had invested in the business was about to run out, and his attempts at finding investors had proved fruitless until he made contact with Matt Dunbar, managing director of the Upstate Carolina Angel Network based in nearby Greenville, South Carolina. The Upstate Carolina Angel Network, an angel capital fund founded in 2008 with 70 investors, invested $343,000 in Cerevellum, enabling Solida to bring Hindsight 35, to market. The angel fund's investment was a vital boost to Cerevellum, but the advice and contacts that its experienced angel members provide to Solida have proved to be just as valuable.[37] ■

The Internet has expanded greatly the ability of entrepreneurs in search of capital and angels in search of businesses to find one another. Dozens of angel networks have set up shop on the Web, many of which are members of the Angel Capital Association (www.angelcapitalassociation .org). The association reports that its average member group has 42 investors and makes investments in four small companies each year.[38] Entrepreneurs can expand the scope of their hunt for financing by including online angel groups and the Angel Capital Association's membership list in their searches.

Angels are an excellent source of "patient money," often willing to wait seven years or longer to cash out their investments. They earn their returns through the increased value of the business, not through dividends and interest. For example, more than 1,000 early investors in Microsoft Inc. are now multimillionaires. Angels' return-on-investment targets tend to be lower than those of professional venture capitalists. Although venture capitalists shoot for 60 to 75 percent returns annually, angel investors usually settle for 20 to 50 percent (depending on the level of risk involved in the venture). A study by the Kauffman Foundation reports that the average return on angels' investments in small companies is 2.6 times the original investment in 3.5 years, which is the equivalent of a 27 percent internal rate of return.[39] Angel investors typically purchase 15 to 30 percent ownership in a small company, leaving the majority ownership to the company founder(s). They look for the same exit strategies that venture capital firms look for: either an initial public offering or a buyout by a larger company. The lesson: If an entrepreneur needs relatively small amounts of money to launch or to grow a company, angels are an excellent source.

Partners

As we saw in Chapter 4, entrepreneurs can take on partners to expand the capital foundation of a business. Before entering into any partnership arrangement, however, entrepreneurs must

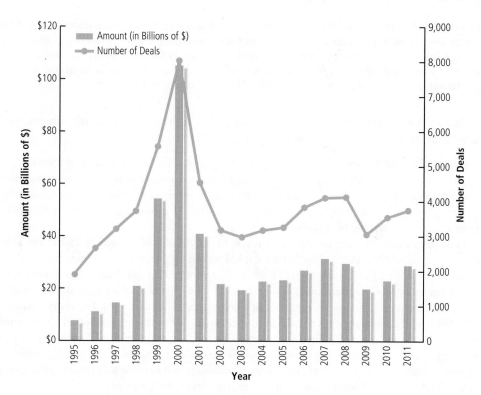

FIGURE 13.3
Venture Capital Funding

Source: Money Tree Survey, PriceWaterhouse Coopers, 2012.

consider the impact of giving up some personal control over operations and of sharing profits with others.

Venture Capital Companies

Venture capital companies are private, for-profit organizations that assemble pools of capital and then use them to purchase equity positions in young businesses that they believe have high-growth and high-profit potential, producing annual returns of 300 to 500 percent within five to seven years. More than 400 venture capital firms operate across the United States today, investing billions of dollars (see Figure 13.3) in promising small companies in a wide variety of industries. Companies in the high-tech hubs in California's Silicon Valley and Boston's high-tech corridor account for nearly half of all venture capital investments, but "secondary" cities, such as Boulder (CO), Salt Lake City (UT), Ann Arbor (MI), Providence (RI), Norwalk (CT), and Stamford (CT), offer thriving venture capital sectors that invests significant sums of money, especially in local small businesses with high growth potential.[40] Venture capital firms have invested billions of dollars in high-potential small companies over the years, including such notable businesses as Google, Apple, FedEx, Netscape, Home Depot, Microsoft, Intel, Starbucks, Whole Foods Market, and Genentech.[41]

venture capital companies
private, for-profit organizations that purchase equity positions in young businesses that they believe have high-growth and high-profit potential.

ENTREPRENEURIAL PROFILE: Niklas Hed, Jarno Väkeväinen, and Kim Dikert: Rovio Mobile In 2003, University of Helsinki students Niklas Hed, Jarno Väkeväinen, and Kim Dikert won a mobile game development competition and started a company, Relude, with financing from an angel investor to market the game. In 2005, the cofounders changed the name of the company to Rovio Mobile and continued to successfully market games for mobile devices, including Darkest Fear and War Diary: Burma. In 2009, Rovio, based in Espoo, Finland, launched the highly popular Angry Birds (in which players destroy green

© Vinod Kurien / Alamy

pigs with avian missiles fired from a slingshot), which became a global phenomenon that has been downloaded more than one billion times and boasts 40 million players per month! In 2011, the founders turned to three venture capital companies for $42 million to finance Rovio's growth strategy, including developing new games, extending the Angry Birds brand, expanding internationally, and opening an Angry Birds retail store in Helsinki.[42] ∎

POLICIES AND INVESTMENT STRATEGIES Venture capital firms usually establish stringent policies to implement their overall investment strategies.

Investment Size and Screening. The average venture capital firm's investment in a small company is $7.4 million.[43] Depending on the size of the venture capital company, minimum investments range from $100,000 to $5 million. Investment ceilings, in effect, do not exist. Most venture capital firms seek investments in the $5 million to $25 million range to justify the cost of screening the large number of proposals they receive.

In a typical year, venture capital firms invest in only 3,600 of the nearly 28 million small businesses in the United States. The venture capital screening process is *extremely* rigorous. According to the Global Entrepreneurship Monitor, only about 1 in 1,000 businesses in the United States receives venture capital during its existence.[44] The typical venture capital firm receives about 1,200 business plans each year (although some receive many more). For every 100 business plans that the average venture capital firm receives, 90 of them are rejected immediately because they do not match the firm's investment criteria or requirements. The firm conducts a thorough due diligence investigation of the remaining 10 companies and typically invests in only one of them (see Figure 13.4). The average time required to close a venture capital deal is 80 days, slightly longer than the time required to complete angel financing.[45]

Ownership and Control. Most venture capitalists prefer to purchase ownership in a small business through common stock or convertible preferred stock. Although many venture capital firms purchase less than 50 percent of a company's stock, others buy a controlling share of a company,

FIGURE 13.4

The Business Plan Funnel

Source: From *Venture Impact: The Economic Importance of Venture Backed Companies to the U.S. Economy.* Copyright © 2007 by the National Venture Capital Association. Reprinted with permission.

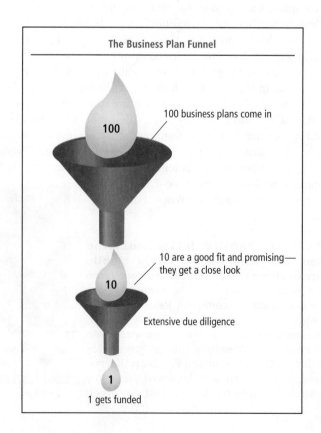

The Business Plan Funnel

100 — 100 business plans come in

10 — 10 are a good fit and promising—they get a close look

Extensive due diligence

1 — 1 gets funded

leaving its founders with a minority share of ownership. Most venture capitalists prefer to let the founding team of managers employ its skills to operate a business *if* they are capable of managing its growth. However, it is quite common for venture capitalists to join the boards of directors of the companies in which they invest. Sometimes venture investors step in and shake up the management teams in the companies in which they invest. "We change management in the companies we fund about 40 percent of the time," says Janet Effland, a partner in the venture capital firm Apax Partners.[46] In other words, entrepreneurs should *not* expect venture capitalists to be passive investors! Some serve only as financial and managerial advisers, but others take an active role managing the company—recruiting employees, providing sales leads, choosing attorneys and advertising agencies, and making daily decisions. The majority of these active venture capitalists say that they are forced to step in because the existing management team lacks the talent and experience to achieve growth targets.

Stage of Investment. Most venture capital firms invest in companies that are either in the early stages of development (called early-stage investing) or in the rapid-growth phase (called expansion-stage investing). About 96 to 98 percent of all venture capital goes to businesses in these stages; very few invest in small companies that are in the start-up phase.[47] According to the Global Entrepreneurship Monitor, only 1 in 10,000 entrepreneurs worldwide receives venture capital funding at start-up.[48] Most venture capital firms do not make just a single investment in a company. Instead, they invest in a company over time across several stages, where their investments often total $10 million to $15 million or more.

Advice and Contacts. In addition to the money they invest, more venture capital companies are providing the small companies in their portfolios with management advice and access to valuable networks of contacts of suppliers, employees, customers, and other sources of capital than they did just a few years ago. One of their goals in doing so is to strengthen the companies in which they have invested, thereby increasing their value.

Investment Preferences. Venture capital firms now are larger, more professional, and more specialized than they were 25 years ago. As the industry matures, venture capital funds increasingly are focusing their investments in niches—everything from information technology to the biotechnology. Some will invest in almost any industry, but most prefer companies in later stages. Traditionally, only 2 to 4 percent of the companies receiving venture capital financing are in the start-up or seed stage, when entrepreneurs are forming a company or developing a product or service and when angels are most likely to invest (see Figure 13.5). Most of the start-up businesses that attract venture capital are technology companies in "hot" fields such as software, biotechnology, energy, medical devices, and media and entertainment.[49]

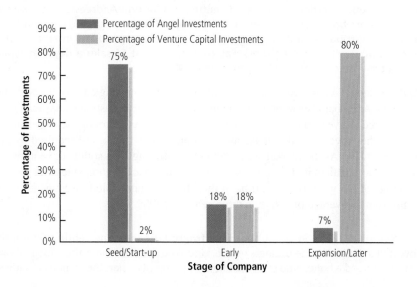

FIGURE 13.5

Angel Investing and Venture Capital Investing

Source: Robert Wiltbank and Warren Boeker, *Returns to Angel Investors in Groups*, Angel Capital Education Foundation, http://www.kauffman.org/Details.aspx?id=1032, and PWC Moneytree Report, PriceWaterhouse Coopers, https://www.pwcmoneytree.com/MTPublic/ns/index.jsp.

WHAT VENTURE CAPITALISTS LOOK FOR Entrepreneurs must realize that it is very difficult for any small business, especially fledgling or struggling firms, to pass the intense screening process of a venture capital company and qualify for an investment. A great elevator pitch and a sound business plan are essential to convincing venture capital firms to invest in a company. "Investors want to see proof that a concept works," says Geeta Vemuri, a principal in a venture capital firm.[50] Two factors make a deal attractive to venture capitalists: high returns and a convenient (and profitable) exit strategy. When evaluating potential investments, venture capitalists look for the following features:

Competent Management. The most important ingredient in the success of any business is the ability of the management team, and venture capitalists understand this. To venture capitalists, the ideal management team has experience, managerial skills, commitment, and the ability to expand the team as the business grows. "If you don't have good management [in place], it's going to bite you," says Phil Soran, CEO of Compellent Technologies, a data storage company that has attracted venture capital successfully.[51]

Competitive Edge. Investors are searching for some factor that will enable a small business to set itself apart from its competitors. This distinctive competence may range from an innovative product or service that satisfies unmet customer needs to a unique marketing or research-and-development (R&D) approach. It must be something with the potential to create a sustainable competitive edge, making the company a leader in its industry. "I look for transformational ideas," says Bill Turner, founder of venture capital firm Signature Capital, explaining his investments in a variety of businesses, including an online music service, a hearing-aid maker, and an HIV-therapy company.[52]

Growth Industry. Hot industries attract profits—and venture capital. Most venture capital funds focus their searches for prospects in rapidly growing fields because they believe that the profit potential is greater in these areas. Venture capital firms are most interested in young companies that have enough growth potential to become at least $100 million businesses within three to five years. Venture capitalists know that most of the businesses they invest in will flop, so their winners have to be *big* winners.

ENTREPRENEURIAL PROFILE: Jason Goldberg: Fab.com After raising start-up financing from angel investors and an early-stage venture fund, Jason Goldberg decided to ditch his original business idea and launched Fab.com, a Web site that conducts flash sales on discounted furniture, jewelry, and art from top designers. Within six weeks of its launch, Fab.com had 400,000 users and was profitable. The company's fast growth attracted the interest of venture capital firms, and Goldberg, who previously had founded job site Jobster.com, was able to raise $8 million to fuel its ascent. Just four months later, Fab.com landed $40 million investment from venture capital firms. "We think there is a really big business in aggregating the world's designers," says Jeffrey Jordan, a partner at venture capital firm Andreessen Horowitz who will be joining Fab.com's board. The company used the capital to meet surging demand for its products, enhance its distribution and customer service operations, expand into international markets, and hire staff. Now with 4 million users, Fab.com runs about 14 sales a day that typically last 72 hours and generates $20 million in annual sales.[53] ∎

Viable Exit Strategy. Venture capitalists not only look for promising companies with the ability to dominate a market but also want to see a plan for a feasible exit strategy, typically to be executed within three to five years. Venture capital firms realize the return on their investments when the companies they invest in either make an initial public offering or are acquired by or merged into another business. As the market for initial public offerings has softened, venture capitalists have had to be more patient in their exit strategies. Venture-backed companies that go public now take an average of 5.3 years from the time of their first venture capital investment to their stock offering, up from an average of less than three years in 1998.[54]

ENTREPRENEURIAL PROFILE: Reid Hoffman: LinkedIn The venture capital firms that invested in LinkedIn, the business networking Web site with more than 135 million users in 200 countries, reaped a handsome return on their investments when the company made an initial public offering in 2011. Founder Reid Hoffman guided LinkedIn through five rounds of venture financing from firms including Sequoia Capital, Greylock Partners, Bessemer Venture Partners, and Bain Capital before making an initial public offering. After the initial public offering, the venture capital firms' investments of $103 million (over several stages) were worth $1.76 billion! Hoffman retained 20.1 percent of LinkedIn's stock, worth $853 million.[55] ∎

Intangible Factors. Some other important factors considered in the screening process are not easily measured; they are the intuitive, intangible factors that the venture capitalist detects by gut feeling. This feeling might be the result of the small firm's solid sense of direction, its strategic planning process, the chemistry of its management team, or other factors. Venture capital firms want to know that entrepreneurs will use their money wisely—for investments that provide profitable results and not those that merely feed entrepreneurial egos. "When I go into a start-up burning $300,000 a month, and they've got posh offices with great furniture, I immediately think the leadership team's priorities are in the wrong place," says Mark Montgomery, a venture capitalist in Nashville, Tennessee. "It is a matter of being practical."[56]

Despite its many benefits, venture capital is not suited for every entrepreneur. "VC money comes at a price," warns one entrepreneur. "Before boarding a one-way money train, ask yourself if this is the best route for your business and personal desires, because investors are like department stores the day after Christmas—they expect a lot of returns in a short period of time."[57]

Corporate Venture Capital

Large corporations have gotten into the business of financing small companies and invest in businesses for both strategic and financial reasons. More than 300 large corporations across the globe, including Google, BMW, Comcast, Amazon, Qualcomm, Intel, General Electric, Dow Chemical, Cisco Systems, UPS, Wal-Mart, Unilever, and Johnson & Johnson, invest in small companies, usually companies that are in the later stage of growth and because of their maturity are less risky. Today, about 14 percent of all venture capital deals involve corporate venture capital. The average investment that large corporations make in small companies is $4 million, which represents 8.7 percent of total venture capital investments.[58] Young companies not only get a boost from the capital injections large companies give them but also stand to gain many other benefits from the relationship. The right corporate partner may share technical expertise, distribution channels, and marketing know-how and provide introductions to important customers and suppliers. Another intangible yet highly important advantage an investment from a large corporate partner gives a small company is credibility, often referred to as "market validation." Doors that otherwise would be closed to a small company magically open when the right corporation becomes a strategic partner.

ENTREPRENEURIAL PROFILE: Google Ventures: Rumble In 2009, Google launched Google Ventures, the company's venture capital division, with the goal of investing $200 million a year in small companies with fast-growth potential across all stages of development. Since its inception, Google Ventures has invested amounts ranging from $200,000 to $33 million promising companies in a variety of industries. Google Ventures recently partnered with another venture capital firm to invest $15 million in Rumble, a developer of games that combines the ease of social gaming with the quality of console games that users can play online, on mobile devices, and in social media. In addition to providing much-needed capital, Google Ventures helps the companies in which it invests with market research, design and engineering, hiring, training, and many other operational issues.[59] ∎

Public Stock Sale ("Going Public")

In some cases, companies can "go public" by selling shares of stock to outside investors. In an **initial public offering (IPO)**, a company raises capital by selling shares of its stock to the general public for the first time. An IPO is an effective method of raising large amounts of capital, but it can be an expensive and time-consuming process filled with regulatory nightmares. Once a company makes an IPO, *nothing* will ever be the same again. Managers must consider the impact

LO3

Describe the process of "going public" as well as its advantages and disadvantages and the various simplified registrations and exemptions from registration that are available to small businesses.

initial public offering (IPO)

a method of raising equity capital in which a company sells shares of its stock to the general public for the first time.

of their decisions not only on the company and its employees but also on its shareholders and the value of their stock.

Going public isn't for every business. In fact, most small companies do not meet the criteria for making a successful public stock offering. Since 2001, the average number of companies that make IPOs each year is 134, and only about 20,000 companies in the United States—less than 1 percent of the total—are publicly held (see Figure 13.6). Few companies with less than $25 million in annual sales manage to go public successfully. Since 2001, 72 percent of the companies that have completed IPOs have had annual sales of $50 million or more.[60] For instance, LinkedIn, the professional networking Web site, was generating sales of $243 million at the time of its IPO. When Zygna, the creator of popular Facebook games such as Farmville, Cityville, and Words with Friends, filed for its IPO, the company's sales were $597 million.[61]

It is almost impossible for a start-up company with no track record of success to raise money with an IPO. Instead, the investment bankers who underwrite public stock offerings typically look for established companies with the following characteristics:

● *Consistently high growth rates.* In the three years prior to its IPO, LinkedIn's revenues grew an impressive 212 percent.[62]

● *Scalability.* Underwriters and institutional investors want proof that a company can maintain or improve its efficiency as it experiences the strain that rapid growth imposes.

● *A strong record of earnings.* Strangely enough, profitability at the time of the IPO is not essential; from 2001 to 2011, 47 percent of companies making IPOs had negative earnings.[63]

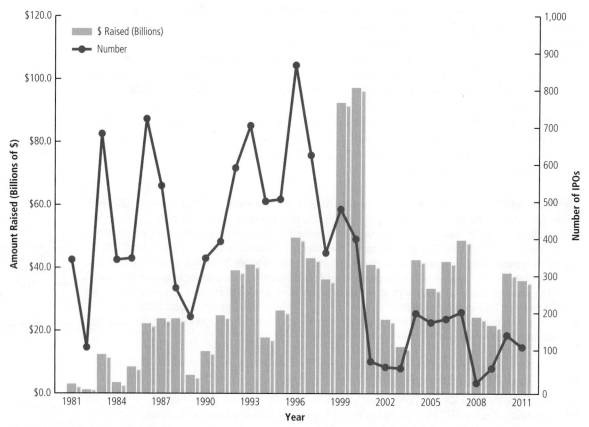

FIGURE 13.6

Initial Public Offerings (IPOs)

Source: Thomson Financial Securities Data.

- *Three to five years of audited financial statements that meet or exceed Securities and Exchange Commission (SEC) standards.* After the Enron and WorldCom scandals, investors are demanding impeccable financial statements.

- *A solid position in a rapidly growing industry.* In 2000, the median age of companies making IPOs was six years; today, it is 10 years.[64]

- *A sound management team with experience and a strong board of directors.*

ENTREPRENEURIAL PROFILE: Adam Miller: Cornerstone OnDemand Cornerstone OnDemand, a human resources software company in Santa Monica, California, with annual sales of $48 million, made its IPO 11 years after the company's founding. "Going public was part of the plan from the outset," says founder and CEO Adam Miller. The offering, led by investment banker Goldman Sachs, raised $136.5 million for Cornerstone OnDemand by selling 10.5 million shares at $13 per share (above the estimated range of $9 to $11 per share). "We went public when we were able to attract top-tier [investment] banks," says Miller. "You have to achieve a certain market capitalization, or the offer is not interesting to them." Even so, Cornerstone OnDemand was one of the smallest companies to make an IPO at the time.[65] ■

THE REGISTRATION PROCESS Taking a company public is a complicated, bureaucratic process that usually takes several months to complete. Many experts compare the IPO process to running a corporate marathon, and both the company and its management team must be in shape and up to the grueling task. The typical entrepreneur *cannot* take his or her company public alone. It requires a coordinated effort from a team of professionals, including company executives, an accountant, a securities attorney, a financial printer, and at least one underwriter. Table 13.1 shows a typical timetable for an IPO. The key steps in taking a company public are discussed in the following sections.

TABLE 13.1 Timetable for an IPO

Time	Action
Week 1	Conduct "all hands" organizational meeting with IPO team, including underwriter, attorneys, accountants, and others. Begin drafting registration statement.
Week 5	Distribute first draft of registration statement to IPO team and make revisions.
Week 6	Distribute second draft of registration statement and make revisions.
Week 7	Distribute third draft of registration statement and make revisions.
Week 8	File registration statement with the SEC. Begin preparing presentations for road show to attract other investment bankers to the underwriting syndicate. Comply with Blue Sky laws in states where offering will be sold. "Quiet period" officially begins and runs until 25 days after the company's stock begins trading.
Week 13	Receive comment letter on registration statement from the SEC* and state authorities. Amend registration statement to satisfy SEC and other regulatory agencies.
Week 14	File amended registration statement with the SEC. Prepare and distribute preliminary offering prospectus (called a "red herring") to members of underwriting syndicate. Begin road show meetings.
Week 16	Receive approval for offering from the SEC (unless further amendments are required). Issuing company and lead underwriter agree on final offering price. Prepare, file, and distribute final offering prospectus.
Week 17	Company and underwriter sign the final agreement. Underwriter issues stock, collects the proceeds from the sale, and delivers proceeds (less commission) to company.

* The SEC's response may require more than five weeks, which will cause all remaining events to be pushed back.

Sources: Adapted from "Initial Public Offering," Entrepreneur, June 14, 2002, http://www.entrepreneur.com/article/0,4621,300892,00.html, and "IPO Basics: IPO ABCs," MSN Money, http://moneycentral.hoovers.com/business-information/–pageid__1960–/global-msn-index.xhtml.

managing underwriter (investment banker)
a financial company that serves two important roles: helping to prepare the registration statement for an issue and promoting the company's stock to potential investors.

Choose the Underwriter. The single most important ingredient in making a successful IPO is selecting a capable **managing underwriter (investment banker)**. The managing underwriter serves two primary roles: helping to prepare the registration statement for the issue and promoting the company's stock to potential investors. The underwriter works with company managers as an adviser to prepare the registration statement that must be filed with the SEC, promotes the issue, prices the stock, and provides aftermarket support. Once the registration statement is finished, the managing underwriter's primary job is selling the company's stock through an underwriting syndicate of other investment bankers it develops. Twenty-five years ago, the average number of managing underwriters involved in an IPO was 1.6; today, it is 7.1.[66] According to a study by Notre Dame professors Shane Corwin and Paul Schultz, the larger the syndicate that supports an IPO, the more likely it is that the company will obtain more favorable pricing and overall results from the offering.[67]

ENTREPRENEURIAL PROFILE: Mark Pincus: Zynga Facebook game creator Zynga, founded by serial entrepreneur Mark Pincus (who named the company after his beloved English bulldog) in 2007, recently completed an IPO. Investment bankers Morgan Stanley and Goldman, Sachs, and Company managed the offering of 100 million shares priced at $10 per share that generated $1 billion to fuel the growth of Zygna, whose shares trade on the NASDAQ under the symbol "ZNGA."[68] ∎

letter of intent
an agreement between the underwriter and the company about to go public that outlines the details of the deal.

Negotiate a Letter of Intent. To begin an offering, the entrepreneur and the underwriter must negotiate a **letter of intent**, which outlines the details of the deal. The letter of intent covers a variety of important issues, including the type of underwriting, its size and price range, the underwriter's commission, and any warrants and options included. It almost always states that the underwriter is not bound to the offering until it is executed—usually the day before or the day of the offering. However, the letter usually creates a binding obligation for the company to pay any direct expenses the underwriter incurs relating to the offer.

The company and the underwriter must decide on the size of the offering and the price of the shares. To keep the stock active in the aftermarket, most underwriters prefer to offer a *minimum* of 400,000 to 500,000 shares. A smaller number of shares inhibits sufficiently broad distribution. Most underwriters recommend selling 25 to 40 percent of the company in the IPO. They also strive to price the issue so that the total value of the offering is at least $8 million to $15 million. (Although there are exceptions; some underwriters, especially regional ones, are interested in doing IPOs in the $2 million to $5 million range.) To meet these criteria and to keep interest in the issue high, the underwriter usually recommends an initial price between $10 and $20 per share. The underwriter establishes an estimated price range for the company's IPO in the underwriting agreement, but it does not establish the final price until the day before the offering takes place. Depending on anticipated demand for the company's shares, the condition of the market, and other factors, the actual price may be outside the estimated range. Since 1980, 72 percent of IPOs have sold within or above the estimated price ranges listed in their SEC filings.[69] In LinkedIn's IPO, managing underwriters Morgan Stanley, BofA Merrill Lynch, and J. P. Morgan originally estimated the stock price to be $32 to $35 per share, but because of strong demand for the issue, the final offering price was $45 per share. LinkedIn's IPO, which sold 7.84 million shares, raised $352.8 million to fund the company's growth.[70]

registration statement
the document a company must file with the SEC that describes both the company and its stock offering and discloses information about the risk of investing.

Prepare the Registration Statement. After a company signs the letter of intent, the next task is to prepare the **registration statement** to be filed with the SEC. This document describes both the company and the stock offering and discloses information about the risks of investing. It includes information on the use of the proceeds, the company's history, its financial position, its capital structure, the risks it faces, its managers' experience, and *many* other details. The statement is extremely comprehensive and may take months to develop. To prepare the statement, entrepreneurs must rely on their team of professionals.

File with the SEC. When the statement is finished (with the exception of pricing the shares, proceeds, and commissions, which cannot be determined until just before the issue goes to market), the company officially files the statement with the SEC and awaits the review of the Division of Corporate Finance, a process that takes 30 to 45 days (or more). The division sends notice of any deficiencies in the registration statement to the company's attorney in a comment letter. The company and its team of professionals must cure all of the deficiencies in the statement noted in the comment letter. Finally, the company files the revised registration statement along with a pricing amendment (giving the price of the shares, the proceeds, and the commissions).

Wait to Go Effective. While waiting for the SEC's approval, the managers and the underwriters are busy. The underwriters are building a syndicate of other underwriters who will market the company's stock. (No stock sales can be made prior to the effective date of the offering, however.) The SEC also limits the publicity and information a company may release during this quiet period (which officially starts when the company reaches a preliminary agreement with the managing underwriter and ends 25 days after the effective date).

Securities laws do permit a **road show**, a gathering of potential syndicate members sponsored by the managing underwriter. Its purpose is to promote interest among potential underwriters in the IPO by featuring the company, its management, and the proposed deal. The managing underwriter and key company officials barnstorm major financial centers at a grueling pace.

road show
a gathering of potential syndicate members sponsored by the managing underwriter for the purpose of promoting a company's IPO.

ENTREPRENEURIAL PROFILE: Walter Allessandrini: Ometric Corporation During the road show for Ometric Corporation, a South Carolina–based company that has developed the technology to provide real-time spectroscopy in a variety of industrial applications, CEO Walter Allessandrini made 140 presentations to potential syndicate members in both Europe and the United States in just two and a half weeks! ■

On the last day before the registration statement becomes effective, the company signs the formal underwriting agreement. The final settlement, or closing, takes place a few days after the effective date for the issue. At this meeting the underwriters receive their shares to sell, and the company receives the proceeds of the offering. Typically, the entire process of going public takes from 120 to 180 days, but it can take much longer if the issuing company is not properly prepared for the process.

Meet State Requirements. In addition to satisfying the SEC's requirements, a company also must meet the securities laws in all states in which the issue is sold. These state laws (or "blue-sky" laws) vary drastically from one state to another, and the company must comply with them.

SIMPLIFIED REGISTRATIONS AND EXEMPTIONS The IPO process just described (called an S-1 filing) requires maximum disclosure in the initial filing and discourages most small businesses from using it. Fortunately, the SEC allows several exemptions from this full-disclosure process for small businesses. Many small businesses that go public choose one of these simplified options the SEC has designed for small companies. The SEC has established simplified registration statements and exemptions from the registration process, discussed in the following sections.

Regulations S-B and S-K. In 2009, the SEC eliminated Regulation S-B but transferred many of its provisions into Regulation S-K, a simplified registration process for small companies seeking to make initial or subsequent public offerings. Not only does this regulation simplify the initial filing requirements with the SEC, but it also reduces the ongoing disclosure and filings required of companies by giving them "smaller-reporting-company" status. Its primary goals are to open the doors to capital markets to smaller companies by cutting the paperwork and the costs of raising capital. To be eligible for the simplified registration process under Regulation S-K, a company must have annual revenues of less than $50 million or have outstanding publicly held stock ("public float") worth no more than $75 million. The goal of Regulation S-K's simplified registration requirements is to enable smaller companies to go public without incurring the expense of a full-blown registration.

Regulation D (Rule 504, 505, and 506). Regulation D rules minimize the expense and the time required to raise equity capital for small businesses by simplifying or eliminating the requirement for registering the offering with the SEC, which often takes months and costs many thousands of dollars. Under Regulation D, the whole process typically costs less than half of what a traditional public offering costs. The SEC's objective in creating Regulation D was to give small companies the access to equity financing that large companies have via the stock market while bypassing many of the costs and filing requirements. A Regulation D offering requires only minimal notification to the SEC. Offerings made under Regulation D do impose limitations and demand certain disclosures, but they only require a company to file a simple form (Form D) with the SEC within 15 days of the first sale of stock. Form D consists of fill-in-the-blank questions about the company, the issue, the use of the proceeds, and other pertinent matters.

Rule 504 is the most popular of the Regulation D exemptions because it is the least restrictive. It allows a company to sell shares of its stock to an unlimited number of investors without regard to their experience or level of sophistication. A business also can make multiple offerings under Rule 504 as long as it waits at least six months between them; however, Rule 504 places a cap of $1 million in a 12-month period on the amount of capital a company can raise. Ligatt Security International, a small cybersecurity company in Norcross, Georgia, recently raised $147,000 under Rule 504 to finance its expansion.[71]

A Rule 505 offering has a higher capital ceiling ($5 million in a 12-month period) than Rule 504 but imposes more restrictions (no more than 35 nonaccredited investors, no advertising of the offer, and more stringent disclosure requirements).

Rule 506 imposes no ceiling on the amount that can be raised, but most companies that make Rule 506 offerings raise between $1 million and $50 million in capital. Like a Rule 505 offering, it limits the issue to no more than 35 nonaccredited investors and prohibits advertising the offer to the public. There is no limit on the number of accredited investors, however. Rule 506 also requires detailed disclosure of relevant information, but the extent depends on the size of the offering.

Section 4(6). Section 4(6) covers private placements and is similar to Regulation D, Rules 505 and 506. It does not require registration on offerings up to $5 million if they are made only to accredited investors.

Intrastate Offerings (Rule 147). Rule 147 governs intrastate offerings, those sold only to investors in a single state by a company doing business in that state. To qualify, a company must be incorporated in the state, maintain its executive offices there, have 50 percent of its assets there, derive 50 percent of its revenues from the state, and use 50 percent of the offering proceeds for business in the state. There is no ceiling on the amount of the offering, but only residents of the state in which the issuing company operates can invest. The maximum number of shareholders is 500, and a company's asset base cannot exceed $10 million.

ENTREPRENEURIAL PROFILE: Ben Cohen and Jerry Greenfield: Ben & Jerry's Home-made Years ago, Ben Cohen and Jerry Greenfield founded a small ice cream manufacturing business named after themselves that struck a chord with customers. Ben & Jerry's Homemade grew rapidly, and the founders needed $600,000 to build a new manufacturing plant in Vermont, where the company was based. They decided to "give the opportunity to our neighbors to grow with our company" by making an intrastate offering under Rule 147. Cohen and Greenfield registered their offering of 73,500 shares of stock with the Vermont Division of Banking and Insurance. Ben & Jerry's Homemade sold the entire offering (mostly to loyal customers) by placing ads in newspapers and stickers on ice cream containers that touted "Get a Scoop of the Action."[72] ■

Regulation A. Regulation A, although currently not used often, allows an exemption for public stock offerings up to $5 million over a 12-month period. Regulation A imposes few restrictions, but it is more costly than the other types of exempted offerings because it requires a company to file a registration statement with the SEC (although its requirements are simpler than those for an S-1 offering). A Regulation A offering allows a company to sell its shares directly to investors.

A small company can sell its stock under Rule 504 of Regulation D, Rule 147, or Regulation A using a Small Corporate Offering Registration (SCOR) by also registering the offering at the state level. The ceiling on a SCOR offering is $1 million in 12 months (except in Texas, where there is no limit), and the issuing price of the stock must be at least $1 per share. Before selling its stock, a company must file Form U-7, a disclosure document that resembles a business plan but also serves as a state securities offering registration, a disclosure document, and a prospectus. A company must register the offering in every state in which it will sell its stock to comply with the states' blue-sky laws, although current regulations allow simultaneous registration in multiple states. Entrepreneurs using SCOR may advertise their companies' offerings and can sell them directly to any investor with no restrictions and no minimums.

Table 13.2 provides a summary of the major types of exemptions and simplified offerings. Of these, the limited offerings and private placements are most commonly used.

TABLE 13.2 Simplified Registrations and Exemptions

Feature	Regulation D Rule 504 (SCOR)	Regulation D Rule 505	Regulation D Rule 506	Private Placements Section 4(6)	Intrastate Offerings	Regulation A	Form S-K (Formerly Forms SB-1 and SB-2)
Ceiling on amount raised	$1 million in any 12-month period	$5 million in any 12-month period	None	$5 million	None	$5 million in any 12-month period	$10 million in any 12-month period
Limit on number of purchasers	No	No, if selling to accredited investors; maximum of 35 nonaccredited investors	No, if selling to accredited investors; maximum of 35 nonaccredited investors	No	No	No	No
Limitation on types of purchasers	Depends	Yes	Yes	Yes. All must be accredited	Yes. Must be residents of the state in which the company is incorporated	No	No
General solicitation and advertising allowed	Yes, if the company sells to accredited investors; otherwise, no	No	No	No	Yes	Yes	Yes
Resale restrictions	Yes	Yes	Yes	Yes	Yes	No	No

Sources: Adapted from "IPO Alternatives: SEC Registration Exemptions," *Inc.*, November 1999, http://www.inc.com/articles/1999/11/15743.html; "Q&A: Small Business and the SEC," U.S. Securities and Exchange Commission, http://www.sec.gov/info/smallbus/qasbsec.htm; and *Small Business: Efforts to Facilitate Equity Capital Formation*, Report to the Chairman, Committee on Small Business, U.S. Senate, Government Accounting Office, Washington, DC, 2000, http://www.gao.gov/archive/2000/gg00190.pdf#search=%22Simplified%20registrations%20exemptions%20SB%22.

In Search of Growth Capital

ShopKeep

In 2010, Jason Richelson and Amy Bennett, co-owners of the Greene Grape, a wine and gourmet food retailer with three locations in New York City, started ShopKeep, a company that provides affordable, reliable point-of-sale software for small businesses, after they grew increasingly frustrated with the point-of-sale systems at the Greene Grape. Richelson and Bennett began shopping for a more user-friendly and more reliable system but could not find one, so they used $800,000 from their investment in the Greene Grape to develop a Web-based point-of-sale system aimed at small businesses. To get the seed capital to start ShopKeep, "we squeezed the Greene Grape," jokes Richelson. ShopKeep charges merchants just $49 to $129 per month per register, much less than some competing systems that cost from $3,000 to $12,000, more than many small businesses can afford. "Because our software runs online, retailers can track sales and manage inventory from anywhere," says Richelson. "What's different about our software is that it also runs locally on the cash register, so that even if a store's Internet connection goes down, the business can still ring up customers." ShopKeep runs on both PCs and Macs and integrates seamlessly with Quickbooks and many e-commerce software packages. The company also released a version that turns an iPad into a cash register.

ShopKeep currently has 60 satisfied customers and generates $300,000 in annual sales. Richelson and Bennett believe that the market potential for ShopKeep is huge, pointing out that sales in the U.S. point-of-sale market are $8.4 billion annually. "I think [ShopKeep] is a billion dollar opportunity," says one industry observer. To capitalize on this opportunity, Richelson and Bennett need $1 million to hire a sales team and to launch an online advertising campaign to raise ShopKeep's visibility.

Keen Guides

In 2008, Catherine McNally, who is deaf, came up with the idea for Keen Guides after she visited a museum and received a 50-page transcript as an alternative to the museum's audio tour for hearing-impaired customers. McNally worked with Karen Borchert and Martin Franklin to start Keen Guides, an Arlington, Virginia–based company that offers captioned video tours of attractions in seven U.S. cities, including Washington, D.C.; Austin, Texas; and Seattle, Washington. Keen Guides uses videos from partners such as public television stations and tour guide companies, adds closed captions, and configures them for mobile devices. "Audio tours of attractions such as museums often aren't accessible to the 36 million people in the United States who are hearing impaired," says McNally. "Our apps our free to download, but we include advertising and offer premium content, such as guided tours of a museum, for a fee." The company has experienced 18,000 downloads and generates $65,000 in annual revenue. With 200 videos currently in their library, the entrepreneurs are seeking $1.2 million to secure more videos and to start guides in other cities.

1. Describe the advantages and the disadvantages of both equity capital and debt capital for the entrepreneurs behind these two businesses.

2. Explain why the following funding sources would or would not be appropriate for these entrepreneurs: family and friends, angel investors, an IPO, a traditional bank loan, asset-based borrowing, or one of the many federal or Small Business Administration (SBA) loans.

3. Assume the role of consultant to these companies. Work with a team of your classmates to brainstorm ways that they could attract the growth capital they need. What steps would you recommend he take before approaching the potential sources of funding you have identified?

Sources: Based on April Joyner, "Elevator Pitch: ShopKeep Makes Cash-Register Software for Small Businesses: Can It Raise $1 Million to Get the Word Out?," *Inc.*, November 2010, pp. 125–126; Spencer Ante, "ShopKeep Raises $2.2 Million for Web-Based iPad Cash Register," *Wall Street Journal*, January 17, 2012, http://blogs .wsj.com/digits/2012/01/17/shopkeep-raises-2-2-million-for-web-based-ipad-cash-register; and April Joyner, "Elevator Pitch: Keen Guide Offers Video Tours for the Hearing Impaired: Can It Get $1.2 Million to Cover More Cities?," *Inc.*, December 2010/January 2011, pp. 137–138.

The Nature of Debt Financing

Debt financing involves the funds that the small business owner borrows and must repay with interest. Debt financing is a popular tool that many entrepreneurs use to acquire capital. In a typical year, small businesses borrow about $1 trillion.[73] Lenders of capital are more numerous than investors, although small business loans can be just as difficult (if not more difficult) to obtain. According to the National Small Business Association, 36 percent of small business owners say that they are unable to obtain adequate financing for their companies.[74] Amy Rhodes, owner of A-2-Z Scuba, a small scuba shop in Puyallup, Washington, says that her company is struggling to survive the aftereffects of an economic downturn and a national credit crisis. "We can't expand, and we can't buy inventory," says the frustrated entrepreneur. "We've had to do everything on credit cards because the banks won't even look at us. Every dime of our $40,000 profit last year

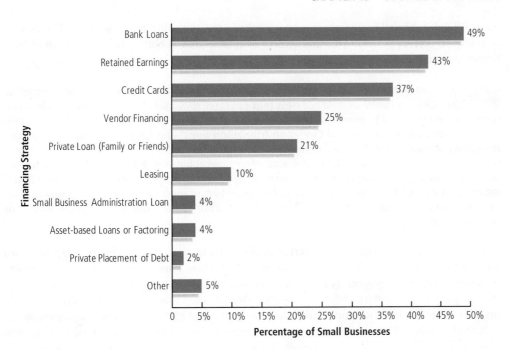

FIGURE 13.7
Small Business Financing Strategies

Source: *2011 Mid-year Economic Report*, National Small Business Association, p. 8.

went right back into the business. Now sales are down, and we're having to make ends meet out of our own pockets."[75]

Although borrowed capital allows entrepreneurs to maintain complete ownership of their businesses, it must be carried as a liability on the balance sheet as well as be repaid with interest at some point in the future. In addition, because small businesses are considered to be greater risks than bigger corporate customers, they must pay higher interest rates because of the risk–return trade-off—the higher the risk, the greater is the return demanded. Most small firms pay well above the **prime rate**, the interest rate that banks charge their most creditworthy customers. A study by David Walker, a professor at Georgetown University, reports that small businesses pay two to three times the prime rate, primarily because they rely heavily on credit cards and other high-cost methods of debt financing. "They are shut out of the markets that are lower cost," he says.[76] Still, the cost of debt financing often is lower than that of equity financing. Because of the higher risks associated with providing equity capital to small companies, investors demand greater returns than lenders. In addition, unlike equity financing, debt financing does not require an entrepreneur to dilute his or her ownership interest in the company.

prime rate
the interest rate that banks charge their most creditworthy customers.

Entrepreneurs seeking debt capital are quickly confronted with an astounding range of credit options varying greatly in complexity, availability, and flexibility. Not all of these sources of debt capital are equally favorable, however. By understanding the various sources of debt capital and their characteristics, entrepreneurs can greatly increase the chances of obtaining a loan.

Figure 13.7 shows the financing strategies that existing small businesses use. We now turn to the various sources of debt capital.

Sources of Debt Capital

Commercial Banks

Commercial banks are the very heart of the financial market for small businesses, providing the greatest number and variety of loans to small companies. Currently, outstanding small business bank loans total $600 billion.[77] For small business owners, banks are lenders of *first* resort. The average microbusiness bank loan (those less than $100,000) is $7,500, and the average small business bank loan (those between $100,000 and $1 million) is $226,400.[78]

Banks tend to be conservative in their lending practices and prefer to make loans to established small businesses rather than to high-risk start-ups. Unfortunately for entrepreneurs, turbulence in the financial markets has caused banks to tighten their lending standards, making it

LO4

Describe the various sources of debt capital and the advantages and disadvantages of each: banks, asset-based lenders, vendors (trade credit), equipment suppliers, commercial finance companies, savings-and-loan associations, stockbrokers, credit unions, bonds, private placements, Small Business Investment Companies (SBICs) and Small Business Lending Companies (SBLCs).

more difficult for small businesses, even established ones, to qualify for loans. The NFIB reports that only 50 percent of small business owners who attempted to borrow had most or all of their borrowing needs met, a decrease from 89 percent in 2005.[79]

ENTREPRENEURIAL PROFILE: Shane Ramsey: RAM-Z LLC Shane Ramsey, owner of RAM-Z LLC, a family-owned business that operates seven Schlotzsky's restaurants in Oklahoma, recently tried to borrow money from five national and regional banks to open an eighth location that includes cobranded Cinnabon (cinnamon buns) and Carvel (soft-serve ice cream) franchises. Although RAM-Z was generating $8.4 million in sales from its seven existing locations, all five banks denied his loan requests. After several months, a frustrated Ramsey turned to a group of angel investors for the capital to open the company's newest location in Tulsa, which produced $1.2 million in sales in its first year. Encouraged by its success, Ramsey is planning to open five more locations within four years but is not counting on bank loans for financing.[80] ■

Because start-up companies are so risky, bankers prefer to make loans to existing businesses with successful track records. They are concerned with a firm's operating past and will scrutinize its financial reports to project its position in the future. They also want proof of the stability of the company's sales and its ability to generate adequate cash flow to repay the loan. If they do make loans to a start-up venture, banks like to see sufficient cash flow to repay the loan, ample collateral to secure it, or an SBA guarantee to insure it. Small banks are more likely than large banks to extend loans to small businesses. Fifty-eight percent of business loans made by small banks (those with less than $1 billion in assets) are to small companies, 32 percent of business loans from midsize banks (those with assets between $1 billion and $10 billion) are small business loans, and only 19 percent of business loans from large banks (those with more than $10 billion in assets) go to small companies.[81] Small banks also tend to be "small business friendly" and are more likely than their larger counterparts to customize the terms of their loans to the particular needs of small businesses, offering, for example, flexible payment terms to match the seasonal pattern of a company's cash flow or interest-only payments until a piece of equipment begins generating revenue. Small and midsize banks approve 45 percent of small business loan requests, but large banks approve only 10 percent of loan requests from small companies.[82]

When evaluating a loan application, especially for a business start-up, banks focus on a company's capacity to create positive cash flow because they know that is where the money to repay their loans will come from. The first question in most bankers' minds when reviewing an entrepreneur's business plan is, "Can this business generate sufficient cash to repay the loan?" Even though they rely on collateral to secure their loans, the last thing banks want is for a borrower to default, forcing them to sell the collateral (often at "fire-sale" prices) and use the proceeds to pay off the loan. *That's* why bankers stress cash flow when analyzing a loan request, especially for a business start-up. "Cash is more important than your mother," jokes one experienced borrower.[83]

Banks and other lenders also require entrepreneurs to sign personal guarantees for any loan they make to small businesses. By making a personal loan guarantee, an entrepreneur is pledging that he or she will be liable *personally* for repaying the loan in the event that the business itself cannot repay the loan. Recall from Chapter 3 that in the eyes of the law, a sole proprietor or a general partner and the business are one and the same; therefore, for them, personal loan guarantees are redundant. However, because the owners of S corporations, corporations, and LLCs are separate from their businesses, they are not automatically responsible for the company's debts. Once the owners of these businesses sign a personal loan guarantee, however, they become liable for their companies' loans. (It is as if these individuals have "cosigned" the loan with the business.)

Short-Term Loans

Short-term loans, extended for less than one year, are the most common type of commercial loan banks make to small companies. These funds typically are used to replenish the working capital account to finance the purchase of inventory, boost output, finance credit sales to customers, or take advantage of cash discounts. As a result, an entrepreneur repays the loan after converting inventory and receivables into cash. There are several types of short-term loans.

HOME EQUITY LOANS Many entrepreneurs use the equity that they have built in their homes to finance their business start-ups. Entrepreneurs borrow from themselves by pledging their homes as collateral for the loans they receive. However, declining real estate values in most parts of the country have reduced or wiped out the equity in many people's homes, making securing home equity loans for their businesses much more difficult. Zalmi Duchman used a $100,000 home equity loan to launch Fresh Diet, a gourmet meal delivery service in Surfside, Florida, in 2006. Eighteen months later, with his company growing fast, Duchman tapped the equity in his home for $200,000 and secured a $900,000 SBA-guaranteed loan to purchase a competitor with locations in Miami and New York City. Fresh Diet now generates $30 million in annual sales.[84]

COMMERCIAL LOANS (OR "TRADITIONAL BANK LOANS") A basic short-term loan is the commercial bank's specialty. Business owners typically repay the loan, which often is unsecured because secured loans are much more expensive to administer and maintain, as a lump sum within three to six months. In other words, the bank grants a loan to a business owner without requiring him or her to pledge any specific collateral to support the loan in case of default. The owner repays the total amount of the loan at maturity. Sometimes the interest due on the loan is prepaid—deducted from the total amount borrowed. Until business owners can prove their companies' creditworthiness to the bank's satisfaction, they are not likely to qualify for unsecured commercial loans.

LINES OF CREDIT One of the most common requests entrepreneurs make of banks and commercial finance companies is to establish a commercial **line of credit**, a short-term loan with a preset limit that provides much-needed cash flow for day-to-day operations. A line of credit is ideal for helping business owners smooth out the uneven flow of cash that results from seasonal sales, slow-moving inventory, rapid growth, extending trade credit, and other factors. With a commercial line of credit, a business owner can borrow up to the predetermined ceiling at any time during the year quickly and conveniently by writing himself or herself a loan. Bankers often require a company to rest its line of credit during the year, maintaining a zero balance, as proof that the line of credit is not a perpetual crutch. Like commercial loans, lines of credit can be secured or unsecured.

> **line of credit**
> a short-term bank loan with a preset limit that provides working capital for day-to-day operations.

Unfortunately, a line of credit is the most difficult type of loan for small business owners to secure; according to a recent NFIB study, only 38 percent of small business owners who sought a line of credit were successful in securing one.[85] Mark Snyder, cofounder of Superior Medical Supply, a Denver-based company whose customers include physicians' offices, surgical centers, and nursing homes, needed a line of credit to bridge the gap in his growing company's cash flow. Superior's customers normally take 60 days to pay for the medical supplies they purchase, but Snyder must pay his vendors within 30 days. To avoid a cash crisis, Snyder convinced a community bank to grant Superior a $100,000 line of credit, which subsequently has increased to $175,000.[86]

FLOOR PLANNING Floor planning is a form of financing frequently employed by retailers of "big-ticket items" that are easily distinguishable from one another (usually by serial number), such as automobiles, boats, and major appliances. For example, a commercial bank finances Auto City's purchase of its inventory of automobiles and maintains a security interest in each car in the order by holding its title as collateral. Auto City pays interest on the loan monthly and repays the principal as it sells the cars. The longer a floor-planned item sits in inventory, the more it costs the business owner in interest expense. Banks and other floor planners often discourage retailers from using their money without authorization by performing spot checks to verify prompt repayment of the principal as items are sold.

Intermediate- and Long-Term Loans

Banks are primarily lenders of short-term capital to small businesses, although they will make intermediate- and long-term loans. Intermediate- and long-term loans, which are normally secured by collateral, are extended for one year or longer. Commercial banks grant these loans for constructing buildings, purchasing real estate and equipment, expanding a business, and other long-term investments. Matching the amount and the purpose of a loan to the appropriate type and length of loan is important. Loan repayments are normally made monthly or quarterly.

"And I want to ask the wizard for a loan."

From *The Wall Street Journal*, permission Cartoon Features Syndicate

INSTALLMENT LOANS One of the most common types of intermediate-term loans is an installment loan, which banks make to small firms for purchasing equipment, facilities, real estate, and other fixed assets. When financing equipment, a bank usually lends the small business from 60 to 80 percent of the equipment's value in return for a security interest in the equipment. The loan's amortization schedule, which is based on a set number of monthly payments, typically coincides with the length of the equipment's usable life. In financing real estate (commercial mortgages), banks typically lend up to 75 to 80 percent of the property's value and allow a lengthier repayment schedule of 10 to 30 years.

Hands On . . . How To

Get a Bank to Say "Yes" to Your Loan Application

Landing a loan to start or expand a small business is much more difficult today than in the past because of stodgy credit markets and upheaval in the banking and financial industries. Entrepreneurs often complain that bankers don't understand the financial needs they face when starting and operating their businesses. In many instances, however, business owners fail to help themselves when they apply for bank loans. Following are the seven most common reasons bankers reject small business loan applications (and how you can avoid them).

Reason 1. "Our bank doesn't make small business loans."

Cure: Select the right bank. Before applying for a bank loan, research banks to find out which ones actively seek the type of loan you need. Some banks don't make loans of less than $500,000, whereas others focus almost exclusively on small company loans. The SBA's reports *Micro-Business-Friendly Banks in the United*

States and *Small Business Lending in the United States* are valuable resources for locating the banks in your area that are most likely to make small business loans. Small, local banks tend to be more receptive to small business loan requests than many large banks, which often rely on formulas and templates to make lending decisions. Other factors that influence the types of loans that banks make include the industry in which the company competes, the company's geographic location, and the length of time it has been in business. Establishing a relationship with a bank before you need a loan also increases the probability that your loan request will be successful. Once you find the right bank for your business, open an account there, seek a small line of credit, and repay it consistently.

Reason 2. "I don't know enough about you or your business."

Cure: Develop a detailed business plan that explains what your company does (or will do) and describes how you will gain a

Hands On . . . How To (continued)

competitive edge over your rivals. The plan should address your company's major competition, what it will take to succeed in the market, and how your business will gain a competitive advantage in the market. In addition, be prepared to supply business credit references and a personal credit history. Finally, make sure you have your "elevator pitch" honed; you should be able to describe your business; what it does, sells, or makes; and its competitive edge in just one or two minutes.

Reason 3. "You haven't told me why you need the money."

Cure: A solid business plan will explain how much money you need and how you plan to use it. Make sure your request is specific; avoid requests for loans "for working capital." Don't make the mistake of answering the question "How much money do you need?" with "How much will you lend me?" "A lot of business owners do themselves a disservice by pulling a number out and saying, 'I think I need $400,000,'" says one lending expert. Instead, know how much money you need and be able to explain how the money will benefit your business. Arm yourself with a sound business plan that includes realistic financial forecasts that support your loan request. Remember that bankers want to make loans (after all, that's how they generate a profit), but they want to make loans only to those people they believe will repay them. Make sure your plan clearly shows how your company will be able to repay the bank loan.

Reason 4. "Your numbers don't support your loan request."

Cure: Include a cash flow forecast in your business plan. Bankers analyze a company's balance sheet and income statement to judge the quality of its assets and its profitability, but they lend primarily on the basis of cash flow. "Can you repay the loan balance?" is the question that most concerns bankers, and they know that repaying a loan requires adequate cash flow. If your business does not generate adequate cash flow, don't expect to get a loan. Prove to the banker that you understand your company's cash flow and how to manage it properly.

As a measure of a company's ability to repay a loan, bankers calculate the company's *cash coverage ratio,* which is its net income plus its noncash expenses (such as depreciation and amortization) divided by the annual payments on the proposed loan. They want to see a cash coverage ratio of at least 1.5:1 before granting a loan. In other words, to support $100,000 of loan payments a company should have net cash flow of at least $150,000.

Reason 5. "You don't have enough collateral."

Cure: Be prepared to pledge your company's assets—and perhaps your personal assets—as collateral for the loan. If a company's cash flow declines to the point that it cannot make loan payments, banks look for other ways to get their money back. To protect themselves in a worst-case scenario (a business that is unable to repay a loan), bankers want the security of collateral before they make a loan. They also expect more than $1 in collateral for every $1 of money they lend a business. Banks typically lend 50 to 90 percent of the value of real estate, 50 to 80 percent of

the value of accounts receivable, and just 10 to 50 percent of the value of inventory and equipment pledged as collateral.

Reason 6. "Your business does not support the loan on its own."

Cure: Be prepared to provide a personal guarantee on the loan. By doing so, you're telling the banker that if your business cannot repay the loan, you will. Many bankers see their small business clients and their companies as one and the same. Even if you choose a form of ownership that provides you with limited personal liability, most bankers will ask you to override that protection by personally guaranteeing the loan. Another way to lower the risk of a bank extending a loan to a small company is to secure a loan guarantee through one of the SBA's programs.

Reason 7: "You don't have enough 'skin' in the game."

Cure: Increase the amount of money you have invested in the project. A few years ago, entrepreneurs were able to get loans for projects by investing as little as 5 to 10 percent of the total amount. Today, depending on the project, bankers expect entrepreneurs to put up at least 20 to 25 percent of the project's cost—and sometimes much more. Be prepared to use your company's retained earnings to pay for a significant portion of the cost of a project.

David Pitts, owner of Classic Graphics, a printing company in Charlotte, North Carolina, knows firsthand how the small business lending environment has changed. In the company's 30-year history, Pitts has relied on many bank loans to finance the company's growth. Recently, however, securing bank loans has been much more difficult despite Classic Graphics's rapid growth (from $39 million in sales to $50 million in sales in just one year) and strong financial performance. Securing several loans that ranged from $200,000 to more than $1 million was "like pulling teeth," says Pitts. "Things that I used to do in three weeks are taking three months to get done. While [Classic Graphics] is dramatically stronger, banks and other lenders are so skittish, so cautious." Although Pitts took realistic financial projections and a strong business plan to banks, several bankers rejected his loan requests for Classic Graphics.

There's no magic to getting a bank to approve your loan request. The secret is proper preparation and building a solid business plan that enhances your credibility as a business owner with your banker. Use your plan to prove that you have what it takes to survive and thrive. "If you have a good business plan and you've already worked with your bank, there's money to be had," says the head of the Independent Community Bankers of America.

Sources: Based on Eileen P. Gunn, "How to Approach Lenders Now," *Entrepreneur,* March 6, 2011, http://www.entrepreneur.com/article/219274; Kirsten Valle Pittman, "Small Businesses Ready for Recovery, Lenders Aren't," *MCT/Joplin Globe,* July 18, 2011, http://www.joplinglobe.com/dailybusiness/x357284366/Small-businesses-ready-for-recovery-but-their-lenders-aren-t; Emily Maltby, "How to Land a Bank Loan, *CNNMoney,* September 17, 2008, http://money.cnn.com/2008/09/16/smallbusiness/land_a_bank_loan.smb/index.htm; Jim Melloan, "Do Not Say 'I Just Want the Money,'" *Inc.,* July 2005, p. 96; Crystal Detamore-Rodman, "Just Your Size," *Entrepreneur,* April 2005, pp. 59–61; Crystal Detamore-Rodman, "Raising Money: Loan Packaging Help," *Entrepreneur,* October 2008, p. 56; C. J. Prince, "Something to Bank on," *Entrepreneur,* August 2008, p. 57; and Kate Lister, "The Numbers That Matter," *Entrepreneur,* November 2010, pp. 98–99.

term loan

a bank loan that imposes restrictions (covenants) on the business decisions an entrepreneur makes concerning the company's operations.

TERM LOANS Another common type of loan banks make to small businesses is a **term loan**. Typically unsecured, banks grant these loans to businesses whose past operating history suggests a high probability of repayment. Some banks make only secured term loans, however. Term loans impose restrictions (called *covenants*) on the business decisions an entrepreneur makes concerning the company's operations. For instance, a term loan may set limits on owners' salaries, prohibit further borrowing without the bank's approval, or maintain certain financial ratios (recall the discussion of ratio analysis in Chapter 11).

The accompanying "Hands On . . . How To" feature describes the six most common reasons bankers reject small business loan applications and how to avoid them.

Nonbank Sources of Debt Capital

Although they usually are the first stop for entrepreneurs in search of debt capital, banks are not the only lending game in town. We now turn our attention to other sources of debt capital that entrepreneurs can tap to feed their cash-hungry companies.

ASSET-BASED LENDERS Across the United States, nearly 3,400 asset-based lenders, which are usually smaller commercial banks, commercial finance companies, or specialty lenders, allow small businesses to borrow money by pledging otherwise idle assets, such as accounts receivable, inventory, or purchase orders, as collateral. This method of financing works especially well for manufacturers, wholesalers, distributors, and other companies that have significant stocks of inventory or accounts receivable. Asset-based borrowing is an efficient method of borrowing because business owners borrow only the money they need when they need it. Even unprofitable companies whose financial statements cannot convince loan officers to make traditional loans often can get asset-based loans. These cash-poor but asset-rich companies can use normally unproductive assets—accounts receivable, inventory, and purchase orders—to finance rapid growth and the cash crises that often accompany it.

advance rate

the percentage of an asset's value that a lender will lend.

Like banks, asset-based lenders consider a company's cash flow, but they are more interested in the quality of the assets pledged as collateral. The amount a small business can borrow through asset-based lending depends on the **advance rate**, the percentage of an asset's value that a lender will lend. For example, a company pledging $100,000 of accounts receivable might negotiate a 70 percent advance rate and qualify for a $70,000 asset-based loan. Advance rates can vary dramatically depending on the quality of the assets pledged and the lender. Because inventory is an illiquid asset (i.e., hard to sell), the advance rate on inventory-based loans is quite low, usually 10 to 50 percent. A business pledging high-quality accounts receivable as collateral, however, may be able to negotiate up to an 85 percent advance rate. The most common types of asset-based financing are discounting accounts receivable, inventory financing, and purchase order financing.

Discounting Accounts Receivable. The most common form of secured credit is accounts-receivable financing. Under this arrangement, a small business pledges its accounts receivable as collateral; in return, the lender advances a loan against the value of approved accounts receivable. The amount of the loan tendered is not equal to the face value of the accounts receivable, however. Even though the lender screens the firm's accounts and accepts only qualified receivables, it makes an allowance for the risk involved because it will have to write off some of them as uncollectible. A small business usually can borrow an amount equal to 55 to 85 percent of its receivables, depending on their quality. Generally, lenders do not accept receivables that are past due.

Inventory Financing. With inventory financing, a small business loan is secured by its inventory of raw materials, work in process, and finished goods. If an owner defaults on the loan, the lender can claim the pledged inventory, sell it, and use the proceeds to satisfy the loan (assuming that the bank's claim is superior to the claims of other creditors). Because inventory usually is not a highly liquid asset and its value can be difficult to determine, lenders are willing to lend only a portion of its worth, usually no more than 50 percent of the inventory's value. Most asset-based lenders avoid inventory-only deals; they prefer to make loans backed by inventory *and* more secure accounts receivable. The key to qualifying for inventory financing is proving that a company has a plan or a process in place to ensure that the inventory securing the loan sells quickly.

ENTREPRENEURIAL PROFILE: Philip Asherian: E & S International Enterprises
Philip Asherian, CEO of E & S International Enterprises, a maker of electronics in Van Nuys, California, knew that the company's $150 million unsecured line of credit from a consortium of five banks was in jeopardy because of a crisis sweeping the financial industry. E & S relied on its line of credit to smooth out the swings in its cash flow that are the result of having to pay its suppliers well before it receives payment from its retail customers. The gap in the company's cash flow cycle can be as long as four months. Asherian turned to Siemens First Capital Commercial Finance Company for an asset-based line of credit that is secured by E & S's inventory and accounts receivable. Although the interest rate on the company's new line of credit is somewhat higher than the rate on its previous one, Asherian knows that the credit that E & S counts on for its success will be there when the company needs it.[87] ∎

To ensure the quality of the assets supporting the loans they make, lenders must monitor borrowers' assets, a task that increases the paperwork requirements on these loans. For example, E & S International Enterprises must submit monthly reports on its inventory and accounts receivable to Siemens First Capital Commercial Finance.

Purchase Order Financing. Small companies that receive orders from large customers can use those purchase orders as collateral for loans. The customer places an order with a small business, which needs financing to fill the order. The small company pledges the future payment from the customer as security for the loan, and the lender verifies the credit rating of the customer (not the small business) before granting the short-term loan, which often carries interest rates of 40 percent or more. Borrowers usually repay the loan within 60 days.

Asset-based loans are more expensive than traditional bank loans because of the cost of originating and maintaining them and the higher risk they involve. Rates usually run from two to seven percentage points (or more) above the prime rate. Because of this rate differential, small business owners should not use asset-based loans for long-term financing; their goal should be to establish their credit through asset-based financing and then to move up to a line of credit.

VENDOR FINANCING Many small companies borrow money from their vendors and suppliers in the form of trade credit. Because of its ready availability, trade credit is an extremely important source of financing to most entrepreneurs. When banks refuse to lend money to a start-up business because they see it as a high credit risk, an entrepreneur may be able to turn to trade credit for capital. Getting vendors to extend credit in the form of delayed payments (e.g., "net 30" credit terms) usually is much easier for small businesses than obtaining bank financing. Essentially, a company receiving trade credit from a supplier is getting a short-term, interest-free loan for the amount of the goods purchased. Vendors and suppliers often are willing to finance a small business's purchases of goods from 30 to 60 days (sometimes longer), interest free.

EQUIPMENT SUPPLIERS Most equipment vendors encourage business owners to purchase their equipment by offering to finance the purchase. This method of financing is similar to trade credit but with slightly different terms. Equipment vendors offer reasonable credit terms with only a modest down payment, with the balance financed over the life of the equipment (often several years). In some cases, the vendor will repurchase equipment for salvage value at the end of its useful life and offer the business owner another credit agreement on new equipment. Start-up companies often use trade credit from equipment suppliers to purchase equipment and fixtures such as display cases, refrigeration units, and machinery. It pays to scrutinize vendors' credit terms, however because they may be less attractive than those of other lenders.

COMMERCIAL FINANCE COMPANIES When denied bank loans, small business owners often look to commercial finance companies for the same types of loans. Commercial finance companies are second only to banks in making loans to small businesses, and, unlike their conservative counterparts, they are willing to tolerate more risk in their loan portfolios. Of course, their primary consideration is collecting their loans, but finance companies tend to rely more on obtaining a security interest in some type of collateral, given the higher-risk loans that make up their portfolios. Because commercial finance companies depend on collateral to recover most of their losses, they are able to make loans to small companies with very irregular cash flows or to those that are not yet profitable.

Approximately 150 large commercial finance companies, such as AT&T Small Business Lending, GE Capital Small Business Finance, and others, make a variety of loans to small companies, ranging from asset-based loans and business leases to construction and SBA loans. Dubbed "the Wal-Marts of finance," commercial finance companies usually offer many of the same credit options as commercial banks do. Because their loans are subject to more risks, finance companies charge a higher interest rate than commercial banks. Their most common methods of providing credit to small businesses are asset based—accounts-receivable financing and inventory loans. Rates on these loans vary but can be as high as 15 to 30 percent (including fees), depending on the risk a particular business presents and the quality of the assets involved. Because many of the loans they make are secured by collateral (if not accounts receivable or inventory, then the business equipment, vehicles, real estate, or inventory purchased with the loan), finance companies often impose more onerous reporting requirements, sometimes requiring weekly (or even daily) information on a small company's inventory levels or accounts-receivable balances. However, entrepreneurs who cannot secure financing from traditional lenders because of their short track records, less-than-perfect credit ratings, or fluctuating earnings often find the loans they need at commercial finance companies.

ENTREPRENEURIAL PROFILE: Gogy and Baljeet Sandher: Saagar Fine Cuisine After emigrating to the United States from India in 1981, Gogy Sandher spent several years picking peaches, working in restaurants in California, and teaching himself to cook in his spare time. In 1981, he and his wife Baljeet started an Indian restaurant in Huntington Beach, California. Twenty years later, the Sandhers were ready to open a second restaurant but needed $2.1 million in financing to complete the project. The Sandhers approached a commercial finance company, CDC Small Business Finance, that partnered with Zions First National Bank to extend the SBA-guaranteed loan they needed to open Saagar Fine Cuisine, an upscale Indian restaurant in Huntington Beach.[88] ∎

SAVINGS-AND-LOAN ASSOCIATIONS Savings-and-loan associations specialize in loans for real property. In addition to their traditional role of providing mortgages for personal residences, savings-and-loan associations offer financing on commercial and industrial property. In the typical commercial or industrial loan, the savings-and-loan association will lend up to 80 percent of the property's value with a repayment schedule of up to 30 years. Most savings-and-loan associations hesitate to lend money for buildings specially designed for a particular customer's needs. They expect the mortgage to be repaid from the company's future earnings.

STOCKBROKERS Stockbrokers also make loans, and many of the loans they make to their customers carry lower interest rates than those from banks. These **margin loans** carry lower rates because the collateral supporting them—the stocks and bonds in the customer's portfolio—is of high quality and is highly liquid. Moreover, brokerage firms make it easy to borrow. Brokers often set up a line of credit for their customers when they open a brokerage account. To tap that line of credit, the customer simply writes a check or uses a debit card. Typically, there is no fixed repayment schedule for a margin loan; the debt can remain outstanding indefinitely as long as the market value of the borrower's portfolio of collateral meets minimum requirements. Aspiring entrepreneurs can borrow up to 50 percent of the value of their stock portfolios, up to 70 percent of their bond portfolios, and up to 90 percent of the value of their government securities.

There is risk involved in using stocks and bonds as collateral on a loan. Brokers typically require a 30 percent cushion on margin loans. If the value of the borrower's portfolio drops, the broker can make a **margin (maintenance) call**, that is, the broker can call the loan and require the borrower to provide more cash and securities as collateral. Recent swings in the stock market have translated into margin calls for many entrepreneurs, requiring them to repay a significant portion of their loan balances within a matter of days—or hours. If an account lacks adequate collateral, the broker can sell off the customer's portfolio to pay off the loan.

CREDIT UNIONS **Credit unions**, nonprofit financial cooperatives that promote saving and provide loans to their members, are best known for making consumer and car loans. However, many are also willing to lend money to their members to launch and operate businesses. More than 7,700 state- and federally-chartered credit unions with some 93 million members operate in the United States, and they make loans to their members totaling more than $584 billion a year. Credit unions make more than $40 billion in small business loans to their members each year,

margin loans
loans from a stockbroker that use the stocks and bonds in the borrower's portfolio as collateral.

margin (maintenance) call
occurs when the value of a borrower's portfolio drops and the broker calls the loan in, requiring the borrower to put up more cash and securities as collateral.

credit union
a nonprofit financial cooperative that promotes saving and provides loans to its members.

and at 53 percent, the approval rates at credit unions for small business loan requests are higher than those at banks.[89] The average credit union business loan is $220,000.[90]

Not every credit union makes business loans (about 30 percent of credit unions do), and credit unions don't make loans to just anyone. To qualify for a loan, an entrepreneur must be a member. Lending practices at credit unions are very much like those at banks, but credit unions usually are willing to make smaller loans. Federal law currently limits a credit union's loans to businesses to 12.25 percent of the credit union's assets, but a bill before Congress proposes raising that cap to 27.5 percent. The SBA also recently opened its 7(a) loan program to credit unions, providing yet another avenue for entrepreneurs in search of financing. Because banks have tightened their lending requirements, many entrepreneurs are turning to credit unions for start-up and operating business loans.

ENTREPRENEURIAL PROFILE: Muhammad Abdullah: Legacy Business Group After his company experienced a sales decline during a recent recession, Muhammad Abdullah, owner of Legacy Business Group, a safety and medical supply company in Des Moines, Iowa, landed several large orders from customers and needed a line of credit to support the company's cash flow while he filled them. After several banks refused his loan requests, Abdullah turned to Veridian Credit Union, which provided Legacy Business Group with a $25,000 line of credit that allows him to take orders that otherwise he would have to refuse.[91] ∎

Entrepreneurs in search of a credit union near them can use the online database at the Credit Union National Association's Web site (www.creditunion.coop).

PRIVATE PLACEMENTS Earlier in this chapter, we saw how companies can raise capital by making private placements of their stock (equity). Private placements are also available for debt instruments. A private placement involves selling debt to one or a small number of investors, usually insurance companies or pension funds. Private placement debt is a hybrid between a conventional loan and a bond. At its heart, it is a bond, but its terms are tailored to the borrower's individual needs as a loan would be.

In addition to making equity investments in small companies, venture capital firms also provide venture debt financing, often in private placements. Interest rates on venture debt typically vary from prime-plus-one-percent to prime-plus-five-percent, and the loan terms range from 24 to 48 months. Venture debt deals often include warrants, which give the venture capital firm the right to purchase shares of stock in a company at a fixed price. Venture debt financing is a hybrid between a loan and venture capital. Most venture loans also come with covenants, requirements that a company must meet or incur a penalty, such as paying a higher interest rate or giving up more stock.

SMALL BUSINESS INVESTMENT COMPANIES Small Business Investment Companies (SBICs), created in 1958 when Congress passed the Small Business Investment Act, are privately owned financial institutions that are licensed and regulated by the SBA. The 292 SBICs operating in the United States use a combination of private capital and federally guaranteed debt to provide growing small businesses with long-term venture capital. Like their venture capital counterparts, most SBICs prefer later-round financing over funding start-ups; about 20 percent of SBIC investments go to start-up businesses.[92] Funding from SBICs helped launch companies such as Apple, Gymboree, Cutter and Buck, Build-a-Bear Workshop, Federal Express, Staples, Sun Microsystems, and Callaway Golf.

Since 1958, SBICs have provided more than $60 billion in long-term debt and equity financing to some 107,000 small businesses, adding hundreds of thousands of jobs to the U.S. economy.[93] SBICs must be capitalized privately with a minimum of $5 million, at which point they qualify for up to $3 (but most often $2) in long-term SBA loans for every $1 of private capital invested in small businesses up to a maximum of $150 million. As a general rule, SBICs may provide financial assistance only to small businesses with a net worth of less than $18 million and average after-tax earnings of $6 million during their last two years. However, employment and total annual sales standards vary from industry to industry. SBICs are limited to a maximum investment or loan amount of 20 percent of their private capital to a single client.

SBICs provide both debt and equity financing to small businesses. Most SBIC financing is in the much-needed range of $250,000 to $5 million, and the average investment is $1.55 million,

Small Business Investment Companies (SBICs) privately owned financial institutions that are licensed by the SBA and use a combination of private capital and federally guaranteed debt to provide long-term venture capital to small businesses.

far below the average investment by venture capital firms of $7.4 million.[94] When they make equity investments, SBICs are prohibited from obtaining a controlling interest in the companies in which they invest (no more than 49 percent ownership). Since 2008, the most common forms of SBIC financing have been debt instruments combined with equity investments (36.7 percent), straight debt instruments (36.5 percent), and equity-only investments (26.8 percent).[95]

ENTREPRENEURIAL PROFILE: Resheda Hagen: Lansinoh Laboratories In 1986, Resheda Hagen started Lansinoh Laboratories, a company that provides a variety of products to breast-feeding mothers, by packaging a lanolin cream in her kitchen and selling it. "It started selling at rates that were unimaginable to me," she recalls. Needing capital to finance the company's growth, Hagen made a pitch to Wayne Clevenger, managing director at Midmark Capital, an SBIC. Within days, Midmark provided a loan that accelerated Lansinoh's sales from $800,000 to $12 million in just 14 months and allowed the company to grow to more than $60 million in sales today.[96] ∎

Small Business Lending Companies

Small business lending companies (SBLCs) make only intermediate- and long-term SBA-guaranteed loans. They specialize in loans that many banks would not consider and operate on a nationwide basis. Most SBLC loans have terms extending for at least 10 years. The maximum interest rate for loans of seven years or longer is 2.75 percent above the prime rate; for shorter-term loans, the ceiling is 2.25 percent above prime. Another feature of SBLC loans is the expertise the SBLC offers borrowing companies in critical areas. Corporations own most of the nation's SBLCs, giving them a solid capital base.

Federally Sponsored Programs

LO5

Identify the various federal loan programs aimed at small businesses.

Federally sponsored lending programs have experienced budget fluctuations over the last several years, but some entrepreneurs have been able to acquire financing from the following programs.

Economic Development Administration

The Economic Development Administration (EDA), a branch of the Commerce Department, offers loan guarantees to create new business and to expand existing businesses in areas with below-average incomes and high unemployment rates. Focusing on economically distressed communities, the EDA often works with local governments to finance long-term investment projects needed to stimulate economic growth and to create jobs by making loan guarantees. The EDA guarantees loans up to 80 percent of business loans between $750,000 and $10 million. Entrepreneurs apply for loans through private lenders, for whom an EDA loan guarantee significantly reduces the risk of lending. Start-ups and existing businesses must make equity investments of at least 15 percent of the guaranteed amount. Small businesses can use the loan proceeds for a variety of ways, from supplementing working capital and purchasing equipment to buying land and renovating buildings.

EDA business loans are designed to help revitalize economically distressed areas by creating or expanding small businesses that provide employment opportunities in local communities. To qualify for a loan, a business must be located in a disadvantaged area, and its presence must directly benefit local residents. Some communities experiencing high unemployment or suffering from the effects of devastating natural disasters have received EDA Revolving Loan Fund Grants to create loan pools for local small businesses.

ENTREPRENEURIAL PROFILE: Natalie Dempsey: Leola Grocery Store With the help of a loan from the EDA-funded Northeast Council of Governments Development Corporation in Aberdeen, South Dakota, Natalie Dempsey purchased the Leola Grocery Store from its retiring owners in tiny Leola, South Dakota. Keeping the store operating means that the Leola's 457 residents do not have to travel nearly an hour to Aberdeen to purchase groceries and other necessities.[97] ∎

Department of Housing and Urban Development

Although the Department of Housing and Urban Development (HUD) does not extend loans or grants directly to entrepreneurs for launching businesses, it does sponsor several programs that can help qualified entrepreneurs to raise the capital they need. Community Development Block Grants

(CDBGs) are extended to cities and counties that, in turn, lend or grant money to entrepreneurs to start or expand small businesses, thereby strengthening the local economy. Grants are aimed at cities and towns that need revitalization and economic stimulation. Some grants are used to construct buildings and factories to be leased to entrepreneurs, sometimes with an option to buy. Others are earmarked for revitalizing a crime-ridden area or making start-up loans to entrepreneurs or expansion loans to existing business owners. No ceilings or geographic limitations are placed on CDBG loans and grants, but projects must benefit low- and moderate-income families.

> **ENTREPRENEURIAL PROFILE: Cheryl and Stephen Kraus: Upcountry Provisions Bakery & Bistro** When Cheryl and Stephen Kraus were renovating a building in downtown Traveler's Rest, South Carolina, to house their retail bakery, the copreneurs received a $5,750 Façade Improvement Grant from a grant funded by HUD's CDBG program. The 1,664-square-foot building on Main Street that serves as the home for the Upcountry Provisions Bakery & Bistro once housed a drugstore but had stood vacant for 20 years. "We wanted a location that would have more foot traffic than one where people are whizzing by in their cars," says Cheryl.[98] ∎

HUD also makes loan guarantees through its Section 108 provision of the CBDG program. These loan guarantees allow a community to transform a portion of CDBG funds into federally guaranteed loans large enough to pursue economic revitalization projects that can lead to the renewal of entire towns.

U.S. Department of Agriculture's Rural Business-Cooperative Service

The U.S. Department of Agriculture provides financial assistance to certain small businesses through its Rural Business-Cooperative Service (RBS). The RBS program is open to all types of businesses (not just farms) and is designed to create nonfarm employment opportunities in rural areas—those with populations below 50,000 and not adjacent to a city where densities exceed 100 people per square mile. Entrepreneurs in many small towns, especially those with populations below 25,000, are eligible to apply for loans through the RBS program, which makes almost $900 million in loan guarantees each year.

The RBS makes a limited number of direct loans to small businesses, but the majority of its activity is in loan guarantees. Through its Business and Industry Guaranteed Loan Program, the RBS will guarantee as much as 80 percent of a commercial lender's loan up to $25 million (although actual guarantee amounts are almost always far less, usually between $200,000 and $1 million) for qualified applicants. Entrepreneurs apply for loans through private lenders, who view applicants with loan guarantees much more favorably than those without such guarantees. The RBS guarantee reduces a lender's risk dramatically because the guarantee means that the government agency would pay off the loan balance (up to the ceiling) if the entrepreneur defaults on the loan.

> **ENTREPRENEURIAL PROFILE: La Rinascente Pasta** La Rinascente Pasta, a small maker of pasta, was founded shortly after World War II in the Bronx, New York, but in 2003, a group investors purchased the company with plans to relocate it to North Dakota. Working with the Hope Development Corporation and the Griggs-Steele Empowerment Zone in Hope, North Dakota, La Rinascente Pasta received a guarantee on a $1.2 million loan from the U.S. Department of Agriculture's Business and Industry Guaranteed Loan Program that allowed the company to purchase the machinery and equipment for its new pasta manufacturing plant.[99] ∎

To make a loan guarantee, the RBS requires much of the same documentation as most banks and most other loan guarantee programs. Because of its emphasis on developing employment in rural areas, the RBS requires an environmental impact statement describing the jobs created and the effect the business has on the area. The Rural-Business Cooperative Service also makes grants available to businesses and communities for the purpose of encouraging small business development and growth.

Small Business Innovation Research Program

Started as a pilot program by the National Science Foundation in the 1970s, the Small Business Innovation Research (SBIR) program has expanded to 11 federal agencies, ranging from NASA to the Department of Defense. The total SBIR budget across all 11 agencies is more than $2 billion annually. These agencies award cash grants or long-term contracts to small companies that want to initiate or to expand their R&D efforts. SBIR grants give innovative small companies the opportunity to attract early-stage capital investments *without* having to give up significant equity stakes or taking on burdensome levels of debt.

The SBIR process involves three phases. Phase I ("proof of concept") grants, which determine the feasibility and commercial potential of a technology or product, last for up to six months and have a ceiling of $150,000. Phase II ("prototype development") grants, designed to develop the concept into a specific technology or product, run for up to 24 months and have a ceiling of $1 million. Approximately one-third of all Phase II applicants receive funding. Phase III is the commercialization phase, in which the company pursues commercial applications of the R&D conducted in Phase I and Phase II and must use private or non-SBIR federal funding to bring a product to market.

Competition for SBIR funding is intense; only 17 percent of the small companies that apply for Phase I grants receive funding. So far, nearly 124,000 SBIR awards totaling more than $30 billion (26 percent in Phase I and 74 percent in Phase II) have gone to more than 18,000 small companies, which traditionally have had difficulty competing with big corporations for federal R&D dollars. The average grant, including Phase I and Phase II, is $242 million.[100] The government's dollars have been well invested. Nearly 45 percent of small businesses receiving Phase II SBIR awards have achieved commercial success with their products.[101]

ENTREPRENEURIAL PROFILE: Walter Bradley, Eliza Guzman-Teipel, and Stanton Greer: Whole Tree Inc. Baylor University professor Walter Bradley and graduate students Eliza Guzman-Teipel and Stanton Greer led a team of students who wanted to alleviate poverty in developing countries to identify abundant natural resources in each nation, develop a product based on those resources, and provide access to the U.S. market for the product. The team of entrepreneurs soon focused on countries that produced coconuts and launched Whole Tree Inc., a company that developed technology to convert coconut husk fibers into trunk liners, floorboards, and interior door covers on cars. The entrepreneurs landed funding from private investors and won a $100,000 Phase I SBIR grant and a $500,000 Phase II SBIR grant to refine their process and products. Not only are the company's coconut-based products all-natural, but they also weigh less than existing synthetic products. In addition, the automotive market represents the potential for the use of up to 100 million pounds of coconut fibers, almost all of which are supplied by farmers that once earned just $2 per day.[102] ■

Small Business Technology Transfer Program

The Small Business Technology Transfer Program (STTR) program complements the SBIR program. Whereas the SBIR focuses on commercially promising ideas that originate in small businesses, the STTR helps companies to utilize the vast reservoir of commercially promising ideas that originate in universities, federally funded R&D centers, and nonprofit research institutions. Researchers at these institutions can join forces with small businesses and can spin off commercially promising ideas while remaining employed at their research institutions. Five federal agencies award grants of up to $750,000 in three phases to these research partnerships.

The Small Business Administration (SBA)

LO6

Describe the various loan programs available from the Small Business Administration.

The SBA has several programs designed to help finance both start-up and existing small companies that cannot qualify for traditional loans because of their thin asset base and their high risk of failure. In its 60 years of operation, the SBA has helped 20 million small businesses through a multitude of programs, enabling many of them to get the financing they need for start-up or for growth. In the wake of the upheaval in the financial markets, banks have tightened their lending standards, and many small businesses cannot qualify for loans. Although SBA loans account for less than 10 percent of all small business lending, tight credit conditions make them all the more important for small companies seeking capital. About 29 percent of SBA-backed loans go to start-up companies.[103]

The SBA's $99 billion portfolio of loans makes it the largest single financial backer of small businesses in the nation.[104] SBA loan programs are aimed at entrepreneurs who do not meet

✓ You Be the Consultant

The Never-Ending Hunt for Financing

Rothman's

Kenneth Giddon has owned Rothman's, the men's clothing store founded by his grandfather in 1926 and located in a former bank building on New York City's Union Square, since 1986. In a recent radio address, Mayor Michael Bloomberg praised Rothman's as a model of the role that small businesses play in the revitalization of once blighted neighborhoods and in creating jobs, portraying Giddon as an entrepreneurial hero.

However, Giddon did not feel like a hero when he applied for a $500,000 loan to expand his business and three banks rejected his loan application.

Giddon applied for the loan after he negotiated a deal with his landlord for a location just one block away from his current store, a site that would allow him to more than double the store's square footage. "We're going big," he says. He approached two banks with whom the company has been doing business for many years and a third bank that had expressed an interest in his business, but all three rejected his loan request. Giddon's business plan emphasized Rothman's track record of success, and his financial projections for the new, larger store were realistic. Rothman's was profitable every year except for 2008 and 2009 when the Great Recession hammered the clothier's sales. The banks, however, focused on the losses the retailer incurred in those two years. Giddon, who offered to sign a personal guarantee for Rothman's loan, responded, "Yes, we lost money in 2008 and 2008, but guess what? So did you. And I didn't get bailed out. I had to own up to it—cut expenses, change my business, retool, be entrepreneurial, and come back."

One banker asked Giddon whether he would simply grant himself a raise if the bank approved his loan request. "No," Giddon replied, "I wouldn't be funding my business." Even though Rothman's has existing accounts that total more than $500,000 at two of the banks, loan officers told Giddon that they would lend him the money if he left it on deposit in a certificate of deposit that would serve as collateral against the loan. The certificate of deposit would earn 1.5 percent, but Giddon would pay 7 percent interest on the loan. "That's just not a good deal," he told them.

The experience has left Giddon frustrated and uncertain about his ability to relocate to the larger store. "A guy who's been in business for 25 years making a decision to upgrade his business, moving to a bigger and better space, and personally guaranteeing the loan," says Giddon reflectively. "I would think that's the kind of loan banks want."

Blazing Onion Burger Company

David Jones, a former Subway franchisee, and his wife Lorri opened the first Blazing Onion Burger Company restaurant in

Mill Creek, Washington, in 2007. Jones once owned six Subway franchises but dreamed of the day that he and Lorri would own a restaurant of their own. The couple collected menus from restaurants they encountered in their travels and in 2004 began researching segments in the restaurant industry to identify those that offered the best opportunities. They settled on the gourmet burger sector and came up with the name Blazing Onion Burger Company in a brainstorming session while traveling to visit their daughter in college. Their commitment to fresh, high-quality ingredients and fast, courteous service won customers' loyalty, and their first Blazing Onion Burger restaurant was a success. Despite a faltering economy, the copreneurs quickly opened two other locations, one in Snohomish and the other in Gig Harbor.

Financing the Gig Harbor restaurant proved to be a challenge, however. Although the Joneses had a good credit rating, a solid business plan, a track record of success in the restaurant business, and a profitable and growing business and were willing to put down 40 percent of the cost of opening the new location, the bank that had provided them with five prior loans rejected their loan request. So did nine other banks. Finally, the Joneses found a community bank, Heritage Bank, in Tacoma, Washington, that approved their loan request with the security of a guarantee from the SBA.

Blazing Onion Burger's sales continued to grow rapidly in the face of a daunting recession, and the Joneses are ready to open another restaurant in Alderwood Mall in Lynnwood, Washington. The business plan for the mall location forecasts annual sales of $4.5 million the first year. The copreneurs also have developed a growth plan for Blazing Onion Burger that calls for opening a new location every 10 months for the next several years.

1. Which of the funding sources described in this chapter do you recommend that Kenneth Giddon and David and Lorri Jones consider for financing the growth of their businesses? Which sources do you recommend that they *not* use? Why?

2. What can entrepreneurs do to increase the probability that bankers will approve their loan requests?

3. Work with a team of your classmates to brainstorm ways that these entrepreneurs could attract the capital they need for their businesses. What steps do you recommend they take before they approach the potential sources of funding you have identified?

Sources: Based on Janean Chun, "Why Aren't Small Businesses Getting Loans from Big Banks?," *Huffington Post*, December 12, 2011, http://www.huffingtonpost.com/2011/12/12/small-business-loans_n_1121955.html; Kurt Batdorf, "Persistence and Technology Give Blazing Onion Burger Sizzle," *Heraldnet*, February 28, 2011, http://www.heraldnet.com/article/20110228/BIZ/702289969; and Alison Pride, "The Blazing Onion Burger Company," *Westsound Home and Garden*, December 2009, pp. 27–29.

lending standards at conventional lending institutions. The SBA does *not* actually lend money to entrepreneurs directly; instead, entrepreneurs borrow money from a traditional lender, and the SBA guarantees repayment of a percentage of the loan (at least 50 percent and sometimes as much as 85 percent) in case the borrower defaults. The loan application process can take from three days to several months, depending on how well prepared the entrepreneur is and which bank or lender is involved.

To reduce the paperwork requirements and processing time involved in its loans, the SBA operates two "express" programs that give entrepreneurs responses to their loan applications within 36 hours.

SBA*EXPRESS* PROGRAM In the SBA*Express* Program, participating lenders use their own loan procedures and applications to make loans of up to $350,000 to small businesses. Because the SBA guarantees 50 percent of the loan, banks often are willing to make smaller loans to entrepreneurs who might otherwise have difficulty meeting lenders' standards. Entrepreneurs can use these flexible term loans for a variety of business purposes, including purchasing equipment, fixtures, land, or buildings; renovating existing structures or building new ones; buying inventory; obtaining a seasonal line of credit; and others. Loan maturities on SBA*Express* loans typically are between 5 and 10 years, but loan maturities for fixed assets can be up to 25 years. The average SBA*Express* loan is $107,000.[105]

PATRIOT *EXPRESS* PROGRAM In 2007, the SBA launched the Patriot *Express* loan program, which is designed to assist some of the nation's 25 million veterans and their spouses or widows who want to become entrepreneurs. The loan ceiling is $500,000, and the SBA guarantees up to 85 percent of the loan amount in case the borrower defaults. Patriot *Express* loans carry interest rates that range from 2.25 percent to 4.75 percent above the prime interest rate. The average Patriot *Express* loan is $83,000.[106]

ENTREPRENEURIAL PROFILE: Jason Kuhn and Evan Kranzley: J&E Technical Services Navy veteran Jason Kuhn knew at age 16 that he wanted to own a business. When he left military service, Kuhn decided to partner with friend Evan Kranzley to launch J&E Technical Services, a company in Martinsburg, Virginia, that performs nondestructive testing for corrosion and cracks on aircraft, the same work that Kuhn had performed in the Navy. Kuhn and Kranzley used a Patriot Express loan to purchase the X-ray technology they needed to expand their fledgling business. "We could see the opportunities they had were real," says Matt Coffey, an executive for BB&T, the lender. "They just needed funding to get started [into X-ray technology]." Kuhn and Kranzley say that the Patriot Express loan has made all the difference in their company, which generates sales of $500,000 annually and has doubled its workforce to six employees. Since receiving the loan, J&E Technical has expanded into other markets, including power-generating wind turbines, petrochemical plants, and pipelines.[107] ∎

Other SBA Loan Programs

7(A) LOAN GUARANTY PROGRAM The SBA works with local lenders (both bank and nonbank) to offer many other loan programs that are designed to help entrepreneurs who cannot get capital from traditional sources gain access to the financing they need to launch and grow their businesses. When they were just small companies, Callaway Golf, Outback Steakhouse, and Intel Corporation borrowed through the SBA's loan programs. The **7(a) loan guaranty program** is the SBA's flagship loan program (see Figure 13.8). More than 3,500 private lenders in the United States make SBA loans to small businesses, but the SBA guarantees them (85 percent of loans up to $150,000 and 75 percent of loans that range from $150,001 up to the loan cap of $5 million). Because the SBA recently increased the ceiling on 7(a) loans from $2 million to $5 million, the average 7(a) loan increased from $264,000 in 2010 to $366,000.[108] Because SBA-guaranteed loans are riskier, their default rate is higher than that of standard bank loans. A recent study reports that the default rate on SBA loans has increased from 2.4 percent in 2004 to 11.9 percent today.[109]

Because the SBA assumes most of the credit risk, lenders are more willing to consider riskier deals that they normally would refuse. With the SBA's guarantee, borrowers also have to come up with less collateral than with a traditional bank loan.

7(a) loan guaranty program

an SBA program in which loans made by private lenders to small businesses are guaranteed up to a ceiling by the SBA.

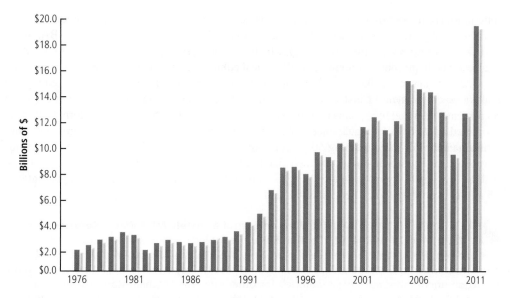

FIGURE 13.8

SBA 7(A) Guaranteed Loans

Source: U.S. Small Business Administration.

ENTREPRENEURIAL PROFILE: Joe Fugere: Tutta Bella Neapolitan Pizzeria Before Joe Fugere opened Tutta Bella Neapolitan Pizzeria in Seattle, Washington, in 2004, he traveled to Naples, Italy, where he studied the intricate details of making authentic Neapolitan pizzas (known as "pizzaiolis" in Naples). Tutta Bella became one of the few pizzerias in the United States to receive certification from the Verace Pizza Napoletana, an association authorized by the Italian government to ensure that only those pizzerias that conform to stringent production methods and specific ingredients are allowed to sell Neapolitan pizzas. Fugere used personal funds and a bank loan to open his first Tutta Bella location. As the business grew, Fugere returned to the same bank for loans to open two more locations in just four years. A year later, when Fugere approached the bank for a loan to open a fourth Tutta Bella pizzeria, the lending officer rejected his loan request. "I thought it was a fluke," says Fugere, but when three other big banks also rejected his loan application, Fugere knew that lending conditions had changed. "I had a successful concept, money in the bank, and a history of making payments," he says, but turmoil in the financial industry had eliminated many banks' appetite for making loans. Finally, Fugere approached a small community bank that offered him an SBA-backed 7(a) loan "almost overnight." The SBA's guarantee lowered the community bank's risk and allowed Fugere to get the financing he needed to open another successful Tutta Bella location.[110] ■

Qualifying for an SBA loan guarantee requires cooperation among the entrepreneur, the participating lender, and the SBA. The participating lender determines the loan's terms and sets the interest rate within SBA limits. Contrary to popular belief, SBA-guaranteed loans do *not* carry special deals on interest rates. Typically, rates are negotiated with the participating lender, with a ceiling of prime-plus-2.25 percent on loans of less than seven years and prime-plus-2.75 percent on loans of 7 to 25 years. Interest rates on loans of less than $25,000 can run up to prime-plus-4.75 percent. The average interest rate on SBA-guaranteed loans is prime-plus-2 percent (compared to prime-plus-1 percent on conventional bank loans). The SBA also assesses a one-time guaranty fee of 0.25 to 3.75 percent for all loan guarantees, depending on the guaranteed amount. The maximum loan available through the 7(a) guaranty program is $5 million.

The average duration of an SBA loan is 12 years—far longer than the average commercial small business loan. In fact, longer loan terms are a distinct advantage of SBA loans. At least half of all bank business loans are for less than one year. By contrast, SBA real estate loans can extend for up to 25 years (compared to just 10 to 15 years for a conventional loan), and working capital loans have maturities of seven years (compared with two to five years at most banks). These longer terms translate into lower loan payments, which are better suited for young, fast-growing, cash-strapped companies.

SECTION 504 CERTIFIED DEVELOPMENT COMPANY PROGRAM The second most popular SBA loan program is the Section 504 program, which is designed to encourage small businesses to purchase fixed assets, expand their facilities, and create jobs. Section 504 loans provide long-term, fixed-asset financing to small companies to purchase land, buildings, or equipment—"brick-and-mortar" loans. Three lenders play a role in every 504 loan: a bank, the SBA, and a **certified development company (CDC)**, which is a nonprofit organization licensed by the SBA and designed to promote economic growth in local communities. Some 270 CDCs operate across the United States and make about 8,000 loans in a typical year. The entrepreneur is required to make a down payment of just 10 percent of the total project cost rather than the typical 20 to 30 percent traditional bank loans require. The CDC provides 40 percent at a long-term fixed rate, supported by an SBA loan guarantee in case the entrepreneur defaults. The bank provides long-term financing for the remaining 50 percent, also supported by an SBA guarantee. The major advantages of Section 504 loans are their fixed rates and terms, their 10- and 20-year maturities, and the low down payment required. The maximum loan amount that the SBA will guarantee is $5 million, and the average Section 504 loan is $607,000.[111]

ENTREPRENEURIAL PROFILE: Ken and Carol Mitchell: MBA Waste Services Ken and Carol Mitchell used a $2.1 million SBA-guaranteed Section 504 loan to build a LEED-certified recycling center for their family business, MBA Waste Services, in Union City, Georgia. The center includes a 41,000-square-foot building that houses a materials sorting center and a reduction grinder that transforms materials for other uses. The Mitchells started MBA Waste Services in 2007 and focused initially on providing portable toilets, on-site dumpsters, and wastewater holding tanks. To build their recycling center, the Mitchells invested 10 percent of the project's cost, the Bank of North Georgia loaned $1.1 million, and an SBA-certified development corporation provided the remaining $949,000. The Mitchells say that the Section 504 loan not only enabled them to expand their successful business but also allowed them to benefit from lower monthly payments than traditional loans because the loan's maturity is 20 years.[112] ■

SMALL LOAN ADVANTAGE AND COMMUNITY ADVANTAGE LOAN PROGRAMS In 2011, the SBA introduced two new loan programs, the Small Loan Advantage and the Community Advantage programs. The Small Loan Advantage program is designed to encourage existing, experienced SBA lenders, known as preferred lenders, to make smaller loans, which are most likely to benefit disadvantaged borrowers. The Community Advantage Loan program encourages new lenders that operate in economically challenged communities that have had little or no access to SBA loans to enter the SBA's 7(a) loan program. Both programs include SBA guarantees of 85 percent on loans up to $150,000 and 75 percent on loans between $150,001 and the ceiling of $250,000 and use a streamlined application process.

MICROLOAN PROGRAM About three-fourths of all entrepreneurs need less than $100,000 to launch their businesses. Indeed, most entrepreneurs require less than $50,000 to start their companies. Unfortunately, loans of that amount can be the most difficult to get. Lending these relatively small amounts to entrepreneurs starting businesses is the purpose of the SBA's Microloan Program. Called **microloans** because they range from just $100 to as much as $50,000, these loans have helped thousands of people take their first steps toward entrepreneurship. Banks typically shun loans in such small amounts because they consider them to be risky and unprofitable. In an attempt to fill the void in small loans to start-up companies, the SBA launched the microloan program in 1992, and it has gone on to become the single largest source of funding for microenterprises. Today, nearly 180 authorized lenders make SBA-backed microloans. The average size of a microloan is $11,800, with a maturity of three years (the maximum term is six years) and maximum interest rates that typically are between 8 and 13 percent. Microloans do not carry SBA guarantees, but lenders' standards are less demanding than those on conventional loans. In fact, 37 percent of all microloans go to business start-ups, and more than half of all microloans go to women- and minority-owned businesses.[113] All microloans are made through nonprofit intermediaries that are approved by the SBA. Entrepreneurs can find a listing of microloan intermediaries at the SBA's Web site (www.sba.gov/content/microloan-program).

ENTREPRENEURIAL PROFILE: Matt Morse: Hot Mama's In 1991, Matt Morse bought Hot Mama's, a company that makes salsa, hummus, and other gourmet food products, and relocated the business from a tiny 500-square-foot building in Millers Falls, Massachusetts, to

Amherst, Massachusetts, with help from a $10,000 microloan from the Western Massachusetts Enterprise Fund. Hot Mama's all-natural product line made with fresh ingredients struck a chord with customers, and the company grew quickly. For a second time, Morse tapped the Western Massachusetts Enterprise Fund for a microloan, this time borrowing $15,000 to expand the company's facilities. Now located in Springfield, Massachusetts, Hot Mama's has $6 million in annual sales and employs 60 people. Looking back, Morse says that those early microloans were essential to his company's success because Hot Mama's was "unbankable." "[The microloans] gave me the chance to take those first few steps and establish some credit," he says. "They enabled me to take the plunge and eventually be able to get bank financing."[114] ∎

THE CAPLINE PROGRAM In addition to its basic 7(a) loan guarantee program (through which the SBA makes about 75 percent of its loans), the SBA provides guarantees on small business loans for start-up, real estate, machinery and equipment, fixtures, working capital, exporting, and restructuring debt through several other methods. About two-thirds of all of the SBA's loan guarantees are for machinery and equipment or working capital. The **CAPLine Program** offers short-term capital to growing companies seeking to finance seasonal buildups in inventory or accounts receivable under five separate programs, each with maturities up to five years: seasonal line of credit (provides advances against inventory and accounts receivable to help businesses weather seasonal sales fluctuations), contract line of credit (finances the cost of direct labor and materials costs associated with performing contracts), builder's line of credit (helps small contractors and builders finance labor and materials costs), standard asset-based line of credit (an asset-based revolving line of credit for financing short-term needs), and small asset-based line of credit (an asset-based revolving line of credit up to $200,000). CAPLine helps cash-hungry small businesses by giving them a credit line to draw on when they need it. A line of credit is what many small companies need most because they are flexible, efficient, and, unfortunately, quite difficult for small businesses to get from traditional lenders.

LOANS INVOLVING INTERNATIONAL TRADE For small businesses going global, the SBA has the **Export *Express* Program**, which, like its other express programs, offers quick turnaround times on applications for guarantees of 75 to 90 percent on loans up to $500,000 to help small companies develop or expand their export initiatives. Loan maturities range from 5 to 25 years.

The SBA also offers the **Export Working Capital (EWC) Program**, which is designed to provide working capital to small exporters. The SBA works in conjunction with the Export-Import Bank to administer this loan guarantee program. Applicants file a one-page loan application, and the response time normally is 10 days or less. The maximum loan is $5 million with a 90 percent guarantee, and proceeds must be used to finance small business exports.

ENTREPRENEURIAL PROFILE: Deborah Smook and Eli Uriel: Turbofil Packaging Machines LLC Copreneurs Deborah Smook and Eli Uriel, both trained as engineers, started Turbofil Packaging Machines LLC in 1999 in Mount Vernon, New York. Sales at their business, which designs and builds custom liquid filling and assembly machines and systems for the cosmetics, pharmaceutical, diagnostic, and chemical industries, started slowly, but the couple persisted. "In the first year, we sold only one machine," recalls Uriel. Turbofil's machines range in price from $1,500 for simple benchtop machines to $500,000 for full-blown filling systems. Today the company employs 10 workers, not counting Pepper, the couple's Chatham Hill retriever, who serves as Turbofil's official greeter. In 2007, Turbofil made its first international sale to a cosmetics company in the Philippines for two nail polish fillers. Two years later, with the help of the SBA's Export Working Capital program, Smook and Uriel landed a $1 million contract to provide machinery to an Israeli defense contractor. The entrepreneurs continue to expand their export sales, which now account for 20 percent of their company's sales.[115] ∎

The **International Trade Program** is for small businesses that are engaging in international trade or are adversely affected by competition from imports. The SBA allows global entrepreneurs to combine loans from the Export Working Capital Program with those from International Trade Program for up to $5 million with a maximum guarantee of $4.5 million. Loan maturities range from one to 25 years.

CAPLine Program
an SBA program that makes short-term capital loans to growing companies needing to finance seasonal buildups in inventory or accounts receivable.

Export *Express* Program
an SBA loan program that offers quick turnaround times to small companies that are developing or expanding their export initiatives.

Export Working Capital Program
an SBA loan program that is designed to provide working capital to small exporters.

Courtesy of Turbofil Packaging Machines

International Trade Program
an SBA loan program for small businesses that are engaging in international trade or are adversely affected by competition from imports.

disaster loans
an SBA loan program that
makes loans to small businesses devastated by some
kind of financial or physical
loss.

DISASTER LOANS As their name implies, **disaster loans** are made to small businesses devastated by some kind of financial or physical losses from hurricanes, floods, earthquakes, tornadoes, and other natural disasters. The maximum disaster loan usually is $2 million, but Congress often raises that ceiling when circumstances warrant. Disaster loans carry below-market interest rates as low as 4 percent and terms as long as 30 years. Loans for physical damage above $14,000 require an entrepreneur to pledge some kind of collateral, usually a lien on the business property. In the aftermath of hurricane-force Santa Ana winds in California that damaged or destroyed many small businesses, the SBA approved disaster loans at just 4 percent interest to help entrepreneurs get their companies back up and running.[116]

Table 13.3 summarizes the features of the major SBA loan programs.

State and Local Loan Development Programs

Many states have created their own loan and economic development programs to provide funds for business start-ups and expansions. They have decided that their funds are better spent encouraging small business growth rather than "chasing smokestacks"—trying to entice large businesses to locate within their boundaries. These programs come in many forms, but they all tend to focus on developing small businesses that create the greatest number of jobs and economic benefits. Entrepreneurs who apply for state and local funding must have patience and be willing to slog through some paperwork, however.

Although each state's approach to economic development is somewhat special, one common element is some kind of small business financing program: loans, loan guarantees, development grants, venture capital pools, and others. One approach many states have had success with is **Capital Access Programs (CAPs)**. First introduced in Michigan in 1986, many states now offer CAPs that are designed to encourage lending institutions to make loans to businesses that do not qualify for traditional financing because of their higher risk. Under a CAP, a bank and a borrower each pay an upfront fee (a portion of the loan amount) into a loan-loss reserve fund at the participating bank, and the state matches this amount. The reserve fund, which normally ranges from 6 to 14 percent of the loan amount, acts as an insurance policy against the potential loss a bank might experience on a loan and frees the bank to make loans that it otherwise might refuse. One study of CAPs found that 55 percent of the entrepreneurs who received loans under a CAP would not have been granted loans without the backing of the program.[117]

**Capital Access
Programs (CAPs)**
a state lending program
that encourages lending
institutions to make loans
to businesses that do
not qualify for traditional
financing because of their
higher risk.

Even cities and small towns have joined in the effort to develop small businesses and help them grow. Many communities across the United States operate **revolving loan funds** that combine private and public funds to make loans to small businesses, often at favorable interest rates, for the purpose of starting or expanding businesses that create jobs and contribute to economic development. As money is repaid into the funds, it is loaned back out to other entrepreneurs.

revolving loan fund
a program offered by
communities that combine
private and public funds
to make loans to small
businesses, often at below-
market interest rates.

ENTREPRENEURIAL PROFILE: Sarah Dvorak: Mission Cheese Launched in 2009 with $680,000, San Francisco's Small Business Revolving Loan Fund has made loans ranging from $5,000 to $50,000 to 27 start-up and existing small businesses that need capital. Sarah Dvorak received a loan from the revolving loan fund to start Mission Cheese, a café and artisan cheese shop, in the city's historic Mission District. "This project would not have been possible without the $25,000 loan and assistance from the Revolving Loan Fund," she says.[118] ■

In addition to revolving loan funds, nearly 1,000 communities across the United States have created **community development financial institutions (CDFIs)** that designate at least some of their loan portfolios to supporting entrepreneurs and small businesses. CDFIs operate through a variety of institutions, including microenterprise loan funds, community development loan funds, and others to provide capital and credit to otherwise "unbankable" business owners and aspiring entrepreneurs in low-income communities across the United States. Because the loans that they make are higher risk, the interest rates that CDFIs charge are higher than those charged by traditional lenders.

**community
development financial
institutions (CDFIs)**
community-based financial
institutions that designate
at least a portion of their
loan portfolios to otherwise
"unbankable" business
owners and aspiring entrepreneurs.

ENTREPRENEURIAL PROFILE: William Ortiz-Cartagena: Gentle Parking William Ortiz-Cartagena borrowed $10,000 from the Opportunity Fund, a California CDFI, to launch his San Francisco–based parking logistics company, Gentle Parking, after

TABLE 13.3 SBA Loan Program Overview

Program	Maximum Loan Amount	Guaranty Percentage	Use of Proceeds	Loan Maturity	Maximum Interest Rates
Standard 7(a)	$5 million	85% on loans up to $150,000; 75 percent on loans between $151,000 and $5 million	Term loan. Purchase land or buildings; expand or renovate existing buildings; acquire equipment and fixtures; make leasehold improvements; refinance existing debt; purchase inventory; establish seasonal line of credit	Working capital—up to 7 years; equipment—5 to 10 years; real estate—up to 25 years	Loans of 7 years or less: prime + 2.25%; loans longer than 7 years: prime + 2.75%; for loans of less than $50,000, rates can be up to prime + 4.25%
SBA*Express*	$350,000	50%	Same as 7(a) loan purposes and revolving line of credit	Up to 7 years for revolving line of credit; otherwise, same as 7(a)	Loans of $50,000 or less: prime + 6.5%; Loans of $50,001 to $350,000: prime + 4.5%
Patriot *Express*	$500,000	Same as 7(a)	Same as SBA*Express*	Same as 7(a)	Same as 7(a)
Export *Express*	$500,000	90% on loans of $350,000 or less; 75% on loans greater than $350,000	Same as SBA*Express*	Same as SBA*Express*	Same as SBA*Express*
CAPLines	$5 million	Same as 7(a)	Working capital needs that are associated with specific contracts	Up to 5 years	Same as 7(a)
International Trade	$2 million	Same as 7(a)	Acquire fixed assets	Up to 25 years	Same as 7(a)
Small Loan Advantage	$250,000	Same as 7(a)	Same as 7(a)	Same as 7(a)	Same as 7(a)
Community Advantage	$250,000	Same as 7(a)	Same as 7(a)	Same as 7(a)	Prime + 4%
Export Working Capital	$5 million (may be combined with International Trade loan)	90%	Short-term working capital for exporting	Generally 1 year or a single transaction cycle (3-year maximum)	No cap
Section 504 Community Development Corporation	$5 to $5.5 million, depending on type of business	40% up to $2.2 million maximum	Long-term, fixed asset projects such as constructing new buildings, purchasing and renovating existing buildings, and purchasing equipment and machinery	Equipment—up to 10 years; real estate—up to 20 years	Fixed rate depends on when SBA's debenture-backed loan is sold
Microloan	$50,000	N/A	Purchase machinery and equipment, fixtures, leasehold improvements, financing receivables, or working capital. Cannot be used to repay existing debt.	Up to 6 years	Variable; generally between 8% and 13%

Source: "Quick Reference to SBA Loan Guaranty Programs," U.S. Small Business Administration, Washington, DC, http://www.sba.gov/sites/default/files/files/Loan%20Chart%20HQ%202011.pdf.

several banks refused his loan request. "It was very hard to start this company because traditional lending institutions said 'no, '" says Ortiz-Cartagena, who also credits the Opportunity Fund with helping him polish his business plan. Gentle Parking is growing and now has 12 employees.[119] ■

LO7

Explain other methods of financing a business, including factoring, leasing assets, and using credit cards.

Other Methods of Financing

Small business owners do not have to rely solely on financial institutions and government agencies for capital; their businesses have the capacity to generate capital. Other common methods of financing, including factoring, leasing rather than purchasing equipment, and using credit cards, are available to almost every small business.

Factoring Accounts Receivable

factor

a financial institution that buys business's accounts receivable at a discount.

Instead of carrying credit sales on its own books (some of which may never be collected), a small business can sell outright its accounts receivable to a factor. A **factor** buys a company's accounts receivable and pays for them in two parts. The first payment, which the factor makes immediately, is for 50 to 80 percent of the accounts' agreed-on (and usually discounted) value. The factor makes the second payment of 15 to 18 percent, which makes up the balance less the factor's service fees, when the original customer pays the invoice. High interest rates (often 36 percent or more) make factoring a more expensive type of financing than loans from either banks or commercial finance companies, but for businesses that cannot qualify for those loans, it may be the only choice! Factoring volume totals more than $74 billion per year.[120]

Factoring deals are either with recourse or without recourse. Under deals arranged with recourse, a small business owner retains the responsibility for customers who fail to pay their accounts. The business owner must take back these uncollectible invoices. Under deals arranged without recourse, however, the owner is relieved of the responsibility for collecting them. If customers fail to pay their accounts, the factor bears the loss. Nearly 70 percent of factoring deals are without recourse.[121] Because the factor assumes the risk of collecting the accounts, it screens a company's credit customers, accepts those judged to be creditworthy, and advances the small business owner a portion of the value of the accounts receivable. Factors discount anywhere from 2 to 40 percent of the face value of a company's accounts receivable, depending on the following factors related to a small company:

- Customers' financial strength and credit ratings
- Industry and its customers' industries because some industries have a reputation for slow payments
- History and financial strength, especially in deals arranged with recourse
- Credit policies[122]

The discount rate on deals without recourse usually is higher than on those with recourse because of the higher level of risk they carry for the factor.

Although factoring is more expensive than traditional bank loans (a 2 percent discount from the face value of an invoice due in 30 days amounts to an annual interest rate of 24.8 percent), it is a source of quick cash and is ideally suited for fast-growing companies, especially start-ups that cannot qualify for bank loans. Small companies that sell to government agencies and large corporations, both famous for stretching out their payments for 60 to 90 days or more, also find factoring attractive because they collect the money from the sale (less the factor's discount) much faster.

Leasing

Leasing is another common bootstrap financing technique. Today, small businesses can lease virtually any kind of asset, including office space, telephones, computers, and heavy equipment. By leasing expensive assets, the small business owner is able to use them without locking in valuable capital for an extended period of time. In other words, entrepreneurs can reduce the long-term capital requirements of their businesses by leasing equipment and facilities and are not investing their capital in depreciating assets. In addition, because no down payment is required and because the cost of the asset is spread over a longer time (lowering monthly payments), a company's cash flow improves.

Credit Cards

Unable to find financing elsewhere, many entrepreneurs launch their companies using the fastest and most convenient source of debt capital available: credit cards. Google cofounders Larry Page and Sergey Brin used three credit cards to purchase the $15,000 worth of hardware that they needed to launch their budding search engine.[123] Kai Huang and his brother Charles maxed out credit cards to finance the launch of the company that developed Guitar Hero, which went on to become one of the best-selling video games of all time.[124] A study by the Kauffman Foundation reports that 7 percent of the capital for start-up companies comes from credit cards. The study also shows that 58 percent of new businesses rely on credit cards to finance operations in their first year of business.[125] Putting business start-up costs on credit cards charging 21 percent or more in annual interest is expensive and risky, especially if sales fail to materialize as quickly as planned, but some entrepreneurs have no other choice.

Chapter Summary by Learning Objective

1. Describe the differences between equity capital and debt capital and the advantages and disadvantages of each.

Capital is any form of wealth employed to produce more wealth. Entrepreneurs have access to two different types of capital:

- Equity financing represents the personal investment of the owner (or owners), and it offers the advantage of not having to be repaid with interest.

- Debt capital is the financing that a small business owner has borrowed and must repay with interest. It does not require entrepreneurs to give up ownership in their companies.

2. Discuss the various sources of equity capital available to entrepreneurs, including personal savings, friends and relatives, crowd funding, angels, partners, venture capital firms, corporate venture capital, public stock offerings, and simplified registrations and exemptions.

- The most common source of financing a business is the owner's personal savings. After emptying their own pockets, the next place entrepreneurs turn for capital is family members and friends. Crowd funding taps the power of social networking and allows entrepreneurs to post their elevator pitches and proposed investment terms on crowd-funding Web sites and raise money to fund their ventures from ordinary people who invest as little as $100. Angels are private investors who not only invest their money in small companies but also offer valuable advice and counsel to them. Some business owners have success financing their companies by taking on limited partners as investors or by forming an alliance with a corporation, often a customer or a supplier. Venture capital companies are for-profit, professional investors looking for fast-growing companies in "hot" industries. When screening prospects, venture capital firms look for competent management, a competitive edge, a growth industry, and important intangibles that will make a business successful. Some owners choose to attract capital by taking their companies public, which requires registering the public offering with the SEC.

3. Describe the process of "going public" as well as its advantages and disadvantages and the various simplified registrations and exemptions from registration available to small businesses.

- Going public involves (1) choosing the underwriter, (2) negotiating a letter of intent, (3) preparing the registration statement, (4) filing with the SEC, and (5) meeting state requirements.

- Rather than go through the complete registration process, some companies use one of the simplified registration options and exemptions available to small companies: Regulations S-B and S-K, Regulation D, SCOR, Section 4(6), Rule 147 intrastate offerings, and Regulation A.

4. Describe the various sources of debt capital and the advantages and disadvantages of each: banks, asset-based lenders, vendors (trade credit), equipment suppliers, commercial finance companies, savings-and-loan associations, stockbrokers, insurance companies, credit unions, bonds, private placements, Small Business Investment Companies (SBICs) and Small Business Lending Companies (SBLCs).

- Commercial banks offer the greatest variety of loans, although they are conservative lenders.

Typical short-term bank loans include commercial loans, lines of credit, discounting accounts receivable, inventory financing, and floor planning.

- Trade credit is used extensively by small businesses as a source of financing. Vendors and suppliers commonly finance sales to businesses for 30, 60, or even 90 days.

- Equipment suppliers offer small businesses financing similar to trade credit but with slightly different terms.

- Commercial finance companies offer many of the same types of loans that banks do, but they are more risk oriented in their lending practices. They emphasize accounts-receivable financing and inventory loans.

- Savings-and-loan associations specialize in loans to purchase real property—commercial and industrial mortgages—for up to 30 years.

- Stock brokerage houses offer loans to prospective entrepreneurs at lower interest rates than banks because they have high-quality, liquid collateral—stocks and bonds in the borrower's portfolio.

- Small Business Investment Companies are privately owned companies licensed and regulated by the SBA that qualify for SBA loans to be invested in or loaned to small businesses.

- Small Business Lending Companies make only intermediate- and long-term loans that are guaranteed by the SBA.

5. Identify the various federal loan programs aimed at small businesses.

- The Economic Development Administration, a branch of the Commerce Department, makes loan guarantees to create and expand small businesses in economically depressed areas.

- The Department of Housing and Urban Development extends grants (such as Community Development Block Grants) to cities that, in turn, lend and grant money to small businesses in an attempt to strengthen the local economy.

- The Department of Agriculture's Rural Business-Cooperative Service loan program is designed to create nonfarm employment opportunities in rural areas through loans and loan guarantees.

- The Small Business Innovation Research Program involves 11 federal agencies that award cash grants or long-term contracts to small companies wanting to initiate or to expand their R&D efforts.

- The Small Business Technology Transfer Program allows researchers at universities, federally funded R&D centers, and nonprofit research institutions to join forces with small businesses and develop commercially promising ideas.

6. Describe the various loan programs available from the Small Business Administration.

- Almost all SBA loan activity is in the form of loan guarantees rather than direct loans. Popular SBA programs include: the SBA *Express* program, the Patriot *Express* program, the 7(a) loan guaranty program, the Section 504 Certified Development Company program, the Microloan program, the CAPLine program, the Export Working Capital program, and the Disaster Loan program.

- Many state and local loan and development programs, such as capital access programs, revolving loan funds, and community development financial institutions, complement those sponsored by federal agencies.

7. Explain other methods of financing a business, including factoring, leasing assets, and using credit cards.

- Business owners can get the capital they need by factoring accounts receivable, leasing equipment instead of buying it, or even using credit cards.

Discussion Questions

1. Why is it so difficult for most small business owners to raise the capital needed to start, operate, or expand their ventures?
2. What is capital?
3. Define equity financing. What advantage does it offer over debt financing?
4. What is the most common source of equity funds in a typical small business? If an owner lacks sufficient equity capital to invest in the firm, what options are available for raising it?
5. What guidelines should an entrepreneur follow if friends and relatives choose to invest in her business?
6. What is an angel investor? Assemble a brief profile of the typical private investor. How can entrepreneurs locate potential angels to invest in their businesses?
7. What advice would you offer an entrepreneur about to strike a deal with a private investor to avoid problems?

8. What types of businesses are most likely to attract venture capital? What investment criteria do venture capitalists use when screening potential businesses? How do these compare to the typical angel's criteria?

9. How do venture capital firms operate? Describe their procedure for screening investment proposals.

10. Summarize the major exemptions and simplified registrations available to small companies wanting to make public offerings of their stock.

11. What role do commercial banks play in providing debt financing to small businesses? Outline and briefly describe the major types of short-, intermediate-, and long-term loans commercial banks offer.

12. What is trade credit? How important is it as a source of debt financing to small firms?

13. What function do SBICs serve? How does an SBIC operate? What methods of financing do SBICs rely on most heavily?

14. Briefly describe the loan programs offered by the following:
    a. Economic Development Administration
    b. Department of Housing and Urban Development
    c. Department of Agriculture
    d. Local development companies

15. Explain the purpose and the methods of operation of the Small Business Innovation Research Program and the Small Business Technology Transfer Program.

16. What is a factor? How does the typical factor operate? Explain the advantages and the disadvantages of using factors as a source of funding.

17. What role do credit cards play in financing business start-ups? Explain the advantages and disadvantages of using credit cards to finance the start-up costs of a small business.

Business Plan Pro™

One reason for creating a business plan is to secure funding. Your business plan can be an excellent communication tool for convincing lenders and investors that your company is an attractive investment with a bright future.

Business Plan Exercises

Consider the financial needs of your company. Do you need start-up funding to purchase equipment, make building improvements, or for other reasons? Will your business require additional working capital based on your cash flow projections? Does your business need additional financing for growth? If there is a need to raise capital, your business plan can help clarify those needs and formulate a strategy for raising it.

On the Web

If you need start-up or growth capital for your venture, visit www.pearsonhighered.com/scarborough, click on Chapter 3, and review these financing options. Determine whether these sources may be of use as you explore financing opportunities. You will also find information regarding bootstrap and nontraditional funding.

Sample Plans

Review your favorite sample plans and note the capital needs in the financial section. If you are creating a start-up plan, you may also want to review these sample plans:

- Elsewares Promotional
- Westbury Storage, Inc.

  If you will be searching for financing for an ongoing business, these plans may be of interest:

- Coach House Bed & Breakfast
- Bioring SA (second-round financing)

These plans present financial information that may give you ideas on how to best communicate your financial needs. Use approaches that your audience will find enticing. Lenders want to confirm that you will be able to repay your loan on time. Investors want to learn about the growth and earning potential of your business. Leverage each aspect of the financial section—the break-even analysis, projected profit and loss, projected cash flow, and projected balance sheet and business ratios—that you deem valuable for your financial audience.

In the Software

Open your business plan in *Business Plan Pro* and go to the Financial Plan section. You may want to begin by providing an overview of your financial situation and needs. State the relevant assumptions about the financial environment. These assumptions will help to identify general facts about your plan, such as anticipated economic conditions, current short- and long-term interest rates, expected tax rates, personnel expenses, cash expenses, sales on credit, or any areas. Let the software lead you through this section. Next, assess the type and the amount of funding that you will need. Do you anticipate that the business will need short- or long-term financing? Are you going to bring in capital through a loan or through investors? If you are adding investors, what will be their percentage of the total ownership? How does this affect your ownership position? What role will the investors play in the business? These questions will be important to address in this section of your business plan. Make certain this section clearly tells your financial story. It is critical to provide relevant information that will be meaningful to others who will review your plan for investment or loan purposes.

Building Your Business Plan

One of the most valuable aspects of developing the financial section of your business plan is to assess the company's financial needs, describe the use of the funds to meet those needs, and make certain that you can live with the consequences of these decisions. Keep in mind that potential lenders and investors will also assess the qualifications of your management team, the growth rate of the industry, your proposed exit strategy, and other factors as they judge the financial stability and potential of your venture. Your business plan may serve as a "financial road map" to analyze your funding alternatives and determine the most attractive options available. Test each alternative against your plan to assess its viability and fit with your venture's financial needs.

Beyond the Classroom...

1. Interview several local business owners about how they financed their businesses. Where did their initial capital come from? Ask the following questions:

   - How did you raise your starting capital? What percentage did you supply?

   - What percentage was debt capital and what percentage was equity capital?

   - Which of the sources of funds described in this chapter do you use?

   - How much money did you need to launch your businesses? Where did subsequent capital come from? What advice do you offer others seeking capital?

2. Contact a local private investor and ask him or her to address your class. (You may have to search to locate one!) What kinds of businesses does this angel prefer to invest in? What screening criteria does he or she use? How are the deals typically structured?

3. Contact a local venture capitalist and ask him or her to address your class. What kinds of businesses does his or her company invest in? What screening criteria does the company use? How are deals typically structured?

4. Invite an investment banker or a financing expert from a local accounting firm to address your class about the process of taking a company public. What do they look for in a potential IPO candidate? What is the process, and how long does it usually take?

5. Describing the changes that a financial crisis created in the banking business, one small business financial adviser says, "Banks may be open to making loans, but they're still scared of making bad loans." How has this attitude affected entrepreneurs' access to bank financing? Contact a local banker who works with small businesses and ask him or her how the small business lending market has changed over the last five years. What steps can entrepreneurs take to increase the likelihood that a bank will approve their loan requests?

6. Interview the administrator of a financial institution program offering a method of financing with which you are unfamiliar and prepare a short report on its method of operation.

7. Contact your state's economic development board and prepare a report on the financial assistance programs it offers small businesses.

8. Go to the "IPO Home" section of the Web site for Renaissance Capital ("www.renaissancecapital.com/ipohome/marketwatch.aspx) and explore the details of a company that is involved in making an initial public offering. View some of the documents the company has filed with the SEC, especially the IPO filing. Prepare a brief report on the company. What is its business? Who are its major competitors? How fast is the industry growing? What risk factors has the company identified? How much money does it plan to raise in the IPO? What is the anticipated IPO stock price? How many shares of stock will the company sell in the IPO? Would you buy this company's stock? Explain.

Endnotes

1. William J. Dennis Jr., *National Small Business Poll: Growth-External Impediments*, National Federation of Independent Businesses, Volume 11, Issue 1, 2011, p. 15.
2. Dayan Gupta, "The Right Fit," *Wall Street Journal*, May 22, 1995, p. R8.
3. Aliza Pilar Sherman, "The Opposite Sex," *Entrepreneur*, September 2002, p. 36.
4. U. N. Umesh and Patrick Criteser, "Venture Capital's Foul Weather Friends," *Wall Street Journal*, January 14, 2003, p. B13; "Press Releases," Northwest Energy Efficiency Alliance, http://www.nwalliance.org/news/pressreleases.asp.
5. Emily Glazer, "Finding New Investors, in 140 Characters or Less," *Wall Street Journal*, August 22, 2011, http://online.wsj.com/article/SB10001424052702304066504576349331437407542.html.
6. Kasey Wehrum, "Angel Investing 2009," *Inc.*, January/February 2009, p. 85.
7. Gwen Moran, "Wardrobe Change," *Entrepreneur*, September 2011, p. 87.
8. *Frequently Asked Questions about Small Business Finance*, Small Business Administration Office of Advocacy, September 2011, p. 2.

9. J. Lynn Lunsford, "Eclipse Ousts Raburn to Win Financing," *Wall Street Journal*, July 29, 2008, p. B3; Eric Anderson, "Sale of Eclipse Aviation's Assets Gets Judge's Approval," *Albany Times Union*, January 20, 2009, http://blogs .timesunion.com/business/?p=7523; Andy Pasztor, "Eclipse Aviation Files for Chapter 11," Wall Street Journal, November 26, 2008, http://online.wsj.com/article/ SB122765456029258007.html.

10. Douglas McMillan, "Google's Historic IPO Run: Beatable," *Business Week*, August 16, 2007, http://www.businessweek .com/technology/content/aug2007/tc20070816_081016 .htm?chan=technology_technology+index+page_top+stories; Robert Andrews, "Google Gamble," *I.T. Wales*, May 17, 2004, http://www.itwales.com/998765.htm.

11. Elizabeth Fenner, "How to Raise the Cash You Need," *Money Guide*, Summer 1991, p. 45.

12. "Start-Ups, Small Firms Tap Savings," *Wall Street Journal*, April 20, 2011, http://blogs.wsj.com/in-charge/2011/04/20/ start-ups-small-firms-tap-savings.

13. Alicia M. Robb and David T. Robinson, *The Kauffman Firm Survey*, Kauffman Foundation, November 2008, p. 10.

14. Wayne Mullins, "7 Rules for Successful Bootstrapping," *American Express OPEN Forum*, July 13, 2011, http://www.openforum.com/articles/7-rules-for-successful-bootstrapping.

15. Josh Hyatt, "Numbers Junkie Changes Career," *Money*, May 25, 2011, http://money.cnn.com/2011/05/25/pf/entreprenuer_ changes_careers.moneymag/index.htm; Kate Lister, "Risky Business," Entrepreneur, April 2011, p. 86.

16. Susan Solovic, "Need Funds: What about Family and Friends?" *Up and Running*, August 2, 2011, http://upandrunning.bplans .com/2011/08/02/need-funds-what-about-family-and-friends; "Profile: Leslie H. Wexner," *Forbes*, 2011, http://people.forbes .com/profile/leslie-h-wexner/49445.

17. *Global Entrepreneurship Monitor: National Entrepreneurship Assessment-United States of America, 2004-2005 Executive Report*, Global Entrepreneurship Research Association, 2006, p. 22.

18. Stephen L. Rosenstein, "Use Caution with Family Loans for Your Business," *Baltimore Sun*, August 10, 2008, http:// www.baltimoresun.com/business/bal-bz.ml .biztip10aug10,cs-bearstoday,6345879.column.

19. Paul Kvinta, "Frogskins, Shekels, Bucks, Moolah, Cash, Simoleans, Dough, Dinero: Everybody Wants It. Your Business Needs It. Here's How to Get It," Smart Business, August 2000, pp. 74–89.

20. Emily Maltby, "Tappnig the Crowd for Funds," *Wall Street Journal*, December 9, 2010, p. B5.

21. Sarah E. Needleman and Angus Loten, "When 'Friending' Becomes a Source of Start-Up Funds," *Wall Street Journal*, November 1, 2011, p. B1.

22. Joseph R. Bell, Kenneth M. Huggins, and Christine McClatchey, "Profiling the Angel Investor," presented at Small Business Institute Director's Association Conference, February 7, 2002, San Diego, CA, p. 1; "Biography: Laurance Spelman Rockefeller," InfoPlease.com, http://www .infoplease.com/ipa/A0771997.html.

23. Mark Whitehouse, "Shortage of Capital Costs Firm," *Wall Street Journal*, November 19, 2010, p. B8.

24. Pamela Sherrid, "Angels of Capitalism," *U.S. News & World Report*, October 13, 1997, pp. 43–45.

25. Jeffrey Sohl, "The Angel Investor Market in 2011: The Recovery Continues," Center for Venture Research, University of New Hampshire, April 3, 2012, p. 1.

26. Gwen Moran, "Looking to Angels," *Entrepreneur*, March 2011, p. 68; Lena Rao, "Daily Grommet Raises $3.4 Million for Invention Marketplace," *Tech Crunch*, April 15, 2010, http://techcrunch.com/2010/04/15/ daily-grommet-raises-3-4-million-for-invention-marketplace.

27. Jeffrey Sohl, "The Angel Investor Market in 2010: A Market on the Rebound," Center for Venture Research, University of New Hampshire, April 12, 2011, p. 1.

28. Robert Wiltbank and Warren Boeker, "Returns to Angel Investors in Groups," Angel Capital Education Foundation, November 2007, http://www.angelcapitaleducation.org/ dir_downloads/resources/RSCH_-_ACEF_-_Returns_to_ Angel_Investor_in_Groups.pdf.

29. "Raising Funds," *Inc.*, November 2008, pp. 69–70.

30. Jeffrey Sohl, "The Angel Investor Market in 2010: A Market on the Rebound," Center for Venture Research, University of New Hampshire, April 12, 2011, p. 2.

31. Robert E. Wilbank and Warren Boeker, "Angel Performance Project," Angel Capital Education Foundation, November 2007, http://www.angelcapitalassociation.org/dir_downloads/ resources/RSCH_-_ACEF_-_Returns_to_Angel_Investors_ PPT.pdf.

32. "What Is the Average Closing Time to Receive Financing?," *Jian Business Power Tools*, http://www.jian.com/ library-of-business-information/f252/venture-capital/what -is-the-average-closing-time-it-takes-between-receiving-a.php.

33. Josh Hyatt, "More Guardian, Less Angel," *CFO*, September 2008, p. 45.

34. Doug Steiner, "Venture Capitalists Died and Became Angels," *Globe and Mail*, September 15, 2011, http://www.theglobeandmail.com/report-on-business/small-business/sb-money/business-funding/ venture-capitalists-died-and-became-angels/article2166990.

35. Josh Hyatt, "More Guardian, Less Angel," *CFO*, September 2008, pp. 41–45.

36. Doug Steiner, "Venture Capitalists Died and Became Angels," *Globe and Mail*, September 15, 2011, http://www.theglobeandmail.com/report-on-business/small-business/sb-money/business-funding/ venture-capitalists-died-and-became-angels/article2166990.

37. Rudolph Bell, "Investors Help Bring a Vision into Focus," *Greenville News*, June 12, 2011, p. 1E–2E.

38. "About ACA," Angel Capital Association, http://www .angelcapitalassociation.org/dir_about/overview.aspx.

39. Robert Wiltbank and Warren Boeker, "Returns to Angel Investors in Groups," Angel Capital Education Foundation, November 2007, http://www.angelcapitaleducation.org/ dir_downloads/resources/RSCH_-_ACEF_-_Returns_to_ Angel_Investor_in_Groups.pdf.

40. Carole Carlson and Prabal Chakrabarti, "Venture Capital Opportunities in Secondary Cities: Issues and Opportunities for Impact," Federal Reserve Bank of Boston, April 2007, p. 3.

41. *Venture Impact: The Economic Importance of Venture Backed Companies to the U.S. Economy*, 4th ed. (Arlington, VA: National Venture Capital Association, 2007), pp. 8–9.

42. Alexander Sliwinski, "Angry Birds Downloaded a Billion Times," *Joystiq*, May 9, 2012, http://www.joystiq .com/2012/05/09/angry-birds-downloaded-a-billion-times; Arild Moen and Nick Wingfield, "Seed Money for Maker of 'Angy Birds,'" *Wall Street Journal*, March 11, 2011, p. B1; "Profile: Rovio Mobile," Crunch Base, http://www.crunch-base.com/company/rovio-mobile; Robin Wauters, "Angry Birds Maker Rovio Raises $42 Million from Accel, Atomico, and Felicis," *Tech Crunch*, March 10, 2011, http://techcrunch .com/2011/03/10/angry-birds-maker-rovio-raises-42-million-from-accel-atomico-and-felicis.

43. "Historical Trend Data," MoneyTree Report, PriceWaterhouseCoopers, National Venture Capital Association, and Thomson Reuters, January 2012, https://www.pwcmoney-tree.com/MTPublic/ns/nav.jsp?page=historical.

44. William D. Bygrave with Mark Quill, *Global Entrepreneurship Monitor: 2006 Financing Report*, Global Entrepreneurship Research Association, 2006, p. 23.

45. Dee Power and Brian E. Hill, "Venture Capital Survey," *The Capital Connection*, 2008, http://www.capital-connection.com/survey-close.html.

46. Janet Effland, "How to Bet on the Next Big Thing," *Business 2.0*, December 2002/January 2003, p. 90.

47. Thea Singer, "Where the Money Is," *Inc.*, September 2000, pp. 52–55; National Venture Capital Association, http://www.nvca.org; PriceWaterhouseCoopers MoneyTree Survey, http://www.pwcmoneytree.com/moneytree/index.jsp.

48. Mabel Brecrick-Okereke, "Report to U.N. Cautions That Focus on Venture Capital Can Hinder Entrepreneurial Economy," United Nations Association of the United States of America, http://unusa.school.aol.com/newsroom/NewsReleases/ean_venture.asp; Cara Cannella, "Where Seed Money Really Comes From," *Inc.*, August 2003, p. 26.

49. "Investments by Industry," PriceWaterhouseCoopers MoneyTree Survey, https://www.pwcmoneytree.com/MTPublic/ns/nav.jsp?page=industry.

50. Kate O'Sullivan, "Not-So-Easy Money, *CFO*, October 2005, p. 20.

51. Rebecca Buckman,"Baby Sitting for Start-Ups," *Wall Street Journal*, March 13, 2006, p. B3.

52. Andrea Poe, "Venturing Out," *Entrepreneur*, September 2008, p. 31.

53. Spencer E. Ante, "Big Price for Flash-Sale Site," *Wall Street Journal*, December 8, 2011, p. B8; Courtney Rubin, "Afer Massive Pivot, Fab.com Raises $40 Million," *American Express OPEN Forum*, December 9, 2011, http://www.openforum.com/articles/after-massive-pivot-fabcom-raises-40-million.

54. John Cook, "Venture-Backed IPOS and M&A Deals Decline in 2011, but It's Not All Bad News," *GeekWire*, January 3, 2012, http://www.geekwire.com/2012/venturebacked-companies-complete-ipos-ma-deals-decline; Rebecca Buckman, "BabySitting for Start-Ups," *Wall Street Journal*, March 13, 2006, pp. B1, B3.

55. Scott Austin, "LinkedIn's IPO: What Everone's Stakes Are Now Worth," *Wall Street Journal*, May 18, 2011, http://blogs.wsj.com/venturecapital/2011/05/18/linkedins-ipo-what-everyones-stakes-are-now-worth; "Profile: LinkedIn," *Crunch Base*, http://www.crunchbase.com/company/linkedin; Rebecca Buckman, "LinkedIn's Venture-Capitalist Connection," *Wall Street Journal*, June 18, 2008, p. B6.

56. Christopher Hann, "The Importance of Aesthetics," *Entrepreneur*, September 2011, p. 26.

57. Dave Pell, "What's Old Is New Again," *FSB*, July/August 2000, p. 122.

58. "Corporate VC Stats," National Venture Capital Association, September 30, 2011, http://www.nvca.org/index.php?option=com_content&view=article&id=344&Itemid=103.

59. Gwen Moran, "Can Google Get Your Back?" *Entrepreneur*, August 2011, p. 76; "Portfolio: Rumble," Google Ventures, http://www.googleventures.com/rumble.html; Josh Constine, "Rumble to Build and Publish Games Using $15M Series A from Google Ventures and Khosla," Tech *Crunch*, December 1, 2011, http://techcrunch.com/2011/12/01/rumble-to-build-and-publish-games-using-15m-series-a-from-google-ventures-and-khosla.

60. Jay R. Ritter, "Initial Public Offerings: Tables Updated through 2011," University of Florida, December 22, 2011, p. 19.

61. Burt Helm, "So, You Think You're Going Public?," *Inc.*, September 2011, pp. 162–168; Julianne Peppitone, "Zynga

Shares Close below IPO Price," *CNN Money*, December 16, 2011, http://money.cnn.com/2011/12/16/technology/zynga_ipo/index.htm.

62. Nathan Olivarez-Giles, "LinkedIn Values Itself at about $3 Billion before IPO," *Los Angeles Times*, May 9, 2011, http://latimesblogs.latimes.com/technology/2011/05/linkedin-value-3-billion.html.

63. Jay R. Ritter, "Initial Public Offerings: Tables Updated through 2011," University of Florida, December 22, 2011, p. 15.

64. Jay R. Ritter, "Initial Public Offerings: Tables Updated through 2011," University of Florida, December 22, 2011, p. 8.

65. Burt Helm, "So, You Think You're Going Public?," *Inc.*, September 2011, pp. 162–168.

66. Jay R. Ritter, "Initial Public Offerings: Tables Updated through 2011," University of Florida, December 22, 2011, p. 18.

67. "The More the Merrier," CFO, October 2005, p. 18.

68. Shayndi Raice and Randall Smith, "Zygna Sets IPO Price," *Wall Street Journal*, December 16, 2011, p. B2; "Zynga Prices High-Profile Deal at $10 in Largest Tech IPO since Google," *Renaissance Capital IPO Home*, December 15, 2011, http://www.renaissancecapital.com/ipohome/news/Zynga-prices-high-profile-deal-at-$10-in-largest-tech-IPO-since-Google-10760.html.

69. Jay R. Ritter, "Initial Public Offerings: Tables Updated through 2011," University of Florida, December 22, 2011, p. 11.

70. Burt Helm, "So, You Think You're Going Public?," *Inc.*, September 2011, pp. 162-168; "LinkedIn Prices IPO at $45, High End of Revised Range," *Renaissance Capital IPO Home*, May 18, 2011, http://www.renaissancecapital.com/ipohome/news/LinkedIn-prices-IPO-at-$45-high-end-of-revised-range-9638.html.

71. Form D: Ligatt Security International, March 23, 2010, http://attrition.org/errata/charlatan/gregory_evans/ligatt04/LIGATT-SEC-Form-D.pdf.

72. Telephone interview with David Barash, Ben & Jerry's Homemade.

73. *Frequently Asked Questions about Small Business Finance*, Small Business Administration Office of Advocacy, September 2011, p. 1.

74. *2011 Mid-Year Economic Report*, National Small Business Association, September 2011, p. 9.

75. Stacy Cowley, "Message to Obama: Send Loans Fast," *CNNMoney*, November 16, 2008, http://money.cnn.com/2008/11/14/smallbusiness/loans_needed_asap.smb/index.htm.

76. John Tozzi, "Credit Cards Replace Small Business Loans," *Business Week*, August 20, 2008, http://www.business-week.com/smallbiz/content/aug2008/sb20080820_288348.htm?chan=smallbiz_smallbiz+index+page_top+small+business+stories.

77. Victoria Williams, "Small Business Lending: Third Quarter 2011," *Quarterly Lending Bulletin*, Small Business Administration Office of Advocacy, December 28, 2011, p.1.

78. *Small Business Lending in the United States, 2009–2010*, Small Business Administration, Office of Advocacy, February 2011, p. 20.

79. William J. Dennis Jr., *Small Business Credit in a Deep Recession*, National Federation of Independent Businesses, February 2010, p. 1.

80. Emily Maltby, "Some Players Still Sidelined in Lending Game," *Wall Street Journal*, November 4, 2010, http://online.wsj.com/article/SB100014240527487044627045755906305996632148.html; Natasha Ball, "Schlotzsky's Goes for a

Triple-Brand Score in Mid-Town," *Tulsa Business Journal*, March 14, 2011, http://tulsabusiness.com/main.asp?SectionID=3&SubSectionID=47&ArticleID=52438.

81. *Small Business Performance and Credit Conditions in the Current Recession*, Democratic Policy Committee, December 2, 2009, p. 10.

82. "Biz2Credit Small Business Lending Index for December 2011 Finds Loan Approval Rates Rose at Small Banks and Alternative Lenders, Dipped at Big Banks," *Biz2Credit*, January 2012, http://www.biz2credit.com/january2012/biz2Credit-small-business-lending-index-for-december2011.

83. Daniel M. Clark, "Banks and Bankability," *Venture*, September 1989, p. 29.

84. Ian Mount, "Why It's Getting Harder, and Riskier, to Bet the House," *New York Times*, November 30, 2011, http://www.nytimes.com/2011/12/01/business/smallbusiness/why-business-owners-routinely-bet-the-house-and-why-its-getting-harder-to-do.html.

85. William J. Dennis Jr., *Small Business Credit in a Deep Recession*, National Federation of Independent Businesses, February 2010, p. 1.

86. Louis Uchitelle, "Small Businesses Feeling the Chill," *New York Times*, October 2, 2008, http://www.nytimes.com/2008/10/02/business/smallbusiness/02sbiz.html?em.

87. Kelly K. Spors and Simona Covel, "When a Bank Loan Isn't an Option," *Wall Street Journal*, May 1, 2008, p. B9.

88. "Featured Success Stories: Dishing Up the American Dream," CDC Small Business Finance, http://cdcloans.com/featured-success-stories.

89. *U.S. Credit Union Profile*, Credit Union National Association, September 2011, p. 5; "Small Business Lending Index for December 2011 Finds Loan Approval Rates Rose at Small Banks and Alternative Lenders, Dipped at Big Banks," *Biz2Credit*, January 2012, http://www.biz2credit.com/january2012/biz2Credit-small-business-lending-index-for-december2011.

90. Gwen Moran, "The Credit Union Option," *Entrepreneur*, July 2010, p. 85.

91. Adam Belz, "Credit Unions Growing Commercial Lending Business," *USA Today*, July 10, 2011, http://www.usatoday.com/money/industries/banking/2011-07-11-credit-unions-small-business_n.htm.

92. *SBIC Program Overview*, National Association of Small Business Investment Companies, February 6, 2012, p. 3.

93. "U.S. Small Business Investment Company Program: History and Highlights," National Association of Small Business Investment Companies, http://www.nasbic.org/?page=SBIC_Program_History.

94. *SBIC Program Overview*, National Association of Small Business Investment Companies, February 6, 2012, p. 3.

95. *SBIC Program Overview*, National Association of Small Business Investment Companies, February 6, 2012, p. 3.

96. "A 50th Anniversary Tribute to the SBIC Program," National Association of Small Business Investment Companies, 2012, http://www.nasbic.org/?page=50th_Video; Melissa Castro, "Milking Lansinoh for mOmma Details," *Washington Business Journal*, January 7, 2011, http://www.bizjournals.com/washington/blog/2011/01/milking-lansinoh-for-momma-details.html.

97. "NECOG-DC Revolving Loan Fund Success Stories: Leola Groceries," Northeast Council of Governments Development Corporation, Aberdeen, SD, http://necog.org/SuccessStories.asp.

98. Angelia Davis, "Filling a Need," *Greenville News*, November 6, 2011, pp. 1E–2E.

99. "Business Programs Success Stories: North Dakota," U.S. Department of Agriculture, Rural Development, http://www.rurdev.usda.gov/rbs/busp/ss/ssbpnd.htm.

100. "Past Awards," Small Business Innovation Research/Small Business Technology Transfer, http://www.sbir.gov/past-awards?program=SBIR.

101. Charles Wessner, "An Assessment of the SBIR Program," National Research Council, http://books.nap.edu/openbook.php?record_id=11989&page=12, pp. 91–107.

102. "Whole Tree Taking a Wholly Different Approach," *NCIIA News*, Spring 2010, p. 2; Lee Dye, "Is a Coconut Car Coming Your Way?," *ABC News*, January 21, 2009, http://abcnews.go.com/Technology/story?id=6694602&page=1.

103. "7(a) Gross Loan Approvals," National Association of Government Guaranteed Lenders, September 30, 2011, http://www.naggl.org/AM/Template.cfm?Section=7_a_Gross_Loan_Approvals&Template=/CM/ContentDisplay.cfm&ContentID=16381.

104. *U.S. Small Business Administration Agency Financial Report Fiscal Year 2011*, U.S. Small Business Administration, Washington, DC, p. i.

105. "7(a) Gross Loan Approvals," National Association of Government Guaranteed Lenders, September 30, 2011, http://www.naggl.org/AM/Template.cfm?Section=7_a_Gross_Loan_Approvals&Template=/CM/ContentDisplay.cfm&ContentID=16381.

106. Marie Hernan, "SBA Patriot Express Loans Top $633 Million," *Small Biz Trends*, July 11, 2011, http://smallbiztrends.com/2011/07/sba-patriot-express-loans.html.

107. "Veteran-Owned Business Receives Patriot Express Loan, Contracting Opportunities," U.S. Small Business Administration, Washington, DC, http://www.sba.gov/about-offices-content/2/3159/success-stories/3987; "Veterans Get Access to Capital," *All Business*, March 30, 2008, http://www.allbusiness.com/government/government-support-business-small-assistance/11954188-1.html.

108. *U.S. Small Business Administration Agency Financial Report Fiscal Year 2011*, U.S. Small Business Administration, Washington, DC, p. 9.

109. Emily Maltby, "Small Biz Loan Failure Rate Hits 12%," *CNNMoney*, February 25, 2009, http://money.cnn.com/2009/02/25/smallbusiness/smallbiz_loan_defaults_soar.smb/index.htm.

110. Daniel P. Smith, "Capital Gains," *Pizza Today*, Critical Issues 2012, http://www.pizzatoday.com/Magazines/Year/2012/capital-gains; "Authenticity," Tutta Bella Neapolitan Pizzeria, http://tuttabella.com/vpn.

111. *U.S. Small Business Administration Agency Financial Report Fiscal Year 2011*, U.S. Small Business Administration, Washington, DC, p. 9.

112. "SBA 504 Loan Financing Materials Recovery Facility (MRF) Being Constructed in Union City, Georgia," U.S. Small Business Administration, Washington, DC, http://www.sba.gov/content/sba-504-loan-financing-materials-recovery-facility-mrf-being-constructed-union-city-georgia.

113. *SBA Microloan Program: FY 2007*, Women Impacting Public Policy, http://www.wipp.org/news_details.asp?story_id=204&memberonly=False.

114. "CDFI Success Story: Western Massachusetts Enterprise Fund, Inc: Hot Mama's, Springfield, Massachusetts," The Next American Opportunity, http://www.nextamericanopportunity.org/ffi/sba/successStory.asp.

115. John Golden, "Small Business Big on Exports," *Westfair Online*, May 26, 2011, http://westfaironline.com/2011/13578-small-business-big-on-exports; "Turbofil Awarded Exporter of the Year," *Healthcare Packaging*, May 11, 2011, http://www.healthcarepackaging.com/archives/2011/05/turbofil_awarded_exporter_of_t.php.

116. "SBA Offers Disaster Assistance to California Residents and Businesses Affected by the Los Angeles High Winds,"

California SBDC, December 20, 2011, http://smallbizla
.org/2011/sba-offers-disaster-assistance-to-california-
residents-and-businesses-affected-by-the-los-angeles-high-
winds-3.

117. Ziona Austrian and Zhongcai Zhang, "An Inventory and
Assessment of Pollution Control and Prevention Financing
Programs," Great Lakes Environmental Finance Center,
Levin College of Urban Affairs, Cleveland State University,
http://www.csuohio.edu/glefc/inventor.htm#sba.

118. "Mayor Lee Celebrates Success of Small Business Revolving
Loan Fund," Office of the Mayor, San Francisco, May 16,
2011, http://www.sfmayor.org/index.aspx?page=397.

119. Catherine Clifford, "Community Lenders Hit the Funding
Jackpot," *CNNMoney*, December 23, 2009, http://money.cnn
.com/2009/12/23/smallbusiness/small_business_cdfi_funding/
index.htm.

120. *Annual Asset-Based Lending and Factoring Survey Highlights*, 2010, Commercial Finance Association, April 27,
2011, p. 7.

121. *Annual Asset-Based Lending and Factoring Survey Highlights, 2010*, Commercial Finance Association, April 27,
2011, p. 9.

122. Roberta Reynes, "A Big Factor in Expansion," *Nation's Business*, January 1999, pp. 31–32; Bruce J. Blechman, "The High
Cost of Credit," *Entrepreneur*, January 1993, pp. 22–25.

123. Rich Karlgaard, "Bootstrappers Rule," Forbes, January 12,
2009, p. 25; "Larry Page and Sergey Brin Boigraphy," *Encyclopedia of World Biography*, http://www.notablebiographies
.com/news/Ow-Sh/Page-Larry-and-Brin-Sergey.html.

124. "Finance Your Start-Up with Credit Cards? Google Did,"
Fox Small Business Center, April 27, 2011, http://small-
business.foxbusiness.com/finance-accounting/2011/04/26/
finance-start-credit-cards-google-did.

125. *Frequently Asked Questions about Small Business Finance*,
U.S. Small Business Administration, Office of Advocacy,
September 2011, p. 3; Robert H. Scott III, *The Use of Credit
Card Debt by New Firms*, Kauffman Foundation, August
2009, p. 2.

14

Choosing the Right Location and Layout

Learning Objectives

On completion of this chapter, you will be able to:

1. Explain the stages in the location decision: choosing the region, the state, the city, and the specific site.

2. Describe the location criteria for retail and service businesses.

3. Outline the location options for retail and service businesses: central business districts, neighborhoods, shopping centers and malls, near competitors, inside large retail stores, nontraditional locations, at home, and on the road.

4. Explain the site selection process for manufacturers.

5. Describe the criteria used to analyze the layout and design considerations of a building, including the Americans with Disabilities Act.

6. Explain the principles of effective layouts for retailers, service businesses, and manufacturers.

The more alternatives, the more difficult the choice.

—Abbe' D'Allanival

Good order is the foundation of all things.

—Edmund Burke

Location: A Source of Competitive Advantage

Much like choosing a form of ownership and selecting particular sources of financing, the location decision has far-reaching and often long-lasting effects on a small company's future. Entrepreneurs who choose their locations wisely—with their customers' preferences and their companies' needs in mind—establish an important competitive advantage over rivals who choose their locations haphazardly. Because the availability of qualified workers, tax rates, quality of infrastructure, traffic patterns, quality of life, and many other factors vary from one site to another, the location decision is an important one that can influence the growth rate and the ultimate success of a company. Thanks to widespread digital connectivity, mobile computing, extensive cellular coverage, and affordable air travel, entrepreneurs have more flexibility when choosing a business location than ever before.

The location selection process is like an interactive computer game in which each decision opens the way to make another decision on the way to solving the puzzle. The answer to the puzzle, of course, is the best location for a business. At each step in the decision process, entrepreneurs must analyze how well the characteristics of a particular location match the unique requirements of their businesses. Because of its significant impact on a company, the location decision can be difficult; however, by conducting research and gathering and analyzing information about potential sites, entrepreneurs can find locations that are ideally suited for their businesses. When screening sites for both Disneyland and Disney World, Walt and Roy Disney hired site selection pioneer Buzz Price to conduct exhaustive studies that included a demographic analysis, population growth projections, future highway construction, accessibility, weather patterns, and other relevant factors. The location analysis successfully pinpointed ideal locations for both theme parks; today the two parks host nearly 33 million guests each year. "Buzz nailed both of those locations dead center," says Chip Cleary, head of the International Association of Amusement Parks and Attractions.[1]

The location decision process resembles an inverted pyramid. The first level of the decision is the broadest, requiring an entrepreneur to select a particular region of the country. (We will address locating a business in a foreign country in Chapter 15.) Then an entrepreneur must choose the right state, the right city, and, finally, the right site within the city. The key to selecting the ideal location lies in knowing the factors that are most important to a company's success and then finding a location that satisfies as many of them as possible, particularly those that are most critical. For instance, one of the most important location factors for high-tech companies is the availability of a skilled labor force, and their choice of location reflects this. If physically locating near customers is vital to a company's success, then an entrepreneur's goal is to find a site that makes it most convenient for his or her target customers to do business with the company.

ENTREPRENEURIAL PROFILE: Tony and John Calamunci: Johnny's Lunch When Tony and John Calamunci began selling franchises of the family-owned diner that their grandparents, Johnny and Minnie Colera, started in Brooklyn Square in Jamestown, New York, in 1936 (and that their parents still operate), they realized that opening outlets in areas in which large concentrations of their target customers lived was essential to their success. They hired an experienced franchise veteran, George Goulson, and worked with Pitney-Bowes Software's MapInfo, using geospatial technology to determine the ideal locations for their restaurants, which sell budget-priced meals such as hot dogs, hamburgers, onion rings, and milkshakes. The Calamuncis started by defining their target customers, which they discovered include people in the lower-middle- to upper-middle-income bracket who fall between the ages of 16 and 24 or over 60. Using the software, they identified 72 types of neighborhoods that best match the demographic and psychographic profile of Johnny's Lunch customers. The next step was to find locations that matched the 72 prototype neighborhoods. Managers identified 4,500 areas across the United States that held large concentrations of potential Johnny's Lunch customers (most of whom lived within one mile of the proposed location) and would be good locations for restaurants. "These models increase our ability to pick 'home-run' locations and avoid the site mistakes that can cripple a budding franchise," says Goulson. Johnny's Lunch is launching its franchising effort in and around Toledo, Ohio, which Goulson says is a microcosm of the United States. "Small restaurant owners like us can use location intelligence to prevent mistakes that could cripple franchising plans from the start. They can't afford not to invest in location intelligence."[2] ■

The characteristics that make for an ideal location often vary dramatically from one company to another because of the nature of their business. In the early twentieth century, companies looked for ready supplies of water, raw materials, or access to railroads; today, they are more likely to look for sites that are close to universities and offer high-speed Internet access and accessible airports. In fact, one study concluded that the factors that make an area most suitable for starting and growing small companies included access to dynamic universities, an ample supply of skilled workers, a nearby airport, a temperate climate, and a high quality of life.[3] The key to finding a suitable location is identifying the characteristics that can give a company a competitive edge and then searching out potential sites that meet those criteria.

Choosing the Region

The first step in selecting the best location is to focus on selecting the right region. This requires entrepreneurs to look at the location decision from the "30,000-foot level," as if he or she were in an airplane looking down. In fact, in the early days of their companies, Sam Walton, founder of retail giant Wal-Mart, and Ray Kroc, who built McDonald's into a fast-food giant, actually used private planes to survey the countryside for prime locations for their stores.

ENTREPRENEURIAL PROFILE: Walt Disney: Disney World In 1963, Walt Disney flew over central Florida in a private plane (which is now on display at Disney World) to look at a tract of nondescript swampland as a potential site for Disney World. Disney lacked sufficient space to expand Disneyland in California and, with the help of site selection expert Buzz Price and a group of top managers, established several criteria for the company's second theme park, including a place with good weather throughout most of the year, plenty of land at bargain prices, a location near a major city, and access to major highways and infrastructure for the company's second theme park (dubbed "Project X"). When Disney flew over the intersection of Interstate 4 and Route 192 near Orlando, he knew that he had found the ideal location for Disney World, which now encompasses 30,000 acres, an area that is about the size of San Francisco![4] ■

Which region of the country has the characteristics necessary for a new business to succeed? Above all, entrepreneurs must place their customers first when considering a location. As the experience of Johnny's Lunch suggests, facts and statistics, not speculation, lead entrepreneurs to the best locations for their businesses. Common requirements may include rapid growth in the population of a certain age-group, rising disposable incomes, the existence of necessary infrastructure, an available workforce, and low operating costs. At the broadest level of the location decision, entrepreneurs prefer to locate in regions of the country that are experiencing substantial growth. Every year, many popular business publications prepare reports on the various regions of the nation—which ones are growing, which are stagnant, and which are declining. Studying overall trends in population and business growth gives entrepreneurs an idea of where the action is—and isn't. Questions to consider include the following: How large is the population? How fast is it growing? What is the makeup of overall population? Which segments are growing fastest? Slowest? What is the trend in the population's income? Are other businesses moving into the region? If so, what kind of businesses? Generally, entrepreneurs want to avoid dying regions; they simply cannot support a broad base of potential customers.

One of the first stops entrepreneurs should make when conducting a regional evaluation is the U.S. Census Bureau. Excellent sources of basic demographic and population data include the *U.S. Statistical Abstract* and the *County and City Data Book*. The *U.S. Statistical Abstract* provides entrepreneurs looking for the right location with a multitude of helpful information, ranging from basic population characteristics and income data to poverty rates and energy consumption. Every state also publishes its own statistical abstract, providing the same type of data for its own population. The *County and City Data Book* contains useful statistics on the populations of all of the nation's 3,141 counties and 12,175 cities with populations of 25,000 or more (and even more data for cities with populations that exceed 100,000). *Counties USA* provides similar information in 6,300 data categories and focuses only on the nation's counties. The *State and Metropolitan Area Data Book* includes more than 1,500 data items for individual states, counties, and metropolitan areas. *State and County QuickFacts* offers entrepreneurs easy access to useful statistics for all states and counties and for cities and towns with populations of at least 5,000 people.

At the Census Bureau's Web site (www.census.gov), entrepreneurs researching potential sites can access vital demographic information, such as age, income, educational level, employment level, occupation, ancestry, commuting times, housing data (house value, number of rooms, mortgage or rent status, number of vehicles owned, and so on), and many other characteristics. The Census Bureau's American FactFinder site (http://factfinder2.census.gov) provides easily accessible demographic fact sheets and maps on nearly every community in the United States, including small towns. The Census Bureau's *American Community Survey* provides important annual updates to the decennial census data for cities with populations of at least 65,000 people and three-year estimates for cities with populations of at least 20,000 people. Both the *American FactFinder* and the *American Community Survey* allow entrepreneurs to produce easy-to-read, customizable tables and maps of the information they generate in their searches. The Census Bureau also offers ZIP Code Tabulation Areas, a database of 33,178 ZIP codes across the United States that allows users to create tables and maps of census data by ZIP code. With a little practice, entrepreneurs can prepare customized reports on the potential sites they are considering. These Web-based resources give entrepreneurs instant access to important site location information that only a few years ago would have taken many hours of intense research to compile!

Entrepreneurs also can use nongovernment sources to research potential locations. Zoom-Prospector (www.zoomprospector.com) is a useful Web site that allows entrepreneurs to search for the ideal location using a multitude of factors, including population size, job growth rate, number of patents issued, venture capital invested, education level, household incomes, and proximity to interstate highways, railroads, and airports. Once entrepreneurs locate a city that matches their customer profiles, they find other cities across the United States that have similar profiles with a single mouse click! Entrepreneurs who are considering a particular region can display "heat maps" that visually display the areas that have the highest concentrations of people who have a particular characteristic, such as a bachelor's degree, or the highest household incomes.

ENTREPRENEURIAL PROFILE: Steve Sarowitz: Paylocity Steve Sarowitz, CEO of Paylocity, a provider of human resources and payroll services to small and medium-size businesses, uses ZoomProspector to find the best locations across the United States for the rapidly expanding company's new offices. Sarowitz says that ZoomProspector helps his company answer the important question, Would this be a good market for us? "What's great about ZoomProspector is that we can get so much information about each individual market we are considering—market demographics, which industries are strongest, education levels, and more, "says Sarowitz. Founded in 1997, Paylocity, which is based in Arlington Heights, Illinois, and has appeared on *Inc.*'s list of the 5,000 fastest-growing companies seven times, now has 14 locations and, with ZoomProspector's help, is looking to add more.[5] ∎

Zipskinny (www.zipskinny.com) is a Web site that provides quick census data profiles of various ZIP codes across the United States and allows users to compare the demographic profiles of the people who live in different ZIP codes. The Population Reference Bureau (www.prb.org) provides a detailed breakdown of the most relevant data collected from the most recent census reports. The Population Reference Bureau's DataFinder is a database that includes 244 variables for the United States and 132 variables for 210 other nations. The site includes easy-to-generate maps and charts and helpful articles that discuss the implications of the changing demographic and economic profile of the nation's (and the world's) population, such as the impact of aging baby boomers on business and the composition of the U.S. workforce.

Other helpful resources merit mention as well. *Demographics USA* is a publication that covers the United States, its counties, and its ZIP code areas. This useful publication provides market surveys on various segments of U.S. demographics, including purchasing power, retail sales by type of merchandise, employment and payroll data, and forecasts of economic conditions at both the ZIP code and the county level. The buying power indices in *Demographics USA* indicate an area's purchasing potential for economy products, midpriced products, and premium products. This publication also indicates consumers' spending on particular types of products and services, such as apparel, entertainment, and appliances. Entrepreneurs can use *Demographics USA* to analyze the level of competition in a particular area, assess the sales potential of a particular location, compare consumers' buying power across a dozen categories, and more.

Lifestyle Market Analyst, a four-part annual publication, matches population demographics with lifestyle interests. Section 1 provides demographics and lifestyle information for 210 "Designated Market Areas" across the United States. Section 2 gives demographic and geographic profiles of 77 lifestyle interests that range from avid readers and dieters to wine aficionados and pet owners. Section 3 describes the dominant lifestyle interests for each of the 210 market areas. Section 4 provides comparisons of other activities that correspond with each lifestyle interest. Entrepreneurs can use *Lifestyle Market Analyst* to determine, for example, how likely members of a particular market segment are to own a dog, collect antiques, play golf, own a vacation home, engage in extreme sports, invest in stocks or bonds, or participate in a host of other activities.

Other sources of demographic data include the *Survey of Buying Power*, the *Editor and Publisher Market Guide*, *The American Marketplace: Demographics and Spending Patterns*, *Rand McNally's Commercial Atlas and Marketing Guide*, and *Site Selection* magazine. Sales and Marketing Management's *Survey of Buying Power*, having recently undergone the most extensive overhaul in its 80-year history, provides statistics, rankings, and projections for every county and media market in the United States with demographics segmented by age, race, city, county, and state. This publication, now available only online, also includes current information on retail spending and forecasts for each spending category. The data are divided into 323 metro markets as defined by the Census Bureau and 210 media markets, which are television or broadcast markets defined by Nielsen Media Research. The *Survey* also includes several unique statistics. Effective buying income (EBI) is a measure of disposable income, and the buying power index (BPI), for which the *Survey* is best known, is a unique, composite measure of spending power that takes population, EBI, and retail sales into account to determine the ability of customers in a particular to buy goods and services.

The *Editor and Publisher Market Guide* is similar to the *Survey of Buying Power* but provides additional information on markets. The *Guide* includes detailed economic and demographic information, ranging from population and income statistics to information on climate and transportation networks for all 3,141 counties in the United States and more than 1,600 key cities in both the United States and Canada.

The American Marketplace: Demographics and Spending Patterns provides useful demographic information in 11 areas: attitudes, education, health, housing, income, labor force, living arrangements, population, spending, time use, and wealth. Most of the tables in the book are derived from government statistics, but *The American Marketplace* also includes a discussion of the data in each table as well as a forecast of future trends. Many users say that the primary advantage of *The American Marketplace* is its ease of use.

The *Commercial Atlas and Marketing Guide* reports on more than 120,000 places in the United States, many of which are not available through Census reports. This guide, which includes two volumes, one an index and the other the actual guide, covers 11 economic indicators for every major geographic market; tables showing population trends, income, buying power, trade, and manufacturing activity; and large cross-reference maps. Its format makes collecting large amounts of valuable data on any region in the country (and specific areas within a region) easy.

Site Selection magazine (www.siteselection.com) is another useful resource for entrepreneurs that helps entrepreneurs determine the best locations for their companies. Issues contain articles that summarize incentive programs offered by various states, profiles of each region of the country, and the implications of locating in different states. One recent issue featured a story on the top "micropolitan" areas in the United States (the 526 rural counties in which the population of the largest city is less than 50,000 people) and the benefits of locating businesses in them.

A growing number of entrepreneurs are relying on geographic information systems (GIS), powerful software programs that combine map drawing with database management capability, to pinpoint the ideal location for their businesses. GIS packages allow users to search through virtually any database containing a wealth of information and plot the results on a map of the country, an individual state, a specific city, or even a single city block. The visual display highlights what otherwise would be indiscernible business trends. For instance, using GIS programs, entrepreneurs can plot their existing customer base on a map with various colors representing the different population densities. Then they can zoom in on those areas with the greatest concentration of customers, mapping a detailed view of ZIP code borders or even city streets. GIS street files originate in the Census Bureau's Topographically Integrated Geographic Encoding Referencing

(TIGER) file, which contains map information broken down for every square foot of Metropolitan Statistical Areas. TIGER files contain the name and location of every street in the country and detailed block statistics for the 345 largest urban areas. In essence, TIGER is a massive database of geographic features such as roads, railways, and political boundaries across the entire United States that, when linked with mapping programs and demographic databases, gives entrepreneurs incredible power to pinpoint existing and potential customers on easy-to-read digital maps. Many states and counties across the United States now provide GIS files online that allow entrepreneurs to identify sites that meet certain location criteria for their businesses.

The Small Business Administration's Small Business Development Center (SBDC) program (www.sba.gov/content/small-business-development-centers-sbdcs) also offers location analysis assistance to entrepreneurs. These centers, numbering 1,000 nationwide, provide training, counseling, research, and other specialized assistance to entrepreneurs and existing business owners on a wide variety of subjects—all at no charge! To locate the SBDC nearest you, contact the Small Business Administration office in your state or go to the Association of Small Business Development Centers Web page at www.asbdc-us.org.

For entrepreneurs interested in demographic and statistical profiles of international cities, Euromonitor International (www.euromonitor.com) and the Organization for Economic Development and Cooperation (www.oecd.org) are excellent resources.

Once an entrepreneur has identified the best region of the country, the next step is to evaluate the individual states in that region.

Choosing the State

Every state has an economic development office working to recruit new businesses. Even though the publications produced by these offices will be biased in favor of locating in that state, they still are an excellent source of information and can help entrepreneurs assess the business climate in each state. Some of the key issues to explore include the laws, regulations, and taxes that govern businesses, costs of operation, workforce availability, and incentives or investment credits the state may offer to businesses that locate there.

ENTREPRENEURIAL PROFILE: Andrew Peykof: Niagara Bottling Company Niagara Bottling Company, a family-owned producer of bottled water founded in Ontario, California, in 1963 by Andrew Peykoff, recently selected Mooresville, North Carolina, as the home for its tenth bottling operation. After exploring locations in at least six other states and other parts of North Carolina, the company, now led by Andy Peykoff II, decided to build a new $45 million, 310,000-square-foot factory in the Mooresville Business Park. "Of the many factors we consider, estimated annual operating costs and start-up costs are two of the most significant," says Niagara's Derieth Sutton. State and local agencies also enticed Niagara with an incentive package. Sutton admits that incentives are "extremely important" in location decisions but that Niagara does not "choose a site based purely on incentives. Although incentives do not make a bad location good, they have an impact on annual operating and start-up costs." The company also cited the available workforce as an attractive feature of its Mooresville location, noting that its "family values, a strong work ethic, and great attitudes" would enable Niagara to build "a world-class team."[6] ∎

Factors that entrepreneurs often consider when choosing a location include proximity to markets, proximity to raw materials, wage rates, quantity and quality of the labor supply, general business climate, tax rates, Internet access, and total operating costs.

PROXIMITY TO MARKETS Locating close to markets they plan to serve is extremely critical for manufacturers, especially when the cost of transformation of finished goods is high relative to their value. Locating near customers is necessary to remain competitive. Service firms also often find that proximity to their clients is essential. If a business is involved in repairing equipment used in a specific industry, it should be located where that industry is concentrated. The more specialized a business or the greater the relative cost of transporting the product to the customer, the more likely it is that proximity to the market will be of critical importance in the location decision.

States in the southwestern corner of the United States have become home to many companies in the growing renewable energy industry, particularly those in the solar power sector.

ENTREPRENEURIAL PROFILE: Richard Thompson: Power-One Power-One, a Camarillo, California–based provider of photovoltaic and wind inverters, which are key components in many solar and wind energy systems, selected Phoenix, Arizona, as the site for its first manufacturing plant in the United States. Power-One considered locations in Texas, New Mexico, California, and states in the north-central United States before settling on Arizona, where the company found an abandoned factory it could remodel for just $11 million. Because Arizona boasts 300 days of sunshine a year, the state is home to many companies that sell solar energy systems, something that proved to be the key factor in Power-One's location decision. "Our equipment is very heavy, and we rely on trucking," says CEO Richard Thompson. "We needed easy access to our customers in the photovoltaic corridor of the Southwest and to the wind-energy corridor in the north-central region." Power-One already is considering building a dedicated wind inverter plant in the Great Lakes region so that it can be closer to its wind-power customers.[7] ■

PROXIMITY TO NEEDED RAW MATERIALS If a business requires raw materials that are difficult or expensive to transport, it may need a location near the source of those raw materials. For instance, the Oil-Dri Corporation of America, a family-controlled business based in Chicago, Illinois, that makes Cat's Pride and Jonny Cat kitty litter, operates factories in Mississippi, Georgia, Illinois, and Oregon that are located near deposits of fuller's earth, the clay-based material from which the product is made.[8] Transporting the heavy, low-value raw material over long distances would be impractical—and unprofitable. For products in which bulk or weight is not a factor, locating manufacturing operations in close proximity to suppliers facilitates quick deliveries and reduces inventory holding costs.

WAGE RATES Existing and anticipated wage rates provide another measure for comparison among states. Wages can sometimes vary from one state or region to another, significantly affecting a company's cost of doing business. For instance, according to the Bureau of Labor Statistics, the average hourly compensation for workers (including wages and benefits) ranges from a low of $25.14 in the South to a high of $32.44 in the Northeast.[9] Wage rate differentials within geographic regions can be even more drastic. When reviewing wage rates, entrepreneurs must be sure to measure the wage rates for jobs that relate to their particular industries or companies. In addition to surveys by the Bureau of Labor Statistics (www.bls.gov), local newspaper ads can give entrepreneurs an idea of the pay scale in an area. In addition, entrepreneurs can obtain the latest wage and salary surveys with an e-mail or telephone call to the local chambers of commerce for cities in the region under consideration. Entrepreneurs should study not only prevailing wage rates but also *trends* in rates. How does the rate of increase in wage rates compare to those in other states? Another factor influencing wage rates is the level of union activity in a state. How much union organizing activity has the state seen within the last two years? Which industries have unions targeted in the recent past?

ENTREPRENEURIAL PROFILE: Bombardier Inc. Montreal, Canada–based Bombardier Inc. recently built a manufacturing plant in what was once dry cactus fields in Querétaro, Mexico, to produce the Learjet 85, the company's newest corporate jet. Bombardier was attracted by lower wage rates, a pool of trained aeronautics engineers from the local National Aeronautics University of Querétaro, and proximity to customers in both North and South America. The availability of a trained labor force and wage rates that are 25 to 30 percent lower than those in the United States were driving factors in the company's location decision.[10] ■

LABOR SUPPLY For many businesses, especially technology-driven companies, one of the most important characteristics of a potential location is the composition of the local workforce. The number of workers available in an area and their levels of education, training, and experience determine a company's ability to fill jobs with qualified workers at reasonable wages. For example, Provo, Utah, home to Brigham Young University, hosts a large concentration of software companies, second only to California's Silicon Valley but without the high costs. One reason that software companies find Provo attractive is the city's high concentration of college graduates; more than 40 percent of its residents have a bachelor's degree or higher (compared to 28 percent in the United States as a whole).[11]

Entrepreneurs should know how many qualified people are available in the area to perform the work required in their businesses. Some states have attempted to attract industry with the promise of cheap labor. Unfortunately, businesses locating in those states find unskilled, low-wage workers who are ill suited for performing the work the companies need and are difficult to train.

Knowing the exact nature of the workforce needed and preparing job descriptions and job specifications in advance help business owners to determine whether there is a good match between their companies' needs and the available labor pool. Reviewing the major industries already operating in an area provides clues about the characteristics of the local workforce as well. Checking educational statistics to determine the number of graduates in relevant fields of study tells entrepreneurs about the available supply of qualified workers.

BUSINESS CLIMATE What is the state's overall attitude toward your kind of business? Has it passed laws that impose restrictions on the way a company can operate? Are there "blue laws" that prohibit certain business activity on Sundays? Does the state offer small business support programs or financial assistance to entrepreneurs?

ENTREPRENEURIAL PROFILE: Riza Berken and Pentti Kouri: Hakia Riza Berken and Pentti Kouri, founders of Hakia, a semantics-based search engine that offers more focused results than traditional search engine, relocated from Washington, D.C., to New York City for the superior business climate it offered their technology start-up. New York offered greater venture capital funding opportunities, a rich pool of talented high-tech workers, and a business climate that offered plenty of business-to-business sales potential for Hakia. Although New York City is one of the cities with the highest cost of doing business, Berken and Kouri say that it offers the ideal location for their company.[12] ■

Some states and cities create policies that are more small business friendly than others. Texas is the birthplace of many business start-ups, especially technology firms, because it offers entrepreneurs access to venture capital; quality colleges and universities; a young, well-educated workforce; and a variety of programs designed to encourage entrepreneurship. Texas was an early participant in the Startup America program, which is designed to encourage start-up companies and to help them succeed. Austin, Texas, is home to SpiceWorks, a social business network for information technology professionals ("kinda' like an iTunes for IT management," say its founders, Francis Sullivan, Jay Hallberg, Scott Abel, and Greg Kattawar). Launched in 2006, the company has landed $54 million in venture capital and has 1.8 million users.[13]

The Small Business & Entrepreneurship Council publishes an annual "small-business-friendly" ranking of the states and the District of Columbia that includes a composite measure of 44 factors, ranging from a variety of taxes and regulations to crime rates and energy costs (see Table 14.1).[14]

TAX RATES Another important factor that entrepreneurs must consider when screening states for potential locations is the tax burden they impose on businesses and individuals. Does the state

TABLE 14.1 Most and Least Small-Business-Friendly States

States *Most* Friendly to Small Businesses

1. South Dakota	6. Alabama
2. Nevada	7. Ohio
3. Texas	8. Florida
4. Wyoming	9. Colorado
5. South Carolina	10. Virginia

States *Least* Friendly to Small Businesses

41. Massachusetts	46. Rhode Island
42. Minnesota	47. Vermont
43. Connecticut	48. New Jersey
44. Maine	49. New York
45. California	50. District of Columbia

Source: Raymond J. Keating, *Small Business Survival Index 2011*, Small Business & Entrepreneurship Council, 16th Annual Edition, November 2011, p. 2.

impose a corporate income tax? How heavy are the state's property, income, and sales taxes? Income taxes may be the most obvious tax that states impose on both business and individuals, but entrepreneurs also must evaluate the impact of payroll taxes, sales taxes, property taxes, and specialized taxes on the cost of their operations. Currently, nine states impose no state individual income tax, and three states have no corporate income tax, but state governments always impose taxes of some sort on businesses and individuals.[15] In some cases, states offer special tax rates or are willing to negotiate fees in lieu of taxes for companies that will create jobs and stimulate the local economy.

ENTREPRENEURIAL PROFILE: Jimmy John Liautaud: Jimmy John's When Illinois raised its individual income tax rate from 3 to 5 percent and its corporate income tax rate from 7.3 to 9.5 percent, Jimmy John Liautaud, founder of Jimmy John's, a chain of sandwich shops with more than 1,000 locations (many of them franchised), announced that he was considering moving his company's headquarters to Florida, which has no individual income tax and a corporate tax rate of 5.3 percent. Liautaud says that officials from "multiple pro-business states" contacted him about relocating the company. "I love it here [in Illinois,] says James North, Jimmy John's president, "but when you do the math, it doesn't add up. Florida looks pretty good right now."[16] ∎

INTERNET ACCESS Speedy, reliable Internet access is an increasingly important factor in the location decision. In fact, 95 percent of small businesses that have computers have broadband Internet access.[17] Fast Internet access is essential for high-tech companies, those that rely on cloud computing, and those that engage in e-commerce; however, even those companies that may not sell to customers over the Internet are finding that they almost certainly use the Internet as a business tool. Companies that fall behind in high-speed Internet access find themselves at a severe competitive disadvantage. According to a recent study, 48 percent of small business owners in rural areas and 37 percent of business owners in metropolitan areas say they are not satisfied with their Internet speed. A high-speed fiber network from Google that runs 100 times faster (1 gigabyte per second) than current broadband is proving to be an important factor in many entrepreneurs' decisions to locate in Kansas City (Kansas and Missouri), which has earned the nickname "Silicon Prairie."[18]

TOTAL OPERATING COSTS When scouting a state in which to locate a company, an entrepreneur must consider the total cost of operating a business. For instance, a state may offer low utility rates, but its labor costs and tax rates may be among the highest in the nation. To select the ideal location, entrepreneurs must consider the impact of a state's total cost of operation on their business ventures. After Feel Golf, a company that makes golf clubs and grips, acquired Pro Line Sports, a Sanford, Florida–based business that markets the IGOTCHA golf ball retriever, CEO Lee Miller decided to relocate Feel Golf to Florida from Salinas, California, where the company had operated for 15 years. Miller made the move because he was concerned about the effect that the "high cost of doing business" in California had on his company.[19]

The state evaluation matrix in Table 14.2 provides a handy tool designed to help entrepreneurs determine which states best suit the most important location criteria for their companies. This same matrix can be adapted to analyze individual cities as well. Claremont McKenna College's Kosmont-Rose Institute Cost of Doing Business Survey reports that Austin, Abilene, and Fort Worth, Texas; Cheyenne, Wyoming; Eugene, Oregon; and Yakima, Washington, are among the cities that offer the lowest cost of doing business and New York City, New York; Los Angeles and San Francisco, California; Philadelphia, Pennsylvania; and Newark, New Jersey, are those with the highest costs of doing business.[20]

Table 14.3 on page 529 shows the states that CEOs rank as the 10 best states and the 10 worst states on factors that include taxes and regulations, quality of workforce, and living environment.

Choosing the City

POPULATION TRENDS Analyzing over time the lists of "best cities for business" compiled annually by many magazines reveals one consistent trend: Successful small companies in a city tend to track a city's population growth. In other words, more potential customers mean that a small business has a better chance of success. The Census Bureau recently named Las Vegas–Paradise,

TABLE 14.2 State Evaluation Matrix

Location Criterion	Weight	Score (Low = 1, High = 5)	State-Weighted Score (Weight × Score)		
			State 1	State 2	State 3
Quality of labor force					
Wage rates					
Union activity					
Property/building costs					
Utility costs					
Transportation costs					
Tax burden					
Educational/training assistance					
Start-up incentives					
Raw material availability					
Quality of life					
Other:					
Other:					
Total Score					

Assign to each location criterion a weight that reflects its relative importance to your company. Then score each state on a scale of 1 (low) to 5 (high). Calculate the weighted score (weight × score) for each state. Finally, add up the total weighted score for each state. The state with the highest total score is the best location for your business.

Nevada; Raleigh–Cary, North Carolina; Austin–Round Rock–San Marcos, Texas; and Charlotte–Gastonia–Rock Hill, North–South Carolina, as the fastest-growing cities in the United States.

ENTREPRENEURIAL PROFILE: Jaime and Elvira Picos: Fiesta Tortillas Jaime and Elvira Picos started Fiesta Tortillas in Del Rio, Texas, as a home-based business and sold their corn and flour tortillas, which they made from an old-fashioned recipe handed down from Jaime's grandmother, Mama Tomasita, to local meat markets. As the company's reputation and sales grew, the Picos moved into a small factory. After 14 years in Del Rio, the Picos noticed the rapid growth that the city of Austin, which had become a magnet for high-tech companies, was experiencing and decided to move their business there, opening a tortilla factory with used equipment in an old shopping center. After they produced a batch of tortillas, the Picos would close their factory and take their products around town to prospective customers. Fiesta Tortillas grew quickly and now operates from a state-of-the-art baking bakery that turns out thousands of tortillas each day, many of them for businesses in the fast-growing Austin area. The company's customer base includes many of the local, family-owned restaurants that have been with Fiesta Tortillas for more than 20 years, large food service companies, and five-star hotels located in the area.[21] ■

By analyzing population and other demographic data, entrepreneurs can examine a city in detail, and the location decision becomes more than just an educated guess or, worse, a shot in the dark. Studying the trends and the demographics of a city, including population size and density, growth trends, family size, age breakdowns, education, income levels, job categories, gender, religion, race, and nationality, gives entrepreneurs the facts they need to make an informed location decision. In fact, using only basic census data, entrepreneurs can determine the value of the homes in an area, how many rooms they contain, how many bedrooms they contain, what percentage of the population own their homes, and how much residents' monthly rental or mortgage payments are. Imagine how useful that information would be to someone about to launch a bed-and-bath shop!

TABLE 14.3 Best and Worst States for Doing Business

Top 10 States for Doing Business

Rank*	State	Taxes and Regulations	Workforce Quality	Living Environment
1	Texas	*****	*****	****
2	Florida	****	****	*****
3	North Carolina	****	****	*****
4	Tennessee	****	****	*****
5	Indiana	****	****	****
6	Virginia	****	****	*****
7	South Carolina	****	****	****
8	Georgia	****	****	****
9	Utah	****	*****	*****
10	Arizona	****	****	****

Bottom 10 States for Doing Business

Rank*	State	Taxes and Regulations	Workforce Quality	Living Environment
41	Hawaii	**	***	*****
42	Oregon	**	***	****
43	Pennsylvania	**	****	****
44	Connecticut	**	****	****
45	New Jersey	**	****	***
46	Michigan	**	***	***
47	Massachusetts	**	****	***
48	Illinois	**	***	***
49	New York	***	****	***
50	California	*	***	****

*Rank is the result of a survey by *Chief Executive* magazine that asked 650 business leaders to rank the states on factors such as taxes, regulatory burden, quality of workforce, and quality of life. Five stars is best; one star is worst.

Source: J. P. Donlon, "Another Triumph for Texas: Best and Worst States for Business 2012," *Chief Executive*, May 2, 2012, http://chiefexecutive .net/best-worst-states-for-business-2012.

A company's location should match the market for its products or services, and assembling a demographic profile tells an entrepreneur how well a particular site measures up to his or her target market's profile. For instance, an entrepreneur planning to open a fine art shop would likely want information on a city's household income, size, age, and education level. To succeed, this art shop should be located in an area where people appreciate its products and have the discretionary income to purchase them.

ENTREPRENEURIAL PROFILE: Bobby Flay: Bobby's Burger Palace Celebrity chef Bobby Flay recently opened a location of his gourmet hamburger restaurant, Bobby's Burger Palace, on K Street in Washington, D.C., just blocks from George Washington University, the National Mall, the White House, and other Washington landmarks. Flay, whose Burger Palace restaurants are a staple in New York and New Jersey, has joined other restaurateurs in opening locations in Washington, D.C., which was recently named the most attractive retail market in the United States by ChainLinks Retail Advisors. Lease rates for restaurants in Washington typically range between $30 and $40 per square foot, compared to as much as $150 per square foot in New York City. "Restaurateurs from New York are coming down here because they can pay half the rent and do 75 percent of the business," says broker Thomas Papadopoulos. Owners of upscale restaurants are drawn to the city's diverse, well-educated, and affluent population.[22] ■

The amount of available data on the population of any city or town is staggering. These statistics allow entrepreneurs to compare a wide variety of cities or towns and to narrow the choices to those few that warrant further investigation. Analyzing all of this data makes it possible to screen out undesirable locations and to narrow the list of suitable locations to a few, but it does not make the final location decision for an entrepreneur. Entrepreneurs must see the potential locations on their "short list" *firsthand*. Only by seeing a potential location can an entrepreneur add the intangible factor of intuition into the decision-making process. Spending time at a potential location tells an entrepreneur not only how many people frequent it but also what they are like, how long they stay, and what they buy. Walking or driving around the area will give an entrepreneur clues about the people who live and work there. What are their houses like? What kinds of cars do they drive? What stage of life are they in? Do they have children? Is the area on the rise, or is it past its prime?

Following are other factors that entrepreneurs should consider when evaluating cities as possible business locations.

COMPETITION For some retailers, locating near competitors makes sense because similar businesses located near one another may serve to increase traffic flow to both. This location strategy works well for products for which customers are most likely to comparison shop. For instance, in many cities, auto dealers locate next to one another in a "motor mile," trying to create a shopping magnet for customers. The convenience of being able to shop for dozens of brands of cars all within a few hundred yards of one another draws customers from a sizable trading area. Locating near competitors is a common strategy for restaurants as well.

ENTREPRENEURIAL PROFILE: George Stathakis: Stax Omega When George Stathakis opened his sixth restaurant, Stax Omega, in Greenville, South Carolina, he chose a site at the intersection of an interstate highway and a busy road where several other popular restaurants were already operating. With years of experience in the restaurant business, Stathakis knows that a cluster of restaurants create business for one another. "I always liked the idea of locating my restaurants near competitors," he says.[23] ■

Of course, this strategy has limits. Overcrowding of businesses of the same type in an area can create an undesirable impact on the profitability of all competing firms.

Studying the size of the market for a product or service and the number of existing competitors helps an entrepreneur determine whether he or she can capture a sufficiently large market share to earn a profit. Again, census reports can be a valuable source of information. *County Business Patterns* gives a breakdown of businesses in manufacturing, wholesale, retail, and service categories and estimates companies' annual payrolls and number of employees broken down by county. *ZIP Code Business Patterns* provides the same data as *County Business Patterns* except it organizes the data by ZIP code. The *Economic Census*, which is produced for years that end in "2" and "7," gives an overview of the businesses in an area—their sales (or other measure of output), employment, payroll, and form of organization. It covers eight industry categories—including retail, wholesale, service, manufacturing, construction, and others—and gives statistics not only at the national level but also by state, Metropolitan Statistical Area, county, places with 2,500 or more inhabitants, and ZIP code. The *Economic Census* is a useful tool for helping entrepreneurs determine whether the areas they are considering as a location are already saturated with competitors.

clusters
geographic concentrations of interconnected companies, specialized suppliers, and service providers that are present in a region.

CLUSTERS Some cities have characteristics that attract certain industries, and, as a result, companies tend to cluster there. **Clusters** are geographic concentrations of interconnected companies, specialized suppliers, distribution networks, and service providers that are present in a region.[24] According to Harvard professor Michael Porter, clusters are important because they allow companies in them to increase their productivity, gain a competitive edge, and increase their likelihood of survival. "Specialization in a region increases the number of patents and business formations and leads to higher wages," adds Harvard's Rich Bryden, who has helped develop a map of business clusters in the United States. Albany, New York, is home to hundreds of companies in the nanotechnology field, many of them inspired by the University of Albany's College of Nanoscale Science and Engineering. With its highly trained, well-educated, and technologically literate workforce, Austin, Texas, has become a mecca for high-tech companies. California's Napa Valley boasts more than 300 wineries, many of them small, family-owned operations that are among the best in the United States. The region's climate and soil, both of which are ideal for growing grapes, led entrepreneurs to establish wineries as early as 1861. As in most clusters, over time these vintners shared both knowledge and best practices, leading to the formation of more wineries, increased productivity and innovation, and the resulting competitive advantages.[25]

Once a concentration of companies takes root in a city, other businesses in those industries tend to spring up there as well. Ogden, Utah, hosted some events for the 2002 Olympics in Salt Lake City. With its bountiful mountains, canyons, and rivers and a population devoted to outdoor activities ranging from hiking and biking to mountain climbing and skiing, Ogden has become the hub of a cluster of outdoor sports companies. It offers the ideal location for testing new products, and a nearby airport provides direct international flights for entrepreneurs who are engaged in international business.

ENTREPRENEURIAL PROFILE: Steve Flagg: Quality Bicycle Products Steve Flagg, founder of Quality Bicycle Products, a small wholesale bicycle distributor based in Bloomington, Minnesota, chose Ogden for his company's second location. Flagg, whose company serves 5,000 independent bicycle shops, was drawn to Ogden by its cluster of companies that make outdoor gear, its strong pool of labor, its growing retail base, and its easy access to the West Coast market.[26] ■

COMPATIBILITY WITH THE COMMUNITY One of the intangibles that can be determined only by a visit to an area is the degree of compatibility a business has with the surrounding community. In other words, a small company's image must fit in with the character of a town and the needs and wants of its residents. For example, Beverly Hills's ritzy Rodeo Drive or Palm Beach's Worth Avenue are home to shops that match the characteristics of the area's wealthy residents. Exclusive shops such as Cartier, Jimmy Choo, Versace, Louis Vuitton, and Tiffany & Company, abound, catering to the area's rich-and-famous residents.

LOCAL LAWS AND REGULATIONS Before settling on a city, entrepreneurs must consider the regulatory burden local government will impose. Government regulations affect many aspects of small business's operation, from acquiring business licenses and building permits to erecting business signs and dumping trash. Some cities are regulatory activists, creating so many rules that they discourage business creation; others take a more laissez-faire approach, imposing few restrictions on businesses.

ENTREPRENEURIAL PROFILE: Juliet Pries: The Ice Cream Bar Entrepreneur Juliet Pries battled a regulatory bureaucracy for two years before she was able to acquire all of the permits, approvals, and licenses required to start her vintage ice cream shop, The Ice Cream Bar, in San Francisco. At one point, the reams of paperwork that she was required to submit (along with thousands of dollars in fees) sat unprocessed in an office for months while Pries continued to pay rent and other expenses so that she would not lose her desired location. Pries persevered, and her shop, which employs 14 people, has become a popular attraction in the Cole Valley neighborhood for both residents and visitors. Inspired by Pries's story, employees of the city's planning department made a YouTube video lampooning the convoluted approval process that discourages entrepreneurs from launching food-related businesses in San Francisco.[27] ■

The Business Journal/Spencer Brown

zoning laws
laws that divide a city or county into small cells or districts to control the use of land, buildings, and sites.

Zoning laws can have a major impact on an entrepreneur's location decision. New York City passed the first comprehensive zoning laws in 1916, and most cities now have **zoning laws** that divide a city or county into cells or districts to control the use of land, buildings, and sites.[28] Their purpose is to contain similar activities in suitable locations. For instance, one section of a city may be zoned residential, whereas the primary retail district may be zoned commercial and another zoned industrial to house manufacturing operations. Before selecting a particular site within a city, entrepreneurs must explore local zoning laws to determine whether there are any ordinances that would place restrictions on business activity or that would prohibit establishing a business altogether. Zoning regulations may make a particular location out of bounds. In 2010, the Los Angeles City Council passed zoning standards that essentially ban quick-service restaurant chains from establishing new locations in a 32-square-mile area of South Los Angeles, where 70 percent of the restaurants are fast-food establishments. The council passed the zoning law because of concerns about the area's higher-than-average rate of obesity and diabetes and the desire to keep sites open for grocery stores and full-service restaurants that offer healthier menus.[29]

variance
a special exemption to a zoning ordinance.

In some cases, an entrepreneur may appeal to the local zoning commission to rezone a site or to grant a **variance** (a special exception to a zoning ordinance), but this is risky and could be devastating if the board disallows the variance. As the number of home-based businesses has increased in the last several years, more entrepreneurs have found themselves at odds with zoning regulations.

Appropriate Infrastructure Business owners must consider the quality of the infrastructure in a potential location. Is an airport located nearby? Are flights available to the necessary cities, and are the schedules convenient? If a company needs access to a railroad spur, is one available in the city? How convenient is the area's access to major highways? What about travel distances to major customers? How long will it take to deliver shipments to them? Are the transportation rates reasonable? In some situations, double or triple handling of merchandise and inventory causes transportation costs to skyrocket. For many businesses, the availability of loading and unloading zones is an important feature of a suitable location. Some downtown locations suffer from a lack of sufficient space for carriers to unload deliveries of merchandise.

ENTREPRENEURIAL PROFILE: Gene Konczal: Providencia USA Providencia USA recently built a $70 million factory that makes nonwoven fabric in Statesville, North Carolina, because the location offered all of the necessary infrastructure that is important to the factory's success. An international airport is just 45 minutes away, and two major interstate highways make transporting finished goods to customers along the East Coast fast and efficient. Railway access was also an important factor because railroad delivery is the least expensive way to deliver the pelletized polypropylene raw material that Providencia uses in its production process. Finally, the availability of low-cost electricity was the "tipping factor" in the location decision. "We are a heavy electricity user," says Gene Konczal, the plant's manager.[30] ■

COST OF UTILITIES AND PUBLIC SERVICES A location should be served by a governmental unit that provides water and sewer services, trash and garage collection, and other necessary utilities at a reasonable cost. The streets should be in good repair with adequate drainage. If a location is not within the jurisdiction of a municipality that provides these services, it imposes additional ongoing costs on a business.

Mike Baldwin/www.CartoonStock.com

INCENTIVES Many states, counties, and cities offer financial and other incentives to encourage businesses that will create jobs to locate within their borders. These incentives range from job training for workers and reduced tax rates to financial grants and loans. One reason that North Carolina has attracted 40 companies in the video game industry is that it is one of 22 states that offer incentives aimed at recruiting companies engaged in digital media production. Qualifying companies receive a 15 percent tax credit on the compensation for full-time employees and a 20 percent credit for research expenses paid to a North Carolina college or university. North Carolina compares favorably on all of the factors that these companies look for in a location, and the incentive packages tend to move the state to the top of the list for many companies, including Epic Games, Electronic Arts, Insomniac Games, Red Storm Entertainment, Virtual Heroes, and Spark Plug Games, all of which have offices in the Cary–Raleigh area. "What often is the tie-breaker in the ultimate [location] decision made by a video game company is an incentive package," says Make Gallagher, CEO of the industry's trade association.[31]

Companies that accept incentives must be aware of "clawback" provisions that require them to repay the state the value of some or all of the incentives if the company fails to create a minimum number of jobs or make a minimum capital investment. State and local government entities approved nearly $270 million in incentives to convince Dell Inc. to build a computer assembly plant in Winston–Salem, North Carolina, on the condition that the company create at least 900 jobs. Four years later, however, in a move to improve its efficiency, Dell decided to close the factory, which required the company to repay $28 million under the contract's clawback provision.[32]

QUALITY OF LIFE A final consideration when selecting a city is the quality of life it offers. For many entrepreneurs, quality of life is one of the key determinants of their choice of locale. Cities that offer comfortable weather, cultural events, colleges and universities, museums, outdoor activities, concerts, unique restaurants, and an interesting nightlife have become magnets for entrepreneurs looking to start companies. Over the last two decades, cities such as Austin, Boston, Seattle, San Francisco, Washington, Dallas, Minneapolis, and others have become incubators for creativity and entrepreneurship as educated young people drawn by the cities' quality of life have moved in.

Not only can a location in a city offering a high quality of life be attractive to an entrepreneur, but it can also make recruiting employees much easier. According to a study of the importance of location on recruiting employees conducted by the Human Capital Institute, the three most important factors in attracting talent are job opportunities, a clean and safe community, and an affordable cost of living.[33]

ENTREPRENEURIAL PROFILE: Earl Overstreet: General Microsystems Inc. Earl Overstreet, founder of General Microsystems Inc., a Bellevue, Washington, computer system supply company, has discovered that the area's high quality of life allows his company to attract the highly qualified employees that his company counts on for success. It is not unusual to see Overstreet and many of his employees walking through Mercer Slough Nature Park, which is located across the street from the company's headquarters. Many of the company's employees spend their free time taking advantage of the outdoor activities that the nearby Cascade Mountains, lakes, streams, and bike trails offer. Bellevue, with a population of 122,000, boasts 90 parks and 50 miles of trails.[34] ∎

Choosing the Site

The final step in the location selection process is choosing the actual site for the business. Once again, entrepreneurs must let the facts guide them to the best location. Every business has its own unique set of criteria for an ideal location. A manufacturer's prime consideration may be access to raw materials, suppliers, labor, transportation, and customers. Service firms need access to customers but can generally survive in lower-rent properties. A retailer's prime consideration is sufficient customer traffic. For example, an entrepreneur who is planning to launch a convenience store should know that generating a sufficient volume of sales requires a population of at least 500 to 1,000 people who live within a one-mile radius of the outlet and choose a location accordingly.[35] The one element common to all three types of businesses is the need to locate where customers want to do business.

Some entrepreneurs test the suitability of potential locations by opening "pop-up" stores, shops that are open for only a few days, weeks, or months before shutting down. These temporary stores open in available spaces, sell their merchandise quickly, close, and move on to the next location.

ENTREPRENEURIAL PROFILE: Bobby Kim and Ben Shenasafar: The Hundreds Before Bobby Kim and Ben Shenasafar, founders of The Hundreds, a store in Los Angeles that sells clothing inspired by skateboarders, opened a location in San Francisco, they opened a pop-up store to test potential customers' level of interest in their product line. Sales from their one-day pop-up store exceeded their expectations, which led Kim and Shenasafar to open a permanent store in San Francisco. The entrepreneurs used the same strategy to test New York City as a potential market for The Hundreds and after a successful weekend of sales decided to open their third location there.[36] ■

Rental or lease rates are an important factor when choosing a site. Of course, entrepreneurs must be sure that the rent or lease payments for a particular location fit comfortably into their financial forecasts. Although "cheap" rental rates can be indicative of a second-class location (and the resulting poor revenues they generate), entrepreneurs should not agree to exorbitant rental rates that jeopardize their ability to surpass their break-even points.

ENTREPRENEURIAL PROFILE: Cipriani Family: Rainbow Room The Cipriani family, owners of New York's famous Rainbow Room since 1998, recently closed the landmark restaurant, which opened in 1934 and was located on the sixty-fifth floor of Rockefeller Center ("30 Rock") because the annual rent had more than doubled from $4 million in 1998 to $8.7 million! A lawsuit filed by the Ciprianis against landlord Tishman Speyer Properties claims that sales at the Rainbow Room, where dinner for two easily topped $600, "could not possibly support" rent that high.[37] ■

Many businesses are downsizing their outlets to lower their start-up and operating costs and to allow for a greater number of location options that are not available to full-size stores. Franchises such as Cinnabon and Burger King are finding success by placing smaller, less expensive outlets in locations that cannot support a full-size store. Burger King recently opened six Whopper Bars in the United States and three international locations in Venezuela and Singapore. At just 700 square feet, a Whopper Bar is one-fifth the size of a traditional Burger King outlet and is ideal for locations in theme parks, airports, museums, casinos, cruise ships, and shopping malls. "It's really [ideal] for any limited-space venue," says Chuck Fallon, president of Burger King North America, "especially where there is a captive audience and the potential for high impact volumes." A Whopper Bar, which sells beer and includes a Whopper topper area in which customers customize the company's signature sandwich with 22 different toppings, cost between $600,000 and $800,000 to build, which is 30 percent less than the smallest traditional Burger King restaurant. Despite its size, the Whopper Bar's sales per square foot exceed those of its full-size franchise outlets.[38]

Finally, an entrepreneur must be careful to select a site that creates the right impression for a business in the customers' eyes. A company's location speaks volumes about a company's "personality."

ENTREPRENEURIAL PROFILE: Charlene Dupray and Pascal Siegler: South'n France When copreneurs Charlene Dupray and Pascal Siegler saw an old diner in downtown Wilmington, North Carolina, with its salmon pink concrete exterior, 13-foot ceilings, and diner stools, they knew that they had found the perfect building to house their chocolate bonbon business, South'n France. In addition to its unique character, the building came equipped with freezers capable of holding 20,000 bonbons, provided sufficient space for Dupray and Siegler to manufacture their chocolate delicacies, and included rooms that they could convert into a retail storefront. Even though their business is on the verge of outgrowing the space, Dupray says, "We love it so much that we're considering adding another story or buying nearby residences because this old luncheonette really is a workhorse for us." ■

Location Criteria for Retail and Service Businesses

LO2

Describe the location criteria for retail and service businesses.

Few decisions are as important for retailers and service firms as the choice of a location. Because their success depends on a steady flow of customers, these businesses must locate their businesses with their target customers' convenience and preferences in mind. The following are important considerations:

You Be the Consultant

"Pop" Goes the Store

Courtesy of Ricky's

Pop-up stores are temporary locations that are open for only a few hours, days, or weeks before shutting down. For entrepreneurs who operate highly seasonal businesses, pop-up stores are a way of life, but other entrepreneurs use them to test new business ideas, to clear out excess inventory, and to promote their full-time locations. Ricky's Halloween Stores, a quintessential seasonal business, opened the chain's first pop-up store in 2005 and now operates about 30 temporary pop-up stores each year not only to generate costume sales during the peak Halloween season but also to test markets for suitability for permanent Ricky's stores in the company's principal line of business, beauty supply shops. "The profit [from the costume sales] is icing on the cake," explains a former top manager. "The real benefit is to study the demographics in an area."

Opening a Ricky's Halloween pop-up store actually requires a year of extensive planning. Managers begin working in early November with a team of employees to scout potential locations for the next Halloween costume sales season and to begin placing orders for inventory. The team members attend the Halloween & Party Expo, a large convention that attracts vendors and retailers from around the world, in January to spot the latest trends and the hottest costumes for the upcoming season. They place orders for costumes in March. In May, the team identifies specific locations that are available in the areas they identified the previous November, looking for vacant spaces in high-traffic locations that do not require extensive renovations. The company negotiates and signs leases, which typically run for just 2 months, from June to September. Over the summer, the company's human resources manager gears up the hiring process, adding as many as 1,000 temporary employees to make the necessary renovations to the pop-up stores and to staff them. The stores open their doors in early September, sell costumes furiously until Halloween, and then close.

The team analyzes sales from the company's pop-up stores, looking for locations that generate above-average sales of women's and children's costumes because they represent the best potential sites for one of the company's permanent beauty supply stores. The team eliminates from contention locations that sell mostly men's costumes because they would be unable to attract a sufficient number of the company's primary target customers:

young women. Typically, the company converts about 10 percent of its pop-up Halloween stores into permanent Ricky's beauty supply stores. Using pop-up stores to test the suitability of potential locations is a key ingredient in the company's location strategy as it expands outside of its New York City base. Ricky's has one store in Miami, and because a pop-up store was very successful in Philadelphia, the company plans to open a permanent Ricky's store there.

Even restaurateurs are using pop-up stores to test the feasibility of their food concepts in various locations. Before investing $100,000 to $500,000 to open a permanent location that may not succeed, entrepreneurs test the waters with temporary pop-up restaurants. Leo Beckerman and Evan Bloom believed that they had spotted an opportunity to sell classic Jewish delicatessen food, such as smoked pastrami and bialy with cream cheese, in San Francisco. "The Bay Area has tons of great food, but there was nowhere to get a great pastrami sandwich," says Beckerman. Because neither Beckerman nor Bloom had been in the restaurant business before, they thought that setting up a temporary restaurant would be the ideal way to determine whether a Jewish deli would thrive in San Francisco. They launched Wise Sons Jewish Delicatessen as a Saturday-only pop-up store in a vacant café or under tents at various outdoor locations at a cost of $2,000 to $2,500 each week, an amount they funded themselves.

Very quickly, Beckerman and Bloom were serving between 300 and 400 customers each Saturday, generating enough revenue to cover their costs and to convince them that a Jewish deli could be successful. They used social media to spread the word among customers about the location and menu offerings of their weekly pop-up, and local media covered their once-weekly venture. Beckerman admits that operating the pop-up was "trial by fire," but the benefits far outweighed the costs. "We got to test our ideas and get the word out and prove our capabilities," he says. "It's doubtful that any of this would have happened without the pop-up." With the help of the successful feasibility study that their pop-up restaurant provided, Beckerman and Bloom raised $100,000 from family members and friends, added another $100,000 of their own money, and opened Wise Sons Jewish Delicatessen in a permanent location in San Francisco's Mission District.

1. What advantages and disadvantages do pop-up stores such as the ones described here offer entrepreneurs?

2. What types of businesses would be successful opening pop-up stores temporarily on your campus or on a nearby campus? What advice would you offer entrepreneurs who are considering opening the store? When should it open and for how long?

3. Would a pop-up store such as the ones that Ricky's and Wise Brothers Jewish Delicatessen used be successful in your community? Explain. Work with a team of your classmates to identify three products or product lines that would be successful in your community if they were sold from a pop-up store.

Sources: Based on Jason Del Ray, "Shop before It All Disappears," *Inc.*, July/August 2010, pp. 126–128; Amy Barrett, "Scream Therapy," *Inc.*, October 2011, pp. 99–100; and Katy McLaughlin, "Pop-Ups Are Taking Over the Kitchen," *Wall Street Journal*, March 23, 2012, pp. B1, B4.

Trade Area Size

Every retail and service business should determine the extent of its **trading area**, the region from which a business can expect to draw customers over a reasonable time span. The primary variables that influence the scope of the trading area are the type and the size of the business. If a retail store specializes in a particular product line and offers a wide selection and knowledgeable salespeople, it may draw customers from a great distance. In contrast, a convenience store with a general line of merchandise has a small trading area because it is unlikely that customers will drive across town to purchase items that are available within blocks of their homes or businesses. As a rule, the larger the store, the greater its selection, and the better its service, the broader is its trading area. Businesses that offer a narrow selection of products and services tend to have smaller trading areas. For instance, the majority of a massage therapist's clients live within three to five miles of the location with a secondary tier of clients who live within 5 to 10 miles. Clients who are willing to travel more than 15 minutes for a session are rare.[39]

ENTREPRENEURIAL PROFILE: Francine Galante: Managed Care Concepts Francine Galante owns Managed Care Concepts, a company that provides employee assistance programs, background checks, and training to businesses in Boca Raton, Florida. As her company grew, Galante noticed that a significant number of her company's clients were clustered in one area on the other side of town and opened a second location there. Because her employees spend most of their time in clients' offices, Galante says that "it's smart for us to be within a quarter mile of the clients we serve." Galante used the same technique to find a good location for a third office in Boca Raton and is considering opening her first out-of-state office in Tennessee, where the company recently landed its largest client.[40] ■

Retail Compatibility

Shoppers tend to be drawn to clusters of related businesses. That's one reason shopping malls and outlet shopping centers are popular destinations for shoppers and are attractive locations for retailers. The concentration of businesses pulls customers from a larger trading area than a single freestanding business does. **Retail compatibility** describes the benefits a company receives by locating near other businesses that sell complementary products and services or that generate high volumes of foot traffic. Clever business owners choose their locations with an eye on the surrounding mix of businesses. For instance, grocery store operators prefer not to locate in shopping centers with movie theaters, offices, and fitness centers, all businesses whose customers occupy parking spaces for extended time periods. Drugstores, nail salons, and ice cream parlors have proved to be much better shopping center neighbors for grocers.

Degree of Competition

The size, location, and activity of competing businesses also influence the size of a company's trading area. If a business will be the first of its kind in a location, its trading area might be quite extensive. However, if the area already has 8 or 10 nearby stores that directly compete with a business, its trading area might be very small because the market is saturated with competitors. Market saturation is a problem for businesses in many industries, ranging from fast-food restaurants to convenience stores. Red Mango, an upscale yogurt chain based in Los Angeles, recently saw four of its franchises in Los Angeles close because of poor location choices. The company is continuing with its expansion plans but will focus them on other cities that are less saturated with frozen yogurt shops.[41]

The Index of Retail Saturation

One of the best measures of the level of saturation in an area is the index of retail saturation (IRS), which takes into account both the number of customers and the intensity of competition in a trading area. The **index of retail saturation** is a measure of the potential sales per square foot of store space for a given product within a specific trading area. It is the ratio of a trading area's sales potential for a particular product or service to its sales capacity:

$$IRS = \frac{C \times RE}{RF}$$

where

C = number of customers in the trading area

RE = retail expenditures, or the average expenditure per person ($) for the product in the trading area

RF = retail facilities, or the total square feet of selling space allocated to the product in the trading area

This computation is an important one for every retailer to make. Locating in an area already saturated with competitors results in dismal sales volume and often leads to failure.

To illustrate the index of retail saturation, suppose that an entrepreneur who is looking at two sites for a shoe store finds that he needs sales of $175 per square foot to be profitable. Site 1 has a trading area with 25,875 potential customers who spend an average of $42 on shoes annually; the only competitor in the trading area has 6,000 square feet of selling space. Site 2 has 27,750 potential customers spending an average of $43.50 on shoes annually; two competitors occupy 8,400 square feet of space:

Site 1

$$\text{Index of retail saturation} = \frac{25,875 \times 42}{6,000}$$
$$= \$181.12 \text{ sales potential per square foot}$$

Site 2

$$\text{Index of retail saturation} = \frac{27,750 \times 43.50}{8,400}$$
$$= \$143.71 \text{ sales potential per square foot}$$

Although site 2 appears to be more favorable on the surface, the index shows that site 1 is preferable; site 2 fails to meet the minimum standard of $175 per square foot.

Reilly's Law of Retail Gravitation

Reilly's Law of Retail Gravitation, a classic work in market analysis published in 1931 by William J. Reilly, uses the analogy of gravity to estimate the attractiveness of a particular business to potential customers. A business's ability to draw customers is directly related to the extent to which customers see it as a "destination" and is inversely related to the distance customers must travel to reach it. Reilly's model also provides a way to estimate the trade boundary between two market areas by calculating the "break point" between them. The break point between two primary market areas is the boundary between the two where customers become indifferent about shopping at one or the other. The key factor in determining this point of indifference is the size of the communities. If two nearby cities have the same population sizes, then the break point lies halfway between them. The following is the equation for Reilly's Law:[42]

$$BP = \frac{d}{1 + \sqrt{\dfrac{P_b}{P_a}}}$$

where

BP = the distance in miles from location A to the break point

d = the distance in miles between locations A and B

P_b = the population surrounding location B

P_a = the population surrounding location A

For example, if city A and city B are 22 miles apart and city A has a population of 25,500 and city B has a population of 42,900, the break point according to Reilly's law is

$$BP = \frac{22}{1 + \sqrt{\dfrac{42,900}{25,500}}} = 9.2 \text{ miles}$$

The outer edge of city A's trading area lies about nine miles between city A and city B. Although only a rough estimate, this simple calculation using readily available data can be useful for screening potential locations.

Transportation Network

For many retail and service businesses, easy customer access from a smoothly flowing network of highways and roads is essential. If a location is inconvenient for customers to reach, a business located there will suffer from a diminished trading area and lower sales. Entrepreneurs should verify that the transportation system works smoothly and is free of barriers that prevent customers from reaching their shopping destinations. Is it easy for customers traveling in the opposite direction to cross traffic? Do traffic signs and lights allow traffic to flow smoothly?

E-commerce companies also must consider accessibility to trucking routes, such as interstate highways, and airports so that they can expedite customers' orders. Zappos, the online shoe retailer, moved its fulfillment center to Louisville, Kentucky, so that the company can ship orders almost anywhere in the United States within one day. The Zappos center is located just 12 miles from the UPS Worldport, the world's largest automated package-sorting facility (it can sort 416,000 packages per hour) in the Louisville International Airport. From this airport, flights can reach 75 percent of the population of the United States in just 2.5 hours and 95 percent of the population in four hours. The city also has three interstate highways and two railways. Because of Zappos's location, a package that leaves UPS Worldport by 12:45 a.m. can arrive at the home or business of any customer in the United States that same day, giving the company a competitive edge in customer service.[43]

Physical and Psychological Barriers

Trading area shape and size also are influenced by physical and psychological barriers. Physical barriers may be parks, rivers, lakes, bridges, or any other natural or man-made obstruction that hinders customers' access to the area. Locating on one side of a large park may reduce the number of customers who will drive around it to get to a store. Psychological barriers include areas that have a reputation for crime and illegal activities. If high crime areas exist near a site, potential customers will not travel through them to reach a business.

Other factors retailers should consider when evaluating potential sites are discussed next.

Customer Traffic

Perhaps the most important screening criterion for a potential retail (and often for a service) location is the number of potential customers passing by the site during business hours. To be successful, a business must be able to generate sufficient sales to surpass its break-even point, and that requires an ample volume of customer traffic going past its doors. The key success factor for many retail stores is a high-volume location with easy accessibility. Entrepreneurs should use traffic counts (pedestrian and/or auto) and traffic pattern studies to confirm that the sites they are considering as potential locations are capable of generating sufficient sales volume.

ENTREPRENEURIAL PROFILE: Seth Smart and Jefferey Agee: Brewed Awakenings Seth Smart and Jefferey Agee, co-owners of Brewed Awakenings, a drive-through coffee kiosk in Tigard, Oregon, selected a location for their business that offers the benefit of high traffic volume. The entrepreneurs credit their location for much of their business's success. Brewed Awakenings is in a highly visible location in a busy shopping complex that sits at the intersection of two major roads, one of which funnels traffic from downtown Portland and the other leads to an upscale mall. "[Finding the ideal location] is all about traffic counts, visual exposure, and means of access," says Ed Arvidson, a consultant to coffee retailers.[44] ■

Adequate Parking

If customers cannot find convenient and safe parking, they are not likely to shop in the area. Many downtown areas have lost customers because of inadequate parking. Although shopping malls average five parking spaces per 1,000 square feet of shopping space, many central business districts get by with 3.5 spaces per 1,000 square feet. Even when free parking is available, some potential customers may not feel safe on the streets, especially after dark. Some large city downtown business districts become virtual ghost towns at the end of the business day. A location where traffic vanishes after 6 p.m. may not be as valuable as mall or shopping center locations that mark the beginning of the prime sales time at 6 p.m.

Reputation

Like people, a site can have a bad reputation. Sites in which businesses have failed repeatedly create negative impressions in customers' minds; many people view the business as just another one that soon will be gone. Sometimes previous failures are indicative of a fundamental problem with the location itself; in other cases, the cause of the previous failure was the result not of a poor location but of a poorly managed business. When entrepreneurs decide to conduct business in a location that has housed pervious failures, it is essential that they make many highly visible changes to the site so that customers perceive the company as a "fresh start."

ENTREPRENEURIAL PROFILE: Peter Sibilia and Damien Vizuete: Sadie's Kitchen Some locals questioned Peter Sibilia and Damien Vizuete's decision to start Sadie's Kitchen, a retro-style diner that serves southern-style dishes, such as mac 'n' cheese and biscuit sandwiches at 243 Degraw Street in Brooklyn's Cobble Hill neighborhood. Over the previous 10 years, the location had been home to five different restaurants, from an oyster bar to a gourmet hamburger and hot dog shop, all of which failed. "The biggest mistake that new operators make is the failure to perform radical renovations," says Jeffrey Angel, a real estate expert. "You have to do a complete overhaul to make sure everyone forgets the last place." Sibilia and Vizuete have made sure that Sadie's Kitchen is a vast departure from its previous tenant, Gourmet Burgers and Dogs. Sibilia and Vizuete say that their business model is consistent with the space's limitations and includes a bakery in the basement that one day could supply Sadie's locations across the city.[45] ∎

Visibility

A final characteristic of a good location is visibility. Highly visible locations simply make it easy for customers to find a business and make purchases. A site that lacks visibility puts a company at a major disadvantage before it ever opens its doors for business.

Location Options for Retail and Service Businesses

LO3

Outline the location options for retail and service businesses: central business districts, neighborhoods, shopping centers and malls, near competitors, inside large retail stores, nontraditional locations, at home, and on the road.

There are eight basic areas where retail and service business owners can locate: the central business district, neighborhoods, shopping centers and malls, near competitors, inside large retail stores, nontraditional locations, at home, and on the road. According to Reis Inc., the average cost to lease space in a shopping center is about $19 per square foot, and at malls, lease rates average $39 per square foot. In central business locations, the average cost is between $22 and $45 per square foot (rental rates vary significantly, depending on the city).[46] Of course, cost is just one factor a business owner must consider when choosing a location.

Central Business District

The central business district (CBD) is the traditional center of town—the downtown concentration of businesses established early in the development of most towns and cities. Entrepreneurs derive several advantages from a downtown location. Because the business is centrally located, it attracts customers from the entire trading area of the city. In addition, a small business usually benefits from the customer traffic generated by the other stores in the district. Many cities have undertaken revitalization efforts in their CBDs and have transformed these areas into thriving, vigorous hubs of economic activity that are proving to be ideal locations for small businesses. However, locating in some CBDs does have certain disadvantages. Many CBDs are characterized by intense competition, high rental rates, traffic congestion, and inadequate parking facilities.

ENTREPRENEURIAL PROFILE: Fran Tate: Pepe's North of the Border One of the most unusual locations for a Mexican restaurant is Barrow, Alaska, the northernmost town in North America, home to Pepe's North of the Border. Entrepreneur Fran Tate chose the central business district of her beloved hometown (population 4,212) at 1204 Agvik Street as the location for her restaurant. Although the low temperature in Barrow is below freezing an average of 324 days of the year, Pepe's North of the Border does a booming business with tourists and with locals, most of whom are native Inupiats. One travel writer has awarded Pepe's North of the Border the Golden Flamingo Award, which goes to "attractions of exceptional concept and scope."[47] ■

Beginning in the 1950s, many cities saw their older downtown business districts begin to decay as residents moved to the suburbs and began shopping at newer, more conveniently located malls. Today, however, many of these CBDs are experiencing rebirth as cities restore them to their former splendor and shoppers return. Many customers find irresistible the charming atmosphere that traditional downtown districts offer with their rich mix of stores, their unique architecture and streetscapes, and their historic character. Cities have begun to reverse the urban decay of their downtown business districts through proactive revitalization programs designed to attract visitors and residents alike to cultural events by locating major theaters and museums in the downtown area. In addition, many cities are providing economic incentives to real estate developers to build apartment and condominium complexes in the heart of the downtown area. Vitality is returning as residents live and shop in the once nearly abandoned downtown areas. The "ghost-town" image is being replaced by both younger and older residents who love the convenience, culture, and excitement of life at the city center.

ENTREPRENEURIAL PROFILE: Nello Gioia: Ristorante Bergamo *Forbes* recently named Greenville, South Carolina, one of America's Best Downtowns, but 30 years ago, the city's central business district was a far different place. Nello Gioia, owner of Ristorante Bergamo, an upscale Italian restaurant, took a chance on a downtown location on Main Street in Greenville in 1985 when the city was just beginning an ambitious revitalization of its central business district. Unlike the busy, vibrant, highly desirable location Greenville's downtown is today, what Gioia saw then was a seedy-looking street spattered with offices, a few longtime resident businesses, and lots of shuttered and vacant stores. "The month before we opened, I got cold feet," recalls Gioia. "But I was up to my neck. I had to do it." Gioia had considered locating in a nearby regional mall and a strip mall but decided that those locations were inconsistent with the image he wanted to create for his restaurant. "The one place that resembled where I came from [Bergamo, Italy] was downtown," says Gioia.[48] ■

Today, Gioia is glad he took the chance on a downtown location; Greenville's central business district, with its eclectic mix of restaurants, small shops, and cultural events, has become a well-known success story, and many other cities across the United States are using it as a model for reclaiming their own downtowns.

Neighborhood Locations

Small businesses that locate near residential neighborhoods rely heavily on the local trading area for business. Businesses that provide convenience as a major attraction for customers find that locating on a street or road just outside major residential areas provides the needed traffic counts essential for success. Gas stations and convenience stores thrive in these high-traffic areas. One study of food stores found that the majority of the typical grocer's customers live within a five-mile radius. The primary advantages of a neighborhood location include relatively low operating rent and close contact with customers.

ENTREPRENEURIAL PROFILE: Bill and Erik Young: Ace Hardware When father and son entrepreneurs Bill and Erik Young opened their second Ace Hardware store in Asheville, North Carolina, they knew that the competition from big-box hardware stores such as Lowe's and Home Depot would be intense. Not only did they stock items and brands that the big-box retailers did not carry, such as pet food and supplies and Benjamin Moore paint, but they also chose their location strategically. The Youngs selected a site that was away from their big-box competitors and between two large neighborhoods, making their independent store the most convenient choice for shoppers.[49] ■

Shopping Centers and Malls

Until the early twentieth century, central business districts were the primary shopping venues in the United States. As cars and transportation networks became more prevalent in the 1920s, shopping centers began popping up outside cities' central business districts. Then in October 1956, the nation's first shopping mall, Southdale, opened in the Minneapolis, Minnesota, suburb of Edina.

Designed by Victor Gruen, the fully enclosed mall featured 72 shops anchored by two competing department stores (a radical concept at the time), a garden courtyard with a goldfish pond, an aviary, hanging plants, and artificial trees. With its multilevel layout and parking garage, Southdale was a huge success and forever changed the way Americans would shop.[50] Today, shopping centers and malls are a mainstay of the American landscape. Approximately 108,500 shopping centers and 1,000 traditional enclosed malls operate in the United States.[51] Because many different types of stores operate under one roof, shopping centers give meaning to the term "one-stop shopping." In a typical month, nearly 187 million adults visit malls or shopping centers, generating $2.25 trillion in annual sales, an amount that represents more than half of all retail sales in the United States.[52] There are eight types of shopping centers (see Table 14.4):

- *Neighborhood shopping centers.* The typical neighborhood shopping center is relatively small, containing from 3 to 12 stores and serving a population of up to 40,000 people who live within a 10-minute drive. The anchor store in these centers is usually a supermarket or a drugstore. Neighborhood shopping centers typically are straight-line strip malls with parking available in front and serve primarily the daily shopping needs of customers in the surrounding area.

- *Community shopping centers.* A community shopping center contains from 12 to 50 stores and serves a population ranging from 40,000 to 150,000 people. The leading tenant often is a large department or variety store, a superdrugstore, or a supermarket. Community shopping centers sell more clothing and other soft goods than do neighborhood shopping centers. Of the eight types of shopping centers, community shopping centers take on the greatest variety of shapes, designs, and tenants.

- *Power centers.* A power center combines the drawing strength of a large regional mall with the convenience of a neighborhood shopping center. Anchored by several large specialty retailers, such as warehouse clubs, discount department stores, or large specialty stores, these centers target older, wealthier baby boomers who want selection and convenience. Anchor stores usually account for 80 percent of power center space, compared with 50 percent in the typical community shopping center. Just as in a shopping mall, small businesses can benefit from the traffic generated by anchor stores, but they must choose their locations carefully so that they are not overshadowed by their larger neighbors. William James recently opened the Arms Room gun shop, which includes a shooting range, in a former Circuit City store in a power center in Houston, Texas. James spent $5 million to purchase and renovate the 20,000-square-foot building, a bargain compared to what it would have cost to build.[53]

- *Theme or festival centers.* Festival shopping centers employ a unifying theme that individual stores display in their decor and sometimes in the merchandise they sell. Entertainment is a common theme for these shopping centers, which often target tourists. Many festival shopping centers are located in urban areas and are housed in older, sometimes historic buildings that have been renovated to serve as shopping centers.

- *Outlet centers.* As their name suggests, outlet centers feature manufacturers' and retailers' outlet stores selling name-brand goods at a discount. Unlike most other types of shopping centers, outlet centers typically have no anchor stores; the discounted merchandise they offer draws sufficient traffic. Most outlet centers are open air and are laid out in strips or in clusters, creating small "villages" of shops.

- *Lifestyle centers.* Typically located near affluent residential neighborhoods where their target customers live, lifestyle centers are designed to look less like shopping centers and malls and more like the busy streets in the central business districts that existed in towns and cities in their heyday. Occupied by many upscale national chain restaurants such as P. F. Chang and specialty stores such as Talbots, Coach, and many others, these centers combine shopping convenience and entertainment ranging from movie theaters and open-air concerts to art galleries and people watching. "Lifestyle centers create a shopping-leisure destination that's an extension of customers' personal lifestyles," says one industry expert. The typical lifestyle center generates between $400 and $500 in sales per square foot compared to $350 in sales per square foot in traditional malls. Lifestyle centers are

TABLE 14.4 Types of Shopping Centers

Type of Shopping Center	Concept	Square Footage (Including Anchors)	Acreage	Typical Anchor		Anchor Ratio (%)[a]	Primary Trade Area (Miles)[b]
				Number	Type		
Malls							
Regional center	General and fashion merchandise; mall (typically enclosed)	480,000–800,000	40–100	2 or more	Full-line department store; junior department store; mass merchant; discount department store; fashion apparel	50–70	5–15
Superregional center	Similar to regional center but offers more variety	>800,000	60–120	3 or more	Full-line department store; junior department store; mass merchant; fashion apparel	50–70	5–25
Open-air centers							
Neighborhood center	Convenience	30,000–150,000	3–15	1 or more	Supermarket	30–50	3
Community center	General merchandise; convenience	100,000–350,000	10–40	2 or more	Discount department store; supermarket; drug; home improvement; large specialty or discount apparel	40–60	3–6
Lifestyle center	Upscale national chain specialty stores, dining, and entertainment in an outdoor setting	150,000–500,000 but can be larger or smaller	10–40	0–2	Not usually anchored in the traditional sense but may include bookstore; large specialty retailers; multiplex cinema; small department store	0–50	8–12
Power center	Category-dominant anchors; few small business tenants	250,000–600,000	25–80	3 or more	Category killer; home improvement; discount; department store; warehouse club; off price	75–90	5–10
Theme/festival center	Leisure; tourist oriented; retail and service	80,000–250,000	5–20	Unspecified	Restaurants; entertainment	N/A	25–75
Outlet center	Manufacturers' outlet stores	50,000–400,000	10–50	N/A	Manufacturers' outlet stores	N/A	25–75

[a] The share of a center's total square footage that is occupied by its anchors.
[b] The area from which 60% to 80% of the center's sales originate.

Source: Table adapted from *U.S. Shopping Center Definitions*, April 2009. Copyright © 2009 by the International Council of Shopping Centers. Reprinted with permission.

among the most popular types of shopping centers being built today, but the first lifestyle center, The Shops of Saddle Creek, opened in Germantown, Tennessee, in 1987.[54]

●   *Regional shopping malls.* The regional shopping mall serves a large trading area, usually from 5 to 15 miles or more in all directions. These enclosed malls contain from 50 to 100 stores and serve a population of 150,000 or more living within a 20- to 40-minute drive. The anchor is typically one or more major department stores with smaller specialty stores occupying the spaces between the anchors. Clothing is one of the most popular items sold in regional shopping malls.

- *Superregional shopping malls.* A superregional mall is similar to a regional mall but is bigger, containing more anchor stores and a greater variety of shops selling deeper lines of merchandise. Its trade area stretches up to 25 or more miles out. Canada's West Edmonton Mall, the largest mall in North America, with more than 800 stores and 100 restaurants, is one of the most famous superregional malls in the world. In addition to its abundance of retail shops, the mall, which draws an average of nearly 31 million visitors a year, contains an ice skating rink, a water park, an amusement park, an aquarium, a bungee tower, miniature golf courses, and a 21-screen movie complex.

Major department or mass merchandising stores serve as anchors and attract a significant volume of customer traffic to malls and shopping centers, allowing small businesses with their unique, sometimes quirky product offerings; boutique atmospheres; and marketing approaches to thrive in their shadows. In fact, as mall vacancy rates have climbed, mall owners are eager to rent space to small businesses, tenants that in the past many of them had shunned in favor of large brand-name retailers.

ENTREPRENEURIAL PROFILE: John Myers: Party Palace John Myers had a successful but highly seasonal business renting inflatable bounce houses and other equipment for backyard parties. His goal was to secure an indoor location, and in 2010, he rented a space that had once housed an Old Navy store in Aviation Mall in Queensbury, New York. Myers converted the 18,000-square-foot space into the ideal home for the Party Palace, which hosts children's parties and offers a full line of inflatables, miniature golf, playhouses, kids' rides, and a stuffed animal center.[55] ∎

When evaluating a mall or shopping center location, an entrepreneur should consider the following questions:

- Is there a good fit with other products and brands sold in the mall or center?
- Who are the other tenants? Which stores are the anchors that will bring people into the mall or center?
- Demographically, is the center a good fit for your products or services? What are its customer demographics? (see Figure 14.1)
- How much foot traffic does the mall or center generate? How much traffic passes the specific site you are considering?
- What is the mall's average sales per square foot (a common metric for measuring a mall's attractiveness)? The average for all malls is $350 per square foot, but one-third of malls generate less than $300 per square foot in sales. Only about 15 percent of malls generate sales per square foot of $400 or more.[56]
- How much vehicle traffic does the mall or center generate? Check its proximity to major population centers, the volume of tourists it draws, and the volume of drive-by freeway traffic. A mall or center that scores well on all three is more likely to be a winner.
- What is the mall's vacancy rate? What is the turnover rate of its tenants?
- How much is the rent, and how is it calculated? Most mall tenants pay a base amount of rent plus a small percentage of their sales above a specified level.

A mall location is no guarantee of business success, however. Malls have been under pressure lately, especially from online retailers and fast-growing discount stores, and mall vacancy rates have been slow to recover from the Great Recession. Many weaker malls (known as "grayfields") have closed or have been redeveloped. The basic problem is an oversupply of mall space; there is about 20 square feet of mall retail space for every person in the United States! The last new indoor shopping mall opened in 2006. Another problem is that many malls are showing their

FIGURE 14.1

Shopping Mall Patterns

Source: International Council of Shopping Centers, 2010.

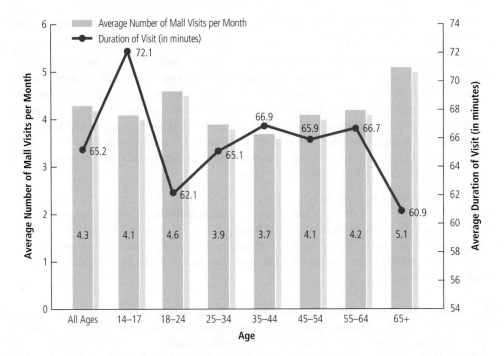

age; in fact, 85 percent of the malls in the United States are more than 20 years old.[57] In addition, the demographic makeup of an area's shoppers often changes over time, creating a new socio-economic customer base that may not be compatible with a small company's target customer profile. As a result, many malls have undergone extensive renovations to transform themselves into "entertailing" destinations, adding entertainment features to their existing retail space in an attempt to generate more traffic. For instance, in addition to its 520 retail shops and 60 restaurants, Minneapolis's Mall of America, the second-largest mall in the United States (located only a few miles from Southdale, the nation's first mall), includes a Nickelodeon Universe amusement park at its center, a 1.2-million-gallon aquarium, and a 14-screen movie complex in its 4.2 million square feet of space.[58]

Near Competitors

One of the most important factors in choosing a retail or service location is the compatibility of nearby stores with the retail or service customer. For example, stores selling high-priced goods find it advantageous to locate near competitors to facilitate comparison shopping. Locating near competitors might be a key factor for success in those businesses selling goods that customers shop for and compare on the basis of price, quality, color, and other factors.

Although some business owners avoid locations near direct competitors, others see locating near rivals as an advantage. For instance, restaurateurs know that successful restaurants attract other restaurants, which, in turn, attract more customers. Many cities have at least one "restaurant row," where restaurants cluster together; each restaurant feeds customers to the others.

Locating near competitors has its limits, however. Clustering too many businesses of a single type into a small area ultimately erodes their sales once the market reaches the saturation point. When an area becomes saturated with competitors, the shops cannibalize sales from one another, making it difficult for any of them to be successful.

Inside Large Retail Stores

Rather than compete against giant retailers, some small business owners are cooperating with them, locating their businesses inside the larger company's stores. These small companies offer products that the large retailers do not and benefit from the large volume of customer traffic the large stores attract. The world's largest retailer, Wal-Mart, is a host to several small businesses, including franchisees of national chains Subway, McDonald's, Seattle's Best Coffee, and others.[59]

Nontraditional Locations

Rather than select a location and try to draw customers to it, many small businesses are discovering where their customers already are and setting up locations there. Many of these are nontraditional locations, such as airports, museums, office buildings, churches, casinos, college and university campuses, athletic arenas, and others, that offer high concentrations of potential customers. In many cases, these locations are smaller and less expensive to build but generate more sales per square foot than traditional, full-size stores. Dunkin' Donuts has more than 500 nontraditional locations out of 6,800 outlets in the United States, including locations in theme parks, military bases, universities, travel centers on interstate highways, and others. About 8,000 of Subway's 35,000 restaurants worldwide are in nontraditional locations, including a high school in Detroit in which students operate the outlet, and account for 20 percent of the chain's total sales. Subway also has an outlet on the MS *Stolzenfels* riverboat that cruises the Rhine River in Germany.[60]

Home-Based Businesses

For millions of entrepreneurs, home is where the business is, and their numbers are swelling. One recent study from the Small Business Administration reports that 52 percent of all small companies are home based.[61] Although a home-based retail business usually is not a good idea, locating a service business at home is quite popular. Many service companies do not have customers come to their places of business, so an expensive office location is unnecessary. For instance, customers typically contact plumbers or exterminators by telephone, and the work is performed in customers' homes.

Entrepreneurs locating their businesses at home reap several benefits. Perhaps the biggest benefit is the low cost of setting up the business. Most often, home-based entrepreneurs set up shop in a spare bedroom or basement, avoiding the cost of renting, leasing, or buying a building. With a few basic pieces of office equipment—a computer or tablet, printer, copier, and smart phone—a lone entrepreneur can perform just like a major corporation.

ENTREPRENEURIAL PROFILE: Paul Morris: CheekyTeez After 15 years, Paul Morris left his corporate job in marketing and advertising and spent a year researching and preparing a business plan for CheekyTeez, a home-based business that sells T-shirts and clothing imprinted with cheeky slogans and custom items that customers design themselves by adding their own text, photos, and graphics. Morris runs the business from his home in Kingsley, Australia, and appreciates the flexibility and low cost that his home-based business allows.[62] ■

Choosing a home location has certain disadvantages, however. Interruptions are more frequent, the refrigerator is all too handy, work is always just a few steps away, and isolation can be a problem. Another difficulty facing some home-based entrepreneurs involves zoning laws. As their businesses grow and become more successful, entrepreneurs' neighbors often begin to complain about the increased traffic, noise, and disruptions from deliveries, employees, and customers who drive through their residential neighborhoods to conduct business. Many communities now face the challenge of passing updated zoning laws that reflect the reality of today's home-based businesses while protecting the interests of residential home owners.

On the Road

Some entrepreneurs are finding that the best location is not a permanent location but a mobile business that takes products and services to its customers. Veterinarians, dentists, restaurants, and others are outfitting mobile units and taking their businesses on the road. Although mobile entrepreneurs avoid the costs of building or renovating permanent locations, they must incur the expense of setting up their mobile businesses. They also face other obstacles, such as finding suitable parking spaces in high-traffic areas, complaints from nearby owners of businesses, and securing the necessary permits to operate. In New York City, entrepreneurs complain that getting one of the 3,100 year-round permits the city issues to operate a food truck or cart can take a decade or more, causing many people to buy permits (which the city issues for a fee of $200) from existing permit holders. One entrepreneur recently paid $144,000 for a permit to operate a food cart at the south entrance of the Central Park Zoo.[63]

LO4

Explain the site selection process for manufacturers.

The Location Decision for Manufacturers

The criteria for the location decision for manufacturers are very different from those of retailers and service businesses; however, the decision can have just as much impact on the company's success. In some cases, a manufacturer has special needs that influence the choice of a location. For instance, when one manufacturer of photographic plates and digital cameras was searching for a location for a new plant, it had to limit its search to those sites with a large supply of available fresh water, a necessary part of its process. In other cases, the location decision is controlled by zoning ordinances. If a manufacturer's process creates offensive odors or excessive noise, it may be even further restricted in its choices.

The type of transportation network required dictates location of a factory in some cases. Some manufacturers may need to locate on a railroad siding, whereas others may need only reliable trucking service. If raw materials are purchased by the carload for economies of scale, the location must be convenient to a railroad siding. Bulk materials are sometimes shipped by barge and consequently require a facility convenient to a navigable river or lake. The added cost of using multiple shipping methods (e.g., rail to truck or barge to truck) can significantly increase shipping costs and make a location unfeasible for a manufacturer.

As fuel costs escalate, the cost of shipping finished products to customers also influences the location decision for many manufacturers, forcing them to open factories or warehouses in locations that are close to their primary markets to reduce transportation costs. Thermo-Pur Technologies, a small company that has developed a new stainless-steel heat exchanger core that makes automotive radiators lighter, more efficient at transferring heat, and less expensive to manufacture, recently selected the Clemson University International Center for Automotive Research in Greenville, South Carolina, as the location for its headquarters and first North American factory. Company managers considered other locations but selected Greenville because of its growing reputation as a knowledge center for automotive products, excellent transportation network, proximity to potential customers (including BMW, Mercedes Benz, Kia, and others), cost of operation, and overall quality of life.[64]

Foreign Trade Zones

foreign trade zone

a specially designated area in or near a U.S. customs port of entry that allows resident companies to import materials and components from foreign countries; assemble, process, manufacture, or package them; and then ship the finished product while either reducing or eliminating tariffs and duties.

Foreign trade zones can be an attractive location for small manufacturers that engage in global trade and are looking to reduce or eliminate the tariffs, duties, and excise taxes they pay on the materials and the parts they import and the goods they export. A **foreign trade zone** (see Figure 14.2) is a specially designated area in or near a U.S. customs port of entry that allows resident companies to import materials and components from foreign countries; assemble, process, manufacture, or package them; and then ship the finished product back out while either reducing or eliminating completely tariffs and duties. As far as tariffs and duties are concerned, a company located in a foreign trade zone is treated as if it is located outside the United States. For instance, a maker of speakers can import components from around the world and assemble them at its plant located in a foreign trade zone. The company pays no duties on the components it imports or on the speakers it exports to other foreign markets. The only duties the manufacturer pays are on the speakers it sells

FIGURE 14.2

How a Foreign Trade Zone Works

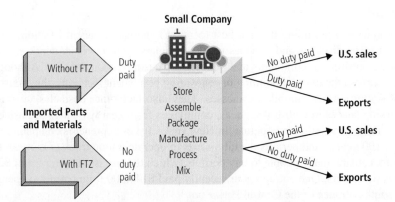

in the United States. There are 256 foreign trade zones and 498 subzones, which are special foreign trade zones that are established for limited purposes, operating in the United States.

Business Incubators

For many start-up companies, a business incubator may make the ideal initial location. A **business incubator** is an organization that combines low-cost, flexible rental space with a multitude of support services for its small business residents. The primary reason for establishing an incubator is to enhance economic development by growing new businesses that create jobs and diversify the local economy. An incubator's goal is to nurture young companies during the volatile start-up period and to help them survive until they are strong enough to go out on their own. Common sponsors of incubators include economic development organizations (31 percent), government entities (21 percent), colleges or universities (20 percent), economic development organizations (15 percent), and others. Most incubators (54 percent) are "mixed use," hosting a variety of start-up companies, followed by incubators that focus on technology companies.[65] A growing number of incubators operate virtually with no physical presence much like a social network, providing entrepreneurs with mentoring and the opportunity to collaborate with other entrepreneurs. Sparkseed, a virtual incubator in San Francisco, focuses on helping start-ups that are solving social and environmental issues. So far, Sparkseed has helped entrepreneurs launch 15 companies.[66]

In addition to discounted lease rates, incubators also offer tenants valuable resources, such as telephone systems, computers and software, high-speed Internet service, meeting and conference rooms, and sometimes management consulting services and financing contacts. Not only do these services save young companies money (reducing a small company's start-up costs in some cases by 40 to 50 percent), but they also save them valuable time. Entrepreneurs can focus on getting their products and services to market faster than competitors rather than searching for the resources they need to build their companies. The typical incubator has entry requirements that prospective residents must meet. Incubators also have criteria that establish the conditions a business must maintain to remain in the facility as well as the expectations for "graduation" into the business community (usually within three to five years).

More than 1,200 incubators operate across the United States, up from just 12 in 1980, and house an estimated 41,000 start-up companies.[67] Perhaps the greatest advantage of choosing to locate a start-up company in an incubator is a greater chance for success; according to the National Business Incubation Association, graduates from incubators have a success rate of 87 percent, and 84 percent of the companies that graduate stay in the local community.[68]

ENTREPRENEURIAL PROFILE: Jenny Britton Bauer and Charly Bauer: Jeni's Splendid Ice Cream Jeni Britton Bauer spotted an opportunity to market artisan ice cream made from fresh, all-natural ingredients in her hometown of Columbus, Ohio, and started Jeni's Splendid Ice Cream with her husband Charly in the North Market, a business incubator located in a 44,000-square-foot space that was once home to Columbus's first public market. Today, Jeni has eight retail locations and a wholesale distribution company that sells her unique menu of flavors, such as Salty Caramel, Thai Chili, and Bourbon Butter Pecan. Although Jeni's Splendid Ice Cream has graduated from the incubator, North Market continues to nurture 35 food-related start-up companies that want to emulate Jeni's success.[69] ∎

Layout and Design Considerations

Once an entrepreneur chooses the best location for his or her business, the next issue to address is designing the proper layout for the space to maximize sales (retail) or productivity (manufacturing or service). **Layout** is the logical arrangement of the physical facilities in a business that contributes to efficient operations, increased productivity, and higher sales. Planning for the most effective and efficient layout in a business environment can produce dramatic improvements in a company's operating effectiveness, efficiency, and overall performance. An attractive, effective layout can help a company's recruiting efforts, reduce absenteeism, and improve employee productivity and satisfaction. The comprehensive *U.S. Workplace Survey* by global design firm Gensler reports that employees believe that the quality and the quantity of their work would increase by an average of 25 percent with better workplace design.[70] The changing nature of work

business incubator an organization that combines low-cost, flexible rental space with a multitude of support services for its small business residents.

The Washington Post/Getty

LO5

Describe the criteria used to analyze the layout and design considerations of a building, including the Americans with Disabilities Act.

layout the logical arrangement of the physical facilities in a business that contributes to efficient operations, increased productivity, and higher sales.

You Be the Consultant

Business Incubators: A Nurturing Environment for Small Companies

A business incubator is a location that provides a safe place for entrepreneurs to start businesses, providing them with low-cost space, access to computers and high-speed Internet connections, office equipment, business services, and sometimes experts willing to offer advice and consulting. In 1956, Joseph Mancuso created the first incubator in an abandoned 85,000-square-foot manufacturing facility in Batavia, New York, that he named the Batavia Industrial Center. Several small business tenants signed up, including a winery, a nonprofit organization, and a chicken processor. When Mancuso saw newly hatched chicks running around the center, he realized that it provided the same kind of nurturing environment for new businesses that an incubator provided for baby chicks and began referring to the center as an incubator. The name stuck (although some people refer to them as business accelerators), and now 1,200 business incubators, most of them nonprofit organizations sponsored by state or local governments or universities, operate across the United States with the goal of attracting and growing entrepreneurial talent.

Some incubators attract a variety of companies, and others specialize in particular niches. As its name implies, Blue Ridge Food Ventures, located in Asheville, North Carolina, is a niche incubator that houses food-oriented businesses in an 11,000-square-foot manufacturing operation that includes wet- and dry-preparation areas (for products ranging from jams, jellies, and sauces to bakery products) and a commercial kitchen. Advisers provide support in areas such as developing products, navigating the maze of regulations governing safe production of food products and dietary supplements, packaging and label design, and others. The incubator also includes a natural products processing area in which entrepreneurs can convert herbs and other plant materials into finished products. Entrepreneurs in the incubator have access to all of the equipment they need, including normal commercial kitchen equipment, bottling machines, labeling machines, and others. Jeannine Buscher and Sarah Schomber, cofounders of Buchi, a company that makes kombucha, a fermented tea that people have been drinking for thousands of years, operated their business from Buscher's dining room before moving into the Blue Ridge Food Ventures incubator. Today, the entrepreneurs process and bottle their tea in a 6,000-square-foot facility of their own but credit the incubator for giving them a strong start. "It's hard to say what kind of business we'd have today if we didn't have Blue Ridge Food Ventures to help us get started," says Buscher. "We could never have afforded the kind of place we have now two years ago."

Innovation Depot, a public–private venture between the city of Birmingham, Alabama, Jefferson County, and the University of Alabama at Birmingham, is housed in a former Sears department store and targets as its tenants young technology companies in areas that include biotechnology, life sciences, business services, information technology, software, and others. At 140,000 square

feet and just three blocks from the university campus, it is the largest business incubator in the Southeast and features equipment that small technology companies need, including wet laboratory space, a high-speed centrifuge, a microscopic optics system, a minus-80-degree freezer, and an autoclave. Currently housing 84 tenants that employ 460 people, Innovation Depot has an estimated $1 billion impact on Birmingham's economy. To become tenants, entrepreneurs must submit their business plans and go through an interview process. "Most of the people here have started or even sold companies before," says Susan Matlock, the incubator's CEO. Vaxin, a company that is developing proprietary vaccines that are administered by application to the skin or to nasal passages, recently secured a $21.7 million contract with the U.S. Department of Health and Human Services. Another tenant, Agenta Biotechnologies, won a $150,000 grant from the National Institutes of Health for its groundbreaking work on molecular processes for generating bone and skin using only DNA.

Highland Partners, a venture capital firm with offices in Boston, Silicon Valley, Shanghai, and Europe, sponsors a special summer business incubator aimed at college students with entrepreneurial aspirations. Founded in 2007, the incubator's goal is to provide collegiate entrepreneurs with the resources they need to launch and grow their companies. The incubator takes no equity in the companies it selects, choosing instead to give each company a $15,000 grant and to provide founders with advice, counsel, and access to a star-studded network of business contacts. More than 200 companies apply for the 10 spots in the summer incubator. Recent companies selected for the prestigious program include Clinkle, a software-based mobile payment platform, and Bard27, a Web site that helps small tour operators create and market unique tours.

1. What advantages does starting a company in a business incubator offer an entrepreneur? What are some of the disadvantages of locating in an incubator?

2. What benefits do business incubators provide for the local communities in which they are housed?

Sources: Adapted from Darren Dahl, "How to Choose and an Incubator," *New York Times*, January 26, 2011, http://www.nytimes.com/2011/01/27/business/smallbusiness/27sbiz.html; Martin Swant, "Alabama Business Incubators Touted for Economic Growth," *Birmingham News*, January 24, 2012, http://blog.al.com/businessnews/2012/01/alabama_business_incubators_to.html; Michael Tomberlin, "Birmingham's Innovation Depot Technology Incubator Posts Best Progress Report Ever," *Birmingham News*, March 23, 2012, http://blog.al.com/businessnews/2012/03/birminghams_innovation_depot_t.html; "Who We Are," Innovation Depot, http://www.innovationdepot.net/#/about; Steve Strauss, "Business Incubator Can Mean a Faster Start for Your Start-Up," *USA Today*, May 9, 2011, http://www.usatoday.com/money/smallbusiness/columnist/strauss/2011-05-08-business-incubator_n.htm; "Innovation Depot Posts $1 Billion in Economic Impact," *Amazing Alabama*, http://www.amazingalabama.com/innovation_depot_post_1_billion_economic_impact.html; Matthew DeLuca, Portrait of an Incubated Summer," *Inc.*, August 2, 2011, http://www.inc.com/articles/201108/a-summer-in-good-company.html; and "Highland Capital Partners Announces 2011 Summer@Highland Teams," July 20, 2011, http://www.hcp.com/news/newsdetails.php/id/92871.

demands that work space design also changes. Although many jobs require the ability to focus on "heads down," individual tasks, collaboration with coworkers is becoming a more significant component of work. An effective work space must be flexible enough to accommodate and encourage both types of work. Increasingly, work is becoming more complex, team based, technology dependent, and mobile; work spaces must change to accommodate these characteristics. The study by Gensler concludes that top-performing companies have work spaces that are more effective than those of average companies, particularly for collaboration. Gensler also reports that employees at top-performing companies spend 23 percent more time collaborating with their coworkers than do employees at average companies.[71]

ENTREPRENEURIAL PROFILE: Mark Zuckerberg: Facebook Facebook recently moved into its new headquarters on a 57-acre tract in Menlo Park, California, whose design encourages creativity, productivity, interaction, and collaboration among its 2,000 workers. Designers took out interior walls, cubicles, and private offices in the existing building to create an open space, covered the walls with whiteboard paint, and sprinkled comfortable sofas and hundreds of small breakout rooms throughout the space where workers can conduct informal meetings and brainstorming sessions. In a tribute to Facebook's "hacker culture," the design features exposed beams and ductwork and plywood-covered corridors to "remind us that our work is never done," says John Tenanes, the company's real estate director. The renovated building features a glass roof that provides plenty of natural light and a central courtyard with cafés, dry cleaners, a fitness center, a medical clinic, and other services to maximize employee convenience. When completed, Facebook's complex will include 10 buildings with a total of 1 million square feet.[72] ∎

When creating a layout, managers must consider its impact on space itself (comfort, flexibility, size, and ergonomics), the people who occupy it (type of work, special requirements, need for interaction, and tasks performed), and the technology they use (communication, Internet access, and equipment).[73] The following factors have a significant impact on a space's layout and design.

Size

A building must be large enough to accommodate a business's daily operations comfortably. If it is too small at the outset of operations, efficiency will suffer. A space must have enough room for customers' movement, inventory, displays, storage, work areas, offices, and restrooms. Haphazard layouts undermine employee productivity and create organizational chaos. Too many small business owners start their operations in locations that are already overcrowded or lack the capacity for expansion. The result is that an owner is forced to make a costly move to a new location within the first few years of operation.

Associated Press

"It'll take a little getting used to, but we're saving a bundle on cubicles, and you'll find you are scratching a lot less."

From The Wall Street Journal, permission Cartoon Features Syndicate.

ENTREPRENEURIAL PROFILE: Alexandra Cirimelli: Serenite Maison When interior designer Alexandra Cirimelli and her music producer husband, Gary, moved to tiny Leiper's Fork, Tennessee, she opened Serenite Maison, a store that sells antique furniture, lighting, accessories, textiles, and jewelry from all over the world, in a small, 300-square-foot space. Within nine months, her company outgrew the space and moved into another store twice the size of the original. Within a year, sales were so strong that Cirimelli was again on the lookout for a larger building. This time, she selected a 3,000-square-foot former general store built in 1914 that provides the ideal backdrop for displaying the shop's eclectic collections and large pieces of antique furniture that her customers want.[74] ■

Construction and External Appearance

Is the construction of the building sound? Having an expert look it over before buying and leasing the property can pay big dividends. Beyond the soundness of construction, does the building have attractive external and internal appearances? The physical appearance of the building provides customers with their first impression of a business. Retailers and service providers, in particular, must recognize the importance of creating the proper image for their stores and how their shops' layouts and physical facilities influence this image. A store's external appearance contributes significantly to establishing its identity among its target customers. Is the building's appearance consistent with the entrepreneur's desired image for the business? In many ways, a building's appearance sets the tone for what the customer expects in the way of quality and service. A building's appearance should reflect a company's "personality." Should the building project an upscale image or an economical one? Is the atmosphere informal and relaxed or formal and businesslike? Physical facilities send important messages to customers.

Communicating the right signals through layout and physical facilities is an important step in attracting a steady stream of customers. Retail consultant Paco Underhill advises merchants to "seduce" passersby with their storefronts. "The seduction process should start a minimum of 10 paces away," he says.[75]

ENTREPRENEURIAL PROFILE: Boston Market Boston Market, a chain of nearly 500 restaurants that serve home-style meals, recently renovated its stores in a format it calls "America's Kitchen Table" after a 10-store test resulted in a 20 percent increase in sales in just five months. The design features an inviting atmosphere with warm colors designed to elicit happy memories of gatherings in the family kitchen. Boston Market added chef's carving stations and replaced stainless-steel holding trays with colorful enamel pots that keep food hot longer and send a message of freshness. The company eliminated disposable plates and utensils, replacing

© America/Alamy

them with real plates and silverware, and added new menu items and "dining room ambassadors" to enhance customer service.[76] ■

A store's window display can be a powerful selling tool if used properly. Often, a store's display window is an afterthought, and many business owners neglect to change their displays often enough. The following tips help entrepreneurs create window displays that sell:

- *Keep displays simple.* Simple, uncluttered, and creative arrangements of merchandise draw the most attention and have the greatest impact on potential customers.

- *Keep displays clean and current.* Dusty, dingy displays or designs that are outdated send a negative message to passersby.

- *Change displays frequently.* Customers do not want to see the same merchandise on display every time they enter a store. Experts recommend changing displays at least quarterly, but stores selling trendy items should change their displays twice a month.

- *Get expert help if necessary.* Not every business owner has a knack for designing window displays. Their best bet is to hire a professional or to work with the design department at a local college or university.

Entrances

Entrances to a business should *invite* customers into a store. Wide entryways and attractive merchandise displays that are set back from the doorway draw customers into a business. A store's entrance should catch passing customers' attention and draw them inside. "That's where you want somebody to slam on the brakes and realize they're going someplace new," says retail consultant Paco Underhill.[77] Retailers with heavy traffic flows, such as supermarkets or drugstores, often install automatic doors to ensure a smooth traffic flow into and out of their stores. Retailers must remove any barriers that interfere with customers' easy access to the storefront. Broken sidewalks, sagging steps, mud puddles, and sticking or heavy doors create not only obstacles that might discourage potential customers but also legal hazards for a business if they cause customers to be injured. The goal is to overcome anything that creates what one expert calls "threshold resistance."[78]

The Americans with Disabilities Act

Approximately 18 percent of people in the United States are disabled.[79] The **Americans with Disabilities Act (ADA)**, passed in 1990, requires practically all businesses, regardless of their

Americans with Disabilities Act (ADA)
a law that requires practically all businesses to make their facilities available to physically challenged customers and employees.

size, to make their facilities available to physically challenged customers and employees. Most states have similar laws, many of them more stringent than the ADA, that apply to small companies as well. The rules of the these state laws and the ADA's Title III are designed to ensure that mentally and physically challenged customers have equal access to a firm's goods or services. For instance, the act requires business owners to remove architectural and communication barriers when "readily achievable" (accomplished without much difficulty or expense). The ADA allows flexibility in how a business achieves this equal access, however. For example, a restaurant could either provide menus in Braille or offer to have a staff member read the menu to blind customers. A small dry cleaner might not be able to add a wheelchair ramp to its storefront without incurring significant expense, but the owner could comply with the ADA by offering curbside pickup and delivery services at no extra charge for disabled customers.

The Department of Justice revised the ADA in 2010, and all newly constructed or renovated buildings that are open to the public and were occupied after March 15, 2012, must comply with the 2010 requirements. For example, in retail stores, checkout aisles must be wide enough—at least 36 inches—to accommodate wheelchairs. Restaurants must have at least 5 percent of their tables accessible to wheelchair-bound patrons. Miniature golf courses must make at least 50 percent of the holes on the course accessible to disabled customers.

Complying with the ADA does not necessarily require businesses to spend large amounts of money. The Department of Justice estimates that more than 20 percent of the cases customers have filed under Title III involved changes the business owners could have made at no cost, and another 60 percent would have cost less than $1,000![80] In addition, companies with $1 million or less in annual sales or with 30 or fewer full-time employees that invest in making their locations more accessible qualify for a tax credit. The credit is 50 percent of their expenses between $250 and $10,250. Businesses that remove physical, structural, and transportation barriers for disabled employees and customers also qualify for a tax deduction of up to $15,000.

Signs

One of the lowest-cost and most effective methods of communicating with customers is a business sign. Signs tell potential customers what a business does, where it is, and what it is selling. The United States is a very mobile society, and a well-designed, well-placed sign can be a powerful tool for reaching potential customers. The Viva McDonald's restaurant on Las Vegas Boulevard (or "the Strip") includes an oversized sign and four jumbo display screens—all with video playback ability—mounted on the front of the store. Designers recognized that a restaurant located in a city known for gaudy neon light displays required a sign that would stand out to attract customers.[81]

A sign should be large enough for passersby to read from a distance, taking into consideration the location and speed of surrounding traffic arteries. To be most effective, the message should be short, simple, and clear. A sign should be legible both in daylight and at night; proper illumination is a must. Contrasting colors and simple typefaces are best. The most common problems with business signs are that they are illegible, poorly designed, improperly located, poorly maintained, and have color schemes that are unattractive or are hard to read.

Before investing in a sign, an entrepreneur should investigate the local community's sign ordinance. In some cities and towns, local regulations impose restrictions on the size, location, height, and construction materials used in business signs.

Building Interiors

Designing a functional, efficient interior layout demands research, planning, and attention to detail. Retailers in particular have known for a long time that their stores' layouts influence their customers' buying behavior. Retailers such as Cabela's, Barnes & Noble, and Starbucks use layouts that encourage customers to linger and spend time (and money). Others, such as Lowe's, Aldi, and Wal-Mart, reinforce their discount images with layouts that communicate a warehouse environment, often complete with pallets, to shoppers. Luxury retailers, such as Tiffany and Company, Coach, and Nordstrom, create opulent layouts in which their upscale customers feel comfortable.

Coordinating an effective layout is not a haphazard process. **Ergonomics**, the science of adapting work and the work environment to complement employees' strengths and to suit

ergonomics
the science of adapting work and the work environment to complement employees' strengths and to suit customers' needs.

customers' needs, is an integral part of a successful design. For example, chairs, desks, and table heights that allow people to work comfortably can help employees perform their job faster and more easily. Design experts claim that improved lighting, better acoustics, and proper climate control benefit the company as well as employees. An ergonomically designed workplace can improve workers' productivity significantly and reduce days lost due to injuries and accidents. A study for the Commission of Architecture and the Built Environment and the British Council for Offices reports that simple features, such as proper lighting, reduce absenteeism by 15 percent and increase productivity between 2.8 and 20 percent.[82]

Unfortunately, many businesses fail to incorporate ergonomic design principles into their layouts, and the result is costly. The most frequent and most expensive workplace injuries are repetitive strain injuries (RSIs), which cost U.S. businesses $20 billion in workers' compensation claims and $600 million in lost productivity each year. According to the Bureau of Labor Statistics, RSIs cause an injured worker to miss an average of 18 days of work per year, more than twice the time missed for the average injury. RSIs also are a major driver of workers' compensation claims.[83] Workers who spend their days staring at computer monitors (a significant and growing proportion of the workforce) often are victims of RSIs.

The most common RSI is carpal tunnel syndrome, which occurs when repetitive motion causes swelling in the wrist that pinches the nerves in the arm and hand. The good news for employers, however, is that preventing injuries, accidents, and lost days does *not* require spending thousands of dollars on ergonomically correct solutions. Most of the solutions to RSIs are actually quite simple and inexpensive, ranging from installing equipment that eliminates workers' repetitive motions to introducing breaks during which workers engage in exercises designed by occupational therapists to combat RSIs.

Sight, Sound, Scent, and Lighting

Retailers can increase sales by sending important subconscious signals to customers using what design experts call "symbolics." For instance, when shoppers enter a Whole Foods supermarket, the first items they see are displays of fresh flowers. Not only are the flowers' colors and the smells pleasing, but they also send a clear message to customers: "You are embarking on an adventure in freshness in our store—flowers, produce, meats, seafood, *everything.*"[84] Layouts that engage all of customers' senses also increase sales. Retail behavioral expert Paco Underhill, founder of Envirosell, a market research company, says that most of customers' unplanned purchases come after they touch, taste, smell, or hear something in a store. For example, stores that sell fresh food see sales increase if they offer free samples to customers. One study reports that offering shoppers free samples increases not only sales of the item offered but also sales of other products.[85] Research also shows that customers are willing to pay more for products they can see, touch, taste, or try.[86] "If somebody doesn't try 'em, they're not going to buy 'em," quips Underhill.[87] Sight, sound, scent, and lighting are particularly important aspects of retail layout.

SIGHT A business can use colors and visual cues in its interior designs to support its brand and image in subtle yet effective ways. At the Vermont Country Deli in Brattleboro, Vermont, wooden bookshelves and odd tables filled with colorful displays of jams, jellies, and desserts greet customers as they enter the store. The mismatched tables and shelves give the store an authentic, down-home look, and signs such as "Life is short. Eat cookies." entice customers to make purchases. At Whole Foods, prices for fresh fruits and vegetables appear to be hand scrawled on fragments of black slate, a tradition in outdoor markets in Europe—as if a farmer had pulled up that morning, unloaded the produce, and posted the price before heading back to the farm. Some of the produce also is sprinkled with water droplets. When customers at the restaurant Tallulah on the Thames in Newport, Rhode Island, are seated, waiters hand them a rustic clipboard with a handwritten list of the daily "farm-to-table menu." [88] The subtle message these symbolics send to customers is *freshness.*[89]

SOUND In an attempt to engage all of their customers' senses, companies are realizing the impact that sound has on shoppers and are incorporating it into their layouts. Research shows that a business's "soundscape" can have an impact on the length of time customers shop and the amount of money they spend. Background music that appeals to a company's target customers can be an effective marketing tool, subtly communicating important messages about its brand to customers. "Music is an extension of a brand, something you can reinforce without the customer looking at it or touching it," says Greg

Sapier, vice president of Melody, a company that provides customized music to businesses. Quaker State & Lube, a chain of 45 casual dining restaurants that feature an automotive theme, hired experts at Ambiance Radio to create playlists for its shops for different parts of the day. "Lunch and dinner have different playlists, and late night has different music from those," says the company's marketing vice president. At peak times, Quaker State & Lube plays upbeat, fast-tempo music to encourage faster dining and to speed up the number of table turns. Freebirds World Burritos, a chain of 76 Mexican restaurants, plays blaring classic rock music because it appeals to the company's target customers, college students.[90] For retail soundscapes, however, one rule is clear: slow is good. People's biorhythms reflect the sounds around them, and soothing classical music encourages shoppers to relax and slow down, meaning that they will shop longer and spend more. Classical music also makes shoppers feel more affluent and increases sales more than any other type of music.[91]

SCENT Research shows that scents can have a powerful effect in retail stores. The Sense of Smell Institute reports that the average human being can recognize 10,000 different odors and can recall scents with 65 percent accuracy after one year, a much higher recall rate than visual stimuli produce. In one experiment, when Eric Spangenberg of Washington State University diffused a subtle scent of vanilla into the women's department of a store and rose maroc into the men's department, he discovered that sales nearly doubled. He also discovered that if he switched the scents, sales in both departments fell well below their normal average.[92] Vanilla connotes warmth and comfort, and citrus scents tend to be energizing and invigorating.

Many companies—from casinos to convenience stores—are beginning to understand the power of using scent as a sales tool. Bakeries use fans to push the smell of fresh-baked breads and sweets into pedestrian traffic lanes, tempting them to sample some of their delectable goodies. A chain of gas stations in California installed a device that emits the aroma of brewing coffee to customers at its gas pumps to increase coffee sales.[93] Select Comfort, the company that markets the Sleep Number mattress in 400 stores across the United States, worked with ScentAir, a company that designs scents for retailers, to infuse its retail outlets with a blend of cashmere wool, amber, cardamom, cinnamon, and bergamot that conveys a sense of "quiet repose."[94]

LIGHTING Good lighting allows employees to work at maximum efficiency. Proper lighting is measured by the amount of light required to do a job properly with the greatest lighting efficiency. Efficiency is essential because lighting consumes 24 percent of the total energy used in the typical commercial building.[95] Traditional incandescent lighting is least efficient. Only 10 percent of the energy it generates is light; the remaining 90 percent is heat. Compact fluorescent lights (CFLs) generate far less heat, use 75 percent less energy, and last 10 times longer than traditional incandescent lights. Technology advances are increasing the popularity of light-emitting-diode (LED) lighting. Although still more expensive to purchase, LEDs use just 20 percent of the electricity of incandescent lights and 50 percent of CFLs. They also last six times longer than CFLs and 25 times longer than incandescent lights. LEDs generate the least amount of heat, reducing business's cooling costs.[96]

Lighting provides a good return on investment given its overall impact on a business. Few people seek out businesses that are dimly lit because they convey an image of untrustworthiness. The use of natural gives a business an open and cheerful look and actually can boost sales. Saladworks, a chain of fast-casual restaurants based in Conshohocken, Pennsylvania, recently redesigned its stores to minimize the use of fluorescent lights and to include a glass front and skylights that allow in more natural light.[97] A series of studies by energy research firm Heschong Mahone Group found that stores using natural light experience sales that are 40 percent higher than those of similar stores using fluorescent lighting.[98] In a retail environment, proper lighting should highlight featured products and encourage customers to stop and look at them.

Sustainability and Environmentally Friendly Design

Businesses are designing their buildings in more environmentally friendly ways not only because it is the right thing to do but also because it saves money. Companies are using recycled materials; installing high-efficiency lighting, fixtures, and appliances; and using Leadership in Energy and Environmental Design (LEED) principles in construction and renovation. McDonald's franchisees recently opened restaurants in Chicago, Illinois; Riverside, California; and Cary, North Carolina, that meet LEED standards. The restaurants generate a portion of their own electricity from photovoltaic solar panels. They also contain high-efficiency appliances; furnishings made from recycled materials (including denim) and renewable resources, such as bamboo and sunflower seed board; water-conserving plumbing fixtures that will save 550,000 gallons of water annually in each outlet; permeable pavement that minimizes the runoff of rainwater into city waterways; and cisterns that collect rainwater for use in landscape irrigation. The restaurants use Solatube lights that provide natural lighting to most of the buildings (and reduce energy consumption by 24 percent) and energy-saving LED lighting that adjusts automatically to complement the level of natural light. A roof garden on the Chicago restaurant not only is attractive but also insulates the building naturally. McDonald's even used paints that do not emit chemical odors. The company plans to build more "green" restaurants in the future.[99]

Layout: Maximizing Revenues, Increasing Efficiency, or Reducing Costs

LO6

Explain the principles of effective layouts for retailers, service businesses, and manufacturers.

The ideal layout for a building depends on the type of business it houses and on the entrepreneur's strategy for gaining a competitive edge. An effective layout can reinforce a brand and contribute to a company's desired image.

ENTREPRENEURIAL PROFILE: John Kunkel: Lime Fresh Mexican Grill John Kunkel, founder of Lime Fresh Mexican Grill, a small chain of casual burrito restaurants that Ruby Tuesday recently purchased, was repulsed by the "cold, hard plastic interiors of other quick-service Mexican restaurants that scream, 'Finish your food and move on.'" Instead, Kunkel wanted to create a comfortable, welcoming environment that supported his company's image. "I took cues from Starbucks and tried to make a 'third place,' a social place where people can come to hang out," he says. A large tub filled with ice and bottled beverages sits on a countertop, reminding customers of a friendly backyard cookout. Large windows that diffuse natural light, golden-toned walls, warm hammered-copper and brick accents, and comfortable chairs invite customers to linger inside, and umbrella-covered sidewalk tables beckon hungry customers to sit and relax. Dining room attendants called "fronters" greet customers and provide café-style service, delivering beverage refills, chips, salsas, and desserts.[100] ■

Retailers design their layouts with the goal of maximizing sales revenue and reinforcing the brand; manufacturers see layout as an opportunity to increase efficiency and productivity and to lower costs.

Layout for Retailers

Retail layout is the arrangement of merchandise and displays in a store. For retailers, layout is all about understanding a company's target customers and crafting every element of a store's design to appeal to those customers. Retail expert Paco Underhill says that "a store's interior architecture is fundamental to the customers' experience—the stage upon which a retail company functions."[101] A retail layout should pull customers into the store and make it easy for them to locate merchandise; compare price, quality, and features; and ultimately make a purchase. This is another area in which small stores may have an advantage over their larger rivals. Small stores allow customers to find the products that they want to purchase quickly and easily. (One study reports that the average shopper in a cavernous Wal-Mart Supercenter spends 21 minutes in the store but finds only 7 out of 10 items on his or her shopping list![102])

In addition, a floor plan should take customers past displays of other items that they may buy on impulse. Customers make a significant percentage of their buying decisions once they enter a store, meaning that the right layout can boost sales significantly. One of the most comprehensive studies of impulse purchases found that one-third of shoppers made impulse purchases. The median impulse purchase amount was $30 but varied by product category, ranging from $6 for food items to $60 for jewelry and sporting goods. Although the urge to take advantage of discounts was the most common driver of unplanned buying decisions, the location and attractiveness of the display also were important factors.[103]

Retailers have always recognized that some locations within a store are superior to others. Customer traffic patterns give the owner a clue to the best location for the highest gross margin items. Generally, prime selling space should be reserved for products that carry the highest

Create the Ideal Layout

As the world shifts to a knowledge-based economy, more workers are engaging in office work, in which measuring productivity sometimes proves difficult. Research shows that a well-designed office is one of the simplest and most cost-effective ways to increase workers' productivity and satisfaction. For instance, if a company builds and operates an office building, the cost of initial construction accounts for just 2 percent of the building's total cost over 30 years. Operating expenses account for 6 percent. The remaining 92 percent of the total cost of operating the building over 30 years goes to paying the salaries and benefits of the people who occupy the space! The implication of this research is that top-performing companies recognize that their employees account for the largest portion of the total cost of a work environment and make adequate investments to ensure that the work space maximizes their efficiency, satisfaction, and productivity. Unfortunately, many other companies remain stuck in the antiquated cubicle culture that provides the fodder for so many Dilbert cartoon strips and that squelches individual expression, collaboration with colleagues, and creativity. Robert Propst, the designer who invented the cubicle in 1968, originally described his creation as a productivity-enhancing "action office" but later lamented the fact that he had contributed unwittingly to "monolithic insanity" as impersonal cubicles became the dominant component of office designs around the world. As real estate prices escalated, companies saw cubicles as an efficient way to pack lots of workers into a limited amount of space, giving cubicles the reputation of housing employees in the same way that a hive houses bees.

What principles make for a good office design and allow a company to get the most out of its investment in designing a work space?

Observe How Employees Use the Existing Space

The nature of employees' work changes over time, and so do their work space needs. A design that was suitable a few years ago may be inappropriate today. Entrepreneurs should take the time to observe employees at work. When do workers use office space? Which spaces are at maximum capacity, and which ones are underutilized? Why? Does the existing design support employees' ability to do their jobs or hinder it? Red flags include the following:

- People whose work requires collaboration do not naturally interact with their colleagues during the course of a day.

- Employees waste a lot of time in transit to meeting rooms, printers, copiers, and other office equipment.

- Workers are competing for the use of certain pieces of office equipment.

- An area is either typically overcrowded or empty.

- Employees schedule meetings at nearby coffee shops or restaurants because these places provide better common space for collaboration.

At Cisco Systems, studies showed that employees' cubicles sat vacant 35 percent of the time; workers came to the office mainly for meetings and to socialize. The company removed the cubicles and converted the office into a flexible, multifunctional "connected work space" where employees can pick almost any spot to do their work. Desks, chairs, and dividers on wheels give employees the flexibility to rearrange the work space to fit their needs. An IP telephone system allows them to transfer their calls to any telephone in the office. Cisco says that the redesign allows 140 employees to work in a space that formerly housed only 88 workers and that both productivity and employee satisfaction have increased.

Involve Employees in the Redesign

One of the worst mistakes designers make is creating a new layout without the input of the people who will be working in the space. Asking employees up front for ideas and suggestions is essential to producing an effective layout. What barriers to their work does the existing design create? How can you eliminate them? One surefire way to alienate employees is to fail to involve them in the redesign of their work space.

Plan the New Design

Redesigning a work space can be a major undertaking. The process goes much more smoothly, and the end result is superior for companies that invest in significant planning than for those companies that do not. Successful designs usually result when entrepreneurs and their employees define two to five priorities, such as increased collaboration, enhanced productivity, reduced absenteeism and turnover, or improved energy efficiency, for design professionals to achieve.

An extensive report, *Innovative Workplace Strategies*, from the General Services Administration, lists the following hallmarks of the productive workplace:

- *Spatial equity.* Do workers have adequate space to accomplish their tasks and have access to privacy, natural light, and aesthetics?

- *Healthfulness.* Is the work space a healthy environment with access to air, light, and water? Is it free of harmful contaminants and excess noise?

- *Flexibility.* Can workers adjust their work environment to respond to important functional changes?

- *Comfort.* Can workers adjust light, temperature, acoustic levels, and furnishings to their individual preferences?

- *Technological connectivity.* Can on-site and off-site workers stay connected with one another and gain access to the information they need? Does technology enhance their ability to collaborate on projects?

- *Reliability.* Does the workplace have dependable mechanical and technological systems that receive proper support?

Hands On . . . How To (continued)

- **Sense of place.** Does the workplace decor and atmosphere reflect the company's mission and brand? Does the space create a culture that is appropriate for accomplishing the tasks at hand?

Create a Design That Helps People Get Their Work Done

A work space should *never* impede employees' productivity— although many designs do. At animated film company Pixar, the work space, which includes large open areas with large couches and high-top tables that encourage impromptu meetings, is designed to encourage collaboration among employees. Even the company's volleyball and basketball courts encourage employee interaction, making Pixar headquarters a haven of creativity.

Rely on Continuous Improvement

A redesign project is not finished just because the work is complete. Smart entrepreneurs resist the temptation to sit back and admire the finished product and think about how happy they are to be "done." Instead, they recognize that no redesign, however well planned, is perfect. They are willing to tweak the project and to make necessary adjustments to meet employees' changing needs.

Sources: Based on Aaron Herrington, "Pixar Is Inspiration for Modea's New Headquarters," Modea, September 19, 2011, http://www.modea.com/blog/pixar-is-inspiration-for-modeas-new-headquarters; Jane Hodges, "How to Build a Better Office," *BNET*, 2007, http://www.bnet.com/2403-13056_23-190221.html; Julie Schlosser, "The Great Escape," *Fortune*, March 20, 2006, pp. 107–110; Michael Lev-Ram, "How to Make Your Workspace Better," *Business 2.0*, November 2006, pp. 58–60; Jeffrey Pfeffer, "Thinking Outside the Cube," *Business 2.0*, April 2007, p. 60; and *Innovative Workplace Strategies*, General Services Administration, Office of Governmentwide Policy, Office of Real Property, Washington, DC, 2003, p. 70.

---

markups. If customers come into the store for specific products and have a tendency to walk directly to those items, placing complementary products in their path boosts sales. Diane Holtz, CEO of Pet Supermarket, a retailer of pet supplies founded in 1962 with 124 locations in the Southeast, redesigned the layout of the company's stores, placing essential items such as pet food and kitty litter at the rear of the store to draw customers past attractive displays of pet toys, treats, and supplies. The new design features a clean, colorful look with space to feature new products each week and to encourage interaction with pets and their owners. One year after the redesign, the company's sales had increased almost 16 percent.[104]

Layout in a retail store evolves from a clear understanding of customers' buying habits. Observing customer behavior helps entrepreneurs identify "hot spots" where merchandise sells briskly and "cold spots" where it may languish indefinitely. Winn-Dixie stores, a supermarket chain, recently remodeled its stores to capitalize on its primary hot spot, the front section of the store to the right of the front door. Because market research shows that produce is the most important factor in choosing a grocery store and winning customer loyalty, Winn-Dixie located its produce section there and expanded it by 30 percent. Bananas, one of the most commonly purchased produce items, are located at the back of the section to draw customers through it. Produce displays also use wood shelves, carts, and display tables as symbolics to send a message of freshness.[105]

Business owners should display merchandise as neatly and attractively as possible. Customers' eyes focus on displays, which tell them the type of merchandise the business sells. It is easier for customers to relate to one display than to a rack or shelf of merchandise. Open displays of merchandise can surround a focal display, creating an attractive selling area. Spacious aisles provide shoppers an open view of merchandise and reduce the likelihood of shoplifting. One study found that shoppers, especially women, are reluctant to enter narrow aisles in a store. Narrow aisles force customers to jostle past one another (experts call this the "butt-brush factor"), making them extremely nervous. The same study also found that placing shopping baskets in several areas around a store can increase sales. Seventy-five percent of shoppers who pick up a basket buy something, compared to just 34 percent of customers who do not pick up a basket.[106]

Retailers can also boost sales by displaying together items that complement each other. For example, displaying ties near dress shirts or handbags next to shoes often leads to multiple sales. Placement of items on store shelves is important, too, and store owners must keep their target customers in mind when stocking shelves. For example, putting hearing aid batteries on bottom shelves where the elderly have trouble getting to them or placing popular children's toys on top shelves where little ones cannot reach them hurts sales. Retailers also must avoid wasting prime selling space on nonselling functions (e.g., storage, office, fitting rooms, and others). For a typical retailer, the ratio of selling to nonselling space is 80/20. Although nonselling activities are necessary for a successful retail operation, they should not occupy a store's most valuable selling space. Shoppers who use fitting rooms to try on garments make purchases 67 percent of the time, compared to a 10 percent purchase rate for shoppers who do not use a fitting room. Clothing retailer Ann Taylor recently revamped its fitting rooms, enhancing their lighting to be more flattering, enlarging them to accommodate shoppers' and their friends, and making them more like a shopper's walk-in closet. The company also added displays of complementary merchandise, such as camisoles, underwear, and shapewear, to its fitting room areas. Many retailers place their nonselling departments in the rear of the building, recognizing the value of each foot of space in a retail store and locating their most profitable items in the best-selling areas.[107]

The checkout process is a particularly important ingredient in customer satisfaction and often ranks as a sore spot with shoppers. Research shows that shoppers tend to be impatient, willing to wait only about four minutes in a checkout line before becoming exasperated. One study reports that 43 percent of customers say that long checkout lines make them less likely to shop at a store.[108] Retailers are discovering that simplifying and speeding up the checkout process increases customer convenience, lowers shoppers' stress levels, and makes them more likely to come back. Some retailers, including Apple, use roving clerks equipped with handheld credit card–swiping devices, especially during peak hours, to hasten the checkout process. Studies conclude that having shoppers form a single line that leads to multiple cashiers results in faster checkout times than having shoppers form multiple lines in front of multiple cashiers.[109]

The value of a store's space for generating sales depends on floor location in a multistory building, location with respect to aisles and walkways, and proximity to entrances. Space values decrease as the distance from the main entry-level floor increases. Selling areas on the main level contribute a greater portion to sales than those on other floors in the building because they offer greater exposure to customers than either basement or higher-level locations. Therefore, main-level locations carry a greater share of rent than other levels.

Space values also depend on their position relative to the store entrance. Typically, the farther away an area is from the entrance, the lower is its value. Another consideration is that in North America, most shoppers turn to the right entering a store and move around it counterclockwise. (This apparently is culturally determined; studies of shoppers in Australia and Great Britain find that they turn *left* on entering a store.) Finally, only about one-fourth of a store's customers will go more than halfway into the store. Based on these characteristics, Figure 14.3 illustrates space values for a typical small store.

FIGURE 14.3

Space Values for a Small Store

Source: From *Retailing*, 6th edition, by Dale M. Lewison. Copyright © 1997 by Dale M. Lewison. Reprinted with permission.

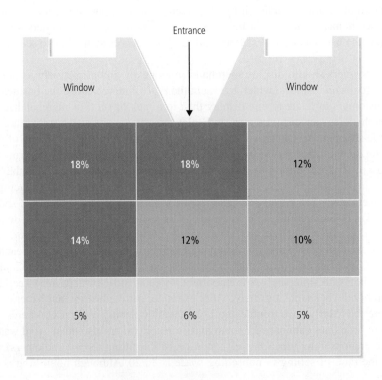

Retail layout is a never-ending experiment in which entrepreneurs learn what works and what doesn't. The accompanying "You Be the Consultant" feature explains how two popular quick-service restaurants are undergoing dramatic physical transformations as they attempt to create new images for their brands among the next generation of customers.

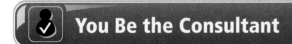

A Fresh New Look

For decades, quick-service restaurants, such as McDonald's and Wendy's, featured fluorescent lighting, garish color schemes, hard, fiberglass booths, and industrial steel chairs that encouraged diners to eat quickly and leave. Recently, however, many restaurant chains have redesigned their outlets, adding hardwood floors; stone and metal accents; natural lighting; rich, subtle colors; and comfortable, flexible seating arrangements reminiscent of European cafés. The goal is to enhance customers' dining experience, encourage them to linger and to return, and to increase traffic, frequency of visits, and sales.

The restaurants' new designs also reflect the new images they are trying to create in the minds of their next generation of customers. Competition in the quick-service sector has grown more intense, and companies such as McDonald's and Wendy's see an opportunity to win customers away from popular fast-casual restaurants, such as Ruby Tuesday, Chipotle Mexican Grill, and Applebee's. "McDonald's has to change with the times," says Jim Carras, a top manager at the fast-food giant, "and we have to do so faster than we ever have before." McDonald's recently embarked on a multi-billion-dollar global initiative, working with franchisees to redesign thousands of restaurants and give them a new, contemporary, more upscale look. Renovations to existing restaurants in the United States cost on average $600,000, of which the franchiser pays 40 to 45 percent.

McDonald's strategy, called Plan to Win, focuses on three pillars: menu innovation, upgrading customers' ordering experience, and giving restaurants a new, modern look and feel. The restaurant renovations are the key to the success of the last two pillars. "People eat with their eyes first," explains McDonald's president Don Thompson. "If you have a restaurant that is appealing, contemporary, and relevant both from the street and interior, the food tastes better." The new design started in France when Pierre Woreczek, chief brand manager for McDonald's Europe, decided that the only way the company could compete on the Continent was to eliminate the carnival atmosphere, including bright red mansard roof, the giant clown, and the prefabricated furniture. The new layout features four distinct seating areas, each designed for a different activity: a slow zone designed for people who want to sip on a McCafé Caramel Mocha and use the free WiFi, a fast zone with high bar tables for single diners who are in a hurry to get back to work, a family zone with carefully arranged booths so that parents can more easily control the movement of their children and keep them from wandering away, and a casual zone for those who want to dine leisurely with their friends. Take away the McDonald's signage, and customers might think they are in a trendy café.

Denis Weil, McDonald's vice president of concept and design, says that cultural differences across the company's far-flung global operations require different exterior designs for its restaurants. Weil has worked with franchisees to design three prototype buildings that serve as models for newly constructed restaurants. The arcade design, which is aimed at the North American market, features a modern, white-block facade; angular yellow awnings; and a stylized singular golden arch structure that is a modern version of McDonald's twin golden arches from the 1950s. The folded design, which is aimed at the European market, has a deconstructed version of the company's mansard roof from the 1970s. The Australasian design is futuristic and features a large red blade shaped like a chimney jutting skyward.

However visually striking a design may be, McDonald's always abides by one cardinal rule: no new design can interfere with the efficiency of "the system." In other words, any layout and design changes cannot impede workers' speed of service or negatively affect customers' experience.

In an attempt to win customer loyalty and increase sales, Wendy's also is creating a new look for its restaurants, one that is quite different from the simple, nostalgic look that founder Dave Thomas created when he opened his first store in 1969. Surveys show that quality food has always been a draw for Wendy's customers but that customers consider the company's restaurants to be "dated." Wendy's executives worked with San Francisco–based design firm Tesser to develop and build 10 new restaurants using four prototype designs to determine which one yields the best response from customers. "People are tired of big boxes that look ordinary," says Tre Musco, Tesser's CEO. Tesser's goal was to transform Wendy's "You know when it's real" brand statement into a physical space. Each of the four designs—the ultramodern, urban, traditional, and classic—has a unique look, but all share certain features. In the dining room, tile floors replace carpet, and, like McDonald's, the seating layout is in zones and includes high-top, bar-style seats; a high-top counter equipped with electrical outlets; café booths; and cushy chairs one might find in a lounge. The ultramodern prototype uses a warm, natural color scheme with bold red accents, brick and wood elements, and large floor-to-ceiling windows that not only make the restaurant look modern but also allow plenty of natural light to filter into the space. Comfortable chairs surround a fireplace in the center of the dining area, and the kitchen is more visible from the dining room. Customers can easily see the food preparation and baking areas and fresh produce in the kitchen. "The whole idea of the layout is to support the food story," explains Musco. "We wanted to

(continued)

You Be the Consultant *(continued)*

reinforce that Wendy's makes the best-quality food, and the best way to do that is to show them."

For both companies, the redesigned restaurants appear to be working. McDonald's reports that restaurants featuring the new designs are experiencing same-store sales increases of 6 to 7 percent. At Wendy's prototypes, traffic and sales have increased, and a higher percentage of customers are eating in the dining room.

1. Why do companies such as McDonald's and Wendy's periodically renovate their restaurants to give them a new look?

2. With its new restaurant design aimed at updating the McDonald's image and appealing to a new generation of customers, does the company risk alienating its traditional core customers—families and children? Explain.

3. Tre Musco, CEO of Tesser, the firm that created new restaurant designs for Wendy's, says that his company's job is to bring Wendy's brand positioning to life by turning it into a store of the future. Musco goes on to say that the real challenge is to convey something new without losing the brand's identity. What does he mean?

Sources: Based on Ben Paynter, "Super Style Me," *Fast Company*, October 2010, pp. 104–112; Bruce Horovitz, "McDonald's Revamps Stores to Look Upscale," *USA Today*, May 29, 2011, http://www.usatoday.com/money/industries/food/2011-05-06-mcdonalds-revamp_n.htm; Emily Bryson York, "McDonald's Pushes Ahead with New Look," *Los Angeles Times*, February 3, 2012, http://articles.latimes.com/2012/feb/03/business/la-fi-mcdonalds-design-20120203; Barney Wolf, "Wendy's Tests Four New Stores," *QSR*, August 10, 2011, http://www.qsrmagazine.com/news/wendy-s-tests-four-new-stores; Alicia Kelso, "Wendy's Testing Store Designs That 'Push the Envelope,'" *QSR*, September 12, 2011, http://www.qsrweb.com/article/184485/Wendy-s-testing-store-designs-that-push-the-envelope; and Joe Satran, "Wendy's Redesigned Restaurants Will Reshape Fast Food Brand," *Huffington Post*, December 20, 2011, http://www.huffingtonpost.com/2011/12/20/wendys-redesign-fast-food-restaurant_n_1159108.html.

Layout for Manufacturers

Manufacturing layout decisions take into consideration the arrangement of departments, work stations, machines, and stock-holding points within a production facility. The objective is to arrange these elements to ensure a smoothly flowing, efficient, and highly productive work flow. Manufacturing facilities have come under increasing scrutiny as firms attempt to improve quality, reduce inventory and increase productivity through layouts that are integrated, flexible, and efficient. Facility layout has a dramatic effect on product processing, material handling, storage, production volume, and quality.

Factors in Manufacturing Layout

The ideal layout for a manufacturing operation depends on several factors, including the following:

- *Type of product.* Product design and quality standards, whether the product is produced for inventory or for order, and the physical properties, such as the size of materials and products, special handling requirements, susceptibility to damage, and perishability.

- *Type of production process.* Technology used, types of materials handled, means of providing a service, and processing requirements in terms of number of operations involved and amount of interaction between departments and work centers.

- *Ergonomic considerations.* Ensure worker safety, avoid injuries and accidents, and increase productivity.

- *Economic considerations.* Volume of production; costs of materials, machines, work stations, and labor; pattern and variability of demand; and minimizing cycle time, the amount of time between receiving a customer's order and delivering the finished product.

- *Space availability within the facility itself.* Ensure that the space will adequately meet current and future manufacturing needs.

Types of Manufacturing Layouts

Manufacturing layouts are categorized either by the work flow in a plant or by the production system's function. There are three basic types of layouts that manufacturers can use separately or in combination—product, process, and fixed position—and they are differentiated by their applicability to different conditions of manufacturing volume.

PRODUCT LAYOUTS In a **product (line) layout**, a manufacturer arranges workers and equipment according to the sequence of operations performed on the product. Conceptually, the flow is an unbroken line from raw material input or customer arrival to finished goods to customer departure. This type of layout is applicable to rigid-flow, high-volume, continuous-process or a mass-production operation or when the service or product is highly standardized. Automobile assembly plants, paper mills, and oil refineries are examples of product layouts. Product layouts offer the advantages of low material handling costs; simplified tasks that can be done with low-cost, lower-skilled labor; small amounts of work-in-process inventory; and relatively simplified production control activities. All units are routed along the same fixed path, and scheduling consists primarily of setting a production rate.

Disadvantages of product layouts are their inflexibility, monotony of job tasks, high fixed investment in specialized equipment, and heavy interdependence of all operations. A breakdown in one machine or at one work station can idle the entire line. This layout also requires business owners to duplicate many pieces of equipment in the manufacturing facility, which for a small firm can be cost prohibitive.

product (line) layout
an arrangement of workers and equipment according to the sequence of operations performed on a product.

PROCESS LAYOUTS In a **process layout**, a manufacturer groups workers and equipment according to the general functions they perform, without regard to any particular product or customer. Process layouts are appropriate when production runs are short, when demand shows considerable variation and the costs of holding finished goods inventory are high, or when the service or product is customized. Process layouts offer the advantages of being flexible for doing custom work and promoting job satisfaction by offering employees diverse and challenging tasks. Its disadvantages are the higher costs of materials handling, requirement of more skilled labor, lower productivity, and more complex production control. Because the work flow is intermittent, each job must be routed individually through the system and scheduled at the various work centers and have its status monitored.

process layout
an arrangement of workers and equipment according to the general function they perform, without regard to any particular product or customer.

FIXED POSITION LAYOUTS In a **fixed position layout**, materials do not move down a line as in a production layout but rather, because of the weight, size, or bulk of the final product, are assembled in one spot. In other words, workers and equipment go to the material rather than having the material flow down a line to them. Aircraft assembly plants and shipyards typify this kind of layout.

fixed position layout
an arrangement in which materials do not move down a production line but rather, because of their weight, size, or bulk, are assembled on the spot.

ANALYZING PRODUCTION LAYOUTS Two important criteria for selecting and designing a layout are workers' productivity and material handling costs. An effective layout allows workers to maximize their productivity by providing them the tools and a system for doing their jobs properly. For example, a layout that requires a production worker to step away from the work area in search of the proper tool is inefficient. An effective manufacturing layout avoids what lean manufacturing principles identify as the seven forms of waste:

- *Transportation.* Unnecessary movement of inventory, materials, and information

- *Inventory.* Carrying unnecessary inventory

- *Motion.* Engaging in motion that does not add value to the product or process

- *Waiting.* Periods of inactivity when people, materials, or information are idle

- *Overproduction.* Producing more than customer demand dictates

- *Processing.* Using tools and procedures that are inappropriate for the job

- *Defects.* Producing poor-quality products, which requires scrapping or reworking material

In its newest factory in Miyagi, Japan, Toyota positioned cars on the assembly line side by side rather than tip to tail, reducing the required length of the production line by 35 percent and increasing worker productivity by allowing employees to walk shorter distances between cars.[110]

Manufacturers can lower materials handling costs by using the following principles that are hallmarks of a lean, efficient manufacturing layout:

- Planned materials flow pattern

- Straight-line layout where possible

- Straight, clearly marked aisles

- "Backtracking" of products kept to a minimum

- Related operations located close together

- Minimum amount of in-process inventory on hand

- Easy adjustment to changing conditions

- Minimum materials handling distances

- Minimum of manual handling of materials and products

- Ergonomically designed work centers

- Minimum distances between work stations and processes

- No unnecessary rehandling of material

- Minimum handling between operations

- Minimum storage

- Materials delivered to production employees just in time

- Materials efficiently removed from the work area

- Maximum visibility; maintain clear lines of site to spot problems and improve safety

- Orderly materials handling and storage

- Good housekeeping; minimize clutter

- Maximum flexibility

- Maximum communication

Using the principles of lean manufacturing can improve efficiency, quality, and productivity and lower costs.

ENTREPRENEURIAL PROFILE: Bensonwood Homes Bensonwood Homes, a premier designer and builder of energy-efficient timber frame homes based in Walpole, New Hampshire, applies "5S" principles (sort, shine, simplify, standardize, and sustain) that world-class automaker Toyota uses in its lean manufacturing process. (Bensonwood also added a sixth "S" principle, safety.) As the company's 65 employees began to buy into the process, improvements quickly became apparent. Employees applied lean and 5S principles to processes for both standard and custom products; productivity increased by 40 percent, setup time for several machining process decreased by 90 percent, and the company experienced dramatic reductions in costs associated with the seven forms of waste.[111] ∎

Chapter Summary by Learning Objective

1. Explain the stages in the location decision: choosing the region, the state, the city, and the final site.

- The location decision is one of the most important decisions an entrepreneur will make given its long-term effects on the company. An entrepreneur should look at the choice as a series of increasingly narrow decisions: Which region of the country? Which state? Which city? Which site? Choosing the right location requires an entrepreneur to evaluate potential sites

with his or her target customers in mind. Demographic statistics are available from a wide variety of sources, but government agencies such as the Census Bureau have a wealth of detailed data that can guide an entrepreneur in her location decision.

2. Describe the location criteria for retail and service businesses.

- For retailers, the location decision is especially crucial. Retailers must consider the size of the trade area, the compatibility of surrounding businesses, the degree of competition, the suitability of the surrounding transportation network, physical and psychological barriers, the volume of customer traffic, the adequacy of parking spots, a site's reputation, and the site's visibility.

3. Outline the location options for retail and service businesses: central business districts, neighborhoods, shopping centers and malls, near competitors, inside large retail stores, nontraditional locations, at home, and on the road.

- Retail and service businesses have eight basic location options: central business districts; neighborhoods; shopping centers and malls; near competitors; inside large retail stores; nontraditional locations, such as museums, sports arenas, and college campuses; at home; and on the road.

4. Explain the site selection process for manufacturers.

- A manufacturer's location decision is strongly influenced by local zoning ordinances. Some areas offer industrial parks designed specifically to attract manufacturers. Two crucial factors for most manufacturers are the reliability (and the cost of transporting) raw materials and the quality and quantity of available labor.

- A foreign trade zone is a specially designated area in or near a U.S. customs port of entry that allows resident companies to import materials and components from foreign countries; assemble, process, manufacture, or package them; and then ship the finished product while either reducing or eliminating tariffs and duties.

- Business incubators are locations that offer flexible, low-cost rental space to their tenants as well as business and consulting services. Their goal is to nurture small companies until they are ready to "graduate" into the business community. Many government agencies and universities sponsor incubator locations.

5. Describe the criteria used to analyze the layout and design considerations of a building, including the Americans with Disabilities Act.

- When evaluating the suitability of a particular building, an entrepreneur should consider several factors: size (Is it large enough to accommodate the business with some room for growth?), construction and external appearance (Is the building structurally sound, and does it create the right impression for the business?), entrances (Are they inviting?), legal issues (Does the building comply with the Americans with Disabilities Act? If not, how much will it cost to bring it up to standard?), signs (Are they legible, well located, and easy to see?), interior (Does the interior design contribute to our ability to make sales? Is it ergonomically designed?), and lights and fixtures (Is the lighting adequate for the tasks that workers will be performing? What is the estimated cost of lighting?).

6. Explain the principles of effective layouts for retailers, service businesses, and manufacturers.

- Layout for retail stores and service businesses depends on the owner's understanding of his or her customers' buying habits. Some areas of a retail store generate more sales per square foot and therefore are more valuable.

- The goal of a manufacturer's layout is to create a smooth, efficient work flow. Three basic options exist: product layout, process layout, and fixed position layout. Two key considerations are worker productivity and materials handling costs.

Discussion Questions

1. Buzz Price, the location expert who helped Disney and other entrepreneurs find the ideal locations for their businesses, described the location decision in the following way: "Guessing is dysfunctional. Using valid numbers to project performance is rational." How can entrepreneurs find "valid numbers" to help them project the performance of their businesses in different locations?
2. What factors should a manager consider when evaluating a region in which to locate a business? Where are such data available?
3. Outline the factors important when selecting a state in which to locate a business.
4. What factors should a seafood processing plant, a beauty shop, and an exclusive jewelry store consider in choosing a location? List factors for each type of business.
5. What intangible factors might enter into the entrepreneur's location decision?
6. What are zoning laws? How do they affect the location decision?
7. What is the trade area? What determines a small retailer's trade area?
8. Why is it important to discover more than just the number of passersby in a traffic count for a potential location?
9. What types of information can the entrepreneur collect from census data?
10. Why may a "cheap location" not be the "best location"?

11. What is a foreign trade zone? A business incubator? What advantages and disadvantages does each one offer a small business locating there?

12. Why is it costly for a small firm to choose a location that is too small?

13. What function does a small company's sign serve? What are the characteristics of an effective business sign?

14. Explain the Americans with Disabilities Act. Which businesses does it affect? What is its purpose?

15. What is ergonomics? Why should entrepreneurs utilize the principles of ergonomics in the design of their facilities?

16. Explain the statement, "Not every portion of a small store's interior space is of equal value in generating sales revenue." What areas are most valuable?

17. According to market research firm NPD Group, in 1985, women purchased 70 percent of all men's clothing; today, women buy just 34 percent of men's apparel. What implications does this have for modern store layouts?

18. What are some of the key features that determine a good manufacturing layout?

Business Plan Pro™

Analyzing the value of a potential business site is critical. Typically, retail or service companies benefit from high-traffic locations with optimal exposure. The location of a manufacturing, repair, or storage business must meet the demands of shipping and receiving logistics. Selecting the wrong location places a business at a disadvantage from the outset.

Business Plan Exercises

This chapter emphasizes that selecting the right location is critical to a retail venture or any business venture in which customers benefit from face-to-face contact and the ability to view, touch, try, and ultimately purchase products.

On the Web

The Web offers valuable information regarding location information. One resource mentioned earlier in the marketing chapter of the text is the PRIZM information from Claritas, Inc. (www.claritas.com/MyBestSegments). This site identifies the most common market segments in a particular ZIP code and can help you verify that your location is in proximity to your target markets. PRIZM categorizes U.S. consumer markets on the basis of demographic and customer segmentation profiling research data by ZIP code. A retail business, for example, will find that locating close to its target customers is a critical success factor. Additional information, such as traffic counts and other location characteristics, will also be important to include in your business plan. Use the many resources described in this chapter to show why the location you have chosen is ideal for reaching your target customers conveniently.

Sample Plans

Identify a sample plan with a business concept that demands a high-traffic location. Now find a sample plan that has specific location needs for other reasons. Note how each plan presents the needs and importance of the location and the facility.

In the Software

Open your business plan and go to the Your Company section. Describe your potential or existing location. If you already have selected a location for your business, you may want to assess whether it is a strength or a weaknesses in your SWOT analysis. If your location possesses some of the positive attributes mentioned in the chapter, identify your location as strength. If your location has negative characteristics, recognize it as a weakness and address how you plan to overcome the challenges your location presents. The location may be so important to the business that you will also list it under the Keys to Success section. Remember to include the expense for your location—rent, lease, or mortgage payments—into the financial section of your plan.

Building Your Business Plan

Selecting your location is an important strategic business decision for most business ventures. Your business plan can help you profile, describe, and ultimately decide on the most attractive business location available. Once you determine a location, your plan can leverage that location's strongest attributes to optimize customer exposure, sales, and profits.

Beyond the Classroom...

1. Select a specific type of business you would like to go into one day and use census data to choose a specific site for the business in the local region. What location factors are critical to the success of this business? Would it be likely to succeed in your hometown?

2. Interview a sample of local small business owners. How did they decide on their particular locations?

What are the positive and negative features of their existing locations?

3. Visit the Web sites for *Entrepreneur* or *Fortune* magazine and find articles about the "best cities for (small) business. (For *Entrepreneur*, it is usually the October issue, and for *Fortune*, it is normally an issue in November).

Which cities are in the top 10? What factors did the magazine use to select these cities? Pick a city and explain what makes it an attractive destination for locating a business there.

4. Select a manufacturing operation, a wholesale business, or a retail store and evaluate their layouts using the guidelines presented in this chapter. What changes would you recommend? Why? How does the new layout contribute to a more effective operation? How much would the changes you suggest cost?

5. Every year, *Site Selection* magazine selects the states with the top business climates. Use the Internet to locate the latest state rankings. Which states top the list? Which states are at the bottom of the list? What factors affect a state's ranking? Why are these factors important to entrepreneurs' location decisions?

6. Visit the Web site for the Census Bureau at www .census.gov. Go to the census data for your town and

use it to discuss its suitability as a location for the following types of businesses:

- A new motel with 25 units
- A bookstore
- An exclusive women's clothing shop
- A Mexican restaurant
- A residential plumber
- A day care center
- A high-quality stereo shop
- A family hair care center

7. Visit the Census Bureau's Web site and use the American FactFinder section to prepare a demographic profile of your hometown or city or of the town or city in which you attend college. Using the demographic profile as an analytical tool, what kinds of businesses do you think would be successful there? Unsuccessful? Explain.

Endnotes

1. Kasey Wehrum, "Strictly by the Numbers," *Inc.*, November 2010, p. 160.
2. Dennis Phillips, "Johnny's Lunch Turns 75 Years Old," *Post-Journal*, September 25, 2011, http://www.post-journal.com/page/content.detail/id/591527/Johnny-s-Lunch-Turns-75-Years-Old.html?nav=5003; Karen E. Klein, "Finding the Perfect Location," *Business Week*, March 24, 2008, http://www.businessweek.com/smallbiz/content/mar2008/sb20080324_098559.htm?chan=smallbiz_smallbiz+index+page_top+small+business+stories; Nora Parker, "Johnny's Lunch Plans Franchise Expansion with LI," Directions Magazine, October 8, 2007, http://www.directionsmag.com/article.php?article_id=2569&trv=1; Chris Knape, "New Diner Downtown Is Johnny on the Spot," *Grand Rapids Press*, May 12, 2008, p. B4.
3. Mark Henricks, "Hot Spots," *Entrepreneur*, October 2005, pp. 68–74.
4. Louis Mongello, "Walt Disney World History 101: How to Buy 27,000 Acres of Land and No One Notice," Gather.com, December 18, 2005, http://www.gather.com/viewArticle.jsp?articleId=281474976719796.
5. "2011 Inc. 5000: Company Profile: Paylocity," *Inc.*, http://www.inc.com/inc5000/profile/paylocity; "Paylocity Talks about ZoomProspector and Fast Growth," *YouTube*, September 25, 2008, http://www.youtube.com/watch?v=QrbI3XmhoMc.
6. "Ron Starner, "A Dynasty of Deals," *Site Selection*, March 2012, http://www.siteselection.com/issues/2012/mar/top-micropolitans-of-2011.cfm.
7. Ann Moline, "Dawn of an Era," *Site Selection*, May 2011, http://www.siteselection.com/issues/2011/may/Alternative-Energy-Hubs.cfm; Catherine Holland, "New Power-One Plant Opens in Phoenix, Brings Hundreds of Jobs," *AZFamily*, January 31, 2011, http://www.azfamily.com/news/local/New-Power-One-plant-opens-in-Phoenix--114931349.html#.
8. "Oil-Dri Corporation of America," *Funding Universe*, http://www.fundinguniverse.com/company-histories/OilDri-Corporation-of-America-company-History.html.
9. "Employer Costs for Employee Compensation for the Regions," Bureau of Labor Statistics, December 2011, http://www.bls.gov/ro7/ro7ecec.htm.
10. Nicholas Casey, "The New Learjet . . . Now Mexican Made," *Wall Street Journal*, July 29, 2011, pp. B1–B2.
11. Jason Ankeny, "Innovation Nation," *Entrepreneur*, August 2010, pp. 58–62.
12. Sara Wilson, "Tech and the City," *Entrepreneur*, February 2009, p. 19.
13. "Spiceworks," *Crunchbase*, http://www.crunchbase.com/company/spiceworks; "The Story of How We Got Here," Spiceworks, http://www.spiceworks.com/about.
14. Victoria Rivers, "100 Best Places to Live and Launch: Manchester, New Hampshire," *FSB*, April 2008, pp. 74–77; "100 Best Places to Live and Launch: Manchester, New Hampshire," *FSB*, April 2008, http://money.cnn.com/galleries/2008/fsb/0803/gallery.best_places_to_launch.fsb/13.html.
15. "States without a State Income Tax," Internal Revenue Service, December 2, 2011, http://www.irs.gov/efile/article/0,,id=130684,00.html; "State Corporate Income Tax Rates," Tax Foundation, February 16, 2012, http://www.taxfoundation.org/taxdata/show/230.html.
16. Don Dodson, "Jimmy John's Founder Contemplates Moving Headquarters Out of Illinois," *News-Gazette*, January 19, 2011, http://www.news-gazette.com/news/business/economy/2011-01-19/jimmy-johns-founder-contemplates-moving-headquarters-out-illinois.h.
17. *The Impact of Broadband Speed and Price on Small Business*, U.S. Small Business Administration Office of Advocacy, November 2010, pp. 1–2.
18. Emily Maltby, "Where the Action Is," *Wall Street Journal*, August 22, 2011, pp. R1, R4.
19. Tami Luhby, "California Companies Fleeing the Golden State," *CNN Money*, July 12, 2011, http://money.cnn.com/2011/06/28/news/economy/California_companies/index.htm.

20. "2011 Kosmont-Rose Institute Cost of Doing Business Survey Report," *Business Wire*, November 28, 2011, http://www.businesswire.com/news/home/20111128006144/en/2011-Kosmont-Rose-Institute-Cost-Business-Survey-Report.

21. "From Our Kitchen to Yours: Our History," Fiesta Tortillas, http://www.fiestatortillas.com/history.html.

22. Danielle Douglas, "Washington Looks Tanatalizing to New York's Restaurateurs," *Washington Post*, August 23, 2010, http://www.washingtonpost.com/wp-dyn/content/article/2010/08/22/AR2010082202018.html; Lisa Jennings, "The 10 Strongest Retail Markets," *Nation's Restaurant News*, March 21, 2011, http://nrn.com/article/10-strongest-retail-markets.

23. Richard Breen, "Stax Omega Joins Pelham Party," *GSA Business*, December 27, 2004, pp. 5, 9.

24. "Clusters and Cluster Development," Institute for Strategy and Competitiveness, Harvard Business School, http://www.isc.hbs.edu/econ-clusters.htm.

25. Mercedes Delagado, Michael Porter, and Scott Stern, "Clusters and Entrepreneurship," *Journal of Economic Geography*, May 2010, http://joeg.oxfordjournals.org/content/early/2010/05/28/jeg.lbq010.abstract; "History of Wine Making in Napa Valley," Golden Haven Hot Springs and Resort, http://www.goldenhaven.com/regions/napa_valley/napa_valley_history.html.

26. Emily Maltby, "Where the Action Is," *Wall Street Journal*, August 22, 2011, pp. R1, R4; "Ogden Partners with Outdoor-Themed Companies," *Utah Business*, August 16, 2011, http://www.utahbusiness.com/issues/articles/11431/2011/08/ogden_partners_with_outdoor-themed_companies.

27. "SF's Own Planning Department Satirizes Convoluted Regulations Deterring Small Businesses," *California City News*, February 2012, http://www.californiacitynews.org/2012/02/sf%E2%80%99s-own-planning-department-satirizes-convoluted-regulations-deterring-small-businesses.htm.

28. Julie V. Iovine, "Zoning Laws Grow Up," *Wall Street Journal*, January 19, 2012, p. D6.

29. Lisa Jennings, "LA Considers Restricting Fast-Food Locations," *Nation's Restaurant News*, September 7, 2010, http://nrn.com/article/la-considers-restricting-fast-food-locations; Hayley Fox, "After a Year, Fast-Food Ban Has 'Virtually No Effect' on Health in South LA, Group Says," *On Central*, Southern California Public Radio, January 6, 2012, http://www.oncentral.org/news/2012/01/06/after-1-year-fast-food-ban-has-virtually-no-impact.

30. Verena Dobnik, "An Immigrant Era Ends: Matzo Factory Closing," *Greenville News*, December 29, 2007, p. 16A; Bonnie Rosenstock, "The Streit Family Dynasty," *The Villager* 73, no. 38 (January 21–27, 2004), http://www.thevillager.com/villager_38/thestreitsfamily.html.

31. John W. McCurry, "Digital Derby," *Site Selection*, January 2011, http://www.siteselection.com/issues/2011/jan/Digital-Media.cfm.

32. Matt Evans, "Controversy Aside, Incentives Usually Deliver as Promised," *Business Journal*, July 5, 2010, http://www.bizjournals.com/triad/stories/2010/07/05/story2.html?page=all.

33. "Worker Relocation Worries," *Inside Training Newsletter*, November 29, 2007, p. 1.

34. Eilene Zimmerman, "100 Best Places to Live and Launch: Bellevue, Washington," *FSB*, April 2008, pp. 68–69.

35. "Starting a Convenience Store," Canada Business: Services for Entrepreneurs, November 25, 2008, http://www.canada-business.ca/servlet/ContentServer?cid=1099483437618&lang=en&pagename=CBSC_FE%2Fdisplay&c=GuideHowto.

36. Jason Del Rey, "Shop Now, before It All Disappears," *Inc.*, July/August 2010, pp. 126–127.

37. "Ciprianis Told to Vacate Rainbow Room," *Nation's Restaurant News*, January 11, 2009, http://www.nrn.com/breakingNews.aspx?id=362066&menu_id=1368; "Rainbow Room's Grill to Close as Economy, Lease Dispute Dull Future," *Nation's Restaurant News*, January 5, 2009, http://www.nrn.com/breakingNews.aspx?id=361810; Oshrat Carmiel and Peter S. Green, "Cipriani Dining Empire Loses BlackRock, Rainbow Room," *Bloomberg*, February 5, 2009, http://www.bloomberg.com/apps/news?pid=20601088&sid=abZWspVJXPSA&refer=muse#.

38. Bruce Horovitz, "Burger King Plans Beer-Selling Whopper Bar in South Beach," *USA Today*, January 22, 2010, http://www.usatoday.com/money/industries/food/2010-01-21-burger-king-beer_N.htm; "Booze Making Its Way into Fast-Food Outlets," *MSNBC*, July 1, 2011, http://www.msnbc.msn.com/id/43608911/ns/business-retail/t/booze-making-its-way-fast-food-outlets/#.T2ejZaG6_AI; Ron Ruggless, "BK Debuts Whopper Bar Concept, Eyes On-Site Arena in Plan to Beef up Growth," *Nation's Restaurant News*, http://www.nrn.com/landingPage.aspx?menu_id=1424&coll_id=676&id=364528; "BK to Debut Whopper Bar Next Year," *Nation's Restaurant News*, October 7, 2008, http://www.nrn.com/breakingNews.aspx?id=359160.

39. Shannon Perez, "6 Tips to Finding the Perfect Location for Your Practice," *Massage Therapy*, http://www.massagetherapy.com/articles/index.php/article_id/1377.

40. Christina Galoozis, "Twice as Nice," *MyBusiness*, November/December 2011, http://www.nfib.com/mybusiness-magazine/article?cmsid=58640.

41. Lisa Jennings, "Upscale Brands Positioned as Less Luxury, More Valuable," *Nation's Restaurant News*, March 16, 2009, http://www.nrn.com/landingPage.aspx?coll_id=554&keyword=%20frozen%20yogurt&id=364242#.

42. Matt Rosenberg, "About Reilly's Law of Retail Gravitation," About.com, http://geography.about.com/cs/citiesurbangeo/a/aa041403a.htm; G. I. Thrall and J. C. del Valle, "The Calculation of Retail Market Areas: The Reilly Model," *GeoInfoSystems* 7, no.4, (1997): 46–49.

43. Alex Konrad, "Louisville Flies High," *Fortune*, October 18, 2010, pp. 32–33.

44. Xylia Buros, "The Improved Grab-and-Go Model," *Fresh Cup*, January 2009, http://www.freshcup.com/featured-article.php?id=84.

45. Anne Kadet, "Don't Mention the 'Curse,'" *Wall Street Journal*, December 10, 2011, http://online.wsj.com/article/SB10001424052970203501304577088303490848564.html.

46. Kris Hudson, "For Malls, Occupancy Firms Up," *Wall Street Journal*, January 9, 2012, http://online.wsj.com/article/SB10001424052970203436904577148813815182788.html.

47. Bill Streever, "Taking the Arctic Plunge," *Wall Street Journal*, July 30–31, 2011, p. D8; Jeffrey Sward, "Pepe's North of the Border, Barrow, Alaska," http://www.jeffreysward.com/tributes/pnotb.htm; Heather Carreiro, "Tours of Barrow, Alaska," *USA Today*, http://traveltips.usatoday.com/tours-barrow-alaska-18216.html.

48. John Giuffo, "America's Best Downtowns," *Forbes*, October 14, 2011, http://www.forbes.com/sites/johngiuffo/2011/10/14/americas-best-downtowns; John C. Stevenson, "Downtown Fixture," *Business*, November 6, 2006, pp. 1, 8–9; Vanessa Sumo, "Downtown Is Dead: Long Live Downtown!" *Region Focus*, Fall 2007, pp. 12–17.

49. Jessica Shambora, "David vs. Goliath," *Fortune*, December 6, 2010, p. 69.

50. Paul Lukas, "Our Malls, Ourselves," *Fortune*, October 18, 2004, pp. 243–256.

51. Stephanie Clifford, "How About Gardening or Golfing at the Mall?," *New York Times*, February 5, 2012, http://www.nytimes.com/2012/02/06/business/making-over-the-mall-in-rough-economic-times.html?pagewanted=all; Kris Hudson, "The Malaise Afflicting America's Malls," *Wall Street Journal*, March 1, 2012, pp. B1–B2.

52. "Shopping Center Facts and Stats," International Council of Shopping Centers, http://www.icsc.org/research/stats.php.

53. Kris Hudson and Miguel Bustillo, "New Tricks for Old Malls," *Wall Street Journal*, October 26, 2011, pp. B1–B2.

54. "ICSC Shopping Center Definitions," International Council of Shopping Centers, http://www.icsc.org; Andrew Blum, "The Mall Goes Undercover," *Washington Post*, April 6, 2005, http://www.slate.com/id/2116246; Parija Bhatnagar, "It's Not a Mall, It's a Lifestyle Center," *CNN/Money*, January 12, 2005, http://money.cnn.com/2005/01/11news/fortune500/retail_lifestylecenter.

55. John Wisely and Greta Guest, "More Big Malls Are Home to Small, Independent Retailers," *USA Today*, December 20, 2011, http://www.usatoday.com/money/industries/retail/story/2011-12-20/small-stores-big-malls/52123450/1.

56. Kris Hudson, "The Malaise Afflicting America's Malls," *Wall Street Journal*, March 1, 2012, pp. B1–B2.

57. Paul Lukas, "Our Malls, Ourselves," *Fortune*, October 18, 2004, pp. 243–256.

58. "Mall of America by the Numbers," Mall of America, http://www.mallofamerica.com/about/moa/facts.

59. Lisa Jennings, "Seattle's Best Testing Outlets in Walmart Stores," *Nation's Restaurant News*, May 12, 2011, http://nrn.com/article/seattle%E2%80%99s-best-testing-outlets-walmart-stores.

60. Alan J. Liddle, "10 Non-Traditional Subway Restaurants," *Nation's Restaurant News*, July 26, 2011, http://nrn.com/article/10-non-traditional-subway-restaurants; Bret Thom, "The New Nontraditional Location," *Nation's Restaurant News*, October 24, 2011, http://nrn.com/article/new-nontraditional-location.

61. "Frequently Asked Questions," Small Business Administration, Office of Advocacy, January 2011, p. 1.

62. "Paul's Cheeky Idea Is a Winner," Small Business Development Corporation, http://www.homebasedbusiness.sbdc.com.au/10_01_casestudies.asp.

63. Sumathi Reddy, "Prices for Food-Cart Permits Skyrocket," *Wall Street Journal*, March 9, 2011, http://online.wsj.com/article/SB10001424052748704758904576188523780657688.html.

64. Rudolph Bell, "ICAR Start-up Predicts Growth," *Greenville News*, March 19, 2011, p. 8A.

65. "Business Incubation FAQ," National Business Incubation Association, http://www.nbia.org/resource_center/bus_inc_facts/index.php.

66. Sarah E. Needleman, "Start-Up Programs Find Niche," *Wall Street Journal*, November 18, 2010, p. B7.

67. Anita Campbell, "Business Incubators: The Next Innovation Engine?," *Open Forum*, September 27, 2010, http://www.openforum.com/idea-hub/topics/innovation/article/business-incubators-the-next-innovation-engine-1.

68. "Business Incubation FAQ," National Business Incubation Association, http://www.nbia.org/resource_center/bus_inc_facts/index.php.

69. "Eric Anderson, "Mumbai by Way of Niskayuna," *Times Union*, February 25, 2009, http://www.timesunion.com/AspStories/story.asp?storyID=773529&category=BUSINESS; "Cinematography Oscar for 'Slumdog' Focuses Attention on Silicon Imaging, a Graduate of RPI Incubator Program," Business Incubator Program of New York State, February 26, 2009, http://bianys.com/node/499.

70. "Workplace Design = Job Performance?," *Inside Training*, October 29, 2008, p. 1.

71. "Workplace Design = Job Performance?," *Inside Training*, October 29, 2008, p. 1.

72. Sam Laird, "Facebook Completes Move into New Menlo Park Headquarters," *Mashable Social Media*, December 19, 2011, http://mashable.com/2011/12/19/facebook-completes-move-into-new-menlo-park-headquarters; Moign Khawaja, "Facebook 'Likes' Its New Cool Space Campus," *Arabian Gazette*, December 20, 2011, http://arabiangazette.com/facebook-likes-its-cool-space-campus; Dan Levy, "Facebook's 'Cool Space' Campus Points to Future of Office Growth," *Business Week*, December 22, 2011, http://www.businessweek.com/news/2011-12-28/facebook-s-cool-space-campus-points-to-future-of-office-growth.html; Matt Rosoff, "The 15 Coolest Offices in Tech: Facebook Menlo Park Headquarters Tour," *Business Insider*, December 19, 2011, http://www.businessinsider.com/15-coolest-offices-in-tech-2012-1.

73. *The Integrated Workplace*, Office of Governmentwide Policy, Office of Real Property, Washington, DC, 2008, pp. 8–9.

74. Margaret Littman, "Fresh Picked," *Entrepreneur*, September 2011, p. 46.

75. Laura Tiffany, "The Rules of . . . Retail," *Business Start-Ups*, December 1999, p. 106.

76. Lisa Jennings, "Boston Market Upgrades Boost Sales, Traffic," *Nation's Restaurant News*, February 22, 2011, http://nrn.com/article/boston-market-upgrades-boost-sales-traffic; "To NY and NJ: Here Comes Boston Market," *QSR*, April 11, 2012, http://m.qsrmagazine.com/news/ny-and-nj-here-comes-boston-market.

77. Laura Tiffany, "The Rules of . . . Retail," *Business Start-Ups*, December 1999, p. 106.

78. A. Alfred Taubman, "Getting over the Threshold," *Inc.*, April 2007, pp. 75–76.

79. *ADA Update: A Primer for Small Business*, U.S. Department of Justice, Civil Rights Division, March 16, 2011, p. 2.

80. "Educational Kit," President's Committee on Employment of People with Disabilities, http://www50.pcepd.gov/pcepd/archives/pubs/ek99/wholedoc.htm#decisions.

81. "McD Unveils One-Off Restaurant in Las Vegas," *Nation's Restaurant News*, December 10, 2008, http://www.nrn.com/breakingNews.aspx?id=361116.

82. Brian Amble, "Poor Workplace Design Damages Productivity," *Management-Issues*, May 23, 2006, http://www.management-issues.com/2006/8/24/research/poor-workplace-design-damages-productivity.asp.

83. Kate Lister, "Office Ergonomics: Lessons Learned from Physical Therapy," *Open Forum*, April 11, 2011, http://www.openforum.com/idea-hub/topics/lifestyle/article/office-ergonomics-lessons-learned-from-physical-therapy-kate-lister.

84. Amanda MacArthur, "Retail Atmospherics: Can You Really Influence Customer Buying Habits?," *Swipely*, September 19, 2011, http://blog.swipelyworks.com/restaurant-store-atmospherics/retail-atmospherics-can-you-really-influence-customer-buying-habits.

85. Eric Markowitz, "How Cinnamon Smells Will Save Holiday Sales," *Inc.*, November 3, 2011, http://www.inc.com/articles/201111/how-cinnamon-smells-will-save-holiday-sales.html.

86. Ned Smith, "Consumers Will Pay More for Products They Can Touch," *Business News Daily*, September 13, 2010, http://www.businessnewsdaily.com/203-consumers-will-pay-more-for-products-they-can-touch.html.

87. "Paco Underhill: Shopping Scientist," *CBC News*, November 7, 2000, http://www.cbc.ca/consumers/market/files/home/shopping/index.html.

88. Amanda MacArthur, "Retail Atmospherics: Can You Really Influence Customer Buying Habits?," *Swipely*, September 19, 2011, http://blog.swipelyworks.com/

restaurant-store-atmospherics/retail-atmospherics-can-you-really-influence-customer-buying-habits.

89. Martin Lindstrom, "How Whole Foods 'Primes' You to Shop," *Fast Company*, September 15, 2011, http://www.fastcompany.com/1779611/priming-whole-foods-derren-brown.

90. Mark Brandau, "Operators in the Mood for Music," *Nation's Restaurant News*, August 3, 2011, http://nrn.com/article/operators-music-mood.

91. Eric Markowitz, "How Cinnamon Smells Will Save Holiday Sales," *Inc.*, November 3, 2011, http://www.inc.com/articles/201111/how-cinnamon-smells-will-save-holiday-sales.html; Michael Morain, "Muzak—It Remains Music to Retailers' Ears," *Greenville News*, December 23, 2007, p. 3F; Theunis Bates,"Volume Control," *Time*, August 2, 2007, http://www.time.com/time/printout/0,8816,1649304,00.html.

92. Linda Tischler, "Smells Like a Brand Spirit," *Fast Company*, August 2005, pp. 52–59.

93. Kara Newman, "How to Sell with Smell," *Business 2.0*, April 2007, p. 36; Linda Tischler, "Smells Like a Brand Spirit," *Fast Company*, August 2005, pp. 52–59.

94. Jeremy Caplan, "Scents and Sensibility," *Time*, October 8, 2006, http://www.time.com/time/magazine/article/0,9171,1543956,00.html.

95. Tiffany Meyers, "Waste Not," *Entrepreneur*, February 2008, p. 75.

96. "Energy Savers," U.S. Department of Energy, http://www.energysavers.gov/your_home/lighting_daylighting/index.cfm/mytopic=11975; *Pizzeria Planning: Designing and Maintaining an Efficient Pizza Kitchen*, Pizza Marketplace, p. 26.

97. Julie Sturgeon, "Fast Casuals Light Up," *Fast Casual*, March 10, 2009, http://www.fastcasual.com/article.php?id=13677.

98. Jennifer Alsever, "Showing Products in a Better Light," *Business 2.0*, September 2005, p. 62.

99. "Quick-Serve Design Takes the LEED," *QSR*, 2012, http://www2.qsrmagazine.com/articles/exclusives/0709/mcdonalds-1.phtml; "McDonald's Signature Arches Go Green," *QSR*, October 15, 2010, http://www.qsrmagazine.com/news/mcdonalds-signature-arches-go-green; Andrew Martin,

"Green Plans in Blueprints of Retailers," *New York Times*, November 8, 2008, http://www.nytimes.com/2008/11/08/business/08build.html?ref=science.

100. Jason Daley, "Stay Awhile," *Entrepreneur*, December 2011, p. 118.

101. Paul Keegan, "The Architect of Happy Customers," *Business 2.0*, August 2002, pp. 85–87.

102. Kris Hudson and Ann Zimmerman, "Big Boxes Aim to Speed Up Shopping," *Wall Street Journal*, June 27, 2007, pp. B1, B8.

103. Annette Elton, "I'll Take That Too: Increasing Impulse Buys," Gift Shop, Spring 2008, http://www.giftshopmag.com/2008/spring/unique_giftware/increasing_impulse_buys.

104. "Marcia Hendroux Pounds, "Pet Supermarket CEO Makes Stores Fashionable," *South Florida Sun-Sentinel*, March 30, 2012, http://articles.sun-sentinel.com/2012-03-30/news/fl-women-business-south-florida-20120330_1_women-owned-businesses-diane-holtz-pet-toys.

105. Sarah Nassauer, "A Food Fight in the Produce Aisle," *Wall Street Journal*, October 20, 2011, pp. D1–D2.

106. Kenneth Labich, "This Man Is Watching You," *Fortune*, July 19, 1999, pp. 131–134.

107. Elizabeth Holmes and Day A. Smith, "Why Are Fitting Rooms So Awful?," *Wall Street Journal*, April 6, 2011, pp. D1–D2.

108. Kris Hudson and Ann Zimmerman, "Big Boxes Aim to Speed Up Shopping," *Wall Street Journal*, June 27, 2007, pp. B1, B8; Tom Ryan, "Checkout Time Limit Around Four Minutes," *Retail Wire*, July 8, 2008, http://www.retailwire.com/discussions/Sngl_Discussion.cfm/13077?.

109. Ray A. Smith, "Find the Best Checkout Line," *Wall Street Journal*, December 8, 2011, pp. D1–D2.

110. Chester Dawson, "For Toyota, Patriotism and Profits May Not Mix," *Wall Street Journal*, November 29, 2011, pp. A1, A16.

111. "The Beam Team Gets Lean," Massachusetts Manufacturing Advancement Center, http://www.massmac.org/newsline/0705/article02.htm.

© Gino Santa Maria/Fotolia

15

Global Aspects of Entrepreneurship

Learning Objectives

On completion of this chapter, you will be able to:

1. Explain why "going global" has become an integral part of many small companies' marketing strategies.

2. Describe the principal strategies small businesses have for going global.

3. Explain how to build a thriving export program.

4. Discuss the major barriers to international trade and their impact on the global economy.

5. Describe the trade agreements that have the greatest influence on foreign trade the World Trade Organization, the North American Free Trade Agreement, and the Central American Free Trade Agreement.

Arguing against globalization is like arguing against the laws of gravity.

—Kofi Annan

If we ignore the opportunities to go internationally, generally the option is to go out of business.

—Matthew Calvage

Until recently, the world of international business was much like astronomy before Copernicus, who revolutionized the study of the planets and the stars with his theory of planetary motion. In the sixteenth century, the Copernican system replaced the Ptolemaic system, which held that the earth was the center of the universe with the sun and all the other planets revolving around it. The Copernican system, however, placed the sun at the center of the solar system with all of the planets revolving around it. Astronomy would never be the same.

In the same sense, business owners across the globe have been guilty of having Ptolemaic tunnel vision when it came to viewing international business opportunities. Like their pre-Copernican counterparts, owners saw an economy that revolved around the nations that served as their home bases. Market opportunities stopped at their homeland's borders. Global trade was only for giant corporations that had the money and the management talent to tap foreign markets and enough resources to survive if the venture flopped. This scenario no longer holds true in the twenty-first century.

Today, the global marketplace is as much the territory of small upstart companies as it is that of giant multinational corporations. The world market for goods and services continues to grow, fueled by a global economy that welcomes consumers with new wealth. By 2025, more than 1 billion people globally will join the ranks of middle-class consumers, creating a tremendous opportunity for small businesses.[1] Powerful, affordable technology; the Internet; increased access to information on conducting global business; and the growing interdependence of the world's economies have made it easier for small companies, many of which had never considered going global, to engage in international trade. These micromultinational companies are proving that even the smallest companies can succeed in the global marketplace. A study of the future of small business by Intuit predicts that nearly half of U.S. small businesses will engage in some kind of global trade by 2018.[2]

ENTREPRENEURIAL PROFILE: Efrem Meretab: MCAP Research LLC Efrem Meretab left his job as a stock analyst to launch MCAP Research LLC, a Montclair, New Jersey–based business that helps investors sift through reams of company earnings reports and display important information in just seconds. When Meretab needed software developers to help him create his company's core product, he went online and hired developers in Belarus, Ukraine, and Pakistan who completed the job at a fraction of the cost of U.S.-based developers. Rather than purchase servers to handle the traffic to his company's Web site, Meretab rents the capacity that he needs from Amazon. "You wouldn't have been able to do this six years ago," says Meretab. "[MCAP is] a global company."[3] ■

As globalization transforms entire industries, even experienced business owners and managers must rethink the rules of competition on which they have relied for years. To thrive, they must develop new business models and new sources of competitive advantages and be bold enough to seize the opportunities that the global marketplace offers. Although opportunities for global trade can come from anywhere, entrepreneurs should focus their attention on the 20 "gateway" countries that account for 70 percent of the world's population and 80 percent of its income. Ten of these countries are industrialized nations: Australia, Canada, France, Germany, Italy, Japan, the Netherlands, Spain, the United Kingdom, and the United States. The other 10 countries are emerging markets: Brazil, China, India, Indonesia, Mexico, Russia, South Africa, South Korea, Thailand, and Turkey.[4]

Entrepreneurs are discovering that the tools of global business are within their reach, the costs of going global are decreasing, and the benefits of conducting global business can be substantial. Nearly 96 percent of the world's population and 67 percent of the world's purchasing power lies *outside* of the borders of the United States![5] By 2020, global middle-class consumption will increase from $21 trillion to $35 trillion, with more than 80 percent of that growth occurring outside of North America and Europe.[6] "The timing has never been better for small businesses to get out of their back yards and become global players," says Laurel Delaney, founder of Globe-Trade.com, a consulting company.[7] Worldwide, countries trade nearly $19 trillion in goods and services annually, a dramatic increase from $58 billion in 1948.[8]

LO1

Explain why "going global" has become an integral part of many small companies' marketing strategies.

Why Go Global?

Failure to cultivate global markets can be a lethal mistake for modern businesses, whatever their size. A few decades ago, small companies had to concern themselves mainly with competitors who were perhaps six blocks away; today, small companies face fierce competition from

© Mike Baldwin / Cornered

"Can Billy come out and compete in the global economy?"

Mike Baldwin/www.CartoonStock.com

companies that may be six *time zones* away! As a result, entrepreneurs find themselves under greater pressure to expand into international markets and to build businesses without borders. Today, the potential for doing business globally for companies of all sizes means that where a business's goods and services originate or where its headquarters is located is insignificant. Operating a successful business increasingly requires entrepreneurs to see their companies as global citizens rather than as companies based in a particular geographic region. For small companies around the world, going global is a matter of survival, not preference. To be successful, small companies must take their place in the world market. Unfortunately, most small companies follow a *reactive* approach to going global (engaging in global sales because foreign customers initiate the contact) rather than pursue a *proactive* global sales strategy that involves researching and analyzing foreign markets that represent the best fit for their products and services.[9]

Going global can put a tremendous strain on a small company, but entrepreneurs who take the plunge into global business can reap many benefits, including the ability to offset sales declines in the domestic market, increase sales and profits, improve the quality of their products to meet the stringent demands of foreign customers, lower the manufacturing cost of their products by spreading fixed costs over a larger number of units, and enhance their competitive positions to become stronger businesses. In fact, companies that sell their goods and services in other countries generate more sales revenue, are more profitable, have higher levels of productivity, and are less likely to fail than those that limit their sales to the domestic market.[10]

Success in a global economy requires constant innovation; staying nimble enough to use speed as a competitive weapon; maintaining a high level of quality and constantly improving it; being sensitive to foreign customers' unique requirements; adopting a more respectful attitude toward foreign habits and customs; hiring motivated, multilingual employees; and retaining a desire to learn constantly about global markets. In short, business owners must strive to become "insiders" rather than just "exporters."

Becoming a global entrepreneur does require a different mind-set. To be successful, entrepreneurs must see their companies from a global perspective and must instill a global culture throughout their companies that permeates everything the business does. To these entrepreneurs and their companies, national boundaries are irrelevant; they see the world as a market opportunity. An absence of global thinking is one of the barriers that most often limit entrepreneurs' ability to move beyond the domestic market. Indeed, learning to *think globally* may be the first—and most challenging—obstacle an entrepreneur must overcome on the way to creating a truly global business. Global thinking is the ability to appreciate, understand, and respect the different beliefs, values, behavior, and business practices of companies and people in different cultures and countries. This requires entrepreneurs to "do their homework" to learn about the people, places, business techniques, potential customers, and culture of the countries in which they intend to do business. Several U.S. government agencies, including the Department of Commerce, offer vast amounts of information about all nations, including economic data that can be useful to entrepreneurs searching for market opportunities. Doing business globally presents extraordinary opportunities only to those who are prepared. "With a little know-how, creativity, and confidence, even the smallest business can find opportunities around the globe," says Donna Sharp, director of the World Trade Institute at Pace University.[11]

LO2

Describe the principal strategies small businesses have for going global.

Strategies for Going Global

Small companies pursuing a global presence have nine principal strategies from which to choose: creating a presence on the Web, relying on trade intermediaries, establishing joint ventures, engaging in foreign licensing arrangements, franchising, using countertrading and bartering, exporting products or services, establishing international locations, and importing and outsourcing (see Figure 15.1).

CREATING A WEB SITE In our technology-rich global environment, the fastest, least expensive, and lowest-cost strategic option to establish a global business presence is to create a Web site. As you saw in Chapter 9 on e-commerce, the Internet gives even the smallest businesses the ability to sell its goods and services all over the globe. By establishing a presence online, a local candy maker or a home-based luxury boat broker gains immediate access to customers around the world. With a well-designed Web site, an entrepreneur can extend his or her reach to customers anywhere in the world—without breaking the budget! A company's Web site is available to potential customers anywhere in the world and provides exposure 24 hours a day to its products or services seven days a week. For many small companies, the Internet has become a tool that is as essential to doing business as the telephone.

Establishing an Internet presence has become an important part of many small companies' strategies for reaching customers outside the United States. Internet World Stats estimates the number of Internet users worldwide to be 2.3 billion. Just 245 million of them live in the United States, leaving more than 2 *billion* potential Internet customers outside this country's borders (see Figure 15.2)![12] A study by the World Retail Congress reports that 23 percent of global retail sales will take place online by 2015.[13] eBay, another popular online channel for entrepreneurs, provides access to international shoppers; 62 percent of all eBay sales take

FIGURE 15.1

Nine Strategies for Going Global

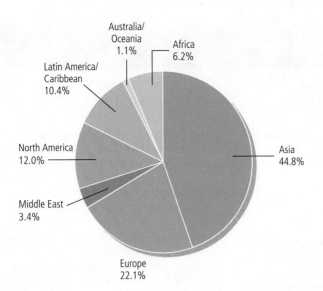

FIGURE 15.2

Internet Users by World Region

Source: "Internet Users by World Region" from Internet World Stats Website. Copyright © 2000–2012 Miniwatts Marketing Group. All rights reserved. Reprinted with permission.

place outside the United States.[14] In addition, more than 80 percent of Facebook users live outside the United States.[15]

ENTREPRENEURIAL PROFILE: Eric Zuziak: JZMK Partners Eric Zuziak co-owner of JZMK Partners, an architectural firm in Irvine, California, was able to weather the economic fallout of a severe recession and downturn in construction activity in the United States by taking on projects in other countries. Zuziak's global push started when a company in Nanjing, China, discovered JZMK Partners' Web site. Impressed by the design awards that JZMK Partners had won, the Chinese company hired JZMK to design a residential community in Nanjing. That successful job led to other international design work, including projects in Costa Rica, Turkey, Morocco, Egypt, and Qatar. Using market research, Zuziak has targeted several international markets and hired locals to work in business development and project management with the goal of acquiring more international work. Today, JZMK Partners generates 85 percent of its $4 million in annual revenue from global markets.[16] ▪

Just as business owners who conduct international business in person must be sensitive to the cultural nuances and differences in the business practices of other countries, entrepreneurs who conduct business online must take these same factors into account when they design their companies' Web sites. Entrepreneurs must "think local" when they create Web sites that target customers in other countries. Although having a single domain name with separate "language" buttons for translations is simpler and less expensive, e-commerce experts say that having separate domain names for each targeted country produces better sales results. The design of Web sites that target foreign customers must reflect the local culture, customs, and language. For instance, not all cultures read from left to right, and colors that may be appropriate in one culture may be offensive to customers in another. An entrepreneur won't have much luck listing "panties" for sale on a Web site aimed at customers in the United Kingdom; customers there would search for "knickers." Google Global Market Finder is a free market research tool that shows entrepreneurs how many times people around the world use particular key words in online searches in 56 different languages. Business owners can use the Global Market Finder as a tool to test the international appeal of key words on their Web sites and to isolate the key words that are likely to produce the best results in their search engine optimization strategies.

Before the advent of the Internet, small businesses usually took incremental steps toward becoming global businesses. They began selling locally and then, after establishing a reputation, expanded regionally and perhaps nationally. Only after establishing themselves domestically did small businesses begin to think about selling their products or services internationally. The Internet makes that business model obsolete because it provides small companies with a low-cost global distribution channel that they can utilize from the day they are launched.

TRADE INTERMEDIARIES Although many small businesses handle their foreign sales efforts in-house, another alternative for getting into international markets with a minimum of cost and effort is to

You Be the Consultant

Going Global from the Outset

Entrepreneurs are discovering that doing business globally is not just for large corporations. Some entrepreneurs take their companies global from the outset, and their micromultinational companies are reaping the benefits.

Zee Wines USA

Roy Goslin and his wife Dianne Ferrandi grew up in South Africa, where both had connections to that country's wine industry. Ferrandi's parents owned vineyards and sold grapes to local vintners, and Goslin worked in materials and process management for one of South Africa's largest wineries. Both Goslin and Ferrandi grew up with wine as an integral part of meals. In 1998, recruited by a large information technology consulting firm, the couple moved to Minneapolis, Minnesota, but they never lost their passion for the fine wines of South Africa. Because few people in the United States knew about the storied winemaking tradition and superb vineyards of South America, Goslin and Ferrandi had difficulty finding wines from their homeland in Minnesota. Their solution: start their own wine import business that specializes in wines from South Africa. They announced their decision at a dinner with friends, where one friend suggested that they name their company "Z Wines." (You've got zee food, and we have zee wine," he joked.)

In 2006, Goslin and Ferrandi started Zee Wines USA as a home-based business with the goal of importing wines from South Africa that they knew were the best the country had to offer and wholesaling them to retail stores. "Some of the wineries we work with have been making wine since the 1600s," says Goslin. With its diverse climate, rich soil, amazing biodiversity, and rich winemaking tradition, South Africa produces some of the world's finest, most unique wines. "South Africa also is the world leader in sustainable wine production," says Ferrandi. The couple knew that they could import wines from South Africa and sell them for just $10 to $15 per bottle in the United States.

In addition to the South African wines they import, Goslin and Ferrandi also sell domestic wines from Washington, Oregon, and California. With $500,000 in annual sales, their total portfolio of wines numbers only about 100. We could have a much larger portfolio," says Ferrandi, "but we accept only 1 or 2 percent of all the wines that cross our path. We don't believe that you can build a sustainable wine business on huge volumes of bulk wines. You have to have exceptional value in the bottle."

Somnio

When Sean Sullivan was an executive at The North Face and Specialized Bicycle Components, he noticed that international sales accounted for the majority of sales in some product categories. Learning from his corporate experience, Sullivan decided that when he launched his own company, he would operate it as a

global business from the start. Sullivan, an avid runner, came up with the idea for his business after visiting his doctor, Andy Pruitt, founder of the Boulder Center for Sports Medicine in Boulder, Colorado, for treatment for chronic foot pain. Pruitt told Sullivan that his running shoes were the cause of his foot problem, and the two worked together to design a better running shoe using biomechanics, custom padding, and inserts to create customized shoes that accommodate runners' foot shape and running style. For instance, they developed insoles that are tailored to fit each customer's arch height. They launched Somnio in 2009 and immediately began developing strategies to sell their running shoes in Europe and Asia.

After a four-month search, Sullivan hired Saskia Stock, who had been in charge of biomechanical research at MBT Shoes, a Swiss footwear maker, to manage Somnia's European division in Zurich, Switzerland. The reason that Sullivan wanted a veteran of the shoe industry to manage the company's European operations was to enable Somnia to enter into direct sales relationships with retailers rather than sell through foreign distributors. "Having worldwide distributors is great for small companies that want to grow quickly," explains Sullivan, "but it can get expensive to get out of those contracts later." When Somnio entered Asian markets, however, Sullivan opted to use foreign distributors there because they had established connections that would take Somnio years to develop and understood the nuances of doing business locally.

Somnio, which is headquartered in La Selva Beach, California, manufactures its running shoes in China and sells them in 20 countries, throughout the Americas, Europe, and Asia. The company generates $10 million in annual sales, more than half of which comes from Europe.

1. "Businesses are increasingly being reordered around addressing consumer needs that transcend national borders," says Eric Ries, an entrepreneur and author. Do you agree? If Ries is correct, what are the implications for small companies that have the potential to conduct business globally?

2. What advice can you offer the founders of Zee Wine USA about selling their products globally?

3. Notice that Sean Sullivan used a direct sales approach to enter the European market but relied on foreign distributors in the Asian market. What are the advantages and the disadvantages of each approach? Why do most small companies that sell internationally use trade intermediaries?

Sources: Adapted from John Garland, "Roy Goslin and Dianne Ferrandi of Z Wines," *Heavy Table*, March 2, 2011, http://heavytable.com/roy-goslin-and-dianne-ferrandi-of-z-wines; Phil Bolsta, "Small Business Success Stories: Z Wines USA," *Twin Cities Business*, December 2008, http://www.tcbmag.com/superstars/smallbusinesssuccessstories/106542p1.aspx; and Ryan Underwood, "Made to Travel: Why More Start-Ups Are Going Beyond Borders, *Inc.*, March 2011, pp. 96–98.

use a trade intermediary. **Trade intermediaries** are domestic agencies that serve as distributors in foreign countries for domestic companies of all sizes. They rely on their networks of contacts, their extensive knowledge of local customs and markets, and their experience in international trade to market products effectively and efficiently all across the globe. These trade intermediaries serve as the export departments for small businesses, enabling the small companies to focus on what they do best and delegate the responsibility for coordinating foreign sales efforts to the intermediaries. They are especially valuable to small companies that are getting started in the global arena, often producing benefits that far outweigh their costs. Lawrence Harding, president of High Street Partners, a trade intermediary that manages foreign sales for small companies, points to the example of a company that imported telecommunications equipment into the United Kingdom to sell to its customers there. The deal triggered a hefty 17.5 percent duty that Harding says the company could have avoided paying if it had imported the equipment in a different way.[17]

Although a broad array of trade intermediaries is available, the following are ideally suited for small businesses.

Export Management Companies **Export management companies (EMCs)** are an important channel of foreign distribution for small companies just getting started in international trade or for those that lack the resources to assign their own people to foreign markets. Most EMCs are merchant intermediaries, working on a buy-and-sell arrangement with domestic small companies, taking title to the goods and then reselling them in foreign markets; others work on commission. More than 1,000 EMCs operate across the United States, and many of them specialize in particular industries, products, or product lines as well as in the foreign countries they target. For instance, Dorian Drake international, an EMC started in 1947, specializes in selling equipment around the world for U.S.-based companies in four industries—automotive, food service, lawn and garden, and environmental. For more than 40 years, Dorian Drake has managed global sales for American Lawn, the leading U.S. maker of manual reel lawn mowers, a family-owned business founded in Shelbyville, Indiana, in 1895.[18]

EMCs provide small businesses with a low-cost, efficient, independent international marketing and export department, offering services that range from conducting market research and giving advice on patent protection to arranging financing and handling shipping. The greatest benefits that EMCs offer small companies are ready access to global markets and an extensive knowledge base on foreign trade, both of which are vital for entrepreneurs who are inexperienced in conducting global business. In return for their services, EMCs usually earn an extra discount on the goods they buy from their clients or, if they operate on a commission rate, a higher commission than domestic distributors earn on what they sell. EMCs charge commission rates of about 10 percent on consumer goods and 15 percent on industrial products. Although EMCs rarely advertise their services, finding one is not difficult. The Federation of International Trade Associations provides useful information for small companies about global business and trade intermediaries on its Web site (http://fita.org), including a listing of EMCs. Industry trade associations and publications and the U.S. Department of Commerce's Export Assistance Centers* also can help entrepreneurs to locate EMCs and other trade intermediaries.

Export Trading Companies Another tactic for getting into international markets with a minimum of cost and effort is through export trading companies. **Export trading companies (ETCs)** are businesses that buy and sell products in a number of countries, and they typically offer a wide range of services, such as exporting, importing, shipping, storing, distributing, and others, to their clients. Unlike EMCs, which tend to focus on exporting, ETCs usually perform both import and export trades across many countries' borders. Although EMCs usually create exclusive contracts with companies for a particular product line, ETCs often represent several companies selling the same product line. However, like EMCs, ETCs lower the risk of exporting for small businesses. Some of the largest ETCs in the world are based in the United States and Japan. In fact, many businesses that have navigated successfully Japan's complex system of distribution have done so with the help of ETCs.

trade intermediaries
domestic agencies that serve as distributors in foreign countries for domestic companies of all sizes.

export management companies (EMCs)
merchant intermediaries that provide small businesses with a low-cost, efficient, off-site international marketing department.

export trading companies (ETCs)
businesses that buy and sell products in a number of countries and offer a wide variety of services to their clients.

---

*A searchable list of the Export Assistance Centers is available at the Export.gov Web site at www.export.gov/comm_svc/eac.html.

In 1982, Congress passed the Export Trading Company Act to allow producers of similar products to form ETC cooperatives without the fear of violating antitrust laws. The goal was to encourage U.S. companies to export more goods by allowing businesses in the same industry to band together to form ETCs.

manufacturer's export agents (MEAs)
businesses that act as international sales representatives in a limited number of markets for noncompeting domestic companies.

export merchants
domestic wholesalers who do business in foreign markets.

resident buying offices
government- or privately owned operations of one country established in another country for the purpose of buying goods made there.

Manufacturer's Export Agents Manufacturer's export agents (MEAs) act as international sales representatives in a limited number of markets for various noncompeting domestic companies. Unlike the close, partnering relationship formed with most EMCs, the relationship between the MEA and a small company is a short-term one, and the MEA typically operates on a commission basis.

Export Merchants Export merchants are domestic wholesalers who do business in foreign markets. They buy goods from many domestic manufacturers and then market them in foreign markets. Unlike MEAs, export merchants often carry competing lines, meaning that they have little loyalty to suppliers. Most export merchants specialize in particular industries, such as office equipment, computers, industrial supplies, and others.

Resident Buying Offices Another approach to exporting is to sell to a **resident buying office**, a government- or privately owned operation of one country established in another country for the purpose of buying goods made there. Many foreign governments and businesses have set up buying offices in the United States. Selling to them is just like selling to domestic customers because the buying office handles all of the details of exporting.

Foreign Distributors Some small businesses work through foreign distributors to reach international markets. Domestic small companies export their products to these distributors, who handle all of the marketing, distribution, support, and service functions in the foreign country. The key to success is screening potential distributors to find those that are reliable, financially sound, and customer focused.

ENTREPRENEURIAL PROFILE: Scott Tuttle: Livin' Lite Recreational Vehicles Scott Tuttle, owner of Livin' Lite Recreational Vehicles, a small company based in Wakarusa, Indiana, that makes off-road, ultralight weight, aluminum and composite campers and trailers, found a reliable distributor for its products in Sydney, Australia. Although shipping campers to the other side of the world is no easy task (a standard 40-foot shopping container can hold just two campers), Livin' Lite Recreational Vehicles sales through its foreign distributor are growing. Even though the company, which has appeared on *Inc.*'s list of the 500 fastest-growing private companies in the United States, charges an additional $1,500 to reconfigure its campers for left-side driving, it recently expanded to four production lines in a new factory.[19] ■

THE VALUE OF USING TRADE INTERMEDIARIES Trade intermediaries such as these are becoming increasingly popular among small businesses attempting to branch out into world markets because they make that transition much faster and easier. Most small business owners simply do not have the knowledge, resources, or confidence to go global alone. Intermediaries' global networks of buyers and sellers allow their small business customers to build their international sales much faster and with fewer hassles and mistakes. Entrepreneurs who are inexperienced in global sales and attempt to crack certain foreign markets alone quickly discover just how difficult the challenge can be. However, with their know-how, experience, and contacts, trade intermediaries can get small companies' products into foreign markets quickly and efficiently. The primary disadvantage of using trade intermediaries is that doing so requires entrepreneurs to surrender control over their foreign sales. However, by maintaining close contact with intermediaries and evaluating their performance regularly, entrepreneurs can avoid major problems.

The key to establishing a successful relationship with a trade intermediary is conducting a thorough screening to determine which type of intermediary—and which one in particular—will best serve a small company's needs. Entrepreneurs should look for intermediaries that specialize in the products their companies sell and that have experience and established contacts in the countries they have targeted. An entrepreneur looking for an intermediary should compile a list of potential candidates using some of the sources listed in Table 15.1. After compiling the list, entrepreneurs should evaluate each one using a list of criteria to narrow the field to the most

TABLE 15.1 Resources for Finding Trade Information and Trade Intermediaries

Trade intermediaries make doing business around the world much easier for small companies, but finding the right one can be a challenge. Fortunately, several government agencies offer a wealth of information to businesses interested in reaching into global markets with the help of trade intermediaries. Entrepreneurs looking for help in breaking into global markets should contact the International Trade Administration, the U.S. Commerce Department, and the Small Business Administration first to take advantage of the following services:

- *Agent/Distributor Service.* Provides customized searches to locate interested and qualified foreign distributors for a product or service. (Search cost, $250 per country)
- *Commercial Service International Contacts List.* Provides contact and product information for more than 82,000 foreign agents, distributors, and importers interested in doing business with U.S. companies.
- *Country Directories of International Contacts List.* Provides the same kind of information as the Commercial Service International Contacts List but is organized by country.
- *Industry Sector Analyses.* Offer in-depth reports on industries in foreign countries, including information on distribution practices, end users, and top sales prospects.
- *International Market Insights.* Include reports on specific foreign market conditions, upcoming opportunities for U.S. companies, trade contacts, trade show schedules, and other information.
- *Trade Opportunity Program.* Provides up-to-the-minute, prescreened sales leads around the world for U.S. businesses, including joint venture and licensing partners, direct sales leads, and representation offers.
- *International Company Profiles.* Commercial specialists will investigate potential partners, agents, distributors, or customers for U.S. companies and will issue profiles on them.
- *Commercial News USA.* A government-published magazine that promotes U.S. companies' products and services to 400,000 business readers in 178 countries at a fraction of the cost of commercial advertising. Small companies can use *Commercial News USA* to reach new customers around the world for as little as $495.
- *Gold Key Service.* For a small fee, business owners wanting to target a specific country can use the Department of Commerce's Gold Key Service, in which experienced trade professionals arrange meetings with prescreened contacts whose interests match their own.
- *Platinum Key Service.* The U.S. Commercial Service's Platinum Key Service is more comprehensive than its Gold Key Service, offering business owners long-term consulting services on topics such as building a global marketing strategy, deciding which countries to target, and how to reach customers in foreign markets.
- *Matchmaker Trade Delegations Program.* This program helps small U.S. companies establish business relationships in major markets abroad by introducing them to the right contacts on foreign trade missions.
- *Multi-State/Catalog Exhibition Program.* Working with state economic development offices, the Department of Commerce presents companies' product and sales literature to hundreds of interested business prospects in foreign countries.
- *Trade Fair Certification Program.* This service promotes U.S. companies' participation in foreign trade shows that represent the best marketing opportunities for them.
- *National Trade Data Bank (NTDB).* Most of the information listed above is available on the NTDB, the U.S. government's most comprehensive database of world trade data. With the NTDB, small companies have access to information that at one time only *Fortune* 500 companies could afford.
- *International Trade Library.* At the Bloomberg Bureau of National Affairs Web site (www.bna.com/international-trade-library-p6709), entrepreneurs can access the International Trade Library, where they can see current developments in trade policy, manage exchange rates risks, find country-specific market research, and access the *Import Reference Guide* and the *Export Reference Guide*.
- *WAND.* The WAND database (www.wand.com) allows entrepreneurs to search globally for suppliers or distributors in 172 countries across 70,000 product categories.
- *U.S. Export Assistance Centers.* The U.S. Department of Commerce has established a network of export specialists in export assistance centers in 100 cities in the United States and 80 countries to serve as one-stop shops for entrepreneurs who need export help (http://export.gov/eac).
- *Office of International Trade.* The U.S. Small Business Administration's Office of International Trade works with other federal agencies to encourage small companies to provides a variety of export assistance, how-to articles and videos, searchable databases, and links to other export resources.
- *Export-U.* A Web site (www.export-u.com/ExportU44) that offers free export training webinars and videos.
- *Tradeport.* This Web site (www.tradeport.org) offers helpful trade tutorials on exporting and importing, a trade library, comprehensive trade information, and access to trade leads.
- *U.S. Commercial Service.* The U.S. Commercial Service, a division of the International Trade Administration (www.trade.gov), provides many of the services listed in this table. Its Web site (www.buyusa.gov/home) is an excellent starting point for entrepreneurs who are interested in exporting.
- *Export.gov.* This Web site from the U.S. Commercial Service is an excellent gateway to myriad resources for entrepreneurs who are interested in learning more about exporting. This site includes market research, trade events, trade leads, and much more.
- *Federation of International Trade Associations (FITA).* The FITA Global Trade Portal (www.fita.org) is an excellent source for international import and export trade leads and events and provides links to about 8,000 Web sites related to international trade.
- *World Trade Centers.* The 320 World Trade Centers (www.wtcaonline.com/cms_wtca) located in 96 countries offer entrepreneurs useful information on local market conditions, government regulations, and business culture. They also offer practical workshops, seminars, and courses on conducting international business.

promising ones. Interviewing a principal from each intermediary on the final list should tell entrepreneurs which ones are best able to meet their companies' needs. Finally, before signing any agreement with a trade intermediary, it is wise to conduct thorough background and credit checks. Entrepreneurs with experience in global trade also suggest entering short-term agreements of about a year with new trade intermediaries to allow time to test their ability and willingness to live up to their promises. Many entrepreneurs begin their global business initiatives with trade intermediaries and then venture into international business on their own as their skill and comfort levels increase.

JOINT VENTURES Joint ventures, both domestic and foreign, lower the risk of entering global markets for small businesses. They also give small companies more clout in foreign lands. In a **domestic joint venture**, two or more U.S. small businesses form an alliance for the purpose of exporting their goods and services. For export ventures, participating companies get antitrust immunity, allowing them to cooperate freely. The businesses share the responsibility and the costs of getting export licenses and permits, and they split the venture's profits. Establishing a joint venture with the right partner has become an essential part of maintaining a competitive position in global markets for a growing number of industries.

In a **foreign joint venture**, a domestic small business forms an alliance with a company in the target nation. The host partner brings to the joint venture valuable knowledge of the local market and its method of operation as well as of the customs and the tastes of local customers, making it much easier to conduct business in the foreign country. Sometimes foreign countries place certain limitations on joint ventures, for example, requiring host companies to hold a majority stake in the venture.

domestic joint venture
an alliance of two or more U.S. small companies for the purpose of exporting their goods and services abroad.

foreign joint venture
an alliance between a U.S. small business and a company in the target nation.

Natcore

ENTREPRENEURIAL PROFILE: Chuck Provini: Natcore Technology Natcore Technology, a small company in Red Bank, New Jersey, that has developed a patented liquid phase deposition technology that allows manufacturers to produce more efficient and more productive solar energy cells at a lower cost, recently entered into two foreign joint ventures. The first joint venture, Natcore China, is with Zhuzhou Hi-Tech Industrial Development Zone, a government-supported zone in Hunan province, and Chuangke Silicon Ltd, a polycrystalline silicon producer. Natcore Technology owns 55 percent of the Chinese joint venture, which is scheduled to last at least 20 years. Natcore also formed a second joint venture with Italy's largest solar panel manufacturer, MX Solar. Founder Chuck Provini plans to use the joint ventures to expand into the chemical business, allowing the company to supply the "magic sauce" used to make solar cells with Natcore's proprietary technology.[20] ∎

The most important ingredient in the recipe for a successful joint venture is choosing the right partner. Taking the following steps will help avoid problems:

- Select a partner that shares their company's values and standards of conduct.

- Define at the outset important issues such as each party's contributions and responsibilities, the distribution of earnings, the expected life of the relationship, and the circumstances under which the parties can terminate the relationship.

- Understand their partner's reasons and objectives for joining the venture.

- Spell out in writing exactly how the venture will work and where decision-making authority lies.

- Select a partner whose skills are different from but compatible with those of their own company's.

- Prepare a "prenuptial agreement" that spells out what will happen in case of a "business divorce."

FOREIGN LICENSING Rather than sell their products or services directly to customers overseas, some small companies enter foreign markets by licensing businesses in other nations to use their patents, trademarks, copyrights, technology, processes, or products. In return for licensing these assets, a small company collects royalties from the sales of its foreign licenses. Licensing is a relatively simple way for even the most inexperienced business owner to extend his or her reach into global markets. Licensing is ideal for companies whose value lies in its intellectual property, unique products or services, recognized name, or proprietary technology. Although many businesses consider licensing only their products to foreign companies, the licensing potential for intangibles, such as processes, technology, copyrights, and trademarks, often is greater. Some entrepreneurs earn more money from licensing their know-how for product design, manufacturing, or quality control than they do from actually selling their finished goods in a highly competitive foreign market with which they are not familiar. Foreign licensing enables a small business to enter foreign markets quickly, easily, and with virtually no capital investment. Risks to the company include the potential loss of control over its manufacturing and marketing processes and creating a competitor if the licensee gains too much knowledge and control. Securing proper patent, trademark, and copyright protection beforehand can minimize those risks, however.

INTERNATIONAL FRANCHISING Franchising has become a major export industry for the United States. Over the last several decades, a growing number of franchises have been attracted to international markets to boost sales and profits as the domestic market has become increasingly saturated with outlets and much tougher to wring growth from. Franchisers should consider expanding into global markets when foreign markets present an important growth opportunity for the franchise. Yum! Brands, the franchiser of KFC, Pizza Hut, and Taco Bell restaurants, has a significant global presence with more than 37,000 restaurants in 117 countries. International franchising, particularly in fast-growing markets such as India and China, has been essential to the company's growth; in fact, China alone accounts for 40 percent of Yum! Brands's profits.[21] To be successful in global markets, a franchiser should have the following characteristics:

- Sufficient managerial and financial resources to devote to globalization

- A solid track record of success in the United States

- Adequate trademark protection for the franchise's brand

- Time-tested training, support, and reporting procedures that help franchisees succeed[22]

Franchisers that decide to expand internationally should take these steps:

1. ***Identify the country or countries that are best suited to the franchiser's business concept.*** Factors to consider include a country's business climate, demographic profile, level of economic development, rate of economic growth, degree of legal protection, language

© Kevin Foy/Alamy

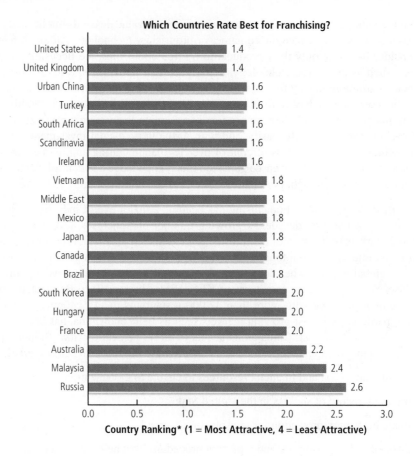

Which Countries Rate Best for Franchising?

Country	Ranking
United States	1.4
United Kingdom	1.4
Urban China	1.6
Turkey	1.6
South Africa	1.6
Scandinavia	1.6
Ireland	1.6
Vietnam	1.8
Middle East	1.8
Mexico	1.8
Japan	1.8
Canada	1.8
Brazil	1.8
South Korea	2.0
Hungary	2.0
France	2.0
Australia	2.2
Malaysia	2.4
Russia	2.6

Country Ranking* (1 = Most Attractive, 4 = Least Attractive)

and cultural barriers, and market potential. Franchisers making their first forays into global markets should consider focusing on a single nation or a small group of similar nations. The International Franchise Association recently ranked nations on their attractiveness for franchises using the results of many global studies, and Figure 15.3 shows the country rankings (a rating of 1 is most attractive, and a rating of 4 is least attractive).

2. *Generate leads for potential franchisees.* Franchisers looking for prospective franchisees in foreign markets have many tools available to them, including international franchise trade shows, their own Web sites, trade missions, and brokers. Many franchisers have had success with trade missions, such as those sponsored by trade groups, including the International Franchise Association or the U.S. Department of Commerce's Gold Key Program. These trade missions are designed to introduce franchisers to qualified franchise candidates in target countries. Others rely on brokers who have extensive business contacts in specific countries.

3. *Select quality candidates.* Just as in any franchise relationship, the real key to success is choosing the right franchisee. Because of the complexity and cost of international franchising, selecting quality franchisees is essential to success. Establishing an intranet allows franchisers to stay in contact with their international franchisees no matter which time zones they are in.

4. *Structure the franchise deal.* Franchisers can structure international franchise arrangements in a variety of ways, but three techniques are most popular: direct franchising, area development, and master franchising.

   - Direct franchising, common in domestic franchise deals, involves selling single-unit franchises to individual operators in foreign countries. Although dealing with individual franchisees makes it easier for the franchiser to maintain control, it also requires more of the franchiser's time and resources.

- Area development is similar to direct franchising except that the franchiser allows the franchisee to develop multiple units in a particular territory, perhaps a province, a county, or even an entire nation. A successful area development strategy depends on a franchiser selecting and then supporting quality franchisees. In 2001, brothers Manpreet and Gurpreet Gulri entered into an area development agreement with Subway to expand the sandwich chain's presence in India and now operate more than 200 stores there. "We work closely with local chefs and regional suppliers to ensure a good balance of vegetarian and non-vegetarian items, along with many traditional Subway menu items, all specifically selected to appeal to the Indian palate," says Manpreet.[23]
- Master franchising is the most popular strategy for companies entering international markets. In a master franchising arrangement, a franchiser grants an experienced master franchisee the right to sell outlets to subfranchisees in a broad geographic area or sometimes in an entire country. Franchisers use this method to expand into international markets quickly and efficiently because their master franchisees understand local laws and customs and the nuances of selling in local markets. Although master franchising simplifies a franchiser's expansion into global markets, it generates less revenue for franchisers than direct franchising and gives them the least amount of control over their international franchisees. Domino's Pizza, with more than 3,500 outlets in 60 countries outside the United States, relies on master franchises, especially in emerging markets such as India, China, Malaysia, and Turkey. Jubilant FoodWorks Limited, Domino's Pizza's master franchisee in India, operates nearly 450 outlets, but Richard Alison, Domino's Pizza's international president, says that the country has the potential to have at least 1,000 locations.[24]

Just as they do in the United States, franchisers in international markets sell virtually every kind of product or service imaginable—from fast food to child day care. In some cases, the products and services sold in international markets are identical to those sold in the United States. However, most franchisers have learned that adaptation is the key to making sure that their goods and services suit local tastes and customs. Traveling the world, one discovers that American fast-food giants such as Domino's, KFC, and McDonald's make significant modifications in their menu to remain attractive to the demands of local customers.

ENTREPRENEURIAL PROFILE: Domino's, KFC, and McDonald's In addition to its 5,050 domestic outlets, Domino's Pizza operates more than 3,500 restaurants in 60 foreign countries, where local franchises offer pizza toppings that are quite different from traditional ones used in the United States, including squid (Japan), pickled ginger (India), tuna and sweet corn (England), green peas (Brazil), and reindeer sausage (Iceland), to cater to customers' palates. In Taiwan, the best-selling pizza is a seafood delight, made with onions, peas, squid, shrimp, and crab toppings. Although the toppings used vary widely around the world, the dough, the sauce, and the cheese are standard in every Domino's location.[25]

McDonald's customers in China and Hong Kong can enjoy seafood soup and red bean sundaes made with soft serve vanilla ice cream topped with green tea-flavored syrups and azuki beans. In Malaysia, for breakfast, McDonald's serves Bubur Ayam McD (known in Singapore as Chicken SingaPorridge), a rice porridge topped with chicken, onions, ginger, shallots, and chili peppers. At McDonald's locations in India, where 80 percent of the population is Hindu and does not eat beef, Maharaja Macs made of chicken share the menu with Vegetable McNuggets and the McAloo Tikki, a vegetarian sandwich, and in Japan, the Koroke Burger (which is made of mashed potatoes and cabbage), a shrimp burger (the Ebi Filet-O), and a green tea–flavored milkshake appear on the menu. McHuevos (a burger topped with a poached egg and mayonnaise) is a popular item in McDonald's in Uruguay.[26] In India, KFC removed mashed potatoes and gravy (too bland for Indian customers!) from its menu, which includes chicken dishes adapted to appeal to Indian palates and a large number of vegetarian items, including a Veg Zinger, a patty made with a blend of vegetables, chickpeas, jalapeño peppers, and panera cheese topped with hot sauce.[27] ∎

COUNTERTRADING AND BARTERING A **countertrade** is a transaction in which a company selling goods in a foreign country agrees to promote investment and trade in that country. The goal of the transaction is to help offset the capital drain from the foreign country's purchases. As entrepreneurs

countertrade
a transaction in which a company selling goods in a foreign country agrees to promote investment and trade in that country.

enter more and more developing countries, they will need to develop skills at implementing this strategy. In some cases, small and medium-size businesses find it advantageous to work together with large corporations that have experience in the implementation of this marketing strategy.

Countertrading suffers numerous drawbacks. Countertrade transactions can be complicated, cumbersome, and time consuming. They also increase the chances that a company will get stuck with merchandise that it cannot move. They can lead to unpleasant surprises concerning the quantity and quality of products required in the countertrade. Still, countertrading offers one major advantage: sometimes it's the only way to make a sale!

Entrepreneurs must weigh the advantages against the disadvantages for their company before committing to a countertrade deal. Because of its complexity and the risks involved, countertrading is not the best choice for a novice entrepreneur looking to break into the global marketplace.

Bartering, the exchange of goods and services for other goods and services, is another way of trading with countries lacking convertible currency. In a barter exchange, a company that manufactures electronics components might trade its products for the coffee that a business in a foreign country processes, which it then sells to a third company for cash. Barter transactions require finding a business with complementary needs, but they are much simpler than countertrade transactions.

bartering
the exchange of goods and services for other goods and services.

LO3

Explain how to build a thriving export program.

EXPORTING For many years, small businesses in the United States focused solely on the domestic market, never venturing beyond its borders. However, growing numbers of small companies, realizing the growth and profit potential that exporting offers, are making globalization part of their marketing plans. Large companies continue to dominate export sales, however. Although only 280,000 companies in the United States—about 1 percent of U.S. small businesses—export, companies with fewer than 20 employees account for 72 percent of all exporters.[28] Small and medium-size companies generate 33 percent of the nation's export sales.[29] Their impact is significant, however; small businesses generate $1.37 billion each day in export sales.[30]

The biggest barrier facing companies that have never exported is not knowing where or how to start, but entrepreneurs have a treasure trove of resources, training, and consulting on which they can draw. The International Trade Administration's *Export Programs Guide* provides entrepreneurs with a comprehensive list of 100 federal programs in 20 agencies designed to help U.S. exporters. The U.S. Commercial Service Web site (www.buyusa.gov) is an excellent starting point for entrepreneurs who are looking for international business partners to help their companies expand into global markets. Many entrepreneurs also find the U.S. Small Business Administration's Export Business Planner (www.sba.gov/exportbusinessplanner), a comprehensive set of worksheets that guides users through the process of building an export business plan, to be a valuable resource.

Another source of useful information are the U.S. Export Assistance Centers (http://export.gov/eac) that serve as single contact points for information on the multitude of federal export programs that are designed to help entrepreneurs who want to start exporting. The U.S. government's export portal (www.export.gov) gives entrepreneurs access to valuable information about exporting in general (finance, shipping, documentation, and others) as well as details on individual nations (market research, trade agreements, statistics, and more). A good place to start is *A Basic Guide to Exporting* (http://export.gov/basicguide/eg_main_017244.asp), which is billed as "the official government resource for small and medium-size businesses." Learning more about exporting and realizing that it is within the realm of possibility for small companies—even *very* small companies—is the first and often most difficult step in breaking the psychological barrier to exporting. The next challenge is to create a sound export strategy:

Step 1. *Recognize that even the tiniest companies and least experienced entrepreneurs have the potential to export.* Many entrepreneurs never considering exporting because they think their companies are too small; however, a business's size has nothing to do with the global potential of its products. In fact, 32 percent of the small companies that are exporters have no employees![31] If a company's products meet the needs of global customers, it has the potential to export. Studies suggest that small companies that export are stronger and grow markedly faster than those that do not. Table 15.2 on page 585 provides nine questions designed to help entrepreneurs assess the export potential of their companies.

✓ You Be the Consultant

A *Really* Bright Future

Loudmouth Golf

Sports Illustrated/Getty Images

Woody Wordsworth never set out to have a global business making and selling golf clothing. While working for a southern California newspaper, Woodsworth learned about graphic design, and when he moved to Sonoma, California, he started his own graphics design company. As his company grew, he began taking clients and potential customers on golf outings. Bored by the mundane styles that dominated golf, Woodsworth decided to use his graphic design skills to come up with his own golf outfits, inspired by the flashy (some might say tacky) styles that Lee Trevino, Bob Hope, and Johnny Miller once wore on the links. "I wanted to be loud and obnoxious," he says.

Woodsworth began scouring fabric stores for outlandish patterns and found pastel prints that featured Bugs Bunny, Daffy Duck, and the Tasmanian Devil riding golf carts that he had made into pants. Whenever he wore them, other golfers would stop him, wanting to know how they could get a pair. (Others sniffed with disdain at his tawdry fashion statement.) In 2000, Woodsworth began taking orders, and as volume swelled, he hired a Sacramento-based apparel company to produce them in volume. "They giggled when they saw the fabric," he recalls.

In 2006, Woodsworth's company, which he aptly named Loudmouth Golf, generated $64,000 in sales but was struggling for traction. One day, Woodsworth played golf with Larry Jackson, a successful Silicon Valley entrepreneur and early customer of Loudmouth Golf, and told him about the young company's struggle for survival. An experienced entrepreneur, Jackson immediately recognized Woodsworth's fundamental problem and offered him some simple yet effective advice that would turn around the company's fortunes: "Go back to what you're good at. Stop all the stuff you are not good at." Woodsworth heeded Jackson's advice and focused his efforts on designing new styles. In 2007, Jackson made an investment in Loudmouth Golf and soon was managing the company's manufacturing and shipping operations and its marketing strategy. A year later, Jackson became the company's CEO. He and Woodsworth embarked on a growth strategy, hiring an independent sales force, a supply-chain manager, a golf-pro liaison, and an international operations director to get Loudmouth Golf into Canada, Europe, Japan, Chile, and South Africa. The company signed a sponsorship deal with pro golfer John Daly, an arrangement that caused sales to increase whenever Daly appeared in tournaments wearing Loudmouth Golf clothing. "Sales bumped 40 percent the day he started," says Jackson.

Another breakout event for the company took place during the 2010 Winter Olympic Games in Vancouver, Canada, when the Norwegian curling team donned matching bright argyle-print pants from Loudmouth Golf. Woodsworth and Jackson were caught by surprise, learning of the team's purchase just eight days before the event. "Eight million eyeballs were seeing our product," recalls Jackson. "Even the king of Norway wanted a pair." Orders began pouring in, and traffic on the Loudmouth Golf Web site increased 10-fold. "We were getting hit so hard that our servers melted," says Jackson. Today, Canada and Norway remain two of the company's top markets. Loudmouth Golf also received exposure in the 2012 Summer Olympic Games in London, where the men's beach volleyball team sported the company's specially designed board shorts.

Loudmouth Golf, now with more than $10 million in annual sales, truly is a global business. The company has no official headquarters. "I run the whole business from Sonoma," says Woodson. "I design patterns in my [home] office, about 40 yards from a vineyard. Factories in China produce the designs (which usually include brightly colored polka dots, shrieking stripes, and dizzying checks) and ship them to the company's fulfillment center in Foster City, California. A global workforce sells Loudmouth Golf's bright, happy clothing in more than 50 golf-crazy countries on six continents. Members of its management team are scattered across the globe, allowing them to stay in close contact with trends and styles in local markets. They use Skype to conduct virtual business meetings, enabling them to operate as if they were in a single location.

Loudmouth Golf has expanded its wild style to other sports, including snowboarding, skiing, skateboarding, and surfing. It also has extended its product line to include shirts, sport coats,

You Be the Consultant (continued)

boxer shorts, hoodies, swimwear, accessories, and women and children's clothing. The company's women's line, which includes skorts, pants, Bermuda shorts, and miniskirts, now accounts for 35 percent of its total sales. Half of Loudmouth Golf's sales originate from its Web site, and half come from golf pro shops and specialty sports stores.

Loudmouth Golf uses its size to its advantage, getting new designs and new products to market faster than its competitors. The company creates six new styles every six weeks to keep customers coming back. Loudmouth Golf's unique, vivid product line, global supply chain, virtual communications, and speed to market give it a distinctive edge in a hotly competitive industry. Woodsworth and Jackson see a future for Loudmouth Golf that is as bright as a pair of its pants. "I think we can be a $100 million company," says Jackson confidently.

1. Identify the risks and the benefits that Loudmouth Golf faces by operating as a global business.

2. Identify some of the barriers that companies such as Loudmouth Golf encounter as they expand internationally. What steps can entrepreneurs take to overcome these obstacles?

3. What steps do you recommend that entrepreneurs such as Woody Woodsworth and Larry Jackson take before they make the decision to take their companies global?

Sources: Adapted from Steve Hart, "Sonoma Company Is Proud to Be Loud," *Press Democrat,* April 29, 2012, http://www.pressdemocrat.com/article/20120429/BUSINESS/120429549/1036/business?Title=Sonoma-company-is-proud-to-be-loud; Marcie Hill, "Lessons from Guys in (Really) Loud Pants," *American Express Open Forum,* January 3, 2012, http://www.openforum.com/articles/lessons-from-guys-in-really-loud-pants; Daniel Kehrer, "New Help for Small Business Exporting,"*BizBest,* July 14, 2011, http://www.bizbest.com/new-help-for-small-business-exporting; and Adam Tschorn, "All the Rage," *Los Angeles Times,* April 18, 2012, http://latimesblogs.latimes.com/alltherage/2012/04/loudmouth-golf-to-outfit-us-two-man-beach-volleyball-team.html.

Sabai Technology

ENTREPRENEURIAL PROFILE: William Haynes: Sabai Technology After William Haynes was laid off during the financial crisis, he started Sabai Technology, a company based in Simpsonville, South Carolina, that develops and sells wireless routers and network equipment, with himself as the sole employee. Initially, Haynes sold only to domestic customers until one of his customers, Strong VPN, opened the door to orders from companies in China. International sales took off after people involved in an Egyptian uprising discovered that Sabai Technology's wireless routers could send and receive information that was blocked by government filters. Haynes began working with the U.S. Commercial Service and U.S. Export Assistance Centers, which led him to advertise his products in *Commercial News USA*, a publication that goes to more than 400,000 readers in 178 countries. Today, international sales account for 80 percent of Sabai Technology's sales, and the company, which exports to 81 countries, has grown to nine employees. Haynes uses superior customer service and speedy delivery to set his company apart from the competition, most of which are much larger businesses.[32] ■

Step 2. *Analyze your product or service.* Is it special? New? Unique? High quality? Priced favorably because of lower costs or favorable exchange rates? Does it fit well with the culture and traditions of a country or region? Southland Log Homes, a small business located in Irmo, South Carolina, that manufactures log homes, has been able to sell its homes in Asia. "Log homes are a natural product, and that makes them a good fit with the culture and values of those countries," says Tim Bradley, the company's CFO. Southland now has a foreign distributor in Japan and has discovered that, because of its proximity to the port of Charleston, shipping a log home to Japan costs less than shipping one to Texas![33]

In many foreign countries, products from the United States are in demand because they have an air of mystery about them! In some cases, entrepreneurs find that they must make slight modifications to their products to accommodate local tastes, customs, and preferences. For instance, when Joseph Zaritski, owner of an Australian juice company, began marketing his company's products in Russia, he met with limited success until he realized that package size was the problem. Willing customers simply could not afford to purchase the two-liter bottles in

TABLE 15.2 Assessing Your Company's Export Potential

1. **Does your company have a product or service that has been successfully sold in the domestic market?** A product's or service's success in the domestic market is a good indicator of its potential success in markets abroad. However, because selling domestically and internationally are entirely different ventures, entrepreneurs should read *A Basic Guide to Exporting* to learn what to expect when selling internationally.

2. **Does your company have or is your company preparing an international marketing plan with defined goals and strategies?** Many companies begin export activities haphazardly, without carefully screening markets or options for market entry. A marketing plan allows your company to find and focus on the best export opportunities. Formulating an export strategy based on good information and proper assessment increases the chances that you will choose the best options, that you will use your company's resources effectively, and, therefore, that your efforts will successful. To find market research on the countries you are interested in selling to, visit the Market Research Library (http://export.gov/mrktresearch/index.asp).

3. **Does your company have sufficient production capacity that can be committed to the export market?** To export successfully, your company must meet the demand that it creates in foreign markets. You may need more space and equipment to manufacture for the specific countries you are selling to (who have their own product standards and regulations). Expanding into the international marketplace will result in a higher number of units to manufacture, and you do not want this increase in production to lower your company's quality of output.

4. **Does your company have the financial resources to actively support the marketing of your products in the targeted overseas markets?** Developing foreign markets requires financial resources. This is a big hurdle for many small companies because it involves activities such as international travel, participation in trade shows, market research, and international business training. However, there are many government programs to help finance companies' export sales, including the Export-Import Bank (Ex-Im Bank) (www.exim.gov), the U.S. Small Business Administration (www.sba.gov/content/export-loan-programs), the U.S. Department of Agriculture (www.fas.usda.gov), and the Overseas Private Investment Corporation (www.opic.gov).

5. **Is your company's management committed to developing export markets and willing and able to dedicate staff, time, and resources to the process?** Management commitment is the number one determining factor for export success. Developing an export market takes time and effort, and managers must be certain that they can afford to allocate sufficient time to exporting. Whether managers are willing to invest the time to build an export business plan is a good indicator of their commitment to an export initiative.

6. **Is your company committed to providing the same level of service to foreign customers that it gives to domestic customers?** This is a commitment that every business must make before it begins selling in foreign markets. Successful exporters treat their foreign customers with the same commitment and service as their domestic customers. They are responsive to inquiries from international customers, work hard to build positive relationships with them, and establish systems to provide the same top-notch service that they provide to their domestic customers.

7. **Does your company have adequate knowledge in modifying product packaging and ingredients to meet foreign import regulations and cultural preferences?** Selecting and preparing your product for export requires not only product knowledge but also knowledge of the unique characteristics of each market your company is targeting. Sound market research and input from foreign representatives tell a company about the potential to sell its products or services in specific target countries. Before the sale can occur, however, a company may have to modify its products and services to satisfy customers' tastes, needs, or preferences and legal requirements in foreign markets. Entrepreneurs can learn about regulations and export controls at http://export.gov/regulation/index.asp.

8. **Does your company have adequate knowledge in shipping its product overseas, such as identifying and selecting international freight forwarders and freight costing?** When shipping a product overseas, entrepreneurs must be aware of packaging, labeling, documentation, and insurance requirements. Violating these requirements often means severe and expensive penalties. This is where international freight forwarders can help. These agents understand the export regulations of the U.S. government, the import rules and regulations of foreign countries, appropriate methods of shipping, and the documents related to foreign trade. Freight forwarders assist exporters in preparing price quotations by advising on freight costs, port charges, consular fees, costs of special documentation, insurance costs, and handling fees. To find a freight forwarder, entrepreneurs can visit the National Customs Brokers and Freight Forwarders Association of America at www.ncbfaa.org.

9. **Does your company have adequate knowledge of export payment mechanisms, such as developing and negotiating letters of credit?** Experienced exporters have extensive knowledge of export payment mechanisms and extend credit cautiously. They evaluate new customers with care and continuously monitor existing customers' accounts. For general information on ways to receive payments, selecting a method of payment, and currency issues and payment problems, see *A Basic Guide to Exporting* and other resources described in this chapter. Conducting a credit check of potential buyers is essential because collecting delinquent accounts receivable from foreign customers is more difficult than collecting them from domestic customers. Exporters can use the U.S. Commercial Service's International Company Profiles (ICPs) to gain insight into the creditworthiness of potential customers. ICPs contain financial profiles of foreign companies and information on their size, capitalization, and number of years in business.

Source: Adapted from: "Export Questionnaire," Export.gov, http://export.gov/begin/assessment.asp.

FIGURE 15.4

Exporting Small Businesses: Number of Countries to Which U.S. Small Business Export

Source: A Basic Guide to Exporting, 10th edition, Washington DC: U.S. Department of Commerce, International Trade Administration, 2008, p. 5.

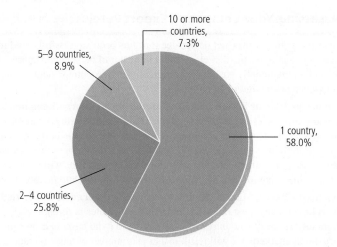

10 or more countries, 7.3%

5–9 countries, 8.9%

1 country, 58.0%

2–4 countries, 25.8%

which the juice was packaged. Zaritski switched to one-liter bottles and saw sales climb by 80 percent within six months![34]

Step 3. *Analyze your commitment.* Are you willing to devote time and energy to develop export markets? Does your company have the necessary resources? Patience is essential. An exporting initiative can take from six to eight months (or longer) to get off the ground, but entering foreign markets isn't as tough as most entrepreneurs think.

Step 4. *Research markets and pick your target.* Fifty-eight percent of small businesses that export sell to just one country (see Figure 15.4). Before investing in a costly sales trip abroad, however, entrepreneurs should search the Internet or make a trip to the local library or the nearest branch of the Department of Commerce. Exporters can choose from a multitude of guides, manuals, books, newsletters, videos, and other resources to help them research potential markets. Market research must include more than just the size of the potential market; it should include a detailed analysis of the demographic and buying habits of the customers in it as well as the cultural nuances of selling there.

ENTREPRENEURIAL PROFILE: Bob Hobe: Orly International Bob Hobe, vice president for international business development at Orly International, a Van Nuys, California–based company that makes nail care products, used the U.S. Department of Commerce's Gold Key Service to identify potential customers in foreign markets. Currently, Orly International exports to 82 countries and is looking to Latin American countries as its next target markets. "We have seen such growth in our export business that we have accelerated our emphasis to build more export markets," says Hobe. For Orly International, the move to exporting has paid off handsomely; sales growth in international markets has outpaced growth in the domestic market.[35] ■

Armed with research, entrepreneurs can avoid wasting time and money on markets with limited potential for their products and can concentrate on those with the greatest promise. The nations that account for the greatest export volume for U.S. businesses are Canada, Mexico, China, Japan, and the United Kingdom.[36] Some of the most helpful tools for researching foreign markets are the Country and Industry Market Reports available at the U.S. government's export Web portal (http://export.gov/mrktresearch/index.asp); these reports provide detailed information on the economic, political, regulatory, and investment environment for countries ranging from Afghanistan to Zimbabwe. Research tells entrepreneurs whether they need to modify their existing products and services to suit the tastes and preferences of their foreign target customers. Sometimes, foreign customers' lifestyles, housing needs, body size, and cultures require exporters to make alterations in their product lines. Making just slight modifications to adapt products and services to local tastes can sometimes spell the difference between success and failure in the global market. Entrepreneurs also should consider traveling to trade shows in the countries they are targeting to witness firsthand customers' responses to their products and services.

Step 5. *Develop a distribution strategy.* Should you use a trade intermediary or sell directly to foreign customers? As you learned earlier in this chapter, many small companies just entering international markets prefer to rely on trade intermediaries to break new ground. Using intermediaries often makes sense until an entrepreneur has the chance to gain experience in exporting and to learn the ground rules of selling in foreign lands.

ENTREPRENEURIAL PROFILE: Dancin' Dogg Golf Managers at Dancin' Dogg Golf, a company in Traverse City, Michigan, that makes an infrared indoor golf simulator called the OptiShot that allows golfers to play golf in their homes or offices, look for foreign markets in which golfers are underserved by traditional golf courses. The company has had success selling the OptiShot in Iceland, which has only 17 18-hole golf courses for its population of 35,000 golfers and fiercely cold winters that make playing golf outside a challenge. Dancin' Dogg Golf is now targeting South Korea, where 7 million golfers vie for tee times on just 400 courses. Dancin' Dogg Golf relies on foreign distributors to sell and service its OptiShot golf simulator in markets outside the United States.[37] ■

Step 6. *Find your customer.* According to a study by U.S. International Trade Commission, one of the most common problems among small business exporters is finding prospective customers (after all, establishing a network of business contacts takes time and resources).[38] Small businesses can rely on a host of export specialists to help them track down foreign customers. The U.S. Department of Commerce and the International Trade Administration should be the first stops on any entrepreneur's agenda for going global. These agencies have the market research available for locating the best target markets for a particular company and specific customers in those markets. Industry Sector Analyses, International Market Insights, and Customized Market Analyses are just some of the reports and services global entrepreneurs find most useful. These agencies also have knowledgeable staff specialists experienced in the details of global trade and in the intricacies of foreign cultures. GlobalEDGE (http://globaledge.msu.edu), an international trade information portal, also offers useful information on doing business in more than 200 countries, including directories, tutorials, online courses, and diagnostic tools

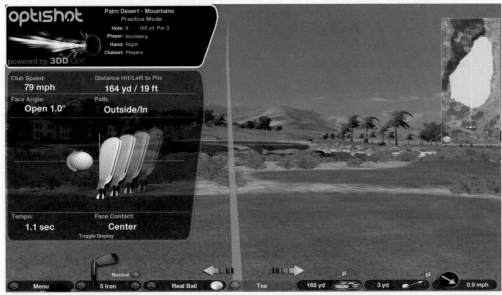

Dancin' Dogg Golf

designed to help companies determine their potential for conducting global business. The International Finance Corporation's Enterprise Surveys (www .enterprisesurveys.org) give entrepreneurs useful profiles of the business environments in 135 countries, ranging from overviews of basic infrastructure and business regulations to corruption and business obstacles. Through its Gold and Platinum Key services, the U.S. Commercial Service provides entrepreneurs who want to take their companies global with a list of prescreened distributors and potential customers and arranges face-to-face meetings with them.

ENTREPRENEURIAL PROFILE: Gary Schmidt: Failsafe Technology Inc. Failsafe Technology Inc., a small company in Bellevue, Washington, that makes safety sensors that detect potentially dangerous shifts in the ground under railroad tracks, bridges, buildings, and other infrastructure, worked with the U.S. Commercial Service to make its first international sale in China. Buoyed by the company's success in China, President Gary Schmidt used the U.S. Commercial Service's office in Australia to find customers there. Failsafe Technology now exports its products to five countries and is looking to enter new global markets.[39] ■

One of the most efficient and least expensive ways for entrepreneurs to locate potential customers for their companies' products and services is to participate in a trade mission. These missions usually are sponsored by either a federal or a state economic development agency or an industry trade association for the purpose of cultivating international trade by connecting domestic companies with potential trading partners overseas. A trade mission may focus on a particular industry or may cover several industries but target a particular country. "Trade missions are a great way to find quality buyers, partners, and agents in international markets," says Maria Cino, who has led many trade mission trips for the U.S. and Foreign Commercial Service.[40] Grain Millers Dairy Products Inc., a small company in Eden Prairie, Minnesota, that markets a full line of dairy products, recently participated in a trade mission sponsored by the Food Export Association of the Midwest to Brazil and Argentina that has resulted in more than $165,000 in new export sales. "Trade missions help you learn more about your markets, your partners, and your competitors," says Liz Perez, the company's director of international sales.[41]

Step 7. *Find financing.* One of the biggest barriers to small business exports is lack of financing. Access to adequate financing is a crucial ingredient in a successful export program because the cost of generating foreign sales often is higher and collection cycles are longer than in domestic markets. The trouble is that bankers and other providers of capital don't always understand the intricacies of international sales and view financing them as excessively risky. In addition, among major industrialized nations, the U.S. government spends the least per capita to promote exports.

Several federal, state, and private programs are operating to fill this export financing void, however. Loan programs from the Small Business Administration's include its Export Working Capital program (90 percent loan guarantees up to $5 million), International Trade Loan program (90 percent loan guarantees up to $5 million) and Export Express program (75 percent loan guarantees up to $500,000). In addition, the Ex-Im Bank (www.exim.gov), the Overseas Private Investment Corporation (www.opic.gov), and a variety of state-sponsored programs offer export-minded entrepreneurs both direct loans and loan guarantees. The Ex-Im Bank, which has been financing the sale of U.S. exports since 1934, provides small exporters with export credit insurance and loans through its working capital line of credit and a variety of preexport loan programs. The Overseas Private Investment Corporation provides loans and loan guarantees up to $250 million to support foreign investments by small and medium-size companies and offers businesses discounted political risk insurance. The Bankers Association for Foreign Trade–International Finance Services (www.baft-ifsa.com) is an association of banks around the world that matches exporters in need of foreign trade financing with interested banks.

ENTREPRENEURIAL PROFILE: Nancy Mercolino: Ceilings Plus With the help of an Ex-Im Bank working capital line of credit and guarantees on loans from Bank of the West, Ceilings Plus, a Los Angeles, California–based manufacturer and installer of high-quality aluminum and wood ceiling and wall panels, was able to finance an $18 million sale to Qatar for an expansion project at the Doha International Airport. The financing from the Ex-Im Bank was an essential component in securing Ceilings Plus's first international sales contract and a second-phase contract of $11 million on the same project. Before its foray into exporting, Ceiling Plus generated annual sales of $10 million. Since going global, sales have more than doubled, and the company's workforce has increased from 86 to 150 employees. "Ex-Im Bank has engaged in a collaboration with our company and our local bank to provide the financial support we needed to venture into the international world," says president Nancy Mercolino.[42] ■

Step 8. *Ship your goods.* Export novices usually rely on international freight forwarders and customs brokers—experienced specialists in overseas shipping—for help in navigating the bureaucratic morass of packaging and regulatory requirements, tariffs, and paperwork demanded by customs. These specialists, also known as transport architects, are to exporters what travel agents are to travelers and normally charge relatively small fees for a valuable service. They not only move shipments of all sizes to destinations all over the world efficiently, saving entrepreneurs many headaches, but also are well versed in the regulations that govern exported products and services. For example, in Canada, product packaging for Ganong Brothers, Canada's oldest candy maker and whose factory is within site of the U.S. border, must read "5 mg" (with a space between the number and the unit of measurement). To sell the same product in the United States, however, the company's packaging must read "5mg" (with no space between the number and the unit of measurement).[43] Exporters can find local freight forwarders and customs brokers at the National Customs Brokers and Freight Forwarders Association of America's Web site (www.ncbfaa.org).

Shipping terms, always important for determining which party in a transaction pays the cost of shipping and bears the risk of loss or damage to the goods while they are in transit, take on heightened importance in international transactions.

Step 9. *Collect your money.* A study by the Ex-Im Bank reports that the top concern of companies that export is collecting payment for the goods and services they sell.[44] Collecting foreign accounts can be more complex than collecting domestic ones; however, by picking their customers carefully and checking their credit references closely, entrepreneurs can minimize bad-debt losses. Businesses that engage in international sales use four primary payment methods (ranked from least risky to most risky): cash in advance, a letter of credit, a bank (or documentary) draft, and an open account. The safest method of selling to foreign customers is to collect cash in advance of the sale because it eliminates the risk of collection problems and provides immediate cash flow. However, requiring cash payments up front severely limits a small company's base of foreign customers.

A **letter of credit** is an agreement between an exporter's bank and the foreign buyer's bank that guarantees payment to the exporter for a specific shipment of goods. In essence, a letter of credit reduces the financial risk for the exporter by substituting a bank's creditworthiness for that of the purchaser (see Figure 15.5). A **bank draft** is a document the seller draws on the buyer, requiring the buyer to pay the face amount (the purchase price of the goods) either on sight (a sight draft) or on a specified date (a time draft) once the goods have been shipped. With either letters of credit or bank drafts, small exporters must be sure that all of the required documentation is present and accurate; otherwise, they may experience delays in the payments due to them from the buyer or the participating banks. Rather than use letters of credit or drafts, some exporters simply sell to foreign customers on open account. In other words, they ship the goods to a foreign

letter of credit
an agreement between an exporter's bank and the foreign buyer's bank that guarantees payment to the exporter for a specific shipment of goods.

bank draft
a document the seller draws on the buyer, requiring the buyer to pay the face amount either on sight or on a specified date.

FIGURE 15.5

How a Letter of Credit Works

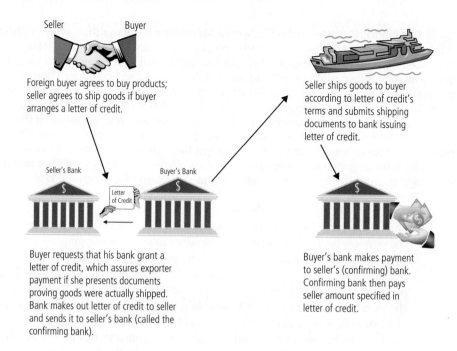

Foreign buyer agrees to buy products; seller agrees to ship goods if buyer arranges a letter of credit.

Seller ships goods to buyer according to letter of credit's terms and submits shipping documents to bank issuing letter of credit.

Buyer requests that his bank grant a letter of credit, which assures exporter payment if she presents documents proving goods were actually shipped. Bank makes out letter of credit to seller and sends it to seller's bank (called the confirming bank).

Buyer's bank makes payment to seller's (confirming) bank. Confirming bank then pays seller amount specified in letter of credit.

customer without any guarantee of payment. This method is riskiest because collecting a delinquent account from a foreign customer is even more difficult than collecting past-due payments from a domestic customer. One way that small exporters can minimize the risk of bad-debt losses on foreign credit sales is to purchase export credit insurance, which protects a company against the nonpayment of its foreign customers' open accounts. The cost of export credit insurance typically is a small percentage of the amount of the foreign sale a company is insuring. Private insurers and the Ex-Im Bank offer export credit insurance.

ESTABLISHING INTERNATIONAL LOCATIONS Once established in international markets, some small businesses set up permanent locations there. Establishing an office or a factory in a foreign land can require a substantial investment reaching beyond the budgets of many small companies. In addition, setting up an international office can be an incredibly frustrating experience in some countries where business infrastructure is in disrepair or is nonexistent. Hayden Hamilton, founder of GreenPrint Technologies, a company that sells software that reduces printing costs by eliminating unnecessary pages, opened an office in India, where he can get bargain rates on quality software programming. He was frustrated when it took three hours to apply for a telephone line—and one month to get it installed. Because power outages in India are common, GreenPrint also had to purchase expensive backup generators.[45]

In some countries, securing necessary licenses and permits from bureaucrats often takes more than filing the necessary paperwork; in some nations, bureaucrats expect payments to "grease the wheels" of commerce. American entrepreneurs consider payments to reduce the amount of red tape involved in an international transaction to be bribery, and many simply avoid doing business in countries where "grease payments" are standard procedure. In fact, the Foreign Corrupt Practice Act, passed in 1977, considers bribing foreign officials to be a criminal act. One study by the World Bank of grease payments for the purpose of minimizing the red tape imposed by foreign regulations concludes that the payments do not work; in fact, companies that actually used them experienced greater government scrutiny and red tape in their international transactions.[46] Finally, finding the right person to manage an international office is crucial to success; it also is a major challenge, especially for small businesses. Small companies usually have lean management staffs and cannot afford to send key people abroad without running the risk of losing their focus.

Small companies that establish international locations can reap significant benefits. Start-up costs are lower in some foreign countries (but not all!), and lower labor costs can produce

You Be the Consultant

A Small Company Goes Global

John Carr, sales manager for Osagian Canoes, a six-employee company in Lebanon, Missouri, never considered selling the company's aluminum canoes in markets outside the United States. After all, he assumed, the cost to ship a 17-foot canoe would be exorbitant. In addition, neither he nor any of his small sales force spoke any foreign languages, and collecting international payments would be extremely complicated.

Then Carr attended a workshop, ExporTech, sponsored by the U.S. Chamber of Commerce and discovered that most of his assumptions about small companies engaging in international business were wrong. "That workshop opened my mind to possibilities," says Carr. "It's not that big of a world out there." Carr learned that Osagian Canoes could purchase export credit insurance to reduce the risk of foreign customers failing to pay invoices. Although learning a foreign language makes conducting international business much easier, he learned that "English is the language of business." He chuckles when he says, "I thought I was going to have to learn to speak German."

Carr's knowledge paid off almost immediately when a kayak distributor in Denmark asked about distributing Osagian's canoes to dealers in Denmark, Norway, and Sweden. The distributor was impressed that Osagian canoes are the only ones whose hull pieces are welded rather than secured by rivets, a process that makes them stronger and more durable. Carr was eager to sign a deal with the Danish distributor because domestic sales, most of which were to camps and resorts, were stagnant because of a recession.

Carr's assumption about shipping costs proved to be correct. A standard shipping container can hold only 20 Osagian canoes.

The cost to ship a container is $5,000, which adds $250 to the cost of each canoe exported. Carr realized, however, that Osagian could ship unassembled canoe pieces at just 10 percent of the cost to ship a fully assembled canoe. "Why don't we set up a small assembly factory in Denmark where a couple of employees can weld the components we ship into finished canoes?" he asked. Osagian did just that.

Carr also attended an outdoor equipment trade show in Neuremberg, Germany, where he met nine sales representatives who now distribute Osagian canoes in Germany, France, England, Switzerland, and Austria. Export sales have increased the company's sales and now account for 15 percent of its revenue. Buoyed by its early success expanding into international markets, Carr is now targeting South America and Australia, where seasons are reversed from those in the Northern Hemisphere. The busy summer season for canoe sales in the Southern Hemisphere would offset the slow winter sales in the Northern Hemisphere. Osagian's foreign sales continue to grow, and the company is already planning to hire more employees.

1. Are John Carr's assumptions about conducting business internationally typical of most small business owners? Explain.

2. What lessons can other entrepreneurs learn from Osagian Canoe's experience in going global?

Source: Adapted from Paul Davidson, "Small Businesses Look across Borders to Add Markets," *USA Today,* April 12, 2011, http://www.usatoday.com/money/economy/2011-04-06-small-businesses-go-international.htm.

---

significant savings. In addition, by locating in a country, a business gains a firsthand understanding of local customers' preferences, tastes, and habits and the nuances of how culture influences business practices. In essence, the business becomes a local corporate citizen.

IMPORTING AND OUTSOURCING In addition to selling their goods in foreign markets, small companies also buy goods from distributors and manufacturers in foreign markets. In the United States alone, companies import more than $3.2 trillion worth of goods and services annually.[47] The intensity of price competition in many industries—from textiles and handbags to industrial machinery and computers—means that more companies now shop the world market looking for the best deals they can find. Because labor costs in countries such as Mexico, Taiwan, and India are far below those in other nations, businesses there offer goods and services at very low prices. Increasingly, these nations are home to well-educated, skilled workers who are paid far less than comparable workers in the United States or western Europe. For instance, a computer programmer in the United States might earn $100,000 a year, but in India, a computer programmer doing the same work earns $20,000 a year or less. As a result, many companies either import goods or outsource work directly to manufacturers in countries where costs are far lower than they would be domestically.

Alibaba.com, an online trading platform started in Hangzhou, China, in 1999, has enabled millions of small companies to find reliable suppliers and vendors around the globe for the products and services they sell. Alibaba.com boasts nearly 80 million registered users in 240 countries.

ENTREPRENEURIAL PROFILE: Lisa and Kevin Hickey: Online Stores Inc. Lisa and Kevin Hickey started Online Stores, Inc., a company that originally sold flags and flag cases, in their basement in 2001. The business grew rapidly, and the Hickeys now operate eight online stores that sell products ranging from flags and work clothing to power tools and promotional gifts. In 2002, Kevin began using Alibaba.com to find suppliers of Online Stores' rapidly growing product line (which now numbers more than 10,000 products), and the company still works with many of those suppliers today. "Finding manufacturers through Alibaba.com was very easy," says Kevin. "I sent an e-mail to a number of suppliers outlining what I wanted and received several replies. I obtained a few samples and placed a small order with a vendor; graduating to larger repeat orders was a natural progression." With its network of global suppliers, Online Stores' sales have grown from $1 million in 2002 to more than $25 million.[48] ■

Entrepreneurs who are considering importing goods and service or outsourcing their manufacturing to foreign countries should follow these steps:

● *Make sure that importing or outsourcing is right for your business.* Even though foreign manufacturers often can provide items at significant cost savings, using them may not always be the best business decision. Some foreign manufacturers require sizable minimum orders, sometimes hundreds of thousands of dollars' worth, before they will produce a product. Entrepreneurs sometimes discover that achieving the lowest price may require a trade-off of other important factors, such as quality and speed of delivery.

● *Establish a target cost for your product.* Before setting off on a global shopping spree, entrepreneurs first should determine exactly what they can afford to spend on manufacturing a product and make a profit on it. Given the low labor costs of many foreign manufacturers, products that are the most labor intensive make good candidates.

● *Do your research before you leave home.* Investing time in basic research about the industry and potential suppliers in foreign lands is essential before setting foot on foreign soil. Useful resources are plentiful, and entrepreneurs should use them, including the Internet, the Federation of International Trade Associations, industry trade associations, government agencies (e.g., the U.S. Commercial Service's Gold Key Matching Service), and consultants.

ENTREPRENEURIAL PROFILE: Dieter Kondek: Moonlight U.S.A. At a dinner party, Dieter Kondek learned about Moonlight, a German company that makes unique polyethylene, globe-shaped lights that can illuminate a pathway, cast an enchanting glow while floating in a pool, or simply light a room. Kondek researched the company and learned that the globes, which range from 13 to 30 inches in diameter and can withstand temperatures from –40° F to 140°F, were popular in upscale homes and businesses in Europe, Asia, and the Middle East but had not yet reached the United States. Within months, Kondek negotiated a deal to become the exclusive U.S. distributor for Moonlight and established Moonlight U.S.A., which the parent company says soon will account for half of its annual sales.[49] ■

● *Be sensitive to cultural differences.* When making contacts, setting up business appointments, or calling on prospective manufacturers in foreign lands, make sure you understand what constitutes accepted business behavior and what does not. This is where your research pays off; be sure to study the cultural nuances of doing business in the countries you will visit.

● *Do your groundwork.* Once you locate potential manufacturers, contact them to set up appointments and go visit them. Preliminary research is essential to finding reliable sources of supply, but "face time" with representatives from various companies allows entrepreneurs to judge the intangible factors that can make or break a relationship. Entrepreneurs who visit foreign suppliers often find that they receive better service because their suppliers know them personally.

● *Protect your company's intellectual property.* A common problem that many entrepreneurs have encountered with outsourcing is "knockoffs." Some foreign manufacturers see nothing wrong with agreeing to manufacture a product for a company and then selling their own knockoff version of it that they manufacture in a "ghost shift." Securing a nondisclosure agreement and a contract that prohibits such behavior helps, but experts say that securing a patent for the item in the source country itself (not just the United States) is a good idea.

● *Select a manufacturer.* Using quality, speed of delivery, level of trust, degree of legal protection, cost, and other factors, select the manufacturer that can do the job for your company.

● *Provide an exact model of the product you want manufactured.* Providing a manufacturer with an actual model of the item to be manufactured will save lots of time, mistakes, and problems. "It's always better to cost something from an actual item rather than an idea of an item," says Jennifer Adams, owner of a consulting firm that helps entrepreneurs to locate foreign manufacturers.[50]

● *Stay in constant contact with the manufacturer and try to build a long-term relationship.* Communication is a key to building and maintaining a successful relationship with a foreign manufacturer. Weekly teleconferences, e-mails, and periodic visits are essential to making sure that your company gets the performance you expect from a foreign manufacturer.

Barriers to International Trade

Governments traditionally have used a variety of barriers to block free trade among nations in an attempt to protect businesses within their own borders. The benefit of protecting their own companies, however, comes at the expense of foreign businesses, which face limited access to global markets. Numerous trade barriers—domestic and international—restrict the freedom of businesses in global trading (see Figure 15.6). Even with these barriers, global trade of goods and services has grown to nearly $19 trillion.[51]

LO4

Discuss the major barriers to international trade and their impact on the global economy.

Domestic Barriers

Sometimes the biggest barriers potential exporters face are those right here at home. Three major domestic roadblocks are common: attitude, information, and financing. Perhaps the biggest

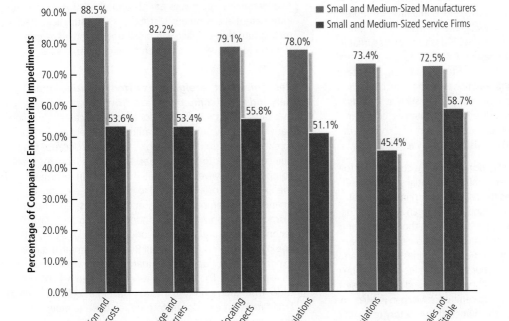

Most Frequently Encountered Impediments to International Trade

- ■ Small and Medium-Sized Manufacturers
- ■ Small and Medium-Sized Service Firms

Percentage of Companies Encountering Impediments (y-axis)

Impediment to International Trade (x-axis)

Categories and values:
- Transportation and shipping costs: 88.5% / 53.6%
- Language and cultural barriers: 82.2% / 53.4%
- Difficulty locating sales prospects: 79.1% / 55.8%
- Foreign regulations: 78.0% / 51.1%
- U.S. regulations: 73.4% / 45.4%
- Foreign sales not sufficiently profitable: 72.5% / 58.7%

FIGURE 15.6

Most Frequently Encountered Impediments to International Trade

Source: U.S. International Trade Commission, *Small and Medium-Sized Enterprises: Characteristics and Performance*, Publication 4189, November 2010, pp. 6–8.

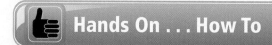

Build a Successful Global Company

Like many entrepreneurs, Darryl Bartlett, cofounder of k-Space, a small company in Dexter, Michigan, that manufactures real-time systems designed to monitor semiconductor, optoelectronic, and photovoltaic manufacturing processes, had not given serious consideration to international sales. Bartlett and a colleague in the University of Michigan's Department of Applied Physics had started the company in 1992 and were focused on selling to domestic companies when a Japanese distributor approached Bartlett at a trade show in 1995. Only then did the realization that high-tech companies around the world could benefit from k-Space's products come to him. "We just fell into it," says Bartlett. Today, k-Space generates more than $8 million in annual sales, 65 percent of which are from foreign countries. Because of k-Space's creative global marketing strategies and success in exporting, the company recently was named the U.S. Small Business Administration's Small Business Exporter of the Year. Following are some of the lessons Bartlett and other entrepreneurs have learned about operating a global small business.

Don't assume that your company has to be big to be an international player. As Darryl Bartlett of k-Space learned, even very small companies have the opportunity to be successful in the global arena. Success in international markets does not require size, but it does require commitment and a sound strategy.

Know what you don't know. Perhaps the most important item in a global entrepreneur's briefcase is *knowledge*. Before embarking on any international business initiative, entrepreneurs should take the time to educate themselves and their employees. This chapter is filled with useful resources, many of which are free, that are designed to help business owners get their global business efforts off to a good start. The starting point for conducting international business successfully is learning about best practices for key issues such as identifying target markets, developing distribution strategies, complying with regulations, adapting products when necessary, collecting payments, and providing customer service.

Build a network of connections. Having a contact in a foreign country who can open doors to potential suppliers and customers greatly reduces the risk involved in international business. Mia Abbruzzese, founder of Morgan & Milo, a children's shoe company, had launched several shoe lines during her days as an executive for three large global shoe companies and knew that success in the shoe business requires an extensive network of connections in all corners of the globe. Using her industry contacts, Abbruzzese found a Taiwanese investor who provided start-up capital for Morgan & Milo and introduced Abbruzzese to the owner of the factory in southern China that makes many of the shoes that Morgan & Milo designs. Two other advisers on whom Abbruzzese relies are industry veterans who have an extensive network of contacts in the shoe industry that have proved to be extremely valuable to her company.

Learn about the cultural aspects of conducting business in the countries in which your company operates. Business dealings are a reflection of a country's culture, and entrepreneurs should educate themselves about the nuances of doing business in the host country to avoid committing embarrassing cultural blunders. In the United States, businesspeople are transaction oriented. They want to set up an appointment, negotiate a deal quickly and efficiently, sign a contract, and leave. In many other countries, landing a deal takes much longer because businesspeople expect to get to know their potential partners first. Particularly in Asia, businesspeople tend to be relationship oriented, doing business only with people they know, like, and respect. Developing relationships can take time, making a network of connections all the more important. When doing business in Asia, entrepreneurs quickly learn that formal contracts, which are the foundation of business deals in the United States, are not as important. They also learn to adjust the speed at which they close deals and take more time to build relationships with reliable suppliers.

Go there. Building a global business usually requires entrepreneurs to travel to the countries in which they plan to do business. It's an excellent way to build a network of contacts. Participating in international trade missions, attending international trade shows, and using matching services such as the U.S. Department of Commerce's Gold Key and Platinum Key services are ideal methods for connecting with potential customers, distributors, and suppliers. Bartlett makes sure that k-Space is represented at three key international trade shows, all of which have generated sales for the company.

Recognize that foreign sales often put additional demands on a company's cash flow. Expanding a company's sales efforts into international markets can strain a company's cash flow, and many traditional lenders are hesitant to extend loans to cover foreign credit sales because they perceive the risk to be too great. Help is available for small companies, however. The Small Business Administration and the Ex-Im Bank offer loan and loan guarantee programs to finance small companies' foreign credit sales. CellAntenna Corporation, a maker of cell phone jamming and control technology in Coral Springs, Florida, secured a $250,000 line of credit through the Small Business Administration's Export Working Capital loan guaranty program to finance its export sales. The company recently landed a $100,000 order from a prison in Australia. "Having a $250,000 line of credit makes it easy for us to produce the equipment while receiving orders from around the world," says CEO Howard Melamed.

Make sure you collect payments from foreign sales. Collecting payments on delinquent foreign sales is more involved than collecting payments on delinquent domestic sales.

Hands On . . . How To *(continued)*

The best way to avoid this problem is to sell to customers who pay their bills on time. That means that conducting credit checks before selling to international customers is just as important as it is before selling to domestic customers. In addition, small companies can reduce the risk of foreign credit sales by purchasing export credit insurance from either private insurers or from the Ex-Im Bank. CellAntenna Corporation routinely sells to foreign customers on open account but purchases export credit insurance from the Ex-Im Bank to mitigate the risk of nonpayment.

Source: Adapted from Diana Ransom, "Five Tips for Getting Started in Exporting," *Entrepreneur,* May 17, 2011, http://www.entrepreneur.com/article/219650; Ian Mount, "Tips for Increasing Sales in International Markets," *New York Times,* April 21, 2010, http://www.nytimes.com/2010/04/22/business/smallbusiness/22sbiz.html; John Jantsch, "Around the Block or around the World," Duct Tape Marketing, September 21, 2010, http://www.ducttapemarketing.com/blog/2010/09/21/around-the-block-or-around-the-world; Anita Campbell, "Preparing Your Business to Go Global," Small Business Trends, November 19, 2010, http://smallbiztrends.com/2010/11/preparing-your-business-to-go-global.html; Allessandra Bianchi, "Small & Global: The World as a Factory," *FSB,* June 2004, pp. 40–42; Sheri Qualters, "Operating on a Shoestring," *Boston Business Journal,* June 10, 2005, http://boston.bizjournals.com/boston/stories/2005/06/13/smallb1.html; and *2011 National Export Strategy: Powering the National Export Initiative,* Trade Promotion Coordinating Committee, Washington, DC, June 2011, p. 23.

barrier to small businesses exporting is the attitude that "My company is too small to export. That's just for big corporations." The first lesson of exporting is "Take nothing for granted about who can export and what you can and cannot export" (see Table 15.3 on page 596). The first step to building an export program is recognizing that the opportunity to export exists. Another reason entrepreneurs neglect international markets is a lack of information about how to get started. The keys to success in international markets are choosing the correct target market and designing the appropriate strategy to reach it. That requires access to information and research. Although a variety of government and private organizations make volumes of exporting and international marketing information available, many small business owners never use it. A successful global marketing strategy also recognizes that not all international markets are the same. Companies must be flexible, willing to make adjustments to their products and services, promotional campaigns, packaging, and sales techniques.

An additional obstacle is the inability of small firms to obtain adequate export financing. Financial institutions that serve small companies often are not experienced in financing international sales and are unwilling to accept the perceived higher levels of risk they create for the lender.

International Barriers

Domestic barriers aren't the only ones that export-minded entrepreneurs must overcome. Trading nations also erect obstacles to free trade. Two types of international barriers are common: tariff and nontariff.

TARIFF BARRIERS A **tariff** is a tax, or duty, that a government imposes on goods and services imported into that country. Imposing tariffs raises the price of the imported goods—making them less attractive to consumers—and protects the domestic makers of comparable product and services. Established in the United States in 1790 by Alexander Hamilton, the tariff system generated the majority of federal revenues for about 100 years. Currently, the *Harmonized Tariff Schedule,* which sets tariffs for products imported into the United States, includes 37,000 categories of goods. The average U.S. tariff on imported goods is 1.78 percent (compared to the global average of 3.70 percent).[52] American tariffs vary greatly and depend on the particular type of good. For instance, inexpensive men's acrylic sweaters imported into the United States carry a 32 percent tariff, but the tariff on cashmere sweaters is 4 percent; cheap sneakers are taxed at 48 percent, but golf shoes carry an 8.5 percent tariff.[53] Tariff rates also vary among nations. Singapore, Switzerland, and Hong Kong impose no tariffs at all on imported goods, but India's average tariff rate is 19.2 percent. Bermuda has the highest average tariff rate in the world at 26.1 percent.[54]

NONTARIFF BARRIERS Many nations have lowered the tariffs they impose on products and services brought into their borders, but they rely on other nontariff structures as protectionist trade barriers.

QUOTAS Rather than impose a direct tariff on certain imported products, nations often use quotas to protect their industries. A **quota** is a limit on the amount of a product imported into a

tariff
a tax, or duty, that a government imposes on goods and services imported into that country.

quota
a limit on the amount of a product imported into a country.

TABLE 15.3 Global Business Assumptions

Old Assumption	New Assumption
Exporting is too risky for my small company.	Exporting to "easy" markets such as Canada is no more risky than selling to companies in the United States. Each international market has its own level of risk. Entrepreneurs can identify the most significant risks their companies face and reduce them by using the extensive amount of affordable export assistance that is available now.
Getting paid is cumbersome, and I'll lose my shirt.	Trade finance and global banking have evolved to the point where buying and selling goods and services internationally is routine, safe, and efficient. Reliable collection methods, including credit cards, online payments, and letters of credit, are readily available. Some delivery firms will collect payment from customers at the time of delivery.
Exporting is too complicated.	Most exporting requires minimal paperwork. Often, entrepreneurs can research markets and find buyers from their computers using free or low-cost information.
My domestic market is secure. I don't need to export.	Globalization has made buying and selling goods in multiple markets easy. Few markets remain static, and new markets are constantly opening. Most U.S. businesses are involved in or affected by international markets, whether they realize it or not. More small and medium-size companies have the potential to benefit from going global, but doing so requires an international marketing strategy.
I'm too small to go global.	No company is too small to go global. In fact, 72 percent of U.S. exporters have fewer than 20 employees.
My product or service probably won't sell outside the United States.	If your product or service sells well in the United States, there is a good chance you can find a foreign market in which it will sell. In addition, help is available for entrepreneurs who want to test the appeal of their products and services in more than 100 countries around the globe. In some markets, entrepreneurs must make modifications to their products and services because of cultural, regulatory, or other differences. However, most modifications are small and simple to make. In addition, by learning to sell successfully in other markets, small companies become stronger and better able to compete in all of their markets.
I won't be successful because I don't speak another language and have never been abroad.	Cultural knowledge and business etiquette are important, but you can learn as you go. English is the language of business in many countries, but you can easily hire translators and interpreters when necessary. Researching cultural differences before engaging in foreign transactions helps prevents embarrassing faux pas, but a friendly disposition, a sense of humor, and a willingness to learn can make up for many unintended mistakes.

Source: Based on "Table 1.1: Global Business Assumptions," *A Basic Guide to Exporting*, 10th ed., 2008, U.S. Department of Commerce, International Trade Administration, p. 7; "U.S. Export Loan Programs," U.S. Small Business Administration, http://www.sba.gov/content/export-loan-programs.

country. Those who favor quotas argue that they protect domestic industries and the jobs they create. Those who oppose quotas say that they artificially raise prices on the restricted goods, imposing a hidden tax on customers who purchase them. China imposes a quota on foreign films, allowing only 34 foreign films to be released each year. Before 2012, the quota was 20 foreign films, even though China's total box office sales are $2.1 billion annually, the third largest in the world, and are predicted to exceed $5 billion by 2015. China has just 9,000 cinema screens, but the number is growing rapidly. Despite pressure from the World Trade Organization (WTO) to eliminate the film quota, Chinese officials have refused, expressing concern that removing the barrier would unleash a flood of foreign films that might wipe out the local film industry.[55]

EMBARGOES An **embargo** is a total ban on imports of certain products. The motivation for embargoes is not always economic; it also can involve political differences, environmental disputes, war, terrorism, and other issues. For instance, the United States imposes embargoes on products from nations it considers to be adversarial, including Cuba, Iran, Iraq, and North Korea, among others. An embargo on trade with Cuba, started in 1962 when Fidel Castro nationalized all U.S. businesses on the island nation and formed an alliance with the Soviet Union, still exists today. In 1994, the United States lifted a total trade embargo on Vietnam that had stood since 1975, when Saigon fell into communist hands at the end of the Vietnam War. Today, the United States imports $17.5 billion worth of goods from Vietnam and exports goods worth $4.3 billion.[56]

Embargoes also originate from cultural differences. For instance, the United States imposes embargoes on any harp seal products from Norway under the Marine Mammal Protection Act. Norway, where seal products make up a multi-million-dollar industry, has pushed for the elimination of the embargo, arguing that harp seals are not an endangered species.[57]

embargo
a total ban on imports of certain products into a country.

DUMPING In an effort to grab market share quickly, some companies have been guilty of **dumping** products: selling large quantities of them at prices that are below cost in foreign countries. The United States has been a dumping ground for steel, televisions, shoes, and computer chips from other nations in the past. Under the U.S. Antidumping Act, a company must prove that the foreign company's prices are lower here than in the home country and that U.S. companies are directly harmed. Disputes over dumping brought before the WTO have increased significantly over the last five years, and China has been the target of most of the complaints from WTO member nations. The U.S. Department of Commerce, without the involvement of the WTO, recently ruled that government-subsidized makers of solar cells and panels in China were guilty of dumping their products in the United States at prices that average 31 percent below "fair value." SolarWorld Industries America and six other U.S.-based solar cell and panel manufacturers initiated the charge, claiming that "artificially low prices on solar products from China are crippling the domestic industry." As part of its ruling, the U.S. Department of Commerce imposed punitive dumping margins (the difference between the fair value of the items and their actual export price) of 31 percent on the Chinese companies.[58]

dumping
selling large quantities of goods at prices that are below cost in foreign countries in an effort to grab market share quickly.

Political Barriers

Entrepreneurs who go global quickly discover a labyrinth of political tangles. Although many U.S. business owners complain of excessive government regulation in the United States, they are often astounded by the onerous web of governmental and legal regulations and barriers they encounter in foreign countries. One entrepreneur who established a business location in Russia says that he had to visit more than two dozen agencies to complete the necessary paperwork and get 90 different documents signed.[59]

Companies doing business in politically risky lands face the very real dangers of government takeovers of private property; coups to overthrow ruling parties; kidnapping, bombings, and other violent acts against businesses and their employees; and other threatening events. Their investments of millions of dollars may evaporate overnight in the wake of a government coup or the passage of a law nationalizing an industry (giving control of an entire industry to the government).

Business Barriers

American companies doing business internationally quickly learn that business practices and regulations in foreign lands can be quite different from those in the United States. Simply duplicating the practices they have adopted (and have used successfully) in the domestic market and using them in foreign markets is not always a good idea. Perhaps the biggest shock comes in the area of human resources management, in which international managers discover that practices common in the United States, such as overtime and employee benefits, are restricted, disfavored, or forbidden in other cultures. Business owners new to international business sometimes are shocked at the wide range of labor costs they encounter and the accompanying wide range of skilled labor available. In some countries, what appear to be "bargain" labor rates turn out to be excessively high after accounting for the quality of the labor force and the benefits their governments mandate: from company-sponsored housing, meals, and clothing to profit sharing and extended vacations. For instance, laws in many European countries mandate a minimum of 20 days of vacation in addition to paid holidays, giving workers there an average of nearly 35 days off per year.[60] Hefty taxes, ineffective legal systems, corruption, and shady business associates can make doing business in foreign countries difficult.

Cultural Barriers

Even though travel and communications technology has increased the ease and the frequency with which entrepreneurs engage in global transactions, the potential for cultural blunders has increased. The **culture** of a nation includes the beliefs, values, views, and mores that its inhabitants share. Differences in cultures among nations create another barrier to international trade. The diversity of languages, business philosophies, practices, and traditions make international trade more complex than selling to the business down the street. Consider the following examples:

- A U.S. entrepreneur, eager to expand into the European Union, arrives at the headquarters of his company's potential business partner in France. Confidently, he strides into the meeting room, enthusiastically pumps his host's hand, slaps him on the back, and says, "Tony, I've heard a great deal about you; please, call me Bill." Eager to explain the benefits of his product, he opens his briefcase and gets right down to business. The French executive politely excuses himself and leaves the room before negotiations ever begin, shocked by the American's rudeness and ill manners. Rudeness and ill manners? Yes—from the French executive's perspective.

- Another American business owner flies to Tokyo to close a deal with a Japanese executive. He is pleased when his host invites him to play a round of golf shortly after he arrives. He plays well and manages to win by a few strokes. The Japanese executive invites him to play again the next day, and again he wins by a few strokes. Invited to play another round the following day, the American asks, "But when are we going to start doing business?" His host, surprised by the question, says, "But we *have* been doing business."

- An American businesswoman in London is invited to a party hosted by an advertising agency. Unsure of her ability to navigate the streets and subways of London alone, she approaches a British colleague who is driving to the party and asks him, "Could I get a ride with you?" After he turns bright red from embarrassment, he regains his composure and politely says, "Lucky for you I know what you meant." Unknowingly, the young woman had requested a sexual encounter with her colleague, not a lift to the party![61]

- One pharmaceutical company was about to market a weight loss pill under the name Tegro, which sounds harmless enough in English. However, phonetically, the word sounds identical to the French phrase *t'es gros*, which translates "You are fat." Another global company attempted to market a technology training system whose name sounded exactly like the Korean phrase for "porn movie."[62]

When American businesspeople enter international markets for the first time, they often are amazed at the differences in foreign cultures' habits and customs. In the first scenario above, for instance, had the entrepreneur done his homework, he would have known that the French are very formal (backslapping is *definitely* taboo!) and do not typically use first names in business relationships (even among longtime colleagues). In the second scenario, a global manager would have known that the Japanese place a tremendous importance on developing personal relationships before committing to any business deals. Thus, he would have seen the golf games for what they really were: an integral part of building a business relationship.

Understanding and heeding these often subtle cultural differences is one of the most important keys to international business success. Conducting a business meeting with a foreign executive in the same manner as one with an American businessperson could doom the deal from the outset. Business customs and behaviors that are acceptable, even expected, in the United States may be taboo in others, and entrepreneurs who fail to learn the differences in the habits and customs of the cultures in which they hope to do business are at a distinct disadvantage.

Culture, customs, and the norms of behavior differ greatly among nations, and making the correct impression is extremely critical to building a long-term business relationship. Consider the following examples:

- In Europe and China, just as in the United States, punctuality for business meetings is important. In Latin America, Africa, and many Middle Eastern countries, however, business meetings rarely start at the scheduled time, something that does not seem to bother locals.

- In Great Britain, businesspeople consider it extremely important to conduct business "properly"—with formality and reserve. Boisterous behavior such as backslapping or overindulging in alcohol and ostentatious displays of wealth are considered ill mannered. The British do not respond to hard-sell tactics but do appreciate well-mannered executives. Politeness and impeccable manners are useful tools for conducting business successfully.

- Japanese executives conduct business much like the British with an emphasis on formality, thoughtfulness, and respect. Don't expect to hear Japanese executives say "no," even during a negotiation; they don't want to offend or to appear confrontational. Instead of "no," the Japanese negotiator will say, "It is very difficult," "Let us think about that," or "Let us get back to you on that." Similarly, "yes" from a Japanese executive doesn't necessarily mean that. It could mean "I understand," "I hear you," or "I don't understand what you mean, but I don't want to embarrass you."

- In India, a limp handshake and avoiding eye contact are not signs of weakness or dislike; they convey respect.[63]

- When doing business in Greece, U.S. executives must be thoughtful of their hand gestures; the hand-waving gesture that means "good-bye" in the United States is considered an insult in Greece.[64]

- In Japan and South Korea, exchanging business cards, known in Japan as *meishi*, is an important business function (unlike in Great Britain, where exchanging business cards is less popular). A Western executive who accepts a Japanese companion's card and then slips it into his pocket or scribbles notes on it has committed a major blunder. Tradition there says that a business card must be treated just as its owner would be—with respect. Travelers should present their own cards using both hands with the card positioned so that the recipient can read it. (The flip side should be printed in Japanese, an expected courtesy.)

- Greeting a Japanese executive properly includes a bow and a handshake—showing respect for both cultures. In many traditional Japanese businesses, exchanging gifts at the first meeting is appropriate. In addition, a love of golf (the Japanese are fanatics about the game) is a real plus for winning business in Japan.

- Exercise caution when giving gifts. Although gift giving is standard practice in Japan, businesspeople in other countries, such as Malaysia, may see a gift as a bribe. In many countries, gifts of flowers are considered inappropriate because they connote romantic attention. In South Korea, giving a clock as a gift is considered good luck, but in China, it is considered a bad omen.[65] Avoid giving gifts to business associates that are traditional symbols of their own cultures, such as chocolates to the Swiss or tea to the Chinese.

- In China, entrepreneurs will need an ample dose of the "three Ps": patience, patience, and patience. Nothing in China—especially business—happens fast, and entrepreneurs wanting to do business there must be persistent! In conversation and negotiations, periods of silence are common; they are a sign of politeness and contemplation. The Chinese view personal space much differently than Americans; in normal conversation, they will stand much closer to their partners. At a business meal, sampling every dish, no matter how exotic, is considered polite. In addition, do not expect to conduct business the week before or after the Chinese New Year ("Yuandan"), whose dates vary from year to year, when many businesses are closed.

- Starting business relationships with customers in the Pacific Rim usually requires a third-party contact because Asian executives prefer to do business with people they know. In addition, building personal relationships is important. Many business deals take place over informal activities in this part of the world. American entrepreneurs doing business in the

Pacific Rim should avoid hard-sell techniques, which are an immediate turnoff to Asian businesspeople. Harmony, patience, and consensus make good business companions in this region. It is also a good idea to minimize the importance of legal documents in negotiations. Although getting deals and trade agreements down in writing always is advisable, attempting to negotiate detailed contracts (as most American businesses tend to do) would insult most Asians, who base their deals on mutual trust and benefits.

International Trade Agreements

With the fundamental assumption that free trade among nations results in enhanced economic prosperity for all parties involved, the last 50 years have witnessed a gradual opening of trade among nations. Hundreds of agreements have been negotiated among nations in this period, with each contributing to free trade across the globe. Although completely free trade across international borders remains elusive, the following trade agreements have reduced some of the barriers to free trade that had stood for many years.

WORLD TRADE ORGANIZATION The World Trade Organization (WTO) was established in January 1995 and replaced the General Agreement of Tariffs and Trade (GATT), the first global tariff agreement, which was created in 1947 and was designed to reduce tariffs among member nations. The WTO, currently with 155 member countries, is the only international organization that establishes rules for trade among nations. Its member countries represent more than 97 percent of all world trade. The rules and agreements of the WTO, called the multilateral trading system, are the result of negotiations among its members. The WTO actively implements the rules established by the Uruguay Round negotiations of GATT from 1986 to 1994 and continues to negotiate additional trade agreements. (Currently, the ninth round of negotiations, the Doha Development Agenda, is under way.) Through the agreements of the WTO, members commit themselves to nondiscriminatory trade practices and to reducing barriers to free trade. The WTO's agreements spell out the rights and obligations of each member country. Each member country receives guarantees that its exports will be treated fairly and consistently in other member countries' markets. The WTO's General Agreement on Trade in Services addresses specific industries, including banking, insurance, telecommunications, and tourism. In addition, the WTO's intellectual property agreement, which covers patents, copyrights, and trademarks, defines rules for protecting ideas and creativity across borders.

In addition to the development of agreements among members, the WTO is involved in the resolution of trade disputes among members. The WTO system is designed to encourage dispute resolutions through consultation. If this approach fails, the WTO has a stage-by-stage procedure that can culminate in a ruling by a panel of experts.

NORTH AMERICAN FREE TRADE AGREEMENT The North American Free Trade Agreement (NAFTA) created a free trade area among Canada, Mexico, and the United States. A **free trade area** is an association of countries that have agreed to eliminate trade barriers, both tariff and nontariff, among partner nations. Under the provisions of NAFTA, these barriers were eliminated for trade among the three countries, but each remained free to set its own tariffs on imports from nonmember nations.

NAFTA forged one of the world's largest free trade areas, a unified United States–Canada–Mexico market of 465 million people with a total annual output of $18.1 trillion in goods and services.[66] This important trade agreement binds together the three nations on the North American continent into a single trading unit stretching from the Yukon to the Yucatan. NAFTA's provisions called for the reduction of tariffs to zero on most goods traded among these three nations. NAFTA's provisions have enhanced trade among the United States, Canada, and Mexico. It also has made that trade more profitable and less cumbersome for companies of all sizes and has opened new opportunities many businesses. Since NAFTA's passage, trade among the three nations has more than tripled; these countries now conduct nearly $2.9 billion in trilateral trade each day![67]

ENTREPRENEURIAL PROFILE: Tanya Shaw: Unique Solutions In 2002, Tanya Shaw launched Unique Solutions, a company based in Dartmouth, Nova Scotia, that markets the Intellifit Virtual Fitting Room, a high-tech scanner that is capable of capturing 200,000 measurements on a fully clothed person in just 20 seconds. After a visit to a mall or retail store for a brief scan, customers receive a report that gives them key body measurements that they can use to purchase made-to-measure garments from a database of companies that Unique Solutions maintains or to make shopping for off-the-rack clothing more a more pleasant and efficient experience. The company's Me-Ality shopping guide matches shoppers' body shapes with specific sizes at retailers ranging from Banana Republic and Coldwater Creek to J. Crew and Talbot's. Shaw decided to leave the company's headquarters in Nova Scotia, but because NAFTA created opportunities in the United States and Mexico, she moved her marketing and sales division to California and partnered with a New Zealand company, TJ's Jeanswear, that has a factory in Parras, Mexico. TJ's Jeanswear produces and delivers custom-made jeans to Unique Solutions customers. "The collaborative business environment that NAFTA has helped to create has been very important for us, especially as a small company trying to form international partnerships," says Shaw.[68] ■

DOMINICAN REPUBLIC–CENTRAL AMERICA FREE TRADE AGREEMENT The Dominican Republic–Central America Free Trade Agreement (CAFTA-DR) is to Central America what NAFTA is to North America. The agreement, which was implemented in stages between 2006 and 2008, is designed to promote free trade among the United States and six Central American countries: Costa Rica, El Salvador, Guatemala, Honduras, the Dominican Republic, and Nicaragua. Annual trade between the United States and these Central American countries has grown from $35 billion before CAFTA-DR to more than $48 billion today.[69] In addition to reducing tariffs among these nations, CAFTA-DR protects U.S. companies' investments and intellectual property in the region, simplifies the export process for U.S. companies, and provides easier access to Central American markets.

ENTREPRENEURIAL PROFILE: Jose Tapia: BKI BKI, a small manufacturer of food service equipment for retail and convenience stores and restaurants located in Simpsonville, South Carolina, started exporting its products in 1958 and recently entered markets in Central America as a result of CAFTA-DR. "Lower [trade] duties make our equipment more affordable" to customers in the region, says Jose Tapia, BKI's international sales manager. "CAFTA-DR has had a positive impact because we are better able to compete with manufacturers from other countries.[70] ■

Conclusion

To remain competitive, small businesses must assume a global posture. Global effectiveness requires entrepreneurs to be able to leverage workers' skills, company resources, and customer know-how across borders and throughout cultures across the world. They also must concentrate on maintaining competitive cost structures and a focus on the core of every business—the *customer!* Although there are no surefire rules for going global, small businesses that want to become successful international competitors should observe these guidelines:

- Take the time to learn about doing business globally before jumping in. Avoiding mistakes is easier and less expensive than cleaning up the results of mistakes later.

- If you have never conducted international business, consider hiring a trade intermediary or finding a local partner to help you.

- Make yourself at home in all three of the world's key markets: North America, Europe, and Asia. This triad of regions is forging a new world order in trade that will dominate global markets for years to come.

- Appeal to the similarities within the various regions in which you operate but recognize the differences in their specific cultures. Although the European Union is a single trading bloc composed of 27 countries, smart entrepreneurs know that each country has its own cultural uniqueness and do not treat the nearly 500 million people in them as a unified market. "Gone are the days when you could just roll out one product for the global market," says Hamad Malik, Middle East marketing director for the South Korean electronics company LG.[71]

- Develop new products for the world market. Make sure your products and services measure up to world-class quality standards.

- Familiarize yourself with foreign customs and languages; constantly scan, clip, and build a file on other cultures: their lifestyles, values, customs, and business practices.

- Learn to understand your customers from the perspective of *their* culture, not your own. Bridge cultural gaps by adapting your business practices to suit their preferences and customs.

- "Glocalize." Make global decisions about products, markets, and management but allow local employees to make tactical decisions about packaging, advertising, and service.

- Recruit and retain multicultural workers who can give your company meaningful insight into the intricacies of global markets. Entrepreneurs with a truly global perspective identify, nurture, and utilize the talents and knowledge multicultural workers possess.

- Train employees to think globally, send them on international trips, and equip them with state-of-the-art communications technology.

- Hire local managers to staff foreign offices and branches.

- Do whatever seems best wherever it seems best, even if people at home lose jobs or responsibilities.

- Consider using partners and joint ventures to break into foreign markets you cannot penetrate on your own.

By its very nature, going global can be a frightening experience. Most entrepreneurs who have already made the jump, however, have found that the benefits outweigh the risks and that their companies are much stronger because of it.

Chapter Summary by Learning Objective

1. **Explain why "going global" has become an integral part of many small companies' marketing strategies.**

   - Companies that move into international business can reap many benefits, including offsetting sales declines in the domestic market, increasing sales and profits; extending their products' life cycles; lowering manufacturing costs; improving competitive position; raising quality levels; and becoming more customer oriented.

2. **Describe the principal strategies small businesses have for going global.**

   - Perhaps the simplest and least expensive way for a small business to begin conducting business globally is to establish a Web site. Companies that sell goods on the Web should establish a secure ordering and payment system for online customers.

   - Trade intermediaries, such as EMCs, ETCs, MEAs, export merchants, resident buying offices, and foreign distributors, can serve as a small company's "export department."

   - In a domestic joint venture, two or more U.S. small companies form an alliance for the purpose of exporting their goods and services abroad. In a foreign joint venture, a domestic small business forms an alliance with a company in the target area.

   - Some small businesses enter foreign markets by licensing businesses in other nations to use their patents, trademarks, copyrights, technology, processes, or products.

   - Franchising has become a major export industry for the United States. Franchisers that enter foreign markets rely on three strategies: direct franchising, area development, and master franchising.

   - Some countries lack a hard currency that is convertible into other currencies, so companies doing business there must rely on countertrading or bartering. A countertrade is a transaction in which a business selling goods in a foreign country agrees to promote investment and trade in that country. Bartering involves trading goods and services for other goods and services.

   - Companies with fewer than 20 employees account for 72 percent of all exporters, but small and medium-size companies generate just 33 percent of the nation's export sales. However, small companies, realizing the incredible profit potential that exporting offers, are making exporting an ever-expanding part of their marketing plans. Success requires a well-conceived export strategy.

   - Once established in international markets, some small businesses set up permanent locations there. Although they can be very expensive to establish and maintain, international locations give businesses the opportunity to stay in close contact with their international customers.

- Many small companies shop the world for the goods and services that they sell. The intensity of price competition has made importing and outsourcing successful strategies for many small businesses.

3. Explain how to build a thriving export business.

- Building a successful export program takes patience and research. Steps include the following: realize that even the tiniest firms have the potential to export, analyze your product or service, analyze your commitment to exporting, research markets and pick your target, develop a distribution strategy, find your customer, find financing, ship your goods, and collect your money.

4. Discuss the major barriers to international trade and their impact on the global economy.

- Three domestic barriers to international trade are common: the attitude that "we're too small to export," lack of information on how to get started in global trade, and a lack of available financing.

- International barriers include tariffs, quotas, embargoes, dumping, and political, business, and cultural barriers.

5. Describe the trade agreements that will have the greatest influence on foreign trade in the twenty-first century—the World Trade Organization, the North American Free Trade Agreement, and the Central American Free Trade Agreement.

- The WTO was established in 1995 to implement the rules established by the Uruguay Round negotiations of GATT from 1986 to 1994, and it continues to negotiate additional trade agreements. The WTO has 155 member nations and represents more than 97 percent of all global trade. The WTO is the governing body that resolves trade disputes among members.

- NAFTA created a free trade area among Canada, Mexico, and the United States. The agreement created an association that knocked down trade barriers, both tariff and nontariff, among the partner nations.

- CAFTA-DR created a free trade area among the United States and six nations in Central America: Costa Rica, El Salvador, Guatemala, Honduras, the Dominican Republic, and Nicaragua. In addition to reducing tariffs among these nations, CAFTA protects U.S. companies' investments and intellectual property in the region, simplifies the export process for U.S. companies, and provides easier access to Central American markets.

Discussion Questions

1. Why must entrepreneurs learn to think globally?
2. What forces are driving small businesses into international markets?
3. What advantages does going global offer a small business owner? Risks?
4. Outline the nine strategies that small businesses can use to go global.
5. Describe the various types of trade intermediaries that small business owners can use. What functions do they perform?
6. What is a domestic joint venture? A foreign joint venture? What advantages does taking on an international partner through a joint venture offer? Disadvantages?
7. What mistake are first-time exporters most likely to make? Outline the steps a small company should take to establish a successful export program.

8. What are the benefits of establishing international locations? Disadvantages?
9. Describe the barriers businesses face when trying to conduct business internationally. How can a small business owner overcome these obstacles?
10. What is a tariff? A quota? What impact do they have on international trade?
11. What impact have the WTO, NAFTA, and CAFTA trade agreements had on small companies that want to go global? What provisions are included in these trade agreements?
12. What advice would you offer an entrepreneur interested in launching a global business effort?

Business Plan Pro™
Do global opportunities exist for your business concept? If so, include those as an "opportunity" in your SWOT analysis. Review the other sections that will benefit from incorporating these global plans into your business strategy. For example, you may need to address your global strategy in the marketing strategy and the Web site sections of your business plan. You may need to include additional expenses into the financial section of your business plan to support your global strategy. If your global strategy increases risk, this is another factor to capture in your business plan.

Business Plan Exercises

A business plan can help to define and clarify global opportunities, resources, and challenges.

On the Web

You will find links to Web resources that address global strategies at www.pearsonhighered.com/scarborough associated with Chapter 15. In addition, a site that may also be helpful is a management portal for global strategy at www.themanager.org/Knowledgebase/Strategy/Global.

Sample Plans

Review the executive summary for the sample plan called Grutzen Watches. Note the information that relates to their global strategy and the additional complexities this introduces to the business plan.

In the Software

If you plan to employ a global strategy, make certain that you have addressed that aspect of your strategy in your business plan. International activity of any kind may have implications for multiple sections of your business plan, including the product and services, market analysis, strategy, implementation, Web site, management, and financial sections.

This is also an excellent time to review your entire plan, paying specific attention to the summary sections at the beginning of each major section. You may have used these areas for notes, but, at this time, review what you have written in the initial stage of each of these sections. Those sections include the following:

- Company
- Product and Services
- Market Analysis
- Strategy and Implementation
- Web Plan
- Management Plan
- Financial Plan

These initial introductory statements will add flow to your plan. You may also want to review each section to avoid redundancy and optimize the efficiency of your overall plan.

Building Your Business Plan

As you near the final stages of creating your business plan, have others review the plan and ask these questions:

- Does the plan tell a complete story about the business, including potential global opportunities?
- Do they have questions that the plan does not address?
- Is the plan compelling?
- Do they find this to be an attractive business investment?

Based on their comments, assess whether the plan succeeds at communicating your message and make any necessary changes.

Beyond the Classroom . . .

1. Go to lunch with a student from a foreign country. Discuss what products and services are most needed there. How does the business system there differ from ours? How much government regulation affects business? What cultural differences exist? What trade barriers has the government erected?
2. Review several current business publications and prepare a brief report on which nations are the most promising for U.S. entrepreneurs. What steps should a small business owner take to break into those markets? Which nations are the least promising? Why?
3. Select a nation that interests you and prepare a report on its business customs and practices. How are they different from those in the United States? How are they similar?

Endnotes

1. John Larsen, "Trade Promotion Coordinating Committee," U.S. Department of Commerce, International Trade Administration, 2011, p. 9.
2. *Intuit Future of Small Business Report, Part Three: The New Artisan Economy*, Institute for the Future, February 2008, p. 24.
3. Mark Whitehouse, "Starting a Global Business, with No U.S. Employees," *Wall Street Journal*, November 19, 2010, p. B8.
4. C. K. Prahalad and Hrishi Bhattacharyya, "How to Be a Truly Global Company," *Strategy + Business*, Autumn 2011, Issue 64, August 23, 2011, http://www.strategy-business.com/article/11308?gko=aaf83.
5. "Commerce, SBA Launch New Online Tool to Help Small Businesses Begin Exporting," U.S. Small Business Administration, November 19, 2010, p. 1.
6. *2011 National Export Strategy: Powering the National Export Initiative*, Trade Promotion Coordinating Committee, Washington, DC, June 2011, p. 1.
7. Edward Iwata, "Small U.S. Firms Make Big Global Sales," *USA Today*, April 7, 2008, http://www.usatoday.com/money/smallbusiness/2008-04-07-small-business-exports_N.htm.
8. *2011 JETRO Global Trade and Investment Report: International Business as a Catalyst for Japan's Reconstruction*, Japan External Trade Organization, Overseas Research Department, p. 8.

9. *Small and Medium-Sized Enterprises: Characteristics and Performance*, U.S. International Trade Commission, Publication 4189, November 2010, pp. 3–4.

10. John Larsen, "Trade Promotion Coordinating Committee," U.S. Department of Commerce, International Trade Administration, 2011, p. 8; "New Markets, New Jobs: The National Export Initiative Small Business Tour," U.S. Department of Commerce, January 27, 2011, http://www.commerce.gov/blog/2011/01/27/new-markets-new-jobs-national-export-initiative-small-business-tour.

11. Jane L. Levere, "A Small Company, a Global Approach," *New York Times*, January 1, 2004, http://www.nytimes.com/2004/01/01/business/small-business-a-small-company-a-global-approach.html?sec=&spon=&pagewanted=all.

12. "Internet Usage Statistics: The Big Picture," Internet World Stats, http://www.internetworldstats.com/stats.htm.

13. *State of the Global Retail Sector*, World Retail Congress and Fusions Communications Ltd, September 2011, p. 24.

14. "eBay Inc. Reports Strong Fourth Quarter and Full 2011 Year Results," *Business Wire*, January 18, 2012, http://www.businesswire.com/news/home/20120118006605/en/eBay-Reports-Strong-Fourth-Quarter-Full-Year.

15. "FaceBook Users in the World," Internet World Stats, http://www.internetworldstats.com/facebook.htm.

16. Verne Harnish, "Step Right Up! Don't Miss the Biggest Opportunity in History! Here Are My Five Strategies for Expanding Globally," *Fortune*, July 26, 2010, p. 54.

17. Phred Dvorak, "Small Firms Hire Guides as They Head Abroad," *Wall Street Journal*, November 5, 2007, p. B3.

18. "About Dorian Drake," Dorian Drake International, http://www.doriandrake.com/frameset.htm.

19. Peggy Olive, "The Future Is Now: U.S. Small Businesses Overcome Export Barriers," ProQuest Discovery Guides, August 2008, http://www.csa.com/discoveryguides/entrepreneur/review.php.

20. Amanda H. Miller, "Lack of Solar Investment Urges Natcore's Second Foreign Joint Venture," *Clean Energy Authority*, October 17, 2011, http://www.cleanenergyauthority.com/solar-energy-news/lack-of-us-solar-investment-for-new-jersey-natcore-101811; "Natcore Finalizes Chinese Production Deal," *Renewable Energy World*, June 23, 2010, http://www.renewableenergyworld.com/rea/news/article/2010/06/natcore-finalizes-chinese-production-deal.

21. Ratna Bhushan and Sarah Jacob, "Pizza Makers Pizza Hut, Domino's Pizza and Others Cut Prices for Higher Sales," *Economic Times*, April 30, 2012, http://articles.economictimes.indiatimes.com/2012-04-30/news/31508319_1_pizza-corner-domino-s-pizza-pizza-makers.

22. William Edwards, "International Expansion: Do Opportunities Outweigh Challenges?" *Franchising World*, February 2008, http://www.franchise.org/Franchise-News-Detail.aspx?id=37992.

23. "Subway Plays to Local Tastes in India," *Nation's Restaurant News*, March 28, 2011, http://nrn.com/article/slide-show-subway-plays-local-tastes-india; Jamie Hartford, "Worldly Advice," *QSR*, 2011, http://www2.qsrmagazine.com/articles/features/125/global_markets-1.phtml.

24. Annie Gasparro, "Domino's Sticks to Its Ways Abroad," *Wall Street Journal*, April 17, 2012, p. B10; "About Us: Domino's in India," Domino's Pizza, http://www.dominos.co.in/dominos-india.php.

25. "International Specialty Regional Toppings," Domino's, http://www.dominos.com/Public-EN/Site+Content/Secondary/Inside+Dominos/Pizza+Particulars/International+Speciality+Toppings.

26. "Fast Foods Gone Global," *Travel Channel*, http://www.travelchannel.com/video/fast-foods-gone-global; "The Hotlist: 10 Unusual Items on McDonald's Menus around the World," *Daily Mail*, January 23, 2009, http://www.dailymail.co.uk/femail/food/article-1126655/The-hotlist-10-unusual-items-McDonalds-menus-world.html; Geoffrey A. Fowler and Ramin Setoodeh, "Outsiders Get Smarter about China's Tastes," *Wall Street Journal*, August 4, 2004, pp. B1, B2.

27. "Fast Foods Gone Global," *Travel Channel*, http://www.travelchannel.com/video/fast-foods-gone-global; Karen Cho, "KFC China's Recipe for Success," *Knowledge*, INSEAD, March 2009, http://knowledge.insead.edu/KFCinChina090323.cfm?vid=195; "Fast Food in China: Here Comes a Whopper," *The Economist*, October 23, 2008, http://www.economist.com/displayStory.cfm?STORY_ID=12488790.

28. "U.S. Trade Officials to Urge Small Businesses to Export," *Fox Business*, January 27, 2011, http://www.foxbusiness.com/markets/2011/01/27/trade-officials-urge-small-businesses-export; Paul Davidson, "Small Businesses Look across Borders to Add Markets," *USA Today*, April 12, 2011, http://www.usatoday.com/money/economy/2011-04-06-small-businesses-go-international.htm.

29. John Larsen, "Trade Promotion Coordinating Committee," U.S. Department of Commerce, International Trade Administration, 2011, p. 10.

30. Karen Mills, "Taking Your Small Business Customers International," U.S. Small Business Administration, October 15, 2010, http://www.sba.gov/administrator/7390/6086.

31. *The Small Business Economy: A Report to the President*, (Washington, DC: U.S. Small Business Administration, Office of Advocacy, U.S. Government Printing Office, 2009), p. 73.

32. Jenny Munro, "World Beats Path to Powers' Door," *Greenville News*, January 18, 2009, p. 1E.

33. Faces of Trade: Southland Log Homes," *Trade Roots*, U.S. Department of Commerce, April 2009, http://blog.illumen.org/traderoots/docs/2009/04/southland-log-homes-inc.pdf.

34. Joseph Zaritski, "15 Tips to Start Successful Export Business," Australian Export Online: Export 61, http://www.export61.com/export-tutorials.asp?ttl=tips.

35. Cyndia Zwahlen, "Exporting Presents Opportunities and Challenges for Small Companies," *Los Angeles Times*, February 21, 2011, http://articles.latimes.com/2011/feb/21/business/la-fi-smallbiz-export-20110221.

36. "U.S. Imports, Exports, and Merchandise Trade Balance by Country," *Statistical Abstract of the United States, 2012*, pp. 808–810.

37. Issie Lapowsky, "Planting the Flag," *Inc.*, September 2011, pp. 148–149.

38. *Small and Medium-Sized Enterprises: Characteristics and Performance*, U.S. International Trade Commission, Publication 4189, November 2010, pp. 6–8.

39. *2011 National Export Strategy: Powering the National Export Initiative*, Trade Promotion Coordinating Committee, Washington, DC, June 2011, p. 11.

40. Erin Butler, "Making the Most of Trade Missions: Advice from Women Who've Been There (and Back)," *Export America*, April 2002, p. 9.

41. "Minnesota Company Expands Export Sales to Brazil through Focused Trade Mission," Food Export Association of the Midwest, 2011, http://www.foodexport.org/Media/SuccessStoryDetail.cfm?itemnumber=1874.

42. "Small Business Success Stories: California Company's First International Deal Due to Ex-Im Bank Guarantee," Export-Import Bank of the United States, http://www.exim.gov/sbgport/SB_success.cfm.

43. Ryan Underwood, "Going Global: Why Borders Still Matter," *Inc.*, May 2011, pp. 120–122.

44. Peggy Olive, "The Future Is Now: U.S. Small Businesses Overcome Export Barriers," ProQuest Discovery Guides, August 2008, http://www.csa.com/discoveryguides/ entrepreneur/review.php.

45. Lee Gimpel, "Global Hot Spots," *Entrepreneur*, June 2008, pp. 62–70.

46. Daniel Kaufmann and Shang-Jin Wei, "Does 'Grease Money' Speed Up the Wheels of Commerce?," World Bank, http:// www.worldbank.org/wbi/governance/pdf/grease.pdf.

47. "U.S. International Transactions," U.S. Department of Commerce, Bureau of Economic Analysis, March 14, 2012, p. 1.

48. "Success Stories: Kevin Hickey, Vice-President, Online Stores Inc.," Alibaba.com, http://www.alibaba.com/activities/ ibdm/fb/stories/kevin_hickey.html, p. 5.

49. Jessica Centers, "Great Balls of Light," *FSB*, April 2008, p. 25; Mark Mavrigian, "An Illuminating Idea," *BizBash*, July/August 2008, p. 19.

50. Joshua Kurlantzick, "On Foreign Soil," *Entrepreneur*, June 2005, p. 92.

51. *2011 JETRO Global Trade and Investment Report: International Business as a Catalyst for Japan's Reconstruction*, Japan External Trade Organization, Overseas Research Department, p. 8.

52. "Tariff Rate, Applied, Weighted Mean, All Products," *Index Mundi*, 2012, http://www.indexmundi.com/facts/ united-states/tariff-rate; "Tariff Rate, Applied, Weighted Mean, All Products (%), in World," *Trading Economics*, 2012, http://www.tradingeconomics.com/world/tariff-rate- applied-weighted-mean-all-products-percent-wb-data.html.

53. *Harmonized Tariff Schedule of the United States, 2012*, U.S. International Trade Commission, pp. 61–45, 61–50, 64–17, and 64–24.

54. "Tariff Rate, Most Favored Nation, Weighted Mean, All Products (%)," World Bank, 2012, http://data.worldbank.org/ indicator/TM.TAX.MRCH.WM.FN.ZS.

55. "China's Quota Change Heralds Reform," *China.org.cn*, February 24, 2012, http://www.china.org.cn/arts/2012-02/24/ content_24721975.htm; "China Film Industry Report, 2011," *PR Newswire*, September 27, 2011, http://www .prnewswire.com/news-releases/china-film-industry- report-2011-130615853.html; Rachel Abrams, "China's Film Quota Cracked," *Variety*, February 20, 2012, http:// www.variety.com/article/VR1118050508?refCatId=13.

56. "Trade in Goods (Imports, Exports, and Trade Balance) with Vietnam," *Foreign Trade Statistics*, U.S. Census Bureau, http://www.census.gov/foreign-trade/balance/c5520.html.

57. Jaime Berkheimer, Stacey Cargile, Gabriel Richards, Erika Palsson, and Inbal Shem-Tov, "Issue Guide: Trade Embargoes, Seals, and More," University of California, Irvine, http:// darwin.bio.uci.edu/~sustain/issueguides/Embargoes/index.html.

58. Cheryl Kaften, "China Caught 'Red-Handed' on U.S. Solar Anti-Dumping Charges," *PV Magazine*, May 18, 2012, http://www.pv-magazine.com/news/details/beitrag/ china-caught-red-handed-on-us-solar-anti-dumping- charges_100006848/#axzz1vbXzfDMB; "China Rejects U.S. Solar Dumping Ruling, Companies Warn Tariffs Might Hurt Clean Energy Industry," *Washington Post*, May 18, 2012, http://www.washingtonpost.com/business/chinese-solar- makers-reject-us-dumping-ruling-say-tariffs-might-hurt- clean-energy-industry/2012/05/18/gIQARwneXU_story .html; Steven Mufson, "U.S. Solar Manufacturers to File Dumping Charges against Chinese Firms," *Washington Post*, October 19, 2011, http://www.washingtonpost.com/business/ economy/us-solar-manufacturers-to-file-dumping-charges- against-chinese-firms/2011/10/19/gIQAlkPrxL_story.html.

59. Gary D. Bruton, David Ahlstrom, Michael N. Young, and Yuri Rubanik, "In Emerging Markets, Know What Your Partners Expect," *Wall Street Journal*, December 15, 2008, p. R5.

60. Mark Scott, "Europe: More Holidays and More Productive?," *Bloomberg Business Week*, August 19, 2009, http://www.businessweek.com/globalbiz/content/aug2009/ gb20090818_398605.htm; Lisa Wade, "Paid Holidays/Vacation Days in the U.S. versus Other OECD Countries," Sociological Images, January 31, 2010, http://thesocietypages.org/ socimages/2010/01/31/paid-holidaysvacation-days-in-the- u-s-versus-other-oecd-countries.

61. Lawrence Van Gelder, "It Pays to Watch Words, Gestures while Abroad," *Greenville News*, April 7, 1996, p. 8E.

62. Malika Zouhali-Worrall, "Watch Your Language!," *FSB*, July/August 2008, pp. 71–72.

63. Scott McCartney, "Teaching Americans How to Behave Abroad," *Wall Street Journal*, April 11, 2006, pp. D1, D4.

64. Aliza Pilar Sherman, "Going Global," *Entrepreneur*, December 2004, p. 34.

65. Aliza Pilar Sherman, "Going Global," *Entrepreneur*, December 2004, p. 34.

66. *Countries of the World: United States: Economy Overview*, Theodora, http://www.theodora.com/wfbcurrent/united_states/ united_states_economy.html; *Countries of the World: Canada: Economy Overview*, Theodora, http://www.theodora.com/ wfbcurrent/canada/canada_economy.html; *Countries of the World: Mexico: Economy Overview*, Theodora, http://www .theodora.com/wfbcurrent/mexico/mexico_economy.html.

67. "Top Trading Partners—Total Trade, Exports, Imports," U.S. Census Bureau, December 2011, http://www.census.gov/ foreign-trade/statistics/highlights/top/top1112yr.html.

68. "Unique Solutions: 'A Pattern for Success,'" *NAFTA Now*, May 2, 2012, http://www.naftanow.org/success/canada_ solutions_en.asp; "Body Scanners," Unique Solutions, http:// www.uniqueltd.com/body_scanners.

69. "Opening CAFTA-DR Export Markets for Small and Medium-Sized U.S. Businesses," Office of the U.S. Trade Representative, May 2011, http://www.ustr.gov/ about-us/press-office/fact-sheets/2011/may/ opening-cafta-dr-export-markets-us-small-and-medium-sized.

70. "Faces of Trade: BKI," *Trade Roots*, U.S. Department of Commerce, April 2009, http://blog.illumen.org/traderoots/ docs/2009/04/bki1.pdf.

71. Elizabeth Esfahani, "Thinking Locally, Succeeding Globally," *Business 2.0*, December 2005, pp. 96–98.

16

Building a New Venture Team and Planning for the Next Generation

Learning Objectives

On completion of this chapter, you will be able to:

1. Explain the challenges involved in the entrepreneur's role as leader and what it takes to be a successful leader.

2. Describe the importance of hiring the right employees and how to avoid making hiring mistakes.

3. Explain how to create a company culture that encourages employee retention.

4. Describe the steps in developing a management succession plan for a growing business that allows a smooth transition of leadership to the next generation.

5. Explain the exit strategies available to entrepreneurs.

Whether your company employs three people or three hundred people, in one office or five, every leader should constantly be working towards a singular company culture where employees feel aligned with the company mission.

—**Eric Markowitz**

I pursue top talent like my success depends on it—because it does.

—**Reggie Aggarwal**

LO1

Explain the challenges
involved in the
entrepreneur's role as leader
and what it takes to be a
successful leader.

leadership

the process of influencing
and inspiring others to work
to achieve a common goal
and then giving them the
power and the freedom
to achieve it.

Leadership in the New Economy

To be successful, an entrepreneur must assume a wide range of roles, tasks, and responsibilities, but none is more important than the role of leader. Some entrepreneurs are uncomfortable assuming this role, but they must learn to be effective leaders if their companies are to grow and reach their potential. **Leadership** is the process of influencing and inspiring others to work to achieve a common goal and then giving them the power and the freedom to achieve it. Without leadership ability, entrepreneurs—and their companies—never rise above mediocrity. Entrepreneurs can learn to be effective leaders, but the task requires dedication, discipline, and hard work. In the past, business owners often relied on an autocratic management style, one built on command and control. Today's workforce is more knowledgeable, has more options, and is more skilled and, as a result, expects a different, more sophisticated style of leadership. Mark Leslie, founder of Veritas Software and under whose leadership the company grew from $95,000 in annual sales to more than $1.5 billion in sales in just 11 years, says that leadership "is not about command and control. You [must] attract the best and brightest people and create an environment where they can use their intelligence and judgment to act autonomously."[1]

The rapid pace of change shaping the economy also is placing new demands on leaders. Technology is changing the ways in which people work, the ways in which the various parts of an organization operate and interconnect, and the ways in which competitors strive for market dominance. To remain competitive, companies must operate at a new, faster speed of business, and that requires a new style of leadership. Leaders of small companies must gather information and make decisions with lightning-fast speed, and they must give workers the resources and the freedom to solve problems and exploit opportunities as they arise. Effective leaders delegate authority and responsibility and empower employees to act in the best interest of the business. In this way, leaders demonstrate trust in employees and respect for their ability to make decisions. Many entrepreneurs have discovered that the old style of leadership has lost its effectiveness and that they must develop a new, more fluid, flexible style of leadership that better fits the needs of modern workers and competitive conditions.

Until recently, experts compared a leader's job to that of a symphony orchestra conductor. Like the symphony leader, an entrepreneur made sure that everyone in the company was playing the same score, coordinated individual efforts to produce a harmonious sound, and directed the orchestra members as they played. The conductor (entrepreneur) retained virtually all of the power and made all of the decisions about how the orchestra would play the music without any input from the musicians themselves. Today's successful entrepreneur, however, is more like the leader of a jazz band, which is known for its improvisation, innovation, creativity, and freewheeling style. "The success of a small [jazz band] rests on the ability to be agile and flexible, skills that are equally central to today's business world," says Michael Gold, founder of Jazz Impact, a company that teaches management skills through jazz.[2] Business leaders, like the leaders of jazz bands, should exhibit the following characteristics:

Innovative. Leaders must step out of their own comfort zones to embrace new ideas; they avoid the comfort of complacency.

Passionate. One of entrepreneurs' greatest strengths is their passion for their businesses. Members of their team feed off of that passion and draw inspiration from it.

Willing to take risks. "[Taking] risk is not an option in jazz or for any company that wants to be solvent ten years from now," says Gold.[3]

Adaptable. Although leaders must stand on a bedrock of resolute values, like jazz band leaders, they must adapt their leadership styles to fit the situation and the people involved.

Management and leadership are not the same, yet both are essential to a company's success. Leadership without management is unbridled; management without leadership is uninspired. Leadership gets a small business going; management keeps it going. In other words, leaders are the architects of small businesses; managers are the builders. Some entrepreneurs are good managers yet are poor leaders; others are powerful leaders but are weak managers. The best bet for the latter is to hire people with solid management skills to help them to execute the vision they have for their companies. Stephen Covey, author of *Principle-Centered Leadership*, explains the difference between management and leadership in this way:

> Leadership deals with people; management deals with things. You manage things; you lead people. Leadership deals with vision; management deals with logistics toward that vision. Leadership deals with doing the right things; management focuses on doing things right. Leadership deals with examining the paradigms on which you are operating; management operates within those paradigms. Leadership comes first, then management, but both are necessary.[4]

Leadership and management are intertwined; one without the other means that a small business is going nowhere. Leadership is especially important for companies in the growth phase, when entrepreneurs are hiring employees (often for the first time) and must keep the company and everyone in it focused on its mission as growth tests every seam in the organizational structure.

Effective leaders exhibit certain behaviors:

- *They create a set of values and beliefs for employees and passionately pursue them.* Values are the foundation on which a company's vision is built. Leaders should be like beacons in the night, constantly shining light on the principles, values, and beliefs on which they founded their companies. Whenever the opportunity presents itself, entrepreneurs must communicate with clarity the company's bedrock values and principles to employees and other stakeholders. Some entrepreneurs may not think that it is necessary to do so, but successful leaders know that they must hammer home the connection between their companies' values and mission and the jobs that workers perform every day.

- *They establish a culture of ethics.* One of the most important tasks facing leaders is to mold a highly ethical culture for their companies. They also must demonstrate the character and the courage necessary to stick to the ethical standards that they create—especially in the face of difficulty.

- *They define and then constantly reinforce the vision they have for the company.* Effective leaders have a clear vision of where they want their companies to go, and they concentrate on communicating that vision to those around them. Unfortunately, this is one area in which employees say their leaders could do a better job. Clarity of purpose is essential to a successful organization because people want to be a part of something that is bigger than they are; however, the purpose must be more than merely achieving continuous quarterly profits.

- *They develop a strategic plan that gives the company a competitive advantage.* Ideally, employees participate in building a successful strategic plan, but the leader is the principal strategic architect of the company. The leader also is responsible for implementing the plan with flexibility and the ability to adapt it to changing conditions.

- *They respect and support their employees.* To gain the respect of their employees, leaders must first respect those who work for them. Successful leaders treat every employee with respect. They know that a loyal, dedicated workforce is a company's most valuable resource, and they treat their employees that way.

- *They set the example for their employees.* Leaders' words ring hollow if they fail to "practice what they preach." Few signals are transmitted to workers faster than a leader who sells employees on one set of values and principles and then acts according to a different set. This behavior quickly undermines a leader's credibility among employees, who expect leaders to "walk their talk." That is why integrity is perhaps the most important determinant of a leader's effectiveness.

- *They are authentic.* Employees quickly see through leaders who only pretend to be what they are not. Authenticity does not make someone a leader, but a leader cannot be successful without it. Authenticity is a vital part in developing trust among employees. Successful leaders follow the philosophy of Popeye,

© Photos 12/Alamy

the spinach-munching, crusty sailor who first appeared in a cartoon strip in 1929 and was famous for saying, "I yam what I yam, and that's all what I yam."[5]

- *They create a climate of trust in the organization.* Leaders who demonstrate integrity win the trust of their employees, an essential ingredient in the success of any organization. Honest, open communication and a consistent pattern of leaders doing what they say they will do serve to build trust in a business. Research suggests that building trust among employees is one of the most important tasks of leaders wherever they may work. One extensive study across 62 nations found that trustworthy leaders were highly valued by employees in every culture studied.[6]

- *They build credibility with their employees.* To be effective, leaders must have credibility with their employees, a sometimes challenging task for entrepreneurs, especially as their companies grow and they become insulated from the daily activities of their businesses. To combat the problem of losing touch with the problems their employees face as they do their jobs, many managers periodically return to the front line to serve customers. *Undercover Boss*, a popular television show, disguises CEOs and sends them to work in frontline jobs in their companies. In addition to seeing just how difficult many jobs can be, all of the CEOs get a superb refresher course in how important every worker's role is to the success of the company and how the policies that they and other top managers create often make workers' jobs harder. Michael Rubin, founder and CEO of GSI Commerce, a company that provides distribution and call center services, learned so much from his frontline experience that he now requires all of the GSI's executives to spend time working in the company's warehouses and call centers. The idea is that top managers will make better decisions about policies and procedures if they see firsthand the impact of those decisions on customers and frontline employees. When 7-Eleven CEO Joe DePinto went undercover, an encounter with a talented night-shift clerk who was considering leaving the company for a brighter future elsewhere led him to implement a "talent identification program" designed to promote promising employees within the company.[7]

- *They focus employees' efforts on challenging goals and keep them driving toward those goals.* When asked by a student intern to define leadership, one entrepreneur said, "Leadership is the ability to convince people to follow a path they have never taken before to a place they have never been—and upon finding it to be successful, to do it over and over again."[8]

- *They provide the resources employees need to achieve their goals.* Effective leaders know that workers cannot do their jobs well unless they have the tools they need. They provide workers not only with the physical resources they need to excel but also with the necessary intangible resources, such as training, coaching, and mentoring.

- *They communicate with their employees.* Leaders recognize that helping workers to see the company's overarching goal is just one part of effective communication; encouraging employee feedback and then *listening* is just as vital. In other words, they know that communication is a two-way street. Open communication takes on even greater importance when a company faces a difficult or uncertain future.

- *They value the diversity of their workers.* Smart business leaders recognize the value of their workers' varied skills, abilities, backgrounds, and interests. When channeled in the right direction, diversity can be a powerful weapon in achieving innovation and maintaining a competitive edge. Good leaders get to know their workers and to understand the diversity of their strengths. Especially important to young workers is a leader's ability capacity for empathy, the ability to see things from another person's viewpoint.

- *They celebrate their workers' successes.* Effective leaders recognize that workers want to be winners, and they do everything they can to encourage top performance among their people. The rewards they give are not always financial; in many cases, it may be as simple as a handwritten congratulatory note.

- *They are willing to take risks.* Entrepreneurs know better than most that launching a business requires taking risks. They also understand that to remain competitive, they must constantly encourage risk taking in their companies. When employees try something innovative and it fails, they don't resort to punishment because they know that doing so would squelch creativity in the organization.

- *They encourage creativity among their workers.* Rather than punish workers who take risks and fail, effective leaders are willing to accept failure as a natural part of innovation and creativity. They know that innovative behavior is the key to future success and do everything they can to encourage it among workers.

- *They maintain a sense of humor.* One of the most important tools a leader can have is a sense of humor. Without it, work can become dull and unexciting for everyone.

ENTREPRENEURIAL PROFILE: Richard Branson: Virgin Group Sir Richard Branson, founder of Virgin Group, a diversified company whose businesses range from airlines and bridal gowns to cosmetics and consumer electronics, is famous for creating a work environment of fun for himself and his employees. "Some 80% of your life is spent working," he says. "You want to have fun at home; why shouldn't you have fun at work?" Branson has put on a wedding dress, bungee jumped, and hosted off-site events designed strictly to allow employees to have fun. The culture of fun at Virgin Group has built an ésprit de corps that gives the company a unique advantage that competitors find difficult to match, and crown prince Richard Branson is its architect.[9] ∎

- *They create an environment in which people have the motivation, the training, and the freedom to achieve the goals they have set.* Leaders know that *their* success is determined by the success of their followers. The goal is to make every employee the manager of his or her job. The leader's role is to provide employees with the resources and support they need to be successful.

- *They create a work climate that encourages maximum performance.* Leaders understand that they play a significant role in shaping a company culture that sets high standards of performance.

- *They become a catalyst for change.* With market and competitive climates changing so rapidly, entrepreneurs must reinvent their companies constantly. Although leaders must cling to the values and principles that form the bedrock of their companies, they must be willing to change, sometimes radically, the policies, procedures, and processes within their businesses. If a company is headed in the wrong direction, the leader's job is to recognize that and to get the company moving in the right direction.

- *They develop leadership talent.* Effective leaders look beyond themselves to spot tomorrow's leaders and take the time to help them grow into their leadership potential. A vital component of every leader's job is to develop the next generation of leaders.

- *They keep their eyes on the horizon.* Effective leaders are never satisfied with what they and their employees accomplished yesterday. They know that yesterday's successes are not enough to sustain their companies indefinitely. They see the importance of building and maintaining sufficient momentum to carry their companies to the next level. "A leader's job is to rally people toward a better future," says Marcus Buckingham, who has spent nearly two decades studying effective leaders.[10] Just like winning athletes, good leaders visualize a successful future and then work to make it happen.

Table 16.1 presents 12 questions that leaders should address if they want their companies to excel.

Leading an organization, whatever its size, is one of the biggest challenges any entrepreneur faces. Yet for an entrepreneur, leadership success is one of the key determinants of a company's success. Research suggests that there is no single "best" style of leadership; the style a leader uses depends, in part, on the situation at hand. Some situations are best suited for a participative leadership style, but in others, an authoritarian style actually may be best. Research by Daniel Goleman and others suggests that today's workers tend to respond more to adaptive, humble leaders who are results oriented and who take the time to cultivate other leaders in the organization.[11] The practice is known as **servant leadership**, a phrase coined by Robert Greenleaf in

servant leadership
a leadership style in which a leader takes on the role of servant first and leader second.

TABLE 16.1 12 Questions That Every Leader Should Address

Jim Collins, coauthor of business best-sellers *Good to Great* and *Great by Choice*, has spent 25 years researching great companies and has integrated the results of his research into 12 questions that leaders must address if they want their companies to excel. Collins advises leaders to discuss one of the following questions every month and repeat the process annually:

1. *Do we want to build a great company, and are we committed to doing the things that are required to make our company great?* Becoming a great company starts by making this fundamental choice, understanding the implications of choosing to build a great company, and then making the commitment to take the necessary steps to achieve greatness.

2. *Do we have the right people on the bus and in the key seats?* Leaders must decide whether the people who will carry the company forward are the *right* people. Are they capable? Motivated? Committed? Leaders must answer this question before they decide *where* they want the business to go, and that sometimes means getting the *wrong* people *off* the bus.

3. *What are the brutal facts?* Leaders cannot make good decisions unless they have access to facts, both good and bad. Confronting the negative, most troubling issues is essential because ignoring them represents a serious threat not only to a company's success but also to its survival. They key is to confront the facts without losing faith.

4. *What are we best at and have an unbounded passion for?* By answering this question, leaders are defining their companies' fundamental economic engine. Isaiah Berlin wrote, "The fox knows many things, but the hedgehog knows one big thing." In other words, a fox is easily distracted, but a hedgehog, like an outstanding company, is focused, determined, and relentless. A company's hedgehog combines its passion and its distinctive competence with what it can make money doing (its economic engine). What is the company's hedgehog?

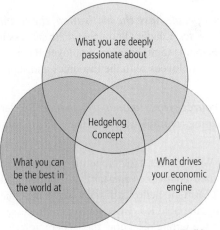

Hedgehog concept Venn diagram, from The Coach Toolkit
website. Copyright © by Neil Phillips. Reprinted with permission.

5. *What is our company's 20-Mile March, and are we hitting it?* Collins refers to Roald Amundsen's successful attempt in 1911 to be the first person to reach the South Pole by committing to traveling 20 miles a day, no matter what the weather or other obstacles he and his team encountered. Every company has a specific performance goal that it must hit year in and year out to be successful. Has the company identified that goal and committed to achieving it? How successful has the company been in achieving the goal? Measuring performance in the 20-Mile March means that leaders must develop a meaningful set of metrics and monitor them constantly.

6. *Where do empirical data tell us that we should be placing our big bets?* A company should invest major resources in a new initiative only if leaders already know that it is likely to succeed. That requires conducting low-cost, low-risk tests on a range of possible options ("shooting bullets") to figure out what works before unleashing the full power of the organization's resources on an initiative ("firing a cannonball"). The empirical evidence from the tests guides leaders' decisions about where to aim the cannon.

7. *What are the core values and core purpose on which we want to build this enterprise over the next 100 years?* The challenge is not only to build a company that can endure the long haul but also to build one that is *worthy* of enduring. Leaders must identify the core values and core purpose that they would be willing have their companies built around 100 years in the future no matter what changes occur in the external environment.

8. *What is our 15- to 25-year BHAG?* A BHAG is "big, hairy audacious goal." To build a great, enduring company, leaders must have a BHAG that is tangible, energizing, and highly focused and that people can understand immediately with little or no explanation. The BHAG should be linked to the company's core values and purpose. In addition, achieving the BHAG should require a company to make a quantum leap in its capabilities and its aptitude.

9. *What could kill our company, and how can we protect our flanks?* Paranoia is productive when it helps a business survive the inevitable bad surprises that come along and avoid the disasters they are capable of producing. The idea is for leaders *not* to be plagued by constant fear but to be sensitive to changing conditions in the environment and ask, "What if . . . ?" Great leaders are always watching the horizon for the threat of storms—and opportunities. They also prepare for the inevitable stormy times by building up cash reserves.

10. ***What should we stop doing to increase our discipline and focus?*** Effective leaders are disciplined when it comes to pursuing business opportunities. They know that determining what their companies should *not* do is as important as determining what they *should* do. Although an "opportunity of a lifetime" may arise, excellent leaders know that pursuing it is meaningless (and downright dangerous) unless it fits inside the three circles of their "hedgehog."

11. ***How can we increase our return on luck?*** All companies are affected by both good luck and bad luck. What counts is what a company does with the luck it encounters—good *and* bad. How can the company glean the greatest benefit from good luck and minimize the damage that a run of bad luck causes?

12. ***Are we becoming a Level 5 leadership team and cultivating a Level 5 management culture?*** Collins calls the highest level of leadership Level 5, which builds enduring greatness in a company through a paradoxical blend of personal humility and professional will. "The central dimension for Level 5 is a leader who is ambitious first and foremost for the cause, for the company, for the work, not for himself or herself; and has an absolutely terrifying iron will to make good on that ambition," says Collins. Are you and your management team providing Level 5 leadership?

Sources: "Bo Burlingham and Jim Collins, "Hedgehogs, Cannonballs, BHAGs, and Bullets," *Inc.*, June 2012, p. 71; Neil Phillips, "The Entrepreneur's Hedgehog," *The Coach Toolkit*, October 20, 2009, http://www.thecoachtoolkit.com/2009/10/the-entrepreneurs-hedgehog; Troy Schrock, "*Great by Choice* and Strategy Execution," *CEO Advantage*, December 8, 2011, http://www.ceoadvantage.com/blog/tag/jim-collins; Jim Collins, *Vision Framework*, 2002, p. 2; Stephen Blandino, "Productive Paranoia: Lesson #3 from Jim Collins' *Good to Great*," *Stephen Blandino*, January 3, 2012, http://stephenblandino.com/2012/01/productive-paranoia-lesson-3-from-jim-collins-great-by-choice.html; Jim Collins, "Jim Collins and Level 5 Leadership," Management-Issues, January 3, 2006, http://www.management-issues.com/2006/5/24/mentors/jim-collins-and-level-5-leadership.asp; and "Roald Amundsen, "Alone on the Ice," WGBH Educational Foundation, 1999, http://www.pbs.org/wgbh/amex/ice/peopleevents/pandeAMEX87.html.

1970. Servant leaders are servants *first* and leaders second, putting their employees and their employees' needs ahead of their own. They are concerned more about empowering others in the organization than about enhancing their own power bases. "Servant-leaders ask, 'What do people need? How can I help them to get it? What does my organization need to do? How can I help my organization to do it?'" explains Kent Keith, CEO of the Greenleaf Center for Servant Leadership. "Rather than embarking on a quest for personal power, servant-leaders embark on a quest to identify and meet the needs of others."[12]

ENTREPRENEURIAL PROFILE: Joel Spolsky and Michael Pryor: Fog Creek Software Joel Spolsky and Michael Pryor started Fog Creek Software, a highly successful software company, in 2000 and built their company on the servant leadership model. "At Fog Creek Software, management, not coding [software], is the support function," they say. When the company moved into its new headquarters in New York City, Spolsky and Pryor spent two afternoons installing window blinds to eliminate the glare on their programmers' computer screens. "I'm well aware that any half-competent handyman could have handled that task for not much money and that Michael and I could have spent the time, in theory, doing something a lot more valuable," says Spolsky. "But I was trying to make a point. In our company, management's job is to get things out of the way so that all the great people we've hired can get work done. Our company was built on the idea of hiring smart and productive people and then clearing the decks."[13] ■

Tyler Hicks-Wright

One business writer explains servant leadership this way:

Real leadership is grounded in a higher level of self-interest that's tied to the interests of those who trust and follow their leader. It [creates] an atmosphere of confidence and light of clarity that flows from and surrounds the leader and that fills the room with the exhilaration of possibility.[14]

To tap into that exhilaration of possibility, an entrepreneurial leader must perform many important tasks, including the following:

● Hire the right employees for the entrepreneurial team and constantly improve their skills.

● Create a culture for motivating and retaining employees.

● Plan for "passing the torch" to the next generation of leadership.

LO2

Describe the importance of
hiring the right employees
and how to avoid making
hiring mistakes.

Building an Entrepreneurial Team: Hiring the Right Employees

The decision to hire a new employee is an important one for every business, but its impact is magnified many times in a small company. Every new hire a business owner makes determines the heights to which the company can climb—or the depths to which it will plunge. "Bad hires" can poison a small company's culture. Unfortunately, hiring mistakes in business are all too common: 68 percent of companies report that they made a bad hire within the last year.[15] The culprit in most cases? The company's selection and hiring process.

Even the best training program cannot overcome a flawed hiring decision. One study reported in the *Harvard Business Review* concludes that 80 percent of employee turnover is caused by bad hiring decisions.[16] The most common causes of a company's poor hiring decisions include the following:

- Managers who rely on candidates' descriptions of themselves rather than requiring candidates to demonstrate their abilities.

- Managers who fail to follow a consistent, evidence-based selection process. Forty-seven percent of managers admit that they make hiring decisions in 30 minutes or less, and 44 percent of managers say that they rely on their intuition to make hiring decisions.

- Managers who fail to provide candidates with sufficient information about what the jobs for which they are hiring actually entail.[17]

- Managers who succumb to the pressure to fill a job quickly.

- Managers who fail to check candidates' references.[18]

As crucial as finding good employees is to a small company's future, it is no easy task because entrepreneurs face a labor shortage, particularly among knowledge-based workers. The severity of this shortage will become more acute as baby boomers retire in increasing numbers and the growth rate of the U.S. labor force slows (see Figure 16.1). According to the National Commission for Employment Policy, the impact of these demographic changes will be a "skilled worker gap" (in which the demand for skilled workers outstrips the supply) of 14 million in 2020.[19] The result is that small businesses already find themselves pursuing the best talent not just across the United States but across the globe. A recent study by ManpowerGroup reports that on average 34 percent of companies around the world have difficulty filling jobs because of a lack of available talent. The United States is well above the global average with 49 percent of companies having difficulty filling jobs because of a lack of talent.[20]

A recent study by IBM reports that 71 percent of CEOs across the globe say that the most important factor in their companies' ability to provide sustained economic value to their customers is the quality of their employees.[21] Smart business owners recognize that the companies that have the most talented, best-trained, and most motivated workforces will be the winners.

FIGURE 16.1

Annual Growth Rate in the U.S. Labor Force

Source: U.S. Census Bureau, 2008.

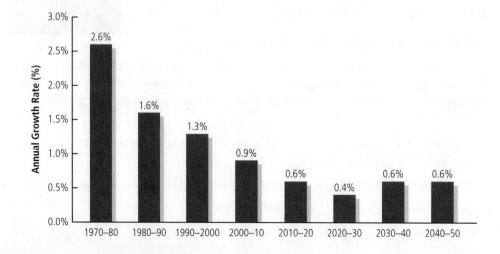

"Winning the war for talent will be the predominant business challenge for this century," says Ian Davis, managing director of McKinsey and Company. "Be thoughtful and diligent about how you recruit and retain talent and about the leadership opportunities you create for your people, especially your younger people."[22]

As a result of the intense competition for quality workers among businesses, employers often feel pressured to hire someone, even if that person is not a good fit for the job. A study by Development Dimensions International reports that 34 percent of hiring managers admit to making bad hiring decisions because they were under pressure to fill a job.[23] The result is the same: an expensive hiring mistake for the company.

ENTREPRENEURIAL PROFILE: Alex Membrillo and Stephen Popov: Cardinal Web Solutions Alex Membrillo, cofounder with Stephen Popov of Cardinal Web Solutions, an Internet marketing agency in Atlanta, Georgia, says that his company recently succumbed to the pressure to fill a sales job quickly even though managers knew that the candidate was not a good fit with the company's culture. As a result, the new hire stayed only three months and cost the company thousands of dollars. "In the future, we will wait as long as it takes to get the perfect fit," says Membrillo.[24] ∎

As Alex Membrillo learned, hiring mistakes are incredibly expensive, and no organization, especially small ones, can afford too many of them. Employers report that their hiring mistakes result in lower productivity (41 percent), time lost to recruit and train another worker (40 percent), additional cost of recruiting and training another worker (37 percent), negative impact on employee morale (36 percent), and diminished customer satisfaction (22 percent).[25]

How to Hire Winners

Even though the importance of hiring decisions is magnified in small companies, small businesses are most likely to make hiring mistakes because they lack the human resources experts and the disciplined hiring procedures that large companies have. In many small businesses, the hiring process is informal, and the results often are unpredictable. In the early days of a company, entrepreneurs rarely take the time to create job descriptions and specifications; instead, they usually hire people because they know or trust them rather than for their job or interpersonal skills. As the company grows, business owners hire people to fit in around these existing employees, often creating a very unusual, inefficient organization structure built around jobs that are poorly planned and designed.

The following guidelines can help entrepreneurs to hire winners and avoid making costly hiring mistakes as they build their team of employees.

COMMIT TO HIRING THE BEST TALENT Smart entrepreneurs follow the old adage, "A players hire A players; B players hire C players." They are not threatened by hiring people who may be smarter and more talented than they are. In fact, they recognize that doing so is the best way to build a quality team. What skill sets do CEOs say are essential to employees' success? According to the IBM study of global CEOs, the most important skills are the ability to collaborate with others (75 percent), the ability to communicate effectively (67 percent), creativity (61 percent), flexibility (61 percent), and analytical and quantitative skills (50 percent).[26]

ELEVATE RECRUITING TO A STRATEGIC POSITION IN THE COMPANY The recruiting process is the starting point for building quality into a company. "After money, the hardest thing [for a start-up company] to find is talent," says Chris McCann, cofounder of NextDigest, a company that publishes newsletters for technology entrepreneurs.[27] Assembling a quality workforce begins with a sound recruiting effort. By investing time and money in the crucial planning phase of the staffing process, entrepreneurs can generate spectacular savings down the road by hiring the best talent. Recruiting is so important that many entrepreneurs are actively involved in the process themselves. Visionary entrepreneurs *never* stop recruiting because top-quality talent is hard to find and is extremely valuable. Tom Bonney, founder of CMF Associates, a fast-growing financial consulting firm in Philadelphia, knows that finding superior talent is essential to the success of his service business. "I never stop recruiting," he says. "Even if I don't have a need, I am always looking."[28]

Attracting a pool of qualified job candidates requires not only constant attention but also creativity, especially among smaller companies that often find it difficult to match the more generous offers large companies make. With a sound recruiting strategy and a willingness to look in new places, however, smaller companies *can* hire and retain high-caliber employees. The following techniques will help:

Look inside the company first. One of the best sources for top prospects is inside the company itself. A promotion-from-within-policy serves as an incentive for existing workers to upgrade their skills and to produce results. In addition, an entrepreneur already knows the employee's work habits, and the employee already understands the company's culture. Unfortunately, companies fill only one-third of their job vacancies from within.[29]

Look for employees with whom your customers can identify. For an entrepreneur whose company sells women's shoes, hiring young women straight out of college to manage the company's social media presence makes sense; however, hiring young women for sales positions in a company that sells makeup to middle-age women does not.

ENTREPRENEURIAL PROFILE: Greg Selkoe: Karmaloop Greg Selkoe, founder and CEO of Karmaloop, a Boston-based e-commerce company that operates a growing hipster media empire representing more than 500 brands, looks for employees who resemble the company's target customers, members of verge culture. "What makes us successful is that our employees reflect the street culture that we market to," says Selkoe. "Some are DJs or musicians or artists. They're young; the median age here is 26, and from almost every race, religion, and ethnicity. Basically, they are the market we sell to."[30] ■

Encourage employee referrals. To cope with the shortage of available talent, many companies are offering their employees (and others) bonuses for referring candidates who come to work and prove to be valuable employees. Employees serve as reliable screens because they do not want to jeopardize their reputations with their employer. At Groupon, the fast-growing online coupon discounter, Dan Jessup, whose title is "head of people strategy," says that 40 percent of the company's new hires originate with employee referrals. "Leveraging our employee base for referrals works especially well with our top performers," says Jessup, who has managed the company's hiring efforts as it grew from just 37 employees to more than 10,000 employees in less than three years.[31] To encourage employee referrals, many companies offer incentives for successful hires. Rewards companies offer to employees for successful referrals range from cash and iPods to big-screen televisions and exotic vacations.

Make employment advertisements stand out. Getting employment ads noticed in traditional media is becoming more difficult because they get lost in the swarm of ads from other companies.

ENTREPRENEURIAL PROFILE: Roger Mody: Signal Corporation Roger Mody, founder and former CEO of Signal Corporation, an information technology services provider, uses humor to make his employment ads stand out and to communicate the sense of fun in the company's culture. One ad ran a photo of Mody after a company pie-eating contest with the tagline "And you should see us on casual day."[32] ■

Use multiple channels to recruit talent. Although newspaper ads still top employers' list of job postings, many businesses are successfully attracting candidates through other media, particularly the Internet. The goal is to spread wide a company's recruiting net. Posting job listings on the company's Web page and on career-oriented Web sites such as Monster, CareerBuilder, and others not only expands a small company's reach far beyond ads in a local newspaper but also is very inexpensive. Employers also are connecting with potential employees (not all of whom are actively seeking new jobs) through their employees' network of contacts, company blogs, online and offline professional organizations, and social media sites, such as Facebook, LinkedIn, and Twitter. A recent survey by Jobvite reports that 80 percent of recruiters use social media to search for job candidates.[33] The strategy works well for technology companies such as Red Hat Inc. (the company that distributes the Linux operating system), which finds 50 percent of its new hires through social networks.[34]

ENTREPRENEURIAL PROFILE: Jeff Greenhouse: Singularity Design Jeff Greenhouse has used LinkedIn with its more than 175 million registered users to recruit top-notch employees to Singularity Design, the digital marketing agency he cofounded in Philadelphia, after attracting applicants who were only marginally qualified with traditional job postings. "One of [LinkedIn's] greatest strengths is the ability to proactively search for people who might be a good fit for your company and then reach out to them to gauge their interest," says Greenhouse. "LinkedIn gets you talking to high-quality candidates who might otherwise not see or respond to a job posting."[35] ■

Recruit on campus. For many employers, college and university campuses remain an excellent source of workers, especially for entry-level positions. After screening résumés, a recruiter can interview a dozen or more high-potential students in just one day.

Forge relationships with schools and other sources of workers. Some employers have found that forging long-term relationships with schools and other institutions can provide a valuable source of workers. As colleges and universities offer students more internship opportunities, a small business can benefit from hosting one or more students for a semester or for the summer. Internships offer companies a low-risk opportunity to "test-drive" potential employees, observe students' work habits, and sell top performers on permanent positions on graduation.

Recruit "retired" workers. By 2020, 20 percent of workers in the United States will reach retirement age.[36] Many of these baby boomers plan to continue working after reaching retirement age to maintain their lifestyles, however. The Bureau of Labor Statistics estimates that 13.2 million people over the age of 65 will be in the workforce in 2022, an increase from 7.3 million today, and small businesses should be ready to hire them.[37] With a lifetime of work experience, time on their hands, and a strong work ethic, "retired" workers can be the ideal solution to many entrepreneurs' labor problems and can be a valuable asset to small firms.

Consider using offbeat recruiting techniques. To attract the workers they need to support their growing businesses, some entrepreneurs have resorted to creative recruiting techniques. As part of its recruiting efforts, Range Resources Corporation, a natural gas company, sponsors a unique float in the local Fourth of July parade, invites prospective employees to mingle with current employees at cookouts, and sends employee representatives prepared to talk about working at the company to more than 1,000 community events each year.[38] Other ideas include the following:

- Sending young recruiters to mingle with college students on spring break.
- Using social networking media, such as Facebook, LinkedIn, Twitter, blogs, and podcasts, to reach potential employees, especially young ones.
- Sponsoring a "job-shadowing" program that gives students and other prospects the opportunity to observe firsthand the nature of the work and the work environment.
- Inviting prospective employees to a company tailgating party at a sports event.
- Inviting potential candidates to participate in a company-sponsored event. Corey Reese, cofounder of Ness Computing, a company that makes practical apps for the iPhone, sponsors "hackathon" events on college campuses that attract the technologically savvy computer software engineers he must hire for the fast-growing company.
- Posting "what it's like to work here" videos created by current employees on the company's Facebook page, YouTube, and other video sites.
- Inviting potential candidates to meet and mingle with a company's workforce at informal, fun events. "It's a good way to get people comfortable and talking—and interested in working for you," says Corey Reese of Ness Computing, which regularly invites potential employees to company-sponsored barbecues and picnics.

• Keeping a file of all of the workers mentioned in the "People on the Move" column in the business section of the local newspaper and then contacting them a year later to see whether they are happy in their jobs.[39]

Offer what workers want. Adequate compensation and benefits are important considerations for job candidates, but other, less tangible factors also weigh heavily in a prospect's decision to accept a job. To recruit effectively, entrepreneurs must consider what a McKinsey and Company study calls the "employee value proposition," the factors that would make the ideal employee want to work for their businesses. Flexible work schedules and telecommuting that allow employees to balance the demands of work and life can attract quality workers to small companies. In fact, a study by staffing firm Robert Half International reports that after salary and benefits, flexible work schedules and telecommuting were the most important incentives in attracting employees.[40] A two-year study of 243 small companies for the Gevity Institutes, confirms the link among effective human resource practices, worker-friendly policies, and superior company performance. Small companies that relied on best-practice human resource policies and worker-friendly strategies produced revenues that were 22 percent higher and profits that were 23 percent higher than those companies that did not do so. They also reported employee turnover rates that were 67 percent lower.[41]

Many of the companies listed on *Fortune*'s "100 Best Companies to Work For" offer low-cost but valuable (from their employees' perspectives) benefits, such as take-home meals, personal concierge services that coordinate everything from dry cleaning to auto maintenance for employees, exercise facilities, and discounts on the merchandise they sell.[42]

ENTREPRENEURIAL PROFILE: April Kumzelman: Fat Wallet Fat Wallet, an online discount retailer, provides employees with a valuable, low-cost benefit—the flexibility they need to achieve work–life balance. The company's "no-miss" policy tells employees not to miss important family or school events because of work. "It doesn't cost us any money, and people really appreciate it," says human resources director April Kunzelman. "Flexibility pays huge benefits for a small company like ours."[43] ∎

Table 16.2 provides examples of affordable alternative benefits that small businesses can offer employees.

TABLE 16.2 Affordable Alternative Benefits

Although small companies typically cannot match their larger rivals on the employee benefits packages they offer, with some creativity entrepreneurs can provide less expensive options that increase employee retention, motivation, and morale.

Perhaps you cannot offer . . .	But you might . . .
Tuition reimbursement for college classes	Implement a flex-time schedule that allows employees to attend classes at a nearby college or university
Paid leave	Use job sharing so that two part-time employees share one full-time job
Comprehensive health insurance	Hold a wellness day in which a local health care provider performs basic health screens for employees
An on-site fitness center	Set up a basketball goal in a corner of the parking lot or a ping-pong table in the office or negotiate a reduced fee for employees at the local YMCA
401(k) retirement plan with employer match	Invite a local investment adviser to provide financial counseling and retirement advice to employees
Counseling services	Allow employees to bring their dogs to work; research shows that allowing pets in the workplace reduces stress and increases job satisfaction
Child care subsidies	Negotiate discounts at a local preschool for employees' children or allow employees to telecommute from home several days a week

Source: Adapted from Paula Andruss, "Affordable Alternatives," *Entrepreneur*, May 2012, p. 57; "Pets at Work Keep Workers Happy," *U.S. News and World Report*, April 2, 2012, http://health.usnews.com/health-news/news/articles/2012/04/02/pets-at-work-keep-workers-happy.

Create Practical Job Descriptions and Job Specifications

Business owners must recognize that what they do *before* they interview candidates for a position determines to a great extent how successful they will be at hiring winners. The first step is to perform a **job analysis**, the process by which a firm determines the duties and nature of the jobs to be filled and the skills and experience required of the people who are to fill them. Without a proper job analysis, a hiring decision is, at best, a coin toss. The first step in conducting a job analysis is to develop a **job description**, a written statement of the duties, responsibilities, reporting relationships, working conditions, and methods and techniques as well as materials and equipment used in a job. A results-oriented job description explains what a job entails and the duties the person filling it is expected to perform. A detailed job description includes a job title, job summary, primary responsibilities and duties, nature of supervision, the job's relationship to others in the company, working conditions, the job's location, definitions of job-specific terms, and a description of the company and its culture.

Preparing job descriptions is a task that most small business owners overlook; however, this may be one of the most important parts of the hiring process because it creates a blueprint for the job. Without this blueprint, a manager tends to hire the person with experience whom they like the best.

ENTREPRENEURIAL PROFILE: Sherri Comstock: The Cheshire Cat and The Spotted Crocodile Sherri Comstock, owner of The Cheshire Cat and The Spotted Crocodile, two jewelry and gift boutiques in Grayslake, Illinois, admits to failing to write meaningful job descriptions. "One of the biggest mistakes we've made is not defining the job as well as we should," she says. "If the position is not well-defined before you hire the person to fill it, a bad fit is all but inevitable."[44] ■

Useful sources of information for writing job descriptions include the manager's knowledge of the job, the worker(s) currently holding the job, and the *Dictionary of Occupational Titles*, available at most libraries. This dictionary, published by the U.S. Department of Labor, lists more than 20,000 job titles and descriptions and serves as a useful tool for getting a small business owner started when writing job descriptions. Internet searches also are a valuable tool for finding templates for writing job descriptions. There, entrepreneurs can find templates and descriptions they can easily modify to fit their companies' needs. Table 16.3 provides an example of the description drawn from the *Dictionary of Occupational Titles* for an unusual job.

The second objective of a job analysis is to create a **job specification**, a written statement of the qualifications and characteristics needed for a job stated in such terms as education, skills, and experience. A job specification shows the small business manager what kind of person to recruit and establishes the standards an applicant must meet to be hired. In essence, it is a written "success profile" of the ideal employee. Does the person have to be a good listener, empathetic, well organized, decisive, and a "self-starter"? Should he or she have experience in Java programming? One of the best ways to develop this success profile is to study the top performers currently working for the company and to identify the characteristics that make them successful. Before hiring new sales representatives, sales managers at Blackboard, Inc., a Washington, D.C., company that sells software for the educational market, study their top sales producers to identify the characteristics they demonstrate in four areas—skills, experience, knowledge, and personality traits. Table 16.4 provides an example that links the tasks for a sales representative's job (drawn from the job description) to the traits or characteristics an entrepreneur identified as necessary to succeed in that job. These traits become the foundation for writing the job specification.

job analysis
the process by which a firm determines the duties and nature of the jobs to be filled and the skills and experience required of the people who are to fill them.

job description
a written statement of the duties, responsibilities, reporting relationships, working conditions, and methods and techniques as well as materials and equipment used in a job.

job specification
a written statement of the qualifications and characteristics needed for a job stated in terms such as education, skills, and experience.

TABLE 16.3 A Sample Job Description from the *Dictionary of Occupational Titles*

Worm Picker—gathers worms to be used as fish bait; walks about grassy areas, such as gardens, parks, and golf courses and picks up earthworms (commonly called dew worms and nightcrawlers). Sprinkles chlorinated water on lawn to cause worms to come to the surface and locates worms by use of lantern or flashlight. Counts worms, sorts them, and packs them into containers for shipment. (# 413.687-014)

TABLE 16.4 Linking Tasks from a Job Description to the Traits Necessary to Perform a Job Successfully

Job Task	Trait or Characteristic
Generate and close new sales	"Outgoing"; persuasive; friendly
Make 15 "cold calls" per week	"Self-starter"; determined; optimistic; independent; confident
Analyze customers' needs and recommend proper equipment	Good listener; patient; empathetic
Counsel customers about options and features needed	Organized; polished speaker; "other oriented"
Prepare and explain financing methods	Honest; "numbers oriented"; comfortable with computers and spreadsheets
Retain existing customers	Customer oriented; relationship builder

Plan an Effective Interview

Once an entrepreneur knows what to look for in a job candidate, he or she can develop a plan for conducting an informative job interview. Research shows that planned interviews produce much more reliable hiring results than unstructured interviews in which interviewers "freewheel" the questions they ask candidates. Unstructured interviews produce no better results than flipping a coin to decide whether to hire a candidate, but structured interviews produce highly valid hiring results.[45] Too often, business owners go into an interview unprepared, and as a result, they fail to get the information they need to judge the candidate's qualifications, qualities, and suitability for the job. A common symptom of failing to prepare for an interview is that the interviewer rather than the candidate does most of the talking. "It's the most common mistake made by interviewers," says one human resource manager.[46]

Conducting an effective interview requires an entrepreneur to know what he or she wants to get out of the interview in the first place and to develop a series of questions to extract that information. The following guidelines will help entrepreneurs develop interview questions that will give them meaningful insight into an applicant's qualifications, personality, and character:

Involve others in the interview process. Solo interviews are prone to errors. A better process is to involve other employees, particularly employees with whom the prospect would be working, in the interview process either individually or as part of a panel.

ENTREPRENEURIAL PROFILE: Richard Sheridan: Menlo Innovations At Menlo Innovations, a successful custom software company in Ann Arbor, Michigan, collaboration among workers is paramount because employees typically work together on projects in pairs all day. Menlo Innovations's hiring process reflects its emphasis on collaboration in what cofounder Richard Sheridan calls "extreme interviewing." Candidates team up in pairs to tackle 20-minute exercises that are typical of the projects they would work on at Menlo Innovations while employees and managers observe them. To drive home the company's focus on teamwork, each team of candidates shares a single pencil. Candidates complete three exercises so that employees can observe them. After an extreme interviewing session, employees collectively decide which candidates to invite back. Those selected spend a day working for pay with two employees on a project. Those who pass that test come back for a three-week trial employment period. Only after completing the trial successfully do they become Menlo Innovations employees.[47] ■

Develop a series of core questions and ask them of every candidate. To give the screening process more consistency, smart business owners rely on a set of relevant questions they ask in every interview. Of course, they also customize each interview using impromptu questions based on an individual candidate's responses. "The most effective way to hire fantastic, loyal employees who will fit into your company culture and help you meet your goals is to hire them for their inherent abilities (which can't be taught), such as personality, learning style, and core values," says Mike Michalowicz, a successful serial entrepreneur who started his first business at age 24. "You do this by identifying behavior patterns during the interview process. If you ask questions designed to identify the patterns, you can predict how prospective employees will behave."[48]

⚖ Ethics and Entrepreneurship

Honesty in Job Descriptions

our time unless thorou..., qualified. M. L. Barker, 1408 Chapman Bldg.

MEN WANTED

for hazardous journey, small wages, bitter cold, long months of complete darkness, constant danger, safe return doubtful, honor and recognition in case of success.

Ernest Shackleton 4 Burlington st.

MEN—Neat-appearing young men of pleasing personality, between a... of 01 and 40 to wor..

Explorer Ernest Shackleton reportedly placed this advertisement in a British newspaper to recruit the crew for his 1914 expedition with the goal of "crossing the South Polar continent from sea to sea," a distance of 1,800 miles in the face of some of the most grueling and dangerous conditions possible. Nearly 5,000 men applied, from which Shackleton selected 28 of the most capable men, carefully matching their skills and abilities to the challenges that the journey would present. On August 1, 1914, Shackleton and his crew left London on their ship, the *Endurance*, to document the largely unexplored Antarctic. On October 27, 1915, after watching the *Endurance* splinter after being stuck in pack ice for 10 months, Shackleton and his crew began a harrowing journey of survival that would not end until August 20, 1916, 22 months after their expedition began. Even though Shackleton's ad stated "safe return doubtful," Shackleton and his entire crew returned safely to London after an amazing adventure.

Like Shackleton, smart entrepreneurs know that writing job descriptions that make jobs sound more interesting, glamorous, and exciting than they really are not only is misleading but also creates problems for their businesses. To avoid high turnover rates, low morale, and abysmal productivity rates among their employees, entrepreneurs must paint realistic pictures of jobs when they create job descriptions. Recruiters at Lindblad Expeditions, a company that takes guests on adventure cruises to exciting destinations around the globe, makes sure that job applicants get an unvarnished picture of what their jobs would entail—warts and all. Prospective employees receive a DVD that shows crew members performing their daily tasks—from serving meals to guests and seeing wildlife on the Galapagos Islands to washing windows and swabbing toilets. "The things you see and the places that you go are amazing, but you're still doing this incredibly hard work,"

says one employee. "You're going to put in 10- to 12-hour days," adds another. The video discourages most applicants, but those who do apply tend to be just the kind of young people Lindblad is looking for to take on a six-month assignment of taking care of guests' safety and comfort. "If they get on board and say, 'This is not what I expected,' then shame on us," says Kris Thompson, vice president of human resources.

Tony Hseih, CEO of Zappos, the online shoe retailer whose 10 core values include "deliver WOW through service" and "create fun and a little weirdness," relies on an unusual policy to make sure that his company hires only those employees who are most committed to fulfilling the company's mission. After the first week of the company's four-week training program, during which employees earn a full salary, Zappos presents them with "The Offer": Stay with the company or take a $4,000 payout to leave, no strings attached. Only about 10 percent of new employees take the money and leave. Hseih says that those who remain are more likely to believe in Zappos's values and to commit themselves to upholding the company's commitment to customer service. Every year, Zappos publishes the *Zappos Culture Book*, in which employees have the opportunity to write anything they want about Zappos's core values and its culture, what the values and culture mean to them, and what they do to uphold them. In the foreword of a recent edition of the *Zappos Culture Book*, Hseih wrote, "For us to succeed as a service company, we need to create, maintain, and grow a culture where employees want to play a part in providing great service. . . . As we grow as a company and hire new people, we need to make sure that they understand and become a part of our culture."

1. Why is it important for entrepreneurs to create honest job descriptions to potential employees? What are the implications for entrepreneurs who fail to do so?

2. Is it ethical for small companies to present to potential employees only the "fun" aspects of a job and to gloss over its less appealing components?

3. Lindblad Expeditions and Zappos sometimes receive criticism for being too extreme in the honesty of their recruiting approaches. Do you agree? Explain.

Sources: Based on *Shackleton's Expedition*, NOVA, http://www.pbs.org/wgbh/nova/shackleton/1914; Boost Retention with Honest Job Previews," *Manager's e-Bulletin*, July 24, 2008, pp. 1–2; "Would You Give an Employee $1,000 to Quit?," *Marketing Profs*, June 2, 2008, pp. 1–2; Lisa Everitt, "Zappos Tells New Employees: Please Go Away," *BNet*, May 21, 2008, http://industry.bnet.com/retail/100066/zappos-tells-new-employees-please-go-away; Bud Bilanich, "Zappos and Employee Engagement and Commitment," Common Sense Solutions to Tough Business Problems, November 20, 1007, http://bbilanich.typepad.com/blog/2007/11/last-week-i-blo.html; and Matt Rosoff, "Tony Hseih: Don't Rule Out a Zappos Airline," *Business Insider*, September 28, 2011, http://articles.businessinsider.com/2011-09-28/tech/30211874_1_customer-service-tony-hsieh-virgin-brand.

"I believe the courts recently ruled that it is illegal to ask questions during a job interview."

Aaron Bacall/Cartoon Bank

Ask open-ended questions (including on-the-job "scenarios") rather than questions calling for "yes or no" answers. These types of questions are most effective because they encourage candidates to talk about their work experience in a way that will disclose the presence or the absence of the traits and characteristics the business owner is seeking. Peter Bregman, CEO of Bregman Partners, a company that helps businesses implement change, says that one of the most revealing questions that an interviewer can ask candidates is, "What do you do in your spare time?" The answer to this question offers unique insight that helps interviewers differentiate between those who are merely competent and those who are stars. "Understand a person's obsessions and you will understand his or her natural motivation," says Bregman, pointing to the example of Captain C. B. "Sully" Sullenberger, the pilot who safely landed a disabled jet with 155 passengers on the Hudson River using skills that he learned from his hobby: flying gliders.[49]

Create hypothetical situations that candidates would be likely to encounter on the job and ask how they would handle them. Building the interview around these kinds of questions gives the owner a preview of the candidate's actual work habits and attitudes. Some companies take this idea a step farther and put candidates into a simulated work environment to see how they prioritize activities and handle mail, e-mail, and a host of "real-world" problems they are likely to encounter on the job, ranging from complaining customers to problematic employees. Known as **situational interviews**, their goal is to give interviewers keener insight into how candidates would perform in the work environment.

Probe for specific examples in the candidate's past work experience that demonstrate the necessary traits and characteristics. A common mistake interviewers make is failing to get candidates to provide the detail they need to make an informed decision. Experienced interviewers use the phrase "Tell me more" to harvest meaningful information about candidates.

Ask candidates to describe a recent success and a recent failure and how they dealt with them. Smart entrepreneurs look for candidates who describe their successes and their failures with equal enthusiasm because they know that peak performers put as much into their failures as they do their successes and usually learn something valuable from their failures.

Arrange a "noninterview" setting that allows several employees to observe the candidate in an informal setting. Taking candidates on a plant tour, setting up a coffee break, or taking them to lunch gives more people a chance to judge a candidate's interpersonal skills and personality outside the formal interview process. These informal settings can be very revealing.

situational interview
an interview in which the interviewer gives candidates a typical job-related situation (e.g., a job simulation) to see how they respond to it.

TABLE 16.5 Interview Questions for Candidates for a Sales Representative Position

Trait or Characteristic	Question
Outgoing; persuasive; friendly; self-starter; determined; optimistic; independent; confident	How do you persuade reluctant prospects to buy?
Good listener; patient; empathetic; organized; polished speaker; "other" oriented	What would you say to a fellow salesperson who was getting more than his share of rejections and was having difficulty getting appointments?
Honest; customer oriented; relationship builder	How do you feel when someone questions the truth of what you say? What do you do in such situations?
Other questions:	If you owned a company, why would you hire yourself?
	If you were head of your department, what would you do differently?
	How do you recognize the contributions of others in your department?
	If you weren't in sales, what other job would you be in?

ENTREPRENEURIAL PROFILE: Jeffrey Swartz: Timberland Before Jeffrey Swartz, CEO of Timberland, the popular shoe and boot maker, makes an offer to a candidate for a management position, he invites the candidate to participate in one of the company's community service projects. "In an interview, I'm sure you're more clever than I am," he says. "But on a service site, you will reveal who you [really] are."[50] ■

Table 16.5 shows an example of some interview questions one business owner uses to uncover the traits and characteristics he was seeking in a top-performing sales representative.

Conduct the Interview

An effective interview contains three phases: breaking the ice, asking questions, and selling the candidate on the company.

BREAKING THE ICE In the opening phase of the interview, the manager's primary job is to diffuse the tension that exists because of the nervousness of both parties. Many skilled interviewers use the job description to explain the nature of the job and the company's culture to the applicant. Then they use "icebreakers," questions about a hobby or special interest, to get the candidate to relax and begin talking.

ASKING QUESTIONS During the second phase of the interview, the employer asks the questions from the question bank to determine the applicant's suitability for the job. The interviewer's primary job at this point is to listen. Effective interviewers spend about 25 percent of the interview talking and about 75 percent listening. They also take notes during the interview to help them ask follow-up questions based on a candidate's comments and to evaluate a candidate after the interview is over. Experienced interviewers also pay close attention to a candidate's nonverbal clues, or body language, during the interview. They know that candidates may be able to say exactly what they want with their words but that their body language does not lie!

Some of the most valuable interview questions are designed to gain insight into a candidate's creativity and capacity for abstract thinking. Known as **puzzle interviews**, their goal is to determine how candidates think by asking them offbeat questions, such as "You are shrunk to the height of a nickel and thrown into a blender. Your mass is reduced so that your density is the same as usual. The blades start moving in 60 seconds. What do you do?" (a classic interview question at Google).[51] Other companies use questions such as "How many different ways can you get water from a lake at the foot of a mountain to the top of the mountain?," "If you could go camping anywhere, where would you put your tent?" (a question asked by interviewers at the travel site Expedia), "How would you design Bill Gates's bathroom?" (a favorite at Microsoft), or "How many people are using Facebook in San Francisco at 2:30 p.m. on a Friday?"[52] The logic and creativity that candidates use to derive an answer is much more important than the answer itself.

puzzle interview
an interview that includes offbeat questions to determine how job candidates think and reason and to judge their capacity for creativity.

Entrepreneurs must be careful to make sure they avoid asking candidates illegal questions. At one time, interviewers could ask wide-ranging questions covering just about every area of an applicant's background. Today, interviewing is a veritable minefield of legal liabilities waiting

TABLE 16.6 Is It Legal?

Some interview questions can lead an employer into legal problems. Test your knowledge concerning which questions are legal to ask in an interview using the following quiz.

Legal	Illegal	Interview Question
☐	☐	1. Are you currently using illegal drugs?
☐	☐	2. Have you ever been arrested?
☐	☐	3. Do you have any children or do you plan to have children?
☐	☐	4. Are you willing to travel as part of this job?
☐	☐	5. When and where were you born?
☐	☐	6. Is there any limit on your ability to work overtime or travel?
☐	☐	7. How tall are you? How much do you weigh?
☐	☐	8. Do you drink alcohol?
☐	☐	9. How much alcohol do you drink each week?
☐	☐	10. Would your religious beliefs interfere with your ability to do the job?
☐	☐	11. What contraceptive practices do you use?
☐	☐	12. Are you HIV positive?
☐	☐	13. Have you ever filed a lawsuit or workers' compensation claim against a former employer?
☐	☐	14. Do you have physical/mental disabilities that would interfere with doing your job?
☐	☐	15. Are you a U.S. citizen?
☐	☐	16. What is your Facebook password?

Answers: 1. Legal. **2.** Illegal. Employers cannot ask about an applicant's arrest record, but they can ask whether a candidate has ever been *convicted* of a crime. **3.** Illegal. Employers cannot ask questions that could lead to discrimination against a particular group (e.g., women, physically challenged, and so on). **4.** Legal. **5.** Illegal. The Civil Rights Act of 1964 bans discrimination on the basis of race, color, sex, religion, or national origin. **6.** Legal. **7.** Illegal. Unless a person's physical characteristics are necessary for job performance (e.g., lifting 100-pound sacks of mulch), employers cannot ask such questions. **8.** Legal. **9.** Illegal. Notice the fine line between question 7 and question 8; this is what makes interviewing so challenging. **10.** Illegal. This question violates the Civil Rights Act of 1964. **11.** Illegal. What relevance would this have to an employee's job performance? **12.** Illegal. Under the Americans with Disabilities Act, which prohibits discrimination against people with disabilities, people who are HIV positive or have AIDS are considered "disabled." **13.** Illegal. Workers who file workers' compensation suits are protected from retribution by a variety of federal and state laws. **14.** Illegal. This question also violates the Americans with Disabilities Act. **15.** Illegal. This question violates the Civil Rights Act of 1964. **16.** Currently legal—but creepy and creates the possibility that employers would have access to information about which they cannot legally ask, such as religion, marital status, and others—creating a potential legal liability.

to explode in the unsuspecting interviewer's face. Although the Equal Employment Opportunity Commission, the government agency responsible for enforcing employment laws, does not outlaw specific questions, it does recognize that some questions can result in employment discrimination. If a candidate files charges of employment discrimination against a company, the burden of proof shifts to the employer to prove that all preemployment questions are job related and nondiscriminatory. In addition, many states have passed laws that forbid the use of certain questions or screening tools in interviews. To avoid trouble, business owners should keep in mind why they are asking a particular question. The goal is to identify individuals who are qualified to do the job well. By steering clear of questions about subjects that are peripheral to the job itself, employers are less likely to ask questions that will land them in court. Wise business owners ask their attorneys to review their bank of questions before using them in an interview. Table 16.6 provides a quiz for you to test your knowledge of the legality of certain interview questions.

SELLING THE CANDIDATE ON THE COMPANY In the final phase of the interview, the employer tries to sell desirable candidates on the company. This phase begins by allowing the candidate to ask questions about the company, the job, or other issues. Again, experienced interviewers note the nature of these questions and the insights they give into the candidate's personality. This part of the interview offers the employer a prime opportunity to explain to the candidate why the company is an attractive place to work. Remember that the best candidates will have other offers, and it's up to you to make sure they leave the interview wanting to work for your company. Finally, before closing the interview, the employer should thank the candidate and tell him or her what happens next (e.g., "We'll be contacting you about our decision within two weeks.").

Contact References and Conduct a Background Check

Business owners should take the time to conduct a background check and contact a candidate's references. Background checks are inexpensive to perform, typically costing between $25 and $100, and identify "red flags" that allow a company to avoid making an expensive hiring mistake. By performing a basic background check, employers can steer clear of candidates with criminal or other high-risk backgrounds. Although a few states ban the practice, conducting credit checks on job candidates (which legally require the candidates' written permission) also can be quite revealing, giving employers insight into candidates' dependability and trustworthiness. A recent study by the Society of Human Resource Managers reports that 60 percent of employers get credit reports as part of some or all of their background checks.[53]

Checking potential employees' social networking pages such as Facebook and LinkedIn also can provide a revealing look at their character. A study by CareerBuilder reports that 37 percent of employers investigate job candidates' social networking sites and that 34 percent have discovered something there that caused them to reject a candidate (see Figure 16.2).[54]

Although many business owners see checking references as a formality and pay little attention to it, others realize the need to protect themselves (and their customers) from hiring unscrupulous workers. Is it really necessary? Yes! According to a survey of hiring professionals, 53 percent of candidates either exaggerate or falsify information on their résumés.[55] Yahoo Inc. recently fired its CEO just five months after hiring him when the company's board of directors discovered that his résumé contained false information about his academic credentials.[56] Checking references thoroughly can help employers uncover false or exaggerated information. Rather than contacting only the references listed, experienced employers call applicants' previous employers and talk to their immediate supervisors to get a clear picture of the applicant's job performance, character, and work habits.

Many employers implement a probationary "trial" period for new hires that may range from two weeks to several months. Doing so increases the probability that the company has found the right person for the job. After two weeks on the job at Whole Foods Market, team members of new hires vote on whether to keep the new employees or to let them go.[57]

Experienced small business owners understand that the hiring process provides them with one of the most valuable raw materials their companies count on for success—capable, hardworking people. They know that hiring an employee is not a single event but rather the beginning of a long-term relationship. Table 16.7 features some strange but true incidents that employers have encountered during the selection process.

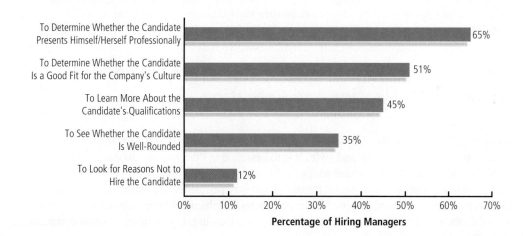

FIGURE 16.2

Why Hiring Managers Check Job Candidates' Social Networking Sites

Source: "Thirty-Seven Percent of Companies Use Social Networking Sites to Research Potential Candidates, According to New CareerBuilder Survey," *CareerBuilder,* April 18, 2012.

TABLE 16.7 Strange but True!

Human resource managers typically review résumés and job applications quickly. In fact, 45 percent of hiring managers say that they spend less than one minute on average reviewing a résumé or application. If you read enough résumés, conduct enough interviews, and check enough references, sooner or later you will encounter something bizarre. Consider the following examples (all true):

- When asked why he had applied for a job, one candidate said that he just wanted the opportunity to show off his new tie.
- One candidate listed the ability to do the moonwalk as a special skill on his résumé. Another candidate included "versatile toes" as a strength on her résumé.
- One applicant listed on her résumé her e-mail address, which included the phrase "shakinmybootie."
- After having lunch with a job candidate, a business owner took the applicant to her office for more discussion. The discussion ended, however, when the applicant dozed off and began snoring.
- On his résumé, one candidate wrote, "It's best for employers if I not work with people." Another included the following note: "Please don't misconstrue my 14 jobs as job hopping. I have never quit a job."
- When asked to provide a writing sample, one candidate said that she could not because all of her previous writing had been for the Central Intelligence Agency and was "classified."
- When asked what person, living or dead, he would most like to meet, one candidate replied, "The living one."
- One candidate answered his cell phone during the interview and asked the interviewer to leave her own office because it was a personal call.
- When asked about his personal interests, one candidate proudly replied, "Donating blood. Fourteen gallons so far!"
- One candidate wore a Boy Scout uniform to his interview but never explained to the interviewers why.
- A candidate explained that promptness was one of her strengths—even though she showed up 10 minutes late for the interview.
- During an interview, one candidate asked the interviewer, "What company is this again?" Another asked the interviewer if he could have a sip of the interviewer's coffee.
- At the end of an interview, the interviewer asked the candidate if he had any questions. His only question: "Is the office close enough so I can run home three times a day to Water Pik my teeth?"
- One candidate asked if he could bring his rabbit to work with him, adding that the rabbit was focused and reliable but that he himself had been fired before.
- One man who forgot to wear socks to his interview remedied the problem by coloring his ankles with a black felt-tip marker.

Recommendations from previous employers can sometimes be quite entertaining too. The following are statements from managers about workers:

- "Works well when under constant supervision and cornered like a rat in a trap."
- "This young lady has delusions of adequacy."
- "A photographic memory but with the lens cover glued on."
- "If you were to give him a penny for his thoughts, you'd get change."
- "If you stand close enough to him, you can hear the ocean."
- "He's so dense that light bends around him."

Sources: Based on "Hiring Managers Share Most Unusual Résumé Mistakes in Annual CareerBuilder Survey," *CareerBuilder*, August 24, 2011, http://www.careerbuilder.com/share/aboutus/pressreleasesdetail.aspx?id=pr653&sd=8/24/2011&ed=8/24/2099; "Survey Reveals Wackiest Job Interview Mistakes," *SmartPros*, March 13, 2008, http://accounting.smartpros.com/x61115.xml; "Hiring Horrors," *Your Company*, April 1999, p. 14; Mike B. Hall, "From Job Applicants," Joke-of-the-Day, December 8, 2000, http://www.jokeoftheday.com; Karen Axelton, "L-L-L-Losers!," *Business Start-Ups*, April 2000, p. 13; "Great Places to Work: Interview Horror Stories," *Washingtonian*, November 1, 2005, http://www.washingtonian.com/articles/businesscareers/2159.html; and "Hiring Managers Share the Most Memorable Interview Mistakes in Annual CareerBuilder Survey," *CareerBuilder*, February 22, 2012, http://www.careerbuilder.com/share/aboutus/pressreleasesdetail.aspx?id=pr680&sd=2/22/2012&ed=12/31/2012.

LO3

Explain how to create a company culture that encourages employee retention.

culture

the distinctive, unwritten, informal code of conduct that governs an organization's behavior, attitudes, relationships, and style.

Creating an Organizational Culture That Encourages Employee Motivation and Retention

Culture

A company's **culture** is the distinctive, unwritten, informal code of conduct that governs its behavior, attitudes, relationships, and style. It is the essence of "the way we do things around here." In many small companies, culture plays as important a part in gaining a competitive edge as strategy does. Culture has a powerful impact on the way people work together in a business, how they do their jobs, and how they treat their customers. Company culture manifests itself in many ways—from how workers dress and act to the language they use. For instance, at some companies, the unspoken dress code requires workers to wear suits and ties, but at others employees routinely come to work in jeans and T-shirts. Although it is an intangible characteristic, a company's culture has a powerful influence on everyone the company touches, especially its employees.

ENTREPRENEURIAL PROFILE: Greg Selkoe: Karmaloop At Karmaloop, the e-commerce company that targets members of the verge culture, founder Greg Selkoe has created a company culture that appeals to his young, hip workers but maintains high performance expectations. "Most people don't arrive at the office until 10 or 10:30," says Selkoe. "There is a lot of joking and camaraderie, but you have to work hard or you won't last here. You are always on duty. I'll call people on a Sunday at 4 in the afternoon because I've thought of something I want to talk about." Many employees at Karmaloop operate part-time businesses of their own, and that's fine with Selkoe. "Part of the fun of working at Karmaloop is that employees have creative outlets, but it can't affect job performance. If you're not doing your job, you can't stay."[58] ∎

An important ingredient in a company's culture is the performance objectives an entrepreneur sets and against which employees are measured. If entrepreneurs want integrity, respect, honesty, customer service, and other important values to be the foundation on which a positive culture can flourish, they must establish measures of success that reflect those core values. *Effective executives know that building a positive organizational culture has a direct, positive impact on the financial performance of an organization.* The intangible factors that make up an organization's culture have an influence, either positive or negative, on the tangible outcomes of profitability, cash flow, return on equity, employee productivity, innovation, and cost control. An entrepreneur's job is to create a culture that has a positive influence on the company's tangible outcomes.

Sustaining a company's culture begins with the hiring process. Beyond the normal requirements of competitive pay and working conditions, the hiring process must focus on finding employees who share the *values* of the organization. In winning workplaces, small companies "treat workers fairly, often generously; respect their personal lives; provide opportunities for development, and endow their jobs with meaning and fun," say the editors of *Inc.* magazine, which works with the nonprofit organization Winning Workplaces to recognize the top small business workplaces in the United States. "In return, those employees bestow their best ideas and efforts on the business. They pull together through change and hard times."[59]

ENTREPRENEURIAL PROFILE: Aaron Levie and Dylan Smith: Box.net At Box.net, a cloud software development company in Los Altos, California, cofounders Aaron Levie and Dylan Smith expect their employees to invest long hours to meet their weekly project deadlines. In their hiring process, they look for software engineers who are highly competitive and hard driving—the "I-can't-rest-until-I've-noodled-out-an-answer" types. To attract those types of workers, Levie and Smith say that they spend "a large portion of [their] management attention building a culture in the right way." They reward their hardworking employees with perks such as free dinners and facilities so that workers can sleep and shower if they stay late to work on a project. Box.net also encourages collaboration and innovation with its semiannual Hackathon, an event in which teams of employees take new product ideas from early stage to implementation in a single night. Levie and Smith have successfully created a culture of "we're all in this together" in which the company's employee approval rating is an impressive 97 percent.[60] ∎

Creating a culture that supports a company's strategy is no easy task, but entrepreneurs who have been most successful at it believe that having a set of overarching beliefs serves as a powerful guide for everyday action. Culture arises from an entrepreneur's consistent and relentless pursuit of a set of core values that everyone in the company can believe in. "Values outlive business models," says management guru Gary Hamel.[61]

Nurturing the right culture in a company can enhance a company's competitive position by improving its ability to attract and retain quality workers and by creating an environment in which workers can grow and develop. As a new generation of employees enters the workforce, companies are discovering that more relaxed, open cultures have an edge in attracting the best workers. These companies embrace nontraditional, fun cultures that incorporate concepts such as casual dress, team-based assignments, telecommuting, flexible work schedules, free meals, company outings, and many other unique options. Barbara Corcoran, a regular on the television show *Shark Tank*, built her company, The Corcoran Group, into the largest residential real

Kristin Callahan—Ace Pictures/
Newscom

estate brokerage firm in New York by creating a fun, engaging culture, which is a reflection of her leadership style. "The more fun I created in the company, the more creative and innovative it became," she says. "Fun is the most underutilized tool in the leadership tool belt," according to Corcoran, who started her business with a $1,000 loan and ultimately sold it for $66 million.[62]

Modern organizational culture relies on several principles that are fundamental to creating a productive, fun workplace that enables employees and the company to excel.

RESPECT FOR WORK AND LIFE BALANCE Successful companies recognize that their employees have lives away from work. One study of Generation X workers found that those companies that people most wanted to work for erased the traditional barriers between home life and work life by making it easier for employees to deal with the pressures they face away from their jobs. These businesses offer flexible work schedules, part-time jobs, job sharing, telecommuting, sabbaticals, on-site day care, and dry cleaning.

ENTREPRENEURIAL PROFILE: Tess Coody: Guerra DeBerry Coody Guerra DeBerry Coody (GDC), an advertising agency based in San Antonio, Texas, not only attracts top-quality talent but also reaps the benefits of high productivity and employee retention by emphasizing work–life balance. The company provides its employees with flexible work schedules, three one-hour exercise sessions with a personal trainer (on company time) each week, and an on-site day care center, benefits that allow employees to more easily balance their work–life demands.[63] ■

A SENSE OF PURPOSE As you learned in Chapter 3, one of the most important jobs an entrepreneur faces is defining the company's vision and then communicating it effectively to everyone the company touches. Effective companies use a strong sense of purpose to make employees feel connected to the company's mission. At motorcycle legend Harley-Davidson, employees are so in tune with the company's mission that some of them have tattooed the company's name on their bodies.

A SENSE OF FUN For some companies, the line between work and play is blurred. The founders of these businesses see no reason for work and fun to be mutually exclusive. In fact, they believe that a workplace that creates a sense of fun makes it easier to recruit quality workers and encourages them to be more productive and more customer oriented. "Healthy and sustainable organizations focus on the fundamentals: quality, service, fiscal responsibility, leadership—but they didn't forget to add fun to that formula," says Leslie Yerkes, a consultant and author.[64] At Kimpton Hotels and Restaurants, a chain of 55 boutique hotels across the United States founded by Bill Kimpton, employees compete in the "Housekeeping Olympics." Events in the morale-building competition include blindfolded bed making, a vacuum dash, and a $10,000 prize to the employee who has provided the best customer service.[65]

ENGAGEMENT Employees who are fully engaged in their work take pride in making valuable contributions to the organization's success and derive personal satisfaction from doing so. Although engaged employees are a key ingredient in superior business performance, just 33 percent of employees in North America are fully engaged in their work. In addition, 18 percent of them actually are disengaged.[66] Research shows that disengaged employees have turnover rates that are three to five times higher than the average employee (and 25 times higher than engaged employees). Disengaged employees also cost their employers 46 percent of their salaries in lost productivity, costing U.S. companies a total of $370 billion a year.[67] What can managers do to improve employee engagement?

- Constantly communicate the purpose and vision of the organization and why it matters.

- Challenge employees to learn and advance in their careers and give them the resources and the incentives to do so.

- Create a culture that encourages and rewards engagement.

Figure 16.3 shows the factors that drive employee engagement.

DIVERSITY Companies with appealing cultures not only accept cultural diversity in their workforces but also embrace it, actively seeking out workers with different backgrounds. Today, businesses must recognize that a workforce that has a rich mix of cultural diversity gives the company more talent, skills, and abilities from which to draw. A study of the demographics

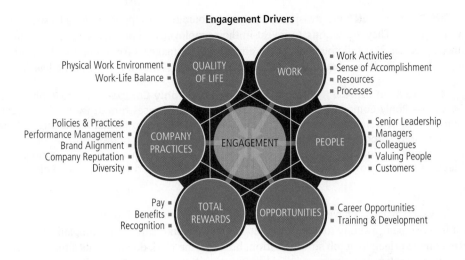

FIGURE 16.3
Drivers of Employee Engagement

Source: From *Trends in Global Employee Engagement*, 2011, p. 7. Copyright © 2011 by Aon-Hewitt Associates. Reprinted with permission from Aon-Hewitt.

of the United States reveals a steady march toward an increasingly diverse population. In fact, demographic trends suggest that by 2050, African Americans, Asians, Hispanics, and other non-white groups will make up nearly one-half of the U.S. population.[68] For companies to remain relevant in this environment, their workforces must reflect this diversity (see Figure 16.4). Who is better equipped to deal with a diverse, multicultural customer base than a diverse, multicultural workforce? Fred Kleisner, chairman and CEO of Wyndham International, a company that operates a chain of hotels, explains his approach to diversity: "I want diversity to be more than a corporate initiative. I want it to be a living part of our culture, a belief system and service philosophy that permeates each of our employees.[69]

INTEGRITY Employees want to work for companies that stand for honesty and integrity. They do not want to check their own personal values systems at the door when they report to work. Indeed, many workers take pride in the fact that they work for companies that are ethical and socially responsible. People want to work for a company that makes a difference in the world rather than merely making a product or providing a service.

PARTICIPATIVE MANAGEMENT Today's workers do not respond well to the autocratic management styles of yesteryear. Company owners and managers must learn to trust and empower employees at all levels of the organization to make decisions and to take the actions they need to do their jobs well. As a company grows, managers must empower employees at all levels to act without direct supervision. A recent study by consulting firm McKinsey and Company reports a strong correlation among the quality of a decision, clarity concerning the person responsible for implementing the decision, and that person's involvement in the decision-making process.[70]

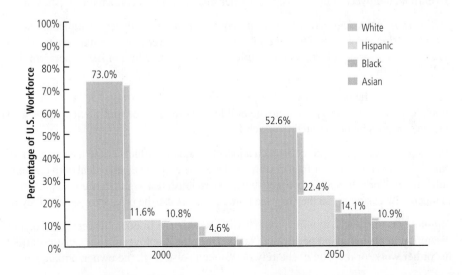

FIGURE 16.4
Composition of U.S. Workforce

Source: Jennifer Cheeseman Day, "Population Profile of the United States," U.S. Census Bureau, July 8, 2008, http://www.census.gov/population/www/pop-profile/natproj.html.

LEARNING ENVIRONMENT Progressive companies encourage and support lifelong learning among their employees. They are willing to invest in their employees, improving their skills and helping them to reach their full potential. These companies are magnets for the best and the brightest young workers who know that to stay at the top of their fields, they must always be learning.

ENTREPRENEURIAL PROFILE: Diana Pohly: The Pohly Company Diana Pohly, founder of The Pohly Company, a marketing and publishing services firm in Boston, understands the importance of training to her company's success. In addition to formal leadership and management training programs for managers at all levels, the company holds monthly "brown-bag" lunch meetings that include training on specific topics. "We invest in a strategic training plan and budget that help us provide the staff with continuous growth opportunities," says Pohly.[71] ■

Job Design

Over the years, managers have learned that the job itself and the way it is designed is an important factor in a company's ability to attract and retain quality workers. In some companies, work is organized on the principle of **job simplification**, breaking the work down into its simplest form and standardizing each task, as in some assembly-line operations. The scope of jobs organized in such a way is extremely narrow, resulting in impersonal, monotonous, and boring work that creates little challenge or motivation for workers. Job simplification invites workers to "check their brains at the door" and offers them little opportunity for excitement, enthusiasm, or pride in their work. The result can be apathetic, unmotivated workers who don't care about quality, customers, or costs.

To break this destructive cycle, some companies have redesigned workers' jobs. The following strategies are common: job enlargement, job rotation, job enrichment, flextime, job sharing, and flexplace.

Job enlargement (horizontal job loading) adds more tasks to a job to broaden its scope. For instance, rather than an employee simply mounting four screws in computers coming down an assembly line, a worker might assemble, install, and test the entire motherboard (perhaps as part of a team). The idea is to make the job more varied and to allow employees to perform a more complete unit of work.

Job rotation involves cross training employees so that they can move from one job in the company to others, giving them a greater number and variety of tasks to perform. As employees learn other jobs within an organization, both their skills and their understanding of the company's purpose and processes rise. Cross-trained workers are more valuable because they give a company the flexibility to shift workers from low-demand jobs to those where they are most needed. As an incentive for workers to learn to perform other jobs within an operation, some companies offer skill-based pay, a system under which the more skills workers acquire, the more they earn.

Job enrichment (vertical job loading) involves building motivators into a job by increasing the planning, decision-making, organizing, and controlling functions—traditionally managerial tasks—that workers perform. The idea is to make every employee a manager (at least one of his or her own job).

To enrich employees' jobs, a business owner must build five core characteristics into them:

- *Skill variety* is the degree to which a job requires a variety of different skills, talents, and activities from the worker. Does the job require the worker to perform a variety of tasks that demand a variety of skills and abilities, or does it force him or her to perform the same task repeatedly?

- *Task identity* is the degree to which a job allows the worker to complete a whole or identifiable piece of work. Does the employee build an entire piece of furniture (perhaps as part of a team), or does he or she merely attach four screws?

- *Task significance* is the degree to which a job substantially influences the lives or work of others—other employees or final customers. Does the employee get to deal with customers, either internal or external? One effective way to establish task significance is to put employees in touch with customers so they can see how customers use the product or service they make.

- *Autonomy* is the degree to which a job gives a worker the freedom, independence, and discretion in planning and performing tasks. Does the employee make decisions affecting his or her work, or must he or she rely on someone else (e.g., the owner, a manager, or a

---

job simplification

the type of job design that breaks work down into its simplest form and standardizes each task.

job enlargement (horizontal job loading)

the type of job design that adds more tasks to a job to broaden its scope.

job rotation

the type of job design that involves cross training employees so that they can move from one job in the company to others, giving them a greater number and variety of tasks to perform.

job enrichment (vertical job loading)

the type of job design that involves building motivators into a job by increasing the planning, decision-making, organizing, and controlling functions that workers perform.

You Be the Consultant

Fired over Facebook

The proliferation of social media has created a legal quagmire for employers when employees post in public forums comments that a few years ago would have been shared among only a few coworkers around the office watercooler. Employers want to protect their public images, and some have fired employees for posting rude, derogatory comments about the company or its managers on their Facebook walls, blogs, or Twitter, where potentially millions of people can read them. Some employees have fought back, claiming that they were wrongfully terminated and that their comments are protected by the First Amendment right to freedom of speech and the National Labor Relations Act (NLRA) of 1935, which guarantees the right of employees to "engage in protected concerted activity" and protects those who engage in protected activities from adverse actions by their employers. Others claim that managers violated their privacy by accessing employees' Facebook or Twitter accounts. "The intersection of social media and the office is a potential minefield," says one attorney who specializes in privacy matters.

The NLRA protects private employees' right to complain about job-related matters such as pay, safety, working conditions, discrimination, illegal activities, and others, but it does not protect simple griping about a job. Although case law in the area of dismissals over social media posts is relatively new and evolving, several significant cases provide employers with guidelines to avoid legal complications. In one case, Robert Becker, a salesman at Karl Knauz BMW in Lake Bluff, Illinois, complained on his Facebook wall about the quality of food that the auto dealership provided at an on-site event promoting a new BMW model. He and several other sales representatives disapproved of serving upscale shoppers "lowbrow food" and expressed to a sales manager their concern that doing so would send the wrong message to potential customers and jeopardize their ability to generate sales of the new model. On the day of the event, Becker took photographs of his coworkers posing next to the food and a banner promoting the new BMW. A week later, Becker posted the photos on his Facebook wall with sarcastic comments mocking the dealership for "going all out" for the most significant model launch in years by serving guests "an overcooked wiener and a stale bun, semifresh apples and oranges, and the $2 cookie plate from Sam's Club."

Becker also posted photos and comments on his Facebook page about an incident that took place at the Land Rover dealership across the street that his employer also owned. A customer had let his 13-year-old son sit in the driver's seat of a new Land Rover, and the boy accidentally stepped on the accelerator and drove the car into a small pond. Becker's comments included "This is your car. This is your car on drugs." and "Finally, some action at our Land Rover store."

A week later, another car dealer in town called the owner of Karl Knauz BMW and told him about the posts on Becker's Facebook page. A part-time employee at the BMW dealership who was one of Becker's Facebook friends also told her supervisor about the posts. The dealership's sales manager, who was Becker's boss, called Becker at home and asked him to remove the posts from his page. Becker agreed and removed the offending posts immediately. When Becker returned to work, however, the sales manager confronted him with copies of the photos and posts, told Becker that they were "embarrassing" to the dealership, and fired him. Becker filed a claim for wrongful termination with the National Labor Relations Board.

Administrative law judge Joel Biblowitz heard testimony from the sales manager that the dealership had decided to fire Becker because of his Facebook post about the Land Rover accident and not his comments about the food at the BMW sales promotion. The sales manager testified that he thought that Becker's comments about the sales promotion were "somewhat comical" and that he was more upset about Becker's comments about the Land Rover incident because Becker had made light of a serious accident. Judge Biblowitz ruled that Becker's Facebook posts about the sales promotion was protected activity under the NLRA and that Becker could not be fired for it. "Although the employee posted the photographs on Facebook and wrote the comments himself, this type of activity was clearly concerted," says the judge. "He was vocalizing the sentiments of his coworkers and continuing the course of concerted activity that began when the salespeople raised their concerns at the staff meeting. Further, this concerted activity clearly was related to the employees' terms and conditions of employment. Since the employees worked entirely on commission, they were concerned about the impact the employer's choice of refreshments would have on sales, and therefore, their commissions."

The judge ruled, however, that Becker's Facebook posts about the Land Rover incident were not "protected concerted activity" and that the dealership had not wrongfully terminated him for it. Because Becker had not discussed the accident with other employees and because the postings about the accident had no connection to employees' terms and conditions of employment, the judge ruled that Becker's posts did not constitute protected concerted activity.

What steps can companies take to minimize the probability that they will violate the law if an employee posts negative comments on social media?

- ***Establish a social media policy.*** Legal experts say that the best defense against legal action is to create a social media policy that defines what is and is not appropriate for social media. Unfortunately, fewer than half of U.S. companies (and fewer still small businesses) have a social media policy.

- ***Make sure the social media policy is legal.*** The ideal social media policy balances respect for employees' privacy with the need for employees to maintain professional standards. A company's social media policy cannot be overly broad—for instance, forbidding employees to post anything about work, prohibiting them from criticizing the company on social media, or preventing them from engaging in activities that are protected by federal labor laws.

- ***Ensure that employees understand the importance of respecting confidential information on social media.*** A company's policy should prohibit employees from posting

(continued)

You Be the Consultant *(continued)*

comments concerning confidential information available to them through their jobs.

- **Train employees.** Once a company has established a policy, management's responsibility is to train employees concerning its implementation. Training employees on the proper use of social media also helps.

1. Do you agree with the judge's ruling in the Karl Knauz BMW case? Explain.

2. Have you observed a post on social media that might (or did) land an employee in trouble with his or her employer? If so, describe the post and why the employer would be upset about it.

3. Conduct an online search for cases in which employees have been fired for their social media posts about the company that employs them or their managers. (The National Labor Relations Board's Web site, www.nlrb.gov, provides useful resources.) Select a case that you find interesting and

prepare a brief summary of the case, outlining the facts, the issues in question, and the judge's ruling. Do you agree with the ruling? Explain.

Sources: Based on David B. Ritter, "NLRB on Social Media: Facebook Firing Didn't Break Law," *Business Management Daily*, February 1, 2012, http://www.businessmanagementdaily.com/28881/nlrb-on-social-media-facebook-firing-didnt-break-law; Report of the Acting General Counsel concerning Social Media Cases within the Last Year, National Labor Relations Board, Division of Operations Management, August 18, 2011, pp. 6–9; Ameet Sachdev, "Judge Backs Car Dealer That Fired Employee over Facebook Post," *Chicago Tribune*, October 1, 2011, http://articles.chicagotribune.com/2011-10-01/business/ct-biz-1001-nlrb-20111001_1_facebook-post-karl-knauz-bmw-dealership; Dave Jameison, "Facebook Posting Led to Workers Unfair Firing: Feds," *Huffington Post*, July 24, 2011, http://www.huffingtonpost.com/2011/05/24/facebook-posting-worker-fired_n_866353.html; Mikal E. Belicove, "Employees' Facebook Posts Give Businesses Heartburn," *Entrepreneur*, October 5, 2011, http://www.entrepreneur.com/blog/220462; Jeannette Borzo, "Employers Tread a Minefield," *Wall Street Journal*, January 21, 2011, p. B6; Kashmir Hill, "When You Can and Can't Fire Employees for Social Media Misbehavior," *Forbes*, August 5, 2011, http://www.forbes.com/sites/kashmirhill/2011/08/25/when-you-can-and-cant-fire-employees-for-social-media-misbehavior; and Lisa Skapinker, "How to Set a Social Media Policy That Won't Get Your Employees Fired," *Rypple*, May 17, 2012, http://rypple.com/blog/2012/05/how-to-set-a-social-media-policy-that-wont-get-your-employees-fired.

---

supervisor) to "call the shots"? At Intuit, employees have the autonomy to spend 10 percent of their time working on projects that they believe will benefit the company.[72]

- *Feedback* is the degree to which a job gives the worker direct, timely information about the quality of his or her performance. Does the job give the employee feedback about the quality of his or her work, or does the product (and all information about it) simply disappear after it leaves the worker's station?

A study conducted by researchers at the University of New Hampshire and the Bureau of Labor Statistics concludes that employees of companies that use job enrichment principles are more satisfied than those who work in jobs designed using principles of simplification.[73]

flextime

an arrangement under which employees work a normal number of hours but have flexibility about when they start and stop work.

Flextime is an arrangement under which employees work a normal number of hours but have flexibility about when they start and stop work. Most flextime arrangements require employees to build their work schedules around a set of "core hours," such as 10 a.m. to 2 p.m., but give them the freedom to set their schedules outside of those core hours. For instance, one worker might choose to come in at 7 a.m. and leave at 3 p.m. to attend her son's soccer game, and another may work from 11 a.m. to 7 p.m. Flextime not only raises worker morale but also makes it easier for companies to attract high-quality young workers who want rewarding careers without sacrificing their lifestyles. In addition, companies using flextime schedules often experience lower levels of tardiness, turnover, and absenteeism.

ENTREPRENEURIAL PROFILE: Pamela Blackwell: Blackwell Consulting Services Pamela Blackwell, president of Blackwell Consulting Services, an information technology consulting firm in Chicago that her father Bob started in 1992, says that flextime plays an important part in attracting skilled, high-tech workers whom the company relies on for its success. "We're more focused on the job and delivering on client expectations than on how, when, and where our employees work," she says.[74] ∎

Flextime is becoming an increasingly popular job design strategy, especially among small companies. A recent study by the Families and Work Institute found that 77 percent of U.S. businesses give at least some of their employees flexible schedules, up from 68 percent in 1998. However, 32 percent of small companies (fewer than 100 employees) offer most or all of their employees flexible schedules, compared to just 16 percent of large companies (more than 1,000 employees).[75] The number of companies using flextime is likely to continue to grow as companies find recruiting capable, qualified full-time workers more difficult and as technology makes working from a dedicated office space less important. Research shows that when considering job offers, candidates, particularly members of Generation Y, weigh heavily the flexibility of the work schedule that companies offer.[76]

Job sharing is a work arrangement in which two or more people share a single full-time job. For instance, two college students might share the same 40-hour-a-week job, one working mornings and the other working afternoons. Salary and benefits are prorated between the workers sharing a job. Because job sharing is a simple solution to the growing challenge of life–work balance, it is becoming more popular. Companies already using it are finding it easier to recruit and retain qualified workers. "Employers get the combined strengths of two people, but they only have to pay for one," says one hotel sales manager, herself a job sharer.[77]

Flexplace is a work arrangement in which employees work at a place other than the traditional office, such as a satellite branch closer to their homes or, in many cases, at home. Flexplace is an easy job design strategy for companies to use because of **telecommuting**. Using modern communication technology such as WiFi, smart phones, texting, e-mail, and instant messaging, employees have more flexibility in choosing where they work. Today, connecting electronically to the workplace (and to all of the people and the information there) from practically anywhere on the planet is quite simple for many workers. The Telework Research Network estimates that 45 percent of workers in the United States have the potential to telecommute at least some of the time.[78] However, a survey by Reuters and the global market research firm Ipsos reports that only 9 percent of employees in North America telecommute frequently, well below the global average of 17 percent.[79] Telecommuting employees get the flexibility they seek, and they also benefit from reduced commuting times and expenses, not to mention a less expensive wardrobe (bathrobes and bunny slippers compared to business suits and wingtips). Companies reap many benefits as well, including improved employee morale, less absenteeism, lower turnover, higher productivity, and more satisfied, more loyal employees. Studies show that telecommuting can reduce employee turnover by 20 percent and increase productivity between 15 and 20 percent.[80] Even though many small companies are ideally suited for telecommuting, large companies use this job design strategy more than small companies.[81]

ENTREPRENEURIAL PROFILE: Jonathan Hilland: MindWave Research Fourteen of 23 employees at MindWave Research, a market research company in Austin, Texas, telecommute either all or most of the time. For a total cost of $30,000, the company installed in their home offices fast computers; reliable, high-speed Internet connections to the company's central computer; and Web cameras for videoconferencing. Because of telecommuting, Jonathan Hilland, CEO of the $5 million company, was able to move MindWave's office to a smaller space, saving $7,000 per month in rent.[82] ∎

Motivating Employees to Higher Levels of Performance: Rewards and Compensation

Another important aspect of creating a culture that attracts and retains quality workers is establishing a robust system of rewards and compensation. The rewards that an employee gets from the job itself are intrinsic rewards, but managers have at their disposal a wide variety of extrinsic rewards (those outside the job itself) to attract, retain, and motivate workers. The keys to using rewards to motivate are linking them to performance and tailoring them to the needs and characteristics of the workers. Entrepreneurs must base rewards and compensation on what is really important to their employees. For instance, to a technician making $25,000, a chance to earn a $3,000 performance bonus would most likely be a powerful motivator. To an executive earning $175,000 a year, it may not be.

One of the most popular rewards is money. Cash is an effective motivator—up to a point. Simple performance bonuses are a common reward at many companies. The closer the bonus payment is to the action that prompted it, the more effective it will be.

ENTREPRENEURIAL PROFILE: Robert Verdun: Computer Facility Integration At Computer Facility Integration (CFI), a technology installation company in Southfield, Michigan, CEO Robert Verdun pays his 75 employees bonuses at the end of every month in which they meet specific performance targets. "We clearly state what everyone should be achieving, and we reward people accordingly," he says. CFI's sales are growing at 30 percent per year, and its employee turnover rate is just 4 percent per year, compared to the industry average of 30 percent.[83] ∎

---

job sharing
a work arrangement in which two or more people share a single full-time job.

flexplace
a work arrangement in which employees work at a place other than the traditional office, such as a satellite branch closer to their homes or at home.

telecommuting
an arrangement in which employees working remotely use modern communications equipment to connect electronically to their workplaces.

pay-for-performance compensation systems compensation systems in which employees' pay depends on how well they perform their jobs.

Other companies have moved to **pay-for-performance compensation systems**, in which employees' pay depends on how well they perform their jobs. In other words, extra productivity equals extra pay. By linking employees' compensation directly to the company's financial performance, a business owner increases the likelihood that workers will achieve performance targets that are in their best interest and in the company's best interest. Pay-for-performance systems work only when employees see a clear connection between their performance and their pay, however. That's where small businesses have an advantage over large businesses. Because they work for small companies, employees can see more clearly the impact that their performances have on the company's profitability and ultimate success than their counterparts at large corporations.

profit-sharing plan a reward system in which employees receive a portion of the company's profits.

Some companies offer their employees financial rewards in the form of **profit-sharing plans** in which employees receive a portion of the company's profits. At Rackspace Hosting, a company that provides Web hosting and cloud computing services, employees (affectionately known as "Rackers") participate in a generous profit-sharing plan and are part owners of the company thanks to stock options they receive.[84] A few companies have gone even farther, coupling profit sharing plans with **open-book management**, a system in which entrepreneurs share openly their companies' financial results with employees. The goal is teach employees how their job performances have a direct impact on profits and to give them an incentive for improving the company's bottom line. "Open book [management] gives everyone the chance to see what we need to do to succeed," says Jack Stack, CEO of SRC Holdings, a holding company of 26 employee-owned businesses and a longtime advocate of open-book management.[85]

open-book management a system in which entrepreneurs share openly their companies' financial results with employees.

ENTREPRENEURIAL PROFILE: Trish Karter: Dancing Deer Baking Company Dancing Deer Baking Company, a Boston-based bakery that sells baked goods made from all-natural ingredients, uses open-book management and distributes 15 percent of the company's after-tax net income to all of the company's 35 employees on a pro rata basis. Managers regularly present the details of the Dancing Deer's financial performance to employees. "We all rise and fall together," says Trish Karter, CEO and cofounder. Employees know that "if they're more productive and efficient, they see it at the end of the year in the profits and in their salaries."[86] ∎

Money isn't the only motivator business owners have at their disposal, of course. In fact, money tends to be only a short-term motivator. In addition to the financial compensation they provide, most companies offer their employees a wide array of benefits, ranging from stock options and medical insurance to retirement plans and tuition reimbursement. **Stock options**, a plan under which the employees can purchase shares of a company's stock at a fixed price, have become a popular benefit for employees. Stock options take on real value once the market price of a company's stock exceeds the exercise price, the price at which employees can purchase stock. (Note that if the fair market price of a stock never exceeds the exercise price, the stock option is useless.) When trying to attract and retain quality employees, many small companies rely on stock options to gain an edge over larger companies offering bigger salaries. Stock options produce a huge payoff for employees when companies succeed. Workers at highly successful companies such as Microsoft, Google, and Dell have retired as multimillionaires thanks to stock options.

stock options a plan under which employees can purchase shares of a company's stock at a fixed price.

Benefits packages also are an important part of attracting and retaining quality workers and achieving high productivity. A recent survey by MetLife shows that employees who are satisfied with their benefits demonstrate more loyalty to their employers and are less likely to leave than those who are not. The most important benefit? Health insurance.[87] Shortly after hiring his first employee, Tim Storm, founder of Fat Wallet, the online discount retailer, realized that to attract the talent he needed to build his company, he would have to enhance its employee benefits package. "We knew we couldn't compete [for talent] if we didn't offer, at the very least, health insurance," says April Kunzelman, the company's human resources director. "So we immediately began putting an employee benefits package in place." Today, Fat Wallet offers its 60 employees an impressive array of benefits, ranging from health, dental, and disability insurance to free lunches.[88]

cafeteria benefit plan a plan under which employers provide certain basic benefits and then allocate a specific dollar amount for employees to select the benefits that suit their needs best.

In an economy in which they must compete aggressively for employees, entrepreneurs must recognize that compensation and benefits no longer follow a "one-size-fits-all" pattern. The diversity of today's workforce requires employers to be highly flexible and innovative with the compensation and benefits they provide. To attract and retain quality workers, creative entrepreneurs offer employees benefits designed to appeal to their employees' particular needs. This diversity has led to the popularity of **cafeteria benefit plans**, in which employers provide certain base benefits and then allocate a specific dollar amount for employees to select the benefits that suit their needs best. To provide the best package of benefits most efficiently, employers should survey their employers periodically to discover which benefits are most important to them and then build their benefits package to include them. Online shoe retailer Zappos, which is consistently listed as one of *Fortune*'s "Top 100 Companies to Work For," conducts benefits surveys of its employees throughout the year and adjusts its benefits package accordingly.[89]

Beyond flexible benefits plans, many small companies are setting themselves apart from others by offering unique benefits, including the following:

- Employees of Clif Bar, a 65-employee company that makes energy bars, can scale the 22-foot-high climbing wall located in the company gym during breaks. Clif Bar also hires trainers to conduct classes in aerobics, weightlifting, and other workouts on company time.

- Employees at Autodesk bring their dogs to work and get a six-week paid sabbatical leave every four years to pursue some topic of interest to them.

- Google, the search engine company based in Mountain View, California, offers free organic food, laundry machines, a gym, massages, volleyball court, bike repairs, and medical care—all on-site. "We provide many unusual benefits to our employees, but we are careful to consider the long-term advantages to the company of these benefits," explain cofounders Sergey Brin and Larry Page.[90]

Many small business owners whose companies may not be able to afford benefits such as these find other ways to reward their employees, including vacation days on their birthdays, an occasional catered lunch (especially after completing a big project successfully), and free tickets to a local game, movie, or performance.

Besides the wages, salaries, and attractive benefits they use as motivators, creative entrepreneurs have discovered that intangible incentives can be more important sources of employee motivation. After its initial impact, money loses its effectiveness; it does not have a lasting motivational effect (which for small businesses, with their limited resources, is a plus). For many workers, the most meaningful motivational factors are the simplest ones—praise, recognition, feedback, job security, promotions, and others—things that any small business, no matter how limited its budget, can do. When the economy is in a downturn, a business that can display its commitment to employees through a record of job security has a powerful tool to recruit good employees.

Praise is another simple yet powerful motivational tool. People enjoy getting praise, especially from a manager or business owner; it's just human nature. As Mark Twain said, "I can live for two months on a good compliment." One recent survey reports that 86 percent of U.S. workers want to be recognized for doing a good job, and 78 percent say that they would work harder if managers recognized and appreciated their efforts.[91] Praise is an easy and inexpensive reward for employees producing extraordinary work. A short note to an employee for a job well done costs practically nothing, yet it can be a potent source of motivation. Barbara Corcoran, founder of The Corcoran Group, awarded her company's top performers each week with colored ribbons and annual "Salesperson of the Year" trophies as if they had just won an Olympic event. Edith Salton, a senior vice president for the company, recalls, "People said, 'This is really silly.' But they loved having those ribbons hanging on their desks." Corcoran realized that recognition often is a better motivator than money after visiting her top salesperson's home and seeing a large cabinet in the middle of her living room in which she proudly displayed the five "Salesperson of the Year" trophies that she had won.[92] How often have you had an employer recognize you and say "thank you" for a job you performed well?

Because they lack the financial resources of bigger companies, small business owners must be more creative when it comes to giving rewards that motivate workers. In many cases, however, using rewards other than money gives small businesses an advantage because they usually have more impact on employee performance over time. Rewards do not have to be expensive to be effective, and managers are not the only ones who can give them. At Interface Software, the CRM software development company, employees hand out STAR (Special Thanks and Recognition) cards that are redeemable for free merchandise to coworkers who go above and beyond the call of duty in their jobs. An employee team selects a weekly winner from the nominees, and every Monday morning that person receives a special glass trophy and a blue ribbon at his or her work space.[93]

Entrepreneurs tend to rely more on nonmonetary rewards, such as praise, recognition, game tickets, dinners, letters of commendation, and others, to create a work environment in which employees take pride in their work, enjoy it, are challenged by it, and get excited about it. In other words, the employees act like owners of the business.

Management Succession: Passing the Torch of Leadership

More than 80 percent of all companies in the world are family owned, and their contributions to the global economy are significant. In the United States alone, family businesses create 57 percent of the nation's gross domestic product, employ 60 percent of the private sector workforce, and account for 65 percent of all wages paid. Not all family-owned businesses are small, however; 35 percent of *Fortune* 500 companies are family businesses. Family-owned companies such as Wal-Mart, Ford, Mars, Cargill, and Winn-Dixie employ thousands of people and generate billions of dollars in annual revenue.[94] Family firms also create 78 percent of the U.S. economy's net new jobs and are responsible for many famous products, including Heinz ketchup, Levi's jeans, and classic toys, such as the Slinky and the Wiffle Ball.[95]

Unfortunately, the stumbling block for most family businesses is management succession. Just when they are ready to make the transition from one generation of leaders to the next, family businesses are most vulnerable. Nearly 70 percent of first-generation businesses fail to survive into the second generation; of those that do survive, only 12 percent make it to the third generation, and just 3 percent make it to the fourth generation and beyond.[96]

ENTREPRENEURIAL PROFILE: James Cooley, Brandi Easler-Cooley, and Bethani Cooley: Strawberry Hill USA Strawberry Hill USA, a family business that operates a 1,000-plus-acre farm, produce stands, and a café in rural Spartanburg County, South Carolina, is in its third generation of family ownership. Gene Cooley started Strawberry Hill USA in 1946, and granddaughters Brandi Cooley-Easler and Bethani Cooley now manage the business with help from their father, James. "I'm very fortunate to have two daughters who want to carry on this tradition," says James.[97] ■

Like Strawberry Hill USA, more family businesses are being handed over to women. Nearly one-fourth of family businesses are led by women, and nearly one-third of family business CEOs say that the next leader will be a woman.[98]

The average life expectancy of a family business is 24 years, although some last *much* longer.[99] For instance, the oldest family business in the world is Houshi Ryokan, an inn and spa that was built near a hot spring in Komatsu, Japan, in 718 by Gengoro Sasakiri. Today, the forty-sixth generation of Sasakiri's descendants operate the inn, which can accommodate 450 guests in its 100 rooms.[100]

The primary causes of lack of continuity among family businesses are inadequate estate planning, failure to create a management succession plan, and lack of funds to pay estate taxes.[101] In addition, sibling rivalries, fights over control of the business, and personality conflicts often lead to nasty battles that can tear families apart and destroy once thriving businesses. The best way to avoid deadly turf battles and conflicts is to develop a succession plan for the company. Numerous studies have found a positive relationship between the existence of a management succession plan and the longevity of family businesses.

Although business founders inevitably want their businesses to survive them and almost 81 percent intend to pass them on to family members, they seldom support their intentions with a plan to accomplish that goal. A recent survey by PriceWaterhouseCoopers reports that 47 percent of family business owners have no management succession plan in place.[102] Often, the reason for failing to develop a succession plan is that the entrepreneur is unwilling to make tough and potentially disruptive family-oriented decisions that require selecting the successor. Family feuds often erupt over who is (and is not) selected as the successor in the family business.

Most of the family businesses in existence today were started after World War II, and their founders are ready to pass the torch of leadership on to the next generation. Experts estimate that by 2055, $41 trillion in wealth will be transferred from one generation to the next, much of it through family businesses.[103] For these companies to have a smooth transition from one

Hands On . . . How To

Make Your Small Business a Great Place to Work

Smart entrepreneurs know that although they may be the driving force behind their businesses, their highly committed and engaged employees are the *real* keys to their companies' success. As a result, these entrepreneurs carefully select their employees, develop their talents through training and education, and create a culture reflects that the central role that their employees play in the success of their businesses. Following are 11 lessons for creating a great workplace drawn from small companies that have been recognized by *Inc.* magazine as Top Small Company Workplaces.

Lesson 1. Take a long-term view of your business. Owners of small, privately held companies have a distinct advantage over managers in large, publicly held firms in that they can make decisions that are in the best interest of their companies for the long haul rather than managing to meet quarterly financial expectations. These companies are willing to sacrifice short-term results for long-term stability and success. Eric Leighton, founder of LoadSpring Solutions, a company that provides customized project management software, recognizes that his company's success hinges on his employees, and the company culture reflects his emphasis on workers. Every employee with at least two years of tenure receives an additional week of vacation and a $5,000 stipend to travel abroad. The policy "sends a message to all new hires and employees that we care about you," says Leighton.

Lesson 2. Recognize your company's responsibility to society. These leading small companies strive for more than profitability; they aim to make a difference in the world, both locally and globally, and they get their employees involved in their efforts. At Golden Artist Colors, an acrylics paint manufacturing company in New Berlin, New York, cofounder Mark Golden encourages his employees to give back to the community by giving them 40 hours of paid time for participating in volunteer service.

Lesson 3. Honest, open, two-way communication helps your company in good times and bad times. Managers at these small companies recognize that good communication is a key to building trust with employees and to encouraging them to participate in making decisions that make the workplace better. At One Call Now, a company that provides a high-speed telephone message delivery service, founder Leib Lurie uses open-book management, sharing with employees all of the company's financial statements and teaching them how to read them. He also works closely with them to set goals and objectives so that they can see how their jobs directly affect the company's profits. At One Call Now, employees also can bring their pets to work, something that Lurie says has helped contribute to the company's below-average employee turnover rate.

Lesson 4. Teamwork counts. Managers at leading small companies understand that a genuine team spirit leads to innovation, unparalleled productivity, and a fun atmosphere of camaraderie. They rely on team-based awards and recognition to encourage a team spirit and help employees understand how their jobs fit into the "big picture." At Jump Associates, an innovation consulting company in San Mateo, California, employees gather every morning for a "scrum," a short meeting in which they learn about company news, do quick yoga exercises, and engage in a short, creativity-stimulating game to get them energized for the day.

Lesson 5. Investing in your employees is one of the best investments you can make. Scott Mitchell, CEO of Southern Rewinding, a small company in Columbus, Georgia, that provides sales and service for electric motors, also uses open-book management with his company's 60-plus employees. The tradition started with informal lunch meetings between Mitchell and employees during which employees could ask questions about the company. Southern Rewinding employees work in cross-functional teams to encourage greater trust, accountability, and communication throughout the company. Mitchell also invests in his employees, offering them extensive technical training opportunities and tuition assistance and paid time off for off-site courses they take.

Lesson 6. Work space design affects teamwork, collaboration, and productivity. At rbb Public Relations in Miami, Florida, CEO Christine Barney recently remodeled the company's office, nicknamed "Casa rbb," eliminating cubicles and creating a communal space that encourages teamwork, interaction, and collaboration, which are vital to stimulating the lifeblood of the company's business: creativity. The design also includes homelike features, including a kitchen/library area, a den that allows employees to collaborate or brainstorm ideas, and an exercise room. The design reflects the company's culture of involvement in which every employee joins one of four operational groups to decide what to buy, what to develop, what to market, and how to make a more cohesive office.

Lesson 7. Give your employees a real sense of ownership. Every employer's dream is to have employees who act like owners of the company. The best way to achieve that is to make them owners of the company! Kim Jordan and Jeff Lebesch, a husband-and-wife team who launched the New Belgium Brewing Company in 1991, believed that allowing their employees to own part of the company would increase their level of engagement. The copreneurs created an employee stock ownership plan (ESOP), and employees now own 43 percent of the company. Jordan and Lebesch also practice open-book management and teach employees how to read the company's financial statements. Even in the leading small companies that do not offer ESOPs, employees receive some kind of performance-based compensation, such as profit sharing or stock options. The result is an ownership

(continued)

Hands On . . . How To *(continued)*

mentality and a workforce that is dedicated to making the company successful.

Lesson 8. Encourage your employees to stay healthy.

With health care costs rising rapidly, smart business owners know that anything they can do to help their employees stay healthy not only lowers costs but also helps their employees lead better personal and work lives. Many of these leading small companies pay 100 percent of the cost of their employees' health insurance. Others provide incentives for employees to improve their health by quitting smoking, reaching and maintaining an ideal weight, or exercising regularly. Some companies provide on-site exercise facilities or pay for employees memberships at local gyms. At ReadyTalk, a Denver, Colorado–based company that provides Web conferencing and international audio conferencing services, employees not only own part of the company through an ESOP but also have the opportunity to participate in on-site yoga classes and massage services. The company also pays a portion of employees' gym memberships. "People who take care of themselves are going to have higher levels of energy and are going to be more balanced in terms of work-life," observes CEO Dan King.

Lesson 9. Recognize your employees' stellar performances publicly and privately—and often. At

Knight Point Systems, a company that solves information technology problems for its clients, cofounder Rober Eisiminger says that every employee embodies the company's "4 Cs" core values—candor, competence, commitment, and confidence—and are rewarded for stellar performance. Employees can nominate other employees for the annual 4C Award that recognizes the worker who best exhibits commitment

to the 4 Cs. The award includes a $1,000 prize and an all-expenses-paid exotic vacation. At Torch Technologies, recognition is not as elaborate but no less effective. CEO Bill Roark recognizes employees' outstanding performances with a handwritten thank-you letter sent to their homes. "I get notes back from kids and wives that bring tears to my eyes," he says.

Lesson 10. Let your employees have fun. Just because

you are at work does not mean that you cannot have fun. At Skullcandy, a company in Park City, Utah, that sells earbuds and earphones, the primarily Generation Y workforce can bring their skateboards to work and practice on the company's half-pipe and miniramp. On big snow days, the company has a "Powder Day Policy" that prohibits work before 11 a.m. to allow employees to spend some quality time on the local ski slopes. In addition to providing medical, dental, and disability insurance, Skullcandy offers flexible work arrangements and Skull Academy, a program designed to encourage lifelong learning among employees and promotion from within.

Lesson 11. Give your employees the flexibility they need for work–life balance. Small companies that offer

flextime, job sharing, telecommuting, and other flexible work arrangements have an edge when it comes to hiring the best workers. At rbb Public Relations, CEO Christine Barney says that her employees "can work from home; they can work from the beach. We have systems in place to make that work."

Sources: Based on Gabrielle M. Blue, Dave Smith, and Drew Gannon, "2011 Top Small Company Workplaces," *Inc.*, June 2011, http://www.inc.com/top-workplaces/index.html; Kelly K. Spors, "Top Small Workplaces 2008," *Wall Street Journal*, February 22, 2009, http://online.wsj.com/article/SB122347733961315417.html; and *2008 Guide to Bold New Ideas for Making Work Work* (New York: Families and Work Institute, 2008), pp. 3–6, 42.

---

generation to the next, they must develop management succession plans. Without a succession plan, family businesses face an increased risk of faltering or failing in the next generation. Family businesses with the greatest probability of surviving are the ones whose owners prepare a succession plan well before it is time to pass the torch of leadership to the next generation. Succession planning also allows business owners to minimize the impact of estate taxes on their businesses and on their successors' wealth as well.

Succession planning reduces the tension and stress of a transition by gradually "changing the guard." A well-developed succession plan is like the smooth, graceful exchange of a baton between runners in a relay race. The new runner still has maximum energy; the concluding runner has already spent his or her his or energy by running at maximum speed. The athletes never come to a stop to exchange the baton; instead, the handoff takes place on the move. The race is a skillful blend of the talents of all team members; the exchange of leadership is so smooth and powerful that the business never falters but accelerates, fueled by a new source of energy at each leg of the race.

HOW TO DEVELOP A MANAGEMENT SUCCESSION PLAN Creating a succession plan involves the following steps:

Step 1. *Select the successor.* There comes a time for even the most dedicated company founder to step down from the helm of the business and hand the reins over to the next generation. Between 2008 and 2018, 12 million business owners will retire from their companies, looking either to sell them or to hand them over to the next generation.[104] Unfortunately, only 41 percent of family business owners have

"Someday, son, over my dead body, all of this will be yours."

Mick Stevens/Cartoon Bank

identified their successors.[105] "Leaving is a subject most business owners would rather not think about, so they put off dealing with it as long as they can," explains a longtime editor of *Inc.* magazine. "But make no mistake: Sooner or later, every entrepreneur leaves the company he or she has built."[106]

Entrepreneurs should never assume that their children want to take control of the family business, however. It is critical to remember at this juncture in the life of a business that children do not necessarily inherit their parents' entrepreneurial skills and interests. By leveling with the children about the business and their options regarding a family succession, the owner will know which heirs, if any, are willing to assume leadership of the business.

When naming a successor, merit is a better standard to use than birth order. When considering a successor, an entrepreneur should consider taking the following actions:

- Let family members, especially children, know that joining the business is not mandatory. Family members' goals, ambitions, and talents should be foremost in their career decisions. "The odds of a good [succession] outcome improve when the child has grown up in the business, helping out on weekends and vacations, and perhaps learns to see a future in it," says Meg Hirshberg, whose husband Gary is the founder of Stonyfield Yogurt.[107]
- Do not assume that a successor must always come from within the family. Simply being born into a family does *not* guarantee that a person will make a good business leader. A recent survey by PriceWaterhouseCoopers reports that 34 percent of leaders of family businesses in North America with succession plans say that the next top manager will come from outside the family.[108]
- Give family members the opportunity to work outside the business first to learn firsthand how others conduct business. Working for others will allow them to develop knowledge, confidence, and credibility before stepping back into the family business. Seventy percent of the successors who have been identified have full-time work experience outside the family business.[109]

One of the worst mistakes entrepreneurs can make is to postpone naming a successor until just before they are ready to step down. The problem is especially acute when more than one family member works for the company and is interested in assuming leadership of it. Sometimes founders avoid naming successors because they don't want to hurt the family members who are not chosen to succeed them. However, both the business and the family will be better off if, after observing the family members as they work in the business, the founder picks a successor on the basis of that person's skills and abilities.

ENTREPRENEURIAL PROFILE: Irwin and James Monroe Smucker: J.M. Smucker Company J.M. Smucker Company, the well-known maker of jams and jellies, has had five CEOs since James Monroe Smucker started the company in Orrville, Ohio, in 1897, and every one of them has been a member of the Smucker family. Well before Paul, the grandson of founder J.M., stepped down from the company's helm in 1961, he named both of his sons, Timothy and Richard Smucker as co-CEOs. Timothy and Richard currently are grooming their sons, Mark Smucker and Paul Smucker Wagstaff, to become the fifth-generation coleaders of the company. Mark and Paul, both in their early forties, have held a variety of positions in the company and currently are in charge of two major divisions. "We would like for them to share the CEO job," says Richard, "but it's not a *fait accompli.*"[110] ∎

Step 2.   *Create a survival kit for the successor.* Once he or she identifies a successor, an entrepreneur should prepare a survival kit and then brief the future leader on its contents, which should include all of the company's critical documents (wills, trusts, insurance policies, financial statements, bank accounts, key contracts, corporate bylaws, and so forth). The founder should be sure that the successor reads and understands all of the relevant documents in the kit.

Step 3.   *Groom the successor.* Typically, founders transfer their knowledge to their successors gradually over time. The discussions that set the stage for the transition of leadership are time consuming and require openness by both parties. In fact, grooming a successor is the founder's greatest teaching and development responsibility, and it takes time and deliberate effort. To create ability and confidence in a successor, a founder must be

- patient, realizing that the transfer of power is gradual and evolutionary and that the successor should earn responsibility and authority one step at a time until the final transfer of power takes place;
- willing to accept that the successor will make mistakes;
- skillful at using the successor's mistakes as a teaching tool;
- an effective communicator and an especially tolerant listener;
- capable of establishing reasonable expectations for the successor's performance; and
- able to articulate the keys to the successor's successful performance.

Grooming a successor can begin at an early age simply by involving children in the family business and observing which ones have the greatest ability and interest in the company.

Susan Weich/St. Louis Post-Dispatch

ENTREPRENEURIAL PROFILE: Kendele Noto: J. Noto's Fine Italian Confections When Kendele Noto was 12 years old, she and her older sister Courtney began working after school in the family-run bakery her grandfather Jasper started in 1973 in St. Louis, Missouri, taking on jobs such as folding pastry boxes and refilling cookie trays. "Kendele always wanted to do more," says her father, the second-generation owner of J. Noto's Fine Italian Confections. After graduating from high school, Kendele enrolled in a culinary arts program at a local school. She decided that she did not want to go into the family business and took a job in the restaurant at a local tennis club. However, Kendele was soon drawn back to the bakery, which is run entirely by family members. Today, Kendele manages J. Noto's Fine Italian Confections, where she balances maintaining traditions, such as family recipes handed down from her Sicilian great-grandparents, with introducing important innovations, such as building a Web site and a Facebook page, marketing through Twitter, and introducing new products, such as cupcakes, minidesserts, and cake pops.[111] ∎

Step 4.   *Promote an environment of trust and respect.* Another priceless gift a founder can leave a successor is an environment of trust and respect. Trust and respect on the part of the founder and others fuel the successor's desire to learn and excel and build the successor's confidence in making decisions. Developing a competent successor typically requires at least 5 to 10 years. Empowering the successor by gradually delegating responsibilities creates an environment in which all parties can objectively view the growth and development of the successor. Customers, creditors, suppliers, and staff members can gradually develop confidence in the successor. The final transfer of power is not a dramatic, wrenching change but a smooth, coordinated passage. Founders must be careful at this stage to avoid the "meddling retiree syndrome" in which they continue to report for work after they have officially stepped down and take control of matters that are no longer their responsibility. Doing so undermines a successor's authority and credibility among workers quickly.

Step 5. ***Cope with the financial realities of estate and gift taxes.*** The final step in developing a workable management succession plan is structuring the transition to minimize the impact of estate, gift, and inheritance taxes on family members and the business. Entrepreneurs who fail to consider the impact of these taxes may force their heirs to sell a successful business just to pay the estate's tax bill. Recent tax legislation may reduce the impact of taxation on the continuity of family businesses. Currently, without proper estate planning, an entrepreneur's family members will incur a painful tax bite that can be as high as 55 percent (or more if the state also imposes an estate tax) when they inherit the business (see Table 16.8). Entrepreneurs should be actively engaged in estate planning no later than age 45; those who start businesses early in their lives or whose businesses grow rapidly may need to begin as early as age 30. A variety of options exist that may prove to be helpful in reducing the estate tax liability. Each operates in a different fashion, but their objective remains the same: to remove a portion of business owners' assets out of their estates so that when they die, those assets will not be subject to estate taxes. Many of these estate planning tools need time to work their magic, so the key is to put them in place early on in the life of the business.

buy-sell agreement
a contract among co-owners of a business stating that each agrees to buy out the others in case of the death or disability of one.

BUY-SELL AGREEMENT One of the most popular estate planning techniques is the buy-sell agreement. A **buy-sell agreement** is a contract that co-owners often rely on to ensure the continuity of a business. In a typical arrangement, the co-owners create a contract stating that each agrees to

TABLE 16.8 Changes in the Estate and Gift Taxes

As the following table illustrates, Congress is constantly tinkering with the often punishing structures of estate and gift taxes. The federal estate tax is actually interwoven with the gift tax; the impact of the two taxes began differing in 2004. Congress repealed the estate tax originally in 2010 but reinstated it in 2011. The following table shows how the exemptions and the maximum tax rates for the estate and gift taxes have changed over time.

Year	Estate Tax Exemption	Gift Tax Exemption	Maximum Tax Rate
2001	$675,000	$675,000	55%
2002	$1 million	$1 million	50%
2003	$1 million	$1 million	49%
2004	$1.5 million	$1 million	48%
2005	$1.5 million	$1 million	47%
2006	$2 million	$1 million	46%
2007	$2 million	$1 million	45%
2008	$2 million	$1 million	45%
2009	$3.5 million	$1 million	45%
2010	Tax repealed	$1 million	35% (gifts only)
2011	$5 million	$1 million	35%
2012	$5.12 million	$5 million	35%
2013 and beyond	$1 million	$1 million	55%

However the federal laws governing estate taxes may change over the next few years, entrepreneurs whose businesses have been successful cannot afford to neglect estate planning.

buy the others out in case of the death or disability of one. That way, the heirs of the deceased or disabled owner can "cash out" of the business while leaving control of the business in the hands of the remaining owners. The buy-sell agreement specifies a formula for determining the value of the business at the time the agreement is to be executed. One problem with buy-sell agreements is that the remaining co-owners may not have the cash available to buy out the disabled or deceased owner. To resolve this issue, many businesses purchase life and disability insurance for each of the owners in amounts large enough to cover the purchase price of their respective shares of the business.

ENTREPRENEURIAL PROFILE: Larry Jaffe and Bob Gross: Jaffe and Gross Larry Jaffe and Bob Gross, co-owners of Jaffe and Gross, a successful jewelry store in Dayton, Ohio, failed to create a buy-sell agreement backed by insurance for their business. When Gross died suddenly of a heart attack, Jaffe did not have enough cash to purchase Gross's share of ownership in the business. "Bob just assumed that I'd be Larry's partner and the business would go on," says Gross's widow. However, Gross's heirs, who inherited his shares of the business, had no interest in operating the jewelry store, and without a buy-sell agreement or a succession plan in place, the 27-year-old company folded. Jaffe has since launched his own jewelry store, Jaffe's Jewelers, but admits that things would have been much easier had he and Gross taken the time to create a succession plan.[112] ■

LIFETIME GIFTING The owner of a successful business may transfer money to his or her children (or other recipients) from the estate throughout his or her life. Current federal tax regulations allow individuals to make gifts of $13,000 per year, per parent, per recipient that are exempt from federal gift taxes. The recipient is not required to pay tax on the $13,000 gift that he or she receives, and the donor must pay a gift tax only on the amount of a gift that exceeds $13,000. For instance, husband-and-wife business owners could give $1,560,000 worth of stock to their three children and their spouses over a period of 10 years without incurring any estate or gift taxes at all. To be an effective estate planning strategy, lifetime gifting requires time to work, meaning that business owners must create a plan for using it early on.

trust
a contract between a grantor (the company founder) and a trustee in which the grantor gives the trustee assets (e.g., company stock) that the trustee holds for the trust's beneficiaries (e.g., the grantor's heirs).

revocable trust
a trust that a grantor can change or revoke during his or her lifetime.

irrevocable trust
a trust in which a grantor cannot require the trustee to return the assets held in trust.

SETTING UP A TRUST A **trust** is a contract between a grantor (the company founder) and a trustee (generally a bank officer or an attorney) in which the grantor gives to the trustee legal title to assets (e.g., stock in the company) that the trustee agrees to hold for the beneficiaries (the founder's children). The beneficiaries can receive income from the trust, the property in the trust, or both at some specified time. Trusts can take a wide variety of forms, but two broad categories of trusts are available: revocable trusts and irrevocable trusts. A **revocable trust** is one that a grantor can change or revoke during his or her lifetime. Under present tax laws, however, the only trust that provides a tax benefit is an **irrevocable trust**, in which the grantor cannot require the trustee to return the assets held in trust. The value of the grantor's estate is lowered because the assets in an irrevocable trust are excluded from the value of the estate. However, an irrevocable trust places severe restrictions on the grantor's control of the property placed in the trust. Although recent changes in tax laws have eliminated certain types of trusts as estate planning tools, business owners use several types of irrevocable trusts to lower their estate tax liabilities:

- *Irrevocable life insurance trust (ILIT).* This type of trust allows business owners to keep the proceeds of a life insurance policy out of their estates and away from estate taxes, freeing up that money to pay the taxes on the remainder of their estates. To get the tax benefit, business owners must be sure that the business or the trust (rather than the owners themselves) owns the insurance policy. The primary disadvantage of an ILIT is that if the owner dies within three years of establishing it, the insurance proceeds become part of the estate and *are* subject to estate taxes. Because the trust is irrevocable, it cannot be amended or rescinded once it is established. Like most trusts, ILITs must meet stringent requirements to be valid, and entrepreneurs should use experienced attorneys to create them.

- *Irrevocable asset trust.* An irrevocable asset trust is similar to a life insurance trust except that it is designed to pass the assets (such as stock in a family business) in the parents' estate on to their children. The children do not have control of the assets while the parents are living, but they do receive the income from those assets. On the parents' death, the assets in the trust go to the children without being subjected to the estate tax.

- *Grantor retained annuity trust (GRAT).* A GRAT is a special type of irrevocable trust and has become one of the most popular tools for entrepreneurs to transfer ownership of a business while maintaining control over it and minimizing estate taxes. Under a GRAT, an owner can put property (such as company stock) in an irrevocable trust for a minimum of two years. While the trust is in effect, the grantor (owner) retains the benefits associated with the assets in the trust (e.g., the voting rights associated with the stock) and receives interest income (calculated at a fixed interest rate that is determined by the Internal Revenue Service [IRS]) from the assets in the trust. At the end of the trust, the property passes to the beneficiaries (heirs). The beneficiaries are required to pay a gift tax on the value of the assets placed in the GRAT. However, the IRS taxes GRAT gifts only according to their discounted present value because the heirs did not receive use of the property while it was in trust. The primary disadvantage of using a GRAT in estate planning is that if the grantor dies during the life of the GRAT, its assets pass back into the grantor's estate. These assets then become subject to the full estate tax. A GRAT is an excellent tool for transferring the appreciation of an asset such as a growing company to heirs with few tax implications.

ENTREPRENEURIAL PROFILE: Mark Zuckerberg: Facebook Mark Zuckerberg, founder of Facebook, and seven other major shareholders in the company recently created GRATs that will save an estimated $240 million in estate taxes in the future. By setting up a GRAT with 3.4 million pre-IPO shares of Facebook stock valued at just $1.85 per share, Zuckerberg alone will avoid nearly $68 million in estate taxes (at current estate tax rates).[113] ■

Establishing a trust requires meeting many specific legal requirements and is not something business owners should do on their own. It is much better to work with experienced attorneys, accountants, and financial advisers to create them. Although the cost of establishing a trust can be high, the tax savings they generate are well worth the expense.

ESTATE FREEZE An **estate freeze** minimizes estate taxes by having family members create two classes of stock for the business: (1) preferred voting stock for the parents and (2) nonvoting common stock for the children. The value of the preferred stock is frozen, whereas the common stock reflects the anticipated increased market value of the business. Any appreciation in the value of the business after the transfer is not subject to estate taxes. However, the parent must pay gift taxes on the value of the common stock given to the children. The value of the common stock is the total value of the business less the value of the voting preferred stock retained by the parent. The parents also must accept taxable dividends at the market rate on the preferred stock they own.

FAMILY LIMITED PARTNERSHIP Creating a **family limited partnership (FLP)** allows business-owning parents to transfer their company to their children and lower their estate taxes while still retaining control over it for themselves. To create an FLP, the parents (or parent) sets up a partnership among themselves and their children. The parents retain the general partnership interest, which can be as low as 1 percent, and the children become the limited partners. As general partners, the parents control both the limited partnership and the family business. In other words, nothing in the way the company operates has to change. Over time, the parents transfer company stock into the limited partnership, ultimately passing ownership of the company to their children.

One of the principal tax benefits of an FLP is that it allows discounts on the value of the shares of company stock that the parents transfer into the limited partnership. Because a family business is closely held, shares of ownership in it, especially minority shares, are not as marketable as those of a publicly held company. As a result, company shares transferred into the limited partnership are discounted at 20 to 50 percent of their full market value, producing a large tax savings for everyone involved. The average discount is 40 percent, but that amount varies, depending on the industry and the individual company involved.

Because of their ability to reduce estate and gift taxes, FLPs became one of the most popular estate planning tools in recent years. The following tips will help entrepreneurs establish an FLP that will withstand legal challenges:

- Establish a legitimate business reason other than avoiding estate taxes—such as transferring a business over time to the next generation of family members—for creating the FLP and document it on paper.

- Make sure that all members of the FLP make contributions and take distributions according to a predetermined schedule. "Don't allow partners to use partnership funds to pay for personal expenses and do not time partnership distributions with personal needs for cash," says one attorney.[114]

estate freeze
a strategy that minimizes estate taxes by creating two classes of stock for a business: preferred voting stock for the parents and nonvoting common stock for the children.

family limited partnership (FLP)
a strategy that allows business-owning parents to transfer their company to their children (lowering their estate taxes) while still retaining control over it for themselves.

- Do not allow members to put all of their personal assets (such as a house, automobiles, or personal property) into the FLP. Commingling personal and business assets in an FLP raises a red flag to the IRS.

- Expect an audit of the FLP. The IRS tends to scrutinize FLPs, so be prepared for a thorough audit.[115]

Developing a succession plan and preparing a successor require a wide variety of skills, some of which the business founder will not have. That's why it is important to bring experts into the process when necessary. Entrepreneurs often call on their attorneys, accountants, insurance agents, and financial planners to help them build a succession plan that works best for their particular situations. Because the issues involved can be highly complex and charged with emotion, bringing in trusted advisers to help improves the quality of the process and provides an objective perspective.

Exit Strategies

LO5

Explain the exit strategies available to entrepreneurs.

Most family business founders want their companies to stay within their families, but in some cases, maintaining family control is not practical. Sometimes, no one in the next generation of family members has an interest in managing the company or has the necessary skills and experience to handle the job. In fact, 25 percent of business owners say that the next generation of family members lacks the competence to manage the family business successfully.[116] Under these circumstances, the founder must look outside the family for leadership if the company is to survive. Whatever the case, entrepreneurs must confront their mortality and plan for the future of their companies. Having a solid management succession plan in place well before retirement is near is absolutely critical to success. Entrepreneurs should examine their options once they decide it is time to step down from the businesses they have founded. Entrepreneurs who are planning to retire often use two strategies: sell to outsiders or sell to (nonfamily) insiders. We turn now to these two exit strategies.

Selling to Outsiders

As you learned in Chapter 5, selling a business to an outsider is no simple task. Done properly, it takes time, patience, and preparation to locate a suitable buyer, strike a deal, and make the transition. Advance preparation, maintaining accurate financial records, and timing are the keys to a successful sale. Too often, however, business owners, like some famous athletes, stay with the game too long until they and their businesses are well past their prime. A "fire-sale" approach rarely yields the maximum value for a business.

A straight sale may be best for those entrepreneurs who want to step down and turn the reins of the company over to someone else. However, selling a business outright is not an attractive exit strategy for those who want to stay on with the company or for those who want to surrender control of the company gradually rather than all at once.

ENTREPRENEURIAL PROFILE: Ernest Oppenheimer: De Beers SA The Oppenheimer family owned De Beers SA, the South African company that accounts for one-third of the world's rough diamond sales, since the 1920s, when Ernest Oppenheimer bought the company from its founder, Cecil Rhodes. Oppenheimer's son Harry and grandson Nicky built the company into a dominant and often controversial diamond empire, opened diamond retail outlets under the De Beers name, and created its legendary advertising slogan, "A diamond is forever." Recently, the Oppenheimer family sold De Beers SA to another diamond mining company, Anglo American PLC, for $5.1 billion. "It's the end of an era," says a spokesperson of the family's unanimous decision to sell. "This has been a very emotional decision for the family."[117] ■

Selling to Insiders

leveraged buyout (LBO)
a situation in which managers and/or employees borrow money from a financial institution to purchase a business, then they use the money from the company's operations to pay off the debt.

When entrepreneurs have no family members to whom they can transfer ownership or who want to assume the responsibilities of running a company, selling the business to employees is often the preferred option. In most situations, the options available to owners are a leveraged buyout and an employee stock ownership plan.

LEVERAGED BUYOUTS In a **leveraged buyout (LBO)**, managers and/or employees borrow money from a financial institution and pay the owner the total agreed-on price at closing; then they use the cash generated from the company's operations to pay off the debt. The drawback of this technique is that it creates a highly leveraged business. Because of the high levels of debt they take on, the new management has very little room for error. Too many management mistakes or a slowing economy has led many highly leveraged businesses into bankruptcy.

If properly structured, LBOs can be attractive to both buyers and sellers. Because they get their money up front, sellers do not incur the risk of loss if the buyers cannot keep the business operating successfully. The managers and employees who buy the company have a strong incentive to make sure the business succeeds because they own a piece of the action and some of their capital is at risk in the business. The result can be a highly motivated workforce that works hard and makes sure that the company operates efficiently.

EMPLOYEE STOCK OWNERSHIP PLANS   Unlike LBOs, **employee stock ownership plans (ESOPs)** allow employees and/or managers (i.e., the future owners) to purchase the business gradually, freeing up enough cash to finance the venture's future growth. With an ESOP, employees contribute a portion of their salaries and wages over time toward purchasing shares of the company's stock from the founder until they own the company outright. In leveraged ESOPs, the ESOP borrows the money to buy the owner's stock either all at once or over time. Then, using employees' contributions, the ESOP repays the loan over time. Another advantage of a leveraged ESOP is that the principal and the interest that the ESOP borrows to buy the business are tax deductible, which can save thousands or even millions of dollars in taxes. Transferring ownership to employees through an ESOP is a long-term exit strategy that benefits everyone involved. The owner sells the business to the people he or she can trust the most—his or her managers and employees. The managers and employees buy a business they already know how to run successfully. In addition, because they own the company, the managers and employees have a huge incentive to see that it operates effectively and efficiently. One study of employee stock ownership plans in privately held companies found that the ESOPs increased sales, employment, and sales per employee by 2.4 percent a year.[118] Approximately 10,900 ESOPs operate in U.S. companies, and they involve 10.3 million employee owners. In half of the companies, the ESOP controls a majority of the ownership.[119]

> **employee stock ownership plan (ESOP)**
> an arrangement in which employees and/or managers contribute a portion of their salaries and wages over time toward purchasing shares of a company's stock from the founder until they own the company outright.

ENTREPRENEURIAL PROFILE: Eileen Fisher: Eileen Fisher Inc. Eileen Fisher started her namesake clothing company in 1984 with $350 and the idea that women wanted chic, simple clothing that made getting dressed easy. Fisher developed a line of "modular" clothing in which all of the pieces could be mixed and matched to create stylish outfits. Today, the Eileen Fisher brand is available in department stores across the United States and in 52 company-owned retail stores in the United States, Canada, and Great Britain. In 2006, Fisher, who is now the company's chief creative officer, sold 31 percent of the company to her 624 employees through an ESOP. "The ESOP is an extension of what I always wanted for my company: a sense of inclusivity," says Fisher. "My employees run the business, and they deserve to own it. Over time it is my intention to move the whole company into the ESOP."[120] ■

ZUMA Press/Newscom

Chapter Summary by Learning Objective

1. **Explain the challenges involved in the entrepreneur's role as leader and what it takes to be a successful leader.**

   - Leadership is the process of influencing and inspiring others to work to achieve a common goal and then giving them the power and the freedom to achieve it.

   - Management and leadership are not the same, yet both are essential to a small company's success. Leadership without management is unbridled; management without leadership is uninspired. Leadership gets a small business going; management keeps it going.

2. **Describe the importance of hiring the right employees and how to avoid making hiring mistakes.**

   - The decision to hire a new employee is an important one for every business, but its impact is magnified many times in a small company. Every new hire a business owner makes determines the heights to which the company can climb—or the depths to which it will plunge.

   - To avoid making hiring mistakes, entrepreneurs should develop meaningful job descriptions and job specifications, plan and conduct an effective interview, and check references before hiring any employee.

3. Explain how to create a company culture that encourages employee retention.

- Company culture is the distinctive, unwritten code of conduct that governs the behavior, attitudes, relationships, and style of an organization. Culture arises from an entrepreneur's consistent and relentless pursuit of a set of core values that everyone in the company can believe in. Small companies' flexible structures can be a major competitive weapon.

- Job design techniques for enhancing employee motivation include job enlargement, job rotation, job enrichment, flextime, job sharing, and flexplace (which includes telecommuting).

- Money is an important motivator for many workers but not the only one. The key to using rewards such as recognition and praise and to motivate involves tailoring them to the needs and characteristics of the workers.

4. Describe the steps in developing a management succession plan for a growing business that allows a smooth transition of leadership to the next generation.

- As their companies grow, entrepreneurs must begin to plan for passing the leadership baton to the next generation well in advance. A succession plan is a crucial element in successfully transferring a company to the next generation. Preparing a succession plan involves five steps: (1) select the successor, (2) create a survival kit for the successor, (3) groom the successor, (4) promote an environment of trust and respect, and (5) cope with the financial realities of estate taxes.

5. Explain the exit strategies available to entrepreneurs.

- Family business owners wanting to step down from their companies can sell to outsiders or to insiders. Common tools for selling to insiders (employees or managers) include LBOs and ESOPs.

Discussion Questions

1. What is leadership? What is the difference between leadership and management?
2. What behaviors do effective leaders exhibit?
3. Why is it so important for small companies to hire the right employees? What can small business owners do to avoid making hiring mistakes?
4. What is a job description? A job specification? What functions do they serve in the hiring process?
5. Outline the procedure for conducting an effective interview.
6. What is company culture? What role does it play in a small company's success? What threats does rapid growth pose for a company's culture?
7. Explain the differences among job simplification, job enlargement, job rotation, and job enrichment.

What impact do these different job designs have on workers?
8. Is money the "best" motivator? How do pay-for-performance compensation systems work? What other rewards are available to small business managers to use as motivators? How effective are they?
9. Why is it so important for a small business owner to develop a management succession plan? Why is it so difficult for most business owners to develop such a plan? What are the steps that are involved in creating a succession plan?
10. Briefly describe the options a small business owner wanting to pass the family business on to the next generation can take to minimize the impact of estate taxes.

Business Plan Pro™

This chapter discusses the importance of people, their roles, and how they influence an organization. The Management section is where you can address these issues in the business plan. This section of the plan captures the key information about your management team, including its strengths and its weaknesses. The Management section of the business plan also addresses other key personnel issues for the venture.

Business Plan Exercises

Review the Management section of your business plan and make certain that it addresses the important management

and personnel issues for your venture. Check to see that your plan includes the relevant concepts presented in this chapter and captures those thoughts. Think about the business culture you want to build. Assess the leadership abilities of your current management team. Are additional managers or other positions needed? Have you accounted for those new hires and the anticipated expenses associated with these additional employees? Does your plan address factors that will encourage retention of existing employees? Your plan may also benefit from succession planning or an exit strategy. Remember that you can add or modify topics of your choice within *Business Plan Pro™* by right-clicking on the outline in the left-hand navigation of the page.

On the Web

Visit www.pearsonhighered.com/scarborough and review the links that are presented under the Web Destinations tab. You will find resources that address leadership issues, interviewing techniques, employee incentive programs, succession planning, exit strategies, and other topics that you may find of value. These areas may offer additional insight for the human resource and managerial aspects of your business that you may choose to incorporate into your business plan.

Sample Plans

Review an executive summary from a sample plan that you have found beneficial. You may also want to consider these options:

- Pegasus Sports
- Sagebrush Sam's
- Salvador's Inc.

Next, review the Management sections of these plans. Note how these plans present information about their owners and their personnel. Incorporate relevant management and personnel information into your plan.

In the Software

The chapters in this book address all key aspects of creating a business plan. The final section you will complete—and one that many consider to be the most important—is the executive summary. The executive summary is the first section presented, and your plan may be judged on its value and impact alone. Your executive summary should be no more than two pages—one is even better—and its intent is to capture the highlights of your plan. In addition to communicating important concepts and ideas about your plan, the executive summary should also include key financial forecasts along with brief summaries of key sections. A concise executive summary enables the reader to quickly grasp the essence of the plan for your business. This section should be compelling, allowing the reader to see your vision for the venture and motivate him or her to want to read the entire plan.

Building Your Business Plan

Write your executive summary in *Business Plan Pro™*. This section incorporates key highlights of information in the plan ahead. Show this executive summary to others and test its effectiveness in describing the most important ideas of your business plan. Remember that the executive summary should be the most powerful and convincing pages of your business plan—a written version of your elevator pitch. Does your executive summary accomplish that goal?

Beyond the Classroom . . .

1. Visit a local business that has experienced rapid growth in the past three years and ask the owner about the specific problems he or she had to face because of the organization's growth. How did the owner handle these problems? Looking back, what would he or she do differently?

2. Contact a local small business with at least 20 employees. Does the company have job descriptions and job specifications? What process does the owner use to hire a new employee? What questions does the owner typically ask candidates in an interview?

3. Ask the owner of a small manufacturing operation to give you a tour of his or her operation. During your tour, observe the way jobs are organized. To what extent does the company use the job design concepts of job simplification, job enlargement, job rotation, job enrichment, flextime, and job sharing? Based on your observations, what recommendations would you make to the owner about the company's job design?

4. Find *Fortune*'s "100 Best Companies to Work For" or *Inc.*'s "Top Small Company Workplaces" issue. Read the profiles of the companies included on the list and develop a list of at least five ideas that you would like to incorporate into the company that you plan to launch.

5. Contact five small business owners about their plans for passing their businesses on to the next generation. Do they intend to pass the business along to a family member? Do they have a management succession plan? When do they plan to name a successor? Have they developed a plan for minimizing the effects of estate taxes? How many more years do they plan to work before retiring?

6. Entrepreneurs say that they have learned much about leadership from the movies! "Films beg to be interpreted and discussed," says one leadership consultant, "and from those discussions businesspeople come up with principles for their own jobs." A recent survey of small company CEOs by *Inc.* magazine* resulted in the following list of the best movies for leadership

---

*Leigh Buchanan and Mike Hofman, "Everything I Know about Leadership, I Learned from the Movies," *Inc.*, March 2000, pp. 58–70.

lessons: *Apollo 13* (1995), *The Bridge on the River Kwai* (1957), *Dead Poets Society* (1989), *Elizabeth* (1998), *Glengarry Glen Ross* (1992), *It's a Wonderful Life* (1946), *Norma Rae* (1979), *One Flew over the Cuckoo's Nest* (1975), *Twelve Angry Men* (1957), and *Twelve O'Clock High* (1949). Rent one of these films and watch it with a group of your classmates. After viewing the movie, discuss the leadership lessons you learned from it and report the results to the other members of your class.

Endnotes

1. Christopher Hann, "The Masters," *Entrepreneur*, March 2012, p. 56.
2. Michael Gold, "Jazzin' CEO," *Manage Smarter*, January 9, 2008, p. 1.
3. Michael Gold, "Jazzin' CEO," *Manage Smarter*, January 9, 2008, p. 1.
4. Francis Huffman, "Taking the Lead," *Entrepreneur*, November 1993, p. 101.
5. Jack Welch and Suzy Welch, "What Do Great Leaders Have in Common? They're Authentic," *Fortune*, April 9, 2012, p. 58.
6. Edward Teach, "Suspicious Minds," *CFO*, June 2006, p. 31.
7. Bill Briggs, "'Undercover Boss' Spurs Shop-Floor Changes," *MSNBC*, March 22, 2010, http://www.msnbc.msn.com/id/35912818/ns/business-careers/t/undercover-boss-spurs-shop-floor-changes/#.T8eRpcqwX3Y.
8. John Mariotti, "The Role of a Leader," *Industry Week*, February 1, 1999, p. 75.
9. Dan Schawbel, "A Sense of Humor Is Worth Big Money in the Workplace," Personal Branding Blog, September 17, 2008, http://personalbrandingblog.com/a-sense-of-humor-is-worth-big-money-in-the-workplace; Evan Carmichael, "Lesson #5: Have Fun," Famous Entrepreneur Advice, http://www.evancarmichael.com/Famous-Entrepreneurs/592/Lesson-5-Have-Fun.html.
10. Bill Breen, "The Clear Leader," *Fast Company*, March 2005, p. 66.
11. Dave Zielinski, "New Ways to Look at Leadership," *Presentations*, June 2005, pp. 26–33.
12. Kent M. Keith, "Servant Leaders Are the Best Leaders during Times of Change," *Branches*, January–February 2009, http://www.greenleaf.org/whatissl/BranchesMagazine.pdf.
13. Joel Spolsky, "My Style of Servant Leadership," *Inc.*, December 1, 2008, http://www.inc.com/magazine/20081201/how-hard-could-it-be-my-style-of-servant-leadership.html.
14. James Lea, "Leadership Is a Choice—One You Should Make Carefully," *Bizjournals*, July 16, 2007, http://sacramento.bizjournals.com/extraedge/consultants/family_business/2007/07/16/column267.html.
15. "More Than Two-Thirds of Businesses Affected by a Bad Hire in the Past Year, According to CareerBuilder Survey-Headline," *CareerBuilder*, December 8, 2011, http://www.pitchengine.com/careerbuilder/more-than-twothirds-of-businesses-affected-by-a-bad-hire-in-the-past-year-according-to-careerbuilder-surveyheadline.
16. David Meyer, "Nine Recruiting and Selection Tips to Ensure Successful Hiring," About.com, http://humanresources.about.com/od/selectemployees/a/staff_selection_p.htm.
17. Hiring Decisions Miss the Mark 50% of the Time," Corporate Executive Board, October 24, 2008, http://ir.executiveboard.com/phoenix.zhtml?c=113226&p=irol-newsArticle&ID=1205091&highlight=; "2 Out of 3 Managers Still Fear a Hiring Decision They'll Regret," DDI, March 16, 2009, http://www.ddiworld.com/about/pr_releases_en.asp?id=211.
18. "More Than Two-Thirds of Businesses Affected by Bad Hire in the Past Year, According to CareerBuilder Survey,"
CareerBuilder, December 8, 2011, http://www.pitchengine.com/careerbuilder/more-than-twothirds-of-businesses-affected-by-a-bad-hire-in-the-past-year-according-to-careerbuilder-surveyheadline.
19. Mark Foster, "The Global Talent Crisis," *Business Week*, September 19, 2008, http://www.businessweek.com/managing/content/sep2008/ca20080919_403840.htm.
20. *2012 Talent Shortage Survey Research Results* (Milwaukee, WI: ManpowerGroup, 2012), p. 5.
21. "CEOs Point to Tech as Most Disruptive External Force," *Marketing Charts*, May 30, 2012, http://www.marketingcharts.com/interactive/ceos-point-to-tech-as-most-disruptive-external-force-22194/ibm-top-external-biz-factors-may2012png.
22. Corey Hajim, "The Top Companies for Leaders," *Fortune*, October 1, 2007, pp. 113–114.
23. Jennifer Gilbert, "Choosing Wisely," *Sales & Marketing Management*, October 2004, p. 9.
24. Darren Dahl, "13 Most Common Mistakes Made When Hiring," *American Express Open Forum*, November 9, 2011, http://www.openforum.com/articles/13-most-common-mistakes-made-when-hiring.
25. "More Than Two-Thirds of Businesses Affected by Bad Hire in the Past Year, According to CareerBuilder Survey," *CareerBuilder*, December 8, 2011, http://www.pitchengine.com/careerbuilder/more-than-twothirds-of-businesses-affected-by-a-bad-hire-in-the-past-year-according-to-careerbuilder-surveyheadline.
26. "CEOs Point to Tech as Most Disruptive External Force," *Marketing Charts*, May 30, 2012, http://www.marketingcharts.com/interactive/ceos-point-to-tech-as-most-disruptive-external-force-22194/ibm-top-external-biz-factors-may2012png.
27. Jennifer Wang, "Hire Powers," *Entrepreneur*, September 2011, p. 108.
28. Chris Pentilla, "Talent Scout," *Entrepreneur*, July 2008, p. 19.
29. Peter Cappelli, "Why Companies Aren't Getting the Employees They Need," *Wall Street Journal*, October 24, 2011, pp. R1, R6.
30. Liz Welch, "The Way I Work: Gary Selkoe, Karmaloop," *Inc.*, May 2012, pp. 121–122.
31. Vickie Elmer, "Hiring without a Net: Groupon's Recruiter Speaks," *Fortune*, July 25, 2011, p. 34.
32. Christopher Caggiano, "Recruiting Secrets of the Smartest Companies Around," *Inc.*, October 1998, http://hiring.inc.com/inc/magazine/19981001/1008.html.
33. Shayndi Raice, "Friend—and Possible Employee," *Wall Street Journal*, October 24, 2011, p. R7.
34. Rita Pyrillis, "The Bait Debate," *Workforce Management*, February 2011, pp. 18–21.
35. "How to Use LinkedIn as a Recruiting Tool," National Federation of Independent Businesses, http://www.nfib.com/business-resources/business-resources-item?cmsid=55492.
36. Melissa Hennessy, "The Retirement Age," *CFO: Human Capital Issue*, 2006, pp. 43–45.

37. Colleen Leahy, "The Workforce of the Future: Older and Healthier," *CNNMoney*, January 9, 2012, http://management .fortune.cnn.com/2012/01/09/workforce-future-older.

38. Kris Maher, "A Tactical Recruiting Effort Pays Off," *Wall Street Journal*, October 24, 2011, p. R6.

39. "Innovating Human Resources," *BrainReactions*, January 16, 2007, http://www.brainreactions.com/whitepapers/ brainreactions_hr_innovation_paper.pdf, pp. 11–14; Christopher Caggiano, "Recruiting Secrets," *Inc.*, October 1998, pp. 30–42.

40. Amy Barrett, "Making Telcommuting Work," *Business Week*, October 17, 2008, http://www.businessweek.com/magazine/ content/08_70/s0810048750962.htm?chan=smallbiz_small- biz+index+page_best+of+small+biz+magazine.

41. Christopher Collins, "Human Resources Management Practices and Firm Performance in Small Business: A Look across Industries," Cornell University/Gevity Institute, March 2007, p. 4.

42. Milton Moskowitz and Robert Levering, "The 100 Best Companies to Work For," *Fortune*, February 6, 2012, pp. 117–127.

43. Paula Andruss, "Perk Up Your Business," *Entrepreneur*, May 2012, pp. 54–58.

44. Darren Dahl, "13 Most Common Mistakes Made When Hiring," *American Express Open Forum*, November 9, 2011, http://www.openforum.com/ articles/13-most-common-mistakes-made-when-hiring.

45. Michael A. McDaniel, Deborah L. Whetzel, Frank L. Schmidt, and Steven D. Maurer, "The Validity of Employment Interviews: A Comprehensive Review and Meta-Analysis," *Journal of Applied Psychology* 79, no. (August 1994): 599–616.

46. Ann Marsh, "Babbling Interviewer Disease," *Business 2.0*, March 2005, p. 54.

47. Leigh Buchanan, "Core Value: Teamwork," *Inc.*, June 2011, pp. 68–69.

48. Mike Michalowicz, "The Best Recruits May Not Be Who You Think They Are," *Wall Street Journal*, October 4, 2011, http://online.wsj.com/article/SB100014240529702045246045 76610961317004204.html.

49. Peter Bregman, "The Interview Question You Should Always Ask," *Harvard Business Publishing*, Janaury 27, 2009, http:// blogs.harvardbusiness.org/cs/2009/01/the_interview_ question_you_sho.html.

50. Kate Bonamici, "The Shoe-In," *Fortune*, January 20, 2006, p. 116.

51. William Poundstone, "How to Ace a Google Interview," *Wall Street Journal*, December 24, 2011, http://online.wsj.com/ article/SB10001424052970204552304577112522982505052 22.html.

52. "Top 25 Oddball Interview Questions of 2011," *Glassdoor*, December 28, 2011, http://www.glassdoor.com/blog/top- 25-oddball-interview-questions-2011; William Poundstone, "How to Ace a Google Interview," *Wall Street Journal*, December 24, 2011, http://online.wsj.com/article/SB100014240 5297020455230457711252298250522.html.

53. Juliette Fairley, "Employers Face Challenges in Screening Candidates," *Workforce Management*, November 2010, pp. 7, 9.

54. "Thirty-Seven Percent of Companies Use Social Networks to Research Potential Candidates, According to New Career- Builder Survey," *CareerBuilder*, April 18, 2012, http://www .careerbuilder.com/share/aboutus/pressreleasesdetail.aspx? id=pr691&sd=4/18/2012&ed=4/18/2099.

55. "Resume Falsification Statistics," *Statistic Brain*, February 16, 2012, http://www.statisticbrain.com/resume-falsification- statistics.

56. Amir Efrati and Joann S. Lublin, "Yahoo's CEO's Downfall," *Wall Street Journal*, May 15, 2012, p. B5.

57. Anne Fisher, "Staying Power: Whole Foods Market," *Fortune* Insert, July 7, 2008, p. 6.

58. Liz Welch, "The Way I Work: Greg Selkoe, Karmaloop," *Inc.*, May 2012, pp. 120–124.

59. "Core Values of the Top Small Company Workplaces," *Inc.*, June 2011, http://www.inc.com/winning-workplaces/ magazine/201106/core-values-top-small-company- workplaces.html.

60. Leigh Buchanan, "Core Values: 2011 Top Small Company Workplaces," *Inc.*, June 2011, pp. 60–74; "Aaron Levie," Stanford Technology Ventures Program, January 19, 2011, *YouTube*, http://www.youtube.com/ watch?v=GZNDnMUrKc0.

61. Damon Darlin, "When Your Start-Up Takes Off," *Business 2.0*, May 2005, p. 127.

62. Christopher Hann, "A Leading Personality," *Entrepreneur*, March 2012, p. 60.

63. "Serving the Greater Familial Good," *Winning Workplaces*, http://www.winningworkplaces.org/library/success/serving_ greater_familial_good.php.

64. Nichole L. Torres, "Let the Good Times Roll," *Entrepreneur*, November 2004, p. 57.

65. Milton Moskowitz and Robert Levering, "The Best Companies to Work For," *Fortune*, February 6, 2012, pp. 117–127.

66. *Employee Engagement Report 2011* (Skillman, NJ: Blessing- White North America, 2011), pp. 3, 9.

67. Elizabeth Lupfer, "Social Knows: Employee Engagement Statistics (August 2011 Edition)," *The Social Workplace*, August 8, 2011, http://www.thesocialworkplace.com/ 2011/08/08/social-knows-employee-engagement-statistics-au- gust-2011-edition; Elizabeth Lupfer, "Frontline Employees: Engaging the Disengaged," *The Social Workplace*, May 7, 2012, http://www.thesocialworkplace.com/2012/05/07/ frontline-employees-engaging-the-dis-engaged.

68. Jennifer Cheeseman Day, "Population Profile of the United States," U.S. Census Bureau, July 8, 2008, http://www .census.gov/population/www/pop-profile/natproj.html.

69. Roy Harris, "The Illusion of Inclusion: Why Most Corporate Diversity Efforts Fail," *CFO*, May, 2001, p. 42.

70. "How Companies Make Good Decisions," McKinsey Global Survey Results, *McKinsey Quarterly*, January 2009, http:// www.mckinseyquarterly.com/How_companies_make_good_ decisions_McKinsey_Global_Survey_Results_2282.

71. "Success Stories: Creative Communications," *Winning Workplaces*, http://www.winningworkplaces.org/library/success/ creative_communications.php.

72. Milton Moskowitz and Robert Levering, "The Best Companies to Work For," *Fortune*, February 6, 2012, pp. 117–127.

73. Robert D. Mohr and Cindy Zoghi, *Is Job Enrichment Really Enriching?* (Washington, DC: U.S. Department of Labor, U.S. Bureau of Labor Statistics, Office of Productivity and Technology, January 2006), pp. 13–15.

74. "Success Stories: A Flexible Workplace," *Winning Workplaces*, http://www.winningworkplaces.org/library/success/a_ flexible_workplace.php.

75. Kenneth Matos and Ellen Galinsky, *2012 National Study of Employers* (New York: Families and Work Institute, 2012), p. 14.

76. "Flex at a Glance," When Work Works, http://www .whenworkworks.org/research/reports.html#gissues, p. 1.

77. Carol Kleiman, "Job Sharing Working Its Way into Mainstream," *Greenville News*, August 6, 2000, p. 3G.

78. Kate Lister and Tom Harnish, *The State of Telework in the U.S.*, Telework Research Network, June 2011, pp. 4–5.

79. Karen Gottfried, "The World of Work: Global Study of Online Employees Shows One in Five (17%) Work from Elsewhere," Ipsos, January 23, 2012, http://www.ipsos-na.com/ news-polls/pressrelease.aspx?id=5486.

80. Meredith Levinson, "Survey: Telecommuting Improves Productivity, Lowers Cost," *CIO*, October 7, 2008, http://www .cio.com/article/453289/Telecommuting_Improves_

Productivity_Lowers_Costs_New_Survey_Finds; Harriet Hagestad, "New Ways to Work: Telecommuting and Job Sharing," *Career Builder*, June 23, 2006, http://www .careerbuilder.com/JobSeeker/careerbytes/CBArticle.aspx? articleID=369&cbRecursionCnt=1&cbsid=49944662f7b64 dc38639d9a3ef87dd18-204624985-R5-4.

81. Kate Lister and Tom Harnish, *The State of Telework in The U.S.*, Telework Research Network, June 2011, pp. 4–5.

82. Amy Barrett, "Making Telcommuting Work," *Business Week*, October 17, 2008, http://www.businessweek.com/magazine/ content/08_70/s0810048750962.htm?chan=smallbiz_ smallbiz+index+page_best+of+small+biz+magazine.

83. Anne Fisher, "Staying Power: Computerized Facility Integration," *Fortune* insert, July 7, 2008, p. 4.

84. Milton Moskowitz and Robert Levering, "The Best Companies to Work For," *Fortune*, February 6, 2012, pp. 117–127.

85. Darren Dahl, "Open Book Management's Lessons for Detroit," *New York Times*, May 20, 2009, http://www.nytimes .com/2009/05/21/business/smallbusiness/21open.html.

86. "On the Rise," *Winning Workplaces*, http://www .winningworkplaces.org/library/success/on_the_rise.php.

87. *Tenth Annual MetLife Study of Employee Benefits Trends*, MetLife, 2012, pp.2—22.

88. Paula Andruss, "Perk Up Your Business," *Entrepreneur*, May 2012, pp. 54–58.

89. Paula Andruss, "Perk Up Your Business," *Entrepreneur*, May 2012, pp. 54–58.

90. Milton Moskowitz and Robert Levering, "The Best Companies to Work For," *Fortune*, February 6, 2012, pp. 117–127.

91. Derek Irvine, "Spring 2012 Workforce Mood Tracker Results," *HR*, May 30, 2012, http://www.hr.com/en/app/ blog/2012/05/spring-2012-workforce-mood-tracker-results_ h2upxeod.html.

92. Christopher Hann, "A Leading Personality," *Entrepreneur*, March 2012, pp. 59–62; "Barbara Corcoran's 8 Lessons for Entrepreneurs," *Inc.Women's Summit*, December 1, 2011, http://www.inc.com/barbara-corcoran/eight-lessons-for-entrepreneurs.html.

93. "Winning Workplaces: Building a Fun Work Culture," *Small Business Review*, http://smallbusinessreview.com/ human_resources/Building_a_fun_work_culture.

94. *Annual Family Business Survey General Results and Conclusions*, Family Enterprise USA, March 2011, p. 1; Karen E. Klein, "Fathers and Daughters: Passing on the Family Business," *Bloomberg Businessweek*, December 27, 2011, http://www.businessweek.com/small-business/fathers-and-daughters-passing-on-the-family-business-12272011.html; Veronica Dagher, "Who Will Run the Family Business?," *Wall Street Journal*, March 12, 2012, p. R6.

95. Chris Arnold, "Wiffle Ball: Born and Still Made in the USA," *National Public Radio*, September 5, 2011, http://www.npr.org/ 2011/09/05/140145711/wiffle-ball-born-and-still-made-in-the-usa.

96. "Passing the Baton," *Fortune* insert, May 28, 2008, p. 60; "Facts and Figures," Family Firm Institute, http://www.ffi .org/genTemplate.asp?cid=186#us.

97. Trevor Anderson, "Young Farmers Are Finding Themselves Bucking the Trend," *Spartanburg Herald Journal*, May 29, 2012, pp. A1, A5.

98. "Family Business Facts," The Family Business Initiative, University of Vermont, http://www.uvm .edu/~vfbi/?Page=facts.html.

99. "Facts and Perspectives on Family Business around the World: United States," Family Business Institute, http://www .ffi.org/looking/fbfacts_us.pdf.

100. "Family Business: The Oldest Family Businesses in the World," Family Business School, http://thefamilybusinessschool.com/node/60.

101. "Passing the Baton," *Fortune* insert, May 28, 2008, p. 60; "Facts and Figures," Family Firm Institute, http://www.ffi .org/genTemplate.asp?cid=186#us.

102. Norbert Winkeljohan and Jacques Lesieur, *Kin in the Game: PwC Family Business Survey 2010/11*, PriceWaterhouseCoopers, p. 22.

103. Passing the Baton," *Fortune* insert, May 28, 2008, p. 60.

104. Patricia B. Gray, "The Stranger among Us," *FSB*, October 2008, pp. 86–90.

105. *Laird Norton Tyee Family Business Survey: Family to Family 2007* (Seattle: Laird Norton Tyee, 2007), p. 12.

106. Bo Burlingham, "What Am I, if Not My Business?" *Inc.*, November 2010, p. 88.

107. Meg Hirshberg, "Passing the Reins," *Inc.*, March 2011, p. 38.

108. Norbert Winkeljohan and Jacques Lesieur, *Kin in the Game: PwC Family Business Survey 2010/11*, PriceWaterhouseCoopers, p. 22.

109. *Laird Norton Tyee Family Business Survey: Family to Family 2007* (Seattle: Laird Norton Tyee, 2007), p. 15.

110. Marc Gunther, "The Making of a Future 500 Company," *Fortune*, August 16, 2010, pp. 94–98.

111. Susan Weich, "'Cake Boss' Emerges at St Charles Family's Bakery," *Stltoday*, February 22, 2012, http://www.stltoday .com/news/local/columns/susan-weich/cake-boss-emerges-at-st-charles-family-s-bakery/article_c875d31d-8aa9-5b59-914e-b651ac45eb54.html.

112. H. G. Stern and Bob Vineyard, "Death of a Salesman (and His Business)," *Insureblog*, December 13, 21, 2005, http:// insureblog.blogspot.com/2005/12/death-of-salesman-and-his-business.html; Tim Tresslar, "Jeweler Jaffe Returning to Downtown . . . Temporarily," *Dayton Business Journal*, June 9, 2006, http://dayton.bizjournals.com/dayton/ stories/2006/06/12/tidbits1.html.

113. Laura Saunders, "How Facebook's Elite Skirt Estate Tax," *Wall Street Journal*, May 12–13, 2012, p. B9.

114. Gay Jervey, "Family Ties," *FSB*, March 2006, p. 60.

115. Gay Jervey, "Family Ties," *FSB*, March 2006, p. 60; Tom Herman, "Court Ruling Bolsters Estate Planning Tool," *Wall Street Journal*, May 27, 2004, p. D1.

116. *Laird Norton Tyee Family Business Survey: Family to Family 2007* (Seattle: Laird Norton Tyee, 2007), p. 15.

117. Devon Maylie and John W. Miller, "Oppenheimer Family Bids Adieu to De Beers," *Wall Street Journal*, November 5–6, 2011, pp. B1, B3; Jana Marais and Thomas Biesheuvel, "Anglo's $5.1 Billion Deal Ends Oppenheimer's De Beers Dynasty," *Bloomberg Businessweek*, November 7, 2011, http://www.businessweek.com/news/2011-11-07/anglo-s-5-1-billion-deal-ends-oppenheimer-s-de-beers-dynasty.html.

118. "Largest Study Yet Shows ESOPs Improve Performance and Employee Benefits," National Center for Employee Ownership, http://www.nceo.org/library/esop_perf.html.

119. "A Statistical Profile of Employee Ownership," National Center for Employee Ownership, February 2012, http://www .nceo.org/articles/statistical-profile-employee-ownership; "ESOP Statistics," ESOP Association, 2010, http://www .esopassociation.org/media/media_statistics.asp.

120. Bruce Edwards, "Carris Reels Wins 'Company of the Year' Award," *Rutland Herald*, June 2, 2008, http://www.rutlandherald .com/apps/pbcs.dll/article?AID=/20080602/BUSINESS/ 806020301/1011/BUSINESS; "Carris Reels Named 2008 Company of the Year by the ESOP Association," ESOP Association, May 13, 2008, http://www.esopassociation.org/media/media_ reels.asp; Loren Rodgers, "'Employee Owned and Governed,' the Carris Community of Companies,'" *ESOP Report*, March 2001, p. 3.

Appendix

The Daily Perc Business Plan*

This sample business plan has been made available to users of *Business Plan Pro*®, business planning software published by Palo Alto Software, Inc. Names, locations, and numbers may have been changed, and substantial portions of the original plan text have been omitted because of space limitations and to preserve confidentiality and proprietary information.

You are welcome to use this plan as a starting point to create your own, but you do not have permission to resell, reproduce, publish, distribute, or even copy this plan as it exists here.

Requests for reprints, academic use, and other dissemination of this sample plan should be e-mailed to the marketing department of Palo Alto Software at marketing@paloalto.com. For product information, visit our Website: www.paloalto.com or call: 1-800-229-7526.

1.0 Executive Summary

The Daily Perc (TDP) is a specialty beverage retailer. TDP uses a system that is new to the beverage and food service industry to provide hot and cold beverages conveniently and efficiently. TDP provides its customers the ability to drive up and order (from a trained Barista) their choice of a custom-blended espresso drink, freshly brewed coffee, or other beverage. TDP offers a high-quality alternative to fast-food, convenience store, or institutional coffee.

The Daily Perc offers its patrons the finest hot and cold beverages, specializing in specialty coffees, blended teas, and other custom drinks. In addition, TDP will offer soft drinks, fresh-baked pastries, and other confections. Seasonally, TDP will add beverages such as hot apple cider, hot chocolate, frozen coffees, and more.

The Daily Perc will focus on two markets:

The Daily Commuter. Someone who is traveling to or from work, shopping, delivering goods or services, or just out for a drive.

The Captive Consumer. Someone who is in a restricted environment that does not allow convenient departure and return for refreshments or where refreshments stands are an integral part of the environment.

The Daily Perc will penetrate the commuter and captive consumer markets by deploying drive-through facilities and Mobile Cafés in highly visible, accessible locations. The drive-through facilities are designed to handle two-sided traffic and dispense customer-designed, specially ordered cups of premium coffee in less time than is required for a visit to a locally owned café or one of the national chains.

In addition to providing a quality product and an extensive menu of delicious items, we will donate up to 7.5 percent of revenue to local charities to increase customer awareness of and loyalty to our business and to generate good publicity coverage and media support.

The Daily Perc's customer service process is labor intensive, and TDP recognizes that a higher level of talent is essential to success. The financial investment in its employees will be one of the greatest differentiators between TDP and its competition. For the purpose of this plan, the capital expenditures of facilities and equipment are financed. We will maintain minimum levels of inventory on hand to keep our products fresh and to take advantage of price decreases when and if they should occur.

The Daily Perc anticipates an initial combination of investments and short- and long-term financing of $365,670 to cover start-up costs. This will require TDP to grow more slowly than might be otherwise possible, but our growth will be solid, financially sound, and tied to customer demand.

The Daily Perc's goal is to become the drive-through version of Starbucks between the mountains, eventually obtaining several million dollars through a private offering that will allow the company to open 20 to 30 facilities per year in metropolitan communities in the North, Midwest, and South with populations of more than 150,000. This is the preferred exit strategy of the management team. The danger in this strategy is that competitors could establish a foothold in a community before the arrival of TDP, causing a potential drain on revenues and a dramatic increase in advertising expenditures to maintain market share. Knowing these risks—and planning for them—gives TDP the edge needed to make the exit strategy viable.

By year 3, we estimate a net worth of $1,075,969, a cash balance of $773,623, and earnings of $860,428, based on 13 drive-throughs and four Mobile Cafés. At that point, a market value of between $3.5 million and $8.6 million for the company is reasonable. At present, coffee chains are trading in multiples of 4 to 10 times earnings. Using the midpoint of that range (7) provides an estimated value of $6 million by the end of year 3.

The figure on page 653 summarizes the forecasts for TDP's sales, gross profit, and net income for the first three years of operation.

1.1 Objectives

The Daily Perc has established three objectives it plans to achieve in the next three years:

1. Thirteen drive-through locations and four fully booked Mobile Cafés by the end of the third year

2. Gross profit margin of 45 percent or more

3. Net after-tax profit above 15 percent of sales

1.2 Mission

The Daily Perc's mission is threefold, with each being as integral to our success as the next.

- *Product Mission.* Provide customers the finest quality beverages in the most efficient way

- *Community Mission.* Support the local communities in which we operate

- *Economic Mission.* Operate and grow at a profitable rate by making sound business decisions

1.3 Keys to Success

There are four keys to success in this business, three of which are virtually the same as in any food service business. It is the fourth key—the Community Mission—that gives TDP the extra measure of respect in the public eye.

1. The greatest locations, characterized by highly visible, high traffic counts, and convenient access

2. The best products, featuring the freshest coffee beans, cleanest equipment, premium serving containers, and most consistent flavor

3. The friendliest servers who are well trained, cheerful, skilled, professional, and articulate

4. The finest reputation that generates word-of-mouth advertising and promotes our community mission and charitable giving

Forecasted Highlights

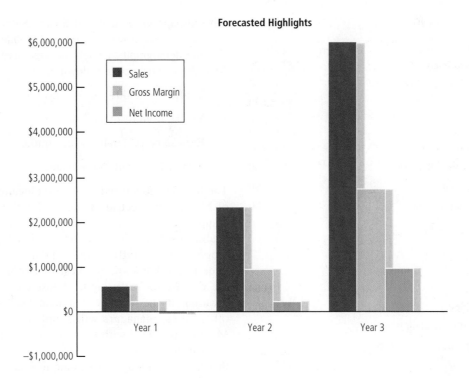

2.0 Company Summary

The Daily Perc is a specialty beverage retailer. TDP uses a system that is new to the beverage and food service industry to provide hot and cold beverages conveniently and efficiently. TDP provides its customers the ability to drive up and order from a trained Barista their choice of a custom-blended espresso drink, freshly brewed coffee, or other beverage. TDP offers a high-quality alternative to fast-food, convenience store, and institutional coffee.

2.1 Company Ownership

The Daily Perc is a limited liability company. All membership shares are currently owned by Bart and Teresa Fisher, who intend to use a portion of the shares to raise capital.

The plan calls for the sale of 100 membership units in the company to family members, friends, and private (angel) investors. Each membership unit in the company is priced at $4,250, with a minimum of five units per membership certificate, or a minimum investment of $21,250 per investor.

If TDP completes its financing goals successfully, Bart and Terri Fisher will maintain ownership of no less than 51 percent of the company.

2.2 Start-Up Summary

The Daily Perc's start-up expenses and funding are shown in the following tables and charts. The majority of these funds will be used to build the first facility, pay deposits, and provide capital for six months of operating expenses, initial inventory, and other one-time expenses. The Daily Perc also will need operating capital for the first few months of operation.

TABLE: START-UP

Start-Up

REQUIREMENTS

Start-Up Expenses:	
Legal	$3,500
Office Equipment	$4,950
Drive-Through Labor (6 months)	$65,000
Drive-Through Finance Payment (6 months)	$12,300
Drive-Through expenses (6 months)	$8,520
Land Lease (6 months)	$7,200
Vehicle Finance (6 months)	$3,700
Administration Labor (6 months)	$54,000
Web Site Development and Hosting	$5,600
Identity/Logos/Stationery	$4,000
Other	$5,000
Total Start-Up Expenses	$173,770
Start-Up Assets:	
Cash Required	$25,500
Start-Up Inventory	$35,000
Other Current Assets	$0
Long-Term Assets	$131,400
Total Assets	$191,900
Total Requirements	$365,670

TABLE: START-UP FUNDING

Start-Up Funding	
Start-Up Expenses to Fund	$173,770
Start-Up Assets to Fund	$191,900
Total Funding Required	$365,670
Assets	
Noncash Assets from Start-Up	$166,400
Cash Requirements from Start-Up	$25,500
Additional Cash Raised	$0
Cash Balance on Starting Date	$25,500
Total Assets	$191,900
Liabilities and Capital	
Liabilities	
Current Borrowing	$9,000
Long-Term Liabilities	$131,400
Accounts Payable (Outstanding Bills)	$0
Other Current Liabilities (Interest Free)	$0
Total Liabilities	$140,400
Capital	
Planned Investment	
Partner 1	$10,000
Partner 2	$10,000
Partner 3	$10,000
Partner 4	$10,000
Partner 5	$11,500
Partner 6	$10,000
Partner 7	$11,500
Partner 8	$10,000
Partner 9	$11,500
Partner 10	$10,000
Partner 11	$11,500
Partner 12	$11,500
Other	$97,770
Additional Investment Requirement	$0
Total Planned Investment	$225,270
Loss at Start-Up (Start-Up Expenses)	($173,770)
Total Capital	$51,500
Total Capital and Liabilities	$191,900
Total Funding	$365,670

2.3 Company Locations and Facilities

The Daily Perc will open its first drive-through facility on Manchester Road in the Colonial Square Shopping Center. We will locate 12 more drive-through facilities throughout the metropolitan area over the next three years. The drive-through in the Colonial Square Shopping Center will serve as the commissary for the first mobile unit.

The demographic and physical requirements for a drive-through location are the following:

- Traffic of 40,000+ cars per day on store side
- Visible from roadway
- Easy entry, preferably with a traffic light
- Established retail shops in area

The founders identified TDP's first location with the help of MapInfo's Spectrum Location Intelligence Module, a mapping and geographic analysis software package that enables users to visualize the relationships between demographic and traffic count data and geography to produce maps that show the best locations for businesses. We will use this software to choose the company's future locations in the metropolitan area. As TDP expands into other cities, managers will supplement the insight that MapInfo provides with the tools in ZoomProspector, another useful location analysis tool, to identify the cities that are most likely to be home to other successful TDP locations.

3.0 Products

The Daily Perc provides its patrons the finest hot and cold beverages, specializing in specialty coffees and custom-blended teas. In addition, TDP will offer select domestic soft drinks, Italian sodas, fresh-baked pastries, and other confections. Seasonally, TDP will add beverages such as hot apple cider, hot chocolate, frozen coffees, and more.

3.1 Product Description

The Daily Perc provides its customers, whether at a drive-through facility or at one of the Mobile Cafés, the ability to custom-order a beverage that will be blended to their exact specifications. Each of TDP's Baristas will be trained in the fine art of brewing, blending, and serving the highest-quality hot and cold beverages with exceptional attention to detail.

Besides its selection of coffees, TDP will offer teas, domestic and Italian sodas, frozen coffee beverages, seasonal specialty drinks, pastries, and other baked goods. Through the Web site and certain locations, TDP will market premium items bearing the TDP logo, such as coffee mugs, T-shirts, sweatshirts, caps, and more.

3.2 Competitive Comparison

The Daily Perc considers itself to be a player in the retail coffeehouse industry. However, we understand that competition for its products range from soft drinks to milk shakes to adult beverages.

The Daily Perc's primary competition will come from three sources:

1. National coffeehouses, such as Starbucks and Panera

2. Locally owned and operated cafés

3. Fast-food chains and convenience stores

Two things make TDP stand out from all its competitors: The Daily Perc will provide products in the most convenient and efficient way, either at one of the two-sided drive-through shops or at one of the Mobile Cafés. This separates TDP from the competition in that its customers won't have to find parking places, wait in a long lines, jockey for seats, and clean up the mess left by previous patrons. The Daily Perc's customers can drive or walk up, order their beverages, receive and pay for them and quickly be on their way.

The second differentiator is TDP's focus on providing a significant benefit to the community through a 7.5 percent contribution to customer-identified charities, schools, or other institutions.

3.3 Sourcing

The Daily Perc purchases its coffees from PJ's Coffee. It also has wholesale purchasing agreements for other products with Major Brands, Coca-Cola, Big Train, Al's Famous Filled Bagels, L&N Products, and Royal Distribution.

The drive-through facilities are manufactured by City Stations, and the Mobile Cafés are manufactured by Tow Tech Industries.

Fulfillment equipment suppliers include PJ's Coffee, City Stations, Talbert Ford, and Retail Image Programs. The Daily Perc's computer equipment and Internet connectivity is provided by NSI Communications.

3.4 Technology

The Daily Perc's delivery system uses state-of-the-art, two-sided drive-through facilities to provide convenience and efficiency for its clientele. An architectural exterior diagram of the drive-through building can be found in the appendix (removed from this sample plan).

The Daily Perc also has designed state-of-the-art Mobile Cafés that will be deployed on high school and college campuses, on corporate campuses, and at special events.

3.5 Future Products

The Daily Perc will offer products that reflect the changing seasons and customers' changing demand for beverages. During the warm summer months, TDP will offset lower hot beverage sales with frozen coffee drinks as well as soft drinks and other cold beverages. The Daily Perc will also have special beverages during holiday seasons, such as eggnog during the Christmas season and hot apple cider in the fall.

The Daily Perc's primary desire will be to listen to its customers to ascertain which products they want and to provide them.

4.0 Market Analysis Summary

The Daily Perc will focus on two markets:

1. *The Daily Commuter.* Someone traveling to or from work, out shopping, delivering goods or services, or just out for a drive

2. *The Captive Consumer.* Someone who is in a restricted environment that does not allow convenient departure and return while searching for refreshments or where refreshment stands are an integral part of the environment

4.1 Market Segmentation

The Daily Perc will focus on two different market segments: commuters and captive consumers. To access both of these markets, TDP has two different delivery systems. For the commuters, TDP offers the drive-through coffeehouse. For the captive consumer, TDP offers the Mobile Café.

Commuters are defined as anyone in a motorized vehicle traveling "from point A to point B." The Daily Perc's principal focus will be on attracting commuters heading to or from work and those on their lunch breaks.

Captive consumers include those who are tethered to a campus environment or to a restricted-entry environment where people's schedules afford limited time to make purchases. Examples include high school and college campuses, where students have limited time between classes, and corporate campuses, where the same time constraints are involved.

The following table and pie chart reflect the number of venues available for the Mobile Cafés and the growth we expect in those markets over the next five years. For an estimate of the number of Captive Consumers, we multiplied the total number of venues by 1,000. For example, in year 1, we estimate that there are 2,582 venues at which we might position a Mobile Café. That would equate to a captive consumer potential of 2,582,000 people.

Similarly, there are more than 2,500,000 commuters in the metropolitan area as well as visitors, vacationers, and others. Some of these commuters make not just one beverage purchase a day but, in many cases, two and even three beverage purchases.

The chart also reflects college and high school campuses, special events, hospital campuses, and various charitable organizations. A segment that the chart does not show (because it would skew the chart greatly) is the number of corporate campuses in the metropolitan area. There are more than 1,700 corporate facilities that employ more than 500 people, giving us an additional 1,700,000 potential customers, or a total of 2,582 locations at which we could place a Mobile Café.

TABLE: MARKET ANALYSIS

Market Analysis

Potential Customers	Growth	Year 1	Year 2	Year 3	Year 4	Year 5	CAGR
Public High School Campuses	1%	80	81	82	83	84	1.23%
Private High Schools	0%	88	88	88	88	88	0.00%
College Campuses	0%	77	77	77	77	77	0.00%
Golf Courses	0%	99	99	99	99	99	0.00%
Special Events	3%	43	44	45	46	47	2.25%
Nonprofits with $500K+ Budgets	2%	362	369	376	384	392	2.01%
Hospital Campuses	0%	100	100	100	100	100	0.00%
Total	1.10%	849	858	867	877	887	1.10%

CHART: MARKET ANALYSIS (PIE)

Source: Based on data from the National Coffee Association.

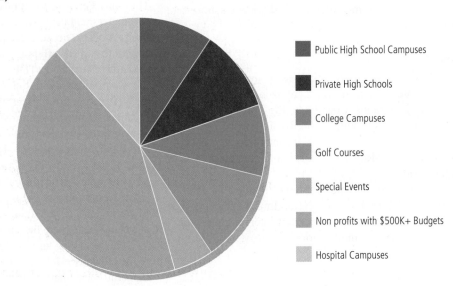

- Public High School Campuses
- Private High Schools
- College Campuses
- Golf Courses
- Special Events
- Non profits with $500K+ Budgets
- Hospital Campuses

4.2 Target Market Segment Strategy

The Daily Perc's target market is the mobile individual who has more money than time and excellent taste in the choice of a beverage but no time to linger in a café. By locating the drive-throughs in high-traffic/high-visibility areas, these customers will patronize TDP and become our regular guests.

Our Mobile Cafés will allow TDP to take the café to the customer! By using the community support program that TDP is instituting, we will make arrangements to visit high schools, college campuses, or corporate campuses once or twice a month. (We also will offer to visit these facilities for special games, tournaments, recruiting events, or corporate open houses.) We will return a portion of the revenue from each beverage or baked goods sold to the high school or college, allowing the institution to reap a financial reward while providing a pleasant and fulfilling benefit to their students or employees.

4.2.1 MARKET TRENDS Nearly 20 years ago, a trend toward more unique coffees began to develop in the United States. There had always been specialty coffee stores, such as Gloria Jeans and others, but people began to buy espresso machines for their homes and offices. Coffee tastings in stores became popular, and later espresso bars began to appear. Then along came Starbucks, the quintessential bastion of upwardly mobile professionals who wanted to take control over how their beverages were made.

Since Starbucks arrived on the scene, people have become more pressed for time. The same customers who helped push Starbucks's sales to nearly $10 billion are now rushing to get their kids to soccer practice and basketball games, running to the grocery store, and trying to get to work on time and back home in time for dinner—or to get to the next soccer game. Yet they still have the desire for that refreshing, specially blended coffee each morning.

Recently, we have seen the introduction of beverage dispensers at convenience stores that spit out overly sweet, poorly blended cappuccinos in flavors such as French vanilla or mocha, and consumers are paying as much as $3.00 for these substandard beverages.

The market is primed for the introduction of a company that offers a superior quality, specially blended product in a convenient, drive-through environment at a price that is competitive with national coffeehouses.

The Daily Perc is a member of the National Coffee Association and the National Specialty Coffee Association. These two trade associations provide useful information on the relevant trends in the industry, information for making comparisons to other companies on financial performance, and educational workshops and seminars.

4.2.2 MARKET GROWTH The 183 million Americans who drink coffee consume 146 *billion* cups of coffee per year. In addition, more than 173 million people in the United States drink tea. According to industry statistics, the consumption of coffee and flavored coffee products is growing rapidly, and 34 percent of coffee drinkers go to "premium" coffee outlets to purchase their beverages.

The segment of that market we are targeting is the commuter, and the number of people who commute to work is increasing by about 6 percent per year. In the metropolitan area, as with many metropolitan areas in the country, there is a migration away from the cities as people choose to live in quiet suburban areas and drive to work in the city.

The United States is home to 128.3 million commuters. Using census data, we estimate that more than 2.5 million commuters drive to and from work each day in our defined market. In addition, research shows that 54 percent of Americans drink coffee every day and that the typical coffee drinker consumes three nine-ounce cups of coffee per day. Nearly 65 percent of coffee consumption takes place in the morning, 30 percent occurs between meals, and 5 percent occurs between meals. Therefore, TDP has a significant daily target for its beverages, particularly during the morning drive time.

4.2.3 MARKET NEEDS The United States is a very mobile society. With the introduction of the automobile, we became a nation that thrived on the freedom of going where we wanted when we wanted. The population of the United States is 315 million people, and there are more licensed vehicles in the country than there are people. The population's mobility has created a unique need in our society for products available "on the go."

Our market is made up of consumers who have busy schedules, a desire for quality, and adequate disposable income. As much as they would like the opportunity to sit in an upscale coffeehouse and sip a uniquely blended coffee beverage and read the morning paper, they don't have the time. However, they still have the desire for a uniquely blended beverage as they hurry through their busy lives.

4.3 Industry Analysis

Consumers in the United States drink *450 million cups* of coffee per *day* and spend *$40 billion* a *year* on coffee-based drinks. The coffee industry in the United States has grown rapidly in the United States over the last five years. Sales of specialty coffees are growing at a rate of 20 percent per year. Even general coffee sales have increased, with international brands such as Folgers, Maxwell House, and Safari coffee reporting higher sales and greater profits. The United States is the leading coffee-consuming nation in the world, and the coffee industry is reaping the rewards.

4.3.1 DISTRIBUTION PATTERNS The café experience comes from the Italian origins of espresso. The customer enters a beautifully decorated facility surrounded by wondrous aromas and finds himself or herself involved in a sensory experience that, more often than not, masks an average product at a premium price. However, the proliferation of cafés in the United States proves the viability of the market. It is a duplication of the same delivery process as currently exists in Europe.

4.3.2 COMPETITION AND BUYING PATTERNS There are four general competitors in TDP's drive-through market. They are the national specialty beverage chains, such as Starbucks and Panera; local coffeehouses—or cafés with an established clientele and a quality product; fast-food restaurants; and convenience stores. There is a dramatic distinction among the patrons of each of these outlets.

Patrons of Starbucks or of one of the local cafés are looking for the "experience" of the coffeehouse. They want the ability to "design" a custom coffee, smell fresh pastries, listen to soothing Italian music, and read a newspaper or visit with a friend. It is a relaxing, slow-paced environment.

Patrons of fast-food restaurants or convenience stores expect just the opposite. They have no time for idle chatter and are willing to overpay for whatever beverage the machine spits out—as long as it's quick. They pay for their gas and are back on the road to work. Although they have ability to differentiate between a good cup of coffee and a bad one, time is more valuable to them than quality.

Competitors of the Mobile Cafés on campuses include fast-food restaurants (assuming that they are close enough so that customers can get there and back in the minimal allotted time), vending machines, and company or school cafeterias. The customers in this environment are looking for a quick, convenient, fairly priced, quality beverage that allows them to purchase the product and return to work, class, or other activity.

Competitors of the Mobile Cafés at events such as festivals and fairs include all the other vendors who are licensed to sell refreshments. Attendees of these events expect to pay a premium price for a quality product.

4.3.3 MAIN COMPETITORS The Daily Perc has no direct competitors in the drive-through segment of the market in the metropolitan area. The Daily Perc will be the first double-sided, drive-through coffeehouse in the city. However, we face significant competition from indirect competitors in the form of traditional coffeehouses, convenience stores, fast-food outlets, and other retailers.

National Chains: In 2011, Starbucks, the national leader, operated more than 9,000 retail outlets that generated operating revenue of $9.6 billion, which represents an increase of 7.5 percent over 2010. The average annual revenue for a Starbucks outlet is $1,078,000, or $81,821 in revenue per employee.

Panera Bread had revenues of $1.59 billion from company-owned stores and $1.83 billion from franchised locations in 2011. Revenue from company-owned stores increased 20.5 percent over 2010. Coffee beverages are not the primary focus of Panera Bread's menu.

Despite its name, Dunkin' Donuts's primary emphasis is on selling coffee. The company has more than 10,000 outlets worldwide, 7,000 of which are in the United States. Constructing a Dunkin' Donuts retail store costs $474,000, and average sales at a Dunkin' Donuts outlet in the United States are $839,000. The company's stronghold on market share is greatest in the Northeast, where it originated.

The Daily Perc believes it has a significant competitive advantage over these chains because of the following benefits:

- Drive-through service
- Superior customer service
- Community benefit
- Mobile Cafés
- Greater selection
- Higher product quality

Local Cafés: The toughest competitor for TDP is the established locally owned café. The Daily Perc knows the quality and pride that the local café has in the products their customers purchase. Local cafés typically benefit from their loyal, highly educated customers. The quality of beverages served at an established café surpasses those of the regional or national chains.

The competitive edge TDP has over local cafés is based on the following:

- Drive-through service
- Supply discounts
- Mobile Café
- Consistent menu
- Community benefit
- Quality product

Drive-Through Coffeehouses: There are no drive-through specialty beverage retailers with a significant market presence in the central United States. The only company with similar depth to that of TDP is Quikava, a wholly owned subsidiary of Chock Full 'o Nuts. However, Quikava has limited its corporate footprint to the East Coast and the Great Lakes region.

In the drive-through specialty beverage market, TDP has a competitive edge over these competitors, including Quikava, because of the following:

- Mobile Cafés
- Consistent menu
- Community benefit
- Quality product
- Supply discounts
- Valued image
- Greater product selection

Fast-Food and Convenience Stores: Most national fast food chains and national convenience store chains already serve coffee, soda, and some breakfast foods. The national fast-food chains understand the benefits and value that drive-through service provides customers; 70 percent of the typical fast-food outlet's sales come from drive-through customers. In addition, nearly 80 percent of the growth in the fast-food industry in the last five years has come through outlets' drive-through windows. Customers who buy coffee at fast-food and convenience stores shop primarily on the basis of price rather than quality and, therefore, are not TDP's primary target customers. The Daily Perc's advantage is that the quality of the products it sells is much higher than those sold at fast-food and convenience stores. Soft-drink sales for the typical quick-serve store account for a large portion of beverage sales. The Daily Perc believes that the quality of its products and the convenience of speedy drive-through service give it a competitive edge over fast-food and convenience stores.

Other Competition: The Daily Perc understands that once it has entered the market and established a presence, others will try to follow. However, TDP believes that although imitators will appear, they cannot duplicate its corporate mission, organizational design, or customer value proposition. The Daily Perc will constantly evaluate its products, locations, service, and mission to ensure that it remains a leader in the specialty beverage industry in its market segment.

4.3.4 INDUSTRY PARTICIPANTS There is only one national drive-through coffee franchise operation in the United States that poses a threat: a subsidiary of Chock Full 'o Nuts called Quikava. Quikava operates primarily on the East Coast and in the upper Great Lakes region. The East and West coasts and even some Mountain and Midwest states have smaller local drive-through chains such as Caffino, Java Espress, Crane Coffee, Java Drive, Sunrise Coffee, and Caffe Diva. However, other players in the premium coffee service industry include Starbucks, Gloria Jean's, Caribou Coffee, Panera Bread, and locally owned and operated coffee shops or "cafés."

5.0 Strategy and Implementation Summary

The Daily Perc will penetrate the commuter and captive consumer markets by deploying drive-through facilities and Mobile Cafés in highly visible, high-volume, accessible locations. The drive-throughs are designed to handle two-sided traffic and dispense customer-designed, specially ordered cups of specialty beverages in less time than required for a visit to the locally owned café or one of the national chains.

The Daily Perc has identified its market as busy, mobile people whose time is already at a premium but who desire a refreshing, high-quality beverage or baked item while commuting to or from work or school.

In addition to providing a quality product and an extensive menu of delicious side items, TDP pledges to donate up to 7.5 percent of revenue from each cup sold in individual drive-throughs to the charities that its customers choose.

5.1 Strategy Pyramid

The Daily Perc's strategy is to offer customers quality products, convenient accessibility, and a community benefit. To execute this strategy, TDP is placing the drive-throughs and Mobile Cafés in well-researched, easily accessible locations throughout the metropolitan area. The Daily Perc is pricing its product competitively and training the production staff to be among the best Baristas in the country. Prices for TDP's products are at or slightly below the national average. Through coupons and display ads at its locations, TDP will involve customers in community support efforts by donating a portion of each sale to a charity of their choosing.

In so doing, TDP has accomplished the following:

1. Provided a customer with a quality product at a competitive price

2. Provided customers with a more convenient method for obtaining their desired product

3. Demonstrated how TDP appreciates their loyalty and patronage by donating money to a meaningful cause

5.2 Value Proposition

The drive-through facilities provide a substantial value proposition because our customers do not have to find parking places, exit their vehicles, stand in long lines to order, pay premium prices for average products, find places to sit, clean up the previous patron's mess, and then enjoy their coffee—assuming that they have sufficient time to linger over the cup.

The Daily Perc's concept is that the customer drives up, places an order that is filled quickly and accurately, receives a high-quality product at a competitive price, and drives away, having invested little time in the process.

The Daily Perc is also providing a significant community value on behalf of customers who patronize TDP. For every purchase a customer makes from us, TDP will donate up to 7.5 percent of each sale to a local charity selected by our customers.

5.3 Competitive Edge

The Daily Perc's competitive edge is simple. TDP provides a high-quality product at a competitive price in a drive-through environment that saves customers valuable time.

5.4 Marketing Strategy

The Daily Perc will be placing its drive-through facilities in highly visible, easily accessible locations. They will be located on high-traffic commuter routes and near shopping centers and concentrations of complementary retail shops to catch customers who are traveling to or from work, going out for lunch, or venturing on a shopping expedition. The drive-throughs' design is very unique and eye-catching, which will be a branding feature of its own.

As the following chart indicates, TDP's target audience skews older.

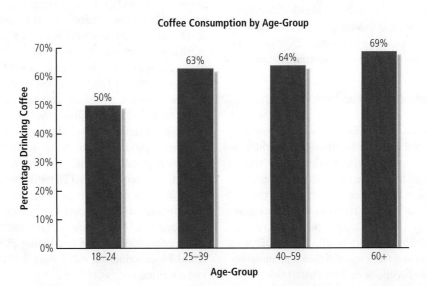

Coffee Consumption by Age-Group

Therefore, TDP will implement a low-cost advertising campaign that includes traditional advertising media, such as drive-time radio and a few strategically located outdoor ads. However, because a significant portion of our target customers is younger than 40, we also will use social media tools extensively.

The Daily Perc will rely on building relationships with schools, charities, and companies to provide significant free publicity through its community support program. When TDP makes charitable contributions to these institutions, they will get the word out to their students/faculty/employees/partners about TDP. Word-of-mouth advertising has long been one of the greatest advertising techniques a company can use. In addition, we will encourage the media to cover the charitable aspects of TDP, giving the company the opportunity for more exposure every time TDP writes a check to a nonprofit organization.

The Daily Perc will use social media marketing tools such as Twitter and Facebook as well, particularly to promote the locations of its Mobile Cafés. We will send tweets to our followers to alert them to the location of our Mobile Cafés. We also will post the Mobile Cafés' locations on Facebook.

5.4.1 PROMOTION STRATEGY The long-range goal is to gain enough visibility to expand the TDP brand into other regions and generate inquiries from potential inventors. To do that, TDP must employ the following:

- A public relations service at $1,000 per month for the next year to generate awareness of TDP among newspapers, magazines, bloggers, and reviews. We anticipate that the school fund-raising program will generate a publicity on its own and eventually will minimize—or even eliminate—the need for a publicist.

- Advertising expenditures of $1,000 per month focused on drive-time radio and strategically selected billboards. The Daily Perc will experiment with different stations, keeping careful track of results. We will select billboards that are near our existing locations to serve as reminders of our locations for passing motorists. As with the school fund-raising program, TDP expects its storefronts and signage to be a substantial portion of our advertising.

- A social media presence on Facebook, Twitter, and YouTube. We can use these tools to reach our target customers at very little expense. We will promote daily specials on selected items on Facebook and Twitter and will post videos of our Best Barista Contest on YouTube. We also plan to involve our customers through a contest that offers free coffee for one year to the customer who posts the best YouTube video promoting TDP. We also will sponsor a "Fan of the Day" contest by randomly drawing one person who likes TDP on Facebook to receive a free cup of coffee and announcing the winner on Facebook and on Twitter.

5.4.2 DISTRIBUTION STRATEGY The Daily Perc will locate its drive-through facilities in high-traffic areas of the city where it knows working commuters will be passing. Our first outlet will be located at the corner of Main Street and Broughton Road, which has a traffic count of 42,200 cars per day.

The Daily Perc will also make arrangements for the Mobile Cafés to be at as many schools, businesses, and events as possible every year to promote TDP to new customers.

5.4.3 MARKETING PROGRAMS
Distinctive Logo: Our logo, "Papo," is a very happy and conspicuous sun. The sun touches every human being every day, and TDP wants to touch its customers every day. Papo is already an award-winning logo, having won the "New Artist Category" of the 2011 Not Just Another Art Director's Club (NJAADC).

Distinctive Buildings: The Daily Perc is using diner-style buildings for its drive-through facilities and has worked closely with the manufacturer to make the building distinctive so that it is easy to recognize and functional.

The Mobile Café: The Mobile Café will be a key marketing tool for TDP. The similarities between the Mobile Cafés and the drive-through facilities will be unmistakable. The exposure that these units provide is difficult to measure directly but is extremely important to the company's growth. The Daily Perc will negotiate visits for its mobile units at schools, hospitals, companies, and special events. A portion of all sales made while at these locations will go to a nonprofit entity of the organization's choice. The organization will promote its presence to its constituency and encourage them to frequent TDP's drive-through establishments to support their charitable cause. This will give those patrons an opportunity to taste the products and become regular customers of the drive-through facilities. The Mobile Cafés will also be appearing at community events, such as fairs, festivals, and other charitable events.

Advertising and Promotion: In the first year, TDP plans to spend moderately on advertising and promotion, with the program beginning in June, prior to the opening of the first drive-through. This would not be considered a serious advertising budget for any business, but TDP believes that the exposure will come from publicity and promotion, so we will spend most of the funds on a good publicist who will get the word out about the charitable contribution program and how it works in conjunction with the Website. The Daily Perc also believes that word-of-mouth advertising and free beverage coupons will be better ways to drive people to the first and second locations.

In the second year, TDP will increase the budget because it will need to promote several locations, with particular emphasis on announcing these openings and all the other locations. The Daily Perc will continue to use publicity as a key component of the marketing program because TDP could be contributing more than $70,000 to local schools and charities.

In the third year, TDP will double its advertising and promotion budget, with the majority of the advertising budget being spent on drive-time radio to reach our commuting target audience. As in the previous years, TDP will get substantial publicity from the donation of nearly $200,000 to local schools and charities.

5.4.4 PRICING STRATEGY The national average price for a cup of brewed coffee is $1.38, and the average price of an espresso-based drink is $2.45. The Daily Perc's pricing will be slightly below those of the national chain coffeehouses but very similar to those of local cafés to reflect the value-added feature of immediate, drive-through service and convenience. Costs to make a 6-ounce cup of coffee are as follows:

Coffee	$0.25
Cup, lid, and sleeve	0.22
Milk	0.21
Total	$0.68

Additional ingredients add anywhere from $0.02 (sugar) to $1.08 (mocha syrup) to the cost of a single 6-ounce cup of coffee for a total cost that ranges from $0.70 for a basic cup of premium coffee to $1.76 for a café mocha.

5.5 Sales Strategy

We will rely on several in-store sales strategies, including posting specials on high-profit items at the drive-up window. The Daily Perc also will use a customer loyalty program that awards a free cup of coffee to customers who have accumulated the required number of points by purchasing 12 cups of coffee. Customers also can earn points by telling others about their purchases at TDP on Facebook, Twitter, and other social media sites. The Daily Perc will also develop window cross-selling techniques, such as the Baristas asking whether customers would like a fresh-baked item with their coffee.

5.5.1 SALES FORECAST In the first year, TDP anticipates having two drive-through locations in operation. The first location will open on July 15. The second drive-through will open six months later. The Daily Perc is building in a few weeks of "ramp-up" time for each facility while commuters become familiar with its presence. The drive-throughs will generate 288,000 checks in the first year of operation.

In the second year, TDP will add two more drive-throughs, and in the third year, TDP will add an additional nine drive-through facilities. The addition of these facilities will increase the revenue from drive-throughs with a total of more than 1,000,000 checks in the second year and 2,675,000 checks in the third.

In addition to the drive-throughs, TDP will deploy one mobile unit in the fourth quarter of the first fiscal year and expects this mobile unit to generate 10,000 checks at an average check of $2.45 (including baked goods).

In the second quarter of the second fiscal year, TDP will deploy its second and third mobile units and expects all three mobile units to generate a total of 150,000 checks in the second year. In the third fiscal year, with the addition of a fourth mobile unit, TDP expects to generate 264,000 mobile unit checks.

The Daily Perc also will generate revenue from the sale of "The Daily Perc" T-shirts, sweatshirts, insulated coffee mugs, prepackaged coffee beans, and other items. The Daily Perc is not expecting this to be a significant profit center, but it is an integral part of the marketing plan and an important part of developing our brand and building product awareness. The Daily Perc expects revenues from this portion, which will begin in the second fiscal year, to reach as much as $3,000 per month in the third fiscal year.

We forecast total first year unit sales will reach 298,402 cups. The second year will see unit sales increase to 1,177,400 cups. The third year, with the addition of a significant number of outlets, we will see unit sales increase to 2,992,000 cups.

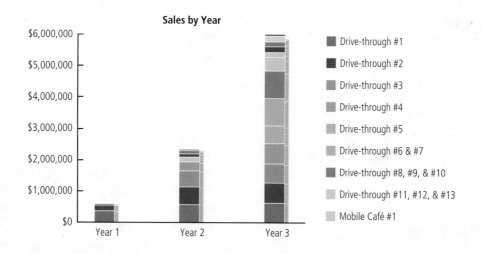

TABLE: SALES FORECAST

Sales Forecast			
	Year 1	Year 2	Year 3
Unit Sales			
Drive-Through 1	202,913	300,000	325,000
Drive-Through 2	85,489	300,000	325,000
Drive-Through 3	0	275,000	325,000
Drive-Through 4	0	150,000	325,000
Drive-Through 5	0	0	300,000
Drive-Throughs 6 and 7	0	0	450,000
Drive-Throughs 8, 9, and 10	0	0	450,000
Drive-Throughs 11, 12, and 13	0	0	225,000
Mobile Café 1	10,000	60,000	66,000
Mobile Café 2	0	45,000	66,000
Mobile Café 3	0	45,000	66,000
Mobile Café 4	0	0	66,000
Web Site Sales/Premium Items	0	2,400	3,000
Total Unit Sales	298,402	1,177,400	2,992,000
Unit Prices	Year 1	Year 2	Year 3
Drive-Through 1	$1.85	$1.90	$1.95
Drive-Through 2	$1.85	$1.90	$1.95
Drive-Through 3	$0.00	$1.90	$1.95
Drive-Through 4	$0.00	$1.90	$1.95
Drive-Through 5	$0.00	$1.90	$1.95
Drive-Throughs 6 and 7	$0.00	$1.90	$1.95
Drive-Throughs 8, 9, and 10	$0.00	$1.90	$1.95
Drive-Throughs 11, 12, and 13	$0.00	$1.90	$1.95
Mobile Café 1	$2.45	$2.50	$2.55
Mobile Café 2	$0.00	$2.50	$2.55
Mobile Café 3	$0.00	$2.50	$2.55
Mobile Café 4	$0.00	$2.50	$2.55
Web Site Sales/Premium Items	$0.00	$11.00	$12.00
Sales			
Drive-Through 1	$375,389	$570,000	$633,750
Drive-Through 2	$158,154	$570,000	$633,750
Drive-Through 3	$0	$522,500	$633,750
Drive-Through 4	$0	$285,000	$633,750
Drive-Through 5	$0	$0	$585,000
Drive-Throughs 6 and 7	$0	$0	$877,500
Drive-Throughs 8, 9, and 10	$0	$0	$877,500
Drive-Throughs 11, 12, and 13	$0	$0	$438,750
Mobile Café 1	$24,500	$150,000	$168,300
Mobile Café 2	$0	$112,500	$168,300
Mobile Café 3	$0	$112,500	$168,300
Mobile Café 4	$0	$0	$168,300
Web Site Sales/Premium Items	$0	$26,400	$36,000
Total Sales	$558,043	$2,348,900	$6,022,950

Sales Forecast

	Year 1	Year 2	Year 3
Direct Unit Costs	Year 1	Year 2	Year 3
Drive-Through 1	$0.64	$0.61	$0.59
Drive-Through 2	$0.64	$0.61	$0.59
Drive-Through 3	$0.00	$0.61	$0.59
Drive-Through 4	$0.00	$0.61	$0.59
Drive-Through 5	$0.00	$0.61	$0.59
Drive-Throughs 6 and 7	$0.00	$0.61	$0.59
Drive-Throughs 8, 9, and 10	$0.00	$0.61	$0.59
Drive-Throughs 11, 12, and 13	$0.00	$0.61	$0.59
Mobile Café 1	$0.64	$0.61	$0.59
Mobile Café 2	$0.00	$0.61	$0.59
Mobile Café 3	$0.00	$0.61	$0.59
Mobile Café 4	$0.00	$0.61	$0.59
Web Site Sales/Premium Items	$0.00	$6.50	$6.50
Direct Cost of Sales			
Drive-Through 1	$129,864	$183,000	$191,750
Drive-Through 2	$54,713	$183,000	$191,750
Drive-Through 3	$0	$167,750	$191,750
Drive-Through 4	$0	$91,500	$191,750
Drive-Through 5	$0	$0	$177,000
Drive-Throughs 6 and 7	$0	$0	$265,500
Drive-Throughs 8, 9, and 10	$0	$0	$265,500
Drive-Throughs 11, 12, and 13	$0	$0	$132,750
Mobile Café #1	$6,400	$36,600	$38,940
Mobile Café #2	$0	$27,450	$38,940
Mobile Café #3	$0	$27,450	$38,940
Mobile Café #4	$0	$0	$38,940
Web Site Sales/Premium Items	$0	$15,600	$19,500
Subtotal Direct Cost of Sales	$190,977	$732,350	$1,783,010

5.5.2 SALES PROGRAMS

Corporate Tasting Events. The Daily Perc plans to host at least one tasting event for customers each quarter. In addition, TDP will adjust its menu to reflect the changing seasons in the flavors it served.

Drink Coupons. At fund-raising events for schools and corporate events, we will give away drink coupons as door prizes or awards. These giveaways are inexpensive and encourage new customers to come in to claim a free beverage and bring a friend or buy a baked item or a package of our premium coffee. The drive-through units will also distribute coupons for special menu items or new product introductions.

Chamber of Commerce and Professional Memberships. Because of the need to promote its drive-through locations and its Mobile Café services, TDP will be an active member in the regional and local chambers of commerce, food service associations, and two national coffee associations. The exposure and education that these organizations provide is outstanding, but equally important are the contacts and opportunities made available for deploying a Mobile Café—or even two—at a special event.

5.6 Milestones

The Milestone table reflects critical dates for occupying headquarters, launching the first drive-through and subsequent drive-throughs as well as deploying the mobile units. The Daily Perc also defines our break-even month, our Web site launch and subsequent visitor interaction function, and other key markers that will help us measure our success.

TABLE: MILESTONES

Milestones					
Milestone	Start Date	End Date	Budget	Manager	Department
Launch Web Site	6/1/2013	8/15/2013	$5,600	COO	Marketing
Open First Drive-Through	7/15/2013	8/31/2013	$105,400	COO	Administration
First Break-Even Month	12/1/2013	12/31/2013	$0	COO	Finance
Open Second Drive-Through	12/15/2013	2/1/2013	$105,400	COO	Administration
Receive First Mobile Unit	3/1/2014	3/30/2014	$86,450	COO	Administration
Launch Web Site Voting	5/1/2014	6/1/2014	$12,500	COO	Marketing
Open Third Drive-Through	4/15/2014	6/1/2014	$105,400	COO	Administration
Receive Second and Third Mobile Units	7/15/2014	9/1/2014	$172,900	COO	Administration
Open Fourth Drive-Through	12/15/2014	2/1/2015	$105,400	COO	Administration
Install Point-of-Sale System	12/1/2014	2/1/2015	$21,000	CIO	MIS
Occupy Headquarters	4/1/2015	5/15/2015	$45,000	COO	Administration
Open Fifth Drive-Through	4/15/2015	6/1/2015	$105,400	COO	Administration
Receive Fourth Mobile Unit	4/15/2015	6/1/2015	$86,450	Equipment	Administration
Open Drive-Throughs 6 and 7	7/15/2015	9/15/2015	$210,800	COO/Director	Management
Open Drive-Through 8, 9, and 10	10/15/2015	12/15/2015	$316,200	COO/Director	Management
Open Drive-Throughs 11, 12, and 13	1/15/2016	3/1/2016	$316,200	COO	Administration
Expand to Kansas City	1/15/2016	6/1/2016	$176,943	COO	Management
Open First Franchise	10/31/2015	9/1/2016	$45,000	CFO	Finance
Initiate Exit Strategy	10/1/2016	1/1/2017	$100,000	CFO	Management
Totals			$2,122,043		

6.0 Management Summary

The Daily Perc will maintain a relatively flat organization. Overhead for management will be kept to a minimum, and all senior managers will be "hands-on" workers. We have no intention of creating a top-heavy organization that drains profits and complicates decision making.

At the end of year 3, TDP will have four executive positions: chief operating officer, chief financial officer, chief information officer, and director of marketing. There will be other midmanagement positions, such as district managers for every four drive-throughs and a facilities manager to oversee the maintenance and stocking of the Mobile Cafés and the equipment in the drive-through facilities.

6.1 Management Team

The Daily Perc has selected Mr. Barton Fisher to perform the duties of chief operating officer. Bart has an entrepreneurial spirit and has already started a company (NetCom Services, Inc.) that was profitable within three months of start-up and paid off all of its initial debt within six months. Bart's experience, leadership, and focus and three years of research in specialty drinks and drive-through service make him the ideal chief operating officer for TDP.

Ms. Mary Jamison will fill the position of bookkeeper and office manager. Mary has been the business administrator of Jones International, Inc., for the last four years. Jones is a $4 million company that retails vitamins and other nutritional products. During her four years with Jones International, Mary has written numerous corporate policies and directed the financial reporting.

Mr. Tony Guy will perform the duties of corporate events coordinator on a part-time basis. Mr. Guy has more than five years of experience in business-to-business sales. Last year he sold more than $250,000 in sales of promotional material to corporate and educational clients.

Mr. Chuck McNulty will fill the position of warehouse/trailer manager. Chuck has been working for Nabisco, Inc., as a service representative for more than 10 years; before that, he was involved in inventory control for a Nabisco factory. His experience in account services, merchandising, and inventory control is a welcome addition to the TDP team. Chuck will use his knowledge to establish inventory and warehouse policies. The warehouse manager is responsible for the inventory of all products sold by TDP. In addition, knowledge of regulations and health requirements are important. Chuck will be responsible for ensuring that TDP maintains proper levels of inventory. He will work closely with the mobile and drive-through Baristas to make sure that all of the products they sell are fresh, appetizing, and available in the appropriate quantities at the right time.

6.2 Management Team Gaps

The Daily Perc will require several additional management team members over the next three years. We will hire one district manager for every four drive-throughs. These district managers will oversee the quality of the products sold, the training of the Baristas, inventory management, and customer satisfaction. Eventually, the goal is to promote from within, particularly from our Mobile Café and drive-through teams, for these positions.

By the beginning of the third year, TDP will have hired three key senior managers: a chief financial officer, a chief information officer, and a director of marketing. We will discuss the roles of each of these managers in subsequent sections of this plan.

6.3 Organizational Structure

The organization will be relatively flat; most of TDP's employees are involved in production, and our goal is to maintain a small core of qualified managers who empower employees to make decisions that are in our customers' best interest.

There are three functioning groups within the company: production, sales and marketing, and general and administrative. For purposes of this plan—and to show the details of adding senior-level management—TDP has broken management down as a separate segment, but it is an integral part of the general and administrative function.

Production involves the Baristas, or customer service specialists, who will be staffing the drive-throughs and Mobile Cafés and blending the beverages for the customers. The sales and marketing staff will coordinate the promotion and scheduling of the Mobile Cafés as well as the promotion of the drive-throughs and the Community Contribution program. General and administrative personnel will manage the facilities, equipment, inventory, payroll, and other basic, operational processes for the company.

6.4 Personnel Plan

The Daily Perc forecasts its first year to be rather lean because we will have only two locations and one mobile unit, none of which will be in operation for the entire year. The total head count for the first year, including management, administrative support, and customer service (production) employees, is 15. The payroll expenditures are shown in the following table.

In the second year, with the addition of two drive-throughs and two mobile units, TDP will add customer service personnel, its first district manager, and some additional support staff at headquarters, including an inventory clerk, equipment technician, and administrative support staff. The head count will increase by nearly 100 percent in the second year to 29, causing a significant increase in payroll expense.

In the third year, we will see the most dramatic growth in head count—180 percent over year 2—because of the addition of nine drive-throughs and another mobile unit. Total payroll for the third year will reflect this increase as well as the significant increase in the senior management team with the addition of a chief financial officer, a chief information officer, and a director of marketing. The Daily Perc also will add two more district managers and a corporate events sales executive. Total personnel will reach 81.

The chief financial officer will be brought in to manage the growing company's finances. The chief information officer will be responsible for the expansion of our existing point-of-sale computerized cash register system that will make tracking and managing receipts, inventory control, and charitable contributions more robust. Ideally, this person will have both point-of-sale and inventory control experience that will allow him or her to provide real-time sales and inventory control information for accurate decision making at every level in the company. In addition, the chief information officer should begin building the foundation for an Internet-based information system that will support franchisees in the future.

The director of marketing will be charged with managing the relationships with advertising agencies, public relations firms, the media; keeping the TDP Web site current; and coordinating the company's social media marketing efforts.

Personnel Plan			
	Year 1	Year 2	Year 3
Production Personnel			
Drive-Through Team	$135,474	$439,250	$1,098,650
Mobile Café Team	$9,400	$172,800	$225,600
Equipment Care Specialist (Headquarters)	$0	$22,000	$77,000
Other	$0	$12,000	$24,000
Subtotal	$144,874	$646,050	$1,425,250
Sales and Marketing Personnel			
District Manager (Four Drive-Throughs)	$0	$22,000	$77,000
Corporate Events Sales Executive	$0	$0	$36,000
Director of Marketing	$0	$0	$72,000
Other	$0	$0	$0
Subtotal	$0	$22,000	$185,000

(continued)

Personnel Plan

	Year 1	Year 2	Year 3
General and Administrative Personnel			
Bookkeeper/Office Administrator	$24,500	$46,000	$54,000
Warehouse/Site Manager	$7,000	$42,000	$48,000
Inventory Clerk	$0	$12,000	$42,000
Other	$0	$6,000	$12,000
Subtotal	$31,500	$106,000	$156,000
Other Personnel			
Chief Operating Officer	$66,000	$72,000	$78,000
Chief Financial Officer	$0	$0	$96,000
Chief Information Officer	$0	$0	$84,000
Other	$0	$0	$0
Subtotal	$66,000	$72,000	$258,000
Total People	15	29	81
Total Payroll	$242,374	$846,050	$2,024,250

7.0 Financial Plan

Although we forecast a loss of about $29,000 for TDP in its first year of operation, the company's long-term financial picture is quite promising. Because TDP is a cash business, its cash requirements are significantly less than other companies that must carry extensive amounts of accounts receivable. However, because our process is labor intensive, TDP recognizes that we must hire employees with more talent. The financial investment in our employees will be one of the greatest differentiators between TDP and its competitors. In this plan, we assume that we are financing the cost of our facilities and equipment. These items are capital expenditures and will be available for financing. We will maintain a minimum of inventory to ensure the freshness of our coffee products and baked goods and to take advantage of price decreases when and if they should occur.

The Daily Perc forecasts that the initial combination of investments and long-term financing will be sufficient without the need for any additional equity or debt investment other than the purchase of additional equipment and facilities as it grows. This strategy will require TDP to grow more slowly than might be otherwise possible, but the company's expansion will be solid, financially sound growth based on its success in meeting customers' needs.

7.1 Important Assumptions

The following table shows the underlying assumptions used to build the financial forecasts for TDP:

- A slow-growth economy but no major recession.

- No unforeseen changes in public health perceptions of its products.

- Access to equity capital and financing sufficient to maintain its financial plan as shown in the tables.

TABLE: GENERAL ASSUMPTIONS

General Assumptions

	Year 1	Year 2	Year 3
Short-Term Interest Rate	8.00%	8.00%	8.00%
Long-Term Interest Rate	9.00%	9.00%	9.00%
Tax Rate (LLC)	0.00%	0.00%	0.00%
Other	0	0	0

7.2 Key Financial Indicators

The following chart shows changes in key financial indicators: sales, gross margin, operating expenses, and inventory turnover. The expected growth in sales exceeds 250 percent each year. The Daily Perc forecasts its gross profit margin in year 1 to be 40 percent; by year 3, we expect it to reach 45 percent.

Projections for inventory turnover show that TDP will maintain a relatively stable amount of inventory in its warehouse so that it has no less than one week of inventory on hand but no more than two weeks of inventory so that products stay fresh. The only time we will consider holding larger stores of inventory is if there is some catastrophic event that would cause shortages in the supplies of its coffees or teas.

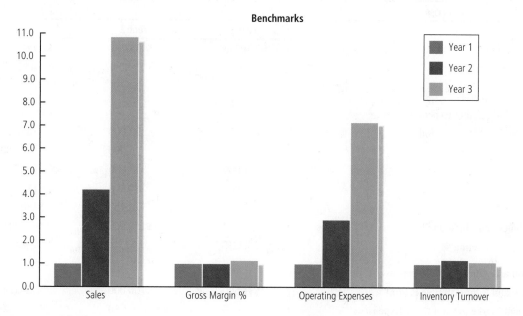

Benchmarks

7.3 Break-Even Analysis

Assuming average revenue per unit of $1.87 and fixed operating costs of $19,457 per month, TDP estimates its break-even point to be $29,580 per month. This is the equivalent of selling 15,817 cups of coffee per month, or 527 cups per day.

Break-Even Analysis	
Monthly Units Break-Even	15,817
Monthly Revenue Break-Even	$29,580
Assumptions:	
Average Per-Unit Revenue	$1.87
Average Per-Unit Variable Cost	$0.64
Estimated Monthly Fixed Cost	$19,457

7.4 Projected Profit and Loss

The Daily Perc is expecting dramatic growth in the next three years, reaching strong sales and a healthy gross profit margin by the end of its first year of operation. Expenses during the first year will, however, produce a net loss of about $29,000.

Aside from production costs of 60 percent, which include actual purchases of products and commissions for sales efforts, the single largest expenditures in the first year

are in the general and administrative (G&A) area, which total 23 percent of sales. G&A includes expenses for rents, equipment leases, utilities, and payroll for all employees.

Sales increase by nearly 400 percent in the second year because of the addition of two more drive-throughs and two more Mobile Cafés. Although operating expenses double in the second year, TDP forecasts a net profit of $217,000, which represents a net profit margin (net income ÷ sales) of 9.24 percent. In that same year, TDP will make substantial charitable contributions in the communities in which it operates.

The third year is when TDP has the opportunity to break into markets outside the metropolitan area. The Daily Perc will open nine additional drive-through facilities in the third year, which will increase sales faster than production costs, which improve the company's gross profit margin. Several expenses increase substantially in year 3, including advertising, charitable donations, and payroll (because TDP will add several key management team members). Once again, the company's two largest expenses are production costs and G&A expenses. However, the G&A expenses decrease from 23 percent of sales in year 1 to 18.5 percent of sales in year 2 and 15.0 percent of sales in year 3. By year 3, operating efficiencies push the company's net profit margin to 16 percent.

Pro Forma Profit and Loss	Year 1	Year 2	Year 3
Sales	$558,043	$2,348,900	$6,022,950
Direct Cost of Sales	$190,977	$732,350	$1,783,010
Production Payroll	$144,874	$646,050	$1,425,250
Sales Commissions	$1,416	$35,234	$90,344
Total Cost of Sales	$337,267	$1,413,634	$3,298,604

(continued)

Pro Forma Profit and Loss

	Year 1	Year 2	Year 3
Gross Margin	$220,776	$935,267	$2,724,346
Gross Margin %	39.56%	39.82%	45.23%
Operating Expenses			
Sales and Marketing Expenses			
Sales and Marketing Payroll	$0	$22,000	$185,000
Advertising/Promotion	$18,000	$36,000	$72,000
Web site	$1,000	$15,000	$22,000
Travel	$4,000	$7,500	$15,000
Donations	$3,332	$70,467	$180,689
Total Sales and Marketing Expenses	$26,332	$150,967	$474,689
Sales and Marketing %	4.72%	6.43%	7.88%
General and Administrative Expenses			
General and Administrative Payroll	$31,500	$106,000	$156,000
Sales and Marketing and Other Expenses	$0	$0	$0
Depreciation	$21,785	$92,910	$196,095
Leased Offices and Equipment	$0	$6,000	$18,000
Utilities	$9,640	$19,800	$41,100
Insurance	$12,570	$32,620	$63,910
Rent	$16,800	$50,400	$126,000
Payroll Taxes	$36,356	$126,908	$303,638
Other General and Administrative Expenses	$0	$0	$0
Total General and Administrative Expenses	$128,651	$434,638	$904,743
General and Administrative %	23.05%	18.50%	15.02%
Other Expenses:			
Other Payroll	$66,000	$72,000	$258,000
Consultants	$0	$0	$0
Legal/Accounting/Consultants	$12,500	$24,000	$36,000
Total Other Expenses	$78,500	$96,000	$294,000
Other %	14.07%	4.09%	4.88%
Total Operating Expenses	$233,483	$681,605	$1,673,431
Profit before Interest and Taxes	($12,707)	$253,662	$1,050,915
EBITDA	$9,078	$346,572	$1,247,010
Interest Expense	$16,165	$36,639	$77,102
Taxes Incurred	$0	$0	$0
Net Income	($28,872)	$217,023	$973,812
Net Income/Sales	-5.17%	9.24%	16.17%

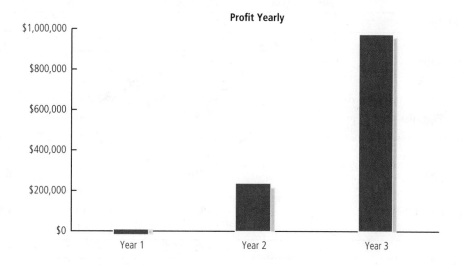

Profit Yearly

7.5 Projected Cash Flow

As in any business, managers must manage cash extremely carefully; however, TDP has the benefit of operating a cash business. Forecasts show that the business generates positive cash flow, even in year 1. The greatest challenge that TDP faces in managing cash flow results from the seasonal dips in coffee sales during warm weather, but TDP will attempt to offset those declines by adding seasonal menu items, such as iced cappuccinos, iced mochas, and others.

With sufficient initial financing, TDP anticipates no cash flow shortfalls for the first year or beyond. In year 1, the months of March and May produce the greatest cash drains because TDP will incur the cost of adding second drive-through and a second mobile unit. In addition, TDP experiences heavier-than-normal cash disbursements in December and January because accounts payable come due then.

Pro Forma Cash Flow			
	Year 1	Year 2	Year 3
Cash Received			
Cash from Operations			
Cash Sales	$558,043	$2,348,900	$6,022,950
Subtotal Cash from Operations	$558,043	$2,348,900	$6,022,950
Additional Cash Received			
Sales Tax, VAT, HST/GST Received	$0	$0	$0
New Current Borrowing	$0	$0	$0
New Other Liabilities (interest Free)	$0	$0	$0
New Long-Term Liabilities	$181,463	$253,970	$729,992
Sales of Other Current Assets	$0	$0	$0
Sales of Long-Term Assets	$0	$0	$0
New Investment Received	$0	$0	$0
Subtotal Cash Received	$739,506	$2,602,870	$6,752,942
Expenditures			
Expenditures from Operations			
Cash Spending	$242,374	$846,050	$2,024,250
Bill Payments	$273,191	$1,236,069	$2,880,058
Subtotal Spent on Operations	$515,565	$2,082,119	$4,904,308

(continued)

Pro Forma Cash Flow

	Year 1	Year 2	Year 3
Additional Cash Spent			
Sales Tax, VAT, HST/GST Paid Out	$0	$0	$0
Principal Repayment of Current Borrowing	$1,500	$2,000	$5,000
Other Liabilities Principal Repayment	$0	$0	$0
Long-Term Liabilities Principal Repayment	$26,469	$27,000	$50,000
Purchase Other Current Assets	$0	$0	$0
Purchase Long-Term Assets	$191,850	$429,700	$1,356,993
Dividends	$0	$0	$0
Subtotal Cash Spent	$735,384	$2,540,819	$6,316,301
Net Cash Flow	$4,122	$62,051	$436,641
Cash Balance	$29,622	$91,673	$528,315

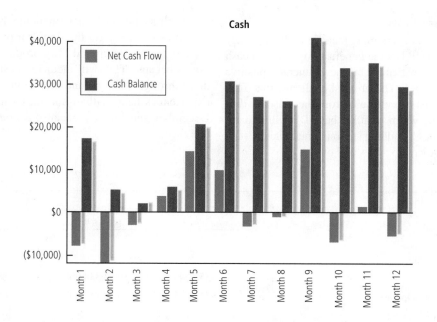

Cash

7.6 Projected Balance Sheet

The Daily Perc's projected balance sheet shows a significant increase in net worth in year 2, at which point the company will generate an impressive 90.5 percent return on investment (ROI). As the financial projections indicate, TDP expects to build a company with strong profit potential and a solid balance sheet that will be asset heavy and flush with cash at the end of the third year. The Daily Perc has no plan to pay dividends before the end of the third year; instead, the company will use the cash it generates to fuel its growth.

Pro Forma Balance Sheet

	Year 1	Year 2	Year 3
Assets			
Current Assets			
Cash	$29,622	$91,673	$528,315
Inventory	$35,159	$134,826	$328,253
Other Current Assets	$0	$0	$0
Total Current Assets	$64,781	$226,499	$856,568

Pro Forma Balance Sheet

	Year 1	Year 2	Year 3
Long-Term Assets			
Long-Term Assets	$323,250	$752,950	$2,109,943
Accumulated Depreciation	$21,785	$114,695	$310,790
Total Long-Term Assets	$301,465	$638,255	$1,799,153
Total Assets	$366,246	$864,754	$2,655,721
Liabilities and Capital			
Current Liabilities			
Accounts Payable	$49,724	$106,240	$248,402
Current Borrowing	$7,500	$5,500	$500
Other Current Liabilities	$0	$0	$0
Subtotal Current Liabilities	$57,224	$111,740	$248,902
Long-Term Liabilities	$286,394	$513,364	$1,193,356
Total Liabilities	$343,618	$625,104	$1,442,258
Paid-In Capital	$225,270	$225,270	$225,270
Retained Earnings	($173,770)	($202,642)	$14,381
Earnings	($28,872)	$217,023	$973,812
Total Capital	$22,628	$239,651	$1,213,463
Total Liabilities and Capital	$366,246	$864,754	$2,655,721
Net Worth	$22,628	$239,651	$1,213,463

7.7 Exit Strategy

There are three scenarios for the investors and managers to recover their investment, two of which produce significant returns on each dollar invested.

Scenario 1: The Daily Perc becomes extremely successful and begins selling franchises. When one considers the wealth that successful franchisers such as McDonald's, Wendy's, Five Guys Burgers and Fries, and others have created, the potential to franchise a well-run system is considerable. However, developing a franchise can be extremely costly, takes years to build, and can be diminished by a few franchisees who fail to deliver the consistency or value on which the founding company has built its reputation.

Scenario 2: The Daily Perc becomes the drive-through version of Starbucks, obtaining several million dollars through private offering that allows the company to open 20 to 30 outlets per year in the region of the country between the mountain ranges in both metropolitan and micropolitan communities. This is the preferred exit strategy of the management team. The danger with this exit strategy is that once TDP becomes successful, competitors will attempt to enter high-potential markets with copycat concepts before TDP can expand into those markets, resulting in lower revenues and a dramatic increase in advertising expenditures to maintain market share. Understanding these risks—and planning for them—gives TDP the edge required to make this scenario work.

Scenario 3: By the third year, the growth and community support for TDP is creating a buzz in cities beyond the metropolitan area. Competitors such as Starbucks or Quikava will realize the value proposition that TDP offers its customers and identify the company an attractive target for buyout.

Taking a conservative approach to valuation, we estimate that TDP would be valued at $7.5 million. Assuming that all 250 units of ownership in TDP are distributed to investors, a cash purchase of TDP would net each unit $30,000. With each unit selling at $4,250, that price constitutes an ROI of 705 percent over the three years. However, any buyout will most likely involve a cash/stock combination, which is preferable because tax consequences of the transaction for the sellers would be more favorable than in an all-cash deal.

Pro Forma Cash Flow

	Month 1	Month 2	Month 3	Month 4	Month 5	Month 6	Month 7	Month 8	Month 9	Month 10	Month 11	Month 12
Cash Received												
Cash from Operations												
Cash Sales	$0	$0	$0	$32,375	$42,637	$44,769	$42,530	$42,637	$77,144	$85,167	$95,392	$95,392
Subtotal Cash from Operations	$0	$0	$0	$32,375	$42,637	$44,769	$42,530	$42,637	$77,144	$85,167	$95,392	$95,392
Additional Cash Received												
Sales Tax, VAT, HST/GST Received 0.00%	$0	$0	$0	$0	$0	$0	$0	$0	$0	$0	$0	$0
New Current Borrowing	$0	$0	$0	$0	$0	$0	$0	$0	$0	$0	$0	$0
New Other Liabilities (Interest Free)	$0	$0	$0	$0	$0	$0	$0	$0	$0	$0	$0	$0
New Long-Term Liabilities	$0	$0	$5,300	$0	$0	$0	$0	$0	$98,184	$0	$77,979	$0
Sales of Other Current Assets	$0	$0	$0	$0	$0	$0	$0	$0	$0	$0	$0	$0
Sales of Long-Term Assets	$0	$0	$0	$0	$0	$0	$0	$0	$0	$0	$0	$0
New Investment Received	$0	$0	$0	$0	$0	$0	$0	$0	$0	$0	$0	$0
Subtotal Cash Received	$0	$0	$5,300	$32,375	$42,637	$44,769	$42,530	$42,637	$175,328	$85,167	$173,371	$95,392
Expenditures												
Expenditures from Operations												
Cash Spending	$5,500	$5,500	$5,500	$16,000	$18,100	$17,050	$18,800	$19,500	$28,624	$30,700	$38,200	$38,900
Bill Payments	$112	$3,349	$2,987	$7,228	$10,030	$17,719	$27,251	$24,342	$26,320	$54,407	$46,831	$52,615
Subtotal Spent on Operations	$5,612	$8,849	$8,487	$23,228	$28,130	$34,769	$46,051	$43,842	$54,944	$85,107	$85,031	$91,515
Additional Cash Spent												
Sales Tax, VAT, HST/GST Paid Out	$0	$0	$0	$0	$0	$0	$0	$0	$0	$0	$500	$1,000
Principal Repayment of Current Borrowing	$0	$0	$0	$0	$0	$0	$0	$0	$0	$0	$0	$0
Other Liabilities Principal Repayment	$0	$0	$0	$0	$0	$0	$0	$0	$0	$0	$0	$0
Long-Term Liabilities Principal Repayment	$2,500	$3,116	$0	$5,166	$0	$0	$0	$0	$0	$7,216	$0	$8,471
Dividends	$0	$0	$0	$0	$0	$0	$0	$0	$0	$0	$0	$0
Purchase Other Current Assets	$0	$0	$0	$0	$0	$0	$0	$0	$0	$0	$0	$0
Purchase Long-Term Assets	$0	$0	$0	$0	$0	$0	$0	$0	$105,400	$0	$86,450	$0
Subtotal Cash Spent	$8,112	$11,965	$8,487	$28,394	$28,130	$34,769	$46,051	$43,842	$160,344	$92,323	$171,981	$100,986
Net Cash Flow	($8,112)	($11,965)	($3,187)	$3,981	$14,507	$10,000	($3,521)	($1,205)	$14,984	($7,156)	$1,390	($5,594)
Cash Balance	$17,388	$5,422	$2,236	$6,217	$20,724	$30,724	$27,203	$25,998	$40,982	$33,826	$35,216	$29,622

Promethean Power

Stick to the Vision or Make a Pivot?

Sorin Grama emigrated to the United States from Romania with his family in 1987 and went on to earn degrees in engineering from the Ohio State University and MIT, where he met Sam White, who was working for a start-up company in Cambridge, Massachusetts. Both men had an interest in solar energy technology, and together they developed a variety of solar-powered applications, including a solar-powered turbine that won second place in MIT's prestigious $100K Entrepreneurship Competition in 2007. That same year, they launched Boston-based Promethean Power Systems with the goal of using solar energy to provide much-needed refrigeration for India's rural dairy industry, which loses billions of dollars of products each year to spoilage. The dairy industry in India relies on a continuous round of pickups by truck from rural collection stations that lack refrigeration. The company's solar-powered chilling systems would allow the pickup stations to store milk safely in areas that lacked electricity or in areas in which the electrical grid was unreliable.

Grama and White attracted a $500,000 investment from a venture capital company and used it to develop a prototype solar-powered chiller that they had convinced R. F. Chandramogan, owner of several dairies in India, to install in his dairy near the rural village of Karumapuram in the Indian state of Tamil Nadu. If the prototype was successful, Chandramogan had committed to purchasing 10 more units for his other dairies. There was just one problem: Chandramogan balked when he learned that installing the $12,000 solar-powered milk-chilling unit would cost an additional $8,000, bringing his total cost to $20,000 per unit. "Too much," he said. In addition to being too expensive, the system was too large and too complex to be practical.

It was a devastating blow to the young company. Grama, White, and Rajat Gupta, the company's agent on the ground in India, sat dejectedly in a cramped office at the dairy and debated their next move. "Why not strip out the solar component of the chilling system and install a simpler, less expensive one powered by electricity?" asked one of the engineers. Doing so would bring down the cost of the chiller from $12,000 to $3,000, and collection centers in areas that lack electricity could use generators to power the unit. "We shouldn't be trying to shove something down the customer's throat," said White. Grama frowned.

Making the change to the chilling system's design would be simple enough from an engineering perspective, but it would mean a mammoth change in the company's vision. "We had developed very good solar technology, and I did not want to give it up without a fight," said Grama. "I had to ask myself, 'Am I going to be as passionate about this business if it is not about renewable energy?'" Gupta argued that dropping the solar-powered technology in favor of the old-fashioned, low-tech electric solution was the only feasible route for the company to take if it was to survive. Redesigning the solar unit to meet customer expectations would take time and lots of money, neither of which the company had. What made sense to Gupta was transforming the chiller from an impractical solar-powered unit that was too expensive to market into an electric-powered unit that could give Indian dairies what they needed: inexpensive but reliable chillers with plenty of storage capacity.

Grama, however, was not yet convinced. He argued that since its inception, the entire premise of Promethean Power was to create solar-powered products. *That* was Grama's passion. Over the next several days, Gupta and White spent time with managers of several dairies in India, explained to them that the changes the company was considering making to its chiller, and asked for their feedback. Every one of them liked the proposed changes and supported the simpler, less expensive product. Grama, however, was still wrestling with letting go of his vision of building a company that specializes in solar-powered energy solutions. White pointed out that if Promethean Power could produce an electric-powered chiller that was successful, the company would have the resources to develop solar-powered technology that was practical and inexpensive. "This could be a bridge," he said.

Questions

1. What steps might Promethean Power have taken as it developed its solar-powered chiller for the Indian dairy market to avoid the problem it now faces?

2. Why is Grama balking at switching the company's chiller from solar power to electricity?

3. Should Promethean Power stick to its original vision and try to sell its solar-powered chilling units or make a "pivot" and convert its chiller to an electric-powered unit? Explain your reasoning.

Sources: Adapted from Amy Barrett, "Case Study: The CEO Had His Sights Set on Solar Technology: Should He Ditch His Dream to Save His Company?," *Inc.*, September 2011, pp. 57–62, and "About Us—Team," Promethean Power Systems, http://www.coolectrica.com/team.

Mixed Chicks

Should a Small Company Battle a Large Competitor in Court over Trademark Infringement?

Best friends Kim Etheridge and Wendi Levy are of mixed race and for years struggled to find the right hair treatments to tame their unruly curls. "When you are multicultural, you have a blend of hair," explains Etheridge, but, she adds, the hair products on the market do not address that fact. Instead, the companies that make them merely target various ethnic groups with products that are not tailored to the particular characteristics of their hair. In 2003, Etheridge and Levy decided that they could create better hair care products for the growing multicultural market and began working with a chemist to create them. Their first product was a conditioner designed specifically to work on their type of hair. Within a year, the duo had created a shampoo and launched a business, Mixed Chicks, from Wendi's garage to sell their hair care products through salons and beauty supply stores nationwide. Five years later, their small company's sales accelerated when star Halle Berry endorsed Mixed Chicks products in an interview that appeared in three national magazines.

A short time later, Etheridge and Levy were working the Mixed Chicks booth at a trade show when a representative from a large national beauty supply company with more than 3,000 stores and $3 billion in annual sales stopped and expressed interest in their products. Although the entrepreneurs initially were excited about the prospects of selling Mixed Chicks products to a large national chain, they decided not to pursue the opportunity when they learned about the retail chain's strict return and liberal discount policies. Neither would be good for their small company.

About a year later, Etheridge received an e-mail from a retail customer telling her that the same large national chain had created its own line of products aimed at mixed-race women. Not only was the product line's name, Mixed Silk, similar to the name that Etheridge and Levy were using for their products, but the bottles the large company was using also had the same shape as Mixed Chicks' bottles. The only significant difference between the products was the price; the large retailer was selling Mixed Silk products for about $8, compared to $14 to $20 for Mixed Chicks products.

Alarmed, Etheridge and Levy purchased samples of the copycat products and began testing them. They were unimpressed. When Etheridge went into one of the chain's stores, she asked an employee about the Mixed Silk products on display near the register. "It's a generic version of Mixed Chicks," explained the clerk. "Virtually the same thing." Over the next several weeks, the entrepreneurs heard from several of their retailers who told them that more customers were balking at purchasing Mixed Chicks products because they had discovered Mixed Silk products, which cost far less.

Etheridge and Levy were furious, and their first reaction was to file a lawsuit against the large retail chain for trademark infringement. Over the next two months, they researched the problem and consulted with several attorneys. They considered sending a "cease-and-desist" letter, demanding that the chain stop selling Mixed Silk products. Although the letter might work, the strategy carries a significant risk: If the chain stopped selling Mixed Silk products and then challenged Etheridge and Levy in court and won, their small company would have to compensate the large chain for its lost revenue. However, if Mixed Chicks filed a lawsuit for trademark infringement and won, the retail chain would be forced to take its Mixed Silk products off the market, and Mixed Chicks would collect damages for lost sales. Filing a trademark infringement suit would be costly, perhaps $250,000 to $500,000 in legal fees per year for, quite possibly, many years. The young entrepreneurs also knew that filing a lawsuit would distract them from managing their growing business, which was now generating annual sales of $7 million. Yet they were concerned that not taking legal action could be more expensive in the long run, perhaps even costing them their entire business. Finally, could they live with themselves if they did not stand up against a larger, more powerful competitor when they knew they were right?

Questions

1. Why is securing proper intellectual property protection such as trademarks, patents, and copyrights important for entrepreneurs?
2. Analyze the advantages and the disadvantages of filing a trademark infringement lawsuit against the large chain selling Mixed Silk products? Conduct the same analysis for not filing the lawsuit.
3. What course of action do you recommend that Etheridge and Levy take? Explain.
4. Can you recommend ways that Etheridge and Levy might be able to use the significant difference in the size of their company and the national retail chain to their advantage, especially for marketing their company?

Sources: Adapted from Jennifer Alsever, "Case Study: The Rival: Enormous. Its Product Disturbingly Similar. The Question: To Sue or Not to Sue?," *Inc.*, February 2012, pp. 81–83; "Have a Curly Hair Conundrum? The Girls at Mixed Chicks Can Solve It," *A Bulls Eye View*, June 6, 2012, http://abullseyeview.com/interview-mixed-chicks-kim-etheredge-wendi-levy; and Janell Hazelwood, "8 Trailblazing Women Then and Now," *Black Enterprise*, March 31, 2011, http://www.blackenterprise.com/small-business/8-trailblazing-women-then-and-now/3.

Case 3

True Body Products

Should a Small Company Extend Its Product Line to Satisfy a Key Customer?

In 2007, after spending 15 years in product development and brand management with large companies such as Procter and Gamble, Welch's, and Seventh Generation, Janice Shade decided to start True Body Products, a company in Richmond, Vermont, that markets all-natural, unscented, affordable soaps. True Body's line of soaps is manufactured to strict quality standards by a New England contract manufacturer and sold in 45 Whole Foods stores in the Northeast, Fred Meyer stores in the Northwest, and several independent natural food stores across the United States and online at alice.com, an online household products marketplace. In its first full year of operation, True Body generated sales of $45,000. Shade was operating the company using the $100,000 that she and private investors had invested in the company at start-up.

The buyer from Whole Foods with whom Shade works recently approached her with an idea for increasing sales of True Body products. "Why not introduce a line of scented soaps?" the buyer asked Shade. Scented soaps would be a natural extension of the small company's product line, would increase its shelf presence in stores, and would lead to more sales. Shade wanted to avoid alienating or confusing existing customers, many of whom suffered from allergies and purchased True Body products *because* the soaps were unscented. "The most ardent and positive consumer feedback I get is from people who are happy to have found an unscented bar soap," she says. However, Shade thought that the idea of adding a scented line was worth considering. "I want my business to grow to a scale where it makes an impression on the world," she says.

Shade began to research scented soaps and consider the options for her company with her advisory board. She asked the company that manufactures her soaps to create samples of soaps scented with fragrances such as lavender and grapefruit. "Then we started costing them out," says Shade. "That's when the red flags came up." Because True Body's soaps are made with all-natural ingredients, the manufacturer would have to use costly pure essential oils rather than cheaper synthetic fragrances to create the line of scented soaps. The result would be higher prices for the scented soaps. Shade estimated that True Body soaps would have to retail for $6.19 for a package of three bars, compared to just $5.49 for a package of three unscented bars. The higher pricing concerned Shade because she built her company on the premise of marketing soaps that are all-natural *and* affordable. In conversations with the buyer, she learned that if she introduced scented soaps, the retailer planned to set the price of both the unscented and the scented soaps at $6.19 for a package of three bars.

Concerned that customers would balk at the price increase, Shade considered selling the scented soap in two-bar packages, a pricing tactic that would allow her to offer a lower price point. She agreed with the Whole Foods buyer that True Body needed more in-store shelf exposure and began to consider other ways to expand her company's product line that would be more consistent with her commitment to all-natural, unscented soaps, including liquid hand soap, shampoos, face soap, and others. "I have every intention of growing," says Shade, "but I want to be intentional about it."

Questions

1. Should Shade introduce scented soaps to True Body's product line? Explain.
2. What steps should Shade take to increase the in-store shelf space of True Body's products?
3. Given Shade's vision for her company (soaps that are all-natural, unscented, and affordable), do you think that her concerns over the proposed higher prices that Whole Foods would charge for her unscented soaps are justified? Explain.
4. Write a one-page memo to Janice Shade outlining the key components of a marketing strategy that will increase her company's in-store shelf space and its sales.

Sources: Adapted from Adriana Gardella, "Can a Small Company Say No to Whole Foods?" *New York Times*, June 1, 2010, http://boss.blogs .nytimes.com/2010/06/01/can-a-small-company-say-no-to-whole-foods; Adriana Gardella, "Yes, You Can Say No to Whole Foods," *New York Times*, June 4, 2010, http://boss.blogs.nytimes.com/2010/06/04/yes-you-can-say-no-to-whole-foods; and Adriana Gardella, "A Start-Up Soap Maker Starts to Get Traction," *New York Times*, January 7, 2011, http://boss.blogs.nytimes.com/2011/01/07/more-of-everything-for-a-start-up-soap-maker.

Case 4

Little Dudes and Divas

Can a Web Site Redesign Accelerate a Small Company's Growth?

In 2004, Steve and Susan Karasanti, a husband-and-wife entrepreneurial team, started Little Dudes and Divas, a company based in Rockaway Park, New York, that sells clothing and accessories for infants and toddlers. In addition to their Web site, the Karasantis operate a brick-and-mortar store in Rockaway Park. "Our business model is based on keeping things fresh and selling only items which are of the highest quality," explains Steve. "If a new bag or print comes out, we want to be the first to have it on our Web site."

The Karasantis know that, to succeed, they must create a competitive advantage for their company, something that differentiates it from a multitude of competitors, many of whom are far bigger with greater resources, including online giants such as Babies "R" Us and Diapers.com and retailers such as Target, Macy's, and Nordstrom. "When we first started selling diaper bags and diaper accessories online, there was much less competition," observes Steve. "It's extremely challenging to compete with well-known Web sites that sell the same items we do. It's very hard to compete with the bigger online companies on price, but we can compete by giving our customers personal attention." For instance, if a customer wants to see a diaper bag packed a particular way, the Karasantis and their three employees will make a video that shows the bag being packed that way and post it on the company's Web site.

Most of Little Dudes and Divas's sales come from the Web site, and the Karasantis have invested heavily in e-mail marketing to tell customers about special sales and promotions. They also have focused on search engine optimization (SEO). "We did extensive research on SEO," explains Steve. "We use only methods that are considered ethical. Our site is filled with meaningful and unique content." Their SEO efforts are focused primarily on Google, and the copreneurs use Google Analytics reports extensively. "These reports help you understand why a customer may click off a page or why they abandoned their shopping cart," says Steve. "You can tell which pages get the most clicks and what page customers are on when they leave the site. If you have a page on the site that gets lots of clicks but customers don't continue to shop and leave, it's an indication that something is wrong."

To drive traffic to their Web site, the Karasantis also are active on social media, including Facebook, Twitter, and YouTube. They post frequently and respond quickly to visitors' comments. "We use [social media] to keep our customers current and give them reasons to come back," says Steve.

The Karasantis would like to generate more sales from their Web site and recently subjected the site to a review by experienced online shoppers. A common criticism of the site by nearly all of the reviewers is that the site is too cluttered and confuses potential customers by offering too much information, particularly on its home page. "Wow! What a mess," wrote one reviewer. Others pointed out the inconsistency in Little Dudes and Divas's emphasis on quality products and the bargain-basement impression its Web site creates. "I don't like the site because they're selling high-end products, but the visual appearance of the store is bargain basement," says one reviewer. Another reviewer notes that although unique products and superior customer service are key components of the small company's strategy, the Web site fails to get that message across. "Why aren't they delivering that message on the home page in a bold, clear way?" he asks.

Questions

1. Visit the Web site for Little Dudes and Divas (www.littledudesanddivas.com) and spend some time exploring it. What is your first impression of the company? Is your impression consistent with the image that the Karasantis want to create for their business? Is the site easy to navigate? Does the site allow shoppers to easily find the items they want? Does the site create an image of trustworthiness?

2. Write a short memo to the Karasantis that includes at least five recommendations for improving their company's Web site.

3. What steps can the Karasantis take to communicate their company's unique selling proposition (USP) to their customers and potential customers through their Web site?

4. What suggestions can you offer the Karasantis for improving their social media marketing strategies?

Sources: Adapted from Gabriel Shaoolian, "Can a Small Retailer Compete Online with the Big Boys?," *New York Times*, December 13, 2011, http://boss.blogs.nytimes.com/2011/12/13/a-small-retailer-tries-to-compete-with-the-big-boys-online; Gabriel Shaoolian, "When a Small Retailer Shoots Itself in the Foot with a Weak Web Site," *New York Times*, December 20, 2011, http://boss.blogs.nytimes.com/2011/12/20/when-a-small-retailer-shoots-itself-in-the-foot-with-a-weak-web-site; and "About Us," Little Dudes and Divas, http://www.littledudesanddivas.com/info.html.

Case 5

Erik Buell Racing

Can an Innovative Designer of Sport Motorcycles Raise the Capital He Needs to Build a Dealer Network and Increase Production to Meet Customer Demand?

In 1983, Erik Buell left his engineering job at iconic motorcycle maker Harley-Davidson to start the first sport bike design and manufacturing company, Buell Motorcycle Company (BMC), in the United States. His goal was to build sport bikes (known as "crotch rockets") capable of surpassing those made by famous Japanese and European brands, which dominated (and still dominate) the market segment. Sport bikes account for 15 percent of total annual motorcycle sales in the United States, which are estimated at 560,000 units and $5.87 billion. Buell worked out of the garage of a rented farmhouse in Mukwonago, Wisconsin, just 40 miles from Harley-Davidson's headquarters in Milwaukee. Ten years later, Harley-Davidson purchased a minority share in Buell's company with the idea of expanding its reach beyond the cruiser motorcycle market. In 1998, Harley-Davidson purchased 98 percent of Buell's company, and Buell thought that with the larger company's resources behind him, he could transform BMC into a global powerhouse in the sport bike market. In 2008, BMC sold 15,000 bikes, but a severe recession caused Harley-Davidson to refocus on its core business, and the motorcycle giant closed BMC, meaning that Buell lost everything, including the rights to the BMC name.

Like a true entrepreneur, Buell never gave up on his dream, however. He had a reputation as one of the most gifted motorcycle designers in the world, 30 years of experience creating championship-winning sports bikes, and $40 million worth of equipment and tooling for manufacturing motorcycles. Eighteen months after Harley-Davidson closed BMC, Buell launched his second motorcycle design and manufacturing business, Erik Buell Racing (EBR), in East Troy, Wisconsin. In 2011, the company, with just 20 talented and devoted employees, produced a limited run of 100 exotic street racing bikes priced between $37,500 and $44,000. His goal is to build EBR into a major competitor in the sport motorcycle market with manufacturing operations in the United States and a network of domestic and international dealers to handle sales and service. "EBR is going to stay focused on invention and intellectual property," Buell declares, "and do radical things that the rest of the world isn't doing. That's how we're going to bring some American flavor to the sport bike industry." EBR's signature model is the 1190RS, a sleek, muscular bike that sports all of Buell's unique styling elements, including sporty, upswept lines from handlebar tips to tail; the innovative Zero Torsional Load braking system that lightens wheel weights; and mufflers located underneath the engine to limit noise and maintain a low center of gravity. "Our design DNA is radically different," says Buell. Indeed, the 175-horsepower 1190RS weighs just 389 pounds, 50 pounds less than most competing bikes. It also is eco-friendly, producing just 25 percent of the exhaust emissions allowed by the Environmental Protection Agency.

The primary obstacle that Buell faces in the growth of EBR is a lack of capital. Buell knows that the customer base for his motorcycles exists, and it is a global market. So far, more than 50 percent of the young company's sales have been to foreign customers, but Buell must establish a dealer network to reach both domestic and foreign customers. Setting up a domestic dealer network takes time and money, and establishing international dealerships is even more complex and expensive. "We had the potential to sell 1,500 bikes in 2011, but we had to revise that down to 900," says Buell, who says that he needs $20 million to achieve his goals for EBR. "I didn't think it would be this hard to raise $20 million," he says with a hint of frustration. Buell has supplemented EBR's revenue from bike sales by performing design consulting for other large motorcycle manufacturers, many of them his competitors, around the world. Buell is holding firmly to his dream for EBR. "We're brave when we make decisions because we all want to be first," he says of himself and his employees. "To be first, we have to get there fast, and we can't make mistakes."

Questions

1. Is Erik Buell's dilemma—lack of capital to fuel a business with growth potential—a common one that entrepreneurs face?
2. What steps should Erik Buell take before he begins the search for capital for his company?
3. How do you recommend that Buell raise the capital he needs to achieve the goals he has set for Erik Buell Racing?
4. Which sources of capital should Buell approach first to raise the money to fuel EBR's growth? Are there sources of capital that you recommend that he avoid? Explain.

Sources: Adapted from Jennifer Wang, "Speed Demons," *Inc.*, March 2012, pp. 28–34, and "About EBR," Erik Buell Racing, http://www.erikbuellracing.com/about-ebr.

James Confectioners— Part 1

Squeezed by Rising Costs, a Confectioner Struggles to Cope

Telford James and his wife Ivey are the second-generation owners of James Confectioners, a family-owned manufacturer of premium chocolates that was started by Telford's father, Frank, in 1964 in Eau Claire, Wisconsin. In its nearly 50 years, James Confectioners has grown from its roots in a converted hardware store into a large, modern factory with sophisticated production and quality control equipment. In the early days, all of Frank's customers were local shops and stores, but the company now supplies customers across the United States and a few in Canada. Telford and Ivey have built on the company's reputation as an honest, reliable supplier of chocolates. The prices they charge for their chocolates are above the industry average but are not anywhere near the highest prices in the industry even though the company is known for producing quality products.

Annual sales for the company have grown to $3.9 million, and its purchases of the base chocolate used as the raw materials for their products have increased from 25,000 pounds 20 years ago to 150,000 pounds. The Jameses are concerned about the impact of the rapidly rising cost of the base chocolate, however. Bad weather in South America and Africa, where most of the world's cocoa is grown, and a workers' strike disrupted the global supply of chocolate, sending prices upward. There appears to be no relief from high chocolate prices in the near future. The International Cocoa Organization, an industry trade association, forecasts world production of cocoa, from which chocolate is made, to decline by 7.2 percent this year.[1] Escalating milk and sugar prices are squeezing the company's profit margins as well. Much to James and Ivey's dismay, James Confectioners's long-term contracts with its chocolate suppliers have run out, and the company is purchasing its raw materials under short-term, variable-price contracts. They are concerned about the impact that these increases in cost will have on the company's financial statements and on its long-term health.

Ivey, who has the primary responsibility for managing James Confectioners's finances, has compiled the balance sheet and the income statement for the fiscal year that just ended. The two financial statements appear below:

[1]"Cocoa Forecasts," International Cocoa Organization, May 27, 2009, http://www.icco.org/about/press2.aspx?Id=0ji12056.

Balance Sheet, James Confectioners
December 31, 20xx

	Assets
CURRENT ASSETS	
Cash	$ 161,254
Accounts Receivable	$ 507,951
Inventory	$ 568,421
Supplies	$ 84,658
Prepaid Expenses	$ 32,251
Total Current Assets	$ 1,354,536
FIXED ASSETS	
Land	$ 104,815
Buildings, net	$ 203,583
Autos, net	$ 64,502
Equipment, net	$ 247,928
Furniture and Fixtures, net	$ 40,314
Total Fixed Assets	$ 661,142
Total Assets	$ 2,015,678

	Liabilities
CURRENT LIABILITIES	
Accounts Payable	$ 241,881
Notes Payable	$ 221,725
Line of Credit Payable	$ 141,097
Accrued Wages/Salaries Payable	$ 40,314
Accrued Interest Payable	$ 20,157
Accrued Taxes Payable	$ 10,078
Total Current Liabilities	$ 675,252
Long-Term Liabilities	
Mortgage	$ 346,697
Loan	$ 217,693
Total Long-Term Liabilities	$ 564,390
	Owner's Equity
James, Capital	$ 776,036
Total Liabilities and Owner's Equity	$ 2,015,678

Income Statement, James Confectioners

Net Sales Revenue		$3,897,564
Cost of Goods Sold		
Beginning Inventory, 1/1/xx	$ 627,853	
+ Purchases	$2,565,908	
Goods Available for Sale	$3,193,761	
− Ending Inventory, 12/31/xx	$ 568,421	
Cost of Goods Sold		$2,625,340
Gross Profit		$1,272,224
Operating Expenses		
Utilities	$163,698	
Advertising	$155,903	
Insurance	$ 74,065	
Depreciation	$ 74,043	
Salaries and Benefits	$381,961	
E-commerce	$ 38,976	
Repairs and Maintenance	$ 58,463	
Travel	$ 23,385	
Supplies	$ 15,590	
Total Operating Expenses		$ 986,084
Other Expenses		
Interest Expense	$119,658	
Miscellaneous Expense	$ 1,248	
Total Other Expenses		$ 120,906
Total Expenses		$1,106,990
Net Income		$ 165,234

To see how the company's financial position changes over time, Ivey calculates 12 ratios. She also compares James Confectioners's ratios to those of the typical firm in the industry. The table below shows the value of each of the 12 ratios from last year and the industry median:

Ratio Comparison

Ratio	James Confectioners		Confectionery Industry Median*
	Current Year	**Last Year**	
Liquidity Ratios			
Current ratio		1.86	1.7
Quick ratio		1.07	0.8
Leverage Ratios			
Debt ratio		0.64	0.7
Debt-to-Net-Worth ratio		1.71	1.0
Times-Interest-Earned ratio		2.49	2.3
Operating Ratios			
Average Inventory Turnover Ratio		4.75	4.9
Average Collection Period Ratio		34.6	23.0 days
Average Payable Period Ratio		31.1	33.5 days
Net-Sales-to-Total-Assets Ratio		2.17	2.1
Profitability Ratios			
Net-Profit-on-Sales Ratio		7.40%	7.1%
Net-Profit-to-Assets Ratio		9.20%	5.6%
Net-Profit-to-Equity Ratio		29.21%	16.5%

*from Risk Management Associates Annual Statement Studies.

"How does the financial analysis look for this year, Hon?" Telford asks.

"I'm about to crunch the numbers now," says Ivey. "I'm sure that rising chocolate prices have cut into our profit margins. The question is 'how much'?"

"I think we're going to have to consider raising prices, but I'm not sure how our customers will respond if we do," says Telford. "What other options do we have?"

Questions

1. Calculate the 12 ratios for James Confectioners for this year.
2. How do the ratios that you calculated for this year compare to those that Ivey calculated for the company last year? What factors are most likely to account for those changes?
3. How do the ratios you calculated for this year compare to those of the typical company in the industry? Do you spot any areas that could cause the company problems in the future? Explain.
4. Develop a set of specific recommendations for improving the financial performance of James Confectioners using the analysis you conducted in questions 1 to 3.
5. What pricing recommendations can you make to Telford and Ivey James?

James Confectioners— Part 2

Forecasting Cash Flow for a Small Confectioner

Telford James and his wife Ivey, the second-generation owners of James Confectioners, a family-owned manufacturer of premium chocolates that was started by Telford's father, Frank, in 1964 in Eau Claire, Wisconsin, have become increasingly concerned that turmoil in the banking and financial industries could have a negative impact on their business. They have read the headlines about bank closures, heightened government scrutiny of the banking industry, and tight credit conditions, especially for small businesses. The company has a $150,000 line of credit with Maple Leaf Bank, but the Jameses want to increase it to $250,000 as a precautionary move. Last week, they contacted Claudia Fernandes, their personal banker at Maple Leaf, about increasing the line of credit. Fernandes said that in addition to reviewing James Confectioners's most recent balance sheet and income statement, she would need a cash flow forecast for the upcoming year.

Although Telford and Ivey have prepared budgets for James Confectioners and have analyzed their financial statements using ratio analysis, they have not created a cash flow forecast before. They expect sales to increase 6.2 percent next year to $4,139,213. Credit sales account for 96 percent of total sales, and the company's collection pattern for credit sales is 8 percent in the same month in which the sale is generated, 54 percent in the first month after the sale is generated, and 34 percent in the second month after the sale is generated. The Jameses have gathered estimates from their budget for the upcoming year (see page 683).

Actual sales for the last two months, November and December, were $459,913 and $553,454, respectively. The company's cash balance as of January 1 is $22,565. The interest rate on James Confectioners's current line of credit is 8.25 percent, and the Jameses have established a minimum cash balance of $10,000.

Questions

1. Develop a monthly cash budget for James Confectioners for the upcoming year.
2. What recommendations can you offer Telford and Ivey James to improve their company's cash flow?
3. If you were Claudia Fernandes, the Jameses' banker, would you be willing to increase the company's line of credit? Explain.

	Jan	Feb	Mar	Apr	May	Jun	Jul	Aug	Sep	Oct	Nov	Dec
Sales	$264,910	$447,035	$289,745	$293,884	$190,404	$318,719	$281,466	$231,796	$335,276	$409,782	$488,427	$587,768
Other cash receipts	105	55	60	75	85	55	65	60	65	85	95	110
Purchases	365,280	174,400	294,300	190,750	193,745	125,350	209,825	185,300	152,600	220,725	269,774	321,549
Utilities	13,600	14,100	13,700	13,200	13,200	13,600	14,800	15,900	14,900	14,100	13,800	14,000
Advertising	18,000	11,000	10,000	7,000	9,000	10,000	12,000	12,000	15,000	20,000	22,000	24,000
Insurance	0	0	19,650	0	0	19,650	0	0	19,650	0	0	19,650
Salaries and benefits	33,583	33,583	33,583	33,583	33,583	33,583	33,583	33,583	33,583	33,583	33,583	33,583
E-commerce	2,700	4,500	2,900	3,000	1,900	2,400	3,200	3,300	3,400	3,900	5,000	6,000
Repairs and maintenance	5,000	5,000	5,000	5,000	5,000	5,000	5,000	5,000	5,000	5,000	5,000	5,000
Travel	4,100	2,700	2,700	2,000	3,000	2,600	2,200	3,100	3,800	4,500	5,500	6,500
Supplies	1,088	1,836	1,190	1,207	782	1,309	1,156	952	1,377	1,683	2,006	2,414
Interest	10,000	10,000	10,000	10,000	10,000	10,000	10,000	10,000	10,000	10,000	10,000	10,000
Other cash disbursements	125	125	125	125	125	125	125	125	125	125	125	125

Case 8

Just Marry

Sales Have Plummeted Because of a Recession, and Susan Southerland Is Cutting Expenses to Save Her Company. Should She Fire Her Best Friend?

After graduating from the University of Florida in 1992 at age 21, Susan Southerland started Just Marry, a wedding planning business, in Orlando, Florida. In 1998, with sales growing fast, Southerland hired her first employee, Michele Butler, as an office assistant. Butler proved to be an outstanding employee with a passion for customer service and a natural ability to connect with clients. Just Marry continued to expand, and Southerland eventually hired four full-time wedding planners and 10 independent contractors to handle 300 events per year. Butler became an integral part of the business, and she and Southerland became best friends. They would work together for 8 to 10 hours a day and then spend time socializing with one another after work. In fact, many clients assumed that Butler and Southerland were business partners. "It seemed like a relationship of equals," says a former employee.

For a decade, Just Marry experienced annual growth rates of 20 percent, and then a recession hit, and sales plummeted 39 percent in just one year as fewer people came to Orlando for destination weddings and those who did cut back on their wedding expenditures. Southerland immediately starting looking for ways to cut expenses. She switched her full-time employees to independent contractors, reduced the commission that she paid them, and shaved operating expenses everywhere she could. Southerland even stopped drawing her normal salary from the business. Even with the cutbacks, Southerland's analysis showed that the cost of Butler's salary and benefits, which was one of the company's biggest expenses, was exerting a severe strain on

Just Marry's financial position. She met with the members of her board of advisers and explained the situation to them. "We looked at many options, but having salaried employees was too difficult to maintain," recalls one adviser.

Southerland agonized over the decision. Butler was a single mother of two with no child support and was struggling to meet her personal expenses on what she earned at Just Marry. Southerland asked Butler if she would take a pay cut or cut back to part-time work until conditions improved, but Butler balked. "I was barely getting by on what I was making," Butler says.

Southerland considered taking out a loan to help the company weather the economic downturn, but banks were restricting their loans to small companies, especially those that were struggling. Southerland began to share the details of Just Marry's financial problems with Butler, even taking her friend to the bank with her while she made another $10,000 transfer from a home equity line of credit to the company's account. She hoped that Butler would get the hint and offer to resign, but that did not happen. As Just Marry's sales and financial position continued to spiral downward, Southerland and Butler found their friendship fraying. Could Southerland fire her best friend to save her company? If she did, would their friendship survive?

Questions

1. Do you recommend that Southerland seek a bank loan to keep the company afloat so that she and Butler can work together to save the company? Explain.
2. Should Susan Southerland fire Michele Butler? Explain.

Source: Adapted from Jennifer Alsever, "Case Study: With Business on the Rocks, Susan Southerland Was Cutting Back on Everything. Could She Really Fire Her Best Friend?," *Inc.*, July/August 2011, pp. 54–57.

Our Town America

Should a Son Take Over the Family Business After his Father's Death Even Though the Company Is Not His Passion?

A few days after delivering his father's eulogy, Michael Plummer Jr. sat at the ornate desk in his father's office and signed paychecks for the 30 employees who worked at Our Town America, the company his father had founded in 1972 in Pinellas Park, Florida. Although Plummer never shared his father's enthusiasm for the family business, which provided welcome packages from local businesses to people who had just relocated, he had spent the last nine years working with his father in the company. Plummer had given up a career that he loved as an army medic to help his father manage the family business after Michael Plummer Sr. had his first heart attack. Sitting at his late father's desk, Plummer, 35, thought about how much he missed the adrenaline rush of emergency medicine and saving lives with split-second decisions. Reflecting on the last nine years, he thought, "Everything is [my father's]. It was his legacy, but I am engulfed by it."

Naturally, Plummer was saddened by his father's sudden death at 57, but he thought it might be the ideal time for him to sell the family business and return to the career that he loved. The decision would be difficult. Our Town America was his father's legacy, and the company employed his sister, aunt, and cousin. Could he sell it and walk away? After all, Plummer had started working in the business when he was just five years old, stuffing envelopes, and continued working there until he graduated from high school, when he turned down a $65,000 salary offer from his father to join the army. Plummer's military service took him to South Korea, where he managed an urgent care clinic. Four years later, he received word that his father had survived a heart attack and needed help running the family business. Without hesitation, Plummer returned to Florida, where his father began grooming him to take over the family business. He started in sales before moving into the company's information technology department, where he improved the company's databases and developed an on-demand printing operation. The work was challenging and fun, but Plummer says that the best part of the job was the time he spent with his father. Still, he never considered Our Town America anything more than a detour from his passion of being a medic.

A few days after his father died, Plummer received a call from a business broker who asked him whether he would be interested in selling Our Town America. Still in shock over his father's sudden death, Plummer said, "No." Now that he had some time to consider the option of selling the family business, however, Plummer began to wonder whether selling was the best option. Several family members, including his father's ex-wife, were quarreling over the ownership and direction of the company. Longtime employees wondered about the security of their jobs, and everyone was looking to Plummer for answers. "A lot of knowledge was lost when Michael Sr. passed away," says Travis Morales, the company's national sales manager. "People wondered if we were going to make it."

In reality, Plummer also was wondering whether the company would be able to survive. He soon discovered that the recession had caused the company's sales to decline by 24 percent. His father's penchant for doling out cash when employees ran into financial problems had created financial problems for the company. Our Town America's payroll was bloated. "[Michael Sr.] was paying people who didn't actually do anything," says Cliff Hallmark, the company's chief financial officer. "Instead of hiring the right person for the job, he hired friends."

The challenges the company faced made Plummer's decision all the more difficult. His father had named him as successor in the family business and had spent nine years grooming him for the job, but was he really ready to take over the company his father had founded and loved so much? What if the company failed under his watch? Should he sell the business outright and share the proceeds with his two sisters? Should he keep the business and hire a professional manager to run it? When Plummer asked Cliff Hallmark for advice, he replied, "If you wrote your obituary, what would you want it to say?"

Questions

1. Outline the various exit strategies that Michael Plummer faces if he decides to sell the business.
2. If Plummer decides to sell the family business, what steps should he take to prepare the company for sale and maximize its value?
3. Do you think that Michael Plummer Sr. adequately prepared his son to take over the family business? What steps should an entrepreneur take to groom his or her successor?
4. Assume the role of adviser to Michael Plummer. What actions do you recommend he take concerning the future of the family business? Explain.

Source: Adapted from Jennifer Alsever, "Case Study: He Dreamed of Leaving the Family Business. Then His Father Died. Could He Really Abandon His Legacy?," *Inc.*, November 2011, pp. 551–556.

Case 10

Liz Corah and Studio-310

An Entrepreneur Overcomes Obstacles to Realize Her Dream

The wood floors creaked and the studio was still warm. Classes had ended hours ago, but there was still work to be done. After teaching eight classes with a fever and surviving her first day as the owner of her own dance studio in San Diego, it was time for Liz Corah to go home and get some much-deserved rest. But who could rest on a day like this, the day your dream comes true?

Slowly she walked to the end of the studio and turned out the lights. She turned around to see the dark, quiet studio that hours ago was filled with dozens of people full of energy and excitement. The room was still buzzing with energy. You could feel it vibrating in the walls. Never had she imagined that so many people would share her vision and join her at her new studio.

Corah walked to the center of the dance floor to take a look around to make sure everything was as it should be. Too busy with classes, customers, phone calls, ballet barre and equipment delivery, and a broken toilet, there had been no time to let any of it sink in. She stared at the walls she had painted herself and the paintings she had hung on them and marveled at the sheer elegance of her dream having come to reality. Then she saw herself in the mirror: business owner, dance/fitness studio owner, teacher, motivator, single mother of two—an entrepreneur who had saved for an entire year for start-up costs and who had achieved a dream that others had told her she would never accomplish. Her knees buckled beneath her, and she fell to the floor. She felt so many emotions—happiness, sadness, exhaustion, and excitement. How else could you feel when you take a leap of faith and succeed?

Corah had been dancing all of her life anywhere there was space or an audience. As a teenager, Corah lacked the money for dance lessons, but she struck a deal with a local studio owner in which she would work in the studio in exchange for lessons. Every night, she would clean the studio and prepare it for lessons for the next day. She also checked in dance students, took telephone messages, and assisted with the day-to-day running of the studio. In exchange, she had unlimited access to the studio's classes. Ballet classes usually were full, and because Corah was a nonpaying student, instructors often moved her away from the barre to the floor to make room for students who paid tuition. Practicing barre work without a barre was incredibly difficult, but it developed Corah into the studio's strongest dancer.

Shortly after Corah married in 2002, her husband was assigned to duty in Iraq. She had her first baby alone in a San Diego Naval Hospital. When her husband returned from active duty, he was transferred to Bethesda Naval Hospital

near Washington, D.C. Soon, Corah was back at work in local fitness clubs in Washington, where she introduced her cardio dance programs. She had a second child and earned an associate's degree before divorcing her abusive husband. Fortified by her courage and independence, she found herself thinking, "Why not follow my dream of owning my own dance-fitness studio? What do I have to lose?" Her classes were so popular that the exercise clubs required reservations for them, but working for someone else, Corah had little room for creativity and self-expression. This felt like the right time to open her own studio.

In 2007, at 24, Corah started Studio-310. With a backpack full of music and a portable stereo in hand, she rented various studios across the county and began advertising, relying on flyers, e-mail lists, demonstrations at community events, and word of mouth to promote her business. Later that year, Corah signed a lease for a commercial store front in a busy shopping center. Previously a women's exercise center, the walls were purple, and the carpet was "Pepto-Bismol" pink. "This will never do," she thought. Corah and a friend replaced the carpet with hardwood flooring, repainted the walls, and hung some inexpensive decorations. In just three weeks, the studio was open for business.

Corah now had a business to manage, but the idea of having more control over her schedule so that she could spend more time with her children pushed her to work harder than she had ever worked. Corah sometimes felt like a juggler with too many balls in the air, but she also was energized by the activity, knowing that she was fulfilling her dream and creating an avenue in which she could be creative and innovative and could grow. Dancing, teaching, and motivating young dancers make her happy. Although like every entrepreneur she continues to encounter challenges in her business, Corah has achieved amazing success with Studio-310. The *Maryland Gazette* recently named Corah one of the women business leaders in Maryland. She also was featured in *Crave D.C.*'s list of the top 100 women in the District of Columbia. Local media has picked up on her entrepreneurial success as well. In addition to realizing her entrepreneurial dream, Corah is raising a happy, healthy family in a new home in Rockville, Maryland.

Questions

1. What characteristics of the typical entrepreneur does Liz Corah exhibit?
2. What traits enable entrepreneurs to start companies even in the most difficult times?
3. Would you characterize Liz Corah as successful? Explain.
4. Develop at least three lessons about entrepreneurship that you can glean from Corah's experience.

Case 11

Ann Bevans Collective

After Losing Her Job in a Corporate Downsizing, a Woman Chooses Entrepreneurship as a Career Path

Heads at the company where Ann Bevans worked had been rolling for some time.

Bevans was the overworked but generally appreciated marketing coordinator at a commercial construction company in Baltimore, Maryland. At age 24, she'd been a marketing coordinator for five years. A writer by training, Ann had become a "Jill of All Trades," making herself indispensable by constantly adding new skills to her repertoire. Writing, designing, programming, managing vendors—she just figured it out as she went along.

After she was downsized, Ann walked out of the small conference room in stunned silence. She packed up her coffee mug and family photos, drove home, opened a beer, and looked around her $615 a month apartment. She thought for a moment and said, "That's never going to happen to me ever again."

At that moment, Ann Bevans Collective was born.

In the beginning, the company was just another job. Ann created Web sites, wrote technical proposals, and ordered paperweights. If a job paid and was tangentially related to marketing, she accepted it.

One day, Ann realized that the Collective could be more than a way to pay the rent. It could be *about* something—a creative expression, a clear reflection of her deepest values. That thought made all the difference.

There were a number of factors working against Ann as she set out on her entrepreneurial adventure. She was young, she was introverted, and she was a woman. In many ways, she was still invisible. Nevertheless, Ann launched her company (initially called the Bevans Group) and got to work. When she ran out of contacts, she stretched out of her comfort zone, joined a networking group, and learned how to sell herself. Eventually, Ann found herself falling farther behind despite working harder than ever. It turned out that doing everything herself limited the revenue her company could generate.

At first, Ann attempted to grow the company the way that most entrepreneurs do: she leased office space and hired employees. She discovered, however, that the "big-agency" model was not for her. The increased responsibility, high overhead, and office politics were exactly what she had sworn off years before. Ann didn't want her business to become just like the companies that had disappointed her in the past. Then two trends changed the industry:

1. Technology made building virtual companies possible and, in many cases, preferable. Having an office and a big staff were no longer prerequisites to being taken seriously.
2. Social media transformed the landscape. Marketers' responsibilities evolved from broadcasting the company line to facilitating access to information. Authenticity and transparency were suddenly seen as vital to marketing success.

In 2009, in response to these market changes, Ann rebranded the company as Ann Bevans Collective. This change put Ann squarely in the center of her company's marketing message. As an introvert, Ann struggled at first with her new role but ultimately decided that she and her clients would be best served by allowing the Collective to be an extension and reflection of her own values. Ann began focusing on the areas she most enjoyed, including marketing strategy and content development. Ann Bevans Collective took on a decidedly global feel with the addition of a creative director based in the United Kingdom and programmers based in Europe, Australia, and the United States.

Just as Ann was making the transition from the Bevans Group to Ann Bevans Collective, tragedy struck. At age 33, Ann was diagnosed with breast cancer. She began to question the amount of energy that the Collective required as well as the impact of her intense work schedule on her family, which included an energetic two-year-old. At the same time, Ann knew intuitively that work and the wonderful relationships she had developed with her clients would keep her sane during her battle.

During her cancer treatments, Ann leaned on her colleagues in the Collective to manage client relationships and counted on them to work independently. When she felt well enough, Ann would return phone calls and e-mails, keeping the lines of communication open.

Ann completed six rounds of chemotherapy and had a mastectomy, and her prognosis is excellent. Thanks to the hard work of her colleagues in the Collective and the patience and understanding of her clients, Ann and her company are continuing to grow and prosper despite personal challenges and difficult economic times.

Questions

1. If you were diagnosed with a life-threatening disease, what would your top three priorities be? Would they be different from your top three priorities today?
2. How has technology changed the entrepreneurial process? Has modern technology made starting a business easier or more difficult? Explain.
3. What lessons about entrepreneurship can you learn from Ann Bevans?

Name Index

Subject Index